T
OXFORD
School
German
DICTIONARY

Editorial Manager: Valerie Grundy
Editors: Neil and Roswitha Morris

OXFORD UNIVERSITY PRESS

Oxford University Press, Great Clarendon Street, Oxford OX2 6DP

Oxford New York
Athens Auckland Bangkok Bogotá Buenos Aires
Calcutta Cape Town Chennai Dar es Salaam
Delhi Florence Hong Kong Istanbul Karachi
Kuala Lumpur Madras Madrid Melbourne
Mexico City Mumbai Nairobi Paris São Paulo
Singapore Taipei Tokyo Toronto

and associated companies in
Berlin Ibadan

Oxford is a trade mark of Oxford University Press

© Oxford University Press 1998

First published 1998
5 7 9 10 8 6 4

A CIP catalogue record for this book is available from the British Library

ISBN 0-19-910-451-4

Typeset by
Selwood Systems, Midsomer Norton

Printed in Spain

INTRODUCTION

Learning a new language is an exciting experience. It can also sometimes seem confusing and difficult. Feeling secure and at ease in using a bilingual dictionary is essential to the building of confidence in understanding and using a foreign language.

This dictionary has been specially written for students who are preparing for exams. We have paid particular attention to making the dictionary as user-friendly as possible. With the help of colour headwords, easy-to-follow signposts and simple example phrases, the right translation can quickly be found. The things students need to know about words in German are clearly shown. These include main parts of irregular verbs, noun plurals, and the case taken by prepositions.

We have adopted a simplified version of traditional bilingual entry layout. This means that the dictionary is ideal for learning basic dictionary skills, which can subsequently be built upon as the student moves towards larger, more complex dictionaries. We have done our best to make this dictionary a practical, easy-to-use tool for learning and understanding German.

Throughout the writing of this dictionary we have worked in close consultation with students, teachers, and examining boards. We gratefully acknowledge the examining boards AQA (NEAB and SEG), OCR, and EDEXCEL, who have read and commented on the dictionary text.

HOW A BILINGUAL DICTIONARY WORKS

A bilingual dictionary is a dictionary that has two languages in it. When you look up a word in one of the languages, the dictionary gives the translation for that word in the other language. The two languages in this dictionary are English and German. This dictionary is divided into two halves separated by red-edged pages in the middle. In the first half you look up German words to find out what they mean in English and in the second half you look up English words and find out how to say them in German.

The words you look up are in red and in the first half of the dictionary you will find **German** words in alphabetical order from a to z and in the second half **English** words from a to z. In a dictionary, these are called **headwords** because each one of them comes at the **head** of an **entry**. In the **entry** you can find **translations** but also other sorts of information which you can use to make sure you get the correct translation. The different sorts of information are typed in different ways to help you see clearly which is which. Here is a guide to the different things you will find in an entry:

headword	a word you look up in the dictionary
translation	translations are the only things that are in 'ordinary' type in an entry. They are always typed like this, and something that is typed in a different way can never be a translation
part of speech	tells you whether the word you are looking up is a verb, an adjective, or another part of speech. One headword can have more than one part of speech. **Book** can be a noun (*she was reading a book*) or a verb (*remember to book a table*)
(signpost)	helpful information to guide you to the right translation, to show you how to use the translation, or to give you essential information about either the headword or the translation
example	a phrase using the word you have looked up. If these appear in the entry you are looking at, you should read through them carefully to see if one of them is close to what you want to understand or say
der/die/das	gender: after a German noun to tell you whether it is masculine (*der*), feminine (*die*), or neuter (*das*)
(PL *die........*)	plural: shows the plural form of a German noun
●	indicates a phrasal verb such as *to carry on*
★	indicates an idiomatic expression such as *to look on the bright side*
✧	indicates an irregular German verb
SEP	indicates that a German verb is separable such as *ablenken* (PERF *lenkt ab*)
Δ	indicates a new spelling of a German word (see page xii)

You can think of a dictionary entry as being made out of different sorts of building bricks. In the entries below you can see how they fit together to help you to find what you need. The more you use your dictionary the more confident you will feel about finding your way around it.

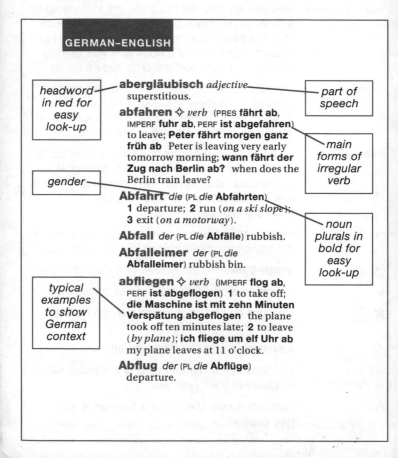

GERMAN–ENGLISH

headword in red for easy look-up

part of speech

abergläubisch *adjective* superstitious.

abfahren ✧ *verb* (PRES **fährt ab**, IMPERF **fuhr ab**, PERF **ist abgefahren**) to leave; **Peter fährt morgen ganz früh ab** Peter is leaving very early tomorrow morning; **wann fährt der Zug nach Berlin ab?** when does the Berlin train leave?

main forms of irregular verb

gender

Abfahrt *die* (PL *die* **Abfahrten**) 1 departure; 2 run (*on a ski slope*); 3 exit (*on a motorway*).

Abfall *der* (PL *die* **Abfälle**) rubbish.

Abfalleimer *der* (PL *die* **Abfalleimer**) rubbish bin.

noun plurals in bold for easy look-up

typical examples to show German context

abfliegen ✧ *verb* (IMPERF **flog ab**, PERF **ist abgeflogen**) 1 to take off; **die Maschine ist mit zehn Minuten Verspätung abgeflogen** the plane took off ten minutes late; 2 to leave (*by plane*); **ich fliege um elf Uhr ab** my plane leaves at 11 o'clock.

Abflug *der* (PL *die* **Abflüge**) departure.

ENGLISH–GERMAN

case governed by German preposition

based *adjective* **1 to be based on** basieren auf (+DAT); **the film is based on a true story** der Film basiert auf einer wahren Geschichte; **2 to be based in** wohnen in (+DAT); **he's based in Bristol** er wohnt in Bristol.

essential structures for expression in German

new spelling

basement *noun* Kellergeschoss △ *das* (PL *die* Kellergeschosse).

plural form

irregular verb

bear *noun* Bär *der* (PL *die* Bären). *verb* **1** ertragen ✧; **I can't bear the idea** ich kann den Gedanken nicht ertragen; **2 to bear something in mind** an etwas +(ACC) denken; **I'll bear it in mind** ich denke daran.

case of 'etwas' shown in translation of example

perfect formed with 'sein'

blush *verb* erröten (PERF *sein*).

bolt *noun* (*on a door*) Riegel *der* (PL *die* Riegel). *verb* **1** (*lock*) verriegeln; **2** (*gobble down*) runterschlingen ✧ SEP (*informal*).

gender

separable verb

informal word or expression

✧ IRREGULAR VERB: *See the verb tables in the centre of the dictionary*

A STEP-BY-STEP GUIDE TO FINDING THE TRANSLATION YOU NEED

Finding a word in the dictionary

You will be using this dictionary to do one of the following things:

1 look up a German word or phrase to find out what it means
2 look up an English word or phrase to find out how to say it in German.

1 Finding out what a German word means

First of all, look for it in the first half of the dictionary where you can find the German words and expressions with their English translations. You will see that the top of every page is marked with this red box.

No matter what you are using the dictionary to find out, you will always start by looking up a headword. Here are the German headwords **Ampel**, **Amsel**, **Amt**, **amtlich**, and **amüsant** with their entries.

> **Ampel** *die* (PL *die* **Ampeln**) traffic lights.
>
> **Amsel** *die* (PL *die* **Amseln**) blackbird.
>
> **Amt** *das* (PL *die* **Ämter**) **1** office; **2** exchange (*telephone*).
>
> **amtlich** *adjective* official.
>
> **amüsant** *adjective* amusing.

Suppose you want to find out what the German word **Bürste** means. You will look through the first half of your dictionary until you come to the bit which has all the German words beginning with **b**. You now need to find the page or pages containing German words beginning with **bu**, then **bur**, then **burs**, then **burst**. The dictionary helps you to do this by showing you the alphabetical range of words that you can find on the two pages you can see when you have the dictionary open.

For instance, if you look at pages 52-53, you will see **Brühwürfel** and **campen** at the top of the pages. If you look down the first column on page 53, you will find **Bürste** between **Büroklammer** and **bürsten**. You will know that all German nouns start with a capital letter. Notice that this makes no difference to the alphabetical order, nor do accented letters like **ü**.

Büro das (PL die **Büros**) office.

Büroklammer die (PL die **Büroklammern**) paper clip.

Bürste die (PL die **Bürsten**) brush.

bürsten verb (PERF **hat gebürstet**) to brush.

When you look at the entry for **Bürste** you will find the translation you are looking for: **Bürste** means **brush**.

Bürste die (PL die **Bürsten**) brush.

You can also see what the gender of **Bürste** is. Nouns in German are either masculine, feminine, or neuter. These are shown in the dictionary as der, die, or das. You can see that **Bürste** says die. **Bürste** is a feminine noun.

It often happens that a German word has more than one translation in English. If you look at the entry for **Tor** on page 235 you will see that it is divided into sections numbered **1** and **2**.

Tor das (PL die **Tore**) **1** gate; **2** goal.

The first translation is **gate** and the second is **goal**. You will need to look at both translations and see which fits best in the German sentence you are trying to understand, so:

Uli hat das Tor geöffnet means Uli opened the gate

BUT

Uli steht im Tor means Uli's in goal

In English, the plural of most nouns is formed by adding **-s**
(**book/books**). In German there are quite a lot of ways of forming
the plural and these are not always easy to recognize. To help
you with this, we show the plural form after every noun headword.

For instance, if you are trying to find out what the German word
Häuser means, you can see immediately that it is the plural of
Haus and so it means **houses**.

> **Haus** *das* (PL *die* **Häuser**) **1** house;
> **2 nach Hause** home; **zu Hause** at
> home.

German like English has certain words that you would use when
chatting with friends but not in more formal situations. German
words like this are marked (*informal*) like **flitzen** here:

> **flitzen** *verb* (*informal*) (PERF **ist**
> **geflitzt**) **1** to dash; **2** to whizz.

2 Finding an English word and how to say it in German

You can see that it is quite easy once you know how the
dictionary works to look up a German word and find out what it
means. Students usually find it harder to use the dictionary to find
out how to say something in German. This dictionary is written
specially to help you do this and to make it easy to find the right
way of saying things in German.

ENGLISH–GERMAN

Suppose you want to know how to say
garden in German. Look up the word in the
second part of the dictionary where the top
of every page is marked with this box
framed in red.

If you follow the same way of going through the alphabetical
order of the headwords as you did when you were looking up a
German word, you will find **garden** on page 417.

Now you can see that the German word for **garden** is **Garten**. But if you want to make a sentence using a noun like **Garten** you need to know its gender. The dictionary shows that it is *der* **Garten** so **in the garden** will be **im Garten**.

It is not always as easy as this to know which German word you need. Sometimes there will be more than one German word for the English word you are looking up. When the dictionary entry gives you more than just one translation, it is very important to take the time to read through the whole entry. If you look up **plug** the entry looks like this:

> **plug** *noun* **1** (*electrical*) Stecker *der* (PL *die* Stecker); **2** (*in a bath or sink*) Stöpsel *der* (PL *die* Stöpsel); **to pull out the plug** den Stöpsel herausziehen.

You can see that **1** tells you that the German word for an electrical plug is **Stecker** and **2** tells you that the word for a plug in a bath or a sink is **Stöpsel**.

Remember that information which is either in brackets or italics or both is there to help you, but it *will never be* the translation itself. Wherever there is more than one translation, depending on what meaning of the English word you are looking for, the dictionary will always help you to choose the right one.

Often it is not enough to find the translation of one word. In the case of more common words the dictionary also gives you a selection of phrases you will often want to use. In the entry for **hair** below you can find out how to use the translation **Haare** in different expressions:

> **hair** *noun* **1** Haare (*plural*); **to comb your hair** sich ←(DAT) die Haare kämmen; **to wash your hair** sich ←(DAT) die Haare waschen; **to have your hair cut** sich ←(DAT) die Haare schneiden lassen; **she's had her hair cut** sie hat sich die Haare schneiden lassen; **2 a hair** ein Haar.

THE GERMAN SPELLING REFORM

The German spelling reform was adopted by German-speaking countries in July 1996. It was agreed that both old and new spellings would be acceptable until 2005, by which time the new spellings should be included in all written texts.

The main changes to the spelling of German words include:
- After a short vowel, **ss** is used instead of **ß**. For example: **daß** becomes **dass**, **Schloß** becomes **Schloss**.
- Capital letters are now used more often, especially for adjectives used as nouns. For example: **recht haben** becomes **Recht haben**, **es tut mir leid** becomes **es tut mir Leid**.
- Words which were previously one word are now often spelt as two words. For example: **stehenlassen** becomes **stehen lassen**, **wieviel** becomes **wie viel**.

In the headword list of this dictionary you will find all the new spellings. They are marked Δ and there is a note at the foot of each page explaining that this symbol signals a new spelling. However, since you may come across old spellings if you are reading pre-reform German material, we have also given as headwords all the most frequent old spellings which could cause problems in looking up. These are cross-referred to the new spellings.

The same symbol Δ is used on the English-German side of the dictionary to signal new spellings in translations of English headwords.

A a

Aal *der* (PL *die* **Aale**) eel.

ab *preposition* ←(+DAT) from; **ab Montag** from Monday; **Kinder ab sechs Jahren** children from the age of six.
adverb 1 off; **der Henkel ist ab** the handle has come off; **ab ins Bett!** (*informal*) off (you go) to bed!; 2 **ab und zu** now and again.

abbiegen ✧ *verb* (IMPERF **bog ab**, PERF **ist abgebogen**) 1 to turn off; **nach rechts abbiegen** to turn off to the right; 2 **biegen Sie an der Ampel (nach) links ab** turn left at the lights.

Abbildung *die* (PL *die* **Abbildungen**) illustration.

abbrechen ✧ *verb* (PRES **bricht ab**, IMPERF **brach ab**, PERF **hat abgebrochen**) 1 to break off (*a branch, negotiations*); **Ruth brach ein paar Zweige ab** Ruth broke off a few branches; 2 to pull down (*a building*); 3 to cut short; **leider mussten wir unsere Ferien vorzeitig abbrechen** unfortunately we had to cut short our holidays; **er hat sein Studium aus finanziellen Gründen abgebrochen** he left university for financial reasons; 4 (PERF **ist abgebrochen**) **der Ast ist abgebrochen** the branch has broken off.

Abend *der* (PL *die* **Abende**) evening;

am Abend in the evening, **heute Abend** △ this evening, tonight; **gestern Abend** △ yesterday evening, last night; **wann esst ihr zu Abend?** when do you have dinner?

Abendessen *das* (PL *die* **Abendessen**) dinner (*in the evening*); **was gibt es zum Abendessen?** what are we having for dinner?

Abendbrot *das* evening meal.

Abendkurs *der* (PL *die* **Abendkurse**) evening course.

abends *adverb* in the evening.

Abenteuer *das* (PL *die* **Abenteuer**) adventure.

aber *conjunction* but; **es ist zwar nützlich, aber zu teuer** it's useful, but too expensive.
adverb really; **das ist aber sehr nett von dir** that's really nice of you; **du bist aber groß!** aren't you tall!; **aber ja!** but of course!; **jetzt ist aber Schluss!** that's it now!

abergläubisch *adjective* superstitious.

abfahren ✧ *verb* (PRES **fährt ab**, IMPERF **fuhr ab**, PERF **ist abgefahren**) to leave; **Peter fährt morgen ganz früh ab** Peter is leaving very early tomorrow morning; **wann fährt der Zug nach Berlin ab?** when does the Berlin train leave?

Abfahrt *die* (PL *die* **Abfahrten**) 1 departure; 2 run (*on a ski slope*); 3 exit (*on a motorway*).

Abfall *der* (PL *die* **Abfälle**) rubbish.

△ NEW SPELLING: *See pag*

Abfalleimer der (PL die
Abfalleimer) rubbish bin.

abfliegen ✧ verb (IMPERF **flog ab**,
PERF **ist abgeflogen**) **1** to take off;
**die Maschine ist mit zehn Minuten
Verspätung abgeflogen** the plane
took off ten minutes late; **2** to leave
(by plane); **ich fliege um elf Uhr ab**
my plane leaves at 11 o'clock.

Abflug der (PL die **Abflüge**)
departure.

abfragen verb (PERF **hat abgefragt**)
1 to test; **sie fragt ihn Vokabeln ab**
she's testing him on his vocabulary;
2 to call up (on a computer);
Adressen am Computer abfragen
to call up addresses on the
computer.

Abgase (plural noun) exhaust
fumes.

abgeben ✧ verb (PRES **gibt ab**,
IMPERF **gab ab**, PERF **hat abgegeben**)
1 to hand in (homework, an
application, lost property); **2** to pass
(in football); **den Ball abgeben** to
pass the ball; **3** **sich mit etwas
abgeben** to spend time on
something; **mit solchen Typen
würde ich mich nicht abgeben** I
wouldn't associate with blokes like
that; **4** **jemandem etwas abgeben**
to give someone something; **gib mir
ein Stück von deiner Schokolade
ab** give me a piece of your
chocolate; **5** **er wird einen guten
Lehrer abgeben** he'll make a good
teacher.

abgelegen adjective remote.

abgemacht adjective agreed.

Abgeordnete der/die (PL die
Abgeordneten) member of
parliament.

Abhang der (PL die **Abhänge**) slope.

abhängen¹ ✧ verb (IMPERF **hing ab**,
PERF **hat abgehangen**) **von
jemandem abhängen** to depend on
somebody; **von etwas abhängen** to
depend on something; **es hängt vom
Wetter ab, ob wir am Wochenende
nach Wales fahren** whether or not
we are going to Wales at the weekend
depends on the weather.

abhängen² verb (PERF **hat
abgehängt**) **1** to unhitch (a trailer);
2 to uncouple (a train carriage);
3 (informal) to shake off; **die
Einbrecher hängten die Polizei
schnell ab** the burglars soon shook
off the police.

abheben ✧ verb (IMPERF **hob ab**,
PERF **hat abgehoben**) **1** to lift off;
2 to withdraw (money); **3** to answer
the phone; **ich habe schon zweimal
angerufen, aber niemand hat
abgehoben** I've rung twice before,
but nobody answered.

abholen verb (PERF **hat abgeholt**)
1 to collect; **2** to pick up; **ich hole
dich am Bahnhof ab** I'll pick you up
at the station.

Abitur das (PL die **Abiture**) A levels
(German students usually take Abitur
at 19, sitting exams in four subjects,
which they have to pass to go on to
university); **sein Abitur machen** to
do your A levels.

Abiturient der (PL die **Abiturienten**)
A-level student.

✧ IRREGULAR VERB: See the verb table in the centre of the dictionary

Abiturientin *die* (PL *die* **Abiturientinnen**) A-level student.

Abkommen *das* (PL *die* **Abkommen**) agreement.

abkürzen *verb* (PERF **hat abgekürzt**) **1** to abbreviate; **wie kürzt man das Wort ab?** how do you abbreviate that word?; **2 den Weg abkürzen** to take a short cut.

Abkürzung *die* (PL *die* **Abkürzungen**) **1** abbreviation; **die Abkürzung für Europäische Union ist EU** the abbreviation for European Union is EU; **2** short cut.

abladen ✧ *verb* (PRES **lädt ab**, IMPERF **lud ab**, PERF **hat abgeladen**) to unload.

ablaufen ✧ *verb* (PRES **läuft ab**, IMPERF **lief ab**, PERF **ist abgelaufen**) **1** to expire (*passport, contract*); **2** to drain off; **das Badewasser ablaufen lassen** to let the bathwater out; **3** to go off; **wie ist die Besprechung abgelaufen?** how did the meeting go?

ablegen *verb* (PERF **hat abgelegt**) **1** to take off; **2 abgelegte Kleidung** cast-offs.

ablehnen *verb* (PERF **hat abgelehnt**) **1** to turn down (*a position, money, an invitation*); **2** to reject (*an applicant, a suggestion*).

ablenken *verb* (PERF **hat abgelenkt**) **1** to distract; **jemanden von seiner Arbeit ablenken** to distract somebody from their work; **2 jemanden von seinen Sorgen ablenken** to take somebody's mind off their worries; **3** to divert (*attention, suspicion*); **vom Thema ablenken** to change the subject.

abliefern *verb* (PERF **hat abgeliefert**) **1** to deliver; **2** to hand in (*an essay, a form, lost property*); **3** to drop off; **die Kinder abliefern** to drop the children off.

abmachen *verb* (PERF **hat abgemacht**) **1** to take off; **kannst du den Deckel abmachen?** can you take off the lid?; **2** to agree; **wir müssen noch einen Termin für unser nächstes Treffen abmachen** we still have to agree on a date for our next meeting; **abgemacht!** agreed!; **3** to sort out; **das müsst ihr untereinander abmachen** you'll have to sort that out amongst yourselves.

Abmachung *die* (PL *die* **Abmachungen**) agreement.

abnehmen ✧ *verb* (PRES **nimmt ab**, IMPERF **nahm ab**, PERF **hat abgenommen**) **1** to take off (*remove*); **2 kann ich dir etwas abnehmen?** (*carry*) can I take something (for you)?; (*help*) can I do anything for you?; **3 jemandem etwas abnehmen** to take something off somebody; **sie nehmen einem schnell zwanzig Mark ab** they'll soon take 20 marks off you; **4** to buy; **5** to decrease (*in number*); **6** to lose weight; **er hat schon vier Kilo abgenommen** he's already lost four kilos; **7** to answer the phone; **8 das nehme ich dir nicht ab** (*informal*) I don't buy that.

Abonnement *das* (PL *die* **Abonnements**) subscription.

△ NEW SPELLING: *See pa*

abonnieren *verb* (PERF **hat abonniert**) to subscribe to.

abraten ♢ *verb* (PRES **rät ab**, IMPERF **riet ab**, PERF **hat abgeraten**) **jemandem von etwas abraten** to advise somebody against something.

abräumen *verb* (PERF **hat abgeräumt**) to clear away.

abreagieren *verb* (PERF **hat abreagiert**) **1 seine Wut an jemandem abreagieren** to take your anger out on somebody; **2 sich abreagieren** to calm down.

Abreise *die* departure.

abreisen *verb* (PERF **ist abgereist**) to leave.

abreißen ♢ *verb* (IMPERF **riss ab** △, PERF **hat abgerissen**) **1** to tear down (*a poster, notice*); **2** (PERF **ist abgerissen**) to come off (*a button, for example*).

Absage *die* (PL *die* **Absagen**) refusal.

absagen *verb* (PERF **hat abgesagt**) **1** to cancel; **2 eine Einladung absagen** to turn down an invitation.

Absatz *der* (PL *die* **Absätze**) **1** heel (*of a shoe*); **2** paragraph.

abschaffen *verb* (PERF **hat abgeschafft**) **1** to abolish (*a regulation, capital punishment*); **2** to get rid of; **wir haben unseren Hund abgeschafft** we got rid of our dog.

abscheulich *adjective* horrible.

abschicken *verb* (PERF **hat abgeschickt**) to send off.

Abschied *der* (PL *die* **Abschiede**) **1** parting; **2** farewell; **3 Abschied nehmen** to say goodbye.

Abschleppdienst *der* breakdown service.

abschleppen *verb* (PERF **hat abgeschleppt**) **1** to tow away; **2 sich mit den Koffern abschleppen** (*informal*) to struggle along with the suitcases; **3 jemanden abschleppen** (*informal*) to pick somebody up.

abschließen ♢ *verb* (IMPERF **schloss ab** △, PERF **hat abgeschlossen**) to lock.

Abschlussprüfung △ *die* (PL *die* **Abschlussprüfungen**) final exam.

abschneiden ♢ *verb* (IMPERF **schnitt ab**, PERF **hat abgeschnitten**) **1** to cut off; **ich schneide dir eine Scheibe Brot ab** I'll cut you a slice of bread; **2 gut/schlecht abschneiden** to do well/badly.

abschrecken *verb* (PERF **hat abgeschreckt**) to deter.

abschreiben ♢ *verb* (IMPERF **schrieb ab**, PERF **hat abgeschrieben**) to copy.

abseits *adverb* **1** far away; **etwas abseits** a little way away; **2** offside (*in soccer*).

Absender *der* (PL *die* **Absender**) sender.

absetzen *verb* (PERF **hat abgesetzt**) **1** to take off (*your hat, glasses*); **2** to put down (*a bag, suitcase*); **3** to drop off; **ich setze euch am Bahnhof ab** I'll drop you off at the station; **4 die**

♢ IRREGULAR VERB: *See the verb table in the centre of the dictionary*

Pille absetzen to stop taking the pill.

Absicht die (PL die **Absichten**) intention.

absichtlich adverb intentionally.

absolut adjective absolute. adverb absolutely; **das ist absolut unmöglich** that's absolutely impossible.

abspülen verb (PERF **hat abgespült**) 1 to rinse, to rinse off; 2 to do the washing up.

Abstand der (PL die **Abstände**) 1 distance; **in zwanzig Meter Abstand** at a distance of 20 metres; **Abstand halten** to keep your distance; 2 interval.

abstauben verb (PERF **hat abgestaubt**) to dust.

abstellen verb (PERF **hat abgestellt**) 1 to turn off (the radio, a tap); 2 to put down (a suitcase, the shopping); 3 to park (the car).

Abstimmung die (PL die **Abstimmungen**) vote.

abstreiten ◇ verb (IMPERF **stritt ab**, PERF **hat abgestritten**) to deny.

abstürzen verb (PERF **ist abgestürzt**) 1 to fall; 2 to crash (a plane).

Abteil das (PL die **Abteile**) compartment.

Abteilung die (PL die **Abteilungen**) department.

Abtreibung die (PL die **Abtreibungen**) abortion.

abtrocknen verb (PERF **hat abgetrocknet**) 1 to dry up; 2 **sich abtrocknen** to dry yourself.

abwägen verb (IMPERF **wog ab**, PERF **hat abgewogen**) to weigh up.

abwärts adverb down.

Abwasch der washing-up.

abwaschen ◇ verb (PRES **wäscht ab**, IMPERF **wusch ab**, PERF **hat abgewaschen**) 1 to wash up (the dishes); 2 to wash off (dirt, marks).

Abwasser das (PL die **Abwässer**) sewage.

Abwechslung die (PL die **Abwechslungen**) change; **zur Abwechslung** for a change.

abwerten verb (PERF **hat abgewertet**) to devalue.

abwertend adjective pejorative.

abwesend adjective absent.

Abwesenheit die absence.

abwischen verb (PERF **hat abgewischt**) to wipe.

abzählen verb (PERF **hat abgezählt**) to count.

Abzeichen das (PL die **Abzeichen**) badge.

abziehen ◇ verb (IMPERF **zog ab**, PERF **hat abgezogen**) 1 to take off (a sheet, backing); **die Betten abziehen** to strip the beds; 2 to take out (a key); 3 to deduct, to take away; 4 to withdraw (troops); 5 (PERF **ist abgezogen**) to escape (steam or smoke, for example); 6 (PERF **ist abgezogen**) sie sind

△ NEW SPELLING: See pag

gleich nach dem Essen abgezogen (*informal*) they pushed off straight after the meal.

abzielen *verb* (PERF **hat abgezielt**) **etwas zielt auf etwas ab** something is aimed at something.

ach *exclamation* oh!

Achsel *die* (PL *die* **Achseln**) shoulder.

acht *number* eight; **um acht (Uhr)** at eight (o'clock); **um halb acht** at half past seven.

Acht[1] *die* (PL *die* **Achten**) eight; **eine Acht schreiben** to write an eight.

Acht[2] *die* **1 Acht geben** △ to pay attention; **er sollte in der Schule besser Acht geben** he should pay more attention at school; **2 auf etwas/jemanden Acht geben** to look after something/somebody; **3 gib Acht!** watch out!; **4 sich in Acht nehmen** △ to be careful; **5 etwas außer Acht lassen** △ to disregard something.

Achtel *das* (PL *die* **Achtel**) eighth.

achten *verb* (PERF **hat geachtet**) **1** to respect (*a person, an opinion*); **2 auf etwas achten** to pay attention to something; **3 auf jemanden achten** to look after somebody; **4 achte nicht darauf!** don't take any notice of it!

achter, achte, achtes *adjective* eighth; **jede achte Kiste** every eighth crate; **mein achter Geburtstag** my eighth birthday; **sie ging als Achte durchs Ziel** she finished eighth.

Achterbahn *die* (PL *die* **Achterbahnen**) roller coaster.

achtgeben SEE **Acht**[2].

achthundert *number* eight hundred.

achtmal *adverb* eight times.

Achtung *die* **1** respect; **Achtung vor jemandem haben** to have respect for somebody; **2 Achtung!** look out!; **Achtung, fertig, los!** on your marks, get set, go!; **'Achtung Stufe'** 'mind the step'.

achtzehn *number* eighteen.

achtzig *number* eighty.

Acker *der* (PL *die* **Äcker**) field.

addieren *verb* (PERF **hat addiert**) to add.

Ader *die* (PL *die* **Adern**) vein.

Adjektiv *das* (PL *die* **Adjektive**) adjective.

Adler *der* (PL *die* **Adler**) eagle.

adoptieren *verb* (PERF **hat adoptiert**) to adopt.

Adoption *die* (PL *die* **Adoptionen**) adoption.

Adoptiveltern *plural noun* adoptive parents.

Adoptivkind *das* (PL *die* **Adoptivkinder**) adopted child.

Adresse *die* (PL *die* **Adressen**) address.

adressieren *verb* (PERF **hat adressiert**) to address; **an wen soll ich den Brief adressieren?** who shall I address the letter to?

Advent *der* Advent.

Adventskalender *der* (PL *die* **Adventskalender**) Advent calendar.

Adventskranz *der* (PL *die* **Adventskränze**) Advent wreath.

Adverb *das* (PL *die* **Adverbien**) adverb.

Aerobic *das* aerobics.

Affe *der* (PL *die* **Affen**) 1 monkey; 2 ape.

Afrika *das* Africa; **aus Afrika** from Africa; **nach Afrika** to Africa.

Afrikaner *der* (PL *die* **Afrikaner**) African.

Afrikanerin *die* (PL *die* **Afrikanerinnen**) African.

afrikanisch *adjective* African.

Agentur *die* (PL *die* **Agenturen**) agency.

aggressiv *adjective* aggressive.

ähneln *verb* (PERF **hat geähnelt**) 1 to resemble; **er ähnelt seinem Vater sehr** he's very like his father; 2 **sich ähneln** to be alike.

ahnen *verb* (PERF **hat geahnt**) 1 to know; **das konnte ich wirklich nicht ahnen** I had no way of knowing that; **wer soll denn ahnen, dass ...?** who would know that ...?; 2 to suspect; **so etwas habe ich doch schon geahnt** I did suspect something like that.

ähnlich *adjective* 1 similar; 2 **jemandem ähnlich sein** to be like somebody; **jemandem ähnlich sehen** to look like somebody;

0 **ähnlich wie** like; 4 **das sieht dir ähnlich!** (*informal*) that's just like you!

Ähnlichkeit *die* (PL *die* **Ähnlichkeiten**) similarity.

Ahnung *die* 1 idea; **hast du eine Ahnung, wie er heißt?** have you got any idea what he's called?; 2 **keine Ahnung!** no idea!; **er hat von Mode absolut keine Ahnung** he doesn't know a thing about fashion; 3 premonition.

ahnungslos *adjective* unsuspecting.

Ahorn *der* (PL *die* **Ahorne**) maple.

Aids *das* Aids.

Akademiker *der* (PL *die* **Akademiker**) university graduate.

Akademikerin *die* (PL *die* **Akademikerinnen**) university graduate.

akademisch *adjective* academic.

Akkusativ *der* (PL *die* **Akkusative**) accusative.

Akne *die* acne.

Akte *die* (PL *die* **Akten**) file.

Aktentasche *die* (PL *die* **Aktentaschen**) briefcase.

Aktion *die* (PL *die* **Aktionen**) 1 action; **in Aktion treten** to go into action; 2 campaign.

aktiv *adjective* active.

Aktiv *das* active.

aktuell *adjective* 1 topical; **ein aktuelles Thema** a topical issue;

△ NEW SPELLING: See page

2 nicht mehr aktuell no longer relevant; **3** current; **eine aktuelle Sendung** a current-affairs programme.

Akzent *der* (PL *die* **Akzente**)
1 accent; **mit starkem Akzent sprechen** to speak with a strong accent; **2** accent (*on a letter*); **3** stress; **den Akzent auf etwas legen** to stress something.

albern *adjective* silly.
adverb in a silly way.

Album *das* (PL *die* **Alben**) album.

Algebra *die* algebra.

Alkohol *der* alcohol.

alkoholfrei *adjective* non-alcoholic.

Alkoholiker *der* (PL *die* **Alkoholiker**) alcoholic.

Alkoholikerin *die* (PL *die* **Alkoholikerinnen**) alcoholic.

alkoholisch *adjective* alcoholic.

All *das* space; **einen Satelliten ins All schicken** to send a satellite into space.

alle SEE **aller**.

Allee *die* (PL *die* **Alleen**) avenue.

allein *adjective, adverb* **1** alone; **sie waren allein im Zimmer** they were alone in the room; **jemanden allein lassen** to leave somebody alone; **2** on your own; **sie hat das ganz allein gezeichnet** she drew it all on her own; **3 von allein** by yourself, by itself (*automatically*); **4 allein stehend** ∆ single; **5 eine allein**

erziehende Mutter ∆ a single mother; **der/die allein Erziehende** ∆ single parent; **6 nicht allein** not only; **7 allein der Gedanke** the mere thought.

alleinerziehend, alleinstehend SEE **allein**.

aller, alle, alles *pronoun* **1** all; **alle meine Freunde** all my friends; **alles Geld** all the money; **alle miteinander** all together; **2 alle Jungen in der Schule** all the boys in the school; **alle Bewohner der Stadt sind dagegen** all the people of the town are against it; **alles Gute!** all the best!; **Getränke aller Art** all kinds of drinks; **3 alle** (*plural*) all; **alle waren da** they were all there; **wir alle** we all, all of us; **wir haben alle gesehen** we saw all of them; **4 ohne allen Grund** without any reason; **5 alle beide** both of them; **6** every; **alle Tage** every day; **alle fünf Minuten** every five minutes; **7 alles** everything, everybody (*people*).
adjective **alle sein** (*informal*) to be all gone.

allerbester, allerbeste, allerbestes *adjective* **1** very best; **2 am allerbesten** best of all.

allerdings *adverb* **1** though; **das Essen ist gut, allerdings ziemlich teuer** the food's good, though rather expensive; **2** certainly (*yes*); **'tut das weh?' – 'allerdings!'** 'does it hurt?' – 'it certainly does!'.

Allergie *die* (PL *die* **Allergien**) allergy.

allergisch *adjective* allergic.

✧ IRREGULAR VERB: *See the verb table in the centre of the dictionary*

Allerheiligen das All Saints' Day.

allerlei *adjective* all sorts of; **allerlei Ausreden** all sorts of excuses.

allerletzter, allerletzte, allerletztes *adjective* very last.

alles SEE **aller**.

allgemein *adjective* 1 general; 2 **im Allgemeinen** ∆ in general.
adverb 1 generally; 2 **es ist allgemein bekannt, dass** ... it is common knowledge that ...

allmählich *adjective* gradual.
adverb gradually; **wir sollten allmählich gehen** it's time we got going.

alltäglich *adjective* everyday (*event, sight*).

Alltag *der* 1 daily routine; 2 weekday.

alltags *adverb* on weekdays.

Alpen *plural noun* **die Alpen** the Alps.

Alphabet *das* (PL *die* **Alphabete**) alphabet.

alphabetisch *adjective* alphabetical.

Alptraum *der* (PL *die* **Alpträume**) nightmare.

als *conjunction* 1 when; **als meine Freundin hier war** when my friend was here; **erst als** only when; 2 than (*as a comparison*); **er ist jünger als sie** he's younger than her; 3 **lieber ... als ...** rather ... than ...; **ich ginge lieber ins Kino als zum Essen** I'd rather go to the cinema than for a meal; 4 as; **als Frau kann ich das verstehen** as a woman, I can sympathize; **gerade als ich gehen wollte** just as I was about to leave; 5 **als ob** as if; **als ob ich das nicht wüsste!** as if I didn't know that!

also *adverb, conjunction* 1 so; **ich konnte ihn telefonisch nicht erreichen, also habe ich ihm ein Fax geschickt** I couldn't get through to him on the phone, so I sent him a fax; 2 then; **also kommst du mit?** you're coming too, then?; **also gut** all right then; 3 well; **also, wie gesagt** well, as I said before; 4 **na also!** there you are!

alt *adjective* 1 old; **wie alt bist du?** how old are you?; **alt werden** to grow old; 2 **alles beim Alten lassen** to leave everything as it was.

Altar *der* (PL *die* **Altäre**) altar.

Alter *das* (PL *die* **Alter**) 1 age; **in deinem Alter** at your age; **im Alter von zwanzig** at the age of twenty; 2 old age; **im Alter** in old age.

älter *adjective* 1 older; **mein Rad ist älter als deins** my bike is older than yours; 2 elder; **mein älterer Bruder** my elder brother; 3 elderly.

altern *verb* (PERF **ist gealtert**) to age.

Alternative *die* (PL *die* **Alternativen**) alternative.

Altersgrenze *die* (PL *die* **Altersgrenzen**) age limit.

Altersheim *das* (PL *die* **Altersheime**) old people's home.

∆ NEW SPELLING: *See page*

ältester, älteste, ältestes
adjective 1 oldest; 2 eldest; **der älteste Sohn** the eldest son.

Altglas *das* used glass.

Altglascontainer *der* (PL *die* **Altglascontainer**) bottle bank.

altmodisch *adjective* old-fashioned.

Altpapier *das* waste paper.

Altstadt *die* (PL *die* **Altstädte**) old town.

Alufolie *die* tin foil.

Aluminium *das* aluminium.

am = **an dem**; 1 **am Freitag** on Friday; 2 **am besten** the best; 3 **am teuersten** (the) most expensive; 4 **am höchsten** the highest; 5 **am Abend** in the evening.

Ameise *die* (PL *die* **Ameisen**) ant.

Amerika *das* America.

Amerikaner *der* (PL *die* **Amerikaner**) American.

Amerikanerin *die* (PL *die* **Amerikanerinnen**) American.

amerikanisch *adjective* American.

Ampel *die* (PL *die* **Ampeln**) traffic lights.

Amsel *die* (PL *die* **Amseln**) blackbird.

Amt *das* (PL *die* **Ämter**) 1 office; 2 exchange (*telephone*).

amtlich *adjective* official.

amüsant *adjective* amusing.

amüsieren *verb* (PERF **hat amüsiert**) 1 to amuse; 2 **sich amüsieren** to enjoy oneself;

amüsier dich gut! enjoy yourself!; 3 **sich über etwas amüsieren** to find something funny.

an *preposition* ←(+DAT *or* +ACC) (*the dative is used when talking about position; the accusative shows movement or a change of place*) 1 at; **an der Spitze** at the top; **sich an den Tisch setzen** to sit down at the table; **er arbeitet an der Schule** he works at the school; 2 on (*attached to, when talking about time*); **das Bild hängt an der Wand** the picture is on the wall; **an dem Tag** on that day; **ich habe am fünften März Geburtstag** my birthday is on the fifth of March; 3 to; **einen Brief an jemanden schicken** to send a letter to somebody; 4 **an einer Krankheit sterben** to die of a disease; 5 **an jemanden denken** to think of somebody; 6 **sich an etwas erinnern** to remember something; 7 **an (und für) sich** actually; **an sich ist das kein Problem** actually, it's no problem; 8 **es liegt an dir, jetzt etwas zu unternehmen** it's up to you to do something now.
adverb 1 on; **das Licht ist an** the light's on; 2 **ohne etwas an** with nothing on; 3 **an die dreißig Mark** about thirty marks; 4 **von heute an** from today.

Ananas *die* (PL *die* **Ananas**) pineapple.

anbieten ✧ *verb* (IMPERF **bot an**, PERF **hat angeboten**) to offer; **Anna bot mir an, mich nach Hause zu bringen** Anna offered to take me home.

✧ IRREGULAR VERB: *See the verb table in the centre of the dictionary*

Anblick *der* (PL die Anblicke) sight.

anbrennen ✧ *verb* (IMPERF **brannte an**, PERF **ist angebrannt**) to burn; **das Essen ist angebrannt** the food's burnt.

Andenken *das* (PL die Andenken) **1** souvenir; **2 zum Andenken an unsere Ferien** to remind us of our holiday.

anderer, andere, anderes *adjective* **1** other; **ich nehme das andere T-Shirt** I'll have the other T-shirt; **2** different; **3 ein anderer/eine andere/ein anderes** another; **ein anderes Mal** another time. *pronoun* **1 der/die/das andere** the other one; **nicht dieses Buch, sondern das andere** not that book, but the other one; **die anderen** the others; **die anderen kommen später** the others are coming later; **2 andere** other ones (*things, toys, etc.*); **3 ein anderer/eine andere/ein anderes** a different one (*thing*); someone else (*person*); **4 kein anderer** no one else; **5 unter anderem** among other things; **6 etwas anderes** something else; **7 alles andere** everything else.

andererseits *adverb* on the other hand.

andermal *adverb* **ein andermal** another time.

ändern *verb* (PERF **hat geändert**) **1** to change; **2** to alter (*a garment*); **3 sich ändern** to change; **sie hat sich sehr geändert** she's changed a lot.

anders *adverb* **1** differently;

2 anders aussehen to look different; **3 niemand anders** nobody else; **jemand anders** somebody else; **4 anders als** different from; **du bist ganz anders als ich** you're quite different from me; **5 irgendwo anders** somewhere else.

anderthalb *number* one and a half.

Anerkennung *die* **1** appreciation; **2** recognition (*of a king, state*).

Anfall *der* (PL die Anfälle) fit.

Anfang *der* (PL die Anfänge) **1** beginning, start; **am Anfang** at the beginning; **von Anfang an** from the start; **2 zu Anfang** at first.

anfangen ✧ *verb* (PRES **fängt an**, IMPERF **fing an**, PERF **hat angefangen**) **1** to begin, to start; **die Schule fängt um acht an** school starts at eight; **mit etwas anfangen** to start (on) something; **2 bei einer Firma anfangen** to start working for a firm; **3 was soll ich damit anfangen?** what am I supposed to do with that?; **4 damit kann ich nichts anfangen** that's no good to me (*it's no use*); it doesn't mean anything to me (*I don't understand it*).

Anfänger *der* (PL die Anfänger) beginner.

Anfängerin *die* (PL die Anfängerinnen) beginner.

anfassen *verb* (PERF **hat angefasst** ∆) **1** to touch; **2** to tackle (*a problem, a task*); **3** to treat (*a person*); **4 mit anfassen** to lend a

∆ NEW SPELLING: See page

hand; **5 sich anfassen** to feel; **es fasst sich weich an** it feels soft; **6 jemanden anfassen** to take somebody's hand; **sie hat ihre Mutter angefasst** she took her mother's hand; **fasst euch an!** hold hands!

anfragen *verb* (PERF **hat angefragt**) to enquire, to ask.

anfreunden *verb* (PERF **hat sich angefreundet**) **1 sich anfreunden** to make friends; **sie freundet sich mit allen möglichen Leuten an** she makes friends with all sorts of people; **2 sich anfreunden** to become friends; **wir haben uns angefreundet** we've become friends.

Anführungszeichen *plural noun* inverted commas.

Angabe *die* (PL *die* **Angaben**) **1** piece of information; **2** serve (*in tennis*); **3** showing off; **das ist nur Angabe** he is/she is/they are only showing off.

angeben ✧ *verb* (PRES **gibt an**, IMPERF **gab an**, PERF **hat angegeben**) **1** to give (*your name, a reason*); **2** to show off; **3** to indicate (*on a map*); **4** to serve (*in tennis*).

Angeber *der* (PL *die* **Angeber**) show-off.

Angeberin *die* (PL *die* **Angeberinnen**) show-off.

Angebot *das* (PL *die* **Angebote**) offer.

angehen ✧ *verb* (IMPERF **ging an**, PERF **ist angegangen**) **1** to come on (*a radio, heating, a light*); **2** to

concern; **das geht auch dich etwas an** it concerns you too; **das geht dich nichts an** it's none of your business; **3** (PERF **hat angegangen**) to tackle (*problems, difficulty, work*).

Angehörige *der/die* (PL *die* **Angehörigen**) relative.

Angel *die* (PL *die* **Angeln**) fishing rod.

Angelegenheit *die* (PL *die* **Angelegenheiten**) **1** matter; **2** business; **das ist meine Angelegenheit** that's my business.

angeln *verb* (PERF **hat geangelt**) **1** to fish; **angeln gehen** to go fishing; **2** to catch (*a fish*).

Angelrute *die* (PL *die* **Angelruten**) fishing rod.

angenehm *adjective* pleasant. *exclamation* pleased to meet you! (*when introduced to somebody*).

Angestellte *der/die* (PL *die* **Angestellten**) employee.

angewiesen *adjective* dependent; **auf etwas angewiesen sein** to be dependent on something; **auf jemanden angewiesen sein** to be dependent on somebody.

angewöhnen *verb* (PERF **hat angewöhnt**) **1 jemandem etwas angewöhnen** to get somebody used to something; **2 sich etwas angewöhnen** to get into the habit of doing something; **ich habe es mir angewöhnt, früh aufzustehen** I've got into the habit of getting up early.

Angewohnheit *die* (PL *die* **Angewohnheiten**) habit.

✧ IRREGULAR VERB: *See the verb table in the centre of the dictionary*

angreifen ⬦ *verb* (IMPERF **griff an**,
PERF **hat angegriffen**) **1** to attack;
2 to affect (*your health, voice*).

Angriff *der* (PL *die* **Angriffe**) attack.

Angst *die* (PL *die* **Ängste**) **1** fear;
2 Angst haben to be afraid; **vor
jemandem Angst haben** to be
afraid of somebody; **mir ist Angst**
I'm afraid; **3 jemandem Angst
machen** to frighten somebody;
4 Angst vor einer Prüfung haben
to be worried about an exam; **Angst
um jemanden haben** to be worried
about somebody.

ängstlich *adjective* **1** nervous;
2 frightened; **3** anxious.

anhaben ⬦ *verb* (*informal*) (PRES
hat an, IMPERF **hatte an**, PERF **hat
angehabt**) to have on; **sie hat heute
das neue Kleid an** she's got her new
dress on today.

anhalten ⬦ *verb* (PRES **hält an**,
IMPERF **hielt an**, PERF **hat angehalten**)
1 to stop; **2 den Atem anhalten** to
hold your breath; **3** to last; **das
schöne Wetter wird nicht lange
anhalten** the nice weather won't last
long; **4 jemanden zur Arbeit
anhalten** to urge somebody to work.

Anhalter *der* (PL *die* **Anhalter**)
hitchhiker; **per Anhalter fahren** to
hitchhike.

Anhalterin *die* (PL *die*
Anhalterinnen) hitchhiker.

Anhang *der* (PL *die* **Anhänge**)
appendix.

Anhänger *der* (PL *die* **Anhänger**)
1 supporter; **2** trailer; **3** label (*on a*

anhängen); **4** pendant, **5** loop (*for
hanging up*).

Anhängerin *die* (PL *die*
Anhängerinnen) supporter.

anhören *verb* (PERF **hat angehört**)
1 to listen to (*music, a CD*); **sich
etwas anhören** to listen to
something; **ich kann ihn mir nicht
länger anhören** I can't listen to him
any longer; **2 sich anhören** to
sound; **sich gut anhören** to sound
good; **3 jemandem etwas anhören**
to hear something in somebody's
voice; **man hörte ihr die
Verzweiflung an** you could hear the
despair in her voice.

anklagen *verb* (PERF **hat angeklagt**)
to accuse.

Ankleidekabine *die* (PL *die*
Ankleidekabinen) changing cubicle.

ankommen ⬦ *verb* (IMPERF **kam an**,
PERF **ist angekommen**) **1** to arrive;
gut ankommen to arrive safely;
2 (bei jemandem) gut ankommen
(*informal*) to go down well (with
somebody); **3 ankommen auf** to
depend on; **es kommt ganz darauf
an** it all depends; **4 es drauf
ankommen lassen** (*informal*) to
take a chance; **5 auf ein paar
Minuten kommt es nicht an** a few
minutes don't matter.

ankündigen *verb* (PERF **hat
angekündigt**) to announce.

Ankunft *die* (PL *die* **Ankünfte**)
arrival.

Ankunftstafel *die* (PL *die*
Ankunftstafeln) arrivals board.

△ NEW SPELLING: *See page*

Ankunftszeit die (PL die Ankunftszeiten) time of arrival.

Anlage die (PL die Anlagen) 1 gardens; 2 investment; **das Haus ist eine gute Anlage** the house is a good investment; 3 plant (*industrial, for recycling, for example*); 4 enclosure; **als Anlage** enclosed; 5 system (*music, loudspeakers, etc.*); 6 installation (*military*).

Anlass Δ der (PL die Anlässe) 1 cause; **der Anlass ihres Streits** the cause of their row; **Anlass zu etwas geben** to give cause for something; 2 occasion; **ein festlicher Anlass** a festive occasion; **aus Anlass ihres Geburtstags** on the occasion of her birthday.

Anleitung die (PL die Anleitungen) instructions.

anmachen *verb* (PERF hat angemacht) 1 to turn on (*the light, radio, TV*); 2 to light (*a fire*); 3 to dress (*salad*); 4 (*informal*) to chat up (*a person*).

Anmeldeformular das (PL die Anmeldeformulare) registration form.

anmelden *verb* (PERF hat angemeldet) 1 to register (*a car, change of address*); 2 **jemanden anmelden** to enrol somebody; 3 **jemanden anmelden** to make an appointment for somebody; **sind Sie angemeldet?** do you have an appointment?; 4 **ein Gespräch anmelden** to book a call (*on the phone*); 5 **sich anmelden** to say that you're coming; 6 **sich anmelden** to register your new address (*in Germany a change of address has to be registered at the 'Einwohnermeldeamt'*); **sich polizeilich anmelden** to register with the police; 7 **sich anmelden** to make an appointment; **sich beim Arzt anmelden** to make an appointment with the doctor; 8 **sich anmelden** to enrol; **sich zu einem Abendkurs anmelden** to enrol for an evening course.

Anmeldung die (PL die Anmeldungen) 1 registration; 2 appointment.

annehmen ✧ *verb* (PRES **nimmt an**, IMPERF **nahm an**, PERF **hat angenommen**) 1 to accept (*an invitation, help, a verdict*); 2 to take (*a call, name*); 3 to adopt (*a child, habit*); 4 to assume; **angenommen, dass** ... assuming that ...; 5 to suppose.

annehmbar *adjective* acceptable.

Annonce die (PL die Annoncen) (small) ad.

anordnen *verb* (PERF hat angeordnet) 1 to arrange; 2 to order.

anpassen *verb* (PERF hat sich angepasst Δ) **sich anpassen** to adapt.

anpassungsfähig *adjective* adaptable.

anprobieren *verb* (PERF hat anprobiert) to try on.

✧ IRREGULAR VERB: *See the verb table in the centre of the dictionary*

Anruf der (PL die Anrufe) (phone) call.

Anrufbeantworter der (PL die Anrufbeantworter) answering machine.

anrufen ✧ verb (IMPERF **rief an**, PERF **hat angerufen**) 1 to ring, to phone; **ich rufe schnell mal meine Mutter an** I'll just quickly ring my mother; 2 to call to (a passer-by).

ans = **an das**; **ans Telefon gehen** to answer the phone.

Ansage die (PL die Ansagen) announcement.

Ansager der (PL die Ansager) announcer.

Ansagerin die (PL die Ansagerinnen) announcer.

anschalten verb (PERF **hat angeschaltet**) to switch on.

anschauen verb (PERF **hat angeschaut**) 1 to look at; 2 **sich etwas anschauen** to look at something, to watch something (on TV); **sie schauten sich den neuen Film an** they saw the new film.

anscheinend adverb apparently.

Anschlag der (PL die Anschläge) 1 notice; 2 attack; **ein Anschlag auf den Präsidenten** an attack on the president.

Anschlagbrett das (PL die Anschlagbretter) notice board.

anschlagen ✧ verb (PRES **schlägt an**, IMPERF **schlug an**, PERF **hat angeschlagen**) 1 to put up (a notice, an announcement); 2 to chip.

anschließen ✧ verb (IMPERF **schloss an** △, PERF **hat angeschlossen**) 1 to connect; 2 **sich an etwas anschließen** to follow something; **an den Vortrag schließt sich eine Diskussion an** the talk will be followed by a discussion; 3 **sich jemandem anschließen** to join somebody; **sich einer Gruppe anschließen** to join a group.

anschließend adverb 1 afterwards; 2 **anschließend an das Essen** after the meal.

Anschluss △ der (PL die Anschlüsse) 1 connection; 2 **Anschluss finden** to make friends; 3 **den Anschluss verlieren** to lose contact; 4 **im Anschluss an** after.

anschnallen verb (PERF **hat sich angeschnallt**) **sich anschnallen** to fasten your seat belt.

Anschrift die (PL die Anschriften) address.

Anschuldigung die (PL die Anschuldigungen) accusation.

ansehen ✧ verb (PRES **sieht an**, IMPERF **sah an**, PERF **hat angesehen**) 1 to look at; **sie sah mich nicht an** she didn't look at me; 2 **sich etwas ansehen** to look at something; (on TV) to watch something; **sich einen Film ansehen** to see a film; 3 **sich eine Stadt ansehen** to look round a town; 4 to regard; **ich sehe ihn als meinen Freund an** I regard him as a friend.

△ NEW SPELLING: See page xii

Ansehen *das* **1** respect;
2 reputation.

Ansicht *die* (PL *die* **Ansichten**) view;
meiner Ansicht nach in my view.

Ansichtskarte *die* (PL *die*
Ansichtskarten) picture postcard.

ansprechen ✧ *verb* (PRES **spricht
an**, IMPERF **sprach an**, PERF **hat
angesprochen**) **1** to speak to; **2** to
appeal to; **die Musik spricht mich
an** the music appeals to me; **3** to
mention; **er hat den Skandal, in den
sie verwickelt war, angesprochen**
he mentioned the scandal she was
involved in; **4** **auf etwas
ansprechen** to respond to
something (*a treatment, for
example*).

Anspruch *der* (PL *die* **Ansprüche**)
1 demand; **keine Ansprüche
stellen** to make no demands;
2 claim; **3** **Anspruch auf etwas
haben** to be entitled to something;
4 **viel Zeit in Anspruch nehmen** to
take up a lot of time; **5** **etwas in
Anspruch nehmen** to take
advantage of something (*an offer, for
example*).

anständig *adjective* **1** decent;
2 respectable.

anstarren *verb* (PERF **hat
angestarrt**) to stare at.

anstatt *preposition* ←(+GEN) instead
of.
conjunction **anstatt zu arbeiten**
instead of working.

ansteckend *adjective* infectious.

anstelle *preposition* ←(+GEN)
instead of.

anstellen *verb* (PERF **hat angestellt**)
1 to employ; **2** to turn on (*the TV,
radio*); **3** to do; **was stellt ihr heute
Abend noch an?** what are you doing
tonight?; **wie kann ich es nur
anstellen, dass …?** what can I do
to …?; **4** **sich anstellen** to queue;
5 **sich anstellen** to make a fuss; **stell
dich nicht so an!** don't make such
a fuss!

anstreichen ✧ *verb* (IMPERF **strich
an**, PERF **hat angestrichen**) to paint.

anstrengen *verb* (PERF **hat
angestrengt**) **1** to tire; **ihr Besuch
hat mich sehr angestrengt** their
visit tired me out; **2** **sich
anstrengen** to make an effort.

anstrengend *adjective* tiring.

Anstrengung *die* (PL *die*
Anstrengungen) effort.

Antarktis *die* **die Antarktis** the
Antarctic.

Anteil *der* (PL *die* **Anteile**) **1** share;
mein Anteil an dem Gewinn my
share of the profit; **2** **Anteil nehmen**
to sympathize; **3** **Anteil nehmen an**
to take an interest in.

Antenne *die* (PL *die* **Antennen**)
aerial.

Antibiotikum *das* (PL *die*
Antibiotika) antibiotic.

antik *adjective* antique.

Antiquitäten *plural noun*
antiques.

Antrag *der* (PL *die* **Anträge**)

✧ IRREGULAR VERB: *See the verb table in the centre of the dictionary*

application; **einen Antrag stellen** to make an application.

Antragsformular das (PL die **Antragsformulare**) application form.

Antwort die (PL die **Antworten**) answer, reply; **jemandem eine Antwort geben** to give somebody an answer.

antworten verb (PERF **hat geantwortet**) to answer, to reply; **auf etwas antworten** to answer something; **jemandem antworten** to reply to somebody.

Anwalt der (PL die **Anwälte**) lawyer.

Anwältin die (PL die **Anwältinnen**) lawyer.

Anweisung die (PL die **Anweisungen**) instruction.

anwenden verb (PERF **hat angewendet**) 1 to use (a method, process, medicine); 2 to apply (a rule, law).

anwesend adjective present.

Anzahl die number.

anzahlen verb (PERF **hat angezahlt**) to pay a deposit; **hundert Mark anzahlen** to pay a hundred marks deposit; **ein Auto anzahlen** to pay a deposit on a car.

Anzahlung die (PL die **Anzahlungen**) deposit.

Anzeichen das (PL die **Anzeichen**) sign.

Anzeige die (PL die **Anzeigen**) 1 advertisement; 2 report (to the police); **(eine) Anzeige gegen jemanden erstatten** to report somebody to the police.

anzeigen verb (PERF **hat angezeigt**) 1 to report; **jemanden anzeigen** to report somebody to the police; 2 to show (the time, a date).

anziehen ✧ verb (IMPERF **zog an**, PERF **hat angezogen**) 1 to attract; 2 to put on (clothes, the brakes); 3 to dress (a child or doll); **gut angezogen** well dressed; 4 **sich anziehen** to get dressed; 5 **was soll ich anziehen?** what shall I wear?

Anzug der (PL die **Anzüge**) suit.

anzünden verb (PERF **hat angezündet**) to light.

Apfel der (PL die **Äpfel**) apple.

Apfelsaft der (PL die **Apfelsäfte**) apple juice.

Apfelsine die (PL die **Apfelsinen**) orange.

Apotheke die (PL die **Apotheken**) chemist's, pharmacy.

Apotheker der (PL die **Apotheker**) chemist, pharmacist.

Apothekerin die (PL die **Apothekerinnen**) chemist, pharmacist.

Apparat der (PL die **Apparate**) 1 set (TV, radio); 2 camera; 3 phone; **am Apparat!** speaking!; 4 gadget.

Appartement das (PL die **Appartements**) flat.

Appetit der appetite; **guten Appetit!** enjoy your meal!

△ NEW SPELLING: See page xii

Aprikose *die* (PL *die* **Aprikosen**) apricot.

April *der* April; **am ersten April** on the first of April; **April, April!** April fool!; **jemanden in den April schicken** to play an April fool trick on somebody.

Äquator *der* equator.

Araber *der* (PL *die* **Araber**) Arab.

Araberin *die* (PL *die* **Araberinnen**) Arab.

arabisch *adjective* 1 Arab; 2 Arabian; 3 Arabic (*number*); **die arabische Sprache** Arabic.

Arbeit *die* (PL *die* **Arbeiten**) 1 work; **viel Arbeit haben** to have a lot of work; **von der Arbeit kommen** to come from work; 2 job; 3 test (*at school*); 4 **sich viel Arbeit machen** to go to a lot of trouble.

arbeiten *verb* (PERF **hat gearbeitet**) to work.

Arbeiter *der* (PL *die* **Arbeiter**) worker.

Arbeiterin *die* (PL *die* **Arbeiterinnen**) worker.

Arbeitgeber *der* (PL *die* **Arbeitgeber**) employer.

Arbeitnehmer *der* (PL *die* **Arbeitnehmer**) employee.

Arbeitsamt *das* (PL *die* **Arbeitsämter**) job centre.

arbeitslos *adjective* unemployed.

Arbeitslose *der/die* (PL *die* **Arbeitslosen**) unemployed person; **die Arbeitslosen** the unemployed.

Arbeitslosigkeit *die* unemployment.

Arbeitspraktikum *das* (PL *die* **Arbeitspraktika**) work experience.

Arbeitsplatz *der* (PL *die* **Arbeitsplätze**) 1 job; 2 desk.

Architekt *der* (PL *die* **Architekten**) architect.

Architektin *die* (PL *die* **Architektinnen**) architect.

Architektur *die* architecture.

Ärger *der* 1 annoyance; 2 trouble; **Ärger mit dem Auto haben** to have trouble with the car.

ärgerlich *adjective* 1 annoying; 2 annoyed; **er war darüber sehr ärgerlich** he was very annoyed about it.

ärgern *verb* (PERF **hat geärgert**) 1 to annoy; 2 **sich ärgern** to be annoyed, to get annoyed; **ich habe mich darüber geärgert** I was annoyed about it; **sich über jemanden ärgern** to get annoyed with somebody.

artig *adjective* well-behaved.

Arktis *die* **die Arktis** the Arctic; **in der Arktis** in the Arctic.

arm *adjective* poor.

Arm *der* (PL *die* **Arme**) arm; **jemanden auf den Arm nehmen** (*informal*) to pull somebody's leg.

Armband *das* (PL *die* **Armbänder**) bracelet.

Armbanduhr *die* (PL *die* **Armbanduhren**) wrist-watch.

✧ IRREGULAR VERB: *See the verb table in the centre of the dictionary*

Armee die (PL die **Armeen**) army.

Ärmel der (PL die **Ärmel**) sleeve.

Ärmelkanal der (English) Channel.

Armut die poverty.

arrangieren verb (PERF **hat arrangiert**) 1 to arrange; 2 sich **arrangieren** to come to an arrangement.

Art die (PL die **Arten**) 1 way; **auf diese Art** in this way; **auf seine Art** in his own way; 2 kind; **diese Art (von) Buch** this kind of book; **Bücher aller Art** all kinds of books; 3 species; 4 nature; **es ist nicht seine Art, das zu tun** it's not (in) his nature to do that.

Artikel der (PL die **Artikel**) article.

Arznei die medicine.

Arzneimittel das (PL die **Arzneimittel**) drug.

Arzt der (PL die **Ärzte**) doctor.

Ärztin die (PL die **Ärztinnen**) doctor.

ärztlich adjective medical. adverb **sich ärztlich behandeln lassen** to have medical treatment.

As SEE **Ass**.

Asche die (PL die **Aschen**) ash.

Aschenbecher der (PL die **Aschenbecher**) ashtray.

Aschermittwoch der Ash Wednesday.

Asiat der (PL die **Asiaten**) Asian.

Asiatin die (PL die **Asiatinnen**) Asian.

asiatisch adjective Asian.

Asien das Asia; **nach Asien** to Asia.

aß SEE **essen**.

Ass △ das (PL die **Asse**) ace.

Assistent der (PL die **Assistenten**) assistant.

Assistentin die (PL die **Assistentinnen**) assistant.

Ast der (PL die **Äste**) branch.

Asthma das asthma.

Astrologie die astrology.

Astronaut der (PL die **Astronauten**) astronaut.

Astronomie die astronomy.

Asyl das (PL die **Asyle**) 1 asylum; **um politisches Asyl bitten** to apply for political asylum; 2 hostel (for the homeless).

Asylant der (PL die **Asylanten**) asylum-seeker.

Atelier das (PL die **Ateliers**) (artist's) studio.

Atem der breath; **außer Atem sein** to be out of breath.

atemlos adjective breathless.

Athlet der (PL die **Athleten**) athlete.

Athletin die (PL die **Athletinnen**) athlete.

Atlantik der der **Atlantik** the Atlantic (Ocean); **im Atlantik** in the Atlantic.

Atlas der (PL die **Atlanten**) atlas.

atmen verb (PERF **hat geatmet**) to breathe.

△ NEW SPELLING: See page xii

Atmosphäre *die* (PL *die* **Atmosphären**) atmosphere.

Atom *das* (PL *die* **Atome**) atom.

atomar *adjective* atomic.

Atomwaffen *plural noun* nuclear weapons.

atomwaffenfrei *adjective* nuclear-free.

attraktiv *adjective* attractive.

ätzend *adjective* 1 corrosive; 2 caustic (*wit, remark*).

au *exclamation* 1 ouch!; 2 oh! (*when surprised or enthusiastic*); **au ja!** oh yes!

auch *adverb* 1 also, too; **Sophie war auch dabei** Sophie was also there, Sophie was there too; **ich auch** me too; **nicht nur ... sondern auch ...** not only ... but also ...; 2 'ich gehe jetzt' – 'ich auch' 'I'm going now' – 'so am I'; 'er schläft' – 'sie auch' 'he's asleep' – 'so is she'; 3 'ich bin nicht müde' – 'ich auch nicht' 'I'm not tired'-'neither am I'; **das weiß ich auch nicht** I don't know either; 4 **auch wenn** even if; 5 **wann auch** whenever; **was auch** whatever; **wo auch** wherever; **wer auch** whoever; 6 **wie dem auch sei** however that may be; 7 **lügst du auch nicht?** you're not lying, are you?

auf *preposition* ←(+DAT *or* +ACC) (*the dative is used when talking about position; the accusative shows movement or a change of place*) 1 on; **das Buch liegt auf dem Tisch** the book's on the table; **er hat das Buch auf den Tisch gelegt** he put the book on the table; 2 **ich war auf der Party** I was at the party; **ich gehe auf eine Party** I'm going to a party; **ich war auf der Post** I was at the post office; **er ist auf die Post gegangen** he went to the post office; 3 **auf der Straße** in the street; 4 **auf diese Art** in this way; **auf Deutsch** in German; 5 for (*indicating time or distance*); **er ist auf ein paar Tage verreist** he's gone away for a few days; 6 **auf seinen Rat hin** on his advice; 7 **auf Wiedersehen!** goodbye!
adverb 1 open; **die Tür ist auf** the door is open; **Mund auf!** open your mouth!; 2 up (*out of bed*); **auf sein** to be up; **er ist schon auf** he's already up; 3 **auf einmal** suddenly; 4 **auf einmal** at once (*at the same time*); 5 **auf und ab** up and down; 6 **sich auf und davon machen** to make off.

aufbekommen ✧ *verb* (IMPERF **bekam auf**, PERF **hat aufbekommen**) 1 to get open; 2 **Hausaufgaben aufbekommen** to be given homework.

aufbewahren *verb* (PERF **hat aufbewahrt**) to keep.

aufblasen ✧ *verb* (PRES **bläst auf**, IMPERF **blies auf**, PERF **hat aufgeblasen**) to blow up.

aufbleiben ✧ *verb* (IMPERF **blieb auf**, PERF **ist aufgeblieben**) 1 to stay open; **wie lange bleiben die Geschäfte auf?** how long do the shops stay open?; 2 to stay up (*not go to bed*).

✧ IRREGULAR VERB: *See the verb table in the centre of the dictionary*

aufbringen ◊ *verb* (IMPERF **brachte auf**, PERF **hat aufgebracht**) 1 to raise (*money*); 2 to find (*patience, strength*); 3 to open; **ich kann die Tür nicht aufbringen** I can't open the door; 4 **jemanden aufbringen** to make somebody angry; 5 **Verständnis für etwas aufbringen** to be able to understand something.

aufeinander *adverb* 1 one on top of the other; **die Bretter aufeinander legen** to put the planks one on top of the other; 2 **aufeinander liegen** △ to lie on top of each other; 3 **aufeinander folgen** △ to follow one another; 4 **aufeinander warten** to wait for each other; 5 **aufeinander schießen** to shoot at each other; 6 **aufeinander fahren** △ to collide with each other.

Aufenthalt *der* (PL **die Aufenthalte**) 1 stay; 2 stop (*pause in a journey*); **zehn Minuten Aufenthalt haben** to stop for ten minutes.

Auffahrt *die* (PL **die Auffahrten**) 1 drive; 2 slip road.

auffallend *adjective* striking.

auffangen ◊ *verb* (PRES **fängt auf**, IMPERF **fing auf**, PERF **hat aufgefangen**) to catch.

aufführen *verb* (PERF **hat aufgeführt**) 1 to perform (*a play*); 2 to list (*words, items*); 3 **sich aufführen** to behave.

Aufführung *die* (PL **die Aufführungen**) performance.

Aufgabe *die* (PL **die Aufgaben**)

1 task; 2 exercise (*at school*); 3 question (*in a test or an exam*); 4 **Aufgaben** homework.

aufgeben ◊ *verb* (PRES **gibt auf**, IMPERF **gab auf**, PERF **hat aufgegeben**) 1 to give up; **ich gebe auf!** I give up!; 2 to post; 3 to check in (*luggage*); 4 to place (*an advertisement, order*); 5 **Hausaufgaben aufgeben** to set homework.

aufgehen ◊ *verb* (IMPERF **ging auf**, PERF **ist aufgegangen**) 1 to open (*of a door or flower, for example*); 2 to come undone (*of a knot or zip, for example*); 3 to rise (*of the sun, moon*); 4 to realize; **es ist mir aufgegangen, dass …** I've realized that …; 5 to work out (*in maths*); **zehn durch drei geht nicht auf** three into ten won't go.

aufgeregt *adjective* excited.

aufgeschlossen *adjective* open-minded.

aufgrund *preposition* ←(+GEN) 1 because of; 2 on the strength of.

aufhaben ◊ *verb* (PRES **hat auf**, IMPERF **hatte auf**, PERF **hat aufgehabt**) 1 to have on (*a hat*); 2 **den Mund aufhaben** to have your mouth open; 3 **etwas aufhaben** to have homework to do; **viel aufhaben** to have a lot of homework; 4 to be open; **der Laden hat abends auf** the shop is open in the evening.

aufhalten ◊ *verb* (PRES **hält auf**, IMPERF **hielt auf**, PERF **hat aufgehalten**) 1 to hold open (*a

△ NEW SPELLING: *See page*

door); **2** to hold up, to keep (*somebody from doing something*); **3 die Hand aufhalten** to hold out your hand; **4 die Augen aufhalten** to keep your eyes open; **5** to check (*inflation, an advance, unemployment*); **6 sich aufhalten** to stay; **7 sich mit etwas aufhalten** to spend your time on something.

aufhängen *verb* (PERF **hat aufgehängt**) **1** to hang up (*washing*); **2 sich aufhängen** to hang yourself.

aufheben ✧ *verb* (IMPERF **hob auf**, PERF **hat aufgehoben**) **1** to pick up (*from the ground*); **2** to keep; **3** to abolish (*a law*); **4 gut aufgehoben sein** to be well looked after.

aufheitern *verb* (PERF **hat aufgeheitert**) **1** to cheer up; **2 sich aufheitern** to brighten up (*of the weather*).

aufhören *verb* (PERF **hat aufgehört**) to stop; **aufhören zu arbeiten** to stop working.

aufklären *verb* (PERF **hat aufgeklärt**) **1** to solve (*a crime*); **2** to explain (*an event, incident*); **3 ein Kind aufklären** to tell a child the facts of life; **4 sich aufklären** to be solved (*a misunderstanding or mystery*); **5 sich aufklären** to clear up; **das Wetter klärt sich auf** the weather is clearing up.

Aufkleber *der* (PL *die* **Aufkleber**) sticker.

auflegen *verb* (PERF **hat aufgelegt**) **1** to put on; **2** to hang up (*when phoning*); **3** to publish; **ein Buch neu auflegen** to reprint a book.

auflösen *verb* (PERF **hat aufgelöst**) **1** to dissolve; **2** to close (*an account*); **3 sich auflösen** to dissolve; **4 sich auflösen** to break up (*of a crowd, demonstration*); **5 der Nebel hat sich aufgelöst** the fog has lifted; **6 in Tränen aufgelöst sein** to be in floods of tears.

aufmachen *verb* (PERF **hat aufgemacht**) **1** to open; **2 jemandem aufmachen** to open the door to somebody; **3** to undo (*a zip, knot*); **4 sich aufmachen** to set out.

aufmerksam *adjective* **1** attentive; **2 auf etwas aufmerksam werden** to notice something; **3 jemanden auf etwas aufmerksam machen** to draw somebody's attention to something.

aufmuntern *verb* (PERF **hat aufgemuntert**) to cheer up.

Aufnahme *die* (PL *die* **Aufnahmen**) **1** photograph; **2** recording; **3** admission (*to hospital, to a club*); **4** welcome.

Aufnahmeprüfung *die* (PL *die* **Aufnahmeprüfungen**) entrance exam.

aufnehmen ✧ *verb* (PRES **nimmt auf**, IMPERF **nahm auf**, PERF **hat aufgenommen**) **1** to receive (*guests*); **2** to take up (*an idea, activity, a theme*); **3** to admit (*to hospital, to a club*); **4** to photograph; **5** to film; **6** to record (*a song*); **7 es mit jemandem aufnehmen können**

✧ **IRREGULAR VERB:** *See the verb table in the centre of the dictionary*

to be a match for somebody; **6** to
take (food, news); **etwas gelassen
aufnehmen** to take something
calmly.

aufpassen verb (PERF **hat
aufgepasst** △) **1** to pay attention;
2 to watch out; **3 auf jemanden
aufpassen** to look after somebody;
4 auf etwas aufpassen to keep an
eye on something; **pass auf meine
Tasche auf** keep an eye on my bag.

aufräumen verb (PERF **hat
aufgeräumt**) to tidy up.

aufrecht adjective upright.

aufregen verb (PERF **hat aufgeregt**)
1 to excite; **2** to annoy; **3 sich
aufregen** to get worked up.

aufregend adjective exciting.

aufs = **auf das**.

Aufsatz der (PL die **Aufsätze**) essay.

aufschieben ◇ verb (IMPERF **schob
auf**, PERF **hat aufgeschoben**) **1** to put
off (an arrangement); **2** to slide
open.

aufschließen ◇ verb (IMPERF
schloss auf △, PERF **hat
aufgeschlossen**) to unlock.

Aufschnitt der sliced cold meat and
cheese.

aufschreiben ◇ verb (IMPERF
schrieb auf, PERF **hat
aufgeschrieben**) to write down.

aufsehen ◇ verb (PRES **sieht auf**,
IMPERF **sah auf**, PERF **hat
aufgesehen**) to look up.

aufsetzen verb (PERF **hat
aufgesetzt**) **1** to put on; **2** to draft;
3 sich aufsetzen to sit up.

Aufsicht die **1** supervision;
2 supervisor.

Aufstand der (PL die **Aufstände**)
rebellion.

aufstehen ◇ verb (IMPERF **stand
auf**, PERF **ist aufgestanden**) **1** to get
up; **2** (PERF **hat aufgestanden**) to be
open.

aufstellen verb (PERF **hat
aufgestellt**) **1** to put up; **2** to set up
(skittles, chess pieces); **3 eine
Mannschaft aufstellen** to pick a
team; **4 eine Liste aufstellen** to
draw up a list; **5 sich aufstellen** to
line up.

auftauen verb (PERF **ist aufgetaut**)
1 to thaw; **2** to defrost; **die
Erdbeeren sind aufgetaut** the
strawberries have defrosted; **3** (PERF
hat aufgetaut) to defrost; **ich habe
die Erbeeren aufgetaut** I've
defrosted the strawberries.

aufteilen verb (PERF **hat aufgeteilt**)
to divide up.

Auftrag der (PL die **Aufträge**) **1** job;
2 order (in business); **etwas in
Auftrag geben** to order something;
3 instructions; **einen Auftrag
ausführen** to carry out an
instruction; **4 im Auftrag von** on
behalf of.

auftreten ◇ verb (PRES **tritt auf**,
IMPERF **trat auf**, PERF **ist aufgetreten**)
1 to appear (on stage); **2** to arise (a
problem, difficulty); **3** to behave;
4 to tread.

△ NEW SPELLING: See page xii

aufwachen *verb* (PERF **ist aufgewacht**) to wake up.

aufwachsen ✧ *verb* (PRES **wächst auf**, IMPERF **wuchs auf**, PERF **ist aufgewachsen**) to grow up.

aufwecken *verb* (PERF **hat aufgeweckt**) to wake up.

aufziehen ✧ *verb* (IMPERF **zog auf**, PERF **hat aufgezogen**) **1** to wind up (*a clock or toy*); **2** to draw (*curtains*); **3 jemanden aufziehen** (*informal*) to tease somebody; **4** to bring up (*a child*).

Aufzug *der* (PL *die* **Aufzüge**) lift; **ich fahre mit dem Aufzug runter** I'm going down in the lift.

Auge *das* (PL *die* **Augen**) **1** eye; **2 unter vier Augen** in private.

Augenblick *der* (PL *die* **Augenblicke**) moment; **im Augenblick** at the moment.

Augenbraue *die* (PL *die* **Augenbrauen**) eyebrow.

August *der* August.

aus *preposition* ←(+DAT) **1** out of; **er hat es aus dem Fenster geworfen** he threw it out of the window; **2** from; **aus Spanien** from Spain; **aus Erfahrung** from experience; **3** made of; **aus Holz** made of wood; **4 aus Spaß** for fun; **5 aus der Mode** out of fashion; **6 aus Versehen** by mistake; **7 aus welchem Grund?** for what reason?; **8 aus ihr ist eine gute Rechtsanwältin geworden** she made a good lawyer; **aus ihm ist nichts geworden** he never made anything of his life. *adverb* **1** off (*of a TV, radio*); **das Licht ist aus** the light is off; **Licht aus!** lights out!; **2** finished; **wenn das Spiel aus ist** when the game has finished; **3 von mir aus** as far as I'm concerned; **4 von sich aus** of your own accord.

ausbeuten *verb* (PERF **hat ausgebeutet**) to exploit.

ausbilden *verb* (PERF **hat ausgebildet**) to train.

Ausbildung *die* **1** training; **2** education.

Ausdruck[1] *der* (PL *die* **Ausdrücke**) expression; **etwas zum Ausdruck bringen** to express something.

Ausdruck[2] *der* (PL *die* **Ausdrucke**) print-out.

ausdrucken *verb* (PERF **hat ausgedruckt**) to print out.

ausdrücken *verb* (PERF **hat ausgedrückt**) **1** to squeeze (*oranges, lemons*); **2** to express; **3 sich ausdrücken** to express oneself.

auseinander *adverb* **1** apart; **etwas auseinander nehmen** △ to take something apart; **auseinander halten** △ to tell apart; **2 auseinander gehen** △ to part; **3 auseinander schreiben** to write as separate words; **4 sich mit einem Problem auseinander setzen** △ to come to grips with a problem; **5 sich mit jemandem auseinander setzen** △ to have it out with somebody.

✧ IRREGULAR VERB: *See the verb table in the centre of the dictionary*

Ausfahrt die (PL die **Ausfahrten**)
1 exit; 2 **'Ausfahrt freihalten'** 'keep
clear'.

ausfallen ⬦ verb (PRES **fällt aus**,
IMPERF **fiel aus**, PERF **ist ausgefallen**)
1 to be cancelled; **etwas ausfallen
lassen** to cancel something; 2 to
fall out (*hair*); 3 to fail (*an engine,
brakes, a signal*); 4 to break down (*a
machine, a car, heating*); 5 to turn
out; **gut ausfallen** to turn out well.

Ausflug der (PL die **Ausflüge**) outing,
trip; **einen Ausflug machen** to go
on an outing.

Ausfuhr die export.

ausführen verb (PERF **hat
ausgeführt**) 1 to carry out (*a plan*);
2 to export (*goods*); 3 to take out; **er
hat seine Freundin zum Essen
ausgeführt** he took his girlfriend
out for a meal; 4 **den Hund
ausführen** to take the dog for a walk.

ausführlich adjective detailed.
adverb in detail.

ausfüllen verb (PERF **hat ausgefüllt**)
1 to fill in; 2 **ihr Beruf als Lehrerin
füllt sie ganz aus** teaching gives her
great satisfaction.

Ausgabe die (PL die **Ausgaben**)
1 edition; 2 issue; 3 **Ausgaben**
expenditure.

Ausgang der (PL die **Ausgänge**)
1 exit; **'kein Ausgang'** 'no exit';
2 end, ending; 3 result (*of a game,
discussion*).

ausgeben ⬦ verb (PRES **gibt aus**,
IMPERF **gab aus**, PERF **hat
ausgegeben**) 1 to spend; 2 to hand

out; 3 **Fahrkarten ausgeben** to
issue tickets; 4 to serve (*food*);
5 **sich ausgeben als** to pretend to
be; 6 **einen ausgeben** (*informal*)
to treat everybody (*to a round of
drinks for example*).

ausgebucht adjective fully booked.

ausgehen ⬦ verb (PRES **geht aus**,
IMPERF **ging aus**, PERF **ist
ausgegangen**) 1 to go out; 2 to run
out (*of supplies*); 3 to end; **schlecht
ausgehen** to end badly; 4 **davon
ausgehen, dass ...** to assume
that ...

ausgerechnet adverb
1 **ausgerechnet heute** today of all
days; 2 **ausgerechnet sie** she of all
people.

ausgeschlossen adjective out of
the question.

ausgezeichnet adjective
excellent.

aushalten ⬦ verb (PRES **hält aus**,
IMPERF **hielt aus**, PERF **hat
ausgehalten**) 1 to stand; 2 **es ist
nicht zum Aushalten** it's
unbearable.

Aushilfe die (PL die **Aushilfen**)
temporary assistant, temp.

auskennen ⬦ verb (IMPERF **kannte
sich aus**, PERF **hat sich ausgekannt**)
1 **sich auskennen** to know your way
around; 2 **sich gut mit etwas
auskennen** to know a lot about
something.

auskommen ⬦ verb (IMPERF **kam
aus**, PERF **ist ausgekommen**) 1 to
manage; **mit fünfzig Mark**

△ NEW SPELLING: *See page xii*

auskommen to manage on fifty marks; **2 mit jemandem gut auskommen** to get on well with somebody.

Auskunft die (PL die **Auskünfte**) **1** information; **2** information desk; **3** enquiries (*when phoning*).

auslachen verb (PERF **hat ausgelacht**) to laugh at.

ausladen✧ verb (PRES **lädt aus**, IMPERF **lud aus**, PERF **hat ausgeladen**) **1** to unload; **2 jemanden ausladen** (*informal*) to put somebody off.

Ausland das **im Ausland** abroad; **ins Ausland reisen** to travel abroad.

Ausländer der (PL die **Ausländer**) foreigner.

Ausländerin die (PL die **Ausländerinnen**) foreigner.

ausländisch adjective foreign.

Auslandsgespräch das (PL die **Auslandsgespräche**) international call.

ausleeren verb (PERF **hat ausgeleert**) to empty.

ausleihen✧ verb (IMPERF **lieh aus**, PERF **hat ausgeliehen**) **1** to lend; **2 sich etwas ausleihen** to borrow something.

ausmachen verb (PERF **hat ausgemacht**) **1** to turn off; **2** to put out; **3** to arrange; **wir haben ausgemacht, dass wir uns heute Abend treffen** we've arranged to meet up this evening; **4 das macht mir nichts aus** I don't mind; **macht es Ihnen etwas aus, wenn ...?**

would you mind if ...?; **5 viel ausmachen** to make a great difference.

Ausnahme die (PL die **Ausnahmen**) exception.

ausnutzen verb (PERF **hat ausgenutzt**) **1** to use; **2** to take advantage of.

auspacken verb (PERF **hat ausgepackt**) to unpack.

Auspuff der (PL die **Auspuffe**) exhaust.

ausrechnen verb (PERF **hat ausgerechnet**) to work out.

Ausrede die (PL die **Ausreden**) excuse.

ausreichend adjective **1** sufficient; **2** fair, pass (*as a mark at school*).

Ausreise die (PL die **Ausreisen**) departure (*from a country*).

ausrichten verb (PERF **hat ausgerichtet**) **jemandem etwas ausrichten** to tell somebody something.

Ausrufezeichen das (PL die **Ausrufezeichen**) exclamation mark.

ausruhen verb (PERF **hat sich ausgeruht**) **sich ausruhen** to have a rest.

Ausrüstung die equipment.

ausschalten verb (PERF **hat ausgeschaltet**) **1** to switch off; **2** to eliminate.

ausschneiden✧ verb (IMPERF **schnitt aus**, PERF **hat ausgeschnitten**) to cut out.

✧ IRREGULAR VERB: *See the verb table in the centre of the dictionary*

Ausschuss Δ *der* (PL *die* **Ausschüsse**) committee.

aussehen ✧ *verb* (PRES **sieht aus**, IMPERF **sah aus**, PERF **hat ausgesehen**) to look.

Aussehen *das* appearance.

außen *adverb* 1 (on the) outside; **von außen** from the outside; 2 **nach außen** outwards.

Außenminister *der* (PL *die* **Außenminister**) Foreign Secretary, Foreign Minister.

außer *preposition* ←(+DAT) 1 apart from, except (for); **alle außer ihm** everyone except (for) him; 2 out of; **außer Sicht** out of sight; **außer Betrieb** out of order; 3 **außer Haus** out; 4 **außer sich sein** to be beside yourself.
conjunction 1 except; **außer sonntags** except Sundays; 2 **außer wenn** unless.

außerdem *adverb* 1 as well; 2 besides.

äußerer, äußere, äußeres *adjective* 1 external (*injury, circumstances*); 2 outer (*layer, circle*); 3 outward (*appearance, effect*).

außergewöhnlich *adjective* unusual.

außerhalb *preposition* ←(+GEN) outside.
adverb **außerhalb wohnen** to live out of town.

äußerlich *adjective* 1 external; 2 outward (*appearance*).

außerordentlich *adjective* extraordinary.

äußerst *adverb* extremely.

Äußerung *die* (PL *die* **Äußerungen**) remark.

Aussicht *die* (PL *die* **Aussichten**) 1 prospect; **etwas in Aussicht haben** to have the prospect of something; **keine Aussichten auf Erfolg haben** to have no chance of success; 2 view; **ein Zimmer mit Aussicht aufs Meer** a room with a view of the sea.

Aussprache *die* (PL *die* **Aussprachen**) 1 pronunciation; 2 talk.

aussprechen ✧ *verb* (PRES **spricht aus**, IMPERF **sprach aus**, PERF **hat ausgesprochen**) 1 to pronounce; 2 to express; 3 **lassen Sie ihn aussprechen** let him finish (*speaking*); 4 **sich aussprechen** to talk; **sich mit jemandem aussprechen** to have a talk with somebody; 5 **sich gegen etwas aussprechen** to come out against something; **sich für etwas aussprechen** to come out in favour of something; 6 **sich lobend über jemanden aussprechen** to speak highly of somebody.

aussteigen ✧ *verb* (IMPERF **stieg aus**, PERF **ist ausgestiegen**) 1 to get out; 2 to get off.

ausstellen *verb* (PERF **hat ausgestellt**) 1 to display (*in a shop*); 2 to exhibit; 3 to make out (*a certificate, bill*); 4 to issue (*a passport*); 5 to switch off.

Δ NEW SPELLING: *See page xii*

Ausstellung die (PL die Ausstellungen) exhibition.

ausstreichen ✧ verb (IMPERF strich aus, PERF hat ausgestrichen) to cross out.

aussuchen verb (PERF hat ausgesucht) 1 to choose; 2 sich etwas aussuchen to choose something.

Austausch der exchange.

austauschen verb (PERF hat ausgetauscht) 1 to exchange; 2 to replace; 3 to substitute (a player).

Auster die (PL die Austern) oyster.

austragen ✧ verb (PRES trägt aus, IMPERF trug aus, PERF hat ausgetragen) to deliver (post); to hold (a race).

Australien das Australia; aus Australien from Australia.

Australier der (PL die Australier) Australian.

Australierin die (PL die Australierinnen) Australian.

australisch adjective Australian.

austreten ✧ verb (PRES tritt aus, IMPERF trat aus, PERF hat ausgetreten) 1 to stamp out (a cigarette or fire); 2 to wear out (shoes); 3 (PERF ist ausgetreten) aus einem Klub austreten to leave a club; ich trete aus I'm leaving; 4 (informal) (PERF ist ausgetreten) to go to the loo.

austrinken ✧ verb (IMPERF trank aus, PERF hat ausgetrunken) to drink up.

Ausverkauf der (PL die Ausverkäufe) sale.

ausverkauft adjective 1 sold out; 2 ein ausverkauftes Haus a full house (at the cinema or theatre).

Auswahl die (PL die Auswahlen) choice, selection; wenig Auswahl haben to have a limited selection.

auswärts adverb 1 away (in sport); auswärts spielen to play away; 2 auswärts essen to eat out; 3 sie arbeitet auswärts she doesn't work locally.

Auswärtsspiel das (PL die Auswärtsspiele) away game.

Ausweg der (PL die Auswege) way out.

Ausweis der (PL die Ausweise) 1 identity card; 2 card (for students or members); 3 pass.

auswendig adverb by heart.

auswirken verb (PERF hat sich ausgewirkt) sich auf etwas auswirken to have an effect on something.

ausziehen ✧ verb (IMPERF zog aus, PERF hat ausgezogen) 1 to take off (clothes); 2 to undress; 3 sich ausziehen to get undressed; 4 (PERF ist ausgezogen) to move out (move house).

Auto das (PL die Autos) car; Auto fahren to drive.

Autobahn die (PL die Autobahnen) motorway.

Autofahrer der (PL die Autofahrer) motorist.

✧ IRREGULAR VERB: See the verb table in the centre of the dictionary

Autogramm das (PL die
Autogramme) autograph.

Automat der (PL die Automaten)
machine.

automatisch adjective automatic.

Autor der (PL die Autoren) author.

Autorin die (PL die Autorinnen)
authoress.

Autorität die authority.

Autostopp der **per Autostopp
fahren** to hitchhike.

Autotelefon das (PL die
Autotelefone) car phone.

Autounfall der (PL die Autounfälle)
car accident.

Autoverleih der (PL die
Autoverleihe) car hire (firm).

Axt die (PL die Äxte) axe.

B b

Baby das (PL die Babys) baby.

Bach der (PL die Bäche) stream.

Backe die (PL die Backen) cheek.

backen ◇ verb (PRES **bäckt**, IMPERF
backte, PERF **hat gebacken**) to bake.

Bäcker der (PL die Bäcker) 1 baker;
2 **beim Bäcker** at the baker's.

Bäckerei die (PL die Bäckereien)
baker's.

Backofen der (PL die Backöfen)
oven.

Backpflaume die (PL die
Backpflaumen) prune.

Bad das (PL die Bäder) 1 bath;
2 bathroom; 3 pool (for
swimming).

Badeanzug der (PL die
Badeanzüge) swimsuit.

Badehose die (PL die Badehosen)
swimming trunks.

Bademütze die (PL die
Bademützen) bathing cap.

baden verb (PERF **hat gebadet**) 1 to
have a bath; 2 to bathe (in the sea);
3 to bath (wash somebody).

Badetuch das (PL die Badetücher)
bath towel.

Badewanne die (PL die
Badewannen) bath (tub).

Badezimmer das (PL die
Badezimmer) bathroom.

Bahn die (PL die Bahnen) 1 railway;
2 train; **mit der Bahn fahren** to go
by train; 3 tram; 4 track (in sport);
5 lane (on a track); 6 path; **auf die
schiefe Bahn geraten** to go off the
rails.

Bahnhof der (PL die Bahnhöfe)
(railway) station.

Bahnsteig der (PL die Bahnsteige)
platform.

Bahnübergang der (PL die
Bahnübergänge) level crossing.

bald adverb 1 soon; **bis bald!** see
you soon!; 2 **wird's bald!**
(informal) get a move on!; 3 almost;
ich hätte bald vergessen, ihn

△ NEW SPELLING: *See page xii*

anzurufen I almost forgot to ring him.

Balken *der* (PL *die* **Balken**) beam.

Balkon *der* (PL *die* **Balkons**) balcony.

Ball *der* (PL *die* **Bälle**) 1 ball; **Ball spielen** to play ball; 2 ball; **auf dem Ball** at the ball.

Ballett *das* (PL *die* **Ballette**) ballet.

Balletttänzer△ *der* (PL *die* **Balletttänzer**) ballet dancer.

Balletttänzerin△ *die* (PL *die* **Balletttänzerinnen**) ballet dancer.

Ballon *der* (PL *die* **Ballons**) balloon.

Banane *die* (PL *die* **Bananen**) banana.

band SEE **binden**.

Band[1] *das* (PL *die* **Bänder**) 1 ribbon; 2 tape (*for recording*); **etwas auf Band aufnehmen** to tape something; 3 production line; **am Band arbeiten** to work on the production line; 4 **am laufenden Band** (*informal*) nonstop.

Band[2] *der* (PL *die* **Bände**) volume.

Band[3] *die* (PL *die* **Bands**) band.

Bank[1] *die* (PL *die* **Bänke**) bench.

Bank[2] *die* (PL *die* **Banken**) bank; **ich muss erst zur Bank gehen** I have to go to the bank first.

Bankkonto *das* (PL *die* **Bankkonten**) bank account.

Banknote *die* (PL *die* **Banknoten**) banknote.

bankrott *adjective* bankrupt;

bankrott gehen/machen to go bankrupt.

bar *adjective* (in) cash.

Bar *die* (PL *die* **Bars**) bar.

Bär *der* (PL *die* **Bären**) bear.

Bardame *die* (PL *die* **Bardamen**) barmaid.

barfuß *adjective* barefoot.

Bargeld *das* cash.

Barkeeper *der* (PL *die* **Barkeeper**) barman.

Barren *der* (PL *die* **Barren**) 1 bar; 2 parallel bars.

Bart *der* (PL *die* **Bärte**) beard.

bärtig *adjective* bearded.

Basel *das* Basle.

Basis *die* (PL *die* **Basen**) basis.

Bass△ *der* (PL *die* **Bässe**) bass.

basta *exclamation* and that's that!

basteln *verb* (PERF **hat gebastelt**) 1 to make (*things*); 2 **sie bastelt gern** she likes making things.

bat SEE **bitten**.

Batterie *die* (PL *die* **Batterien**) battery.

Bau *der* (PL *die* **Bauten**) 1 construction; **im Bau sein** to be under construction; 2 building; 3 building site; **auf dem Bau arbeiten** to work on a building site.

Bauarbeiter *der* (PL *die* **Bauarbeiter**) builder.

Bauch *der* (PL *die* **Bäuche**) stomach, belly.

✦ IRREGULAR VERB: *See the verb table in the centre of the dictionary*

Bauchschmerzen *plural noun* stomachache.

bauen *verb* (PERF **hat gebaut**) 1 to build; 2 **einen Unfall bauen** (*informal*) to have an accident.

Bauer *der* (PL *die* **Bauern**) 1 farmer; 2 pawn (*in chess*).

Bäuerin *die* (PL *die* **Bäuerinnen**) 1 farmer; 2 farmer's wife.

Bauernhof *der* (PL *die* **Bauernhöfe**) farm.

Baum *der* (PL *die* **Bäume**) tree.

Baumwolle *die* cotton.

Bausparkasse *die* (PL *die* **Bausparkassen**) building society.

Baustelle *die* (PL *die* **Baustellen**) building site.

Bayer *der* (PL *die* **Bayern**) Bavarian.

Bayerin *die* (PL *die* **Bayerinnen**) Bavarian.

Bayern *das* Bavaria; **aus Bayern** from Bavaria.

bayrisch *adjective* Bavarian.

beabsichtigen *verb* (PERF **hat beabsichtigt**) to intend.

beachten *verb* (PERF **hat beachtet**) 1 to take notice of; **beachte ihn einfach nicht** just don't take any notice of him; 2 to observe; 3 to follow (*a rule, advice*); 4 to obey; **die Verkehrsregeln beachten** to obey traffic regulations.

Beamte *der* (PL *die* **Beamten**) 1 civil servant (*in Germany all public employees, such as teachers and policemen, are 'Beamte'*); 2 official.

Beamtin *die* (PL *die* **Beamtinnen**) 1 civil servant; 2 official.

beanspruchen *verb* (PERF **hat beansprucht**) 1 to claim (*benefit*); 2 to take up (*time, space*); **jemanden beanspruchen** to take up somebody's time; 3 to demand (*energy, attention*); **die Arbeit beansprucht sie sehr** her work is very demanding; 4 to take advantage of (*hospitality, services, help*); **ich möchte Ihre Geduld nicht zu sehr beanspruchen** I don't want to try your patience.

Beanstandung *die* (PL *die* **Beanstandungen**) complaint.

beantragen *verb* (PERF **hat beantragt**) to apply for.

beantworten *verb* (PERF **hat beantwortet**) to answer.

bearbeiten *verb* (PERF **hat bearbeitet**) 1 to deal with; **einen Antrag bearbeiten** to deal with an application; 2 to adapt (*a play*); 3 to treat (*wood, for example*); **er hat die Oberfläche mit Wachs bearbeitet** he's treated the surface with wax; 4 **jemanden bearbeiten, dass er etwas macht** (*informal*) to work on somebody so that he does something (*persuade*).

beaufsichtigen *verb* (PERF **hat beaufsichtigt**) to supervise.

Becher *der* (PL *die* **Becher**) 1 beaker, mug; 2 pot, carton (*of yoghurt, cream*).

△ NEW SPELLING: *See page xii*

Becken das (PL die **Becken**)
1 basin; 2 pool (for swimming);
3 pelvis.

bedanken verb (PERF **hat sich bedankt**) **sich bedanken** to say thank you; **vergiss nicht, dich zu bedanken** don't forget to say thank you; **ich habe mich bei ihm bedankt** I thanked him.

Bedarf der 1 need; 2 **bei Bedarf** if required; 3 demand; **je nach Bedarf** according to demand.

bedauerlicherweise adverb unfortunately.

bedauern verb (PERF **hat bedauert**)
1 to regret; **ich bedaure kein Wort** I don't regret a single word; 2 **ich bedaure sehr, dass du nicht kommen kannst** I'm very sorry that you can't come; **bedaure!** sorry!; 3 **jemanden bedauern** to feel sorry for somebody.

bedecken verb (PERF **hat bedeckt**) to cover.

bedeckt adjective 1 covered; 2 overcast (weather); **gestern war es den ganzen Tag bedeckt** it was overcast all day yesterday.

bedenken ♦ verb (IMPERF **bedachte**, PERF **hat bedacht**) to consider.

Bedenken plual noun 1 doubts; **Bedenken haben** to have doubts; 2 **ohne Bedenken** without hesitation.

bedenklich adjective 1 worrying; **die Situation ist sehr bedenklich** the situation is very worrying; 2 dubious; **er hat bedenkliche Mittel angewendet, um sein Ziel zu**

erreichen he's used dubious methods to achieve his aims; 3 serious.

bedeuten verb (PERF **hat bedeutet**) to mean.

bedeutend adjective 1 important; 2 considerable.

Bedeutung die (PL die **Bedeutungen**) 1 meaning; 2 importance.

bedienen verb (PERF **hat bedient**)
1 to serve; **hier wird man sehr schnell bedient** you get served very quickly here; 2 to operate; 3 **sich bedienen** to help oneself.

Bedienung die (PL die **Bedienungen**) 1 service; **Bedienung inbegriffen** service included; 2 waiter, waitress; 3 shop assistant; 4 operation (of a machine).

Bedingung die (PL die **Bedingungen**) condition; **nur unter der Bedingung, dass du mitkommst** only on condition that you're coming with us.

bedrohen verb (PERF **hat bedroht**) to threaten.

Bedrohung die (PL die **Bedrohungen**) threat.

beeilen verb (PERF **hat sich beeilt**) **sich beeilen** to hurry (up); **beeilt euch!** hurry up!

beeindrucken verb (PERF **hat beeindruckt**) to impress.

beeinflussen verb (PERF **hat beeinflusst**) to influence.

♦ IRREGULAR VERB: See the verb table in the centre of the dictionary

beenden *verb* (PERF **hat beendet**) to end.

Beerdigung *die* (PL *die* **Beerdigungen**) funeral.

Beere *die* (PL *die* **Beeren**) berry.

Beet *das* (PL *die* **Beete**) 1 bed (*of flowers*); 2 patch (*of vegetables*).

befahl SEE **befehlen**.

Befehl *der* (PL *die* **Befehle**) 1 order; 2 command; **den Befehl über etwas haben** to be in command of something.

befehlen ◇ *verb* (PRES **befiehlt**, IMPERF **befahl**, PERF **hat befohlen**) 1 **jemandem etwas befehlen** to order somebody to do something; 2 to give orders.

befestigen *verb* (PERF **hat befestigt**) 1 to fix; **etwas an der Wand befestigen** to fix something to the wall; 2 to fasten.

befinden ◇ *verb* (IMPERF **befand sich**, PERF **hat sich befunden**) **sich befinden** to be; **sie befindet sich zur Zeit in Deutschland** she's in Germany at the moment.

befolgen *verb* (PERF **hat befolgt**) to follow.

befördern *verb* (PERF **hat befördert**) 1 to carry (*people by bus or train*); 2 to transport (*goods by train or lorry*); 3 to promote; **er ist zum Kommissar befördert worden** he's been promoted to superintendent.

befragen *verb* (PERF **hat befragt**) to question.

befreien *verb* (PERF **hat befreit**) 1 to free; 2 to exempt; **jemanden vom Wehrdienst befreien** to exempt somebody from military service; 3 **sich befreien** to free oneself.

Befreiung *die* liberation.

befreunden *verb* (PERF **hat sich befreundet**) **sich befreunden** to make friends.

befreundet *adjective* **mit jemandem befreundet sein** to be friends with somebody; **wir sind schon lange gut befreundet** we've been close friends for a long time.

befriedigen *verb* (PERF **hat befriedigt**) to satisfy.

befriedigend *adjective* satisfactory.

Befugnis *die* (PL *die* **Befugnisse**) authority.

begabt *adjective* gifted, talented.

Begabung *die* gift, talent.

begann SEE **beginnen**.

begegnen *verb* (PERF **ist begegnet**) 1 **jemandem begegnen** to meet somebody; **etwas begegnen** to meet something; 2 **sich begegnen** to meet (each other).

Begegnung *die* (PL *die* **Begegnungen**) meeting.

begehen ◇ *verb* (IMPERF **beging**, PERF **hat begangen**) to commit.

begeistern *verb* (PERF **hat begeistert**) 1 **jemanden für etwas begeistern** to fill somebody with enthusiasm for something; 2 **sich begeistern** to get enthusiastic.

△ NEW SPELLING: *See page xii*

begeistert *adjective* enthusiastic.

Begeisterung *die* enthusiasm.

Beginn *der* beginning; **zu Beginn** at the beginning.

beginnen ◇ *verb* (IMPERF **begann**, PERF **hat begonnen**) to begin, to start.

begleiten *verb* (PERF **hat begleitet**) to accompany; **er hat mich nach Hause begleitet** he took me home.

beglückwünschen *verb* (PERF **hat beglückwünscht**) to congratulate.

begonnen SEE **beginnen**.

begraben ◇ *verb* (PRES **begräbt**, IMPERF **begrub**, PERF **hat begraben**) to bury.

begreifen ◇ *verb* (IMPERF **begriff**, PERF **hat begriffen**) to understand.

Begriff *der* (PL *die* **Begriffe**)
1 concept; **davon kann ich mir keinen Begriff machen** I can't imagine that; 2 term; **ein Begriff aus der Malerei** a painting term; 3 **im Begriff sein, etwas zu tun** to be about to do something; 4 **für meine Begriffe** to my mind; 5 **schwer von Begriff** (*informal*) slow on the uptake.

Begründung *die* (PL *die* **Begründungen**) reason.

begrüßen *verb* (PERF **hat begrüßt**)
1 to greet; 2 to welcome.

Begrüßung *die* welcome.

begünstigen *verb* (PERF **hat begünstigt**) to favour.

behaglich *adjective* cosy.

behalten ◇ *verb* (PRES **behält**, IMPERF **behielt**, PERF **hat behalten**)
1 to keep; **du kannst die CD behalten** you can keep the CD; 2 to remember (*a name*).

Behälter *der* (PL *die* **Behälter**) container.

behandeln *verb* (PERF **hat behandelt**) 1 to treat; **er ist sehr schlecht behandelt worden** he's been treated very badly; **einen Patienten behandeln** to treat a patient; 2 to deal with (*a subject, question*).

Behandlung *die* (PL *die* **Behandlungen**) treatment.

behaupten *verb* (PERF **hat behauptet**) 1 to claim; 2 **sich behaupten** to assert oneself.

Behauptung *die* (PL *die* **Behauptungen**) claim.

beherrschen *verb* (PERF **hat beherrscht**) 1 to rule over (*a country, people*); 2 to control; 3 to know; 4 **sich beherrschen** to control oneself.

behilflich *adjective* **jemandem behilflich sein** to help somebody.

behindert *adjective* disabled, handicapped.

Behinderte *der/die* (PL *die* **Behinderten**) disabled person, handicapped person.

Behinderung *die* 1 obstruction; 2 handicap, disability.

Behörde *die* (PL *die* **Behörden**) authority, authorities.

◇ IRREGULAR VERB: *See the verb table in the centre of the dictionary*

behüten *verb* (PERF **hat behütet**) to protect.

bei *preposition* ←(+DAT) **1** near; **die Diskothek beim Bahnhof** the disco near the station; **2** at (*indicating a place or time*); **bei mir** at my place; **beim Arzt** at the doctor's; **bei Beginn** at the beginning; **3 bei seinen Eltern wohnen** to live with your parents; **4 bei uns in der Firma** in our firm; **bei guter Gesundheit** in good health; **5 bei einem Verlag arbeiten** to work for a publisher; **6 bei Regen** if it rains; **bei Nebel** in fog; **bei Tag** by day; **7 etwas bei sich haben** to have something on you; **8 bei Morris** c/o Morris; **9 sich bei jemandem entschuldigen** to apologize to somebody; **10 bei der hohen Miete** with the high rent; **11 beim Fahren** while driving; **beim Lesen sein** to be reading; **beim Frühstück** at breakfast; **12 bei der Ankunft** on arrival.

beibringen ◊ *verb* (PRES **bringt bei**, IMPERF **brachte bei**, PERF **hat beigebracht**) **jemandem etwas beibringen** to teach somebody something.

Beichte *die* (PL *die* **Beichten**) confession.

beichten *verb* (PERF **hat gebeichtet**) to confess.

beide *adjective, pronoun* **1** both; **ihr beide** both of you; **er hat seine beiden Eltern verloren** he has lost both his parents; **2 die ersten beiden** the first two; **eins von beiden** one of the two; **3 keiner von**

beiden neither (of them), **4 beides** both; **er kann beides – Klavier und Gitarre spielen** he can do both – play the piano and the guitar; **5 dreißig beide** thirty all (*in tennis*).

beieinander *adverb* together.

Beifahrer *der* (PL *die* **Beifahrer**) passenger.

Beifahrerin *die* (PL *die* **Beifahrerinnen**) passenger.

Beifall *der* applause.

Beil *das* (PL *die* **Beile**) axe.

Beilage *die* (PL *die* **Beilagen**) **1** supplement (*to a paper*); **2** side-dish; **als Beilage Reis und Spinat** served with rice and spinach.

beiläufig *adjective* casual.

beilegen *verb* (PERF **hat beigelegt**) to enclose.

beiliegen ◊ *verb* (PRES **liegt bei**, IMPERF **lag bei**, PERF **hat beigelegen**) to be enclosed; **ein Scheck liegt bei** please find enclosed a cheque.

beiliegend *adjective* enclosed.

Beileid *das* condolences; **jemandem sein Beileid aussprechen** to offer your condolences to somebody.

beim = **bei dem**.

Bein *das* (PL *die* **Beine**) leg.

beinahe *adverb* almost.

Beinbruch *der* (PL *die* **Beinbrüche**) broken leg; **das ist doch kein Beinbruch** (*informal*) it's not the end of the world.

△ NEW SPELLING: *See page xii*

beisammen *adverb* together.

beiseite *adverb* 1 aside; **etwas beiseite schieben** to push something aside; 2 **etwas beiseite legen** to put something by; 3 **das Geld beiseite schaffen** to hide the money away.

Beispiel *das* (PL **die Beispiele**) example; **zum Beispiel** for example; **mit gutem Beispiel vorangehen** to set a good example.

beispielsweise *adverb* for example.

beißen ✧ *verb* (IMPERF **biss** △, PERF **hat gebissen**) 1 to bite; 2 to sting (*of smoke, for example*); 3 **sich beißen** to clash; **die Farben beißen sich** the colours clash.

Beitrag *der* (PL **die Beiträge**) 1 contribution; 2 subscription; 3 premium (*insurance fee*); 4 article (*in a newspaper*).

beitragen ✧ *verb* (PRES **trägt bei**, IMPERF **trug bei**, PERF **hat beigetragen**) **zu etwas beitragen** to contribute to something.

beitreten ✧ *verb* (PRES **tritt bei**, IMPERF **trat bei**, PERF **ist beigetreten**) to join; **ich trete dem Fußballverein bei** I'm joining the football club.

bekam SEE **bekommen**.

bekämpfen *verb* (PERF **hat bekämpft**) 1 to fight; 2 **sich bekämpfen** to fight.

bekannt *adjective* 1 well known; 2 familiar; **das kommt mir bekannt vor** that seems familiar; 3 **mit jemandem bekannt sein** to know

somebody; 4 **für etwas bekannt sein** to be (well) known for something; 5 **jemanden bekannt machen** to introduce somebody; 6 **das ist mir bekannt** I know that; 7 **etwas bekannt geben/machen** to announce something; 8 **bekannt werden** to become known.

Bekannte *der/die* (PL **die Bekannten**) 1 acquaintance; 2 friend.

bekanntlich *adverb* **Rauchen ist bekanntlich schädlich** as you know, smoking is bad for you.

beklagen *verb* (PERF **hat sich beklagt**) **sich beklagen** to complain.

Bekleidung *die* clothes, clothing.

bekommen ✧ *verb* (IMPERF **bekam**, PERF **hat bekommen**) 1 to get; **Angst bekommen** to get frightened; 2 to catch (*a cold, the train*); 3 **ein Kind bekommen** to have a baby; 4 **was bekommen Sie?** (*in a shop*) can I help you?; (*in a restaurant*) what would you like?; 5 **was bekommen Sie dafür?** how much is it?; 6 (PERF **ist bekommen**) **fettes Essen bekommt mir nicht** fatty food doesn't agree with me; 7 (PERF **ist bekommen**) **die Ferien sind mir gut bekommen** the holiday did me good.

Belag *der* (PL **die Beläge**) 1 covering; 2 coating; 3 topping (*on bread*); 4 lining (*of brakes*).

belasten *verb* (PERF **hat belastet**) 1 to burden; 2 to put weight on (*foot*); 3 to pollute (*the*

✧ IRREGULAR VERB: *See the verb table in the centre of the dictionary*

atmosphere)' **4** to debit (*an account*); **5** to incriminate.

belästigen *verb* (PERF **hat belästigt**) **1** to bother; **2** to harass.

Belastung *die* **1** strain; **2** load; **3** burden; **4** pollution.

belegen *verb* (PERF **hat belegt**) **1** to cover; **2** **eine Scheibe Brot mit Käse belegen** to put some cheese on a slice of bread; **3** to enrol for (*a course*); **4** to reserve (*a seat*); **5** **den ersten Platz belegen** to come first; **6** to prove (*facts*).

belegt *adjective* **1** occupied; **2** **der Platz ist belegt** this seat is taken; **3** **ein belegtes Brot** an open sandwich; **4** **die Nummer ist belegt** (*when phoning*) the number's engaged.

beleidigen *verb* (PERF **hat beleidigt**) to insult.

Beleidigung *die* (PL *die* **Beleidigungen**) insult.

Beleuchtung *die* lighting.

Belgien *das* Belgium.

Belgier *der* (PL *die* **Belgier**) Belgian.

Belgierin *die* (PL *die* **Belgierinnen**) Belgian.

belgisch *adjective* Belgian.

Belichtung *die* exposure.

beliebig *adjective* any; **eine beliebige Zahl** any number you like.
adverb **beliebig lange** as long as you like; **beliebig viele** as many as you like.

beliebt *adjective* popular.

Beliebtheit *die* popularity.

bellen *verb* (PERF **hat gebellt**) to bark.

belohnen *verb* (PERF **hat belohnt**) to reward.

Belohnung *die* (PL *die* **Belohnungen**) reward.

belügen *verb* (IMPERF **belog**, PERF **hat belogen**) to lie to.

bemerkbar *adjective* **sich bemerkbar machen** to attract attention, to become noticeable.

bemerken *verb* (PERF **hat bemerkt**) **1** to notice; **2** to remark; **3** **nebenbei bemerkt** by the way.

Bemerkung *die* (PL *die* **Bemerkungen**) remark.

bemitleiden *verb* (PERF **hat bemitleidet**) to pity.

bemühen *verb* (PERF **hat sich bemüht**) **1** **sich bemühen** to try; **sich sehr bemühen** to try hard; **er bemüht sich um eine Stelle** he's trying to get a job; **2** **sich um jemanden bemühen** to try to help somebody; **3** **bitte, bemühen Sie sich nicht** please don't trouble yourself.

Bemühung *die* (PL *die* **Bemühungen**) effort.

benachrichtigen *verb* (PERF **hat benachrichtigt**) **1** to inform; **2** to notify (*officially*).

benachteiligt *adjective* disadvantaged.

△ NEW SPELLING: *See page xii*

benehmen ✧ verb (PRES **benimmt sich**, IMPERF **benahm sich**, PERF **hat sich benommen**) **sich benehmen** to behave; **benimm dich!** behave yourself!

Benehmen das behaviour.

beneiden verb (PERF **hat beneidet**) to envy; **jemanden um etwas beneiden** to envy somebody something.

benoten verb (PERF **hat benotet**) to mark.

benutzen verb (PERF **hat benutzt**) to use.

Benutzer der (PL die **Benutzer**) user.

Benutzung die use.

Benzin das petrol.

beobachten verb (PERF **hat beobachtet**) to observe, to watch.

bequem adjective **1** comfortable; **2 machen Sie es sich bequem** make yourself at home; **3** lazy; **4** easy; **eine bequeme Lösung finden** to find an easy way out.

beraten ✧ verb (PRES **berät**, IMPERF **beriet**, PERF **hat beraten**) **1** to advise; **2 jemanden gut/schlecht beraten** to give somebody good/bad advice; **3 sich beraten lassen** to get advice; **4 gut beraten sein** to be well advised; **5** to discuss (a plan, matter); **6 sich über etwas beraten** to discuss something.

Berater der (PL die **Berater**) adviser.

Beratung die (PL die **Beratungen**) **1** advice; **2** discussion; **3** consultation (with a doctor).

berauben verb (PERF **hat beraubt**) to rob.

berechnen verb (PERF **hat berechnet**) **1** to charge; **jemandem zehn Mark für etwas berechnen** to charge somebody ten marks for something; **2 jemandem zuviel berechnen** to overcharge somebody; **3** to calculate.

Bereich der (PL die **Bereiche**) **1** area; **2** field (in a profession).

bereit adjective ready.

bereiten verb (PERF **hat bereitet**) **1** to make (coffee, tea); **2** to cause (trouble, difficulty); **leider hat es uns Schwierigkeiten bereitet** unfortunately it caused us some trouble; **3** to give (a surprise, pleasure).

bereits adverb already.

bereuen verb (PERF **hat bereut**) to regret.

Berg der (PL die **Berge**) **1** mountain; **2** hill.

bergab adverb downhill.

Bergarbeiter der (PL die **Bergarbeiter**) miner.

bergauf adverb uphill.

bergen ✧ verb (PRES **birgt**, IMPERF **barg**, PERF **hat geborgen**) to rescue.

Bergsteigen das mountaineering.

Bergsteiger der (PL die **Bergsteiger**) mountaineer, climber.

Bergsteigerin die (PL die **Bergsteigerinnen**) mountaineer, climber.

✧ IRREGULAR VERB: *See the verb table in the centre of the dictionary*

Bergwacht *die* mountain rescue.

Bergwerk *das* (PL *die* **Bergwerke**) mine.

Bericht *der* (PL *die* **Berichte**) report.

berichten *verb* (PERF **hat berichtet**)
1 to report; **die Zeitungen haben nichts davon berichtet** the newspapers didn't report anything about it; 2 **jemandem über etwas berichten** to tell somebody about something; **er hat mir über seine Ferien in Amerika berichtet** he told me about his holiday in America.

berücksichtigen *verb* (PERF **hat berücksichtigt**) to take into account.

Beruf *der* (PL *die* **Berufe**)
1 occupation; 2 profession; **ich bin Lehrerin von Beruf** I'm a teacher by profession; 3 trade; 4 **was sind Sie von Beruf?** what do you do for a living?

beruflich *adjective* 1 professional;
2 vocational (*training*).
adverb 1 **beruflich erfolgreich sein** to be successful in your career; 2 **viel beruflich unterwegs sein** to be away a lot on business.

Berufsberatung *die* careers advice.

Berufsschule *die* (PL *die* **Berufsschulen**) technical college.

berufstätig *adjective* working.

Berufsverkehr *der* rush-hour traffic.

beruhigen *verb* (PERF **hat beruhigt**)
1 to calm down; 2 to reassure;
3 **sich beruhigen** to calm down.

Beruhigungsmittel *das* (PL *die* **Beruhigungsmittel**) sedative, tranquillizer.

berühmt *adjective* famous.

berühren *verb* (PERF **hat berührt**)
1 to touch; 2 to touch on (*a topic, an issue*); 3 to affect; **ihre Geschichte berührte ihn seltsam** he was strangely affected by her story; 4 **sich berühren** to touch.

besaß SEE **besitzen**.

beschädigen *verb* (PERF **hat beschädigt**) to damage.

beschaffen[1] *verb* (PERF **hat beschafft**) to get; **kannst du mir nicht einen Job beschaffen?** can't you get me a job?

beschaffen[2] *adjective* **so beschaffen sein, dass …** to be such that …

beschäftigen *verb* (PERF **hat beschäftigt**) 1 to occupy (*keep busy*); 2 to employ (*people*); 3 **sich beschäftigen** to occupy yourself;
4 **ich beschäftige mich mit den Kindern** I'm busy with the children;
5 **sich mit einem Fall beschäftigen** to deal with a case; **sein Aufsatz beschäftigt sich mit der Umweltverschmutzung** his essay deals with environmental pollution.

beschäftigt *adjective* 1 busy;
2 employed.

Beschäftigung *die* (PL *die* **Beschäftigungen**) 1 occupation;
2 activity.

Bescheid *der* (PL *die* **Bescheide**)
1 information; 2 **jemandem**

△ NEW SPELLING: *See page*

Bescheid sagen to let somebody know; **3 über etwas Bescheid wissen** to know about something.

bescheiden *adjective* modest.

Bescheinigung *die* (PL *die* **Bescheinigungen**) 1 certificate; **eine Bescheinigung des Arztes** a doctor's certificate; 2 (written) confirmation.

beschimpfen *verb* (PERF **hat beschimpft**) to abuse.

beschlagnahmen *verb* (PERF **hat beschlagnahmt**) to confiscate.

beschleunigen *verb* (PERF **hat beschleunigt**) 1 to speed up; 2 to accelerate; **der Lastwagen hinter uns hat plötzlich beschleunigt** the lorry behind us suddenly accelerated.

beschließen ✧ *verb* (IMPERF **beschloss** Δ, PERF **hat beschlossen**) to decide.

Beschluss Δ *der* (PL *die* **Beschlüsse**) decision.

beschreiben ✧ *verb* (IMPERF **beschrieb**, PERF **hat beschrieben**) to describe.

Beschreibung *die* (PL *die* **Beschreibungen**) description.

beschuldigen *verb* (PERF **hat beschuldigt**) to accuse.

beschützen *verb* (PERF **hat beschützt**) to protect.

Beschwerde *die* (PL *die* **Beschwerden**) complaint.

beschweren *verb* (PERF **hat sich beschwert**) **sich beschweren** to complain; **ich habe mich bei den Nachbarn über ihn beschwert** I've complained to the neighbours about him.

beschwipst *adjective* tipsy.

beseitigen *verb* (PERF **hat beseitigt**) to remove.

Besen *der* (PL *die* **Besen**) broom.

besetzen *verb* (PERF **hat besetzt**) 1 to occupy; 2 to fill (*a post, role*); 3 to trim, to edge (*with lace or fur*).

besetzt *adjective* 1 occupied; 2 **besetzt sein** to be engaged (*a phone, toilet*); 3 taken (*a table, seat*); **der Platz ist besetzt** this seat is taken; 4 full (*of a train, bus*); **der Zug ist voll besetzt** the train is full up.

Besetztzeichen *das* (PL *die* **Besetztzeichen**) engaged tone.

besichtigen *verb* (PERF **hat besichtigt**) 1 to look round (*a town, museum*); 2 to see (*sights, a house*).

Besichtigung *die* (PL *die* **Besichtigungen**) visit.

besinnungslos *adjective* unconscious.

Besitz *der* 1 property; 2 **im Besitz einer Sache sein** to be in possession of something.

besitzen ✧ *verb* (IMPERF **besaß**, PERF **hat besessen**) 1 to own; **sie besitzen ein Haus in Italien** they own a house in Italy; 2 to have (*talent, a quality*).

Besitzer *der* (PL *die* **Besitzer**) owner.

✧ IRREGULAR VERB: *See the verb table in the centre of the dictionary*

Besitzerin die (PL die Besitzerinnen) owner.

besonderer, besondere, besonderes adjective 1 special; **unter besonderen Umständen** in special circumstances; 2 particular; **ohne besondere Begeisterung** without any particular enthusiasm; 3 **keine besonderen Kennzeichen** no distinguishing features.

Besonderheit die (PL die Besonderheiten) 1 special feature; 2 peculiarity.

besonders adverb particularly.

besorgen verb (PERF hat besorgt) to get; **ich kann dir Karten besorgen** I can get you tickets.

besorgt adjective worried.

besprechen ◇ verb (PRES bespricht, IMPERF besprach, PERF hat besprochen) 1 to discuss; **ich muss es erst mit meinen Eltern besprechen** I'll have to discuss it with my parents first; 2 to review (a book, film).

Besprechung die (PL die Besprechungen) 1 meeting (at work); 2 discussion; 3 review (of a film, play).

besser adjective, adverb better; **alles besser wissen** to know better.

Besserung die 1 improvement; 2 **gute Besserung!** get well soon!

beständig adjective 1 constant; 2 settled (weather).

Bestandteil der (PL die Bestandteile) component.

bestätigen verb (PERF hat bestätigt) 1 to confirm; 2 to acknowledge (receipt); 3 **sich bestätigen** to be confirmed, to prove to be true.

beste SEE **bester**.

Bestechung die (PL die Bestechungen) bribery.

Besteck das (PL die Bestecke) cutlery.

bestehen ◇ verb (IMPERF bestand, PERF hat bestanden) 1 to exist; 2 **es besteht die Gefahr, dass** … there is a danger that …; **noch besteht die Hoffnung, dass** … there is still hope that …; 3 to pass; **eine Prüfung bestehen** to pass an exam; 4 **auf etwas bestehen** to insist on something; 5 **aus etwas bestehen** to consist of something; 6 **aus etwas bestehen** to be made of something.

bestellen verb (PERF hat bestellt) 1 to order (goods); 2 to reserve (tickets); 3 to tell; **jemandem etwas bestellen** to tell somebody something; 4 **bestell ihm schöne Grüße** give him my regards; 5 **kann ich etwas bestellen?** can I take a message?; 6 to send for; **jemanden zu sich bestellen** to send for somebody.

Bestellung die (PL die Bestellungen) 1 order (for goods); 2 reservation (for tickets).

bestens adverb very well; **das hat ja bestens geklappt** that worked out very well.

△ NEW SPELLING: See page

bester, beste, bestes *adjective*
1 best; **sein bestes Buch** his best
book; **2 ich halte es für das Beste** △,
wenn … I think it would be best if
…; **sein Bestes tun** to do your best;
3 einen Witz zum Besten geben △
to tell a joke; **4 jemanden zum
Besten halten** △ to pull somebody's
leg.
adverb **am besten** best; **du bleibst
am besten zu Hause** you'd best stay
at home; **es ist am besten, wenn wir
gleich anfangen** it's best if we get
started straight away.

bestimmen *verb* (PERF **hat
bestimmt**) **1** to fix (*a time, price*);
2 to decide (on); **etwas allein
bestimmen** to decide (on)
something on your own; **er bestimmt
immer, was wir machen** he always
decides what we're going to do; **3** to
be in charge; **4 für jemanden
bestimmt sein** to be meant for
somebody; **5 für etwas bestimmt
sein** to be intended for something
(*a donation for a good cause, for
example*).

bestimmt *adjective* **1** certain; **zu
einer bestimmten Zeit** at a certain
time; **2** particular; **suchen Sie
etwas Bestimmtes?** are you
looking for anything in particular?;
3 definite.
adverb **1** certainly, definitely; **ich
komme ganz bestimmt** I'm
definitely coming; **2 er hat es
bestimmt vergessen** he's bound to
have forgotten; **3 du weißt es doch
bestimmt noch** surely you must
remember it.

Bestimmung *die* (PL *die*
Bestimmungen) regulation.

bestrafen *verb* (PERF **hat bestraft**)
to punish.

bestreiten ✧ *verb* (IMPERF **bestritt**,
PERF **hat bestritten**) **1** to deny; **2** to
dispute; **das möchte ich nicht
bestreiten** I'm not disputing it; **3** to
pay for.

bestürzt *adjective* upset.

Besuch *der* (PL *die* **Besuche**) **1** visit;
2 attendance (*at school*); **3 Besuch
haben** to have visitors/a visitor;
4 bei Freunden zu Besuch sein to
be staying with friends; **zu Besuch
kommen** to be visiting.

besuchen *verb* (PERF **hat besucht**)
1 to visit; **2** to go to (*an exhibition,
the theatre*); **die Schule besuchen**
to go to school; **3** to attend (*a
lecture*).

Besucher *der* (PL *die* **Besucher**)
visitor.

Besucherin *die* (PL *die*
Besucherinnen) visitor.

betätigen *verb* (PERF **hat betätigt**)
1 to operate; **2 die Bremse
betätigen** to apply the brakes;
3 sich politisch betätigen to be
involved in politics; **4 sich
künstlerisch betätigen** to do art;
5 sich als Reporter betätigen to
work as a reporter.

Betäubungsmittel *das* (PL *die*
Betäubungsmittel) anaesthetic.

Bete *die* **Rote Bete** △ beetroot.

beteiligen *verb* (PERF **hat beteiligt**)
1 to give a share to; **jemanden mit**

✧ IRREGULAR VERB: *See the verb table in the centre of the dictionary*

zehn Prozent an einem Geschäft beteiligen to give somebody a ten percent share of a business; **2 sich an etwas beteiligen** to take part in something; **3 kann ich mich an eurem Spiel beteiligen?** can I join in your game?

beten *verb* (PERF **hat gebetet**) to pray.

Beton *der* concrete.

betonen *verb* (PERF **hat betont**) to stress.

Betonung *die* (PL *die* **Betonungen**) stress.

Betrag *der* (PL *die* **Beträge**) amount.

betragen✧ *verb* (PRES **beträgt**, IMPERF **betrug**, PERF **hat betragen**) **1** to amount to, to come to; **2 sich betragen** to behave; **haben sich die Kinder gut betragen?** did the children behave well?

Betragen *das* behaviour.

betreffen✧ *verb* (PRES **betrifft**, IMPERF **betraf**, PERF **hat betroffen**) to concern; **was mich betrifft** as far as I'm concerned.

betreten✧ *verb* (PRES **betritt**, IMPERF **betrat**, PERF **hat betreten**) **1** to enter; **2 'Betreten verboten'** 'keep out', 'keep off' (*the grass, for example*).

Betrieb *der* (PL *die* **Betriebe**) **1** business, firm; **2** activity; **es war viel Betrieb** it was very busy; **3 in Betrieb sein** to be working (*of a machine*); **4 außer Betrieb sein** to be out of order; **5 eine Maschine in**

Betrieb setzen to start up a machine.

Betriebsferien *plural noun* firm's holiday; **'Betriebsferien'** 'closed for the holidays'.

betrinken✧ *verb* (IMPERF **betrank sich**, PERF **hat sich betrunken**) **sich betrinken** to get drunk.

betrog SEE **betrügen**.

Betrug *der* **1** deception; **2** fraud.

betrügen✧ *verb* (IMPERF **betrog**, PERF **hat betrogen**) **1** to cheat; **jemanden um tausend Mark betrügen** to cheat somebody out of a thousand marks; **2** to be unfaithful to, to cheat on; **sie hat ihren Mann betrogen** she's been unfaithful to her husband.

betrunken *adjective* drunk.

Bett *das* (PL *die* **Betten**) bed; **ins Bett gehen** to go to bed.

Bettbezug *der* (PL *die* **Bettbezüge**) duvet cover.

betteln *verb* (PERF **hat gebettelt**) to beg.

Bettlaken *das* (PL *die* **Bettlaken**) sheet.

Bettler *der* (PL *die* **Bettler**) beggar.

Bettlerin *die* (PL *die* **Bettlerinnen**) beggar.

Bettwäsche *die* bed linen.

Bettzeug *das* bedding.

beugen *verb* (PERF **hat gebeugt**) **1** to bend; **2** to decline, to conjugate (*in grammar*); **3 sich nach vorn beugen** to bend forwards; **sich über**

∆ NEW SPELLING: See pa

etwas **beugen** to bend over something; **4 sich aus dem Fenster beugen** to lean out of the window; **5 sich beugen** to submit.

Beule die (PL die **Beulen**) **1** bump; **2** lump; **3** dent.

beurteilen verb (PERF **hat beurteilt**) to judge.

Beutel der (PL die **Beutel**) bag.

Bevölkerung die (PL die **Bevölkerungen**) population.

bevor conjunction **1** before; **2 bevor nicht** until; **bevor er nicht unterschrieben hat** until he has signed.

bevorzugen verb (PERF **hat bevorzugt**) to prefer.

bewachen verb (PERF **hat bewacht**) to guard.

bewaffnen verb (PERF **hat bewaffnet**) to arm.

bewaffnet adjective armed.

bewährt adjective **1** reliable; **2** proven (method, design); **3 ein bewährtes Rezept** a well-tried recipe.

bewegen[1] verb (PERF **hat bewegt**) **1** to move; **2 sich bewegen** to take exercise; **3 sich bewegen** to move.

bewegen[2] ◇ verb (IMPERF **bewog**, PERF **hat bewogen**) **jemanden dazu bewegen, etwas zu tun** to persuade somebody to do something.

bewegt adjective eventful.

Bewegung die (PL die **Bewegungen**) **1** movement;

2 exercise; **3 eine Maschine in Bewegung setzen** to start (up) a machine; **4 sich in Bewegung setzen** to start to move.

Beweis der (PL die **Beweise**) **1** proof; **2 belastende Beweise** incriminating evidence; **3** token, sign.

beweisen ◇ verb (IMPERF **bewies**, PERF **hat bewiesen**) **1** to prove; **2** to show.

bewerben ◇ verb (PRES **bewirbt sich**, IMPERF **bewarb sich**, PERF **hat sich beworben**) **sich bewerben** to apply; **sich um eine Stelle bewerben** to apply for a job.

Bewerber der (PL die **Bewerber**) applicant.

Bewerberin die (PL die **Bewerberinnen**) applicant.

Bewerbung die (PL die **Bewerbungen**) application.

bewohnen verb (PERF **hat bewohnt**) to live in.

Bewohner der (PL die **Bewohner**) **1** resident; **2** inhabitant (of a region).

Bewohnerin die (PL die **Bewohnerinnen**) **1** resident; **2** inhabitant (of a region).

bewölkt adjective cloudy.

Bewölkung die clouds.

bewundern verb (PERF **hat bewundert**) to admire.

Bewunderung die admiration.

bewusst ∆ adjective **1** conscious;

◇ IRREGULAR VERB: *See the verb table in the centre of the dictionary*

2 deliberate; **3 sich etwas bewusst sein** to be aware of something; **ich war mir der Folgen bewusst** I was aware of the consequences.

bewusstlos△ *adjective* unconscious.

Bewusstsein△ *das*
1 consciousness; **2 bei vollem Bewusstsein sein** to be fully conscious; **3 mir kam zu(m) Bewusstsein, dass …** I realized that …

bezahlen *verb* (PERF **hat bezahlt**)
1 to pay; **2** to pay for (*goods, food*); **er hat das Essen bezahlt** he paid for the meal.

Bezahlung *die* payment.

bezeichnend *adjective* typical.

beziehen✧ *verb* (IMPERF **bezog**, PERF **hat bezogen**) **1** to cover; **2 das Bett frisch beziehen** to put clean sheets on the bed; **3** to move into; **wann kannst du die neue Wohnung beziehen?** when will you be able to move into the new flat?; **4** to get (*goods, a pension*); **5** to take (*a newspaper*); **6 sich auf etwas/jemanden beziehen** to refer to something/somebody; **7 es bezieht sich** it's clouding over.

Beziehung *die* (PL *die* **Beziehungen**) **1** connection; **2** relationship; **3 Beziehungen** contacts; **Anna hat gute Beziehungen** Anna has good contacts; **4 diplomatische Beziehungen** diplomatic relations; **5 in dieser Beziehung** in this respect; **6 eine Beziehung zu etwas**

haben to be able to relate to something (*to art, pop music, for example*).

beziehungsweise *conjunction*
1 or rather; **2** respectively.

Bezirk *der* (PL *die* **Bezirke**) district.

Bezug *der* (PL *die* **Bezüge**) **1** cover (*of a cushion, duvet, etc.*); **2** connection; **keinen Bezug zu etwas haben** to be unable to relate to something; **3 auf etwas Bezug nehmen** to refer to something; **4 in Bezug auf** regarding; **5 mit Bezug auf Ihr Angebot** with reference to your offer.

bezweifeln *verb* (PERF **hat bezweifelt**) to doubt.

BH *der* (PL *die* **BHs**) bra.

Bibel *die* (PL *die* **Bibeln**) bible; **die Bibel** the Bible.

Bibliothek *die* (PL *die* **Bibliotheken**) library.

biegen✧ *verb* (IMPERF **bog**, PERF **hat gebogen**) **1** to bend; **2 sich biegen** to bend; **3** (PERF **ist gebogen**) to turn; **um die Ecke biegen** to turn the corner.

Biene *die* (PL *die* **Bienen**) bee.

Bier *das* (PL *die* **Biere**) beer.

Bierdeckel *der* (PL *die* **Bierdeckel**) beer mat.

bieten✧ *verb* (IMPERF **bot**, PERF **hat geboten**) **1** to offer; **2** to bid (*at an auction*); **3 es bietet sich die Möglichkeit** there is a possibility; **4** to present (*a sight*); **5 das lasse**

ich mir nicht bieten! I won't put up
with it!

Bikini der (PL die **Bikinis**) bikini.

Bild das (PL die **Bilder**) 1 picture;
jemanden ins Bild setzen to put
somebody in the picture; 2 scene.

bilden verb (PERF **hat gebildet**) 1 to
form; 2 sich bilden to form; 3 sich
bilden to educate yourself.

Bildschirm der (PL die **Bildschirme**)
screen.

bildschön adjective (very)
beautiful.

Bildung die 1 formation;
2 education.

billig adjective cheap.

Billion die (PL die **Billionen**) billion (a
million million).

bin SEE sein.

Binde die (PL die **Binden**)
1 bandage; 2 sanitary towel.

binden ◇ verb (IMPERF **band**, PERF
hat gebunden) 1 to tie; 2 to bind (a
book); 3 to make up (a bouquet);
4 to thicken (a sauce); 5 sich
binden to commit oneself.

Bindestrich der (PL die
Bindestriche) hyphen.

Bindfaden der (PL die **Bindfäden**)
(piece of) string.

Bindung die (PL die **Bindungen**)
1 tie; 2 relationship; 3 binding (on
a ski).

Biokost die health food.

Biologie die biology.

biologisch adjective biological.

Birke die (PL die **Birken**) birch tree.

Birne die (PL die **Birnen**) 1 pear;
2 bulb.

bis preposition ←(+ACC) 1 as far as;
dieser Zug fährt nur bis Passau
this train only goes as far as Passau;
2 up to; Kinder bis zehn zahlen die
Hälfte children up to ten pay half;
bis jetzt up to now; bis zu up to;
3 until, till (with time); 4 by; bis
dahin by then; 5 bis auf except
for; alle sind durchgefallen bis auf
die zwei Mädchen everyone failed
except for the two girls; 6 bis bald!
see you soon!; 7 von München bis
Salzburg from Munich to Salzburg;
von Montag bis Freitag from
Monday to Friday; zwei bis drei
Mark two to three marks.
conjunction until, till; sie bleibt, bis
es dunkel wird she's staying until it
gets dark.

Bischof der (PL die **Bischöfe**) bishop.

bisher adverb so far.

bisherig adjective previous.

biss △ SEE beißen.

Biss △ der (PL die **Bisse**) bite.

bisschen △ pronoun 1 ein
bisschen a bit; ein bisschen Brot
a bit of bread; 2 kein bisschen not
a bit.

bissig adjective 1 vicious; 'Vorsicht
bissiger Hund!' 'beware of the
dog!'; 2 cutting (remark, tone).

bist SEE sein.

bitte adverb 1 please; 'möchten Sie

◇ IRREGULAR VERB: See the verb table in the centre of the dictionary

Kuchen?' – 'ja bitte' 'would you
like some cake?' – 'yes please';
2 you're welcome (*in reply to
thanks*); **3** come in (*after a knock on
the door*); **4** (*in a shop*) **bitte?** yes,
please?; **5 wie bitte?** sorry?

Bitte *die* (PL *die* **Bitten**) request.

bitten ✧ *verb* (IMPERF **bat**, PERF **hat
gebeten**) to ask; **jemanden um
etwas bitten** to ask somebody for
something.

bitter *adjective* bitter.

blamieren *verb* (PERF **hat blamiert**)
1 to disgrace; **2 jemanden
blamieren** to embarrass somebody;
3 sich blamieren to make a fool of
yourself.

Blase *die* (PL *die* **Blasen**) **1** bubble;
2 blister; **3** bladder.

blasen ✧ *verb* (PRES **bläst**, IMPERF
blies, PERF **hat geblasen**) to blow.

Blasinstrument *das* (PL *die*
Blasinstrumente) wind instrument.

Blaskapelle *die* (PL *die*
Blaskapellen) brass band.

blass △ *adjective* pale.

Blatt *das* (PL *die* **Blätter**) **1** leaf;
2 sheet; **ein Blatt Papier** a sheet of
paper; **3** page; **4** newspaper.

blau *adjective* **1** blue; **ein blau
gestreiftes Kleid** a dress with blue
stripes; **2 ein blaues Auge haben**
to have a black eye; **3 ein blauer
Fleck** a bruise; **4 blau sein**
(*informal*) to be tight; **5 eine Fahrt
ins Blaue** a mystery tour.

Blech *das* (PL *die* **Bleche**) **1** sheet

metal; **2** tin; **3** baking tray; **4** brass
(*in music*).

Blei *das* lead.

bleiben ✧ *verb* (IMPERF **blieb**, PERF **ist
geblieben**) **1** to stay, to remain; **2** to
be left; **3 bleiben Sie am Apparat**
hold the line; **4 bei etwas bleiben**
to stick to something; **5 ruhig
bleiben** to keep calm; **6 wo bleibt
er so lange?** where has he got to?;
7 etwas bleiben lassen to not do
something; **wenn du nicht
mitkommen willst, dann lass es
eben bleiben** if you don't want to
come, then don't.

bleich *adjective* pale.

Bleichmittel *das* (PL *die*
Bleichmittel) bleach.

bleifrei *adjective* unleaded.

Bleistift *der* (PL *die* **Bleistifte**) pencil.

Bleistiftspitzer *der* (PL *die*
Bleistiftspitzer) pencil sharpener.

blenden *verb* (PERF **hat geblendet**)
1 to dazzle; **2** to blind.

blendend *adjective* **1** marvellous;
2 es geht mir blendend I feel great;
wir haben uns blendend amüsiert
we had a great time.

Blick *der* (PL *die* **Blicke**) **1** look;
2 glance; **3 auf den ersten Blick** at
first sight; **4** view; **ein Zimmer mit
Blick aufs Meer** a room with a sea
view.

blicken *verb* (PERF **hat geblickt**) **1** to
look; **2 sich blicken lassen** to show
your face.

blieb SEE **bleiben**.

△ NEW SPELLING: *See pa*

blies SEE **blasen**.

blind *adjective* blind.

Blinddarm *der* (PL *die* **Blinddärme**) appendix.

Blinddarmentzündung *die* (PL *die* **Blinddarmentzündungen**) appendicitis.

Blinde *der/die* (PL *die* **Blinden**) blind person, blind man/woman.

blinzeln *verb* (PERF **hat geblinzelt**) to blink.

blinken *verb* (PERF **hat geblinkt**) 1 to flash; 2 to indicate (*of a car*).

Blinker *der* (PL *die* **Blinker**) indicator.

Blitz *der* (PL *die* **Blitze**) 1 (flash of) lightning; 2 flash.

blitzen *verb* (PERF **hat geblitzt**) 1 to flash; 2 to sparkle; 3 **es hat geblitzt** there was a flash of lightning.

Block *der* (PL *die* **Blöcke**) 1 pad (*for writing on*); 2 (PL *die* **Blocks**) block (*of flats*).

Blockflöte *die* (PL *die* **Blockflöten**) recorder.

blöd *adjective* stupid.

Blödsinn *der* nonsense.

blond *adjective* blonde, fair-haired.

bloß *adverb* 1 only; **es kostet bloß fünf Mark** it's only five marks; 2 **warum hat er das bloß gemacht?** why on earth did he do it?; 3 **was mache ich bloß?** whatever shall I do?; 4 **fass das bloß nicht an!** don't touch it!
adjective 1 bare (*feet*); **mit bloßem Auge** with the naked eye; 2 mere (*words, suspicion*); **der bloße Gedanke daran** the mere thought of it.

Blume *die* (PL *die* **Blumen**) flower.

Blumenkohl *der* cauliflower.

Bluse *die* (PL *die* **Blusen**) blouse.

Blut *das* blood.

Blutdruck *der* blood pressure.

Blüte *die* (PL *die* **Blüten**) blossom.

bluten *verb* (PERF **hat geblutet**) to bleed.

Blutprobe *die* (PL *die* **Blutproben**) blood test.

Bock *der* (PL *die* **Böcke**) 1 buck; 2 billy-goat; 3 ram; 4 **Bock auf etwas haben** (*informal*) to fancy something; 5 **einen Bock schießen** (*informal*) to make a blunder.

Bockwurst *die* (PL *die* **Bockwürste**) frankfurter.

Boden *der* (PL *die* **Böden**) 1 ground; 2 floor; 3 bottom (*of a container*); 4 loft, attic.

Bodensee *der* Lake Constance.

bog SEE **biegen**.

Bogen *der* (PL *die* **Bögen**) 1 curve; 2 arch; 3 turn (*in skiing*).

Bohne *die* (PL *die* **Bohnen**) bean.

bohren *verb* (PERF **hat gebohrt**) to drill.

Bohrer *der* (PL *die* **Bohrer**) drill.

Bohrinsel *die* (PL *die* **Bohrinseln**) oil rig.

✧ IRREGULAR VERB: *See the verb table in the centre of the dictionary*

Bohrmaschine die (PL die Bohrmaschinen) electric drill.

Bombe die (PL die **Bomben**) bomb.

Bonbon der (PL die **Bonbons**) sweet.

Boot das (PL die **Boote**) boat.

Bord[1] das (PL die **Borde**) shelf.

Bord[2] der **an Bord** on board; **über Bord** overboard.

Bordkarte die (PL die **Bordkarten**) boarding card.

borgen (PERF **hat geborgt**) 1 to borrow; 2 **sich etwas borgen** to borrow something; **ich habe es mir von ihr geborgt** I borrowed it from her; 3 **jemandem etwas borgen** to lend somebody something; **Evi hat mir ihr Buch geborgt** Evi lent me her book.

Börse die (PL die **Börsen**) stock exchange.

Borste die (PL die **Borsten**) bristle.

böse adjective 1 bad; 2 wicked; 3 naughty (child); 4 angry; **böse werden** to get angry; **ich bin ihm böse** I'm angry with him; 5 **auf jemanden böse sein** to be cross with somebody.

boshaft adjective malicious.

bot SEE **bieten**.

Bote der (PL die **Boten**) messenger.

Botin die (PL die **Botinnen**) messenger.

Botschaft die (PL die **Botschaften**) 1 message; 2 embassy.

Botschafter der (PL die **Botschafter**) ambassador.

Botschafterin die (PL die **Botschafterinnen**) ambassador.

Bowle die (PL die **Bowlen**) punch (for drinking).

boxen verb (PERF **hat geboxt**) 1 to box; 2 to punch.

Boxer der (PL die **Boxer**) boxer.

brach SEE **brechen**.

brachte SEE **bringen**.

Branche die (PL die **Branchen**) (line of) business.

Branchenverzeichnis das (PL die **Branchenverzeichnisse**) classified directory.

Brand der (PL die **Brände**) fire.

Brandung die surf.

brannte SEE **brennen**.

braten ✧ verb (PRES **brät**, IMPERF **briet**, PERF **hat gebraten**) 1 to fry; 2 to roast.

Braten der (PL die **Braten**) 1 roast; 2 joint.

Brathähnchen das (PL die **Brathähnchen**) roast chicken.

Bratkartoffeln plural noun fried potatoes.

Bratpfanne die (PL die **Bratpfannen**) frying pan.

Bratwurst die (PL die **Bratwürste**) fried sausage.

Brauch der (PL die **Bräuche**) custom.

△ NEW SPELLING: See page xii

brauchbar *adjective* 1 usable; 2 useful.

brauchen *verb* (PERF **hat gebraucht**) 1 need; **ich brauche eine neue Birne für meine Lampe** I need a new bulb for my light; **du brauchst nur auf den Knopf zu drücken** all you need to do is press the button; **du brauchst nicht zu gehen** you needn't go; 2 **sie braucht es nur zu sagen** she only has to say; 3 to take (*time*); **wie lange brauchst du mit dem Auto?** how long does it take you by car?; 4 **ich könnte es gut brauchen** I could do with it.

brauen *verb* (PERF **hat gebraut**) to brew.

Brauerei *die* (PL *die* **Brauereien**) brewery.

braun *adjective* 1 brown; 2 **braun werden** to get a tan; **braun (gebrannt) sein** to be tanned.

Bräune *die* tan.

Brause *die* (PL *die* **Brausen**) fizzy drink.

Braut *die* (PL *die* **Bräute**) bride.

Bräutigam *der* (PL *die* **Bräutigame**) bridegroom.

Brautjungfer *die* (PL *die* **Brautjungfern**) bridesmaid.

Brautpaar *das* (PL *die* **Brautpaare**) bride and groom.

brav *adjective* good.

BRD *die* (*Bundesrepublik Deutschland*) FRG (*Federal Republic of Germany*).

brechen ✧ *verb* (PRES **bricht**, IMPERF **brach**, PERF **hat gebrochen**) 1 to break (*an agreement, a record*); 2 **sich den Arm brechen** to break your arm; 3 to vomit; 4 (PERF **ist gebrochen**) to break; **der Ast ist gebrochen** the branch broke.

breit *adjective* 1 wide; 2 broad; 3 **die breite Masse** the general public.

Breite *die* (PL *die* **Breiten**) width.

Bremse *die* (PL *die* **Bremsen**) 1 brake; 2 horsefly.

bremsen *verb* (PERF **hat gebremst**) 1 to brake; 2 to slow down (*development, production*); 3 **jemanden bremsen** (*informal*) to stop somebody; **er ist nicht mehr zu bremsen** there's no stopping him.

Bremslicht *das* (PL *die* **Bremslichter**) brake light.

Bremspedal *das* (PL *die* **Bremspedale**) brake pedal.

brennen ✧ *verb* (IMPERF **brannte**, PERF **hat gebrannt**) 1 to burn; 2 to be on (*of a light*); **das Licht brennen lassen** to leave the light on; 3 to sting (*of a wound or sore*); 4 **das Haus brennt** the house is on fire; **es brennt!** fire!; 5 **darauf brennen, etwas zu tun** to be dying to do something.

Brennnessel △ *die* (PL *die* **Brennnesseln**) stinging nettle.

Brennpunkt *der* (PL *die* **Brennpunkte**) focus.

Brett *das* (PL *die* **Bretter**) 1 board; 2 plank; 3 shelf.

✧ IRREGULAR VERB: *See the verb table in the centre of the dictionary*

Brezel *die* (PL *die* **Brezeln**) pretzel.

bricht SEE **brechen**.

Brief *der* (PL *die* **Briefe**) letter.

Brieffreund *der* (PL *die* **Brieffreunde**) pen friend.

Brieffreundin *die* (PL *die* **Brieffreundinnen**) pen friend.

Briefkasten *der* (PL *die* **Briefkästen**) 1 letterbox; 2 postbox.

Briefmarke *die* (PL *die* **Briefmarken**) stamp.

Brieftasche *die* (PL *die* **Brieftaschen**) wallet.

Briefträger *der* (PL *die* **Briefträger**) postman.

Briefträgerin *die* (PL *die* **Briefträgerinnen**) postwoman.

Briefumschlag *der* (PL *die* **Briefumschläge**) envelope.

Briefwechsel *der* correspondence.

briet SEE **braten**.

Brillant *der* (PL *die* **Brillanten**) diamond.

Brille *die* (PL *die* **Brillen**) glasses, spectacles.

bringen ◇ *verb* (IMPERF **brachte**, PERF **hat gebracht**) 1 to bring; 2 to take; **Peter bringt dich nach Hause** Peter will take you home; 3 **die Kinder ins Bett bringen** to put the children to bed; 4 **einen Film im Fernsehen bringen** to show a film on television; 5 to publish (*an article*); 6 to yield (*interest, a profit*);

7 **jemanden dazu bringen, etwas zu tun** to get somebody to do something; 8 **mit sich bringen** to entail; 9 **etwas hinter sich bringen** to get something over and done with; 10 **es weit bringen** to go far; 11 **jemanden auf eine Idee bringen** to give somebody an idea; 12 **es zu nichts bringen** to get nowhere; 13 **das bringt's nicht!** (*informal*) that's no use!

Brise *die* (PL *die* **Brisen**) breeze.

Brite *der* (PL *die* **Briten**) Briton; **die Briten** the British.

Britin *die* (PL *die* **Britinnen**) Briton.

britisch *adjective* British.

Brokkoli *der* broccoli.

Brombeere *die* (PL *die* **Brombeeren**) blackberry.

Brosche *die* (PL *die* **Broschen**) brooch.

Broschüre *die* (PL *die* **Broschüren**) brochure.

Brot *das* (PL *die* **Brote**) 1 bread; **ein Brot** a loaf of bread; 2 **ein Brot** a slice of bread.

Brötchen *das* (PL *die* **Brötchen**) roll.

Bruch *der* (PL *die* **Brüche**) 1 break; 2 fracture; 3 hernia; 4 fraction.

Bruchteil *der* (PL *die* **Bruchteile**) fraction.

Brücke *die* (PL *die* **Brücken**) bridge.

Bruder *der* (PL *die* **Brüder**) brother.

Brühe *die* (PL *die* **Brühen**) 1 broth; 2 stock (*for cooking*).

△ NEW SPELLING: *See page xii*

Brühwürfel der (PL die **Brühwürfel**) stock cube.

brüllen verb (PERF **hat gebrüllt**) to roar.

brummen verb (PERF **hat gebrummt**) 1 to buzz; 2 to growl (of a bear); 3 to hum (of an engine).

Brunnen der (PL die **Brunnen**) 1 well; 2 fountain.

Brust die (PL die **Brüste**) 1 chest; 2 breast.

Brustschwimmen das breaststroke.

brutto adverb gross.

BSE das (bovine spongiforme Enzephalopathie) BSE.

Bub der (PL die **Buben**) boy.

Buch das (PL die **Bücher**) book.

Buche die (PL die **Buchen**) beech.

buchen verb (PERF **hat gebucht**) to book.

Bücherei die (PL die **Büchereien**) library.

Bücherregal das (PL die **Bücherregale**) bookcase.

Buchhalter der (PL die **Buchhalter**) accountant, bookkeeper.

Buchhalterin die (PL die **Buchhalterinnen**) accountant, bookkeeper.

Buchhandlung die (PL die **Buchhandlungen**) bookshop.

Büchse die (PL die **Büchsen**) tin, can.

Büchsenöffner der (PL die **Büchsenöffner**) tin opener.

Buchstabe der (PL die **Buchstaben**) letter (of the alphabet); **ein großer Buchstabe** a capital letter; **ein kleiner Buchstabe** a small letter.

buchstabieren verb (PERF **hat buchstabiert**) to spell.

Bucht die (PL die **Buchten**) bay.

bücken (PERF **hat sich gebückt**) **sich bücken** to bend down.

Buddhismus der Buddhism.

Bude die (PL die **Buden**) 1 hut; 2 stall; 3 **meine Bude** (informal) my room, my pad.

Büfett das (PL die **Büfetts**) buffet.

Bügel der (PL die **Bügel**) hanger.

Bügeleisen das (PL die **Bügeleisen**) iron.

bügeln verb (PERF **hat gebügelt**) to iron.

Bühne die (PL die **Bühnen**) stage.

Bulle der (PL die **Bullen**) 1 bull; 2 (informal) cop.

Bummel der (PL die **Bummel**) stroll (around town).

bummeln verb (PERF **ist gebummelt**) 1 to stroll; **wir sind durch die Stadt gebummelt** we strolled around town; 2 (PERF **hat gebummelt**) to dawdle.

Bund[1] der (PL die **Bünde**) 1 association; 2 waistband.

Bund[2] das (PL die **Bunde**) bunch.

$\diamond$ IRREGULAR VERB: See the verb table in the centre of the dictionary

Bundesbürger der (PL die Bundesbürger) German citizen.

Bundeskanzler der (PL die Bundeskanzler) Federal Chancellor.

Bundesland das (PL die Bundesländer) (federal) state.

Bundesliga die (PL die Bundesligen) (German) national league.

Bundesrat der Upper House (of the German Parliament).

Bundesrepublik die Federal Republic.

Bundesstraße die (PL die Bundesstraßen) A road, major road.

Bundestag der Lower House (of the German Parliament).

Bundeswehr die (German) Army.

bunt adjective colourful.

Buntstift der (PL die Buntstifte) coloured pencil.

Burg die (PL die Burgen) castle.

Bürger der (PL die Bürger) citizen.

Bürgerin die (PL die Bürgerinnen) citizen.

Bürgermeister der (PL die Bürgermeister) mayor.

Bürgersteig der (PL die Bürgersteige) pavement.

Büro das (PL die Büros) office.

Büroklammer die (PL die Büroklammern) paper clip.

Bürste die (PL die Bürsten) brush.

bürsten verb (PERF hat gebürstet) to brush.

Bus der (PL die Busse) bus; **ich fahre mit dem Bus** I'm going by bus.

Busbahnhof der (PL die Busbahnhöfe) bus station.

Busch der (PL die Büsche) bush.

Busen der (PL die Busen) bosom.

Busfahrer der (PL die Busfahrer) bus driver.

Busfahrerin die (PL die Busfahrerinnen) bus driver.

Busfahrkarte die (PL die Busfahrkarten) bus ticket.

Bushaltestelle die (PL die Bushaltestellen) bus stop.

Bußgeld das (PL die Bußgelder) fine.

Buslinie die (PL die Buslinien) bus route.

Büstenhalter der (PL die Büstenhalter) bra.

Butter die butter.

Butterbrot das (PL die Butterbrote) sandwich, bread and butter.

bzw. = beziehungsweise.

C c

Café das (PL die Cafés) café.

Cafeteria die (PL die Cafeterias) cafeteria.

campen verb (PERF hat gecampt) to camp.

△ NEW SPELLING: See page xii

Camping *das* camping.

Campingkocher *der* (PL *die* **Campingkocher**) camping stove.

Campingplatz *der* (PL *die* **Campingplätze**) campsite.

CD *die* (PL *die* **CDs**) CD.

CD-Spieler *der* (PL *die* **CD-Spieler**) CD player.

Cello *das* (PL *die* **Cellos**) cello.

Champignon *der* (PL *die* **Champignons**) mushroom.

Chance *die* (PL *die* **Chancen**) chance.

Chaos *das* chaos.

chaotisch *adjective* chaotic.

Charakter *der* (PL *die* **Charaktere**) character.

charmant *adjective* charming.

Charterflug *der* (PL *die* **Charterflüge**) charter flight.

Chauvinist *der* (PL *die* **Chauvinisten**) chauvinist.

Chef *der* (PL *die* **Chefs**) 1 head (*of a firm*); 2 boss.

Chefin *die* (PL *die* **Chefinnen**) 1 head (*of a firm*); 2 boss.

Chemie *die* chemistry.

Chemiker *der* (PL *die* **Chemiker**) chemist.

Chemikerin *die* (PL *die* **Chemikerinnen**) chemist.

chemisch *adjective* 1 chemical; 2 chemische Reinigung dry-cleaning; dry-cleaner's.

China *das* China.

Chinese *der* (PL *die* **Chinesen**) Chinese; **die Chinesen** the Chinese.

Chinesin *die* (PL *die* **Chinesinnen**) Chinese.

chinesisch *adjective* Chinese.

Chipkarte *die* (PL *die* **Chipkarten**) smart card.

Chips *plural noun* crisps.

Chirurg *der* (PL *die* **Chirurgen**) surgeon.

Chirurgin *die* (PL *die* **Chirurginnen**) surgeon.

Chlor *das* chlorine.

Chor *der* (PL *die* **Chöre**) choir.

Christ *der* (PL *die* **Christen**) Christian.

Christin *die* (PL *die* **Christinnen**) Christian.

christlich *adjective* Christian.

Christus *der* Christ.

circa *adverb* approximately.

Clown *der* (PL *die* **Clowns**) clown.

Cola™ *die* (PL *die* **Colas**) Coke™.

Comic *der* (PL *die* **Comics**) cartoon.

Comic-Heft *das* (PL *die* **Comic-Hefte**) comic.

Computer *der* (PL *die* **Computer**) computer.

Computerspiel *das* (PL *die* **Computerspiele**) computer game.

Container *der* (PL *die* **Container**) 1 container; 2 skip.

✧ IRREGULAR VERB: *See the verb table in the centre of the dictionary*

Cordsamt *der* corduroy.

Couch *die* (PL *die* **Couchs**) sofa.

Couchtisch *der* (PL *die* **Couchtische**) coffee table.

Cousin *der* (PL *die* **Cousins**) cousin.

Cousine *die* (PL *die* **Cousinen**) cousin.

Creme *die* (PL *die* **Cremes**) 1 cream; 2 cream dessert.

Curry *das* 1 curry; 2 curry powder.

Currywurst *die* (PL *die* **Currywürste**) curried sausage.

Cursor *der* (PL *die* **Cursors**) cursor.

D d

da *adverb* 1 there; **da draußen** out there; **da drüben** over there; **da sein** to be there; **man muss pünktlich da sein** you have to be there on time; 2 **ist noch Brot da?** is there any bread left?; 3 here; **sind alle da?** is everyone here?; **da sind deine Handschuhe** here are your gloves; 4 **ist Sabine da?** is Sabine about?; 5 **von da an** from then on; 6 **ich bin wieder da** I'm back; 7 so (*therefore*); **der Bus war weg, da bin ich gelaufen** the bus had gone, so I walked; 8 **da kann man nichts machen** there's nothing you can do about it; 9 **da, wo die Straße nach Stuttgart abzweigt** at the turning for Stuttgart.
conjunction as, since; **da es gerade regnet** as it's raining.

dabei *adverb* 1 (*included or next to*) with it/him/her/them; **sie hatten die Kinder dabei** they had the children with them; 2 **dicht dabei** close by; 3 (*referring to something already mentioned*) about it; **das Wichtigste dabei** the most important thing about it; 4 at the same time; **er malte ein Bild und sang dabei** he painted a picture and sang at the same time; 5 during this; 6 **jemandem dabei helfen, etwas zu tun** to help somebody do something; 7 **was hast du dir denn dabei gedacht?** what were you thinking of?; 8 **dabei sein** △ to be there; **er ist dabei gewesen** he was there; 9 **was ist denn dabei?** so what?; 10 **dabei sein, etwas zu tun** to be just doing something; **ich war gerade dabei zu gehen** I was just about to leave; 11 **dabei bleiben** to stick with it (*an opinion, for example*); 12 and yet, even though.

dabeibleiben ◇ *verb* (IMPERF **blieb dabei**, PERF **ist dabeigeblieben**) 1 to stay on (*at an organisation*); 2 **er hat mit dem Training begonnen, ist aber nicht dabeigeblieben** he started training, but didn't keep it up.

dabeisein SEE **dabei**.

Dach *das* (PL *die* **Dächer**) roof.

Dachboden *der* (PL *die* **Dachböden**) loft, attic.

dachte SEE **denken**.

Dackel *der* (PL *die* **Dackel**) dachshund.

dadurch *adverb* 1 through it/them; **das Wasser muss dadurch**

gelaufen sein the water must have run through it; **2** as a result; **3** in this way; **ich nehme die U-Bahn, dadurch bin ich eine halbe Stunde eher da** I'll take the tube, that way I'll be there half an hour earlier. *conjunction* **dadurch, dass** because.

dafür *adverb* **1** for it/them; **dafür kriegt man nicht viel** you won't get much for it/them; **2** instead; **wenn er schon nicht auf die Party gehen will, kann er dich dafür zum Essen einladen** if he doesn't want to go to the party he can take you for a meal instead; **3** but then (*on the other hand*); **4 dafür, dass** considering (that); **5 ich kann nichts dafür** it's not my fault.

dagegen *adverb* **1** against it/them; **ich bin dagegen** I'm against it; **2** for it/them (*when swapping*); **3** into it; **das Auto ist dagegen gefahren** the car drove into it; **4** by comparison; **5 hast du was dagegen?** do you mind?; **6** however.

daheim *adverb* at home.

daher *adverb* **1** from there; **2** that's why.

dahin *adverb* **1** there; **2 bis dahin** (*in the past*) until then; (*in the future*) by then; **3 jemanden dahin bringen, dass er etwas tut** to get somebody to do something.

dahinten *adverb* over there.

dahinter *adverb* **1** behind it/them; **2 dahinter kommen** △ to get to the bottom of it; **ich bin endlich dahinter**

gekommen I finally got to the bottom of it.

dalassen ✧ *verb* (PRES **lässt da** △, IMPERF **ließ da**, PERF **hat dagelassen**) to leave there.

damals *adverb* at that time; then; **wir wohnten damals in Berlin** we were then living in Berlin.

Dame *die* (PL *die* **Damen**) **1** lady; **2** queen (*in chess or cards*); **3** draughts.

Damenbinde *die* (PL *die* **Damenbinden**) sanitary towel.

damit *adverb* **1** with it/them; **ich will damit spielen** I want to play with it; **hör auf damit!** stop it!; **2** by it; **was meinst du damit?** what do you mean by that?; **3 damit hat es noch Zeit** there's no hurry (about that); **4** therefore, because of that; **sie hat den zweiten Satz verloren und damit das Spiel** she lost the second set and because of that the match. *conjunction* so that; **ich habe es aufgeschrieben, damit du es nicht vergisst** I wrote it down so that you won't forget.

Damm *der* (PL *die* **Dämme**) **1** dam; **2** embankment.

dämmern *verb* (PERF **hat gedämmert**) **es dämmert** it is getting light; it is getting dark.

Dämmerung *die* **1** dawn; **2** dusk.

Dampf *der* (PL *die* **Dämpfe**) steam.

dampfen *verb* (PERF **hat gedampft**) to steam.

dämpfen *verb* (PERF **hat gedämpft**)

✧ IRREGULAR VERB: *See the verb table in the centre of the dictionary*

1 to steam (in cooking); 2 to muffle
(a sound); 3 to dampen (somebody's
enthusiasm).

Dampfer der (PL die **Dampfer**)
steamer.

danach adverb 1 after it/them;
2 afterwards; **kurz danach** shortly
afterwards; 3 **danach suchen** to
look for it/them; 4 **danach riechen**
to smell of it; 5 accordingly; 6 **es
sieht danach aus** it looks like it.

Däne der (PL die **Dänen**) Dane.

daneben adverb 1 next to it/them;
2 by comparison.

Dänemark das Denmark.

Dänin die (PL die **Däninnen**) Dane.

dänisch adjective Danish.

dank preposition ←(+GEN or +DAT)
thanks to.

Dank der 1 thanks; **mit Dank
zurück** thanks for the loan; 2 **vielen
Dank** thank you very much.

dankbar adjective 1 grateful;
2 rewarding.

danke exclamation thank you,
thanks; **danke schön** thank you
very much; **(nein) danke** no thank
you, no thanks.

danken verb (PERF **hat gedankt**) 1 to
thank; 2 **nichts zu danken** don't
mention it.

dann adverb then.

daran adverb 1 on it/them; 2 **daran
denken** to think of it/them; 3 **dicht
daran** close to it/them; 4 **nahe
daran sein, etwas zu tun** to be on

the point of doing something;
5 about it/them; **daran ist nichts zu
machen** there is nothing you can do
about it; 6 **es liegt daran, dass ...**
it is because ...; 7 **er ist daran
gestorben** he died of it.

darauf adverb 1 on it/them;
2 **darauf warten** to wait for it;
3 **darauf antworten** to reply to it;
4 after that; **kurz darauf** shortly
after that; 5 **am Tag darauf** the day
after; 6 **am darauf folgenden Tag** Δ
the following day; 7 **es kommt
darauf an, ob ...** it depends
whether ...

daraufhin adverb as a result.

daraus adverb 1 out of it/them, from
it/them; 2 **was ist daraus
geworden?** what has become of
it/them?; 3 **mach dir nichts daraus**
don't worry about it.

darf, darfst SEE **dürfen**.

darin adverb 1 in it/them; 2 in that
respect; **der Unterschied liegt
darin, dass ...** the difference is
that ...

Darm der (PL die **Därme**) intestine(s).

darstellen verb (PERF **hat
dargestellt**) 1 to represent; 2 to
portray; **dieses Gemälde stellt
Szenen aus dem Bürgerkrieg dar**
this painting portrays scenes from
the civil war; 3 to describe; **er stellt
es so dar, als sei es meine Schuld**
the way he describes it, it's all my
fault; 4 to play (in the theatre).

Darsteller der (PL die **Darsteller**)
actor.

Δ NEW SPELLING: See page xii

Darstellerin *die* (PL *die* **Darstellerinnen**) actress.

darüber *adverb* **1** over it/them; **2** about it; **darüber sprechen** to talk about it; **3** more; **dreißig Mark oder darüber** thirty marks or more.

darum *adverb* **1** round it/them; **2 darum bitten** to ask for it; **3** that's why; **darum komme ich nicht** that's why I'm not coming; **4 ich sorge mich darum** I worry about it; **5 es geht darum, zu gewinnen** the main thing is to win; **6 darum geht es nicht** that's not the point; **7** because of that; **darum, weil** because.

darunter *adverb* **1** under it/them; **2 im Stock darunter** on the floor below; **3** among them; **mehrere Schüler, darunter zwei Zehnjährige** a number of pupils, among them two ten year olds; **4** less; **dreißig Mark oder darunter** thirty marks or less; **5 was verstehen Sie darunter?** what do you understand by that?

das *article* (*neuter*) **1** the; **das Haus** the house; **2** that; **das Mädchen war es** it was that girl; **das da** that one. *pronoun* **1** which, that; **das Kleid, das ich im Schaufenster gesehen habe** the dress which I saw in the window; **2 das mit der Spitze** the one with the lace; **3** who; **das Mädchen, das gegenüber wohnt** the girl who lives opposite; **4** that; **das wusste ich nicht** I didn't know that; **das geht** that's all right.

dasein SEE **da**.

Dasein *das* existence.

dass △ *conjunction* **1** that; **ich freue mich, dass …** I'm very pleased that …; **2 ich verstehe nicht, dass Karin ihn mag** I don't understand why Karin likes him.

dasselbe *pronoun* the same, the same one.

Daten *plural noun* data.

Datenbank *die* (PL *die* **Datenbanken**) database.

Datenverarbeitung *die* data processing.

datieren *verb* (PERF **hat datiert**) to date.

Dativ *der* (PL *die* **Dative**) dative.

Datum *das* (PL *die* **Daten**) date.

Dauer *die* **1** duration; **2** length; **3 für die Dauer von fünf Jahren** for (a period of) five years; **4 von Dauer sein** to last; **5 auf die Dauer** in the long run; **auf Dauer** permanently.

Dauerkarte *die* (PL *die* **Dauerkarten**) season ticket.

dauern *verb* (PERF **hat gedauert**) **1** to last; **2 lange dauern** to take a long time; **es hat vier Wochen gedauert, bis der Brief hier ankam** it took four weeks for the letter to arrive.

dauernd *adjective* constant. *adverb* constantly.

Dauerwelle *die* (PL *die* **Dauerwellen**) perm.

Daumen *der* (PL *die* **Daumen**) thumb.

✧ IRREGULAR VERB: *See the verb table in the centre of the dictionary*

Daunendecke *die* (PL *die* Daunendecken) duvet.

davon *adverb* **1** from it/them; **2** about it; **ich weiß nichts davon** I don't know anything about it; **3** of it/them; **die Hälfte davon** half of it/them; **4** **das kommt davon** (*informal*) it serves you right; **5** **was habe ich davon?** what's the point?; **6** **abgesehen davon** apart from that.

davor *adverb* **1** in front of it/them; **2** beforehand; **3** **Angst davor haben** to be frightened of it/them; **4** **kurz davor sein, etwas zu tun** to be on the point of doing something.

dazu *adverb* **1** to it/them; **2** in addition; **noch dazu** in addition (to it); **3** with it; **was isst du dazu?** what are you having with it?; **4** **ich habe keine Lust dazu** I don't feel like it; **5** **jemanden dazu bringen, etwas zu tun** to get somebody to do something; **6** **ich bin nicht dazu gekommen** I didn't get round to it; **7** **er ist nicht dazu bereit** he's not prepared to do it.

dazugeben ◇ *verb* (PRES **gibt dazu**, IMPERF **gab dazu**, PERF **hat dazugegeben**) to add.

dazugehören *verb* (PERF **hat dazugehört**) **1** to belong to it/them; **2** to go with it/them (*of accessories*); **alles, was dazugehört** everything that goes with it.

dazukommen ◇ *verb* (IMPERF **kam dazu**, PERF **ist dazugekommen**) **1** to arrive; **2** to be added; **3** **kommt noch etwas dazu?** would you like anything else?

dazwischen *adverb* **1** in between; **2** between them; **der Unterschied dazwischen** the difference between them.

dazwischenkommen ◇ *verb* (PRES **kommt dazwischen**, IMPERF **kam dazwischen**, PERF **ist dazwischengekommen**) to crop up.

DB *die* (*Deutsche Bundesbahn*) German railways.

DDR *die* (*Deutsche Demokratische Republik*) GDR, East Germany; **in der ehemaligen DDR** in the former East Germany.

Debatte *die* (PL *die* **Debatten**) debate.

Decke *die* (PL *die* **Decken**) **1** blanket, cover; **2** (table)cloth; **ich habe eine neue Decke aufgelegt** I've put on a new tablecloth; **3** ceiling.

Deckel *der* (PL *die* **Deckel**) **1** lid; **2** top.

decken *verb* (PERF **hat gedeckt**) **1** to cover; **2** **ein Tuch über etwas decken** to spread a cloth over something; **3** **den Tisch decken** to lay the table; **4** **jemanden decken** to cover up for somebody; **5** **einen Spieler decken** to mark a player (*in sport*).

definieren *verb* (PERF **hat definiert**) to define.

dehnbar *adjective* elastic.

dehnen *verb* (PERF **hat gedehnt**) to stretch.

dein *adjective* your.

△ NEW SPELLING: *See page xii*

deiner, deine, deins *pronoun* yours; **meine Uhr ist kaputt, kann ich deine haben?** my watch is broken, can I take yours?

deinetwegen *adverb* **1** because of you; **2** for your sake.

deins SEE **deiner**.

deklinieren *verb* (PERF **hat dekliniert**) to decline.

Delle *die* (PL *die* **Dellen**) dent.

Delphin *der* (PL *die* **Delphine**) dolphin.

dem *article* (*dative*) **1** (to) the; **2 es liegt auf dem Tisch** it's on the table. *pronoun* **1** to him; **gib es dem** give it to him; **2** to it, to that one; **3** to whom; **der Mann, dem ich das Geld gegeben habe** the man I gave the money to; **4** which; **das Messer, mit dem ich die Zwiebeln schneide** the knife that I cut onions with.

demnächst *adverb* shortly.

Demokratie *die* (PL *die* **Demokratien**) democracy.

demokratisch *adjective* democratic.

Demonstrant *der* (PL *die* **Demonstranten**) demonstrator.

Demonstrantin *die* (PL *die* **Demonstrantinnen**) demonstrator.

Demonstration *die* (PL *die* **Demonstrationen**) demonstration.

demonstrieren *verb* (PERF **hat demonstriert**) to demonstrate.

den *article* (*accusative*) **1** the; **2 ich habe mir den Arm gebrochen** I've broken my arm.

pronoun **1** him; **kennst du den?** do you know him?; **2** it, that one; **den kannst du gerne haben** you're welcome to it; **ich nehme den** I'll take that one; **3** who(m); **4** which; **der Mantel, den ich mir gekauft habe** the coat I bought.

denen *pronoun* (*dative plural*) **1** (to) them; **2** that, (to) whom; **die Menschen, denen sie geholfen hat** the people she helped.

denkbar *adjective* conceivable.

denken ✧ *verb* (IMPERF **dachte**, PERF **hat gedacht**) **1** to think; **ich denke oft an dich** I often think of you; **2 das kann ich mir denken** I can imagine.

Denkmal *das* (PL *die* **Denkmäler**) monument.

denn *conjunction* **1** because, for; **2 mehr denn je** more than ever. *adverb* **1 wo denn?** where?; **2 was ist denn los?** so what's the matter?; **3 warum denn nicht?** why ever not?; **4 es sei denn** unless.

dennoch *conjunction* nevertheless.

deprimiert *adjective* depressed.

der *article* **1** (*masculine*) the; **der Mann** the man; **2** (*feminine and plural genitive*) of the; **die Katze der Frau** the woman's cat; **der Ball der Kinder** the children's ball; **3** (*dative*) (to) the; **ich gab es der Frau** I gave it to the woman.
pronoun **1** who; **der Mann, der hier wohnt** the man who lives here; **2** which; **der Regenschirm, der mir**

gehört the umbrella which is mine;
3 der da that one; **4** him, he.

deren *pronoun* **1** their; **die Kinder
und deren Hund** the children and
their dog; **2** whose; **3** of which.

derselbe *pronoun* the same, the
same one.

des *article* **1** of the; **das Klingeln des
Telefons** the ringing of the phone;
2 der Ball des Jungen the boy's ball.

deshalb *adverb* **1** therefore; **2** that's
why.

desinfizieren *verb* (PERF **hat
desinfiziert**) to disinfect.

dessen *pronoun* **1** his; **2** its;
3 whose; **der Junge, dessen Mutter
weint** the boy whose mother is
crying; **4** of which.

desto *adverb* the; **je mehr, desto
besser** the more the better.

deswegen *conjunction*
1 therefore; **2** that's why.

Detektiv *der* (PL *die* **Detektive**)
detective.

deutlich *adjective* clear.
adverb **ich konnte ihn deutlich
sehen** I could clearly see him.

deutsch *adjective* German.

Deutsch *das* German; **auf Deutsch**
in German; **fließend Deutsch
sprechen** to speak fluent German.

Deutsche *der/die* (PL *die*
Deutschen) German; **er ist
Deutscher** he's German.

Deutschland *das* Germany; **nach
Deutschland** to Germany.

Devisen *plural noun* foreign
currency.

Dezember *der* December; **am
ersten Dezember** on the first of
December; **im Dezember** in
December.

Dezimalzahl *die* (PL *die*
Dezimalzahlen) decimal (number).

d.h. (*das heißt*) i.e.

Dia *das* (PL *die* **Dias**) slide.

diagonal *adjective* diagonal.

Diagramm *das* (PL *die* **Diagramme**)
diagram.

Dialekt *der* (PL *die* **Dialekte**) dialect.

Dialog *der* (PL *die* **Dialoge**) dialogue.

Diamant *der* (PL *die* **Diamanten**)
diamond.

Diät *die* (PL *die* **Diäten**) diet;
jemanden auf Diät setzen
(*informal*) to put somebody on a
diet.

dich *pronoun* **1** you; **2** yourself.

dicht *adjective* **1** thick (*fog*);
2 dense; **3** watertight; **4** airtight;
5 er ist nicht ganz dicht (*informal*)
he's off his head.
adverb **1** densely; **2** tightly; **3** close;
geh nicht so dicht an den Käfig
don't go so close to the cage; **dicht
bei** close to.

Dichter *der* (PL *die* **Dichter**) poet.

Dichterin *die* (PL *die* **Dichterinnen**)
poet.

Dichtung *die* (PL *die* **Dichtungen**)
1 poetry; **2** seal, washer.

△ NEW SPELLING: *See page xii*

dick *adjective* **1** thick; **2** swollen (*ankle, tonsils*); **3** fat (*person*).

Dickkopf *der* (PL *die* **Dickköpfe**) **1** stubborn person; **2 einen Dickkopf haben** to be stubborn.

die *article* (*feminine and plural*) the; **die Frau** the woman; **die Bücher** the books.
pronoun (*feminine and plural*) **1** who; **die Frau, die hier wohnt** the woman who lives here; **die Frau, die ich kenne** the woman I know; **die Kinder, die ich gefragt habe** the children I asked; **2** which; **die Tasche, die ich gekauft habe** the bag I bought; **3** she, her; **4** them; **ich meine die** I mean them; **5 die da** that one; (*plural*) those.

Dieb *der* (PL *die* **Diebe**) thief.

Diebin *die* (PL *die* **Diebinnen**) thief.

Diebstahl *der* (PL *die* **Diebstähle**) theft.

Diele *die* (PL *die* **Dielen**) **1** hall; **2** floorboard.

dienen *verb* (PERF **hat gedient**) to serve.

Dienst *der* (PL *die* **Dienste**) service; **Dienst haben** to work, to be on duty (*of a soldier or doctor*).

Dienstag *der* (PL *die* **Dienstage**) Tuesday; **am Dienstag** on Tuesday.

dienstags *adverb* on Tuesdays.

dienstfrei *adjective* **1 ein dienstfreier Tag** a day off; **2 dienstfrei haben** to have time off, to be off duty.

dienstlich *adverb* on business.

Dienstreise *die* (PL *die* **Dienstreisen**) business trip.

diese SEE **dieser**.

Diesel *der* diesel.

dieselbe *pronoun* the same, the same one.

dieser, diese, dieses *adjective* **1** this; **2** these; **diese Äpfel** these apples.
pronoun **1** this one; **mir gefällt dieses am besten** I like this one best; **2** these ones.

diesmal *adverb* this time.

Digitaluhr *die* (PL *die* **Digitaluhren**) **1** digital watch; **2** digital clock.

Diktat *das* (PL *die* **Diktate**) dictation.

Ding *das* (PL *die* **Dinge**) thing; **vor allen Dingen** above all; **das war ein Ding** (*informal*) that was quite something.

Dings *der/die/das* thingummy.

Dinosaurier *der* (PL *die* **Dinosaurier**) dinosaur.

Diplom *das* (PL *die* **Diplome**) diploma.

dir *pronoun* **1** you, to you; **sie hat es dir gegeben** she gave it to you; **ich verspreche dir, dass ...** I promise you that ...; **2 Freunde von dir** friends of yours; **3** yourself.

direkt *adjective* direct.

Direktor *der* (PL *die* **Direktoren**) **1** director; **2** headmaster, principal; **3** manager (*of a bank, theatre*).

Direktorin *die* (PL *die* **Direktorinnen**) **1** director;

✧ IRREGULAR VERB: *See the verb table in the centre of the dictionary*

a headmistress, principal;
3 manager (*of a bank, theatre*).

Direktübertragung *die* (PL *die*
Direktübertragungen) live
transmission.

Dirigent *der* (PL *die* **Dirigenten**)
conductor.

dirigieren *verb* (PERF **hat dirigiert**)
to conduct.

Diskette *die* (PL *die* **Disketten**)
floppy disk.

Diskothek *die* (PL *die* **Diskotheken**)
disco, discotheque.

Diskriminierung *die*
discrimination; **die Diskriminierung
von Frauen** discrimination against
women.

Diskussion *die* (PL *die*
Diskussionen) discussion; **zur
Diskussion stehen** to be under
discussion.

diskutieren *verb* (PERF **hat
diskutiert**) to discuss.

Disziplin *die* (PL *die* **Disziplinen**)
discipline.

DJH *die* (*Deutsche Jugendherberge*)
German youth hostel (association).

DM *die* (*Deutsche Mark*) DM,
Deutschmark.

D-Mark *die* (PL *die* **D-Mark**)
Deutschmark, German mark.

doch *adverb* **1** yes (*when you are
contradicting somebody*); **'hast du
keinen Hunger?' – 'doch!'** 'aren't
you hungry?' – 'yes, I am!'; **2** after
all; **sie hat ihn doch eingeladen** she

invited him after all; **sie ist doch
nicht gekommen** she hasn't come
after all; **3 er hat doch meinen Brief
bekommen?** he did get my letter,
didn't he?; **sie kommt doch?** she's
coming, isn't she?; **4** anyway; **du
hörst ja doch nicht auf mich** you
won't listen to me anyway; **5 pass
doch auf!** do be careful!
conjunction but.

Doktor *der* (PL *die* **Doktoren**) doctor;
den Doktor machen to do a
doctorate.

Dokument *das* (PL *die* **Dokumente**)
document.

Dokumentarfilm *der* (PL *die*
Dokumentarfilme) documentary.

Dokumentarsendung *die* (PL *die*
Dokumentarsendungen)
documentary (programme).

dolmetschen *verb* (PERF **hat
gedolmetscht**) to interpret.

Dolmetscher *der* (PL *die*
Dolmetscher) interpreter.

Dolmetscherin *die* (PL *die*
Dolmetscherinnen) interpreter.

Dom *der* (PL *die* **Dome**) cathedral.

Donau *die* Danube.

Donner *der* thunder.

donnern *verb* (PERF **hat gedonnert**)
to thunder.

Donnerstag *der* (PL *die*
Donnerstage) Thursday; **am
Donnerstag** on Thursday.

donnerstags *adverb* on Thursdays.

doof *adjective* (*informal*) stupid.

△ NEW SPELLING: *See page xii*

Doppel *das* (PL *die* **Doppel**)
1 duplicate; **2** doubles (*in sport*).

Doppelbett *das* (PL *die*
Doppelbetten) double bed.

Doppelfenster *das* (PL *die*
Doppelfenster) double-glazed
window; **wir haben Doppelfenster**
we've got double glazing.

Doppelhaus *das* (PL *die*
Doppelhäuser) semi-detached
house.

doppelt *adjective* **1** double; **2 in
doppelter Ausführung** in
duplicate; **3 die doppelte Menge**
twice the amount.
adverb **1** doubly; **2** twice; **doppelt
so viel** twice as much; **sich doppelt
anstrengen** to try twice as hard.

Doppelzimmer *das* (PL *die*
Doppelzimmer) double room.

Dorf *das* (PL *die* **Dörfer**) village.

Dorn *der* (PL *die* **Dornen**) thorn.

dort *adverb* there; **dort drüben** over
there.

dorther *adverb* from there.

dorthin *adverb* there; **geht ihr jetzt
dorthin?** are you going there now?

Dose *die* (PL *die* **Dosen**) tin, can.

Dosenöffner *der* (PL *die*
Dosenöffner) tin opener.

Dosis *die* (PL *die* **Dosen**) dose.

Dotter *der* (PL *die* **Dotter**) yolk.

Dozent *der* (PL *die* **Dozenten**)
lecturer.

Dozentin *die* (PL *die* **Dozentinnen**)
lecturer.

Drache *der* (PL *die* **Drachen**) dragon.

Drachen *der* (PL *die* **Drachen**) kite.

Drachenfliegen *das* hang-gliding.

Draht *der* (PL *die* **Drähte**) **1** wire; **2 er
ist auf Draht** (*informal*) he's on the
ball.

Drama *das* (PL *die* **Dramen**) drama.

Dramatik *die* drama.

dran *adverb* SEE **daran**; **1 ich bin
dran** it's my turn; **wer ist dran?**
whose turn is it?; **2 gut dran sein** to
be well off; **3 arm dran sein** to be
in a bad way; **4 spät dran sein** to
be late.

drängen *verb* (PERF **hat gedrängt**)
1 to push; **2** to press, to urge
(*somebody*); **3 sich drängen** to
crowd; **die Leute drängten sich vor
der Kasse** people crowded around
the box-office.

drankommen ✧ *verb* (IMPERF **kam
dran**, PERF **ist drangekommen**) to
have your turn; **wer kommt dran?**
whose turn is it?

drauf *adverb* SEE **darauf**; **1 drauf
und dran sein, etwas zu tun** to be
on the point of doing something;
2 gut drauf sein (*informal*) to be in
a good mood.

draußen *adverb* outside.

Dreck *der* dirt.

dreckig *adjective* dirty, filthy.

Drehbuch *das* (PL *die* **Drehbücher**)
1 screenplay; **2** script.

drehen *verb* (PERF **hat gedreht**) **1** to
turn; **an etwas drehen** to turn

✧ IRREGULAR VERB: *See the verb table in the centre of the dictionary*

something, **2** to shoot (*a film*),
3 sich drehen to turn; **4 sich im
Kreis drehen** to rotate; **5 es dreht
sich um ihr Taschengeld** it's about
her pocket money.

drei *number* three.

Drei *die* (PL *die* **Dreien**) three.

Dreieck *das* (PL *die* **Dreiecke**)
triangle.

dreieckig *adjective* triangular.

dreifach *adjective* triple.

dreihundert *number* three
hundred.

dreimal *adverb* three times.

dreißig *number* thirty.

dreiviertel *number* three-quarters.

Dreiviertelstunde *die* (PL *die*
Dreiviertelstunden) three-quarters
of an hour.

dreizehn *number* thirteen.

drin *adverb* SEE **darin**; **drin sein** to
be inside.

dringend *adjective* urgent.

drinnen *adverb* **1** inside; **2** indoors.

dritt *adverb* **sie sind zu dritt** there
are three of them.

dritte SEE **dritter**.

Drittel *das* (PL *die* **Drittel**) third.

drittens *adverb* thirdly.

dritter, dritte, drittes *adjective*
third; **zum dritten Mal** for the third
time; **ein Dritter** a third person;
jeder Dritte, der mitwollte every

third person who wanted to come,
die Dritte Welt the Third World.

Droge *die* (PL *die* **Drogen**) drug.

drogenabhängig *adjective*
addicted to drugs.

Drogenabhängige *der/die* (PL *die*
Drogenabhängigen) drug addict.

Drogenabhängigkeit *die* drug
addiction.

drogensüchtig *adjective* addicted
to drugs.

Drogensüchtige *der/die* (PL *die*
Drogensüchtigen) drug addict.

Drogerie *die* (PL *die* **Drogerien**)
chemist's.

Drogist *der* (PL *die* **Drogisten**)
chemist.

Drogistin *die* (PL *die* **Drogistinnen**)
chemist.

drohen *verb* (PERF **hat gedroht**) to
threaten; **jemandem drohen** to
threaten somebody.

Drohung *die* (PL *die* **Drohungen**)
threat.

drüben *adverb* over there.

Druck *der* **1** pressure; **jemanden
unter Druck setzen** to put pressure
on somebody; **2** printing; **3** (PL *die*
Drucke) print.

drucken *verb* (PERF **hat gedruckt**) to
print.

drücken *verb* (PERF **hat gedrückt**)
1 to press; **2 an der Tür drücken** to
push the door; **'bitte drücken'**
'push'; **3** to hug; **4** to pinch (*of
shoes*); **5 die Preise drücken** to

force down prices; **6 sich vor etwas drücken** (*informal*) to get out of something; **du hast dich mal wieder vor dem Aufräumen gedrückt** you've got out of tidying up again.

Drucker *der* (PL *die* **Drucker**) printer.

Druckknopf *der* (PL *die* **Druckknöpfe**) press stud.

Drucksache *die* (PL *die* **Drucksachen**) printed matter.

Druckschrift *die* (PL *die* **Druckschriften**) 1 block letters; 2 type; 3 pamphlet.

Drüse *die* (PL *die* **Drüsen**) gland.

Dschungel *der* (PL *die* **Dschungel**) jungle.

du *pronoun* 1 you; 2 **du sagen** to say 'du' (to each other); **per du sein** to be on familiar terms (*'du' is used when talking to family members, close friends, or people of your own age; otherwise 'Sie' is used*).

Dudelsack *der* (PL *die* **Dudelsäcke**) bagpipes.

Duft *der* (PL *die* **Düfte**) fragrance, scent.

duften *verb* (PERF **hat geduftet**) to smell; **nach Lavendel duften** to smell of lavender.

dumm *adjective* 1 stupid; 2 **das wird mir jetzt zu dumm** (*informal*) I've had enough of it; 3 **so etwas Dummes!** how annoying!; 4 **der Dumme sein** to draw the short straw.

dummerweise *adverb* stupidly.

Dummheit *die* (PL *die*

Dummheiten) 1 stupidity; 2 stupid thing; **mach keine Dummheiten** don't do anything stupid.

Dummkopf *der* (PL *die* **Dummköpfe**) fool.

Dünger *der* (PL *die* **Dünger**) fertilizer.

dunkel *adjective* 1 dark; **ein dunkler Anzug** a dark suit; 2 **im Dunkeln** in the dark; 3 vague (*idea*); 4 shady (*business*); 5 deep (*voice*).

Dunkelheit *die* darkness, dark.

dünn *adjective* 1 thin; 2 weak (*coffee, tea*).

Dunst *der* (PL *die* **Dünste**) haze.

Duo *das* (PL *die* **Duos**) duet.

durch *preposition* ←(+ACC) 1 through; **er ist durch das Fernsehen bekannt geworden** he's become famous through television; 2 by; **durch Boten** by courier; 3 **acht durch zwei ist vier** eight divided by two is four; 4 due to. *adverb* 1 through; **die ganze Nacht durch** all through the night; 2 **den Winter durch** throughout the winter; 3 **durch und durch** completely; 4 **es war acht Uhr durch** (*informal*) it was gone eight o'clock.

durcharbeiten *verb* (PERF **hat durchgearbeitet**) 1 to work through; **die Nacht durcharbeiten** to work through the night; 2 **sich durch etwas durcharbeiten** to work your way through something.

durchaus *adverb* absolutely.

durchblicken *verb* (PERF **hat**

✧ IRREGULAR VERB: *See the verb table in the centre of the dictionary*

durchgeblickt) 1 (*informal*) to understand; 2 **durchblicken lassen, dass …** to hint that …

durchbrechen ✧ *verb* (PRES **bricht durch**, IMPERF **brach durch**, PERF **hat durchgebrochen**) 1 to snap, to break in two; 2 (PERF **ist durchgebrochen**) **das Brett ist durchgebrochen** the board has snapped.

durcheinander *adverb* 1 in a mess; **mein Zimmer ist durcheinander** my room is (in) a mess; 2 **die Akten durcheinander bringen** △ to muddle up the files; **Karl hat ihre Namen durcheinander gebracht** Karl got their names mixed up; 3 confused; **bring mich nicht durcheinander** don't confuse me; 4 **sie haben alle durcheinander geredet** they all talked at once.

Durcheinander *das* 1 muddle; 2 mess; **in der Wohnung herrschte ein fürchterliches Durcheinander** the flat was a terrible mess; 3 confusion; **im allgemeinen Durcheinander** in the general confusion.

durcheinanderbringen SEE **durcheinander**.

durchfahren ✧ *verb* (PRES **fährt durch**, IMPERF **fuhr durch**, PERF **ist durchgefahren**) 1 to drive through; 2 to go through; 3 **der Zug fährt (in Stuttgart) durch** the train doesn't stop (in Stuttgart).

Durchfall *der* diarrhoea.

durchfallen ✧ *verb* (PRES **fällt durch**, IMPERF **fiel durch**, PERF **ist**

durchgefallen) 1 to fall through; 2 to fail (*an exam*).

durchführen *verb* (PERF **hat durchgeführt**) to carry out.

Durchgang *der* (PL *die* **Durchgänge**) 1 passage; 2 **'Durchgang verboten'** 'no entry'; 3 round (*in sport*).

Durchgangsverkehr *der* through traffic.

durchgehen ✧ *verb* (IMPERF **ging durch**, PERF **ist durchgegangen**) 1 to go through; 2 (*informal*) to escape; 3 **jemandem etwas durchgehen lassen** to let somebody get away with something.

durchkommen ✧ *verb* (IMPERF **kam durch**, PERF **ist durchgekommen**) 1 to come through; 2 to get through (*on the phone, in an exam*); 3 to pull through (*after an illness*).

durchlassen ✧ *verb* (PRES **lässt durch** △, IMPERF **ließ durch**, PERF **hat durchgelassen**) 1 to let through; 2 to let in.

durchmachen *verb* (PERF **hat durchgemacht**) 1 to go through; 2 to work through (*your lunch break, for example*); 3 **wir haben die Nacht durchgemacht** we made a night of it.

Durchmesser *der* (PL *die* **Durchmesser**) diameter.

durchnehmen ✧ *verb* (PRES **nimmt durch**, IMPERF **nahm durch**, PERF **hat durchgenommen**) to do (*a topic at school*).

△ NEW SPELLING: *See page xii*

durchs = durch das.

Durchsage die (PL die **Durchsagen**) announcement.

Durchschnitt der (PL die **Durchschnitte**) average; **im Durchschnitt** on average.

durchschnittlich adjective average.
adverb on average.

durchsetzen verb (PERF **hat durchgesetzt**) 1 to carry through; 2 **sich durchsetzen** to assert yourself; 3 **sich durchsetzen** to catch on (of a fashion, an idea).

durchsichtig adjective transparent.

durchstreichen ✧ verb (IMPERF **strich durch**, PERF **hat durchgestrichen**) to cross out.

Durchzug der draught.

dürfen ✧ verb (PRES **darf**, IMPERF **durfte**, PERF **hat gedurft** or **hat dürfen**) 1 to be allowed; **sie darf das nicht** she's not allowed to do that; **er hat nicht gedurft** he wasn't allowed to; 2 **Klaus hat sie im Krankenhaus besuchen dürfen** Klaus was allowed to visit her in hospital; 3 **darf ich?** may I?; 4 **das dürfen Sie nicht vergessen** you mustn't forget that; **du darfst es nicht alles so ernst nehmen** you mustn't take it all so seriously; 5 **du darfst froh sein, dass sonst nichts passiert ist** you should be glad that nothing else happened; **das darf einfach nicht passieren** that just shouldn't happen; **das dürfte nicht schwierig sein** that shouldn't be

difficult; 6 **das darf nicht wahr sein!** I don't believe it!; 7 **was darf es sein?** can I help you?; 8 **das dürfte der Grund sein** that's probably the reason.

durfte, durften, durftest, durftet SEE **dürfen**.

Dürre die (PL die **Dürren**) drought.

Durst der thirst; **Durst haben** to be thirsty.

durstig adjective thirsty.

Dusche die (PL die **Duschen**) shower.

duschen verb (PERF **hat geduscht**) 1 to have a shower; 2 **sich duschen** to have a shower.

Düsenflugzeug das (PL die **Düsenflugzeuge**) jet (plane).

düster adjective 1 gloomy (future, thoughts); 2 dark.

Dutzend das (PL die **Dutzende**) dozen.

duzen verb (PERF **hat geduzt**) to call somebody 'du'; **wollen wir uns duzen?** shall we say 'du' to each other? ('du' is used when talking to family members, close friends, or people of your own age).

dynamisch adjective dynamic.

D-Zug der (PL die **D-Züge**) fast train, express.

✧ IRREGULAR VERB: See the verb table in the centre of the dictionary

E e

Ebbe *die* (PL *die* **Ebben**) low tide.

eben *adjective* 1 flat; 2 level.
adverb 1 just; **Gabi war eben hier**
Gabi was just here; **eben noch** just
now; 2 **eben!** exactly!

Ebene *die* (PL *die* **Ebenen**) 1 plain;
2 level; 3 plane (*in geometry*).

ebenso *adverb* just as; **Ulla hat den
Film ebenso oft gesehen wie du**
Ulla's seen the film just as often as
you; **ich habe ebenso viel Arbeit
wie du** I've got just as much work as
you.

Echo *das* (PL *die* **Echos**) echo.

echt *adjective* real, genuine; **die
Kette ist aus echtem Gold** the
necklace is real gold.
adverb (*informal*) really; **das ist
echt gut** that's really good.

Eckball *der* (PL *die* **Eckbälle**) corner
(kick).

Ecke *die* (PL *die* **Ecken**) corner; **um
die Ecke** round the corner.

eckig *adjective* square.

Edelstein *der* (PL *die* **Edelsteine**)
precious stone.

EDV *die* (*elektronische
Datenverarbeitung*) electronic data
processing, EDP.

Efeu *der* (PL *die* **Efeus**) ivy.

EG *die* (*Europäische Gemeinschaft*)
EC.

egal *adjective* 1 **das ist mir egal** it's
all the same to me; 2 **egal, wie groß**
no matter how big; **egal, ob er es will
oder nicht** (it doesn't matter)
whether he wants to or not.

egoistisch *adjective* selfish.

ehe *conjunction* before; **ehe ich
nicht weiß, was er will, mache ich
nichts** I won't do anything before I
know what he wants.

Ehe *die* (PL *die* **Ehen**) marriage.

Ehefrau *die* (PL *die* **Ehefrauen**) wife.

ehemalig *adjective* former.

Ehemann *der* (PL *die* **Ehemänner**)
husband.

Ehepaar *das* (PL *die* **Ehepaare**)
married couple.

eher *adverb* 1 earlier, sooner; **je
eher, desto besser** the sooner the
better; 2 rather; **eher gehe ich zu
Fuß, als Geld für ein Taxi
auszugeben** I'd rather walk than
pay for a taxi; 3 more; **das ist schon
eher möglich** that's more likely.

Ehre *die* (PL *die* **Ehren**) honour.

Ehrgeiz *der* ambition.

ehrgeizig *adjective* ambitious.

ehrlich *adjective* honest.

Ehrlichkeit *die* honesty.

Ei *das* (PL *die* **Eier**) egg.

Eiche *die* (PL *die* **Eichen**) oak.

△ NEW SPELLING: *See page xii*

Eichhörnchen *das* (PL *die* **Eichhörnchen**) squirrel.

Eid *der* (PL *die* **Eide**) oath.

Eidechse *die* (PL *die* **Eidechsen**) lizard.

Eierbecher *der* (PL *die* **Eierbecher**) egg-cup.

Eierschale *die* (PL *die* **Eierschalen**) eggshell.

Eifer *der* eagerness.

Eifersucht *die* jealousy.

eifersüchtig *adjective* jealous; **auf jemanden eifersüchtig sein** to be jealous of somebody.

eifrig *adjective* eager.

Eigelb *das* (PL *die* **Eigelb(e)**) egg yolk.

eigen *adjective* own; **sie ist erst siebzehn und hat schon ihr eigenes Auto** she's only seventeen and she's already got her own car.

Eigenart *die* (PL *die* **Eigenarten**) peculiarity.

eigenartig *adjective* peculiar.

Eigenschaft *die* (PL *die* **Eigenschaften**) 1 quality; 2 characteristic.

eigensinnig *adjective* obstinate.

eigentlich *adjective* actual. *adverb* actually; **eigentlich habe ich keine Lust, heute ins Kino zu gehen** actually I don't fancy going to the cinema today.

Eigentum *das* property.

Eigentümer *der* (PL *die* **Eigentümer**) owner.

eignen *verb* (PERF **hat sich geeignet**) **sich eignen** to be suitable.

Eile *die* hurry.

eilen *verb* 1 (PERF **ist geeilt**) to hurry; 2 (PERF **hat geeilt**) to be urgent; **das eilt nicht** it's not urgent.

eilig *adjective* 1 urgent; 2 hurried; 3 **es eilig haben** to be in a hurry.

Eilzug *der* (PL *die* **Eilzüge**) fast stopping train.

Eimer *der* (PL *die* **Eimer**) bucket.

ein, eine, ein *article* a, an; **ein Haus** a house; **eine Allergie** an allergy; **ein bisschen mehr** a bit more; **was für ein Kleid hast du gekauft?** what sort of dress did you buy?
adjective 1 one; **sie haben nur ein Kind** they've got just one child; **eines Abends** one evening; 2 **einer Meinung sein** to be of the same opinion; 3 **ein für allemal** once and for all.

einander *pronoun* each other, one another.

Einbahnstraße *die* (PL *die* **Einbahnstraßen**) one-way street.

Einband *der* (PL *die* **Einbände**) cover.

einbauen *verb* (PERF **hat eingebaut**) 1 to fit; 2 to install.

Einbauküche *die* (PL *die* **Einbauküchen**) fitted kitchen.

einbiegen ⟡ *verb* (IMPERF **bog ein**, PERF **ist eingebogen**) to turn; **der Radfahrer bog langsam in die Seitenstraße ein** the cyclist turned slowly down the side street.

⟡ IRREGULAR VERB: *See the verb table in the centre of the dictionary*

einbilden verb (PERF hat sich
eingebildet) **1 sich einbilden** to
imagine; **das bildest du dir nur ein**
you're only imagining it; **2 Till bildet
sich viel ein** Till is very conceited.

Einbildung die imagination; **das ist
alles nur Einbildung** it's all in the
mind.

einbrechen ✧ verb (PRES **bricht
ein**, IMPERF **brach ein**, PERF **ist
eingebrochen**) to break in; **in
unserem Haus sind Diebe
eingebrochen** thieves broke into
our house; **bei unseren Nachbarn
ist eingebrochen worden** our
neighbours have been burgled.

Einbrecher der (PL die **Einbrecher**)
burglar.

Einbruch der (PL die **Einbrüche**)
1 burglary; **2 vor Einbruch der
Dunkelheit** before it gets dark; **3 bei
Einbruch der Nacht** at nightfall.

eindeutig adjective **1** clear;
2 definite (proof).

Eindruck der (PL die **Eindrücke**)
impression.

eindrucksvoll adjective
impressive.

eine SEE **ein, einer**.

eineinhalb number one and a half.

einer, eine, ein(e)s pronoun
1 one; **einer von uns** one of us; **wie
soll das einer wissen?** how is one
supposed to know?; **2** somebody;
3 kaum einer hardly anyone; **4 you**;
das macht einen müde it makes
you tired.

einerseits adverb on the one hand;

**einerseits sagt sie, dass sie kein
Geld hat, andererseits kauft sie
sich dauernd neue Sachen** on the
one hand she claims to have no
money, on the other hand she's
constantly buying new things.

eines SEE **einer**.

einfach adjective **1** simple; **2** easy;
3 single (ticket, knot).
adverb simply.

Einfachheit die simplicity.

Einfahrt die (PL die **Einfahrten**)
1 entrance; **2** arrival (of a train);
3 slip road (on a motorway).

Einfall der (PL die **Einfälle**) idea.

einfallen ✧ verb (PRES **fällt ein**,
IMPERF **fiel ein**, PERF **ist eingefallen**)
1 jemandem einfallen to occur to
somebody; **2 ihr Name fällt mir
nicht ein** I can't think of her name;
3 was fällt dir eigentlich ein? what
do you think you're doing?; **4 sich
etwas einfallen lassen** to think of
something.

Einfamilienhaus das (PL die
Einfamilienhäuser) detached family
house.

Einfluss ∆ der (PL die **Einflüsse**)
influence.

einfrieren ✧ verb (IMPERF **fror ein**,
PERF **ist eingefroren**) **1** to freeze;
2 (PERF **hat eingefroren**) to freeze
(food in the freezer).

Einfuhr die (PL die **Einfuhren**)
import.

einführen verb (PERF **hat**

eingeführt) 1 to import; 2 to introduce.

Einführung *die* (PL *die* **Einführungen**) introduction.

Eingabe *die* input (*of data*).

eingeben ✧ *verb* (PRES **gibt ein**, IMPERF **gab ein**, PERF **hat eingegeben**) 1 to hand in; 2 to input, to key in.

eingebildet *adjective* 1 conceited; 2 imaginary (*illness*).

Eingeborene *der/die* (PL *die* **Eingeborenen**) native.

eingehen ✧ *verb* (IMPERF **ging ein**, PERF **ist eingegangen**) 1 to shrink (*of clothes*); 2 to die (*of plants*); 3 to arrive (*of goods*); 4 **auf etwas eingehen** to go into something; **sie ging näher darauf ein** she went into it in more detail; 5 **auf etwas nicht eingehen** to ignore something; 6 **auf etwas eingehen** to agree to something; **Oliver ist auf unseren Plan eingegangen** Oliver agreed to our plan; 7 **ein Risiko eingehen** to take a risk.

eingeschrieben *adjective* registered; **ein eingeschriebener Brief** a registered letter.

eingestellt *adjective* 1 **auf etwas eingestellt sein** to be prepared for something; 2 **fortschrittlich eingestellt sein** to be progressively minded.

eingewöhnen *verb* (PERF **hat sich eingewöhnt**) **sich eingewöhnen** to settle in.

eingießen ✧ *verb* (IMPERF **goss ein** △, PERF **hat eingegossen**) to pour.

Eingriff *der* (PL *die* **Eingriffe**) 1 intervention; 2 operation (*surgical*).

einheimisch *adjective* 1 native; 2 local.

Einheit *die* (PL *die* **Einheiten**) 1 unity; 2 unit (*of drink, soldiers*).

Einheitspreis *der* (PL *die* **Einheitspreise**) 1 standard price; 2 flat fare.

einholen *verb* (PERF **hat eingeholt**) 1 to catch up with; 2 to make up (*time, a delay*); 3 to buy; **einholen gehen** to go shopping.

einhundert *number* one hundred.

einige SEE **einiger**.

einigen *verb* (PERF **hat sich geeinigt**) **sich einigen** to come to an agreement; **sich auf etwas einigen** to agree on something.

einiger, einige, einiges *adjective, pronoun* 1 some; **vor einiger Zeit** some time ago; 2 several; 3 **nur einige waren noch da** there were only a few left; 4 **einiges** quite a lot; **wir haben einiges gesehen** we saw quite a lot (of things); 5 **einiges** some things; **einiges hat uns nicht gefallen** there were some things we didn't like.

einigermaßen *adverb* 1 fairly; 2 fairly well; 3 'wie geht es dir?' – 'einigermaßen' 'how are you?' – 'so-so'.

einiges SEE **einiger**.

✧ IRREGULAR VERB: *See the verb table in the centre of the dictionary*

Einigung *die* agreement.

Einkauf *der* (PL *die* **Einkäufe**)
1 purchase; 2 shopping; **Einkäufe
machen** to do some shopping.

einkaufen *verb* (PERF **hat
eingekauft**) 1 to buy; **ich habe
vergessen Milch einzukaufen** I
forgot to buy milk; 2 to shop; **wir
kaufen meist im Supermarkt ein**
we usally shop at the supermarket;
einkaufen gehen to go shopping.

Einkaufsbummel *der* (PL *die*
Einkaufsbummel) shopping spree.

Einkaufswagen *der* (PL *die*
Einkaufswagen) shopping trolley.

Einkaufszentrum *das* (PL *die*
Einkaufszentren) shopping centre.

Einkommen *das* (PL *die*
Einkommen) income.

einladen ✧ *verb* (PRES **lädt ein**,
IMPERF **lud ein**, PERF **hat eingeladen**)
1 to invite; **jemanden zum
Abendessen einladen** to invite
somebody for dinner; 2 **jemanden
ins Kino einladen** to take sombody
to the cinema; 3 to treat; **ich lade
euch ein** I'll treat you; 4 to load
(*goods*).

Einladung *die* (PL *die* **Einladungen**)
invitation.

einleben *verb* (PERF **hat sich
eingelebt**) **sich einleben** to settle
down.

Einleitung *die* (PL *die* **Einleitungen**)
introduction.

einlösen *verb* (PERF **hat eingelöst**)
to cash.

einmal *adverb* 1 once (*in the past*);
es war einmal ... once upon a
time ...; 2 one day (*in the future*);
3 **auf einmal** suddenly; 4 **auf
einmal** at the same time; **sie kamen
alle auf einmal** they all came at the
same time; 5 **nicht einmal** not
even; 6 **noch einmal** again;
7 **es geht nun einmal nicht** it's just
not possible.

einmalig *adjective* 1 unique;
2 fantastic; 3 single, one-off
(*payment*).

einmischen *verb* (PERF **hat sich
eingemischt**) **sich einmischen** to
interfere.

einordnen *verb* (PERF **hat
eingeordnet**) 1 to put in order;
2 **sich einordnen** to fit in (*with other
people*); 3 **sich einordnen** to get in
lane (*when driving*).

einpacken *verb* (PERF **hat
eingepackt**) 1 to pack; 2 to wrap.

einreichen *verb* (PERF **hat
eingereicht**) to hand in.

Einreise *die* (PL *die* **Einreisen**) entry.

einreisen *verb* (PERF **ist eingereist**)
to enter a country; **er reiste nach
Italien ein** he entered Italy.

einrichten *verb* (PERF **hat
eingerichtet**) 1 to furnish; 2 to set
up (*an organisation*); 3 to arrange;
**kannst du es so einrichten, dass
du vormittags da bist?** can you
arrange to be here in the morning?;
4 **sich einrichten** to furnish your
home; 5 **sich einrichten** to
economize; 6 **sich auf etwas**

△ NEW SPELLING: *See page xii*

einrichten to prepare for something.

Einrichtung die (PL die Einrichtungen) 1 furnishing; 2 furnishings; 3 setting up; 4 institution; **staatliche Einrichtungen** state institutions.

eins *number* one; **eins zu eins** one all; **es ist eins** it's one o'clock. *pronoun* SEE **einer**. *adjective* **mir ist alles eins** it's all the same to me.

Eins die (PL die Einsen) one.

einsam *adjective* lonely.

einsammeln *verb* (PERF **hat eingesammelt**) to collect.

Einsatz der 1 use; 2 stake (*when betting*).

einschalten *verb* (PERF **hat eingeschaltet**) 1 to switch on (*a radio, TV*); 2 **sich einschalten** to intervene.

einschlafen ✧ *verb* (PRES **schläft ein**, IMPERF **schlief ein**, PERF **ist eingeschlafen**) to go to sleep.

einschließen ✧ *verb* (IMPERF **schloss ein** △, PERF **hat eingeschlossen**) 1 to lock in; 2 to include; 3 **sich einschließen** to lock yourself in.

einschließlich *preposition* ←(+GEN) including; **einschließlich der Unkosten** including expenses. *adverb* inclusive.

einschränken *verb* (PERF **hat eingeschränkt**) 1 to restrict; 2 to cut back; 3 **sich einschränken** to economize.

einschreiben ✧ *verb* (IMPERF **schrieb sich ein**, PERF **hat sich eingeschrieben**) 1 **sich einschreiben** to enrol (*at university*); 2 **sich einschreiben** to put your name down.

Einschreiben das (PL die Einschreiben) registered letter, registered parcel; **per Einschreiben** registered.

einsehen ✧ *verb* (PRES **sieht ein**, IMPERF **sah ein**, PERF **hat eingesehen**) 1 to realize; 2 to see; **das sehe ich nicht ein** I don't see why.

einseitig *adjective* one-sided.

einsenden ✧ *verb* (IMPERF **sendete ein/sandte ein**, PERF **hat eingesendet/hat eingesandt**) to send in.

einsetzen *verb* (PERF **hat eingesetzt**) 1 to put in (*a missing part*), to insert; 2 to use; **während der Weltmeisterschaft wurden Sonderzüge eingesetzt** special train were put on during the World Cup; 3 to stake (*money*); 4 to start (*of rain, snow*); 5 **sich für jemanden einsetzen** to support somebody.

Einsicht die 1 insight; 2 sense; 3 **zu der Einsicht kommen, dass ...** to come to realize that ...

einsperren *verb* (PERF **hat eingesperrt**) to lock up.

Einspruch der (PL die Einsprüche) objection.

✧ IRREGULAR VERB: *See the verb table in the centre of the dictionary*

einst *adverb* **1** once; **2** one day (*in the future*).

einstecken *verb* (PERF **hat eingesteckt**) **1** to put in (*a coin*); **2 einen Brief einstecken** to post a letter; **3** to plug in; **4 etwas einstecken** to put something in your pocket or bag, to take something; **5** (*informal*) to take (*insults*).

einsteigen ◇ *verb* (IMPERF **stieg ein**, PERF **ist eingestiegen**) **1** to get in; **2** to get on (*a bus or train*).

einstellen *verb* (PERF **hat eingestellt**) **1** to employ (*in a job*); **2** to adjust (*a machine*); **3** to focus (*a camera*); **4** to tune into (*a radio station*); **5** to stop; **6 sich auf etwas einstellen** to prepare yourself for something; **7 sich schnell auf eine neue Situation einstellen** to adjust quickly to a new situation.

Einstellung *die* (PL *die* **Einstellungen**) **1** employment; **2** adjustment; **3** stopping; **4** take (*of a film*); **5** attitude; **seine politische Einstellung** his political views.

Einstieg *der* (PL *die* **Einstiege**) entrance.

einstürzen *verb* (PERF **ist eingestürzt**) to collapse.

einstweilen *adverb* **1** for the time being; **2** meanwhile.

eintausend *number* one thousand.

einteilen *verb* (PERF **hat eingeteilt**) **1** to divide up; **2 sich seine Zeit gut einteilen** to organize your time well.

Eintopf *der* (PL *die* **Eintöpfe**) stew.

Eintrag *der* (PL *die* **Einträge**) entry.

eintragen ◇ *verb* (PRES **trägt ein**, IMPERF **trug ein**, PERF **hat eingetragen**) **1** to enter, to write; **2 sich eintragen** to put your name down.

einträglich *adjective* profitable.

eintreffen ◇ *verb* (PRES **trifft ein**, IMPERF **traf ein**, PERF **ist eingetroffen**) **1** to arrive; **2** to come true.

eintreten ◇ *verb* (PRES **tritt ein**, IMPERF **trat ein**, PERF **ist eingetreten**) **1** to enter; **2 in einen Klub eintreten** to join a club; **für jemanden eintreten** to stand up for somebody.

Eintritt *der* **1** entrance; **2** admission; **'Eintritt frei'** 'admission free'.

Eintrittskarte *die* (PL *die* **Eintrittskarten**) (admission) ticket.

Eintrittspreis *der* (PL *die* **Eintrittspreise**) admission charge.

einverstanden *adjective* **1 einverstanden sein** to agree; **einverstanden!** okay!; **2 mit jemandem einverstanden sein** to approve of somebody.

Einwand *der* (PL *die* **Einwände**) objection.

Einwanderer *der* (PL *die* **Einwanderer**) immigrant.

Einwanderin *die* (PL *die* **Einwanderinnen**) immigrant.

einwandern *verb* (PERF **ist eingewandert**) to immigrate.

△ NEW SPELLING: *See page xii*

einweichen *verb* (PERF **hat eingeweicht**) to soak (*washing*).

einwerfen ✧ *verb* (PRES **wirft ein**, IMPERF **warf ein**, PERF **hat eingeworfen**) 1 to post; 2 to put in (*a coin, money*); 3 to throw in; 4 to smash.

Einwohner *der* (PL *die* **Einwohner**) inhabitant.

Einzahl *die* singular.

einzahlen *verb* (PERF **hat eingezahlt**) to pay in.

Einzel *das* (PL *die* **Einzel**) singles (*in sport*).

Einzelheit *die* (PL *die* **Einzelheiten**) detail.

Einzelkarte *die* (PL *die* **Einzelkarten**) single ticket.

Einzelkind *das* (PL *die* **Einzelkinder**) only child.

einzeln *adjective* 1 single; 2 individual; 3 odd (*sock, for example*).
adverb 1 individually; 2 separately, one at a time; **bitte einzeln eintreten** please enter one at a time.

Einzelne △ *der/die/das* (PL *die* **Einzelnen**) 1 *der/die* **Einzelne** the individual; 2 **Einzelne** some; 3 **ein Einzelner/eine Einzelne/ein Einzelnes** a single one; **jeder/jede/jedes Einzelne** every single one; 4 **im Einzelnen** in detail; **ins Einzelne gehen** to go into detail.

Einzelzimmer *das* (PL *die* **Einzelzimmer**) single room.

einziehen ✧ *verb* (IMPERF **zog ein**, PERF **hat eingezogen**) 1 to collect (*payment*); 2 to draw in (*its feelers, claws*); 3 **den Kopf einziehen** to duck; 4 (PERF **ist eingezogen**) to move in; **wann zieht ihr in die neue Wohnung ein?** when are you moving into your new flat?; 5 (PERF **ist eingezogen**) to soak in.

einzig *adjective* only; **ein einziges Mal** only once.

Einzige △ *der/die/das* (PL *die* **Einzigen**) 1 *der/die/das* **Einzige** the only one; 2 **ein Einziger/eine Einzige/ein Einziges** a single one; **kein Einziger/keine Einzige/kein Einziges** not a single one; 3 **das Einzige, was mich stört** the only thing that bothers me.

Eis *das* 1 ice; 2 ice cream.

Eisbahn *die* (PL *die* **Eisbahnen**) skating rink.

Eisbär *der* (PL *die* **Eisbären**) polar bear.

Eisbecher *der* (PL *die* **Eisbecher**) ice-cream sundae.

Eisdiele *die* (PL *die* **Eisdielen**) ice-cream parlour.

Eisen *das* iron.

Eisenbahn *die* (PL *die* **Eisenbahnen**) railway.

eisern *adjective* iron.

Eishockey *das* ice hockey.

eisig *adjective* icy.

eiskalt *adjective* 1 ice-cold (*drink*); 2 freezing cold.

Eislaufen *das* ice-skating.

✧ IRREGULAR VERB: *See the verb table in the centre of the dictionary*

Eiswürfel der (PL die **Eiswürfel**) ice cube.

Eiszapfen der (PL die **Eiszapfen**) icicle.

eitel *adjective* vain.

Eitelkeit die vanity.

Eiter der pus.

Eiweiß das 1 egg-white; 2 protein.

Ekel der disgust.

ekelhaft *adjective* disgusting.

ekeln *verb* (PERF **hat sich geekelt**) **sich vor etwas ekeln** to find something disgusting.

eklig *adjective* disgusting.

Ekzem das (PL die **Ekzeme**) eczema.

Elefant der (PL die **Elefanten**) elephant.

elegant *adjective* elegant.

Elektriker der (PL die **Elektriker**) electrician.

elektrisch *adjective* electrical.

Elektrizität die electricity.

Elektroherd der (PL die **Elektroherde**) electric cooker.

Elektronik die electronics.

elektronisch *adjective* electronic.

Elektrorasierer der (PL die **Elektrorasierer**) electric razor.

elend *adjective* 1 miserable; 2 terrible.

Elend das misery.

elf *number* eleven.

Elfe die (PL die **Elfen**) fairy.

Elfmeter der (PL die **Elfmeter**) penalty (*in soccer*).

Ellbogen der (PL die **Ellbogen**) elbow.

Eltern *plural noun* parents.

Email das (PL die **Emails**) enamel.

E-Mail die (PL die **E-Mails**) E-mail.

empfahl SEE **empfehlen**.

Empfang der (PL die **Empfänge**) 1 reception; 2 receipt (*of goods or a letter*).

empfangen ◇ *verb* (PRES **empfängt**, IMPERF **empfing**, PERF **hat empfangen**) to receive.

Empfängnisverhütung die contraception.

Empfangsdame die (PL die **Empfangsdamen**) receptionist.

empfehlen ◇ *verb* (PRES **empfiehlt**, IMPERF **empfahl**, PERF **hat empfohlen**) to recommend.

empfindlich *adjective* 1 sensitive; 2 delicate; 3 touchy.

empfing SEE **empfangen**.

empfohlen SEE **empfehlen**.

empört *adjective* indignant.

Ende das (PL die **Enden**) 1 end; **Ende April** at the end of April; **am Ende der Straße** at the end of the road; 2 **am Ende** in the end; 3 ending (*of a film, novel*); 4 **zu Ende sein** to be finished, to be over; 5 **Ende gut, alles gut** all's well that ends well.

△ NEW SPELLING: *See page xii*

enden *verb* (PERF **hat geendet**) to end.

endgültig *adjective* 1 final (*consent, decision*); 2 definite.

Endivie *die* (PL *die* **Endivien**) endive.

endlich *adverb* finally, at last; **na endlich!** at last!

endlos *adjective* endless.

Endspiel *das* (PL *die* **Endspiele**) final.

Endstation *die* (PL *die* **Endstationen**) terminus.

Endung *die* (PL *die* **Endungen**) ending.

Energie *die* energy.

energisch *adjective* energetic.

eng *adjective* 1 narrow; 2 tight; 3 close; **eng befreundet sein** to be close friends.

Engel *der* (PL *die* **Engel**) angel.

England *das* England; **aus England** from England.

Engländer *der* (PL *die* **Engländer**) Englishman.

Engländerin *die* (PL *die* **Engländerinnen**) Englishwoman.

englisch *adjective* English; **auf Englisch** in English.

Enkel *der* (PL *die* **Enkel**) grandson.

Enkelin *die* (PL *die* **Enkelinnen**) granddaughter.

Enkelkind *das* (PL *die* **Enkelkinder**) grandchild.

entdecken *verb* (PERF **hat entdeckt**) to discover.

Entdeckung *die* (PL *die* **Entdeckungen**) discovery.

Ente *die* (PL *die* **Enten**) duck.

entfernen *verb* (PERF **hat entfernt**) to remove.

entfernt *adjective* 1 distant; 2 **zehn Kilometer entfernt** ten kilometres away.
adverb **entfernt verwandt sein** to be distantly related.

Entfernung *die* (PL *die* **Entfernungen**) distance.

entführen *verb* (PERF **hat entführt**) 1 to kidnap; 2 to hijack.

entgegen *preposition* ←(+DAT) contrary to.

entgegengesetzt *adjective* 1 opposite; 2 opposing (*views*).

entgegenkommen ◇ *verb* (IMPERF **kam entgegen**, PERF **ist entgegengekommen**) 1 to come towards; 2 **jemandem entgegenkommen** to come to meet somebody; 3 **jemandem auf halbem Wege entgegenkommen** to meet somebody halfway; 4 **jemandem freundlich entgegenkommen** to be accommodating towards somebody.

entgegenkommend *adjective* 1 obliging; 2 **der entgegen-kommende Verkehr** the oncoming traffic.

Entgelt *das* payment.

Enthaarungsmittel *das* (PL *die*

Enthaarungsmittel) hair remover, depilatory.

nthalten ✧ *verb* (PRES **enthält**, IMPERF **enthielt**, PERF **hat enthalten**) 1 to contain; 2 **sich einer Sache enthalten** to abstain from something; **sich der Stimme enthalten** to abstain; 3 (PERF **ist enthalten**) **in etwas enthalten sein** to be included in something; **im Preis enthalten** included in the price.

ntkommen ✧ *verb* (IMPERF **entkam**, PERF **ist entkommen**) to escape.

ntlang *preposition* ←(+ACC or +DAT) along; **die Straße entlang** along the road; **am Fluss entlang** along the river.

ntlanggehen ✧ *verb* (IMPERF **ging entlang**, PERF **ist entlanggegangen**) to walk along.

ntlanglaufen ✧ *verb* (PRES **läuft entlang**, IMPERF **lief entlang**, PERF **ist entlanggelaufen**) to run along.

ntlassen ✧ *verb* (PRES **entlässt** Δ, IMPERF **entließ**, PERF **hat entlassen**) 1 to dismiss (*from a job*); 2 to discharge (*from hospital*); 3 to release (*from prison*).

ntlassung *die* (PL *die* **Entlassungen**) 1 dismissal; 2 discharge; 3 release.

ntmutigen *verb* (PERF **hat entmutigt**) to discourage.

ntschädigen *verb* (PERF **hat entschädigt**) to compensate.

Entschädigung *die* compensation.

entscheiden ✧ *verb* (IMPERF **entschied**, PERF **hat entschieden**) 1 to decide (on); 2 **sich entscheiden** to decide.

Entscheidung *die* (PL *die* **Entscheidungen**) decision.

entschließen ✧ *verb* (IMPERF **entschloss sich** Δ, PERF **hat sich entschlossen**) 1 **sich entschließen** to decide; 2 **sich anders entschließen** to change your mind; **Karl hat sich anders entschlossen** Karl has changed his mind.

entschlossen *adjective* determined.

Entschluss Δ *der* (PL *die* **Entschlüsse**) decision.

entschuldigen *verb* (PERF **hat entschuldigt**) 1 to excuse; **entschuldigen Sie bitte** excuse me; 2 **sich entschuldigen** to apologize; **ich habe mich bei Michi entschuldigt** I apologized to Michi.

Entschuldigung *die* (PL *die* **Entschuldigungen**) 1 apology; 2 **jemanden um Entschuldigung bitten** to apologize to somebody; 3 **Entschuldigung!** sorry!; 4 **Entschuldigung** (*with a question or request*) excuse me; **Entschuldigung, können Sie mir sagen, wie ich zum Bahnhof komme?** excuse me, could you tell me the way to the station?; 5 excuse.

Entsetzen *das* horror.

Δ NEW SPELLING: *See page xii*

entsetzlich *adjective* 1 horrible;
2 terrible.

entsetzt *adjective* horrified.

entspannen *verb* (PERF **hat sich
entspannt**) 1 **sich entspannen** to
relax; 2 **sich entspannen** to ease (*of
a situation*).

entsprechen ◇ *verb* (PRES
entspricht, IMPERF **entsprach**, PERF
hat entsprochen) 1 **den
Anforderungen entsprechen** to
meet the requirements; 2 **einer
Sache entsprechen** to correspond
to something; 3 to agree with (*the
truth, a description*); 4 to comply
with (*certain standards*).

entsprechend *adjective*
1 corresponding; 2 appropriate.
preposition ←(+DAT) in accordance
with.

entstehen ◇ *verb* (IMPERF
entstand, PERF **ist entstanden**) 1 to
develop; 2 to result (*of damage*).

enttäuschen *verb* (PERF **hat
enttäuscht**) to disappoint.

Enttäuschung *die* (PL *die*
Enttäuschungen) disappointment.

entweder *conjunction* either;
entweder heute oder morgen
either today or tomorrow.

entwerten *verb* (PERF **hat
entwertet**) 1 to devalue; 2 to punch
(*a ticket in a machine found on
trains, trams, buses, and on the
platform; you have to punch your
ticket before each journey*).

Entwerter *der* (PL *die* **Entwerter**)
ticket-punching machine (*these
machines are found on trains, trams
buses, and on the platform; you have
to punch your ticket before each
journey*).

entwickeln *verb* (PERF **hat
entwickelt**) 1 to develop; 2 to
display (*ability, a characteristic*);
3 **sich entwickeln** to develop.

Entwicklung *die* (PL *die*
Entwicklungen) 1 development;
2 developing.

Entwicklungsland *das* (PL *das*
Entwicklungsländer) developing
country.

Entwurf *der* (PL *die* **Entwürfe**)
1 design; 2 draft.

entzückend *adjective* delightful.

entzünden *verb* (PERF **hat
entzündet**) 1 to light (*a fire, match*)
2 **sich entzünden** to become
inflamed; 3 **sich entzünden** to
ignite.

Entzündung *die* (PL *die*
Entzündungen) inflammation.

Enzian *der* (PL *die* **Enziane**) gentian

Epidemie *die* (PL *die* **Epidemien**)
epidemic.

er *pronoun* 1 he; 2 it; '**wo ist mein
Mantel?**' – '**er liegt auf dem Stuhl**'
'where's my coat?' – 'it's on the
chair'; 3 him (*stressed*); **er war es**
it was him.

erben *verb* (PERF **hat geerbt**) to
inherit.

erblich *adjective* hereditary.

Erbschaft *die* (PL *die* **Erbschaften**)
inheritance.

◇ IRREGULAR VERB: *See the verb table in the centre of the dictionary*

Erbse die (PL die **Erbsen**) pea.

Erdbeben das (PL die **Erdbeben**) earthquake.

Erdbeere die (PL die **Erdbeeren**) strawberry.

Erde die 1 earth, soil; 2 ground; **auf der Erde** on the ground; 3 Earth; 4 earth (*for electricity*).

Erdgeschoss △ das (PL die **Erdgeschosse**) ground floor; **im Erdgeschoss** on the ground floor.

Erdkunde die geography.

Erdnuss △ die (PL die **Erdnüsse**) peanut.

ereignen verb (PERF **hat sich ereignet**) **sich ereignen** to happen.

Ereignis das (PL die **Ereignisse**) event.

erfahren ✧ verb (PRES **erfährt**, IMPERF **erfuhr**, PERF **hat erfahren**) 1 to hear, to learn; 2 to experience. *adjective* experienced.

Erfahrung die (PL die **Erfahrungen**) experience.

erfinden ✧ verb (IMPERF **erfand**, PERF **hat erfunden**) to invent.

Erfindung die (PL die **Erfindungen**) invention.

Erfolg der (PL die **Erfolge**) 1 success; **Erfolg haben** to be successful; 2 **Erfolg versprechend** △ promising; 3 **viel Erfolg!** good luck!

erfolglos adjective unsuccessful.

erfolgreich adjective successful.

erfolgversprechend SEE **Erfolg**.

erforderlich adjective necessary.

erforschen verb (PERF **hat erforscht**) 1 to explore; 2 to investigate.

erfreulicherweise adverb happily.

erfreut adjective pleased.

Erfrischung die (PL die **Erfrischungen**) refreshment.

erfüllen verb (PERF **hat erfüllt**) to fulfil; **sich erfüllen** to come true.

Ergebnis das (PL die **Ergebnisse**) result.

ergreifen ✧ verb (IMPERF **ergriff**, PERF **hat ergriffen**) 1 to seize, to grab; 2 to take (*measures, an opportunity*); 3 to take up (*a job, career*); 4 to move; **die Nachricht von ihrem Tod hat uns tief ergriffen** the news of her death moved us deeply; 5 **die Flucht ergreifen** to flee.

ergreifend adjective moving.

erhalten ✧ verb (PRES **erhält**, IMPERF **erhielt**, PERF **hat erhalten**) 1 to receive; 2 to preserve.

erhältlich adjective obtainable.

erheben ✧ verb (IMPERF **erhob**, PERF **hat erhoben**) 1 to raise; 2 to charge (*a fee*); 3 **Protest erheben** to protest; 4 **sich erheben** to rise up (*in a rebellion*).

erheblich adjective considerable.

erheitern verb (PERF **hat erheitert**) to amuse.

erhitzen *verb* (PERF **hat erhitzt**) to heat.

erhöhen *verb* (PERF **hat erhöht**) **1** to increase; **2 sich erhöhen** to rise.

Erhöhung *die* (PL *die* **Erhöhungen**) increase.

erholen *verb* (PERF **hat sich erholt**) **1 sich erholen** to have a rest; **ich habe mich in den Ferien gut erholt** I had a good rest on holiday; **2 sich von einer Krankheit erholen** to recover from an illness.

erholsam *adjective* restful.

Erholung *die* rest; **Iris ist zur Erholung in die Berge gefahren** Iris went to the mountains for a rest.

erinnern *verb* (PERF **hat erinnert**) **1** to remind; **2 sich erinnern** to remember.

Erinnerung *die* (PL *die* **Erinnerungen**) **1** memory; **2** souvenir.

erkälten *verb* (PERF **hat sich erkältet**) **1 sich erkälten** to catch a cold; **2 erkältet sein** to have a cold; **Ben ist erkältet** Ben has a cold.

Erkältung *die* (PL *die* **Erkältungen**) cold.

erkennen ✧ *verb* (IMPERF **erkannte**, PERF **hat erkannt**) **1** to recognize; **2** to realize.

erklären *verb* (PERF **hat erklärt**) **1** to explain; **2** to declare; **3 sich zu etwas bereit erklären** to agree to something.

Erklärung *die* (PL *die* **Erklärungen**)

1 explanation; **2** declaration; **3 eine öffentliche Erklärung** a public statement.

erkundigen *verb* (PERF **hat sich erkundigt**) **1** to enquire; **2** to ask about; **Susi hat sich nach dir erkundigt** Susi was asking about you.

Erkundigung *die* (PL *die* **Erkundigungen**) enquiry.

erlauben *verb* (PERF **hat erlaubt**) **1** to allow; **jemandem etwas erlauben** to allow somebody to do something; **2 sich etwas erlauben** to allow yourself something; **3 sich alles erlauben** to do as you please; **4 erlauben Sie mal!** (*informal*) do you mind!

Erlaubnis *die* permission.

erleben *verb* (PERF **hat erlebt**) **1** to experience; **2** to have (*a disappointment, an experience*); **eine Überraschung erleben** to have a surprise; **3 er hat die Geburt seines Enkels nicht mehr erlebt** he didn't live to see the birth of his grandson.

Erlebnis *das* (PL *die* **Erlebnisse**) experience.

erledigen *verb* (PERF **hat erledigt**) to deal with, to do.

erledigt *adjective* **1** settled; **2** (*informal*) worn out.

Erleichterung *die* relief.

erleiden ✧ *verb* (IMPERF **erlitt**, PERF **hat erlitten**) to suffer.

Erlös *der* (PL *die* **Erlöse**) proceeds.

✧ IRREGULAR VERB: *See the verb table in the centre of the dictionary*

ermäßigen verb (PERF hat ermäßigt) to reduce.

Ermäßigung die (PL die Ermäßigungen) reduction.

ermorden verb (PERF hat ermordet) to murder.

ermutigen verb (PERF hat ermutigt) to encourage.

ernähren verb (PERF hat ernährt) 1 to feed; 2 **sich von Nudeln ernähren** to live on pasta; 3 to support (a family).

Ernährung die 1 diet; **eine gesunde Ernährung** a healthy diet; 2 nutrition.

erneuern verb (PERF hat erneuert) to renew.

erneut adjective renewed. adverb once again.

ernst adjective serious.

Ernst der 1 seriousness; 2 **im Ernst** seriously; 3 **ist das dein Ernst?** are you serious?

ernsthaft adjective serious.

ernstlich adjective serious.

Ernte die (PL die Ernten) harvest.

ernten verb (PERF hat geerntet) to harvest.

erobern verb (PERF hat erobert) to conquer.

Eroberung die (PL die Eroberungen) conquest.

eröffnen (PERF hat eröffnet) to open.

Eröffnung die (PL die Eröffnungen) opening.

erraten ⌂ verb (PRES errät IMPERF erriet, PERF hat erraten) to guess.

Erreger der (PL die Erreger) germ.

Erregung die excitement.

erreichen verb (PERF hat erreicht), 1 to reach; 2 **den Zug erreichen** to catch the train; 3 to achieve (a goal, aim); 4 **Irene ist telefonisch zu erreichen** Irene can be contacted by phone.

erröten verb (PERF ist errötet) to blush.

Ersatz der replacement, substitute.

Ersatzreifen der (PL die Ersatzreifen) spare tyre.

Ersatzteil das (PL die Ersatzteile) spare part.

erscheinen ✧ verb (IMPERF erschien, PERF ist erschienen) to appear.

erschöpft adjective exhausted.

erschrecken verb 1 (PERF hat erschreckt) to scare; 2 ✧ (PRES erschrickt, IMPERF erschrak, PERF ist erschrocken) to get a fright.

erschreckend adjective alarming.

erschrocken adjective 1 frightened; 2 startled.

ersetzen verb (PERF hat ersetzt) to replace; **jemandem einen Schaden ersetzen** to compensate somebody for damages.

Ersparnisse plural noun savings.

erst adverb 1 first; **erst einmal** first of all; 2 only; **eben erst** only just; 3 not until; **erst nächste Woche** not

△ NEW SPELLING: See page xii

until next week; **Oma war erst zufrieden, als die ganze Familie da war** granny was not happy until all the family were there.

erstaunen *verb* (PERF **hat erstaunt**) to astonish.

erstaunlich *adjective* astonishing.

erstaunt *adjective* amazed; **über etwas erstaunt sein** to be amazed about something.

Erste △ *der/die/das* (PL *die* **Ersten**) 1 *der/die* **Erste** the first (one); *das* **Erste** the first (thing); 2 **Dirk kam als Erster** Dirk arrived first; **Marianne ging als Erste** Marianne left first; 3 **als Erster/Erste etwas tun** to be the first to do something; 4 **als Erstes** first of all; 5 **fürs Erste** for the time being.

erstens *adverb* firstly.

erster, erste, erstes *adjective* first; **mein erstes Rad war rot** my first bike was red; **der erste April** the first of April; **erste Hilfe** △ first aid.

erstklassig *adjective* first-class.

erstmals *adverb* for the first time.

erteilen *verb* (PERF **hat erteilt**) to give (*advice, information*).

ertragen ⟡ *verb* (PRES **erträgt**, IMPERF **ertrug**, PERF **hat ertragen**) to bear.

ertrinken ⟡ *verb* (IMPERF **ertrank**, PERF **ist ertrunken**) to drown.

erwachsen *adjective* grown-up.

Erwachsene *der/die* (PL *die* **Erwachsenen**) adult, grown-up.

Erwachsenenbildung *die* adult education.

erwähnen *verb* (PERF **hat erwähnt**) to mention.

erwarten *verb* (PERF **hat erwartet**) to expect.

Erwartung *die* (PL *die* **Erwartungen**) expectation.

erzählen *verb* (PERF **hat erzählt**) to tell.

Erzählung *die* (PL *die* **Erzählungen**) story.

Erzeugnis *das* (PL *die* **Erzeugnisse**) product.

erziehen ⟡ *verb* (IMPERF **erzog**, PERF **hat erzogen**) 1 to bring up; 2 to educate.

Erziehung *die* 1 upbringing; 2 education.

es *pronoun* 1 it; **es regnet** it is raining; 2 **es gibt** there is, there are; 3 **'wo ist das Baby?' – 'es schläft'** 'where's the baby?' – 'he's/she's asleep'.

Esel *der* (PL *die* **Esel**) donkey.

essbar △ *adjective* edible.

essen ⟡ *verb* (PRES **isst** △, IMPERF **aß**, PERF **hat gegessen**) to eat.

Essen *das* 1 meal; 2 food.

Essig *der* vinegar.

Essiggurke *die* (PL *die* **Essiggurken**) gherkin.

Esskastanie △ *die* (PL *die* **Esskastanien**) sweet chestnut.

⟡ IRREGULAR VERB: *See the verb table in the centre of the dictionary*

Esszimmer△ das (PL die
Esszimmer) dining room.

Etage die (PL die Etagen) floor; **in der
zweiten Etage** on the second floor.

Etagenbett das (PL die
Etagenbetten) bunk beds.

ethnisch adjective ethnic.

Etikett das (PL die Etikette) label.

Etui das (PL die Etuis) case.

etwa adverb **1** about; **er ist etwa so
groß wie du** he's about as tall as
you; **2** for example; **3 nicht etwa,
dass** ... not that ...; **4 hat Klaus
etwa Angst gehabt?** Klaus wasn't
scared, was he?

etwas pronoun, adverb
1 something; **2** anything; **sonst
noch etwas?** anything else?;
3 some; **etwas von dem Geld** some
of the money; **noch etwas Kaffee?**
(some) more coffee?; **4** a little; **nur
etwas Zucker** only a little sugar;
etwas lauter singen to sing a little
louder.

EU die (Europäische Union) EU.

euch pronoun **1** you; **ich habe euch
eingeladen** I've invited you; **2** to
you; **Eva hat es euch geschenkt**
Eva gave it to you; **3** (reflexive)
yourselves.

euer adjective your.

Eule die (PL die Eulen) owl.

eurer, eure, eures pronoun
yours.

Euro der (PL die Euros) (European
currency) Euro.

Europa das Europe.

Europäer der (PL die Europäer)
European.

Europäerin die (PL die
Europäerinnen) European.

europäisch adjective European.

evangelisch adjective Protestant.

eventuell adjective possible.
adverb possibly.

ewig adjective eternal.
adverb forever.

Ewigkeit die eternity.

Examen das (PL die Examen)
examination, exam.

Exemplar das (PL die Exemplare)
1 copy; **2** specimen.

existieren verb (PERF **hat existiert**)
to exist.

explodieren verb (PERF **ist
explodiert**) to explode.

Explosion die (PL die Explosionen)
explosion.

extra adverb **1** separately; **2** extra;
3 specially; **4** (informal) on
purpose.

extrem adjective extreme.

F f

fabelhaft adjective fabulous,
fantastic.

Fabrik die (PL die Fabriken) factory.

Fach das (PL die Fächer)
1 compartment; **2** drawer;
3 subject (at school).

△ NEW SPELLING: See page xii

Facharzt der (PL die **Fachärzte**) specialist.

Fachärztin die (PL die **Fachärztinnen**) specialist.

Fachfrau die (PL die **Fachfrauen**) expert.

Fachmann der (PL die **Fachleute**) expert.

Faden der (PL die **Fäden**) thread.

fähig adjective 1 capable; 2 able.

Fähigkeit die (PL die **Fähigkeiten**) ability.

Fahne die (PL die **Fahnen**) flag.

Fahrausweis der (PL die **Fahrausweise**) ticket.

Fahrbahn die (PL die **Fahrbahnen**) 1 carriageway; 2 road.

Fähre die (PL die **Fähren**) ferry.

fahren ◆ verb (PRES **fährt**, IMPERF **fuhr**, PERF **ist gefahren**) 1 to go; **mit dem Zug nach Wien fahren** to go to Vienna by train; **ich bin mit dem Auto gefahren** I went by car; 2 to drive; **Hanna ist sehr schnell gefahren** Hanna drove very fast; 3 to ride (of a cyclist); 4 to run (of a train, bus); **der Zug fährt nicht an Sonn- und Feiertagen** the train doesn't run on Sundays and public holidays; 5 to leave; **wann fahrt ihr?** when are you leaving?; 6 **was ist in sie gefahren?** (informal) what's got into her?; 7 (PERF **hat gefahren**) to drive; **er hat Doris nach Hause gefahren** he drove Doris home; **ich**

habe das Auto in die Garage gefahren I drove the car into the garage.

Fahrer der (PL die **Fahrer**) driver.

Fahrerflucht die hit-and-run driving; **Fahrerflucht begehen** to be involved in a hit-and-run.

Fahrerin die (PL die **Fahrerinnen**) driver.

Fahrgast der (PL die **Fahrgäste**) passenger.

Fahrkarte die (PL die **Fahrkarten**) ticket.

Fahrkartenausgabe die ticket office.

Fahrkartenautomat der (PL die **Fahrkartenautomaten**) ticket machine.

Fahrkartenschalter der (PL die **Fahrkartenschalter**) ticket office.

fahrlässig adjective negligent.

Fahrlehrer der (PL die **Fahrlehrer**) driving instructor.

Fahrplan der (PL die **Fahrpläne**) timetable.

Fahrpreis der (PL die **Fahrpreise**) fare.

Fahrprüfung die (PL die **Fahrprüfungen**) driving test; **die Fahrprüfung machen** to take your driving test.

Fahrrad das (PL die **Fahrräder**) bicycle.

Fahrradweg der (PL die **Fahrradwege**) cycle lane.

◆ IRREGULAR VERB: See the verb table in the centre of the dictionary

Fahrschein der (PL die Fahrscheine) ticket.

Fahrschule die (PL die Fahrschulen) driving school.

Fahrstuhl der (PL die Fahrstühle) lift.

Fahrt die (PL die Fahrten) 1 journey; **gute Fahrt!** have a good journey!; 2 trip; 3 drive; 4 **in voller Fahrt** at full speed.

Fahrzeug das (PL die Fahrzeuge) vehicle.

fair adjective fair.

Faktor der (PL die Faktoren) factor.

Falke der (PL die Falken) falcon.

Fall der (PL die Fälle) 1 case; **in diesem Fall** in this case; **auf alle Fälle, auf jeden Fall** in any case; **für alle Fälle** just in case; 2 **auf jeden Fall** definitely; 3 **auf keinen Fall** on no account; 4 fall.

Falle die (PL die Fallen) trap.

fallen ◇ verb (PRES **fällt**, IMPERF **fiel**, PERF **ist gefallen**) 1 to fall; 2 **etwas fallen lassen** △ to drop something; **wir haben den Plan fallen lassen** we've dropped the idea; 3 **eine Bemerkung fallen lassen** △ to make a comment.

fallenlassen SEE **fallen**.

fällig adjective due.

falls conjunction 1 if; 2 in case.

Fallschirm der (PL die Fallschirme) parachute.

falsch adjective 1 wrong; **du hast ihn falsch verstanden** you got him wrong, 2 false (teeth, etc.); 0 forged.

fälschen verb (PERF **hat gefälscht**) to forge.

Fälschung die (PL die Fälschungen) 1 fake; 2 forgery.

Falte die (PL die Falten) 1 fold; 2 crease; 3 pleat; 4 wrinkle.

falten verb (PERF **hat gefaltet**) to fold.

faltig adjective 1 wrinkled; 2 creased.

familiär adjective familiar.

Familie die (PL die Familien) family.

Familienname der (PL die Familiennamen) surname.

Fan der (PL die Fans) fan.

fand SEE **finden**.

fangen ◇ verb (PRES **fängt**, IMPERF **fing**, PERF **hat gefangen**) to catch.

fantastisch adjective fantastic.

Farbe die (PL die Farben) 1 colour; 2 paint; 3 dye; 4 suit (*in playing cards*).

farbecht adjective colour fast.

färben verb (PERF **hat gefärbt**) 1 to dye; 2 **sich die Haare färben** to dye your hair; 3 **das Sweatshirt färbt** this sweatshirt runs.

Farbfilm der (PL die Farbfilme) colour film.

farbig adjective coloured.

farblos adjective colourless.

Farbstift der (PL die Farbstifte) coloured pencil.

△ NEW SPELLING: *See page xii*

Farbstoff *der* (PL *die* **Farbstoffe**)
1 dye; 2 colouring (*for food*).

Farbton *der* (PL *die* **Farbtöne**) shade.

Fasan *der* (PL *die* **Fasane**) pheasant.

Fasching *der* (PL *die* **Faschinge**)
carnival.

Faser *die* (PL *die* **Fasern**) fibre.

Fass Δ *das* (PL *die* **Fässer**) barrel; **Bier
vom Fass** draught beer.

fassen *verb* (PERF **hat gefasst** Δ) 1 to
grasp; 2 **einen Dieb fassen** to catch
a thief; 3 to hold (*of a container*);
4 to understand; 5 **nicht zu fassen**
unbelievable; 6 **sich fassen** to
compose yourself; 7 **einen
Entschluss fassen** to make a
decision; 8 **sich kurz fassen** to be
brief.

Fassung *die* (PL *die* **Fassungen**)
1 version; 2 composure;
3 **jemanden aus der Fassung
bringen** to throw somebody, to upset
somebody; 4 setting (*for gems*).

fassungslos *adjective* speechless.

fast *adverb* 1 almost; 2 **fast nie**
hardly ever.

Fastenzeit *die* (PL *die*
Fastenzeiten) Lent.

Fastnacht *die* carnival.

faul *adjective* 1 lazy; 2 rotten; 3 **eine
faule Ausrede** a lame excuse; 4 **an
der Sache ist etwas faul** (*informal*)
there's something fishy about it.

faulen *verb* (PERF **ist gefault**) to rot.

faulenzen *verb* (PERF **hat
gefaulenzt**) to laze about.

Faust *die* (PL *die* **Fäuste**) 1 fist; 2 **auf
eigene Faust** off your own bat.

Fax *das* (PL *die* **Fax(e)**) fax.

faxen *verb* (PERF **hat gefaxt**) to fax;
ich faxe Ihnen die Liste I'll fax you
the list.

Februar *der* February.

fechten ✧ *verb* (PRES **ficht**, IMPERF
focht, PERF **hat gefochten**) to fence.

Feder *die* (PL *die* **Federn**) 1 feather;
2 spring; 3 nib (*of a pen*).

Federball *der* (PL *die* **Federbälle**)
1 badminton; 2 shuttlecock.

Federmäppchen *das* (PL *die*
Federmäppchen) pencil case.

Fee *die* (PL *die* **Feen**) fairy.

fegen *verb* (PERF **hat gefegt**) to
sweep.

fehl *adjective* **fehl am Platz** out of
place.

fehlen *verb* (PERF **hat gefehlt**) 1 to
be missing; 2 to be lacking; 3 to be
absent (*from school*); 4 **mir fehlt die
Zeit** I haven't got the time; 5 **es fehlt
ihnen einfach das Geld für ein
neues Auto** they simply haven't got
the money for a new car; 5 **was fehlt
dir?** what's the matter?; 6 **Rudi fehlt
mir** I miss Rudi.

Fehler *der* (PL *die* **Fehler**) 1 mistake;
2 fault.

Feier *die* (PL *die* **Feiern**) 1 party;
2 celebration.

Feierabend *der* (PL *die*
Feierabende) 1 finishing time;
2 **nach Feierabend** after work.

✧ IRREGULAR VERB: *See the verb table in the centre of the dictionary*

Feierlichkeiten *plural noun* festivities.

feiern *verb* (PERF **hat gefeiert**) to celebrate.

Feiertag *der* (PL *die* **Feiertage**) 1 holiday; **ein gesetzlicher Feiertag** a public holiday; 2 **am ersten Feiertag** on Christmas Day; **der zweite Feiertag** Boxing Day.

feige *adjective* cowardly; **du bist feige** you're a coward.

Feige *die* (PL *die* **Feigen**) fig.

Feigling *der* (PL *die* **Feiglinge**) coward.

Feile *die* (PL *die* **Feilen**) file.

fein *adjective* 1 fine; 2 delicate; 3 refined; 4 **sich fein machen** △ to dress up.

Feind *der* (PL *die* **Feinde**) enemy.

feindlich *adjective* hostile.

Feld *das* (PL *die* **Felder**) 1 field; 2 pitch; 3 box (*on a form*); 4 square (*on a board game*).

Fell *das* (PL *die* **Felle**) fur, skin.

Fels *der* rock.

Felsen *der* (PL *die* **Felsen**) cliff.

feminin *adjective* feminine.

Feminist *der* (PL *die* **Feministen**) feminist.

Feministin *die* (PL *die* **Feministinnen**) feminist.

Fenster *das* (PL *die* **Fenster**) window.

Fensterladen *der* (PL *die* **Fensterläden**) shutter.

Ferien *plural noun* holidays; **Ferien haben** to be on holiday.

fern *adjective* 1 distant; 2 **sich fern halten** △ to keep away; **jemanden von etwas fern halten** △ to keep somebody away from something. *adverb* far away.

Fernbedienung *die* remote control.

Ferngespräch *das* (PL *die* **Ferngespräche**) long-distance call.

fernhalten SEE **fern**.

Fernglas *das* (PL *die* **Ferngläser**) binoculars.

Fernsehapparat *der* (PL *die* **Fernsehapparate**) television set.

fernsehen ◇ *verb* (PRES **sieht fern**, IMPERF **sah fern**, PERF **hat ferngesehen**) to watch television.

Fernsehen *das* television; **im Fernsehen** on television.

Fernseher *der* (PL *die* **Fernseher**) television (set).

Fernsprecher *der* (PL *die* **Fernsprecher**) telephone.

Ferse *die* (PL *die* **Fersen**) heel.

fertig *adjective* 1 finished; **mit den Hausaufgaben fertig werden** to finish your homework; **fertig sein** to be finished; 2 **mit jemandem fertig sein** (*informal*) to be through with somebody; 3 **völlig fertig sein** to be completely worn out; 4 **mit etwas fertig werden** to cope with something (*problems, for example*); 5 ready; **das Essen ist fertig** food's ready; 6 **etwas fertig machen** △

△ NEW SPELLING: *See page xii*

(*prepare*) to get something ready; (*complete*) to finish something; **sich fertig machen** △ to get ready; **7 jemanden fertig machen** △ to wear somebody out, to wear somebody down; **der ständige Stress macht mich fertig** this constant stress is wearing me down; **8 es fertig bringen** △, **etwas zu tun** to bring yourself to do something; **ich bringe es einfach nicht fertig** I just can't bring myself to do it. *adverb* **fertig essen** to finish eating.

fertigbringen SEE **fertig**.

Fertiggericht *das* (PL *die* **Fertiggerichte**) ready-to-serve meal.

fertigmachen SEE **fertig**.

Fest *das* (PL *die* **Feste**) 1 party; 2 celebration; 3 festival.

fest *adjective* 1 firm; 2 fixed (*salary, address*); 3 solid; **feste Nahrung** solids; 4 **fest werden** to harden. *adverb* 1 **fest schlafen** to be fast asleep; 2 **fest befreundet sein** to be close friends; 3 **fest angestellt sein** to be in permanent employment.

festbinden ✧ *verb* (IMPERF **band fest**, PERF **hat festgebunden**) to tie (up).

festhalten ✧ *verb* (PRES **hält fest**, IMPERF **hielt fest**, PERF **hat festgehalten**) 1 to hold on to; 2 **sich festhalten** to hold on; **halt dich an mir fest** hold on to me.

Festigkeit *die* strength.

festlegen *verb* (PERF **hat**

festgelegt) 1 to fix; 2 **sich auf etwas festlegen** to commit yourself to something.

festlich *adjective* festive.

festmachen *verb* (PERF **hat festgemacht**) 1 to fix; **ich mache gleich einen Termin fest** I'll fix a date straight away; 2 to fasten.

festnehmen ✧ *verb* (PRES **nimmt fest**, IMPERF **nahm fest**, PERF **hat festgenommen**) to arrest.

feststehen ✧ *verb* (IMPERF **stand fest**, PERF **hat festgestanden**) to be certain; **eins steht fest, Daniel lade ich nicht mehr ein** one thing's certain, I'm not going to invite Daniel again.

feststellen *verb* (PERF **hat festgestellt**) 1 to establish; 2 to notice.

Fett *das* (PL *die* **Fette**) 1 fat; 2 grease.

fett *adjective* 1 fat (*person*); 2 greasy, fatty (*food*); 3 bold (*type*).

fettarm *adjective* low-fat.

fettig *adjective* greasy.

Fetzen *der* (PL *die* **Fetzen**) 1 scrap; 2 rag.

feucht *adjective* 1 damp; 2 humid.

Feuchtigkeit *die* 1 moisture; 2 humidity.

Feuer *das* 1 fire; 2 **hast du Feuer?** have you got a light?

Feuerlöscher *der* (PL *die* **Feuerlöscher**) fire extinguisher.

Feuermelder *der* (PL *die* **Feuermelder**) fire alarm.

✧ IRREGULAR VERB: *See the verb table in the centre of the dictionary*

Feuertreppe die (PL die
Feuertreppen) fire escape.

Feuerwehr die (PL die
Feuerwehren) fire brigade.

Feuerwehrauto das (PL die
Feuerwehrautos) fire engine.

Feuerwehrmann der (PL die
Feuerwehrleute) fireman.

Feuerwerk das fireworks.

Feuerzeug das (PL die Feuerzeuge)
lighter.

ficht SEE **fechten**.

Fieber das (high) temperature,
fever; **Fieber haben** to have a
temperature.

fiel SEE **fallen**.

fies adjective (informal) nasty.

Figur die (PL die Figuren) 1 figure;
2 character.

Filiale die (PL die Filialen) branch.

Film der (PL die Filme) film.

filmen verb (PERF hat gefilmt) to film.

Filter der (PL die Filter) filter.

Filzstift der (PL die Filzstifte) felt pen.

finanziell adjective financial.

finanzieren verb (PERF hat
finanziert) to finance.

finden ✧ verb (IMPERF fand, PERF hat
gefunden) 1 to find; 2 to think; **wie
findest du das?** what do you think
of it?; **findest du?** do you think so?;
3 **ich finde nichts dabei** I don't mind.

fing SEE **fangen**.

Finger der (PL die Finger) finger.

Fingernagel der (PL die
Fingernägel) fingernail.

Finne der (PL die Finnen) Finn.

Finnin die (PL die Finninnen) Finn.

Finnland das Finland.

finster adjective 1 dark; **im Finstern**
in the dark; 2 sinister.

Finsternis die darkness.

Firma die (PL die Firmen) firm,
company.

Fisch der (PL die Fische) 1 fish;
2 **Fische** Pisces; **Helmut ist Fisch**
Helmut is Pisces.

Fischer der (PL die Fischer)
fisherman.

fit adjective fit; **er hält sich durch
Jogging fit** he keeps fit by jogging.

Fitnesstraining △ das keep fit.

fix adjective 1 quick; 2 **fix und fertig**
all finished, all ready; 3 **ich bin fix
und fertig** (informal) I'm shattered.

flach adjective 1 flat; 2 low;
3 shallow; **die Erdbeeren kommen
in die flache Schüssel** the
strawberries go into the shallow
bowl.

Fläche die (PL die Flächen)
1 surface; 2 area.

flackern verb (PERF hat geflackert)
to flicker.

Flagge die (PL die Flaggen) flag.

Flamme die (PL die Flammen) flame.

Flasche die (PL die Flaschen) bottle.

△ NEW SPELLING: *See page xii*

Flaschenöffner *der* (PL *die* **Flaschenöffner**) bottle opener.

flauschig *adjective* **1** fluffy; **2** fleecy.

Fleck *der* (PL *die* **Flecken**) **1** stain; **2** spot; **3 ein blauer Fleck** a bruise.

fleckig *adjective* **1** stained; **2** blotchy (*skin*).

Fledermaus *die* (PL *die* **Fledermäuse**) bat.

Fleisch *das* **1** meat; **2** flesh.

Fleischer *der* (PL *die* **Fleischer**) butcher.

Fleischerei *die* (PL *die* **Fleischereien**) butcher's.

Fleiß *der* hard work.

fleißig *adjective* hard-working.

flicken *verb* (PERF **hat geflickt**) to mend.

Fliege *die* (PL *die* **Fliegen**) **1** fly; **2** bow tie.

fliegen ✧ *verb* (IMPERF **flog**, PERF **ist geflogen**) **1** to fly; **2 ich bin geflogen** (*informal*) I fell; **3 Manfred ist geflogen** (*informal*) Manfred has been fired; **4** (PERF **hat geflogen**) to fly (*a plane*).

fliehen ✧ *verb* (IMPERF **floh**, PERF **ist geflohen**) to flee.

Fliese *die* (PL *die* **Fliesen**) tile.

Fließband *das* (PL *die* **Fließbänder**) **1** conveyor belt; **2** assembly line.

fließen ✧ *verb* (IMPERF **floss** △, PERF **ist geflossen**) to flow.

fließend *adjective* **1** running;
2 fluent; **fließendes Deutsch** fluent German; **3** moving (*traffic*).

Flitterwochen *plural noun* honeymoon.

flitzen *verb* (*informal*) (PERF **ist geflitzt**) **1** to dash; **2** to whizz.

Flocke *die* (PL *die* **Flocken**) flake.

flog SEE **fliegen**.

floh SEE **fliehen**.

Floh *der* (PL *die* **Flöhe**) flee.

Flohmarkt *der* (PL *die* **Flohmärkte**) flea market.

floss △ SEE **fließen**.

Flosse *die* (PL *die* **Flossen**) **1** fin; **2** flipper.

Flöte *die* (PL *die* **Flöten**) flute.

fluchen *verb* (PERF **hat geflucht**) to curse.

Flüchtling *der* (PL *die* **Flüchtlinge**) refugee.

Flug *der* (PL *die* **Flüge**) flight.

Flugblatt *das* (PL *die* **Flugblätter**) pamphlet.

Flügel *der* (PL *die* **Flügel**) **1** wing; **2** grand piano.

Fluggast *der* (PL *die* **Fluggäste**) (air) passenger.

Fluggesellschaft *die* (PL *die* **Fluggesellschaften**) airline.

Flughafen *der* (PL *die* **Flughäfen**) airport.

Flugplatz *der* (PL *die* **Flugplätze**) **1** airport; **2** airfield.

✧ IRREGULAR VERB: *See the verb table in the centre of the dictionary*

Flugzeug *das* (PL *die* **Flugzeuge**)
aeroplane.

Fluor *das* fluoride.

Flur *der* (PL *die* **Flure**) **1** hall;
2 corridor.

Fluss Δ *der* (PL *die* **Flüsse**) river.

flüssig *adjective* liquid.

Flüssigkeit *die* (PL *die*
Flüssigkeiten) liquid.

flüstern *verb* (PERF **hat geflüstert**)
to whisper.

Flut *die* (PL *die* **Fluten**) **1** high tide;
2 flood (*of letters, complaints*).

Flutlicht *das* floodlight.

focht SEE **fechten**.

Föhn Δ *der* (PL *die* **Föhne**) hair drier.

föhnen Δ *verb* (PERF **hat geföhnt**) to
blow-dry.

Folge *die* (PL *die* **Folgen**)
1 consequence; **2** episode; **3 etwas
zur Folge haben** to result in
something; **4 an den Folgen eines
Unfalls sterben** to die as the result
of an accident.

folgen *verb* (PERF **ist gefolgt**) **1** to
follow; **daraus folgt, dass** … it
follows that …; **ich kann dir nicht
folgen** I can't follow what you're
saying; **2** (PERF **hat gefolgt**) to obey.

folgend *adjective* **1** following;
2 Folgendes the following.

Folgerung *die* (PL *die* **Folgerungen**)
conclusion.

folgsam *adjective* obedient.

Folie *die* (PL *die* **Folien**) foil.

Fön™ = **Föhn**.

tönen = **tonnen**.

fordern *verb* (PERF **hat gefordert**) to
demand.

fördern *verb* (PERF **hat gefördert**)
1 to promote; **2** to sponsor.

Forderung *die* (PL *die*
Forderungen) **1** demand; **2** claim.

Forelle *die* (PL *die* **Forellen**) trout.

Form *die* (PL *die* **Formen**) **1** shape;
2 form; **in Form sein** to be on form;
3 tin (*for baking*).

Format *das* (PL *die* **Formate**) format.

formatieren *verb* (PERF **hat
formatiert**) to format.

formen *verb* (PERF **hat geformt**) **1** to
form; **2 sich formen** to take shape.

förmlich *adjective* formal.
adverb **1** formally; **2 jemanden
förmlich zwingen, etwas zu tun** to
positively force somebody to do
something; **ich hätte förmlich
schreien können** I really could have
screamed.

Formular *das* (PL *die* **Formulare**)
form.

Forscher *der* (PL *die* **Forscher**)
1 researcher, research scientist;
2 explorer.

Forschung *die* (PL *die*
Forschungen) research.

Forst *der* (PL *die* **Forste**) forest.

Förster *der* (PL *die* **Förster**) forester.

fort *adverb* **1** away; **2 fort sein** to
have gone; **3 und so fort** and so
on; **4 in einem fort** on and on.

Δ NEW SPELLING: *See page xii*

fortbewegen *verb* (PERF **hat fortbewegt**) 1 to move; 2 **sich fortbewegen** to move.

fortfahren✧ *verb* (PRES **fährt fort**, IMPERF **fuhr fort**, PERF **ist fortgefahren**) 1 to leave; **wann fahrt ihr fort?** when are you leaving?; 2 to continue.

fortgeschritten *adjective* advanced.

Fortschritt *der* (PL **die Fortschritte**) progress; **Fortschritte machen** to make progress.

fortsetzen *verb* (PERF **hat fortgesetzt**) to continue.

Fortsetzung *die* (PL **die Fortsetzungen**) 1 continuation; 2 instalment.

Foto *das* (PL **die Fotos**) photo.

Fotoapparat *der* (PL **die Fotoapparate**) camera.

Fotograf *der* (PL **die Fotografen**) photographer.

Fotografie *die* (PL **die Fotografien**) 1 photography; 2 photograph.

fotografieren *verb* (PERF **hat fotografiert**) 1 to photograph, to take a photograph of; 2 to take photographs.

Fotografin *die* (PL **die Fotografinnen**) photographer.

Fotokopie *die* (PL **die Fotokopien**) photocopy.

Fracht *die* (PL **die Frachten**) freight, cargo.

Frage *die* (PL **die Fragen**) question;

etwas in Frage stellen to question something; **das kommt nicht in Frage** that's out of the question.

Fragebogen *der* (PL **die Fragebogen**) questionnaire.

fragen *verb* (PERF **hat gefragt**) 1 to ask; 2 **sich fragen** to wonder.

Fragezeichen *das* (PL **die Fragezeichen**) question mark.

fraglich *adjective* doubtful.

Franken[1] *der* (PL **die Franken**) (Swiss) franc.

Franken[2] *das* Franconia.

Frankreich *das* France.

Franzose *der* (PL **die Franzosen**) Frenchman.

Französin *die* (PL **die Französinnen**) Frenchwoman.

französisch *adjective* French.

Französisch *das* French.

fraß SEE **fressen**.

Frau *die* (PL **die Frauen**) 1 woman; 2 wife; 3 Mrs, Ms (*'Frau' is usually used to address both married and unmarried women*).

Fräulein *das* (PL **die Fräulein**) 1 young lady; 2 Miss; **Fräulein Schmidt** Miss Schmidt.

frech *adjective* cheeky.

Frechheit *die* (PL **die Frechheiten**) 1 cheek; 2 cheeky remark.

frei *adjective* 1 free; 2 freelance; 3 **ist dieser Platz frei?** is this seat taken?; 4 **ein freier Tag** a day off;

✧ **IRREGULAR VERB: See the verb table in the centre of the dictionary**

sich frei nehmen to take a day off;
5 '**Zimmer frei**' 'vacancies'.

Freibad *das* (PL *die* **Freibäder**) open-air swimming pool.

Freie *das* **im Freien** in the open air.

freigebig *adjective* generous.

Freiheit *die* (PL *die* **Freiheiten**)
1 freedom; 2 liberty; **sich
Freiheiten erlauben** to take
liberties.

freimachen *verb* (PERF **hat
freigemacht**) 1 to take time off;
2 **sich freimachen** to take time off.

Freistoß *der* (PL *die* **Freistöße**) free
kick.

Freitag *der* (PL *die* **Freitage**) Friday.

freitags *adverb* on Fridays.

freiwillig *adjective* voluntary.

Freizeit *die* 1 spare time; 2 leisure.

fremd *adjective* 1 foreign; 2 strange;
fremde Leute strangers; **ich bin hier
fremd** I'm a stranger here.

Fremde *der/die* (PL *die* **Fremden**)
1 foreigner; 2 stranger.

Fremdenverkehr *der* tourism.

Fremdenverkehrsbüro *das* (PL
die **Fremdenverkehrsbüros**) tourist
office.

Fremdenzimmer *das* (PL *die*
Fremdenzimmer) room (to let).

Fremdsprache *die* (PL *die*
Fremdsprachen) foreign language.

fressen ✧ *verb* (PRES **frisst** ∆, IMPERF
fraß, PERF **hat gefressen**) to eat.

Freude *die* (PL *die* **Freuden**) 1 joy,
2 pleasure; **mit Freuden** with
pleasure; 3 **an etwas Freude haben**
to be delighted with something;
4 **jemandem eine Freude machen**
to please somebody.

freuen *verb* (PERF **hat sich gefreut**)
1 **sich freuen** to be pleased; **sich
über etwas freuen** to be pleased
about something; 2 **sich auf etwas
freuen** to look forward to
something.

Freund *der* (PL *die* **Freunde**)
1 friend; 2 boyfriend.

Freundin *die* (PL *die* **Freundinnen**)
1 friend; 2 girlfriend.

freundlich *adjective* 1 friendly;
2 kind.

freundlicherweise *adverb* kindly.

Freundlichkeit *die* friendliness.

Freundschaft *die* (PL *die*
Freundschaften) friendship.

Frieden *der* peace.

Friedhof *der* (PL *die* **Friedhöfe**)
cemetery.

friedlich *adjective* peaceful.

frieren ✧ *verb* (IMPERF **fror**, PERF **hat
gefroren**) 1 to be cold; **frierst du?**
are you cold?; 2 **es friert** it's
freezing, it's frosty; 3 (PERF **ist
gefroren**) to freeze.

Frikadelle *die* (PL *die* **Frikadellen**)
rissole.

frisch *adjective* fresh; **sich frisch
machen** to freshen up.
adverb freshly; '**frisch gestrichen**'
'wet paint'.

∆ NEW SPELLING: *See page xii*

Friseur *der* (PL *die* **Friseure**)
hairdresser.

Friseuse *die* (PL *die* **Friseusen**)
hairdresser.

frisieren *verb* (PERF **hat frisiert**)
1 jemanden frisieren to do
somebody's hair; **2 sich frisieren** to
do your hair.

frisst △ SEE **fressen**.

Frisur *die* (PL *die* **Frisuren**) hairstyle,
hairdo.

froh *adjective* **1** happy; **frohe
Weihnachten!** happy Christmas!;
2 über etwas froh sein to be glad
about something.

fröhlich *adjective* cheerful.

Fröhlichkeit *die* cheerfulness.

fromm *adjective* devout.

fror SEE **frieren**.

Frosch *der* (PL *die* **Frösche**) frog.

Frost *der* (PL *die* **Fröste**) frost.

frostig *adjective* frosty.

Frottee *das* (PL *die* **Frottees**)
towelling.

Frottiertuch *das* (PL *die*
Frottiertücher) towel.

Frucht *die* (PL *die* **Früchte**) fruit.

fruchtbar *adjective* fertile.

Fruchtsaft *der* (PL *die* **Fruchtsäfte**)
fruit juice.

früh *adjective, adverb* **1** early; **von
früh auf** from an early age; **2 heute
früh** this morning.

Frühe *die* **in aller Frühe** at the crack
of dawn.

früher *adjective* **1** earlier; **2** former.
adverb **1** earlier; **2** formerly;
3 früher war sie ganz anders she
used to be quite different; **das war
früher ein Blumengeschäft** it used
to be a florist's.

frühestens *adverb* at the earliest.

Frühjahr *das* (PL *die* **Frühjahre**)
spring; **im Frühjahr** in spring.

Frühling *der* (PL *die* **Frühlinge**)
spring; **im Frühling** in spring.

Frühstück *das* (PL *die* **Frühstücke**)
breakfast.

frühstücken *verb* (PERF **hat
gefrühstückt**) to have breakfast.

frühzeitig *adjective* early.

Fuchs *der* (PL *die* **Füchse**) fox.

fühlen *verb* (PERF **hat gefühlt**) **1** to
feel; **2 sich krank fühlen** to feel ill.

fuhr SEE **fahren**.

führen *verb* (PERF **hat geführt**) **1** to
lead; **sie führt mit fünf Punkten** she
is five points in the lead; **unsere
Mannschaft führt** our team's
winning; **2** to run (*a shop or
business*); **3** to show round; **4** to
keep (*a diary, list*); **5 ein
Telefongespräch führen** to make a
phone call.

Führer *der* (PL *die* **Führer**) **1** leader;
2 guide.

Führerschein *der* (PL *die*
Führerscheine) driving licence; **den
Führerschein machen** to take your
driving test.

✧ IRREGULAR VERB: *See the verb table in the centre of the dictionary*

Führung die (PL die **Führungen**)
1 leadership; 2 guided tour;
3 management (*of a shop*); 4 **in
Führung** in the lead.

füllen *verb* (PERF **hat gefüllt**) 1 to
fill; 2 to stuff (*a turkey, peppers*);
3 **sich füllen** to fill (up).

Füller der (PL die **Füller**) fountain
pen.

Füllfederhalter der (PL die
Füllfederhalter) fountain pen.

Füllung die (PL die **Füllungen**) filling.

Fundament das (PL die
Fundamente) foundations.

Fundbüro das (PL die **Fundbüros**)
lost property office.

fünf *number* five.

fünfhundert *number* five hundred.

Fünftel das (PL die **Fünftel**) fifth.

fünfter, fünfte, fünftes *adjective*
fifth.

fünfzehn *number* fifteen.

fünfzig *number* fifty.

Funke der (PL die **Funken**) spark.

funkeln *verb* (PERF **hat gefunkelt**)
1 to sparkle; 2 to twinkle (*of a star*).

funktionieren *verb* (PERF **hat
funktioniert**) to work.

für *preposition* ←(+ACC) 1 for; 2 **was
für ein …?** what sort of … ?; 3 **für
sich** by yourself; **jetzt habe ich das
Haus ganz für mich** now I've got
the house to myself; 4 **das Für und
Wider** the pros and cons.

Furcht die fear.

furchtbar *adjective* terrible.

fürchten *verb* (PERF **hat gefürchtet**)
1 to fear; 2 **sich fürchten** to be
afraid; **ich fürchte mich vor ihm** I'm
afraid of him; **ich fürchte, das geht
nicht** I'm afraid that's not possible.

fürchterlich *adjective* dreadful.

füreinander *adverb* for each other.

fürs = **für das**.

Fürsorge die 1 care; 2 welfare;
3 (*informal*) social security.

Fuß der (PL die **Füße**) 1 foot; **zu Fuß**
on foot; **zu Fuß gehen** to walk;
2 base.

Fußball der (PL die **Fußbälle**)
football.

Fußballplatz der (PL die
Fußballplätze) football pitch.

Fußballspiel das (PL die
Fußballspiele) football match.

Fußballspieler der (PL die
Fußballspieler) footballer.

Fußboden der (PL die **Fußböden**)
floor.

Fußgänger der (PL die **Fußgänger**)
pedestrian.

Fußgängerzone die (PL die
Fußgängerzonen) pedestrian
precinct.

Fußweg der (PL die **Fußwege**)
footpath.

Futter das 1 feed; **ich habe dem
Hund schon Futter gegeben** I've

△ NEW SPELLING: *See page xii*

already given the dog his food;
2 lining (*of clothes*).

füttern *verb* (PERF **hat gefüttert**) **1** to
feed; **2** to line.

Futur *das* (PL *die* **Future**) future
(*tense*).

G g

gab SEE **geben**.

Gabel *die* (PL *die* **Gabeln**) fork.

gähnen *verb* (PERF **hat gegähnt**) to
yawn.

Galerie *die* (PL *die* **Galerien**) gallery.

galoppieren *verb* (PERF **ist**
galoppiert) to gallop.

Gammler *der* (PL *die* **Gammler**)
drop-out.

Gammlerin *die* (PL *die*
Gammlerinnen) drop-out.

Gang *der* (PL *die* **Gänge**) **1** walk;
2 errand; **3** corridor; **4 ein Platz am**
Gang an aisle seat; **5** course (*of a*
meal); **6** gear (*of a car*); **7 in Gang**
setzen to get going; **8 im Gange** in
progress.

gängig *adjective* **1** common;
2 popular (*goods*).

Gans *die* (PL *die* **Gänse**) goose.

Gänseblümchen *das* (PL *die*
Gänseblümchen) daisy.

Gänsehaut *die* goose pimples.

ganz *adjective* whole; **1 ganz**

Deutschland the whole of
Germany; **2 im Großen und Ganzen**
on the whole; **3 eine ganze Menge**
quite a lot; **4** all; **mein ganzes Geld**
all my money; **die ganzen Leute** all
the people; **5 etwas wieder ganz**
machen to mend something.
adverb **1** quite; **es war ganz gut** it
was quite good; **2 ganz und gar**
completely; **3 ganz und gar nicht**
not at all.

ganztägig *adjective, adverb* **1** full-
time; **2** all-day; **ganztägig geöffnet**
open all day.

ganztags *adverb* **1** full time; **2** all
day.

gar *adjective* done, cooked.
adverb **1 gar nicht** not at all; **gar**
nichts nothing; **2 oder gar** or
even.

Garage *die* (PL *die* **Garagen**) garage.

Garantie *die* (PL *die* **Garantien**)
guarantee.

garantieren *verb* (PERF **hat**
garantiert) to guarantee.

Garderobe *die* (PL *die* **Garderoben**)
cloakroom; **wir können die Mäntel**
an der Garderobe abgeben we can
leave the coats in the cloakroom.

Gardine *die* (PL *die* **Gardinen**)
curtain.

Garn *das* (PL *die* **Garne**) thread.

Garnele *die* (PL *die* **Garnelen**)
1 shrimp; **2** prawn.

Garten *der* (PL *die* **Gärten**) garden.

Gärtner *der* (PL *die* **Gärtner**)
gardener.

✧ IRREGULAR VERB: *See the verb table in the centre of the dictionary*

Gärtnerin die (PL die **Gärtnerinnen**) gardener.

Gas das (PL die **Gase**) 1 gas; 2 **Gas geben** to accelerate.

Gasherd der (PL die **Gasherde**) gas cooker.

Gaspedal das (PL die **Gaspedale**) accelerator.

Gasse die (PL die **Gassen**) lane.

Gast der (PL die **Gäste**) 1 guest; **wir haben heute Abend Gäste** we've got guests tonight; 2 **bei jemandem zu Gast sein** to be staying with somebody.

Gastarbeiter der (PL die **Gastarbeiter**) foreign worker, guest worker.

Gästezimmer das (PL die **Gästezimmer**) 1 (hotel) room; 2 spare room.

gastfreundlich adjective hospitable.

Gastfreundschaft die hospitality.

Gastgeber der (PL die **Gastgeber**) host.

Gastgeberin die (PL die **Gastgeberinnen**) host.

Gasthaus das (PL die **Gasthäuser**) inn.

Gasthof der (PL die **Gasthöfe**) inn.

Gaststätte die (PL die **Gaststätten**) restaurant.

Gauner der (PL die **Gauner**) crook.

Gebäck das 1 pastries; 2 biscuits.

gebären ◇ verb (IMPERF **gebar**, PERF **hat geboren**) 1 to give birth to; 2 **geboren werden** to be born.

Gebäude das (PL die **Gebäude**) building.

geben ◇ verb (PRES **gibt**, IMPERF **gab**, PERF **hat gegeben**) 1 to give; 2 to deal (cards); 3 to teach (at school); 4 **geben Sie mir bitte Frau Scheck** please put me through to Mrs Scheck; 5 **es gibt** there is, there are; **es gibt viele gute Restaurants in München** there are lots of good restaurants in Munich; **was gibt's im Kino?** what's on at the cinema?; **was gibt es zum Mittagessen?** what are we having for lunch?; 6 **was gibt's Neues?** what's the news?, what's new?; 7 **sich geschlagen geben** to admit defeat; 8 **das gibt sich wieder** it'll get better; 9 **das gibt's doch nicht!** I don't believe it!

Gebet das (PL die **Gebete**) prayer.

gebeten SEE **bitten**.

Gebiet das (PL die **Gebiete**) 1 area; 2 field.

gebildet adjective educated.

Gebirge das (PL die **Gebirge**) mountain range; **im Gebirge** in the mountains.

Gebiss △ das (PL die **Gebisse**) 1 teeth; 2 false teeth, dentures.

gebissen SEE **beißen**.

geblieben SEE **bleiben**.

geboren verb SEE **gebären**. adjective 1 born; 2 née; **Frau Hahn, geborene Müller** Mrs Hahn, née Müller.

geborgen *adjective* safe.

geboten SEE **bieten**.

gebracht SEE **bringen**.

gebraten *adjective* fried.

Gebrauch *der* (PL *die* **Gebräuche**)
1 use; **vor Gebrauch schütteln**
shake before use; 2 custom.

gebrauchen *verb* (PERF **hat
gebraucht**) to use.

Gebrauchsanweisung *die* (PL *die*
Gebrauchsanweisungen)
instructions (for use).

gebraucht *adjective* used, second-hand.

Gebrauchtwagen *der* (PL *die*
Gebrauchtwagen) second-hand
car.

gebrochen SEE **brechen**.

Gebühr *die* (PL *die* **Gebühren**) fee,
charge.

gebührenfrei *adjective* free (of
charge).

gebührenpflichtig *adjective*
1 subject to a charge; 2 **eine
gebührenpflichtige Straße** a toll
road.

gebunden SEE **binden**.

Geburt *die* (PL *die* **Geburten**) birth.

Geburtenregelung *die* birth
control.

Geburtsdatum *das* (PL *die*
Geburtsdaten) date of birth.

Geburtsort *der* (PL *die*
Geburtsorte) place of birth.

Geburtstag *der* (PL *die*
Geburtstage) birthday.

Geburtsurkunde *die* (PL *die*
Geburtsurkunden) birth certificate.

gedacht SEE **denken**.

Gedächtnis *das* (PL *die*
Gedächtnisse) memory.

Gedanke *der* (PL *die* **Gedanken**)
1 thought; **in Gedanken versunken
sein** to be lost in thought; 2 **sich
Gedanken machen** to worry;
3 **jemanden auf andere Gedanken
bringen** to take somebody's mind
off things.

gedankenlos *adjective*
thoughtless.
adverb without thinking.

Gedeck *das* (PL *die* **Gedecke**)
1 place setting; 2 set meal.

Gedicht *das* (PL *die* **Gedichte**) poem.

Geduld *die* patience.

geduldig *adjective* patient.

gedurft SEE **dürfen**.

geehrt *adjective* 1 honoured;
2 **Sehr geehrte Frau Ross** Dear
Mrs Ross.

geeignet *adjective* 1 suitable;
2 right.

Gefahr *die* (PL *die* **Gefahren**)
1 danger; **außer Gefahr** out of
danger; 2 **auf eigene Gefahr** at your
own risk; **Gefahr laufen, etwas zu
tun** to run the risk of doing
something.

gefährlich *adjective* dangerous.

gefallen[1] SEE **fallen**.

◇ IRREGULAR VERB: *See the verb table in the centre of the dictionary*

gefallen[2] ✧ *verb* (PRES **gefällt**, IMPERF **gefiel**, PERF **hat gefallen**) 1 **es gefällt mir** I like it; **es hat mir sehr gut gefallen** I liked it a lot; 2 **sich etwas gefallen lassen** to put up with something.

Gefallen[1] *der* (PL *die* **Gefallen**) favour.

Gefallen[2] *das* pleasure; **dir zu Gefallen** to please you.

Gefangene *der/die* (PL *die* **Gefangenen**) prisoner.

Gefängnis *das* (PL *die* **Gefängnisse**) prison.

Gefäß *das* (PL *die* **Gefäße**) container.

gefasst ∆ *adjective* 1 calm, composed; 2 **auf etwas gefasst sein** to be prepared for something.

gefiel SEE **gefallen**.

geflogen SEE **fliegen**.

geflossen SEE **fließen**.

Geflügel *das* poultry.

gefochten SEE **fechten**.

gefräßig *adjective* (*informal*) greedy.

gefrieren ✧ *verb* (IMPERF **gefror**, PERF **ist gefroren**) to freeze.

Gefrierfach *das* (PL *die* **Gefrierfächer**) freezer (compartment).

gefroren *adjective* frozen.

Gefühl *das* (PL *die* **Gefühle**) 1 feeling; 2 **etwas im Gefühl haben** to have a feel for something.

gefüllt *adjective* stuffed (*peppers, for example*).

gefunden SEE **finden**.

gegangen SEE **gehen**.

gegeben SEE **geben**.

gegebenenfalls *adverb* if need be.

gegen *preposition* ←(+ACC) 1 against; 2 **gegen die Mauer fahren** to drive into the wall; 3 **ein Mittel gegen Grippe** a cure for flu; 4 towards; **gegen Abend** towards evening; 5 **gegen vier Uhr** around four o'clock; 6 compared with; 7 versus (*in sport*).

Gegend *die* (PL *die* **Gegenden**) 1 area; 2 neighbourhood.

gegeneinander *adverb* against each other, against one another.

Gegenmittel *das* (PL *die* **Gegenmittel**) 1 remedy; 2 antidote.

Gegensatz *der* (PL *die* **Gegensätze**) 1 contrast; 2 opposite; 3 **im Gegensatz zu mir** unlike me.

gegenseitig *adjective* mutual. *adverb* **sich gegenseitig helfen** to help each other.

Gegenstand *der* (PL *die* **Gegenstände**) 1 object; 2 subject (*in grammar or of a discussion*).

Gegenteil *das* (PL *die* **Gegenteile**) 1 opposite; 2 **im Gegenteil** on the contrary.

gegenüber *preposition* ←(+DAT) 1 opposite; **Susi saß mir gegenüber** Susi sat opposite me; 2 compared with; 3 towards; **jemandem gegenüber freundlich sein** to be friendly towards

∆ NEW SPELLING: *See page xii*

somebody.
adverb opposite; **meine Freundin wohnt gegenüber** my friend lives opposite.

Gegenwart *die* **1** present; **2** presence.

gegessen SEE **essen**.

Gegner *der* (PL *die* **Gegner**) opponent.

gegrillt *adjective* grilled.

Gehackte *das* mince.

Gehalt *das* (PL *die* **Gehälter**) salary.

gehässig *adjective* spiteful.

geheim *adjective* secret.

Geheimnis *das* (PL *die* **Geheimnisse**) secret.

geheimnisvoll *adjective* mysterious.

gehen ✧ *verb* (IMPERF **ging**, PERF **ist gegangen**) **1** to go; **schlafen gehen** to go to bed; **2** to walk; **3** über die Straße gehen to cross the road; **4** es geht ihr gut she's well; wie geht es Ihnen? how are you?; es geht it's not too bad; **5** das geht nicht that's impossible; **6** um etwas gehen to be about something; worum geht's hier? what's it all about?; **7** die Uhr geht falsch the clock's wrong.

Gehirn *das* (PL *die* **Gehirne**) brain.

Gehirnerschütterung *die* (PL *die* **Gehirnerschütterungen**) concussion.

gehoben SEE **heben**.

geholfen SEE **helfen**.

Gehör *das* hearing.

gehorchen *verb* (PERF **hat gehorcht**) to obey.

gehören *verb* (PERF **hat gehört**) **1** to belong; **es gehört mir** it belongs to me; **2** dazu gehört Mut that takes courage; **3** es gehört sich nicht it isn't done.

gehorsam *adjective* obedient.

Gehsteig *der* (PL *die* **Gehsteige**) pavement.

Geige *die* (PL *die* **Geigen**) violin.

Geisel *die* (PL *die* **Geiseln**) hostage.

Geist *der* (PL *die* **Geister**) **1** mind; **2** ghost; **3** wit.

geistesabwesend *adjective* absent-minded.

Geisteskrankheit *die* (PL *die* **Geisteskrankheiten**) mental illness.

Geisteswissenschaften (*plural noun*) arts, humanities.

geistig *adjective* mental.

geizig *adjective* mean.

gekannt SEE **kennen**.

gekonnt SEE **können**.

Gel *das* (PL *die* **Gele**) gel.

Gelächter *das* (PL *die* **Gelächter**) laughter.

geladen SEE **laden**.

gelähmt *adjective* paralysed.

Geländer *das* (PL *die* **Geländer**) **1** banister(s); **2** railing(s).

gelangweilt *adjective* bored.

✧ IRREGULAR VERB: *See the verb table in the centre of the dictionary*

gelassen *verb* SEE **lassen**.
adjective calm.

geläufig *adjective* 1 common; 2 **das ist mir nicht geläufig** I'm not familiar with it.

gelaunt *adjective* **gut gelaunt sein** to be in a good mood.

gelb *adjective* yellow.

Geld *das* (PL *die* **Gelder**) money.

Geldautomat *der* (PL *die* **Geldautomaten**) cash dispenser.

Geldbörse *die* (PL *die* **Geldbörsen**) purse.

Geldschein *der* (PL *die* **Geldscheine**) banknote.

Geldstrafe *die* (PL *die* **Geldstrafen**) fine.

Geldwechsel *der* 1 bureau de change; 2 currency exchange.

gelegen SEE **liegen**.

Gelegenheit *die* (PL *die* **Gelegenheiten**) 1 opportunity; 2 occasion.

gelegentlich *adverb* occasionally.

Gelenk *das* (PL *die* **Gelenke**) joint.

Geliebte *der/die* (PL *die* **Geliebten**) lover.

geliehen SEE **leihen**.

gelingen ◇ *verb* (IMPERF **gelang**, PERF **ist gelungen**) to succeed; **es ist mir gelungen, sie zu überreden** I succeeded in persuading her.

gelten ◇ *verb* (PRES **gilt**, IMPERF **galt**, PERF **hat gegolten**) 1 to be valid; 2 to apply (*of a rule*); 3 **jemandem**

gelten to be directed at somebody; 4 **sein Wort gilt viel** his word is worth a lot; 5 **das gilt nicht** that doesn't count; 6 **als etwas gelten** to be regarded as something.

gelungen *verb* SEE **gelingen**.
adjective successful.

Gemälde *das* (PL *die* **Gemälde**) painting.

gemein *adjective* mean.

Gemeinde *die* (PL *die* **Gemeinden**) 1 community; 2 congregation.

gemeinsam *adjective* 1 common; 2 joint.
adverb together; **gemeinsam essen** to eat together.

Gemeinschaft *die* (PL *die* **Gemeinschaften**) community.

gemischt *adjective* mixed.

gemocht SEE **mögen**.

Gemüse *das* (PL *die* **Gemüse**) vegetables.

Gemüsehändler *der* (PL *die* **Gemüsehändler**) greengrocer.

gemusst △ SEE **müssen**.

gemustert *adjective* patterned.

gemütlich *adjective* 1 cosy; 2 **mach es dir gemütlich** make yourself comfortable.

genannt SEE **nennen**.

genau *adjective* 1 exact; 2 accurate (*scales, description*); 3 meticulous; 4 **ich weiß nichts Genaues** I don't know any details.
adverb 1 exactly; 2 **genau genommen** △ strictly speaking.

△ NEW SPELLING: *See page xii*

Genauigkeit *die* accuracy.

genauso *adverb* 1 just the same;
2 **genauso gut** just as good;
genauso viel just as much, just as
many; **genauso lange** just as long.

Genehmigung *die* (PL *die*
Genehmigungen) 1 permission;
2 permit; 3 licence.

generell *adjective* general.

Genetik *die* genetics.

Genf *das* Geneva.

Genfer See *der* Lake Geneva.

genial *adjective* brilliant.

Genick *das* (PL *die* **Genicke**) (back of
the) neck.

Genie *das* (PL *die* **Genies**) genius.

genießbar *adjective* edible.

genießen ✧ *verb* (IMPERF **genoss** Δ,
PERF **hat genossen**) to enjoy.

genommen SEE **nehmen**.

genug *adverb* enough.

genügen *verb* (PERF **hat genügt**) to
be enough.

genügend *adjective* 1 enough;
2 sufficient.

Genuss Δ *der* (PL *die* **Genüsse**)
1 enjoyment; 2 consumption (*of
alcohol*).

geöffnet *adjective* open.

Geometrie *die* geometry.

Gepäck *das* luggage.

Gepäckausgabe *die* left-luggage
office.

Gepäckaufbewahrung *die* left-
luggage office.

Gepäckträger *der* (PL *die*
Gepäckträger) 1 porter; 2 roof
rack; 3 carrier (*on a bike*).

gerade *adjective* 1 straight; 2 **etwas
gerade biegen** Δ to straighten
something; 3 upright; 4 **eine
gerade Zahl** an even number.
adverb 1 just; **gerade erst** only
just; 2 **es war nicht gerade billig** it
wasn't exactly cheap.

geradeaus *adverb* straight ahead.

geradebiegen SEE **gerade**.

gerannt SEE **rennen**.

Gerät *das* (PL *die* **Geräte**)
1 appliance; 2 set (*TV or radio*);
3 tool; 4 gadget; 5 **die Geräte**
apparatus (*in gymnastics*).

geraten ✧ *verb* (PRES **gerät**, IMPERF
geriet, PERF **ist geraten**) 1 to get
(*somewhere, the wrong side of the
road etc.*); **in etwas geraten** to get
into something; **in Wut geraten** to
get angry; 2 **an den Richtigen
geraten** to come to the right person;
3 **gut/schlecht geraten** to turn out
well/badly; 4 **nach jemandem
geraten** to take after somebody.

geräuchert *adjective* smoked.

geräumig *adjective* spacious.

Geräusch *das* (PL *die* **Geräusche**)
noise.

gerecht *adjective* 1 just; 2 fair.

✧ IRREGULAR VERB: *See the verb table in the centre of the dictionary*

Gerechtigkeit *die* justice.

Gerede *das* gossip.

Gericht *das* (PL *die* **Gerichte**)
1 court; 2 dish.

gerieben SEE **reiben**.

gering *adjective* 1 small (*amount*);
2 low (*value*); 3 short (*time, distance*).

Gerippe *das* (PL *die* **Gerippe**)
skeleton.

gerissen *adjective* crafty.

geritten SEE **reiten**.

gern(e) *adverb* 1 gladly;
2 **jemanden gern haben** to like
somebody; **etwas gern tun** to like
doing something; **ich tanze gern** I
like dancing; **ich hätte gerne einen
Kaffee** I'd like a coffee; 3 **ja, gern!**
yes, I'd love to!; 4 **das glaube ich
gern** I can well believe that.

Gerste *die* barley.

Geruch *der* (PL *die* **Gerüche**) smell.

Gerücht *das* (PL *die* **Gerüchte**)
rumour.

Gerümpel *das* junk.

gesalzen *verb* SEE **salzen**.
adjective 1 salted; 2 **gesalzene
Preise** (*informal*) steep prices.

gesamt *adjective* 1 whole; 2 **die
gesamten Kosten** the total cost;
3 **die gesamten Werke** the
complete works.

Gesamtschule *die* (PL *die*
Gesamtschulen) comprehensive
school.

gesandt SEE **senden**.

Geschäft *das* (PL *die* **Geschäfte**)
1 shop; 2 business; 3 deal.

Geschäftsführer *der* (PL *die*
Geschäftsführer) manager.

Geschäftsführerin *die* (PL *die*
Geschäftsführerinnen)
manageress.

Geschäftszeiten *plural noun*
business hours.

geschehen ✧ *verb* (PRES
geschieht, IMPERF **geschah**, PERF **ist
geschehen**) to happen.

gescheit *adjective* clever.

Geschenk *das* (PL *die* **Geschenke**)
present, gift.

Geschichte *die* (PL *die*
Geschichten) 1 story; 2 history;
3 **mach bloß keine große
Geschichte daraus** don't make such
a thing of it.

Geschick *das* 1 skill; 2 fate.

geschickt *adjective* 1 skilful;
2 clever.

geschieden *verb* SEE **scheiden**.
adjective divorced.

geschienen SEE **scheinen**.

Geschirr *das* 1 crockery; 2 dishes.

Geschirrspülmaschine *die* (PL
die **Geschirrspülmaschinen**)
dishwasher.

Geschirrtuch *das* (PL *die*
Geschirrtücher) tea towel.

Geschlecht *das* (PL *die*
Geschlechter) 1 sex; 2 gender.

△ NEW SPELLING: *See page xii*

geschlossen *verb* SEE **schließen**. *adjective* closed.

Geschmack *der* (PL *die* **Geschmäcke**) taste.

geschmacklos *adjective* 1 tasteless; 2 **geschmacklos sein** to be in bad taste.

geschnitten SEE **schneiden**.

geschossen SEE **schießen**.

geschrieben SEE **schreiben**.

geschrien SEE **schreien**.

Geschwätz *das* talk.

geschwätzig *adjective* talkative.

Geschwindigkeit *die* (PL *die* **Geschwindigkeiten**) speed.

Geschwindigkeitsbeschränkung *die* (PL *die* **Geschwindigkeitsbeschränkungen**) speed limit.

Geschwister *plural noun* brothers and sisters, siblings.

geschwommen SEE **schwimmen**.

gesellig *adjective* sociable.

Gesellschaft *die* (PL *die* **Gesellschaften**) 1 society; 2 company; **ich leiste dir Gesellschaft** I'll keep you company; 3 party.

gesessen SEE **sitzen**.

Gesetz *das* (PL *die* **Gesetze**) law.

gesetzlich *adjective* legal; **ein gesetzlicher Feiertag** a public holiday.

Gesicht *das* (PL *die* **Gesichter**) face.

Gesichtsausdruck *der* (facial) expression.

gesollt SEE **sollen**.

gespannt *adjective* 1 eager; 2 **auf etwas gespannt sein** to look forward eagerly to something; **auf jemanden gespannt sein** to look forward to seeing somebody; 3 **ich bin gespannt, ob …** I wonder whether …; 4 tense; **in Südafrika is die Lage immer noch gespannt** the situation in South Africa is still tense

Gespenst *das* (PL *die* **Gespenster**) ghost.

Gespräch *das* (PL *die* **Gespräche**) 1 conversation; 2 call (*on the phone*).

gesprächig *adjective* talkative.

gesprochen SEE **sprechen**.

gesprungen SEE **springen**.

Gestalt *die* (PL *die* **Gestalten**) 1 figure; 2 form.

gestanden SEE **stehen**, **gestehen**.

Geständnis *das* (PL *die* **Geständnisse**) confession.

gestatten *verb* (PERF **hat gestattet**) 1 to permit; 2 **nicht gestattet** prohibited; 3 **gestatten Sie?** may I?

Geste *die* (PL *die* **Gesten**) gesture.

gestehen ✧ *verb* (IMPERF **gestand**, PERF **hat gestanden**) to confess.

Gestell *das* (PL *die* **Gestelle**) 1 rack; 2 stand; 3 frame.

gestern *adverb* 1 yesterday; 2 **gestern Nacht** last night.

✧ IRREGULAR VERB: *See the verb table in the centre of the dictionary*

gestohlen SEE **stehlen**.

gestorben SEE **sterben**.

gestreift *adjective* striped.

gesund *adjective* 1 healthy;
2 **wieder gesund werden** to get
well again; 3 **Schwimmen ist
gesund** swimming is good for you.

Gesundheit *die* 1 health;
2 **Gesundheit!** bless you! (*said after
a sneeze*).

gesungen SEE **singen**.

getan SEE **tun**.

Getränk *das* (PL *die* **Getränke**) drink.

Getränkekarte *die* (PL *die*
Getränkekarten) wine list.

getrauen *verb* (PERF **hat sich
getraut**) **sich getrauen** to dare.

Getreide *das* grain.

Getriebe *das* (PL *die* **Getriebe**)
gearbox.

getrieben SEE **treiben**.

getroffen SEE **treffen**.

getrunken SEE **trinken**.

Getue *das* fuss.

geübt *adjective* 1 accomplished;
2 **mit geübtem Auge** with a
practised eye.

Gewächshaus *das* (PL *die*
Gewächshäuser) greenhouse.

Gewalt *die* 1 power; 2 force; **mit
Gewalt** by force; 3 violence.

gewaltig *adjective* enormous.

gewalttätig *adjective* violent.

gewann SEE **gewinnen**.

Gewebe *das* (PL *die* **Gewebe**)
1 fabric; 2 tissue.

Gewehr *das* (PL *die* **Gewehre**) rifle,
gun.

Gewerkschaft *die* (PL *die*
Gewerkschaften) trade union.

gewesen SEE **sein**.

Gewicht *das* (PL *die* **Gewichte**)
weight.

Gewinn *der* (PL *die* **Gewinne**)
1 profit; 2 winnings; 3 prize.

gewinnen ◇ *verb* (IMPERF **gewann**,
PERF **hat gewonnen**) 1 to win; 2 to
gain (*time or influence*); **an
Bedeutung gewinnen** to gain in
importance.

Gewinner *der* (PL *die* **Gewinner**)
winner.

Gewinnerin *die* (PL *die*
Gewinnerinnen) winner.

gewiss △ *adjective* certain; **ein
gewisser Herr Schmidt möchte Sie
sprechen** a Mr Schmidt would like
to speak to you.
adverb certainly; **'darf ich?' 'aber
gewiss doch'** 'may I?' 'but of
course'.

Gewissen *das* (PL *die* **Gewissen**)
conscience.

gewissenhaft *adjective*
conscientious.

gewissermaßen *adverb* 1 more or
less; 2 as it were.

Gewitter *das* (PL *die* **Gewitter**)
thunderstorm.

△ NEW SPELLING: *See page xii*

gewöhnen *verb* (PERF **hat gewöhnt**) **1 jemanden an etwas gewöhnen** to get somebody used to something; **2 an etwas gewöhnt sein** to be used to something; **3 sich an etwas gewöhnen** to get used to something.

Gewohnheit *die* (PL *die* **Gewohnheiten**) habit.

gewöhnlich *adjective* **1** usual; **2** ordinary.
adverb usually; **wie gewöhnlich** as usual.

gewohnt *adjective* **1** usual; **2 etwas gewohnt sein** to be used to something; **Renate ist es nicht gewohnt, früh aufzustehen** Renate isn't used to getting up early.

gewollt SEE **wollen**.

gewonnen SEE **gewinnen**.

geworden SEE **werden**.

geworfen SEE **werfen**.

Gewürz *das* (PL *die* **Gewürze**) spice.

gewusst △ SEE **wissen**.

Gezeiten *plural noun* tides.

gezogen SEE **ziehen**.

gezwungen SEE **zwingen**.

gibt SEE **geben**.

gierig *adjective* greedy.

gießen ✧ *verb* (IMPERF **goss** △, PERF **hat gegossen**) **1** to pour; **es gießt** it's pouring; **2** to water; **vergiss nicht, die Blumen zu gießen** don't forget to water the flowers.

Gießkanne *die* (PL *die* **Gießkannen**) watering can.

Gift *das* (PL *die* **Gifte**) poison.

giftig *adjective* **1** poisonous; **2** toxic

ging SEE **gehen**.

Gipfel *der* (PL *die* **Gipfel**) **1** peak, summit; **2 der Gipfel der Geschmacklosigkeit** the height of bad taste.

Gips *der* plaster.

Girokonto *das* (PL *die* **Girokonten**) current account.

Giraffe *die* (PL *die* **Giraffen**) giraffe.

Gitarre *die* (PL *die* **Gitarren**) guitar.

Gitter *das* (PL *die* **Gitter**) **1** grid; **2** bars.

glänzen *verb* (PERF **hat geglänzt**) to shine.

glänzend *adjective* **1** shining; **2** brilliant; **ein glänzender Erfolg** a brilliant success.

Glas *das* (PL *die* **Gläser**) **1** glass; **2** jar

Glasscheibe *die* (PL *die* **Glasscheiben**) pane (of glass).

glatt *adjective* **1** smooth; **2** slippery; **3 eine glatte Absage** a flat refusal.
adverb **1** smoothly; **2** flatly; **etwas glatt ablehnen** to flatly reject something; **3 das ist glatt gelogen** that's a downright lie; **4 ich habe ihren Geburtstag glatt vergessen** I totally forgot about her birthday.

Glatteis *das* (black) ice.

Glatze *die* (PL *die* **Glatzen**) **eine Glatze haben** to be bald; **eine Glatze bekommen** to go bald.

✧ IRREGULAR VERB: *See the verb table in the centre of the dictionary*

glauben *verb* (PERF **hat geglaubt**)
1 to believe; **an Gott glauben** to
believe in God; **2** to think; **3 nicht
zu glauben!** incredible!

gleich *adjective* **1** same; **2** identical;
3 gleich bleibend △ constant;
4 das ist mir gleich it's all the same
to me; **ganz gleich, wer anruft** no
matter who calls.
adverb **1** the same; **2** equally;
3 immediately; **4 gleich neben**
right next to; **5 er ist gleich fertig**
he'll be ready in a minute.

gleichartig *adjective* similar.

gleichberechtigt *adjective* equal.

Gleichberechtigung *die* equality.

gleichbleibend SEE **gleich**.

gleichen ◇ *verb* (IMPERF **glich**, PERF
hat geglichen) **1** to be like; **2 sich
gleichen** to be alike.

gleichfalls *adverb* **1** also; **2 danke
gleichfalls!** the same to you!

Gleichgewicht *das* balance.

gleichgültig *adjective* indifferent;
das ist doch gleichgültig it's not
important.

gleichzeitig *adverb* at the same
time.

Gleis *das* (PL *die* **Gleise**) **1** track,
line; **2** platform; **Gleis vier**
platform four.

glich SEE **gleichen**.

Glied *das* (PL *die* **Glieder**) **1** limb;
2 link.

glitschig *adjective* slippery.

glitzern *verb* (PERF **hat geglitzert**) to
glitter.

Glocke *die* (PL *die* **Glocken**) bell.

Glück *das* **1** luck; **viel Glück!** good
luck!; **Glück haben** to be lucky; **zum
Glück** luckily; **2** happiness.

glücklich *adjective* **1** lucky; **es war
ein glücklicher Zufall, dass ich ihn
heute in der Stadt getroffen habe**
it was a lucky coincidence that I met
him in town today; **2** happy.

glücklicherweise *adverb* luckily,
fortunately.

Glückwunsch *der* (PL *die*
Glückwünsche) congratulations;
**herzlichen Glückwunsch zum
Geburtstag!** happy birthday!

Glückwunschkarte *die* (PL *die*
Glückwunschkarten) greetings
card.

Glühbirne *die* (PL *die* **Glühbirnen**)
light bulb.

glühen *verb* (PERF **hat geglüht**) to
glow.

Gold *das* gold.

golden *adjective* **1** gold; **2** golden.

Goldfisch *der* (PL *die* **Goldfische**)
goldfish.

Golf[1] *der* (PL *die* **Golfe**) gulf.

Golf[2] *das* golf.

Golfplatz *der* (PL *die* **Golfplätze**) golf
course.

Golfschläger *der* (PL *die*
Golfschläger) golf club.

goss △ SEE **gießen**.

Gott *der* (PL *die* **Götter**) god.

△ NEW SPELLING: *See page xii*

Gottesdienst *der* (PL *die* **Gottesdienste**) service.

Göttin *die* (PL *die* **Göttinnen**) goddess.

Grab *das* (PL *die* **Gräber**) grave.

graben △ *verb* (PRES **gräbt**, IMPERF **grub**, PERF **hat gegraben**) to dig.

Grad *der* (PL *die* **Grade**) degree.

Gramm *das* (PL *die* **Gramme**) gram.

Grammatik *die* (PL *die* **Grammatiken**) grammar.

grantig *adjective* grumpy.

Gras *das* (PL *die* **Gräser**) grass.

grässlich △ *adjective* horrible.

Gräte *die* (PL *die* **Gräten**) (fish)bone.

gratis *adverb* free of charge.

gratulieren *verb* (PERF **hat gratuliert**) 1 to congratulate; 2 ich habe Gabi zum Geburtstag gratuliert I wished Gabi happy birthday; 3 **wir gratulieren!** congratulations!

grau *adjective* grey.

Gräuel △ *der* horror.

grauen *verb* (PERF **hat gegraut**) **mir graut es davor** I dread it.

grauhaarig *adjective* grey-haired.

grausam *adjective* cruel.

Grausamkeit *die* cruelty.

graziös *adjective* graceful.

greifen ✧ *verb* (IMPERF **griff**, PERF **hat gegriffen**) 1 to take hold of; 2 to catch; 3 **nach etwas greifen** to reach for something; 4 **um sich greifen** to spread (*of fire*).

grell *adjective* 1 glaring; 2 garish; 3 shrill.

Grenze *die* (PL *die* **Grenzen**) 1 border; 2 boundary; 3 limit.

grenzen *verb* (PERF **hat gegrenzt**) a**r** **etwas grenzen** to border on something.

Greuel SEE **Gräuel**.

Grieche *der* (PL *die* **Griechen**) Greek.

Griechenland *das* Greece.

Griechin *die* (PL *die* **Griechinnen**) Greek.

griechisch *adjective* Greek.

griff SEE **greifen**.

Griff *der* (PL *die* **Griffe**) 1 grasp; 2 handle.

griffbereit *adjective* handy; **sie hat den Korkenzieher immer griffbereit** she always keeps the corkscrew handy.

Grill *der* (PL *die* **Grills**) 1 grill; 2 barbecue.

Grille *die* (PL *die* **Grillen**) cricket (*the insect*).

grillen *verb* (PERF **hat gegrillt**) 1 to grill; 2 to have a barbecue.

Grillfest *das* (PL *die* **Grillfeste**) barbecue.

grinsen *verb* (PERF **hat gegrinst**) to grin.

Grippe *die* (PL *die* **Grippen**) flu.

grob *adjective* 1 coarse; 2 rough;

✧ IRREGULAR VERB: *See the verb table in the centre of the dictionary*

3 rude; **4 ein grober Fehler** a bad mistake.

Groschen *der* (PL *die* **Groschen**)
1 (*Austrian money*) groschen;
2 (*informal*) ten-pfennig piece;
3 der Groschen ist gefallen the penny's dropped.

groß *adjective* 1 big; 2 great; **Gisela hatte große Angst** Gisela was very frightened; 3 tall; **4 ein großer Buchstabe** a capital letter; **5 groß werden** to grow up; **6 die großen Ferien** the summer holidays; **7 im Großen und Ganzen** △ on the whole; **8 Groß und Klein** △ young and old.
adverb **was soll man da schon groß machen?** what are you supposed to do?

großartig *adjective* great.

Großbritannien *das* Great Britain.

Großbuchstabe *der* (PL *die* **Großbuchstaben**) capital (letter).

Größe *die* (PL *die* **Größen**) 1 size;
2 height; 3 greatness.

Großeltern *plural noun* grandparents.

großenteils *adverb* largely.

Großmarkt *der* (PL *die* **Großmärkte**) hypermarket.

Großmutter *die* (PL *die* **Großmütter**) grandmother.

Großstadt *die* (PL *die* **Großstädte**) city.

großschreiben ◇ *verb* (IMPERF **schrieb groß**, PERF **hat großgeschrieben**) **ein Wort**

großschreiben to write a word with a capital.

Großvater *der* (PL *die* **Großväter**) grandfather.

großzügig *adjective* generous.

grub SEE **graben**.

grün *adjective* 1 green; **2 im Grünen** in the country; **3 die Grünen** the Greens.

Grund *der* (PL *die* **Gründe**) 1 ground;
2 bottom; 3 reason; **aus diesem Grund** for this reason; **4 im Grunde genommen** basically.

gründen *verb* (PERF **hat gegründet**)
1 to set up, to found; **2 sich auf etwas gründen** to be based on something.

Grundlage *die* (PL *die* **Grundlagen**) basis.

gründlich *adjective* thorough.

grundsätzlich *adjective*
1 fundamental; 2 basic.
adverb 1 basically; 2 on principle.

Grundschule *die* (PL *die* **Grundschulen**) primary school.

Grundstück *das* (PL *die* **Grundstücke**) plot (of land).

Gruppe *die* (PL *die* **Gruppen**) group.

Gruß *der* (PL *die* **Grüße**) greeting; **einen schönen Gruß an Lars** give my regards to Lars; **mit herzlichen Grüßen** with best wishes.

grüßen *verb* (PERF **hat gegrüßt**) 1 to greet; 2 to say hello; **3 grüß Gott!** hello; **4 grüße Thomas von mir** give Thomas my regards; **Gisela lässt grüßen** Gisela sends her regards.

△ NEW SPELLING: *See page xii*

gucken *verb* (PERF **hat geguckt**) to look.

gültig *adjective* valid.

Gummi *der* (PL *die* **Gummis**) rubber.

Gummiband *das* (PL *die* **Gummibänder**) rubber band.

Gummistiefel *der* (PL *die* **Gummistiefel**) wellington (boot).

günstig *adjective* 1 favourable; 2 convenient.

Gurgel *die* (PL *die* **Gurgeln**) throat.

gurgeln *verb* (PERF **hat gegurgelt**) to gargle.

Gurke *die* (PL *die* **Gurken**) 1 cucumber; 2 gherkin.

Gürtel *der* (PL *die* **Gürtel**) belt.

Gürteltasche *die* (PL *die* **Gürteltaschen**) bum bag.

gut *adjective* 1 good; 2 **guten Appetit!** enjoy your meal!; 3 **schon gut** that's all right; **also gut** all right; 4 **im Guten** △ amicably; 5 **alles Gute!** all the best!
adverb 1 well; 2 **gut schmecken** to taste good; 3 **gut zwei Stunden** a good two hours; 4 **uns geht's gut** we're fine; **ihm geht es nicht gut** he's not well.

Güte *die* 1 goodness; **du meine Güte!** my goodness!; 2 quality.

Güterzug *der* (PL *die* **Güterzüge**) goods train.

gutgehen SEE **gut**.

gutmütig *adjective* good-natured.

Gutschein *der* (PL *die* **Gutscheine**) 1 voucher; 2 coupon.

Gymnasium *das* (PL *die* **Gymnasien**) grammar school.

Gymnastik *die* 1 gymnastics; 2 keep-fit (exercises).

H h

Haar *das* (PL *die* **Haare**) 1 hair; **sich die Haare waschen** to wash your hair; 2 **um ein Haar** (*informal*) very nearly.

Haarbürste *die* (PL *die* **Haarbürsten**) hairbrush.

haarig *adjective* hairy.

Haarschnitt *der* (PL *die* **Haarschnitte**) haircut.

Haarwaschmittel *das* (PL *die* **Haarwaschmittel**) shampoo.

haben ◇ *verb* (PRES **hat**, IMPERF **hatte**, PERF **hat gehabt**) 1 to have (got); **ich habe ein neues Auto** I have (*or* I've got) a new car; **etwas gegen jemanden haben** to have something against somebody; 2 (*used with another verb, like 'have' in English, to form past tenses*) **ich habe Werners Adresse verloren** I've lost Werner's address; **ich habe deine Mutter gestern angerufen** I rang your mother yesterday; 3 **Angst haben** to be frightened; **Hunger haben** to be hungry; 4 **heute haben wir Mittwoch** it's Wednesday today; 5 **die Kinder haben Ferien** the children are on holiday; 6 **was hat sie?** what's the

◇ IRREGULAR VERB: *See the verb table in the centre of the dictionary*

matter with her?; **7 ich hätte gern
…** I'd like …; **ich hätte ihr geholfen**
I would have helped her; **8 sich
haben** (*informal*) to make a fuss.

hacken *verb* (PERF **hat gehackt**) **1** to
chop (up); **2** to peck (*of a bird*).

Hackfleisch *das* minced meat.

Hafen *der* (PL *die* **Häfen**) harbour.

Haferflocken *plural noun*
porridge oats.

haftbar *adjective* **für etwas haftbar
sein** to be liable for something.

haften *verb* (PERF **hat gehaftet**) **1** to
stick; **2 für etwas haften** to be
responsible for something.

Hagel *der* hail.

hageln *verb* (PERF **hat gehagelt**) to
hail.

Hagelschauer *der* (PL *die*
Hagelschauer) hailstorm.

Hahn *der* (PL *die* **Hähne**) **1** cock;
2 tap.

Hähnchen *das* (PL *die* **Hähnchen**)
chicken.

Hai *der* (PL *die* **Haie**) shark.

Haken *der* (PL *die* **Haken**) **1** hook;
2 tick; **3** catch; **da muss ein Haken
dran sein** there must be a catch.

halb *adjective* half; **zum halben
Preis** at half price; **halb eins** half
past twelve.

Halbfinale *das* (PL *die* **Halbfinale**)
semi-final.

halbieren *verb* (PERF **hat halbiert**)
to halve.

Halbkreis *der* (PL *die* **Halbkreise**)
semicircle.

Halbpension *die* half board.

halbtags *adverb* part-time.

halbwegs *adverb* **1** half-way;
2 more or less.

Halbzeit *die* (PL *die* **Halbzeiten**)
1 half; **2** half-time; **während der
Halbzeit** during half-time.

half SEE **helfen**.

Hälfte *die* (PL *die* **Hälften**) half; **zur
Hälfte** half.

Halle *die* (PL *die* **Hallen**) **1** hall;
2 foyer.

Hallenbad *das* (PL *die* **Hallenbäder**)
indoor swimming pool.

hallo *exclamation* hello!

Hals *der* (PL *die* **Hälse**) **1** neck;
2 throat; **mir tut der Hals weh** I've
got a sore throat; **3 aus vollem Hals
schreien** to shout at the top of your
voice; **4 Hals über Kopf** in a rush.

Halsband *das* (PL *die* **Halsbänder**)
collar.

Halsschmerzen *plural noun* sore
throat; **Paul hat Halsschmerzen**
Paul's got a sore throat.

Halstuch *das* (PL *die* **Halstücher**)
scarf.

halt *exclamation* stop!

Halt *der* **1** hold; **jetzt hat es einen
besseren Halt** it holds better now;
2 Halt machen △ to stop.

haltbar *adjective* **1** hard-wearing;

2 durable; **3 mindestens haltbar bis …** best before …

halten ✧ *verb* (PRES **hält**, IMPERF **hielt**, PERF **hat gehalten**) **1** to hold; **2** to keep; **sein Versprechen halten** to keep your promise; **warm halten** ∆ to keep warm; **3** to stop; **der Bus hält direkt vor seiner Haustür** the bus stops right outside his door; **4** to save (*in sport*); **5** to take (*a paper, magazine*); **6 ich habe ihn für deinen Bruder gehalten** I took him for your brother; **7 viel von jemandem halten** to think a lot of somebody; **jemanden für ehrlich halten** to think somebody is honest; **8 zu jemandem halten** to stand by somebody; **9 eine Rede halten** to make a speech; **10 sich halten** to keep (*of milk, fruit, etc.*); **11 sich links/rechts halten** to keep left/right; **12 sich gut halten** to do well; **13 sich an etwas halten** to keep to something.

Haltestelle *die* (PL *die* **Haltestellen**) stop.

haltmachen SEE **Halt**.

Haltung *die* (PL *die* **Haltungen**) **1** posture; **2** attitude; **3** composure.

Hammelfleisch *das* mutton.

Hammer *der* (PL *die* **Hämmer**) hammer.

hämmern *verb* (PERF **hat gehämmert**) to hammer.

Hamster *der* (PL *die* **Hamster**) hamster.

Hand *die* (PL *die* **Hände**) hand;

jemandem die Hand geben to shake hands with somebody.

Handarbeit *die* (PL *die* **Handarbeiten**) **1** handicraft; **2** hand-made article.

Handball *der* handball.

Handbremse *die* (PL *die* **Handbremsen**) handbrake; **die Handbremse ziehen** to pull the handbrake.

Handbuch *das* (PL *die* **Handbücher**) manual.

Handel *der* **1** trade; **2** deal; **3 in den Handel kommen** to come on the market.

handeln *verb* (PERF **hat gehandelt**) **1** to trade, to deal; **2 mit jemandem handeln** to bargain with somebody; **3** to act; **4 von etwas handeln** to be about something; **5 es handelt sich um …** it's about …; **worum handelt es sich?** what's it about?

Handelsschule *die* (PL *die* **Handelsschulen**) business school, vocational college.

Handfläche *die* (PL *die* **Handflächen**) palm.

Handgelenk *das* (PL *die* **Handgelenke**) wrist.

Handgepäck *das* hand luggage.

handhaben *verb* (PERF **hat gehandhabt**) to handle.

Händler *der* (PL *die* **Händler**) dealer.

handlich *adjective* handy.

Handlung *die* (PL *die* **Handlungen**) **1** act; **2** action; **3** plot.

✧ IRREGULAR VERB: *See the verb table in the centre of the dictionary*

Handschellen (*plural noun*)
handcuffs.

Handschrift die (PL die
Handschriften) handwriting.

Handschuh der (PL die
Handschuhe) glove.

Handtasche die (PL die
Handtaschen) bag.

Handtuch das (PL die Handtücher)
towel.

Handwerker der (PL die
Handwerker) 1 craftsman;
2 workman.

Handwerkszeug das tools.

Handy das (PL die Handys) mobile
(phone).

Hang der (PL die Hänge) slope.

Hängematte die (PL die
Hängematten) hammock.

hängen[1] *verb* (PERF hat gehängt)
1 to hang; **Florian hat das Bild an
die Wand gehängt** Florian hung the
picture on the wall; **sie hängte ihren
Mantel in den Schrank** she hung
her coat up in the cupboard; **2 sie
haben den Wohnwagen an das
Auto gehängt** they attached the
caravan to the car; **3 sich an
jemanden hängen** to latch on to
somebody.

hängen[2] ⬦ *verb* (IMPERF **hing**, PERF
hat gehangen) 1 to hang; **mein Bild
hat immer hier gehangen** my
picture used to hang here; **2 an
seinen Eltern hängen** to be
attached to your parents; **sie hängt
sehr an ihrer Mutter** she's very
attached to her mother; **3 an etwas**

hängen bleiben ⬦ *to catch on
something*, to stick to something;
**ich bin mit dem Ärmel am Zaun
hängen geblieben** I got my sleeve
caught on the fence.

hängenbleiben SEE **hängen**[2].

Hansaplast™ das plaster.

Happen der (PL die Happen)
mouthful; **ich habe heute keinen
Happen gegessen** I haven't had a
bite to eat all day.

Harfe die (PL die Harfen) harp.

Harke die (PL die Harken) rake.

harmlos *adjective* harmless.

hart *adjective* 1 hard; 2 harsh.

hartgekocht *adjective* hard-
boiled.

Hase der (PL die Hasen) hare.

Haselnuss ⬦ die (PL die
Hasselnüsse) hazelnut.

Hass ⬦ der hatred.

hassen *verb* (PERF **hat gehasst** ⬦) to
hate.

hässlich ⬦ *adjective* 1 ugly; **sie hat
ein hässliches Gesicht** she's got an
ugly face; **2 nasty; das war sehr
hässlich von dir** that was very nasty
of you.

hast SEE **haben**.

hastig *adjective* hasty.

**hat, hatte, hatten, hattest,
hattet** SEE **haben**.

Haube die (PL die Hauben)
1 bonnet; 2 cap.

⬦ NEW SPELLING: *See page xii*

hauen ✧ *verb* (PRES **haut**, IMPERF **haute**, PERF **hat gehauen**) 1 to beat; 2 to thump, to bang; 3 **sich hauen** to fight; 4 **jemanden übers Ohr hauen** (*informal*) to cheat somebody.

Haufen *der* (PL *die* **Haufen**) 1 heap; 2 crowd (*of people*); 3 **ein Haufen** (*informal*) heaps of; **ein Haufen Geld** heaps of money.

haufenweise *adverb* heaps of; **Gabi hat haufenweise CDs** Gabi has heaps of CDs.

häufig *adjective* frequent.

Hauptbahnhof *der* (PL *die* **Hauptbahnhöfe**) main station.

Hauptrolle *die* (PL *die* **Hauptrollen**) lead.

Hauptsache *die* (PL *die* **Hauptsachen**) main thing.

hauptsächlich *adjective* main. *adverb* mainly.

Hauptschule *die* secondary school.

Hauptstadt *die* (PL *die* **Hauptstädte**) capital.

Hauptstraße *die* (PL *die* **Hauptstraßen**) main road.

Hauptverkehrszeit *die* (PL *die* **Hauptverkehrszeiten**) rush hour.

Hauptwort *das* (PL *die* **Hauptwörter**) noun.

Haus *das* (PL *die* **Häuser**) 1 house; 2 **nach Hause** home; **zu Hause** at home.

Hausarbeit *die* (PL *die* **Hausarbeiten**) 1 housework; **die** Kinder müssen bei der Hausarbeit helfen the children have to help with the housework; 2 homework.

Hausaufgaben *plural noun* homework; **hast du deine Hausaufgaben gemacht?** have you done your homework?

Hausfrau *die* (PL *die* **Hausfrauen**) housewife.

Haushalt *der* (PL *die* **Haushalte**) 1 household; 2 **den Haushalt machen** to do the housework; 3 budget.

Haushaltswarengeschäft *das* (PL *die* **Haushaltswarengeschäfte**) hardware shop.

Hausmeister *der* (PL *die* **Hausmeister**) caretaker.

Hausnummer *die* house number.

Hausschlüssel *der* (PL *die* **Hausschlüssel**) front-door key.

Hausschuh *der* (PL *die* **Hausschuhe**) slipper.

Haustier *das* (PL *die* **Haustiere**) pet.

Haustür *die* (PL *die* **Haustüren**) front door.

Haut *die* (PL *die* **Häute**) skin; **aus der Haut fahren** (*informal*) to go up the wall.

Hebamme *die* (PL *die* **Hebammen**) midwife.

Hebel *der* (PL *die* **Hebel**) lever.

heben ✧ *verb* (IMPERF **hob**, PERF **hat gehoben**) 1 to lift; 2 **sich heben** to rise.

Hecke *die* (PL *die* **Hecken**) hedge.

✧ IRREGULAR VERB: *See the verb table in the centre of the dictionary*

Heer das (PL die **Heere**) army.

Hefe die (PL die **Hefen**) yeast.

Heft das (PL die **Hefte**) 1 exercise book; 2 issue (*of a magazine*).

heften verb (PERF **hat geheftet**) 1 to pin; 2 to tack (*by sewing*); 3 to clip; 4 to staple.

heftig adjective 1 violent; 2 heavy (*snow, rain*).

Heftklammer die (PL die **Heftklammern**) staple.

Heftpflaster das (PL die **Heftpflaster**) sticking plaster.

Heftzwecke die (PL die **Heftzwecken**) drawing pin.

Heide die heath.

Heidekraut das heather.

Heidelbeere die (PL die **Heidelbeeren**) bilberry.

heilen verb (PERF **hat geheilt**) 1 to cure; 2 to heal.

heilig adjective 1 holy; 2 **heilig halten** to hold sacred; 3 **der heilige Franz von Assisi** Saint Francis of Assisi.

Heiligabend der (PL die **Heiligabende**) Christmas Eve.

Heilige der/die (PL die **Heiligen**) saint.

Heilmittel das (PL die **Heilmittel**) remedy.

heim adverb home.

Heim das (PL die **Heime**) 1 home; 2 hostel.

Heimat die (PL die **Heimaten**) 1 home; 2 native land.

Heimatstadt die home town.

Heimfahrt die (PL die **Heimfahrten**) 1 journey home; 2 way home.

heimgehen ◇ verb (IMPERF **ging heim**, PERF **ist heimgegangen**) to go home.

heimlich adjective secret. adverb secretly.

Heimspiel das (PL die **Heimspiele**) home game.

Heimweg der (PL die **Heimwege**) way home.

Heimweh das homesickness; **Heimweh haben** to be homesick.

Heirat die (PL die **Heiraten**) marriage.

heiraten verb (PERF **hat geheiratet**) to marry.

heiser adjective hoarse.

heiß adjective hot.

heißen ◇ verb (IMPERF **hieß**, PERF **hat geheißen**) 1 to be called; **wie heißt du?** what's your name?; 2 to mean; 3 **das heißt** that is; 4 **es heißt** it is said; 5 **wie heißt 'dog' auf Deutsch?** what's the German for 'dog'?

heiter adjective 1 bright; 2 cheerful.

heizen verb (PERF **hat geheizt**) 1 to heat (*a room*); 2 to put the heating on; 3 to have the heating on.

Heizung die heating.

hektisch adjective hectic.

Held der (PL die **Helden**) hero.

△ NEW SPELLING: *See page xii*

Heldin *die* (PL *die* **Heldinnen**)
heroine.

helfen ◈ *verb* (PRES **hilft**, IMPERF **half**,
PERF **hat geholfen**) 1 to help; **Lisa
hilft mir** Lisa is helping me; 2 **es
hilft nichts** it's no good; 3 **sich zu
helfen wissen** to know what to do;
ich weiß mir nicht zu helfen I don't
know what to do.

Helfer *der* (PL *die* **Helfer**) 1 helper;
2 assistant.

Helferin *die* (PL *die* **Helferinnen**)
1 helper; 2 assistant.

hell *adjective* 1 light (*colour*);
2 bright; 3 **eine helle Stimme** a
clear voice; 4 **helles Bier** lager;
5 **da ist heller Wahnsinn**
(*informal*) that's sheer madness.

hellwach *adjective* wide awake.

Helm *der* (PL *die* **Helme**) helmet.

Hemd *das* (PL *die* **Hemden**) 1 shirt;
2 vest.

Henkel *der* (PL *die* **Henkel**) handle.

Henne *die* (PL *die* **Hennen**) hen.

her *adverb* 1 here; **komm her** come
here; 2 **vor jemandem her** in front
of somebody; 3 **hinter etwas her
sein** to be after something; 4 **von
der Farbe her** as far as the colour is
concerned; 5 **wo bist du her?**
where do you come from?; 6 **wo hat
Klaus das her?** where did Klaus get
it from?; 7 **her damit!** (*informal*)
give it to me!; 8 ago; **das ist schon
lange her** it was a long time ago; **das
ist drei Tage her** it was three days
ago.

herab *adverb* down.

herablassend *adjective*
condescending.

herabsetzen *verb* (PERF **hat
herabgesetzt**) 1 to reduce; 2 to
belittle.

heran *adverb* 1 **an etwas heran**
close to something, right up to
something; **bis an die Wand heran**
up to the wall; 2 **immer heran!**
come closer!

herankommen ◈ *verb* (IMPERF
kam heran, PERF **ist
herangekommen**) 1 to come near;
2 **herankommen an** to come up to;
3 **ich komme nicht heran** I can't get
at it.

herauf *adverb* up.

heraufkommen ◈ *verb* (IMPERF
kam herauf, PERF **ist
heraufgekommen**) to come up.

heraus *adverb* out.

herausbekommen ◈ *verb* (IMPERF
bekam heraus, PERF **hat
herausbekommen**) 1 to get out;
2 to find out; 3 to solve; 4 **Geld
herausbekommen** to get change.

herausfinden ◈ *verb* (IMPERF **fand
heraus**, PERF **hat herausgefunden**)
1 to find out; 2 to find your way out.

herausgeben ◈ *verb* (PRES **gibt
heraus**, IMPERF **gab heraus**, PERF **hat
herausgegeben**) 1 to hand over;
2 to bring out.

herauskommen ◈ *verb* (IMPERF
kam heraus, PERF **ist
herausgekommen**) to come out.

herausnehmen ◈ *verb* (PRES

◈ IRREGULAR VERB: *See the verb table in the centre of the dictionary*

nimmt heraus, IMPERF **nahm heraus**, PERF **hat herausgenommen**) **1** to take out; **sie hat ihren Lippenstift aus der Tasche herausgenommen** she took her lipstick out of the bag; **2 sich die Mandeln herausnehmen lassen** to have your tonsils out; **3 es sich herausnehmen, etwas zu tun** to have the nerve to do something; **du nimmst dir zu viel heraus** you're going too far.

herausstellen *verb* (PERF **hat herausgestellt**) **1** to put out; **2 sich herausstellen** to turn out; **es stellte sich heraus, dass …** it turned out that …

herausziehen ✧ *verb* (IMPERF **zog heraus**, PERF **hat herausgezogen**) to pull out.

herb *adjective* **1** sharp; **2** dry (*wine*).

herbei *adverb* over (here); **kommt herbei!** come over here!

Herberge *die* (PL *die* **Herbergen**) hostel.

Herbergsmutter *die* (PL *die* **Herbergsmütter**) warden (*in a youth hostel*).

Herbergsvater *der* (PL *die* **Herbergsväter**) warden (*in a youth hostel*).

herbringen ✧ *verb* (IMPERF **brachte her**, PERF **hat hergebracht**) to bring (here).

Herbst *der* (PL *die* **Herbste**) autumn; **im Herbst** in autumn.

Herd *der* (PL *die* **Herde**) cooker.

Herde *die* (PL *die* **Herden**) **1** herd; **2** flock.

herein *adverb* in; **herein!** come in!

hereinfallen ✧ *verb* (PRES **fällt herein**, IMPERF **fiel herein**, PERF **ist hereingefallen**) to be taken in; **auf einen Betrüger hereinfallen** to be taken in by a swindler.

hereinkommen ✧ *verb* (IMPERF **kam herein**, PERF **ist hereingekommen**) to come in.

hereinlassen ✧ *verb* (PRES **lässt herein** △, IMPERF **ließ herein**, PERF **hat hereingelassen**) to let in; **Max lässt mich nicht ins Zimmer herein** Max won't let me into the room.

Herfahrt *die* (PL *die* **Herfahrten**) **1** journey here; **2** way here.

hergeben ✧ *verb* (PRES **gibt her**, IMPERF **gab her**, PERF **hat hergegeben**) **1** to hand over; **gib die Tasche her!** hand over the bag!; **2** to give away; **3 sich für etwas hergeben** to get involved in something; **dazu gebe ich mich nicht her** I won't have anything to do with it.

Hering *der* (PL *die* **Heringe**) herring.

herkommen ✧ *verb* (IMPERF **kam her**, PERF **ist hergekommen**) to come (here); **wo kommt das her?** where does it come from?

Herkunft *die* (PL *die* **Herkünfte**) **1** origin; **2** background.

Heroin *das* heroin.

Herr *der* (PL *die* **Herren**) **1** gentleman; **2 Herr Huber** Mr Huber; **3 Sehr geehrte Herren** Dear Sirs (*in a letter*); **4 meine Herren!**

△ NEW SPELLING: *See page xii*

gentlemen!; **5** master; **6 der Herr** the Lord.

herrichten *verb* (PERF **hat hergerichtet**) to get ready, to prepare; **sie richtet die Betten für die Gäste her** she's getting the beds for the guests ready.

herrlich *adjective* marvellous.

herrschen *verb* (PERF **hat geherrscht**) **1** to rule; **2** to be; **es herrschte große Aufregung** there was great excitement.

herstellen *verb* (PERF **hat hergestellt**) to manufacture, to make; **in Deutschland hergestellt** made in Germany.

Herstellung *die* (PL *die* **Herstellungen**) manufacture, production.

herüber *adverb* over (here).

herum *adverb* **um … herum** round; **falsch herum** the wrong way round; **im Kreis herum** in a circle.

herumdrehen *verb* (PERF **hat herumgedreht**) **1** to turn (over or round); **2 sich herumdrehen** to turn round.

herumführen *verb* (PERF **hat herumgeführt**) to show around.

herumgehen ✧ *verb* (IMPERF **ging herum**, PERF **ist herumgegangen**) **1** to go round; **2** to walk around; **im Park herumgehen** to walk around the park; **3** to pass (*of time*).

herunter *adverb* down; **die Treppe herunter** down the stairs.

herunterfallen ✧ *verb* (PRES **fällt**

herunter, IMPERF **fiel herunter**, PERF **ist heruntergefallen**) **1** to fall down; **2** to fall off.

herunterkommen ✧ *verb* (IMPERF **kam herunter**, PERF **ist heruntergekommen**) **1** to come down; **2** (*informal*) to go to rack and ruin.

herunterlassen ✧ *verb* (PRES **lässt herunter** Δ, IMPERF **ließ herunter**, PERF **hat heruntergelassen**) to let down, to lower.

hervor *adverb* out.

hervorragend *adjective* outstanding.
adverb outstandingly well.

hervorrufen ✧ *verb* (IMPERF **rief hervor**, PERF **hat hervorgerufen**) to cause.

Herz *das* (PL *die* **Herzen**) **1** heart; **2** hearts (*in cards*).

Herzanfall *der* (PL *die* **Herzanfälle**) heart attack.

herzlich *adjective* **1** warm; **2** sincere; **3 herzlichen Dank** many thanks; **4 herzliche Grüße** best wishes; **5 herzlichen Glückwunsch!** congratulations!; **6 herzlich willkommen in Passau!** welcome to Passau!

herzlos *adjective* heartless.

Herzschlag *der* (PL *die* **Herzschläge**) **1** heartbeat; **2** heart failure; **er hat einen Herzschlag bekommen** he had a heart attack.

heterosexuell *adjective* heterosexual.

✧ IRREGULAR VERB: *See the verb table in the centre of the dictionary*

Heterosexuelle der/die (PL die **Heterosexuellen**) heterosexual.

Heu das hay.

heulen verb (PERF **hat geheult**) **1** to howl; **2** (informal) to cry.

Heuschnupfen der hay fever.

heute adverb today; **heute Abend** this evening; **heute Morgen** this morning.

heutig adjective **1** today's; **2 in der heutigen Zeit** nowadays.

heutzutage nowadays.

Hexe die (PL die **Hexen**) witch.

Hexenschuss △ der lumbago.

hielt SEE **halten**.

hier adverb here.

hierher adverb here; **komm sofort hierher!** come here immediately!

hierhin adverb here.

hiesig adjective local.

hieß SEE **heißen**.

Hilfe die (PL die **Hilfen**) **1** help; **2** aid.

hilflos adjective helpless.

hilfsbereit adjective helpful.

hilft SEE **helfen**.

Himbeere die (PL die **Himbeeren**) raspberry.

Himmel der (PL die **Himmel**) **1** sky; **2** heaven.

himmlisch adjective heavenly.

hin adverb **1** there; **hin und zurück** there and back; **2 hin und wieder** now and again; **3 hin und her** back and forth, to and fro; **4 auf meinen Rat hin** on my advice; **auf Ihren Brief hin** in reply to your letter; **5 wo ist Dominik hin?** where's Dominik gone?; **6 es ist nicht mehr lange hin** it's not long to go; **7 ich bin hin** (informal) I'm worn out.

hinauf adverb up; **die Straße hinauf** up the road.

hinaufgehen ✧ verb (IMPERF **ging hinauf**, PERF **ist hinaufgegangen**) to go up.

hinaus adverb **1** out; **2 auf Jahre hinaus** for years to come.

hinausgehen ✧ verb (IMPERF **ging hinaus**, PERF **ist hinausgegangen**) **1** to go out; **2 über etwas hinausgehen** to exceed something; **3 das Zimmer geht nach Norden hinaus** the room faces north.

hindern verb (PERF **hat gehindert**) to stop; **jemanden daran hindern, etwas zu tun** to stop somebody from doing something.

Hindernis das (PL die **Hindernisse**) obstacle.

hinduistisch adjective Hindu.

hindurch adverb **1** through it/them; **2 das ganze Jahr hindurch** throughout the year.

hinein adverb **1** in; **2 in etwas hinein** into something.

hineingehen ✧ verb (IMPERF **ging hinein**, PERF **ist hineingegangen**) **1** to go in; **2 in etwas hineingehen** to go into something.

△ NEW SPELLING: See page xii

hinfahren ✧ *verb* (PRES **fährt hin**, IMPERF **fuhr hin**, PERF **ist hingefahren**) **1** to go/drive there; **2** (PERF **hat hingefahren**) to take/drive there.

Hinfahrt *die* (PL *die* **Hinfahrten**) **1** journey there, way there; **2** outward journey.

hinfallen ✧ *verb* (PRES **fällt hin**, IMPERF **fiel hin**, PERF **ist hingefallen**) to fall over.

hing SEE **hängen**.

hingehen ✧ *verb* (IMPERF **ging hin**, PERF **ist hingegangen**) **1** to go there; **wo geht ihr hin?** where are you going?; **2** to go by (*of time*).

hinken *verb* (PERF **hat/ist gehinkt**) to limp.

hinkommen ✧ *verb* (IMPERF **kam hin**, PERF **ist hingekommen**) **1** to get there; **2** to go; **wo kommt das Buch hin?** where does the book go?; **3** **mit etwas hinkommen** (*informal*) to manage (with something).

hinlegen *verb* (PERF **hat hingelegt**) **1** to put down; **leg die Zeitung unten hin** put the paper down there; **2** **sich hinlegen** to lie down.

hinsetzen *verb* (PERF **hat sich hingesetzt**) **sich hinsetzen** to sit down; **Petra setzte sich neben ihm hin** Petra sat down next to him.

hinten *adverb* at the back; **von hinten** from behind.

hinter *preposition* ←(+DAT *or* +ACC) **1** behind; **2** **etwas hinter sich bringen** to get something over with.

hintere SEE **hinterer**.

hintereinander *adverb* **1** one behind the other; **2** one after the other; **dreimal hintereinander** three times in a row.

hinterer, hintere, hinteres *adjective* **1** back; **2** **am hinteren Ende** at the far end.

Hintergrund *der* (PL *die* **Hintergründe**) background.

hinterher *adverb* afterwards.

Hintern *der* (PL *die* **Hintern**) bottom.

Hinterrad *das* (PL *die* **Hinterräder**) back wheel.

hinters = **hinter das**.

hinüber *adverb* **1** over (there), across (there); **2** **das Radio ist hinüber** (*informal*) the radio has had it.

hinübergehen ✧ *verb* (IMPERF **ging hinüber**, PERF **ist hinübergegangen**) to go over, to go across.

hinunter *adverb* down.

Hinweg *der* (PL *die* **Hinwege**) way there; **auf dem Hinweg** on the way there.

Hinweis *der* (PL *die* **Hinweise**) **1** hint; **das war ein deutlicher Hinweis, dass er lieber allein fährt** it was an obvious hint that he prefers to go on his own; **2** reference; **3** **Hinweise zur Bedienung** operating instructions.

hinweisen ✧ *verb* (IMPERF **wies hin**, PERF **hat hingewiesen**) to point; **jemanden auf etwas hinweisen** to point something out to somebody.

Hirn *das* (PL *die* **Hirne**) brain.

✧ IRREGULAR VERB: *See the verb table in the centre of the dictionary*

Hirsch *der* (PL *die* **Hirsche**) 1 deer;
2 stag; 3 venison.

historisch *adjective* historical.

Hitze *die* heat.

hitzefrei *adjective* **hitzefrei haben**
to have the day off school because of
hot weather.

Hitzewelle *die* (PL *die* **Hitzewellen**)
heatwave.

Hitzschlag *der* (PL *die* **Hitzschläge**)
heatstroke.

hob SEE **heben**.

Hobby *das* (PL *die* **Hobbys**) hobby.

hoch *adjective* (*with endings 'hoch'*
becomes 'hoher/hohe/hohes') 1 high;
der Zaun ist zu hoch the fence is
too high; **ein hoher Zaun** a high
fence; 2 deep (*snow*); 3 great (*age,*
weight).
adverb 1 highly; **hoch begabt** highy
gifted; 2 **die Treppe hoch** up the
stairs.

Hoch *das* (PL *die* **Hochs**) 1 cheer; **ein**
dreifaches Hoch für das
Geburtstagskind three cheers for
the birthday girl/boy; 2 high
(*pressure*).

hochachtungsvoll *adverb*
Hochachtungsvoll Yours faithfully.

hochhackig *adjective* high-heeled;
hochhackige Schuhe high-heeled
shoes.

Hochhaus *das* (PL *die* **Hochhäuser**)
high-rise building.

hochheben◇ *verb* (IMPERF **hob**
hoch, PERF **hat hochgehoben**) to lift
up; **sie hob das Kind hoch** she lifted
up the child.

hochmäsig *adjective* stuck-up.

Hochschule *die* (PL *die*
Hochschulen) university, college.

Hochsprung *der* (PL *die*
Hochsprünge) high jump.

höchst *adverb* extremely.

höchstens *adverb* 1 at most;
2 except perhaps.

höchster, höchste, höchstes
adjective highest; **Mount Everest**
ist der der höchste Berg der Welt
Mount Everest is the highest
mountain in the world; **es ist**
höchste Zeit it is high time.

Höchstgeschwindigkeit *die*
maximum speed.

Höchsttemperatur *die* (PL *die*
Höchsttemperaturen) maximum
temperature.

Hochzeit *die* (PL *die* **Hochzeiten**)
wedding.

Hochzeitstag *der* (PL *die*
Hochzeitstage) 1 wedding day;
2 wedding anniversary.

Hocker *der* (PL *die* **Hocker**) stool.

Hockey *das* hockey.

Hockeyschläger *der* (PL *die*
Hockeyschläger) hockey stick.

Hof *der* (PL *die* **Höfe**) 1 yard; 2 farm.

hoffen *verb* (PERF **hat gehofft**) to
hope; **auf etwas hoffen** to hope for
something.

hoffentlich *adverb* hopefully;
hoffentlich nicht I hope not.

Hoffnung *die* (PL *die* **Hoffnungen**)
hope.

△ NEW SPELLING: *See page xii*

hoffnungslos *adjective* hopeless.

höflich *adjective* polite.

Höflichkeit *die* (PL *die* **Höflichkeiten**) politeness, courtesy.

Höhe *die* (PL *die* **Höhen**) 1 height; 2 **das ist die Höhe!** (*informal*) that's the limit!

hoher, hohe, hohes SEE **hoch**.

höher *adjective* 1 higher; 2 deeper.

hohl *adjective* hollow.

Höhle *die* (PL *die* **Höhlen**) 1 cave; 2 den.

holen *verb* (PERF **hat geholt**) 1 to get, to fetch; 2 **jemanden holen lassen** to send for somebody; 3 **sich etwas holen** to get something.

Holland *das* Holland.

Holländer *der* (PL *die* **Holländer**) Dutchman.

Holländerin *die* (PL *die* **Holländerinnen**) Dutchwoman.

holländisch *adjective* Dutch.

Hölle *die* (PL *die* **Höllen**) hell.

Holz *das* (PL *die* **Hölzer**) wood.

Holzkohle *die* charcoal.

homöopathisch *adjective* homeopathic.

homosexuell *adjective* homosexual.

Homosexuelle *der/die* (PL *die* **Homosexuellen**) homosexual.

Honig *der* (PL *die* **Honige**) honey.

horchen *verb* (PERF **hat gehorcht**) 1 to listen; 2 to eavesdrop.

hören *verb* (PERF **hat gehört**) 1 to hear; 2 to listen (to).

Hörer *der* (PL *die* **Hörer**) 1 listener; 2 receiver (*of a phone*).

Hörerin *die* (PL *die* **Hörerinnen**) listener.

Horizont *der* (PL *die* **Horizonte**) horizon.

Horn *das* (PL *die* **Hörner**) horn.

Horoskop *das* (PL *die* **Horoskope**) horoscope.

Hose *die* (PL *die* **Hosen**) trousers.

Hosenträger *plural noun* braces.

Hotel *das* (PL *die* **Hotels**) hotel.

Hotelverzeichnis *das* (PL *die* **Hotelverzeichnisse**) list of hotels.

hübsch *adjective* 1 pretty; 2 nice.

Hubschrauber *der* (PL *die* **Hubschrauber**) helicopter.

Huf *der* (PL *die* **Hufe**) hoof.

Hufeisen *das* (PL *die* **Hufeisen**) horseshoe.

Hüfte *die* (PL *die* **Hüften**) hip.

Hügel *der* (PL *die* **Hügel**) hill.

Huhn *das* (PL *die* **Hühner**) 1 chicken; 2 hen.

Hummel *die* (PL *die* **Hummeln**) bumble-bee.

Hummer *der* (PL *die* **Hummer**) lobster.

Humor *der* humour; **Humor haben** to have a sense of humour.

Hund *der* (PL *die* **Hunde**) dog.

✧ IRREGULAR VERB: *See the verb table in the centre of the dictionary*

Hundehütte *die* (PL *die* **Hundehütten**) kennel.

hundemüde *adjective* (*informal*) dog-tired.

hundert *number* a hundred, one hundred.

Hunger *der* hunger; **Hunger haben** to be hungry.

hungrig *adjective* hungry.

Hupe *die* (PL *die* **Hupen**) horn.

hurra *exclamation* hooray!

husten *verb* (PERF **hat gehustet**) to cough.

Husten *der* cough.

Hut *der* (PL *die* **Hüte**) hat.

hüten *verb* (PERF **hat gehütet**) **1** to look after (*a child, children*); **2 sich hüten** to be on your guard; **3 sich hüten, etwas zu tun** to take care not to do something.

Hütte *die* (PL *die* **Hütten**) hut.

hygienisch *adjective* hygienic.

hypnotisieren *verb* (PERF **hat hypnotisiert**) to hypnotize.

Hypothek *die* (PL *die* **Hypotheken**) mortgage.

hysterisch *adjective* hysterical.

I i

ich *pronoun* I.

IC-Zug *der* (PL *die* **IC-Züge**) (*Intercityzug*) intercity train.

ideal *adjective* ideal.

Idee *die* (PL *die* **Ideen**) idea.

identifizieren *verb* (PERF **hat identifiziert**) to identify.

identisch *adjective* identical.

Idiot *der* (PL *die* **Idioten**) idiot.

idiotisch *adjective* idiotic.

idyllisch *adjective* idyllic.

Igel *der* (PL *die* **Igel**) hedgehog.

ihm *pronoun* **1** him, to him; **2** it, to it.

ihn *pronoun* **1** him; **2** it.

ihnen *pronoun* them, to them.

ihr *pronoun* **1** you (*plural*); **2** her, to her; **3** (*standing for an object*) it, to it.
adjective **1** her; **2** its; **3** their; **sie haben ihr Auto verkauft** they sold their car.

Ihr *adjective* your; **Ihr Sohn hat mir geschrieben** your son wrote to me.

ihrer, ihre, ihr(e)s *pronoun* **1** hers; **mein Rad ist rot, ihrs ist blau** my bike is red, hers is blue; **2** theirs; **das ist nicht ihre Katze, ihre ist**

△ NEW SPELLING: *See page xii*

schwarz that's not their cat, theirs is black.

Ihrer, Ihre, Ihr(e)s *pronoun* yours; **mein Job ist nicht so interessant wie Ihrer** my job's not as interesting as yours.

ihretwegen *adverb* 1 for her sake; 2 for their sake; 3 because of her; 4 because of them.

Ihretwegen *adverb* 1 for your sake; 2 because of you.

Illusion *die* (PL die **Illusionen**) illusion.

Illustration *die* (PL die **Illustrationen**) illustration.

Illustrierte *die* (PL die **Illustrierten**) magazine.

im = in dem; **was läuft im Kino?** what's on at the cinema?; **im August** in August.

Imbiss △ *der* (PL die **Imbisse**) 1 snack; 2 snack bar.

Imbissstube △ *die* (PL die **Imbissstuben**) snack bar.

imitieren *verb* (PERF **hat imitiert**) to imitate.

immer *adverb* 1 always; 2 **immer wieder** again and again; 3 **immer mehr** more and more; **immer dunkler** darker and darker; 4 **immer noch** still; 5 **immer, wenn er anruft** every time he rings; 6 **wo/wer/wann immer** wherever/whoever/whenever; 7 **für immer** for ever.

immerhin *adverb* at least.

immerzu *adverb* all the time.

impfen *verb* (PERF **hat geimpft**) to vaccinate.

Impfung *die* (PL die **Impfungen**) vaccination.

imponieren *verb* (PERF **hat imponiert**) to impress; **jemandem imponieren** to impress somebody.

Import *der* (PL die **Importe**) import.

importieren *verb* (PERF **hat importiert**) to import.

imprägniert *adjective* waterproof.

imstande *adverb* **imstande sein, etwas zu tun** to be able to do something; **er ist nicht imstande, seine Hausaufgaben allein zu machen** he's not able to do his homework on his own.

in *preposition* ←(+DAT *or* +ACC) (*the dative is used when talking about position; the accusative shows movement towards something*) 1 in; **es ist in der Küche** it's in the kitchen; 2 into, in; **ich habe es in meine Tasche gesteckt** I've put it in my bag; 3 **in die Schule gehen** to go to school; 4 **Susi ist in der Schule** Susi is at school; 5 **in diesem Jahr** this year; 6 **in sein** to be in; **der Rap ist in** rap is in.

inbegriffen *adjective* included; **Essen ist inbegriffen** food is included.

indem *conjunction* 1 while; 2 by.

Inder *der* (PL die **Inder**) Indian.

Inderin *die* (PL die **Inderinnen**) Indian.

Indianer *der* (PL die **Indianer**)

✧ IRREGULAR VERB: *See the verb table in the centre of the dictionary*

(American) Indian, native American.

Indianerin *die* (PL *die* **Indianerinnen**) (American) Indian, native American.

indianisch *adjective* (American) Indian, native American.

Indien *das* India.

indisch *adjective* Indian.

indiskutabel *adjective* out of the question.

individuell *adjective* individual.

Individuum *das* (PL *die* **Individuen**) individual.

Industrie *die* (PL *die* **Industrien**) industry.

industriell *adjective* industrial.

Infektion *die* (PL *die* **Infektionen**) infection.

Infinitiv *der* (PL *die* **Infinitive**) infinitive.

infizieren *verb* (PERF **hat infiziert**) 1 to infect; 2 **sich bei jemandem infizieren** to be infected by somebody.

infolge *preposition* ←(+GEN) as a result of.

infolgedessen *adverb* consequently.

Informatik *die* computer science.

Informatiker *der* (PL *die* **Informatiker**) computer scientist.

Informatikerin *die* (PL *die* **Informatikerinnen**) computer scientist.

Information *die* (PL *die* **Informationen**) (piece of) information.

Informationsbüro *das* (PL *die* **Informationsbüros**) (tourist) information office.

informieren *verb* (PERF **hat informiert**) 1 to inform; 2 **informiert sein** to be aware; **da bist du falsch informiert** you've been wrongly informed; 3 **sich über etwas informieren** to find out about something; **ich habe mich darüber genau informieren lassen** I found out all about it.

Ingenieur *der* (PL *die* **Ingenieure**) engineer.

Ingenieurin *die* (PL *die* **Ingenieurinnen**) engineer.

Ingwer *der* ginger.

Inhaber *der* (PL *die* **Inhaber**) 1 owner (*of a shop*); 2 holder (*of an office*).

Inhaberin *die* (PL *die* **Inhaberinnen**) 1 owner (*of a shop*); 2 holder (*of a position*).

Inhalt *der* (PL *die* **Inhalte**) 1 contents; **den Inhalt der Dose mit etwas Wasser verdünnen** dilute the contents of the tin with a little water; 2 content (*of a story, film*); **er hat uns eine kurze Zusammenfassung des Inhalts der Geschichte gegeben** he gave us a quick summary of the content of the story; 3 volume; 4 area (*of a rectangle, circle, etc.*).

△ NEW SPELLING: *See page xii*

inklusive *preposition* ←(+GEN)
including.
adverb inclusive.

innen *adverb* inside; **nach innen**
inwards.

Innenstadt *die* (PL *die* **Innenstädte**)
town centre, city centre.

Innere *das* 1 interior; 2 inside.

innerer, innere, inneres
adjective 1 inner; 2 inside;
3 internal (*injuries*).

innerhalb *preposition* ←(+GEN)
1 within; 2 during.
adverb **innerhalb von** within.

innerlich *adjective* 1 internal;
2 inner.
adverb 1 internally; 2 inwardly.

ins = **in das**; **ins Theater gehen** to go
to the theatre.

Insekt *das* (PL *die* **Insekten**) insect.

Insel *die* (PL *die* **Inseln**) island.

Inserat *das* (PL *die* **Inserate**)
advertisement.

inserieren *verb* (PERF **hat inseriert**)
to advertise.

insgesamt *adverb* in all.

Instinkt *der* (PL *die* **Instinkte**)
instinct.

instinktiv *adjective* instinctive.

Instrument *das* (PL *die*
Instrumente) instrument.

intelligent *adjective* intelligent.

Intelligenz *die* intelligence.

Intercityzug *der* (PL *die*
Intercityzüge) intercity train.

interessant *adjective* interesting.

Interesse *das* (PL *die* **Interessen**)
interest.

interessieren *verb* (PERF **hat
interessiert**) 1 to interest; 2 **sich
für etwas interessieren** to be
interested in something.

Internat *das* (PL *die* **Internate**)
boarding school.

international *adjective*
international.

Internet *das* internet.

Interview *das* (PL *die* **Interviews**)
interview.

inzwischen *adverb* in the
meantime, meanwhile.

Ire *der* (PL *die* **Iren**) Irishman; **die Iren**
the Irish.

irgend *adverb* 1 at all; **wenn irgend
möglich** if at all possible; **wenn du
irgend kannst** if you could possibly
manage it; 2 **irgend so ein Idiot**
some such idiot.

irgendein *adjective* 1 some; 2 any;
3 **irgendein anderer** someone else,
anyone else.

**irgendeiner, irgendeine,
irgendein(e)s** *pronoun* 1 any
one; **'welche möchten Sie?'** –
'irgendeine' 'which one would you
like?' – 'any one'; 2 somebody,
someone; 3 anybody, anyone; **hat
irgendeiner angerufen?** has
anybody phoned?

✧ IRREGULAR VERB: *See the verb table in the centre of the dictionary*

irgendetwas Δ *pronoun*
1 something; 2 anything.

irgendjemand Δ *pronoun*
1 somebody; 2 anybody, anyone.

irgendwann *adverb* 1 some time, at some time; 2 any time, at any time.

irgendwas (*informal*) = **irgendetwas**.

irgendwie *adverb* somehow.

irgendwo *adverb* 1 somewhere; 2 anywhere.

Irin *die* (PL die **Irinnen**) Irishwoman.

irisch *adjective* Irish.

Irland *das* Ireland.

ironisch *adjective* ironic.

irre *adjective* 1 mad; 2 (*informal*) incredible, fantastic (*party, song*). *adverb* **irre gut** incredibly good.

irren *verb* (PERF **ist geirrt**) 1 to wander (about) (*when lost*); 2 (PERF **hat sich geirrt**) **sich irren** to be mistaken, to be wrong.

irrsinnig *adjective* 1 mad; 2 (*informal*) incredible.

Irrtum *der* (PL die **Irrtümer**) mistake.

Islam *der* Islam.

isst Δ SEE **essen**.

ist SEE **sein**.

Italien *das* Italy.

Italiener *der* (PL die **Italiener**) Italian.

Italienerin *die* (PL die **Italienerinnen**) Italian.

italienisch *adjective* Italian.

J j

ja *adverb* 1 yes; 2 **ich glaube ja** I think so; 3 **du kommst doch, ja?** you'll come, won't you?; **es passt doch, ja?** it fits, doesn't it?; 4 **sag's ihm ja nicht!** don't (you dare) tell him, whatever you do!; **seid ja vorsichtig!** do be careful!; 5 **es ist ja noch früh** it's still early; **ich kann ihn ja mal fragen, ob er mitkommen will** I could always ask him if he wants to come.

Jacht *die* (PL die **Jachten**) yacht.

Jacke *die* (PL die **Jacken**) 1 jacket; 2 cardigan.

Jackett *das* (PL die **Jacketts**) jacket.

Jagd *die* (PL die **Jagden**) 1 hunt; 2 hunting.

jagen *verb* (PERF **hat gejagt**) 1 to hunt; 2 to chase; **drei Polizisten jagten den Einbrecher, aber er hängte sie schnell ab** three policemen chased the burglar, but he soon shook them off; **meine Mutter hat mich aus dem Bett gejagt** (*informal*) my mother chased me out of bed; 3 **jemanden aus dem Haus jagen** to throw somebody out of the house; 4 **damit kannst du mich jagen** (*informal*) I can't stand that.

Jahr *das* (PL die **Jahre**) year; **in den sechziger Jahren** in the sixties;

Kinder bis zu zwölf Jahren children up to the age of twelve.

jahrelang *adverb* for years.

Jahrestag *der* (PL *die* **Jahrestage**) anniversary.

Jahreszeit *die* (PL *die* **Jahreszeiten**) season.

Jahrgang *der* (PL *die* **Jahrgänge**) 1 year; 2 vintage.

Jahrhundert *das* (PL *die* **Jahrhunderte**) century.

jährlich *adjective, adverb* yearly; **zweimal jährlich** twice a year.

Jahrmarkt *der* (PL *die* **Jahrmärkte**) fair.

Jahrtausend *das* (PL *die* **Jahrtausende**) millennium.

Jahrzehnt *das* (PL *die* **Jahrzehnte**) decade.

jähzornig *adjective* hot-tempered.

jammern *verb* (PERF **hat gejammert**) to moan.

Januar *der* January.

Japan *das* Japan.

Japaner *der* (PL *die* **Japaner**) Japanese.

Japanerin *die* (PL *die* **Japanerinnen**) Japanese.

japanisch *adjective* Japanese.

jawohl *adverb* 1 yes; 2 certainly.

je *adverb* 1 ever; **besser denn je** better than ever; 2 each; **sie kosten je zwanzig Mark** they are twenty marks each; 3 **seit eh und je** always; 4 **je nach** depending on.

preposition ←(+ACC) per.
conjunction 1 **je mehr, desto besser** the more the better; 2 **je nachdem** it depends.

Jeans *plural noun* jeans.

jede SEE **jeder**.

jedenfalls *adverb* in any case.

jeder, jede, jedes *adjective* 1 every; **jedes Mal** △ every time; 2 each; 3 any; **ohne jeden Grund** without any reason.
pronoun 1 everybody, everyone; 2 each one; 3 anybody, anyone; **das kann jeder** anybody can do that.

jedermann *pronoun* everybody, everyone.

jederzeit *adverb* at any time.

jedes SEE **jeder**.

jedesmal SEE **jeder**.

jedoch *adverb* however.

jemals *adverb* ever.

jemand *pronoun* 1 somebody, someone; **jemand hat das für dich abgegeben** sombody left this for you; 2 anybody, anyone; **hat jemand angerufen?** did anybody call?

jener, jene, jenes *adjective* (*used in elevated language and in literature*) 1 that; 2 those (*plural*).
pronoun 1 that one; 2 those (*plural*).

jenseits *preposition* ←(+GEN) (on) the other side of.

jetzt *adverb* now.

✧ IRREGULAR VERB: *See the verb table in the centre of the dictionary*

Job *der* (PL die **Jobs**) job.

jobben *verb* (*informal*) (PERF **hat gejobbt**) to work.

joggen *verb* (PERF **ist gejoggt**) to jog.

Jogginganzug *der* (PL die **Jogginganzüge**) tracksuit.

Joghurt *der* (PL die **Joghurt**) yoghurt.

Johannisbeere *die* (PL die **Johannisbeeren**) 1 **rote Johannisbeeren** redcurrants; 2 **schwarze Johannisbeeren** blackcurrants.

Journalist *der* (PL die **Journalisten**) journalist.

Journalistin *die* (PL die **Journalistinnen**) journalist.

jubeln *verb* (PERF **hat gejubelt**) 1 to cheer; 2 **Beifall jubeln** to applaud.

Jubiläum *das* (PL die **Jubiläen**) 1 anniversary; 2 jubilee.

Jude *der* (PL die **Juden**) Jew.

Jüdin *die* (PL die **Jüdinnen**) Jew.

jüdisch *adjective* Jewish.

Jugend *die* youth.

Jugendherberge *die* (PL die **Jugendherbergen**) youth hostel.

Jugendklub *der* (PL die **Jugendklubs**) youth club.

Jugendliche *der/die* (PL die **Jugendlichen**) 1 young man/woman; 2 **die Jugendlichen** youth, young people.

Jugoslawien *das* Yugoslavia.

jugoslawisch *adjective* Yugoslavian.

Juli *der* July.

jung *adjective* 1 young; 2 **Jung und Alt** △ young and old.

Junge[1] *der* (PL die **Jungen**) boy.

Junge[2] *das* (PL die **Jungen**) young (animal).

Jungfrau *die* (PL die **Jungfrauen**) 1 virgin; 2 Virgo.

jüngster, jüngste, jüngstes *adjective* 1 youngest; 2 latest (*news, developments*); 3 **in jüngster Zeit** recently.

Juni *der* June.

Jury *die* (PL die **Jurys**) 1 jury; 2 judges (*in sport*).

Juwelier *der* (PL die **Juweliere**) jeweller.

Jux *der* (*informal*) laugh; **aus Jux** for a laugh.

K k

Kabel *das* (PL die **Kabel**) 1 cable; 2 wire.

Kabelfernsehen *das* cable television.

Kabeljau *der* (PL die **Kabeljaus**) cod.

Kabine *die* (PL die **Kabinen**) 1 cabin; 2 cubicle (*for changing*); 3 car (*of a cable car*).

Kachel *die* (PL die **Kacheln**) tile.

Käfer der (PL die **Käfer**) beetle.

Kaffee der (PL die **Kaffee(s)**) coffee; **zwei Kaffee mit Milch bitte** two white coffees please.

Kaffeekanne die (PL die **Kaffeekannen**) coffee-pot.

Käfig der (PL die **Käfige**) cage.

kahl adjective **1** bald (head); **2** bare (tree, walls).

Kaiser der (PL die **Kaiser**) emperor.

Kaiserin die (PL die **Kaiserinnen**) empress.

Kakao der (PL die **Kakao(s)**) cocoa; **zwei Kakao bitte** two cups of cocoa please.

Kakerlak der (PL die **Kakerlaken**) cockroach.

Kaktus der (PL die **Kakteen**) cactus.

Kalb das (PL die **Kälber**) **1** calf; **2** veal.

Kalbfleisch das veal.

Kalender der (PL die **Kalender**) **1** calendar; **2** diary.

Kalk der **1** lime; **2** limescale; **3** calcium.

Kalorie die (PL die **Kalorien**) calorie.

kalorienarm adjective low-calorie.

kalt adjective cold; **ist dir kalt?** are you cold?; **stell die Heizung an, den Kindern ist kalt** put on the heating, the children are cold; **abends essen wir kalt** we have a cold meal in the evening; **den Wein kalt stellen** to chill the wine.

Kälte die **1** cold; **2** coldness; **3 fünf**

Grad Kälte five degrees below zero.

kam SEE **kommen**.

Kamel das (PL die **Kamele**) camel.

Kamera die (PL die **Kameras**) camera.

Kamerad der (PL die **Kameraden**) friend.

Kameramann der (PL die **Kameramänner**) cameraman.

Kamin der (PL die **Kamine**) fireplace; **wir saßen am Kamin** we sat by the fire.

Kamm der (PL die **Kämme**) **1** comb; **2** ridge (of a mountain).

kämmen verb (PERF **hat gekämmt**) **1** to comb; **2 sich kämmen** to comb your hair.

Kammer die (PL die **Kammern**) **1** store room; **2** chamber.

Kampf der (PL die **Kämpfe**) **1** fight; **2** contest; **3** struggle.

kämpfen verb (PERF **hat gekämpft**) to fight.

Kanada das Canada.

Kanadier der (PL die **Kanadier**) Canadian.

Kanadierin die (PL die **Kanadierinnen**) Canadian.

kanadisch adjective Canadian.

Kanal der (PL die **Kanäle**) **1** canal; **2** channel (radio, TV); **3 der Kanal** the (English) Channel; **4** sewer, drain.

Kanalinseln plural noun Channel Islands.

✧ IRREGULAR VERB: See the verb table in the centre of the dictionary

Kanalisation *die* sewers, drains

Kanarienvogel *der* (PL *die* **Kanarienvögel**) canary.

Kandidat *der* (PL *die* **Kandidaten**) candidate.

Kandidatin *die* (PL *die* **Kandidatinnen**) candidate.

Känguru △ *das* (PL *die* **Kängurus**) kangaroo.

Kaninchen *das* (PL *die* **Kaninchen**) rabbit.

kann SEE **können**.

Kännchen *das* (PL *die* **Kännchen**) 1 pot; **ein Kännchen Kaffee bitte** a pot of coffee please; 2 jug (*of milk*).

Kanne *die* (PL *die* **Kannen**) 1 pot (*for coffee, tea*); 2 jug (*for water*); 3 can (*for oil*); 4 churn (*for milk*); 5 watering can.

kannst SEE **können**.

kannte SEE **kennen**.

Kante *die* (PL *die* **Kanten**) edge.

Kantine *die* (PL *die* **Kantinen**) canteen; **wir essen immer in der Kantine zu Mittag** we always have lunch in the canteen.

Kanu *das* (PL *die* **Kanus**) canoe; **Kanu fahren** to go canoeing.

Kapelle *die* (PL *die* **Kapellen**) chapel.

kapieren *verb* (*informal*) (PERF **hat kapiert**) to understand; **er hat es mir schon dreimal erklärt, aber ich kapier es einfach nicht** he's already explained it to me three times, but I still don't get it.

Kapital *das* capital

Kapitalismus *der* capitalism.

Kapitän *der* (PL *die* **Kapitäne**) captain.

Kapitel *das* (PL *die* **Kapitel**) chapter.

Kappe *die* (PL *die* **Kappen**) cap.

kaputt *adjective* 1 broken; 2 **an meinem Computer ist etwas kaputt** there's something wrong with my computer; 3 **ich bin kaputt** (*informal*) I'm shattered.

kaputtgehen ◇ *verb* (IMPERF **ging kaputt**, PERF **ist kaputtgegangen**) 1 to break; 2 to pack up; **mein Fernseher ist mitten im Fußballspiel kaputtgegangen** the television packed up in the middle of the football match; 3 to wear out (*of clothing*); 4 to break up (*of a marriage or friendship*).

kaputtmachen *verb* (PERF **hat kaputtgemacht**) 1 to break; **er macht alle seine Spielsachen kaputt** he breaks all his toys; 2 to ruin (*clothes, furniture*); 3 to finish off (*a person*); **die viele Arbeit macht mich ganz kaputt** all this work is wearing me out; 4 **sich kaputtmachen** to wear yourself out.

Kapuze *die* (PL *die* **Kapuzen**) hood.

Karamell △ *der* (PL *die* **Karamells**) caramel.

Karfreitag *der* Good Friday.

Karibik *die* **die Karibik** the Caribbean.

karibisch *adjective* Caribbean.

kariert *adjective* 1 check; **ein**

△ NEW SPELLING: *See page xii*

karierter Rock a check skirt;
2 squared (*paper*).

Karneval *der* (PL *die* **Karnevale**)
carnival.

Karo *das* (PL *die* **Karos**) 1 square;
2 diamonds (*in cards*).

Karotte *die* (PL *die* **Karotten**) carrot.

Karriere *die* (PL *die* **Karrieren**)
career; **Karriere machen** to get to
the top.

Karte *die* (PL *die* **Karten**) 1 card; **ich
schicke euch eine Karte aus
Italien** I'll send you a card from
Italy; 2 card (*for playing*); **wir haben
den ganzen Abend Karten gespielt**
we played cards all evening;
gute/schlechte Karten haben to
have a good/bad hand; 3 ticket; **gibt
es noch Karten für das
Popfestival?** can you still get tickets
for the pop festival?; 4 menu; 5 map;
**ich kann Oberammergau nicht auf
der Karte finden** I can't find
Oberammergau on the map; 6 **alles
auf eine Karte setzen** to put all your
eggs in one basket.

Kartenspiel *das* (PL *die*
Kartenspiele) 1 card game; 2 pack
of cards.

Kartoffel *die* (PL *die* **Kartoffeln**)
potato.

Kartoffelbrei *der* mashed
potatoes.

Karton *der* (PL *die* **Kartons**)
1 cardboard; 2 cardboard box.

Karussell *das* (PL *die* **Karussells**)
merry-go-round; **Karussell fahren**
to go on the merry-go-round.

Käse *der* cheese.

Käsekuchen *der* (PL *die*
Käsekuchen) cheesecake.

Kasse *die* (PL *die* **Kassen**) 1 till;
2 checkout; **an der Kasse zahlen**
pay at the checkout; 3 cash desk (*in
a bank*); 4 box-office; **Sie können
die Karten an der Kasse abholen**
you can collect the tickets from the
box office; 5 ticket office (*at a sports
stadium*); **Sie müssen sich an der
Kasse anstellen** you have to queue
at the ticket office; 6 health
insurance; 7 **knapp bei Kasse sein**
(*informal*) to be short of money; **gut
bei Kasse sein** (*informal*) to be in
the money.

Kassenzettel *der* (PL *die*
Kassenzettel) receipt.

Kassette *die* (PL *die* **Kassetten**)
1 cassette, tape; **ich habe den neuen
Song auf Kassette aufgenommen**
I've taped the new song; 2 box (*for
money, jewellery*).

Kassettenrekorder *der* (PL *die*
Kassettenrekorder) cassette
recorder.

kassieren *verb* (PERF **hat kassiert**)
1 to collect the money; 2 to collect
the fares; 3 **wie viel hat er kassiert?**
how much did he charge you?;
4 **darf ich bei Ihnen kassieren?**
would you like to pay now? (*your bill
in a restaurant*); 5 (*informal*) to take
away (*a driving licence, for
example*).

Kassierer *der* (PL *die* **Kassierer**)
cashier.

✧ IRREGULAR VERB: *See the verb table in the centre of the dictionary*

Kassiererin die (PL die **Kassiererinnen**) cashier.

Kastanie die (PL die **Kastanien**) chestnut.

Kasten der (PL die **Kästen**) 1 box; 2 crate; **ein Kasten Bier** a crate of beer; 3 bin; 4 letter-box; 5 **was auf dem Kasten haben** (*informal*) to be brainy.

Katalog der (PL die **Kataloge**) catalogue.

Katalysator der (PL die **Katalysatoren**) catalytic converter.

Katastrophe die (PL die **Katastrophen**) catastrophe.

katastrophal *adjective, adverb* 1 catastrophic; 2 **sie hat katastrophal schlecht abgeschnitten** she came out terribly badly.

Kategorie die (PL die **Kategorien**) category.

Kater der (PL die **Kater**) 1 tom-cat; 2 **einen Kater haben** (*informal*) to have a hangover.

Kathedrale die (PL die **Kathedralen**) cathedral.

Katholik der (PL die **Katholiken**) Catholic.

Katholikin die (PL die **Katholikinnen**) Catholic.

katholisch *adjective* Catholic.

Kätzchen das (PL die **Kätzchen**) kitten.

Katze die (PL die **Katzen**) cat.

kauen verb (PERF **hat gekaut**) to chew.

Kauf der (PL die **Käufe**) 1 purchase; 2 **ein guter Kauf** a bargain; 3 **etwas in Kauf nehmen** to put up with something.

kaufen *verb* (PERF **hat gekauft**) to buy.

Käufer der (PL die **Käufer**) buyer.

Käuferin die (PL die **Käuferinnen**) buyer.

Kauffrau die (PL die **Kauffrauen**) businesswoman.

Kaufhaus das (PL die **Kaufhäuser**) department store.

Kaufmann der (PL die **Kaufleute**) businessman.

Kaugummi der (PL die **Kaugummis**) chewing gum.

kaum *adverb* hardly, scarcely.

kauern *verb* (PERF **hat gekauert**) to crouch.

Kaution die (PL die **Kautionen**) 1 deposit; 2 bail.

Kegel der (PL die **Kegel**) 1 cone; 2 skittle.

Kegelbahn die skittle alley.

kegeln *verb* (PERF **hat gekegelt**) to play skittles.

Kehle die (PL die **Kehlen**) throat.

Keim der (PL die **Keime**) 1 shoot; 2 germ.

kein *adjective* 1 no; **auf keinen Fall** on no account; 2 **ich habe keine Zeit** I haven't got any time; **er hat**

△ NEW SPELLING: *See page xii*

kein Geld he hasn't got any money; **3 keine zehn Minuten** less than ten minutes.

keiner, keine, kein(e)s *pronoun* **1** nobody, no one; **2** none, not one; **3 von diesen Kleidern gefällt mir keins** I don't like any of these dresses; **4 keiner von beiden** neither (of them).

keinesfalls *adverb* on no account.

keineswegs *adverb* by no means.

keinmal *adverb* not once.

keins SEE **keiner**.

Keks *der* (PL *die* **Kekse**) biscuit.

Keller *der* (PL *die* **Keller**) cellar.

Kellergeschoss △ *das* (PL *die* **Kellergeschosse**) basement.

Kellner *der* (PL *die* **Kellner**) waiter.

Kellnerin *die* (PL *die* **Kellnerinnen**) waitress.

kennen ✧ *verb* (IMPERF **kannte**, PERF **hat gekannt**) **1** to know; **2 kennen lernen** △ to get to know; **sich kennen lernen** to get to know each other; **3 kennen lernen** △ to meet; **ich habe Ulrike in London kennen gelernt** I met Ulrike in London; **wo habt ihr euch kennen gelernt?** where did you meet?

kennenlernen SEE **kennen**.

Kenntnis *die* (PL *die* **Kenntnisse**) **1** knowledge; **2 etwas zur Kenntnis nehmen** to take note of something.

Kennzeichen *das* (PL *die* **Kennzeichen**) **1** mark;

2 characteristic; **3** registration (number) (*of a vehicle*).

Kerl *der* (PL *die* **Kerle**) **1** bloke; **2 Eva ist ein netter Kerl** Eva's a nice girl.

Kern *der* (PL *die* **Kerne**) **1** pip; **2** stone (*of an apricot, peach*); **3** kernel (*of a nut*).

Kernenergie *die* nuclear power.

Kernkraftwerk *das* (PL *die* **Kernkraftwerke**) nuclear power station.

Kernwaffen *plural noun* nuclear weapons.

Kerze *die* (PL *die* **Kerzen**) candle.

Kerzenhalter *der* (PL *die* **Kerzenhalter**) candlestick.

Kessel *der* (PL *die* **Kessel**) **1** kettle; **2** boiler.

Kette *die* (PL *die* **Ketten**) chain.

Keule *die* (PL *die* **Keulen**) **1** club; **2** leg (*of lamb*); **3** drumstick (*of chicken*).

kichern *verb* (PERF **hat gekichert**) to giggle.

Kiefer[1] *der* (PL *die* **Kiefer**) jaw.

Kiefer[2] *die* (PL *die* **Kiefern**) pine tree.

Kieselstein *der* (PL *die* **Kieselsteine**) pebble.

Kilo *das* (PL *die* **Kilo(s)**) kilo.

Kilogramm *das* (PL *die* **Kilogramme**) kilogram.

Kilometer *der* (PL *die* **Kilometer**) kilometre.

Kind *das* (PL *die* **Kinder**) child.

✧ IRREGULAR VERB: *See the verb table in the centre of the dictionary*

Kindergarten der (PL die Kindergärten) nursery school.

Kindergeld das child benefit.

kinderleicht adjective very easy; das ist kinderleicht it's child's play.

Kindertagesstätte die (PL die Kindertagesstätten) day nursery.

Kinderwagen der (PL die Kinderwagen) pram.

Kindheit die childhood.

kindisch adjective childish.

Kinn das (PL die Kinne) chin.

Kino das (PL die Kinos) cinema.

kippen verb (PERF hat gekippt) 1 to tip; 2 (PERF ist gekippt) to topple.

Kirche die (PL die Kirchen) church.

Kirsche die (PL die Kirschen) cherry.

Kissen das (PL die Kissen) 1 cushion; 2 pillow.

Kiste die (PL die Kisten) 1 crate; 2 box.

kitzeln verb (PERF hat gekitzelt) to tickle.

kitzlig adjective ticklish.

Kiwi die (PL die Kiwis) kiwi fruit.

klagen verb (PERF hat geklagt) to complain.

Klammer die (PL die Klammern) 1 peg (for washing); 2 grip (for hair); 3 bracket.

klang SEE klingen.

Klang der (PL die Klänge) sound.

Klappe die (PL die Klappen) 1 flap;

2 clapperboard; 3 (informal) trap (mouth); halt die Klappe! shut up!

klappen verb (PERF hat geklappt) 1 nach vorne klappen to tilt forward; 2 nach hinten klappen to tip back; 3 nach oben klappen to lift up; 4 nach unten klappen to put down; 5 to work out; hoffentlich klappt es I hope it'll work out.

Klappstuhl der (PL die Klappstühle) folding chair.

klar adjective 1 clear (water, answer); klar werden △ to become clear; 2 jetzt ist mir alles klar now I understand; 3 sich klar werden △ to make up your mind; 4 sich über etwas im Klaren sein △ to realize something. adverb clearly; na klar! (informal) of course!

klären verb (PERF hat geklärt) 1 to clarify; 2 to sort out; 3 to purify (sewage); 4 sich klären to clear (of the weather or the sky); 5 sich klären to resolve itself, to be settled.

Klarinette die (PL die Klarinetten) clarinet.

klarwerden SEE klar.

klasse adjective (informal) great, smashing.

Klasse die (PL die Klassen) 1 class; erster Klasse reisen to travel first class; 2 year; in die sechste Klasse gehen to be in year six.

Klassenarbeit die (PL die Klassenarbeiten) (written) test.

Klassenbuch das register (kept by

the teacher, it also contains notes about students' achievements).

Klassenkamerad *der* (PL *die* **Klassenkameraden**) class-mate.

Klassenkameradin *die* (PL *die* **Klassenkameradinnen**) class-mate.

Klassensprecher *der* (PL *die* **Klassenprecher**) class representative.

Klassensprecherin *die* (PL *die* **Klassensprecherinnen**) class representative.

Klassenzimmer *das* (PL *die* **Klassenzimmer**) classroom.

klassisch *adjective* classical.

Klatsch *der* gossip.

klatschen *verb* (PERF **hat geklatscht**) **1** to clap; **jemandem Beifall klatschen** to clap somebody, to applaud somebody; **2** to slap; **3** to gossip.

klauen *verb* (*informal*) (PERF **hat geklaut**) to pinch.

Klavier *das* (PL *die* **Klaviere**) piano.

kleben *verb* (PERF **hat geklebt**) **1** to stick; **2** to glue; **3** **jemandem eine kleben** (*informal*) to belt somebody one.

klebrig *adjective* sticky.

Klebstoff *der* (PL *die* **Klebstoffe**) glue.

Klebstreifen *der* (PL *die* **Klebstreifen**) sticky tape.

Klecks *der* (PL *die* **Kleckse**) stain.

Kleid *das* (PL *die* **Kleider**) **1** dress;

Uschi hat sich zwei neue Kleider gekauft Uschi bought two new dresses; **2 Kleider** clothes.

Kleiderbügel *der* (PL *die* **Kleiderbügel**) coat hanger.

Kleiderschrank *der* (PL *die* **Kleiderschränke**) wardrobe.

Kleidung *die* clothes, clothing.

klein *adjective* **1** small, little; **etwas klein schneiden** △ to cut something up small; **2** short; **Peter ist kleiner als Klaus** Peter is shorter than Klaus.

Kleingeld *das* change.

Klempner *der* (PL *die* **Klempner**) plumber.

klettern *verb* (PERF **ist geklettert**) to climb.

Klima *das* (PL *die* **Klimas**) climate.

Klimaanlage *die* (PL *die* **Klimaanlagen**) air conditioning.

Klinge *die* (PL *die* **Klingen**) blade.

Klingel *die* (PL *die* **Klingeln**) bell.

klingeln *verb* (PERF **hat geklingelt**) to ring; **es klingelt** there's a ring at the door.

klingen ✧ *verb* (IMPERF **klang**, PERF **hat geklungen**) to sound.

Klinik *die* (PL *die* **Kliniken**) clinic.

Klinke *die* (PL *die* **Klinken**) handle.

Klippe *die* (PL *die* **Klippen**) rock.

Klo *das* (*informal*) (PL *die* **Klos**) loo.

klopfen *verb* (PERF **hat geklopft**) **1** to knock; **2** to beat.

✧ IRREGULAR VERB: *See the verb table in the centre of the dictionary*

Klosett das (PL die **Klosetts**) lavatory.

Kloster das (PL die **Kloster**) 1 monastery; 2 convent.

Klotz der (PL die **Klötze**) block.

Klub der (PL die **Klubs**) club.

klug adjective 1 clever; 2 **ich werde daraus nicht klug** I don't understand it.

Klugheit die cleverness.

Klumpen der (PL die **Klumpen**) lump.

knabbern verb (PERF **hat geknabbert**) to nibble.

Knäckebrot das (PL die **Knäckebrote**) crispbread.

knacken verb (PERF **hat geknackt**) to crack.

Knall der (PL die **Knalle**) bang.

knallen verb (PERF **hat geknallt**) 1 to go bang; 2 to pop (of a cork); 3 to slam (of a door); 4 to crack (of a whip).

knapp adjective 1 scarce; 2 tight (skirt, top); 3 **knapp bei Kasse sein** to be short of money; 4 **mit knapper Mehrheit** by a narrow majority; 5 just; **eine knappe Stunde** just under an hour; **sie haben knapp verloren** they only just lost; 6 **das war knapp** (informal) that was a close shave.

knarren verb (PERF **hat geknarrt**) to creak.

Knauf der (PL die **Knäufe**) knob.

knautschen verb (PERF **hat geknautscht**) 1 to crumple; 2 to crease.

kneifen ◇ verb (IMPERF **kniff**, PERF **hat gekniffen**) 1 to pinch; 2 (informal) to chicken out; **sie hat mal wieder gekniffen und nichts gesagt** she's chickened out yet again and didn't say anything.

Kneipe die (PL die **Kneipen**) pub.

kneten verb (PERF **hat geknetet**) to knead.

knicken verb (PERF **hat geknickt**) 1 to bend; 2 to fold.

Knie das (PL die **Knie**) knee.

knien verb (PERF **hat gekniet**) 1 to kneel; 2 **sich knien** to kneel down.

kniff SEE **kneifen**.

knipsen verb (PERF **hat geknipst**) (to photograph) to take a snap, to take snaps.

Knoblauch der garlic.

Knoblauchzehe die (PL die **Knoblauchzehen**) clove of garlic.

Knöchel der (PL die **Knöchel**) 1 ankle; 2 knuckle; **Mario hat sich beim Jogging den Knöchel verstaucht** Mario sprained his ankle when jogging.

Knochen der (PL die **Knochen**) bone.

Knopf der (PL die **Knöpfe**) button.

Knoten der (PL die **Knoten**) 1 knot; 2 bun (as a hairstyle); 3 lump.

knurren verb (PERF **hat geknurrt**) 1 to growl; 2 to rumble; 3 to grumble.

knusprig adjective crisp, crusty (bread).

△ NEW SPELLING: See page xii

Koch der (PL die **Köche**) 1 cook;
2 chef.

Kochbuch das (PL die **Kochbücher**)
cookery book.

kochen verb (PERF **hat gekocht**) 1 to
cook; 2 to boil; **das Wasser kocht**
the water's boiling.

Köchin die (PL die **Köchinnen**) cook.

Kochtopf der (PL die **Kochtöpfe**)
saucepan.

Koffer der (PL die **Koffer**) suitcase.

Kofferkuli der (PL die **Kofferkulis**)
baggage trolley.

Kofferraum der (PL die
Kofferräume) boot.

Kohl der 1 cabbage; 2 (informal)
rubbish; **rede keinen Kohl** don't
talk rubbish.

Kohle die (PL die **Kohlen**) coal.

Kokosnuss △ die (PL die
Kokosnüsse) coconut.

Kollege der (PL die **Kollegen**)
colleague.

Kollegin die (PL die **Kolleginnen**)
colleague.

Köln das Cologne.

Kölnischwasser das eau de
cologne.

Kombination die (PL die
Kombinationen) combination.

Komfort der comfort.

Komiker der (PL die **Komiker**)
comedian.

komisch adjective funny.

Komma das (PL die **Kommas**)
1 comma; 2 decimal point; **zwei
Komma fünf** two point five.

kommen ◇ verb (IMPERF **kam**, PERF
ist gekommen) 1 to come; 2 to get;
wie komme ich zur U-Bahn? how
do I get to the tube station?; **kommt
gut nach Hause!** have a safe
journey home!; 3 **etwas kommen
lassen** to send for something; 4 **wie
kommst du darauf?** what gave you
that idea?; 5 **hinter etwas kommen**
to find out about something; 6 **zur
Schule kommen** to start school;
7 to go; **die Gabeln kommen in die
Schublade** the forks go in the
drawer; **ins Krankenhaus kommen**
to go to hospital; 8 **wer kommt
zuerst?** who's first?; **du kommst an
die Reihe** it's your turn; 9 **wie
kommt das?** why is that?; 10 **zu
etwas kommen** to acquire
something; 11 **wieder zu sich
kommen** to come round (after
fainting or anaesthetic); 12 **dazu
kommen, etwas zu tun** to get round
to doing something; **ich komme
einfach nicht zum Einkaufen** I just
can't get round to doing the
shopping; 13 **das kommt davon!**
see what happens!

Kommissar der (PL die
Kommissare) superintendent.

Kommode die (PL die **Kommoden**)
chest of drawers.

Kommunismus der communism.

Kommunist der (PL die
Kommunisten) communist.

Kommunistin die (PL die
Kommunistinnen) communist.

◇ IRREGULAR VERB: See the verb table in the centre of the dictionary

Komödie *die* (PL *die* **Komödien**) comedy.

Kompass △ *der* (PL *die* **Kompasse**) compass.

komplett *adjective* complete.

Kompliment *das* (PL *die* **Komplimente**) compliment.

kompliziert *adjective* complicated.

Komponist *der* (PL *die* **Komponisten**) composer.

Komponistin *die* (PL *die* **Komponistinnen**) composer.

Kompott *das* (PL *die* **Kompotte**) stewed fruit.

Kompromiss △ *der* (PL *die* **Kompromisse**) compromise; **einen Kompromiss schließen** to compromise.

Konditorei *die* (PL *die* **Konditoreien**) patisserie, cake shop.

Kondom *das* (PL *die* **Kondome**) condom.

Konfektion *die* ready-made clothes.

Konferenz *die* (PL *die* **Konferenzen**) conference.

Konflikt *der* (PL *die* **Konflikte**) conflict.

König *der* (PL *die* **Könige**) king.

Königin *die* (PL *die* **Königinnen**) queen.

königlich *adjective* royal.

Königreich *das* (PL *die* **Königreiche**) kingdom.

Konjunktion *die* (PL *die* **Konjunktionen**) conjunction.

Konkurrent *der* (PL *die* **Konkurrenten**) competitor.

Konkurrentin *die* (PL *die* **Konkurrentinnen**) competitor.

Konkurrenz *die* competition.

können ✧ *verb* (PRES **kann**, IMPERF **konnte**, PERF **hat gekonnt**) **1** can; **kann ich Ihnen helfen?** can I help you?; **kannst du Auto fahren?** can you drive?; **kannst du Deutsch?** can you speak German?; **ich konnte nicht früher kommen** I couldn't come any earlier; **das kann ich nicht** I can't do that; **2 etwas können** to be able to do something; **er wird es vor Dienstag nicht machen können** he won't be able to do it before Tuesday; **3 das kann gut sein** that may well be so; **es kann sein, dass …** it may be that …; **4 ich kann nichts dafür** it's not my fault.

Können *das* ability.

Könner *der* (PL *die* **Könner**) expert.

könnt SEE **können**.

konnte, konnten, konntest, konntet SEE **können**.

Konserven *plural noun* tinned food.

Konsonant *der* (PL *die* **Konsonanten**) consonant.

Korsika *das* Corsica.

Kontakt *der* (PL *die* **Kontakte**) contact.

Kontaktlinse *die* (PL *die* **Kontaktlinsen**) contact lens.

△ NEW SPELLING: *See page xii*

Kontinent *der* (PL *die* **Kontinente**) continent.

Konto *das* (PL *die* **Konten**) account.

Kontrolle *die* (PL *die* **Kontrollen**) 1 check; 2 control.

Kontrolleur *der* (PL *die* **Kontrolleure**) inspector.

kontrollieren *verb* (PERF **hat kontrolliert**) 1 to check; 2 to control.

konzentrieren *verb* (PERF **hat konzentriert**) 1 to concentrate; 2 **sich konzentrieren** to concentrate.

Konzert *das* (PL *die* **Konzerte**) 1 concert; 2 concerto.

Kopf *der* (PL *die* **Köpfe**) 1 head; 2 **sich den Kopf zerbrechen** to rack your brains; 3 **seinen Kopf durchsetzen** to get your own way; 4 **sich den Kopf waschen** to wash your hair; 5 **auf dem Kopf** upside down; 6 **ein Kopf Salat** a lettuce.

köpfen *verb* (PERF **hat geköpft**) 1 to head (*in football*); 2 to behead.

Kopfhörer *der* (PL *die* **Kopfhörer**) headphones.

Kopfkissen *das* (PL *die* **Kopfkissen**) pillow.

Kopfsalat *der* (PL *die* **Kopfsalate**) lettuce.

Kopfschmerzen *plural noun* headache.

Kopie *die* (PL *die* **Kopien**) copy.

kopieren *verb* (PERF **hat kopiert**) to copy.

Kopiergerät *das* (PL *die* **Kopiergeräte**) photocopier.

Korb *der* (PL *die* **Körbe**) 1 basket; 2 **jemandem einen Korb geben** to turn somebody down.

Kork *der* (PL *die* **Korke**) cork.

Korken *der* (PL *die* **Korken**) cork.

Korkenzieher *der* (PL *die* **Korkenzieher**) corkscrew.

Korn *das* (PL *die* **Körner**) corn.

Körper *der* (PL *die* **Körper**) body.

körperbehindert *adjective* disabled.

körperlich *adjective* physical.

Korrektur *die* (PL *die* **Korrekturen**) correction.

korrigieren *verb* (PERF **hat korrigiert**) to correct.

koscher *adjective* kosher.

Kosmetik *die* (PL *die* **Kosmetika**) 1 cosmetics; 2 beauty care.

Kost *die* food.

kostbar *adjective* precious.

kosten *verb* (PERF **hat gekostet**) 1 to cost; 2 **wie viel kostet es?** how much is it?; 3 to taste.

Kosten *plural noun* 1 cost; 2 expenses.

kostenlos *adjective* free (of charge).

köstlich *adjective* 1 delicious; 2 funny.

Kostüm *das* (PL *die* **Kostüme**) 1 suit; 2 costume.

Kotelett *das* (PL *die* **Koteletts**) chop.

◇ IRREGULAR VERB: *See the verb table in the centre of the dictionary*

Krabbe *die* (PL *die* **Krabben**) **1** crab; **2** shrimp.

krabbeln *verb* (PERF **ist gekrabbelt**) to crawl.

Krach *der* **1** row; **2** noise; **3** crash.

krachen *verb* (PERF **hat gekracht**) **1** to crash; **2** (PERF **ist gekracht**) to crack; **er ist gegen die Mauer gekracht** he crashed into the wall.

krächzen *verb* (PERF **hat gekrächzt**) to croak.

Kraft *die* (PL *die* **Kräfte**) **1** strength; **er hat nicht viel Kraft** he's not very strong; **2** force; **in Kraft treten** to come into force; **3 geistige Kräfte** mental powers; **4** worker.

kräftig *adjective* **1** strong; **2** nourishing.
adverb **1** strongly; **2** hard; **kräftig schütteln** shake hard.

Kraftwerk *das* (PL *die* **Kraftwerke**) power station.

Kragen *der* (PL *die* **Kragen**) collar.

Krähe *die* (PL *die* **Krähen**) crow.

Kralle *die* (PL *die* **Krallen**) claw.

Kram *der* stuff; **mach deinen Kram allein!** (*informal*) do it yourself!

kramen *verb* (PERF **hat gekramt**) to rummage about.

Krampf *der* (PL *die* **Krämpfe**) cramp.

Kran *der* (PL *die* **Kräne**) crane (*machine*).

Kranich *der* (PL *die* **Kraniche**) crane (*bird*).

krank *adjective* ill, sick; **krank werden** to fall ill.

Kranke *der/die* (PL *die* **Kranken**) patient.

kränken *verb* (PERF **hat gekränkt**) to hurt.

Krankenhaus *das* (PL *die* **Krankenhäuser**) hospital; **sie haben ihn gestern ins Krankenhaus eingeliefert** he was taken to hospital yesterday.

Krankenkasse *die* health insurance; **bei welcher Krankenkasse sind Sie versichert?** what health insurance have you got?

Krankenpfleger *der* (PL *die* **Krankenpfleger**) (male) nurse.

Krankenpflegerin *die* (PL *die* **Krankenpflegerinnen**) nurse.

Krankenschwester *die* (PL *die* **Krankenschwestern**) nurse; **Ulrike ist Krankenschwester** Ulrike is a nurse.

Krankenwagen *der* (PL *die* **Krankenwagen**) ambulance.

Krankheit *die* (PL *die* **Krankheiten**) illness, disease.

kratzen *verb* (PERF **hat gekratzt**) to scratch.

Kratzer *der* (PL *die* **Kratzer**) scratch.

kraus *adjective* frizzy.

Kraut *das* (PL *die* **Kräuter**) **1** herb; **2** sauerkraut; **3** cabbage.

Krawall *der* (PL *die* **Krawalle**) **1** riot; **2** row.

Krawatte *die* (PL *die* **Krawatten**) tie.

kreativ *adjective* creative.

△ NEW SPELLING: *See page xii*

Krebs der (PL die **Krebse**) 1 crab; 2 cancer; 3 Cancer.

Kredit der (PL die **Kredite**) credit; **auf Kredit** on credit.

Kreditkarte die (PL die **Kreditkarten**) credit card.

Kreide die (PL die **Kreiden**) chalk.

kreieren verb (PERF **hat kreiert**) to create.

Kreis der (PL die **Kreise**) 1 circle; 2 district.

Kreislauf der 1 cycle; 2 circulation.

Kreuz das (PL die **Kreuze**) 1 cross; 2 (small of the) back; 3 intersection (of a motorway); 4 clubs (in cards).

kreuzen verb (PERF **hat gekreuzt**) 1 to cross; 2 **sich kreuzen** to cross.

Kreuzung die (PL die **Kreuzungen**) 1 crossroads; 2 cross (of plants, animals).

Kreuzfahrt die (PL die **Kreuzfahrten**) 1 cruise; **eine Kreuzfahrt machen** to go on a cruise; 2 crusade.

Kreuzworträtsel das (PL die **Kreuzworträtsel**) crossword (puzzle).

kriechen ◇ verb (IMPERF **kroch**, PERF **ist gekrochen**) to crawl.

Krieg der (PL die **Kriege**) war.

kriegen verb (informal) (PERF **hat gekriegt**) 1 to get; 2 **ein Kind kriegen** to have a baby.

Krimi der (PL die **Krimis**) thriller.

Kriminalroman der (PL die **Kriminalromane**) crime novel.

kriminell adjective criminal.

Kriminelle der/die (PL die **Kriminellen**) criminal.

Krippe die (PL die **Krippen**) 1 manger; 2 crib; 3 crèche.

Krise die (PL die **Krisen**) crisis.

Kristall[1] der (PL die **Kristalle**) crystal.

Kristall[2] das (glass) crystal.

kritisch adjective critical.

kritisieren verb (PERF **hat kritisiert**) 1 to criticize; 2 to review.

kroch SEE **kriechen**.

Krokodil das (PL die **Krokodile**) crocodile.

Krone die (PL die **Kronen**) crown.

Kröte die (PL die **Kröten**) toad.

Krücke die (PL die **Krücken**) crutch.

Krug der (PL die **Krüge**) 1 jug; 2 mug.

Krümel der (PL die **Krümel**) crumb.

krümelig adjective crumbly.

krumm adjective 1 bent; 2 crooked.

Kruste die (PL die **Krusten**) crust.

Küche die (PL die **Küchen**) 1 kitchen; 2 cooking; **die italienische Küche** Italian cooking; 3 **warme Küche** hot food.

Kuchen der (PL die **Kuchen**) cake.

Kuckuck der (PL die **Kuckucke**) cuckoo.

Kugel die (PL die **Kugeln**) 1 ball; 2 bullet; 3 sphere.

◇ IRREGULAR VERB: See the verb table in the centre of the dictionary

Kugelschreiber der (PL die **Kugelschreiber**) ballpoint pen, biro™.

Kuh die (PL die **Kühe**) cow.

kühl adjective cool.

kühlen verb (PERF **hat gekühlt**) 1 to cool, to chill; 2 to refrigerate.

Kühler der (PL die **Kühler**) radiator.

Kühlerhaube die (PL die **Kühlerhauben**) bonnet.

Kühlschrank der (PL die **Kühlschränke**) fridge.

Kühltruhe die (PL die **Kühltruhen**) freezer.

Küken das (PL die **Küken**) chick.

Kuli der (PL die **Kulis**) biro™.

Kultur die (PL die **Kulturen**) 1 culture; 2 civilization.

Kulturbeutel der (PL die **Kulturbeutel**) toilet bag.

kulturell adjective cultural.

Kummer der 1 sorrow; 2 worry; 3 trouble.

kümmern verb (PERF **hat gekümmert**) 1 to concern; 2 **sich um jemanden kümmern** to look after somebody; **sich um den Garten kümmern** to look after the garden; 3 **sich darum kümmern, dass …** to see to it that …; 4 **kümmere dich um deine eigenen Angelegenheiten** mind your own business.

Kunde der (PL die **Kunden**) 1 customer; 2 client.

kündigen verb (PERF **hat gekündigt**) 1 to cancel; 2 to give notice; **die Firma hat ihm gekündigt** the company gave him his notice; 3 **seine Stellung kündigen** to hand in your notice.

Kundin die (PL die **Kundinnen**) 1 customer; 2 client.

Kundschaft die customers.

Kunst die (PL die **Künste**) 1 art; 2 skill.

Künstler der (PL die **Künstler**) artist.

Künstlerin die (PL die **Künstlerinnen**) artist.

künstlerisch adjective artistic.

künstlich adjective artificial.

Kunststoff der (PL die **Kunststoffe**) plastic.

Kunststück das (PL die **Kunststücke**) 1 trick; 2 feat.

Kunstwerk das (PL die **Kunstwerke**) work of art.

Kupfer das copper.

Kupplung die (PL die **Kupplungen**) 1 clutch (of a car); 2 coupling.

Kürbis der (PL die **Kürbisse**) pumpkin.

Kurort der (PL die **Kurorte**) health resort.

Kurs der (PL die **Kurse**) 1 course; 2 exchange rate; 3 price (of shares).

Kurve die (PL die **Kurven**) 1 curve; 2 bend.

kurz adjective 1 short; **vor kurzem** a short time ago; 2 **zu kurz kommen**

△ NEW SPELLING: *See page xii*

to get less than your fair share, to come off badly.
adverb **1** shortly; **2** briefly; **3 kurz gesagt** in a word.

Kurzarbeit *die* short-time working.

kurzärmelig *adjective* short-sleeved.

kürzen *verb* (PERF **hat gekürzt**) **1** to shorten; **2** to cut.

kurzfristig *adjective* short-term.
adverb at short notice.

kürzlich *adverb* recently.

kurzsichtig *adjective* short-sighted.

Kurzwaren *plural noun* haberdashery.

Kusine *die* (PL *die* **Kusinen**) cousin.

Kuss Δ *der* (PL *die* **Küsse**) kiss.

küssen *verb* (PERF **hat geküsst** Δ) **1** to kiss; **2 sich küssen** to kiss.

Küste *die* (PL *die* **Küsten**) coast.

Kuvert *das* (PL *die* **Kuverts**) envelope.

L l

Labor *das* (PL *die* **Labors**) laboratory.

Lache *die* (PL *die* **Lachen**) pool.

lächeln *verb* (PERF **hat gelächelt**) to smile.

lachen *verb* (PERF **hat gelacht**) to laugh.

lächerlich *adjective* ridiculous.

Lachs *der* (PL *die* **Lachse**) salmon.

Lack *der* (PL *die* **Lacke**) **1** varnish; **2** paint.

lackieren *verb* (PERF **hat lackiert**) **1** to varnish; **2** to spray (*with paint*).

laden ♦ *verb* (PRES **lädt**, IMPERF **lud**, PERF **hat geladen**) **1** to load; **wir haben die Möbel in den Möbelwagen geladen** we loaded the furniture into the removal van; **2 eine Batterie laden** to charge a battery; **3** to summon; **mein Bruder wurde als Zeuge geladen** my brother was summoned as a witness.

Laden *der* (PL *die* **Läden**) **1** shop; **wann macht der Laden zu?** when does the shop close?; **2** shutter; **wenn es heiß ist, lassen wir die Läden den ganzen Tag zu** when it's hot we keep the shutters closed all day.

Ladendieb *der* (PL *die* **Ladendiebe**) shoplifter.

Ladung *die* (PL *die* **Ladungen**) **1** cargo; **2** charge (*of dynamite or shot*); **3** summons; **4** load.

lag SEE **liegen**.

Lage *die* (PL *die* **Lagen**) **1** situation; **nicht in der Lage sein, etwas zu tun** not be in a position to do something; **2** layer.

Lager *das* (PL *die* **Lager**) **1** camp; **2** warehouse; **3** stock; **etwas auf Lager haben** to have something in stock; **4** stock-room; **5** bearing (*in a machine*).

lagern *verb* (PERF **hat gelagert**) **1** to store; **2** to camp.

♦ **IRREGULAR VERB:** *See the verb table in the centre of the dictionary*

ahm *adjective* lame.

ähmen *verb* (PERF **hat gelähmt**) to paralyse.

ähmung *die* paralysis.

aib *der* (PL *die* **Laibe**) loaf.

aken *das* (PL *die* **Laken**) sheet.

akritze *die* liquorice.

amm *das* (PL *die* **Lämmer**) lamb.

ampe *die* (PL *die* **Lampen**) lamp.

ampenschirm *der* (PL *die* **Lampenschirme**) lampshade.

and *das* (PL *die* **Länder**) 1 country; **auf dem Land** in the country; 2 land; 3 state (*there are 16 Länder in Germany*).

andebahn *die* (PL *die* **Landebahnen**) runway.

anden *verb* (PERF **ist gelandet**) 1 to land; 2 **im Krankenhaus landen** (*informal*) to end up in hospital.

andkarte *die* (PL *die* **Landkarten**) map.

andkreis *der* (PL *die* **Landkreise**) district.

ändlich *adjective* rural.

Landschaft *die* (PL *die* **Landschaften**) 1 countryside; 2 landscape.

Landstraße *die* (PL *die* **Landstraßen**) country road.

Landtag *der* state parliament.

Landwirtschaft *die* agriculture, farming.

lang *adjective* 1 long; **seit langem**

for a long time; 2 tall. *adverb* **eine Woche lang** for a week.

langärmelig *adjective* long-sleeved.

lange *adverb* 1 a long time; **lange nicht** not for a long time; 2 **so lange wie möglich** as long as possible; 3 **er ist lange nicht so reich** he's nowhere near as rich.

Länge *die* (PL *die* **Längen**) 1 length; 2 longitude.

langen *verb* (PERF **hat gelangt**) 1 to be enough; **das Geld langt nicht** it's not enough money; **mir langt's** (*informal*) I've had enough; 2 to reach; **nach etwas langen** to reach for something; 3 **jemandem eine langen** (*informal*) to slap somebody's face.

Langlauf *der* cross-country (*in skiing*).

langsam *adjective, adverb* slow; **die Musik geht mir langsam auf die Nerven** the music is slowly getting on my nerves.

längst *adverb* 1 a long time ago; **das habe ich schon längst gemacht** I did it a long time ago; 2 for a long time; **er weiß es schon längst** he's known it for a long time; 3 **längst nicht** nowhere near, not nearly.

längster, längste, längstes *adjective* longest; **Marion hat den längsten Aufsatz geschrieben** Marion wrote the longest essay.

langweilen *verb* (PERF **hat gelangweilt**) 1 to bore; 2 **sich langweilen** to be bored.

△ NEW SPELLING: *See page xii*

langweilig *adjective* boring.

Lappen *der* (PL *die* **Lappen**) cloth, rag.

Laptop *der* (PL *die* **Laptops**) laptop.

Lärm *der* noise.

las SEE **lesen**.

Laser *der* (PL *die* **Laser**) laser.

Laserdrucker *der* (PL *die* **Laserdrucker**) laser printer.

lassen ◇ *verb* (PRES **lässt** △, IMPERF **ließ**, PERF **hat gelassen**) **1** to let; **jemanden schlafen lassen** to let somebody sleep; **lass uns jetzt gehen** let's go now; **2 jemandem etwas lassen** to let somebody have something; **3** to leave; **die Kinder zu Hause lassen** to leave the children at home; **lass mich!** leave me!; **4 jemanden warten lassen** to keep somebody waiting; **5 etwas reparieren lassen** to have something repaired; **6 lass das!** stop it!; **7 die Tür lässt sich leicht öffnen** the door opens easily; **das lässt sich alles machen** that can all be arranged.

lässig *adjective* casual.

Last *die* (PL *die* **Lasten**) **1** load; **2 jemandem zur Last fallen** to be a burden on somebody.

lästig *adjective* troublesome.

Lastwagen *der* (PL *die* **Lastwagen**) lorry, truck.

Latein *das* Latin.

Laterne *die* (PL *die* **Laternen**) **1** lantern; **2** street lamp.

Laub *das* leaves.

Lauch *der* leek(s).

Lauf *der* (PL *die* **Läufe**) **1** run; **2** course; **im Laufe der Zeit** in the course of time; **im Laufe der Jahre** over the years; **3** race; **4** barrel (*of a gun*).

Laufbahn *die* (PL *die* **Laufbahnen**) career.

laufen ◇ *verb* (PRES **läuft**, IMPERF **lief** PERF **ist gelaufen**) **1** to run; **sie kann viel schneller laufen als ihr Bruder** she can run much faster than her brother; **2** to walk; **du kannst nach Hause laufen oder mit dem Bus fahren** you can walk home or go on the bus; **3** to be valid; **4 Ski laufen** to ski; **5** to be on (*of a film, programme, or machine*).

laufend *adjective* **1** running; **2** current (*issue, month*); **3 auf dem Laufenden sein** △ to be up to date; **Anita hält mich auf dem Laufenden** △ Anita keeps me up to date.
adverb continually, constantly.

Läufer *der* (PL *die* **Läufer**) **1** runner; **2** rug; **3** bishop (*in chess*).

Läuferin *die* (PL *die* **Läuferinnen**) runner.

Laufmasche *die* (PL *die* **Laufmaschen**) ladder (*in your tights*).

Laufwerk *das* (PL *die* **Laufwerke**) drive (*on a computer*).

Laune *die* (PL *die* **Launen**) mood.

launisch *adjective* moody.

◇ IRREGULAR VERB: *See the verb table in the centre of the dictionary*

Laus *die* (PL *die* **Läuse**) louse.

laut *adjective* 1 loud; 2 noisy.
adverb 1 loudly; 2 **laut lesen** to
read aloud; 3 **lauter stellen** to turn
up.
preposition ←(+GEN *or* +DAT)
according to.

Laut *der* (PL *die* **Laute**) sound.

lauten *verb* (PERF **hat gelautet**) 1 to
be; 2 to go.

läuten *verb* (PERF **hat geläutet**) to
ring.

lauter *adjective* nothing but.

Lautsprecher *der* (PL *die*
Lautsprecher) (loud)speaker.

Lautstärke *die* volume.

lauwarm *adjective* lukewarm.

Lavendel *der* lavender.

Lawine *die* (PL *die* **Lawinen**)
avalanche.

leben *verb* (PERF **hat gelebt**) 1 to
live; 2 to be alive; 3 **leb wohl!**
farewell!

Leben *das* (PL *die* **Leben**) life; **am
Leben sein** to be alive; **ums Leben
kommen** to lose your life.

lebend *adjective* living.

lebendig *adjective* 1 living;
2 **lebendig sein** to be alive; 3 lively.

Lebensgefahr *die* mortal danger;
sein Vater ist in Lebensgefahr his
father is critically ill.

lebensgefährlich *adjective*
1 extremely dangerous; 2 critical;

lebensgefährlich verletzt critically
injured.

Lebenshaltungskosten *plural
noun* cost of living.

lebenslänglich *adjective* life.
adverb for life.

Lebenslauf *der* (PL *die*
Lebensläufe) CV.

Lebensmittel *plural noun* food,
groceries.

Lebensmittelgeschäft *das* (PL
die **Lebensmittelgeschäfte**)
grocer's (shop).

Lebensunterhalt *der* livelihood;
seinen Lebensunterhalt verdienen
to earn one's living.

Leber *die* (PL *die* **Lebern**) liver.

Leberfleck *der* (PL *die* **Leberflecke**)
mole.

Leberwurst *die* liver sausage.

Lebewesen *das* (PL *die*
Lebewesen) living being, living
thing.

lebhaft *adjective* 1 lively; 2 vivid
(*idea, colour*).

Lebkuchen *der* (PL *die* **Lebkuchen**)
gingerbread.

leblos *adjective* lifeless.

Leck *das* (PL *die* **Lecks**) leak.

lecken *verb* (PERF **hat geleckt**) 1 to
lick; **die Katze leckte ihre Jungen**
the cat licked the kittens; **an etwas
lecken** to lick something; 2 to leak.

lecker *adjective* delicious.

Leder *das* (PL *die* **Leder**) leather.

△ NEW SPELLING: *See page xii*

ledig *adjective* single.

lediglich *adverb* merely.

leer *adjective* empty; **leer machen** to empty.

leeren *verb* (PERF **hat geleert**) 1 to empty; 2 **ein leeres Blatt Papier** a blank sheet of paper; 3 **sich leeren** to empty.

Leerlauf *der* neutral (*gear*).

Leerung *die* (PL *die* **Leerungen**) collection.

legal *adjective* legal.

legen *verb* (PERF **hat gelegt**) 1 to put; 2 to lay; 3 **sich legen** to lie down; 4 **sich legen** to die down (*of a storm, noise*); **unsere Begeisterung hat sich gelegt** our enthusiasm has worn off.

leger *adjective, adverb* casual; **leger gekleidet sein** to be casually dressed.

Lehm *der* clay.

Lehne *die* (PL *die* **Lehnen**) 1 back (*of a chair*); 2 arm (*of a sofa or chair*).

lehnen *verb* (PERF **hat gelehnt**) 1 to lean; 2 **sich an etwas lehnen** to lean against something.

Lehrbuch *das* (PL *die* **Lehrbücher**) textbook.

lehren *verb* (PERF **hat gelehrt**) to teach.

Lehrer *der* (PL *die* **Lehrer**) 1 teacher; 2 instructor.

Lehrerin *die* (PL *die* **Lehrerinnen**) 1 teacher; 2 instructor.

Lehrerzimmer *das* (PL *die* **Lehrerzimmer**) staffroom.

Lehrling *der* (PL *die* **Lehrlinge**) 1 apprentice; 2 trainee.

Lehrplan *der* (PL *die* **Lehrpläne**) syllabus.

Lehrstelle *die* (PL *die* **Lehrstellen**) apprenticeship.

Leibwächter *der* (PL *die* **Leibwächter**) bodyguard.

Leiche *die* (PL *die* **Leichen**) (dead) body, corpse.

leicht *adjective* 1 light; 2 easy; **jemandem leicht fallen** △ to be easy for somebody; **es ist ihm nicht leicht gefallen** it wasn't easy for him; **Markus macht es sich immer leicht** Markus always takes the easy way out; 3 **ein leichter Akzent** a slight accent.

Leichtathletik *die* athletics.

leichtfallen SEE **leicht**.

Leichtsinn *der* 1 carelessness; 2 recklessness.

leichtsinnig *adjective* 1 careless; 2 reckless.

leid *adjective* **jemanden leid sein** △ to be fed up with somebody; **etwas leid sein** △ to be fed up with something.

Leid *das* 1 sorrow; 2 harm; 3 **es tut mir Leid** △ I'm sorry; **Andreas tut mir Leid** △ I feel sorry for Andreas.

leiden ◇ *verb* (IMPERF **litt**, PERF **hat gelitten**) 1 to suffer; 2 **jemanden gut leiden können** to like

---

◇ **IRREGULAR VERB:** *See the verb table in the centre of the dictionary* somebody; **3 ich kann Erika nicht leiden** I can't stand Erika.

leider *adverb* **1** unfortunately; **2 leider ja** I'm afraid so; **leider nicht** I'm afraid not.

leihen ◇ *verb* (IMPERF **lieh**, PERF **hat geliehen**) **1** to lend; **2 sich etwas leihen** to borrow something; **ich habe mir das Buch von Alex geliehen** I borrowed the book from Alex.

Leihwagen *der* (PL **die Leihwagen**) hire car.

Leim *der* (PL **die Leime**) glue.

Leine *die* (PL **die Leinen**) **1** rope; **2** line (*for washing*); **3** lead (*for a dog*).

Leinen *das* (PL **die Leinen**) linen.

Leinwand *die* screen (*in a cinema*).

leise *adjective* quiet.
adverb **1** quietly; **2 die Musik leiser stellen** to turn the music down.

leisten *verb* (PERF **hat geleistet**) **1** to achieve; **2 jemandem Hilfe leisten** to help somebody; **3 jemandem Gesellschaft leisten** to keep somebody company; **4 sich etwas leisten** to treat yourself to something; **5 sich etwas leisten können** to be able to afford something; **ich kann mir kein neues Auto leisten** I can't afford a new car.

Leistung *die* (PL **die Leistungen**) **1** achievement; **2** performance; **3 Leistungen** payment.

leiten *verb* (PERF **hat geleitet**) **1** to lead; **2** to direct; **3** to manage, run (*a business*); **4** to conduct.

Leiter¹ *die* (PL **die Leitern**) ladder.

Leiter² *der* (PL **die Leiter**) **1** leader; **2** head; **3** manager; **4** director; **5** conductor (*of an orchestra or electricity*).

Leiterin *die* (PL **die Leiterinnen**) **1** leader; **2** head; **3** manageress; **4** director.

Leitung *die* (PL **die Leitungen**) **1** direction; **2** management; **3** (*phone*) line; **4** (*electric*) lead; **5** cable; **6** pipe; **7 unter der Leitung von** conducted by.

Leitungswasser *das* tap water.

Lektion *die* (PL **die Lektionen**) lesson.

lenken *verb* (PERF **hat gelenkt**) **1** to steer; **2** to guide; **3 den Verdacht auf jemanden lenken** to throw suspicion on somebody.

Lenkrad *das* (PL **die Lenkräder**) steering wheel.

Lenkstange *die* (PL **die Lenkstangen**) handlebars.

lernen *verb* (PERF **hat gelernt**) **1** to learn; **schwimmen lernen** to learn to swim; **2** to study.

lesen ◇ *verb* (PRES **liest**, IMPERF **las**, PERF **hat gelesen**) to read.

Leser *der* (PL **die Leser**) reader.

Leserin *die* (PL **die Leserinnen**) reader.

letzte SEE **letzter**.

Letzte △ *der/die/das* (PL **die Letzten**) **1 der/die Letzte** the last (one); **das**

Letzte the last (thing); **2 Boris kam als Letzter** Boris arrived last.

letztens *adverb* **1** recently; **2** lastly.

letzter, letzte, letztes *adjective* **1** last; **zum letzten Mal** for the last time; **das letzte Mal** the last time; **2** latest (*news, information*); **3 in letzter Zeit** recently.

leuchten *verb* (PERF **hat geleuchtet**) to shine.

Leuchter *der* (PL *die* **Leuchter**) candlestick.

Leuchtreklame *die* neon sign.

Leuchtturm *der* (PL *die* **Leuchttürme**) lighthouse.

leugnen *verb* (PERF **hat geleugnet**) to deny.

Leute *plural noun* people.

Lexikon *das* (PL *die* **Lexika**) **1** encyclopedia; **2** dictionary.

Licht *das* (PL *die* **Lichter**) light.

Lichtbild *das* (PL *die* **Lichtbilder**) photograph.

Lichtschalter *der* (PL *die* **Lichtschalter**) light switch.

Lid *das* (PL *die* **Lider**) (eye)lid.

Lidschatten *der* (PL *die* **Lidschatten**) eye shadow.

lieb *adjective* **1** dear; **liebe Gabi** dear Gabi; **2** nice; **das ist lieb von euch** that's nice of you; **3 jemanden lieb haben** △ to be fond of somebody; **4 es wäre mir lieber, wenn** … I'd prefer it if …; **5 ihr liebstes Spielzeug** her favourite toy.

Liebe *die* (PL *die* **Lieben**) love.

lieben *verb* (PERF **hat geliebt**) to love

liebenswürdig *adjective* kind.

lieber *adverb* **1** rather; **2 lieber mögen** to like better; **3 lass das lieber** you'd better not do that; **4 ich trinke lieber Kaffee** I prefer coffee.

Liebesbrief *der* (PL *die* **Liebesbriefe**) love letter.

Liebeskummer *der* **Liebeskummer haben** to be lovesick.

liebevoll *adjective* loving.

liebhaben SEE **lieb**.

Liebling *der* (PL *die* **Lieblinge**) **1** darling; **2** favourite.

Lieblings- *prefix* favourite.

liebster, liebste, liebstes *adjective* **1** dearest; **2** favourite. *adverb* **am liebsten** best (of all); **ich mag Max am liebsten** I like Max best.

Lied *das* (PL *die* **Lieder**) song.

lief SEE **laufen**.

liefern *verb* (PERF **hat geliefert**) **1** to deliver; **2** to supply.

Lieferung *die* (PL *die* **Lieferungen**) delivery.

Lieferwagen *der* (PL *die* **Lieferwagen**) (delivery) van.

liegen ✧ *verb* (IMPERF **lag**, PERF **hat gelegen**) **1** to lie; **der Brief liegt auf dem Tisch** the letter is on the table; **es liegt viel Schnee** there's lots of snow; **2** to be, to be situated; **3 liegen bleiben** △ to stay (*in bed*); **er ist liegen geblieben** he didn't get

✧ IRREGULAR VERB: *See the verb table in the centre of the dictionary*

up; **4 etwas bleibt liegen**
something is left behind; **die Arbeit
ist liegen geblieben** the job was left
undone; **5 der Schnee bleibt liegen**
the snow is settling; **6 liegen
lassen**△ to leave; **7 es liegt mir
nicht** it doesn't suit me; **8 an etwas
liegen** to be due to something;
9 das liegt an ihm it's up to him.

iegenbleiben, liegenlassen
SEE **liegen**.

Liegestuhl *der* (PL *die* **Liegestühle**)
deckchair.

Liegewagen *der* (PL *die*
Liegewagen) couchette (car).

ieß SEE **lassen**.

iest SEE **lesen**.

Lift *der* (PL *die* **Lifte**) lift.

Liga *die* (PL *die* **Ligen**) league.

ila *adjective* **1** purple; **2** mauve.

Limo *die* (PL *die* **Limo(s)**) = **Limonade**.

Limonade *die* (PL *die* **Limonaden**)
1 fizzy drink; **2** lemonade.

Limone *die* (PL *die* **Limonen**) lime.

Lineal *das* (PL *die* **Lineale**) ruler.

Linie *die* (PL *die* **Linien**) **1** line;
2 route (*of a bus*); **Linie 6**
number 6.

Linke *die* **1** left; **zu meiner Linken**
on my left; **2** left hand; **3** left side;
4 die Linke the left (*in politics*).

linker, linke, linkes *adjective*
1 left; **2** left-wing.

links *adverb* **1** on the left; **links
fahren** to drive on the left; **links
abbiegen** to turn left; **nach links**
left; **von links** from the left; **2 links
sein** to be left-wing; **3 zwei links,
zwei rechts stricken** to purl two,
knit two; **4** (*clothing*) inside out.

Linkshänder *der* (PL *die*
Linkshänder) left-hander.

Linkshänderin *die* (PL *die*
Linkshänderinnen) left-hander.

Linse *die* (PL *die* **Linsen**) **1** lens;
2 lentil.

Lippe *die* (PL *die* **Lippen**) lip.

Lippenstift *der* (PL *die* **Lippenstifte**)
lipstick.

Liste *die* (PL *die* **Listen**) list.

listig *adjective* cunning.

Liter *der* (PL *die* **Liter**) litre.

Literatur *die* literature.

litt SEE **leiden**.

Livesendung △ *die* (PL *die*
Livesendungen) live programme.

Lizenz *die* (PL *die* **Lizenzen**) licence.

Lkw *der* (PL *die* **Lkws**)
(*Lastkraftwagen*) lorry, truck.

Lob *das* praise.

loben *verb* (PERF **hat gelobt**) to
praise.

Loch *das* (PL *die* **Löcher**) hole.

Locke *die* (PL *die* **Locken**) curl.

locken *verb* (PERF **hat gelockt**) **1** to
tempt; **2** to curl.

locker *adjective* **1** loose; **2** slack
(*rope*); **3** relaxed (*atmosphere,
person*).

△ NEW SPELLING: *See page xii*

lockerlassen ✧ *verb* (PRES **lässt locker** △, IMPERF **ließ locker**, PERF **hat lockergelassen**) **nicht lockerlassen** (*informal*) not to let up.

lockig *adjective* curly.

Löffel *der* (PL *die* **Löffel**) 1 spoon; 2 **ein Löffel Mehl** a spoonful of flour.

log SEE **lügen**.

Logik *die* logic.

logisch *adjective* 1 logical; 2 **ja, logisch!** yes, of course!

Lohn *der* (PL *die* **Löhne**) 1 wages; 2 reward.

lohnen *verb* (PERF **hat sich gelohnt**) **sich lohnen** to be worth it.

Lokal *das* (PL *die* **Lokale**) 1 bar; 2 restaurant.

Lokomotive *die* (PL *die* **Lokomotiven**) locomotive, engine.

Lorbeerblatt *das* (PL *die* **Lorbeerblätter**) bay leaf.

los *adjective* 1 **der Hund ist los** the dog is off the lead; 2 **die Schraube ist los** the screw's loose; 3 **es ist viel los** there's a lot going on; 4 **etwas los sein** to be rid of something; 5 **was ist los?** what's the matter?
adverb 1 **los!** go on!; 2 **Achtung, fertig, los!** ready, steady, go!

Los *das* (PL *die* **Lose**) 1 (lottery) ticket; 2 **das große Los ziehen** to hit the jackpot; 3 lot.

losbinden ✧ *verb* (IMPERF **band los**, PERF **hat losgebunden**) to untie.

löschen *verb* (PERF **hat gelöscht**) 1 to put out; 2 **seinen Durst löschen** to quench your thirst; 3 to delete, to cancel; 4 to erase.

lose *adjective* loose.

lösen *verb* (PERF **hat gelöst**) 1 to solve; 2 to undo; 3 **eine Fahrkarte lösen** to buy a ticket; 4 **sich lösen** to come undone; 5 **sich lösen** to be solved (*of a puzzle or mystery*); **sich von selbst lösen** to be resolved (*of a problem*); 6 **sich in Wasser lösen** to dissolve in water.

losfahren ✧ *verb* (PRES **fährt los**, IMPERF **fuhr los**, PERF **ist losgefahren**) 1 to set off; 2 to drive off.

losgehen ✧ *verb* (IMPERF **ging los**, PERF **ist losgegangen**) 1 to set off; 2 to start; 3 to come off (*of a button*); 4 to go off (*of a bomb*); 5 **auf jemanden losgehen** to go for somebody.

loslassen ✧ *verb* (PRES **lässt los** △, IMPERF **ließ los**, PERF **hat losgelassen**) 1 to let go of; 2 to let go.

Lösung *die* (PL *die* **Lösungen**) solution.

loswerden ✧ *verb* (PRES **wird los**, IMPERF **wurde los**, PERF **ist losgeworden**) to get rid of.

Lotterie *die* (PL *die* **Lotterien**) lottery.

Lotto *das* (PL *die* **Lottos**) (national) lottery.

Löwe *der* (PL *die* **Löwen**) 1 lion; 2 Leo.

✧ IRREGULAR VERB: *See the verb table in the centre of the dictionary*

Lücke die (PL die **Lücken**) gap.

Luft die (PL die **Lüfte**) 1 air; 2 die Luft
anhalten to hold your breath; 3 **in
die Luft gehen** (*informal*) to blow
your top; 4 **jemanden wie Luft
behandeln** to ignore somebody.

Luftballon der (PL die **Luftballons**)
balloon.

Luftdruck der air pressure.

Luftmatratze die (PL die
Luftmatratzen) air-bed.

Luftpost die airmail; **per Luftpost**
by airmail.

Luftverschmutzung die air
pollution.

Luftwaffe die air force.

Lüge die (PL die **Lügen**) lie.

lügen ✧ verb (IMPERF **log**, PERF **hat
gelogen**) to lie.

Lügner der (PL die **Lügner**) liar.

Lügnerin die (PL die **Lügnerinnen**)
liar.

Lunge die (PL die **Lungen**) lungs.

Lungenentzündung die
pneumonia.

Lupe die (PL die **Lupen**) magnifying
glass.

Lust die 1 pleasure; 2 **Lust haben,
etwas zu tun** to feel like doing
something; **ich habe keine Lust** I
don't feel like it; **Lust auf etwas
haben** to feel like something.

lustig adjective 1 jolly; 2 funny;
3 **Dieter hat sich über mich lustig
gemacht** Dieter made fun of me.

lutschen verb (PERF **hat gelutscht**)
to suck.

Lutscher der (PL die **Lutscher**)
lollipop.

Luxemburg das Luxembourg.

Luxus der luxury.

M m

machen verb (PERF **hat gemacht**)
1 to make; 2 to do; **was machst du
da?** what are you doing?; 3 **was
macht die Arbeit?** how's work?;
was macht Karin? how's Karin?;
4 **sich an die Arbeit machen** to get
down to work; 5 **schnell machen** to
hurry; 6 **das macht nichts** it
doesn't matter; 7 **das macht fünf
Mark** that's five marks; 8 **sich
nichts aus etwas machen** to not be
very keen on something; **Roswitha
macht sich nichts aus Schokolade**
Roswitha isn't keen on chocolate.

Macht die (PL die **Mächte**) power; **an
die Macht kommen** to come to
power.

Mädchen das (PL die **Mädchen**) girl.

Made die (PL die **Maden**) maggot.

Mädchenname der (PL die
Mädchennamen) maiden name.

mag SEE **mögen**.

Magazin das (PL die **Magazine**)
magazine.

Magen der (PL die **Mägen**) stomach.

△ NEW SPELLING: *See page xii*

Magenschmerzen *plural noun* stomach-ache.

mager *adjective* **1** thin; **2** lean; **3** low-fat.

Magie *die* magic.

Magnet *der* (PL *die* **Magneten**) magnet.

magnetisch *adjective* magnetic.

magst SEE **mögen**.

Mahagoni *das* mahogany.

mähen *verb* (PERF **hat gemäht**) to mow; **den Rasen mähen** to mow the lawn.

mahlen ◇ *verb* (PERF **hat gemahlen**) to grind.

Mahlzeit *die* (PL *die* **Mahlzeiten**) meal; **Mahlzeit!** enjoy your meal!

Mai *der* May; **der Erste Mai** May Day.

Maiglöckchen *das* (PL *die* **Maiglöckchen**) lily of the valley.

Mais *der* maize.

Majonäse△ *die* mayonnaise.

Majoran *der* marjoram.

Makkaroni (*plural noun*) macaroni.

Makler *der* (PL *die* **Makler**) estate agent.

Makrele *die* (PL *die* **Makrelen**) mackerel.

mal *adverb* **1** times; **zwei mal drei** two times three; **2** by (*with measurements*); **3** sometime (*in the future*); **ich möchte mal nach Brasilien fahren** I'd like to go to Brazil sometime; **4 schon mal** ever; **5 ich war schon mal da** I've been once before; **6 nicht mal** not even; **7 komm mal her!** come here

Mal *das* (PL *die* **Male**) **1** time; **nächstes Mal** next time; **zum ersten Mal** for the first time; **2** mark; **3** mole.

malen *verb* (PERF **hat gemalt**) to paint.

Maler *der* (PL *die* **Maler**) painter.

Malerei *die* painting.

Malerin *die* (PL *die* **Malerinnen**) painter.

Mallorca *das* Majorca.

Mama *die* (PL *die* **Mamas**) mum.

Mami *die* (PL *die* **Mamis**) mummy.

man *pronoun* **1** you, one; **wie macht man das?** how do you do it?; **man kann ja nie wissen** one can never tell; **2** they, people; **man sagt** they say; **3 man hat mir gesagt** I was told.

mancher, manche, manches *adjective* **1** many a; **so manchen Tag** many a day; **2 manche** (*plural*) some; **an manchen Tagen** some days.
pronoun **1** many a person; **2 manche** (*plural*) some people; **3 manches** some things.

manchmal *adverb* sometimes.

Mandarine *die* (PL *die* **Mandarinen**) mandarin.

Mandel *die* (PL *die* **Mandeln**) **1** almond; **2** tonsil.

◇ IRREGULAR VERB: *See the verb table in the centre of the dictionary*

Mandelentzündung *die*
tonsillitis.

Mangel *der* (PL *die* **Mängel**) 1 lack;
2 shortage; 3 defect, fault.

mangelhaft *adjective* 1 faulty;
2 unsatisfactory (*school mark*).

Manie *die* (PL *die* **Manien**) mania.

Manieren *plural noun* manners; **er
hat keine Manieren** he's got no
manners.

Mann *der* (PL *die* **Männer**) 1 man;
2 husband.

Männchen *das* (PL *die* **Männchen**)
male (*animal*).

Mannequin *das* (PL *die*
Mannequins) model.

männlich *adjective* 1 male;
2 manly; 3 masculine.

Mannschaft *die* (PL *die*
Mannschaften) 1 team; 2 crew.

Manschette *die* (PL *die*
Manschetten) cuff.

Mantel *der* (PL *die* **Mäntel**) coat.

Mappe *die* (PL *die* **Mappen**) 1 folder;
2 briefcase; 3 bag.

Märchen *das* (PL *die* **Märchen**) fairy
tale.

Margarine *die* margarine.

Marienkäfer *der* (PL *die*
Marienkäfer) ladybird.

Marine *die* (PL *die* **Marinen**) navy.

Mark *die* (PL *die* **Mark**) mark.

Marke *die* (PL *die* **Marken**) 1 make,
brand; **meine Mutter fährt seit**

Jahren die gleiche Marke my
mother has been driving the same
make of car for years; **Adidas ist eine
führende Marke** Adidas is a leading
brand; 2 tag; 3 stamp (*for letters*);
4 coupon.

markieren *verb* (PERF **hat markiert**)
1 to mark; 2 to fake.

Markstück *das* (PL *die* **Markstücke**)
one-mark piece.

Markt *der* (PL *die* **Märkte**) market.

Marktplatz *der* (PL *die* **Marktplätze**)
market-place.

Marmelade *die* (PL *die*
Marmeladen) jam.

Marmor *der* marble.

Marokko *das* Morocco.

Marsch *der* (PL *die* **Märsche**) march.

März *der* March.

Masche *die* (PL *die* **Maschen**)
1 stitch; 2 mesh; 3 (*informal*) trick;
die Masche raushaben to know
how to do it; **das is die neueste
Masche** that's the latest thing.

Maschine *die* (PL *die* **Maschinen**)
1 machine; 2 plane; 3 typewriter;
Maschine schreiben △ to type.

Masern *plural noun* measles.

Maske *die* (PL *die* **Masken**) mask.

maskieren *verb* (PERF **hat sich
maskiert**) 1 **sich maskieren** to
dress up; 2 **sich maskieren** to
disguise yourself.

maß SEE **messen**.

Maß[1] *das* (PL *die* **Maße**) 1 measure;
2 measurement; 3 extent; **in hohem**

△ NEW SPELLING: *See page xii*

Maße to a high degree; **4 Maß halten** to show moderation.

Maß² *die* (PL *die* **Maß**) litre (of beer).

Masse *die* (PL *die* **Massen**) **1** mass; **eine Masse Arbeit** masses of work; **2** crowd; **3** mixture (*in cooking*).

massenhaft *adjective* masses of.

massieren *verb* (PERF **hat massiert**) to massage.

mäßig *adjective* moderate.

Maßnahme *die* (PL *die* **Maßnahmen**) measure.

Maßstab *der* (PL *die* **Maßstäbe**) **1** standard; **2** scale.

Mast *der* (PL *die* **Masten**) **1** mast; **2** pole; **3** pylon.

Material *das* (PL *die* **Materialien**) **1** material; **2** materials.

Mathe *die* (*informal*) maths.

Mathematik *die* mathematics.

Matratze *die* (PL *die* **Matratzen**) mattress.

Matrose *der* (PL *die* **Matrosen**) sailor.

Matsch *der* **1** mud; **2** slush.

matschig *adjective* **1** muddy; **2** slushy.

matt *adjective* **1** weak; **2** matt; **3** dull; **4** matt! checkmate!

Matte *die* (PL *die* **Matten**) mat.

Mauer *die* (PL *die* **Mauern**) wall.

Maul *das* (PL *die* **Mäuler**) mouth; **halt's Maul!** (*informal*) shut up!

Maulkorb *der* (PL *die* **Maulkörbe**) muzzle.

Maulwurf *der* (PL *die* **Maulwürfe**) mole.

Maurer *der* (PL *die* **Maurer**) bricklayer.

Maus *die* (PL *die* **Mäuse**) mouse.

Mayonnaise *die* mayonnaise.

Mechaniker *der* (PL *die* **Mechaniker**) mechanic.

mechanisch *adjective* mechanical.

meckern *verb* (PERF **hat gemeckert**) **1** to bleat; **2** to grumble.

Medaille *die* (PL *die* **Medaillen**) medal.

Medien *plural noun* media.

Medikament *das* (PL *die* **Medikamente**) medicine, drug.

Medizin *die* (PL *die* **Medizinen**) medicine.

Meer *das* (PL *die* **Meere**) sea.

Meeresfrüchte *plural noun* seafood.

Meerschweinchen *das* (PL *die* **Meerschweinchen**) guinea pig.

Mehl *das* flour.

mehr *adverb, pronoun* more; **nichts mehr** no more; **nie mehr** never again.

mehrere *pronoun* several.

mehreres *pronoun* several things.

mehrfach *adjective* **1** multiple, many; **2** repeated. *adverb* several times.

Mehrheit die (PL die Mehrheiten) majority.

mehrmalig *adjective* repeated.

mehrmals *adverb* several times.

Mehrwertsteuer die value added tax.

Mehrzahl die 1 majority; 2 plural.

meiden ◇ *verb* (IMPERF **mied**, PERF **hat gemieden**) to avoid.

Meile die (PL die Meilen) mile.

mein *adjective* my.

meine SEE **meiner**.

meinen *verb* (PERF **hat gemeint**) 1 to think; 2 to mean; **es gut meinen** to mean well; 3 to say.

meiner, meine, mein(e)s *pronoun* mine.

meinetwegen *adverb* 1 for my sake; 2 because of me; 3 as far as I'm concerned; **'kann ich das Auto haben?' – 'meinetwegen'** 'can I take the car?' – 'I don't mind'.

meins SEE **meiner**.

Meinung die (PL die Meinungen) opinion.

meist *adverb* 1 mostly; 2 usually.

meiste *adjective, pronoun* **der/die/das meiste** most; **die meisten** most; **am meisten** most, the most.

meistens *adverb* 1 mostly; 2 usually.

Meister der (PL die Meister) 1 master; 2 champion.

Meisterin die (PL die Meisterinnen) champion.

Meisterschaft die (PL die Meisterschaften) championship.

Meisterwerk das (PL die Meisterwerke) masterpiece.

melden *verb* (PERF **hat gemeldet**) 1 to report; 2 to register; 3 **sich melden** to report; (*on the phone*) to answer; **Luise hat sich gemeldet** (*in school*) Luise put up her hand; 4 **sich bei jemandem melden** to get in touch with somebody.

Melodie die (PL die Melodien) melody, tune.

Melone die (PL die Melonen) 1 melon; 2 bowler (hat).

Menge die (PL die Mengen) 1 quantity; **eine Menge Geld** a lot of money; 2 crowd; 3 set (*in maths*).

Mensch der (PL die Menschen) 1 human being; 2 person; **kein Mensch** nobody; **jeder Mensch** everybody; 3 **die Menschen** people; **wie viele Menschen?** how many people?; 4 (*as an exclamation*) **Mensch!** (*informal*) wow!, hey!; **Mensch, hab ich mich geärgert!** (*informal*) I was damn annoyed.

menschenleer *adjective* deserted.

Menschenverstand der **gesunder Menschenverstand** common sense.

Menschheit die mankind.

menschlich *adjective* 1 human; 2 humane.

△ NEW SPELLING: *See page xii*

Mentalität *die* (PL *die* **Mentalitäten**) mentality.

Menü *das* (PL *die* **Menüs**) 1 menu; 2 set meal.

merken *verb* (PERF **hat gemerkt**) 1 to notice; 2 **sich etwas merken** to remember something.

Merkmal *das* (PL *die* **Merkmale**) feature.

merkwürdig *adjective* strange, odd.

Messe *die* (PL *die* **Messen**) 1 mass; 2 trade fair.

messen ✧ *verb* (PRES **misst** △, IMPERF **maß**, PERF **hat gemessen**) 1 to measure; **(bei jemandem) Fieber messen** to take somebody's temperature; 2 **sich mit jemandem messen können** to be as good as somebody.

Messer *das* (PL *die* **Messer**) knife.

Messing *das* brass.

Metall *das* (PL *die* **Metalle**) metal.

Meter *der* (PL *die* **Meter**) metre.

Metermaß *das* (PL *die* **Metermaße**) tape measure.

Methode *die* (PL *die* **Methoden**) method.

metrisch *adjective* metric.

Metzger *der* (PL *die* **Metzger**) butcher.

Metzgerei *die* (PL *die* **Metzgereien**) butcher's (shop).

Mexiko *das* Mexico.

miauen *verb* (PERF **hat miaut**) to miaow.

mich *pronoun* 1 me; 2 myself.

mied SEE **meiden**.

Miete *die* (PL *die* **Mieten**) 1 rent; **zur Miete wohnen** to live in rented accommodation; 2 hire charge.

mieten *verb* (PERF **hat gemietet**) 1 to rent; 2 to hire.

Mieter *der* (PL *die* **Mieter**) tenant.

Mieterin *die* (PL *die* **Mieterinnen**) tenant.

Mietshaus *das* (PL *die* **Mietshäuser**) block of rented flats.

Mietvertrag *der* (PL *die* **Mietverträge**) lease.

Mietwagen *der* (PL *die* **Mietwagen**) hire car.

Mikrofon *das* (PL *die* **Mikrofone**) microphone.

Mikroskop *das* (PL *die* **Mikroskope**) microscope.

Mikrowellenherd *der* (PL *die* **Mikrowellenherde**) microwave oven.

Milch *die* milk.

mild *adjective* mild.

Militär *das* army.

militärisch *adjective* military.

Milliarde *die* (PL *die* **Milliarden**) thousand million, billion.

Millimeter *der* (PL *die* **Millimeter**) millimetre.

Million *die* (PL *die* **Millionen**) million.

✧ IRREGULAR VERB: *See the verb table in the centre of the dictionary*

Millionär der (PL die **Millionäre**) millionaire.

Millionärin die (PL die **Millionärinnen**) millionairess.

Minderheit die (PL die **Minderheiten**) minority.

minderjährig adjective under age.

mindestens adverb at least.

mindester, mindeste, mindestes adjective least.
pronoun 1 der/die/das Mindeste Δ the least; zum Mindesten Δ at least; 2 nicht im Mindesten Δ not in the least.

Mine die (PL die **Minen**) 1 mine; 2 lead (in a pencil); 3 refill (for a ball-point).

Mineralwasser das (PL die **Mineralwasser**) mineral water.

Minirock der (PL die **Miniröcke**) miniskirt.

Minister der (PL die **Minister**) minister.

Ministerin die (PL die **Ministerinnen**) minister.

Ministerium das (PL die **Ministerien**) ministry, department.

minus adverb minus.

Minute die (PL die **Minuten**) minute.

mir pronoun 1 me, to me; 2 myself.

mischen verb (PERF hat gemischt) 1 to mix; 2 die Karten mischen to shuffle the cards; 3 sich mischen to mix.

Mischung die (PL die **Mischungen**) 1 mixture; 2 blend.

miserabel adjective (informal) 1 hopeless; 2 dreadful.

missbilligen Δ verb (PERF hat missbilligt) to disapprove.

Missbrauch Δ der abuse.

missbrauchen Δ verb (PERF hat missbraucht) to abuse.

Misserfolg Δ der (PL die **Misserfolge**) failure.

Missgeschick Δ das (PL die **Missgeschicke**) 1 misfortune; 2 mishap.

misshandeln Δ verb (PRES hat misshandelt) to ill-treat.

misslingen Δ ◇ verb (IMPERF misslang, PERF ist misslungen) to fail; es misslang ihr she failed.

misst Δ SEE **messen**.

Misstrauen Δ das 1 mistrust; 2 distrust.

misstrauen Δ verb (PERF hat misstraut) jemandem misstrauen to mistrust somebody.

misstrauisch Δ adjective suspicious.

Missverständnis Δ das (PL die **Missverständnisse**) misunderstanding.

missverstehen Δ ◇ verb (IMPERF missverstand, PERF hat missverstanden) to misunderstand.

Mist der 1 manure; 2 (informal) rubbish.

Mistel die (PL die **Misteln**) mistletoe.

Δ NEW SPELLING: See page xii

mit *preposition* ←(+DAT) **1** with; **2 mit der Bahn fahren** to go by train; **3 mit sechs Jahren** at the age of six; **4 mit jemandem sprechen** to speak to somebody; **5 mit Bleistift** in pencil; **6 mit lauter Stimme** in a loud voice. *adverb* as well, too; **warst du mit dabei?** were you there too?

Mitarbeiter *der* (PL *die* **Mitarbeiter**) **1** colleague; **2** employee.

Mitarbeiterin *die* (PL *die* **Mitarbeiterinnen**) **1** colleague; **2** employee.

mitbringen ✧ *verb* (IMPERF **brachte mit**, PERF **hat mitgebracht**) to bring, to bring along; **ich bringe den Kindern Schokolade mit** I'm taking the children some chocolate.

miteinander *adverb* with each other, with one another.

Mitesser *der* (PL *die* **Mitesser**) blackhead.

mitfahren ✧ *verb* (PRES **fährt mit**, IMPERF **fuhr mit**, PERF **ist mitgefahren**) **1 mit jemandem mitfahren** to go with somebody; **die Kinder fahren mit uns mit** the children are coming with us; **2 bei jemandem mitfahren** to get a lift with somebody; **jemanden mitfahren lassen** to give somebody a lift.

mitgeben ✧ *verb* (PRES **gibt mit**, IMPERF **gab mit**, PERF **hat mitgegeben**) to give.

Mitglied *das* (PL *die* **Mitglieder**) member.

mithalten ✧ *verb* (PRES **hält mit**, IMPERF **hielt mit**, PERF **hat mitgehalten**) to keep up.

mitkommen ✧ *verb* (IMPERF **kam mit**, PERF **ist mitgekommen**) **1** to come too; **2** to keep up.

Mitleid *das* pity; **kein Mitleid mit jemandem haben** not to feel any sympathy for somebody.

mitmachen *verb* (PERF **hat mitgemacht**) **1** to join in; **hast du Lust, bei dem Spiel mitzumachen?** do you want to join in the game?; **2** to take part in; **3** to go through (*experiences, troubles*); **sie hat viel mitgemacht** she's gone through a lot.

mitnehmen ✧ *verb* (PRES **nimmt mit**, IMPERF **nahm mit**, PERF **hat mitgenommen**) **1** to take, to take along; **Anni hat die Kinder auf den Spielplatz mitgenommen** Anni has taken the children to the playground; **2** to give a lift to; **3** to affect (badly); **4 zum Mitnehmen** to take away.

Mitschüler *der* (PL *die* **Mitschüler**) schoolfriend.

Mitschülerin *die* (PL *die* **Mitschülerinnen**) schoolfriend.

mitspielen *verb* (PERF **hat mitgespielt**) **1** to play; **wer spielt bei dem Fußballspiel mit?** who's playing in the football match?; **willst du mitspielen?** do you want to join in?; **2 in einem Film mitspielen** to be in a film.

Mittag *der* (PL *die* **Mittage**) **1** midday; **2** lunch; **zu Mittag essen** to have lunch; **3** lunch-break.

✧ IRREGULAR VERB: *See the verb table in the centre of the dictionary*

Mittagessen *das* (PL *die* Mittagessen) lunch; **beim Mittagessen** at lunch.

mittags *adverb* **1** at lunchtime, at midday; **2 um zwölf Uhr mittags** at noon.

Mittagspause *die* (PL *die* Mittagspausen) lunch-break.

Mitte *die* (PL *die* Mitten) **1** middle; **2** centre.

Mitteilung *die* (PL *die* Mitteilungen) **1** announcement; **2** communication.

Mittel *das* (PL *die* Mittel) **1** means; **2 ein Mittel gegen Husten** a cough remedy; **3 öffentliche Mittel** public funds.

Mittelalter *das* Middle Ages.

mittelgroß *adjective* medium-sized.

mittelmäßig *adjective* mediocre.

Mittelmeer *das* Mediterranean.

Mittelpunkt *der* (PL *die* Mittelpunkte) centre; **im Mittelpunkt stehen** to be the centre of attention.

Mittelstand *der* middle class.

Mittelstürmer *der* (PL *die* Mittelstürmer) centre-forward.

mitten *adverb* **mitten in/auf** in the middle of; **mitten in der Nacht** in the middle of the night.

Mitternacht *die* midnight.

mittlerer, mittlere, mittleres *adjective* **1** middle; **2** medium (*quality, size*); **3** average.

mittlerweile *adverb* **1** meanwhile; **2** by now.

Mittwoch *der* (PL *die* Mittwoche) Wednesday.

mittwochs *adverb* on Wednesdays.

Möbel *plural noun* furniture.

Möbelwagen *der* (PL *die* Möbelwagen) removal van.

Mobiltelefon *das* (PL *die* Mobiltelefone) mobile phone.

möbliert *adjective* furnished.

mochte, möchte SEE **mögen**.

Mode *die* (PL *die* Moden) fashion.

Modell *das* (PL *die* Modelle) model.

Moderator *der* (PL *die* Moderatoren) presenter (*on TV*).

Moderatorin *die* (PL *die* Moderatorinnen) presenter (*on TV*).

modern *adjective* modern.

modernisieren *verb* (PERF **hat modernisiert**) to modernize.

modisch *adjective* fashionable.

Mofa *die* (PL *die* Mofas) moped.

mogeln *verb* (PERF **hat gemogelt**) to cheat.

mögen ◇ *verb* (PRES **mag**, IMPERF **mochte**, PERF **hat gemocht**) **1** to like; **ich mag ihn nicht** I don't like him; **ich möchte** I'd like; **ich möchte gern wissen** I'd like to know; **möchtest du nach Hause?** would you like to go home?; **2 lieber mögen** to prefer; **ich möchte lieber Tee** I would prefer tea; **3 etwas nicht tun mögen** not to want to do

△ NEW SPELLING: *See page xii*

something; **ich mag nicht fragen** I don't want to ask; **ich mag nicht mehr** I've had enough; **4 das mag sein** maybe; **5 was mag das sein?** whatever can it be?

möglich *adjective* possible; **alles Mögliche** all sorts of things.

möglicherweise *adverb* possibly.

Möglichkeit *die* (PL *die* **Möglichkeiten**) possibility.

möglichst *adverb* if possible; **möglichst früh** as early as possible.

Möhre *die* (PL *die* **Möhren**) carrot.

Molekül *das* (PL *die* **Moleküle**) molecule.

Moment *der* (PL *die* **Momente**) moment; **im Moment** at the moment; **Moment (mal)!** just a moment!

Monat *der* (PL *die* **Monate**) month.

monatelang *adverb* for months.

monatlich *adjective, adverb* monthly.

Mönch *der* (PL *die* **Mönche**) monk.

Mond *der* (PL *die* **Monde**) moon.

Mondschein *der* moonlight; **im Mondschein** by moonlight.

Montag *der* (PL *die* **Montage**) Monday.

montags *adverb* on Mondays.

Moped *das* (PL *die* **Mopeds**) moped.

Moral *die* **1** moral; **2** morale; **3** morals.

moralisch *adjective* moral.

Mord *der* (PL *die* **Morde**) murder.

Mörder *der* (PL *die* **Mörder**) murderer.

Mörderin *die* (PL *die* **Mörderinnen**) murderer.

morgen *adverb* tomorrow; **morgen Abend** tomorrow evening.

Morgen *der* (PL *die* **Morgen**) morning; **am Morgen** in the morning; **heute Morgen** △ this morning; **guten Morgen!** good morning!

morgens *adverb* in the morning.

Moschee *die* (PL *die* **Moscheen**) mosque.

Mosel *die* (River) Moselle.

Moslem *der* (PL *die* **Moslems**) Muslim.

moslemisch *adjective* Muslim.

Moskau *das* Moscow.

Moslime *die* (PL *die* **Moslimen**) Muslim.

Motiv *das* (PL *die* **Motive**) **1** motive; **2** motif.

Motor *der* (PL *die* **Motoren**) engine, motor.

Motorrad *das* (PL *die* **Motorräder**) motorcycle, motorbike.

Möwe *die* (PL *die* **Möwen**) seagull.

Mücke *die* (PL *die* **Mücken**) **1** midge; **2** mosquito.

müde *adjective* tired.

Müdigkeit *die* tiredness.

Mühe *die* (PL *die* **Mühen**) **1** effort;

✧ IRREGULAR VERB: *See the verb table in the centre of the dictionary*

sich Muhe geben to make an effort, 2 trouble; **machen Sie sich keine Mühe** don't go to any trouble; **3 mit Müh und Not** only just.

Mühle *die* (PL *die* **Mühlen**) 1 mill; 2 grinder (*for coffee*).

mühsam *adjective* laborious.

Müll *der* rubbish.

Müllabfuhr *die* refuse collection.

Mülleimer *der* (PL *die* **Mülleimer**) rubbish bin.

Mülltonne *die* (PL *die* **Mülltonnen**) dustbin.

Mumps *der* mumps.

München *das* Munich.

Mund *der* (PL *die* **Münder**) mouth; **halt den Mund!** (*informal*) shut up!

Mundharmonika *die* (PL *die* **Mundharmonikas**) mouth organ.

mündlich *adjective* oral.

Münster *das* (PL *die* **Münster**) cathedral.

Münze *die* (PL *die* **Münzen**) coin.

Münzfernsprecher *der* (PL *die* **Münzfernsprecher**) payphone.

murmeln *verb* (PERF **hat gemurmelt**) to mumble.

mürrisch *adjective* surly.

Muschel *die* (PL *die* **Muscheln**) 1 mussel; 2 (sea) shell; 3 mouthpiece (*of a phone*).

Museum *das* (PL *die* **Museen**) museum.

Musik *die* music.

musikalisch *adjective* musical.

Musiker *der* (PL *die* **Musiker**) musician.

Musikerin *die* (PL *die* **Musikerinnen**) musician.

Muskat *der* nutmeg.

Muskel *der* (PL *die* **Muskeln**) muscle.

Müsli *das* muesli.

muss △ SEE **müssen**.

müssen ✧ *verb* (PRES **muss** △, IMPERF **musste** △, PERF **hat gemusst** △) 1 **etwas tun müssen** to have to do something; **sie muss es tun** she's got to do it, she must do it; **muss ich?** do I have to?; **muss das sein?** is that necessary?; 2 **Sie müssten es mal versuchen** you should try it; 3 **sie müssen gleich hier sein** they'll be here at any moment; 4 **ich muss mal** (*informal*) I need (to go to) the loo.

Muster *das* (PL *die* **Muster**) 1 pattern; 2 sample.

Mut *der* courage; **jemandem Mut machen** to encourage somebody.

mutig *adjective* courageous.

Mutter[1] *die* (PL *die* **Mütter**) mother.

Mutter[2] *die* (PL *die* **Muttern**) nut.

Muttersprache *die* (PL *die* **Muttersprachen**) mother tongue, native language.

Muttertag der (PL die **Muttertage**)
Mother's Day.

Mutti die (PL die **Muttis**) mum.

Mütze die (PL die **Mützen**) cap.

MwSt. (*Mehrwertsteuer*) VAT.

Mythos der (PL die **Mythen**) myth.

N n

na *exclamation* well; **na und?** so
what?; **na gut** all right then.

Nabel der (PL die **Nabel**) navel.

nach *preposition* ←(+DAT) **1** to; **nach
Hause gehen** to go home; **nach
oben** up; **nach hinten** back; **nach
rechts abbiegen** to turn right;
2 after; **nach Ihnen** after you; **zehn
nach eins** ten past one; **nach etwas
greifen** to reach for something;
3 according to; **meiner Meinung
nach** in my opinion.
adverb **nach und nach** bit by bit,
gradually; **nach wie vor** still.

nachahmen *verb* (PERF **hat
nachgeahmt**) to imitate.

Nachbar der (PL die **Nachbarn**)
neighbour.

Nachbarin die (PL die
Nachbarinnen) neighbour.

Nachbarschaft die
neighbourhood.

nachdem *conjunction* **1** after; **2 je
nachdem** it depends; **je nachdem,
wie schnell du damit fertig wirst** it

depends on how quicky you can
finish it.

nachdenken ✧ *verb* (IMPERF
dachte nach, PERF **hat
nachgedacht**) to think; **über etwas
nachdenken** to think about
something; **ich habe lange über ihr
Angebot nachgedacht und mich
schließlich dagegen entschieden**
I've thought a long time about her
offer and finally decided against it.

nachdenklich *adjective*
thoughtful.

nacheinander *adverb* one after the
other; **die Bewerber kamen
nacheinander herein** the
applicants came in one after the
other.

Nachfrage die (PL die **Nachfragen**)
demand; **es besteht keine
Nachfrage** there's no demand for it.

nachgehen ✧ *verb* (IMPERF **ging
nach**, PERF **ist nachgegangen**) **1** to
be slow; **meine Uhr geht nach** my
watch is slow; **2 jemandem
nachgehen** to follow somebody;
einer Sache nachgehen to look
into something.

nachher *adverb* afterwards; **erst
gehen wir ins Kino und nachher
könnten wir essen gehen** we go to
the cinema first and afterwards we
could go for a meal; **bis nachher!**
see you later!

nachholen *verb* (PERF **hat
nachgeholt**) **1** to catch up on; **ich
hatte Grippe und muss jetzt viel
Mathe nachholen** I've had flu and
now I've got a lot of maths to catch
up on; **2** to make up for (*something*

✧ IRREGULAR VERB: *See the verb table in the centre of the dictionary*

missed); **3 eine Prüfung nachholen** to do an exam at a later date.

Nachtklub *der* (PL *die* **Nachtklubs**) night club.

nachkommen ✧ *verb* (IMPERF **kam nach**, PERF **ist nachgekommen**) **1** to come later, to follow; **2 ich komme nicht nach** I can't keep up; **3 einem Versprechen nachkommen** to carry out a promise; **seinen Verpflichtungen nachkommen** to meet your commitments.

nachlassen ✧ *verb* (PRES **lässt nach** △, IMPERF **ließ nach**, PERF **hat nachgelassen**) **1** to ease; **meine Zahnschmerzen lassen langsam nach** my toothache is getting better; **2** to let up; **sobald die Kälte nachlässt** as soon as it gets warmer; **3** to deteriorate; **4 etwas vom Preis nachlassen** to take something off the price; **jemandem zwanzig Mark nachlassen** to give somebody twenty marks off.

nachlässig *adjective* careless.

nachlaufen ✧ *verb* (PRES **läuft nach**, IMPERF **lief nach**, PERF **ist nachgelaufen**) **jemandem nachlaufen** to run after somebody; **Philipp läuft allen Mädchen nach** (*informal*) Philipp chases all the girls.

nachmachen *verb* (PERF **hat nachgemacht**) to copy.

Nachmittag *der* (PL *die* **Nachmittage**) afternoon.

nachmittags *adverb* in the afternoon.

Nachnahme *die* **per Nachnahme** cash on delivery.

Nachname *der* (PL *die* **Nachnamen**) surname.

nachprüfen *verb* (PERF **hat nachgeprüft**) to check; **er prüft nach, ob es stimmt** he's going to check if it is correct.

Nachricht *die* (PL *die* **Nachrichten**) **1** news; **ich warte noch immer auf eine Nachricht von ihm** I'm still waiting for news of him; **eine Nachricht hinterlassen** to leave a message; **2 die Nachrichten** the news; **das kam in den Nachrichten** it was on the news.

Nachrichtensprecher *der* (PL *die* **Nachrichtensprecher**) newsreader.

Nachrichtensprecherin *der* (PL *die* **Nachrichtensprecherinnen**) newsreader.

nachschlagen ✧ *verb* (PRES **schlägt nach**, IMPERF **schlug nach**, PERF **hat nachgeschlagen**) to look up.

nachsehen ✧ *verb* (PRES **sieht nach**, IMPERF **sah nach**, PERF **hat nachgesehen**) **1** to check; **sieh nach, wer da ist** go and see who's there; **2** to look up; **3 jemandem etwas nachsehen** to let somebody get away with something.

nachsitzen ✧ *verb* (IMPERF **saß nach**, PERF **hat nachgesessen**) to be in detention; **Jan muss nachsitzen** Jan has detention.

Nachspeise *die* (PL *die* **Nachspeisen**) dessert, pudding.

△ NEW SPELLING: *See page xii*

nächste SEE **nächster**.

nächstens *adverb* shortly.

nächster, nächste, nächstes
adjective 1 next; 2 nearest; **am nächsten sein** to be nearest; 3 **in nächster Nähe** close by.
pronoun **der/die/das Nächste** △ (the) next; **als Nächstes** △ next.

Nacht *die* (PL *die* **Nächte**) night.

Nachteil *der* (PL *die* **Nachteile**) disadvantage.

Nachtfalter *der* (PL *die* **Nachtfalter**) moth.

Nachthemd *das* (PL *die* **Nachthemden**) nightdress, nightshirt.

Nachtigall *die* (PL *die* **Nachtigallen**) nightingale.

Nachtisch *der* (PL *die* **Nachtische**) dessert, pudding.

Nachtleben *das* nightlife.

nachträglich *adjective*
1 subsequent; 2 belated.
adverb 1 later; 2 belatedly.

nachts *adverb* at night; **um zwei Uhr nachts** at two o'clock in the morning.

Nacken *der* (PL *die* **Nacken**) neck.

nackt *adjective* 1 naked; 2 bare.

Nadel *die* (PL *die* **Nadeln**) 1 needle; 2 pin.

Nagel *der* (PL *die* **Nägel**) nail.

Nagelbürste *die* (PL *die* **Nagelbürsten**) nailbrush.

Nagelfeile *die* (PL *die* **Nagelfeilen**) nailfile.

Nagellack *der* (PL *die* **Nagellacke**) nail varnish.

nagelneu *adjective* brand-new.

Nagelschere *die* (PL *die* **Nagelscheren**) nail scissors.

nahe, nah *adjective, adverb* 1 near, nearby; **der Nahe Osten** the Middle East; **nahe daran sein, etwas zu tun** to nearly do something; 2 close; **nahe bei** close to; **nahe verwandt sein** to be closely related; 3 **jemandem nahe legen** △, **etwas zu tun** to urge somebody to do something; 4 **nahe liegend** △ obvious.
preposition ←(+DAT) near, close to.

Nähe *die* 1 proximity; 2 **in der Nähe der Kirche** near the church; **ganz in der Nähe** nearby; 3 **aus der Nähe** close up.

nahelegen, naheliegend SEE **nahe**.

nähen *verb* (PERF **hat genäht**) 1 to sew; 2 to stitch (*a wound*).

näher *adjective* 1 closer; 2 **nähere Einzelheiten** further details; 3 shorter (*way, road*).
adverb 1 closer; **näher kommen** to come closer; 2 more closely; 3 **Näheres** further details.

nähern *verb* (PERF **hat sich genähert**) **sich nähern** to approach.

Nähgarn *das* cotton.

nahm SEE **nehmen**.

✧ IRREGULAR VERB: *See the verb table in the centre of the dictionary*

Nähmaschine *die* (PL *die* **Nähmaschinen**) sewing machine.

Nahrung *die* food.

Naht *die* (PL *die* **Nähte**) seam.

Nahverkehrszug *der* (PL *die* **Nahverkehrszüge**) local train.

Name *der* (PL *die* **Namen**) name.

nämlich *adverb* 1 because; 2 namely; 3 **das war nämlich ganz anders** it was quite different actually.

nannte SEE **nennen**.

nanu *exclamation* well, well!

Narbe *die* (PL *die* **Narben**) scar.

Narr *der* (PL *die* **Narren**) fool.

Närrin *die* (PL *die* **Närrinnen**) fool.

Nase *die* (PL *die* **Nasen**) nose; **die Nase voll haben** (*informal*) to have had enough.

Nasenbluten *das* nosebleed.

Nashorn *das* (PL *die* **Nashörner**) rhinoceros.

nass △ *adjective* wet.

Nation *die* (PL *die* **Nationen**) nation.

Nationalhymne *die* (PL *die* **Nationalhymnen**) national anthem.

Nationalität *die* (PL *die* **Nationalitäten**) nationality.

Natur *die* 1 nature; **von Natur aus** by nature; 2 **die freie Natur** the open countryside.

natürlich *adjective* natural. *adverb* of course, naturally.

Naturschutzgebiet *das* (PL *die* **Naturschutzgebiete**) nature reserve.

Naturwissenschaft *die* natural science.

Nebel *der* (PL *die* **Nebel**) 1 fog; 2 mist.

nebelig *adjective* = **neblig**.

neben *preposition* ←(+DAT, *or* +ACC *with movement towards a place*) 1 next to; **er hat neben mir gesessen** he sat next to me; **er hat sich neben mich gesetzt** he sat down next to me; 2 apart from.

nebenan *adverb* next door.

nebenbei *adverb* 1 as well, at the same time; **er liest die Zeitung und hört nebenbei Musik** he reads the newspaper and listens to music at the same time; 2 on the side; **nebenbei arbeite ich noch in einem Blumengeschäft** I work in a florist's on the side; **das mache ich so nebenbei** (*informal*) that's just a sideline; 3 in passing; **nebenbei bemerkt** by the way.

nebeneinander *adverb* next to each other.

nebenhergehen ◇ *verb* (IMPERF **ging nebenher**, PERF **ist nebenhergegangen**) to walk alongside.

neblig *adjective* 1 foggy; 2 misty.

necken *verb* (PERF **hat geneckt**) to tease.

Neffe *der* (PL *die* **Neffen**) nephew.

negativ *adjective* negative.

Negativ *das* (PL *die* **Negative**) negative.

nehmen ✧ *verb* (PRES **nimmt**, IMPERF **nahm**, PERF **hat genommen**) **1** to take; **2 ich nehme eine Suppe** I'll have soup; **3 was nehmen Sie dafür?** how much do you want for it?; **4 jemanden zu sich nehmen** to have somebody live with you; **5 sich etwas nehmen** to take something; **nimm dir ein Stück Kuchen** help yourself to a piece of cake.

Neid *der* envy, jealousy.

neidisch *adjective* envious, jealous.

nein *adverb* no.

Nelke *die* (PL *die* **Nelken**) carnation.

nennen ✧ *verb* (IMPERF **nannte**, PERF **hat genannt**) **1** to call; **2** to name; **3 ihr Name wurde nicht genannt** her name wasn't mentioned; **4 sich nennen** to call yourself.

Nerv *der* (PL *die* **Nerven**) nerve; **Gabi geht mir auf die Nerven** Gabi gets on my nerves.

nervös *adjective* nervous.

Nervosität *die* nervousness.

Nessel *die* (PL *die* **Nesseln**) nettle.

Nest *das* (PL *die* **Nester**) **1** nest; **2** little place (*a village*).

nett *adjective* nice.

netto *adverb* net.

Netz *das* (PL *die* **Netze**) **1** net; **2** network; **3** string bag; **4** (*spider's*) web.

neu *adjective* **1** new; **wie neu** as good as new; **neue Sprachen** modern

languages; **2 seit neuestem** recently; **3 die neueste Mode** the latest fashion; **das Neueste** the latest news; **4 das ist mir neu** that's news to me.
adverb **1** newly; **2** only just; **es ist neu eingetroffen** it has only just come in; **3 etwas neu schreiben** to rewrite something.

neuartig *adjective* new; **ein neuartiger Flaschenöffner** a new kind of bottle opener.

neuerdings *adverb* recently.

Neugier *die* curiosity.

neugierig *adjective* curious, inquisitive.

Neuigkeit *die* (PL *die* **Neuigkeiten**) piece of news; **gibt es irgendwelche Neuigkeiten?** is there any news?

Neujahr *das* New Year, New Year's Day.

neulich *adverb* the other day.

neun *number* nine.

neunter, neunte, neuntes *adjective* ninth.

neunzehn *number* nineteen.

neunzig *number* ninety.

Neuseeland *das* New Zealand.

nicht *adverb* **1** not; **ich kann nicht** I can't; **Iris hat nicht angerufen** Iris didn't ring; **bitte nicht** please don't; **nicht!** don't!; **nicht berühren!** don't touch!; **2 'ich mag das nicht'** – **'ich auch nicht'** 'I don't like it' – 'neither do I'; **3 nicht (wahr)?** isn't he/she/it?; **du kennst ihn doch,**

✧ IRREGULAR VERB: *See the verb table in the centre of the dictionary*

nicht? you know him, don't you?;
4 gar nicht not at all; **5 nicht mehr**
no more.

Nichte *die* (PL *die* **Nichten**) niece.

Nichtraucher *der* (PL *die*
Nichtraucher) non-smoker.

nichts *pronoun* **1** nothing; **2 ich
habe nichts gewusst** I didn't know
anything; **3 nichts mehr** no more;
4 das macht nichts it doesn't
matter; **5 nichts ahnend** Δ
unsuspecting.

nichtsahnend SEE **nichts**.

nicken *verb* (PERF **hat genickt**) to
nod.

Nickerchen *das* (PL *die*
Nickerchen) nap; **ein Nickerchen
machen** to have a nap.

nie *adverb* never.

nieder *adjective* low.
adverb down.

Niederlage *die* (PL *die* **Niederlagen**)
defeat.

Niederlande *plural noun* **die
Niederlande** the Netherlands.

Niederländer *der* (PL *die*
Niederländer) Dutchman; **die
Niederländer** the Dutch.

Niederländerin *die* (PL *die*
Niederländerinnen) Dutchwoman.

niederländisch *adjective* Dutch.

niedlich *adjective* sweet.

niedrig *adjective* **1** low; **2** base.

niemals *adverb* never.

niemand *pronoun* nobody; **wir
haben niemand** *or* **niemanden
gesehen** we didn't see anybody.

Niere *die* (PL *die* **Nieren**) kidney.

nieseln *verb* (PERF **hat genieselt**) to
drizzle; **es nieselt** it's drizzling.

niesen *verb* (PERF **hat geniest**) to
sneeze.

Nilpferd *das* (PL *die* **Nilpferde**)
hippopotamus.

nimmt SEE **nehmen**.

nirgends, nirgendwo *adverb*
nowhere.

Niveau *das* (PL *die* **Niveaus**) **1** level;
2 standard.

noch *adverb* **1** still; **immer noch**
still; **2** even; **noch besser** even
better; **3 noch nicht** not yet; **noch
nie** never; **4 gerade noch** only
just; **5 wer war noch da?** who else
was there?; **was noch?** what else?;
6 noch einmal again; **7 noch ein
Bier** another beer; **noch etwas
Kaffee?** (would you like some) more
coffee?; **8 noch gestern** only
yesterday; **9 noch und noch Geld**
loads of money.
conjunction nor; **weder ... noch**
neither ... nor

nochmals *adverb* again.

Nominativ *der* (PL *die* **Nominative**)
nominative.

Nordamerika *das* North America.

Norden *der* north.

Nordirland *das* Northern Ireland.

nördlich *adjective* **1** northern;
2 northerly (*direction*).

Δ NEW SPELLING: *See page xii*

adverb, preposition ←(+GEN)
nördlich von Wien to the north of
Vienna; **nördlich der Stadt** north of
the town.

Nordosten *der* north-east.

Nordpol *der* North Pole.

Nordsee *die* North Sea.

Nordwesten *der* north-west.

nörgeln *verb* (PERF **hat genörgelt**) to
grumble.

Norm *die* (PL *die* **Normen**) 1 norm;
2 standard.

normal *adjective* normal.

normalerweise *adverb* normally.

Norwegen *das* Norway.

Norweger *der* (PL *die* **Norweger**)
Norwegian.

Norwegerin *die* (PL *die*
Norwegerinnen) Norwegian.

norwegisch *adjective* Norwegian.

Not *die* (PL *die* **Nöte**) 1 need; **zur Not**
if necessary, at a pinch; **mit knapper
Not** only just; 2 hardship.

Notausgang *der* (PL *die*
Notausgänge) emergency exit.

Notdienst *der* **Notdienst haben** to
be on call.

Note *die* (PL *die* **Noten**) 1 note; **Noten
lesen** to read music; 2 mark.

Notfall *der* (PL *die* **Notfälle**)
emergency.

notfalls *adverb* if need be.

notieren *verb* (PERF **hat notiert**) 1 to

note down; **2 sich etwas notieren**
to make a note of something.

nötig *adjective* necessary.
adverb urgently.

Notiz *die* (PL *die* **Notizen**) 1 note;
2 keine Notiz von etwas nehmen
to take no notice of something;
3 item (*in a newspaper*).

Notizblock *der* (PL *die* **Notizblöcke**)
notepad.

Notizbuch *das* (PL *die* **Notizbücher**)
notebook.

Notlage *die* (PL *die* **Notlagen**) crisis.

Notruf *der* (PL *die* **Notrufe**)
1 emergency call; 2 emergency
number.

notwendig *adjective* necessary.

November *der* November.

nüchtern *adjective* 1 sober; **wieder
nüchtern werden** to sober up;
2 auf nüchternen Magen on an
empty stomach; 3 down-to-earth.

Nudeln *plural noun* 1 noodles;
2 pasta.

null *number* 1 nought; **unter null**
below zero; 2 nil; **zwei zu null** two
nil; 3 love (*in tennis*); **4 null Fehler
haben** to have no mistakes; **ich habe
null Ahnung** (*informal*) I haven't
got a clue; **5 in null Komma nichts**
(*informal*) in less than no time.

Null *die* (PL *die* **Nullen**) 1 zero,
nought; 2 failure.

numerieren = **nummerieren**.

Nummer *die* (PL *die* **Nummern**)
1 number; 2 issue (*of a magazine*);

◇ IRREGULAR VERB: *See the verb table in the centre of the dictionary*

3 size (*of clothing*); 4 act; 5 auf
Nummer sicher gehen to play safe.

nummerieren△ *verb* (PERF **hat
nummeriert**) to number.

Nummernschild *das* (PL *die*
Nummernschilder) number plate.

nun *adverb* now.
exclamation well; **nun ja** ... well,
yes ...

nur *adverb* 1 only; 2 **was sollen wir
nur tun?** what on earth are we going
to do?; **sie soll es nur versuchen!**
just let her try!; 3 **nur zu!** go ahead!

Nürnberg *das* Nuremberg.

Nuss△ *die* (PL *die* **Nüsse**) nut.

Nutzen *der* benefit; **von Nutzen
sein** to be useful.

nutzen, nützen *verb* (PERF **hat
genutzt/genützt**) 1 to use; **etwas
nutzen** to take advantage of
something; 2 to be useful; 3 **nichts
nutzen** to be no use; **das nutzt mir
nichts** that won't help me; 4 **das
nutzt ja doch nichts** it's pointless.

nützlich *adjective* useful.

nutzlos *adjective* useless.

O o

ob *conjunction* 1 whether; **wissen
Sie, ob heute noch ein Zug nach
Freising fährt?** do you know if there
is another train to Freising today?;
2 **ob Alex noch anruft?** I wonder if
Alex will ring; 3 **und ob!** you bet!

obdachlos *adjective* homeless.

Obdachlose *der/die* (PL *die*
Obdachlosen) homeless person; **die
Obdachlosen** the homeless.

oben *adverb* 1 on top; **oben auf** on
top of; **die Vase steht oben auf dem
Schrank** the vase is on top of the
cupboard; 2 at the top; **von oben bis
unten** from top to bottom; **er hat
uns von oben bis unten gemustert**
he looked us up and down;
3 upstairs; 4 **nach oben** up,
upstairs; **er ist nach oben in sein
Zimmer gegangen** he went up into
his room; **geht der Fahrstuhl nach
oben?** is the lift going up?; **hier
oben** up here; **da oben** up there;
5 **siehe oben** see above (*on a page*);
oben erwähnt△ above mentioned;
6 **oben ohne** (*informal*) topless.

obenerwähnt SEE **oben**.

Ober *der* (PL *die* **Ober**) waiter; **Herr
Ober!** waiter!

oberer, obere, oberes *adjective*
upper, top.

Oberfläche *die* (PL *die*
Oberflächen) surface.

oberflächlich *adjective*
superficial.

Oberhaupt *das* (PL *die*
Oberhäupter) head.

Oberhemd *das* (PL *die*
Oberhemden) shirt.

Oberschenkel *der* (PL *die*
Oberschenkel) thigh.

Oberschule *die* (PL *die*
Oberschulen) secondary school.

△ NEW SPELLING: *See page xii*

oberster, oberste, oberstes
adjective top.

Oberstufe *die* (PL *die* **Oberstufen**)
upper school.

Oberweite *die* (PL *die* **Oberweiten**)
chest size, bust measurement.

Objekt *das* (PL *die* **Objekte**) object.

objektiv *adjective* objective.

Objektiv *das* (PL *die* **Objektive**) lens.

Obst *das* fruit.

Obstbaum *der* (PL *die* **Obstbäume**)
fruit tree.

Obstsalat *der* (PL *die* **Obstsalate**)
fruit salad.

obszön *adjective* obscene.

obwohl *conjunction* although.

öde *adjective* **1** desolate; **2** dreary;
das ist so ein furchtbar öder Job
it's such terribly dull job.

oder *conjunction* **1** or; **2 du kennst
sie doch, oder?** you know her, don't
you?

Ofen *der* (PL *die* **Öfen**) **1** oven;
2 stove; **3** heater.

offen *adjective* **1** open; **offen haben**
to be open; **Tag der offenen Tür**
open day; **2** frank; **3** vacant; **eine
offene Stelle** a vacancy; **4 offen
bleiben**△ to stay open; **5 offen
bleiben**△ to remain open (*of a
question, possibility*).
adverb **1** openly; **2** frankly; **offen
gesagt** frankly.

offenbar *adjective* obvious.
adverb **1** apparently; **2 da hast du
dich offenbar geirrt** you seem to

have made a mistake; **sie hat
offenbar den Zug verpasst** she
must have missed the train.

offenbleiben SEE **offen**.

offensichtlich *adjective* obvious.

öffentlich *adjective* public.

Öffentlichkeit *die* public; **in aller
Öffentlichkeit** in public.

offiziell *adjective* official.

Offizier *der* (PL *die* **Offiziere**) officer.

öffnen *verb* (PERF **hat geöffnet**) to
open; **jemandem die Tür öffnen** to
open the door for somebody.

Öffner *der* (PL *die* **Öffner**) opener.

Öffnung *die* (PL *die* **Öffnungen**)
opening.

Öffnungszeiten *plural noun*
opening times.

oft *adverb* often.

öfter, öfters *adverb* quite often; **ich
habe ihn öfters mal getroffen** I
used to meet him quite often.

ohne *preposition* ←(+ACC) **1** without;
ohne mich count me out; **2 ohne
weiteres** easily; **3 oben ohne**
(*informal*) topless; **4 das ist nicht
ohne** (*informal*) it's not bad.
conjunction without; **ohne zu
überlegen** without thinking.

Ohnmacht *die* **in Ohnmacht fallen**
to faint.

ohnmächtig *adjective*
1 unconscious; **2 ohnmächtig
werden** to faint; **Roswitha ist
ohnmächtig** Roswitha's fainted.

✧ IRREGULAR VERB: *See the verb table in the centre of the dictionary*

Ohr das (PL die Ohren) ear.

Ohrenschmerzen *plural noun* earache.

Ohrring der (PL die Ohrringe) earring.

oje *exclamation* oh dear!

Ökoladen der (PL die Ökoläden) health-food shop.

Ökologie die ecology.

ökologisch *adjective* ecological.

Oktober der October.

Öl das (PL die Öle) oil.

Ölfarbe die (PL die Ölfarben) oil-paint.

Ölgemälde das (PL die Ölgemälde) oil painting.

ölig *adjective* oily.

Olive die (PL die Oliven) olive.

Olivenöl das (PL die Olivenöle) olive oil.

Olympiade die (PL die Olympiaden) Olympic Games; **die Olympiade findet alle vier Jahre statt** the Olympic Games take place every four years.

olympisch *adjective* Olympic.

Oma die (PL die Omas) granny.

Omelett das (PL die Omeletts) omelette.

Omi die (PL die Omis) granny.

Onkel der (PL die Onkel) uncle.

Opa der (PL die Opas) grandpa.

Oper die (PL die Opern) opera.

Operation die (PL die Operationen) operation.

Operationssaal der (PL die Operationssäle) operating theatre.

operieren *verb* (PERF **hat operiert**) 1 to operate on; **sich operieren lassen** to have an operation; **sie wurde am Magen operiert** she had a stomach operation; 2 to operate.

Opfer das (PL die Opfer) 1 sacrifice; 2 victim; **das Erdbeben forderte viele Opfer** the earthquake claimed many victims.

Optiker der (PL die Optiker) optician.

Optikerin die (PL die Optikerinnen) optician.

Optimist der (PL die Optimisten) optimist.

optimistisch *adjective* optimistic.

orange *adjective* orange.

Orange die (PL die Orangen) orange.

Orangensaft der (PL die Orangensäfte) orange juice.

Orchester das (PL die Orchester) orchestra.

ordentlich *adjective* 1 tidy; 2 respectable; 3 proper (*meal, job, salary*); 4 **eine ordentliche Tracht Prügel** (*informal*) a good hiding. *adverb* 1 tidily; **ordentlich schreiben** to write neatly; 2 respectably; 3 properly; 4 **ordentlich feiern** (*informal*) to have a really good celebration; **wir sind ordentlich nass geworden** (*informal*) we got soaked.

ordinär *adjective* vulgar.

△ NEW SPELLING: *See page xii*

ordnen *verb* (PERF **hat geordnet**)
1 to arrange; 2 to put in order.

Ordner *der* (PL *die* **Ordner**) file.

Ordnung *die* 1 order; **Ordnung
halten** to keep order; 2 **Ordnung
machen** to tidy up; **die Wohnung in
Ordnung bringen** to tidy up the flat;
3 **mit der Waschmaschine ist etwas
nicht in Ordnung** there's something
wrong with the washing machine;
4 **etwas in Ordnung bringen** to put
something right; **die
Waschmaschine in Ordnung
bringen** to repair the washing
machine; 5 **in Ordnung!** okay!;
6 **er ist in Ordnung** he's all right.

Organ *das* (PL *die* **Organe**) 1 organ;
2 (*informal*) voice.

Organisation *die* (PL *die*
Organisationen) organization.

organisch *adjective* organic.

organisieren *verb* (PERF **hat
organisiert**) 1 to organize;
2 (*informal*) to get (hold of).

Orgel *die* (PL *die* **Orgeln**) organ.

orientieren *verb* (PERF **hat sich
orientiert**) 1 **sich orientieren** to get
your bearings; 2 **sich über etwas
orientieren** to inform yourself
about something.

Orientierung *die* 1 orientation;
die Orientierung verlieren to lose
your bearings; 2 **zu Ihrer
Orientierung** for your information.

Orientierungssinn *der* sense of
direction.

originell *adjective* original.

Orkan *der* (PL *die* **Orkane**) hurricane.

Ort *der* (PL *die* **Orte**) 1 place; **an Ort
und Stelle** on the spot; 2 (small)
town.

Orthografie △, **Orthographie**
die spelling.

örtlich *adjective* local.

Ortschaft *die* (PL *die* **Ortschaften**)
village.

Ortsgespräch *das* (PL *die*
Ortsgespräche) local call.

Ossi *der* (*informal*) (PL *die* **Ossis**)
East German.

Osten *der* east.

Osterei *das* (PL *die* **Ostereier**) Easter
egg.

Ostern *das* Easter.

Österreich *das* Austria.

Österreicher *der* (PL *die*
Österreicher) Austrian.

Österreicherin *die* (PL *die*
Österreicherinnen) Austrian.

österreichisch *adjective* Austrian.

östlich *adjective* 1 eastern;
2 easterly.
adverb, preposition ←(+GEN) **östlich
von Wien** to the east of Vienna;
östlich der Stadt east of the town.

Ostsee *die* Baltic (Sea).

oval *adjective* oval.

Ozean *der* (PL *die* **Ozeane**) ocean.

Ozon *das* ozone.

Ozonschicht *die* ozone layer.

✧ IRREGULAR VERB: *See the verb table in the centre of the dictionary*

P p

paar *pronoun* **ein paar** a few; **ein paar Mal** △ a few times; **alle paar Tage** every few days.

Paar *das* (PL *die* **Paare**) 1 pair; **ein Paar Schuhe** a pair of shoes; 2 couple.

paarmal SEE **paar**.

paarweise *adjective* in pairs; **die Kinder stellten sich paarweise auf** the children lined up in pairs.

Päckchen *das* (PL *die* **Päckchen**) 1 package, packet; 2 small parcel.

packen *verb* (PERF **hat gepackt**) 1 to pack; **ich muss jetzt meinen Koffer packen** I must pack my case now; 2 to grab (hold of); **von Furcht gepackt** seized with fear.

Packung *die* (PL *die* **Packungen**) packet, pack.

Pädagoge *der* (PL *die* **Pädagogen**) 1 educationalist; 2 teacher.

pädagogisch *adjective* educational.

Paddel *das* (PL *die* **Paddel**) paddle.

Paket *das* (PL *die* **Pakete**) 1 parcel; **Gabi hat mir ein Paket geschickt** Gabi sent me a parcel; 2 packet; **kaufe bitte ein Paket Waschpulver für mich** can you please buy a packet of washing powder for me.

Palast *der* (PL *die* **Paläste**) palace.

Palme *die* (PL *die* **Palmen**) palm (tree).

Pampelmuse *die* (PL *die* **Pampelmusen**) grapefruit.

Panik *die* panic; **in Panik geraten** to panic.

Panne *die* (PL *die* **Pannen**) 1 breakdown; **wir haben auf dem Rückweg eine Panne gehabt** we had a breakdown on the way back; 2 mishap; **uns ist eine Panne passiert** we had a mishap.

Papa *der* (PL *die* **Papas**) daddy.

Papagei *der* (PL *die* **Papageien**) parrot.

Papier *das* (PL *die* **Papiere**) paper.

Papierkorb *der* (PL *die* **Papierkörbe**) waste-paper basket.

Papiertüte *die* (PL *die* **Papiertüten**) paper bag.

Pappe *die* (PL *die* **Pappen**) cardboard.

Paprika *der* (PL *die* **Paprikas**) 1 pepper; 2 paprika.

Papst *der* (PL *die* **Päpste**) pope.

Parabolantenne *die* (PL *die* **Parabolantennen**) satellite dish.

Paradies *das* paradise.

Paragraph *der* (PL *die* **Paragraphen**) 1 section; 2 clause.

parallel *adjective* parallel.

Pärchen *das* (PL *die* **Pärchen**) couple.

Parfüm *das* (PL *die* **Parfüms**) perfume.

△ NEW SPELLING: *See page xii*

Park *der* (PL *die* **Parks**) park.

Parkanlage *die* (PL *die* **Parkanlagen**) park.

parken *verb* (PERF **hat geparkt**) to park.

Parkett *das* (PL *die* **Parkette**) 1 (*in a theatre*) stalls; 2 parquet floor.

Parkhaus *das* (PL *die* **Parkhäuser**) multi-storey car park.

Parklücke *die* (PL *die* **Parklücken**) parking space.

Parkplatz *der* (PL *die* **Parkplätze**) 1 car park; 2 parking space.

Parkschein *der* (PL *die* **Parkscheine**) car-park ticket.

Parkuhr *die* (PL *die* **Parkuhren**) parking meter.

Parkverbot *das* '**Parkverbot**' 'no parking'; **in der Innenstadt ist Parkverbot** you can't park in the town centre.

Parlament *das* (PL *die* **Parlamente**) parliament.

Parole *die* (PL *die* **Parolen**) slogan.

Partei *die* (PL *die* **Parteien**) 1 party; 2 **für jemanden Partei ergreifen** to side with somebody.

Parterre *das* (PL *die* **Parterres**) ground floor.

Partie *die* (PL *die* **Partien**) 1 part; 2 game (*of tennis, chess*).

Partner *der* (PL *die* **Partner**) partner.

Partnerin *die* (PL *die* **Partnerinnen**) partner.

Partnerstadt *die* (PL *die* **Partnerstädte**) twin town.

Party *die* (PL *die* **Partys**) party.

Pass △ *der* (PL *die* **Pässe**) 1 passport 2 pass.

Passagier *der* (PL *die* **Passagiere**) passenger.

Passant *der* (PL *die* **Passanten**) passer-by.

Passantin *die* (PL *die* **Passantinnen**) passer-by.

passen (PERF **hat gepasst** △) 1 to fit; **jemandem passen** to fit somebody; 2 to suit; **jemandem passen** to suit somebody; **Freitag passt mir nicht** Friday doesn't suit me; **seine Art passt mir nicht** I don't like his manner; 3 **zu etwas passen** to go with something; **zu jemandem passen** to be right for somebody.

passend *adjective* 1 suitable; 2 matching.

passieren *verb* (PERF **ist passiert**) to happen.

passiv *adjective* passive.

Passiv *das* passive.

Passkontrolle △ *die* passport control.

Paste *die* (PL *die* **Pasten**) paste.

Pastete *die* (PL *die* **Pasteten**) pie.

Pate *der* (PL *die* **Paten**) godfather.

Patenkind *das* (PL *die* **Patenkinder**) godchild.

patent *adjective* capable, clever.

✧ IRREGULAR VERB: *See the verb table in the centre of the dictionary*

Patentante der (PL die **Patentanten**) godmother.

Patient der (PL die **Patienten**) patient.

Patientin die (PL die **Patientinnen**) patient.

Patin die (PL die **Patinnen**) godmother.

patschnass Δ *adjective* soaking wet.

pauken *verb* (*informal*) (PERF **hat gepaukt**) to swot.

Pauschalreise die (PL die **Pauschalreisen**) package tour.

Pause die (PL die **Pausen**) 1 break; 2 pause; 3 interval.

Pazifik der **der Pazifik** the Pacific (Ocean).

PC der (PL die **PCs**) PC.

Pech das 1 bad luck; **Pech haben** to be unlucky; 2 pitch.

Pedal das (PL die **Pedale**) pedal.

peinlich *adjective* 1 embarrassing; **es war mir sehr peinlich** I felt very embarrassed about it; 2 awkward; 3 meticulous.

Peitsche die (PL die **Peitschen**) whip.

Pelle die skin.

Pelz der (PL die **Pelze**) fur.

pendeln *verb* 1 (PERF **ist gependelt**) to commute; 2 (PERF **hat gependelt**) to swing.

Pendler der (PL die **Pendler**) commuter.

penetrant *adjective* 1 overpowering (*odour, perfume*); 2 pushy (*person*).

Penis der (PL die **Penisse**) penis.

pennen *verb* (*informal*) (PERF **hat gepennt**) to sleep, to kip.

Pension die (PL die **Pensionen**) 1 guesthouse; 2 **bei voller Pension** with full board; 3 pension; **eine schöne Pension haben** to get a good pension; **in Pension gehen** to retire.

pensioniert *adjective* retired.

per *preposition* ←(+ACC) 1 by; **per Luftpost** by airmail; 2 per.

perfekt *adjective* perfect.

Perfekt das (PL die **Perfekte**) perfect.

Periode die (PL die **Perioden**) period.

Perle die (PL die **Perlen**) 1 pearl; 2 bead.

Person die (PL die **Personen**) person; **für vier Personen** for four people; **ich für meine Person** personally.

Personal das staff, personnel.

Personenzug der (PL die **Personenzüge**) stopping train.

Personalausweis der (PL die **Personalausweise**) identity card.

persönlich *adjective* personal. *adverb* 1 personally; 2 in person.

Perücke die (PL die **Perücken**) wig.

Pessimist der (PL die **Pessimisten**) pessimist.

Δ NEW SPELLING: *See page xii*

pessimistisch *adjective* pessimistic.

Petersilie *die* parsley.

Petroleum *das* paraffin.

Pfad *der* (PL *die* **Pfade**) path.

Pfadfinder *der* (PL *die* **Pfadfinder**) (Boy) Scout.

Pfadfinderin *die* (PL *die* **Pfadfinderinnen**) (Girl) Guide.

Pfand *das* (PL *die* **Pfänder**) 1 forfeit; 2 deposit (*on a bottle*); 3 pledge.

Pfanne *die* (PL *die* **Pfannen**) (frying) pan.

Pfannkuchen *der* (PL *die* **Pfannkuchen**) pancake.

Pfarrer *der* (PL *die* **Pfarrer**) 1 vicar; 2 priest.

Pfau *der* (PL *die* **Pfauen**) peacock.

Pfeffer *der* pepper.

Pfefferkorn *das* (PL *die* **Pfefferkörner**) peppercorn.

Pfefferkuchen *der* gingerbread.

Pfefferminzbonbon *der* (PL *die* **Pfefferminzbonbons**) mint.

Pfefferminze *die* peppermint.

Pfeffermühle *die* (PL *die* **Pfeffermühlen**) peppermill.

Pfeife *die* (PL *die* **Pfeifen**) 1 whistle; 2 pipe.

pfeifen ◇ *verb* (IMPERF **pfiff**, PERF **hat gepfiffen**) to whistle.

Pfeil *der* (PL *die* **Pfeile**) arrow.

Pfeiler *der* (PL *die* **Pfeiler**) 1 pillar; 2 pier.

Pfennig *der* (PL *die* **Pfennige**) pfennig; **ein Kaugummi kostet zwanzig Pfennig** a chewing gum is twenty pfennigs; **ich habe keinen Pfennig mehr** I haven't got a penny left.

Pferd *das* (PL *die* **Pferde**) horse.

Pferdeschwanz *der* (PL *die* **Pferdeschwänze**) ponytail.

pfiff SEE **pfeifen**.

Pfingsten *das* (PL *die* **Pfingsten**) Whitsun.

Pfirsich *der* (PL *die* **Pfirsiche**) peach.

Pflanze *die* (PL *die* **Pflanzen**) plant.

pflanzen *verb* (PERF **hat gepflanzt**) to plant.

Pflaster *das* (PL *die* **Pflaster**) 1 pavement; 2 plaster.

Pflaume *die* (PL *die* **Pflaumen**) plum.

Pflege *die* 1 care; 2 nursing; 3 **ein Kind in Pflege nehmen** to foster a child.

Pflegeeltern *plural noun* foster parents.

Pflegeheim *das* (PL *die* **Pflegeheime**) nursing home.

Pflegekind *das* (PL *die* **Pflegekinder**) foster child.

pflegeleicht *adjective* easy-care (*fabric*).

pflegen *verb* (PERF **hat gepflegt**) 1 to look after, to care for; **eine Freundschaft pflegen** to foster a friendship; 2 to nurse.

◇ IRREGULAR VERB: *See the verb table in the centre of the dictionary*

Pfleger der (PL die **Pfleger**) (male) nurse.

Pflicht die (PL die **Pflichten**) duty; **Pflicht sein** to be compulsory.

pflichtbewusst Δ adjective conscientious.

Pflichtfach das (PL die **Pflichtfächer**) compulsory subject.

pflücken verb (PERF **hat gepflückt**) to pick.

Pflug der (PL die **Pflüge**) plough.

Pforte die (PL die **Pforten**) gate.

Pförtner der (PL die **Pförtner**) porter.

Pfosten der (PL die **Pfosten**) post.

Pfote die (PL die **Pfoten**) paw.

pfui exclamation ugh!

Pfund das (PL die **Pfund(e)**) pound.

Pfütze die (PL die **Pfützen**) puddle.

Phantasie die 1 imagination; 2 **Phantasien** (plural) fantasies.

phantasievoll adjective imaginative.

phantastisch adjective fantastic.

Philosoph der (PL die **Philosophen**) philosopher.

Philosophie die (PL die **Philosophien**) philosophy.

Photo das (PL die **Photos**) photo.

Physik die physics.

Physiker der (PL die **Physiker**) physicist.

Physikerin die (PL die **Physikerinnen**) physicist.

Pickel der (PL die **Pickel**) spot, pimple.

Picknick das (PL die **Picknicks**) picnic.

Pik das spades (in cards).

pikant adjective spicy.

Pille die (PL die **Pillen**) pill.

Pilot der (PL die **Piloten**) pilot.

Pilz der (PL die **Pilze**) 1 mushroom; 2 fungus.

Pinguin der (PL die **Pinguine**) penguin.

pinkeln verb (informal) (PERF **hat gepinkelt**) to pee.

Pinnwand die (PL die **Pinnwände**) noticeboard.

Pinsel der (PL die **Pinsel**) brush.

Pinzette die (PL die **Pinzetten**) tweezers.

Pirat der (PL die **Piraten**) pirate.

Piste die (PL die **Pisten**) 1 run, piste; 2 track; 3 runway.

Pizza die (PL die **Pizzas**) pizza.

Pkw der (PL die **Pkws**) (Personenkraftwagen) car.

plagen verb (PERF **hat geplagt**) 1 to bother, to torment; 2 to pester; 3 **sich plagen** to struggle; **sich in der Schule plagen** to struggle at school; **er muss sich plagen** he has to work hard.

Plakat das (PL die **Plakate**) poster.

Plan der (PL die **Pläne**) 1 plan; 2 map.

Δ NEW SPELLING: See page xii

planen *verb* (PERF **hat geplant**) to plan.

planmäßig *adjective* scheduled. *adverb* 1 according to plan; **alles läuft planmäßig** everything is going according to plan; 2 on schedule; **der Zug ist planmäßig abgefahren** the train left on schedule.

Plastik[1] *das* plastic.

Plastik[2] *die* (PL *die* **Plastiken**) sculpture.

Plastiktüte *die* (PL *die* **Plastiktüten**) plastic bag.

platt *adjective* flat; **platt sein** (*informal*) to be flabbergasted.

plattdeutsch *adjective* low German.

Platte *die* (PL *die* **Platten**) 1 plate; 2 dish; **kalte Platte** cold meats and cheeses; 3 hotplate; 4 record; 5 board (*made of wood*); 6 slab (*made of stone*); 7 sheet (*made of metal or glass*); 8 top (*of a table*).

Plattenspieler *der* (PL *die* **Plattenspieler**) record player.

Platz *der* (PL *die* **Plätze**) 1 place; **viel Platz haben** to have a lot of room; **Platz lassen** to leave room; **auf die Plätze, fertig, los!** on your marks, get set, go!; 2 seat; **Platz nehmen** to take a seat; 3 square (*in a town*); 4 ground, pitch; **einen Spieler vom Platz stellen** to send a player off; 5 court (*for tennis*); 6 course (*for golf*).

Plätzchen *das* (PL *die* **Plätzchen**) 1 biscuit; 2 spot.

platzen *verb* (PERF **ist geplatzt**) 1 to burst; 2 **der Plan ist geplatzt** (*informal*) the plan fell through; 3 **vor Neugier platzen** to be bursting with curiosity.

plaudern *verb* (PERF **hat geplaudert**) to chat.

pleite *adjective* (*informal*) broke.

Plombe *die* (PL *die* **Plomben**) filling.

plombieren *verb* (PERF **hat plombiert**) to fill.

plötzlich *adjective* sudden. *adverb* suddenly.

plump *adjective* 1 plump; 2 clumsy.

Plural *der* (PL *die* **Plurale**) plural.

plus *adverb* plus.

Plus *das* 1 plus; 2 profit; 3 advantage.

PLZ = **Postleitzahl**.

Po *der* (*informal*) (PL *die* **Pos**) bottom.

Poesie *die* poetry.

Pokal *der* (PL *die* **Pokale**) 1 cup; 2 goblet.

Pokalspiel *das* (PL *die* **Pokalspiele**) cup-tie.

Pole *der* (PL *die* **Polen**) Pole.

Polen *das* Poland.

polieren *verb* (PERF **hat poliert**) to polish.

Polin *die* (PL *die* **Polinnen**) Pole.

Politik *die* 1 politics; 2 policy.

Politiker *der* (PL *die* **Politiker**) politician.

♢ IRREGULAR VERB: *See the verb table in the centre of the dictionary*

Politikerin die (PL die
Politikerinnen) politician.

politisch adjective political.

Politur die (PL die Polituren) polish.

Polizei die police.

polizeilich adjective police.
adverb by the police; **sich
polizeilich anmelden** to register
with the police.

Polizeiwache die (PL die
Polizeiwachen) police station.

Polizist der (PL die Polizisten)
policeman.

Polizistin die (PL die Polizistinnen)
policewoman.

polnisch adjective Polish.

Pommes frites plural noun chips,
French fries.

Pony[1] das (PL die Ponys) pony.

Pony[2] der (PL die Ponys) fringe.

Popmusik die pop music.

poppig adjective bright; **Natalie hat
immer poppige Socken an** Natalie
always wears bright socks.

Porree der leeks; **eine Stange
Porree** a leek.

Portemonnaie das = **Portmonee**.

Portier der (PL die Portiers) porter.

Portion die (PL die Portionen)
portion.

Portmonee △ das (PL die
Portmonees) purse.

Porto das postage.

Porträt das (PL die Porträts) portrait.

Portugal das Portugal.

Portugiese der (PL die
Portugiesen) Portuguese.

Portugiesin die (PL die
Portugiesinnen) Portuguese.

portugiesisch adjective
Portuguese.

Posaune die (PL die Posaunen)
trombone.

Post die 1 post; **mit der Post** by
post; 2 post office.

Postamt das (PL die Postämter) post
office.

Postbote der (PL die Postboten)
postman.

Poster das (PL die Poster) poster.

Postkarte die (PL die Postkarten)
postcard.

Postleitzahl die (PL die
Postleitzahlen) postcode.

prächtig adjective splendid.

prahlen verb (PERF **hat geprahlt**) to
boast.

praktisch adjective 1 practical;
praktische Erfahrung practical
experience; 2 handy; 3 **ein
praktischer Arzt** a general
practitioner.
adverb 1 practically; 2 in practice.

Praline die (PL die Pralinen)
chocolate.

Präposition die (PL die
Präpositionen) preposition.

Präsens das present (tense).

△ NEW SPELLING: See page xii

Präservativ das (PL die Präservative) condom.

Präsident der (PL die Präsidenten) president.

Präsidentin die (PL die Präsidentinnen) president.

Praxis die (PL die Praxen) 1 practice; 2 practical experience; 3 surgery.

Preis der (PL die Preise) 1 price; **um keinen Preis** not at any price; 2 prize.

Preisausschreiben das (PL die Preisausschreiben) competition.

Preiselbeere die (PL die Preiselbeeren) cranberry.

preiswert adjective reasonable, cheap.

Prellung die (PL die Prellungen) bruise.

Premierminister der (PL die Premierminister) prime minister.

Presse die press.

Priester der (PL die Priester) priest.

prima adjective (informal) brilliant.

Prinz der (PL die Prinzen) prince.

Prinzessin die (PL die Prinzessinnen) princess.

Prise die (PL die Prisen) pinch; **eine Prise Salz** a pinch of salt.

privat adjective private.

Privileg das (PL die Privilegien) privilege.

pro preposition ←(+ACC) per.

Probe die (PL die Proben) 1 test; **jemanden auf die Probe stellen** to test somebody; **ein Auto Probe fahren** △ to test-drive a car; 2 sample; 3 rehearsal.

probefahren SEE **Probe**.

probieren verb (PERF **hat probiert**) 1 to try; 2 to taste.

Problem das (PL die Probleme) problem.

Produkt das (PL die Produkte) product.

Produzent der (PL die Produzenten) producer.

produzieren verb (PERF **hat produziert**) to produce.

Profi der (PL die Profis) pro.

Profil das (PL die Profile) 1 profile; 2 tread (of a tyre).

Programm das (PL die Programme) 1 programme; 2 program (in computing); 3 channel (on TV).

programmieren verb (PERF **hat programmiert**) to program.

Programmierer der (PL die Programmierer) programmer.

Projekt das (PL die Projekte) project.

Promille das alcohol level; **zuviel Promille haben** to be over the limit.

Pronomen das (PL die Pronomen or Pronomina) pronoun.

Prospekt der (PL die Prospekte) brochure.

prost exclamation cheers!

⬦ IRREGULAR VERB: *See the verb table in the centre of the dictionary*

Protein das (PL die Proteine) protein.

Protest der (PL die Proteste) protest.

protestantisch adjective Protestant.

protestieren verb (PERF hat protestiert) to protest.

Protokoll das (PL die Protokolle) 1 minutes, transcript; 2 record (in court); 3 protocol.

protzen verb (PERF hat geprotzt) to show off; **Klaus protzt mit seinem neuen Auto** Klaus is showing off with his new car.

Proviant der provisions.

Prozent das (PL die Prozente) 1 per cent; **zehn Prozent** ten per cent; 2 **Prozente bekommen** (informal) to get a discount.

Prozentsatz der (PL die Prozentsätze) percentage.

Prozess △ der (PL die Prozesse) 1 court case; **einen Prozess gewinnen** to win a case; 2 trial; 3 process.

prüfen verb (PERF hat geprüft) 1 to test, to examine (at school); 2 to check; **hast du die Reifen geprüft?** have you checked the tyres?

Prüfung die (PL die Prüfungen) 1 examination, exam; **eine Prüfung bestehen** to pass an examination; **sie ist durch die Prüfung gefallen** she failed the exam; 2 check.

Prügel der (PL die Prügel) 1 stick; 2 **Prügel bekommen** to get a beating.

Prügelei die (PL die Prügeleien) fight.

prügeln verb (PERF hat geprügelt) 1 to beat; 2 **sich prügeln** to fight; **sich um etwas prügeln** to fight for something.

Psychiater der (PL die Psychiater) psychiatrist.

Psychiaterin die (PL die Psychiaterinnen) psychiatrist.

psychisch adjective psychological.

Psychologe der (PL die Psychologen) psychologist.

Psychologie die psychology.

Psychologin die (PL die Psychologinnen) psychologist.

Publikum das 1 audience, crowd; 2 public.

Pudding der (PL die Puddings) 1 blancmange; 2 pudding (steamed).

Pudel der (PL die Pudel) poodle.

Puder der (PL die Puder) powder.

Puffmais der popcorn.

Pulli der (PL die Pullis) pullover.

Pullover der (PL die Pullover) pullover.

Puls der (PL die Pulse) pulse.

Pult das (PL die Pulte) desk.

Pulver das (PL die Pulver) powder.

Pulverkaffee der instant coffee.

Pumpe die (PL die Pumpen) pump.

pumpen verb (PERF hat gepumpt) 1 to pump; 2 (informal) to lend;

△ NEW SPELLING: *See page xii*

jemandem Geld pumpen to lend somebody money; **3** (*informal*) to borrow; **sich etwas pumpen** to borrow something.

Punker *der* (PL *die* **Punker**) punk.

Punkerin *die* (PL *die* **Punkerinnen**) punk.

Punkt *der* (PL *die* **Punkte**) **1** dot, spot; **Punkt sechs Uhr** at six o'clock on the dot; **2** full stop; **3** point; **nach Punkten siegen** to win on points.

pünktlich *adjective* punctual.

Puppe *die* (PL *die* **Puppen**) **1** doll; **2** puppet.

pur *adjective* **1** pure; **2 Whisky pur** neat whisky.

Purzelbaum *der* (PL *die* **Purzelbäume**) somersault.

pusten *verb* (PERF **hat gepustet**) to blow.

Pute *die* (PL *die* **Puten**) turkey.

putzen *verb* (PERF **hat geputzt**) **1** to clean; **putz dir die Zähne** clean your teeth; **putzen gehen** to work as a cleaner; **2 sich die Nase putzen** to blow your nose.

Putzfrau *die* (PL *die* **Putzfrauen**) cleaning lady, cleaner.

putzig *adjective* cute.

Puzzle *das* (PL *die* **Puzzles**) jigsaw (puzzle).

Pyjama *der* (PL *die* **Pyjamas**) pyjamas.

Pyramide *die* (PL *die* **Pyramiden**) pyramid.

Pyrenäen (*plural noun*) **die Pyrenäen** the Pyrenees.

Q q

Quadrat *das* (PL *die* **Quadrate**) square.

quadratisch *adjective* square.

Quadratmeter *der* (PL *die* **Quadratmeter**) square metre.

quaken *verb* (PERF **hat gequakt**) **1** to quack; **2** to croak (*of a frog*).

Qual *die* (PL *die* **Qualen**) **1** torment; **2** agony; **es war eine Qual, das ansehen zu müssen** it was agony to watch.

quälen *verb* (PERF **hat gequält**) **1** to torment; **2** to torture; **3** to pester; **4 sich quälen** to suffer; **5 sich mit etwas quälen** to struggle with something; **sich durch ein Buch quälen** to struggle (your way) through a book.

Quälgeist *der* (*informal*) (PL *die* **Quälgeister**) pest.

Qualifikation *die* (PL *die* **Qualifikationen**) qualification.

Qualität *die* (PL *die* **Qualitäten**) quality.

Qualle *die* (PL *die* **Quallen**) jellyfish.

Qualm *der* thick smoke.

qualmen *verb* (PERF **hat gequalmt**) to give off clouds of smoke; **sie**

◇ IRREGULAR VERB: *See the verb table in the centre of the dictionary*

qualmt wie ein Schlot (*informal*) she smokes like a chimney.

Quarantäne *die* quarantine.

Quark *der* (*curd cheese*) quark.

Quartett *das* (PL *die* **Quartette**) quartet.

Quartier *das* (PL *die* **Quartiere**) 1 accommodation; 2 quarters.

quasseln *verb* (*informal*) (PERF **hat gequasselt**) to natter.

Quatsch *der* (*informal*) rubbish.

quatschen *verb* (*informal*) (PERF **hat gequatscht**) to chat.

Quelle *die* (PL *die* **Quellen**) 1 source; 2 spring.

quer *adverb* 1 across; 2 crosswise; 3 diagonally; **quer gestreift** △ with diagonal stripes; 4 **quer durch** straight through.

quergestreift SEE **quer**.

Querstraße *die* (PL *die* **Querstraßen**) side street; **die erste Querstraße rechts** the first turning on the right.

quetschen *verb* (PERF **hat gequetscht**) 1 to crush; 2 to squash; 3 **ich habe mich in meine Jeans gequetscht** I squeezed into my jeans.

Quetschung *die* (PL *die* **Quetschungen**) bruise.

quietschen *verb* (PERF **hat gequietscht**) to squeak.

quitt *adjective* quits.

Quittung *die* (PL *die* **Quittungen**) receipt.

Quiz *das* (PL *die* **Quiz**) quiz.

R r

Rabatt *der* (PL *die* **Rabatte**) discount.

Rache *die* revenge.

rächen *verb* (PERF **hat gerächt**) 1 to avenge; 2 **sich an jemandem rächen** to take revenge on somebody; 3 **das wird sich rächen** you'll have to pay for it.

Rad *das* (PL *die* **Räder**) 1 wheel; 2 bike; **Julia ist mit dem Rad gekommen** Julia came by bike; 3 **Rad fahren** △ to cycle.

Radar *der* radar.

Radarschirm *der* (PL *die* **Radarschirme**) radar screen.

radfahren SEE **Rad**.

Radfahrer *der* (PL *die* **Radfahrer**) cyclist.

Radfahrerin *die* (PL *die* **Radfahrerinnen**) cyclist.

Radfahrweg *der* (PL *die* **Radfahrwege**) cycle lane.

radeln *verb* (PERF **ist geradelt**) to cycle; **Max ist ins Dorf geradelt** Max cycled into the village.

Radiergummi *der* (PL *die* **Radiergummis**) rubber.

Radieschen *das* (PL *die* **Radieschen**) radish.

△ NEW SPELLING: *See page xii*

Radio das (PL die **Radios**) radio.

radioaktiv adjective radioactive.

Radler der (PL die **Radler**) cyclist.

Radlerin die (PL die **Radlerinnen**) cyclist.

Radrennen das 1 cycle race; **Maria hat das Radrennen gewonnen** Maria won the cycle race; 2 cycle racing.

raffiniert adjective crafty.

Rahm der cream.

Rahmen der (PL die **Rahmen**) 1 frame; 2 framework; 3 limits; **im Rahmen des Möglichen** within the bounds of possibility.

rahmen verb (PERF **hat gerahmt**) to frame (a picture).

Rakete die (PL die **Raketen**) rocket.

ran (informal) SEE **heran**.

Rand der (PL die **Ränder**) 1 edge; 2 rim; **der Rand der Tasse war angeschlagen** the rim of the cup was chipped; 3 ring, mark; 4 margin (of a page); **du musst einen Rand für die Korrekturen lassen** you must leave a margin for the corrections; 5 outskirts (of a town); 6 **etwas am Rande erwähnen** to mention something in passing; 7 **am Rande der Pleite sein** to be on the verge of bankruptcy; 8 **außer Rand und Band geraten** (informal) to go wild.

Randstreifen der (PL die **Randstreifen**) hard shoulder.

Rang der (PL die **Ränge**) 1 rank; 2 (in a theatre) circle.

rannte SEE **rennen**.

rasch adjective quick.

Rasen der (PL die **Rasen**) lawn, grass.

rasen verb (PERF **ist gerast**) to tear along, to rush; **gegen eine Mauer rasen** to career into a wall.

Rasenmäher der (PL die **Rasenmäher**) lawnmower.

Rasierapparat der (PL die **Rasierapparate**) 1 shaver; 2 razor.

Rasiercreme die (PL die **Rasiercremes**) shaving cream.

rasieren verb (PERF **hat rasiert**) 1 to shave; 2 **sich rasieren** to shave.

Rasierklinge die (PL die **Rasierklingen**) razor blade.

Rasierwasser das aftershave.

Rasse die (PL die **Rassen**) 1 race; 2 breed; **ich weiß nicht, was für eine Rasse unser Hund ist** I don't know what breed our dog is.

Rassenhass △ der racial hatred.

rassisch adjective racial.

Rassismus der racism.

Rassist der (PL die **Rassisten**) racist.

Rassistin die (PL die **Rassistinnen**) racist.

rassistisch adjective racist.

rasten verb (PERF **hat gerastet**) to rest.

Rastplatz der (PL die **Rastplätze**) picnic area (on a motorway).

Raststätte die (PL die **Raststätten**) services (on a motorway).

✧ IRREGULAR VERB: *See the verb table in the centre of the dictionary*

Rat *der* 1 advice; **ein Rat** a piece of advice; **jemanden zu Rate ziehen** to ask somebody's advice; **2 sich keinen Rat wissen** not to know what to do; **3** council.

Rate *die* (PL *die* **Raten**) instalment; **in monatlichen Raten abzahlen** to pay in monthly instalments.

raten ✧ *verb* (PRES **rät**, IMPERF **riet**, PERF **hat geraten**) **1 jemandem raten** to advise somebody; **was rätst du mir?** what do you advise me to do?; **2** to guess; **richtig raten** to guess right.

Rathaus *das* (PL *die* **Rathäuser**) town hall.

rationell *adjective* efficient.

ratlos *adjective* helpless; **Emma hat mich ratlos angesehen** Emma gave me a helpless look; **ratlos sein** not to know what to do.

ratsam *adjective* advisable; **es wäre ratsam, früher zu fahren** it would be advisable to leave earlier.

Ratschlag *der* (PL *die* **Ratschläge**) piece of advice, advice; **deine klugen Ratschläge kannst du dir sparen** you can keep your advice to yourself.

Rätsel *das* (PL *die* **Rätsel**) **1** puzzle; **2** mystery.

rätselhaft *adjective* mysterious.

Ratte *die* (PL *die* **Ratten**) rat.

rau Δ *adjective* **1** rough; **2** harsh; **3 eine raue Stimme** a husky voice; **4 einen rauen Hals haben** to have a sore throat.

Raub *der* robbery.

Räuber *der* (PL *die* **Räuber**) robber.

Rauch *der* smoke.

rauchen *verb* (PERF **hat geraucht**) to smoke; **'Rauchen verboten'** 'no smoking'.

Raucher *der* (PL *die* **Raucher**) smoker.

Raucherin *die* (PL *die* **Raucherinnen**) smoker.

räuchern *verb* (PERF **hat geräuchert**) to smoke (*fish, meat*).

rauf (*informal*) SEE **herauf**, **hinauf**.

rauh *adjective* = **rau**.

Raum *der* (PL *die* **Räume**) **1** room; **das Haus hat sehr große Räume** the house has very big rooms; **2** space; **wir brauchen mehr Raum** we need more space; **3 die Rakete ist im Raum explodiert** the rocket exploded in space; **4** area; **im Raum Berlin** in the area of Berlin.

räumen *verb* (PERF **hat geräumt**) **1** to clear; **das Geschirr vom Tisch räumen** to clear away the dishes; **2 die Hemden in den Schrank räumen** to put the shirts in the cupboard; **seine Sachen beiseite räumen** to put your things to one side; **die Akten aus dem Schrank räumen** to take the files out of the cabinet; **3** to vacate.

Raumfahrt *die* space travel.

Raumschiff *das* (PL *die* **Raumschiffe**) space ship.

Raupe *die* (PL *die* **Raupen**) caterpillar.

raus (*informal*) SEE **heraus, hinaus**.

Rauschgift *das* (PL *die* **Rauschgifte**) drug; **Rauschgift nehmen** to take drugs.

Rauschgiftsüchtige *der/die* (PL *die* **Rauschgiftsüchtigen**) drug addict.

rauskriegen *verb* (*informal*) (PERF **hat rausgekriegt**) 1 to get out; 2 **ein Geheimnis rauskriegen** to find out a secret; 3 **ich kann die Aufgabe nicht rauskriegen** I can't do the exercise.

räuspern *verb* (PERF **hat sich geräuspert**) **sich räuspern** to clear your throat.

reagieren *verb* (PERF **hat reagiert**) to react.

Reaktion *die* (PL *die* **Reaktionen**) reaction.

realisieren *verb* (PERF **hat realisiert**) 1 to realize; 2 to implement.

Realschule *die* (PL *die* **Realschulen**) secondary school.

rebellieren *verb* (PERF **hat rebelliert**) to rebel.

rechnen *verb* (PERF **hat gerechnet**) 1 to do arithmetic; **Peter kann gut rechnen** Peter's good at arithmetic, Peter's good at figures; 2 to reckon; **mit etwas rechnen** to reckon with something; 3 **er wird zu den besten Schauspielern gerechnet** he's reckoned to be one of the best actors; 4 to count; **jemanden zu seinen Freunden rechnen** to count somebody as a friend; 5 **mit etwas rechnen** to expect something; 6 **auf jemanden rechnen** to count on somebody.

Rechner *der* (PL *die* **Rechner**) 1 calculator; 2 computer.

Rechnung *die* (PL *die* **Rechnungen**) 1 bill; 2 invoice; **die Rechnung liegt bei** the invoice is enclosed; 3 calculation.

recht *adjective* 1 right; **jemandem recht sein** to be all right with somebody; **wenn es dir recht ist** if it's all right with you; 2 **der/die Rechte** the right man/woman; 3 **das Rechte** the right thing; **etwas Rechtes** something proper; **ich habe nichts Rechtes gegessen** I haven't had a proper meal; **etwas Rechtes lernen** to learn something useful; 4 real; **ich habe keine rechte Lust** I don't really feel like it. *adverb* 1 correctly; 2 quite; **recht einfach** quite simple; 3 really; 4 **recht vielen Dank** many thanks; 5 **das geschieht dir recht!** (it) serves you right!; 6 **man kann es nicht allen recht machen** you can't please everyone.

Recht *das* (PL *die* **Rechte**) 1 law; **nach deutschem Recht** under German law; 2 right; **Recht haben** △ to be right; **im Recht sein** to be in the right; **Recht bekommen** △ to be proved right; 3 **jemandem Recht geben** △ to agree with somebody; 4 **mit Recht** rightly; **du hast dich mit Recht beschwert** you were right to complain.

rechte SEE **rechter**.

Rechte *die* 1 right (side); **zu meiner**

Rechten on my right; **2** right hand;
3 die Rechte the right (*in politics*).

rechteckig *adjective* rectangular.

Rechteck *das* (PL *die* **Rechtecke**)
rectangle.

rechter, rechte, rechtes
adjective **1** right; **auf der rechten
Seite** on the right; **2** right-wing.

rechtfertigen *verb* (PERF **hat
gerechtfertigt**) to justify; **2 sich
rechtfertigen** to justify yourself.

rechtlich *adjective* legal.

rechts *adverb* **1** on the right; **von
rechts** from the right; **rechts
abbiegen** to turn right; **2 rechts
sein** to be right-wing; **3 zwei
rechts, zwei links stricken** to knit
two, purl two.

Rechtsanwalt *der* (PL *die*
Rechtsanwälte) lawyer.

Rechtsanwältin *die* (PL *die*
Rechtsanwältinnen) lawyer.

Rechtschreibung *die* spelling.

Rechtshänder *der* (PL *die*
Rechtshänder) **Klaus ist
Rechtshänder** Klaus is right-
handed.

Rechtshänderin *die* (PL *die*
Rechtshänderinnen) **Beate ist
Rechtshänderin** Beate is right-
handed.

rechtzeitig *adjective* timely.
adverb in time; **wir sind gerade
noch rechtzeitig angekommen** we
got there just in time.

Redakteur *der* (PL *die* **Redakteure**)
editor.

Redakteurin *die* (PL *die*
Redakteurinnen) editor.

Rede *die* (PL *die* **Reden**) **1** speech;
eine Rede halten to make a speech;
2 nicht der Rede wert not worth
mentioning; **davon kann keine
Rede sein** it's out of the question;
jemanden zur Rede stellen to take
somebody to task.

reden *verb* (PERF **hat geredet**) **1** to
talk; **2** to speak; **mit jemandem
reden** to speak to somebody; **3 sie
hat kein Wort geredet** she didn't
say a word; **4 mir ist egal, was über
mich geredet wird** I don't care what
people say about me.

reduzieren *verb* (PERF **hat
reduziert**) to reduce.

reflexiv *adjective* reflexive.

Reformhaus *das* (PL *die*
Reformhäuser) health-food shop.

Regal *das* (PL *die* **Regale**) **1** shelf;
2 shelves, bookcase.

Regel *die* (PL *die* **Regeln**) **1** rule; **in
der Regel** as a rule; **2** period
(*menstruation*).

regelmäßig *adjective* regular.

regeln *verb* (PERF **hat geregelt**) **1** to
regulate; **2** to direct (*the traffic*);
3 to settle (*a matter*); **wir haben die
Sache so geregelt, dass** … we've
arranged things so that …; **4 sich
von selbst regeln** to sort itself out.

Regelung *die* (PL *die* **Regelungen**)
1 regulation; **2** settlement.

Regen *der* rain.

△ NEW SPELLING: *See page xii*

Regenbogen der (PL die Regenbogen) rainbow.

Regenmantel der (PL die Regenmäntel) raincoat.

Regenschirm der (PL die Regenschirme) umbrella.

Regenwurm der (PL die Regenwürmer) earthworm.

regieren verb (PERF hat regiert) 1 to govern; 2 to rule, to reign.

Regierung die (PL die Regierungen) 1 government; 2 reign.

Regisseur der (PL die Regisseure) director.

Regisseurin die (PL die Regisseurinnen) director.

regnen verb (PERF hat geregnet) to rain.

regnerisch adjective rainy.

Reh das (PL die Rehe) deer.

reiben ✧ verb (IMPERF rieb, PERF hat gerieben) 1 to rub; 2 to grate.

reibungslos adjective smooth.

reich adjective rich.

Reich das (PL die Reiche) 1 empire; 2 kingdom, realm.

reichen verb (PERF hat gereicht) 1 to hand, to pass; 2 to be enough; **mit dem Geld reichen** to have enough money; 3 **bis zu etwas reichen** to reach up to something; **er reicht seinem Vater bis zur Schulter** he comes up to his father's shoulder; **die Felder reichen bis zum Wald** the fields extend as far as or go right up to the forest; 4 **mir reicht's!** (informal) I've had enough!

reichlich adjective 1 large; 2 ample (space).
adverb plenty of.

Reichtum der (PL die Reichtümer) wealth.

Reichweite die 1 reach; **außer Reichweite** out of reach; 2 range.

reif adjective 1 ripe; 2 mature.

Reifen der (PL die Reifen) 1 tyre; 2 hoop.

Reifenpanne die (PL die Reifenpannen) puncture.

Reifendruck der tyre pressure.

Reihe die (PL die Reihen) 1 row; 2 series; 3 **der Reihe nach** in turn; **außer der Reihe** out of turn; **du bist an der Reihe** it's your turn.

Reihenfolge die (PL die Reihenfolgen) order.

Reihenhaus das (PL die Reihenhäuser) terraced house.

Reim der (PL die Reime) rhyme.

reimen verb (PERF hat gereimt) 1 to rhyme; 2 **sich reimen** to rhyme.

rein[1] adjective 1 pure; 2 clean; 3 sheer (madness); 4 **etwas ins Reine schreiben** △ to make a fair copy of something; **etwas ins Reine bringen** △ to sort something out.
adverb 1 purely; 2 absolutely; **rein gar nichts** absolutely nothing.

rein[2] (informal) SEE **herein**, **hinein**.

✧ IRREGULAR VERB: See the verb table in the centre of the dictionary

reinigen *verb* (PERF **hat gereinigt**) to clean.

Reinigung *die* (PL *die* **Reinigungen**) 1 cleaning; 2 cleaner's.

Reis *der* rice.

Reise *die* (PL *die* **Reisen**) 1 journey, trip; **gute Reise !** have a good journey!; **auf meinen Reisen** on my travels; 2 voyage.

Reiseandenken *das* (PL *die* **Reiseandenken**) souvenir.

Reisebüro *das* (PL *die* **Reisebüros**) travel agency.

Reisebus *der* (PL *die* **Reisebusse**) coach.

Reiseführer *der* (PL *die* **Reiseführer**) 1 guidebook; 2 (travel) guide.

Reiseleiter *der* (PL *die* **Reiseleiter**) (travel) guide.

reisen *verb* (PERF **ist gereist**) to travel.

Reisende *der/die* (PL *die* **Reisenden**) traveller.

Reisepass △ *der* (PL *die* **Reisepässe**) passport.

Reisescheck *der* (PL *die* **Reiseschecks**) traveller's cheque.

Reiseziel *das* (PL *die* **Reiseziele**) destination.

reißen ✧ *verb* (IMPERF **riss** △, PERF **hat gerissen**) 1 to tear; 2 to snatch; 3 to pull; **an etwas reißen** to pull at something; 4 **mit sich reißen** to sweep away; 5 **etwas an sich reißen** to snatch something; **die Macht an sich reißen** to seize power; **6 Witze reißen** to crack jokes; **7 sich um etwas reißen** to fight for something; **8 hin und her gerissen sein** to be torn; 9 (PERF **ist gerissen**) to tear, to break.

Reißverschluss △ *der* (PL *die* **Reißverschlüsse**) zip.

Reißzwecke *die* (PL *die* **Reißzwecken**) drawing pin.

reiten ✧ *verb* (IMPERF **ritt**, PERF **hat/ist geritten**) to ride.

Reiter *der* (PL *die* **Reiter**) rider.

Reiterin *die* (PL *die* **Reiterinnen**) rider.

Reitschule *die* (PL *die* **Reitschulen**) riding school.

Reiz *der* (PL *die* **Reize**) 1 attraction, appeal; 2 charm.

reizen *verb* (PERF **hat gereizt**) 1 to appeal to, to tempt; **das reizt mich sehr** it's very tempting; 2 to annoy; **jemanden zum Zorn reizen** to provoke somebody to anger; 3 to irritate (*the skin, eyes*); 4 to bid (*when playing cards*).

reizend *adjective* charming.

reizvoll *adjective* attractive.

Reklame *die* (PL *die* **Reklamen**) 1 advertisement, advert; **für etwas Reklame machen** to advertise something; 2 commercial (*on TV*).

Rekord *der* (PL *die* **Rekorde**) record.

Rektor *der* (PL *die* **Rektoren**) 1 head (*of a school*); 2 vice-chancellor (*of a university*).

△ NEW SPELLING: *See page xii*

Religion die (PL die **Religionen**) religion.

religiös adjective religious.

Rendezvous das (PL die **Rendezvous**) date.

Rennbahn die (PL die **Rennbahnen**) racetrack.

rennen ◇ verb (IMPERF **rannte**, PERF **ist gerannt**) to run.

Rennen das (PL die **Rennen**) race.

Rennfahrer der (PL die **Rennfahrer**) racing driver.

Rennwagen der (PL die **Rennwagen**) racing car.

renovieren verb (PERF **hat renoviert**) to renovate, to redecorate.

rentabel adjective profitable.

Rente die (PL die **Renten**) pension; **in Rente gehen** to retire.

Rentner der (PL die **Rentner**) pensioner.

Rentnerin die (PL die **Rentnerinnen**) pensioner.

Reparatur die (PL die **Reparaturen**) repair.

reparieren verb (PERF **hat repariert**) to repair.

Reportage die (PL die **Reportagen**) 1 report; 2 live commentary.

Reporter der (PL die **Reporter**) reporter.

Reporterin die (PL die **Reporterinnen**) reporter.

Reptil das (PL die **Reptile**) reptile.

Republik die (PL die **Republiken**) republic.

Reservat das (PL die **Reservate**) reservation.

Reserverad das (PL die **Reserveräder**) spare wheel.

reservieren verb (PERF **hat reserviert**) to reserve.

Reservierung die (PL die **Reservierungen**) reservation.

Respekt der respect.

respektieren verb (PERF **hat respektiert**) to respect.

Rest der (PL die **Reste**) 1 rest, remainder; 2 left-over; **zum Mittagessen gibt's die Reste** we're having the leftovers for lunch; 3 **die Reste** the remains.

Restaurant das (PL die **Restaurants**) restaurant.

restlich adjective remaining.

restlos adjective complete.

Resultat das (PL die **Resultate**) result.

retten verb (PERF **hat gerettet**) 1 to save, to rescue; **jemandem das Leben retten** to save somebody's life; 2 **sich retten** to escape.

Rettich der (PL die **Rettiche**) radish.

Rettung die rescue.

Rettungsring der (PL die **Rettungsringe**) lifebelt.

Rettungswagen der (PL die **Rettungswagen**) ambulance.

◇ IRREGULAR VERB: *See the verb table in the centre of the dictionary*

Rezept *das* (PL *die* **Rezepte**)
1 prescription; 2 recipe.

Rezeption *die* (PL *die* **Rezeptionen**)
reception; **bitte geben Sie Ihren
Schlüssel an der Rezeption ab**
please leave your key at reception.

R-Gespräch *das* (PL *die* **R-
Gespräche**) reverse-charge call.

Rhabarber *der* rhubarb.

Rhein *der* Rhine.

Rheuma *das* rheumatism.

Rhythmus *der* (PL *die* **Rhythmen**)
rhythm.

richten *verb* (PERF **hat gerichtet**)
1 to direct, to point (*a torch,
telescope, gun*); 2 **eine Frage an
jemanden richten** to put a question
to somebody; 3 to address (*a letter,
remarks*); 4 to prepare (*a meal,
room*); 5 **sich auf etwas richten** to
be directed towards something;
6 **sich nach jemandem richten** to
fit in with somebody's wishes; **sich
nach den Vorschriften richten** to
follow the rules; 7 **sich nach etwas
richten** to depend on something.

Richter *der* (PL *die* **Richter**) judge.

richtig *adjective* 1 right; 2 **das
Richtige** the right thing; **der/die
Richtige** the right man/woman;
3 real, proper.
adverb 1 correctly; 2 really;
3 **richtig stellen** △ to put right; **die
Uhr geht richtig** the clock is right.

Richtung *die* (PL *die* **Richtungen**)
1 direction; 2 trend.

rieb SEE **reiben**.

riechen ◇ *verb* (IMPERF **roch**, PERF
hat gerochen) 1 to smell; 2 **ich
kann ihn nicht riechen** (*informal*)
I can't stand him.

rief SEE **rufen**.

Riegel *der* (PL *die* **Riegel**) 1 bolt;
2 **ein Riegel Schokolade** a bar of
chocolate.

Riemen *der* (PL *die* **Riemen**) strap.

Riese *der* (PL *die* **Riesen**) giant.

riesengroß *adjective* gigantic.

riesig *adjective* huge.

riet SEE **raten**.

Rind *das* (PL *die* **Rinder**) 1 ox; 2 cow;
Rinder cattle; 3 beef.

Rinde *die* (PL *die* **Rinden**) 1 bark;
2 rind; 3 crust.

Rindfleisch *das* beef.

Ring *der* (PL *die* **Ringe**) ring.

Ringbuch *das* (PL *die* **Ringbücher**)
ring binder.

Ringen *das* wrestling.

Rippe *die* (PL *die* **Rippen**) rib.

Risiko *das* (PL *die* **Risiken**) risk.

riskant *adjective* risky.

riskieren *verb* (PERF **hat riskiert**) to
risk.

riss △ SEE **reißen**.

Riss △ *der* (PL *die* **Risse**) 1 tear;
2 crack.

ritt SEE **reiten**.

Rivale *der* (PL *die* **Rivalen**) rival.

Rivalin *die* (PL *die* **Rivalinnen**) rival.

△ NEW SPELLING: *See page xii*

Robbe *die* (PL *die* **Robben**) seal.

Roboter *der* (PL *die* **Roboter**) robot.

roch SEE **riechen**.

Rock *der* (PL *die* **Röcke**) skirt.

Roggen *der* rye.

roh *adjective* 1 raw; 2 rough;
3 brutal.

Rohr *das* (PL *die* **Rohre**) 1 pipe;
2 reed; 3 cane.

Rolladen = **Rollladen**.

Rolle *die* (PL *die* **Rollen**) 1 roll;
2 reel; 3 role, part; 4 **es spielt keine
Rolle** it doesn't matter.

rollen *verb* (PERF **hat gerollt**) 1 to
roll; 2 (PERF **ist gerollt**) to roll.

Roller *der* (PL *die* **Roller**) scooter.

Rollkragen *der* (PL *die* **Rollkrägen**)
polo neck.

Rollladen △ *der* (PL *die* **Rolllläden**)
shutter.

Rollschuh *der* (PL *die* **Rollschuhe**)
roller-skate.

Rollschuhlaufen *das* roller-
skating.

Rollstuhl *der* (PL *die* **Rollstühle**)
wheelchair.

Rolltreppe *die* (PL *die* **Rolltreppen**)
escalator.

Rom *das* Rome.

Roman *der* (PL *die* **Romane**) novel.

romantisch *adjective* romantic.

röntgen *verb* (PERF **hat geröntgt**) to
X-ray.

rosa *adjective* pink.

Rose *die* (PL *die* **Rosen**) rose.

Rosenkohl *der* (Brussels) sprouts.

Rosine *die* (PL *die* **Rosinen**) raisin.

Rosmarin *der* rosemary.

Rosskastanie △ *die* (PL *die*
Rosskastanien) horse-chestnut.

Rost *der* (PL *die* **Roste**) 1 rust;
2 grate, grill.

rosten *verb* (PERF **ist gerostet**) to
rust.

rösten (PERF **hat geröstet**) 1 to roast;
2 to toast.

rostig *adjective* rusty.

rot *adjective* red.

Röteln *plural noun* German
measles.

rothaarig *adjective* red-haired.

Rotkehlchen *das* (PL *die*
Rotkehlchen) robin.

Rotwein *der* (PL *die* **Rotweine**) red
wine.

rüber *adverb* (*informal*) over;
komm zu uns rüber come over to
us.

rücken *verb* (PERF **hat gerückt**) to
move; **kannst du ein wenig
rücken?** can you move over a bit?

Rücken *der* (PL *die* **Rücken**) 1 back;
2 spine (*of a book*).

Rückfahrkarte *die* (PL *die*
Rückfahrkarten) return ticket; **eine
Rückfahrkarte nach München** a
return ticket to Munich.

⟡ IRREGULAR VERB: *See the verb table in the centre of the dictionary*

Rückfahrt die return journey; **auf der Rückfahrt** on the way back.

Rückgabe die (PL die **Rückgaben**) return.

rückgängig adjective **etwas rückgängig machen** to cancel something.

Rückkehr die return.

Rückreise die return journey.

Rucksack der (PL die **Rucksäcke**) rucksack.

Rückseite die (PL die **Rückseiten**) back.

Rücksicht die consideration.

rücksichtslos adjective
1 inconsiderate; **ein rücksichtsloser Fahrer** a reckless driver; **2** ruthless.

rücksichtsvoll adjective considerate.

Rücksitz der (PL die **Rücksitze**) back seat.

rückwärts adverb backwards.

Rückwärtsgang der (PL die **Rückwärtsgänge**) reverse (gear).

Rückweg der (PL die **Rückwege**)
1 way back; **2** return journey.

Rückzahlung die (PL die **Rückzahlungen**) refund, repayment.

Ruder das (PL die **Ruder**) **1** oar; **2** rudder.

Ruderboot das (PL die **Ruderboote**) rowing boat.

rudern verb (PERF **ist gerudert**) **1** to row; **ich bin über den See gerudert** I rowed across the lake; **2** (PERF **hat gerudert**) to row; **ich habe Monika über den See gerudert** I rowed Monika across the lake.

Ruf der (PL die **Rufe**) **1** call, shout; **2** reputation; **3** phone number.

rufen ◇ verb (IMPERF **rief**, PERF **hat gerufen**) to call; **den Arzt rufen** to send for the doctor.

Rufnummer die (PL die **Rufnummern**) phone number.

Ruhe die **1** silence; **Ruhe bitte!** quiet please!; **2** rest; **3** peace; **jemanden in Ruhe lassen** to leave somebody in peace; **in aller Ruhe** calmly; **4 sich nicht aus der Ruhe bringen lassen** to not get worked up; **5 sich zur Ruhe setzen** to retire.

ruhen verb (PERF **hat geruht**) to rest; **hier ruht …** here lies …

Ruhestand der **im Ruhestand** retired.

Ruhetag der (PL die **Ruhetage**) closing day; **'Dienstag Ruhetag'** 'closed on Tuesdays'.

ruhig adjective **1** quiet; **2** peaceful; **3** calm.
adverb **1** quietly; **sich ruhig verhalten** to keep quiet; **2** calmly; **ruhig bleiben** to remain calm; **3 sehen Sie sich ruhig um** you're welcome to look around; **du kannst es ihm ruhig sagen** it's OK, you can tell him.

Ruhm der fame.

Rührei das scrambled eggs.

△ NEW SPELLING: *See page xii*

rühren *verb* (PERF **hat gerührt**) **1** to move; **2** to stir; **3** **sich rühren** to move; **4** **an etwas rühren** to touch, to touch on.

Ruine *die* (PL *die* **Ruinen**) ruin.

ruinieren *verb* (PERF **hat ruiniert**) to ruin.

rülpsen *verb* (PERF **hat gerülpst**) to belch.

Rumänien *das* Romania.

rumänisch *adjective* Romanian.

Rummel *der* **1** hustle and bustle; **2** fuss; **3** fair.

Rummelplatz *der* (PL *die* **Rummelplätze**) fairground.

rund *adjective* round.
adverb about; **rund um** around.

Runde *die* (PL *die* **Runden**) **1** round; **2** lap; **3** circle, group; **4** **über die Runden kommen** (*informal*) to get by.

Rundfahrt *die* (PL *die* **Rundfahrten**) tour.

Rundfrage *die* (PL *die* **Rundfragen**) poll.

Rundfunk *der* radio; **im Rundfunk** on the radio.

rundherum *adverb* all around.

runter *adverb* (*informal*) SEE **herunter, hinunter**; **runter da !** get off!

runzlig *adjective* wrinkled.

Rüsche *die* (PL *die* **Rüschen**) frill.

Russe *der* (PL *die* **Russen**) Russian.

Rüssel *der* (PL *die* **Rüssel**) trunk.

Russin *die* (PL *die* **Russinnen**) Russian.

russisch *adjective* Russian.

Russland ∆ *das* Russia.

Rüstung *die* (PL *die* **Rüstungen**) **1** armament; **2** arms; **3** (suit of) armour.

Rutschbahn *die* (PL *die* **Rutschbahnen**) slide.

rutschen *verb* (PERF **ist gerutscht**) **1** to slide; **2** to slip; **3** **rutsch mal !** move over !

rutschig *adjective* slippery.

rütteln *verb* (PERF **hat gerüttelt**) to shake; **an der Tür rütteln** to rattle a[t] the door.

S s

Saal *der* (PL *die* **Säle**) hall.

Sabbat *der* (PL *die* **Sabbate**) Sabbath.

Sache *die* (PL *die* **Sachen**) **1** matter; **das ist eine andere Sache** that's a different matter; **2** business; **das ist seine Sache** that's his business; **3** thing; **meine Sachen** my things (*clothing*); **sie räumt nie ihre Sachen weg** she never puts away her things; **4** **zur Sache kommen** to get to the point; **5** **das ist so'ne Sache** (*informal*) it's a bit tricky.

Sachgebiet *das* (PL *die* **Sachgebiete**) field, area.

⬧ IRREGULAR VERB: *See the verb table in the centre of the dictionary*

sachlich *adjective* **1** objective;
2 factual.

sächlich *adjective* neuter.

Sachsen *das* Saxony.

Sack *der* (PL *die* **Säcke**) **1** sack;
2 bag.

Sackgasse *die* (PL *die* **Sackgassen**)
cul-de-sac.

Saft *der* (PL *die* **Säfte**) **1** juice; **2** sap.

saftig *adjective* juicy.

Säge *die* (PL *die* **Sägen**) saw.

Sägemehl *das* sawdust.

sagen *verb* (PERF **hat gesagt**) **1** to
say; **man sagt, dass** ... it's said that
...; **2 was ich noch sagen wollte** by
the way; **unter uns gesagt** between
you and me; **3** to tell; **jemandem
etwas sagen** to tell somebody
something; **sag mal** tell me; **was
sagen Sie dazu?** what do you think
about it?; **4** to mean; **das hat nichts
zu sagen** it doesn't mean anything;
5 zu jemandem Tante sagen to call
somebody aunt; **6 ihr Gesicht
sagte alles** it was written all over
her face.

sägen *verb* (PERF **hat gesägt**) to saw.

sagenhaft *adjective* **1** legendary;
2 (*informal*) brilliant.

sah SEE **sehen**.

Sahne *die* cream.

Saison *die* (PL *die* **Saisons**) season.

Saite *die* (PL *die* **Saiten**) string.

Sakko *das* (PL *die* **Sakkos**) jacket.

Salat *der* (PL *die* **Salate**) **1** lettuce;
2 salad.

Salatsoße *die* (PL *die* **Salatsoßen**)
salad dressing.

Salbe *die* (PL *die* **Salben**) ointment.

Salbei *der* sage.

salopp *adjective* casual, informal.

Salz *das* salt.

salzen *verb* (PERF **hat gesalzen**) to
salt.

salzig *adjective* salty.

Salzkartoffeln *plural noun* boiled
potatoes.

Salzwasser *das* **1** salt water;
2 salted water (*for cooking*).

Samen *der* (PL *die* **Samen**) **1** seed;
2 sperm, semen.

sammeln *verb* (PERF **hat
gesammelt**) **1** to collect; **Martin
sammelt Briefmarken** Martin
collects stamps; **2** to gather; **3 sich
sammeln** to gather; **seine
Gedanken sammeln** to gather your
thoughts.

Sammlung *die* (PL *die*
Sammlungen) collection; **eine
Sammlung für einen guten Zweck**
a collection for charity.

Samstag *der* (PL *die* **Samstage**)
Saturday.

samstags *adverb* on Saturdays.

samt *preposition* ←(+DAT) (together)
with; **Mimi kam samt Puppen und
Katze** Mimi arrived with her dolls
and cat.

△ NEW SPELLING: *See page xii*

Samt *der* (PL *die* **Samte**) velvet.

sämtlicher, sämtliche, sämtliches *adjective* all the; **meine sämtlichen Bücher** all my books.

Sand *der* sand.

Sandale *die* (PL *die* **Sandalen**) sandal.

sandig *adjective* sandy.

sandte SEE **senden**.

sanft *adjective* gentle; **eine sanfte Stimme** a soft voice.

sang SEE **singen**.

Sänger *der* (PL *die* **Sänger**) singer.

Sängerin *die* (PL *die* **Sängerinnen**) singer.

sank SEE **sinken**.

Sardelle *die* (PL *die* **Sardellen**) anchovy.

Sardine *die* (PL *die* **Sardinen**) sardine.

Sarg *der* (PL *die* **Särge**) coffin.

Sarkasmus *der* sarcasm.

sarkastisch *adjective* sarcastic.

saß SEE **sitzen**.

Satellit *der* (PL *die* **Satelliten**) satellite.

Satellitenfernsehen *das* satellite television.

satt *adjective* 1 full (up); **bist du satt geworden?** have you had enough to eat?; **sich satt essen** to eat as much as one wants; **satt machen** to be filling; 2 **etwas satt haben** (*informal*) to be fed up with something.

Sattel *der* (PL *die* **Sättel**) saddle.

Satz *der* (PL *die* **Sätze**) 1 sentence; 2 set (*of things or in tennis*); **ein Satz Reifen** a set of tyres; 3 movement (*in music*); 4 rate (*of tax, interest*); 5 leap.

sauber *adjective* 1 clean; 2 neat; 3 (*informal*) fine (*expressing irony*); 4 **sauber machen** Δ to clean.

Sauberkeit *die* cleanliness, cleanness.

saubermachen SEE **sauber**.

Sauce *die* (PL *die* **Saucen**) = **Soße**.

sauer *adjective* 1 sour; 2 pickled; 3 acid; **saurer Regen** acid rain; 4 **sauer sein** (*informal*) to be annoyed; **ich bin sauer auf Eva** I'm annoyed with Eva.

Sauerei *die* (*informal*) (PL *die* **Sauereien**) 1 mess; 2 disgrace, scandal; 3 obscenity.

Sauerstoff *der* oxygen.

saufen ✧ *verb* (*informal*) (PRES **säuft**, IMPERF **soff**, PERF **hat gesoffen**) to drink, to booze.

saugen *verb* (PERF **hat gesaugt**) 1 to suck; 2 to vacuum, to hoover.

Säugetier *das* (PL *die* **Säugetiere**) mammal.

Säugling *der* (PL *die* **Säuglinge**) baby, infant.

Säule *die* (PL *die* **Säulen**) column.

Säure *die* (PL *die* **Säuren**) acid.

✧ IRREGULAR VERB: *See the verb table in the centre of the dictionary*

axofon Δ *das* (PL *die* **Saxofone**) saxophone.

-Bahn *die* (PL *die* **S-Bahnen**) city and suburban railway.

chäbig *adjective* shabby.

chach *das* chess; **Schach!** check!

chachbrett *das* (PL *die* **Schachbretter**) chessboard.

chachfigur *die* (PL *die* **Schachfiguren**) chess piece.

chachtel *die* (PL *die* **Schachteln**) box.

chade *adjective* 1 **schade sein** to be a pity; **schade!** (what a) pity!; 2 **zu schade für jemanden sein** to be too good for somebody.

chaden *verb* (PERF **hat geschadet**) 1 to damage; **das hat seinem Ruf geschadet** it damaged his reputation; 2 **jemandem schaden** to harm somebody; 3 **das schadet nichts** it doesn't matter.

chaden *der* (PL *die* **Schäden**) 1 damage; 2 disadvantage.

chädlich *adjective* harmful.

chaf *das* (PL *die* **Schafe**) sheep.

chäfer *der* (PL *die* **Schäfer**) shepherd.

chäferhund *der* (PL *die* **Schäferhunde**) sheepdog.

chaffen¹ ◇ *verb* (IMPERF **schuf**, PERF **hat geschaffen**) to create; **wie geschaffen für** made for.

chaffen² *verb* (PERF **hat geschafft**) 1 to manage; **es schaffen, etwas zu tun** to manage to do something;

2 **eine Prüfung schaffen** to pass an exam; 3 **jemandem zu schaffen machen** to cause somebody trouble; 4 **geschafft sein** (*informal*) to be worn out.

Schaffner *der* (PL *die* **Schaffner**) 1 conductor; 2 (ticket) inspector.

Schaffnerin *die* (PL *die* **Schaffnerinnen**) 1 conductress; 2 (ticket) inspector.

Schal *der* (PL *die* **Schals**) scarf.

Schale *die* (PL *die* **Schalen**) 1 skin; 2 peel; 3 shell; 4 dish, bowl; **eine Schale Obst** a bowl of fruit.

schälen *verb* (PERF **hat geschält**) 1 to peel; **er hat ihr eine Orange geschält** he peeled an orange for her; 2 **sich schälen** to peel; **mein Rücken schält sich** my back's peeling.

Schall *der* sound.

Schallplatte *die* (PL *die* **Schallplatten**) record.

schalten *verb* (PERF **hat geschaltet**) 1 to switch; **auf etwas schalten** to turn to something; 2 to change gear; 3 **schnell schalten** (*informal*) to catch on quickly.

Schalter *der* (PL *die* **Schalter**) 1 switch; 2 counter.

Schaltjahr *das* (PL *die* **Schaltjahre**) leap year.

schämen *verb* (PERF **hat sich geschämt**) **sich schämen** to be ashamed.

Schampon *das* (PL *die* **Schampons**) shampoo.

Δ NEW SPELLING: See p

Schande *die* 1 disgrace; 2 shame.

scharf *adjective* 1 sharp; 2 hot (*food*); **ein scharfer Wind** a biting wind; 3 fierce (*dog, frost*); 4 **scharf nachdenken** to think hard; 5 (*in photography*) **scharf sein** to be in focus; **scharf einstellen** to focus; 6 **scharf schießen** to fire live ammunition; 7 **scharf auf etwas sein** (*informal*) to be really keen on something; **sie ist scharf auf Bernd** (*informal*) she fancies Bernd.

Schaschlik *der* (PL *die* **Schaschliks**) kebab.

Schatten *der* (PL *die* **Schatten**) 1 shadow; 2 shade.

schattig *adjective* shady.

Schatz *der* (PL *die* **Schätze**) 1 treasure; 2 darling.

Schätzchen *das* (PL *die* **Schätzchen**) darling.

schätzen *verb* (PERF **hat geschätzt**) 1 to estimate; 2 to value; 3 to reckon, to guess; **schätz mal!** guess!; 4 **etwas zu schätzen wissen** to appreciate something.

Schau *die* (PL *die* **Schauen**) show.

schauen *verb* (PERF **hat geschaut**) to look.

Schauer *der* (PL *die* **Schauer**) shower.

Schauergeschichte *die* (PL *die* **Schauergeschichten**) horror story.

Schaufel *die* (PL *die* **Schaufeln**) 1 shovel; 2 dustpan.

Schaufenster *das* (PL *die* **Schaufenster**) shop window.

Schaukel *die* (PL *die* **Schaukeln**) swing.

schaukeln *verb* (PERF **hat geschaukelt**) to swing.

Schaukelstuhl *der* (PL *die* **Schaukelstühle**) rocking chair.

Schaum *der* 1 foam; 2 froth; 3 lather.

schäumen *verb* (PERF **hat geschäumt**) 1 to foam; 2 to froth (up).

Schauplatz *der* (PL *die* **Schauplätze**) scene.

Schauspiel *das* (PL *die* **Schauspiele**) 1 play; 2 spectacle.

Schauspieler *der* (PL *die* **Schauspieler**) actor.

Schauspielerin *die* (PL *die* **Schauspielerinnen**) actress.

Scheck *der* (PL *die* **Schecks**) cheque

Scheckbuch *das* (PL *die* **Scheckbücher**) chequebook.

Scheckkarte *die* (PL *die* **Scheckkarten**) cheque card.

Scheibe *die* (PL *die* **Scheiben**) 1 pane (*of a window, car*); 2 slice; **eine Scheibe Schinken** a slice of ham; **die Salami in Scheiben schneiden** to slice the salami; **du könntest dir eine Scheibe von ihr abschneiden** (*informal*) you could take a leaf out of her book; 3 disc.

Scheibenwischer *der* (PL *die*

$\diamondsuit$ **IRREGULAR VERB:** *See the verb table in the centre of the dictionary*

Scheibenwischer) windscreen
wiper.

cheiden ✧ *verb* (IMPERF **schied**,
PERF **hat geschieden**) **1** to separate;
sich scheiden lassen to get
divorced; **2 geschieden sein** to be
divorced.

cheidung *die* (PL *die*
Scheidungen) divorce.

chein *der* (PL *die* **Scheine**) **1** light;
2 appearance; **etwas nur zum
Schein machen** to only pretend to
do something; **3** certificate; **4** note
(*money*).

cheinbar *adverb* apparently.

cheinen ✧ *verb* (IMPERF **schien**,
PERF **hat geschienen**) **1** to shine;
2 to seem; **mir scheint** it seems to
me.

cheinwerfer *der* (PL *die*
Scheinwerfer) **1** headlamp,
headlight; **2** floodlight, spotlight.

cheitern *verb* (PERF **ist
gescheitert**) to fail.

chenkel *der* (PL *die* **Schenkel**)
thigh.

chenken *verb* (PERF **hat
geschenkt**) **1** to give; **etwas
geschenkt bekommen** to be given
something; **2 sich etwas schenken**
to give something a miss; **3 das ist
ja geschenkt!** (*informal*) it's a gift!

chere *die* (PL *die* **Scheren**) **1** (pair
of) scissors; **2** shears; **3** claw (*of a
crab*).

cheren *verb* (*informal*) (PERF **hat
geschert**) to bother; **sich nicht um
etwas scheren** not to care about

something; **scher dich um deine
eigenen Angelegenheiten!** mind
your own business!; **scher dich zum
Teufel!** go to hell!

Scherz *der* (PL *die* **Scherze**) joke.

scheu *adjective* shy.

scheuern *verb* (PERF **hat
gescheuert**) **1** to scrub; **2** to rub.

Scheune *die* (PL *die* **Scheunen**)
barn.

scheußlich *adjective* horrible.

Schi *der* (PL *die* **Schi(er)**) = **Ski**.

Schicht *die* (PL *die* **Schichten**)
1 layer; **2** class; **3** shift.

schick *adjective* **1** stylish, smart;
2 (*informal*) great.

schicken *verb* (PERF **hat geschickt**)
to send.

Schicksal *das* (PL *die* **Schicksale**)
fate.

schieben ✧ *verb* (IMPERF **schob**,
PERF **hat geschoben**) **1** to push;
2 etwas auf etwas schieben to
blame something for something; **die
Schuld auf jemanden schieben** to
put the blame on somebody.

schied SEE **scheiden**.

Schiedsrichter *der* (PL *die*
Schiedsrichter) referee, umpire.

schief *adjective* crooked; **ein
schiefer Blick** a funny look.
adverb **1 das Bild hängt schief** the
picture is not straight; **2 schief
gehen** △ to go wrong.

Schiefer *der* slate.

schiefgehen SEE **schief**.

schielen *verb* (PERF **hat geschielt**) to squint.

schien SEE **scheinen**.

Schienbein *das* (PL *die* **Schienbeine**) shin.

Schiene *die* (PL *die* **Schienen**) 1 rail; 2 splint.

schießen ◇ *verb* (IMPERF **schoss** Δ, PERF **hat geschossen**) 1 to shoot; **auf jemanden schießen** to shoot at somebody; **ein Tor schießen** to score a goal; 2 (PERF **ist geschossen**) to shoot (along); **Andrea ist in die Höhe geschossen** Andrea's shot up (*has got a lot taller*).

Schiff *das* (PL *die* **Schiffe**) ship.

schikanieren *verb* (PERF **hat schikaniert**) to bully.

Schikoree Δ *der* chicory.

Schild *das* (PL *die* **Schilder**) 1 sign; 2 badge; 3 label.

Schildkröte *die* (PL *die* **Schildkröten**) 1 tortoise; 2 turtle.

Schilling *der* (PL *die* **Schilling(e)**) Schilling.

Schimmel *der* (PL *die* **Schimmel**) 1 mould; 2 white horse.

Schimpanse *der* (PL *die* **Schimpansen**) chimpanzee.

schimpfen *verb* (PERF **hat geschimpft**) 1 to tell off; 2 to grumble.

Schinken *der* (PL *die* **Schinken**) ham.

Schirm *der* (PL *die* **Schirme**) 1 umbrella; 2 sunshade; 3 shade (*a lamp*); 4 peak (*of a cap*).

Schlaf *der* sleep.

Schlafanzug *der* (PL *die* **Schlafanzüge**) pyjamas.

schlafen ◇ *verb* (PRES **schläft**, IMPERF **schlief**, PERF **hat geschlafen**) 1 to sleep; 2 to be asleep; 3 **schlafen gehen** to go to bed.

Schlafcouch *die* (PL *die* **Schlafcouchs**) sofa bed.

schlaff *adjective* 1 slack (*rope*); 2 limp (*handshake, body*); 3 lethargic.

Schlafsaal *der* (PL *die* **Schlafsäle**) dormitory.

Schlafsack *der* (PL *die* **Schlafsäcke**) sleeping bag.

Schlafzimmer *das* (PL *die* **Schlafzimmer**) bedroom.

Schlafwagen *der* (PL *die* **Schlafwagen**) sleeper.

Schlag *der* (PL *die* **Schläge**) 1 blow, punch; **Schläge kriegen** to get a beating; 2 stroke; 3 (*electric*) shock; 4 **Schlag auf Schlag** in quick succession; **auf einen Schlag** all at once.

schlagen ◇ *verb* (PRES **schlägt**, IMPERF **schlug**, PERF **hat geschlagen**) 1 to hit; **einen Nagel in die Wand schlagen** to knock a nail into the wall; 2 to beat; 3 to bang; **mit dem Kopf gegen etwas schlagen** to bang your head against something; 4 to strike (*of a clock*); 5 to whip (*cream*); 6 **sich schlagen** to fight;

7 sich geschlagen geben to admit defeat.

chlager der (PL die **Schlager**) hit.

chläger der (PL die **Schläger**) 1 racket (*in tennis*); 2 bat (*in baseball*); 3 club (*in golf*); 4 stick (*in hockey*); 5 thug.

chlägerei die (PL die **Schlägereien**) fight.

chlagsahne die 1 whipping cream; 2 whipped cream.

chlagzeile die (PL die **Schlagzeilen**) headline.

chlagzeug das (PL die **Schlagzeuge**) drums.

chlagzeuger der (PL die **Schlagzeuger**) drummer.

chlamm der mud.

chlampen verb (PERF **hat geschlampt**) to be sloppy.

chlamperei die (PL die **Schlampereien**) 1 sloppiness; 2 mess.

chlampig adjective sloppy.

chlange die (PL die **Schlangen**) 1 snake; 2 queue; **Schlange stehen** to queue.

chlank adjective slim.

chlankheitskur die (PL die **Schlankheitskuren**) diet; **eine Schlankeitskur machen** to be on a diet.

chlapp adjective worn out, tired out.

chlau adjective 1 crafty; 2 clever;

ich werde nicht schlau daraus I can't make head nor tail of it.

Schlauch der (PL die **Schläuche**) hose.

schlecht adjective 1 bad; **schlecht werden** to go bad; 2 **mir ist schlecht** I feel sick; 3 **jemanden schlecht machen** △ to run somebody down.
adverb 1 badly; **schlecht gelaunt** in a bad mood; 2 **es geht ihm schlecht** he's not well.

schleichen ✧ verb (IMPERF **schlich**, PERF **ist geschlichen**) 1 to creep; 2 to crawl (*in traffic*); 3 **sich schleichen** to creep.

Schleife die (PL die **Schleifen**) 1 bow; 2 loop.

Schleuder die (PL die **Schleudern**) 1 catapult; 2 spin-dryer.

schleudern verb (PERF **hat geschleudert**) 1 to hurl; 2 to spin (*washing*); 3 (PERF **ist geschleudert**) to skid.

schlich SEE **schleichen**.

schlicht adjective plain, simple.

schlief SEE **schlafen**.

schließen ✧ verb (IMPERF **schloss** △, PERF **hat geschlossen**) 1 to close, to shut; 2 to close down; 3 to lock; 4 to conclude; **aus etwas schließen, dass ...** to conclude from something that ...; 5 **einen Vertrag schließen** to enter into a contract; 6 **Freundschaft mit jemandem schließen** to make friends with somebody; 7 **sich schließen** to close.

△ NEW SPELLING: *See page xii*

Schließfach das (PL die Schließfächer) locker.

schließlich adverb 1 finally; 2 after all; **er hat sie schließlich doch eingeladen** he's invited her after all.

schlimm adjective bad.

schlimmstenfalls adverb if the worst comes to the worst.

Schlips der (PL die Schlipse) tie.

Schlitten der (PL die Schlitten) sledge; **Schlitten fahren gehen** to go sledging.

Schlittschuh der (PL die Schlittschuhe) skate; **Schlittschuh laufen** to skate.

Schlittschuhlaufen das ice-skating.

Schlitz der (PL die Schlitze) 1 slit; 2 flies (in trousers); 3 slot.

schloss △ SEE **schließen**.

Schloss △ das (PL die Schlösser) 1 lock; 2 castle.

Schluck der (PL die Schlucke) 1 mouthful; 2 gulp.

Schluckauf der hiccups.

schlucken verb (PERF **hat geschluckt**) to swallow.

schlug SEE **schlagen**.

Schlüpfer der (PL die Schlüpfer) knickers.

Schluss △ der (PL die Schlüsse) 1 end, ending; **zum Schluss** in the end; **Schluss machen** to stop; **mit jemandem Schluss machen** to finish with somebody; 2 conclusion.

Schlüssel der (PL die Schlüssel) 1 key; 2 spanner.

Schlussverkauf △ der sales.

schmal adjective 1 narrow; 2 thin (face, nose); 3 **sie ist schmäler geworden** she's lost weight.

schmecken verb (PERF **hat geschmeckt**) to taste; **die Suppe schmeckt gut** the soup tastes good; **das schmeckt mir nicht** I don't like it; **das Eis schmeckt nacht Zitrone** the ice cream tastes of lemon.

schmeicheln verb (PERF **hat geschmeichelt**) to flatter; **jemandem schmeicheln** to flatter somebody.

schmeißen ✧ verb (informal) (IMPERF **schmiss** △, PERF **hat geschmissen**) to chuck; **mit etwas schmeißen** to chuck something.

schmelzen ✧ verb (PRES **schmilzt**, IMPERF **schmolz**, PERF **ist geschmolzen**) 1 to melt; **der Schnee ist geschmolzen** the snow has melted; 2 (PERF **hat geschmolzen**) to melt (snow, ice); 3 (PERF **hat geschmolzen**) to smelt (ore).

Schmerz der (PL die Schmerzen) 1 pain; 2 grief.

schmerzen verb (PERF **hat geschmerzt**) to hurt.

schmerzhaft adjective painful.

Schmerzmittel das (PL die Schmerzmittel) painkiller.

Schmetterling der (PL die Schmetterlinge) butterfly.

✧ IRREGULAR VERB: *See the verb table in the centre of the dictionary*

chmieren *verb* (PERF **hat geschmiert**) **1** to lubricate; **2** to spread (*butter, jam*); **Brote schmieren** to spread slices of bread; **jemandem eine schmieren** (*informal*) to clout somebody; **3** to scrawl; **4** to smudge.

chmilzt SEE **schmelzen**.

chminke *die* make-up.

chminken *verb* (PERF **hat geschminkt**) **1** to make up; **2 sich schminken** to put on make-up.

chmiss △ SEE **schmeißen**.

chmolz SEE **schmelzen**.

chmuck *der* **1** jewellery; **2** decoration.

chmücken *verb* (PERF **hat geschmückt**) to decorate.

chmuggeln *verb* (PERF **hat geschmuggelt**) to smuggle.

chmusen *verb* (PERF **hat geschmust**) to cuddle; **Gabi hat mit Max geschmust** Gabi cuddled Max.

chmutz *der* dirt.

chmutzig *adjective* dirty.

chnabel *der* (PL *die* **Schnäbel**) beak.

chnalle *die* (PL *die* **Schnallen**) buckle.

chnarchen *verb* (PERF **hat geschnarcht**) to snore.

chnauze *die* (PL *die* **Schnauzen**) **1** muzzle; **eine kalte Schnauze** a cold nose; **2 die Schnauze halten** (*informal*) to keep your mouth shut.

schnäuzen △ (PERF **hat sich geschnäuzt**) **sich schnäuzen** to blow your nose.

Schnecke *die* (PL *die* **Schnecken**) snail.

Schnee *der* snow.

Schneeregen *der* sleet.

schneiden ✧ *verb* (IMPERF **schnitt**, PERF **hat geschnitten**) **1** to cut; **ich kann dir die Haare schneiden** I can cut your hair; **Evi hat sich die Haare kurz schneiden lassen** Evi had her hair cut short; **in Scheiben schneiden** to slice; **2 sich schneiden** to cut yourself; **ich habe mich in den Finger geschnitten** I've cut my finger; **3 sich schneiden** to intersect; **4 Gesichter schneiden** to pull faces.

Schneider *der* (PL *die* **Schneider**) tailor.

Schneiderin *die* (PL *die* **Schneiderinnen**) dressmaker.

schneien *verb* (PERF **hat geschneit**) to snow; **es schneit** it's snowing.

schnell *adjective* quick, fast. *adverb* quickly; **mach schnell!** hurry up!

Schnelligkeit *die* speed.

Schnellimbiss △ *der* (PL *die* **Schnellimbisse**) snack bar.

schnellstens *adverb* as quickly as possible.

Schnellzug *der* (PL *die* **Schnellzüge**) express (train).

schneuzen = **schnäuzen**.

△ NEW SPELLING: *See page xii*

schnitt SEE **schneiden**.

Schnitt der (PL die **Schnitte**) 1 cut;
**er hat einen tiefen Schnitt im
Finger** he's got a deep cut in his
finger; **das Kostüm hat einen sehr
guten Schnitt** the suit is well cut;
2 cutting (of a film); 3 **im Schnitt**
on average; 4 pattern.

Schnittlauch der chives.

Schnitzel das (PL die **Schnitzel**)
1 escalope; 2 scrap.

schnitzen verb (PERF **hat
geschnitzt**) to carve.

Schnorchel der (PL die
Schnorchel) snorkel.

schnüffeln verb (PERF **hat
geschnüffelt**) 1 to sniff; 2 to snoop
around.

Schnuller der (PL die **Schnuller**)
dummy.

Schnupfen der (PL die **Schnupfen**)
cold.

Schnur die (PL die **Schnüre**) 1 (piece
of) string; 2 flex; 3 cord.

Schnurrbart der (PL die
Schnurrbärte) moustache.

schnurren verb (PERF **hat
geschnurrt**) to purr.

Schnürsenkel der (PL die
Schnürsenkel) shoelace.

schob SEE **schieben**.

Schock der (PL die **Schocks**) shock.

schockieren verb (PERF **hat
schockiert**) to shock.

Schokolade die (PL die
Schokoladen) chocolate.

schon adverb 1 already ('schon' is
often not translated); **schon wieder**
again; **schon oft** often; **du wirst
schon sehen** you'll see; **ja schon,
aber ...** well yes, but ...; **nun geh
schon!** go on then!; 2 yet; **hast du
sie schon gesehen?** have you see
her yet?; **du weißt schon** you know
3 even; 4 **komm schon!** come on
5 **schon deshalb** for that reason
alone; 6 **das ist schon möglich**
that's quite possible; 7 **er war schon
mal da** he's been there before.

schön adjective 1 beautiful; 2 nice
schönes Wochenende! have a nice
weekend!; 3 good; **na schön** all
right then; 4 **schönen Dank** thank
you very much; **schöne Grüße** best
wishes.

schonen verb (PERF **hat geschont**)
1 to look after; 2 **sich schonen** to
take things easy.

Schönheit die (PL die **Schönheiten**)
beauty.

Schornstein der (PL die
Schornsteine) chimney, funnel.

schoss △ SEE **schießen**.

Schoß der (PL die **Schöße**) lap.

Schotte der (PL die **Schotten**) Scot,
Scotsman.

Schottin die (PL die **Schottinnen**)
Scot, Scotswoman.

schottisch adjective Scottish.

Schottland das Scotland.

schräg adjective 1 diagonal;

✧ IRREGULAR VERB: See the verb table in the centre of the dictionary

2 sloping.
adverb **etwas schräg halten** to tilt something; **etwas schräg stellen** to put something at an angle.

Schrank *der* (PL die **Schränke**)
1 cupboard; 2 wardrobe.

Schranke *die* (PL die **Schranken**)
barrier.

Schraube *die* (PL die **Schrauben**)
screw.

schrauben *verb* (PERF **hat geschraubt**) to screw.

Schraubenschlüssel *der* (PL die **Schraubenschlüssel**) spanner.

Schraubenzieher *der* (PL die **Schraubenzieher**) screwdriver.

Schreck *der* fright; **jemandem einen Schreck einjagen** to give somebody a fright; **ich habe einen Schreck bekommen** I got a fright.

schrecklich *adjective* terrible.

Schrei *der* (PL die **Schreie**) 1 cry, shout; 2 scream; 3 **der letzte Schrei** (*informal*) the latest thing.

Schreibblock *der* (PL die **Schreibblöcke**) writing pad.

schreiben ◇ *verb* (IMPERF **schrieb**, PERF **hat geschrieben**) 1 to write; **David hat mir einen Brief geschrieben** David wrote a letter to me; **einen Test schreiben** to do a test; 2 to spell; **wie schreibt man das?** how is it spelt?; 3 to type.

Schreibmaschine *die* (PL die **Schreibmaschinen**) typewriter.

Schreibpapier *das* writing paper.

Schreibtisch *der* (PL die **Schreibtische**) desk.

Schreibwaren *plural noun* stationery.

schreien ◇ *verb* (IMPERF **schrie**, PERF **hat geschrien**) 1 to cry, to shout; **das Baby schreit** the baby's crying; 2 to scream; **vor Lachen schreien** to scream with laughter; **zum Schreien sein** (*informal*) to be a scream.

Schreiner *der* (PL die **Schreiner**) joiner.

schrie SEE **schreien**.

schrieb SEE **schreiben**.

Schrift *die* (PL die **Schriften**) 1 writing; 2 type; 3 script.

schriftlich *adjective* written.
adverb in writing; **das lasse ich mir schriftlich geben** I'll get that in writing; **jemanden schriftlich einladen** to send somebody a written invitation.

Schriftsteller *der* (PL die **Schriftsteller**) writer.

Schriftstellerin *die* (PL die **Schriftstellerinnen**) writer.

Schritt *der* (PL die **Schritte**) step.

schrumpfen *verb* (PERF **ist geschrumpft**) 1 to shrink; 2 to shrivel.

Schublade *die* (PL die **Schubladen**) drawer.

schubsen *verb* (PERF **hat geschubst**) to shove.

schüchtern *adjective* shy.

schuf SEE **schaffen**.

△ NEW SPELLING: *See page xii*

Schuh der (PL die **Schuhe**) shoe.

Schuhgröße die (PL die **Schuhgrößen**) shoe size.

Schularbeiten plural noun homework.

Schulaufgaben plural noun homework.

Schulbuch das (PL die **Schulbücher**) schoolbook.

Schuld die (PL die **Schulden**)
1 blame; **Schuld haben** △ to be to blame; **jemandem Schuld geben** to blame somebody; 2 fault; **es war seine Schuld** it was his fault; 3 guilt; 4 debt; **Schulden haben** to be in debt; **Schulden machen** to get into debt.

schuld adjective **schuld sein** to be to blame; **du bist schuld daran** it's your fault.

schulden verb (PERF **hat geschuldet**) to owe.

schuldig adjective 1 guilty; 2 **jemandem etwas schuldig sein** to owe somebody something.

Schule die (PL die **Schulen**) school.

schulen verb (PERF **hat geschult**) to train.

Schüler der (PL die **Schüler**) pupil, student.

Schülerin die (PL die **Schülerinnen**) pupil, student.

Schulferien plural noun school holidays.

schulfrei adjective **ein schulfreier Tag** a day off school; **wir haben**

heute schulfrei there's no school today.

Schulfreund der (PL die **Schulfreunde**) schoolfriend.

Schulfreundin die (PL die **Schulfreundinnen**) schoolfriend.

Schulhof der (PL die **Schulhöfe**) playground.

Schulstunde die (PL die **Schulstunden**) period.

Schultasche die (PL die **Schultaschen**) schoolbag.

Schulter die (PL die **Schultern**) shoulder.

schummeln verb (PERF **hat geschummelt**) to cheat.

Schuppe die (PL die **Schuppen**) 1 scale; 2 **Schuppen** dandruff.

Schuppen der (PL die **Schuppen**) shed.

Schürze die (PL die **Schürzen**) apron.

Schuss △ der (PL die **Schüsse**) 1 shot; 2 dash (of brandy, vinegar); 3 schuss (in skiing).

Schüssel die (PL die **Schüsseln**) bowl, dish.

Schuster der (PL die **Schuster**) shoemaker.

schütten verb (PERF **hat geschüttet**) 1 to pour; **es schüttet** (informal) it's pouring (down); 2 to tip; 3 to spill.

schütteln verb (PERF **hat geschüttelt**) 1 to shake; 2 **sich**

schütteln to shake yourself; **sich vor Ekel schütteln** to shudder.

Schutz der 1 protection; 2 shelter.

Schütze der (PL die **Schützen**) 1 marksman; 2 Sagittarius; **Daniel ist Schütze** Daniel's Sagittarius.

schützen verb (PERF **hat geschützt**) 1 to protect; **die meisten Cremes schützen die Haut gegen Sonnenbrand** most creams protect the skin from sunburn; 2 **gesetzlich geschützt** registered (*as a trademark*).

schwach adjective 1 weak; 2 poor (*performance, memory*).

Schwäche die (PL die **Schwächen**) weakness.

schwachsinnig adjective idiotic.

Schwager der (PL die **Schwäger**) brother-in-law.

Schwägerin die (PL die **Schwägerinnen**) sister-in-law.

Schwalbe die (PL die **Schwalben**) swallow.

schwamm SEE **schwimmen**.

Schwamm der (PL die **Schwämme**) sponge.

Schwan der (PL die **Schwäne**) swan.

schwanger adjective pregnant.

schwanken verb (PERF **hat geschwankt**) 1 to sway; 2 to fluctuate; 3 to waver; 4 (PERF **ist geschwankt**) to stagger.

Schwanz der (PL die **Schwänze**) tail.

schwänzen verb (PERF **hat geschwänzt**) to skip, to skive off; **die Schule schwänzen** to play truant.

Schwarm der (PL die **Schwärme**) swarm.

schwarz adjective, adverb 1 black; **schwarz gekleidet** dressed in black; **ein schwarz gestreiftes Kleid** a dress with black stripes; **das habe ich schwarz auf weiß** I have it in black and white; 2 **ins Schwarze treffen** to hit the nail on the head, to score a bull's eye; 3 **schwarz sehen** Δ to be pessimistic; 4 **etwas schwarz machen** to do something illegally.

Schwarze der/die (PL die **Schwarzen**) black.

schwarzsehen SEE **schwarz**.

Schwarzwald der Black Forest.

schwätzen verb (PERF **hat geschwätzt**) to chatter.

Schwede der (PL die **Schweden**) Swede.

Schweden das Sweden.

Schwedin die (PL die **Schwedinnen**) Swede.

schwedisch adjective Swedish.

schweigen ◇ verb (IMPERF **schwieg**, PERF **hat geschwiegen**) to be silent; **ganz zu schweigen von …** not to mention …

Schwein das (PL die **Schweine**) 1 pig; 2 pork; 3 **du Schwein!** (*informal*) you swine!; **Schwein haben** (*informal*) to be lucky.

Schweinefleisch das pork.

Δ NEW SPELLING: *See page xii*

Schweiß *der* sweat.

Schweiz *die* **die Schweiz** Switzerland.

Schweizer *der* (PL *die* **Schweizer**) Swiss.

Schweizerin *die* (PL *die* **Schweizerinnen**) Swiss.

schweizerisch *adjective* Swiss.

schwer *adjective* 1 heavy; **zwei Pfund schwer sein** to weigh two pounds; 2 difficult; 3 serious. *adverb* 1 heavily; 2 seriously; **schwer krank** seriously ill; 3 **schwer arbeiten** to work hard; **jemandem schwer fallen** △ to be hard for somebody; 4 **sich mit etwas schwer tun** △ to have difficulty with something.

schwerfallen SEE **schwer**.

schwerhörig *adjective* hard of hearing.

Schwert *das* (PL *die* **Schwerter**) sword.

schwertun SEE **schwer**.

Schwester *die* (PL *die* **Schwestern**) sister.

schwieg SEE **schweigen**.

Schwiegereltern *plural noun* parents-in-law.

Schwiegermutter *die* (PL *die* **Schwiegermütter**) mother-in-law.

Schwiegersohn *der* (PL *die* **Schwiegersöhne**) son-in-law.

Schwiegertochter *die* (PL *die* **Schwiegertöchter**) daughter-in-law.

Schwiegervater *der* (PL *die* **Schwiegerväter**) father-in-law.

schwierig *adjective* difficult.

Schwierigkeit *die* (PL *die* **Schwierigkeiten**) difficulty.

Schwimmbad *das* (PL *die* **Schwimmbäder**) swimming baths.

Schwimmbecken *das* (PL *die* **Schwimmbecken**) swimming pool.

schwimmen ✧ (IMPERF **schwamm**, PERF **ist/hat geschwommen**) 1 to swim; 2 to float.

Schwimmweste *die* (PL *die* **Schwimmwesten**) life-jacket.

schwindlig *adjective* dizzy; **mir ist schwindlig** I feel dizzy.

Schwips *der* (PL *die* **Schwipse**) **einen Schwips haben** to be tipsy.

schwitzen *verb* (PERF **hat geschwitzt**) to sweat.

schwören ✧ *verb* (IMPERF **schwor**, PERF **hat geschworen**) to swear.

schwul *adjective* gay.

schwül *adjective* close.

Schwule *der* (PL *die* **Schwulen**) gay.

Schwung *der* (PL *die* **Schwünge**) 1 swing; 2 drive; **die Party in Schwung bringen** to get the party going.

sechs *number* six.

sechster, sechste, sechstes *adjective* sixth.

sechzehn *number* sixteen.

sechzig *number* sixty.

✧ IRREGULAR VERB: *See the verb table in the centre of the dictionary*

See[1] *der* (PL *die* Seen) lake.

See[2] *die* sea.

Seehund *der* (PL *die* **Seehunde**) seal.

seekrank *adjective* seasick.

Seele *die* (PL *die* **Seelen**) soul.

Seemann *der* (PL *die* **Seeleute**) seaman, sailor.

Seetang *der* seaweed.

Segel *das* (PL *die* **Segel**) sail.

Segelboot *das* (PL *die* **Segelboote**) sailing boat.

Segelfliegen *das* gliding.

Segelflugzeug *das* (PL *die* **Segelflugzeuge**) glider.

segeln *verb* (PERF **ist gesegelt**) to sail.

sehen ✧ *verb* (PRES **sieht**, IMPERF **sah**, PERF **hat gesehen**) 1 to see; **jemanden wieder sehen** △ to see somebody again; **mal sehen, ob ...** let's see if ...; 2 to look; 3 **eine Fernsehsendung sehen** to watch a television programme; 4 **gut/schlecht sehen** to have good/bad eyesight; 5 **nach jemandem sehen** to look after somebody.

sehenswert *adjective* worth seeing.

Sehenswürdigkeiten *plural noun* sights.

Sehnsucht *die* longing; **Sehnsucht nach jemandem haben** to long to see somebody.

sehr *adverb* 1 very, **sehr gut** very good; 2 **danke sehr** thank you very much; 3 **ich habe Karin sehr gern** I like Karin a lot; 4 **Sehr geehrte Frau Huber** Dear Mrs Huber.

seid SEE **sein**.

Seide *die* (PL *die* **Seiden**) silk.

Seife *die* (PL *die* **Seifen**) soap.

Seil *das* (PL *die* **Seile**) 1 rope; 2 cable.

Seilbahn *die* (PL *die* **Seilbahnen**) cable railway.

sein[1] ✧ *verb* (PRES **ist**, IMPERF **war**, PERF **ist gewesen**) 1 to be; **wir sind in der Küche** we're in the kitchen; **Rosi ist krank** Rosi is ill; **mir ist schlecht** I feel sick; **mir ist kalt** I'm cold; 2 **sie ist Lehrerin** she's a teacher; 3 **es ist drei Uhr** it's three o'clock; **Karl ist aus München** Karl's from Munich; **es war viel zu tun** there was a lot to be done; 4 **aus Seide sein** to be made of silk; 5 **etwas sein lassen** △ to stop something; **lass das sein!** stop it!; 6 **es sei denn, dass ...** unless ...; 7 (*used with certain verbs to form past tenses*) **ich bin nach Berlin gefahren** I went to Berlin; **wir sind kurz vor acht nach Hause gekommen** we got home shortly before eight o'clock; **er ist abgeholt worden** he's been collected.

sein[2] *adjective* 1 his; 2 (*of a thing or animal*) its; **der Hund ist in seiner Hütte** the dog is in its kennel; 3 (*after the pronoun 'man'*) your, one's; **wenn man sich seine Eltern aussuchen könnte** if you could choose your parents.

△ NEW SPELLING: *See page xii*

seiner, seine, sein(e)s *pronoun*
1 his; **das ist nicht meine CD, das ist seine** it's not my CD, it's his; **du kannst seins nehmen** you can take his; **2** (*after the pronoun 'man'*) your own, one's own; **das Seine tun** to do one's share.

seinetwegen *adverb* **1** for his sake; **2** because of him; **3** on his account.

seinlassen SEE **sein**.

seins SEE **seiner**.

seit *preposition* ←(+DAT),
conjunction **1** since; **seit etwa einer Woche** since about a week; **seit du hier wohnst** since you've been living here; **seit wann?** since when?; **2 ich bin seit zwei Wochen hier** I've been here for two weeks; **seit einiger Zeit** for some time.

seitdem *adverb* since then; **ich habe sie seitdem nicht mehr gesehen** I haven't seen her since.
conjunction since.

Seite *die* (PL *die* **Seiten**) **1** side; **auf der einen Seite** on the one hand; **2** page; **das steht auf Seite zwanzig** it's on page twenty.

Seitenstechen *das* stich; **ich habe Seitenstechen** I've got a stitch.

Seitenstraße *die* (PL *die* **Seitenstraßen**) side street.

seither *adverb* since then.

Sekretärin *die* (PL *die* **Sekretärinnen**) secretary.

Sekt *der* (PL *die* **Sekte**) sparkling wine.

Sekte *die* (PL *die* **Sekten**) sect.

Sekunde *die* (PL *die* **Sekunden**) second.

selbst *pronoun* **1 ich selbst** I myself; **er selbst** he himself; **wir selbst** we ourselves; **Sie selbst** you yourself, you yourselves; **2 von selbst** by itself; **3 sie schneidet sich die Haare selbst** she cuts her own hair; **4** on one's own; **ich kann es selbst machen** I can do it on my own; **5 selbst gemacht** △ home-made.
adverb even; **selbst wenn** even if.

selbständig = **selbstständig**.

Selbstbedienung *die* self-service.

selbstbewusst △ *adjective* self-confident.

Selbstbewusstsein △ *das* self-confidence.

selbstgemacht SEE **selbst**.

Selbstmord *der* (PL *die* **Selbstmorde**) suicide; **Selbstmord begehen** to commit suicide.

selbstständig △ *adjective*
1 independent; **2** self-employed; **sich selbstständig machen** to set up on your own.

selbstverständlich *adjective* natural; **etwas für selbstverständlich halten** to take something for granted; **das ist selbstverständlich** it goes without saying.
adverb naturally, of course; **wir haben ihn selbstverständlich auf die Party eingeladen** of course we invited him to the party.

⬦ IRREGULAR VERB: *See the verb table in the centre of the dictionary*

selten *adjective* rare.
adverb rarely.

seltsam *adjective* strange, odd.

Semester *das* (PL *die* **Semester**) semester, term.

Semikolon *das* (PL *die* **Semikolons**) semicolon.

Semmel *die* (PL *die* **Semmeln**) roll.

senden *verb* (PERF **hat gesendet**) 1 to send; **etwas an jemanden senden** to send something to somebody; 2 to broadcast; **seine Rede wird im ersten Programm gesendet** his speech will be broadcast on channel one; 3 to transmit.

Sendung *die* (PL *die* **Sendungen**) 1 programme; 2 consignment.

Senf *der* (PL *die* **Senfe**) mustard.

Senior *der* (PL *die* **Senioren**) 1 senior; 2 **Senioren** senior citizens.

sensationell *adjective* sensational.

sensibel *adjective* sensitive.

September *der* September.

Serie *die* (PL *die* **Serien**) 1 series; 2 serial.

Service[1] *das* (PL *die* **Service**) set (*of china, for example*).

Service[2] *der* service; **das Essen im Hotel ist gut, aber der Service ist furchtbar** the food in the hotel is good but the service is appalling.

servieren *verb* (PERF **hat serviert**) to serve.

Serviette *die* (PL *die* **Servietten**) napkin.

Sessel *der* (PL *die* **Sessel**) armchair.

Sessellift *der* (PL *die* **Sessellifte**) chair-lift.

setzen *verb* (PERF **hat gesetzt**) 1 to put; **ein Komma setzen** to put a comma; **vergiss nicht, deinen Namen auf die Liste zu setzen** don't forget to put your name on the list; 2 to move (*a counter in games*); 3 **auf etwas setzen** to bet on something; **auf ein Pferd setzen** to back a horse; 4 **sich setzen** to sit down; **sich auf einen Stuhl setzen** to sit down on a chair.

seufzen *verb* (PERF **hat geseufzt**) to sigh.

Seufzer *der* (PL *die* **Seufzer**) sigh.

Sex *der* sex.

Sexismus *der* sexism.

sexistisch *adjective* sexist.

sexuell *adjective* sexual.

Shampoo *das* (PL *die* **Shampoos**) shampoo.

sich *pronoun* 1 (*with 'er/sie/es'*) himself/herself/itself; **sie hat sich eingeschlossen** she locked herself in; 2 (*with plural 'sie'*) themselves; 3 (*with 'Sie'*) yourself, yourselves (*plural*); 4 each other, one another; **sich kennen** to know each other; **Petra und Werner lieben sich** Petra and Werner love each other; 5 (*not translated with certain verbs*) **sich freuen** to be pleased; **sich wundern** to be surprised; 6 **Anita wäscht sich**

△ NEW SPELLING: *See page xii*

die Haare Anita is washing her hair;
sich den Arm brechen to break your
arm; 7 sich gut verkaufen to sell
well; 8 von sich aus of your own
accord.

sicher *adjective* 1 safe; 2 certain;
bist du sicher? are you sure?
adverb 1 safely; 2 certainly, surely;
sicher! certainly!

Sicherheit *die* 1 safety; **zur
Sicherheit** for safety's sake;
**schnallen Sie sich zur Ihrer eigenen
Sicherheit an** fasten your seat belt
for your own safety; **etwas in
Sicherheit bringen** to rescue
something; **in Sicherheit sein** to be
safe; 2 security; **die Sicherheit der
Arbeitsplätze** job security;
3 certainty; **mit Sicherheit!**
certainly! (*as a reply*).

Sicherheitsgurt *der* (PL die
Sicherheitsgurte) seatbelt.

Sicherheitsnadel *die* (PL die
Sicherheitsnadeln) safety pin.

sicherlich *adverb* certainly.

sichern *verb* (PERF **hat gesichert**) to
secure; **jemandem etwas sichern**
to secure something for somebody.

Sicherung *die* (PL die **Sicherungen**)
1 fuse; **die Sicherung is
durchgebrannt** the fuse has blown;
2 safeguard; **die Sicherung der
Arbeitsplätze** safeguarding jobs;
3 safety catch.

Sicht *die* 1 view; **ich hatte eine gute
Sicht auf den See** I had a good view
of the lake; **auf lange Sicht** in the
long term; 2 **aus meiner Sicht** as I

see it; 3 visibility; **gute/schlechte
Sicht** good/poor visibility.

sichtbar *adjective* visible.

sie *pronoun* 1 she; 2 her; **ich kenne
sie** I know her; 3 it; **so eine
hübsche Bluse, war sie teuer?**
what a pretty blouse, was it
expensive?; 4 they; **sie sind in der
Küche** they're in the kitchen;
5 them; **ich habe sie gestern
abgeschickt** I posted them
yesterday.

Sie *pronoun* you; **kommen Sie
herein!** come in!

Sieb *das* (PL die **Siebe**) 1 sieve;
2 strainer.

sieben *number* seven.

siebter, siebte, siebtes
adjective seventh.

siebzehn *number* seventeen.

siebzig *number* seventy.

Siedlung *die* (PL die **Siedlungen**)
1 (housing) estate; 2 settlement.

Sieg *der* (PL die **Siege**) victory, win.

Siegel *das* (PL die **Siegel**) seal.

siegen *verb* (PERF **hat gesiegt**) to
win.

Sieger *der* (PL die **Sieger**) winner.

Siegerin *die* (PL die **Siegerinnen**)
winner.

sieht SEE **sehen**.

Silbe *die* (PL die **Silben**) syllable.

Silber *das* silver.

silbern *adjective* silver.

✧ IRREGULAR VERB: *See the verb table in the centre of the dictionary*

Silvester *das* New Year's Eve.

sind SEE **sein**.

Sinfonie *die* (PL *die* **Sinfonien**) symphony.

singen ✧ *verb* (IMPERF **sang**, PERF **hat gesungen**) to sing.

sinken ✧ *verb* (IMPERF **sank**, PERF **ist gesunken**) **1** to sink; **2** to go down.

Sinn *der* (PL *die* **Sinne**) **1** sense; **2** meaning; **3** point; **das hat keinen Sinn** there's no point.

sinnlos *adjective* pointless.

sinnvoll *adjective* **1** sensible; **2** meaningful.

Situation *die* (PL *die* **Situationen**) situation.

Sitz *der* (PL *die* **Sitze**) **1** seat; **2** fit (*of clothes*).

sitzen ✧ *verb* (IMPERF **saß**, PERF **hat gesessen**) **1** to sit; **sitzen bleiben** △ to remain seated; **2 sitzen bleiben** △ to have to repeat a year, to stay down (*at school*); **3 er sitzt** (*informal*) he's in jail; **4 jemanden sitzen lassen** △ to leave somebody in the lurch; **5** to fit (*of clothes*); **der Mantel sitzt gut** the coat fits well.

Sitzplatz *der* (PL *die* **Sitzplätze**) seat.

Sitzung *die* (PL *die* **Sitzungen**) **1** meeting; **2** session.

Sizilien *das* Sicily.

Skandal *der* (PL *die* **Skandale**) scandal.

Skandinavien *das* Scandinavia.

skandinavisch *adjective* Scandinavian.

Skelett *das* (PL *die* **Skelette**) skeleton.

Ski *der* (PL *die* **Ski(er)**) ski; **Ski fahren/laufen** to ski.

Skifahren *das* skiing.

Skifahrer *der* (PL *die* **Skifahrer**) skier.

Skifahrerin *die* (PL *die* **Skifahrerinnen**) skier.

Skilaufen *das* skiing.

Skiläufer *der* (PL *die* **Skiläufer**) skier.

Skiläuferin *die* (PL *die* **Skiläuferinnen**) skier.

Skilehrer *der* (PL *die* **Skilehrer**) ski instructor.

Skizze *die* (PL *die* **Skizzen**) sketch.

Skorpion *der* (PL *die* **Skorpione**) **1** scorpion; **2** Scorpio.

Skulptur *die* (PL *die* **Skulpturen**) sculpture.

Slip *der* (PL *die* **Slips**) briefs, pants.

Slowake *der* (PL *die* **Slowaken**) Slovak.

Slowakei *die* Slovakia.

Slowakin *die* (PL *die* **Slowakinnen**) Slovak.

slowakisch *adjective* Slovak.

Smoking *der* (PL *die* **Smokings**) dinner jacket.

so *adverb* **1** so; **nicht so viel** not so much; **und so weiter** and so on; **2** like this, like that; **so nicht** not like

△ NEW SPELLING: *See page xii*

that; **3** as; **so bald wie** as soon as;
4 such; **so ein Zufall!** what a
coincidence!; **5 das kriegst du so**
(*informal*) you get it for nothing;
6 so um zwanzig Mark (*informal*)
about twenty marks.
conjunction **so dass** so that.
exclamation right!, well!; **so?**
really?

sobald *conjunction* as soon as.

Socke *die* (PL *die* **Socken**) sock.

Sofa *das* (PL *die* **Sofas**) sofa.

sofort *adverb* immediately.

sogar *adverb* even.

sogleich *adverb* at once.

Sohle *die* (PL *die* **Sohlen**) sole.

Sohn *der* (PL *die* **Söhne**) son.

solange *conjunction* as long as.

solch *pronoun* such; **solch
einer/eine/eins** one like that,
somebody like that.

solcher, solche, solches
adjective, pronoun **1** such; **ich habe
solche Angst** I'm so frightened;
2 ein solcher Mann a man like that;
eine solche Frage a question like
that; **ein solches Haus** a house like
that; **3 solche** (*plural*) those;
solche wie die people like that.

Soldat *der* (PL *die* **Soldaten**) soldier.

solide *adjective* **1** solid;
2 respectable.

Solist *der* (PL *die* **Solisten**) soloist.

Solistin *die* (PL *die* **Solistinnen**)
soloist.

sollen ✧ *verb* (PRES **soll**, IMPERF
sollte, PERF **hat gesollt**) **1** should;
sollte es regnen if it should rain;
2 to be supposed to; **was soll das
heißen?** what's that supposed to
mean?; **3 sagen Sie ihr, sie soll
anrufen** tell her to ring; **4 was soll
ich machen?** what shall I do?; **soll
ich?** shall I?; **5 was soll's!** so what

sollte, sollten, solltest, solltet
SEE **sollen**.

Sommer *der* (PL *die* **Sommer**)
summer.

sommerlich *adjective* summery,
summer.

Sommersprossen *plural noun*
freckles.

Sonderangebot *das* (PL *die*
Sonderangebote) special offer; **im
Sonderangebot** on special offer.

sonderbar *adjective* strange, odd.

sondern *conjunction* but; **nicht nur
..., sondern auch ...** not only ..., but
also ...

Song *der* (PL *die* **Songs**) song.

Sonnabend *der* (PL *die*
Sonnabende) Saturday.

sonnabends *adverb* on Saturdays.

Sonne *die* (PL *die* **Sonnen**) sun.

sonnen *verb* (PERF **hat sich gesonnt**)
sich sonnen to sun yourself.

Sonnenaufgang *der* sunrise.

Sonnenbrand *der* sunburn.

Sonnenbrille *die* (PL *die*
Sonnenbrillen) sunglasses.

✧ IRREGULAR VERB: *See the verb table in the centre of the dictionary*

Sonnencreme die (PL die Sonnencremes) suntan lotion.

Sonnenenergie die solar energy.

Sonnenmilch die suntan lotion.

Sonnenöl das suntan oil.

Sonnenschein der sunshine.

Sonnenstich der sunstroke.

sonnig adjective sunny.

Sonntag der (PL die Sonntage) Sunday.

sonntags adverb on Sundays.

sonst adverb 1 usually; 2 else; **wer sonst?** who else?; **was sonst?** what else?; **3 sonst noch etwas?** anything else?; **sonst noch jemand?** anybody else?; **4 sonst wo** △ somewhere; **es kann sonst wo sein** it could be anywhere; **5** otherwise; **geh jetzt, sonst verpasst du den Bus** go now, otherwise you'll miss the bus.

sonstwo SEE **sonst**.

sooft conjunction whenever.

Sorge die (PL die Sorgen) worry; **sich Sorgen machen** to worry.

sorgen verb (PERF **hat gesorgt**) **1 für etwas sorgen** to take care of something; **für die Musik sorgen** to see to the music; **für jemanden sorgen** to look after somebody; **2 dafür sorgen, dass ...** to make sure that ...; **3 sich sorgen** to worry; **ich sorge mich um meine Eltern** I worry about my parents.

sorgfältig adjective careful.

Sorte die (PL die Sorten) **1** kind; **2** brand.

Soße die (PL die Soßen) **1** sauce; **2** gravy; **3** dressing.

Souvenir das (PL die Souvenirs) souvenir.

soviel conjunction as far as; **soviel ich weiß** as far as I know.
adverb SEE **viel**.

soweit conjunction as far as; **soweit ich weiß, ist er in Ferien** as far as I know, he's on holiday.
adverb SEE **weit**.

sowenig SEE **wenig**.

sowie conjunction **1** as well as; **2** as soon as.

sowieso adverb anyway.

sowohl adverb **sowohl ... als auch ...** both ... and ...; **sowohl er wie auch sein Freund** both he and his friend.

sozial adjective social.

Sozialarbeiter der (PL die Sozialarbeiter) social worker.

Sozialarbeiterin die (PL die Sozialarbeiterinnen) social worker.

Sozialhilfe die social security.

Sozialismus der socialism.

sozialistisch adjective socialist.

Sozialkunde die social studies.

Sozialwohnung die (PL die Sozialwohnungen) council flat.

Soziologie die sociology.

sozusagen adverb so to speak.

Spalte die (PL die **Spalten**) 1 crack;
2 column (in text).

spalten verb (PERF **hat gespalten**) to
split.

Spanien das Spain.

Spanier der (PL die **Spanier**)
Spaniard.

Spanierin die (PL die **Spanierinnen**)
Spaniard.

spanisch adjective Spanish.

spann SEE **spinnen**.

spannend adjective exciting.

Spannung die (PL die **Spannungen**)
1 tension; 2 suspense (in a film or
novel, for example); **ich erwarte
seine Antwort mit Spannung** I can't
wait for his answer; 3 voltage.

sparen verb (PERF **hat gespart**) 1 to
save; **auf etwas sparen** to save up
for something; 2 **sich etwas sparen**
not to bother with something; **sich
die Mühe sparen** to save yourself
the trouble; 3 **an etwas sparen** to
economize on something.

Spargel der asparagus.

Sparkasse die savings bank.

sparsam adjective 1 economical;
2 thrifty.

Spaß der (PL die **Späße**) 1 fun;
zum/aus Spaß for fun; **das macht
Spaß** it's fun; **Segeln macht mir
keinen Spaß** I don't like sailing;
2 **viel Spaß!** have a good time!;
3 joke; **er macht nur Spaß** he's only
joking.

spät adjective, adverb late; **zu spät**

kommen to be late; **wie spät ist
es?** what time is it?

Spaten der (PL die **Spaten**) spade.

später adjective later.

spätestens adverb at the latest.

Spatz der (PL die **Spatzen**) sparrow.

spazieren verb (PERF **ist spaziert**)
1 to stroll; 2 **spazieren gehen** △ to
go for a walk; **hast du Lust,
spazieren zu gehen?** would you
like to go for a walk?

spazierengehen SEE **spazieren**.

Spaziergang der (PL die
Spaziergänge) walk; **einen
Spaziergang machen** to go for a
walk.

Speck der bacon.

Speiche die (PL die **Speichen**) spoke.

Speicher der (PL die **Speicher**)
1 loft, attic; 2 memory (in
computing).

speichern verb (PERF **hat
gespeichert**) 1 to store; 2 to save
(in computing).

Speise die (PL die **Speisen**) 1 food;
2 dish.

Speisekarte die (PL die
Speisekarten) menu.

Speisesaal der (PL die **Speisesäle**)
1 dining hall; 2 dining room.

Speisewagen der (PL die
Speisewagen) dining car.

Spende die (PL die **Spenden**)
donation.

✧ IRREGULAR VERB: *See the verb table in the centre of the dictionary*

spenden *verb* (PERF **hat gespendet**)
1 to donate; 2 to give.

spendieren *verb* (PERF **hat spendiert**) **jemandem etwas spendieren** to treat somebody to something.

Sperre *die* (PL *die* **Sperren**)
1 barrier; 2 ban.

sperren *verb* (PERF **hat gesperrt**)
1 to close; 2 to block (*an entrance, access*); 3 **den Strom sperren** to cut off the electricity; 4 **einen Scheck sperren** to stop a cheque; 5 **ein Tier in einen Käfig sperren** to shut an animal (up) in a cage.

Spezialität *die* (PL *die* **Spezialitäten**) speciality.

speziell *adjective* special.

Spiegel *der* (PL *die* **Spiegel**) mirror.

Spiegelbild *das* (PL *die* **Spiegelbilder**) reflection.

Spiegelei *das* (PL *die* **Spiegeleier**) fried egg.

spiegeln *verb* (PERF **hat gespiegelt**)
1 to reflect; 2 **sich spiegeln** to be reflected.

Spiel *das* (PL *die* **Spiele**) 1 game; 2 **ein Spiel Karten** a pack of cards; 3 **es steht viel auf dem Spiel** there's a lot at stake.

spielen *verb* (PERF **hat gespielt**) 1 to play; **wir spielen morgen Tennis** we're going to play tennis tomorrow; 2 to gamble; 3 to act; **das Stück war gut gespielt** the play was well acted; 4 **der Film spielt in Rom** the film is set in Rome.

spielend *adverb* easily.

Spieler *der* (PL *die* **Spieler**) 1 player; 2 gambler.

Spielerin *die* (PL *die* **Spielerinnen**) 1 player; 2 gambler.

Spielfeld *das* (PL *die* **Spielfelder**) pitch, field.

Spielhalle *die* (PL *die* **Spielhallen**) amusement arcade.

Spielplatz *der* (PL *die* **Spielplätze**) playground.

Spielverderber *der* (PL *die* **Spielverderber**) spoilsport.

Spielverderberin *die* (PL *die* **Spielverderberinnen**) spoilsport.

Spielwaren *plural noun* toys.

Spielzeug *das* 1 toy; 2 toys.

Spinat *der* spinach.

Spinne *die* (PL *die* **Spinnen**) spider.

spinnen ✧ *verb* (IMPERF **spann**, PERF **hat gesponnen**) 1 to spin; 2 **du spinnst!** (*informal*) you're mad!

Spinnennetz *das* (PL *die* **Spinnennetze**) cobweb.

Spion *der* (PL *die* **Spione**) spy.

Spionage *die* spying, espionage.

spionieren *verb* (PERF **hat spioniert**) to spy.

Spirituosen *plural noun* spirits (*alcohol*).

spitz *adjective* pointed.

Spitze *die* (PL *die* **Spitzen**) 1 point; 2 top; **Schalke liegt jetzt an der Spitze** Schalke is top of the league

△ NEW SPELLING: *See page xii*

at the moment; **3** peak; **von hier kann man die schneebedeckten Spitzen sehen** you can see the snow-covered peaks from here; **4** front; **an der Spitze liegen** to be in the lead; **5** lace; **6 Spitze sein** (*informal*) to be great.

spitzen *verb* (PERF **hat gespitzt**) **1** to sharpen; **2 sich auf etwas spitzen** (*informal*) to look forward to something.

Spitzname *der* (PL *die* **Spitznamen**) nickname.

Splitter *der* (PL *die* **Splitter**) splinter.

sponsern *verb* (PERF **hat gesponsert**) to sponsor.

Sport *der* sport.

Sporthalle *die* (PL *die* **Sporthallen**) sports hall.

Sportler *der* (PL *die* **Sportler**) sportsman.

Sportlerin *die* (PL *die* **Sportlerinnen**) sportswoman.

sportlich *adjective* **1** sporting; **2** sporty.

Sportplatz *der* (PL *die* **Sportplätze**) sports field, sports ground.

Sportschuh *der* (PL *die* **Sportschuhe**) trainer.

Sportverein *der* (PL *die* **Sportvereine**) sports club.

Sportwagen *der* (PL *die* **Sportwagen**) **1** sports car; **2** pushchair.

Sportzentrum *das* (PL *die* **Sportzentren**) sports centre.

spotten *verb* (PERF **hat gespottet**) to mock.

sprach SEE **sprechen**.

Sprache *die* (PL *die* **Sprachen**) **1** language; **2** speech; **etwas zur Sprache bringen** to bring something up.

sprachlos *adjective* speechless.

sprang SEE **springen**.

sprechen ✧ *verb* (PRES **spricht**, IMPERF **sprach**, PERF **hat gesprochen**) **1** to speak; **Deutsch sprechen** to speak German; **mit wem spreche ich?** who's speaking? (*on the phone*); **jemanden sprechen** to speak to somebody; **2 Frau Hahn ist nicht zu sprechen** Mrs Hahn is not available; **3** to talk; **mit jemandem über etwas sprechen** to talk to somebody about something; **4** to say (*a word, sentence*).

Sprecher *der* (PL *die* **Sprecher**) **1** spokesman; **2** (*on TV*) announcer; **3** (*in a film*) narrator; **4** speaker.

Sprecherin *die* (PL *die* **Sprecherinnen**) **1** spokeswoman; **2** (*on TV*) announcer; **3** (*in a film*) narrator; **4** speaker.

Sprechstunde *die* (PL *die* **Sprechstunden**) surgery.

spricht SEE **sprechen**.

Sprichwort *das* (PL *die* **Sprichwörter**) proverb.

springen ✧ *verb* (IMPERF **sprang**, PERF **ist gesprungen**) **1** to jump;

✧ IRREGULAR VERB: *See the verb table in the centre of the dictionary*

2 to bounce (*of a ball*); 3 to dive;
4 to crack.

Spritze die (PL die **Spritzen**)
1 syringe; 2 injection; 3 hose.

spritzen verb (PERF **hat gespritzt**)
1 to inject; 2 to splash; **du hast mich
nass gespritzt** you've splashed me;
3 to spray; 4 to spit (*of fat*); 5 (PERF
ist gespritzt) to splash up.

Sprudel der (PL die **Sprudel**)
sparkling mineral water.

sprühen verb (PERF **hat gesprüht**)
1 to spray; 2 to sparkle (*of eyes*);
3 (PERF **ist gesprüht**) to fly (*of
sparks*); **die Funken sind in alle
Richtungen gesprüht** sparks flew in
all directions.

Sprung der (PL die **Sprünge**)
1 jump; 2 dive; 3 crack (*in china,
glass*).

Sprungbrett das (PL die
Sprungbretter) diving board.

spucken verb (PERF **hat gespuckt**)
to spit.

Spülbecken das (PL die
Spülbecken) sink.

spülen verb (PERF **hat gespült**) 1 to
rinse; 2 to wash up; 3 to flush.

Spülmaschine die (PL die
Spülmaschinen) dishwasher.

Spülmittel das (PL die **Spülmittel**)
washing-up liquid.

Spur die (PL die **Spuren**) 1 track; **auf
der falschen Spur sein** to be on the
wrong track; **jemandem auf die Spur
kommen** to get on to somebody;

2 lane; **in der Spur bleiben** to keep
in lane; 3 trail; 4 trace.

spüren verb (PERF **hat gespürt**) 1 to
feel; 2 to sense.

Staat der (PL die **Staaten**) state.

staatlich adjective state; **eine
staatliche Schule** a state school.
adverb by the state.

Staatsangehörigkeit die (PL die
Staatsangehörigkeiten) nationality.

stabil adjective 1 stable; 2 sturdy.

stach SEE **stechen**.

Stachel der (PL die **Stacheln**)
1 spine; 2 spike; 3 sting.

Stachelbeere die (PL die
Stachelbeeren) gooseberry.

Stacheldraht der barbed wire.

Stadion das (PL die **Stadien**)
stadium.

Stadium das (PL die **Stadien**) stage.

Stadt die (PL die **Städte**) town, city.

städtisch adjective 1 urban;
2 municipal.

Stadtmitte die town centre.

Stadtplan der (PL die **Stadtpläne**)
street map.

Stadtrand der outskirts (of town);
am Stadtrand on the outskirts.

Stadtrundfahrt die (PL die
Stadtrundfahrten) sightseeing tour
(*of a town*).

Stadtteil der (PL die **Stadtteile**)
district.

stahl SEE **stehlen**.

△ NEW SPELLING: *See page xii*

Stahl *der* steel.

Stall *der* (PL *die* **Ställe**) **1** stable;
2 cowshed; **3** pigsty.

Stamm *der* (PL *die* **Stämme**)
1 trunk; **2** tribe; **3** stem (*of a word*).

stammen *verb* (PERF **hat gestammt**)
aus Deutschland stammen to
come from Germany.

Stammgast *der* (PL *die*
Stammgäste) regular customer (*in
a pub or restaurant*).

stand SEE **stehen**.

Stand *der* (PL *die* **Stände**) **1** state;
**etwas auf den neuesten Stand
bringen** to bring something up to
date; **2** score (*in a game*); **3** stall;
4 level.

ständig *adjective* constant.

Standort *der* (PL *die* **Standorte**)
position, location; **von ihrem
Standort aus konnte sie nichts
sehen** she couldn't see anything
from where she was standing.

Stange *die* (PL *die* **Stangen**) **1** bar;
2 pole.

stank SEE **stinken**.

starb SEE **sterben**.

stark *adjective* **1** strong; **2** heavy
(*rain, traffic*); **3** severe (*frost, pain*);
4 (*informal*) great; **das ist stark!**
that's great!

Stärke *die* (PL *die* **Stärken**)
1 strength; **2** starch.

starrsinnig *adjective* obstinate.

Start *der* (PL *die* **Starts**) **1** start;
2 take-off.

Startbahn *die* (PL *die* **Startbahnen**)
runway.

starten *verb* (PERF **ist gestartet**)
1 (*of a plane*) to take off; **2** (PERF **hat
gestartet**) to start, to launch (*a
campaign*).

Station *die* (PL *die* **Stationen**)
1 station; **2** stop; **Station machen**
to stop over; **3** ward.

statt *conjunction, preposition*
←(+GEN) instead of; **statt zu
arbeiten** instead of working; **sie
ging statt ihrer Schwester** she went
instead of her sister.

stattdessen Δ *conjunction* instead.

stattfinden ✧ *verb* (IMPERF **fand
statt**, PERF **hat stattgefunden**) to
take place.

Stau *der* (PL *die* **Staus**) **1** congestion;
2 traffic jam.

Staub *der* dust.

staubig *adjective* dusty.

staubsaugen *verb* (PERF **hat
staubgesaugt**) to vacuum.

Staubsauger *der* (PL *die*
Staubsauger) vacuum cleaner.

staunen *verb* (PERF **hat gestaunt**) to
be amazed.

stechen ✧ *verb* (PRES **sticht**, IMPERF
stach, PERF **hat gestochen**) **1** to
prick; **sich in den Finger stechen** to
prick your finger; **2** to sting, to bite
(*of an insect*); **3** **mit etwas in etwas
stechen** to jab something into
something.

✧ IRREGULAR VERB: *See the verb table in the centre of the dictionary*

Steckdose die (PL die Steckdosen) socket.

stecken verb (PERF **hat gesteckt**) 1 to put; **du musst die Münze in den Schlitz stecken** put the coin into the slot; 2 to pin; 3 **wo steckt er?** where is he?; 4 **stecken bleiben** △ to get stuck; **den Schlüssel stecken lassen** △ to leave the key in the lock.

Stecker der (PL die Stecker) plug.

Stecknadel die (PL die Stecknadeln) pin.

stehen ✧ verb (IMPERF **stand**, PERF **hat gestanden**) 1 to stand; 2 to be; **es steht zwei zu zwei** the score is two all; **wie steht's?** what's the score?; 3 to have stopped (of a clock or a machine); 4 **es steht schlecht um ihn** he's in a bad way; **na, wie steht's?** how are you?; 5 **stehen bleiben** △ to stop; **die Uhr ist stehen geblieben** the clock has stopped; 6 **in der Zeitung steht, dass ...** it says in the paper that ...; 7 **jemandem (gut) stehen** to suit somebody; 8 **zu jemandem stehen** to stand by somebody; 9 **sich gut stehen** to be on good terms; 10 **zum Stehen kommen** to come to a standstill.

stehenbleiben SEE **stehen**.

stehlen ✧ verb (PRES **stiehlt**, IMPERF **stahl**, PERF **hat gestohlen**) to steal.

steif adjective stiff.

steigen verb (IMPERF **stieg**, PERF **ist gestiegen**) 1 to climb; **auf eine Leiter steigen** to climb up a ladder; **auf ein Fahrrad steigen** to get on a bike; **in den Bus steigen** to get on the bus; 2 to rise.

steil adjective steep.

Stein der (PL die Steine) stone.

Steinbock der (PL die Steinböcke) 1 ibex; 2 Capricorn; **Petra ist Steinbock** Petra's Capricorn.

Stelle die (PL die Stellen) 1 place; **an deiner Stelle** in your place; 2 job; 3 authority; 4 **auf der Stelle** immediately.

stellen verb (PERF **hat gestellt**) 1 to put; 2 to set (a watch, task); 3 **zur Verfügung stellen** to provide; 4 **lauter stellen** to turn up; **leiser stellen** to turn down; **die Heizung höher stellen** to turn the heating up; 5 **sich krank stellen** to pretend to be ill; 6 **sich stellen** to give yourself up; 7 **die Kinder stellten sich an die Wand** the children stood against the wall.

Stellenanzeige die (PL die Stellenanzeigen) job advertisement.

Stellung die (PL die Stellungen) position.

Stempel der (PL die Stempel) 1 stamp; 2 postmark.

stempeln verb (PERF **hat gestempelt**) to stamp.

Steppdecke die (PL die Steppdecken) quilt.

sterben ✧ verb (PRES **stirbt**, IMPERF **starb**, PERF **ist gestorben**) to die.

Stereoanlage die (PL die Stereoanlagen) stereo (system).

△ NEW SPELLING: See page xii

Stern der (PL die **Sterne**) star.

Sternzeichen das (PL die **Sternzeichen**) star sign; **was ist dein Sternzeichen?** what star sign are you?

Steuer[1] das (PL die **Steuer**) 1 (steering) wheel; 2 helm.

Steuer[2] die (PL die **Steuern**) tax.

steuern verb (PERF **hat gesteuert**) 1 to steer; 2 to control; 3 (PERF **ist gesteuert**) to head.

Stewardess △ die (PL die **Stewardessen**) stewardess, air hostess.

Stich der (PL die **Stiche**) 1 prick; 2 stab; 3 sting, bite (of an insect); 4 stitch; 5 trick (when playing cards); 6 engraving; 7 **jemanden im Stich lassen** to leave somebody in the lurch.

sticht SEE **stechen**.

sticken verb (PERF **hat gestickt**) to embroider.

Stickstoff der nitrogen.

Stiefbruder der (PL die **Stiefbrüder**) stepbrother.

Stiefel der (PL die **Stiefel**) boot.

Stiefkind das (PL die **Stiefkinder**) stepchild.

Stiefmutter die (PL die **Stiefmütter**) stepmother.

Stiefschwester die (PL die **Stiefschwestern**) stepsister.

Stiefvater der (PL die **Stiefväter**) stepfather.

stieg SEE **steigen**.

stiehlt SEE **stehlen**.

Stiel der (PL die **Stiele**) 1 handle; 2 stem.

Stier der (PL die **Stiere**) 1 bull; 2 Taurus; **Andrea ist Stier** Andrea's Taurus.

stieß SEE **stoßen**.

Stift der (PL die **Stifte**) 1 pencil; 2 crayon; 3 tack (nail).

Stil der (PL die **Stile**) style.

still adjective 1 quiet; 2 still.

stillen verb (PERF **hat gestillt**) 1 to quench; 2 to breast-feed.

stillhalten ✧ verb (PRES **hält still**, IMPERF **hielt still**, PERF **hat stillgehalten**) to keep still.

Stimme die (PL die **Stimmen**) 1 voice; 2 vote.

stimmen verb (PERF **hat gestimmt**) 1 to be right; **stimmt das?** is that right?; 2 to vote; 3 to tune.

Stimmung die (PL die **Stimmungen**) 1 mood; 2 atmosphere.

stinken ✧ verb (IMPERF **stank**, PERF **hat gestunken**) to smell, to stink.

Stipendium das (PL die **Stipendien**) 1 scholarship; 2 grant.

stirbt SEE **sterben**.

Stirn die (PL die **Stirnen**) forehead.

Stock[1] der (PL die **Stöcke**) stick.

Stock[2] der (PL die **Stock**) floor.

Stockwerk das (PL die **Stockwerke**) floor.

✧ IRREGULAR VERB: See the verb table in the centre of the dictionary

Stoff der (PL die **Stoffe**) 1 material, fabric; 2 substance.

stöhnen verb (PERF **hat gestöhnt**) to groan.

stolpern verb (PERF **ist gestolpert**) 1 to stumble; 2 to trip; **ich bin über einen Stein gestolpert** I tripped on a stone.

stolz adjective proud.

stoppen verb (PERF **hat gestoppt**) to stop.

Stöpsel der (PL die **Stöpsel**) 1 plug; 2 stopper.

stören verb (PERF **hat gestört**) 1 to disturb; 2 to bother; **das stört mich nicht** that doesn't bother me; 3 **stört es Sie, wenn ich das Fenster aufmache?** do you mind if I open the window?; **der Empfang ist gestört** there's interference (on a TV).

Störung die (PL die **Störungen**) 1 disturbance, interruption; **entschuldigen Sie die Störung** I'm sorry to bother you; 2 interference; **eine technische Störung** a technical fault.

Stoß der (PL die **Stöße**) 1 push; 2 pile; **ein Stoß Handtücher** a pile of towels.

stoßen ◇ verb (PRES **stößt**, IMPERF **stieß**, PERF **hat gestoßen**) 1 to push; 2 to kick; 3 **sich den Kopf stoßen** to hit your head; **ich habe mir den Kopf an dem Balken gestoßen** I hit my head on the beam; **sich stoßen** to bump yourself; 4 **sich an etwas stoßen** to object to something;

5 (PERF **ist gestoßen**) **gegen etwas stoßen** to bump into something; 6 (PERF **ist gestoßen**) **auf etwas stoßen** to come across something.

Stoßstange die (PL die **Stoßstangen**) bumper.

Stoßzeit die (PL die **Stoßzeiten**) rush hour.

stottern verb (PERF **hat gestottert**) to stutter.

Strafe die (PL die **Strafen**) 1 punishment; 2 fine; 3 penalty.

Straftat die (PL die **Straftaten**) crime.

Strahl der (PL die **Strahlen**) 1 ray, beam; 2 jet.

strahlen verb (PERF **hat gestrahlt**) 1 to shine; 2 to beam.

Strand der (PL die **Strände**) beach.

Straße die (PL die **Straßen**) street, road; **in welcher Straße ist der Supermarkt?** which street is the supermarket in?; **über die Straße gehen** to cross the road; **jemanden auf die Straße setzen** (informal) to give somebody the sack; **mein Wirt hat mich einfach auf die Straße gesetzt** (informal) my landlord just turned me out (of a flat or room).

Straßenbahn die (PL die **Straßenbahnen**) tram; **mit der Straßenbahn fahren** to go by tram.

Strauch der (PL die **Sträucher**) bush.

Strauß[1] der (PL die **Sträuße**) bunch of flowers, bouquet.

Strauß[2] der (PL die **Strauße**) ostrich.

△ NEW SPELLING: See page xii

Streber der (PL die **Streber**) swot.

Strecke die (PL die **Strecken**)
1 distance; 2 route; 3 line (*rail*).

strecken verb (PERF **hat gestreckt**)
1 to stretch (*your arms, legs*); 2 **sich strecken** to stretch.

Streich der (PL die **Streiche**) trick.

streicheln verb (PERF **hat gestreichelt**) to stroke.

streichen ◇ verb (IMPERF **strich**,
PERF **hat gestrichen**) 1 to paint;
'**frisch gestrichen**' 'wet paint'; 2 to spread (*with butter*); 3 to delete;
4 to cancel (*a flight*); 5 **jemandem über den Kopf streichen** to stroke somebody's head.

Streichholz das (PL die **Streichhölzer**) match.

Streifen der (PL die **Streifen**)
1 stripe; 2 strip.

Streik der (PL die **Streiks**) strike.

streiken verb (PERF **hat gestreikt**) to strike.

Streit der (PL die **Streite**) quarrel, argument.

streiten ◇ verb (IMPERF **stritt**, PERF **hat gestritten**) 1 to quarrel, to argue; 2 **sich streiten** to quarrel, to argue.

streng adjective strict.

Stress Δ der stress.

stressig adjective stressful.

streuen verb (PERF **hat gestreut**)
1 to spread; **die Straßen streuen** to grit the roads; 2 to sprinkle.

strich SEE **streichen**.

Strich der (PL die **Striche**) 1 line;
2 stroke.

Strichpunkt der (PL die **Strichpunkte**) semicolon.

stricken verb (PERF **hat gestrickt**) to knit.

Strickjacke die (PL die **Strickjacken**) cardigan.

stritt SEE **streiten**.

Stroh das straw.

Strohhalm der (PL die **Strohhalme**) straw (*for drinking*).

Strom der (PL die **Ströme**) 1 river;
2 stream (*of people or blood*); **es regnet in Strömen** it's pouring with rain; 3 current.

strömen verb (PERF **ist geströmt**) to stream.

Strömung die (PL die **Strömungen**) current.

Strumpf der (PL die **Strümpfe**)
1 stocking; 2 sock.

Strumpfhose die (PL die **Strumpfhosen**) tights.

Stube die (PL die **Stuben**) room.

Stück das (PL die **Stücke**) 1 piece;
2 item; **eine Mark das Stück** one mark each; 3 play.

Stückchen das (PL die **Stückchen**) little piece.

Student der (PL die **Studenten**) student.

Studentin die (PL die **Studentinnen**) student.

◇ IRREGULAR VERB: *See the verb table in the centre of the dictionary*

studieren *verb* (PERF **hat studiert**) to study; **Horst studiert Mathematik** Horst is studying mathematics.

Studium *das* (PL *die* **Studien**) studies.

Stufe *die* (PL *die* **Stufen**) **1** step; **'Vorsicht Stufe'** 'mind the step'; **2** stage (*of development*).

Stuhl *der* (PL *die* **Stühle**) chair.

stumm *adjective* **1** dumb; **2** silent.

stumpf *adjective* **1** blunt; **2** dull; **3 ein stumpfer Winkel** an obtuse angle.

Stunde *die* (PL *die* **Stunden**) **1** hour; **2** lesson.

stundenlang *adverb* for hours.

Stundenplan *der* (PL *die* **Stundenpläne**) timetable.

stündlich *adjective* hourly.

stur *adjective* stubborn.

Sturm *der* (PL *die* **Stürme**) storm.

stürmisch *adjective* stormy.

Sturz *der* (PL *die* **Stürze**) **1** fall; **2** overthrow.

stürzen *verb* (PERF **ist gestürzt**) **1** to fall; **2** to rush (*into a room*); **3** (PERF **hat gestürzt**) to overthrow; **4** (PERF **hat sich gestürzt**) **er hat sich aus dem Fenster gestürzt** he threw himself out of the window; **sich auf jemanden stürzen** to pounce on somebody.

Sturzhelm *der* (PL *die* **Sturzhelme**) crash helmet.

stützen *verb* (PERF **hat gestützt**) to support; **sich auf jemanden stützen** to lean on somebody.

Subjekt *das* (PL *die* **Subjekte**) subject.

Substantiv *das* (PL *die* **Substantive**) noun.

subventionieren *verb* (PERF **hat subventioniert**) to subsidize.

Suche *die* (PL *die* **Suchen**) search.

suchen *verb* (PERF **hat gesucht**) **1** to look for; **'Zimmer gesucht'** 'room wanted'; **2** to search.

süchtig *adjective* addicted.

Süchtige *der/die* (PL *die* **Süchtigen**) addict.

Südafrika *das* South Africa.

Südamerika *das* South America.

Süden *der* south.

südlich *adjective* **1** southern; **2** southerly.
adverb, preposition ←(+GEN) **südlich von Wien** south of Vienna; **südlich der Stadt** to the south of the town.

Südosten *der* south-east.

Südpol *der* South Pole.

Südwesten *der* south-west.

Summe *die* (PL *die* **Summen**) sum.

summen *verb* (PERF **hat gesummt**) **1** to hum; **2** to buzz.

super *adjective* (*informal*) great.

Supermarkt *der* (PL *die* **Supermärkte**) supermarket.

Suppe *die* (PL *die* **Suppen**) soup.

△ NEW SPELLING: *See page xii*

surfen verb (PERF **hat gesurft**) to surf.

süß adjective sweet.

Süßigkeit die (PL die **Süßigkeiten**) sweet.

sympathisch adjective likeable.

Synagoge die (PL die **Synagogen**) synagogue.

synthetisch adjective synthetic.

System das (PL die **Systeme**) system.

Szene die (PL die **Szenen**) scene.

T t

Tabak der (PL die **Tabake**) tobacco.

Tabelle die (PL die **Tabellen**) table.

Tablett das (PL die **Tabletts**) tray.

Tablette die (PL die **Tabletten**) tablet.

Tafel die (PL die **Tafeln**) 1 board, blackboard; **ein Wort an die Tafel schreiben** to write a word on the blackboard; 2 **eine Tafel Schokolade** a bar of chocolate.

Tag der (PL die **Tage**) day; **guten Tag** hello; **am Tag** in the daytime.

Tagebuch das (PL die **Tagebücher**) diary.

tagelang adverb for days.

Tagesanbruch der dawn.

Tageskarte die (PL die **Tageskarten**) 1 today's menu; 2 day ticket.

Tageslicht das daylight.

Tageslichtprojektor der (PL die **Tageslichtprojektoren**) overhead projector.

Tagesmutter die (PL die **Tagesmütter**) childminder.

Tagesschau die (PL die **Tagesschauen**) news (on television)

Tageszeitung die (PL die **Tageszeitungen**) daily paper.

täglich adverb, adjective daily; **zweimal täglich** twice a day.

tagsüber adverb during the day.

Taille die (PL die **Taillen**) waist.

Takt der (PL die **Takte**) 1 tact; 2 time; **im Takt** in time to the music; 3 rhythm.

taktlos adjective tactless.

taktvoll adjective tactful.

Tal das (PL die **Täler**) valley.

Talent das (PL die **Talente**) talent.

Tampon der (PL die **Tampons**) tampon.

Tank der (PL die **Tanks**) tank.

tanken verb (PERF **hat getankt**) to fill up (with petrol), to get petrol.

Tankstelle die (PL die **Tankstellen**) petrol station.

Tankwart der (PL die **Tankwarte**) petrol-pump attendant.

Tanne die (PL die **Tannen**) fir.

Tannenbaum der (PL die **Tannenbäume**) 1 fir tree; 2 Christmas tree.

◇ IRREGULAR VERB: *See the verb table in the centre of the dictionary*

ante die (PL die Tanten) aunt.

anz der (PL die Tänze) dance.

anzen verb (PERF hat getanzt) to dance.

änzer der (PL die Tänzer) dancer.

änzerin die (PL die Tänzerinnen) dancer.

apete die (PL die Tapeten) wallpaper.

apezieren verb (PERF hat tapeziert) to (wall)paper.

apfer adjective brave.

arif der (PL die Tarife) 1 tariff; 2 rate.

asche die (PL die Taschen) 1 bag; 2 pocket; **er hat es aus eigener Tasche bezahlt** he paid for it out of his own pocket; **Max hat mir fünf Mark aus der Tasche gezogen** (informal) Max wangled five marks out of me.

aschenbuch das (PL die Taschenbücher) paperback.

aschendieb der (PL die Taschendiebe) pickpocket.

aschengeld das pocket money.

aschenlampe die (PL die Taschenlampen) torch.

aschenmesser das (PL die Taschenmesser) penknife.

aschenrechner der (PL die Taschenrechner) pocket calculator.

aschentuch das (PL die Taschentücher) handkerchief.

asse die (PL die Tassen) cup.

Tastatur die (PL die Tastaturen) keyboard.

Taste die (PL die Tasten) 1 key; 2 button (on a phone or a machine).

tasten verb (PERF hat getastet) 1 to feel; 2 **sich tasten** to feel your way.

tat SEE **tun**.

Tat die (PL die Taten) 1 action; 2 **eine gute Tat** a good deed; 3 crime; 4 **in der Tat** indeed.

Täter der (PL die Täter) 1 culprit; 2 offender.

Täterin die (PL die Täterinnen) 1 culprit; 2 offender.

Tätigkeit die (PL die Tätigkeiten) 1 activity; 2 job.

Tätowierung die (PL die Tätowierungen) tattoo.

Tatsache die (PL die Tatsachen) fact.

tatsächlich adjective actual. adverb 1 actually; 2 really.

Tau¹ der dew.

Tau² das (PL die Taue) rope.

taub adjective deaf.

Taube die (PL die Tauben) 1 pigeon; 2 dove.

tauchen verb (PERF hat getaucht) 1 to dip; 2 (PERF hat/ist getaucht) ('ist getaucht' is used when movement is described) to dive.

Taucher der (PL die Taucher) diver.

Taucherin die (PL die Taucherinnen) diver.

△ NEW SPELLING: See page xii

tauen *verb* (PERF **ist getaut**) **1** to melt; **2 es taut** it's thawing.

Taufe *die* (PL *die* **Taufen**) christening.

taufen *verb* (PERF **hat getauft**) **1** to christen; **2** to baptize.

taugen *verb* (PERF **hat getaugt**) **nichts taugen** to be no good.

tauschen *verb* (PERF **hat getauscht**) to exchange, to swap.

tausend *number* a thousand.

Taxi *das* (PL *die* **Taxis**) taxi.

Taxifahrer *der* (PL *die* **Taxifahrer**) taxi driver.

Taxifahrerin *die* (PL *die* **Taxifahrerinnen**) taxi driver.

Taxistand *der* (PL *die* **Taxistände**) taxi rank.

Technik *die* (PL *die* **Techniken**) **1** technology; **2** technique.

Techniker *der* (PL *die* **Techniker**) technician.

Technikerin *die* (PL *die* **Technikerinnen**) technician.

technisch *adjective* **1** technical; **2** technological.

Technologie *die* technology.

technologisch *adjective* technological.

Teddybär *der* (PL *die* **Teddybären**) teddy bear.

Tee *der* (PL *die* **Tee(s)**) tea; **Tee mit Zitrone** lemon tea.

Teebeutel *der* (PL *die* **Teebeutel**) tea bag.

Teekanne *die* (PL *die* **Teekannen**) teapot.

Teelöffel *der* (PL *die* **Teelöffel**) teaspoon.

Teenager *der* (PL *die* **Teenager**) teenager.

Teich *der* (PL *die* **Teiche**) pond.

Teig *der* (PL *die* **Teige**) **1** dough; **2** pastry; **3** mixture.

Teigwaren *plural noun* pasta.

Teil[1] *der* (PL *die* **Teile**) **1** part; **der zweite Teil** the second part; **zum größten Teil** for the most part; **2 zum Teil** partly; **3** share; **mein Teil am Gewinn** my share of the profit.

Teil[2] *das* (PL *die* **Teile**) **1** spare part; **2** part (*of a car, machine*); **3** unit (*o furniture*).

teilen *verb* (PERF **hat geteilt**) **1** to divide; **2 sich etwas mit jemanden teilen** to share something with somebody.

teilnehmen ✧ *verb* (PRES **nimmt teil**, IMPERF **nahm teil**, PERF **hat teilgenommen**) **an etwas teilnehmen** to take part in something.

Teilnehmer *der* (PL *die* **Teilnehmer**) **1** participant; **2** competitor.

Teilnehmerin *die* (PL *die* **Teilnehmerinnen**) **1** participant; **2** competitor.

teils *adverb* partly.

Teilung *die* (PL *die* **Teilungen**) division.

✧ IRREGULAR VERB: *See the verb table in the centre of the dictionary*

Teilzeitarbeit *die* part-time work.

Telefax *das* (PL *die* **Telefax(e)**) fax.

Telefon *das* (PL *die* **Telefone**) telephone.

Telefonanruf *der* (PL *die* **Telefonanrufe**) phone call.

Telefonbuch *das* (PL *die* **Telefonbücher**) telephone directory, phone book.

Telefongespräch *das* (PL *die* **Telefongespräche**) telephone call.

Telefonhörer *der* (PL *die* **Telefonhörer**) receiver.

telefonieren *verb* (PERF **hat telefoniert**) to telephone, to make a phone call.

telefonisch *adjective* telephone. *adverb* by telephone; **er ist telefonisch nicht erreichbar** he can't be contacted by phone.

Telefonkarte *die* (PL *die* **Telefonkarten**) phone card.

Telefonnummer *die* (PL *die* **Telefonnummern**) telephone number.

Telefonzelle *die* (PL *die* **Telefonzellen**) phone box, call box.

Teller *der* (PL *die* **Teller**) plate.

Temperatur *die* (PL *die* **Temperaturen**) temperature.

Tempo *das* (PL *die* **Tempos**) speed; **Tempo Tempo!** (*informal*) hurry up!

Tendenz *die* (PL *die* **Tendenzen**) 1 trend; 2 tendency.

tendieren *verb* (PERF **hat tendiert**) **zu etwas tendieren** to tend towards something.

Tennis *das* tennis.

Tennisplatz *der* (PL *die* **Tennisplätze**) tennis court.

Tennisschläger *der* (PL *die* **Tennisschläger**) tennis racket.

Tennisspieler *der* (PL *die* **Tennisspieler**) tennis player.

Tennisspielerin *die* (PL *die* **Tennisspielerinnen**) tennis player.

Teppich *der* (PL *die* **Teppiche**) 1 carpet; 2 rug.

Termin *der* (PL *die* **Termine**) 1 date; **einen Termin vereinbaren** to fix a date; 2 appointment; 3 **der letzte Termin** the deadline.

Terminal[1] *der* (PL *die* **Terminals**) terminal.

Terminal[2] *das* (PL *die* **Terminals**) (computer) terminal.

Terrasse *die* (PL *die* **Terrassen**) terrace.

Terror *der* terror.

Terrorismus *der* terrorism.

Terrorist *der* (PL *die* **Terroristen**) terrorist.

Terroristin *die* (PL *die* **Terroristinnen**) terrorist.

Tesafilm™ *der* Sellotape™.

Test *der* (PL *die* **Tests**) test.

testen *verb* (PERF **hat getestet**) to test.

△ NEW SPELLING: *See page xii*

teuer *adjective* expensive; **wie teuer?** how much?

Teufel *der* (PL *die* **Teufel**) devil.

Text *der* (PL *die* **Texte**) **1** text; **2** lyrics; **3** caption.

Textverarbeitung *die* word processing.

Theater *das* (PL *die* **Theater**) **1** theatre; **2** (*informal*) fuss.

Theaterstück *das* (PL *die* **Theaterstücke**) play.

Theke *die* (PL *die* **Theken**) **1** bar; **2** counter.

Thema *das* (PL *die* **Themen**) subject, topic.

Themse *die* Thames.

theoretisch *adjective* theoretical. *adverb* in theory.

Theorie *die* (PL *die* **Theorien**) theory.

Therapie *die* (PL *die* **Therapien**) therapy.

Thermometer *das* (PL *die* **Thermometer**) thermometer.

Thron *der* (PL *die* **Throne**) throne.

Thunfisch *der* (PL *die* **Thunfische**) tuna.

Thymian *der* thyme.

tief *adjective* **1** deep; **2** low.

Tiefe *die* (PL *die* **Tiefen**) depth.

Tiefgarage *die* (PL *die* **Tiefgaragen**) underground car park.

Tiefkühlfach *das* (PL *die* **Tiefkühlfächer**) freezer compartment.

Tiefkühlkost *die* frozen food.

Tiefkühltruhe *die* (PL *die* **Tiefkühltruhen**) freezer.

Tiefsttemperatur *die* (PL *die* **Tiefsttemperaturen**) minimum temperature.

Tier *das* (PL *die* **Tiere**) animal.

Tierarzt *der* (PL *die* **Tierärzte**) vet.

Tierärztin *die* (PL *die* **Tierärztinnen**) vet.

Tiergarten *der* (PL *die* **Tiergärten**) zoo.

Tierkreis *der* zodiac.

Tiger *der* (PL *die* **Tiger**) tiger.

Tinte *die* (PL *die* **Tinten**) ink.

Tintenfisch *der* (PL *die* **Tintenfische**) **1** octopus; **2** squid.

Tipp Δ *der* (PL *die* **Tipps**) tip.

tippen *verb* (PERF **hat getippt**) **1** to type; **2** to tap; **3 auf etwas tippen** to bet on something; **ich tippe auf ihn** I'm tipping him to win; **im Lotto tippen** to do the lottery.

Tisch *der* (PL *die* **Tische**) **1** table; **2 nach Tisch** after the meal.

Tischdecke *die* (PL *die* **Tischdecken**) tablecloth.

Tischler *der* (PL *die* **Tischler**) joiner, carpenter.

Tischtennis *das* table tennis.

Tischtuch *das* (PL *die* **Tischtücher**) tablecloth.

Titel *der* (PL *die* **Titel**) title.

Toast *der* (PL *die* **Toasts**) toast.

✧ IRREGULAR VERB: *See the verb table in the centre of the dictionary*

toben *verb* (PERF **hat getobt**) **1** to rage; **2** to go mad; **3** to charge about.

Tochter *die* (PL *die* **Töchter**) daughter.

Tod *der* (PL *die* **Tode**) death.

Todesstrafe *die* death penalty.

tödlich *adjective* **1** fatal; **2** deadly.

todmüde *adjective* dead tired.

todschick *adjective* trendy.

Toilette *die* (PL *die* **Toiletten**) toilet; **auf die Toilette gehen** to go to the toilet.

Toilettenpapier *das* toilet paper.

toll *adjective* (*informal*) brilliant.

Tollwut *die* rabies.

Tomate *die* (PL *die* **Tomaten**) tomato.

Tomatenmark *das* tomato purée.

Ton[1] *der* (PL *die* **Töne**) **1** sound; **er hat keinen Ton gesagt** he didn't make a sound; **2 große Töne spucken** (*informal*) to talk big; **3** tone; **einen frechen Ton anschlagen** to adopt a cheeky tone; **4** note; **5** shade (*of colour*); **6** stress (*in pronunciation*).

Ton[2] *der* clay.

Tonband *das* (PL *die* **Tonbänder**) tape.

Tonbandgerät *das* (PL *die* **Tonbandgeräte**) tape recorder.

Tonne *die* (PL *die* **Tonnen**) **1** barrel; **2** bin (*for rubbish*); **3** tonne, ton.

Topf *der* (PL *die* **Töpfe**) **1** pot; **2** pan.

Töpferei *die* (PL *die* **Töpfereien**) pottery.

Tor *das* (PL *die* **Tore**) **1** gate; **2** goal.

Torte *die* (PL *die* **Torten**) **1** gateau; **2** cake.

Torwart *der* (PL *die* **Torwarte**) goalkeeper.

tot *adjective* dead.

total *adjective* complete. *adverb* completely; **du bist total verrückt** you're totally mad.

Tote *der/die* (PL *die* **Toten**) **1** dead man/woman; **die Toten** the dead; **2** fatality.

töten *verb* (PERF **hat getötet**) to kill.

totlachen *verb* (*informal*) (PERF **hat sich totgelacht**) **sich totlachen** to laugh your head off.

Tour *die* (PL *die* **Touren**) **1** tour; **2** trip; **3 auf diese Tour** (*informal*) in this way.

Tourismus *der* tourism.

Tourist *der* (PL *die* **Touristen**) tourist.

Touristin *die* (PL *die* **Touristinnen**) tourist.

Tournee *die* (PL *die* **Tournees**) tour.

traben *verb* (PERF **ist getrabt**) to trot.

Tradition *die* (PL *die* **Traditionen**) tradition.

traditionell *adjective* traditional.

traf SEE **treffen**.

tragbar *adjective* **1** portable; **2** wearable.

tragen ◇ *verb* (PRES **trägt**, IMPERF **trug**, PERF **hat getragen**) **1** to carry; **2** to wear; **sie trug ein weißes Kleid** she wore a white dress; **man trägt**

△ NEW SPELLING: *See page xii*

wieder kurz short skirts are in fashion again; **3** to bear; **die Verantwortung für etwas tragen** to be responsible for something; **4** to support; **die Organisation trägt sich selbst** the organization is self-supporting.

Träger der (PL die **Träger**) **1** porter; **2** bearer (*of a name, title*); **3** strap (*of a dress*); **4** girder.

Tragetasche die (PL die **Tragetaschen**) carrier bag.

tragisch adjective tragic.

Tragödie die (PL die **Tragödien**) tragedy.

Trainer der (PL die **Trainer**) coach, trainer.

trainieren verb (PERF hat **trainiert**) **1** to coach; **2** to train.

Training das training.

Trainingsanzug der (PL die **Trainingsanzüge**) tracksuit.

Traktor der (PL die **Traktoren**) tractor.

trampen verb (PERF ist **getrampt**) to hitchhike.

Tramper der (PL die **Tramper**) hitchhiker.

Tramperin die (PL die **Tramperinnen**) hitchhiker.

Träne die (PL die **Tränen**) tear.

trank SEE **trinken**.

Transport der (PL die **Transporte**) **1** transport; **2** consignment.

transportieren verb (PERF hat **transportiert**) to transport.

trat SEE **treten**.

Traube die (PL die **Trauben**) grape.

trauen verb (PERF hat **getraut**) **1** to trust; **jemandem trauen** to trust somebody; **2** sich trauen to dare; **Ich trau mich nicht** I don't dare; **3** to marry.

Trauer die **1** grief; **2** mourning.

Traum der (PL die **Träume**) dream.

träumen verb (PERF hat **geträumt**) to dream.

traumhaft adjective fabulous.

traurig adjective sad.

Traurigkeit die sadness.

Trauung die (PL die **Trauungen**) wedding.

treffen ◇ verb (PRES **trifft**, IMPERF **traf**, PERF hat **getroffen**) **1** to hit; **2** to meet; **3** to make (*arrangements, a decision*); **4** sich mit jemandem treffen to meet somebody; **5** sich gut treffen to be convenient; **6** (PERF ist **getroffen**) auf etwas treffen to meet with (*resistance, difficulties*).

Treffen das (PL die **Treffen**) meeting.

Treffer der (PL die **Treffer**) **1** hit; **2** winner; **3** goal.

Treffpunkt der (PL die **Treffpunkte**) meeting place.

treiben ◇ verb (IMPERF **trieb**, PERF hat **getrieben**) **1** to drive; **2** to do; **viel Sport treiben** to do a lot of sport;

◇ IRREGULAR VERB: *See the verb table in the centre of the dictionary*

Handel treiben to trade;
3 jemanden zur Eile treiben to
hurry somebody up; **4 Unsinn
treiben** to mess about; **5** (PERF **ist
getrieben**) to drift.

Treibhaus das (PL die **Treibhäuser**)
hothouse.

Treibhauseffekt der greenhouse
effect.

Treibstoff der fuel.

trennen verb (PERF **hat getrennt**)
1 to separate; **2** to divide (words,
parts of a room); **3 sich trennen** to
separate; **wir haben uns getrennt**
we've separated; **Jutta hat sich von
ihm getrennt** Jutta has left him;
4 sich von etwas trennen to part
with something.

Trennung die (PL die **Trennungen**)
1 separation; **2** division.

Treppe die (PL die **Treppen**) stairs;
eine Treppe a flight of stairs.

Treppenhaus das stairwell; **im
Treppenhaus** on the stairs.

treten ◇ verb (PRES **tritt**, IMPERF **trat**,
PERF **ist getreten**) **1** to step; **2** to
tread; **3** to kick; **4 mit jemandem in
Verbindung treten** to get in touch
with somebody.

treu adjective faithful.

Tribüne die (PL die **Tribünen**)
1 stand (in a stadium); **2** platform.

Trick der (PL die **Tricks**) trick.

Trickfilm der (PL die **Trickfilme**)
cartoon.

trieb SEE **treiben**.

trifft SEE **treffen**.

Trimm-dich-Pfad der (PL die
Trimm-dich-Pfade) keep-fit trail.

trimmen verb (PERF **hat getrimmt**)
1 to trim; **2 sich trimmen** to keep
fit.

trinken ◇ verb (IMPERF **trank**, PERF
hat getrunken) to drink.

Trinkgeld das (PL die **Trinkgelder**)
tip.

Trinkwasser das drinking water.

tritt SEE **treten**.

Tritt der (PL die **Tritte**) **1** step; **2** kick.

Triumph der (PL die **Triumphe**)
triumph.

trocken adjective dry.

trocknen verb (PERF **hat
getrocknet**) to dry.

Trockner der (PL die **Trockner**) drier.

Trödel der (informal) junk.

Trödelmarkt der (PL die
Trödelmärkte) flea market.

Trommel die (PL die **Trommeln**)
drum.

trommeln verb (PERF **hat
getrommelt**) to drum.

Trompete die (PL die **Trompeten**)
trumpet.

Tropen (plural noun) **die Tropen**
the tropics.

tropfen verb (PERF **hat getropft**) to
drip.

Tropfen der (PL die **Tropfen**) drop.

△ NEW SPELLING: See page xii

Trophäe die (PL die **Trophäen**) trophy.

tropisch adjective tropical.

trösten verb (PERF **hat getröstet**) to console, to comfort.

trotz preposition ←(+GEN) despite, in spite of.

trotzdem adverb nevertheless.

trüb adjective **1** dull, dismal; **2** cloudy (liquid).

trübsinnig adjective gloomy.

trug SEE **tragen**.

Truhe die (PL die **Truhen**) chest.

Trümmer plural noun ruins.

Trumpf der (PL die **Trümpfe**) **1** trump (card); **2** trumps.

Trunkenheit die drunkenness; **Trunkenheit am Steuer** drink-driving.

Truppen plural noun troops.

Truthahn der (PL die **Truthähne**) turkey.

Tscheche der (PL die **Tschechen**) Czech.

Tschechin die (PL die **Tschechinnen**) Czech.

tschechisch adjective Czech.

Tschechische Republik die Czech Republic.

tschüss Δ exclamation bye!

T-Shirt das (PL die **T-Shirts**) T-shirt.

Tube die (PL die **Tuben**) tube.

Tuberkulose die tuberculosis.

Tuch das (PL die **Tücher**) **1** cloth; **2** scarf.

tüchtig adjective **1** competent; **2** big.

Tulpe die (PL die **Tulpen**) tulip.

Tumor der (PL die **Tumoren**) tumour.

tun ✧ verb (PRES **tut**, IMPERF **tat**, PERF **hat getan**) **1** to do; **das tut man nicht** it isn't done; **das tut's** (informal) that'll do; **2** to put; **die Butter in den Kühlschrank tun** to put the butter in the fridge; **3** to pretend; **er tut nur so** he's only pretending; **4** to act; **freundlich tun** to act friendly; **5** jemandem etwas **tun** to hurt somebody; **6** mit jemandem etwas zu tun haben to have dealings with somebody; **das hat nichts damit zu tun** it's got nothing to do with it; **7** das tut nichts it doesn't matter; **es hat sich viel getan** lots has happened.

Tunfisch Δ der (PL die **Tunfische**) tuna.

Tunesien das Tunisia.

Tunesier der (PL die **Tunesier**) Tunisian.

Tunesierin die (PL die **Tunesierinnen**) Tunisian.

tunesisch adjective Tunisian.

Tunnel der (PL die **Tunnel**) tunnel.

tupfen verb (PERF **hat getupft**) to dab.

Tupfen der (PL die **Tupfen**) dot.

Tür die (PL die **Türen**) door.

Türke der (PL die **Türken**) Turk.

✧ IRREGULAR VERB: See the verb table in the centre of the dictionary

Türkei die Turkey.

Türkin die (PL die **Türkinnen**) Turk.

türkis adjective turquoise.

türkisch adjective Turkish.

Turm der (PL die **Türme**) 1 tower;
2 steeple; 3 rook, castle (in chess).

turnen verb (PERF **hat geturnt**) to do
gymnastics.

Turnen das 1 gymnastics;
2 physical education, PE.

Turnhalle die (PL die **Turnhallen**)
gymnasium, gym.

Turnier das (PL die **Turniere**)
tournament.

Turnschuh der (PL die **Turnschuhe**)
1 trainer; 2 gym shoe.

Turnverein der (PL die **Turnvereine**)
gymnastics club.

tuscheln verb (PERF **hat getuschelt**)
to whisper.

tut SEE **tun**.

Tüte die (PL die **Tüten**) bag.

Typ der (PL die **Typen**) 1 type;
2 (informal) bloke.

typisch adjective typical.

U u

U-Bahn die (PL die **U-Bahnen**)
underground.

übel adjective 1 bad; 2 **mir ist übel**
I feel sick; 3 **etwas übel nehmen** △
to take offence at something;
jemandem etwas übel nehmen △ to
hold something against somebody.

Übelkeit die nausea.

übelnehmen SEE **übel**.

üben verb (PERF **hat geübt**) to
practise.

über preposition ←(+DAT, or +ACC with
movement towards a place) 1 over;
über Weihnachten over Christmas;
2 above; **er wohnt über uns** he lives
above us; **fünf Grad über Null** five
degrees above zero; 3 about; **über
etwas schreiben** to write about
something; 4 for; **ein Scheck über
hundert Mark** a cheque for one
hundred marks; 5 across (a field, the
street); 6 **über Frankfurt fahren** to
go via Frankfurt; 7 **über die Straße
gehen** to cross the road.
adverb 1 **über und über** over and
over; 2 **jemandem über sein** to be
better than somebody; 3 **über sein**
(informal) to be left over;
4 **jemandem ist etwas über**
(informal) somebody is fed up with
something; 5 **etwas über haben** △
(informal) to be fed up with
something; **Nudeln habe ich über**
I'm getting fed up with pasta.

△ NEW SPELLING: See page xii

überall *adverb* everywhere.

Überblick *der* (PL *die* **Überblicke**)
1 **einen guten Überblick über
etwas haben** to have a good view of
something; 2 overall view; **den
Überblick verlieren** to lose track of
things; 3 summary.

überblicken *verb* (PERF **hat
überblickt**) 1 to overlook; 2 to
assess.

Überdruss Δ *der* **bis zum
Überdruss** ad nauseam.

übereinander *adverb* 1 one on top
of the other; 2 **übereinander
sprechen** to talk about each other.

übereinstimmen *verb* (PERF **hat
übereingestimmt**) to agree.

überempfindlich *adjective*
hypersensitive.

überfahren ◇ *verb* (PRES
überfährt, IMPERF **überfuhr**, PERF **hat
überfahren**) to run over; **das Kind ist
von einem Auto überfahren
worden** the child was run over by a
car.

Überfahrt *die* (PL *die* **Überfahrten**)
crossing.

Überfall *der* (PL *die* **Überfälle**)
1 attack; 2 raid.

überfallen ◇ *verb* (PRES **überfällt**,
IMPERF **überfiel**, PERF **hat überfallen**)
1 to attack, to mug; 2 to raid;
3 **jemanden mit Fragen überfallen**
to bombard somebody with
questions.

überfällig *adjective* overdue.

überflüssig *adjective* superfluous.

Überführung *die* (PL *die*
Überführungen) 1 transfer;
2 flyover; 3 footbridge.

überfüllt *adjective* 1 crowded;
2 oversubscribed.

Übergang *der* (PL *die* **Übergänge**)
1 crossing; 2 transition.

übergeben ◇ *verb* (PRES **übergibt**,
IMPERF **übergab**, PERF **hat
übergeben**) 1 to hand over; 2 **sich
übergeben** to be sick.

überhaben SEE **über**.

überhaupt *adverb* 1 in general;
2 anyway; **was will er überhaupt?**
what does he want anyway?;
3 **überhaupt nicht** not at all;
überhaupt nichts nothing at all;
überhaupt keine Zeit haben to
have no time at all.

überholen *verb* (PERF **hat überholt**)
1 to overtake; 2 to overhaul.

überholt *adjective* out-of-date.

überlassen ◇ *verb* (PRES
überlässt Δ, IMPERF **überließ**, PERF
hat überlassen) 1 **jemandem etwas
überlassen** to let somebody have
something; 2 **etwas jemandem
überlassen** to leave something up
to somebody (*a decision, for
example*); **das bleibt dir
überlassen** it's up to you.

überlaufen ◇ *verb* (PRES **läuft über**,
IMPERF **lief über**, PERF **ist
übergelaufen**) to overflow.

überleben *verb* (PERF **hat überlebt**)
to survive.

überlegen[1] *verb* (PERF **hat**

◇ IRREGULAR VERB: *See the verb table in the centre of the dictionary*

überlegt) 1 to think; **sich etwas überlegen** to think something over; **ohne zu überlegen** without thinking; **2 ich habe es mir anders überlegt** I've changed my mind.

überlegen[2] *adjective* **1** superior; **jemandem überlegen sein** to be superior to somebody; **2** convincing (*victory*).

überm = **über dem**.

übermäßig *adjective* excessive.

übermorgen *adverb* the day after tomorrow.

übernächster, übernächste, übernächstes *adjective* next but one; **übernächstes Jahr** the year after next.

übernachten *verb* (PERF **hat übernachtet**) to stay the night; **bei jemandem übernachten** to stay the night at somebody's house.

übernehmen ✧ *verb* (PRES **übernimmt**, IMPERF **übernahm**, PERF **hat übernommen**) **1** to take over; **2** to take on; **3 sich übernehmen** to take on too much.

überqueren *verb* (PERF **hat überquert**) to cross.

überraschen *verb* (PERF **hat überrascht**) to surprise.

Überraschung *die* (PL *die* **Überraschungen**) surprise.

überreden *verb* (PERF **hat überredet**) to persuade.

übers = **über das**.

Überschrift *die* (PL *die* **Überschriften**) heading.

überschüssig *adjective* surplus.

überschütten *verb* (PERF **hat überschüttet**) **jemanden mit etwas überschütten** to shower somebody with something.

Überschwemmung *die* (PL *die* **Überschwemmungen**) flood.

übersehen[1] ✧ *verb* (PRES **übersieht**, IMPERF **übersah**, PERF **hat übersehen**) **1** to overlook; **einen Fehler übersehen** to overlook a mistake; **2** to assess (*consequences, damages*).

übersehen[2] ✧ *verb* (PRES **sieht sich über**, IMPERF **sah sich über**, PERF **hat sich übersehen**) **sich etwas übersehen** to get fed up of seeing something.

übersetzen *verb* (PERF **hat übersetzt**) to translate.

Übersetzer *der* (PL *die* **Übersetzer**) translator.

Übersetzerin *die* (PL *die* **Übersetzerinnen**) translator.

Übersetzung *die* (PL *die* **Übersetzungen**) translation.

Übersicht *die* **1** overall view; **2** summary.

überspringen ✧ *verb* (IMPERF **übersprang**, PERF **hat übersprungen**) **1** to jump (over); **2** to skip (*a chapter*).

überstehen ✧ *verb* (IMPERF **überstand**, PERF **hat überstanden**) **1** to get over; **2** to survive.

△ NEW SPELLING: *See page xii*

Überstunden *plural noun*
overtime; **Überstunden machen** to
work overtime.

übertragen ✧ *verb* (PRES
überträgt, IMPERF **übertrug**, PERF **hat
übertragen**) 1 to transfer; 2 to
transmit; 3 to broadcast; 4 **etwas
ins Reine übertragen** to make a fair
copy of something; 5 **sich auf
jemanden übertragen** to
communicate itself to somebody (*of
enthusiasm or nervousness*).

Übertragung *die* (PL *die*
Übertragungen) 1 broadcast;
2 transmission.

übertreiben ✧ *verb* (IMPERF
übertrieb, PERF **hat übertrieben**)
1 to exaggerate; 2 to overdo.

Übertreibung *die* (PL *die*
Übertreibungen) exaggeration.

überwältigend *adjective*
overwhelming.

überweisen ✧ *verb* (IMPERF
überwies, PERF **hat überwiesen**)
1 to transfer; 2 to refer (*a patient*).

überzeugen *verb* (PERF **hat
überzeugt**) 1 to convince; 2 **sich
selbst überzeugen** to satisfy
yourself.

überzeugend *adjective*
convincing.

Überzeugung *die* (PL *die*
Überzeugungen) conviction.

überziehen¹ ✧ *verb* (IMPERF **zog
über**, PERF **hat übergezogen**) to put
on (*a cardigan, jacket*).

überziehen² ✧ *verb* (IMPERF

überzog, PERF **hat überzogen**) 1 to
overdraw; 2 to cover (*with icing, fo
example*).

üblich *adjective* usual.

übrig *adjective* 1 remaining; 2 **übri
sein** to be left over; 3 **etwas übrig
lassen** △ to leave something (over);
4 **uns blieb nichts anderes übrig**
we had no other choice; 5 **alles
Übrige** the rest; **die Übrigen** the
others; 6 **im Übrigen** besides.

übrigens *adverb* by the way.

übriglassen SEE **übrig**.

Übung *die* (PL *die* **Übungen**)
1 exercise; 2 practice; **aus der
Übung sein** to be out of practice.

Ufer *das* (PL *die* **Ufer**) 1 bank (*of a
river*); 2 shore.

Uhr *die* (PL *die* **Uhren**) 1 clock;
2 watch; 3 (*in time phrases*) **es ist
ein Uhr** it's one o'clock; **wie viel Uh
ist es?** what's the time?; **um
sechzehn Uhr** at four o'clock (in th
afternoon).

Uhrzeiger *der* (PL *die* **Uhrzeiger**)
hand (*of a clock or watch*).

Uhrzeigersinn *der* **im
Uhrzeigersinn** clockwise;
entgegen dem Uhrzeigersinn anti-
clockwise.

Uhrzeit *die* time; **jemanden nach
der Uhrzeit fragen** to ask
somebody the time.

ulkig *adjective* funny.

um *preposition* ←(+ACC) 1 round,
around; **um das Haus herum**
around the house; 2 at; **um fünf Uhr**

✧ IRREGULAR VERB: *See the verb table in the centre of the dictionary*

at five o'clock; **3** around (about); **4** for; **um etwas bitten** to ask for something; **um seinetwillen** for his sake; **5 sich um jemanden sorgen** to worry about somebody; **6** by (*indicating difference*); **um vieles besser** better by far; **um so besser** so much the better.
adverb **1** about, around; **um die dreihundert Mark herum** about three hundred marks; **um Weihnachten** around Christmas; **2 um sein** (*informal*) to be over. *conjunction* **um zu** (in order) to; **er ist noch zu klein, um in die Schule zu gehen** he's too young to go to school.

umarmen *verb* (PERF **hat umarmt**) to hug.

Umbau *der* (PL *die* **Umbauten**) **1** renovation; **2** conversion.

umbinden ⬦ *verb* (IMPERF **band um**, PERF **hat umgebunden**) to put on.

umblättern *verb* (PERF **hat umgeblättert**) to turn over.

umbringen ⬦ *verb* (IMPERF **brachte um**, PERF **hat umgebracht**) to kill.

umdrehen *verb* (PERF **hat umgedreht**) **1** to turn (round); **2 sich umdrehen** to turn round, to turn over.

umfallen ⬦ *verb* (PRES **fällt um**, IMPERF **fiel um**, PERF **ist umgefallen**) to fall down.

Umfrage *die* (PL *die* **Umfragen**) survey.

umgänglich *adjective* sociable.

Umgangsformen *plural noun* manners.

Umgangssprache *die* slang, colloquial language.

umgeben ⬦ *verb* (PRES **umgibt**, IMPERF **umgab**, PERF **hat umgeben**) to surround.

Umgebung *die* (PL *die* **Umgebungen**) **1** surroundings; **2** neighbourhood.

umgehen[1] ⬦ *verb* (IMPERF **ging um**, PERF **ist umgegangen**) **1** to go round (*of a rumour, an illness*); **2 mit jemandem streng umgehen** to treat somebody strictly; **3 er kann mit Geld nicht umgehen** he can't handle money; **mit seinen Sachen sorgfältig umgehen** to handle one's things carefully.

umgehen[2] ⬦ *verb* (IMPERF **umging**, PERF **hat umgangen**) to avoid.

umgekehrt *adjective* **1** opposite; **2** reverse (*order*); **3 es war umgekehrt** it was the other way round.
adverb **1 und umgekehrt** and vice versa; **2** the other way round; **warum machst du es nicht umgekehrt?** why don't you do it the other way round?

umkehren *verb* (PERF **ist umgekehrt**) **1** to turn back; **nach zehn Minuten sind wir wieder umgekehrt** ten minutes later we turned back again; **2** to turn round (*a picture, book*); **3** to turn inside out (*a bag, for example*); **4 sie hat das ganze Zimmer umgekehrt**

△ NEW SPELLING: *See page xii*

(*informal*) she turned the whole room upside down.

Umkleidekabine die (PL die **Umkleidekabinen**) changing cubicle.

Umkleideraum der (PL die **Umkleideräume**) changing room.

umkommen ✧ verb (IMPERF **kam um**, PERF **ist umgekommen**) to be killed.

Umlaut der (PL die **Umlaute**) umlaut.

umlegen verb (PERF **hat umgelegt**) 1 to put on (*a scarf*); 2 to transfer (*a patient, call*); 3 **jemanden umlegen** (*informal*) to bump somebody off.

Umleitung die (PL die **Umleitungen**) diversion.

umrechnen verb (PERF **hat umgerechnet**) to convert.

Umrechnung die conversion.

Umrechnungskurs der exchange rate.

Umriss △ der (PL die **Umrisse**) outline.

umrühren verb (PERF **hat umgerührt**) to stir.

ums = um das.

umschalten verb (PERF **hat umgeschaltet**) 1 to turn over; **vom ersten aufs zweite Programm umschalten** to turn from channel one to channel two; 2 **auf Rot umschalten** to change to red.

Umschlag der (PL die **Umschläge**) 1 envelope; 2 cover.

umsehen ✧ verb (PRES **sieht sich um**, IMPERF **sah sich um**, PERF **hat sic umgesehen**) **sich umsehen** to loo round.

umso △ adverb **umso besser** all th better; **je mehr, umso besser** the more the better.

umsonst adverb 1 in vain; 2 free, for nothing.

Umstand der (PL die **Umstände**) 1 circumstance; 2 **unter Umständen** possibly; 3 **jemanden Umstände machen** to put somebody to trouble; **das macht ga keine Umstände** it's no trouble at all; 4 **in anderen Umständen sein** to be pregnant.

umständlich adjective 1 laborious; 2 complicated.

umsteigen ✧ verb (IMPERF **stieg um**, PERF **ist umgestiegen**) to change

umstellen¹ verb (PERF **hat umgestellt**) 1 to rearrange; 2 to reset; 3 to change over; 4 **sich umstellen** to adjust.

umstellen² verb (PERF **hat umstellt** to surround.

Umtausch der exchange.

umtauschen verb (PERF **hat umgetauscht**) to change, to exchange.

Umweg der (PL die **Umwege**) detour.

Umwelt die environment.

umweltfreundlich adjective environmentally friendly.

Umweltschützer der (PL die **Umweltschützer**) environmentalist.

✧ IRREGULAR VERB: *See the verb table in the centre of the dictionary*

Umweltverschmutzung *die*
pollution.

umwerfen ✧ *verb* (PRES **wirft um**,
IMPERF **warf um**, PERF **hat
umgeworfen**) **1** to knock over; **2** to
upset (*a plan*); **das hat mich
umgeworfen** it's thrown me.

umwerfend *adjective* fantastic.

umziehen ✧ *verb* (IMPERF **zog um**,
PERF **ist umgezogen**) **1** to move; **sie
ziehen nächste Woche um** they're
moving next week; **2** (PERF **hat
umgezogen**) to change; **3** (PERF **hat
sich umgezogen**) **sich umziehen**
to get changed.

Umzug *der* (PL *die* **Umzüge**) move.

unabhängig *adjective*
independent.

Unabhängigkeit *die*
independence.

unangenehm *adjective*
1 unpleasant; **2** embarrassing
(*question, situation*).

unartig *adjective* naughty.

unbedeutend *adjective*
insignificant.
adverb slightly.

unbedingt *adjective* absolute.
adverb really; **ich muss ihn
unbedingt sprechen** I really must
talk to him; **nicht unbedingt** not
necessarily.

unbefriedigend *adjective*
unsatisfactory.

unbefriedigt *adjective* unsatisfied.

unbehaglich *adjective*
1 uncomfortable; **2** uneasy.

unbekannt *adjective* unknown.

unbeliebt *adjective* unpopular.

unbequem *adjective*
uncomfortable.

unbestimmt *adjective* **1** indefinite;
auf unbestimmte Zeit for an
indefinite period; **2** uncertain.
adverb vaguely; **etwas unbestimmt
lassen** to leave something open.

unbewusst Δ *adjective*
unconscious.

und *conjunction* and; **und so weiter**
and so on; **na und?** so what?

undankbar *adjective* ungrateful.

undeutlich *adjective* unclear.

undicht *adjective* leaking, leaky;
eine undichte Stelle a leak.

uneben *adjective* uneven.

unempfindlich *adjective* **1** hard-
wearing, easy-care; **2** immune;
gegen Kälte unempfindlich sein
not to feel the cold.

unentbehrlich *adjective*
indispensable.

unentschieden *adjective*
undecided; **unentschieden spielen**
to draw.

unerträglich *adjective* unbearable.

unerwartet *adjective* unexpected.

unfähig *adjective* **1** incompetent;
2 unfähig sein, etwas zu tun to be
incapable of doing something.

Δ NEW SPELLING: *See page xii*

unfair *adjective* unfair.

Unfall *der* (PL *die* **Unfälle**) accident.

unfreundlich *adjective* unfriendly.

Unfug *der* 1 nonsense; 2 mischief; **Unfug machen** to get up to mischief.

Ungar *der* (PL *die* **Ungarn**) Hungarian.

Ungarin *die* (PL *die* **Ungarinnen**) Hungarian.

ungarisch *adjective* Hungarian.

Ungarn *das* Hungary.

Ungeduld *die* impatience.

ungeduldig *adjective* impatient.

ungeeignet *adjective* unsuitable.

ungefähr *adjective* approximate. *adverb* approximately, about.

ungefährlich *adjective* safe, harmless.

ungeheuer *adjective* enormous.

Ungeheuer *das* (PL *die* **Ungeheuer**) monster.

ungehorsam *adjective* disobedient.

ungelegen *adjective* inconvenient.

ungemütlich *adjective* uncomfortable.

ungenau *adjective* 1 inaccurate; 2 vague.

ungenießbar *adjective* 1 inedible; 2 undrinkable; 3 **Bernd ist heute aber ungenießbar** (*informal*) Bernd is quite unbearable today.

ungenügend *adjective* 1 insufficient; 2 unsatisfactory (*mark at school*).

ungerade *adjective* **eine ungerade Zahl** an odd number.

ungerecht *adjective* unjust.

ungern *adverb* reluctantly.

ungeschickt *adjective* clumsy.

ungesund *adjective* unhealthy.

ungewöhnlich *adjective* unusual.

Ungeziefer *das* vermin.

ungezwungen *adjective* 1 informal; 2 natural.

unglaublich *adjective* incredible.

Unglück *das* (PL *die* **Unglücke**) 1 accident; 2 misfortune; 3 bad luck; **das bringt Unglück** that's unlucky.

unglücklich *adjective* 1 unhappy; 2 unfortunate.

unglücklicherweise *adverb* unfortunately.

unheilbar *adjective* incurable.

unheimlich *adjective* eerie. *adverb* 1 eerily; 2 (*informal*) incredibly; **unheimlich viel** an incredible amount.

unhöflich *adjective* impolite.

Uniform *die* (PL *die* **Uniformen**) uniform.

uninteressant *adjective* uninteresting.

Universität *die* (PL *die* **Universitäten**) university.

Unkenntnis *die* ignorance.

✧ IRREGULAR VERB: *See the verb table in the centre of the dictionary*

unklar *adjective* unclear.

Unkosten *plural noun* expenses.

Unkraut *das* weed.

unmodern *adjective* old-fashioned.

unleserlich *adjective* illegible.

unlogisch *adjective* illogical.

unmittelbar *adjective* immediate, direct.

unmöglich *adjective* impossible.

Unmöglichkeit *die* impossibility.

unnötig *adjective* unnecessary.

unordentlich *adjective* untidy.

Unordnung *die* 1 disorder; 2 mess.

unpraktisch *adjective* impractical.

unpünktlich *adjective* unpunctual; **unpünktlich sein** to be late.

unrecht *adjective* wrong; **jemandem unrecht tun** to do somebody an injustice.

Unrecht *das* 1 wrong; **zu Unrecht** wrongly; **Unrecht haben** Δ to be wrong; 2 **jemandem Unrecht geben** Δ to disagree with somebody.

unregelmäßig *adjective* irregular.

unreif *adjective* 1 unripe; 2 immature.

Unruhe *die* (PL *die* **Unruhen**) 1 restlessness; 2 agitation; 3 **Unruhen** unrest.

Unruhestifter *der* (PL *die* **Unruhestifter**) troublemaker.

unruhig *adjective* restless.

uns *pronoun* 1 us; **gib es uns** give it

to us; **sie kommen mit uns** they're coming with us; 2 ourselves; **wir waschen uns die Hände** we are washing our hands; 3 each other; **wir kennen uns** we know each other.

unschuldig *adjective* innocent.

unser our.

unserer, unsere, unser(e)s *pronoun* ours.

unsertwegen *adverb* 1 for our sake; 2 because of us; 3 as far as we're concerned.

unsicher *adjective* 1 uncertain; 2 insecure.
adverb unsteadily.

unsichtbar *adjective* invisible.

Unsinn *der* nonsense.

unsrer SEE **unserer**.

unsympathisch *adjective* unpleasant; **Tobias ist mir unsympathisch** I don't like Tobias.

unten *adverb* 1 at the bottom; 2 underneath; 3 downstairs; **hier unten** down here; **nach unten** down.

unter *preposition* ←(+DAT *or* +ACC *with movement towards a place*) 1 under, below; 2 among; **unter anderem** among other things; 3 **unter sich** by themselves; **unter uns gesagt** between ourselves; 4 **unter der Woche** during the week.

Unterbewusstsein Δ *das* subconscious.

unterbrechen ◆ *verb* (PRES **unterbricht**, IMPERF **unterbrach**, PERF **hat unterbrochen**) to interrupt.

Δ NEW SPELLING: *See page xii*

Unterbrechung die (PL die Unterbrechungen) interruption.

unterbringen ✧ verb (IMPERF **brachte unter**, PERF **hat untergebracht**) 1 to put; 2 to put up (a guest).

untere SEE **unterer**.

untereinander adverb 1 among ourselves/yourselves/themselves; 2 one below the other.

unterer, untere, unteres adjective lower.

Unterführung die (PL die Unterführungen) subway.

untergehen ✧ verb (IMPERF **ging unter**, PERF **ist untergegangen**) 1 to set (of the sun); 2 to sink, to drown; 3 to come to an end.

Untergrundbahn die (PL die Untergrundbahnen) underground.

unterhalb preposition ←(+GEN) below.

unterhalten ✧ verb (PRES **unterhält**, IMPERF **unterhielt**, PERF **hat unterhalten**) 1 to support; 2 to run (a hotel, leisure centre); 3 to entertain; 4 **sich über etwas unterhalten** to talk about something; 5 **sich unterhalten** to enjoy yourself.

unterhaltsam adjective entertaining.

Unterhaltung die (PL die Unterhaltungen) 1 conversation; 2 entertainment.

Unterhemd das (PL die Unterhemden) vest.

Unterhose die (PL die Unterhosen) underpants.

Unterkunft die (PL die Unterkünfte) accommodation.

Unterlagen plural noun documents, papers.

Untermieter der (PL die Untermieter) lodger.

Untermieterin die (PL die Untermieterinnen) lodger.

unternehmen ✧ verb (PRES **unternimmt**, IMPERF **unternahm**, PERF **hat unternommen**) 1 to undertake; 2 **nichts unternehmen** to do nothing; **was unternehmt ihr heute?** what are you doing today?

Unternehmen das (PL die Unternehmen) 1 enterprise; 2 concern.

Unterricht der 1 lessons; **heute haben wir keinen Unterricht** we've got no lessons today; 2 teaching.

unterrichten verb (PERF **hat unterrichtet**) 1 to teach; 2 to inform; 3 **sich unterrichten** to inform yourself.

Unterrichtsfach das (PL die Unterrichtsfächer) subject.

Unterrock der (PL die Unterröcke) slip.

unterscheiden ✧ verb (IMPERF **unterschied**, PERF **hat unterschieden**) 1 to distinguish, to tell apart; 2 **sich unterscheiden** to differ.

Unterschied der (PL die Unterschiede) difference.

✧ IRREGULAR VERB: See the verb table in the centre of the dictionary

unterschiedlich *adjective*
different; **das ist unterschiedlich**
it varies.

unterschreiben ◇ *verb* (IMPERF
unterschrieb, PERF **hat
unterschrieben**) to sign.

Unterschrift *die* (PL *die*
Unterschriften) signature.

unterster, unterste, unterstes
adjective bottom, lowest.

unterstreichen ◇ *verb* (IMPERF
unterstrich, PERF **hat unterstrichen**)
to underline.

unterstützen *verb* (PERF **hat
unterstützt**) to support.

Unterstützung *die* support.

untersuchen *verb* (PERF **hat
untersucht**) 1 to examine; 2 to
investigate.

Untersuchung *die* (PL *die*
Untersuchungen) 1 examination,
check-up; 2 investigation.

Untertasse *die* (PL *die*
Untertassen) saucer.

Untertitel *der* (PL *die* **Untertitel**)
subtitle.

Unterwäsche *die* underwear.

unterwegs *adverb* on the way; **den
ganzen Tag unterwegs sein** to be
out all day.

untreu *adjective* 1 unfaithful;
2 disloyal.

ununterbrochen *adjective*
uninterrupted.

unverbleit *adjective* unleaded.

unvergleichlich *adjective*
incomparable.

unverheiratet *adjective*
unmarried.

unverkäuflich *adjective* not for
sale; **ein unverkäufliches Muster**
a free sample.

unverschämt *adjective*
impertinent.

unverständlich *adjective*
incomprehensible.

unvorsichtig *adjective* careless.

unwahr *adjective* untrue.

unwahrscheinlich *adjective*
1 unlikely; 2 incredible.
adverb (*informal*) incredibly;
unwahrscheinlich schön
incredibly beautiful.

Unwetter *das* storm.

unwichtig *adjective* unimportant.

unzählig *adjective* countless.

unzerbrechlich *adjective*
unbreakable.

unzertrennlich *adjective*
inseparable.

unzufrieden *adjective* dissatisfied.

üppig *adjective* lavish.

uralt *adjective* ancient.

Urenkel *der* (PL *die* **Urenkel**) great-
grandson; **die Urenkel** the great-
grandchildren.

Urenkelin *die* (PL *die* **Urenkelinnen**)
great-granddaughter.

△ NEW SPELLING: *See page xii*

Urkunde *die* (PL *die* **Urkunden**) certificate.

Urlaub *der* (PL *die* **Urlaube**) holiday; **Urlaub haben** to be on holiday; **auf/im Urlaub** on holiday.

Urlauber *der* (PL *die* **Urlauber**) holidaymaker.

Ursache *die* (PL *die* **Ursachen**) cause; **keine Ursache!** don't mention it!

Ursprung *der* (PL *die* **Ursprünge**) origin.

ursprünglich *adjective* original. *adverb* originally.

Urteil *das* (PL *die* **Urteile**) 1 judgement; 2 opinion; 3 verdict.

urteilen *verb* (PERF **hat geurteilt**) to judge.

Urwald *der* (PL *die* **Urwälder**) jungle.

USA *plural noun* USA.

usw. (*und so weiter*) etc.

V v

vage *adjective* vague.

Vagina *die* (PL *die* **Vaginen**) vagina.

Valentinstag *der* Valentine's Day.

Vanille *die* vanilla.

Vase *die* (PL *die* **Vasen**) vase.

Vater *der* (PL *die* **Väter**) father.

Vaterunser *das* Lord's Prayer.

Vati *der* (PL *die* **Vatis**) dad.

Veganer *der* (PL *die* **Veganer**) vegan.

Vegetarier *der* (PL *die* **Vegetarier**) vegetarian.

Vegetarierin *die* (PL *die* **Vegetarierinnen**) vegetarian.

vegetarisch *adjective* vegetarian.

Veilchen *das* (PL *die* **Veilchen**) violet.

Vene *die* (PL *die* **Venen**) vein.

Ventil *das* (PL *die* **Ventile**) valve.

Ventilator *der* (PL *die* **Ventilatoren**) fan.

verabreden *verb* (PERF **hat verabredet**) 1 to arrange; **was habt ihr verabredet?** what did you arrange?; **mit jemandem verabredet sein** to have arranged to meet somebody; 2 **sich mit jemandem verabreden** to arrange to meet somebody; **ich habe mich mit Oliver zum Tennis verabredet** I've arranged to play tennis with Oliver.

Verabredung *die* (PL *die* **Verabredungen**) 1 appointment; 2 date; 3 arrangement.

verabschieden *verb* (PERF **hat verabschiedet**) 1 to say goodbye to; 2 **sich verabschieden** to say goodbye.

Verachtung *die* contempt.

verallgemeinern *verb* (PERF **hat verallgemeinert**) to generalize.

veralten *verb* (PERF **ist veraltet**) to become obsolete.

veränderlich *adjective* changeable.

⟡ IRREGULAR VERB: *See the verb table in the centre of the dictionary*

verändern *verb* (PERF **hat verändert**) 1 to change; 2 **sich verändern** to change.

Veränderung *die* (PL *die* **Veränderungen**) change.

veranstalten *verb* (PERF **hat veranstaltet**) to organize.

Veranstalter *der* (PL *die* **Veranstalter**) organizer.

Veranstaltung *die* (PL *die* **Veranstaltungen**) event.

verantwortlich *adjective* responsible.

Verantwortung *die* responsibility.

verantwortungsbewusstΔ *adjective* responsible.

verantwortungslos *adjective* irresponsible.

verarbeiten *verb* (PERF **hat verarbeitet**) 1 to process; **etwas zu etwas verarbeiten** to make something into something; 2 to digest (*food, information*).

verärgern *verb* (PERF **hat verärgert**) to annoy.

Verb *das* (PL *die* **Verben**) verb.

verband SEE **verbinden**.

Verband *der* (PL *die* **Verbände**) 1 association; **sich zu einem Verband zusammenschließen** to form an associaton; 2 bandage, dressing; **einen Verband anlegen** to apply a dressing.

verbergen ✧ *verb* (PRES **verbirgt**, IMPERF **verbarg**, PERF **hat verborgen**) 1 to hide; 2 **sich verbergen** to hide.

verbessern *verb* (PERF **hat verbessert**) 1 to improve; 2 to correct; 3 **sich verbessern** to improve.

Verbesserung *die* (PL *die* **Verbesserungen**) 1 improvement; 2 correction.

verbiegen ✧ *verb* (IMPERF **verbog**, PERF **hat verbogen**) 1 to bend; 2 **sich verbiegen** to bend.

verbieten ✧ *verb* (IMPERF **verbot**, PERF **hat verboten**) 1 to forbid; **sie hat ihm verboten, das Haus zu betreten** she forbade him to enter the house; **meine Eltern verbieten mir, am Abend wegzugehen** my parents don't allow me to go out in the evening; 2 to ban.

verbilligt *adjective* reduced.

verbinden ✧ *verb* (IMPERF **verband**, PERF **hat verbunden**) 1 to connect, to join; 2 to combine; 3 to bandage, to dress (*a wound*); **jemandem die Augen verbinden** to blindfold somebody; 4 **jemanden verbinden** to put somebody through (*on the phone*); **ich verbinde** I'm putting you through.

verbindlich *adjective* 1 friendly; 2 binding (*agreement, decision*).

Verbindung *die* (PL *die* **Verbindungen**) 1 connection; 2 **gute Verbindungen haben** to have good contacts; **sich mit jemandem in Verbindung setzen** to get in touch with somebody; 3 combination; 4 **eine chemische Verbindung** a chemical compound.

verbirgt SEE **verbergen**.

Δ NEW SPELLING: *See page xii*

verbleit *adjective* leaded.

verblüffen *verb* (PERF **hat verblüfft**) to amaze.

verbog SEE **verbiegen**.

verbogen *adjective* hidden.

verbot SEE **verbieten**.

Verbot *das* (PL *die* **Verbote**) ban.

verboten *adjective* forbidden; **'Rauchen verboten'** 'no smoking'.

verbracht, verbrachte SEE **verbringen**.

verbrannt, verbrannte SEE **verbrennen**.

Verbrauch *der* consumption.

verbrauchen *verb* (PERF **hat verbraucht**) to use, to use up; **die Waschmaschine verbraucht nicht viel Strom** the washing machine doesn't use up much electricity.

Verbraucher *der* (PL *die* **Verbraucher**) consumer.

Verbrechen *das* (PL *die* **Verbrechen**) crime.

Verbrecher *der* (PL *die* **Verbrecher**) criminal.

verbreiten *verb* (PERF **hat verbreitet**) 1 to spread; **eine Krankheit verbreiten** to spread an illness; 2 **eine Meldung über den Rundfunk verbreiten** to broadcast a message; 3 **sich verbreiten** to spread; **die Neuigkeit hat sich schnell verbreitet** the news spread quickly.

verbreitet *adjective* widespread.

verbrennen ✧ *verb* (IMPERF **verbrannte**, PERF **ist verbrannt**) 1 to burn; 2 (PERF **hat verbrannt**) to burn (*rubbish, leaves*); 3 to cremate; 4 **sich die Hand verbrennen** to burn your hand.

verbringen ✧ *verb* (IMPERF **verbrachte**, PERF **hat verbracht**) to spend; **wir haben schöne Ferien in Bayern verbracht** we spent a nice holiday in Bavaria.

verbunden SEE **verbinden**.

Verdacht *der* suspicion.

verdächtig *adjective* suspicious.

verdächtigen *verb* (PERF **hat verdächtigt**) to suspect.

verdammt *adjective, adverb* (*informal*) damned; **verdammt!** damn!

verdarb SEE **verderben**.

Verdauung *die* digestion.

verderben ✧ *verb* (PRES **verdirbt**, IMPERF **verdarb**, PERF **hat verdorben**) 1 to spoil, to ruin; **das hat mir den Abend verdorben** it ruined the evening for me; **ich habe mir den Magen verdorben** I have an upset stomach; 2 **es sich mit jemandem verderben** to get into somebody's bad books; 3 (PERF **ist verdorben**) to go off; **die Milch verdirbt, wenn du sie nicht in den Kühlschrank stellst** the milk will go off if you don't put it in the fridge.

verdienen *verb* (PERF **hat verdient**) 1 to earn; 2 to deserve.

✧ IRREGULAR VERB: *See the verb table in the centre of the dictionary*

Verdienst der (PL die **Verdienste**)
1 salary; 2 achievement.

verdirbt SEE **verderben**.

verdoppeln verb (PERF **hat
verdoppelt**) 1 to double; 2 **sich
verdoppeln** to double.

verdorben SEE **verderben**.

verdünnen verb (PERF **hat
verdünnt**) to dilute.

verehren verb (PERF **hat verehrt**) to
worship.

Verehrer der (PL die **Verehrer**)
admirer.

Verehrerin die (PL die
Verehrerinnen) admirer.

Verein der (PL die **Vereine**) 1 society;
2 organization; 3 club.

vereinbaren verb (PERF **hat
vereinbart**) to arrange.

Vereinbarung die (PL die
Vereinbarungen) 1 agreement;
2 arrangement.

vereinfachen verb (PERF **hat
vereinfacht**) to simplify.

vereinigen verb (PERF **hat vereinigt**)
to unite; **ein Land wieder
vereinigen** ∆ to reunify a country.

Vereinigte Staaten plural noun
United States.

Vereinigung die (PL die
Vereinigungen) organization.

verfahren ◇ verb (PRES **verfährt**,
IMPERF **verfuhr**, PERF **ist verfahren**)
1 to proceed; 2 **ich habe mich
verfahren** I've lost my way.

verfallen ◇ verb (PRES **verfällt**,
IMPERF **verfiel**, PERF **ist verfallen**) 1 to
decay; 2 to expire (of a passport or
ticket).

Verfassung die (PL die
Verfassungen) 1 constitution;
2 state (of a person).

verfaulen verb (PERF **ist verfault**) to
rot.

verfiel SEE **verfallen**.

verfolgen verb (PERF **hat verfolgt**)
1 to follow; 2 to persecute.

Verfolgung die (PL die
Verfolgungen) 1 pursuit, hunt;
2 persecution.

verfügbar adjective available.

Verfügung die **jemandem etwas
zur Verfügung stellen** to put
something at somebody's disposal;
jemandem zur Verfügung stehen
to be at somebody's disposal.

verfuhr SEE **verfahren**.

verführen verb (PERF **hat verführt**)
1 to tempt; 2 to seduce.

Verführung die (PL die
Verführungen) 1 temptation;
2 seduction.

vergab SEE **vergeben**.

vergangen verb SEE **vergehen**.
adjective last.

Vergangenheit die 1 past; 2 past
tense.

vergaß SEE **vergessen**.

vergeben ◇ verb (PRES **vergibt**,
IMPERF **vergab**, PERF **hat vergeben**)
1 to forgive; **jemandem etwas
vergeben** to forgive somebody for

∆ NEW SPELLING: See page xii

something; **2** to give away, to award;
3 vergeben sein to be taken; **das
Zimmer ist schon vergeben** the
room's already taken.

vergeblich *adverb* in vain.

vergehen ✧ *verb* (IMPERF **verging**,
PERF **ist vergangen**) to pass.

vergessen ✧ *verb* (PRES **vergisst** Δ,
IMPERF **vergaß**, PERF **hat vergessen**)
to forget.

vergesslich Δ *adjective* forgetful.

vergewaltigen *verb* (PERF **hat
vergewaltigt**) to rape.

Vergewaltigung *die* (PL *die*
Vergewaltigungen) rape.

vergibt SEE **vergeben**.

vergiften *verb* (PERF **hat vergiftet**)
to poison.

verging SEE **vergehen**.

vergisst Δ SEE **vergessen**.

Vergleich *der* (PL *die* **Vergleiche**)
comparison.

vergleichen ✧ *verb* (IMPERF
verglich, PERF **hat verglichen**) to
compare.

Vergnügen *das* (PL *die* **Vergnügen**)
pleasure; **viel Vergnügen!** have
fun!

vergnügt *adjective* cheerful.

vergrößern *verb* (PERF **hat
vergrößert**) **1** to enlarge; **2** to
increase; **3** to magnify; **4** to extend
(*a room, building*); **5 sich
vergrößern** to expand, to grow
bigger.

Vergrößerung *die* (PL *die*
Vergrößerungen) **1** expansion;
2 enlargement (*of a photograph*).

verhaften *verb* (PERF **hat verhaftet**)
to arrest; **er ist verhaftet worden** h‹
was arrested.

verhalten ✧ *verb* (PRES **verhält
sich**, IMPERF **verhielt sich**, PERF **hat
sich verhalten**) **sich verhalten** to
behave.

Verhalten *das* behaviour.

Verhältnis *das* (PL *die* **Verhältnisse**)
1 relationship; **sie hat ein gutes
Verhältnis zu ihren Eltern** she has ‹
good relationship with her parents;
2 affair; **Gabi hat ein Verhältnis mit
einem verheirateten Mann** Gabi is
having an affair with a married man;
3 ratio (*in maths*); **4 in keinem
Verhältnis zu etwas stehen** to be
out of all proportion to something;
5 Verhältnisse conditions; **über
seine Verhältnisse leben** to live
beyond your means.

verhältnismäßig *adverb*
relatively.

verhandeln *verb* (PERF **hat
verhandelt**) to negotiate; **über
etwas verhandeln** to negotiate
something.

Verhandlung *die* (PL *die*
Verhandlungen) **1** negotiation;
2 hearing; **3** trial.

verhauen *verb* (PERF **hat verhauen**)
1 to beat up; **2 die Prüfung
verhauen** (*informal*) to make a
mess of the exam.

verheimlichen *verb* (PERF **hat
verheimlicht**) to keep secret.

✧ IRREGULAR VERB: *See the verb table in the centre of the dictionary*

verheiratet *adjective* married.

verhielt SEE **verhalten**.

verhindern *verb* (PERF **hat verhindert**) 1 to prevent; 2 **verhindert sein** to be unable to make it; **Petra ist verhindert** Petra won't be able to make it.

verhungern *verb* (PERF **ist verhungert**) to starve.

Verhütungsmittel *das* (PL *die* **Verhütungsmittel**) contraceptive.

verirren *verb* (PERF **hat sich verirrt**) **sich verirren** to get lost.

verkam SEE **verkommen**.

Verkauf *der* (PL *die* **Verkäufe**) sale; **zum Verkauf** for sale.

verkaufen *verb* (PERF **hat verkauft**) to sell; **zu verkaufen** for sale.

Verkäufer *der* (PL *die* **Verkäufer**) 1 seller; 2 sales assistant.

Verkäuferin *die* (PL *die* **Verkäuferinnen**) 1 seller; 2 sales assistant.

Verkehr *der* traffic.

Verkehrsampel *die* (PL *die* **Verkehrsampeln**) traffic lights.

Verkehrsamt *das* (PL *die* **Verkehrsämter**) tourist office.

Verkehrsunfall *der* (PL *die* **Verkehrsunfälle**) road accident.

Verkehrszeichen *das* (PL *die* **Verkehrszeichen**) traffic sign, road sign.

verkehrt *adjective* 1 wrong;

2 **verkehrt herum** inside out, the wrong way round.

verklagen *verb* (PERF **hat verklagt**) to sue.

verkleiden *verb* (PERF **hat sich verkleidet**) **sich verkleiden** to dress up.

Verkleidung *die* (PL *die* **Verkleidungen**) disguise, fancy dress.

verkommen ◇ *verb* (IMPERF **verkam**, PERF **ist verkommen**) 1 to go off (*of food*); 2 to become dilapidated (*of a house*); 3 to go to the bad.

verkratzt *adjective* scratched.

Verlag *der* (PL *die* **Verlage**) publisher's.

verlangen *verb* (PERF **hat verlangt**) 1 to ask for, to require; **am Telefon verlangt werden** to be wanted on the phone; 2 to demand; 3 to charge.

verlängern *verb* (PERF **hat verlängert**) 1 to extend; 2 to lengthen; 3 to renew (*a passport, driving licence*).

Verlängerung *die* (PL *die* **Verlängerungen**) 1 extension; 2 renewal; 3 extra time (*in sport*).

verlassen[1] ◇ *verb* (PRES **verlässt** Δ, IMPERF **verließ**, PERF **hat verlassen**) 1 to leave; **jemanden verlassen** to leave somebody; 2 **sich auf etwas verlassen** to rely on something; **du kannst dich auf ihn verlassen** you can rely on him.

verlassen[2] *adjective* deserted.

verlaufen ✧ *verb* (PRES **verläuft**, IMPERF **verlief**, PERF **ist verlaufen**) **1** to go; **es ist gut verlaufen** it went well; **2 sich verlaufen** to lose your way; **3 die Menge verlief sich schnell** the crowd quickly dispersed.

verlegen[1] *adjective* embarrassed.

verlegen[2] *verb* (PERF **hat verlegt**) **1** to mislay; **2** to postpone; **3** to publish; **4** to lay (*a carpet, cable*).

Verlegenheit *die* embarrassment.

Verleih *der* (PL *die* **Verleihe**) **1** renting out, hiring out; **2** rental firm, hire shop.

verleihen ✧ *verb* (IMPERF **verlieh**, PERF **hat verliehen**) **1** to hire out; **2** to lend; **3** to award.

verlernen *verb* (PERF **hat verlernt**) to forget.

verletzen *verb* (PERF **hat verletzt**) **1** to injure; **2** to hurt; **3** to violate (*a law*); **4 sich verletzen** to hurt yourself.

Verletzte *der/die* (PL *die* **Verletzten**) **1** injured person; **2** casualty.

Verletzung *die* (PL *die* **Verletzungen**) injury.

verlieben *verb* (PERF **hat sich verliebt**) **sich verlieben** to fall in love.

verlief SEE **verlaufen**.

verlieh SEE **verleihen**.

verlieren ✧ *verb* (IMPERF **verlor**, PERF **hat verloren**) to lose.

verließ SEE **verlassen**.

verloben *verb* (PERF **hat sich verlobt**) **sich verloben** to get engaged.

Verlobte *der/die* (PL *die* **Verlobten**) fiancé, fiancée.

Verlobung *die* (PL *die* **Verlobungen**) engagement.

verlor, verloren SEE **verlieren**.

Verlosung *die* (PL *die* **Verlosungen**) prize draw.

Verlust *der* (PL *die* **Verluste**) loss.

vermeiden ✧ *verb* (IMPERF **vermied**, PERF **hat vermieden**) to avoid.

vermieten *verb* (PERF **hat vermietet**) **1** to rent out, to hire out; **2** to let; **Zimmer zu vermieten** rooms to let.

Vermieter *der* (PL *die* **Vermieter**) landlord.

Vermieterin *die* (PL *die* **Vermieterinnen**) landlady.

vermissen *verb* (PERF **hat vermisst** △) to miss.

Vermittlung *die* (PL *die* **Vermittlungen**) **1** arrangement; **2** agency; **3** switchboard; **4** telephone exchange; **5** mediation.

Vermögen *das* (PL *die* **Vermögen**) fortune.

vermuten *verb* (PERF **hat vermutet**) to suspect.

vermutlich *adjective* probable. *adverb* probably.

vernichten *verb* (PERF **hat vernichtet**) **1** to destroy; **2** to exterminate.

✧ IRREGULAR VERB: *See the verb table in the centre of the dictionary*

Vernunft *die* reason.

vernünftig *adjective* sensible.

verpacken *verb* (PERF **hat verpackt**) 1 to pack; 2 to wrap up.

Verpackung *die* (PL *die* **Verpackungen**) packaging.

verpassen *verb* (PERF **hat verpasst** △) to miss.

Verpflegung *die* food; **Unterkunft und Verpflegung** board and lodging.

verpflichten *verb* (PERF **hat verpflichtet**) 1 **sich verpflichten** to promise; 2 **sich vertraglich verpflichten** to sign a contract; 3 **verpflichtet sein, etwas zu tun** to be obliged to do something; **jemandem zu Dank verpflichtet sein** to be obliged to somebody; 4 **verpflichtend** binding.

Verpflichtung *die* (PL *die* **Verpflichtungen**) 1 obligation; 2 commitment.

verprügeln *verb* (PERF **hat verprügelt**) to beat up.

verraten ✧ *verb* (PRES **verrät**, IMPERF **verriet**, PERF **hat verraten**) 1 to betray; 2 to give away; 3 to tell; 4 **sich verraten** to give yourself away.

verrechnen *verb* (PERF **hat sich verrechnet**) **sich verrechnen** to make a mistake.

verregnet *adjective* rainy.

verreisen *verb* (PERF **ist verreist**) to go away; **verreist sein** to be away.

verriet SEE **verraten**.

verrosten *verb* (PERF **ist verrostet**) to rust.

verrostet *adjective* rusty.

verrückt *adjective* mad, crazy.

Verrückte *der/die* (PL *die* **Verrückten**) maniac.

versagen *verb* (PERF **hat versagt**) to fail.

versammeln *verb* (PERF **hat versammelt**) 1 to assemble; 2 **sich versammeln** to assemble.

Versammlung *die* (PL *die* **Versammlungen**) meeting.

versäumen *verb* (PERF **hat versäumt**) to miss; **es versäumen, etwas zu tun** to fail to do something.

verschenken *verb* (PERF **hat verschenkt**) to give away.

verschieben ✧ *verb* (IMPERF **verschob**, PERF **hat verschoben**) to postpone.

verschieden *adjective* 1 different; 2 various.

verschlafen ✧ *verb* (PRES **verschläft**, IMPERF **verschlief**, PERF **hat verschlafen**) 1 to oversleep; 2 to sleep through (*the day*); 3 to miss (*a date, the train*).

verschlechtern *verb* (PERF **hat verschlechtert**) 1 to make worse; 2 **sich verschlechtern** to get worse.

verschlief SEE **verschlafen**.

verschließen ✧ *verb* (IMPERF **verschloss** △, PERF **hat verschlossen**) 1 to close (*a tin,* *package*); **2** to lock (*a door, drawer*).

verschlimmern *verb* (PERF **hat verschlimmert**) **1** to make worse; **2 sich verschlimmern** to get worse.

verschloss △ SEE **verschließen**.

verschlucken *verb* (PERF **hat verschluckt**) **1** to swallow; **2 sich verschlucken** to choke.

Verschluss △ *der* (PL *die* **Verschlüsse**) **1** fastener, clasp; **2** top (*of a bottle*).

verschmutzen *verb* (PERF **hat verschmutzt**) to soil; **die Umwelt verschmutzen** to pollute the environment.

Verschmutzung *die* pollution.

verschob SEE **verschieben**.

verschreiben ✧ *verb* (IMPERF **verschrieb**, PERF **hat verschrieben**) **1** to prescribe; **2 sich verschreiben** to make a mistake.

verschütten *verb* (PERF **hat verschüttet**) to spill.

verschwand SEE **verschwinden**.

verschwenden *verb* (PERF **hat verschwendet**) to waste.

Verschwendung *die* waste.

verschwinden ✧ *verb* (IMPERF **verschwand**, PERF **ist verschwunden**) to disappear.

Versehen *das* (PL *die* **Versehen**) oversight; **aus Versehen** by mistake.

versehentlich *adverb* by mistake.

versetzen *verb* (PERF **hat versetzt**) **1** to move, to transfer (*a person*);

2 to move up (*into the next class at school*); **3 jemanden versetzen** to stand somebody up; **4 jemandem einen Schreck versetzen** to give somebody a fright; **jemandem einen Tritt versetzen** to kick somebody; **5 sich in jemandes Lage versetzen** to put yourself in somebody's position.

versichern *verb* (PERF **hat versichert**) **1** to insure; **2** to assert; **jemandem versichern, dass** … to assure somebody that …

Versicherung *die* (PL *die* **Versicherungen**) **1** insurance; **2** assurance.

versöhnen *verb* (PERF **hat sich versöhnt**) **sich versöhnen** to make up; **sich mit jemandem versöhnen** to make it up with somebody.

versorgen *verb* (PERF **hat versorgt**) **1** to supply; **2** to provide for; **3** to look after.

verspäten *verb* (PERF **hat sich verspätet**) **sich verspäten** to be late.

Verspätung *die* lateness, delay; **Verspätung haben** to be late.

versprechen ✧ *verb* (PRES **verspricht**, IMPERF **versprach**, PERF **hat versprochen**) **1** to promise; **2 sich viel von etwas versprechen** to have high hopes of something; **3 sich versprechen** to make a slip of the tongue.

Versprechen *das* (PL *die* **Versprechen**) promise.

verstand SEE **verstehen**.

✧ IRREGULAR VERB: *See the verb table in the centre of the dictionary*

verstand der 1 mind; **den verstand verlieren** to go out of your mind; 2 reason.

verstanden SEE **verstehen**.

verständigen verb (PERF **hat verständigt**) 1 to notify; 2 **sich verständigen** to communicate, to make yourself understood; 3 **sich über etwas verständigen** to agree on something.

verständlich adjective 1 understandable; **jemandem etwas verständlich machen** to make something clear to somebody; 2 comprehensible.

Verständigung die 1 communication; 2 notification.

Verstärker der (PL die **Verstärker**) amplifier.

verstauchen verb (PERF **hat verstaucht**) to sprain; **sich den Fuß verstauchen** to sprain your ankle.

Versteck das (PL die **Verstecke**) hiding place.

verstecken verb (PERF **hat versteckt**) 1 to hide; 2 **sich verstecken** to hide.

verstehen ✧ verb (IMPERF **verstand**, PERF **hat verstanden**) 1 to understand; **etwas falsch verstehen** to misunderstand something; 2 **sich gut verstehen** to get on well; 3 **das versteht sich von selbst** that goes without saying.

verstellbar adjective adjustable.

verstellen verb (PERF **hat verstellt**) 1 to adjust; 2 to block; 3 to disguise; 4 **sich verstellen** to pretend.

verstimmt adjective 1 out of tune; 2 peeved; 3 **ein verstimmter Magen** an upset stomach.

Versuch der (PL die **Versuche**) 1 attempt; 2 experiment.

versuchen verb (PERF **hat versucht**) to try.

verteidigen verb (PERF **hat verteidigt**) to defend.

Verteidiger der (PL die **Verteidiger**) 1 defender; 2 defence counsel.

Verteidigung die defence.

verteilen verb (PERF **hat verteilt**) to distribute.

Vertrag der (PL die **Verträge**) 1 contract; 2 treaty.

vertragen ✧ verb (PRES **verträgt**, IMPERF **vertrug**, PERF **hat vertragen**) 1 to stand, to take; 2 **ich vertrage keinen Kaffee** coffee disagrees with me; 3 **sich vertragen** to get on; **sich wieder vertragen** to make it up.

vertrat SEE **vertreten**.

vertrauen verb (PERF **hat vertraut**) to trust.

Vertrauen das trust; **im Vertrauen** in confidence.

vertraulich adjective 1 confidential; 2 familiar.

vertreten ✧ verb (PRES **vertritt**, IMPERF **vertrat**, PERF **hat vertreten**) 1 to stand in for; 2 to represent; 3 **eine Meinung vertreten** to hold an opinion; 4 **sich die Beine vertreten** to stretch your legs.

△ NEW SPELLING: See page xii

Vertreter der (PL die **Vertreter**)
1 representative; 2 deputy.

Vertreterin die (PL die
Vertreterinnen) 1 representative;
2 deputy.

vertritt SEE **vertreten**.

vertrug SEE **vertragen**.

verunglücken verb (PERF **ist
verunglückt**) to have an accident.

verursachen verb (PERF **hat
verursacht**) to cause.

verurteilen verb (PERF **hat
verurteilt**) 1 to sentence; 2 to
condemn.

Verwaltung die (PL die
Verwaltungen) administration.

verwandt adjective related.

Verwandte der/die (PL die
Verwandten) relative.

Verwandtschaft die relatives.

verwechseln verb (PERF **hat
verwechselt**) to mix up, to confuse;
**jemanden mit jemandem
verwechseln** to mistake somebody
for somebody.

verwenden verb (PERF **hat
verwendet**) to use.

Verwendung die use.

verwickelt adjective complicated.

verwirren verb (PERF **hat verwirrt**)
1 to confuse; 2 to tangle up.

verwirrt adjective confused.

verwöhnen verb (PERF **hat
verwöhnt**) to spoil.

verwunden verb (PERF **hat
verwundet**) to wound.

Verwundete der/die (PL die
Verwundeten) casualty, injured
person.

Verwundung die (PL die
Verwundungen) injury, wound.

verzählen verb (PERF **hat sich
verzählt**) **sich verzählen** to
miscount.

Verzeichnis das (PL die
Verzeichnisse) 1 list; 2 index.

verzeihen verb (IMPERF **verzieh**, PERF
hat verziehen) to forgive; **verzeihen
Sie, können Sie mir sagen …?**
excuse me, could you tell me …?

Verzeihung die forgiveness;
jemanden um Verzeihung bitten to
apologize to somebody;
Verzeihung! sorry!

verzieh, verziehen SEE **verzeihen**.

verzichten verb (PERF **hat
verzichtet**) 1 to do without; **ich
verzichte auf deine Hilfe** I can do
without your help; 2 **auf etwas
verzichten** to give up something
(*smoking or your share of
something*); to relinquish something
(*a right or privilege*).

verzögern verb (PERF **hat
verzögert**) 1 to delay; 2 **sich
verzögern** to be delayed.

Verzögerung die (PL die
Verzögerungen) delay.

verzollen verb (PERF **hat verzollt**) to
pay duty on; **haben Sie etwas zu**

♦ IRREGULAR VERB: *See the verb table in the centre of the dictionary*

verzollen? have you anything to declare?

verzweifeln *verb* (PERF **ist verzweifelt**) to despair.

verzweifelt *adjective* desperate.

Verzweiflung *die* despair.

Vetter *der* (PL *die* **Vettern**) cousin.

Video *das* (PL *die* **Videos**) video.

Videokamera *die* (PL *die* **Videokameras**) video camera.

Videokassette *die* (PL *die* **Videokassetten**) video cassette.

Videorekorder *der* (PL *die* **Videorekorder**) video recorder.

Videospiel *das* (PL *die* **Videospiele**) video game.

Videothek *die* (PL *die* **Videotheken**) video shop.

Vieh *das* cattle.

viel *adjective, pronoun* **1** a lot of; **Erika hat viel Arbeit** Erika's got a lot of work; **2 viele** (*plural*) many, a lot of; **viele Leute** many people; **3** much, a lot; **wie viel?** how much?, how many?; **zu viel** too much; **vielen Dank** thank you very much; **viel Spaß!** have fun!; **viel Glück!** good luck!; **4 das viele Geld** all that money.
adverb **1** much, a lot; **viel weniger** much less; **so viel wie möglich** as much as possible; **sie redet viel** she talks a lot; **2 viel zu groß** far too big, much too big; **das dauert viel zu lange** it'll take far too long.

vielleicht *adverb* perhaps.

vielmals *adverb* **danke vielmals** thanks a lot.

vier *number* four.

Viereck *das* (PL *die* **Vierecke**) **1** rectangle; **2** square.

viereckig *adjective* **1** rectangular; **2** square.

vierte SEE **vierter**.

Viertel *das* (PL *die* **Viertel**) quarter; **es ist Viertel vor acht** it's quarter to eight.

viertel *adjective* quarter; **wir treffen uns um viertel acht** △ we'll meet at quarter past seven; **um drei viertel acht** △ at quarter to eight.

Viertelstunde *die* (PL *die* **Viertelstunden**) quarter of an hour.

vierter, vierte, viertes *adjective* fourth.

vierzehn *number* fourteen.

vierzig *number* forty.

Villa *die* (PL *die* **Villen**) villa.

virtuell *adjective* virtual; **virtuelle Realität** virtual reality.

Virus *das* (PL *die* **Viren**) virus.

visuell *adjective* visual.

Visum *das* (PL *die* **Visa**) visa.

Vitamin *das* (PL *die* **Vitamine**) vitamin.

Vogel *der* (PL *die* **Vögel**) bird.

Vokabel *die* (PL *die* **Vokabeln**) word; **Vokabeln** vocabulary.

Vokal *der* (PL *die* **Vokale**) vowel.

Volk *das* (PL *die* **Völker**) people.

△ NEW SPELLING: *See page xii*

Volkshochschule *die* adult education centre; **ein Kurs an der Volkshochschule** an adult education class.

Volkslied *das* (PL *die* **Volkslieder**) folk song.

Volkswirtschaft *die* economics.

voll *adjective* 1 full; **ein Korb voll Äpfel** a basket full of apples; **die volle Wahrheit** the whole truth; 2 **etwas voll machen** Δ to fill something up; **voll tanken** Δ to fill up with petrol.
adverb 1 fully, completely; **voll und ganz** completely; 2 **jemanden nicht für voll nehmen** (*informal*) not to take somebody seriously.

völlig *adjective* complete.
adverb completely.

vollkommen *adjective* 1 perfect; 2 complete.
adverb completely.

Vollkornbrot *das* wholemeal bread.

vollmachen SEE **voll**.

Vollpension *die* full board.

vollständig *adjective* complete.

volltanken SEE **voll**.

vom = **von dem**.

von *preposition* ←(+DAT) 1 from; **von heute an** from today; **von hier bis …** from here to …; 2 of; **eine Freundin von mir** a friend of mine; 3 about; **Peter hat mir von dem neuen Haus erzählt** Peter told me about the new house; 4 by; **ein**

Theaterstück von Brecht a play by Brecht; 5 **von mir aus** I don't mind

voneinander *adverb* from each other; **sie sind voneinander abhängig** they depend on each other.

vor *preposition* ←(+DAT *or* +ACC *with movement towards a place*) 1 in front of; 2 before; **Manfred war vor euch da** Manfred arrived before you; **kurz vor der Ampel** shortly before the lights; 3 with; **vor Angst zittern** to tremble with fear; 4 (*with clock time*) **zehn vor fünf** ten to five; 5 ago; **vor zwei Jahren** two years ago; 6 **sich vor jemandem fürchten** to be frightened of somebody; 7 **vor allen Dingen** above all; 8 **vor sich hin summen** to hum to yourself.
adverb forward; **vor und zurück** backwards and forwards.

voraus *adverb* 1 ahead; 2 **im Voraus** Δ in advance.

vorausgehen ◇ *verb* (IMPERF **ging voraus**, PERF **ist vorausgegangen**) 1 to go on ahead; 2 to precede.

voraussetzen *verb* (PERF **hat vorausgesetzt**) 1 to take for granted; 2 to require; 3 **vorausgesetzt, dass …** provided that …

Voraussetzung *die* (PL *die* **Voraussetzungen**) 1 condition; 2 assumption.

vorbei *adverb* 1 past; 2 over; **vorbei sein** to be over.

vorbeifahren ◇ *verb* (PRES **fährt vorbei**, IMPERF **fuhr vorbei**, PERF **ist**

◇ IRREGULAR VERB: *See the verb table in the centre of the dictionary*

vorbeigefahren) to drive past, to pass.

vorbeigehen ◇ *verb* (IMPERF **ging vorbei**, PERF **ist vorbeigegangen**) 1 to go past, to pass; 2 to drop in; **ich gehe bei Anne vorbei** I'll drop in on Anne.

vorbeikommen ◇ *verb* (IMPERF **kam vorbei**, PERF **ist vorbeigekommen**) 1 to pass; 2 to get past; 3 to drop in.

vorbereiten *verb* (PERF **hat vorbereitet**) 1 to prepare; 2 **sich vorbereiten** to prepare.

Vorbereitung *die* (PL *die* **Vorbereitungen**) preparation.

vorbeugen *verb* (PERF **hat vorgebeugt**) 1 to prevent; 2 **sich vorbeugen** to lean forward.

Vorbild *das* (PL *die* **Vorbilder**) example.

vorderer, vordere, vorderes *adjective* front.

Vorderseite *die* front.

vorderster, vorderste, vorderstes *adjective* front.

Vorfahrt *die* right of way; **'Vorfahrt beachten/gewähren'** 'give way'.

Vorfall *der* (PL *die* **Vorfälle**) incident.

Vorführung *die* (PL *die* **Vorführungen**) 1 performance; 2 demonstration.

Vorgänger *der* (PL *die* **Vorgänger**) predecessor.

Vorgängerin *die* (PL *die* **Vorgängerinnen**) predecessor.

vorgehen ◇ *verb* (IMPERF **ging vor**, PERF **ist vorgegangen**) 1 to go on ahead; 2 to go forward; 3 to proceed; 4 **die Uhr geht vor** the clock is fast; 5 **was geht hier vor?** what's going on here?

vorgestern *adverb* the day before yesterday.

vorhaben ◇ *verb* (PRES **hat vor**, IMPERF **hatte vor**, PERF **hat vorgehabt**) 1 to intend; 2 **etwas vorhaben** to have something planned.

Vorhang *der* (PL *die* **Vorhänge**) curtain.

vorher *adverb* beforehand, before.

Vorhersage *die* (PL *die* **Vorhersagen**) 1 forecast; 2 prediction.

vorhin *adverb* just now.

voriger, vorige, voriges *adjective* last.

vorkommen ◇ *verb* (IMPERF **kam vor**, PERF **ist vorgekommen**) 1 to happen; 2 to occur; 3 to come forward; 4 to come out (*from behind somewhere*); 5 to seem; **jemandem bekannt vorkommen** to seem familiar to somebody; 6 **sich alt vorkommen** to feel old.

vorlesen ◇ *verb* (PRES **liest vor**, IMPERF **las vor**, PERF **hat vorgelesen**) 1 to read (out); 2 **jemandem vorlesen** to read to somebody.

vorletzter, vorletzte, vorletztes *adjective* last but one; **vorletztes Jahr** the year before last.

△ NEW SPELLING: *See page xii*

Vormittag *der* (PL *die* **Vormittage**) morning.

vormittags *adverb* in the morning.

vorn *adverb* 1 at the front; **nach vorn** to the front; 2 **von vorn** from the beginning; **wieder von vorn anfangen** to start again at the beginning; **da vorn** over there.

Vorname *der* (PL *die* **Vornamen**) first name.

vorne = **vorn**.

vornehm *adjective* 1 elegant; 2 distinguished.

vornehmen ✧ *verb* (PRES **nimmt vor**, IMPERF **nahm vor**, PERF **hat vorgenommen**) 1 to carry out; 2 **sich vornehmen, etwas zu tun** to plan to do something.

Vorort *der* (PL *die* **Vororte**) suburb.

Vorrat *der* (PL *die* **Vorräte**) supply, stock.

Vorsatz *der* (PL *die* **Vorsätze**) intention.

Vorschau *die* 1 preview; 2 trailer (*of a film*).

Vorschlag *der* (PL *die* **Vorschläge**) suggestion.

vorschlagen ✧ *verb* (PRES **schlägt vor**, IMPERF **schlug vor**, PERF **hat vorgeschlagen**) to suggest.

Vorschrift *die* (PL *die* **Vorschriften**) 1 regulation; 2 instruction.

Vorschule *die* (PL *die* **Vorschulen**) infant school.

vorsehen ✧ *verb* (PRES **sieht sich vor**, IMPERF **sah sich vor**, PERF **hat**

sich vorgesehen) **sich vorsehen** to be careful.

Vorsicht *die* care; **Vorsicht!** careful!; (*on a sign*) caution!

vorsichtig *adjective* careful.

vorsichtshalber *adverb* to be on the safe side.

Vorspeise *die* (PL *die* **Vorspeisen**) starter.

Vorsprung *der* (PL *die* **Vorsprünge**) 1 ledge (*of a rock*); 2 lead (*over somebody*).

vorstellen *verb* (PERF **hat vorgestellt**) 1 to introduce; **darf ich Ihnen Herrn Schulz vorstellen?** may I introduce Mr Schulz?; 2 **die Uhr vorstellen** to put the clock forward; 3 **sich vorstellen** to introduce yourself; 4 **sich beim Personalchef vorstellen** to go for an interview with the personnel manager; 5 **sich etwas vorstellen** to imagine something; **stell dir vor!** can you imagine?

Vorstellung *die* (PL *die* **Vorstellungen**) 1 performance; 2 introduction; 3 interview (*for a job*); 4 idea; 5 imagination.

Vorteil *der* (PL *die* **Vorteile**) advantage.

Vortrag *der* (PL *die* **Vorträge**) talk.

vorüber *adverb* **vorüber sein** to be over.

vorübergehend *adjective* temporary.
adverb temporarily.

✧ IRREGULAR VERB: *See the verb table in the centre of the dictionary*

Vorurteil *das* (PL *die* **Vorurteile**)
prejudice.

Vorwahl *die* (PL *die* **Vorwahlen**)
dialling code.

vorwärts *adverb* forward(s).

vorwiegend *adverb*
predominantly.

Vorwurf *der* (PL *die* **Vorwürfe**)
reproach; **jemandem Vorwürfe
machen** to reproach somebody.

vorzeigen *verb* (PERF **hat
vorgezeigt**) to show.

vorziehen ✧ *verb* (PRES **zieht vor**,
IMPERF **zog vor**, PERF **hat
vorgezogen**) 1 to prefer; 2 to pull
up (*a chair*); 3 **den Vorhang
vorziehen** to draw the curtain.

vorzüglich *adjective* excellent.

vulgär *adjective* vulgar.

Vulkan *der* (PL *die* **Vulkane**) volcano.

W w

Waage *die* (PL *die* **Waagen**) 1 scales;
2 Libra; **Gabi ist Waage** Gabi's
Libra.

waagerecht *adjective* horizontal.

wach *adjective* awake; **wach sein** to
be awake; **wach werden** to wake up.

Wache *die* (PL *die* **Wachen**) 1 guard;
2 (police) station.

Wachhund *der* (PL *die* **Wachhunde**)
guard dog.

Wachs *das* wax.

wachsen ✧ *verb* (PRES **wächst**,
IMPERF **wuchs**, PERF **ist gewachsen**)
to grow.

Wachstum *das* growth.

wackelig *adjective* wobbly.

wackeln *verb* (PERF **hat gewackelt**)
to wobble.

Wade *die* (PL *die* **Waden**) calf.

Waffe *die* (PL *die* **Waffen**) weapon.

Waffel *die* (PL *die* **Waffeln**) waffle.

wagen *verb* (PERF **hat gewagt**) 1 to
risk; 2 **es wagen, etwas zu tun** to
dare to do something; **sich nicht
irgendwohin wagen** not dare to go
somewhere.

Wagen *der* (PL *die* **Wagen**) 1 car;
nimmst du den Wagen? are you
going by car?; 2 carriage (*of a train*);
3 cart.

Wagenheber *der* (PL *die*
Wagenheber) jack.

Wahl *die* (PL *die* **Wahlen**) 1 choice; **er
hat die Wahl** it's his choice;
2 election; **die nächsten Wahlen
sind im Herbst** the next election is
in autumn.

wählen *verb* (PERF **hat gewählt**) 1 to
choose; **zwischen zwei
Möglichkeiten wählen** to choose
between two possibilities; 2 **haben
Sie schon gewählt?** are you ready
to order? (*in a restaurant*); 3 to
elect; 4 to vote; **wählt Schröder!**
vote for Schröder; 5 to dial; **ich
muss die falsche Nummer gewählt**

△ NEW SPELLING: *See page xii*

haben I must have dialled the wrong number.

Wahlfach *das* (PL *die* **Wahlfächer**) optional subject, option.

Wahnsinn *der* madness.

wahnsinnig *adjective* **1** mad; **wahnsinnig werden** to go mad; **2 wahnsinnigen Durst haben** to be terribly thirsty; **der Film war wahnsinnig gut** the film was incredibly good.

wahr *adjective* **1** true; **2 du kommst doch, nicht wahr?** you're coming, aren't you?

während *preposition* ←(+GEN) during.
conjunction **1** while; **2** whereas.

Wahrheit *die* (PL *die* **Wahrheiten**) truth.

Wahrsager *der* (PL *die* **Wahrsager**) fortune-teller.

Wahrsagerin *die* (PL *die* **Wahrsagerinnen**) fortune-teller.

wahrscheinlich *adjective* probable, likely.
adverb probably.

Währung *die* (PL *die* **Währungen**) currency.

Waise *die* (PL *die* **Waisen**) orphan.

Wal *der* (PL *die* **Wale**) whale.

Wald *der* (PL *die* **Wälder**) wood, forest.

Waliser *der* (PL *die* **Waliser**) Welshman.

Waliserin *die* (PL *die* **Waliserinnen**) Welshwoman.

walisisch *adjective* Welsh.

Walkman™ *der* (PL *die* **Walkmen**) walkman™.

Walnuss△ *die* (PL *die* **Walnüsse**) walnut.

Wand *die* (PL *die* **Wände**) wall.

wandern *verb* (PERF **ist gewandert**) **1** to hike; **2** to go walking.

Wanderung *die* (PL *die* **Wanderungen**) **1** hike; **2** walking tour.

wann *adverb* when.

Wanne *die* (PL *die* **Wannen**) **1** tub; **2** bath.

war SEE **sein**.

warb SEE **werben**.

Ware *die* (PL *die* **Waren**) **1** article; **2 Waren** goods.

waren SEE **sein**.

Warenhaus *das* (PL *die* **Warenhäuser**) department store.

warf SEE **werfen**.

warm *adjective* warm; **eine warme Mahlzeit** a hot meal; **das Essen warm machen** to heat up the food.

Wärme *die* warmth.

wärmen *verb* (PERF **hat gewärmt**) to warm, to heat.

Warndreieck *das* (PL *die* **Warndreiecke**) warning triangle.

warnen *verb* (PERF **hat gewarnt**) to warn; **jemanden vor etwas warnen** to warn somebody of something.

✧ IRREGULAR VERB: *See the verb table in the centre of the dictionary*

Warnung *die* (PL *die* **Warnungen**) warning.

warst, wart SEE **sein**.

Warteliste *die* (PL *die* **Wartelisten**) waiting list.

warten *verb* (PERF **hat gewartet**) 1 to wait; **auf jemanden warten** to wait for somebody; **2 auf sich warten lassen** to take your time.

Wärter *der* (PL *die* **Wärter**) 1 keeper; 2 attendant; 3 warder.

Warteraum *der* (PL *die* **Warteräume**) waiting room.

Wärterin *die* (PL *die* **Wärterinnen**) 1 keeper; 2 attendant; 3 warder.

Wartezeit *die* wait; **eine Stunde Wartezeit** an hour's wait.

Wartezimmer *das* (PL *die* **Wartezimmer**) waiting room.

warum *adverb* why.

was *pronoun* 1 what; **was für ein/eine …?** what kind of …?; **was für ein Fahrrad hast du?** what kind of bike do you have?; **was für ein Glück!** what luck!; **was kostet das?** how much is it?; 2 that; **alles, was wir brauchen** all (that) we need; **alles, was du willst** all (that) you want; 3 (*short for 'etwas'*) something; **heute gibt's was Gutes im Fernsehen** there's something good on television today; 4 (*short for 'etwas' in questions and negatives*) anything; **hast du was für mich?** have you got anything for me?

Waschbecken *das* (PL *die* **Waschbecken**) washbasin.

Wäsche *die* 1 washing; 2 underwear.

waschen ◇ *verb* (PRES **wäscht**, IMPERF **wusch**, PERF **hat gewaschen**) 1 to wash; **2 sich waschen** to have a wash; **sich die Hände waschen** to wash your hands.

Wäscherei *die* (PL *die* **Wäschereien**) laundry.

Waschlappen *der* (PL *die* **Waschlappen**) flannel.

Waschmaschine *die* (PL *die* **Waschmaschinen**) washing machine.

Waschsalon *der* (PL *die* **Waschsalons**) launderette.

Waschpulver *das* (PL *die* **Waschpulver**) washing powder.

Wasser *das* water.

wasserdicht *adjective* waterproof.

Wasserfall *der* (PL *die* **Wasserfälle**) waterfall.

Wasserfarbe *die* (PL *die* **Wasserfarben**) watercolour.

Wasserhahn *der* (PL *die* **Wasserhähne**) tap.

Wassermann *der* Aquarius; **Lisa ist Wasserman** Lisa's Aquarius.

Wasserskifahren *das* water-skiing.

Watte *die* cotton wool.

wattiert *adjective* padded.

WC *das* (PL *die* **WCs**) WC, toilet.

weben *verb* (PERF **hat gewebt**) to weave.

△ NEW SPELLING: *See page xii*

Wechselkurs der (PL die Wechselkurse) exchange rate.

wechseln verb (PERF **hat gewechselt**) 1 to change; **kannst du mir zehn Mark wechseln?** have you got change for ten marks?; 2 to exchange (glances, letters).

Wechselstube die (PL die Wechselstuben) bureau de change.

wecken verb (PERF **hat geweckt**) to wake (up).

Wecker der (PL die Wecker) alarm clock; **Max geht mir auf den Wecker** (informal) Max gets on my nerves.

weder conjunction **weder … noch** neither … nor.

weg adverb 1 away; **geh weg!** go away!; **Hände weg!** hands off!; 2 gone; **der Ring ist weg** the ring's gone; **Heidi ist schon weg** Heidi's already gone.

Weg der (PL die Wege) 1 way; **auf dem Weg nach Hause** on the way home; 2 path; 3 **sich auf den Weg machen** to set off; 4 **im Weg sein** to be in the way.

wegen preposition ←(+GEN) because of.

wegfahren ✧ verb (PRES **fährt weg**, IMPERF **fuhr weg**, PERF **ist weggefahren**) 1 to leave; **sie fahren gerade weg** they are leaving just now; 2 (PERF **hat weggefahren**) to drive away (a car or things).

weggehen ✧ verb (IMPERF **ging weg**, PERF **ist weggegangen**) 1 to go away; 2 to leave; 3 to go out; **wir gehen heute Abend weg** we're going out tonight; 4 to come out (of a stain).

weglassen ✧ verb (PRES **lässt weg** Δ, IMPERF **ließ weg**, PERF **hat weggelassen**) 1 to let go; 2 to leave out.

weglaufen ✧ verb (PRES **läuft weg**, IMPERF **lief weg**, PERF **ist weggelaufen**) to run away.

weglegen verb (PERF **hat weggelegt**) 1 to put down; 2 to put away.

wegmachen verb (PERF **hat weggemacht**) to get rid of (a stain or wart, for example).

wegmüssen ✧ verb (informal) (PRES **muss weg** Δ, IMPERF **musste weg** Δ, PERF **hat weggemusst** Δ) to have to go.

wegnehmen ✧ verb (PRES **nimmt weg**, IMPERF **nahm weg**, PERF **hat weggenommen**) to take away.

wegräumen verb (PERF **hat weggeräumt**) to clear away.

wegschicken verb (PERF **hat weggeschickt**) 1 to send away; 2 to send off.

wegtun ✧ verb (IMPERF **tat weg**, PERF **hat weggetan**) to put away.

Wegweiser der (PL die Wegweiser) signpost.

wegwerfen ✧ verb (PRES **wirft weg**, IMPERF **warf weg**, PERF **hat weggeworfen**) to throw away.

✧ IRREGULAR VERB: See the verb table in the centre of the dictionary

weh *adjective* **1** sore; **2 oh weh!** oh dear!; **3 es tut weh** it hurts.

wehen *verb* (PERF **hat geweht**) to blow.

Wehrdienst *der* military service.

wehren *verb* (PERF **hat sich gewehrt**) **sich wehren** to defend yourself.

wehrlos *adjective* defenceless.

wehtun △ ✧ *verb* (PRES **tut weh**, IMPERF **tat weh**, PERF **hat wehgetan**) **1** to hurt; **mein Arm tut weh** my arm hurts; **jemandem wehtun** to hurt somebody; **2 sich wehtun** to hurt yourself.

Weibchen *das* (PL *die* **Weibchen**) female.

weiblich *adjective* **1** female; **2** feminine (*noun*).

weich *adjective* soft.

Weide *die* (PL *die* **Weiden**) **1** willow; **2** pasture.

weigern *verb* (PERF **hat sich geweigert**) **sich weigern** to refuse.

Weihnachten *das* (PL *die* **Weihnachten**) Christmas; **Frohe Weihnachten!** Merry Christmas!

Weihnachtslied *das* (PL *die* **Weihnachtslieder**) Christmas carol.

Weihnachtsmann *der* (PL *die* **Weihnachtsmänner**) Father Christmas.

Weihnachtstag *der* (PL *die* **Weihnachtstage**) Christmas Day; **zweiter Weihnachtstag** Boxing Day.

weil *conjunction* because.

Weile *die* while.

Wein *der* (PL *die* **Weine**) wine.

Weinberg *der* (PL *die* **Weinberge**) vineyard.

Weinbergschnecke *die* (PL *die* **Weinbergschnecken**) snail.

Weinbrand *der* brandy.

weinen *verb* (PERF **hat geweint**) to cry.

Weinkarte *die* (PL *die* **Weinkarten**) wine list.

Weinkeller *der* (PL *die* **Weinkeller**) wine cellar.

Weinstube *die* (PL *die* **Weinstuben**) wine bar.

Weintraube *die* (PL *die* **Weintrauben**) grape.

weise *adjective* wise.

Weise *die* (PL *die* **Weisen**) way; **auf diese Weise** in this way.

Weisheit *die* (PL *die* **Weisheiten**) wisdom.

weiß[1] SEE **wissen**.

weiß[2] *adjective* white.

Weißwein *der* (PL *die* **Weißweine**) white wine.

weit *adjective, adverb* **1** wide, loose (*clothes*); **2** long; **eine weite Reise** a long journey; **3** far; **wie weit ist es?** how far is it?; **ist es noch weit?** is it much further?; **so weit wie möglich** as far as possible; **bei weitem** by far; **4 von weitem** from a distance; **5 ich bin so weit** I'm ready; **6 weit verbreitet**

△ NEW SPELLING: *See page xii*

widespread; **7 zu weit gehen** to go too far.

weiten *verb* (PERF **hat sich geweitet**) **sich weiten** to stretch.

weiter *adjective, adverb* **1** further; **2** in addition; **3 etwas weiter tun** to go on doing something; **weiter nichts** nothing else; **weiter niemand** nobody else; **4 und so weiter** and so on.

weiterer, weitere, weiteres *adjective* **1** further; **2 ohne weiteres** just like that, easily; **3 bis auf weiteres** for the time being.

weiterfahren ✧ *verb* (PRES **fährt weiter**, IMPERF **fuhr weiter**, PERF **ist weitergefahren**) to go on.

weitergehen ✧ *verb* (IMPERF **ging weiter**, PERF **ist weitergegangen**) to go on.

weiterhin *adverb* **1** still; **2** in future; **3 etwas weiterhin tun** to go on doing something.

weitermachen *verb* (PERF **hat weitergemacht**) to carry on.

Weitsprung *der* long jump.

Weizen *der* wheat.

welcher, welche, welches *adjective* which; **welches Kleid?** which dress?; **um welche Zeit?** at what time?
pronoun **1** which (one); **2** some; **brauchst du Briefmarken? ich habe welche** do you need stamps? I've got some; **3** any; **hast du welche?** have you got any?

Welle *die* (PL *die* **Wellen**) wave.

Wellensittich *der* (PL *die* **Wellensittiche**) budgerigar.

wellig *adjective* wavy.

Welt *die* (PL *die* **Welten**) world; **auf der ganzen Welt** in the whole world.

Weltall *das* universe.

Weltkrieg *der* (PL *die* **Weltkriege**) world war.

Weltmeister *der* (PL *die* **Weltmeister**) world champion.

Weltmeisterin *die* (PL *die* **Weltmeisterinnen**) world champion.

Weltmeisterschaft *die* (PL *die* **Weltmeisterschaften**) **1** world championship; **2 die Weltmeisterschaft** (*football*) the World Cup.

Weltraum *der* space.

wem *pronoun* to whom; **wem hat er das Geld gegeben?** who did he give the money to?

wen *pronoun* whom, who; **wen hast du eingeladen?** who did you invite?

Wende *die* **1** change; **2** reunification (*of Germany*).

wenig *pronoun, adjective* **1** little; **zu wenig** too little, not enough; **2 wenige** few; **in wenigen Wochen** in a few weeks.
adverb little; **so wenig wie möglich** as little as possible.

weniger *pronoun, adjective* less, fewer; **sie hat weniger Geschenke bekommen** she got fewer presents;

✧ IRREGULAR VERB: *See the verb table in the centre of the dictionary*

immer weniger Geld less and less money; **immer weniger Häuser** fewer and fewer houses. *adverb, conjunction* less; **zehn weniger fünf** ten minus five.

wenigste SEE **wenigster**.

wenigstens *adverb* at least.

wenigster, wenigste, wenigstes *adjective, pronoun* least; **am wenigsten** least; **sein Geschenk hat mir am wenigsten gefallen** I liked his present least.

wenn *conjunction* 1 when; **wenn ich in München bin, schreibe ich dir** I'll write to you when I'm in Munich; **immer, wenn** whenever; 2 if; **wenn es regnet** if it rains; 3 **außer wenn** unless.

wer *pronoun* who.

werben ◇ *verb* (PRES **wirbt**, IMPERF **warb**, PERF **hat geworben**) 1 to advertise; 2 to recruit (*members*).

Werbespot *der* (PL *die* **Werbespots**) advert, commercial.

Werbung *die* 1 advertising; **in der Werbung arbeiten** to work in advertising; 2 advert; **im Fernsehen kommt viel Werbung** there are many adverts on television; **Werbung für etwas machen** to advertise something.

werden ◇ *verb* (PRES **wird**, IMPERF **wurde**, PERF **ist geworden**) 1 to become; **Arzt werden** to become a doctor; 2 **müde werden** to get tired; **alt werden** to get old; **mir wird kalt** I'm getting cold; 3 **mir wurde schlecht** I felt sick; **blass werden**

to turn pale; 4 **wach werden** to wake up; 5 (*used to form the future tense*) will, shall; **sie wird anrufen** she'll ring; **sie wird gleich da sein** she'll be here in a minute; 6 (*used to form the passive*) to be; **gerufen werden** to be called; **er wurde gefragt** he was asked; 7 (*used to form the conditional*) **sie würde kommen** she would come; **ich würde gern kommen, aber …** I'd like to come but …

werfen ◇ *verb* (PRES **wirft**, IMPERF **warf**, PERF **hat geworfen**) to throw.

Werk *das* (PL *die* **Werke**) 1 work; 2 works (*a factory*).

Werken *das* handicraft.

Werkstatt *die* (PL *die* **Werkstätten**) workshop.

Werktag *der* (PL *die* **Werktage**) weekday.

werktags *adverb* on weekdays.

Werkzeug *das* (PL *die* **Werkzeuge**) tool.

wert *adjective* **viel wert sein** to be worth a lot; **nichts wert sein** to be worthless.

Wert *der* (PL *die* **Werte**) 1 value; **im Wert von hundert Mark** worth one hundred marks; 2 **auf etwas Wert legen** to attach importance to something; 3 **es hat doch keinen Wert** there's no point.

wertlos *adjective* worthless.

wertvoll *adjective* valuable.

Wesen *das* (PL *die* **Wesen**) 1 nature, manner; 2 creature.

△ NEW SPELLING: *See page xii*

wesentlich *adjective* essential; **im Wesentlichen** △ essentially.
adverb considerably.

weshalb *adverb* why.

Wespe *die* (PL *die* **Wespen**) wasp.

wessen *pronoun* whose.

Wessi *der* (*informal*) (PL *die* **Wessis**) West German.

Weste *die* (PL *die* **Westen**) waistcoat.

Westen *der* west.

Westinder *der* (PL *die* **Westinder**) West Indian.

Westinderin *die* (PL *die* **Westinderinnen**) West Indian.

westlich *adjective* 1 western; 2 westerly.
adverb, preposition ←(+GEN)
westlich von Wien west of Vienna; **westlich der Stadt** to the west of the town.

weswegen *adverb* why.

Wettbewerb *der* (PL *die* **Wettbewerbe**) competition, contest.

Wette *die* (PL *die* **Wetten**) bet; **mit jemandem um die Wette laufen** to race somebody.

wetten *verb* (PERF **hat gewettet**) to bet; **mit jemandem um etwas wetten** to bet somebody something.

Wetter *das* weather.

Wetterbericht *der* (PL *die* **Wetterberichte**) weather report.

Wettervorhersage *die* weather forecast.

Wettkampf *der* (PL *die* **Wettkämpfe**) contest.

Wettlauf *der* race.

wichtig *adjective* important.

wickeln *verb* (PERF **hat gewickelt**) 1 to wind; 2 **ein Kind wickeln** to change a baby.

Widder *der* (PL *die* **Widder**) 1 ram; 2 Aries; **Jan ist Widder** Jan's Aries.

widerlich *adjective* disgusting.

widersprechen ✧ *verb* (PRES **widerspricht**, IMPERF **widersprach**, PERF **hat widersprochen**) to contradict.

Widerspruch *der* (PL *die* **Widersprüche**) contradiction.

Widerstand *der* resistance.

widerstehen ✧ *verb* (IMPERF **widerstand**, PERF **hat widerstanden**) to resist.

widmen *verb* (PERF **hat gewidmet**) 1 to dedicate; 2 to devote; 3 **sich einer Sache widmen** to devote yourself to something.

wie *adverb* 1 how; **wie geht's?** how are you?; **wie viel?** △ how much?, how many?; **um wie viel** △ **Uhr kommst du?** (at) what time are you coming?; 2 **wie ist Ihr Name?** what is your name?; **wie ist das Wetter?** what's the weather like?; 3 **wie bitte?** sorry?
conjunction 1 as; **so schnell wie möglich** as quickly as possible; 2 like; **wie du** like you; 3 **wie zum Beispiel** such as.

wieder *adverb* 1 again; **sie ist**

wieder da she's back again,
2 jemanden wieder erkennen △ to
recognize somebody; **etwas wieder
finden** △ to find something (again);
etwas wieder verwerten △ to
recycle something.

wiederbekommen ✧ *verb* (IMPERF
bekam wieder, PERF **hat
wiederbekommen**) to get back.

wiedererkennen SEE **wieder**.

wiederfinden SEE **wieder**.

wiederholen *verb* (PERF **hat
wiederholt**) **1** to repeat; **2** to revise
(*work at school*); **3 sich
wiederholen** to recur; **er hat sich
wiederholt** he's repeated himself.

Wiederholung *die* (PL *die*
Wiederholungen) **1** repetition;
2 repeat; **3** revision (*at school*).

Wiederhören *das* **auf
Wiederhören!** (*said on the phone*)
goodbye!

wiederkommen ✧ *verb* (IMPERF
kam wieder, PERF **ist
wiedergekommen**) **1** to come back;
2 to come again.

wiedersehen SEE **sehen**.

Wiedersehen *das* (PL *die*
Wiedersehen) **1** reunion; **2 auf
Wiedersehen!** goodbye!

wiedervereinigen SEE **vereinigen**.

Wiedervereinigung *die*
reunification.

wiederverwerten SEE **wieder**.

Wiege *die* (PL *die* **Wiegen**) cradle.

wiegen ✧ *verb* (IMPERF **wog**, PERF **hat
gewogen**) to weigh.

Wiegenlied *das* (PL *die*
Wiegenlieder) lullaby.

Wien *das* Vienna.

Wiese *die* (PL *die* **Wiesen**) meadow.

wieso *adverb* why.

wieviel SEE **wie**.

wievielmal *adverb* how often.

**wievielter, wievielte,
wievieltes** *adjective* **1** which;
**2 die wievielte Querstraße ist das
von hier aus?** how many roads is
that from here?; **der Wievielte ist
heute?** what's the date today?

wild *adjective* wild.

Wildleder *das* suede.

Wildpark *der* (PL *die* **Wildparks**)
wildlife park.

will SEE **wollen**.

Wille *der* will; **seinen Willen
durchsetzen** to get your own way.

willkommen *adjective* welcome.

willst SEE **wollen**.

Wimper *die* (PL *die* **Wimpern**)
eyelash.

Wimperntusche *die* (PL *die*
Wimperntuschen) mascara.

Wind *der* (PL *die* **Winde**) wind.

Windel *die* (PL *die* **Windeln**) nappy.

Windhund *der* (PL *die* **Windhunde**)
greyhound.

windig *adjective* windy.

△ NEW SPELLING: *See page xii*

Windmühle die (PL die **Windmühlen**) windmill.

Windpocken plural noun chickenpox.

Windschutzscheibe die (PL die **Windschutzscheiben**) windscreen.

Winkel der (PL die **Winkel**) 1 angle; 2 corner.

winken verb (PERF **hat gewinkt**) to wave.

Winter der (PL die **Winter**) winter.

winzig adjective tiny.

wir pronoun we; **wir sind es** it's us; **wir alle** all of us.

Wirbelsäule die (PL die **Wirbelsäulen**) spine.

wirbt SEE **werben**.

wird SEE **werden**.

wirft SEE **werfen**.

wirken verb (PERF **hat gewirkt**) 1 to have an effect; 2 **gegen etwas wirken** to be effective against something; 3 to seem (sad, happy).

wirklich adjective real. adverb really.

Wirklichkeit die reality.

wirksam adjective effective.

Wirkung die (PL die **Wirkungen**) effect.

wirst SEE **werden**.

Wirt der (PL die **Wirte**) landlord.

Wirtin die (PL die **Wirtinnen**) landlady.

Wirtschaft die (PL die **Wirtschaften**) 1 economy; 2 pub.

wirtschaftlich adjective economic.

Wirtshaus das (PL die **Wirtshäuser**) pub.

wischen verb (PERF **hat gewischt**) to wipe.

wissen ✧ verb (PRES **weiß**, IMPERF **wusste** Δ, PERF **hat gewusst** Δ) to know; **ich weiß, dass er in London wohnt** I know he lives in London; **ich wüsste gern …** I'd like to know …; **von etwas wissen** to know about something; **weißt du was?** you know what?

Wissen das knowledge.

Wissenschaft die (PL die **Wissenschaften**) science.

Wissenschaftler der (PL die **Wissenschaftler**) scientist.

Wissenschaftlerin die (PL die **Wissenschaftlerinnen**) scientist.

wissenschaftlich adjective scientific.

Witwe die (PL die **Witwen**) widow.

Witwer der (PL die **Witwer**) widower.

Witz der (PL die **Witze**) joke.

witzig adjective funny.

wo adverb where; **wo seid ihr gewesen?** where have you been?; **in München, wo Markus seit einem Jahr lebt** in Munich, where Markus has been living for a year; **wo immer** wherever. conjunction 1 seeing that;

✧ IRREGULAR VERB: See the verb table in the centre of the dictionary

2 although; **jetzt ist sie mir böse,
wo ich doch so nett zu ihr war** now
she's angry with me, although I've
been so nice to her.

woanders *adverb* elsewhere.

Woche *die* (PL *die* **Wochen**) week.

Wochenende *das* (PL *die*
Wochenenden) weekend.

wochenlang *adverb* for weeks.

Wochentag *der* (PL *die*
Wochentage) weekday.

wochentags *adverb* on weekdays.

wöchentlich *adjective* weekly.

wofür *adverb* what ... for; **wofür
brauchst du das Geld?** what do you
need the money for?

wog SEE **wiegen**.

woher *adverb* where ... from; **woher
ist er?** where does he come from?;
woher weißt du das? how do you
know?

wohin *adverb* where ... (to); **wohin
geht ihr?** where are you going?

wohl *adverb* 1 well; **sich wohl fühlen**
to feel well; **ich fühle mich heute
nicht wohl** I don't feel well today;
2 **sich wohl fühlen** to be happy;
Anni fühlt sich in London wohl Anni
is happy in London; 3 **jemandem
wohl tun** △ to do somebody good;
4 probably; **er hat den Zug wohl
verpasst** he probably missed the
train; **du bist wohl verrückt!** you
must be mad!; 5 **wohl kaum** hardly.

Wohl *das* 1 welfare, well-being; 2 **zu**

seinem Wohl for his benefit; 3 **zum
Wohl!** cheers!

wohlhabend *adjective* well-off.

wohltun SEE **wohl**.

wohnen *verb* (PERF **hat gewohnt**)
1 to live; 2 to stay (*for a short time*).

Wohngemeinschaft *die* (PL *die*
Wohngemeinschaften) people
sharing a flat/house; **wir wohnen in
einer Wohngemeinschaft** we share
a flat.

wohnhaft *adjective* resident.

Wohnheim *das* (PL *die* **Wohnheime**)
1 hostel; 2 home (*for old people*).

Wohnort *der* (PL *die* **Wohnorte**)
place of residence.

Wohnsitz *der* (PL *die* **Wohnsitze**)
place of residence.

Wohnung *die* (PL *die* **Wohnungen**)
flat.

Wohnwagen *der* (PL *die*
Wohnwagen) caravan.

Wohnzimmer *das* (PL *die*
Wohnzimmer) living room.

Wolf *der* (PL *die* **Wölfe**) wolf.

Wolke *die* (PL *die* **Wolken**) cloud.

Wolkenkratzer *der* (PL *die*
Wolkenkratzer) skyscraper.

wolkig *adjective* cloudy.

Wolldecke *die* (PL *die* **Wolldecken**)
blanket.

Wolle *die* wool.

wollen ◇ *verb* (PRES **will**, IMPERF
wollte, PERF **hat gewollt**) 1 to want;
Anne will einen Hund Anne wants a

△ NEW SPELLING: *See page xii*

dog; **ich will nach Hause** I want to go home; **2 sie wollte gerade gehen** she was just about to go; **3 ganz wie du willst** as you like.

womit *adverb* **1** what ... with; **womit hast du das gewaschen?** what did you wash it with?; **2** with which.

womöglich *adverb* possibly.

wonach *adverb* **1** what ... for; **wonach suchst du?** what are you looking for?; **wonach riecht es?** what does it smell of?; **2** after which, according to which; **eine Regelung, wonach wir eine Stunde mehr arbeiten müssen** a rule according to which we have to work an extra hour.

woran *adverb* what ... of; **1 woran denkst du?** what are you thinking of?; **woran hast du ihn erkannt?** how did you recognize him?; **2** on which, of which; **nichts, woran man sich verletzen könnte** nothing you could hurt yourself on.

worauf *adverb* **1** what ... on, what ... for; **worauf hast du die Vase gestellt?** what did you put the vase on?; **worauf wartet ihr?** what are you waiting for?; **2** on which, for which; **das Regal, worauf das Radio steht** the shelf the radio is on; **das Einzige, worauf ich mich freue** the only thing I'm looking forward to.

woraus *adverb* **1** what ... from, what ... of; **woraus ist das?** what's it made of?; **2** from which; **es gibt nichts, woraus wir trinken können** there isn't anything we can drink out of.

worin *adverb* **1** what ... in, in what; **2** in which; **die Punkte, worin ich mit dir übereinstimme** the points I agree with you on.

Wort *das* (PL *die* **Worte/Wörter**) word; **mir fehlen die Worte** I'm lost for words; **ich habe heute zwanzig neue Wörter gelernt** I've learnt twenty new words today.

Wörterbuch *das* (PL *die* **Wörterbücher**) dictionary.

wörtlich *adjective* word for word.

Wortschatz *der* vocabulary.

Wortspiel *das* (PL *die* **Wortspiele**) pun.

worüber *adverb* **1** what ... over, what ... about; **worüber lacht ihr?** what are you laughing about?; **2** over which, about which.

worum *adverb* **1** about what; **worum geht es?** what's it about?; **worum hat sie dich gebeten?** what did she ask you for?; **2** for which; **3** round which.

wovon *adverb* **1** what ... from, what ... about; **wovon redet ihr?** what are you talking about?; **2** from which, about which; **der Geruch, wovon mir schlecht geworden ist** the smell which made me feel sick.

wovor *adverb* **1** what ... of; **wovor hast du Angst?** what are you frightened of?; **2** in front of what; **3** of which; **4** in front of which; **der Turm, wovor wir stehen** the tower we are standing in front of.

wozu *adverb* **1** what ... for, why; **wozu brauchst du das?** what do

you need it for?; **wozu?** what for?;
2 to which, for which; **wozu ich dir
raten würde** which I would advise.

Wrack *das* (PL *die* **Wracks**) wreck.

wuchs SEE **wachsen**.

Wuchs *der* growth.

wund *adjective* sore.

Wunde *die* (PL *die* **Wunden**) wound.

Wunder *das* (PL *die* **Wunder**) miracle;
kein Wunder! no wonder!

wunderbar *adjective* wonderful.

wundern *verb* (PERF **hat sich
gewundert**) **sich wundern** to be
surprised.

wunderschön *adjective* beautiful.

wundervoll *adjective* wonderful.

Wunsch *der* (PL *die* **Wünsche**) wish;
auf Wunsch on request; **haben Sie
sonst noch einen Wunsch?** will
there be anything else?

wünschen *verb* (PERF **hat
gewünscht**) **1** to wish; **ich wünsche
dir alles Gute zum Geburtstag** I
wish you a happy birthday; **ich
wünschte, ich könnte ...** I wish I
could ...; **was wünschen Sie?** can I
help you?; **2 sich etwas wünschen**
to want something.

wünschenswert *adjective*
desirable.

**wurde, würde, wurden,
würden, wurdest, würdest,
wurdet, würdet** SEE **werden**.

Wurf *der* (PL *die* **Würfe**) throw.

Würfel *der* (PL *die* **Würfel**) **1** dice (*in
games*); **2** cube.

würfeln *verb* (PERF **hat gewürfelt**) to
throw the dice.

Wurm *der* (PL *die* **Würmer**) worm.

Wurst *die* (PL *die* **Würste**) **1** sausage;
2 das ist mir Wurst (*informal*) I
couldn't care less.

Würstchen *das* (PL *die* **Würstchen**)
(little) sausage.

Wurzel *die* (PL *die* **Wurzeln**) root.

würzen *verb* (PERF **hat gewürzt**) to
season.

würzig *adjective* spicy.

wusch SEE **waschen**.

wusste △ SEE **wissen**.

Wüste *die* (PL *die* **Wüsten**) desert.

Wut *die* rage; **eine Wut auf jemanden
haben** to be furious with somebody.

wütend *adjective* furious.

X x

x-beliebig *adjective* (*informal*)
any; **eine x-beliebige Zahl** any
number (you like).

x-mal *adverb* (*informal*) umpteen
times; **zum x-ten Mal** for the
umpteenth time.

Xylophon *das* (PL *die* **Xylophone**)
xylophone.

Y y

Yoga *das* yoga.

Ypsilon *das* (PL *die* **Ypsilons**) Y.

Z z

zaghaft *adjective* 1 timid;
2 tentative.

zäh *adjective* tough.

Zahl *die* (PL *die* **Zahlen**) 1 number;
2 figure.

zahlen *verb* (PERF **hat gezahlt**) 1 to
pay; **hast du schon gezahlt?** have
you paid?; 2 to pay for; **bitte zahlen!**
the bill please!

zählen *verb* (PERF **hat gezählt**) 1 to
count; **auf jemanden zählen** to
count on somebody; **jemanden zu
seinen Freunden zählen** to count
somebody among your friends;
2 **zählen zu** to be one of.

Zähler *der* (PL *die* **Zähler**) meter.

zahlreich *adjective* numerous.

Zahlung *die* (PL *die* **Zahlungen**)
payment.

Zählung *die* (PL *die* **Zählungen**)
1 count; 2 census.

zahm *adjective* tame.

Zahn *der* (PL *die* **Zähne**) tooth.

Zahnarzt *der* (PL *die* **Zahnärzte**)
dentist.

Zahnärztin *die* (PL *die*
Zahnärztinnen) dentist.

Zahnbürste *die* (PL *die*
Zahnbürsten) toothbrush.

Zahnfleisch *das* gums.

Zahnpasta *die* (PL *die* **Zahnpasten**)
toothpaste.

Zahnschmerzen *plural noun*
toothache.

Zange *die* (PL *die* **Zangen**) pliers.

zanken *verb* (PERF **hat sich gezankt**)
sich zanken to squabble.

zappeln *verb* (PERF **hat gezappelt**)
1 to wriggle; 2 to fidget.

zart *adjective* 1 delicate, soft;
2 gentle; 3 tender.

zärtlich *adjective* affectionate.

Zauber *der* 1 magic; 2 spell.

Zauberer *der* (PL *die* **Zauberer**)
magician, conjurer.

zauberhaft *adjective* enchanting.

zaubern *verb* (PERF **hat gezaubert**)
to do magic.

Zaun *der* (PL *die* **Zäune**) fence.

z.B. (*zum Beispiel*) e.g.

Zebra *das* (PL *die* **Zebras**) zebra.

Zebrastreifen *der* (PL *die*
Zebrastreifen) zebra crossing.

Zeh *der* (PL *die* **Zehen**) toe.

Zehe *die* (PL *die* **Zehen**) 1 toe;
2 clove (*of garlic*).

✧ IRREGULAR VERB: *See the verb table in the centre of the dictionary*

ehn *number* ten.

ehntel *das* (PL *die* **Zehntel**) tenth.

ehnter, zehnte, zehntes
adjective tenth.

eichen *das* (PL *die* **Zeichen**)
1 sign; 2 signal.

eichnen *verb* (PERF **hat
gezeichnet**) to draw.

eichnung *die* (PL *die*
Zeichnungen) drawing.

eigefinger *der* (PL *die*
Zeigefinger) index finger.

eigen *verb* (PERF **hat gezeigt**) 1 to
show; **Peter hat uns sein neues Auto
gezeigt** Peter showed us his new
car; 2 to point; **auf jemanden
zeigen** to point at somebody; 3 **sich
zeigen** to appear; 4 **es hat sich
gezeigt, dass** … it has become clear
that …; **es wird sich zeigen** time
will tell.

eiger *der* (PL *die* **Zeiger**) hand.

eile *die* (PL *die* **Zeilen**) line.

eit *die* (PL *die* **Zeiten**) 1 time; **sich
Zeit lassen** to take your time; **ich
habe keine Zeit mehr** I haven't got
any more time; **eine Zeit lang** △ for
a time; 2 **es hat Zeit** there's no
hurry; **die erste Zeit** at first; **in
nächster Zeit** in the near future.

Zeitalter *das* (PL *die* **Zeitalter**) age.

Zeitlang *die* SEE **Zeit**.

Zeitlupe *die* slow motion; **in
Zeitlupe** in slow motion.

Zeitraum *der* (PL *die* **Zeiträume**)
period.

Zeitschrift *die* (PL *die*
Zeitschriften) magazine.

Zeitung *die* (PL *die* **Zeitungen**)
newspaper.

Zeitverschwendung *die* waste of
time.

zeitweise *adverb* at times.

Zeitungshändler *der* (PL *die*
Zeitungshändler) newsagent.

Zelle *die* (PL *die* **Zellen**) 1 cell;
2 booth.

Zelt *das* (PL *die* **Zelte**) tent.

zelten *verb* (PERF **hat gezeltet**) to
camp.

Zeltplatz *der* (PL *die* **Zeltplätze**)
campsite.

Zement *der* cement.

Zentimeter *der* (PL *die* **Zentimeter**)
centimetre.

Zentimetermaß *das* (PL *die*
Zentimetermaße) tape measure.

zentral *adjective* central.

Zentrale *die* (PL *die* **Zentralen**)
1 central office, head office;
2 headquarters; 3 (telephone)
exchange, switchboard.

Zentralheizung *die* central
heating.

Zentrum *das* (PL *die* **Zentren**) centre.

zerbrechen ◇ *verb* (PRES
zerbricht, IMPERF **zerbrach**, PERF **hat
zerbrochen**) 1 to break; **Irene hat
meine Vase zerbrochen** Irene
broke my vase; 2 (PERF **ist
zerbrochen**) to break; **die**

Untertasse ist zerbrochen the saucer broke.

zerbrechlich *adjective* fragile.

Zeremonie *die* (PL *die* **Zeremonien**) ceremony.

zerreißen ✧ *verb* (IMPERF **zerriss** Δ, PERF **hat zerrissen**) 1 to tear; **sie hat sich das Kleid zerrissen** she tore her dress; 2 to tear up; **Anna hat seinen Brief zerrissen** Anna tore up his letter; 3 (PERF **ist zerrissen**) to tear; **das Hemd ist in der Wäsche zerrissen** the shirt got torn in the washing.

zerschlagen ✧ *verb* (PRES **zerschlägt**, IMPERF **zerschlug**, PERF **hat zerschlagen**) 1 to smash, to smash up; 2 **sich zerschlagen** to fall through (*of plans*); **meine Hoffnungen haben sich zerschlagen** my hopes were dashed.

zerschneiden ✧ *verb* (IMPERF **zerschnitt**, PERF **hat zerschnitten**) to cut, to cut up.

zerstören *verb* (PERF **hat zerstört**) to destroy.

Zerstörung *die* destruction.

zerstreuen *verb* (PERF **hat zerstreut**) 1 to scatter; 2 **jemanden zerstreuen** to entertain somebody; 3 **sich zerstreuen** to take your mind off things; 4 **die Menge hat sich zerstreut** the crowd's dispersed.

zerstreut *adjective* absent-minded.

Zettel *der* (PL *die* **Zettel**) 1 piece of paper; 2 note; 3 leaflet.

Zeug *das* (*informal*) 1 stuff; 2 things, gear; 3 **dummes Zeug** nonsense.

Zeuge *der* (PL *die* **Zeugen**) witness.

Zeugin *die* (PL *die* **Zeuginnen**) witness.

Zeugnis *das* (PL *die* **Zeugnisse**) 1 certificate; 2 report (*at school*).

Zickzack *der* (PL *die* **Zickzacke**) zigzag; **im Zickzack laufen** to zigzag.

Ziege *die* (PL *die* **Ziegen**) goat.

Ziegel *der* (PL *die* **Ziegel**) 1 brick; 2 tile.

ziehen ✧ *verb* (IMPERF **zog**, PERF **hat gezogen**) 1 to pull; **an etwas ziehen** to pull on something; **einen Zahn ziehen** to pull out a tooth; 2 to draw; **einen Strich ziehen** to draw a line; **eine Niete ziehen** to draw a blank; 3 **die Bremse ziehen** to put on the brakes; 4 to grow (*vegetables, flowers*); 5 **sich ziehen** to run (*of a path, road*); 6 (PERF **ist gezogen**) to move; **sie sind nach Berlin gezogen** they've moved to Berlin.

Ziel *das* (PL *die* **Ziele**) 1 destination; 2 goal, aim; 3 finish (*in sport*).

zielen *verb* (PERF **hat gezielt**) to aim; **auf etwas zielen** to aim at something.

Zielscheibe *die* (PL *die* **Zielscheiben**) target.

ziemlich *adjective* fair. *adverb* 1 quite; **ziemlich viel** quite a lot; 2 fairly; **ihre Eltern haben ein**

ziemlich großes Haus her parents have a fairly large house.

zierlich *adjective* dainty.

Ziffer *die* (PL *die* **Ziffern**) figure.

Zifferblatt *das* (PL *die* **Zifferblätter**) face, dial.

zig *adjective* (*informal*) umpteen.

Zigarette *die* (PL *die* **Zigaretten**) cigarette.

Zigarre *die* (PL *die* **Zigarren**) cigar.

Zigeuner *der* (PL *die* **Zigeuner**) gypsy.

Zigeunerin *die* (PL *die* **Zigeunerinnen**) gypsy.

Zimmer *das* (PL *die* **Zimmer**) room; **Zimmer mit Frühstück** bed and breakfast; **'Zimmer frei'** 'vacancies'.

Zimmermädchen *das* (PL *die* **Zimmermädchen**) chambermaid.

Zimt *der* cinnamon.

Zink *das* zinc.

zirka *adverb* about.

Zirkel *der* (PL *die* **Zirkel**) pair of compasses.

Zirkus *der* (PL *die* **Zirkusse**) circus.

zischen *verb* (PERF **hat gezischt**) to hiss.

Zitat *das* (PL *die* **Zitate**) quotation.

zitieren *verb* (PERF **hat zitiert**) to quote.

Zitrone *die* (PL *die* **Zitronen**) lemon.

Zitronensaft *der* (PL *die* **Zitronensäfte**) lemon juice.

zittern *verb* (PERF **hat gezittert**) to tremble; **vor Kälte zittern** to shiver.

Zivildienst *der* community service.

Zivilisation *die* (PL *die* **Zivilisationen**) civilization.

zog SEE **ziehen**.

zögern *verb* (PERF **hat gezögert**) to hesitate.

Zoll *der* (PL *die* **Zölle**) 1 customs; **am Zoll** at customs; 2 duty; **Zoll auf etwas bezahlen** to pay duty on something.

Zollbeamte *der* (PL *die* **Zollbeamten**) customs officer.

Zollbeamtin *die* (PL *die* **Zollbeamtinnen**) customs officer.

zollfrei *adjective* duty-free.

Zollkontrolle *die* (PL *die* **Zollkontrollen**) customs check.

Zone *die* (PL *die* **Zonen**) zone.

Zoo *der* (PL *die* **Zoos**) Zoo.

Zoomobjektiv *das* (PL *die* **Zoomobjektive**) zoom lens.

Zopf *der* (PL *die* **Zöpfe**) plait.

Zorn *der* anger.

zornig *adjective* angry.

zu *preposition* ←(+DAT) 1 to; **ich gehe zum Arzt** I'm going to the doctor's; **zu einer Party eingeladen sein** to be invited to a party; 2 **zu … hin** towards; **zum Fenster hin** towards the window; **er kam zu dieser Tür herein** he came in through this door; 3 with; **das passt nicht zu meinem Mantel** it doesn't go with

△ NEW SPELLING: *See page xii*

my coat; **es gab Wein zum Käse** there was wine with the cheese; **4** at; **zu Weihnachten** at Christmas; **zu Hause** at home; **5 zu etwas werden** to turn into something; **6 zu diesem Zweck** for this purpose; **was schenkst du Karin zum Geburtstag?** what are you giving Karin for her birthday?; **zum Spaß** for fun; **zum ersten Mal** for the first time; **7 sich zu etwas äußern** to comment on something; **Papier zum Schreiben** paper to write on; **8 nett zu jemandem sein** to be nice to somebody; **9 sie waren zu zweit** there were two of them; **eine Marke zu achtzig Pfennig** an 80-pfennig stamp; **es steht drei zu zwei** the score is 3–2; **10 zu Fuß** on foot.
adverb **1** too; **zu groß** too big; **2** closed; **zu haben** △ to be closed; **Tür zu!** (*informal*) shut the door!; **3 zu sein** △ to be closed; **alle Läden sind zu gewesen** the shops were all closed; **4** towards (*indicating direction*); **5 mach zu!** (*informal*) hurry up!
conjunction to; **nichts zu essen** nothing to eat; **zu verkaufen** for sale.

zuallererst *adverb* first of all.

zuallerletzt *adverb* last of all.

Zubehör *das* accessories.

zubereiten *verb* (PERF **hat zubereitet**) to prepare; **sie bereitet das Essen zu** she's preparing the meal.

zubinden ✧ *verb* (IMPERF **band zu**, PERF **hat zugebunden**) to tie, to tie up.

zubringen ✧ *verb* (IMPERF **brachte zu**, PERF **hat zugebracht**) to spend; **sie bringt viel Zeit bei ihrem Freund zu** she spends a lot of time with her boyfriend.

Zucchini *plural noun* courgettes.

züchten *verb* (PERF **hat gezüchtet**) to breed.

zucken *verb* (PERF **hat gezuckt**) to twitch.

Zucker *der* sugar.

Zuckerguss △ *der* icing.

zuckerkrank *adjective* diabetic.

zudecken *verb* (PERF **hat zugedeckt**) **1** to cover up, to cover; **2** to tuck up (*in bed*).

zueinander *adverb* **1** to one another; **lieb zueinander sein** to be nice to one another; **2** together; **zueinander passen** to go together; **zueinander halten** △ to stick together.

zuerst *adverb* **1** first; **2** at first.

Zufahrt *die* (PL *die* **Zufahrten**) **1** access; **2** drive(way).

Zufall *der* (PL *die* **Zufälle**) **1** chance; **durch Zufall** by chance; **2** coincidence; **so ein komischer Zufall** such a strange coincidence; **per Zufall traf ich ihn in der U-Bahn** I happened to meet him on the tube.

zufällig *adjective* chance; **das war rein zufällig** it was purely by chance. *adverb* by chance; **kannst du mir zufällig zehn Mark leihen?** could

---

✧ IRREGULAR VERB: *See the verb table in the centre of the dictionary*

you lend me ten marks by any chance?

zufrieden *adjective* 1 content; 2 satisfied; **mit etwas zufrieden sein** to be satisfied with something. *adverb* **jemanden zufrieden lassen** ∆ to leave somebody in peace; **jemanden zufrieden stellen** ∆ to satisfy somebody.

zufriedenlassen, zufriedenstellen SEE **zufrieden**.

Zug *der* (PL *die* **Züge**) 1 train; 2 procession; 3 characteristic, trait; 4 move (*in games*); 5 swig (*when drinking*); 6 drag (*when smoking*); 7 **in einem Zug** in one go.

Zugabe *die* (PL *die* **Zugaben**) 1 free gift; 2 encore.

Zugang *der* (PL *die* **Zugänge**) access.

zugeben ◆ *verb* (PRES **gibt zu**, IMPERF **gab zu**, PERF **hat zugegeben**) 1 to add; 2 to admit.

zugehen ◆ *verb* (IMPERF **ging zu**, PERF **ist zugegangen**) 1 to close, to shut; **die Tür geht nicht zu** the door won't shut; 2 **auf etwas zugehen** to go towards something; **auf jemanden zugehen** to walk up to somebody; 3 **jemandem zugehen** to be sent to somebody; 4 **auf der Party ging es lustig zu** the party was good fun; 5 **dem Ende zugehen** to be nearing the end.

zügig *adjective* quick.

zugreifen ◆ *verb* (IMPERF **griff zu**, PERF **hat zugegriffen**) 1 to grab it/them; 2 to help yourself; 3 to lend a hand.

zugunsten *preposition* ←(+GEN) in favour of.

zuhaben SEE **zu**.

Zuhause *das* home.

zuhören *verb* (PERF **hat zugehört**) to listen.

Zuhörer *der* (PL *die* **Zuhörer**) listener.

Zuhörerin *die* (PL *die* **Zuhörerinnen**) listener.

zukommen ◆ *verb* (IMPERF **kam zu**, PERF **ist zugekommen**) 1 **auf jemanden zukommen** to come up to somebody; **nächstes Jahr kommt eine Menge Arbeit auf mich zu** I'm in for a lot of work next year; 2 **jemandem etwas zukommen lassen** to give somebody something; 3 **etwas auf sich zukommen lassen** to take things as they come.

Zukunft *die* future.

zukünftig *adjective* future.

zulassen ◆ *verb* (PRES **lässt zu** ∆, IMPERF **ließ zu**, PERF **hat zugelassen**) 1 to allow; 2 to register (*a car*); 3 to leave closed.

Zulassung *die* (PL *die* **Zulassungen**) 1 registration; 2 admission.

zuletzt *adverb* 1 last; 2 in the end.

zum = **zu dem**; 1 **etwas zum Lesen** something to read; 2 **spätestens zum fünften März** by 5 March at the latest; 3 **er hat es zum Fenster hinausgeworfen** he threw it out of the window.

∆ NEW SPELLING: *See page xii*

zumachen *verb* (PERF **hat zugemacht**) **1** to close, to shut; **2** to fasten.

zumindest *adverb* at least.

zunächst *adverb* **1** first (of all); **2** at first.

Zuname *der* (PL *die* **Zunamen**) surname.

zunehmen ✧ *verb* (PRES **nimmt zu**, IMPERF **nahm zu**, PERF **hat zugenommen**) **1** to increase; **2** to put on weight.

Zunge *die* (PL *die* **Zungen**) tongue.

zur = **zu der**.

zurechtkommen ✧ *verb* (IMPERF **kam zurecht**, PERF **ist zurechtgekommen**) to cope, to manage.

zurechtlegen *verb* (PERF **hat zurechtgelegt**) **1** to put out ready; **2 sich eine Ausrede zurechtlegen** to think up an excuse.

zurück *adverb* **1** back; **2 Hamburg, hin und zurück** a return to Hamburg.

zurückbekommen ✧ *verb* (IMPERF **bekam zurück**, PERF **hat zurückbekommen**) to get back; **zehn Pfennig zurückbekommen** to get 10 pfennigs change.

zurückbringen ✧ *verb* (IMPERF **brachte zurück**, PERF **hat zurückgebracht**) **1** to bring back; **2** to take back.

zurückfahren ✧ *verb* (PRES **fährt zurück**, IMPERF **fuhr zurück**, PERF **ist zurückgefahren**) **1** to go back; **2** to drive back; **3** (PERF **hat zurückgefahren**) to drive back; **jemanden zurückfahren** to drive somebody back.

zurückgeben ✧ *verb* (PRES **gibt zurück**, IMPERF **gab zurück**, PERF **hat zurückgegeben**) to give back.

zurückgehen ✧ *verb* (IMPERF **ging zurück**, PERF **ist zurückgegangen**) **1** to go back; **zurückgehen auf** to go back to; **2** to go down; **3** to decrease.

zurückhalten ✧ *verb* (PRES **hält zurück**, IMPERF **hielt zurück**, PERF **hat zurückgehalten**) **1** to hold back; **2 sich zurückhalten** to restrain yourself.

zurückkommen ✧ *verb* (IMPERF **kam zurück**, PERF **ist zurückgekommen**) **1** to come back; **2** to get back.

zurücklassen ✧ *verb* (PRES **lässt zurück** △, IMPERF **ließ zurück**, PERF **hat zurückgelassen**) to leave behind.

zurücklegen *verb* (PERF **hat zurückgelegt**) **1** to put back; **2** to keep, to put aside; **3 Geld für etwas zurücklegen** to put money by for something; **4** to cover (*a distance*); **5 sich zurücklegen** to lie back.

zurücknehmen ✧ *verb* (PRES **nimmt zurück**, IMPERF **nahm zurück**, PERF **hat zurückgenommen**) to take back.

zurückrufen ✧ *verb* (IMPERF **rief zurück**, PERF **hat zurückgerufen**) to call back.

zurücktreten ✧ *verb* (PRES **tritt zurück**, IMPERF **trat zurück**, PERF **ist**

✧ IRREGULAR VERB: *See the verb table in the centre of the dictionary*

zurückgetreten) **1** to step back, **2** to resign.

zurückzahlen *verb* (PERF **hat zurückgezahlt**) to pay back.

zurückziehen ✧ *verb* (IMPERF **zog zurück**, PERF **hat zurückgezogen**) **1** to draw back; **2** to withdraw (*an offer*); **3 sich zurückziehen** to withdraw, to retire.

zurzeit △ *adverb* at the moment.

Zusage *die* (PL *die* **Zusagen**) acceptance.

zusammen *adverb* **1** together; **zusammen sein** to be together; **2** altogether.

Zusammenarbeit *die* co-operation.

zusammenarbeiten *verb* (PERF **hat zusammengearbeitet**) to co-operate.

zusammenbleiben ✧ *verb* (IMPERF **blieb zusammen**, PERF **ist zusammengeblieben**) to stay together.

zusammenbrechen ✧ *verb* (PRES **bricht zusammen**, IMPERF **brach zusammen**, PERF **ist zusammengebrochen**) to collapse.

zusammenfassen *verb* (PERF **hat zusammengefasst** △) to summarize.

Zusammenfassung *die* (PL *die* **Zusammenfassungen**) summary.

zusammenhalten ✧ *verb* (PRES **hält zusammen**, IMPERF **hielt zusammen**, PERF **hat zusammengehalten**) **1** to hold together; **2** to keep together; **3 die**

Kinder haben zusammengehalten the children stuck together.

Zusammenhang *der* (PL *die* **Zusammenhänge**) **1** context; **2** connection.

zusammenkommen ✧ *verb* (IMPERF **kam zusammen**, PERF **ist zusammengekommen**) **1** to meet; **2** to accumulate.

Zusammenkunft *die* (PL *die* **Zusammenkünfte**) meeting.

zusammenlegen *verb* (PERF **hat zusammengelegt**) **1** to put together; **2** to fold up; **3** to club together.

zusammennehmen ✧ *verb* (PRES **nimmt zusammen**, IMPERF **nahm zusammen**, PERF **hat zusammengenommen**) **1** to gather up; **2** to summon up, to collect; **3 sich zusammennehmen** to pull yourself together.

zusammenpassen *verb* (PERF **hat zusammengepasst** △) **1** to match; **2** to be well matched (*of people*); **3** to fit together.

Zusammensein *das* get-together.

Zusammenstoß *der* (PL *die* **Zusammenstöße**) collision, crash.

zusammenstoßen ✧ *verb* (PRES **stößt zusammen**, IMPERF **stieß zusammen**, PERF **ist zusammengestoßen**) to collide, to crash.

zusammenzählen *verb* (PERF **hat zusammengezählt**) to add up.

△ NEW SPELLING: *See page xii*

zusätzlich *adjective* additional, extra.
adverb in addition, extra.

zuschauen *verb* (PERF **hat zugeschaut**) to watch.

Zuschauer *der* (PL *die* **Zuschauer**) 1 spectator; 2 viewer; 3 **die Zuschauer** the audience.

Zuschauerin *die* (PL *die* **Zuschauerinnen**) 1 spectator; 2 viewer.

Zuschlag *der* (PL *die* **Zuschläge**) 1 surcharge; 2 supplement.

Zuschuss △ *der* (PL *die* **Zuschüsse**) 1 contribution; 2 grant.

zusehen ✧ *verb* (PRES **sieht zu**, IMPERF **sah zu**, PERF **hat zugesehen**) 1 to watch; 2 **zusehen, dass ...** to see (to it) that ...

zusein SEE **zu**.

zusenden *verb* (PERF **hat zugesendet**) to send; **jemandem etwas zusenden** to send something to somebody.

Zustand *der* (PL *die* **Zustände**) 1 condition; 2 state.

zustande *adverb* **zustande bringen** to bring about; **zustande kommen** to come about.

zuständig *adjective* responsible.

Zustellung *die* (PL *die* **Zustellungen**) delivery.

zustimmen *verb* (PERF **hat zugestimmt**) to agree.

Zustimmung *die* (PL *die*

Zustimmungen) 1 agreement; 2 approval.

zustoßen ✧ *verb* (PRES **stößt zu**, IMPERF **stieß zu**, PERF **ist zugestoßen**) to happen.

Zutat *die* (PL *die* **Zutaten**) ingredient.

zutreffen ✧ *verb* (PRES **trifft zu**, IMPERF **traf zu**, PERF **hat zugetroffen**) **auf etwas zutreffen** to apply to something.

Zutritt *der* entry; **Zutritt haben** to have access.

zuverlässig *adjective* reliable.

zuviel SEE **viel**.

zuvor *adverb* 1 before; **der Tag zuvor** the day before; 2 first.

zuwenig SEE **wenig**.

zuzahlen *verb* (PERF **hat zugezahlt**) to pay extra.

zuziehen ✧ *verb* (IMPERF **zog zu**, PERF **hat zugezogen**) 1 to pull tight; 2 to draw (*curtains*); 3 to call in (*an expert etc.*); 4 (PERF **ist zugezogen**) to move into an area; 5 **sich eine Verletzung zuziehen** to sustain an injury; **sich eine Erkältung zuziehen** to catch a cold.

zuzüglich *preposition* ←(+GEN) plus.

zwang SEE **zwingen**.

Zwang *der* (PL *die* **Zwänge**) 1 compulsion; 2 urge; 3 obligation.

zwängen *verb* (PERF **hat gezwängt**) to squeeze.

zwanglos *adjective* casual, informal.

✧ IRREGULAR VERB: *See the verb table in the centre of the dictionary*

zwar *adverb* **1** admittedly; **2 ich war zwar dabei, habe aber nichts gesehen** I was there, but I didn't see anything; **3 und zwar** to be exact.

Zweck *der* (PL *die* **Zwecke**)
1 purpose; **2** point; **es hat keinen Zweck** there's no point.

zwecklos *adjective* pointless.

zwei *number* two.

zweideutig *adjective* ambiguous.

zweifach *adjective* twice.

Zweifel *der* (PL *die* **Zweifel**) doubt.

zweifelhaft *adjective* **1** doubtful; **2** dubious.

zweifellos *adverb* undoubtedly.

zweifeln *verb* (PERF **hat gezweifelt**) to doubt; **an etwas zweifeln** to doubt something.

Zweig *der* (PL *die* **Zweige**) branch.

zweihundert *number* two hundred.

zweimal *adverb* twice.

zweisprachig *adjective* bilingual.

zweit *adverb* **zu zweit** in twos; **wir sind zu zweit** there are two of us.

zweite SEE **zweiter**.

zweitens *adverb* secondly.

zweiter, zweite, zweites *adjective* second; **Mario kam als Zweiter** Mario was the second to arrive.

Zwerg *der* (PL *die* **Zwerge**) dwarf.

Zwiebel *die* (PL *die* **Zwiebeln**)
1 onion; **2** bulb.

Zwilling *der* (PL *die* **Zwillinge**)
1 twin; **2 Zwillinge** Gemini; **Markus ist Zwilling** Markus is Gemini.

zwingen ◇ *verb* (IMPERF **zwang**, PERF **hat gezwungen**) **1** to force; **2 sich zwingen** to force yourself.

zwinkern *verb* (PERF **hat gezwinkert**) to wink.

zwischen *preposition* ←(+DAT, *or* +ACC *with movement towards a place*)
1 between; **2** among (*a crowd*).

zwischendurch *adverb* **1** in between; **2** now and again.

Zwischenfall *der* (PL *die* **Zwischenfälle**) incident.

Zwischenlandung *die* (PL *die* **Zwischenlandungen**) stop-over.

Zwischenraum *der* (PL *die* **Zwischenräume**) gap, space.

Zwischenzeit *die* **in der Zwischenzeit** in the meantime.

zwo *number* two.

zwölf *number* twelve.

zwoter, zwote, zwotes *adjective* second.

△ NEW SPELLING: *See page xii*

VERB TABLES
AND FORMS

On the following pages you will find forms for
a regular German verb **machen** followed by
the forms for a reflexive verb **sich waschen**
and then the forms for the twelve most
important irregular verbs in alphabetical order:
**dürfen, essen, fahren, gehen, haben,
kommen, können, müssen, sein, sollen,
werden, wissen.**

After these are given the main forms for other
irregular verbs. Note that the forms for
separable verbs such as **aufstehen** are not
given as they can be looked up under the
base form (**stehen**).

machen
to do *or* to make

Imperative

mach!
macht!
machen Sie!

Past participle

hat gemacht

Present

ich mache
du machst
er* macht
wir machen
ihr macht
sie machen

Present subjunctive

ich mache
du machest
er mache
wir machen
ihr machet
sie machen

Perfect

ich habe gemacht
du hast gemacht
er hat gemacht
wir haben gemacht
ihr habt gemacht
sie haben gemacht

Imperfect

ich machte
du machtest
er machte
wir machten
ihr machtet
sie machten

Future

ich werde machen
du wirst machen
er wird machen
wir werden machen
ihr werdet machen
sie werden machen

Conditional

ich würde machen
du würdest machen
er würde machen
wir würden machen
ihr würdet machen
sie würden machen

* er *should be read as* er/sie/es

2

sich waschen
to wash (oneself)

Imperative

wasch dich!
wascht euch!
waschen Sie sich!

Past participle

hat sich
gewaschen

Present

ich wasche mich
du wäschst dich
er wäscht sich
wir waschen uns
ihr wascht euch
sie waschen sich

Perfect

ich habe mich gewaschen
du hast dich gewaschen
er hat sich gewaschen
wir haben uns gewaschen
ihr habt euch gewaschen
sie haben sich gewaschen

Future

ich werde mich waschen
du wirst dich waschen
er wird sich waschen
wir werden uns waschen
ihr werdet euch waschen
sie werden sich waschen

Present subjunctive

ich wasche mich
du waschest dich
er wasche sich
wir waschen uns
ihr waschet euch
sie waschen sich

Imperfect

ich wusch mich
du wuschst dich
er wusch sich
wir wuschen uns
ihr wuscht euch
sie wuschen sich

Conditional

ich würde mich waschen
du würdest dich waschen
er würde sich waschen
wir würden uns waschen
ihr würdet euch waschen
sie würden sich waschen

Note: New German spellings are
used throughout this verb table.
For a general note on the
German spelling reform see
page xii.

dürfen
to be allowed

Imperative

—

Past participle

hat gedurft

Present
ich darf
du darfst
er darf
wir dürfen
ihr dürft
sie dürfen

Perfect
ich habe gedurft
du hast gedurft
er hat gedurft
wir haben gedurft
ihr habt gedurft
sie haben gedurft

Future
ich werde dürfen
du wirst dürfen
er wird dürfen
wir werden dürfen
ihr werdet dürfen
sie werden dürfen

Present subjunctive
ich dürfe
du dürfest
er dürfe
wir dürfen
ihr dürfet
sie dürfen

Imperfect
ich durfte
du durftest
er durfte
wir durften
ihr durftet
sie durften

Conditional
ich würde dürfen
du würdest dürfen
er würde dürfen
wir würden dürfen
ihr würdet dürfen
sie würden dürfen

Imperative	Past participle	**essen**
iss!	hat gegessen	to eat
esst!		
essen Sie!		

Present
ich esse
du isst
er isst
wir essen
ihr esst
sie essen

Perfect
ich habe gegessen
du hast gegessen
er hat gegessen
wir haben gegessen
ihr habt gegessen
sie haben gegessen

Future
ich werde essen
du wirst essen
er wird essen
wir werden essen
ihr werdet essen
sie werden essen

Present subjunctive
ich esse
du essest
er esse
wir essen
ihr esset
sie essen

Imperfect
ich aß
du aßest
er aß
wir aßen
ihr aßt
sie aßen

Conditional
ich würde essen
du würdest essen
er würde essen
wir würden essen
ihr würdet essen
sie würden essen

fahren
to drive *or* to go

Imperative	Past participle
fahr!	ist gefahren
fahrt!	
fahren Sie!	

Present

ich fahre
du fährst
er fährt
wir fahren
ihr fahrt
sie fahren

Perfect

ich bin gefahren
du bist gefahren
er ist gefahren
wir sind gefahren
ihr seid gefahren
sie sind gefahren

Future

ich werde fahren
du wirst fahren
er wird fahren
wir werden fahren
ihr werdet fahren
sie werden fahren

Present subjunctive

ich fahre
du fahrest
er fahre
wir fahren
ihr fahret
sie fahren

Imperfect

ich fuhr
du fuhrst
er fuhr
wir fuhren
ihr fuhrt
sie fuhren

Conditional

ich würde fahren
du würdest fahren
er würde fahren
wir würden fahren
ihr würdet fahren
sie würden fahren

Imperative	**Past participle**	**gehen**
geh!	ist gegangen	to go
geht!		
gehen Sie!		

Present

ich gehe
du gehst
er geht
wir gehen
ihr geht
sie gehen

Present subjunctive

ich gehe
du gehest
er gehe
wir gehen
ihr gehet
sie gehen

Perfect

ich bin gegangen
du bist gegangen
er ist gegangen
wir sind gegangen
ihr seid gegangen
sie sind gegangen

Imperfect

ich ging
du gingst
er ging
wir gingen
ihr gingt
sie gingen

Future

ich werde gehen
du wirst gehen
er wird gehen
wir werden gehen
ihr werdet gehen
sie werden gehen

Conditional

ich würde gehen
du würdest gehen
er würde gehen
wir würden gehen
ihr würdet gehen
sie würden gehen

haben
to have

Imperative	Past participle
hab!	hat gehabt
habt!	
haben Sie!	

Present

ich habe
du hast
er hat
wir haben
ihr habt
sie haben

Perfect

ich habe gehabt
du hast gehabt
er hat gehabt
wir haben gehabt
ihr habt gehabt
sie haben gehabt

Future

ich werde haben
du wirst haben
er wird haben
wir werden haben
ihr werdet haben
sie werden haben

Present subjunctive

ich habe
du habest
er habe
wir haben
ihr habet
sie haben

Imperfect

ich hatte
du hattest
er hatte
wir hatten
ihr hattet
sie hatten

Imperfect subjunctive

ich hätte
du hättest
er hätte
wir hätten
ihr hättet
sie hätten

Conditional

ich würde haben
du würdest haben
er würde haben
wir würden haben
ihr würdet haben
sie würden haben

8

Imperative	Past participle	**kommen**
komm!	ist gekommen	to come
kommt!		
kommen Sie!		

Present

ich komme
du kommst
er kommt
wir kommen
ihr kommt
sie kommen

Present subjunctive

ich komme
du kommest
er komme
wir kommen
ihr kommet
sie kommen

Perfect

ich bin gekommen
du bist gekommen
er ist gekommen
wir sind gekommen
ihr seid gekommen
sie sind gekommen

Imperfect

ich kam
du kamst
er kam
wir kamen
ihr kamt
sie kamen

Future

ich werde kommen
du wirst kommen
er wird kommen
wir werden kommen
ihr werdet kommen
sie werden kommen

Conditional

ich würde kommen
du würdest kommen
er würde kommen
wir würden kommen
ihr würdet kommen
sie würden kommen

können
can *or* to be able to

Imperative

—

Past participle

hat gekonnt *or*
hätte können

Present

ich kann
du kannst
er kann
wir können
ihr könnt
sie können

Present subjunctive

ich könne
du könnest
er könne
wir können
ihr könnet
sie können

Perfect

ich habe gekonnt
du hast gekonnt
er hat gekonnt
wir haben gekonnt
ihr habt gekonnt
sie haben gekonnt

Imperfect

ich konnte
du konntest
er konnte
wir konnten
ihr konntet
sie konnten

Future

ich werde können
du wirst können
er wird können
wir werden können
ihr werdet können
sie werden können

Imperfect subjunctive

ich könnte
du könntest
er könnte
wir könnten
ihr könntet
sie könnten

Conditional

ich würde können
du würdest können
er würde können
wir würden können
ihr würdet können
sie würden können

Imperative	Past participle	**müssen**
—	hat gemusst *or* hätte müssen	must *or* to have to

Present

ich muss
du musst
er muss
wir müssen
ihr müsst
sie müssen

Perfect

ich habe gemusst
du hast gemusst
er hat gemusst
wir haben gemusst
ihr habt gemusst
sie haben gemusst

Future

ich werde müssen
du wirst müssen
er wird müssen
wir werden müssen
ihr werdet müssen
sie werden müssen

Present subjunctive

ich müsse
du müssest
er müsse
wir müssen
ihr müsset
sie müssen

Imperfect

ich musste
du musstest
er musste
wir mussten
ihr musstet
sie mussten

Imperfect subjunctive

ich müsste
du müsstest
er müsste
wir müssten
ihr müsstet
sie müssten

Conditional

ich würde müssen
du würdest müssen
er würde müssen
wir würden müssen
ihr würdet müssen
sie würden müssen

sein
to be

Imperative

sei!
seid!
seien Sie!

Past participle

ist gewesen

Present

ich bin
du bist
er ist
wir sind
ihr seid
sie sind

Perfect

ich bin gewesen
du bist gewesen
er ist gewesen
wir sind gewesen
ihr seid gewesen
sie sind gewesen

Future

ich werde sein
du wirst sein
er wird sein
wir werden sein
ihr werdet sein
sie werden sein

Present subjunctive

ich sei
du sei(e)st
er sei
wir seien
ihr seiet
sie seien

Imperfect

ich war
du warst
er war
wir waren
ihr wart
sie waren

Imperfect subjunctive

ich wäre
du wär(e)st
er wäre
wir wären
ihr wär(e)t
sie wären

Conditional

ich würde sein
du würdest sein
er würde sein
wir würden sein
ihr würdet sein
sie würden sein

Imperative	Past participle
—	hat gesollt

sollen
should

Present

ich soll
du sollst
er soll
wir sollen
ihr sollt
sie sollen

Perfect

ich habe gesollt
du hast gesollt
er hat gesollt
wir haben gesollt
ihr habt gesollt
sie haben gesollt

Future

ich werde sollen
du wirst sollen
er wird sollen
wir werden sollen
ihr werdet sollen
sie werden sollen

Present subjunctive

ich solle
du sollest
er solle
wir sollen
ihr sollet
sie sollen

Imperfect

ich sollte
du solltest
er sollte
wir sollten
ihr solltet
sie sollten

Imperfect subjunctive

ich sollte
du solltest
er sollte
wir sollten
ihr solltet
sie sollten

Conditional

ich würde sollen
du würdest sollen
er würde sollen
wir würden sollen
ihr würdet sollen
sie würden sollen

werden
to become *or* to get

Imperative
werde!
werdet!
werden Sie!

Past participle
ist geworden

Present
ich werde
du wirst
er wird
wir werden
ihr werdet
sie werden

Present subjunctive
ich werde
du werdest
er werde
wir werden
ihr werdet
sie werden

Perfect
ich bin geworden
du bist geworden
er ist geworden
wir sind geworden
ihr seid geworden
sie sind geworden

Imperfect
ich wurde
du wurdest
er wurde
wir wurden
ihr wurdet
sie wurden

Future
ich werde werden
du wirst werden
er wird werden
wir werden werden
ihr werdet werden
sie werden werden

Conditional
ich würde werden
du würdest werden
er würde werden
wir würden werden
ihr würdet werden
sie würden werden

Imperative	Past participle	**wissen**
wisse!	hat gewusst	to know
wisst!		
wissen Sie!		

Present

ich weiß
du weißt
er weiß
wir wissen
ihr wisst
sie wissen

Perfect

ich habe gewusst
du hast gewusst
er hat gewusst
wir haben gewusst
ihr habt gewusst
sie haben gewusst

Future

ich werde wissen
du wirst wissen
er wird wissen
wir werden wissen
ihr werdet wissen
sie werden wissen

Present subjunctive

ich wisse
du wissest
er wisse
wir wissen
ihr wisset
sie wissen

Imperfect

ich wusste
du wusstest
er wusste
wir wussten
ihr wusstet
sie wussten

Conditional

ich würde wissen
du würdest wissen
er würde wissen
wir würden wissen
ihr würdet wissen
sie würden wissen

German irregular verb forms

This list shows the main forms of other irregular verbs.

Infinitive	Present ich, du, er/sie/es	Imperfect er/sie/es	Perfect er/sie/es
bekommen	bekomme, bekommst, bekommt	bekam	hat bekommen
bergen	berge, birgst, birgt	barg	hat geborgen
besitzen	besitze, besitzst, besitzt	besaß	hat besessen
betrügen	betrüge, betrügst, betrügt	betrog	hat betrogen
biegen	biege, biegst, biegt	bog	hat *or* ist gebogen
bieten	biete, bietest, bietet	bot	hat geboten
binden	binde, bindest, bindet	band	hat gebunden
bitten	bitte, bittest, bittet	bat	hat gebeten
blasen	blase, bläst, bläst	blies	hat geblasen
bleiben	bleibe, bleibst, bleibt	blieb	ist geblieben
braten	brate, brätst, brät	briet	hat gebraten
brechen	breche, brichst, bricht	brach	hat *or* ist gebrochen
brennen	brenne, brennst, brennt	brannte	hat gebrannt
bringen	bringe, bringst, bringt	brachte	hat gebracht
denken	denke, denkst, denkt	dachte	hat gedacht
dürfen	darf, darfst, darf	durfte	hat gedurft
einladen	lade ein, lädst ein, lädt ein	lud ein	hat eingeladen
empfangen	empfange, empfängst, empfängt	empfing	hat empfangen
empfehlen	empfehle, empfiehlst, empfiehlt	empfahl	hat empfohlen
entscheiden	entscheide, entscheidest, entscheidet	entschied	hat entschieden

Infinitive	Present ich, du, er/sie/es	Imperfect er/sie/es	Perfect er/sie/es
erfahren	erfahre, erfährst, erfährt	erfuhr	hat erfahren
erfinden	erfinde, erfindest, erfindet	erfand	hat erfunden
erschrecken	erschrecke, erschrickst, erschrickt	erschrak	ist erschrocken
ertrinken	ertrinke, ertrinkst, ertrinkt	ertrank	ist ertrunken
essen	esse, isst, isst	aß	hat gegessen
fahren	fahre, fährst, fährt	fuhr	ist *or* hat gefahren
fallen	falle, fällst, fällt	fiel	ist gefallen
fangen	fange, fängst, fängt	fing	hat gefangen
fechten	fechte, fichtst, ficht	focht	hat gefochten
finden	finde, findest, findet	fand	hat gefunden
fliegen	fliege, fliegst, fliegt	flog	ist *or* hat geflogen
fliehen	fliehe, fliehst, flieht	floh	ist geflohen
fließen	fließe, fließt, fließt	floss	ist geflossen
fressen	fresse, frisst, frisst	fraß	hat gefressen
frieren	friere, frierst, friert	fror	hat *or* ist gefroren
geben	gebe, gibst, gibt	gab	hat gegeben
gefallen	gefalle, gefällst, gefällt	gefiel	hat gefallen
gehen	gehe, gehst, geht	ging	ist gegangen
gelingen	es gelingt mir/dir/ihm/ihr/ihm	gelang	ist gelungen
gelten	gelte, giltst, gilt	galt	hat gegolten
genießen	genieße, genießt, genießt	genoss	hat genossen
geraten	gerate, gerätst, gerät	geriet	ist geraten
geschehen	es geschieht	geschah	ist geschehen
gewinnen	gewinne, gewinnst, gewinnt	gewann	hat gewonnen
gießen	gieße, gießt, gießt	goss	hat gegossen
gleichen	gleiche, gleichst, gleicht	glich	hat geglichen
graben	grabe, gräbst, gräbt	grub	hat gegraben
greifen	greife, greifst, greift	griff	hat gegriffen

Infinitive	Present ich, du, er/sie/es	Imperfect er/sie/es	Perfect er/sie/es
haben	habe, hast, hat	hatte	hat gehabt
halten	halte, hältst, hält	hielt	hat gehalten
hängen	hänge, hängst, hängt	hing	hat gehangen
heben	hebe, hebst, hebt	hob	hat gehoben
heißen	heiße, heißt, heißt	hieß	hat geheißen
helfen	helfe, hilfst, hilft	half	hat geholfen
hinweisen	weise hin, weist hin, weist hin	wies hin	hat hingewiesen
kennen	kenne, kennst, kennt	kannte	hat gekannt
klingen	klinge, klingst, klingt	klang	hat geklungen
kneifen	kneife, kneifst, kneift	kniff	hat gekniffen
kommen	komme, kommst, kommt	kam	ist gekommen
können	kann, kannst, kann	konnte	hat gekonnt
kriechen	krieche, kriechst, kriecht	kroch	ist gekrochen
lassen	lasse, lässt, lässt	ließ	hat gelassen
laufen	laufe, läufst, läuft	lief	ist gelaufen
leiden	leide, leidest, leidet	litt	hat gelitten
leihen	leihe, leihst, leiht	lieh	hat geliehen
lesen	lese, liest, liest	las	hat gelesen
liegen	liege, liegst, liegt	lag	hat gelegen
lügen	lüge, lügst, lügt	log	hat gelogen
mahlen	mahle, mahlst, mahlt	mahlte	hat gemahlen
meiden	meide, meidest, meidet	mied	hat gemieden
messen	messe, mißt, mißt	maß	hat gemessen
misslingen Δ	misslinge, misslingst, misslingt	misslang	ist misslungen
mögen	mag, magst, mag	mochte	hat gemocht
müssen	muss, musst, muss	musste	hat gemusst

Infinitive	Present ich, du, er/sie/es	Imperfect er/sie/es	Perfect er/sie/es
nehmen	nehme, nimmst, nimmt	nahm	hat genommen
nennen	nenne, nennst, nennt	nannte	hat genannt
pfeifen	pfeife, pfeifst, pfeift	pfiff	hat gepfiffen
raten	rate, rätst, rät	riet	hat geraten
reiben	reibe, reibst, reibt	rieb	hat gerieben
reißen	reiße, reißt, reißt	riss	hat or ist gerissen
reiten	reite, reitest, reitet	ritt	hat or ist geritten
rennen	renne, rennst, rennt	rannte	ist gerannt
riechen	rieche, riechst, riecht	roch	hat gerochen
rufen	rufe, rufst, ruft	rief	hat gerufen
saufen	saufe, säufst, säuft	soff	hat gesoffen
schaffen	schaffe, schaffst, schafft	schuf	hat geschaffen
scheiden	scheide, scheidest, scheidet	schied	hat or ist geschieden
scheinen	scheine, scheinst, scheint	schien	hat geschienen
schieben	schiebe, schiebst, schiebt	schob	hat geschoben
schießen	schieße, schießt, schießt	schoss	hat or ist geschossen
schlafen	schlafe, schläfst, schläft	schlief	hat geschlafen
schlagen	schlage, schlägst, schlägt	schlug	hat geschlagen
schleichen	schleiche, schleichst, schleicht	schlich	ist geschlichen
schließen	schließe, schließt, schließt	schloss	hat geschlossen
schmeißen	schmeiße, schmeißt, schmeißt	schmiss	hat geschmissen
schmelzen	schmelze, schmilzt, schmilzt	schmolz	ist geschmolzen
schneiden	schneide, schneidest, schneidet	schnitt	hat geschnitten

Infinitive	Present ich, du, er/sie/es	Imperfect er/sie/es	Perfect er/sie/es
schreiben	schreibe, schreibst, schreibt	schrieb	hat geschrieben
schreien	schreie, schreist, schreit	schrie	hat geschrien
schweigen	schweige, schweigst, schweigt	schwieg	hat geschwiegen
schwimmen	schwimme, schwimmst, schwimmt	schwamm	ist or hat geschwommen
schwören	schwöre, schwörst, schwört	schwor	hat geschworen
sehen	sehe, siehst, sieht	sah	hat gesehen
sein	bin, bist, ist	war	ist gewesen
singen	singe, singst, singt	sang	hat gesungen
sinken	sinke, sinkst, sinkt	sank	ist gesunken
sitzen	sitze, sitzt, sitzt	saß	hat gesessen
sollen	soll, sollst, soll	sollte	hat gesollt
spinnen	spinne, spinnst, spinnt	spann	hat gesponnen
sprechen	spreche, sprichst, spricht	sprach	hat gesprochen
springen	springe, springst, springt	sprang	ist gesprungen
stechen	steche, stichst, sticht	stach	hat gestochen
stehen	stehe, stehst, steht	stand	hat gestanden
stehlen	stehle, stiehlst, stiehlt	stahl	hat gestohlen
steigen	steige, steigst, steigt	stieg	ist gestiegen
sterben	sterbe, stirbst, stirbt	starb	ist gestorben
stinken	stinke, stinkst, stinkt	stank	hat gestunken
stoßen	stoße, stößt, stößt	stieß	hat or ist gestoßen
streichen	streiche, streichst, streicht	strich	hat gestrichen
streiten	streite, streitest, streitet	stritt	hat gestritten
tragen	trage, trägst, trägt	trug	hat getragen
treffen	treffe, triffst, trifft	traf	hat getroffen
treiben	treibe, treibst, treibt	trieb	hat getrieben
treten	trete, trittst, tritt	trat	hat or ist getreten
trinken	trinke, trinkst, trinkt	trank	hat getrunken
tun	tue, tust, tut	tat	hat getan

Infinitive	Present ich, du, er/sie/es	Imperfect er/sie/es	Perfect er/sie/es
überweisen	überweise, überweist, überweist	überwies	hat überwiesen
umziehen	ziehe um, ziehst um, zieht um	zog um	ist *or* hat umgezogen
verbieten	verbiete, verbietest, verbietet	verbot	hat verboten
verderben	verderbe, verdirbst, verdirbt	verdarb	hat *or* ist verdorben
vergessen	vergesse, vergißt, vergißt	vergaß	hat vergessen
verlieren	verliere, verlierst, verliert	verlor	hat verloren
verschwinden	verschwinde, verschwindest, verschwindet	verschwand	ist verschwunden
verstehen	verstehe, verstehst, versteht	verstand	hat verstanden
verzeihen	verzeihe, verzeihst, verzeiht	verzieh	hat verziehen
wachsen	wachse, wächst, wächst	wuchs	ist gewachsen
waschen	wasche, wäscht, wäscht	wusch	hat gewaschen
werben	werbe, wirbst, wirbt	warb	hat geworben
werden	werde, wirst, wird	wurde	ist geworden
werfen	werfe, wirfst, wirft	warf	hat geworfen
wiegen	wiege, wiegst, wiegt	wog	hat gewogen
wissen	weiß, weißt, weiß	wusste	hat gewusst
wollen	will, willst, will	wollte	hat gewollt
ziehen	ziehe, ziehst, zieht	zog	hat *or* ist gezogen
zwingen	zwinge, zwingst, zwingt	zwang	hat gezwungen

Note: New German spellings are used throughout this verb table. For a general note on the German spelling reform see page xii.

A a

a *indefinite article* 1 (*before a noun which is masculine in German*) ein; **a tree** ein Baum; 2 (*before a noun which is feminine in German*) eine; **a story** eine Geschichte; 3 (*before a noun which is neuter in German*) ein; **a dress** ein Kleid; 4 **not a** kein; **the party was not a success** die Party war kein Erfolg; **he didn't say a word** er hat kein Wort gesagt; 5 **six marks a kilo** sechs Mark das Kilo; 6 **fifty kilometres an hour** fünfzig Stundenkilometer; 7 **three times a day** dreimal täglich.

abandon *verb* 1 aufgeben ✧ SEP; **they abandoned the plan** sie gaben den Plan auf; 2 verlassen ✧; **they abandoned the city** sie verließen die Stadt.

abbey *noun* Abtei *die* (PL *die* Abteien).

abbreviation *noun* Abkürzung *die* (PL *die* Abkürzungen).

ability *noun* Fähigkeit *die* (PL *die* Fähigkeiten); **to have the ability to do something** etwas tun können.

about *preposition* 1 über (+ACC); **a film about space** ein Film über den Weltraum; **to talk about something/somebody** über etwas/jemanden reden; **what is she talking about?** worüber redet sie?; 2 um (+ACC); **to be about something**

um etwas gehen; **what's it about?** worum geht es?; 3 **to know about something** von etwas ←(DAT) wissen; **she didn't know about the party** sie wusste nichts von der Party; **he knows nothing about it** er weiß nichts davon; 4 **to think about something/somebody** an etwas/jemanden ←(ACC) denken; **I'm thinking about you** ich denke an dich.
adverb 1 (*approximately*) ungefähr; **about sixty people** ungefähr sechzig Leute; **in about a week** in ungefähr einer Woche; 2 (*when talking about time*) gegen; **about three o'clock** gegen drei Uhr; 3 **to be about to do something** gerade etwas tun wollen; **I was (just) about to leave** ich wollte gerade gehen.

above *preposition* 1 über (+DAT); **the lamp above the table** die Lampe über dem Tisch; 2 **above all** vor allem.

abroad *adverb* im Ausland; **to live abroad** im Ausland leben; **to go abroad** ins Ausland fahren.

absent *adjective* abwesend; **to be absent from school** in der Schule fehlen.

absent-minded *adjective* zerstreut.

absolute *adjective* absolut; **an absolute disaster** eine absolute Katastrophe.

absolutely *adverb* 1 wirklich; **it's absolutely dreadful** das ist wirklich furchtbar; 2 völlig; **you're**

△ NEW SPELLING: *See page xii*

absolutely right du hast völlig recht.

abuse *noun* 1 Missbrauch △ *der*; **drug abuse** Missbrauch von Drogen; 2 (*insults*) Beschimpfungen (*plural*). *verb* 1 **to abuse somebody** jemanden missbrauchen; 2 (*to insult*) beschimpfen.

accelerator *noun* Gaspedal *das* (PL *die* Gaspedale).

accent *noun* Akzent *der* (PL *die* Akzente); **to speak with a German accent** mit deutschem Akzent sprechen.

accept *verb* annehmen ✧ SEP; **he accepted the invitation** er nahm die Einladung an.

acceptable *adjective* annehmbar.

access *noun* Zugang *der*. *verb* **to access data** auf Daten zugreifen.

accessory *noun* 1 Zubehörteil *das*; **accessories** Zubehör *das*; 2 **accessories** (*fashion items*) Accessoires (*plural*).

accident *noun* 1 Unfall *der* (PL *die* Unfälle); **to have an accident** einen Unfall haben; **road accident** der Verkehrsunfall; **car accident** der Autounfall; 2 Zufall *der* (PL *die* Zufälle); **by accident** zufällig; **I found it by accident** ich habe es zufällig gefunden.

accidental *adjective* zufällig; **an accidental discovery** eine zufällige Entdeckung.

accidentally *adverb* 1 (*without meaning to*) versehentlich; **I accidentally threw it away** ich habe es versehentlich weggeworfen; 2 (*by chance*) zufällig; **I accidentally discovered that …** ich habe zufällig herausgefunden, dass …

accommodation *noun* Unterkunft *die*; **accommodation is free** Unterkunft ist kostenlos; **I'm looking for accommodation** (*when looking for a room*) ich suche ein Zimmer.

according *in phrase* **according to** laut (+DAT); **according to Sophie** laut Sophie.

accordion *noun* Akkordeon *das* (PL *die* Akkordeons).

account *noun* 1 (*in a bank, shop, or post office*) Konto *das* (PL *die* Konten); **bank account** *das* Bankkonto; **to open an account** ein Konto eröffnen; **I have fifty pounds in my account** ich habe fünfzig Pfund auf meinem Konto; 2 (*an explanation*) Darstellung *die* (PL *die* Darstellungen); **I want to hear his account of what happened** ich möchte seine Darstellung der Ereignisse hören; 3 **on account of** wegen (+GEN); 4 **to take something into account** etwas berücksichtigen.

accountant *noun* Buchhalter *der* (PL *die* Buchhalter), Buchhalterin *die* (PL *die* Buchhalterinnen); **she's an accountant** sie ist Buchhalterin.

accurate *adjective* genau.

accurately *adverb* genau.

✧ IRREGULAR VERB: *See the verb table in the centre of the dictionary*

accuse *verb* beschuldigen; **she accused me of stealing her pen** sie beschuldigte mich, ihren Kugelschreiber gestohlen zu haben.

ace *noun* Ass △ *das* (PL die Asse); **the ace of hearts** das Herzass. *adjective* klasse (*informal*); **he's an ace drummer** er spielt klasse Schlagzeug.

achieve *verb* 1 leisten; **she's achieved a great deal** sie hat eine Menge geleistet; 2 erreichen (*an aim*); **he achieved what he wanted** er hat erreicht, was er wollte.

achievement *noun* Leistung *die* (PL die Leistungen); **it's a great achievement** das ist eine große Leistung.

acid *noun* Säure *die* (PL die Säuren).

acne *noun* Akne *die*.

across *preposition* 1 (*over to the other side of*) über (+ACC); **to run across the road** über die Straße laufen; **we walked across the park** wir sind durch den Park gegangen; 2 (*on the other side of*) auf der anderen Seite (+GEN); **he lives across the river** er wohnt auf der anderen Seite des Flusses; 3 **they live across the street** sie wohnen gegenüber.

act *noun* (*deed*) Tat *die* (PL die Taten). *verb* (*in a play or film*) spielen; **to act the part of the hero** die Rolle des Helden spielen.

action *noun* 1 Handlung *die* (PL die Handlungen); 2 **to take action** etwas unternehmen.

active *adjective* aktiv.

activity *noun* Aktivität *die* (PL die Aktivitäten).

actor *noun* Schauspieler *der* (PL die Schauspieler).

actress *noun* Schauspielerin *die* (PL die Schauspielerinnen).

actual *adjective* **what were his actual words?** was genau hat er gesagt?; **in actual fact** eigentlich.

actually *adverb* 1 (*in fact, as it happens*) eigentlich; **actually, I've changed my mind** ich habe mich eigentlich anders entschlossen; 2 (*really and truly*) wirklich; **did she actually say that?** hat sie das wirklich gesagt?

ad *noun* 1 (*on TV*) Werbespot *der* (PL die Werbespots); 2 (*in a newspaper*) Anzeige *die* (PL die Anzeigen); **to put an ad in the paper** eine Anzeige in die Zeitung setzen; **the small ads** die Kleinanzeigen.

AD (*Anno Domini*) n.Chr. (*nach Christus*); **in 400 AD** 400 n.Chr.

adapt *verb* 1 **to adapt something** (*a book or film*) etwas bearbeiten; 2 **to adapt to** sich anpassen SEP (+DAT); **she's adapted to her new surroundings** sie hat sich der neuen Umgebung angepasst.

adaptor *noun* 1 Adapter *der* (PL die Adapter); 2 (*for two plugs*) Doppelstecker *der* (PL die Doppelstecker).

add *verb* 1 hinzufügen SEP; **to add an introduction to something** etwas ←(DAT) eine Einleitung hinzufügen; 2 dazugeben ◇ SEP; **add three eggs** geben Sie drei Eier dazu.
● **to add up** zusammenzählen SEP.

addict *noun* 1 (*drug addict*)
Süchtige *der/die* (PL *die* Süchtigen);
2 **she's a telly addict** sie ist
fernsehsüchtig; **he's a football
addict** er hat die Fußballsucht.

addicted *adjective* 1 **to become
addicted to drugs** drogensüchtig
werden; 2 **he's addicted to football**
Fußball ist bei ihm zur Sucht
geworden; 3 **I'm addicted to
sweets** ich bin nach Süßigkeiten
süchtig.

addition *noun* 1 (*adding up*)
Addition *die*; 2 **in addition**
außerdem; 3 **in addition to**
zusätzlich zu (+DAT).

additional *adjective* zusätzlich.

additive *noun* Zusatz *der* (PL *die*
Zusätze).

address *noun* Adresse *die* (PL *die*
Adressen); **do you know his
address?** weißt du seine Adresse?;
to change address die Adresse
wechseln.

address book *noun*
Adressbuch △ *das* (PL *die*
Adressbücher).

adhesive *noun* Klebstoff *der*.
adjective **adhesive tape** *der*
Klebstreifen.

adjective *noun* Adjektiv *das* (PL *die*
Adjektive).

adjust *verb* 1 **to adjust something**
etwas einstellen SEP; **he adjusted the
set** er stellte das Gerät ein; **to adjust
the distance** auf die richtige
Entfernung einstellen; 2 **to adjust**

to something sich an etwas ←(ACC)
gewöhnen.

adjustable *adjective* verstellbar.

administration *noun*
Verwaltung *die*.

admiration *noun*
Bewunderung *die*.

admire *verb* bewundern.

admission *noun* Eintritt *der*;
'admission free' 'Eintritt frei'.

admit *verb* 1 (*confess, concede*)
zugeben ✧ SEP; **she admits she lied**
sie gibt zu, dass sie gelogen hat;
2 (*allow to enter*) hereinlassen ✧
SEP; **to admit somebody to a
restaurant** jemanden in ein
Restaurant hereinlassen; 3 **to be
admitted to hospital** ins
Krankenhaus eingeliefert werden.

adolescence *noun* Jugend *die*.

adolescent *noun*
Jugendliche *der/die* (PL *die*
Jugendlichen).

adopt *verb* adoptieren.

adopted *adjective* adoptiert.

adoption *noun* Adoption *die* (PL *die*
Adoptionen).

adore *verb* lieben.

adult *noun* Erwachsene *der/die* (PL
die Erwachsenen).
adjective **the adult population**
Erwachsene (*plural*).

Adult Education *noun*
Erwachsenenbildung *die*.

advance *noun* Fortschritt *der* (PL
die Fortschritte); **advances in**

technology technologische Fortschritte.
verb 1 (*make progress*) Fortschritte machen; 2 (*move forward*) (*of a group or an army*) vorrücken SEP (PERF *sein*).

advanced *adjective* fortgeschritten (*student, age*).

advantage *noun* 1 Vorteil *der* (PL *die* Vorteile); **there are several advantages** es gibt verschiedene Vorteile; 2 **to take advantage of something** etwas ausnutzen SEP; **I always take advantage of the sales to buy myself some shoes** ich nutze immer den Ausverkauf aus, um mir Schuhe zu kaufen; 3 **to take advantage of somebody** (*unfairly*) jemanden ausnutzen SEP.

Advent *noun* Advent *der*.

adventure *noun* Abenteuer *das* (PL *die* Abenteuer).

adverb *noun* Adverb *das* (PL *die* Adverbien).

advert, advertisement *noun* 1 (*at the cinema or on television*) Werbespot *der* (PL *die* Werbespots); 2 (*in a newspaper for a job, article for sale, etc.*) Anzeige *die* (PL *die* Anzeigen); **she answered a job advertisement** sie meldete sich auf eine Stellenanzeige.

advertise *verb* **to advertise something in the newspaper** (*in the small ads*) etwas in der Zeitung inserieren; **I saw a bike advertised in the paper** ich habe ein Rad in der Zeitung inseriert gesehen.

advertising *noun* Werbung *die*.

advice *noun* Rat *der*; **to ask somebody's advice** jemanden um Rat fragen; **a piece of advice** ein Ratschlag.

advise *verb* raten ✧ (+DAT); **to advise somebody to do something** jemandem raten, etwas zu tun; **I advised him to stop** ich riet ihm anzuhalten; **I advised her not to buy the car** ich habe ihr geraten, das Auto nicht zu kaufen.

aerial *noun* Antenne *die* (PL *die* Antennen).

aerobics *noun* Aerobic *das*; **to do aerobics** Aerobic machen.

aeroplane *noun* Flugzeug *das* (PL *die* Flugzeuge).

aerosol *noun* **an aerosol can** eine Spraydose.

affair *noun* 1 Angelegenheit *die* (PL *die* Angelegenheiten); **international affairs** internationale Angelegenheiten; **current affairs** *die* Tagespolitik; 2 **love affair** *das* Liebesverhältnis.

affect *verb* beeinflussen.

affectionate *adjective* liebevoll.

afford *verb* **to be able to afford something** sich ←(DAT) etwas leisten können; **we can't afford to go out much** wir können es uns nicht leisten, oft auszugehen; **I can't afford a new bike** ich kann mir kein neues Rad leisten.

afraid *adjective* 1 **to be afraid of something** Angst vor etwas ←(DAT) haben; **she's afraid of dogs** sie hat vor Hunden Angst; 2 **I'm afraid I**

△ NEW SPELLING: *See page xii*

can't help you ich kann dir leider nicht helfen; **I'm afraid so** leider ja; **I'm afraid not** leider nicht.

Africa *noun* Afrika *das*; **to Africa** nach Afrika.

African *noun* Afrikaner *der* (PL *die* Afrikaner), Afrikanerin *die* (PL *die* Afrikanerinnen).
adjective afrikanisch; **she is African** sie ist Afrikanerin.

after *preposition, adverb* **1** nach (+DAT); **after 10 o'clock** nach zehn Uhr; **after lunch** nach dem Mittagessen; **after school** nach der Schule; **2 the day after tomorrow** übermorgen; **soon after** kurz danach; **3 to run after somebody** jemandem hinterherlaufen ◇ SEP.
conjunction nachdem; **after I'd finished my homework** nachdem ich meine Hausaufgaben gemacht hatte.

after all *adverb* schließlich; **after all, she's only six** sie ist schließlich erst sechs.

afternoon *noun* **1** Nachmittag *der* (PL *die* Nachmittage); **in the afternoon** am Nachmittag; **every afternoon** jeden Nachmittag; **2 this afternoon** heute Nachmittag; **on Sunday afternoon** am Sonntagnachmittag; **3 on Saturday afternoons** samstagsnachmittags; **at four o' clock in the afternoon** um vier Uhr nachmittags.

after-shave *noun* Rasierwasser *das*.

afterwards *adverb* danach; **shortly afterwards** kurz danach.

again *adverb* **1** wieder; **she's ill again** sie ist wieder krank; **2 I saw her again yesterday** ich habe sie gestern wieder gesehen; **3 never again!** nie wieder!; **again and again** immer wieder; **4** (*one more time*) noch einmal; **try again** versuche es noch einmal; **you should ask her again** du solltest sie noch einmal fragen.

against *preposition* gegen (+ACC); **against the wall** gegen die Wand; **to lean against the wall** sich gegen die Wand lehnen; **I'm against the idea** ich bin gegen die Idee.

age *noun* **1** Alter *das*; **at the age of fifty** im Alter von fünfzig; **she's the same age as me** sie ist genauso alt wie ich; **to be under age** minderjährig sein; **2 I haven't seen Johnny for ages** ich habe Johnny schon ewig nicht mehr gesehen; **I haven't been to London for ages** ich bin schon ewig nicht mehr in London gewesen.

agent *noun* Vertreter *der* (PL *die* Vertreter); **an estate agent** ein Immobilienmakler; **a travel agent's** ein Reisebüro.

aggressive *adjective* aggressiv.

ago *adverb* vor (+DAT); **an hour ago** vor einer Stunde; **three days ago** vor drei Tagen; **a long time ago** vor langer Zeit; **not long ago** vor kurzem; **how long ago was it?** wie lange ist das her?

agree *verb* **1 to agree with somebody** mit jemandem übereinstimmen SEP; **I agree with**

◇ IRREGULAR VERB: *See the verb table in the centre of the dictionary*

Laura ich stimme mit Laura überein; **2 I agree** ich bin der gleichen Meinung; **I don't agree** ich bin anderer Meinung; **3 to agree that ...** zugeben ◇ SEP, dass ...; **I agree that it's too late now** ich gebe zu, dass es jetzt zu spät ist; **4 to agree to something** mit etwas einverstanden sein; **Steve's agreed to help me** Steve war damit einverstanden, mir zu helfen; **5 coffee doesn't agree with me** Kaffee bekommt mir nicht.

agreement *noun* **1** (*when sharing an opinion*) Übereinstimmung *die*; **2** (*contract*) Abkommen *das* (PL *die* Abkommen).

agriculture *noun* Landwirtschaft *die*.

ahead *adverb* **1 go ahead!** bitte !; **2 straight ahead** geradeaus; **keep going straight ahead until you get to the crossroads** gehen Sie immer geradeaus bis zur Kreuzung; **3 our team was ten points ahead** unsere Mannschaft hatte zehn Punkte Vorsprung; **4 ahead of time** früher als geplant; **5 the people ahead of me** die Leute vor mir.

aid *noun* **1** Hilfe *die*; **aid to developing countries** die Entwicklungshilfe; **2 in aid of** zugunsten (+GEN); **in aid of the homeless** zugunsten der Obdachlosen.

Aids *noun* Aids *das*; **to have Aids** Aids haben.

aim *noun* Ziel *das* (PL *die* Ziele); **their aim is to control pollution** ihr Ziel

ist es, die Verschmutzung unter Kontrolle zu bringen.
verb **1 to aim to do something** beabsichtigen, etwas zu tun; **we're aiming to finish it today** wir beabsichtigen, es heute fertig zu machen; **2 the campaign is aimed at young people** die Kampagne ist auf junge Leute abgezielt.

air *noun* **1** Luft *die*; **in the open air** im Freien; **to go out for a breath of air** frische Luft schöpfen gehen; **2 to travel by air** fliegen ◇ (PERF *sein*).

air-conditioned *adjective* klimatisiert.

air conditioning *noun* Klimaanlage *die*.

Air Force *noun* Luftwaffe *die*.

air hostess *noun* Stewardess △ *die* (PL *die* Stewardessen); **she's an air hostess** sie ist Stewardess.

airline *noun* Fluggesellschaft *die* (PL *die* Fluggesellschaften).

airmail *noun* **by airmail** per Luftpost.

airport *noun* Flughafen *der* (PL *die* Flughäfen).

alarm *noun* Alarm *der* (PL *die* Alarme); **fire alarm** *der* Feuermelder; **burglar alarm** *die* Alarmanlage.

alarm clock *noun* Wecker *der* (PL *die* Wecker).

album *noun* Album *das* (PL *die* Alben).

alcohol *noun* Alkohol *der*.

△ NEW SPELLING: *See page xii*

alcoholic noun Alkoholiker der (PL die Alkoholiker), Alkoholikerin die (PL die Alkoholikerinnen).
adjective alkoholisch.

A levels noun Abitur das (Students who want to go on to university do Abitur at the end of secondary school; they are examined in four subjects).

alike adjective 1 gleich; 2 they're all alike sie sind alle gleich; 3 to look alike sich ←(DAT) ähnlich sehen; the two brothers look alike die beiden Brüder sehen sich ähnlich.

alive adjective 1 to be alive leben; to stay alive am Leben bleiben; 2 (lively) lebendig.

all adjective 1 (with a singular noun) ganz; all the time die ganze Zeit; all day den ganzen Tag; 2 (with a plural noun) alle; all the knives alle Messer; all our friends alle unsere Freunde.
pronoun 1 (everything) alles; they've eaten it all sie haben alles aufgegessen; 2 (everybody) alle; all of us wir alle; they're all there sie sind alle da; 3 not at all gar nicht.
adverb 1 ganz; all alone ganz allein; 2 three all drei zu drei.

all along adverb die ganze Zeit; I knew it all along ich habe es die ganze Zeit gewusst.

allergic adjective allergisch; to be allergic to something gegen etwas ←(ACC) allergisch sein.

allow verb 1 to allow somebody to do something jemandem erlauben, etwas zu tun; the teacher allowed them to go home der Lehrer erlaubte ihnen, nach Hause zu gehen; 2 to be allowed to dürfen ✧; I'm not allowed to go to the cinema during the week ich darf während der Woche nicht ins Kino gehen.

all right adverb 1 (yes) ist gut, okay (informal); 'come round to my house around six' – 'all right' 'komm um sechs bei mir vorbei' – 'okay'; 2 (fine) in Ordnung, okay (informal); is everything all right? ist alles okay?; she's all right now sie ist jetzt okay; it's all right by me das geht in Ordnung; is it all right if I come later? geht es in Ordnung, wenn ich später komme?; 3 (not bad) gut, okay (informal); the meal was all right das Essen war okay; 4 'how are you?' – 'I'm all right' 'wie geht's dir?' – 'mir geht's gut'.

almost adverb fast; almost every day fast jeden Tag; almost everybody fast alle.

alone adjective 1 allein; he lives alone er lebt allein; 2 leave me alone! lass mich in Ruhe!

along preposition 1 entlang (+ACC, or +DAT); there are trees all along the river den ganzen Fluss entlang stehen Bäume; to go for a walk along the beach am Strand entlang spazieren gehen; 2 (there is often no direct translation for 'along', so the sentence has to be expressed differently) she lives along the road from me sie wohnt in der gleichen Straße wie ich; I'll bring it along ich bringe es mit.

✧ IRREGULAR VERB: See the verb table in the centre of the dictionary

aloud *adverb* laut; **to read something aloud** etwas vorlesen ✧ SEP.

alphabet *noun* Alphabet *das* (PL *die* Alphabete).

Alps *plural noun* **the Alps** die Alpen.

already *adverb* schon; **they've already left** sie sind schon weggefahren; **it's six o'clock already** es ist schon sechs Uhr.

Alsatian *noun* Schäferhund *der* (PL *die* Schäferhunde).

also *adverb* auch; **I've also invited Karen** ich habe Karen auch eingeladen.

alternative *noun* 1 Alternative *die* (PL *die* Alternativen); **there are several alternatives** es gibt mehrere Alternativen; 2 **we have no alternative** wir haben keine andere Wahl.
adjective anderer/andere/anderes (*masculine/feminine/neuter*); **to find an alternative solution** eine andere Lösung finden.

alternative medicine *noun* Alternativmedizin *die*.

although *conjunction* obwohl; **although she's ill, she wants to help us** obwohl sie krank ist, will sie uns helfen.

altogether *adverb* 1 insgesamt; **I've spent thirty pounds altogether** insgesamt habe ich dreißig Pfund ausgegeben; 2 (*completely*) ganz; **I'm not altogether convinced** ich bin nicht ganz überzeugt.

always *adverb* immer; **I always leave at five** ich gehe immer um fünf weg.

am *verb* SEE **be**.

a.m. *abbreviation* vormittags; **at 8 a.m.** um acht Uhr morgens.

amateur *noun* 1 Amateur *der* (PL *die* Amateure); 2 **amateur dramatics** *das* Laientheater.

amaze *verb* erstaunen; **what amazes me is...** was mich erstaunt, ist...

amazed *adjective* erstaunt; **I was amazed to see her** ich war erstaunt, sie zu sehen.

amazing *adjective* 1 (*terrific*) fantastisch △; **they've got an amazing house** sie haben ein fantastisches Haus; 2 (*extraordinary*) erstaunlich; **she has an amazing number of friends** sie hat erstaunlich viele Freunde.

ambition *noun* Ehrgeiz *der*.

ambitious *adjective* ehrgeizig.

ambulance *noun* Krankenwagen *der* (PL *die* Krankenwagen).

America *noun* Amerika *das*; **in America** in Amerika; **to America** nach Amerika.

American *noun* Amerikaner *der* (PL *die* Amerikaner), Amerikanerin *die* (PL *die* Amerikanerinnen).
adjective amerikanisch; **she's American** sie ist Amerikanerin.

among, amongst *preposition* 1 unter (+DAT); **I found it amongst my books** ich habe das unter

meinen Büchern gefunden;
amongst other things unter
anderem; **2** (*between*) **among
yourselves** untereinander.

amount *noun* **1** Menge *die* (PL *die*
Mengen); **a huge amount of work**
eine Menge Arbeit; **2** (*of money*)
Betrag *der* (PL *die* Beträge); **a large
amount of money** ein sehr hoher
Betrag.

amp *noun* (*amplifier*)
Verstärker *der* (PL *die* Verstärker).

amplifier *noun* Verstärker *der* (PL
die Verstärker).

amuse *verb* amüsieren.

amusement arcade *noun*
Spielhalle *die* (PL *die* Spielhallen).

amusing *adjective* amüsant.

an *article* SEE **a**.

anchovy *noun* Sardelle *die* (PL *die*
Sardellen).

ancient *adjective* **1** alt; **ancient
Greece** *das* alte Griechenland;
2 (*very old*) uralt; **an ancient pair of
jeans** uralte Jeans.

and *conjunction* **1** und; **Rosie and I**
Rosie und ich; **girls and boys**
Mädchen und Jungen; **2** **louder and
louder** immer lauter; **3** **try and
come** versuche zu kommen.

angel *noun* Engel *der* (PL *die* Engel).

anger *noun* Zorn *der*.

angle *noun* Winkel *der* (PL *die*
Winkel).

angrily *adverb* wütend.

angry *adjective* **to be angry** böse
sein; **she was angry with me** sie
war böse auf mich; **to get angry**
böse werden.

animal *noun* Tier *das* (PL *die* Tiere).

ankle *noun* Knöchel *der* (PL *die*
Knöchel).

anniversary *noun* **1** Jahrestag *der*
(PL *die* Jahrestage); **2** **our wedding
anniversary** unser Hochzeitstag.

annoy *verb* **to be annoyed** verärgert
sein; **to get annoyed with
somebody** sich über jemanden
ärgern; **she got annoyed about it**
sie hat sich darüber geärgert.

annoying *adjective* ärgerlich.

annual *adjective* jährlich.

anorak *noun* Anorak *der* (PL *die*
Anoraks).

anorexia *noun* Magersucht *die*.

another *adjective* **1** (*additional*)
noch ein/noch eine/noch ein;
would you like another cup of tea?
möchtest du noch eine Tasse Tee?;
we need another three chairs wir
brauchen noch drei Stühle;
2 (*different*) ein anderer/eine
andere/ein anderes; **we saw
another film** wir haben einen
anderen Film gesehen; **3** **in another
two years** in zwei weiteren Jahren.

answer *noun* **1** Antwort *die* (PL *die*
Antworten); **the right answer** die
richtige Antwort; **the wrong answer**
die falsche Antwort; **2** **the answer
to a problem** die Lösung eines
Problems.
verb **1** antworten (+DAT); **why don't
you answer him?** warum

✧ IRREGULAR VERB: *See the verb table in the centre of the dictionary*

antwortest du ihm nicht?;
2 beantworten (*a letter, a question*);
he hasn't answered our letter er
hat unseren Brief nicht beantwortet.

answering machine *noun*
Anrufbeantworter *der* (PL *die*
Anrufbeantworter).

anthem *noun* **the national anthem**
die Nationalhymne.

antibiotic *noun* Antibiotikum *das*
(PL *die* Antibiotika).

antique *noun* **antiques**
Antiquitäten (*plural*).
adjective antik; **an antique table**
ein antiker Tisch.

antique shop *noun*
Antiquitätengeschäft *das* (PL *die*
Antiquitätengeschäfte).

anxious *adjective* **1** (*worried*)
besorgt; **2** (*keen*) **she was anxious
to see him** sie wollte ihn unbedingt
sehen.

anxiously *adverb* ängstlich.

any *adjective* **1** irgendein; **if they had
any plan** wenn sie irgendeinen Plan
hätten; **2** (*with plural nouns*)
irgendwelche; **if they had any plans**
wenn sie irgendwelche Pläne hätten;
3 (*in questions 'any' is often not
translated*) **have you got any
stamps?** haben Sie Briefmarken?;
have we got any milk? haben wir
Milch?; **4** not any **kein**; **they
haven't made any plans** sie haben
keine Pläne gemacht; **we haven't
got any milk** wir haben keine Milch;
5 (*no matter which*) jeder
beliebige/jede beliebige/jedes

beliebige; **you can have any colour**
du kannst jede beliebige Farbe
haben.
pronoun **1** (*in questions, replacing
the noun*) welcher/welche/welches;
(*replacing a plural noun*) welche;
**I need some flour, have you got
any?** ich brauche Mehl, hast du
welches?; **2** not any keiner/keine/
keins; (*replacing a plural noun*)
keine; **I don't want any** ich will
keins haben; **there aren't any** es gibt
keine; **3** (*no matter which one*)
irgendein; **'which chair can I take?'**
– **' take any of them '** 'welchen
Stuhl kann ich nehmen?' – 'nimm
irgendeinen'.
adverb **1** (*in questions*) noch; **would
you like any more?** möchtest du
noch etwas?; **2** (*with negatives*) **I
can't see him any more** ich kann
ihn nicht mehr sehen.

anybody, anyone *pronoun* **1** (*in
questions*) jemand; **does anybody
want some tea?** möchte jemand
Tee?; **is anybody in?** ist
irgendjemand da?; **2** not anybody
niemand; **there isn't anybody in the
office** niemand ist im Büro;
3 (*absolutely anybody*) jeder;
anybody can do it das kann jeder.

anyhow *adverb* SEE **anyway**.

anyone *pronoun* SEE **anybody**.

anything *pronoun* **1** (*in questions*)
irgendetwas △; **is there anything I
can do to help?** kann ich irgendwie
helfen?; **2** not anything nichts;
there isn't anything on the table
auf dem Tisch liegt nichts;
3 (*anything at all*) alles; **I'll do**

△ NEW SPELLING: *See page xii*

anything to help him ich werde alles tun, um ihm zu helfen.

anyway, anyhow *adverb*
1 jedenfalls; **anyway, I'll ring you before I leave** jedenfalls ruf ich dich an, bevor ich fahre; 2 sowieso.

anywhere *adverb* 1 (*in questions*) irgendwo; **have you seen my keys anywhere?** hast du meine Schlüssel irgendwo gesehen?; 2 **not anywhere** nirgends; **I can't find my keys anywhere** ich kann meine Schlüssel nirgends finden; 3 (*to any place*) irgendwohin; **are you going anywhere tomorrow?** fahrt ihr morgen irgendwohin?; **put your cases down anywhere** stell deine Koffer irgendwohin; 4 (*in any place*) überall; **you can get that anywhere** das kann man überall kriegen.

apart *adjective, adverb* 1 (*separate*) auseinander; **they've been apart for some time** sie sind schon lange auseinander; 2 **to be two metres apart** zwei Meter auseinander liegen; 3 **apart from** außer (+DAT); **apart from my brother everybody was there** außer meinem Bruder waren alle da.

apologize *verb* sich entschuldigen; **he apologized for his mistake** er enschuldigte sich für seinen Fehler; **he apologized to Sam** er hat sich bei Sam entschuldigt.

apology *noun* Entschuldigung *die* (PL *die* Entschuldigungen).

apostrophe *noun* Apostroph *der* (PL *die* Apostrophe).

apparent *adjective* offensichtlich.

apparently *adverb* offensichtlich.

appeal *noun* Appell *der* (PL *die* Appelle).
verb 1 **to appeal for something** um etwas ←(ACC) bitten ✧; 2 **to appeal to somebody** sich an jemanden wenden ✧; **horror films don't appeal to me** Horrorfilme sind nicht mein Geschmack.

appear *verb* 1 erscheinen ✧ (PERF *sein*); **Mick appeared at breakfast** Mick erschien zum Frühstück; 2 **to appear on television** im Fernsehen auftreten ✧ SEP (PERF *sein*); 3 (*seem*) scheinen ✧; **it appears that somebody has stolen the key** es scheint, dass jemand den Schlüssel gestohlen hat.

appendicitis *noun* Blinddarmentzündung *die*.

appetite *noun* Appetit *der*; **it'll spoil your appetite** das verdirbt dir den Appetit.

applaud *verb* Beifall klatschen.

applause *noun* Beifall *der*.

apple *noun* Apfel *der* (PL *die* Äpfel).

apple tree *noun* Apfelbaum *der* (PL *die* Apfelbäume).

applicant *noun* Bewerber *der* (PL *die* Bewerber), Bewerberin *die* (PL *die* Bewerberinnen).

application *noun* Bewerbung *die* (PL *die* Bewerbungen).

application form *noun* (*for a job*) Bewerbungsformular *das* (PL *die* Bewerbungsformulare).

✧ IRREGULAR VERB: *See the verb table in the centre of the dictionary*

apply *verb* **1 to apply for a job** sich um eine Stellung bewerben ◇; **2 to apply for university** sich um einen Studienplatz bewerben ◇; **3 to apply for a passport** einen Pass beantragen; **4 to apply to** zutreffen ◇ SEP auf (+ACC); **that doesn't apply to students** das trifft nicht auf Studenten zu.

appointment *noun* Termin *der* (PL die Termine); **to make a dental appointment** einen Termin mit dem Zahnarzt vereinbaren; **I've got a hair appointment at four** ich bin um vier beim Friseur angemeldet.

appreciate *verb* **I appreciate your advice** ich bin dir für deinen Rat dankbar; **I'd appreciate it if you could tidy up afterwards** es wäre nett von dir, wenn du danach aufräumen würdest.

apprentice *noun* Lehrling *der* (PL die Lehrlinge).

apprenticeship *noun* Lehre *die* (PL die Lehren).

approve *verb* **to approve of something** mit etwas ←(DAT) einverstanden sein; **they don't approve of her friends** sie sind nicht mit ihren Freunden einverstanden.

approximate *adjective* ungefähr.

approximately *adverb* ungefähr; **approximately fifty people** ungefähr fünfzig Personen.

apricot *noun* Aprikose *die* (PL die Aprikosen).

April *noun* April *der*; **in April** im April.

April Fool *noun* (*trick*) Aprilscherz *der* (PL die Aprilscherze); **April fool!** April, April!

April Fool's Day *noun* der erste April.

apron *noun* Schürze *die* (PL die Schürzen).

Aquarius *noun* Wassermann *der*; **Sharon's Aquarius** Sharon ist Wassermann.

archaeologist *noun* Archäologe *der* (PL die Archäologen), Archäologin *die* (PL die Archäologinnen); **she's an archaeologist** sie ist Archäologin.

archaeology *noun* Archäologie *die*.

architect *noun* Architekt *der* (PL die Architekten), Architektin *die* (PL die Architektinnen); **he's an architect** er ist Architekt.

architecture *noun* Architektur *die*.

are *verb* SEE **be**.

area *noun* **1** (*part of a town, a region*) Gegend *die* (PL die Gegenden); **a nice area** eine nette Gegend; **in the Leeds area** in der Gegend von Leeds; **2 picnic area** der Picknickplatz.

argue *verb* sich streiten ◇; **to argue about something** sich über etwas ←(ACC) streiten; **they're arguing about the result** sie streiten sich über das Ergebnis.

argument *noun* Streit *der* (PL die Streite); **to get into an argument with somebody** mit jemandem in

△ NEW SPELLING: *See page xii*

Streit geraten ✧; **to have an argument** sich streiten ✧.

Aries *noun* Widder *der*; **Pauline's Aries** Pauline ist Widder.

arm *noun* Arm *der* (PL *die* Arme); **arm in arm** Arm in Arm; **to break your arm** sich ←(DAT) den Arm brechen.

armchair *noun* Sessel *der* (PL *die* Sessel).

armed *adjective* bewaffnet.

army *noun* 1 Heer *das* (PL *die* Heere); 2 (*profession*) Militär *das*; **to join the army** zum Militär gehen.

around *preposition, adverb* 1 (*with time of day*) gegen (+ACC); **we'll be there around ten** wir werden gegen zehn da sein; 2 (*with ages or amounts*) etwa; **she's around fifteen** sie ist etwa fünfzehn; **we need around six kilos** wir brauchen etwa sechs Kilo; 3 (*with dates*) um (+ACC); **around 10 August** um den 10. August; 4 (*surrounding*) um ... herum; **the countryside around Edinburgh** die Landschaft um Edinburgh herum; 5 (*near*) **is there a post office around here?** gibt es hier in der Gegend eine Post?; **is Phil around?** ist Phil da?

arrange *verb* **to arrange something** etwas vereinbaren; **we've arranged to go to the cinema on Saturday** wir haben vereinbart, am Samstag ins Kino zu gehen.

arrest *noun* **to be under arrest** verhaftet sein.
verb verhaften.

arrival *noun* Ankunft *die* (PL *die* Ankünfte).

arrive *verb* ankommen ✧ SEP (PERF *sein*); **they arrived at 3 p.m.** sie kamen um fünfzehn Uhr an.

art *noun* 1 Kunst *die* (PL *die* Künste); **modern art** moderne Kunst; 2 (*school subject*) Kunsterziehung *die*.

art gallery *noun* Kunstgalerie *die* (PL *die* Kunstgalerien).

article *noun* 1 (*in a newspaper or magazine*) Artikel *der* (PL *die* Artikel); 2 (*object*) Stück *das* (PL *die* Stücke).

artificial *adjective* künstlich.

artist *noun* Künstler *der* (PL *die* Künstler), Künstlerin *die* (PL *die* Künstlerinnen); **he's an artist** er ist Künstler.

artistic *adjective* künstlerisch.

art school *noun* Kunsthochschule *die* (PL *die* Kunsthochschulen).

as *conjunction, adverb* 1 wie; **as you know** wie du weißt; **as usual** wie üblich; **as I told you** wie ich dir gesagt habe; 2 (*because*) da; **as there was no bus, we took a taxi** da es keinen Bus gab, nahmen wir ein Taxi; 3 **as ... as** so ... wie; **he's as tall as his brother** er ist so groß wie sein Bruder; **come as quickly as possible** komm so schnell wie möglich; 4 **as much ... as** so viel ... wie; **you have as much time as I do** du hast so viel Zeit wie ich; 5 **as many ... as** so viele ... wie; **we have**

✧ IRREGULAR VERB: *See the verb table in the centre of the dictionary*

as many problems as he does wir
haben so viele Probleme wie er; **6 as
long as** vorausgesetzt; **we'll go
tomorrow, as long as it's a nice day**
wir gehen morgen, vorausgesetzt es
ist schönes Wetter; **7 for as long as**
solange; **you can stay for as long as
you like** du kannst bleiben, solange
du willst; **8 as soon as possible** so
bald wie möglich; **9 to work as**
arbeiten als; **he works as a waiter in
the evenings** abends arbeitet er als
Kellner; **as well** auch.

ash noun **1** Asche die (PL die
Aschen); **2** (tree) Esche die (PL die
Eschen).

ashamed adjective **to be ashamed
of something** sich über etwas
←(ACC) schämen; **you should be
ashamed of yourself!** du solltest
dich schämen!

ashtray noun Aschenbecher der (PL
die Aschenbecher).

Asia noun Asien das; **in Asia** in
Asien.

ask verb **1** fragen; **to ask somebody
something** jemanden nach etwas
←(DAT) fragen; **I asked him the way**
ich fragte ihn nach dem Weg; **2 to
ask something** um etwas ←(ACC)
bitten; **to ask somebody a favour**
jemanden um einen Gefallen bitten;
to ask somebody to do something
jemanden bitten, etwas zu tun; **ask
Danny to give you a hand** bitte
Danny, dir zu helfen; **3 to ask
somebody a question** jemandem
eine Frage stellen; **I asked him a few
questions** ich habe ihm ein paar
Fragen gestellt; **4** einladen ♦ SEP;

they've asked us to a party sie
haben uns auf eine Party eingeladen;
Paul's asked Janie out on Friday
Paul hat Janie Freitag eingeladen;
5 to ask for verlangen; **how much
are they asking for the car?** wieviel
verlangen sie für das Auto?

asparagus noun Spargel der (PL die
Spargel).

aspirin noun Aspirin das.

assembly noun (at school)
Morgenandacht die (PL die
Morgenandachten).

assignment noun (at school)
Aufgabe die (PL die Aufgaben).

assistance noun Hilfe die.

assistant noun **1** Helfer der (PL die
Helfer), Helferin die (PL die
Helferinnen); **2** (in school)
Assistent der (PL die Assistenten),
Assistentin die (PL die
Assistentinnen); **3 shop assistant**
der Verkäufer, die Verkäuferin.

association noun Verband der (PL
die Verbände).

assorted adjective gemischt.

assortment noun Auswahl die.

assume verb annehmen ♦ SEP;
I assume ich nehme an.

asthma noun Asthma das.

astrology noun Astrologie die.

astronaut noun Astronaut der (PL
die Astronauten), Astronautin die
(PL die Astronautinnen).

astronomy noun Astronomie die.

at *preposition* **1** in (+DAT); **at school** in der Schule; **at my office** in meinem Büro; **at the supermarket** im Supermarkt; **2** an (+DAT); **at the station** am Bahnhof; **at the bus stop** an der Bushaltestelle; **3** bei (+DAT); **at the dentist** beim Zahnarzt; **at discussions** bei Besprechungen; **at Emma's** bei Emma; **she's at her brother's this evening** sie ist heute Abend bei ihrem Bruder; **at the hairdresser's** beim Friseur; **4 at a party** auf einer Party; **5 at home** zu Hause; **6** (*talking about the time*) um; **at eight o'clock** um acht Uhr; **7 at night** nachts; **at Christmas** zu Weihnachten; **at the weekend** am Wochenende; **8 at last** endlich; **she's found a job at last** sie hat endlich einen Job gefunden.

athlete *noun* Athlet *der* (PL die Athleten), Athletin *die* (PL die Athletinnen).

athletic *adjective* sportlich.

athletics *noun* Leichtathletik *die*.

Atlantic *noun* **the Atlantic (Ocean)** der Atlantik.

atlas *noun* Atlas *der* (PL die Atlanten).

atmosphere *noun* Atmosphäre *die* (PL die Atmosphären).

attach *verb* befestigen.

attached *adjective* (*emotionally*) **to be attached to somebody/ something** an jemandem/ etwas ←(DAT) hängen ✧.

attack *noun* Angriff *der* (PL die Angriffe).
verb **1** angreifen ✧ SEP; **2** (*mug or raid*) überfallen ✧.

attempt *noun* Versuch *der* (PL die Versuche); **at the first attempt** beim ersten Versuch.
verb **to attempt to do something** versuchen, etwas zu tun.

attend *verb* teilnehmen ✧ SEP an (+DAT); **to attend a meeting** an einer Besprechung teilnehmen; **to attend an evening class** einen Abendkurs besuchen.

attention *noun*
1 Aufmerksamkeit *die*; **to pay attention** aufpassen SEP; **I wasn't paying attention** ich habe nicht aufgepasst; **2 he wasn't paying attention to the teacher** er hörte dem Lehrer nicht zu.

attic *noun* Dachboden *der* (PL die Dachböden); **in the attic** auf dem Dachboden.

attitude *noun* **1** (*way of thinking*) Einstellung *die*; **2** (*way of acting*) Haltung *die*.

attract *verb* anziehen ✧ SEP.

attraction *noun* **1** Anziehung *die*; **2** (*a thing that attracts*) Attraktion *die* (PL die Attraktionen); **the whale was a big attraction** der Wal war eine große Attraktion.

attractive *adjective* attraktiv.

aubergine *noun* Aubergine *die* (PL die Auberginen).

audience *noun* Publikum *das*; **the television audience** die Fernsehzuschauer (*plural*).

✧ IRREGULAR VERB: *See the verb table in the centre of the dictionary*

August noun August der, **in August** im August.

aunt, auntie noun Tante die (PL die Tanten).

au pair noun Aupairmädchen △ das (PL die Aupairmädchen); **I'm looking for a job as an au pair** ich suche eine Aupair-Stelle.

Australia noun Australien das; **to Australia** nach Australien.

Australian noun Australier der (PL die Australier), Australierin die (PL die Australierinnen).
adjective australisch; **she's Australian** sie ist Australierin.

Austria noun Österreich das; **in Austria** in Österreich.

Austrian noun Österreicher der (PL die Österreicher), Österreicherin die (PL die Österreicherinnen).
adjective österreichisch; **he's Austrian** er ist Österreicher.

author noun Autor der (PL die Autoren), Autorin die (PL die Autorinnen).

autograph noun Autogramm das (PL die Autogramme).

automatic adjective automatisch.

automatically adverb automatisch.

autumn noun Herbst der (PL die Herbste); **in autumn** im Herbst.

available adjective (on sale) erhältlich.

average noun Durchschnitt der (PL die Durchschnitte); **on average** im Durchschnitt; **above average** über

dem Durchschnitt.
adjective durchschnittlich; **the average height** die durchschnittliche Größe.

avocado noun Avocado die (PL die Avocados).

avoid verb 1 vermeiden ✧; **to avoid doing something** es vermeiden, etwas zu tun; **I avoid speaking to him** ich vermeide es, mit ihm zu reden; **2** (keep away from somebody or a place) meiden ✧; **she avoids me** sie meidet mich.

awake adjective **to be awake** wach sein; **are you still awake?** bist du noch wach?

award noun Preis der (PL die Preise); **to win an award** einen Preis gewinnen.

aware adjective **to be aware of a problem** sich ←(DAT) eines Problems bewusst △ sein; **I'm aware of the danger** ich bin mir der Gefahr bewusst; **as far as I'm aware** soweit ich weiß.

away adverb 1 **to be away** nicht da sein; **I'll be away next week** ich bin nächste Woche nicht da; **2 to go away** verreisen (PERF sein); **Laura's gone away for a week** Laura ist auf eine Woche verreist; **go away!** geh weg!; **3 to run away** weglaufen ✧ SEP (PERF sein); **the thieves ran away** die Diebe liefen weg; **4 the school is two kilometres away** die Schule ist zwei Kilometer entfernt; **how far away is it?** wie weit entfernt ist es?; **not far away** nicht weit entfernt; **5 to put something away** etwas wegräumen SEP; **I'm just putting my**

△ NEW SPELLING: See page xii

books away ich räume gerade meine Bücher weg; **6 to give something away** etwas weggeben ✧ SEP; (*as a present*) etwas verschenken; **she's given away all her cassettes** sie hat alle ihre Kassetten verschenkt.

awful *adjective* furchtbar; **the film was awful** der Film war furchtbar; **I feel awful** (*ill*) ich fühle mich furchtbar; **I feel awful about it** es ist mir furchtbar unangenehm; **an awful lot of mistakes** furchtbar viele Fehler.

awkward *adjective* **1** schwierig; **it's an awkward situation** das ist eine schwierige Situation; **it's a bit awkward** das ist ein bisschen schwierig; **an awkward child** ein schwieriges Kind; **2 an awkward question** eine peinliche Frage.

B b

baby *noun* Baby *das* (PL *die* Babys).

babysit *verb* babysitten.

babysitter *noun* Babysitter *der* (PL *die* Babysitter).

babysitting *noun* Babysitten *das*.

back *noun* **1** (*of a person or animal*) Rücken *der* (PL *die* Rücken); **he did it behind my back** er hat es hinter meinem Rücken getan; **2** (*of a piece of paper, cheque, or building*) Rückseite *die* (PL *die* Rückseiten); **on the back** auf der Rückseite; **3 the**

back of your hand der Handrücken; **4 at the back** hinten; **at the back of the room** hinten im Zimmer; **we sat at the back** wir saßen hinten; **a garden at the back of the house** ein Garten hinter dem Haus; **5** (*of a chair or sofa*) Rückenlehne *die* (PL *die* Rückenlehnen); **6** (*in football or hockey*) Verteidiger *der* (PL *die* Verteidiger); **left back** *der* Linksverteidiger.
adjective **1 the back seat** (*of a car*) der Rücksitz; **2 the back door** die Hintertür; **the back garden** der Garten hinter dem Haus.
adverb **1** zurück; **there and back** hin und zurück; **to go back** (*on foot*) zurückgehen ✧ SEP (PERF *sein*) (*in a vehicle*) zurückfahren ✧ SEP (PERF *sein*); **2 to come back** zurückkommen ✧ SEP (PERF *sein*); **they've come back from Italy** sie sind aus Italien zurückgekommen; **I'll be back at 8 o'clock** ich bin um acht Uhr zurück; **Sue's not back yet** Sue ist noch nicht zurück; **3 to phone back** zurückrufen ✧ SEP; **I'll ring back later** ich rufe dich später zurück; **4 to give something back to somebody** jemandem etwas zurückgeben ✧ SEP; **give it back!** gib es zurück!
verb (*bet on*) setzen auf (+ACC).
● **to back up** (*computing*) sichern; **to back up a file** eine Sicherungsdatei machen.
● **to back somebody up** jemanden unterstützen.

backache *noun* Rückenscherzen (*plural*).

✧ IRREGULAR VERB: *See the verb table in the centre of the dictionary*

background *noun* 1 (*of a person*) Verhältnisse (*plural*); **she comes from a poor background** sie kommt aus ärmlichen Verhältnissen; 2 (*in a picture, view, or situation*) Hintergrund *der* (PL *die* Hintergründe); **background noise** Hintergrundgeräusche (*plural*); 3 (*to events or problems*) Hintergründe (*plural*).

backing *noun* 1 (*on sticky-back plastic, for example*) Verstärkung *die* (PL *die* Verstärkungen); 2 (*moral support*) Unterstützung *die*; 3 (*in music*) Begleitung *die*; **a backing group** eine Begleitband.

backpack *noun* Rucksack *der* (PL *die* Rucksäcke).
verb **to go backpacking** trampen (PERF *sein*).

back seat *noun* Rücksitz *der* (PL *die* Rücksitze).

backstroke *noun* Rückenschwimmen *das*.

back to front *adverb* verkehrt herum; **your jumper's back to front** du hast deinen Pullover verkehrt herum an.

backup *noun* 1 (*support*) Unterstützung *die*; 2 (*in computing*) Sicherungskopie *die* (PL *die* Sicherungskopien); **a backup disk** eine Sicherungsdiskette.

backwards *adverb* 1 rückwärts; 2 **to lean backwards** sich nach hinten lehnen; **to fall backwards** nach hinten fallen.

bacon *noun* Speck *der*; **bacon and eggs** Eier mit Speck.

bad *adjective* 1 (*not good*) schlecht; **a bad idea** eine schlechte Idee; **a bad meal** ein schlechtes Essen; **his new film's not bad** sein neuer Film ist nicht schlecht; **it's bad for your health** das ist ungesund; **I'm bad at physics** ich bin schlecht in Physik; 2 (*serious*) schlimm; **a bad mistake** ein schlimmer Fehler; **a bad cold** eine schlimme Erkältung; 3 **a bad accident** ein schwerer Unfall; 4 (*rotten*) schlecht; **to go bad** schlecht werden; 5 **a bad apple** ein fauler Apfel; 6 **bad language** Kraftausdrücke (*plural*); ★ **too bad!** schade!, so ein Pech!

badge *noun* Abzeichen *das* (PL *die* Abzeichen).

badly *adverb* 1 (*poorly*) schlecht; **he writes badly** er schreibt schlecht; **I slept badly** ich habe schlecht geschlafen; 2 (*seriously*) schwer; **they were badly injured** sie waren schwer verletzt; 3 (*very much*) dringend; **to need something badly** etwas dringend brauchen.

bad-mannered *adjective* **to be bad-mannered** schlechte Manieren haben.

badminton *noun* Badminton *das*.

bad-tempered *adjective* schlecht gelaunt △; **a bad-tempered old man** ein schlecht gelaunter alter Mann.

bag *noun* 1 Tasche *die* (PL *die* Taschen); 2 (*made of paper or plastic*) Tüte *die* (PL *die* Tüten).

△ NEW SPELLING: *See page xii*

baggage *noun* Gepäck *das*.

bagpipes *plural noun* Dudelsack *der*.

bags *plural noun* Gepäck *das*; **to pack your bags** sein Gepäck packen; ★ **to have bags under your eyes** Ringe unter den Augen haben (*informal*).

bake *verb* 1 backen; **to bake a cake** einen Kuchen backen; 2 **to bake vegetables** Gemüse backen.

baked *adjective* 1 (*fish or fruit*) überbacken; **baked apples** Bratäpfel; 2 **a baked potato** eine (in der Schale) gebackene Kartoffel.

baked beans *plural noun* Bohnen in Tomatensoße.

baker *noun* Bäcker *der* (PL *die* Bäcker); **to go to the baker's** zum Bäcker gehen.

balance *noun* 1 Gleichgewicht *das*; **to lose your balance** das Gleichgewicht verlieren; 2 (*in a bank account*) Kontostand *der*.

balanced *adjective* ausgeglichen.

balcony *noun* Balkon *der* (PL *die* Balkons).

bald *adjective* 1 kahl; 2 (*of a person*) kahlköpfig; **to go bald** eine Glatze bekommen.

ball *noun* 1 (*for tennis, football, or golf*) Ball *der* (PL *die* Bälle); 2 (*for billiards, croquet*) Kugel *die* (PL *die* Kugeln); 3 (*of string or wool*) Knäuel *das* (PL *die* Knäuel).

ballet *noun* Ballett *das* (PL *die* Ballette).

ballet dancer *noun* Balletttänzer △ *der* (PL *die* Balletttänzer), Balletttänzerin △ *die* (PL *die* Balletttänzerinnen).

balloon *noun* 1 Luftballon *der* (PL *die* Luftballons); 2 (*hot-air*) Ballon *der* (PL *die* Ballons).

ballpoint (pen) *noun* Kugelschreiber *der* (PL *die* Kugelschreiber).

ban *noun* Verbot *das* (PL *die* Verbote); **a ban on smoking** ein Rauchverbot.
verb verbieten ✧; **to ban someone from smoking** jemandem verbieten zu rauchen.

banana *noun* 1 Banane *die* (PL *die* Bananen); 2 **a banana yoghurt** ein Bananenjoghurt.

band *noun* 1 (*playing music*) Band *die* (PL *die* Bands); **rock band** *die* Rockband; **brass band** *die* Blaskapelle; 2 **rubber band** *das* Gummiband.

bandage *noun* Verband *der* (PL *die* Verbände).
verb verbinden ✧.

bang *noun* (*noise*) Knall *der* (PL *die* Knalle).
verb 1 (*hit, knock*) schlagen ✧; **he banged his fist on the table** er hat mit der Faust auf den Tisch geschlagen; **to bang on the door** gegen die Tür schlagen; 2 **I banged my head on the door** ich habe mir den Kopf an der Tür gestoßen; 3 **to bang into something** gegen etwas ←(ACC) knallen; 4 (*shut loudly*) zuknallen SEP; **he banged the door**

✧ IRREGULAR VERB: *See the verb table in the centre of the dictionary*

er knallte die Tür zu.
exclamation peng!

bank *noun* 1 (*for money*) Bank *die*
(PL *die* Banken); **I'm going to the
bank** ich gehe auf die Bank; 2 (*of a
river or lake*) Ufer *das* (PL *die* Ufer).

bank account *noun*
Bankkonto *das* (PL *die* Bankkonten).

bank balance *noun*
Kontostand *der* (PL *die*
Kontostände).

bank card *noun* Scheckkarte *die*
(PL *die* Scheckkarten).

bank holiday *noun* gesetzliche
Feiertag *der* (PL *die* gesetzlichen
Feiertage).

banknote *noun* Geldschein *der* (PL
die Geldscheine).

bank statement *noun*
Kontoauszug *der* (PL *die*
Kontoauszüge).

bar *noun* 1 (*selling drinks*) Bar *die*
(PL *die* Bars); **Janet works in a bar**
Janet arbeitet in einer Bar;
2 (*counter*) Theke *die* (PL *die*
Theken); **on the bar** auf der Theke;
3 **a bar of chocolate** eine Tafel
Schokolade; 4 **a bar of soap** ein
Stück Seife; 5 (*made of wood or
metal*) Stange *die* (PL *die* Stangen);
an iron bar eine Eisenstange;
6 (*in music*) Takt *der* (PL *die* Takte).

barbecue *noun* 1 (*apparatus*)
Grill *der* (PL *die* Grills); 2 (*party*)
Grillfest *das* (PL *die* Grillfeste).
verb **to barbecue a chicken** ein
Hühnchen grillen; **barbecued
chicken** gegrilltes Hühnchen.

bare *adjective* nackt.

barefoot *adjective* **to be barefoot**
barfuß sein; **to walk barefoot**
barfuß gehen.

bargain *noun* (*a good buy*) gute
Kauf *der* (PL *die* guten Käufe); **I got
a bargain** ich habe einen guten Kauf
gemacht; **it's a bargain!** ein guter
Kauf!

bark *noun* 1 (*of a tree*) Rinde *die* (PL
die Rinden); 2 (*of a dog*) Bellen *das*.
verb bellen.

barmaid *noun* Bardame *die* (PL *die*
Bardamen).

barman *noun* Barkeeper *der* (PL *die*
Barkeeper).

barn *noun* Scheune *die* (PL *die*
Scheunen).

barrel *noun* Fass △ *das* (PL *die*
Fässer).

barrier *noun* Absperrung *die* (PL *die*
Absperrungen).

base *noun* (*bottom part*) Fuß *der*
(PL *die* Füße).

baseball *noun* Baseball *der*.

based *adjective* 1 **to be based on**
basieren auf (+DAT); **the film is
based on a true story** der Film
basiert auf einer wahren
Geschichte; 2 **to be based in**
wohnen in (+DAT); **he's based in
Bristol** er wohnt in Bristol.

basement *noun*
Kellergeschoss △ *das* (PL *die*
Kellergeschosse).

bash *noun* 1 Schlag *der* (PL *die* Schläge); 2 **I'll have a bash** ich probier's mal.
verb **I bashed my head** ich habe mir den Kopf angehauen.

basic *adjective* 1 grundlegend, Grund-; **basic knowledge** Grundkenntnisse (*plural*); **her basic salary** ihr Grundgehalt; 2 **the basic problem** das Hauptproblem; 3 (*not luxurious*) einfach.

basically *adverb* 1 grundsätzlich; **it's basically all right** grundsätzlich ist es okay; 2 **basically, I don't want to come** eigentlich will ich nicht kommen.

basics *plural noun* **the basics** das Wesentliche.

basin *noun* Becken *das* (PL *die* Becken).

basis *noun* 1 Basis *die*; 2 **on a regular basis** regelmäßig.

basket *noun* Korb *der* (PL *die* Körbe); **a basket of apples** ein Korb Äpfel; **waste-paper basket** *der* Papierkorb.

basketball *noun* Basketball *der*.

bass *noun* 1 Bass Δ *der* (PL *die* Bässe); 2 **double bass** *der* Kontrabass Δ.

bass guitar *noun* Bassgitarre Δ *die* (PL *die* Bassgitarren).

bassoon *noun* Fagott *das* (PL *die* Fagotte).

bat *noun* 1 (*for games*) Schläger *der* (PL *die* Schläger); 2 (*animal*) Fledermaus *die* (PL *die* Fledermäuse).

bath *noun* 1 Bad *das* (PL *die* Bäder); **to have a bath** baden; 2 (*tub*) Badewanne *die* (PL *die* Badewannen).

bathroom *noun* Badezimmer *das* (PL *die* Badezimmer).

baths *plural noun* Badeanstalt *die* (PL *die* Badeanstalten).

bath towel *noun* Badetuch *das* (PL *die* Badetücher).

batter *noun* Teig *der* (PL *die* Teige); **fish in batter** ausgebackener Fisch.

battery *noun* Batterie *die* (PL *die* Batterien).

battle *noun* 1 (*in war*) Schlacht *die* (PL *die* Schlachten); 2 (*contest*) Kampf *der* (PL *die* Kämpfe).

Bavaria *noun* Bayern *das*.

bay *noun* Bucht *die* (PL *die* Buchten).

BC (*before Christ*) v.Chr. (*vor Christus*).

be *verb* 1 sein ◇ (PERF *sein*); **Melanie is in the kitchen** Melanie ist in der Küche; **where is the butter?** wo ist die Butter?; **I'm tired** ich bin müde; **when we were in Germany** als wir in Deutschland waren; 2 (*with jobs and professions*) sein ◇ (PERF *sein*); **she's a teacher** sie ist Lehrerin; **he's a taxi driver** er ist Taxifahrer; 3 (*in clock times, days of the week, dates, and age*) sein ◇ (PERF *sein*); **it's three o'clock** es ist drei Uhr; **it's half past five** es ist halb sechs; **what day is it today?** welcher Tag ist heute?; **it's Tuesday today** heute ist Dienstag; **it's the twentieth of May** heute ist der zwanzigste Mai; **what's**

the date today? der Wievielte ist heute?; **how old are you?** wie alt bist du?; **I'm fifteen** ich bin fünfzehn; **4** (*cold, hot, ill*) sein ✧ (PERF *sein*); **I'm hot** mir ist heiß; **I'm cold** mir ist kalt; **to be ill** krank sein; **5** (*weather*) sein ✧ (PERF *sein*); **it's cold today** heute ist es kalt; **it's a nice day** es ist schönes Wetter; **it's raining** es regnet; **6 I'm hungry** ich habe Hunger; **she's thirsty** sie hat Durst; **7** (*saying how much something costs*) kosten; **how much are the bananas?** wie viel kosten die Bananen?; **8** (*go, come, or visit*) sein ✧ (PERF *sein*); **I've never been to Berlin** ich bin noch nie in Berlin gewesen; **have you been to England before?** bist du schon einmal in England gewesen?; **has the postman been?** war der Briefträger schon da?; **9** (*forming the passive*) werden ✧ (PERF *sein*); **to be loved** geliebt werden; **he has been promoted** er ist befördert worden; **10 there is/are** es gibt; **are there any shops near here?** gibt es hier in der Nähe Geschäfte?

beach *noun* Strand *der* (PL *die* Strände); **to go to the beach** zum Strand gehen; **on the beach** am Strand.

bead *noun* Perle *die* (PL *die* Perlen).

beam *noun* **1** (*of light*) Strahl *der* (PL *die* Strahlen); **2** (*for a roof*) Balken *der* (PL *die* Balken).

bean *noun* Bohne *die* (PL *die* Bohnen); **green beans** grüne Bohnen.

bear *noun* Bär *der* (PL *die* Bären). *verb* **1** ertragen ✧; **I can't bear the idea** ich kann den Gedanken nicht ertragen; **2 to bear something in mind** an etwas ←(ACC) denken; **I'll bear it in mind** ich denke daran.

beard *noun* Bart *der* (PL *die* Bärte).

bearded *adjective* bärtig.

bearings *plural noun* **to get one's bearings** sich orientieren.

beast *noun* **1** (*animal*) Tier *das* (PL *die* Tiere); **2 you beast!** du Biest!

beat *noun* (*in music*) Takt *der*. *verb* **1** schlagen ✧; (*defeat*) **we beat them!** wir haben sie geschlagen; **2 you can't beat a good meal** es geht doch nichts über ein gutes Essen.
● **to beat somebody up** jemanden verprügeln.

beautiful *adjective* schön.

beauty *noun* **1** Schönheit *die* (PL *die* Schönheiten); **2 the beauty of it is that …** das Schöne daran ist, dass …

because *conjunction* **1** weil; **because it's cold** weil es kalt ist; **2 because of** wegen (+GEN); **because of the accident** wegen des Unfalls; **because of you** deinetwegen.

become *verb* werden ✧ (PERF *sein*); **she's become a painter** sie ist Malerin geworden.

bed *noun* **1** Bett *das* (PL *die* Betten); **double bed** *das* Doppelbett; **in bed** im Bett; **to go to bed** ins Bett gehen; **2** (*flower bed*) Beet *das* (PL *die* Beete).

△ NEW SPELLING: *See page xii*

bedclothes *plural noun*
Bettwäsche *die*.

bedding *noun* Bettzeug *das*.

bedroom *noun* Schlafzimmer *das*
(PL *die* Schlafzimmer); **bedroom
furniture** Schlafzimmermöbel
(*plural*); **my bedroom window**
mein Schlafzimmerfenster.

bedside table *noun* Nachttisch
der.

bedsit, bedsitter *noun* möblierte
Zimmer *das* (PL *die* möblierten
Zimmer).

bedspread *noun* Tagesdecke *die*
(PL *die* Tagesdecken).

bedtime *noun* Schlafenszeit *die*; **at
bedtime** vor dem Schlafengehen.

bee *noun* Biene *die* (PL *die* Bienen).

beech *noun* Buche *die* (PL *die*
Buchen).

beef *noun* Rindfleisch *das*; **we had
roast beef** wir haben Rinderbraten
gegessen.

beefburger *noun* Hamburger *der*
(PL *die* Hamburger).

beer *noun* Bier *das* (PL *die* Biere);
two beers please zwei Bier bitte;
beer can *die* Bierdose.

beetle *noun* Käfer *der* (PL *die* Käfer).

beetroot *noun* Rote Bete △ *die*.

before *preposition* 1 vor (+DAT);
before Monday vor Montag; **he left
before me** er ist vor mir gegangen;
the day before the wedding am Tag
vor der Hochzeit; 2 **the day before**
am Tag zuvor; **the day before**
yesterday vorgestern; **the week
before** in der Woche zuvor;
3 (*already*) schon einmal; **I've seen
him before somewhere** ich habe
ihn schon einmal irgendwo gesehen;
I had seen the film before ich hatte
den Film schon einmal gesehen.
conjunction bevor; **I closed the
windows before leaving** (*or* **before
I left**) ich habe die Fenster
zugemacht, bevor ich wegging;
before the train leaves bevor der
Zug abfährt; **oh, before I forget** …
bevor ich es vergesse …

beforehand *adverb* (*ahead of time*)
vorher; **phone beforehand** rufe
vorher an.

beg *verb* 1 betteln; **to beg for money**
um Geld betteln; 2 (*ask*) bitten ✧;
he begged her not to say anything
er bat sie, nichts zu sagen; 3 **I beg
your pardon** entschuldigen Sie
bitte.

begin *verb* anfangen ✧ SEP,
beginnen ✧; **the meeting begins at
ten** die Besprechung fängt um zehn
an; **the words beginning with P** die
Wörter, die mit P anfangen; **to begin
to do something** anfangen, etwas
zu tun; beginnen, etwas zu tun; **I'm
beginning to understand why** …
ich beginne zu verstehen, warum …

beginner *noun* Anfänger *der* (PL *die*
Anfänger), Anfängerin *die* (PL *die*
Anfängerinnen).

beginning *noun* Anfang *der* (PL *die*
Anfänge); **at the beginning** am
Anfang; **at the beginning of the
holidays** am Anfang der Ferien.

✧ IRREGULAR VERB: *See the verb table in the centre of the dictionary*

behave *verb* **1** sich benehmen ✧; **he behaved badly** er hat sich schlecht benommen; **2 to behave oneself** sich benehmen ✧; **behave yourself!** benimm dich!

behaviour *noun* Benehmen *das*.

behind *noun* Hintern *der* (*informal*) (PL *die* Hintern). *preposition, adverb* **1** hinter (+DAT, *or* +ACC *when there is movement towards a place*); **behind the sofa** hinter dem Sofa; **behind them** hinter ihnen; **the car behind** das Auto hinter ihnen/uns; **2 to leave something behind** (*belongings*) etwas vergessen.

beige *adjective* beige.

Belgian *noun* Belgier *der* (PL *die* Belgier), Belgierin *die* (PL *die* Belgierinnen). *adjective* belgisch; **he's Belgian** er ist Belgier.

Belgium *noun* Belgien *das*; **to Belgium** nach Belgien.

belief *noun* Glaube *der* (PL *die* Glauben); **his political beliefs** seine politische Überzeugung.

believe *verb* **1** glauben; **I believe so** ich glaube schon; **they believed what I said** sie glaubten, was ich sagte; **I don't believe you** das glaube ich dir nicht; **2 to believe in something** an etwas ←(ACC) glauben; **to believe in God** an Gott glauben.

bell *noun* **1** (*in a church*) Glocke *die* (PL *die* Glocken); **2** (*on a door*) Klingel *die* (PL *die* Klingeln); **to ring the bell** klingeln; **3** (*for a cat or toy*) Glöckchen das (PL *die* Glöckchen); ★ **that name rings a bell** der Name sagt mir etwas (*literally: says something to me*).

belong *verb* **1 to belong to** gehören (+DAT); **that belongs to my mother** das gehört meiner Mutter; **2 to belong to a club** einem Klub angehören; **3** (*go*) gehören; **where does this vase belong?** wo gehört diese Vase hin?

belongings *plural noun* Sachen (*plural*); **all my belongings** alle meine Sachen.

below *preposition* unter (+DAT, *or* +ACC *when there is movement towards a place*); **below the window** unter dem Fenster; **the flat below yours** die Wohnung unter dir. *adverb* **1** (*further down*) unten; **he called from below** er rief von unten; **2 the flat below** die Wohnung darunter.

belt *noun* Gürtel *der* (PL *die* Gürtel).

bench *noun* Bank *die* (PL *die* Bänke).

bend *noun* **1** (*in a road*) Kurve *die* (PL *die* Kurven); **2** (*in a river*) Biegung *die* (PL *die* Biegungen). *verb* **1** (*make a bend in*) biegen ✧ (*a pipe or wire*), beugen (*your knee, arm, or head*); **2** (*curve*) eine Biegung machen; **3 to bend down** sich bücken.

beneath *preposition* unter (+DAT).

benefit *noun* **1** Vorteil *der* (PL *die* Vorteile); **2 unemployment benefit** *die* Arbeitslosenunterstützung.

bent *adjective* verbogen.

△ NEW SPELLING: See page xii

beret *noun* Baskenmütze *die* (PL *die* Baskenmützen).

beside *preposition* (*next to*) neben (+DAT, *or* +ACC *when there is movement towards a place*); **she was sitting beside me** sie saß neben mir; **she sat down beside me** sie hat sich neben mich gesetzt; ★ **that's beside the point** das hat nichts damit zu tun.

besides *adverb* (*anyway*) außerdem; **besides, it's too late** außerdem ist es zu spät; (*as well*) **four dogs, and six cats besides** vier Hunde und außerdem sechs Katzen.

best *adjective* 1 bester/beste/bestes; **she's my best friend** sie ist meine beste Freundin; 2 **she's the best at tennis** im Tennis ist sie die Beste; **it's best to wait** das Beste ist zu warten.
adverb am besten; **he plays best** er spielt am besten; **I like Munich best** München gefällt mir am besten; **best of all** am allerbesten; **I like grapes best** ich mag Weintrauben am liebsten; ★ **all the best!** alles Gute!; ★ **to make the best of it** das Beste daraus machen; ★ **to do your best** sein Bestes tun; **I did my best to help her** ich habe mein Bestes getan, um ihr zu helfen.

bet *noun* Wette *die* (PL *die* Wetten).
verb wetten; **to bet on a horse** auf ein Pferd wetten; **I bet you'll forget it** ich wette mit dir, dass er es vergisst.

better *adjective, adverb* 1 besser; **she's found a better flat** sie hat eine bessere Wohnung gefunden; 2 **it works better than the other one** dieser geht besser als der andere; **even better** noch besser; **it's even better than before** das ist noch besser als vorher; 3 (*less ill*) **I'm better** es geht mir besser; **he's a bit better today** es geht ihm heute ein bisschen besser; **I feel better** ich fühle mich besser; 4 **to get better** besser werden; **my German is getting better** mein Deutsch wird besser; 5 **so much the better** umso besser; **the sooner the better** je eher, desto besser.
adverb **it's better to phone at once** es wäre besser, sofort anzurufen; **he'd better not go** er sollte besser nicht gehen; **I'd better go now** ich gehe jetzt besser.

better off *adjective* 1 (*richer*) besser gestellt; **they're better off than us** sie sind besser gestellt als wir; 2 (*more comfortable*) **to be better off** besser dran sein; **you'd be better off in bed** du wärst im Bett besser dran.

between *preposition* 1 zwischen (+DAT, *or* +ACC *when there is movement towards a place*); **between London and Dover** zwischen London und Dover; **between Monday and Friday** zwischen Montag und Freitag; 2 (*sharing*) unter (+DAT); **between ourselves** unter uns; **between the two of them** unter sich.

beyond *preposition* 1 (*in space*)

jenseits (IDEN)¦ **beyond the border**
jenseits der Grenze; **2** (*in time*) nach
(+DAT); **beyond midnight** nach
Mitternacht; **3 it's beyond me!** das
ist mir unverständlich.

bicycle *noun* Fahrrad *das* (PL *die*
Fahrräder); **she rides a bicycle** sie
fährt Rad.

big *adjective* groß; **a big house** ein
großes Haus; **my big sister** meine
große Schwester; **a big mistake** ein
großer Fehler; **it's too big for me**
das ist mir zu groß.

big toe *noun* große Zehe *die* (PL *die*
großen Zehen).

bike *noun* Rad *das* (PL *die* Räder); **by
bike** mit dem Rad.

bilingual *adjective* zweisprachig.

bill *noun* Rechnung *die* (PL *die*
Rechnungen); **can we have the bill,
please?** die Rechnung bitte.

billiards *noun* Billard *das*; **to play
billiards** Billard spielen.

bin *noun* Mülleimer *der* (PL *die*
Mülleimer).

biochemistry *noun*
Biochemie *die*.

biology *noun* Biologie *die*.

bird *noun* Vogel *der* (PL *die* Vögel).

bird sanctuary *noun*
Vogelschutzgebiet *das* (PL *die*
Vogelschutzgebiete).

Biro™ *noun* Kugelschreiber *der* (PL
die Kugelschreiber).

birth *noun* Geburt *die* (PL *die*
Geburten).

birth certificate *noun*
Geburtsurkunde *die* (PL *die*
Geburtsurkunden).

birthday *noun* Geburtstag *der* (PL
die Geburtstage); **happy birthday!**
herzlichen Glückwunsch zum
Geburtstag!

birthday party *noun*
Geburtstagsfeier *die* (PL *die*
Geburtstagsfeiern).

biscuit *noun* Keks *der* (PL *die*
Kekse).

bit *noun* **1** (*piece*) Stückchen *das*; **a
bit of chocolate** ein Stückchen
Schokolade; **2** (*a small amount*) **a
bit of** ein bisschen △; **a bit of sugar**
ein bisschen Zucker; **3** (*in a book,
film, etc.*) Teil *der* (PL *die* Teile); **this
bit is brilliant** dieser Teil ist
glänzend; **4 a bit** ein bisschen △; **a
bit too early** ein bisschen zu früh;
wait a bit! warte ein bisschen!;
5 he's a bit of a show-off er ist ein
ziemlicher Angeber; **6 bit by bit**
nach und nach.

bite *noun* **1** (*snack*) Happen *der* (PL
die Happen); **we'll just have a bite
before we go** wir essen noch einen
kleinen Happen, bevor wir gehen;
2 (*from an insect*) Stich *der* (PL *die*
Stiche); **mosquito bite** *der*
Mückenstich; **3** (*from a dog*)
Biss △ *der* (PL *die* Bisse).
verb **1** (*person or dog*) beißen ✧;
2 (*insect*) stechen ✧.

bitter *adjective* (*taste*) bitter.

black *adjective* **1** schwarz; **my black
jacket** meine schwarze Jacke; **2 a
black man** ein Schwarzer; **a black
woman** eine Schwarze.

△ NEW SPELLING: *See page xii*

blackberry noun Brombeere die
(PL die Brombeeren).

blackbird noun Amsel die (PL die
Amseln).

blackboard noun Tafel die (PL die
Tafeln).

blackcurrant noun schwarze
Johannisbeere die (PL die schwarzen
Johannisbeeren).

blame noun Schuld die; **to take the
blame for something** die Schuld für
etwas ←(ACC) auf sich ←(ACC) nehmen;
to put the blame on somebody die
Schuld auf jemanden schieben.
verb **to blame somebody for
something** jemandem die Schuld
an etwas ←(DAT) geben; **they blamed
him for the accident** sie haben ihm
die Schuld an dem Unfall gegeben;
she is to blame for it sie ist daran
schuld; **I blame the parents** ich
gebe den Eltern Schuld; **I don't
blame you** ich kann es dir nicht
verdenken.

blank noun Lücke die (PL die
Lücken).
adjective **1** (page) leer; (tape or
disk) unbespielt; **2 blank cheque**
der Blankoscheck.

blanket noun Decke die (PL die
Decken).

blaze noun Feuer das (PL die Feuer).
verb brennen ✧.

bleach noun Bleichmittel das (PL
die Bleichmittel).

bleed verb bluten; **my nose is
bleeding** meine Nase blutet.

blend verb mischen.

blender noun Mixer der (PL die
Mixer).

bless verb segnen; **bless you!** (after
a sneeze) Gesundheit!

blind noun (in a window) Rollo das
(PL die Rollos).
adjective blind.

blister noun Blase die (PL die
Blasen).

block noun (a building or buildings)
Block der (PL die Blocks); **block of
flats** der Wohnblock; **office block**
das Bürohaus; **to drive round the
block** um den Block fahren.
verb **1** sperren (an exit or a road);
2 the sink's blocked das
Spülbecken ist verstopft.

blonde adjective blond.

blood noun Blut das.

blood test noun Blutprobe die (PL
die Blutproben).

blouse noun Bluse die (PL die
Blusen).

blow noun Schlag der (PL die
Schläge).
verb **1** (a person) blasen ✧; **2** (the
wind) wehen; **3 the bomb blew the
bridge to pieces** die Bombe hat die
Brücke in die Luft gesprengt; **4 to
blow your nose** sich ←(DAT) die Nase
putzen.
● **to blow something out** etwas
ausblasen ✧ SEP.
● **to blow up** (explode) explodieren
(PERF sein).
● **to blow something up** (a tyre or
balloon) etwas aufblasen ✧ SEP;
(with explosives) etwas sprengen.

✧ IRREGULAR VERB: See the verb table in the centre of the dictionary

blow-dry noun Föhnen △ das; **a cut and blow-dry** Schneiden und Föhnen.

blue adjective blau; **blue eyes** blaue Augen.

blunder noun Fehler der (PL die Fehler).

blunt adjective 1 (a knife, pencil, or scissors) stumpf; 2 (a person or question) direkt.

blush verb erröten (PERF sein).

board noun 1 (plank, notice board, game) Brett das (PL die Bretter); **chess board** das Schachbrett; 2 (blackboard) Tafel die (PL die Tafeln); 3 (accommodation in a hotel) **full board** die Vollpension; **half board** die Halbpension; **board and lodging** Unterkunft und Verpflegung.

boarder noun (in a school) Internatsschüler der (PL die Internatsschüler), Internatsschülerin die (PL die Internatsschülerinnen).

board game noun Brettspiel das (PL die Brettspiele).

boarding noun (on a plane, train) Einsteigen das.

boarding card noun Bordkarte die (PL die Bordkarten).

boarding school noun Internat das (PL die Internate).

boast verb prahlen; **he was boasting about his new bike** er prahlte mit seinem neuen Rad.

boat noun 1 Boot das (PL die Boote), **rowing boat** das Ruderboot; 2 (larger boat) Schiff das (PL die Schiffe); **to go by boat** mit dem Schiff fahren.

body noun 1 Körper der (PL die Körper); 2 (corpse) Leiche die (PL die Leichen).

bodybuilding noun Bodybuilding das.

bodyguard noun Leibwächter der (PL die Leibwächter).

boil noun 1 **to bring the water to the boil** das Wasser zum Kochen bringen; 2 (swelling) Furunkel der (PL die Furunkel). verb 1 kochen; **the water's boiling** das Wasser kocht; **to boil vegetables** Gemüse kochen; 2 (put the kettle on) **to boil some water** Wasser aufsetzen SEP.
● **to boil over** überkochen SEP (PERF sein).

boiled egg noun gekochte Ei das (PL die gekochten Eier).

boiled potato noun Salzkartoffel die (PL die Salzkartoffeln).

boiler noun (for central heating) Heizkessel der (PL die Heizkessel).

boiling adjective 1 (water) kochend; 2 **it's boiling hot today** heute ist es wahnsinnig heiß.

bolt noun (on a door) Riegel der (PL die Riegel). verb 1 (lock) verriegeln; 2 (gobble down) runterschlingen ◇ SEP (informal).

△ NEW SPELLING: *See page xii*

bomb *noun* Bombe *die* (PL *die* Bomben).
verb bombardieren.

bombing *noun* 1 (*in war*) Bombardierung *die* (PL *die* Bombardierungen); 2 (*a terrorist attack*) Bombenattentat *das* (PL *die* Bombenattentate).

bone *noun* 1 Knochen *der* (PL *die* Knochen); 2 (*of a fish*) Gräte *die* (PL *die* Gräten).

bonfire *noun* Feuer *das* (PL *die* Feuer).

book *noun* 1 Buch *das* (PL *die* Bücher); **a book about dinosaurs** ein Buch über Dinosaurier; **my biology book** mein Biologiebuch; 2 (*of stamps, tickets*) Heft *das* (PL *die* Hefte); 3 **exercise book** *das* Heft; **cheque book** *das* Scheckbuch.
verb 1 buchen (*holiday, flight*); 2 bestellen (*a table, theatre, or cinema tickets*); **I booked a table for 8 p.m.** ich habe einen Tisch für zwanzig Uhr bestellt.

bookcase *noun* Bücherregal *das* (PL *die* Bücherregale).

booking *noun* (*for a flight or a holiday, for example*) Buchung *die* (PL *die* Buchungen).

booking office *noun* 1 (*at a train station*) Fahrkartenschalter *der* (PL *die* Fahrkartenschalter); 2 (*in a theatre or cinema*) Kasse *die* (PL *die* Kassen).

booklet *noun* Broschüre *die* (PL *die* Broschüren).

bookshelf *noun* Bücherregal *das* (PL *die* Bücherregale).

bookshop *noun* Buchhandlung *die* (PL *die* Buchhandlungen).

boot *noun* 1 Stiefel *der* (PL *die* Stiefel); 2 (*for football, walking, climbing, or skiing*) Schuh *der* (PL *die* Schuhe); **football boots** Fußballschuhe; 3 (*of a car*) Kofferraum *der* (PL *die* Kofferräume).

border *noun* (*between countries*) Grenze *die* (PL *die* Grenzen); **at the border** an der Grenze.

bore *noun* 1 (*a boring person*) langweiliger Mensch *der* (PL *die* langweiligen Menschen); 2 (*a nuisance*) **what a bore!** wie ärgerlich!

bored *adjective* **to be bored** sich langweilen; **I'm bored** ich langweile mich.

boring *adjective* langweilig.

born *adjective* geboren; **to be born** geboren werden; **she was born in Germany** sie ist in Deutschland geboren.

borrow *verb* sich ←(DAT) borgen; **can I borrow your bike?** kann ich mir dein Rad borgen?; **to borrow something from somebody** sich etwas von jemandem borgen; **I borrowed some money from Dad** ich habe mir Geld von Vati geborgt.

boss *noun* Chef *der* (PL *die* Chefs), Chefin *die* (PL *die* Chefinnen).

bossy *adjective* herrisch.

⬧ IRREGULAR VERB: *See the verb table in the centre of the dictionary*

both *pronoun* beide; **they both came** sie kamen beide; **both my sisters were there** meine beiden Schwestern waren da; **both of us** wir beide; **they are both sold** beide sind verkauft.
adverb **both at home and at school** sowohl zu Hause als auch in der Schule; **both in summer and in winter** sowohl im Sommer als auch im Winter.

bother *noun* 1 (*minor trouble*) Ärger *der*; **I've had a lot of bother with the car** ich hatte viel Ärger mit dem Auto; 2 **if it isn't too much bother** wenn es nicht zuviel Mühe macht; **it's no bother** das ist kein Problem; **the children were no bother** die Kinder waren kein Problem; **without any bother** ohne irgendwelche Schwierigkeiten.
verb 1 (*disturb*) stören; **I'm sorry to bother you** es tut mir leid, dich zu stören; 2 (*worry*) stören; **what's bothering you?** was stört dich?; **it doesn't bother me at all** das stört mich überhaupt nicht; 3 (*take trouble*) **don't bother to write** du brauchst nicht zu schreiben; **she didn't even bother to wait** sie hat nicht einmal gewartet; **don't bother!** lass es sein! (*informal*); **I can't be bothered** ich habe keine Lust.

bottle *noun* Flasche *die* (PL *die* Flaschen).

bottle bank *noun* Altglascontainer *der* (PL *die* Altglascontainer).

bottle opener *noun* Flaschenöffner *der* (PL *die* Flaschenöffner).

bottom *noun* 1 (*of a bag, bottle, hole, or stretch of water*) Boden *der* (PL *die* Böden); **at the bottom of the lake** am Boden des Sees; 2 (*of a hill or building*) Fuß *der* (PL *die* Füße); **at the bottom of the tower** am Fuß des Turms; 3 (*of a garden, street, list*) Ende *das* (PL *die* Enden); **at the bottom of the street** am Ende der Straße; 4 **at the bottom of the page** unten auf der Seite; 5 (*buttocks*) Hintern *der* (*informal*) (PL *die* Hintern).
adjective 1 unterster/unterste/ unterstes; **the bottom shelf** das unterste Regal; 2 **the bottom flat** die Wohnung im Erdgeschoss.

bounce *verb* (*jump*) springen ◇ (PERF *sein*).

bouncer *noun* Rausschmeißer *der* (PL *die* Rausschmeißer).

bound *adjective* (*certain*) **he's bound to be late** er kommt ganz bestimmt zu spät; **that was bound to happen** das musste ja kommen.

bow *noun* 1 (*in a shoelace or ribbon*) Schleife *die* (PL *die* Schleifen); 2 (*for a violin or with arrows*) Bogen *der* (PL *die* Bogen); **with bow and arrow** mit Pfeil und Bogen.

bowl *noun* 1 (*large, for salad, mixing, or washing up*) Schüssel *die* (PL *die* Schüsseln); 2 (*smaller*) Schale *die* (PL *die* Schalen).

bowler *noun* (*in cricket*) Werfer *der* (PL *die* Werfer), Werferin *die* (PL *die* Werferinnen).

bowling *noun* (*tenpin*) Bowling *das*; **to go bowling** bowlen gehen.

△ NEW SPELLING: *See page xii*

bow tie *noun* Fliege *die* (PL *die* Fliegen).

box *noun* **1** Schachtel *die* (PL *die* Schachteln); **a box of chocolates** eine Schachtel Pralinen; **2 cardboard box** *der* Karton; **3** (*on a form*) Kästchen *das* (PL *die* Kästchen).

boxer *noun* Boxer *der* (PL *die* Boxer).

boxing *noun* **1** Boxen *das*; **2 boxing match** *der* Boxkampf.

Boxing Day *noun* zweite Weihnachtsfeiertag *der*.

boy *noun* Junge *der* (PL *die* Jungen); **a little boy** ein kleiner Junge.

boyfriend *noun* Freund *der* (PL *die* Freunde).

bra *noun* BH *der* (PL *die* BHs).

brace *noun* (*for teeth*) Spange *die* (PL *die* Spangen).

bracelet *noun* Armband *das* (PL *die* Armbänder).

bracket *noun* Klammer *die* (PL *die* Klammern); **in brackets** in Klammern.

brain *noun* Gehirn *das* (PL *die* Gehirne).

brainwave *noun* Geistesblitz *der* (PL *die* Geistesblitze).

brake *noun* Bremse *die* (PL *die* Bremsen).
verb bremsen.

branch *noun* **1** (*of a tree*) Ast *der* (PL *die* Äste); **2** (*of a shop*) Filiale *die* (PL *die* Filialen); **3** (*of a bank*) Zweigstelle *die* (PL *die* Zweigstellen).

brand *noun* Marke *die* (PL *die* Marken).

brand new *adjective* nagelneu.

brass *noun* **1** (*metal*) Messing *das*; **2** (*in an orchestra*) **the brass** das Blech.

brass band *noun* Blaskapelle *die* (PL *die* Blaskapellen).

brave *adjective* tapfer.

bread *noun* Brot *das* (PL *die* Brote); **a slice of bread** eine Scheibe Brot; **a piece of bread and butter** ein Butterbrot.

break *noun* **1** (*a short rest or at school*) Pause *die* (PL *die* Pausen); **ten minutes' break** eine Pause von zehn Minuten; **to take a break** Pause machen; **at break** in der Pause; **2 the Christmas break** die Weihnachtsferien (*plural*):
verb **1** zerbrechen ✧, kaputtmachen SEP (*informal*); **he broke a glass** er hat ein Glas zerbrochen; **don't break the doll** mach die Puppe nicht kaputt; **2** (*get damaged*) zerbrechen ✧ (PERF *sein*), kaputtgehen ✧ SEP (*informal*) (PERF *sein*); **the glass broke** das Glas zerbrach; **the eggs broke** die Eier sind kaputtgegangen; **3 to break your arm** sich ←(DAT) den Arm brechen; **4** brechen ✧ (*rules, promise*); **to break one's promise** sein Versprechen brechen; **5 to break the record** den Rekord brechen ✧; **6 to break the news that** … melden, dass …
● **to break down 1** (*car*) eine Panne haben; **the car broke down** das

Auto hatte eine Panne; **2** (*talks, negotiations*) scheitern (PERF *sein*).
● **to break in** einbrechen ✧ SEP (PERF *sein*).
● **to break up 1** (*couple*) sich trennen; **2** (*crowd*) sich auflösen SEP; **3 we break up on Thursday** die Ferien fangen Donnerstag an.

breakdown *noun* **1** (*of a vehicle*) Panne *die* (PL *die* Pannen); **we had a breakdown on the motorway** wir hatten eine Panne auf der Autobahn; **2** (*in talks or negotiations*) Scheitern *das*; **3** (*a nervous collapse*) Zusammenbruch *der* (PL *die* Zusammenbrüche); **to have a nervous breakdown** einen Nervenzusammenbruch haben.

breakfast *noun* Frühstück *das* (PL *die* Frühstücke); **we have breakfast at eight** wir frühstücken um acht Uhr.

break-in *noun* Einbruch *der* (PL *die* Einbrüche).

breast *noun* Brust *die* (PL *die* Brüste).

breath *noun* Atem *der*; **out of breath** außer Atem; **to hold your breath** den Atem anhalten; **to get your breath back** wieder zu Atem kommen; **to take a deep breath** tief einatmen.

breathe *verb* atmen.

breed *noun* (*of animal*) Rasse *die* (PL *die* Rassen).

breeze *noun* Brise *die* (PL *die* Brisen).

brew *verb* **1** brauen (*beer*); **2** aufbrühen SEP (*tea*); **the tea's brewing** der Tee zieht noch.

brick *noun* Ziegel *der* (PL *die* Ziegel); **a brick wall** eine Ziegelmauer.

bride *noun* Braut *die* (PL *die* Bräute); **the bride and groom** das Brautpaar.

bridegroom *noun* Bräutigam *der* (PL *die* Bräutigame).

bridesmaid *noun* Brautjungfer *die* (PL *die* Brautjungfern).

bridge *noun* **1** (*over a river*) Brücke *die* (PL *die* Brücken); **2** (*card game*) Bridge *das*.

brief *adjective* kurz.

briefcase *noun* Aktentasche *die* (PL *die* Aktentaschen).

briefly *adverb* kurz.

briefs *plural noun* Slip *der* (PL *die* Slips).

bright *adjective* **1** (*colour*) leuchtend; **bright green socks** leuchtend grüne Socken; **2** (*eyes, sunshine*) strahlend; **3** (*light*) hell; **4** (*clever*) intelligent; **she's not very bright** sie ist nicht sehr intelligent; ★ **to look on the bright side** die Sache positiv sehen (*literally: to see things positively*).

brilliant *adjective* **1** (*very clever*) glänzend; **he's a brilliant surgeon** er ist ein glänzender Chirurg; **2** (*wonderful*) toll; **the party was brilliant!** die Party war toll!

bring *verb* **1** mitbringen ✧ SEP; **he brought a present** er brachte ein Geschenk mit; **bring your camera**

bring deinen Fotoapparat mit; **2** (*to a place*) bringen ✧; **she's bringing the children home** sie bringt die Kinder nach Hause.

● **to bring somebody up** jemanden großziehen ✧ SEP; **he was brought up by his aunt** er wurde von seiner Tante großgezogen.

Britain *noun* Großbritannien *das*; **to Britain** nach Großbritannien.

British *plural noun* **the British** die Briten.
adjective **1** britisch; **the British Isles** die Britischen Inseln; **2 he's British** er ist Brite; **she's British** sie ist Britin.

broad *adjective* **1** (*wide*) breit; **2** (*extensive*) weit.

broad bean *noun* dicke Bohne *die* (PL *die* dicken Bohnen).

broadcast *noun* Sendung *die* (PL *die* Sendungen).
verb senden.

broccoli *noun* Brokkoli *der* (PL *die* Brokkoli).

brochure *noun* Broschüre *die* (PL *die* Broschüren).

broke *adjective* **to be broke** pleite sein (*informal*).

broken *adjective* zerbrochen, kaputt (*informal*); **the window's broken** das Fenster ist kaputt; **to have a broken leg** ein gebrochenes Bein haben.

bronchitis *noun* Bronchitis *die*.

brooch *noun* Brosche *die* (PL *die* Broschen).

brother *noun* Bruder *der* (PL *die* Brüder); **my mother's brother** der Bruder meiner Mutter.

brother-in-law *noun* Schwager *der* (PL *die* Schwäger).

brown *adjective* braun; **my brown shoes** meine braunen Schuhe; **light brown** hellbraun; **dark brown** dunkelbraun; **to go brown** (*suntanned*) braun werden.

brown bread *noun* Mischbrot *das* (PL *die* Mischbrote).

bruise *noun* **1** (*on a person*) blaue Fleck *der* (PL *die* blauen Flecken); **2** (*on fruit*) Druckstelle *die* (PL *die* Druckstellen).

brush *noun* **1** (*for your hair, clothes, nails, or shoes*) Bürste *die* (PL *die* Bürsten); **my hair brush** meine Haarbürste; **2** (*for sweeping*) Besen *der* (PL *die* Besen); **3** (*for paint*) Pinsel *der* (PL *die* Pinsel).
verb **1** bürsten; **to brush your hair** sich ←(DAT) die Haare bürsten; **I brushed my hair** ich habe mir die Haare gebürstet; **2 to brush your teeth** sich ←(DAT) die Zähne putzen.

Brussels *noun* Brüssel *das*.

Brussels sprout *noun* Rosenkohl *der*; **he likes Brussels sprouts** er mag Rosenkohl.

bubble *noun* Blase *die* (PL *die* Blasen).

bubble bath *noun* Badeschaum *der*.

bucket *noun* Eimer *der* (PL *die* Eimer).

✧ IRREGULAR VERB: *See the verb table in the centre of the dictionary*

buckle *noun* Schnalle *die* (PL *die* Schnallen).

Buddhism *noun* Buddhismus *der*.

Buddhist *noun* Buddhist *der* (PL *die* Buddhisten), Buddhistin *die* (PL *die* Buddhistinnen).

budget *noun* Budget *das* (PL *die* Budgets).

buffet car *noun* Speisewagen *der* (PL *die* Speisewagen).

bug *noun* 1 (*insect*) Wanze *die* (PL *die* Wanzen); 2 (*germ*) Bazillus *der* (PL *die* Bazillen); **a stomach bug** eine Magengrippe; 3 **a computer bug** ein Programmierfehler.

build *verb* bauen.

builder *noun* Bauarbeiter *der* (PL *die* Bauarbeiter).

building *noun* Gebäude *das* (PL *die* Gebäude).

building site *noun* Baustelle *die* (PL *die* Baustellen).

built-up *adjective* 1 bebaut; 2 **built-up area** *das* Wohngebiet.

bulb *noun* 1 (*lightbulb*) Birne *die* (PL *die* Birnen); 2 (*flower bulb*) Zwiebel *die* (PL *die* Zwiebeln).

bull *noun* Bulle *der* (PL *die* Bullen).

bullet *noun* Kugel *die* (PL *die* Kugeln).

bulletin *noun* 1 (*written*) Bulletin *das* (PL *die* Bulletins); 2 (*on TV, radio*) **news bulletin** *die* Kurzmeldung.

bully *noun* 1 (*in school*) Rabauke *der* (PL *die* Rabauken);

2 (*adult*) Tyrann *der* (PL *die* Tyrannen).
verb schikanieren.

bum *noun* Hintern *der* (*informal*) (PL *die* Hintern).

bump *noun* 1 (*on a surface*) Unebenheit *die* (PL *die* Unebenheiten); **there are lots of bumps in the road** die Straße hat viele Unebenheiten; 2 (*swelling*) Beule *die* (PL *die* Beulen); **a bump on the head** eine Beule am Kopf; 3 (*jolt*) Stoß *der* (PL *die* Stöße); 4 (*noise*) Bums *der* (PL *die* Bumse).
verb 1 (*bang*) stoßen ✧; **I bumped my head** ich habe mir den Kopf gestoßen; **to bump into something** gegen etwas ←(ACC) stoßen; 2 **to bump into somebody** (*meet by chance*) jemanden zufällig treffen.

bumper *noun* Stoßstange *die* (PL *die* Stoßstangen).

bumpy *adjective* holperig.

bun *noun* 1 (*for a burger*) Brötchen *das* (PL *die* Brötchen), Semmel *die* (PL *die* Semmeln); 2 (*sweet*) süße Brötchen *das* (PL *die* süßen Brötchen), süße Semmel *die* (PL *die* süßen Semmeln).

bunch *noun* 1 (*of flowers*) Strauß *der* (PL *die* Sträuße); 2 (*of carrots, radishes, or keys*) Bund *das* (PL *die* Bunde); 3 **a bunch of grapes** eine ganze Weintraube.

bundle *noun* Bündel *das* (PL *die* Bündel).

bunk *noun* 1 (*on a boat*) Koje *die* (PL *die* Kojen); 2 (*on a train*) Bett *das* (PL *die* Betten).

△ NEW SPELLING: *See page xii*

bunk beds *plural noun*
Etagenbett *das* (*singular*).

burger *noun* Hamburger *der* (PL *die*
Hamburger).

burglar *noun* Einbrecher *der* (PL *die*
Einbrecher).

burglar alarm *noun*
Alarmanlage *die* (PL *die*
Alarmanlagen).

burglary *noun* Einbruch *der* (PL *die*
Einbrüche).

burn *noun* 1 (*on the skin*)
Verbrennung *die* (PL *die*
Verbrennungen); 2 (*on fabric,
object*) Brandstelle *die* (PL *die*
Brandstellen).
verb 1 verbrennen ✧; **she burnt his
letters** sie hat seine Briefe
verbrannt; 2 (*fire, candle*)
brennen ✧; 3 (*injure*)
verbrennen ✧; **to burn yourself**
sich verbrennen; **you'll burn your
fingers!** du verbrennst dir die
Finger!; 4 (*cake, meat, etc.*)
anbrennen ✧ SEP; **Mum's burnt the
cake** Mutti hat den Kuchen
anbrennen lassen.

burnt *adjective* 1 (*papers, rubbish*)
verbrannt; 2 (*cake, meat, etc.*)
angebrannt.

burst *verb* 1 platzen lassen (*a
balloon*); **the tyre has burst** der
Reifen ist geplatzt; 2 **to burst out
laughing** in Lachen ausbrechen ✧
SEP (PERF *sein*); **to burst into tears** in
Tränen ausbrechen ✧ SEP (PERF
sein); 3 **to burst into flames** in
Flammen aufgehen ✧ SEP (PERF
sein).

bury *verb* 1 begraben ✧ (*a dead
person*); 2 vergraben ✧ (*a treasure
or a bone*).

bus *noun* Bus *der* (PL *die* Busse); **on
the bus** im Bus; **by bus** mit dem
Bus.

bus driver *noun* Busfahrer *der* (PL
die Busfahrer), Busfahrerin *die* (PL
die Busfahrerinnen).

bush *noun* Busch *der* (PL *die*
Büsche).

business *noun* 1 (*commercial
dealings*) Geschäfte (*plural*);
business is bad die Geschäfte
gehen schlecht; **he's in Leeds on
business** er ist geschäftlich in
Leeds; 2 (*a line of business or
profession*) Branche *die* (PL *die*
Branchen); **he's in the insurance
business** er ist in der
Versicherungsbranche; 3 (*firm or
company*) Betrieb *der* (PL *die*
Betriebe); **small businesses** kleine
Betriebe; 4 (*personal concern*)
Angelegenheit *die* (PL *die*
Angelegenheiten); **mind your own
business!** kümmere dich um deine
eigenen Angelegenheiten!

businessman *noun*
Geschäftsmann *der* (PL *die*
Geschäftsleute).

business trip *noun*
Geschäftsreise *die* (PL *die*
Geschäftsreisen).

businesswoman *noun*
Geschäftsfrau *die* (PL *die*
Geschäftsfrauen).

bus pass *noun* Zeitkarte *die* (PL *die*
Zeitkarten).

✧ IRREGULAR VERB: *See the verb table in the centre of the dictionary*

bus route *noun* Buslinie *die* (PL *die* Buslinien).

bus shelter *noun* Wartehäuschen *das* (PL *die* Wartehäuschen).

bus station *noun* Busbahnhof *der* (PL *die* Busbahnhöfe).

bus stop *noun* Bushaltestelle *die* (PL *die* Bushaltestellen).

bus ticket *noun* Busfahrkarte *die* (PL *die* Busfahrkarten).

busy *adjective* 1 beschäftigt; **he's busy** er ist beschäftigt; **she was busy packing** sie war mit Packen beschäftigt; 2 **to have a busy day** viel zu tun haben; 3 **the shops were busy** die Läden waren sehr voll; 4 (*phone*) besetzt.

but *conjunction* 1 aber; **small but strong** klein aber stark; 2 (*after a negative statement*) sondern; **not Thursday but Friday** nicht Donnerstag, sondern Freitag; **not only … but also** nicht nur … sondern auch.
preposition 1 außer (+DAT); **everyone but Winston** alle außer Winston; **anything but that!** nur das nicht!; 2 **the last but one** der/die/das Vorletzte.

butcher *noun* 1 Fleischer *der* (PL *die* Fleischer), Metzger *der* (PL *die* Metzger); **he's a butcher** er ist Fleischer, er ist Metzger; 2 **the butcher's** die Fleischerei, die Metzgerei.

butter *noun* Butter *die*.
verb buttern.

butterfly *noun* Schmetterling *der* (PL *die* Schmetterlinge).

button *noun* Knopf *der* (PL *die* Knöpfe).

buttonhole *noun* Knopfloch *das* (PL *die* Knopflöcher).

buy *noun* Kauf *der* (PL *die* Käufe); **a bad buy** ein schlechter Kauf.
verb kaufen; **I bought the tickets** ich habe die Karten gekauft; **to buy something for somebody** jemandem etwas kaufen; **Sarah bought him a sweater** Sarah hat ihm einen Pullover gekauft.

buzz *verb* (*a fly or bee*) summen.

buzzer *noun* Summer *der* (PL *die* Summer).

by *preposition* 1 von (+DAT); **I was bitten by a dog** ich bin von einem Hund gebissen worden; **by Mozart** von Mozart; 2 **by mistake** versehentlich; 3 (*travel*) mit (+DAT); **to come by bus** mit dem Bus kommen; **to go by train** mit dem Zug fahren; **by bike** mit dem Rad; 4 (*near*) an (+DAT); **by the sea** am Meer; **the stop by the school** die Haltestelle an der Schule; 5 (*before*) bis; **it'll be ready by Monday** es wird bis Montag fertig sein; **I'll be back by four** ich bin bis vier Uhr zurück; 6 **by now** inzwischen; 7 **by yourself** ganz allein; **I was by myself in the house** ich war ganz allein im Haus; **she did it by herself** sie hat es ganz allein gemacht; 8 **by the way** übrigens; 9 **to go by** vorbeigehen ◇ SEP (PERF *sein*).

bye *exclamation* tschüs! (*informal*).

△ NEW SPELLING: See page xii

C c

cab *noun* **1** Taxi *das* (PL *die* Taxis); **to call a cab** ein Taxi rufen; **2** (*on a lorry*) Führerhaus *das* (PL *die* Führerhäuser).

cabbage *noun* Kohl *der*.

café *noun* Café *das* (PL *die* Cafés).

cage *noun* Käfig *der* (PL *die* Käfige).

cake *noun* Kuchen *der* (PL *die* Kuchen); **would you like a piece of cake?** möchtest du ein Stück Kuchen?

calculate *verb* berechnen.

calculation *noun* Rechnung *die* (PL *die* Rechnungen).

calculator *noun* Taschenrechner *der* (PL *die* Taschenrechner).

calendar *noun* Kalender *der* (PL *die* Kalender).

calf *noun* **1** (*animal*) Kalb *das* (PL *die* Kälber); **2** (*of your leg*) Wade *die* (PL *die* Waden).

call *noun* (*telephone*) Anruf *der* (PL *die* Anrufe); **I had several calls this morning** ich erhielt heute Morgen mehrere Anrufe; **thank you for your call** danke für deinen Anruf; **a phone call** ein Telefonanruf.
verb **1** rufen ✧; **to call a taxi** ein Taxi rufen; **to call the doctor** einen Arzt rufen; **they called the police** sie riefen die Polizei; **2** (*phone*)

anrufen ✧ SEP; **call me later** ruf mich später an; **thank you for calling** danke für deinen Anruf; **I'll call you back later** ich rufe dich später zurück; **3** nennen ✧; **they've called the baby Julie** sie haben das Baby Julie genannt; **4 to be called** heißen ✧; **her brother is called Dan** ihr Bruder heißt Dan; **what's he called?** wie heißt er?

call box *noun* Telefonzelle *die* (PL *die* Telefonzellen).

calm *adjective* ruhig.
verb beruhigen.
● **to calm down** sich beruhigen; **he's calmed down a bit** er hat sich etwas beruhigt.
● **to calm somebody down** jemanden beruhigen; **I tried to calm her down** ich habe versucht, sie zu beruhigen.

calmly *adverb* ruhig.

camcorder *noun* Camcorder *der* (PL *die* Camcorder).

camera *noun* **1** Fotoapparat *der* (PL *die* Fotoapparate); **2** (*film or video camera*) Kamera *die* (PL *die* Kameras).

camp *noun* Lager *das* (PL *die* Lager).
verb campen, zelten.

camper van *noun* Camper *der* (PL *die* Camper).

camping *noun* Camping *das*; **to go camping** zelten; **we're going camping in Bavaria this summer** diesen Sommer zelten wir in Bayern.

campsite *noun* Campingplatz *der* (PL *die* Campingplätze).

can¹ *noun* **1** Dose *die* (PL *die* Dosen);

✧ IRREGULAR VERB: *See the verb table in the centre of the dictionary*

a can of tomatoes eine Dose Tomaten; **2** (*for petrol or oil*) Kanister *der* (PL *die* Kanister).

can² *verb* **1** können ◇; **I can't be there before ten** ich kann vor zehn Uhr nicht da sein; **can you open the door, please?** kannst du die Tür bitte aufmachen?; **can I help you?** kann ich Ihnen helfen?; **they couldn't come** sie konnten nicht kommen; **you could have told me** das hättest du mir wirklich sagen können; **I can't see him** ich kann ihn nicht sehen; **I can't remember it** ich kann mich nicht daran erinnern; **she can't drive** sich kann nicht Auto fahren; **2** (*be allowed*) dürfen ◇; **you can't smoke here** Sie dürfen hier nicht rauchen.

Canada *noun* Kanada *das*; **to Canada** nach Kanada.

Canadian *noun* Kanadier *der* (PL *die* Kanadier), Kanadierin *die* (PL *die* Kanadierinnen).
adjective kanadisch; **he is Canadian** er ist Kanadier.

canal *noun* Kanal *der* (PL *die* Kanäle).

cancel *verb* absagen SEP; **the concert's been cancelled** das Konzert ist abgesagt worden.

cancer *noun* Krebs *der*; **to have lung cancer** Lungenkrebs haben.

Cancer *noun* Krebs *der* (PL *die* Krebse); **I'm Cancer** ich bin Krebs.

candidate *noun* Kandidat *der* (PL *die* Kandidaten), Kandidatin *die* (PL *die* Kandidatinnen).

candle *noun* Kerze *die* (PL *die* Kerzen).

candlestick *noun* Kerzenhalter *der* (PL *die* Kerzenhalter).

canned *adjective* in Dosen; **canned tomatoes** Tomaten in Dosen.

canoe *noun* Kanu *das* (PL *die* Kanus).

canoeing *noun* **to go canoeing** Kanu fahren ◇ (PERF *sein*); **I like canoeing** ich fahre gerne Kanu.

can-opener *noun* Dosenöffner *der* (PL *die* Dosenöffner).

canteen *noun* Kantine *die* (PL *die* Kantinen).

canvas *noun* **1** (*of a tent or bag*) Segeltuch *das*; **2** (*for painting on*) Leinwand *die*.

cap *noun* **1** (*hat*) Kappe *die* (PL *die* Kappen); **baseball cap** die Baseballkappe; **2** (*on a bottle or tube*) Verschluss △ *der* (PL *die* Verschlüsse).

capable *adjective* fähig.

capital *noun* **1** (*city*) Hauptstadt *die* (PL *die* Hauptstädte); **Berlin is the capital of Germany** Berlin ist die Hauptstadt von Deutschland; **2** (*letter*) Großbuchstabe *der* (PL *die* Großbuchstaben); **in capitals** mit Großbuchstaben.

capitalism *noun* Kapitalismus *der*.

Capricorn *noun* Steinbock *der* (PL die Steinböcke); **Linda's Capricorn** Linda ist Steinbock.

captain *noun* Kapitän *der* (PL die Kapitäne).

car *noun* Auto *das* (PL die Autos); **to park the car** das Auto einparken; **we're going by car** wir fahren mit dem Auto; **car crash** der Autounfall.

caramel *noun* Karamell∆ *der* (PL die Karamells).

caravan *noun* Wohnwagen *der* (PL die Wohnwagen).

card *noun* Karte *die* (PL die Karten); **card game** das Kartenspiel; **to have a game of cards** Karten spielen.

cardboard *noun* Pappe *die*.

cardigan *noun* Strickjacke *die* (PL die Strickjacken).

cardphone *noun* Kartentelefon *das* (PL die Kartentelefone).

care *noun* 1 Vorsicht *die*; **to take care crossing the road** vorsichtig beim Überqueren der Straße sein; **take care!** (*be careful*) sei vorsichtig!; (*when saying goodbye*) mach's gut!; 2 **to take care to do something** aufpassen SEP, dass man etwas tut; **to take care of somebody** auf jemanden aufpassen.
verb 1 **to care about something** sich um etwas ←(ACC) kümmern; **she cares about the environment** sie kümmert sich um die Umwelt; 2 **she doesn't care** es ist ihr egal; **I couldn't care less!** das ist mir völlig egal!

careful *adjective* vorsichtig; **a careful driver** ein vorsichtiger Fahrer, eine vorsichtige Fahrerin; **be careful!** sei vorsichtig!

carefully *adverb* 1 sorgfältig; **to read the instructions carefully** die Anweisungen sorgfältig lesen; 2 vorsichtig; **she put the vase down carefully** sie stellte die Vase vorsichtig hin; **drive carefully!** fahr vorsichtig!; 3 **listen carefully!** hören Sie gut zu!

careless *adjective* 1 **he's very careless** er ist sehr nachlässig; **this is careless work** das ist eine nachlässige Arbeit; 2 **a careless mistake** ein Flüchtigkeitsfehler; 3 **a careless driver** ein leichtsinniger Fahrer.

car ferry *noun* Autofähre *die* (PL die Autofähren).

car hire *noun* Autovermietung *die*.

Caribbean *noun* **the Caribbean (islands)** die Karibik (*singular*).

carnation *noun* Nelke *die* (PL die Nelken).

carnival *noun* Karneval *der* (PL die Karnevale).

car park *noun* Parkplatz *der* (PL die Parkplätze); (*multi-storey*) Parkhaus *das* (PL die Parkhäuser).

carpenter *noun* Tischler *der* (PL die Tischler).

carpentry *noun* Tischlerhandwerk *das*.

carpet *noun* Teppich *der* (PL die Teppiche).

✧ **IRREGULAR VERB:** *See the verb table in the centre of the dictionary*

car phone *noun* Autotelefon *das* (PL *die* Autotelefone).

car radio *noun* Autoradio *das* (PL *die* Autoradios).

carriage *noun* (*of a train*) Abteil *das* (PL *die* Abteile).

carrier bag *noun* Tragetasche *die* (PL *die* Tragetaschen).

carrot *noun* Karotte *die* (PL *die* Karotten), Möhre *die* (PL *die* Möhren).

carry *verb* tragen; **she was carrying a case** sie trug einen Koffer.
● **to carry on** weitermachen SEP; **they carried on working** sie machten ihre Arbeit weiter.

carrycot *noun* Babytragetasche *die* (PL *die* Babytragetaschen).

carsick *adjective* **he gets carsick** ihm wird beim Autofahren schlecht.

carton *noun* 1 (*of cream or yoghurt*) Becher *der* (PL *die* Becher); 2 (*of milk or orange*) Tüte *die* (PL *die* Tüten).

cartoon *noun* 1 (*a film*) Zeichentrickfilm *der* (PL *die* Zeichentrickfilme); 2 (*a comic strip*) Cartoon *der* (PL *die* Cartoons); 3 (*a drawing*) Karikatur *die* (PL *die* Karikaturen).

cartridge *noun* (*for a pen*) Patrone *die* (PL *die* Patronen).

case[1] *noun* 1 (*suitcase*) Koffer *der* (PL *die* Koffer); **to pack a case** einen Koffer packen; 2 (*a large wooden box*) Kiste *die* (PL *die* Kisten); 3 (*for spectacles or small things*) Etui *das* (PL *die* Etuis).

case[2] *noun* 1 Fall *der* (PL *die* Fälle); **in that case** in dem Fall; **that's not the case** das ist nicht der Fall; **in case of fire** bei Feuer; 2 **in case** falls; **in case he comes** falls er kommt; 3 **just in case** für alle Fälle; 4 **in any case** sowieso; **in any case, it's too late** es ist sowieso zu spät.

cash *noun* 1 (*money in general*) Geld *das*; **I haven't any cash on me** ich habe kein Geld dabei; 2 (*money rather than a cheque*) Bargeld *das*; **to pay in cash** bar zahlen; **£50 in cash** fünfzig Pfund in bar.

cash card *noun* Bankkarte *die* (PL *die* Bankkarten).

cash desk *noun* Kasse *die* (PL *die* Kassen); **to pay at the cash desk** an der Kasse zahlen.

cash dispenser *noun* Geldautomat *der* (PL *die* Geldautomaten).

cashier *noun* Kassierer *der* (PL *die* Kassierer), Kassiererin *die* (PL *die* Kassiererinnen).

cash point *noun* Geldautomat *der* (PL *die* Geldautomaten).

cassette *noun* Kassette *die* (PL *die* Kassetten).

cassette recorder *noun* Kassettenrekorder *der* (PL *die* Kassettenrekorder).

cast *noun* (*of a play*) Besetzung *die*.

castle *noun* 1 Burg *die* (PL *die* Burgen); 2 (*in chess*) Turm *der* (PL *die* Türme).

casual *adjective* zwanglos.

△ NEW SPELLING: *See page xii*

casualty noun 1 (in an accident) Verletzte der/die (PL die Verletzten); 2 (hospital department) Unfallstation die (PL die Unfallstationen); **he's in casualty** er ist auf der Unfallstation.

cat noun Katze die (PL die Katzen); (tomcat) Kater der (PL die Kater); ★ **it's raining cats and dogs** es regnet in Strömen (literally: it's raining in streams).

catalogue noun Katalog der (PL die Kataloge).

catastrophe noun Katastrophe die (PL die Katastrophen).

catch noun 1 (on a door) Schnapper der (PL die Schnapper); 2 (a drawback) Haken der (PL die Haken); **where's the catch?** wo ist der Haken? verb 1 fangen ✧; **Tom caught the ball** Tom hat den Ball gefangen; **she caught a fish** sie hat einen Fisch gefangen; **catch me!** fang mich!; 2 **to catch somebody doing something** jemanden bei etwas ←(DAT) erwischen; **he was caught stealing money** er wurde beim Geldstehlen erwischt; 3 (be in time for) noch erreichen; **did Tim catch his plane?** hat Tim sein Flugzeug noch erreicht?; 4 (become ill with) bekommen ✧; **she's caught chickenpox** sie hat die Windpocken bekommen; 5 verstehen ✧ (what somebody says); **I didn't catch your name** ich habe Ihren Namen nicht verstanden.
• **to catch up with somebody** jemanden einholen SEP.

catering noun 1 (trade) Gastronomie die; 2 **who's doing the catering?** wer liefert das Essen und die Getränke?

cathedral noun Kathedrale die (PL die Kathedralen); **Cologne cathedral** der Kölner Dom.

Catholic noun Katholik der (PL die Katholiken), Katholikin die (PL die Katholikinnen). adjective katholisch.

cattle plural noun Vieh das.

cauliflower noun Blumenkohl der; **cauliflower cheese** der Blumenkohlauflauf.

cause noun 1 Ursache die (PL die Ursachen); **the cause of the accident** die Unfallursache; 2 **for a good cause** für eine gute Sache. verb verursachen; **to cause difficulties** Schwierigkeiten verursachen.

cave noun Höhle die (PL die Höhlen).

caving noun Höhlenforschung die; **to go caving** auf Höhlenforschung gehen.

CD noun CD die (PL die CDs).

CD player noun CD-Spieler der (PL die CD-Spieler).

CD-ROM noun CD-ROM die (PL die CD-ROMs).

ceiling noun Decke die (PL die Decken); **on the ceiling** an der Decke.

✧ IRREGULAR VERB: See the verb table in the centre of the dictionary

celebrate *verb* feiern; **he's celebrating his birthday** er feiert seinen Geburtstag.

celebrity *noun* Berühmtheit *die* (PL die Berühmtheiten).

celery *noun* Sellerie *der* (PL die Sellerie).

cell *noun* Zelle *die* (PL die Zellen).

cellar *noun* Keller *der* (PL die Keller).

cello *noun* Cello *das* (PL die Cellos); **to play the cello** Cello spielen.

cement *noun* Zement *der*.

cemetery *noun* Friedhof *der* (PL die Friedhöfe).

centigrade *adjective* Celsius; **ten degrees centigrade** zehn Grad Celsius.

centimetre *noun* Zentimeter *der* (PL die Zentimeter).

central *adjective* 1 zentral; **the office is very central** das Büro ist sehr zentral gelegen; 2 **in central London** im Zentrum von London.

central heating *noun* Zentralheizung *die*.

centre *noun* Zentrum *das* (PL die Zentren); **in the centre of** im Zentrum von (+DAT); **in the town centre** im Stadtzentrum; **a shopping centre** ein Einkaufszentrum.

century *noun* Jahrhundert *das* (PL die Jahrhunderte); **in the twentieth century** im zwanzigsten Jahrhundert.

cereal *noun* **breakfast cereal** Frühstücksflocken (*plural*).

certain *adjective* 1 (*definite*) bestimmt; **a certain number of** eine bestimmte Zahl von (+DAT); 2 (*confident*) sicher; **to be certain** sich ←(DAT) sicher sein; **are you certain of the address?** bist du dir der Adresse sicher?; **I'm absolutely certain** ich bin mir ganz sicher; **to be certain that** … sicher sein, dass …; 3 **nobody knows for certain** niemand weiß es genau.

certainly *adverb* bestimmt; **certainly not** bestimmt nicht.

certificate *noun* 1 Bescheinigung *die* (PL die Bescheinigungen); 2 **birth certificate** *die* Geburtsurkunde; 3 (*at school*) Zeugnis *das* (PL die Zeugnisse).

chain Kette *die* (PL die Ketten).

chair *noun* 1 (*upright*) Stuhl *der* (PL die Stühle); **a kitchen chair** ein Küchenstuhl; 2 (*with arms*) Sessel *der* (PL die Sessel).

chair lift *noun* Sessellift *der* (PL die Sessellifte).

chalet *noun* 1 (*in the mountains*) Chalet *das* (PL die Chalets); 2 (*in a holiday camp*) Ferienhaus *das* (PL die Ferienhäuser).

challenge *noun* Herausforderung *die* (PL die Herausforderungen).

champion *noun* Meister *der* (PL die Meister), Meisterin *die* (PL die Meisterinnen); **the world slalom champion** der Weltmeister im Slalom, die Weltmeisterin im Slalom.

△ NEW SPELLING: *See page xii*

chance noun 1 (*opportunity*) Gelegenheit die (PL die Gelegenheiten); **to have the chance to do something** die Gelegenheit haben, etwas zu tun; **if you have the chance to go to New York** wenn du die Gelegenheit hast, nach New York zu fahren; **I had no chance to speak to him** ich hatte keine Gelegenheit, mit ihm zu reden; 2 (*likelihood*) Aussicht die (PL die Aussichten); **he's got no chance of winning** er hat keine Aussicht zu gewinnen; 3 (*luck*) **by chance** zufällig; **do you have her address, by any chance?** hast du zufällig ihre Adresse?

change noun 1 (*from one thing to another*) Änderung die (PL die Änderungen); **a change of address** eine Adressenänderung; **there's been a change of plan** der Plan ist geändert worden; 2 (*alteration*) Veränderung die (PL die Veränderungen); **they've made some changes to the house** sie haben im Haus ein paar Veränderungen vorgenommen; **a change in the weather** eine Wetterveränderung; 3 (*for the sake of variety*) **for a change, we could go to a restaurant** zur Abwechslung könnten wir in ein Restaurant gehen; **it makes a change from hamburgers** das ist mal etwas anderes als Hamburger; **a change of clothes** etwas anderes zum Anziehen; 4 (*cash*) Wechselgeld das; **I haven't any change** ich habe kein Wechselgeld. verb 1 (*make different*) ändern; **you can't change her** du kannst sie nicht ändern; **to change your address** seine Adresse ändern; 2 (*become different*) sich verändern; **Liz has changed a lot** Liz hat sich sehr verändert; 3 (*transform completely*) verwandeln; **the prince changed into a frog** der Prinz hat sich in einen Frosch verwandelt; 4 (*exchange in a shop*) umtauschen SEP; **just change it for a larger size** tauschen Sie es einfach gegen eine größere Größe um; 5 (*change clothes*) sich umziehen ✧ SEP; **Mike's just changing** Mike zieht sich gerade um; 6 (*switch from one train or bus to another*) umsteigen ✧ SEP (PERF *sein*); **we changed trains at Crewe** wir sind in Crewe umgestiegen; 7 (*switch one thing for another*) wechseln; **I want to change my job** ich möchte meine Stellung wechseln; **they changed places** sie haben die Plätze gewechselt; 8 **to change your mind** sich anders entschließen ✧.

changing room noun (*for sport or swimming*) Umkleideraum der (PL die Umkleideräume).

channel noun 1 (*on TV*) Kanal der (PL die Kanäle); **to change channels** auf einen anderen Kanal schalten; 2 **the Channel** der Kanal.

Channel Tunnel noun Eurotunnel der.

chaos noun Chaos das; **it was chaos!** das war ein Chaos!

chapel noun Kapelle die (PL die Kapellen).

chapter *noun* Kapitel das (PL die Kapitel); **in chapter two** im zweiten Kapitel.

character *noun* 1 (*personality*) Charakter der; 2 (*somebody in a book*) Charakter der (PL die Charaktere); 3 (*part in a play or film*) Rolle die (PL die Rollen); **the main character** die Hauptrolle.

charcoal *noun* 1 (*for burning*) Holzkohle die; 2 (*for drawing*) Kohlestift der (PL die Kohlestifte).

charge *noun* 1 (*what you pay*) Gebühr die (PL die Gebühren); **a booking charge** Buchungskosten (*plural*); **an extra or additional charge** eine zusätzliche Gebühr; **there's no charge** das ist kostenlos; **2 to be in charge** für etwas ←(ACC) verantwortlich sein; **who's in charge of the children?** wer ist für die Kinder verantwortlich?; **3 to be on a charge of theft** wegen Diebstahls angeklagt sein.
verb 1 (*ask to pay*) berechnen; **they charge us fifteen pounds an hour** sie berechnen uns fünfzehn Pfund pro Stunde; **they didn't charge for delivery** sie haben die Lieferung nicht berechnet; **we won't charge you for it** wir berechnen Ihnen nichts dafür; **2 to charge somebody with something** jemanden wegen etwas ←(GEN) anklagen SEP.

charity *noun* Wohltätigkeitsverein der (PL die Wohltätigkeitsvereine).

charming *adjective* reizend.

chart *noun* 1 (*table*) Tabelle die (PL die Tabellen); 2 **the weather chart** die Wetterkarte; 3 **the charts** die Hitparade.

charter flight *noun* Charterflug der (PL die Charterflüge).

chase *noun* Verfolgungsjagd die (PL die Verfolgungsjagden); **a car chase** eine Verfolgungsjagd im Auto.
verb jagen.

chat *noun* Plauderei die (PL die Plaudereien); **to have a chat with somebody** mit jemandem plaudern.

chat show *noun* Talkshow die (PL die Talkshows).

chatter *verb* 1 (*talk*) schwatzen; **2 my teeth were chattering** ich habe mit den Zähnen geklappert.

cheap *adjective* billig; **cheap shoes** billige Schuhe; **that's very cheap** das ist sehr billig.

cheaply *adverb* billig; **to eat cheaply** billig essen.

cheap-rate *adjective* verbilligt; **a cheap-rate phone call** ein Gespräch zum Spartarif.

cheat *noun* 1 Betrüger der (PL die Betrüger), Betrügerin die (PL die Betrügerinnen); 2 (*in games*) Mogler der (PL die Mogler), Moglerin die (PL die Moglerinnen).
verb 1 betrügen ✧; 2 (*in games*) mogeln.

check *noun* 1 (*in a factory or at a border control*) Kontrolle die (PL die Kontrollen); **passport check** die

△ NEW SPELLING: *See page xii*

Passkontrolle; 2 (*in chess*) **check!**
Schach!
verb 1 (*make sure*) prüfen; **he
checked their statements** er prüfte
ihre Aussage; 2 (*make sure by
looking*) nachsehen ✧ SEP; **to check
the time** nachsehen, wie viel Uhr es
ist; **check they're all back** sieh
nach, ob alle wieder da sind;
3 (*inspect*) kontrollieren; **to check
the tickets** die Fahrkarten
kontrollieren.

check in *verb* (*for a flight*)
einchecken SEP.

check-in *noun*
Abfertigungsschalter *der* (PL *die*
Abfertigungsschalter).

checkout *noun* Kasse *die* (PL *die*
Kassen); **at the checkout** an der
Kasse.

check-up *noun* Untersuchung *die*
(PL *die* Untersuchungen).

cheek *noun* 1 (*part of face*)
Backe *die* (PL *die* Backen); 2 (*nerve*)
Frechheit *die*; **what a cheek!** so
eine Frechheit!

cheer *noun* 1 **three cheers for
Tom!** ein dreifaches Hurra für
Tom!; 2 (*when drinking*) **cheers!**
prost!
verb (*shout hurray*) Hurra
schreien ✧.
• **to cheer somebody up** jemanden
aufmuntern SEP; **your visits always
cheer me up** dein Besuch muntert
mich immer auf; **cheer up!** Kopf
hoch!

cheerful *adjective* fröhlich.

cheese *noun* Käse *der*; **a cheese
sandwich** ein Käsebrot.

chef *noun* Koch *der* (PL *die* Köche),
Köchin *die* (PL *die* Köchinnen).

chemist *noun* 1 (*in a pharmacy*)
Apotheker *der* (PL *die* Apotheker),
Apothekerin *die* (PL *die*
Apothekerinnen); 2 **chemist's**
(*dispensing*) Apotheke *die* (PL *die*
Apotheken); **at the chemist's** in der
Apotheke; 3 (*scientist*)
Chemiker *der* (PL *die* Chemiker),
Chemikerin *die* (PL *die*
Chemikerinnen).

chemistry *noun* Chemie *die*.

cheque *noun* Scheck *der* (PL *die*
Schecks); **to pay by cheque** mit
Scheck bezahlen; **to write a cheque**
einen Scheck austellen.

cheque book *noun*
Scheckbuch *das* (PL *die*
Scheckbücher).

cherry *noun* Kirsche *die* (PL *die*
Kirschen).

chess *noun* Schach *das*; **to play
chess** Schach spielen.

chessboard *noun*
Schachbrett *das* (PL *die*
Schachbretter).

chest *noun* 1 (*part of the body*)
Brust *die* (PL *die* Brüste); 2 (*box*)
Truhe *die* (PL *die* Truhen); 3 **a chest
of drawers** eine Kommode.

chestnut *noun* Esskastanie △ *die*
(PL *die* Esskastanien).

chestnut tree *noun* 1 (*horse-
chestnut*) Rosskastanie △ *die* (PL *die*
Rosskastanien); 2 (*sweet chestnut*)

✧ IRREGULAR VERB: *See the verb table in the centre of the dictionary*

Edelkastanie die (PL die
Edelkastanien).

chew verb kauen.

chewing gum noun
Kaugummi der (PL die Kaugummis).

chicken noun Huhn das (PL die
Hühner); **roast chicken** das
Brathähnchen; **chicken breast** die
Hühnerbrust.

chickenpox noun Windpocken
(plural).

child noun Kind das (PL die Kinder);
when I was a child … als Kind …

childish adjective kindisch.

childminder noun
Tagesmutter die (PL die
Tagesmütter).

chill noun 1 Kälte die; 2 **to have a
chill** eine Erkältung haben.

chilled adjective gekühlt.

chilli noun Chili der.

chimney noun Schornstein der (PL
die Schornsteine).

chimpanzee noun
Schimpanse der (PL die
Schimpansen).

chin noun Kinn das (PL die Kinne).

china noun Porzellan das; **china
bowl** die Porzellanschüssel.

China noun China das.

Chinese noun 1 **the Chinese**
(people) die Chinesen;
2 (language) Chinesisch das.
adjective 1 chinesisch; **a Chinese
man** ein Chinese; **a Chinese**

woman eine Chinesin; 2 **to have a
Chinese meal** chinesisch essen.

chip noun 1 (fried potato) **chips**
Pommes frites (plural); **fish and
chips** ausgebackener Fisch mit
Pommes frites; 2 (microchip)
Chip der (PL die Chips); 3 (in glass or
china) angeschlagene Stelle die (PL
die angeschlagenen Stellen).

chipped adjective angeschlagen.

chocolate noun 1 Schokolade die;
a box of chocolates eine Schachtel
Pralinen; 2 **chocolate ice cream**
das Schokoladeneis; 3 **a cup of hot
chocolate** eine Tasse Kakao.

choice noun 1 Wahl die (PL die
Wahlen); **to make a good choice**
eine gute Wahl treffen; 2 (variety)
Auswahl die; **you have a choice of
two flights** du hast zwei Flüge zur
Auswahl.

choir noun Chor der (PL die Chöre).

choke noun (on a car) Choke der
(PL die Chokes).
verb (by yourself) sich verschlucken;
she choked on a bone sie hat sich
an einer Gräte verschluckt.

choose verb 1 wählen; **you chose
well** du hast gut gewählt; **it's hard to
choose from all these colours** es
ist schwer, unter allen diesen Farben
zu wählen; 2 (select from a group of
things) sich ←(DAT) aussuchen SEP;
Cathy chose the red skirt Cathy
suchte sich den roten Rock aus.

chop noun Kotelett das (PL die
Koteletts); **a pork chop** ein

△ NEW SPELLING: See page xii

Schweinekotelett.
verb hacken.

chord *noun* Akkord der (PL die Akkorde).

chorus *noun* 1 (*when you all join in the song*) Refrain der (PL die Refrains); 2 (*a group of singers*) Chor der (PL die Chöre).

Christ *noun* Christus der.

christening *noun* Taufe die (PL die Taufen).

Christian *noun* Christ der (PL die Christen), Christin die (PL die Christinnen).
adjective christlich.

Christian name *noun* Vorname der (PL die Vornamen).

Christmas *noun* Weihnachten das (PL die Weihnachten); **at Christmas** zu Weihnachten; **what did you get for Christmas?** was hast du zu Weihnachten bekommen?; **Happy Christmas!** Frohe Weihnachten!

Christmas card *noun* Weihnachtskarte die (PL die Weihnachtskarten).

Christmas carol *noun* Weihnachtslied das (PL die Weihnachtslieder).

Christmas cracker *noun* Knallbonbon der (PL die Knallbonbons).

Christmas Day *noun* erste Weihnachtstag der.

Christmas Eve *noun* Heiligabend der; **on Christmas Eve** Heiligabend.

Christmas present *noun* Weihnachtsgeschenk das (PL die Weihnachtsgeschenke).

Christmas tree *noun* Weihnachtsbaum der (PL die Weihnachtsbäume).

church *noun* Kirche die (PL die Kirchen); **to go to church** in die Kirche gehen.

chute *noun* (*in a swimming pool or playground*) Rutsche die (PL die Rutschen).

cider *noun* Apfelwein der (PL die Apfelweine).

cigar *noun* Zigarre die (PL die Zigarren).

cigarette *noun* Zigarette die (PL die Zigaretten).

cinema *noun* Kino das (PL die Kinos); **to go to the cinema** ins Kino gehen.

circle *noun* Kreis der (PL die Kreise); **to sit in a circle** im Kreis sitzen; **to go round in circles** sich im Kreis drehen.

circus *noun* Zirkus der (PL die Zirkusse).

citizen *noun* Bürger der (PL die Bürger), Bürgerin die (PL die Bürgerinnen).

city *noun* Stadt die (PL die Städte); **the city of Berlin** die Stadt Berlin.

city centre *noun* Stadtzentrum das (PL die Stadtzentren); **in the city centre** im Stadtzentrum.

✧ IRREGULAR VERB: *See the verb table in the centre of the dictionary*

civilization noun Zivilisation die
(PL die Zivilisationen).

civil servant noun Beamte der (PL
die Beamten), Beamtin die (PL die
Beamtinnen); **she's a civil servant**
sie ist Beamtin.

claim verb behaupten; **he claims to
know who ...** er behauptet zu
wissen, wer ...

clap verb 1 klatschen; **everyone
clapped** alle klatschten; **2 to clap
your hands** in die Hände klatschen.

clarinet noun Klarinette die (PL die
Klarinetten); **to play the clarinet**
Klarinette spielen.

clash noun (between two groups)
Zusammenstoß der (PL die
Zusammenstöße).
verb 1 (rival groups)
zusammenstoßen ✧ SEP; 2 (colours)
sich beißen ✧; **the curtains clash
with the wallpaper** die Vorhänge
beißen sich mit der Tapete.

class noun 1 (a group of students or
pupils) Klasse die (PL die Klassen);
she's in my class sie geht in meine
Klasse; **2** (a lesson) Stunde die (PL
die Stunden); **history class** die
Geschichtsstunde; **in class** im
Unterricht; **3** (category) Klasse die
(PL die Klassen); **social class** die
gesellschaftliche Klasse.

classical adjective klassisch;
classical music die klassische Musik.

classroom noun
Klassenzimmer das (PL die
Klassenzimmer).

clay noun Ton der.

clean adjective sauber; **a clean shirt**
ein sauberes Hemd; **my hands are
clean** ich habe saubere Hände.
verb 1 putzen; **I cleaned the
windows** ich habe die Fenster
geputzt; **2 to clean your teeth** sich
←(DAT) die Zähne putzen; **I'm going
to clean my teeth** ich putze mir jetzt
die Zähne.

cleaner noun 1 (cleaning lady)
Putzfrau die (PL die Putzfrauen);
2 (in a public place)
Reinigungskraft die (PL die
Reinigungskräfte); **3 dry cleaner's**
die chemische Reinigung.

cleaning noun **to do the cleaning**
putzen.

cleanser noun 1 (for the house)
Reinigungsmittel das (PL die
Reinigungsmittel); **2** (for your face)
Reinigungsmilch die.

clear adjective 1 (that you can see
through) klar; **clear water** klares
Wasser; **2** (cloudless) klar; **3** (easy to
understand) klar; **clear
instructions** klare Anweisungen; **is
that clear?** ist das klar? (informal);
to make something clear etwas
klarmachen.
verb 1 räumen; **have you cleared
your stuff out of your room?** hast
du deine Sachen aus deinem Zimmer
geräumt?; **2 can I clear the table?**
kann ich den Tisch abräumen SEP?;
3 to clear your throat sich
räuspern.
● **to clear up 1** (tidy up) aufräumen
SEP; **2** (the weather) sich aufklären
SEP; **the weather's clearing up a bit**

das Wetter klärt sich ein bisschen auf.

clearly adverb 1 (to think, speak, or hear) deutlich; 2 (obviously) eindeutig; **she was clearly better** sie war eindeutig besser.

clementine noun Klementine die (PL die Klementinen).

clever adjective 1 klug; **their children are all very clever** ihre Kinder sind alle sehr klug; 2 (ingenious) clever; **a clever idea** eine clevere Idee.

cliff noun Klippe die (PL die Klippen).

climate noun Klima das (PL die Klimas).

climb verb 1 (the stairs, a hill) hinaufgehen ◇ SEP (PERF sein); **to climb a mountain** auf einen Berg steigen ◇ (PERF sein); 2 (a wall, tree, or rock) klettern (PERF sein) auf (+ACC); **to climb a tree** auf einen Baum klettern.

climber noun Bergsteiger der (PL die Bergsteiger), Bergsteigerin die (PL die Bergsteigerinnen).

climbing noun Bergsteigen das; **they go climbing in Italy** sie gehen in Italien bergsteigen.

clinic noun Klinik die (PL die Kliniken).

clip noun 1 (from a film) Ausschnitt der (PL die Ausschnitte); 2 (for your hair) Klammer die (PL die Klammern).

cloakroom noun (for coats) Garderobe die (PL die Garderoben).

clock noun 1 Uhr die (PL die Uhren) **to put the clocks forward an hour** die Uhr eine Stunde vorstellen; **to put the clocks back** die Uhr zurückstellen; 2 **an alarm clock** ei Wecker.

close[1] adjective, adverb 1 (result) knapp; 2 (friend, connection) eng; 3 (relation or acquaintance) nahe; 4 (near) in der Nähe; **the station's very close** der Bahnhof ist ganz in der Nähe; **she lives close by** sie wohnt in der Nähe; 5 **close to** nahe nah (informal) (+DAT); **close to the cinema** nahe am Kino; **not very close** nicht sehr nah.

close[2] noun Ende das; **at the close** am Ende. verb zumachen SEP, schließen ◇; **close your eyes!** mach die Augen zu!; **she closed the door** sie macht die Tür zu; **the post office closes at six** die Post macht um sechs zu, die Post schließt um sechs.

closed adjective geschlossen; **'closed on Mondays'** 'Montags geschlossen'.

closing date noun **the closing date for entries** (for a competition) der Einsendeschluss △; (for a sportin event) der Meldeschluss △.

closing time noun 1 Ladenschluss △ der; 2 (of a pub) Polizeistunde die.

cloth noun 1 (for drying up and polishing) Tuch das (PL die Tücher) 2 (for the floor) Lappen der (PL die

◇ IRREGULAR VERB: See the verb table in the centre of the dictionary

Lappen); 3 (*fabric*) Stoff *der* (PL *die* Stoffe).

clothes *plural noun* 1 Kleider (*plural*); 2 **to put your clothes on** sich anziehen ✧ SEP; **to take your clothes off** sich ausziehen ✧ SEP; **to change your clothes** sich umziehen ✧ SEP.

clothes peg *noun* Wäscheklammer *die* (PL *die* Wäscheklammern).

clothing *noun* Kleidung *die*.

cloud *noun* Wolke *die* (PL *die* Wolken).

cloudy *adjective* bewölkt.

clown *noun* Clown *der* (PL *die* Clowns).

club *noun* 1 (*association, for tennis-players, golfers*) Klub *der* (PL *die* Klubs); (*for footballers*) Verein *der* (PL *die* Vereine); **a football club** ein Fußballverein; 2 (*in cards*) Kreuz *das* (PL *die* Kreuze); **the four of clubs** die Kreuz-Vier; 3 (*golfing iron*) Schläger *der* (PL *die* Schläger).

clue *noun* 1 Anhaltspunkt *der* (PL *die* Anhaltspunkte); **they have a few clues** sie haben ein paar Anhaltspunkte; 2 (*in a crossword*) Frage *die* (PL *die* Fragen); ★ **I haven't a clue** ich habe keine Ahnung.

clumsy *adjective* ungeschickt.

clutch *noun* (*in a car*) Kupplung *die* (PL *die* Kupplungen). *verb* **to clutch something** etwas festhalten ✧ SEP.

coach *noun* 1 (*bus*) Bus *der* (PL *die* Busse); **on the coach** im Bus; **to travel by coach** mit dem Bus fahren; 2 (*sports trainer*) Trainer *der* (PL *die* Trainer), Trainerin *die* (PL *die* Trainerinnen); 3 (*railway carriage*) Wagen *der* (PL *die* Wagen).

coach station *noun* Busbahnhof *der* (PL *die* Busbahnhöfe).

coach trip *noun* Busausflug *der* (PL *die* Busausflüge); **to go on a coach trip** einen Busausflug machen.

coal *noun* Kohle *die* (PL *die* Kohlen).

coarse *adjective* grob.

coast *noun* Küste *die* (PL *die* Küsten); **on the east coast** an der Ostküste.

coat *noun* 1 Mantel *der* (PL *die* Mäntel); 2 **coat of paint** *der* Anstrich.

coat hanger *noun* Kleiderbügel *der* (PL *die* Kleiderbügel).

cock *noun* Hahn *der* (PL *die* Hähne).

cocoa *noun* Kakao *der*.

coconut *noun* Kokosnuss △ *die* (PL *die* Kokosnüsse).

cod *noun* Kabeljau *der* (PL *die* Kabeljaue).

code *noun* 1 (*in law*) Gesetzbuch *das*; **the highway code** die Straßenverkehrsordnung; 2 **the dialling code for Hull** die Vorwahl für Hull.

coffee *noun* Kaffee *der* (PL *die* Kaffees); **a cup of coffee** eine Tasse

Kaffee; **a black coffee, please** einen Kaffee ohne Milch bitte; **a white coffee, please** einen Kaffee mit Milch bitte.

coffee break *noun* Kaffeepause *die* (PL *die* Kaffeepausen).

coffee cup *noun* Kaffeetasse *die* (PL *die* Kaffeetassen).

coffee machine *noun* Kaffeemaschine *die* (PL *die* Kaffeemaschinen).

coin *noun* 1 Münze *die* (PL *die* Münzen); **she collects old coins** sie sammelt alte Münzen; 2 **a pound coin** ein Einpfundstück.

coincidence *noun* Zufall *der* (PL *die* Zufälle).

Coke™ *noun* Cola *die*; **two Cokes™ please** zwei Cola bitte.

cold *noun* 1 (*cold weather*) Kälte *die*; **to be out in the cold** draußen in der Kälte sein; 2 (*illness*) Schnupfen *der* (PL *die* Schnupfen), Erkältung *die* (PL *die* Erkältungen); **to have a cold** Schnupfen haben; **Carol's got a cold** Carol hat Schnupfen; **a bad cold** eine schlimme Erkältung.
adjective 1 kalt; **your hands are cold** du hast kalte Hände; **cold milk** kalte Milch; 2 (*weather, temperature*) **it's cold today** heute ist es kalt; 3 (*feeling*) **I'm cold** mir ist kalt.

collapse *verb* 1 (*a roof or wall*) einstürzen SEP (PERF *sein*); 2 (*a person*) zusammenbrechen ✧ SEP (PERF *sein*); **he collapsed in his office** er brach in seinem Büro zusammen.

collar *noun* 1 (*on a garment*) Kragen *der* (PL *die* Kragen); 2 (*for a animal*) Halsband *das* (PL *die* Halsbänder).

colleague *noun* Kollege *der* (PL *die* Kollegen), Kollegin *die* (PL *die* Kolleginnen).

collect *verb* 1 (*as a hobby*) sammeln; **do you collect stamps?** sammelst du Briefmarken?; 2 (*fetch*) abholen SEP; **she collects the children from school** sie holt die Kinder von der Schule ab; 3 **to collect up the exercise books** die Hefte einsammeln SEP.

collection *noun* (*of stamps, CDs, money, etc.*) Sammlung *die* (PL *die* Sammlungen).

college *noun* 1 (*for higher education*) Hochschule *die* (PL *die* Hochschulen); **to go to college** studieren; 2 (*a school*) College *das* (PL *die* Colleges).

Cologne *noun* Köln *das*.

colour *noun* Farbe *die* (PL *die* Farben); **what colour is it?** welche Farbe hat es?; **do you have it in a different colour?** haben Sie es in einer anderen Farbe?
verb 1 (*with paints or crayons*) anmalen SEP; **to colour something red** etwas rot anmalen; 2 (*with dye*) färben.

colour film *noun* Farbfilm *der* (PL *die* Farbfilme).

colourful *adjective* bunt.

✧ IRREGULAR VERB: *See the verb table in the centre of the dictionary*

column noun 1 (of a building)
Säule die (PL die Säulen); 2 (on
a page) Spalte die (PL die
Spalten).

comb noun Kamm der (PL die
Kämme).
verb kämmen; **to comb your hair**
sich ←(DAT) die Haare kämmen; **I'll
just comb my hair** ich kämme mir
nur die Haare.

come verb 1 kommen ✧ (PERF sein);
come quick! komm schnell!; **come
here!** komm mal her!; **Nick came
by car** Nick kam mit dem Auto; **can
you come over for a coffee?** kannst
du auf eine Tasse Kaffe kommen?;
**did Jess come to school
yesterday?** war Jess gestern in der
Schule?; 2 (arrive) **coming!** ich
komme schon!; **the bus is coming**
der Bus kommt gerade; **come along!**
komm schon!
to come back zurückkommen ✧ SEP
(PERF sein); **he's coming back to
collect us** er kommt zurück, um uns
abzuholen.
to come down herunterkommen ✧
SEP (PERF sein).
to come for (collect) abholen SEP; **my
father's coming for me** mein Vater
holt mich ab.
to come in hereinkommen ✧ SEP
(PERF sein); **come in!** herein!; **she
came into the kitchen** sie kam in
die Küche.
to come off (a button) abgehen ✧
SEP (PERF sein).
to come out herauskommen ✧ SEP
(PERF sein); **they came out
when I called** als ich rief, kamen sie
heraus; **the new CD's coming**

out soon die neue CD kommt
bald heraus.
● **to come up** heraufkommen ✧ SEP
(PERF sein); **can you come up a
moment?** kannst du eine Sekunde
heraufkommen?
● **to come up to somebody** auf
jemanden zukommen ✧ SEP (PERF
sein).

comedian noun Komiker der (PL die
Komiker), Komikerin die (PL die
Komikerinnen).

comedy noun Komödle die (PL die
Komödien), Komikerin die (PL die
Komikerinnen).

comfortable adjective 1 bequem;
this chair's really comfortable
dieser Sessel ist wirklich bequem;
2 **to feel comfortable** (a person)
sich wohl fühlen.

comfortably adverb bequem.

comic noun (magazine) Comic-
Heft das (PL die Comic-Hefte).

comic strip noun Comic der (PL die
Comics).

comma noun Komma das (PL die
Kommas).

comment noun (remark)
Bemerkung die (PL die
Bemerkungen); **he made some rude
comments about my friends** er hat
ein paar unhöfliche Bemerkungen
über meine Freunde gemacht.

commentary noun Reportage die
(PL die Reportagen); **the
commentary on the soccer match**
die Reportage über das Fußballspiel.

commentator noun Reporter der
(PL die Reporter), Reporterin die (PL

die Reporterinnen); **sports commentator** *der* Sportreporter.

commercial *noun* Werbespot *der* (PL *die* Werbespots).
adjective kommerziell.

committee *noun* Ausschuss △ *der* (PL *die* Ausschüsse).

common *adjective* **1** häufig; **it's a common problem** das Problem kommt häufig vor; **2 in common** gemeinsam; **they have nothing in common** sie haben nichts gemeinsam.

common sense *noun* gesunde Menschenverstand *der*.

communication *noun* Verständigung *die*.

communion *noun* (*in a Catholic church*) Kommunion *die*; (*in a Protestant church*) Abendmahl *das*.

communism *noun* Kommunismus *der*.

community *noun* Gemeinschaft *die* (PL *die* Gemeinschaften); **the European Community** die Europäische Gemeinschaft.

commute *verb* **to commute between Oxford and London** zwischen Oxford und London pendeln (PERF *sein*).

commuter *noun* Pendler *der* (PL *die* Pendler), Pendlerin *die* (PL *die* Pendlerinnen).

compact disc *noun* Compactdisc △ *die* (PL *die* Compactdiscs).

compact disc player *noun* Compactdisc Spieler △ *der* (PL *die* Compactdisc Spieler).

company *noun* **1** (*business*) Gesellschaft *die* (PL *die* Gesellschaften); **an airline company** eine Fluggesellschaft; **she's set up a company** sie hat ein Firma gegründet; **2** (*group*) Truppe *die* (PL *die* Truppen); **a theatre company** eine Theatertruppe; **3 to keep somebody company** jemandem Gesellschaft leisten; **the dog keeps me company** der Hund leistet mir Gesellschaft.

compare *verb* vergleichen ✧; **if you compare the German phrase with the English** wenn man den deutschen mit dem englischen Ausdruck vergleicht; **our house is small compared with yours** unser Haus ist klein verglichen mit eurem.

compass *noun* Kompass △ *der* (PL *die* Kompasse).

compatible *adjective* **1** zueinander passend; **2** (*in computing*) kompatibel.

compete *verb* **1 to compete in something** (*race, event*) an etwas ←(DAT) teilnehmen ✧ SEP; **2 to compete with each other** miteinander konkurrieren; **3 to compete for something** um etwas ←(ACC) kämpfen; **thirty people are competing for one job** dreißig Leute kämpfen um eine Stelle.

competent *adjective* fähig.

✧ IRREGULAR VERB: *See the verb table in the centre of the dictionary*

competition *noun* **1** (*a contest*)
Wettbewerb *der* (PL *die*
Wettbewerbe); **2** (*in a magazine*)
Preisausschreiben *das* (PL *die*
Preisausschreiben).

competitor *noun* Konkurrent *der*
(PL *die* Konkurrenten), Konkurrentin
die (PL *die* Konkurrentinnen).

complain *verb* sich beschweren; **we
complained about the meals** wir
haben uns über das Essen beschwert.

complete *adjective* **1** (*whole*)
vollständig; **the complete
collection** die vollständige
Sammlung; **2** (*absolute*) völlig; **a
complete idiot** ein völliger Idiot
(*informal*).
verb (*to finish*) beenden.

completely *adverb* völlig.

complexion *noun* Teint *der* (PL *die*
Teints).

complicated *adjective*
kompliziert.

compliment *noun*
Kompliment *das* (PL *die*
Komplimente); **to pay somebody a
compliment** jemandem ein
Kompliment machen.

composer *noun* Komponist *der* (PL
die Komponisten), Komponistin *die*
(PL *die* Komponistinnen).

comprehensive school *noun*
Gemeinschaftsschule *die* (PL *die*
Gemeinschaftsschulen).

compulsory *adjective*
1 obligatorisch; **2** (*at school*)
compulsory subject *das* Pflichtfach.

computer *noun* Computer *der* (PL
die Computer); **to work on a**

computer mit einem Computer
arbeiten; **to have something on
computer** etwas im Computer
gespeichert haben.

computer engineer *noun*
Computeringenieur *der* (PL *die*
Computeringenieure),
Computeringenieurin *die* (PL *die*
Computeringenieurinnen).

computer game *noun*
Computerspiel *das* (PL *die*
Computerspiele).

computer programmer *noun*
Programmierer *der* (PL *die*
Programmierer), Programmiererin
die (PL *die* Programmiererinnen).

computer science *noun*
Informatik *die*.

computing *noun*
Computertechnik *die*.

concentrate *verb* sich
konzentrieren; **I can't concentrate**
ich kann mich nicht konzentrieren;
I was concentrating on the film ich
konzentrierte mich auf den Film.

concentration *noun*
Konzentration *die*.

concern *verb* (*to affect*)
betreffen ◇; **this doesn't concern
you** das betrifft Sie nicht; **as far as
I'm concerned** was mich betrifft.

concert *noun* **1** Konzert *das* (PL *die*
Konzerte); **to go to a concert** ins
Konzert gehen; **2 concert ticket** *die*
Konzertkarte.

conclusion *noun* Schluss △ *der* (PL
die Schlüsse).

△ NEW SPELLING: *See page xii*

concrete *noun* Beton *der*;
concrete floor der Betonboden.

condemn *verb* verurteilen; **to
condemn somebody to death**
jemanden zum Tode verurteilen.

condition *noun* 1 Zustand *der* (PL
die Zustände); **in good condition** in
gutem Zustand; **weather conditions**
die Wetterlage; 2 (*something you
insist on*) Bedingung *die* (PL *die*
Bedingungen); **on condition that
you let me pay** unter der
Bedingung, dass du mich zahlen
lässt.

conditioner *noun* (*for your hair*)
Spülung *die* (PL *die* Spülungen).

condom *noun* Kondom *das* (PL *die*
Kondome).

conduct *noun* Benehmen *das*.
verb dirigieren (*an orchestra or a
piece of music*).

conductor *noun* (*of an orchestra*)
Dirigent *der* (PL *die* Dirigenten),
Dirigentin *die* (PL *die* Dirigentinnen).

cone *noun* 1 (*for ice-cream*)
Eistüte *die* (PL *die* Eistüten); 2 (*for
traffic*) Kegel *der* (PL *die* Kegel).

conference *noun* Konferenz *die*
(PL *die* Konferenzen).

confess *verb* gestehen ✧.

confession *noun* Geständnis *das*
(PL *die* Geständnisse).

confidence *noun* 1 (*self-
confidence*) Selbstvertrauen *das*; **to
be lacking in confidence** kein
Selbstvertrauen haben; 2 (*faith in
somebody else*) Vertrauen *das*; **to**

have confidence in somebody zu
jemandem Vertrauen haben.

confident *adjective* 1 (*sure of
yourself*) selbstbewusst ∆; 2 (*sure
that something will happen*)
zuversichtlich.

confirm *verb* bestätigen; **he
confirmed the date** er bestätigte
das Datum.

confused *adjective* 1 wirr; **a
confused story** eine wirre
Geschichte; 2 durcheinander; **I'm
confused about the holiday plans**
ich bin mit den Ferienplänen
durcheinander; **now I'm completel**
confused jetzt bin ich völlig
durcheinander.

confusing *adjective* verwirrend;
the instructions are confusing die
Anweisungen sind verwirrend.

confusion *noun* Verwirrung *die*.

congratulate *verb* gratulieren; **I
congratulated Tim on passing his
exam** ich gratulierte Tim zur
bestandenen Prüfung.

congratulations *plural noun*
Glückwünsche (*plural*);
congratulations on the baby!
herzlichen Glückwunsch zum Baby!

connect *verb* (*to plug in to the
mains*) anschließen ✧ SEP (*a
dishwasher or TV, for example*).

connection *noun* 1 (*between two
ideas or events*) Zusammenhang
der (PL *die* Zusammenhänge);
**there's no connection between his
letter and my decision** es besteht
kein Zusammenhang zwischen

✧ IRREGULAR VERB: *See the verb table in the centre of the dictionary*

seinem Brief und meiner Entscheidung; **2** (*between trains, planes, on phone, and electrical*) Anschluss ∆ der (PL die Anschlüsse); **Sally missed her connection** Sally hat ihren Anschluss verpasst.

onscience noun Gewissen das; **to have a guilty conscience** ein schlechtes Gewissen haben.

onservation noun (*of nature*) Schutz der; **environmental conservation** der Umweltschutz.

onservative noun Konservative der/die (PL die Konservativen). adjective konservativ.

onservatory noun Wintergarten der (PL die Wintergärten).

onsider verb **1** sich ←(DAT) überlegen; (*a suggestion or idea*) **all things considered** alles in allem; **2** (*think about* (*doing*)) erwägen ✧; **we are considering buying a flat** wir erwägen, eine Wohnung zu kaufen.

onsiderate adjective rücksichtsvoll.

onsidering preposition wenn man bedenkt; **considering her age** wenn man ihr Alter bedenkt; **considering he did it all himself** wenn man bedenkt, dass er es ganz allein gemacht hat.

onsist verb **to consist of** bestehen ✧ aus (+DAT).

onstant adjective ständig.

construct verb bauen.

consumer noun Verbraucher der (PL die Verbraucher), Verbraucherin die (PL die Verbraucherinnen).

contact noun Kontakt der (PL die Kontakte); **to be in contact with somebody** mit jemandem in Kontakt sein; **we've lost contact** wir haben den Kontakt verloren; **Rob has contacts in the music business** Rob hat Kontakte zur Musikindustrie. verb sich in Verbindung setzen mit (+DAT); **I'll contact you tomorrow** ich setze mich morgen mit dir in Verbindung.

contact lens noun Kontaktlinse die (PL die Kontaktlinsen).

contain verb enthalten ✧.

container noun Behälter der (PL die Behälter).

contemporary adjective **1** (*around today*) zeitgenössisch; **2** (*modern*) modern.

contents plural noun Inhalt der; **the contents of my suitcase** der Inhalt meines Koffers.

contest noun Wettbewerb der (PL die Wettbewerbe).

contestant noun Teilnehmer der (PL die Teilnehmer), Teilnehmerin die (PL die Teilnehmerinnen).

continent noun Kontinent der (PL die Kontinente).

continue verb **1** fortsetzen SEP; **we continued (with) our journey** wir setzten unsere Reise fort; **2 to**

continue to do something etwas
weiter tun; **Jill continued talking** Jill
redete weiter; **3 'to be continued'**
'Fortsetzung folgt'.

continuous *adjective*
ununterbrochen.

contraceptive *noun*
Verhütungsmittel *das* (PL *die*
Verhütungsmittel).

contract *noun* Vertrag *der* (PL *die*
Verträge).

contradict *verb* widersprechen ✧
(+DAT).

contradiction *noun*
Widerspruch *der* (PL *die*
Widersprüche).

contrary *noun* Gegenteil *das*; **on
the contrary** im Gegenteil.

contrast *noun* Kontrast *der* (PL *die*
Kontraste).

contribute *verb* beisteuern SEP
(*money*).

contribution *noun* (*to charity or an
appeal*) Spende *die* (PL *die*
Spenden).

control *noun* (*of a crowd or
animals*) Kontrolle *die*; **the police
are in control of the situation** die
Polizei hat die Situation unter
Kontrolle; **keep your dogs under
control** halten Sie Ihre Hunde unter
Kontrolle; **everything's under
control** alles ist unter Kontrolle; **to
get out of control** außer Kontrolle
geraten.
verb **to control yourself** sich
beherrschen.

convenient *adjective* **1** praktisch;
frozen food is very convenient
Tiefkühlkost ist sehr praktisch; **2 to
be convenient for somebody**
jemandem passen; **whenever's
convenient for you** wann immer es
dir passt.

conventional *adjective*
konventionell.

conversation *noun* Gespräch *das*
(PL *die* Gespräche).

convert *verb* **1** umwandeln SEP;
2 (*adapt a building*) umbauen SEP;
**we're going to convert the garage
into a workshop** wir wollen die
Garage zu einer Werkstatt umbauen.

convince *verb* überzeugen; **I'm
convinced he's wrong** ich bin
davon überzeugt, dass er sich irrt.

convincing *adjective* überzeugend

cook *noun* Koch *der* (PL *die* Köche),
Köchin *die* (PL *die* Köchinnen).
verb **1** kochen; **who's cooking
tonight?** wer kocht heute Abend?;
I like cooking ich koche gern; **to
cook vegetables and pasta**
Gemüse und Nudeln kochen; **cook
the cabbage for five minutes** lass
den Kohl fünf Minuten kochen;
2 (*prepare food or a meal*) machen;
Fran's busy cooking supper Fran
macht gerade Abendessen; **how do
you cook duck?** wie macht man
Ente?; **3** (*boil*) kochen; (*fry or roast*)
braten ✧; **the potatoes are cooking**
die Kartoffeln kochen; **the sausages
are cooking** die Würstchen braten.

cooker *noun* Herd *der* (PL *die*
Herde); **electric cooker** *der*

✧ IRREGULAR VERB: *See the verb table in the centre of the dictionary*

Elektroherd; **gas cooker** der Gasherd.

ookery noun Kochen das.

ookery book noun
Kochbuch das (PL die Kochbücher).

ooking noun 1 (preparing food)
Kochen das; **cooking is fun**
Kochen macht Spaß; **who's doing
the cooking?** wer kocht?; 2 (food)
Küche die; **Italian cooking** die
italienische Küche.

ool noun 1 (coldness) Kühle die;
2 (calm) **to lose one's cool**
durchdrehen SEP (PERF sein)
(informal); **don't lose your cool!**
dreh nicht durch!; **he kept his cool**
er blieb gelassen.
adjective 1 (cold) kühl; **it's cool
inside** es ist kühl drinnen; 2 (laid
back) gelassen; **to stay cool**
gelassen bleiben (PERF sein).
verb abkühlen SEP (PERF sein).

op noun Polizist der (PL die
Polizisten).

ope verb zurechtkommen ◇ SEP
(PERF sein); **she copes well** sie
kommt gut zurecht; **to cope with the
children** mit den Kindern
zurechtkommen; **she's had a lot to
cope with** sie musste mit viel
zurechtkommen.

opy noun 1 (photocopy) Kopie die
(PL die Kopien); 2 (of a book)
Exemplar das (PL die Exemplare).
verb 1 (imitate) kopieren; 2 (make
a copy of) abschreiben ◇ SEP; **I
copied (down) the address** ich
habe die Adresse abgeschrieben; (in

an exam) **to copy from somebody**
bei jemandem abschreiben.

cord noun (for a blind, for example)
Schnur die (PL die Schnüre).

cordless telephone noun
schnurlose Telefon das (PL die
schnurlosen Telefone).

core noun (of an apple or a pear)
Kerngehäuse das (PL die
Kerngehäuse).

cork noun 1 (in a bottle) Korken der
(PL die Korken); 2 (material)
Kork der.

corkscrew noun Korkenzieher der
(PL die Korkenzieher).

corn noun 1 (wheat) Korn das;
2 (sweetcorn) Mais der.

corner noun 1 Ecke die (PL die
Ecken); **at the corner of the street**
an der Straßenecke; **it's just round
the corner** es ist gleich um die
Ecke; 2 (of mouth, eye) Winkel der
(PL die Winkel); **out of the corner of
your eye** aus dem Augenwinkel
heraus; 3 (bend in the road)
Kurve die (PL die Kurven); 4 (in
football) Eckball der (PL die
Eckbälle).

corpse noun Leiche die (PL die
Leichen).

correct adjective 1 richtig; **the
correct answer** die richtige
Antwort; 2 **yes, that's correct**
ja, das stimmt.
verb 1 verbessern; 2 (teacher)
korrigieren; **the teacher has
already corrected our homework**

△ NEW SPELLING: *See page xii*

der Lehrer hat unsere Hausaufgaben schon korrigiert.

correction *noun* Verbesserung *die* (PL *die* Verbesserungen).

corridor *noun* Korridor *der* (PL *die* Korridore).

cosmetics *plural noun* Kosmetik *die*.

cost *noun* 1 Kosten (*plural*); **the cost of living** die Lebenshaltungskosten (*plural*); 2 **the cost of a new computer** der Preis für einen neuen Computer. *verb* kosten; **how much does it cost?** was kostet es?; **the tickets cost £10** die Karten kosten zehn Pfund; **it costs too much** das ist zu teuer.

costume *noun* Kostüm *das* (PL *die* Kostüme).

cosy *adjective* (*a room*) gemütlich.

cot *noun* Kinderbett *das* (PL *die* Kinderbetten).

cottage *noun* Häuschen *das* (PL *die* Häuschen).

cotton *noun* 1 (*fabric*) Baumwolle *die*; **cotton shirt** *das* Baumwollhemd; 2 (*thread*) Nähgarn *das* (PL *die* Nähgarne).

cotton wool *noun* Watte *die*.

couch *noun* Couch *die* (PL *die* Couchs).

cough *noun* Husten *der*; **a nasty cough** ein schlimmer Husten; **to have a cough** Husten haben. *verb* husten.

could *verb* 1 (*the past tense of können is used to translate 'was able to'*) **I couldn't open it** ich konnte es nicht aufmachen; **they couldn't come** si konnten nicht kommen; **she did all she could** sie hat getan, was sie konnte; **he couldn't drive** er konnt nicht Auto fahren; **she couldn't see anything** sie konnte überhaupt nichts sehen; 2 (*the past tense of dürfen is used to translate 'was allowed to'*) **they couldn't smoke there** sie durften da nicht rauchen; 3 (*might*) (*the subjunctive of können is used to translate a wish or suggestion*) **could I speak to David?** könnte ich David sprechen?; **you could try phoning** du könntest versuchen anzurufen; **if he could pay** wenn er zahlen könnte; **he could be right** er könnte recht haben.

count *verb* 1 (*reckon up*) zählen; **I counted my money** ich habe mein Geld gezählt; 2 (*include*) mitzählen SEP; **thirty-five not counting the children** fünfunddreißig, die Kinder nicht mitgezählt.

counter *noun* 1 (*in a shop*) Ladentisch *der* (PL *die* Ladentische); 2 (*in a post office or bank*) Schalter *der* (PL *die* Schalter); 3 (*in a bar or café*) Theke *die* (PL *die* Theken); 4 (*for board games*) Spielmarke *die* (PL *die* Spielmarken).

country *noun* 1 (*Germany, England, etc.*) Land *das* (PL *die* Länder); **a foreign country** ein fremdes Land; **from another country** aus einem anderen Land; 2 (*not town*)

✧ IRREGULAR VERB: *See the verb table in the centre of the dictionary*

country das, **in the country** auf dem Land; **country road** die Landstraße.

country dancing noun Volkstanz der.

countryside noun 1 (not town) Land das; 2 (scenery) Landschaft die.

county noun Grafschaft die (PL die Grafschaften).

couple noun 1 (a pair) Paar das (PL die Paare); 2 **a couple of** ein paar; **a couple of times** ein paar Mal; **I've got a couple of things to do** ich habe ein paar Sachen zu tun.

courage noun Mut der.

course noun 1 (lessons) Kurs der (PL die Kurse); **computer course** der Computerkurs; **to go on a course** einen Kurs machen; 2 (part of a meal) Gang der (PL die Gänge); **the main course** der Hauptgang; 3 **golf course** der Golfplatz; 4 **of course** natürlich; **yes, of course!** ja, natürlich!; **he's forgotten, of course** er hat es natürlich vergessen.

court noun 1 (for playing sports) Platz der (PL die Plätze); 2 (lawcourt) Gericht das; **to go to court** vor Gericht gehen.

cousin noun Vetter der (PL die Vettern), Kusine die (PL die Kusinen); **my cousin Sonia** meine Kusine Sonia.

cover noun 1 (of a book) Einband der (PL die Einbände); 2 (for a duvet or cushion) Bezug der (PL die Bezüge).

verb 1 (to cover up) zudecken SEP, **he covered her with a blanket** er hat sie mit einer Decke zugedeckt; 2 **he was covered in spots** er war völlig verpickelt; **the room was covered in dust** das Zimmer war völlig verstaubt; 3 (with leaves, snow, or for protection) bedecken; **the ground was covered with snow** der Boden war mit Schnee bedeckt; 4 (with fabric) beziehen ◇.

cow noun Kuh die (PL die Kühe); **mad cow disease** der Rinderwahn.

coward noun Feigling der (PL die Feiglinge).

cowboy noun Cowboy der (PL die Cowboys).

crack noun 1 (in a glass or cup) Sprung der (PL die Sprünge); 2 (in wood or a wall) Riss △ der (PL die Risse); 3 (a cracking noise) Knack der (PL die Knacke). verb 1 (to make a crack in) anschlagen ◇ SEP; 2 (to break) zerbrechen ◇; 3 (to make a noise) (a twig) knacken.

cracker noun 1 (biscuit) Cracker der (PL die Cracker); 2 (Christmas cracker) Knallbonbon der (PL die Knallbonbons).

craft noun (at school) Werken das.

cramp noun Krampf der (PL die Krämpfe); **to have cramp in your leg** einen Krampf im Bein haben.

crash noun 1 (an accident) Unfall der (PL die Unfälle); **car crash** der Autounfall; 2 (a noise) Krachen das.

verb **1** (*a plane*) abstürzen SEP (PERF *sein*); **the plane crashed** das Flugzeug ist abgestürzt; **2** (*have a collision in a car*) einen Unfall haben; **3 to crash into something** gegen etwas ←(ACC) krachen (PERF *sein*); **the car crashed into a tree** das Auto krachte gegen einen Baum.

crash course *noun* Schnellkurs *der* (PL *die* Schnellkurse).

crash helmet *noun* Sturzhelm *der* (PL *die* Sturzhelme).

crate *noun* Kiste *die* (PL *die* Kisten).

crawl *noun* (*in swimming*) Kraul *das.*
verb **1** (*a person*) kriechen ✧ (PERF *sein*); (*a baby*) krabbeln (PERF *sein*); **2** (*cars in a jam*) im Schneckentempo fahren ✧ (PERF *sein*); **we were crawling along** wir fuhren im Schneckentempo.

crayon *noun* **1** (*wax*) Wachsstift *der* (PL *die* Wachsstifte); **2** (*coloured pencil*) Buntstift *der* (PL *die* Buntstifte).

craze *noun* Mode *die*; **the craze for rollerblades** die Inlinermode.

crazy *adjective* verrückt; **to be crazy for something** verrückt auf etwas ←(ACC) sein.

cream *noun* Sahne *die*; **strawberries and cream** Erdbeeren mit Sahne.

cream cheese *noun* Frischkäse *der.*

creased *adjective* zerknittert.

creative *adjective* kreativ.

creature *noun* Geschöpf *das* (PL *d* Geschöpfe).

credit *noun* Kredit *der*; **to buy something on credit** etwas auf Kredit kaufen.

credit card *noun* Kreditkarte *die* (PL *die* Kreditkarten).

cress *noun* Kresse *die.*

crew *noun* **1** (*on a ship or plane*) Besatzung *die*; **2 camera crew** da Kamerateam; **3** (*in water sports*) Mannschaft *die* (PL *die* Mannschaften).

crew cut *noun* Bürstenschnitt *der* (PL *die* Bürstenschnitte).

cricket *noun* **1** (*game*) Kricket *das* **to play cricket** Kricket spielen; **2** (*insect*) Grille *die* (PL *die* Grillen).

cricket bat *noun* Kricketschläger *der.*

crime *noun* **1** Verbrechen *das* (PL *die* Verbrechen); **theft is a crime** Diebstahl ist ein Verbrechen; **2** (*criminality*) Kriminalität *die*; **to fight crime** die Kriminalität bekämpfen.

criminal *noun* Kriminelle *der/die* (PL *die* Kriminellen).
adjective kriminell.

crisis *noun* Krise *die* (PL *die* Krisen).

crisp *noun* Chip *der* (PL *die* Chips); **a packet of potato crisps** eine Tüte Kartoffelchips.
adjective **1** (*biscuit*) knusprig; **2** (*apple*) knackig.

✧ IRREGULAR VERB: *See the verb table in the centre of the dictionary*

criticism noun Kritik die (PL die Kritiken).

criticize verb kritisieren.

crocodile noun Krokodil das (PL die Krokodile).

crook noun (criminal) Schwindler der (PL die Schwindler).

crop noun Ernte die.

cross noun Kreuz das (PL die Kreuze).
adjective ärgerlich; **she was very cross** sie war sehr ärgerlich; **I'm cross with you** ich bin sehr ärgerlich auf dich.
verb 1 (to cross over) überqueren; **to cross the road** die Straße überqueren; 2 **to cross your legs** die Beine übereinanderschlagen ✧ SEP; 3 (to cross each other) sich kreuzen; **the two roads cross here** die beiden Straßen kreuzen sich hier.
● **to cross out** ausstreichen ✧ SEP.

cross-Channel adjective **a cross-Channel ferry** eine Fähre über den Kanal.

cross-country noun 1 Cross der; 2 **cross-country skiing** der Langlauf.

crossing noun 1 (from one place to another) Überquerung die (PL die Überquerungen); 2 (a sea journey) Überfahrt die (PL die Überfahrten); **Channel crossing** die Überfahrt über den Kanal; 3 **pedestrian crossing** der Fußgängerübergang; **level crossing** der Bahnübergang.

crossroads noun Kreuzung die (PL die Kreuzungen); **at the crossroads** an der Kreuzung.

crossword noun Kreuzworträtsel das (PL die Kreuzworträtsel); **to do the crossword** ein Kreuzworträtsel machen.

crow noun Krähe die (PL die Krähen).
verb (a cock) krähen.

crowd noun 1 Menschenmenge die (PL die Menschenmengen); **in the crowd** in der Menschenmenge; 2 (spectators) **a crowd of five thousand** fünftausend Zuschauer (plural).
verb **to crowd into** or **onto something** sich in etwas ←(ACC) drängen; **we all crowded into the train** wir drängten uns alle in den Zug.

crowded adjective überfüllt.

crown noun Krone die (PL die Kronen).

crude adjective 1 (rough and ready) primitiv; 2 (vulgar) ordinär.

cruel adjective grausam.

crumb noun Krümel der (PL die Krümel).

crumpled adjective zerknittert.

crunchy adjective knusprig.

crush verb zerquetschen.

crust noun Kruste die (PL die Krusten).

crusty adjective knusprig.

△ NEW SPELLING: See page xii

crutch *noun* Krücke *die* (PL *die* Krücken); **to be on crutches** an Krücken gehen.

cry *noun* Schrei *der* (PL *die* Schreie). *verb* **1** (*weep*) weinen; **2** (*call out*) schreien ✧.

cub *noun* **1** (*animal*) Junge *das* (PL *die* Jungen); **2** (*boy scout*) Wölfling *der* (PL *die* Wölflinge).

cube *noun* Würfel *der* (PL *die* Würfel); **ice cube** *der* Eiswürfel.

cubic *adjective* (*in measurements*) Kubik-; **three cubic metres** drei Kubikmeter.

cubicle *noun* **1** (*in a changing room*) Kabine *die*; **2** (*in a public lavatory*) Toilette *die* (PL *die* Toiletten).

cuckoo *noun* Kuckuck *der* (PL *die* Kuckucke).

cucumber *noun* Gurke *die* (PL *die* Gurken).

cuddle *noun* **to give somebody a cuddle** jemanden in den Arm nehmen. *verb* schmusen.

cue *noun* (*billiards, pool, snooker*) Queue *das* (PL *die* Queues).

cuff *noun* (*on a shirt*) Manschette *die* (PL *die* Manschetten).

cul-de-sac *noun* Sackgasse *die* (PL *die* Sackgassen).

culture *noun* Kultur *die* (PL *die* Kulturen).

cunning *adjective* listig.

cup *noun* **1** (*for drinking*) Tasse *die* (PL *die* Tassen); **a cup of tea** eine Tasse Tee; **2** (*a trophy*) Pokal *der* (PL *die* Pokale).

cupboard *noun* Schrank *der* (PL *die* Schränke); **in the kitchen cupboard** im Küchenschrank.

cup tie *noun* Pokalspiel *das* (PL *die* Pokalspiele).

cure *noun* Heilmittel *das* (PL *die* Heilmittel). *verb* heilen.

curiosity *noun* Neugier *die*.

curious *adjective* neugierig.

curl *noun* Locke *die* (PL *die* Locken). *verb* **1** locken (*hair*); **2** (*of hair*) sich locken.

currant *noun* Korinthe *die* (PL *die* Korinthen).

currency *noun* Währung *die* (PL *die* Währungen); **the Japanese currency** die japanische Währung; **foreign currencies** Devisen (*plural*).

current *noun* **1** (*electricity*) Strom *der*; **2** (*in water or air*) Strömung *die* (PL *die* Strömungen). *adjective* aktuell.

current affairs *noun* Tagespolitik *die*.

curriculum *noun* Lehrplan *der* (PL *die* Lehrpläne).

curry *noun* Curry *das*; **vegetable curry** *das* Gemüse in Currysoße.

curtain *noun* Vorhang *der* (PL *die* Vorhänge).

cushion *noun* Kissen *das* (PL *die* Kissen).

✧ IRREGULAR VERB: *See the verb table in the centre of the dictionary*

custard *noun* Vanillesoße *die* (PL die Vanillesoßen).

custom *noun* Brauch *der* (PL die Bräuche).

customer *noun* Kunde *der* (PL die Kunden), Kundin *die* (PL die Kundinnen).

customs *plural noun* Zoll *der*; **to go through customs** durch den Zoll gehen.

customs hall *noun* Zollabfertigung *die*.

customs officer *noun* Zollbeamte *der* (PL die Zollbeamten), Zollbeamtin *die* (PL die Zollbeamtinnen).

cut *noun* 1 (*injury*) Schnittwunde *die* (PL die Schnittwunden); 2 (*haircut*) Schnitt *der* (PL die Schnitte).
verb 1 schneiden ✧; **can you cut the bread please?** kannst du bitte Brot schneiden?; **you'll cut yourself!** du schneidest dich!; **Kevin's cut his finger** Kevin hat sich in den Finger geschnitten; 2 **to cut the grass** den Rasen mähen; 3 **to get your hair cut** sich ←(DAT) die Haare schneiden lassen; **I had my hair cut** ich habe mir die Haare schneiden lassen; 4 **to cut prices** die Preise senken.
● **to cut down** 1 fällen (*a tree*); 2 **to cut down on cigarettes** seinen Zigarettenkonsum einschränken SEP.
● **to cut out something** 1 etwas ausschneiden ✧ SEP (*a shape, a newspaper article*); 2 etwas streichen ✧ (*sugar, fatty food, holidays, for example*).

● **to cut something up** etwas zerschneiden ✧ (*food*).

cutlery *noun* Besteck *das* (PL die Bestecke).

CV *noun* Lebenslauf *der* (PL die Lebensläufe).

cycle *noun* (*bike*) Rad *das* (PL die Räder).
verb Rad fahren ✧ Δ (PERF *sein*); **do you like cycling?** fährst du gerne Rad?; **we cycle to school** wir fahren mit dem Rad zur Schule.

cycle lane *noun* Fahrradspur *die* (PL die Fahrradspuren).

cycle race *noun* Radrennen *das* (PL die Radrennen).

cycling *noun* Radfahren *das*.

cycling shorts *noun* Radlerhose *die* (PL die Radlerhosen).

cyclist *noun* Radfahrer *der* (PL die Radfahrer), Radfahrerin *die* (PL die Radfahrerinnen).

D d

dad *noun* Vati *der* (PL die Vatis).

daffodil *noun* Osterglocke *die* (PL die Osterglocken).

daily *adjective* täglich.

dairy products *plural noun* Milchprodukte (*plural*).

daisy *noun* Gänseblümchen *das* (PL die Gänseblümchen).

damage *noun* Schaden *der* (PL die Schäden); **to do a lot of damage** großen Schaden anrichten.
verb beschädigen.

damn *noun* **I don't give a damn** das ist mir piepegal (*informal*).
exclamation **damn!** verdammt!

damp *adjective* feucht.
noun Feuchtigkeit *die*.

dance *noun* Tanz *der* (PL die Tänze); **a folk dance** ein Volkstanz.
verb tanzen; **I like dancing** ich tanze gerne.

dancer *noun* Tänzer *der* (PL die Tänzer), Tänzerin *die* (PL die Tänzerinnen).

dancing *noun* Tanzen *das*.

dancing class *noun* Tanzstunde *die* (PL die Tanzstunden); **to go to dancing classes** in die Tanzstunde gehen.

dandruff *noun* Schuppen (*plural*).

danger *noun* Gefahr *die* (PL die Gefahren); **to be in danger** in Gefahr sein.

dangerous *adjective* gefährlich; **it's dangerous to drive too fast** es ist gefährlich, zu schnell zu fahren.

Danish *noun* Dänisch *das*.
adjective dänisch; **he's Danish** er ist Däne; **she's Danish** sie ist Dänin.

dare *verb* **1** wagen; **to dare to do something** es wagen, etwas zu tun; **I didn't dare suggest it** ich habe es nicht gewagt, das vorzuschlagen; **2 don't you dare tell her I'm here!** untersteh dich, ihr zu sagen, dass ich da bin!; **3 I dare you!** trau dich!; **I**

dare you to tell him! sag's ihm, trau dich doch!

daring *adjective* gewagt; **that was a bit daring** das war etwas gewagt.

dark *noun* **in the dark** im Dunkeln; **after dark** nach Einbruch der Dunkelheit; **to be afraid of the dark** Angst im Dunkeln haben.
adjective **1** (*colour*) dunkel (*adjectives ending in -el drop the e when followed by a vowel, which means that dunkel becomes dunkler/dunkle/dunkles*); **a dark colour** eine dunkle Farbe; **it gets dark around five** es wird gegen fünf dunkel; **2 a dark blue skirt** ein dunkelblauer Rock; **she has dark brown hair** sie hat dunkelbraune Haare.

darkness *noun* Dunkelheit *die*; **in darkness** in der Dunkelheit.

darling *noun* Liebling *der* (PL die Lieblinge); **see you later, darling!** bis später, Liebling!

dart *noun* **1** Wurfpfeil *der* (PL die Wurfpfeile); **2** (*game*) **darts** Darts *das*; **to play darts** Darts spielen.

data *plural noun* Daten (*plural*).

database *noun* Datenbank *die* (PL die Datenbanken).

date *noun* **1** Datum *das* (PL die Daten); **what's the date today?** welches Datum haben wir heute?; **the date of the meeting** das Datum für das Treffen; **what date is he coming?** wann kommt er?; **2** Termin *der* (PL die Termine); **the**

last date for payment der letzte
Zahlungstermin; **3 out of date**
ungültig; **my passport's out of date**
mein Pass ist ungültig; **4** (*fruit*)
Dattel *die* (PL *die* Datteln).

date of birth *noun*
Geburtsdatum *das* (PL *die*
Geburtsdaten).

daughter *noun* Tochter *die* (PL *die*
Töchter); **Tina's daughter** Tinas
Tochter.

daughter-in-law *noun*
Schwiegertochter *die* (PL *die*
Schwiegertöchter).

dawn *noun* Morgendämmerung *die*
(PL *die* Morgendämmerungen).

day *noun* **1** Tag *der* (PL *die* Tage);
three days later drei Tage später; **a
few days ago** vor ein paar Tagen;
the day I went to London an dem
Tag, an dem ich nach London
gefahren bin; **we spent the day in
London** wir haben den Tag in
London verbracht; **it rained all day**
es hat den ganzen Tag geregnet; **the
day after** am Tag danach; **the day
after the wedding** am Tag nach der
Hochzeit; **the day before** am Tag
davor; **the day before the wedding**
am Tag vor der Hochzeit; **2 the day
after tomorrow** übermorgen; **my
sister's arriving the day after
tomorrow** meine Schwester kommt
übermorgen an; **3 the day before
yesterday** vorgestern; **my brother
arrived the day before yesterday**
mein Bruder kam vorgestern an;
4 during the day tagsüber.

dead *adjective* tot; **her father's
dead** ihr Vater ist tot.

adverb (*really*) irre (*informal*); **he's
dead nice** er ist irre nett; **it was
dead good** es war irre gut; **it was
dead easy** es war kinderleicht;
you're dead right du hast völlig
Recht; **she arrived dead on time** sie
kam auf die Minute pünktlich an.

deadline *noun* letzte Termin *der*
(PL *die* letzten Termine).

deaf *adjective* taub.

deafening *adjective*
ohrenbetäubend.

deal *noun* **1** (*involving money*)
Geschäft *das* (PL *die* Geschäfte); **it's
a good deal** das ist ein gutes
Geschäft; **2** (*agreement*)
Vereinbarung *die* (PL *die*
Vereinbarungen); **to make a deal
with somebody** mit jemandem eine
Vereinbarung treffen; **it's a deal!**
abgemacht!; **3 a great deal of** viel;
I don't have a great deal of time
ich habe nicht viel Zeit.
verb (*in cards*) geben; **it's you to
deal** du gibst.
● **to deal with something** sich um
etwas ←(ACC) kümmern; **Linda deals
with the accounts** Linda kümmert
sich um die Buchführung; **I'll deal
with it as soon as possible** ich
kümmere mich so schnell wie
möglich darum.

dear *adjective* **1** lieb; **Dear Franz**
Lieber Franz; **Dear Mr Smith** Sehr
geehrter Herr Smith; **2** (*expensive*)
teuer.

death *noun* Tod *der*; **after his
father's death** nach dem Tod seines
Vaters; **three deaths** drei

△ NEW SPELLING: *See page xii*

Todesfälle; ★ **I was bored to death** ich habe mich zu Tode gelangweilt; ★ **I'm sick to death of it** ich habe es gründlich satt.

death penalty *noun* Todesstrafe *die*.

debate *noun* Debatte *die* (PL *die* Debatten). *verb* debattieren.

debt *noun* (*money owed*) Schulden (*plural*); **to get into debt** in Schulden geraten.

decaffeinated *adjective* koffeinfrei.

deceive *verb* betrügen ✧.

December *noun* Dezember *der* (PL *die* Dezember); **in December** im Dezember.

decent *adjective* anständig; **a decent salary** ein anständiges Gehalt; **a decent meal** ein anständiges Essen.

decide *verb* 1 entscheiden ✧; **to decide on something** sich für etwas ←(ACC) entscheiden; **he's decided against buying a new car** er hat sich entschieden, kein neues Auto zu kaufen; 2 **to decide to do something** sich entschließen ✧, etwas zu tun; **they've decided to buy a house** sie haben sich entschlossen, ein Haus zu kaufen.

decimal *adjective* Dezimal-; **decimal number** die Dezimalzahl.

decimal point *noun* Komma *das* (PL *die* Kommas).

decision *noun* Entscheidung *die* (PL *die* Entscheidungen); **to make a**

decision eine Entscheidung treffen

deckchair *noun* Liegestuhl *der* (PL *die* Liegestühle).

declare *verb* 1 erklären; 2 (*at customs*) **nothing to declare** nichts zu verzollen.

decorate *verb* 1 schmücken; **to decorate the Christmas tree** den Weihnachtsbaum schmücken; 2 (*with paint*) streichen ✧; (*with wallpaper*) tapezieren; **we're decorating the kitchen this weekend** wir streichen dieses Wochenende die Küche.

decoration *noun* Verzierung *die* (PL *die* Verzierungen); **Christmas decorations** *der* Weihnachtsschmuck.

deep *adjective* tief; **a deep feeling of gratitude** ein tiefes Dankbarkeitsgefühl; **how deep is the swimming pool?** wie tief ist das Schwimmbecken?; **a hole two metres deep** ein zwei Meter tiefes Loch.

deep freeze *noun* Tiefkühltruhe *die* (PL *die* Tiefkühltruhen); (*upright*) Tiefkühlschrank *der* (PL *die* Tiefkühlschränke).

deeply *adverb* tief.

deer *noun* 1 Hirsch *der* (PL *die* Hirsche); 2 (*roe deer*) Reh *das* (PL *die* Rehe).

defeat *noun* Niederlage *die* (PL *die* Niederlagen). *verb* schlagen ✧.

defence *noun* Verteidigung *die*.

✧ IRREGULAR VERB: *See the verb table in the centre of the dictionary*

defend *verb* verteidigen.

defender *noun* Verteidiger *der* (PL die Verteidiger), Verteidigerin *die* (PL die Verteidigerinnen).

definite *adjective* 1 eindeutig; **a definite improvement** eine eindeutige Besserung; 2 (*certain*) sicher; **it's not definite yet** es ist noch nicht sicher; 3 (*exact*) klar; **a definite answer** eine klare Antwort.

definitely *adverb* 1 (*when giving your opinion about something*) eindeutig; **your German is definitely better than mine** dein Deutsch ist eindeutig besser als meins; 2 (*without doubt*) bestimmt; **she's definitely going to be there** sie wird bestimmt dort sein; **I'm definitely not coming** ich komme ganz bestimmt nicht; 3 '**are you sure you like this one better?' – 'definitely!'** 'gefällt dir diese wirklich besser?' – 'klar!' (*informal*).

degree *noun* 1 Grad *der* (PL die Grade); **thirty degrees** dreißig Grad; 2 **a university degree** ein akademischer Grad.

delay *noun* Verspätung *die* (PL die Verspätungen); **a two-hour delay** eine zweistündige Verspätung.
verb 1 (*hold up*) aufhalten ◇ SEP; **she was delayed in the office** sie ist im Büro aufgehalten worden; 2 (*train, plane*) **to be delayed** Verspätung haben; **the flight was delayed by bad weather** der Flug hatte wegen des schlechten Wetters Verspätung; 3 (*postpone*) aufschieben ◇ SEP; **the decision has been delayed until Thursday** die

Entscheidung wurde bis Donnerstag aufgeschoben.

delete *verb* 1 streichen ◇; 2 (*in computing*) löschen.

deliberate *adjective* absichtlich.

deliberately *adverb* absichtlich; **she did it deliberately** sie hat das absichtlich getan.

delicate *adjective* 1 (*fabric, health*) zart; 2 (*situation, question*) heikel; 3 (*taste, smell*) fein.

delicatessen *noun* Feinkostgeschäft *das* (PL die Feinkostgeschäfte).

delicious *adjective* köstlich.

delighted *adjective* hocherfreut; **to be delighted** begeistert sein; **they're delighted with their new flat** sie sind von ihrer neuen Wohnung begeistert; **I'm delighted that you can come** ich freue mich sehr, dass ihr kommen könnt.

deliver *verb* 1 liefern; **they're delivering the washing machine tomorrow** die Waschmaschine wird morgen geliefert; 2 (*mail, newspapers*) zustellen SEP.

delivery *noun* 1 Lieferung *die* (PL die Lieferungen); 2 (*of mail, newspapers*) Zustellung *die* (PL die Zustellungen).

demand *noun* Nachfrage *die* (PL die Nachfragen); **much in demand** sehr gefragt.
verb verlangen.

demo *noun* (*protest*) Demo *die* (*informal*) (PL die Demos).

△ NEW SPELLING: *See page xii*

democracy noun Demokratie die
(PL die Demokratien).

democratic adjective
demokratisch.

demonstrate verb 1 (a machine,
product, or technique) vorführen SEP;
2 (protest) demonstrieren; **to
demonstrate against something**
gegen etwas ←(ACC) demonstrieren.

demonstration noun 1 (of a
machine, product, or technique)
Vorführung die (PL die
Vorführungen); 2 (protest)
Demonstration die (PL die
Demonstrationen).

demonstrator noun
Demonstrant der (PL die
Demonstranten), Demonstrantin
die (PL die Demonstrantinnen).

denim noun Jeansstoff der (PL die
Jeansstoffe); **a denim jacket** eine
Jeansjacke.

Denmark noun Dänemark das.

dental adjective 1 Zahn-; **dental
floss** die Zahnseide; **dental hygiene**
die Zahnpflege; 2 **to have a dental
appointment** beim Zahnarzt
angemeldet sein.

dentist noun Zahnarzt der (PL die
Zahnärzte), Zahnärztin die (PL die
Zahnärztinnen); **my mum's a
dentist** meine Mutter ist
Zahnärztin.

deny verb bestreiten ✧.

deodorant noun Deodorant das
(PL die Deodorants).

depart verb 1 (set out on a journey)
abreisen SEP (PERF sein); 2 (train,
coach) abfahren ✧ SEP (PERF sein);
3 (plane) abfliegen ✧ SEP (PERF sein)

department noun 1 (in a shop,
firm, or hospital) Abteilung die (PL
die Abteilungen); **the men's
department** die Herrenabteilung;
2 (of a university) Seminar das (PL
die Seminare); **the history
department** das Seminar für
Geschichte; 3 (in school)
Fachbereich der (PL die
Fachbereiche).

department store noun
Kaufhaus das (PL die Kaufhäuser).

departure noun 1 (of a person)
Abreise die; 2 (of a car, train)
Abfahrt die; 3 (of a plane)
Abflug der.

departure lounge noun
Abflughalle die (PL die
Abflughallen).

depend verb 1 **to depend on**
abhängen ✧ SEP von (+DAT); **it
depends on the price** das hängt
vom Preis ab; **it depends on what
you want** das hängt davon ab, was
du willst; 2 **it depends** es kommt
darauf an.

deposit noun 1 (when renting or
hiring) Kaution die (PL die
Kautionen); 2 (when booking a
holiday or hotel room)
Anzahlung die (PL die Anzahlungen)
to pay a deposit eine Anzahlung
leisten; 3 (on a bottle) Pfand das.

depressed adjective deprimiert.

depressing adjective
deprimierend.

✧ IRREGULAR VERB: See the verb table in the centre of the dictionary

depth noun Tiefe die.

deputy noun Stellvertreter der (PL die Stellvertreter), Stellvertreterin die (PL die Stellvertreterinnen).

describe verb beschreiben ◇.

description noun Beschreibung die (PL die Beschreibungen).

desert noun Wüste die (PL die Wüsten).

desert island noun verlassene Insel die (PL die verlassenen Inseln).

deserve verb verdienen.

design noun 1 Konstruktion die (PL die Konstruktionen); **the design of the plane** die Flugzeugkonstruktion; 2 (artistic design) Design das (PL die Designs); **modern design** modernes Design; 3 (pattern) Muster das (PL die Muster); **a floral design** ein Blumenmuster; 4 (sketch) Entwurf der (PL die Entwürfe).
verb 1 konstruieren (a machine, plane, system); 2 entwerfen ◇ (costumes, fabric, scenery).

designer noun Designer der (PL die Designer), Designerin die (PL die Designerinnen).

desk noun 1 (in an office or at home) Schreibtisch der (PL die Schreibtische); 2 (pupil's) Pult das (PL die Pulte); 3 **the reception desk** die Rezeption; **the information desk** die Auskunft.

despair noun Verzweiflung die.
verb **to despair of doing**

something alle Hoffnung aufgeben ◇ SEP, etwas zu tun.

desperate adjective 1 verzweifelt; **a desperate attempt** ein verzweifelter Versuch; 2 **to be desperate to do something** etwas dringend tun müssen; **I'm desperate to speak to you** ich muss dich dringend sprechen; **to be desperate for something** etwas dringend brauchen.

dessert noun Nachtisch der (PL die Nachtische); **what's for dessert?** was gibt's zum Nachtisch?

destination noun Ziel das (PL die Ziele).

destroy verb zerstören.

destruction noun Zerstörung die.

detached house noun Einzelhaus das (PL die Einzelhäuser).

detail noun Einzelheit die (PL die Einzelheiten).

detailed adjective ausführlich.

detective noun 1 (in the police) Kriminalbeamte der (PL die Kriminalbeamten), Kriminalbeamtin die (PL die Kriminalbeamtinnen); 2 **private detective** der Detektiv, die Detektivin.

detective story noun Detektivgeschichte die (PL die Detektivgeschichten).

detention noun 1 (at school) Nachsitzen das; 2 (in prison) Haft die.

△ NEW SPELLING: See page xii

detergent noun Waschmittel das (PL die Waschmittel).

determined adjective entschlossen; **he's determined to leave** er ist fest entschlossen zu gehen.

detour noun Umweg der (PL die Umwege).

develop verb 1 entwickeln; **to get a film developed** einen Film entwickeln lassen; 2 sich entwickeln; **how children develop** wie Kinder sich entwickeln.

developing country noun Entwicklungsland das (PL die Entwicklungsländer).

development noun Entwicklung die (PL die Entwicklungen).

devil noun Teufel der (PL die Teufel).

devoted adjective treu.

diabetes noun Zuckerkrankheit die.

diabetic noun Diabetiker der (PL die Diabetiker), Diabetikerin die (PL die Diabetikerinnen). adjective zuckerkrank; **to be diabetic** zuckerkrank sein.

diagonal adjective diagonal.

diagram noun Diagramm das (PL die Diagramme).

dial verb wählen; **I dialled the wrong number** ich habe die falsche Nummer gewählt.

dialling tone noun Freizeichen das.

dialogue noun Dialog der (PL die Dialoge).

diamond noun 1 Diamant der (PL die Diamanten); (gemstone) Brillant der (PL die Brillanten); 2 (in cards) Karo das; **the jack of diamonds** der Karobube; 3 (shape) Raute die (PL die Rauten).

diarrhoea noun Durchfall der.

diary noun 1 (for appointments) Terminkalender der (PL die Terminkalender); 2 Tagebuch das (PL die Tagebücher); **to keep a diary** ein Tagebuch führen.

dice noun Würfel der (PL die Würfel); **to throw the dice** würfeln.

dictation noun Diktat das (PL die Diktate).

dictionary noun Wörterbuch das (PL die Wörterbücher).

did verb SEE **do**.

die verb 1 sterben ✧ (PERF sein); **my grannie died in January** meine Oma starb im Januar; 2 **to be dying to do something** darauf brennen, etwas zu tun; **I'm dying to meet her** ich brenne darauf, sie kennen zu lernen.

diesel noun 1 Dieselöl das; 2 **diesel engine** der Dieselmotor; **diesel car** der Diesel.

diet noun 1 Ernährung die; **a healthy diet** eine gesunde Ernährung; 2 (slimming or special) Diät die (PL die Diäten); **to be on a diet** Diät machen.

✧ IRREGULAR VERB: See the verb table in the centre of the dictionary

difference *noun* 1 Unterschied *der* (PL *die* Unterschiede); **I can't see any difference between the two** ich finde, es besteht kein Unterschied zwischen den beiden; **what's the difference between …?** was ist der Unterschied zwischen …?; 2 **it makes a difference** es ist ein Unterschied; **it makes no difference** es ist egal; **it makes no difference what I say** es ist egal, was ich sage.

different *adjective* 1 verschieden; **the two sisters are very different** die beiden Schwestern sind sehr verschieden; 2 **to be different from** anders sein als; **she's very different from her sister** sie ist ganz anders als ihre Schwester; 3 (*separate*) anderer/andere/anderes; **she reads a different book every day** sie liest jeden Tag ein anderes Buch.

difficult *adjective* schwer; **it's really difficult** es ist sehr schwer; **he finds it difficult** es fällt ihm schwer.

difficulty *noun* Schwierigkeit *die* (PL *die* Schwierigkeiten); **to have difficulty doing something** Schwierigkeiten haben, etwas zu tun; **I had difficulty finding your house** ich hatte Schwierigkeiten, dein Haus zu finden.

dig *verb* graben ✧; **to dig a hole** ein Loch graben.

digital *adjective* digital; **digital watch** *die* Digitaluhr; **digital recording** *die* Digitalaufnahme.

din *noun* Lärm *der*; **stop making such a din!** hör auf, so einen Lärm zu machen!

dinghy *noun* 1 **sailing dinghy** *das* Dingi; 2 **rubber dinghy** *das* Schlauchboot.

dining room *noun* Esszimmer △ *das* (PL *die* Esszimmer); **in the dining room** im Esszimmer.

dinner *noun* 1 (*evening*) Abendessen *das* (PL *die* Abendessen); **to invite somebody to dinner** jemanden zum Abendessen einladen; 2 (*midday*) Mittagessen *das* (PL *die* Mittagessen); **to have school dinner** in der Schulkantine zu Mittag essen.

dinner party *noun* Abendessen *das* (PL *die* Abendessen).

dinner time *noun* Essenszeit *die*.

dinosaur *noun* Dinosaurier *der* (PL *die* Dinosaurier).

diploma *noun* Diplom *das* (PL *die* Diplome).

direct *adjective* direkt. *verb* 1 **to direct a film or a play** bei einem Film oder einem Theaterstück Regie führen; 2 regeln (*traffic*).

direction *noun* 1 Richtung *die* (PL *die* Richtungen); **to go in the other direction** in die andere Richtung gehen; 2 **to ask somebody for directions** jemanden nach dem Weg fragen; 3 **directions for use** *die* Gebrauchsanweisung (*singular*).

director *noun* 1 (*of a company*) Direktor *der* (PL *die* Direktoren), Direktorin *die* (PL *die* Direktorinnen); 2 (*of a programme,*

△ NEW SPELLING: See page xii

play, or film) Regisseur *der* (PL *die* Regisseure), Regisseurin *die* (PL *die* Regisseurinnen).

directory *noun* Telefonbuch *das* (PL *die* Telefonbücher); **he's ex-directory** seine Nummer steht nicht im Telefonbuch.

dirt *noun* Schmutz *der*.

dirty *adjective* schmutzig; **my hands are dirty** ich habe schmutzige Hände; **to get something dirty** etwas schmutzig machen; **you'll get your dress dirty** du machst dir das Kleid schmutzig; **to get dirty** schmutzig werden; **the curtains get dirty quickly** die Vorhänge werden sehr schnell schmutzig.

disabled *adjective* behindert; **disabled people** Behinderte (*plural*).

disadvantage *noun* 1 Nachteil *der* (PL *die* Nachteile); 2 **to be at a disadvantage** im Nachteil sein.

disagree *verb* 1 **I disagree** ich bin anderer Meinung; 2 **to disagree with somebody** mit jemandem nicht übereinstimmen SEP; **I disagree with James** ich stimme mit James nicht überein.

disappear *verb* verschwinden ◇ (PERF *sein*).

disappearance *noun* Verschwinden *das*.

disappointed *adjective* enttäuscht; **I'm disappointed with my marks** ich bin über meine Noten enttäuscht.

disappointment *noun* Enttäuschung *die* (PL *die* Enttäuschungen).

disaster *noun* Katastrophe *die* (PL *die* Katastrophen); **it was a complete disaster** es war eine komplette Katastrophe.

disastrous *adjective* katastrophal.

disc *noun* 1 **compact disc** *die* Compact disc; 2 **tax disc** (*for a vehicle*) *die* Steuerplakette; 3 **slipped disc** *der* Bandscheibenvorfall.

discipline *noun* Disziplin *die*.

disc-jockey *noun* Diskjockey *der* (PL *die* Diskjockeys).

disco *noun* 1 Diskoparty *die* (PL *die* Diskopartys); **they're having a disco** sie machen eine Diskoparty; 2 (*club*) Disko *die* (PL *die* Diskos); **to go to a disco** in eine Disko gehen.

discount *noun* Rabatt *der* (PL *die* Rabatte).

discover *verb* entdecken.

discovery *noun* Entdeckung *die* (PL *die* Entdeckungen).

discreet *adjective* diskret.

discrimination *noun* Diskriminierung *die*; **discrimination against women** die Diskriminierung von Frauen; **racial discrimination** *die* Rassendiskriminierung.

discuss *verb* **to discuss something** etwas besprechen ◇; **we'll discuss the problem tomorrow** wir besprechen das Problem morgen;

◇ IRREGULAR VERB: *See the verb table in the centre of the dictionary*

I'm going to discuss it with Phil ich werde es mit Phil besprechen.

discussion *noun* Gespräch *das* (PL die Gespräche).

disease *noun* Krankheit *die* (PL die Krankheiten).

disguise *noun* Verkleidung *die* (PL die Verkleidungen); **to be in disguise** verkleidet sein. *verb* verkleiden; **disguised as a woman** als Frau verkleidet.

disgust *noun* Ekel *der*.

disgusted *adjective* 1 (*filled with indignation*) empört; 2 (*nauseated*) angeekelt.

disgusting *adjective* eklig.

dish *noun* 1 Schüssel *die* (PL die Schüsseln); **a large white dish** eine große weiße Schüssel; **satellite dish** die Satellitenschüssel; 2 (*type of food*) Gericht *das* (PL die Gerichte); **risotto is my favourite dish** Risotto ist mein Lieblingsgericht; 3 (*crockery*) **the dishes** das Geschirr; **to do the dishes** Geschirr spülen.

dishonest *adjective* unehrlich.

dishonesty *noun* Unehrlichkeit *die*.

dishwasher *noun* Geschirrspülmaschine *die* (PL die Geschirrspülmaschinen).

disinfectant *noun* Desinfektionsmittel *das*.

disk *noun* Diskette *die* (PL die Disketten); **floppy disk** die Diskette; **hard disk** die Festplatte.

diskette *noun* Diskette *die* (PL die Disketten).

dismiss *verb* entlassen ✧ (*an employee*).

disobedient *adjective* ungehorsam.

display *noun* 1 Ausstellung *die* (PL die Ausstellungen); **handicrafts display** die Handarbeitsausstellung; **to be on display** ausgestellt sein; 2 **window display** die Auslage; 3 **firework display** das Feuerwerk. *verb* ausstellen SEP.

disposable *adjective* Wegwerf-; **disposable towel** das Wegwerfhandtuch.

disqualify *verb* disqualifizieren.

dissolve *verb* auflösen SEP.

distance *noun* Entfernung *die* (PL die Entfernungen); **from this distance** aus dieser Entfernung; **from a distance** von weitem; **in the distance** in der Ferne; **it's within walking distance** es ist zu Fuß erreichbar.

distant *adjective* fern.

distinct *adjective* deutlich.

distinctly *adverb* 1 deutlich; 2 **it's distinctly odd** es ist äußerst komisch.

distract *verb* ablenken SEP.

distribute *verb* verteilen.

district *noun* 1 (*of a town*) Stadtteil *der* (PL die Stadtteile); **a poor district of Berlin** ein ärmlicher Stadtteil von Berlin; 2 (*in the country*) Gebiet *das* (PL die Gebiete).

△ NEW SPELLING: *See page xii*

disturb *verb* stören; **sorry to disturb you** Entschuldigung, dass ich störe.

dive *noun* Kopfsprung *der* (PL *die* Kopfsprünge).
verb 1 einen Kopfsprung machen; 2 (*swim underwater*) tauchen (PERF *sein*).

diver *noun* 1 (*underwater*) Taucher *der* (PL *die* Taucher), Taucherin *die* (PL *die* Taucherinnen); 2 (*from a diving board*) Springer *der* (PL *die* Springer), Springerin *die* (PL *die* Springerinnen).

diversion *noun* (*of traffic*) Umleitung *die* (PL *die* Umleitungen).

divide *verb* teilen.

diving *noun* 1 (*underwater*) Tauchen *das*; 2 (*from a diving board*) Kopfspringen *das*.

diving board *noun* Sprungbrett *das* (PL *die* Sprungbretter).

division *noun* 1 Teilung *die* (PL *die* Teilungen); 2 (*in maths*) Division *die* (PL *die* Divisionen); 3 (*sports league*) Liga *die* (PL *die* Ligen).

divorce *noun* Scheidung *die* (PL *die* Scheidungen).

divorced *adjective* geschieden.

DIY *noun* 1 Heimwerken *das*; 2 **to do DIY** heimwerken; 3 **DIY shop** *der* Baumarkt (PL *die* Baumärkte).

dizzy *adjective* **I feel dizzy** mir ist schwindlig.

DJ *noun* DJ *der* (PL *die* DJs).

do *verb* 1 tun ✧, machen; **what are you doing?** was machst du?; **I'm doing my homework** ich mache meine Hausaufgaben; **what have you done with the hammer?** was hast du mit dem Hammer gemacht?; **can you do me a favour?** kannst du mir einen Gefallen tun?; **do as I say** tu was ich sage; 2 **she's doing the cleaning** sie putzt; **I'll do the washing up** ich wasche ab; **I must do the shopping** ich muss einkaufen gehen; 3 (*in questions*) **do you like it?** gefällt es dir?; **when does the film start?** wann fängt der Film an?; **how do you open the door?** wie macht man die Tür auf?; **do you know him?** kennst du ihn?; 4 (*in negative sentences*) **I don't like mushrooms** ich mag keine Pilze; **Rosie doesn't like spinach** Rosie mag keinen Spinat; **you didn't shut the door** du hast die Tür nicht zugemacht; **it doesn't matter** das macht nichts; 5 (*when it refers back to another verb, 'do' is not translated*) **'do you live here?' – 'yes, I do'** 'wohnst du hier?' -'ja'; **she has more money than I do** sie hat mehr Geld als ich; **'I live in Oxford' – 'so do I'** 'ich wohne in Oxford' – 'ich auch'; **'I didn't phone Gemma' – 'neither did I'** 'ich habe Gemma nicht angerufen' – 'ich auch nicht'; 6 **don't you?, doesn't he?,** *etc.* nicht wahr?; **you know Helen, don't you?** du kennst Helen, nicht wahr?; **she left on Thursday, didn't she?** sie ist Donnerstag abgefahren, nicht

---

✧ IRREGULAR VERB: *See the verb table in the centre of the dictionary*

wahr?; **/ that'll do** das reicht; **it'll do like that** das geht so.

- **to do something up 1** etwas zubinden ✧ SEP (*shoes*); **2** etwas zumachen SEP (*a cardigan, jacket*); **3** etwas renovieren (*a house*).
- **to do without something** ohne etwas ←(ACC) auskommen ✧ SEP (PERF *sein*); **we can do without knives** wir können ohne Messer auskommen.

doctor *noun* Arzt *der* (PL *die* Ärzte), Ärztin *die* (PL *die* Ärztinnen); **her mother's a doctor** ihre Mutter ist Ärztin.

documentary *noun* Dokumentarfilm *der* (PL *die* Dokumentarfilme).

dog *noun* Hund *der* (PL *die* Hunde).

do-it-yourself *noun* Heimwerken *das*.

dole *noun* Stempelgeld *das*; **to be on the dole** stempeln gehen (*informal*).

doll *noun* Puppe *die* (PL *die* Puppen).

dollar *noun* Dollar *der* (PL *die* Dollars).

domino *noun* **1** Dominostein *der* (PL *die* Dominosteine); **2** (*game*) **dominoes** Domino *das*; **to play dominoes** Domino spielen.

donkey *noun* Esel *der* (PL *die* Esel).

don't SEE **do**.

door *noun* Tür *die* (PL *die* Türen); **to open the door** die Tür aufmachen; **to shut the door** die Tür zumachen.

doorbell *noun* Türklingel *die* (PL *die* Türklingeln); **to ring the doorbell** klingeln.

dot *noun* **1** Punkt *der* (PL *die* Punkte); **at ten on the dot** Punkt zehn Uhr; **2** (*small dot on fabric*) Pünktchen *das* (PL *die* Pünktchen).

double *adjective, adverb* **1** doppelt; **a double helping** eine doppelte Portion; **double the size** doppelt so groß; **double the time** doppelt so viel Zeit; **at double the price** zum doppelten Preis; **2 double room** *das* Doppelzimmer; **3 double bed** *das* Doppelbett.

double bass *noun* Kontrabass △ *der* (PL *die* Kontrabässe).

double-decker bus *noun* Doppeldeckerbus *der* (PL *die* Doppeldeckerbusse).

doubles *noun* (*in tennis*) Doppel *das* (PL *die* Doppel).

doubt *noun* Zweifel *der* (PL *die* Zweifel); **there's no doubt about it** es besteht kein Zweifel daran; **I have my doubts** ich habe gewisse Zweifel.
verb **to doubt something** etwas bezweifeln; **I doubt it** das bezweifle ich; **I doubt that …** ich bezweifle, dass …; **I doubt they'll buy it** ich bezweifle, dass sie es kaufen.

doubtful *adjective* **1** fraglich; **it's doubtful** es ist fraglich; **2 to be doubtful about doing something** Bedenken haben, ob man etwas tun soll; **I'm doubtful about inviting them together** ich habe Bedenken, ob ich sie zusammen einladen soll.

△ NEW SPELLING: *See page xii*

dough *noun* Teig *der*.

doughnut *noun* Krapfen *der* (PL *die* Krapfen).

down *adverb, preposition* 1 unten; **he's down in the cellar** er ist unten im Keller; **it's down there** es ist da unten; 2 **down the road** (*nearby*) in der Nähe; **there's a chemist's just down the road** eine Apotheke ist ganz in der Nähe; 3 **to go down** nach unten gehen; **I went down to open the door** ich bin nach unten gegangen, um die Tür aufzumachen; **to walk down the street** die Straße entlanggehen ✧ SEP (PERF *sein*); **to run down the stairs** die Treppe runterrennen SEP (PERF *sein*) (*informal*); 4 **to come down** herunterkommen ✧ SEP (PERF *sein*); **she came down into the kitchen** sie kam in die Küche herunter; 5 **to sit down** sich setzen; **she sat down on the chair** sie setzte sich auf den Stuhl; 6 **to write something down** etwas aufschreiben ✧ SEP.

downstairs *adverb* 1 unten; **she's downstairs** sie ist unten; 2 (*with movement*) nach unten; **to go downstairs** nach unten gehen; 3 im Erdgeschoss Δ; **the flat downstairs** die Wohnung im Erdgeschoss.

dozen *noun* Dutzend *das* (PL *die* Dutzende).

drag *noun* 1 **what a drag!** so'n Mist! (*informal*); 2 **what a drag she is!** Mann, ist die langweilig! (*informal*). *verb* schleppen.

drama *noun* 1 (*play*) Drama *das* (PL *die* Dramen); **he made a big drama out of it** er hat ein großes Drama daraus gemacht (*informal*); 2 (*dramatic nature*) Dramatik *die*.

dramatic *adjective* dramatisch.

draught *noun* Luftzug *der*; **there's a draught in here** hier zieht es.

draughts *noun* Damespiel *das*; **to play draughts** Dame spielen.

draw *noun* 1 (*in a match*) Unentschieden *das*; **to end in a draw** mit einem Unentschieden enden; 2 (*lottery*) Ziehung *die* (PL *die* Ziehungen). *verb* 1 zeichnen; **she can draw really well** sie kann wirklich sehr gut zeichnen; 2 **to draw the curtains** (*open*) die Vorhänge aufziehen ✧ SEP; (*close*) die Vorhänge zuziehen ✧ SEP; 3 (*in a match*) unentschieden spielen; **we drew three all** wir haben drei zu drei unentschieden gespielt.

drawer *noun* Schublade *die* (PL *die* Schubladen).

drawing *noun* Zeichnung *die* (PL *die* Zeichnungen).

drawing pin *noun* Reißzwecke *die* (PL *die* Reißzwecken).

dreadful *adjective* furchtbar.

dreadfully *adverb* furchtbar; **I'm dreadfully late** ich habe mich furchtbar verspätet; **I'm dreadfully sorry** es tut mir furchtbar Leid.

dream *noun* Traum *der* (PL *die* Träume); **to have a dream** einen Traum haben. *verb* träumen; **to dream about something** von etwas ←(DAT) träumen.

✧ IRREGULAR VERB: *See the verb table in the centre of the dictionary*

dress *noun* Kleid *das* (PL *die* Kleider).
verb **to dress a child** ein Kind anziehen ✧ SEP.
to dress up sich verkleiden; **to dress up as a vampire** sich als Vampir verkleiden.

dressed *adjective* **1** angezogen; **is Tom dressed yet?** ist Tom schon angezogen?; **2 she was dressed in black trousers and a yellow shirt** sie trug schwarze Hosen und ein gelbes Hemd; **3 to get dressed** sich anziehen ✧ SEP; **I got dressed quickly** ich zog mich schnell an.

dressing gown *noun* Morgenrock *der* (PL *die* Morgenröcke).

dressing table *noun* Frisierkommode *die* (PL *die* Frisierkommoden).

drier *noun* **hair drier** *der* Föhn △; **tumble drier** *der* Wäschetrockner.

drill *noun* Bohrer *der* (PL *die* Bohrer).

drink *noun* Getränk *das* (PL *die* Getränke); **1 to have a drink** etwas trinken; **would you like a drink of water?** möchtest du etwas Wasser trinken?; **2** (*an alcoholic drink*) Drink *der* (PL *die* Drinks); **they've invited us round for drinks** sie haben uns auf einen Drink eingeladen; **let's have a drink!** trinken wir einen! (*informal*).
verb trinken ✧; **he drank a glass of water** er trank ein Glas Wasser.

drive *noun* **1 to go for a drive** eine Autofahrt machen; **2** (*in front of a house*) Einfahrt *die* (PL *die* Einfahrten).

verb **1** fahren ✧ (PERF *sein*); **she drives very fast** sie fährt sehr schnell; **to drive a car** Auto fahren; **I'd like to learn to drive** ich möchte Autofahren lernen; **can you drive?** kannst du Auto fahren?; **2 we drove to Berlin** wir sind mit dem Auto nach Berlin gefahren; **3 to drive somebody (to a place)** jemanden (irgendwohin) fahren (PERF *haben*); **Mum drove me to the station** Mutti hat mich zum Bahnhof gefahren; **to drive somebody home** jemanden nach Hause fahren; ★ **she drives me mad!** sie macht mich verrückt!

driver *noun* **1** Fahrer *der* (PL *die* Fahrer), Fahrerin *die* (PL *die* Fahrerinnen); **2** (*of a locomotive*) Führer *der* (PL *die* Führer), Führerin *die* (PL *die* Führerinnen).

driving instructor *noun* Fahrlehrer *der* (PL *die* Fahrlehrer), Fahrlehrerin *die* (PL *die* Fahrlehrerinnen).

driving lesson *noun* Fahrstunde *die* (PL *die* Fahrstunden).

driving licence *noun* Führerschein *der*.

driving test *noun* Fahrprüfung *die*; **to take your driving test** die Fahrprüfung machen; **Jenny's passed her driving test** Jenny hat den Führerschein gemacht.

drop *noun* Tropfen *der* (PL *die* Tropfen).
verb **1 to drop something** etwas fallen lassen; **I dropped my glasses**

ich habe meine Brille fallen lassen;
2 drop it! lass das!; **3 I'm going to
drop history next year** nächstes
Jahr lege ich Geschichte ab;
4 absetzen SEP (*a person*); **could you
drop me at the station?** könntest
du mich am Bahnhof absetzen?

drug *noun* **1** (*medicine*)
Medikament *das* (PL *die*
Medikamente); **2** (*illegal*) **drugs**
Drogen (*plural*).

drug abuse *noun*
Drogenmissbrauch △ *der*.

drug addict *noun*
Drogenabhängige *der/die* (PL *die*
Drogenabhängigen).

drug addiction *noun*
Drogenabhängigkeit *die*.

drum *noun* **1** Trommel *die* (PL *die*
Trommeln); **2 drums** *das*
Schlagzeug; **to play drums**
Schlagzeug spielen.

drummer *noun* Schlagzeuger *der*
(PL *die* Schlagzeuger).

drunk *noun* Betrunkene *der/die* (PL
die Betrunkenen).
adjective betrunken; **to get drunk**
sich betrinken ✧.

dry *adjective* trocken.
verb **1** trocknen; **to let something
dry** etwas trocknen lassen; **to dry
your hair** sich ←(DAT) die Haare
trocknen; **to dry the washing** die
Wäsche trocknen; **2 to dry your
hands** sich ←(DAT) die Hände
abtrocknen SEP; **I dried my feet** ich
trocknete mir die Füße ab; **to dry the
dishes** das Geschirr abtrocknen .

dry cleaner's *noun* chemische
Reinigung *die*.

dryer *noun* SEE **drier**.

dubbed *adjective* **a dubbed film** ein
synchronisierter Film.

duck *noun* Ente *die* (PL *die* Enten).

due *adjective, adverb* **1 to be due to
do something** etwas tun müssen;
Paul's due back soon Paul muss
bald zurück sein; **we're due to leave
on Thursday** wir müssen
Donnerstag abfahren; **2 due to**
wegen (+GEN); **due to bad weather**
wegen schlechten Wetters.

dull *adjective* **1 dull weather** trübes
Wetter; **it's a dull day today** heute
ist ein trüber Tag; **2** (*boring*)
langweilig.

dumb *adjective* **1** stumm; **2** (*stupid*)
dumm; **he asked some dumb
questions** er hat ein paar dumme
Fragen gestellt.

dump *verb* **1** abladen ✧ SEP
(*rubbish*); **2** (*put down*)
hinwerfen ✧ SEP; **he dumped it in the
rubbish** er hat es in den Müll
geworfen; **3** abschieben ✧ SEP (*a
person*) (*informal*); **she's dumped
her boyfriend** sie hat ihren Freund
abgeschoben.

dungarees *plural noun*
Latzhose *die* (PL *die* Latzhosen).

during *preposition* während (+GEN);
during the night während der
Nacht; **I saw her during the
holidays** ich habe sie während der
Ferien gesehen.

✧ IRREGULAR VERB: *See the verb table in the centre of the dictionary*

dust *noun* Staub *der.*
verb **1** abstauben SEP (*furniture, objects*); **2** (*in a room*) Staub wischen; **she's dusting** sie wischt Staub.

dustbin *noun* Mülltonne *die* (PL *die* Mülltonnen).

dustman *noun* Müllmann *der* (PL *die* Müllmänner).

dusty *adjective* staubig.

Dutch *noun* **1** (*language*) Holländisch *das*; **2 the Dutch** (*people*) die Holländer.
adjective holländisch; **he's Dutch** er ist Holländer; **she's Dutch** sie ist Holländerin.

duty *noun* **1** Pflicht *die* (PL *die* Pflichten); **to have a duty to do something** die Pflicht haben, etwas zu tun; **you have a duty to inform us** du hast die Pflicht, uns zu benachrichtigen; **2 to be on duty** Dienst haben; **to be on night duty** Nachtdienst haben; **I'm off duty tonight** ich habe heute Abend keinen Dienst.

duty-free *adjective* zollfrei; **duty-free shop** *der* Dutyfreeshop; **duty-free goods** zollfreie Waren (*plural*).

duvet *noun* Federbett *das* (PL *die* Federbetten).

duvet cover *noun* Bettbezug *der* (PL *die* Bettbezüge).

dye *noun* Farbe *die* (PL *die* Farben).
verb färben; **to dye your hair** sich ←(DAT) die Haare färben; **I'm going to have my hair dyed pink** ich lasse mir die Haare rosa färben.

dynamic *adjective* dynamisch.

dyslexia *noun* Legasthenie *die.*

dyslexic *adjective* legasthenisch; **to be dyslexic** Legastheniker sein, Legasthenikerin sein.

E e

each *adjective, pronoun*
1 jeder/jede/jedes; **each Sunday** jeden Sonntag; **each time** jedes Mal; **at the beginning of each year** am Anfang jedes Jahres; **we each have an invitation** jeder von uns hat eine Einladung; **my sisters each have a computer** meine Schwestern haben alle einen Computer; **she gave us an apple each** sie hat jedem von uns einen Apfel gegeben; **each of you** jeder von euch/jede von euch; **we each got a present** jeder Einzelne hat ein Geschenk bekommen; **2 the tickets cost ten pounds each** die Karten kosten je zehn Pfund; **£5 each** (*per person*) fünf Pfund pro Person; (*per item*) fünf Pfund pro Stück.

each other *pronoun* (*'each other' is usually translated using a reflexive pronoun*) **they love each other** sie lieben sich; **we know each other** wir kennen uns; **do you see each other often?** seht ihr euch oft?

ear *noun* Ohr *das* (PL *die* Ohren).

earache *noun* **to have earache** Ohrenschmerzen haben.

△ NEW SPELLING: *See page xii*

earlier *adverb* 1 (*a while ago*) vor kurzem; **your brother phoned earlier** dein Bruder hat vor kurzem angerufen; 2 (*not as late*) früher; **we should have started earlier** wir hätten früher anfangen sollen.

early *adverb* 1 (*in the morning*) früh; **to get up early** früh aufstehen; **it's too early** es ist zu früh; 2 (*for an appointment*) **to be early** früh dran sein; **we're early, the train doesn't leave until ten** wir sind früh dran, der Zug fährt erst um zehn Uhr ab. *adjective* 1 (*one of the first*) **in the early months** während der ersten Monate; **I'm getting the early train** ich nehme den früheren Zug; 2 **to have an early lunch** früh zu Mittag essen; **Jan's having an early night** Jan geht früh zu Bett; 3 **in the early afternoon** am frühen Nachmittag; **in the early hours** in den frühen Morgenstunden.

earn *verb* verdienen; **Richard earns four pounds an hour** Richard verdient vier Pfund die Stunde.

earring *noun* Ohrring *der* (PL *die* Ohrringe).

earth *noun* Erde *die*; **life on earth** das Leben auf der Erde; ★ **what on earth are you doing?** was in aller Welt machst du da?

easily *adverb* leicht; **he's easily the best** er ist mit Abstand der Beste.

east *noun* Osten *der*; **in the east** im Osten. *adjective, adverb* östlich, Ost-; **the east side** die Ostseite; **an east**

wind ein Ostwind; **east of Munich** östlich von München.

Easter *noun* Ostern *das* (PL *die* Ostern); **they're coming at Easter** sie kommen zu Ostern; **Happy Easter** Frohe Ostern.

Easter Day *noun* Ostersonntag *de* (PL *die* Ostersonntage).

Easter egg *noun* Osterei *das* (PL *die* Ostereier).

Eastern Europe *noun* Osteuropa *das*.

easy *adjective* leicht; **it's easy!** das ist leicht!; **it was easy to decide** es war leicht zu entscheiden.

eat *verb* 1 essen ✧; **he was eating a banana** er aß eine Banane; **we're going to have something to eat** wir essen jetzt etwas; 2 **to eat your breakfast** frühstücken.

EC *noun* EG *die* (*Europäische Gemeinschaft*).

ecological *adjective* ökologisch.

ecology *noun* Ökologie *die*.

economical *adjective* sparsam.

economics *noun* Wirtschaftswissenschaften (*plural*).

economy *noun* Wirtschaft *die*.

edge *noun* 1 Kante *die* (PL *die* Kanten); **the edge of the table** die Tischkante; 2 (*of a road, sheet of paper, or cliff*) Rand *der* (PL *die* Ränder); **at the edge of the forest** am Waldrand.

editor *noun* 1 (*of a newspaper or magazine*) Chefredakteur *der* (PL

die Chefredakteure),
Chefredakteurin *die* (PL *die*
Chefredakteurinnen); **2** (*of a book*)
Redakteur *der* (PL *die* Redakteure),
Redakteurin *die* (PL *die*
Redakteurinnen).

educate *verb* erziehen ✧.

education *noun* Ausbildung *die*.

effect *noun* **1** Wirkung *die* (PL *die*
Wirkungen); **the effect of the
explosion was horrific** die Wirkung
der Explosion war entsetzlich; **2 to
have an effect on something** eine
Auswirkung auf etwas ←(ACC) haben;
**it had a good effect on the whole
family** es hatte eine gute
Auswirkung auf die ganze Familie;
3 (*in a film*) Effekt *der* (PL *die*
Effekte); **special effects** besondere
Effekte.

efficient *adjective* **1** (*person*)
tüchtig; **2** (*machine or
organization*) leistungsfähig.

effort *noun* **1** Mühe *die* (PL *die*
Mühen); **2 to make an effort** sich
bemühen; **Toya made an effort to
help us** Toya hat sich bemüht, uns
zu helfen; **he didn't even make the
effort to apologize** er hat sich nicht
einmal die Mühe gemacht, sich zu
entschuldigen.

e.g. *abbreviation* z.B. (*zum Beispiel*).

egg *noun* Ei *das* (PL *die* Eier); **a fried
egg** ein Spiegelei; **a hard-boiled
egg** ein hart gekochtes Ei.

egg-cup *noun* Eierbecher *der* (PL
die Eierbecher).

eggshell *noun* Eierschale *die* (PL *die*
Eierschalen).

egg-white *noun* Eiweiß *das* (PL *die*
Eiweiße).

egg-yolk *noun* Eigelb *das* (PL *die*
Eigelbe).

eight *number* acht; **Maya's eight**
Maya ist acht; **at eight o'clock** um
acht Uhr.

eighteen *number* achtzehn;
Jason's eighteen Jason ist
achtzehn.

eighth *number* achter/achte/
achtes; **on the eighth of July** am
achten Juli.

eighty *number* achtzig; **eighty-five**
fünfundachtzig.

either *pronoun* **1** (*one or the other*)
einer von beiden/eine von
beiden/eins von beiden; **take either
(of them)** nimm einen von
beiden/eine von beiden/eins von
beiden; **I don't like either (of them)**
ich mag keinen von beiden/keine
von beiden/keins von beiden;
2 (*both*) beide (*plural*); **either is
possible** beide sind möglich; **on
either side** auf beiden Seiten.
conjunction **1 either … or** entweder
… oder; **either Susie or Judy**
entweder Susie oder Judy; **2 either
… or** (*with a negative*) weder …
noch; **he didn't ring either Sam or
Emma** er hat weder Sam noch
Emma angerufen; **3 I don't know
them either** ich kenne sie auch
nicht.

elastic *noun* Gummiband *das* (PL
die Gummibänder).

elastic band *noun*
Gummiband *das* (PL *die*
Gummibänder).

△ NEW SPELLING: *See page xii*

elbow *noun* Ellbogen *der* (PL *die* Ellbogen).

elder *adjective* älterer/ältere/älteres; **her elder brother** ihr älterer Bruder.

elderly *adjective* alt; **the elderly** ältere Menschen (*plural*).

eldest *adjective* ältester/älteste/ältestes; **her eldest brother** ihr ältester Bruder.

elect *verb* wählen; **she has been elected** sie ist gewählt worden.

election *noun* Wahl *die* (PL *die* Wahlen); **in the election** bei den Wahlen.

electric *adjective* elektrisch.

electrical *adjective* elektrisch, Elektro-; **electrical equipment** Elektrogeräte (*plural*).

electrician *noun* Elektriker *der* (PL *die* Elektriker), Elektrikerin *die* (PL *die* Elektrikerinnen).

electricity *noun* Strom *der*.

electronic *adjective* elektronisch.

electronics *noun* Elektronik *die*.

elephant *noun* Elefant *der* (PL *die* Elefanten).

eleven *number* elf; **Josh is eleven** Josh ist elf; **at eleven o'clock** um elf Uhr; **a football eleven** eine Fußballelf.

eleventh *number* elfter/elfte/elftes; **the eleventh of May** der elfte Mai; **on the eleventh floor** im elften Stock.

else *adverb* **1** (*in addition*) sonst; **who else?** wer sonst?; **did you see anyone else?** hast du sonst noch jemanden gesehen?; **nothing else** sonst nichts; **I don't want anything else** ich will sonst nichts; **2 would you like something else?** möchten Sie sonst noch etwas?; **3** (*instead or different*) anderer/andere/anderes; **somewhere else** irgendwo anders; **everyone else** alle anderen; **somebody else** jemand anders; **something else** etwas anderes; **4 or else** sonst; **hurry up, or else we'll be late** beeil dich, sonst kommen wir zu spät.

E-mail *noun* E-Mail *die* (PL *die* E-Mails).

embarrassed *adjective* verlegen; **he was very embarrassed** er war ganz verlegen.

embarrassing *adjective* peinlich.

emergency *noun* Notfall *der* (PL *die* Notfälle).

emergency exit *noun* Notausgang *der* (PL *die* Notausgänge).

emotion *noun* Gefühl *das* (PL *die* Gefühle).

emotional *adjective* **1** (*person*) empfindsam; **2** (*speech or occasion*) emotionsgeladen.

emphasize *verb* betonen; **he emphasized that it was voluntary** er betonte, dass es freiwillig war.

employ *verb* **1** (*have working for you*) beschäftigen; **2** (*take on a worker*) einstellen SEP.

IRREGULAR VERB: *See the verb table in the centre of the dictionary*

employee *noun*
Angestellte *der/die* (PL *die*
Angestellten).

employer *noun* Arbeitgeber *der* (PL
die Arbeitgeber), Arbeitgeberin *die*
(PL *die* Arbeitgeberinnen).

employment *noun* Arbeit *die*.

empty *adjective* leer; **an empty
bottle** eine leere Flasche.
verb 1 (*empty out*) ausleeren SEP;
2 (*pour*) schütten.

enclose *verb* (*in a letter*) beilegen
SEP; **please find enclosed a cheque**
ein Scheck liegt bei.

encourage *verb* ermutigen; **to
encourage somebody to do
something** jemanden dazu
ermutigen, etwas zu tun; **Mum
encouraged me to try again** Mutti
hat mich dazu ermutigt, es noch
einmal zu versuchen.

encouragement *noun*
Ermutigung *die* (PL *die*
Ermutigungen).

encouraging *adjective*
ermutigend.

encyclopedia *noun* Lexikon *das*
(PL *die* Lexika).

end *noun* 1 Ende *das* (PL *die* Enden);
'The End' 'Ende'; **at the end of the
film** am Ende des Films; **by the end
of the lesson** als die Stunde zu Ende
war; **in the end I went home**
schließlich bin ich nach Hause
gegangen; **Sally's coming at the end
of June** Sally kommt Ende Juni; **I
read to the end of the page** ich
habe die Seite zu Ende gelesen; **hold

the other end** halte das andere Ende
fest; **at the end of the street** am
Ende der Straße; 2 (*in sports*)
Spielfeldhälfte *die* (PL *die*
Spielfeldhälften); **to change ends**
die Seiten wechseln.
verb 1 (*to put an end to*) beenden;
they've ended the strike sie haben
den Streik beendet; 2 (*to come to an
end*) enden; **the day ended with a
meal** der Tag endete mit einem
Essen.

● **to end up** 1 **to end up doing
something** am Ende etwas tun; **we
ended up taking a taxi** am Ende
haben wir ein Taxi genommen; 2 **to
end up somewhere** irgendwo
landen (PERF *sein*) (*informal*); **Rob
ended up in Berlin** Rob ist in Berlin
gelandet.

ending *noun* 1 Ende *das* (PL *die*
Enden); 2 (*in grammar*)
Endung *die* (PL *die* Endungen).

endless *adjective* endlos (*day or
journey, for example*).

enemy *noun* Feind *der* (PL *die*
Feinde); **to make enemies** sich
←(DAT) Feinde machen.

energetic *adjective*
energiegeladen.

energy *noun* Energie *die*.

engaged *adjective* 1 (*to be married*)
verlobt; **they're engaged** sie sind
verlobt; **to get engaged** sich
verloben; 2 (*a phone or toilet*)
besetzt; **it's engaged, I'll ring later**
es ist besetzt, ich rufe später an.

engagement *noun* (*to marry*)
Verlobung *die* (PL *die* Verlobungen).

△ NEW SPELLING: *See page xii*

engagement ring *noun*
Verlobungsring *der* (PL *die*
Verlobungsringe).

engine *noun* 1 (*in a car*) Motor *der*
(PL *die* Motoren); 2 (*pulling a train*)
Lokomotive *die* (PL *die*
Lokomotiven).

engineer *noun* 1 (*who comes for
repairs*) Techniker *der* (PL *die*
Techniker), Technikerin *die* (PL *die*
Technikerinnen); 2 (*who builds
roads and bridges*) Ingenieur *der* (PL
die Ingenieure), Ingenieurin *die* (PL
die Ingenieurinnen).

England *noun* England *das*; **I'm
from England** ich bin Engländer,
ich bin Engländerin.

English *noun* 1 (*the language*)
Englisch *das*; **do you speak
English?** sprechen Sie Englisch?; **he
answered in English** er hat auf
Englisch geantwortet; 2 (*the people*)
the English die Engländer.
adjective 1 (*of or from England*)
englisch; **the English team** die
englische Mannschaft; **he's English**
er ist Engländer; **she's English** sie
ist Engländerin; **an English
lesson** eine Englischstunde; **our
English teacher** unser
Englischlehrer.

English Channel *noun* **the
English Channel** der Ärmelkanal.

Englishman *noun* Engländer *der*
(PL *die* Engländer).

Englishwoman *noun*
Engländerin *die* (PL *die*
Engländerinnen).

enjoy *verb* 1 **did you enjoy the
party?** hat dir die Party gefallen?; **we**
really enjoyed the concert das
Konzert hat uns wirklich gut
gefallen; 2 **to enjoy doing
something** etwas gerne tun ◇; **I
enjoy reading** ich lese gerne; **do you
enjoy living in York?** wohnst du
gerne in York?; 3 **to enjoy oneself**
sich gut amüsieren; **we really
enjoyed ourselves** wir haben uns
richtig gut amüsiert; **enjoy
yourselves!** viel Vergnügen!; **did
you enjoy yourself?** hast du dich
gut amüsiert?

enjoyable *adjective* nett.

enormous *adjective* riesig.

enough *adverb, adjective, pronoun*
1 genug; **there's enough for
everyone** es gibt genug für alle; **big
enough** groß genug; **have we got
enough bread?** haben wir genug
Brot?; 2 **that's enough** das reicht.

enrol *verb* sich anmelden SEP; **I want
to enrol on the course** ich möchte
mich zu dem Kurs anmelden.

enter *verb* 1 (*to go inside*) gehen ◇
(PERF *sein*) in (+ACC) (*a room or a
building*); **we all entered the
church** wir gingen alle in die
Kirche; 2 (*in computing*)
eingeben ◇ SEP; 3 **to enter for** sich
anmelden SEP zu (+DAT) (*an exam or
a race*); **to enter for a competition**
an einem Preisausschreiben
teilnehmen ◇ SEP.

entertain *verb* 1 (*to keep amused*)
unterhalten ◇; 2 (*to have people
round*) Gäste haben ◇; **they don't
entertain much** sie haben selten
Gäste.

◇ IRREGULAR VERB: *See the verb table in the centre of the dictionary*

entertainment *noun* (*fun*)
Unterhaltung *die*; **there wasn't
much entertainment in the
evenings** abends wurde wenig
Unterhaltung geboten.

enthusiasm *noun*
Begeisterung *die*.

enthusiast *noun* 1 Enthusiast *der*
(PL *die* Enthusiasten), Enthusiastin
die (PL *die* Enthusiastinnen); 2 (*for
sports*) Fan *der* (PL *die* Fans); **he's a
rugby enthusiast** er ist ein
Rugbyfan.

enthusiastic *adjective* begeistert.

entire *adjective* ganz; **the entire
class** die ganze Klasse.

entirely *adverb* ganz.

entrance *noun* 1 (*fee*) Eintritt *der*;
2 (*way in*) Eingang *der* (PL *die*
Eingänge).

entry *noun* 1 (*way in*) Eingang *der*
(PL *die* Eingänge); (*for cars*)
Einfahrt *die* (PL *die* Einfahrten);
2 **'no entry'** 'Zutritt verboten'; (*to
cars*) 'Einfahrt verboten'.

entry phone *noun*
Sprechanlage *die* (PL *die*
Sprechanlagen).

envelope *noun* Briefumschlag *der*
(PL *die* Briefumschläge).

environment *noun* Umwelt *die*.

environmental *adjective* Umwelt-;
environmental pollution die
Umweltverschmutzung.

environment-friendly *adjective*
umweltfreundlich.

epidemic *noun* Epidemie *die* (PL
die Epidemien).

epileptic *adjective* epileptisch.

episode *noun* 1 (*an event*)
Episode *die* (PL *die* Episoden);
2 (*on TV or radio*) Folge *die* (PL *die*
Folgen).

equal *adjective* gleich; **milk and
water in equal quantities** gleich
viel Milch und Wasser.
verb gleichen ✧ (+DAT).

equality *noun*
Gleichberechtigung *die*.

equally *adverb* (*to share*)
gleichmäßig; **we divided it equally**
wir haben es gleichmäßig verteilt.

equator *noun* Äquator *der*.

equip *verb* ausrüsten SEP; **well
equipped for the hike** für die
Wanderung gut ausgerüstet;
equipped with rucksacks mit
Rucksäcken ausgerüstet.

equipment *noun* 1 (*for sport*)
Ausrüstung *die* (PL *die*
Ausrüstungen); 2 Ausstattung *die*
(PL *die* Ausstattungen); **laboratory
equipment** *die* Laborausstattung;
3 (*something needed for an activity*)
Geräte (*plural*); **recording
equipment** Aufnahmegeräte.

error *noun* 1 (*in spelling, typing, on
a computer, or in maths*) Fehler *der*
(PL *die* Fehler); **spelling error** *der*
Schreibfehler; 2 (*wrong opinion*)
Irrtum *der* (PL *die* Irrtümer).

error message *noun*
Fehlermeldung *die* (PL *die*
Fehlermeldungen).

△ NEW SPELLING: *See page xii*

escalator *noun* Rolltreppe *die* (PL *die* Rolltreppen).

escape *noun* (*from prison*) Ausbruch *der* (PL *die* Ausbrüche). *verb* **1** (*from prison*) ausbrechen ✧ SEP (PERF *sein*); **2** entkommen ✧ (PERF *sein*); **to escape from somebody** jemandem entkommen.

especially *adverb* besonders.

essay *noun* Aufsatz *der* (PL *die* Aufsätze); **an essay on German reunification** ein Aufsatz über die deutsche Wiedervereinigung.

essential *adjective* unbedingt erforderlich; **it's essential to reply quickly** es ist unbedingt erforderlich, sofort zu antworten.

estate *noun* **1** (*a housing estate*) Wohnsiedlung *die* (PL *die* Wohnsiedlungen); **2** (*a big house and grounds*) Landsitz *der* (PL *die* Landsitze).

estate agent *noun* Immobilienmakler *der* (PL *die* Immobilienmakler).

estate car *noun* Kombiwagen *der* (PL *die* Kombiwagen).

estimate *noun* **1** (*a quote for work*) Kostenvoranschlag *der* (PL *die* Kostenvoranschläge); **2** (*a rough guess*) Schätzung *die* (PL *die* Schätzungen). *verb* schätzen.

etc. *abbreviation* usw. (*und so weiter*).

ethnic *adjective* ethnisch; **an ethnic minority** eine ethnische Minderheit.

EU *noun* EU *die* (*Europäische Union*).

Europe *noun* Europa *das*.

European *noun* Europäer *der* (PL *die* Europäer), Europäerin *die* (PL *die* Europäerinnen). *adjective* europäisch.

European Union *noun* Europäische Union *die*.

even[1] *adverb* **1** sogar; **even Lisa is coming** sogar Lisa kommt; **2** *not even* nicht einmal; **I don't like animals, not even dogs** ich mag keine Tiere, nicht einmal Hunde; **3** *without even asking* ohne wenigstens zu fragen; **4** *even if* selbst wenn; **even if they arrive late** selbst wenn sie spät ankommen; **5** (*with a comparison*) (sogar) noch; **even bigger** sogar noch größer; **even faster** noch schneller; **even better than** sogar noch besser als; **the song is even better than their last one** das Lied ist sogar noch besser als ihr letztes; **6** *even so* trotzdem; **even so, we had a good time** trotzdem haben wir uns amüsiert.

even[2] *adjective* **1** (*surface or layer*) eben; **2** (*number*) gerade; **six is an even number** sechs ist eine gerade Zahl; **3** (*equal*) gleich (*distance, value*); **the score is even** die Punktzahl ist gleich; **4** *to get even with somebody* es jemandem heimzahlen.

evening *noun* **1** Abend *der* (PL *die* Abende); **in the evening** am Abend; **this evening** heute Abend;

tomorrow evening morgen Abend;
on Monday evening am
Montagabend; **every Thursday
evening** jeden Donnerstagabend;
the evening before am Abend
zuvor; **the evening meal** das
Abendessen; **2 at six o'clock in the
evening** um sechs Uhr abends; **the
other evening** neulich abends; **I
work in the evening(s)** ich arbeite
abends.

evening class noun
Abendkurs der (PL die Abendkurse).

event noun **1** (a happening)
Ereignis das (PL die Ereignisse);
2 (in athletics) Disziplin die (PL die
Disziplinen).

eventually adverb schließlich.

ever adverb **1** (at any time) je; **have
you ever noticed that?** hast du das
je bemerkt?; **more than ever** mehr
denn je; **colder than ever** kälter
denn je; **he drove more slowly than
ever** er fuhr langsamer als je zuvor;
2 not ever nie; **nobody ever came**
es kam nie jemand; **hardly ever** fast
nie; **3** (always) immer; **as cheerful
as ever** so vergnügt wie immer; **the
same as ever** so wie immer; **4 ever
since** seitdem; **and it's been
raining ever since** und seitdem
regnet es.

every adjective **1** jeder/jede/jedes;
every house has a garden jedes
Haus hat einen Garten; **every day**
jeden Tag; **every Monday** jeden
Montag; **every time** jedes Mal;
2 every few days alle paar Tage;
every ten kilometres alle zehn
Kilometer; **3 every one** jeder

Einzelne/jede Einzelne/jedes
Einzelne △; **I've seen every one of
his films** ich habe jeden Einzelnen
seiner Filme gesehen; **4 every now
and then** ab und zu.

everybody, everyone pronoun
1 alle (plural); **everybody knows
that ...** alle wissen, dass ...;
everyone else alle anderen;
2 (each one) jeder; **not everybody
can afford it** das kann sich nicht
jeder leisten.

everything pronoun alles;
everything is ready es ist alles
fertig; **everything's fine** alles ist
okay (informal); **everything else**
alles andere; **he gets everything
he wants** er bekommt alles, was
er will.

everywhere adverb **1** überall; **there
was dirt everywhere** überall war
Dreck; **she went everywhere** sie ist
überall hingegangen; **everywhere
else** sonst überall; **2 everywhere
she went** wohin sie auch ging.

evidently adverb offensichtlich.

exact adjective genau; **the exact
fare** das genaue Fahrgeld; **it's the
exact opposite** das ist genau das
Gegenteil.

exactly adverb genau; **they're
exactly the right age** sie sind genau
im richtigen Alter; **yes, exactly!** ja,
genau!

exaggerate verb übertreiben ◇.

exaggeration noun
Übertreibung die (PL die
Übertreibungen).

exam noun Prüfung die (PL die Prüfungen); **history exam** die Geschichtsprüfung; **to sit an exam** eine Prüfung machen; **to pass an exam** eine Prüfung bestehen; **to fail an exam** durch eine Prüfung fallen.

examination noun Prüfung die (PL die Prüfungen).

examine verb 1 (at school or university) prüfen; 2 (at the doctor's) untersuchen.

examiner noun Prüfer der (PL die Prüfer), Prüferin die (PL die Prüferinnen).

example noun Beispiel das (PL die Beispiele); **for example** zum Beispiel; **to set a good example** ein gutes Beispiel geben.

excellent adjective ausgezeichnet.

except preposition 1 außer (+DAT); **every day except Tuesday** täglich außer Dienstag; **we play except when it rains** wir spielen, außer wenn es regnet; **except in March** außer März; 2 **except for** außer (+DAT); **except for the children** außer den Kindern.

exception noun Ausnahme die (PL die Ausnahmen); **without exception** ohne Ausnahme; **with the exception of** mit Ausnahme von (+DAT).

exchange noun 1 Austausch der; **the students are coming to London on an exchange** die Studenten kommen im Austausch nach London; **exchange student** der Austauschstudent, die Austauschstudentin; **an exchange of** pupils ein Schüleraustausch; 2 **in exchange for his help** für seine Hilfe.
verb umtauschen SEP; **can I exchange this shirt for a smaller one?** kann ich dieses Hemd gegen ein kleineres umtauschen?

exchange rate noun Wechselkurs der (PL die Wechselkurse).

excite verb 1 (thrill) begeistern; 2 (agitate) aufregen SEP.

excited adjective 1 aufgeregt; **the children are excited** die Kinder sind aufgeregt; **the dogs get excited when they hear the car** die Hunde sind aufgeregt, wenn sie das Auto hören; 2 (annoyed or angry) **to get excited** sich aufregen SEP.

exciting adjective aufregend; **a very exciting film** ein sehr aufregender Film.

exclamation mark noun Ausrufezeichen das (PL die Ausrufezeichen).

excursion noun Ausflug der (PL die Ausflüge).

excuse noun Entschuldigung die (PL die Entschuldigungen).
verb (apologizing) **excuse me!** Entschuldigung!

exercise noun 1 Übung die (PL die Übungen); **a maths exercise** eine Übung in Mathe; 2 **physical exercise** körperliche Bewegung; **to get exercise** Bewegung haben.

exercise bike noun Heimtrainer der (PL die Heimtrainer).

exercise book *noun* Heft *das* (PL die Hefte); **my German exercise book** mein Deutschheft.

exhausted *adjective* erschöpft.

exhaust fumes *noun* Abgase (*plural*).

exhaust (pipe) *noun* Auspuff *der* (PL die Auspuffe).

exhibition *noun* Ausstellung *die* (PL die Ausstellungen); **the Dürer exhibition** die Dürer-Ausstellung.

exist *verb* existieren.

exit *noun* 1 Ausgang *der* (PL die Ausgänge); 2 (*from a motorway*) Ausfahrt *die* (PL die Ausfahrten).

expect *verb* 1 erwarten (*guests or a baby*); **we're expecting thirty visitors** wir erwarten dreißig Besucher; 2 (*require something*) **to expect somebody to do something** von jemandem erwarten, dass er etwas tut; 3 rechnen mit (+DAT) (*something to happen*); **I didn't expect that** damit habe ich nicht gerechnet; **I didn't expect it at all** damit habe ich überhaupt nicht gerechnet; 4 (*suppose*) glauben; **I expect she'll bring her boyfriend** ich glaube, sie bringt ihren Freund mit; **yes, I expect so** ich glaube ja.

expel *verb* **to be expelled** (*from school*) von der Schule verwiesen werden.

expensive *adjective* teuer; **those shoes are too expensive for me** diese Schuhe sind mir zu teuer; **the most expensive CDs** die teuersten CDs.

experience *noun* 1 Erfahrung *die* (PL die Erfahrungen); 2 (*an event*) Erlebnis *das* (PL die Erlebnisse).

experienced *adjective* erfahren.

experiment *noun* Experiment *das* (PL die Experimente); **to do an experiment** ein Experiment machen.

expert *noun* Experte *der* (PL die Experten), Expertin *die* (PL die Expertinnen); **he's a computer expert** er ist ein Computerexperte.

expire *verb* ablaufen ◇ SEP (PERF sein).

explain *verb* erklären.

explanation *noun* Erklärung *die* (PL die Erklärungen).

explode *verb* explodieren (PERF sein).

explore *verb* erforschen.

explosion *noun* Explosion *die* (PL die Explosionen).

exposure *noun* (*of a film*) Belichtung *die*; **a 24-exposure film** ein Film mit 24 Aufnahmen.

express *noun* (*train*) Schnellzug *der* (PL die Schnellzüge). *verb* 1 ausdrücken SEP; 2 **to express yourself** sich ausdrücken.

expression *noun* Ausdruck *der* (PL die Ausdrücke).

extension *noun* 1 (*to a house*) Anbau *der* (PL die Anbauten); 2 (*telephone*) Apparat *der* (PL die Apparate); **can I have extension 2347 please?** bitte verbinden Sie mich mit Apparat 2347 (*note that in* *spoken German telephone numbers are usually broken down into groups of two figures*); **3** (*electrical*) Verlängerung *die* (PL *die* Verlängerungen).

extension number *noun* Apparatnummer *die* (PL *die* Apparatnummern).

exterior *adjective* äußerer/äußere/äußeres.

extinguish *verb* **1** löschen (*a fire*); **2 to extinguish a cigarette** eine Zigarette ausmachen SEP.

extinguisher *noun* Feuerlöscher *der* (PL *die* Feuerlöscher).

extra *adjective* **1** zusätzlich, extra (*informal*) (*extra never has an ending*); **extra homework** zusätzliche Hausaufgaben; **wine is extra** Wein ist extra; **you have to pay extra** das wird extra berechnet; **2 at no extra charge** ohne Aufschlag.
adverb **1** besonders; **he was extra careful** er war besonders vorsichtig; **2 extra large** extragroß.

extraordinary *adjective* außerordentlich.

extra time *noun* (*in football*) Verlängerung *die* (PL *die* Verlängerungen); **to go into extra time** in die Verlängerung gehen.

extravagant *adjective* verschwenderisch (*person*).

extreme *noun* Extrem *das* (PL *die* Extreme); **to go from one extreme to another** von einem Extrem ins andere fallen.
adjective extrem.

extremely *adverb* äußerst; **extremely fast** äußerst schnell.

eye *noun* Auge *das* (PL *die* Augen); **a girl with blue eyes** ein Mädchen mit blauen Augen; **shut your eyes!** mach die Augen zu!; ★ **to keep an eye on something** auf etwas ←(ACC) aufpassen SEP.

eyebrow *noun* Augenbraue *die* (PL *die* Augenbrauen).

eyelash *noun* Augenwimper *die* (P *die* Augenwimpern).

eyelid *noun* Augenlid *das* (PL *die* Augenlider).

eyeliner *noun* Eyeliner *der* (PL *die* Eyeliner).

eye shadow *noun* Lidschatten *de* (PL *die* Lidschatten).

eyesight *noun* **to have good eyesight** gute Augen haben; **to have bad eyesight** schlechte Augen haben.

F f

fabric *noun* (*cloth*) Stoff *der* (PL *die* Stoffe).

fabulous *adjective* phantastisch.

face *noun* **1** (*of a person*) Gesicht *das* (PL *die* Gesichter); **to pull a face** ein Gesicht machen; **2** (*of a clock or watch*) Zifferblatt *das* (PL *die* Zifferblätter).

✧ IRREGULAR VERB: *See the verb table in the centre of the dictionary*

verb 1 gegenüberstehen ✧ SEP (PERF *sein*) (+DAT); **she was facing him** sie stand ihm gegenüber; **2 the house faces the park** das Haus ist gegenüber dem Park; 3 (*to stand the idea of*) verkraften; **I can't face going back** ich kann es nicht verkraften zurückzugehen; **4 to face up to something** sich etwas ←(DAT) stellen.

acilities *plural noun* **1 the school has good sports facilities** die Schule hat gute Sportanlagen; **2 the flat has no cooking facilities** die Wohnung hat keine Kochgelegenheit.

act *noun* Tatsache *die* (PL *die* Tatsachen); **the fact is that ...** Tatsache ist, dass ...; **in fact** tatsächlich; **is that a fact?** Tatsache?

actory *noun* Fabrik *die* (PL *die* Fabriken).

ade *verb* 1 (*fabric*) verbleichen ✧ (PERF *sein*); **faded jeans** ausgeblichene Jeans; 2 (*a colour or memory*) verblassen (PERF *sein*); **the colours have faded** die Farben sind verblasst.

ail *verb* 1 nicht bestehen ✧ (*a test or an exam*); **I failed my driving test** ich habe meine Fahrprüfung nicht bestanden; **2** (*in a test or an exam*) durchfallen ✧ SEP (PERF *sein*); **three students failed** drei Studenten sind durchgefallen; **3 to fail to do something** etwas nicht tun; **he failed to inform us** er hat uns nicht benachrichtigt; ★ **without fail** auf

jeden Fall, **ring me without fail** ruf mich auf jeden Fall an.

faint *adjective* 1 (*slight*) leicht; **a faint smell of gas** ein leichter Gasgeruch; **I haven't the faintest idea** ich habe keine blasse Ahnung (*informal*); 2 (*voice or sound*) leise. *verb* ohnmächtig werden; **Lisa fainted** Lisa wurde ohnmächtig.

fair *noun* Jahrmarkt *der* (PL *die* Jahrmärkte). *adjective* 1 (*not unfair*) gerecht; 2 (*hair*) blond; **he's fair-haired** er ist blond; 3 (*skin*) hell; **fair-skinned** hellhäutig; 4 (*fairly good*) ganz gut (*chance, condition, or performance*); 5 (*weather*) schön; **if it's fair tomorrow** wenn es morgen schön ist.

fairground *noun* Jahrmarkt *der* (PL *die* Jahrmärkte).

fairly *adverb* (*quite*) ziemlich.

fairy *noun* Fee *die* (PL *die* Feen).

fairy tale *noun* Märchen *das* (PL *die* Märchen).

faith *noun* 1 (*trust*) Vertrauen *das*; **to have faith in somebody** Vertrauen zu jemandem haben; 2 (*religious belief*) Glaube *der* (PL *die* Glauben).

faithful *adjective* treu; **to be faithful to somebody** jemandem treu sein.

faithfully *adverb* **Yours faithfully** Hochachtungsvoll.

fake *noun* 1 Imitation *die* (PL *die* Imitationen); **the diamonds were fakes** die Brillanten waren eine Imitation; 2 (*a painting or money*)

Fälschung die (PL die Fälschungen).
adjective gefälscht; **a fake passport**
ein gefälschter Pass.

fall *noun* Fall der (PL die Fälle); **to
have a fall** stürzen (PERF *sein*).
verb 1 fallen ✧ (PERF *sein*); **mind,
you'll fall** pass auf, dass du nicht
hinfällst; **Tony fell off his bike** Tony
ist vom Rad gefallen; **she fell down
the stairs** sie ist die Treppe
heruntergefallen; 2 (*of temperature,
prices*) sinken ✧ (PERF *sein*).

false *adjective* falsch; **a false alarm**
ein falscher Alarm.

fame *noun* Ruhm der.

familiar *adjective* bekannt; **his face
is familiar** sein Gesicht kommt mir
bekannt vor.

family *noun* Familie die (PL die
Familien); **a family of six** eine
sechsköpfige Familie; **Ben's one of
the family** Ben gehört zur Familie;
the Morris family Familie Morris.

famous *adjective* berühmt.

fan *noun* 1 (*a supporter*) Fan der (PL
die Fans); **Will's a Chelsea fan** Will
ist ein Fan von Chelsea; 2 (*electric,
for cooling*) Ventilator der (PL die
Ventilatoren); 3 (*hand-held*)
Fächer der (PL die Fächer).

fanatic *noun* Fanatiker der (PL die
Fanatiker), Fanatikerin die (PL die
Fanatikerinnen).

fancy *noun* **to take somebody's
fancy** jemandem gefallen ✧; **the
picture took his fancy** das Bild hat
es ihm angetan.
adjective (*equipment*) ausgefallen.

verb 1 (*to want*) **(do you) fancy a
coffee?** hast du Lust auf einen
Kaffee?; **do you fancy going to the
cinema?** hast du Lust, ins Kino zu
gehen?; 2 **I really fancy him** ich ma[g]
ihn wirklich sehr gern; 3 (*just*) **fancy
that!** stell dir vor!; **fancy you being
here!** na so was, dich hier zu
treffen!

fancy dress *noun* **in fancy dress**
verkleidet; **fancy-dress party** das
Kostümfest.

fantastic *adjective* fantastisch △;
really? that's fantastic! wirklich?
das ist ja fantastisch!; **a fantastic
holiday** fantastische Ferien.

far *adverb, adjective* 1 weit; **it's not
far** es ist nicht weit; **is it far to
Carlisle?** ist Carlisle weit von hier?;
how far is it to Bristol? wie weit ist
es bis nach Bristol?; 2 **he took us as
far as Newport** er hat uns bis
Newport mitgenommen; 3 **by far**
bei weitem; **the prettiest by far** bei
weitem das hübscheste; 4 (*much*)
viel; **far better** viel besser; **far
faster** viel schneller; **far too many
people** viel zu viele Leute; 5 **so far**
bis jetzt; **so far everything's going
well** bis jetzt läuft alles gut; 6 **as far
as I know** soweit ich weiß.

fare *noun* 1 (*on a bus, train, or the
underground*) Fahrpreis der (PL
die Fahrpreise); 2 (*on a plane*)
Flugpreis der (PL die Fahrpreise);
half fare der halbe Fahrpreis; **full
fare** der volle Fahrpreis.

farm *noun* Bauernhof der (PL die
Bauernhöfe).

✧ IRREGULAR VERB: *See the verb table in the centre of the dictionary*

farmer *noun* Bauer *der* (PL *die* Bauern), Bäuerin *die* (PL *die* Bäuerinnen).

fascinating *adjective* faszinierend.

fashion *noun* Mode *die* (PL *die* Moden); **in fashion** in Mode; **to go out of fashion** aus der Mode kommen.

fashionable *adjective* modisch.

fashion model *noun* Mannequin *das* (PL *die* Mannequins).

fashion show *noun* Modenschau *die* (PL *die* Modenschauen).

fast *adjective* 1 schnell; **a fast car** ein schnelles Auto; 2 (*of a clock or watch*) **to be fast** vorgehen ◇ SEP (PERF *sein*); **my watch is fast** meine Uhr geht vor; **you're ten minutes fast** deine Uhr geht zehn Minuten vor.
adverb 1 schnell; **he swims fast** er schwimmt schnell; 2 **to be fast asleep** fest schlafen.

fat *noun* Fett *das* (PL *die* Fette). *adjective* 1 (*meat*) fett; 2 (*person*) dick, fett (*informal*); **a fat man** ein dicker Mann; **to get fat** fett werden (*informal*).

father *noun* Vater *der* (PL *die* Väter); **my father's office** das Büro von meinem Vater.

Father Christmas *noun* der Weihnachtsmann.

father-in-law *noun* Schwiegervater *der* (PL *die* Schwiegerväter).

fault *noun* 1 (*when you are responsible*) Schuld *die*; **it's Stephen's fault** Stephen ist Schuld; **it's not my fault** es ist nicht meine Schuld; 2 (*in tennis*) **double fault** *der* Doppelfehler.

favour *noun* 1 (*a kindness*) Gefallen *der* (PL *die* Gefallen); **to do somebody a favour** jemandem einen Gefallen tun; **can you do me a favour?** kannst du mir einen Gefallen tun?; **to ask a favour of somebody** jemanden um einen Gefallen bitten; 2 **to be in favour of something** für etwas ←(ACC) sein.

favourite *adjective* Lieblings-; **my favourite band** meine Lieblingsband.

fax *noun* Fax *das* (PL *die* Faxe). *verb* faxen.

fear *noun* Angst *die* (PL *die* Ängste). *verb* fürchten.

feather *noun* Feder *die* (PL *die* Federn).

feature *noun* 1 (*of your face*) Gesichtszug *der* (PL *die* Gesichtszüge); **to have delicate features** feine Gesichtszüge haben; 2 (*of a car or a machine*) Merkmal *das* (PL *die* Merkmale).

February *noun* Februar *der*; **in February** im Februar.

fed up *adjective* 1 **I'm fed up** ich habe die Nase voll (*informal*); **he's fed up with her** er hat die Nase voll von ihr; 2 **to be fed up with something** etwas ←(ACC) satt haben (*informal*); **I'm fed up with working**

△ NEW SPELLING: *See page xii*

every day ich habe es satt, jeden Tag zu arbeiten.

feed *verb* füttern; **have you fed the dog?** hast du den Hund gefüttert?

feel *verb* 1 sich fühlen; **I don't feel well** ich fühle mich nicht gut; 2 spüren; **I didn't feel a thing** ich habe nichts gespürt; 3 **I feel tired** ich bin müde; **I feel cold** mir ist kalt; 4 **to feel afraid** Angst haben; **to feel thirsty** Durst haben; 5 **to feel like doing something** Lust haben, etwas zu tun; **I feel like going to the cinema** ich habe Lust, ins Kino zu gehen; 6 (*touch*) fühlen; 7 (*to the touch*) sich anfühlen SEP; **to feel soft** sich weich anfühlen.

feeling *noun* 1 Gefühl *das* (PL *die* Gefühle); **to show your feelings** seine Gefühle zeigen; **a dizzy feeling** ein Schwindelgefühl; **I have the feeling James doesn't like me** ich habe das Gefühl, dass James mich nicht mag; 2 **to hurt somebody's feelings** jemanden verletzen.

felt-tip (pen) *noun* Filzstift *der* (PL *die* Filzstifte).

female *noun* (*animal*) Weibchen *das* (PL *die* Weibchen). *adjective* weiblich.

feminine *adjective* weiblich.

feminist *noun* Feministin *die* (PL *die* Feministinnen), Feminist *der* (PL *die* Feministen). *adjective* feministisch.

fence *noun* Zaun *der* (PL *die* Zäune).

ferry *noun* Fähre *die* (PL *die* Fähren).

festival *noun* (*of films, art, or music*) Festspiele (*plural*).

fetch *verb* 1 (*collect*) abholen SEP; **Tom's fetching the children** Tom holt die Kinder ab; 2 holen; **fetch me the other knife** hol mir das andere Messer.

fever *noun* Fieber *das*.

few *adjective, pronoun* 1 wenige; **few people know that …** wenige Leute wissen, dass …; 2 **a few** (*several*) ein paar (*ein paar never changes*); **a few weeks** ein paar Wochen; **in a few minutes** in ein paar Minuten; **have you got any tomatoes? we want a few for the salad** haben Sie Tomaten? wir brauchen ein paar für den Salat; 3 **quite a few** eine ganze Menge; **there were quite a few questions** es gab eine ganze Menge Fragen.

fewer *adjective* weniger; **there are fewer mosquitoes this year** dieses Jahr gibt es weniger Mücken.

field *noun* 1 (*with grass or crops*) Feld *das* (PL *die* Felder); **a field of wheat** ein Kornfeld; 2 (*for sport*) Spielfeld *das* (PL *die* Spielfelder).

fierce *adjective* 1 wild (*animal or person*); 2 heftig (*storm or battle*).

fifteen *number* fünfzehn.

fifth *number* fünfter/fünfte/fünftes; **the fifth of January** der fünfte Januar; **on the fifth floor** im fünften Stock.

fifty *number* fünfzig.

⬥ IRREGULAR VERB: *See the verb table in the centre of the dictionary*

ight noun **1** (*a scuffle*) Schlägerei die (PL die Schlägereien); **2** (*in boxing or against illness*) Kampf der (PL die Kämpfe).
verb **1** (*to have a fight*) sich prügeln; **they were fighting** sie haben sich geprügelt; **2** (*to quarrel*) sich streiten ✧; **they're always fighting** sie streiten sich immer; **3** (*struggle against*) kämpfen gegen (+ACC) (*poverty or a disease*).

igure noun **1** (*number*) Zahl die (PL die Zahlen); **a four-figure number** eine vierstellige Zahl; **2** (*body shape*) Figur die; **good for your figure** gut für die Figur; **3** (*a person*) Gestalt die (PL die Gestalten).
verb **to figure something out** etwas herausfinden ✧ SEP (*the answer or reason*).

file noun **1** (*for records of a person or case*) Akte die (PL die Akten); **2** (*ring binder or folder*) Ordner der (PL die Ordner); **3** (*on a computer*) Datei die (PL die Dateien); **4 a nail file** eine Nagelfeile.
verb **1** ablegen SEP (*documents*); **2 to file your nails** sich ←(DAT) die Nägel feilen.

fill verb **1** füllen (*a container*); **she filled my glass** sie füllte mein Glas; **2 to be filled with people** voller Menschen sein; **filled with smoke** voller Rauch.
• **to fill in** ausfüllen SEP (*a form*).

film noun (*in a cinema and for a camera*) Film der (PL die Filme); **shall we go and see the new film about Freud?** wollen wir uns den neuen Film über Freud ansehen?; **to make a film** einen Film drehen; **a**

24-exposure colour film ein Farbfilm mit 24 Aufnahmen.

film star noun Filmstar der (PL die Filmstars).

filter noun Filter der (PL die Filter).

filthy adjective dreckig.

final noun (*in sport*) Endspiel das (PL die Endspiele).
adjective letzter/letzte/letztes; **the final instalment** die letzte Folge; **the final result** das Endergebnis.

finally adverb schließlich.

find verb finden ✧; **did you find your passport?** hast du deinen Pass gefunden?; **I can't find my keys** ich kann meine Schlüssel nicht finden.
• **to find out 1** (*to enquire*) sich informieren; **I don't know, I'll find out** das weiß ich nicht, ich werde mich informieren; **2 to find something out** etwas ←(ACC) herausfinden ✧ SEP (*the facts or an answer*); **when she found out the truth** als sie die Wahrheit herausfand.

fine noun Bußgeld das (PL die Bußgelder) (*for parking or speeding*).
adjective **1** (*in good health*) gut; **'how are you?' – 'fine, thanks'** 'wie geht's?' – 'danke, gut'; **I'm fine** mir geht es gut; **2** (*convenient*) in Ordnung; **ten o'clock? yes, that's fine** zehn Uhr? ja, in Ordnung!; **Friday will be fine** Freitag geht in Ordnung; **3** (*sunny*) schön; (*weather or day*) **if it's fine** wenn es schön ist; **in fine weather** bei schönem Wetter; **4** (*not coarse or thick*) fein.

△ NEW SPELLING: *See page xii*

finely *adverb* fein (*chopped or grated*).

finger *noun* Finger *der* (PL *die* Finger); ★ **I'll keep my fingers crossed for you** ich drücke dir den Daumen.

fingernail *noun* Fingernagel *der* (PL *die* Fingernägel).

finish *noun* 1 (*end*) Schluss △ *der* (PL *die* Schlüsse); 2 (*in a race*) Ziel *das* (PL *die* Ziele).
verb 1 beenden (*a conversation or quarrel*); **to finish a discussion** ein Gespräch beenden; **to be finished with something** mit etwas ←(DAT) fertig sein (*work or a project*); **have you finished your homework?** bist du mit den Hausaufgaben fertig?; **wait, I haven't finished!** warte, ich bin noch nicht fertig!; 2 (*to finish off*) **to finish doing something** etwas zu Ende tun; **have you finished (reading) the letter?** hast du den Brief zu Ende gelesen?; **he hasn't yet finished (writing) the report** er hat den Bericht noch nicht zu Ende geschrieben; 3 (*come to an end*) zu Ende sein, aus sein △ (*informal*) (*a meeting or performance*); **the film finishes at ten o'clock** der Film ist um zehn Uhr zu Ende; **when does school finish?** wann ist die Schule aus?
● **to finish with** (*complete your use of*) nicht mehr brauchen; **when you've finished with these clothes, give them back to me** wenn du die Sachen nicht mehr brauchst, gib sie mir zurück; **have you finished with**

the computer? brauchen Sie den Computer noch?

Finland *noun* Finnland *das*.

Finnish *noun* (*the language*) Finnisch *das*.
adjective finnisch; **he's Finnish** er ist Finne; **she's Finnish** sie ist Finnin.

fire *noun* 1 (*in a grate*) Kaminfeuer *das* (PL *die* Kaminfeuer); **to light the fire** das Feuer im Kamin anmachen; 2 (*accidental*) Feuer *das* (PL *die* Feuer); **to catch fire** (*fabric, furnishings*) Feuer fangen; 3 (*in a building or forest*) Brand *der* (PL *die* Brände); **to set fire to a factory** eine Fabrik in Brand stecken; 4 **to be on fire** brennen ✧.
verb 1 (*with a gun*) schießen ✧; **to fire at somebody** auf jemanden schießen; 2 abfeuern SEP (*a gun*).

fire alarm *noun* Feuermelder *der* (PL *die* Feuermelder).

fire brigade *noun* Feuerwehr *die*.

fire engine *noun* Feuerwehrauto *das* (PL *die* Feuerwehrautos).

fire escape *noun* Feuertreppe *die* (PL *die* Feuertreppen).

fire extinguisher *noun* Feuerlöscher *der* (PL *die* Feuerlöscher).

firefighter *noun* Feuerwehrmann *der* (PL *die* Feuerwehrleute).

fireplace *noun* Kamin *der* (PL *die* Kamine).

✧ IRREGULAR VERB: *See the verb table in the centre of the dictionary*

fire station noun Feuerwache die (PL die Feuerwachen).

firework noun
Feuerwerkskörper der (PL die Feuerwerkskörper); **firework display** das Feuerwerk.

firm noun (business) Firma die (PL die Firmen).
adjective **1** fest; **2** (strict) streng.

first adjective erster/erste/erstes; **the first of May** der erste Mai; **for the first time** zum ersten Mal; **I was the first to arrive** ich kam als Erster/Erste an; **Susan was first** Susan war die Erste; **to come first in the 100 metres** beim Hundertmeterlauf Erster/Erste werden.
adverb **1** (to begin with) zuerst; **first, I'm going to make some tea** zuerst mache ich Tee; **2 at first** zuerst; **at first he was shy** er war zuerst schüchtern.

first aid noun erste Hilfe △ die.

first class adjective (ticket, carriage, or hotel) erster Klasse (goes after the noun); **a first-class hotel** ein Hotel erster Klasse; **he always travels first class** er reist immer erster Klasse; **a first-class compartment** ein Erste-Klasse-Abteil.

first floor noun erste Stock der; **on the first floor** im ersten Stock.

first name noun Vorname der (PL die Vornamen).

fir tree noun Tanne die (PL die Tannen).

fish noun Fisch der (PL die Fische).
verb fischen; (with a rod) angeln.

fish and chips noun ausgebackener Fisch mit Pommes frites.

fishing noun Fischen das; (with a rod) Angeln das; **to go fishing** fischen/angeln gehen.

fishing rod noun Angel die (PL die Angeln).

fishing tackle noun Angelgeräte (plural).

fist noun Faust die (PL die Fäuste).

fit noun **1** (of rage) Anfall der (PL die Anfälle); **your dad'll have a fit when he sees your hair** dein Vater kriegt bestimmt einen Anfall, wenn er deine Haare sieht; **2 an epileptic fit** ein epileptischer Anfall.
adjective (healthy) fit; **I feel really fit** ich fühle mich richtig fit; **to keep fit** fit bleiben.
verb **1** (be the right size for) (of shoes or a garment) passen (+DAT); **this skirt doesn't fit me** der Rock passt mir nicht; **2** (be able to be put into) passen in (+ACC); **will my cases all fit in the car?** passen meine Koffer alle in das Auto?; **the key doesn't fit in the lock** der Schlüssel passt nicht ins Schloss; **3** (install) einbauen SEP.

fitted carpet noun
Teppichboden der (PL die Teppichböden).

fitted kitchen noun
Einbauküche die (PL die Einbauküchen).

five *number* fünf; **it's five o'clock** es ist fünf Uhr.

fix *verb* 1 (*repair*) reparieren; **Mum's fixed the computer** Mutti hat den Computer repariert; 2 (*decide on*) festlegen ✧ SEP; **to fix a date** einen Termin festlegen; 3 machen (*a meal*); **I'll fix supper** ich mache Abendessen.

fizzy *adjective* sprudelnd; **fizzy water** *das* Sprudelwasser.

flag *noun* Fahne *die* (PL die Fahnen).

flame *noun* Flamme *die* (PL die Flammen).

flan *noun* Torte *die* (PL die Torten); **fruit flan** *die* Obsttorte.

flap *verb* (*of a bird*) **to flap its wings** mit den Flügeln schlagen ✧.

flash *noun* (*on a camera*) Blitz *der* (PL die Blitze); **flash of lightning** *der* Blitz.
verb 1 (*a light*) aufleuchten SEP; (*repeatedly*) blinken; 2 **to flash by** or **past** vorbeiflitzen SEP (*informal*).

flat *noun* Wohnung *die* (PL die Wohnungen); **a third-floor flat** eine Wohnung im dritten Stock.
adjective 1 flach; **flat shoes** flache Schuhe; **a flat landscape** eine flache Landschaft; 2 **a flat tyre** ein platter Reifen.

flatmate *noun* Mitbewohner *der* (PL die Mitbewohner), Mitbewohnerin *die* (PL die Mitbewohnerinnen).

flavour *noun* 1 Geschmack *der* (PL die Geschmäcke); **the sauce has a bitter flavour** die Soße hat einen bitteren Geschmack; **strawberry flavour** Erdbeergeschmack; 2 (*of drinks, coffee, or tea*) Aroma *das* (PL die Aromen).
verb abschmecken SEP; **vanilla-flavoured** mit Vanillegeschmack.

flea *noun* Floh *der* (PL die Flöhe).

flight *noun* 1 Flug *der* (PL die Flüge); **the flight was delayed** der Flug hatte Verspätung; **charter flight** *der* Charterflug; **the flight from Munich to London takes an hour and a half** die Flugzeit von München nach London beträgt eineinhalb Stunden; 2 **flight of stairs** *die* Treppe.

flipper *noun* Flosse *die* (PL die Flossen).

flirt *verb* flirten.

float *verb* 1 (*on water*) treiben ✧; 2 (*in the air*) schweben.

flood *noun* 1 (*of water*) Überschwemmung *die* (PL die Überschwemmungen); 2 **to be in floods of tears** in Tränen aufgelöst sein; 3 (*of letters or complaints*) Flut *die*.
verb überschwemmen.

floodlight *noun* Flutlicht *das*.

floor *noun* 1 Boden *der* (PL die Böden); **your glasses are on the floor** deine Brille liegt auf dem Boden; 2 **to sweep the floor** ausfegen SEP; **to sweep the kitchen floor** die Küche ausfegen; 3 (*a storey*) Stock *der* (PL die Stock); **on the second floor** im zweiten Stock.

floppy disk *noun* Diskette *die* (PL die Disketten).

✧ IRREGULAR VERB: *See the verb table in the centre of the dictionary*

florist *noun* Blumenhändler *der* (PL die Blumenhändler), Blumenhändlerin *die* (PL die Blumenhändlerinnen).

flour *noun* Mehl *das*.

flower *noun* Blume *die* (PL die Blumen); **bunch of flowers** *der* Blumenstrauß.
verb blühen.

flu *noun* Grippe *die* (PL die Grippen); **to have flu** die Grippe haben.

fluent *adjective* **she speaks fluent Italian** sie spricht fließend Italienisch.

fluently *adverb* fließend.

flute *noun* Flöte *die* (PL die Flöten); **to play the flute** Flöte spielen.

fly *noun* Fliege *die* (PL die Fliegen).
verb 1 fliegen ✧ (PERF *sein*); **we flew to Berlin** wir sind nach Berlin geflogen; **2** steigen lassen (*a kite*); **3** fliegen ✧ (PERF *haben*) (*a plane or helicopter*); **4** (*to pass quickly*) schnell vergehen ✧ (PERF *sein*).

foam *noun* 1 (*foam rubber*) Schaumgummi *der*; **foam mattress** *die* Schaumgummimatratze; **2** (*on a drink*) Schaum *der*.

fog *noun* Nebel *der*.

foggy *adjective* neblig.

foil *noun* (*kitchen foil*) Alufolie *die*.

fold *noun* 1 (*in fabric or skin*) Falte *die* (PL die Falten); **2** (*in paper*) Kniff *der* (PL die Kniffe).
verb falten; **to fold something up** etwas zusammenfalten SEP.

folder *noun* Mappe *die* (PL die Mappen).

follow *verb* 1 folgen (PERF *sein*) (+DAT); **follow me!** folgen Sie mir!; **2 do you follow me?** verstehst du, was ich meine?

following *adjective* folgend; **the following evening** am folgenden Abend.

fond *adjective* **to be fond of somebody** jemanden gern haben; **I'm very fond of him** ich habe ihn sehr gern.

food *noun* 1 Essen *das*; **I have to buy some food** ich muss noch etwas zu essen einkaufen; **2 I like German food** ich mag die deutsche Küche; **3** (*stocks*) Lebensmittel (*plural*); **we bought food for the holiday** wir haben Lebensmittel für die Ferien eingekauft.

fool *noun* Dummkopf *der* (PL die Dummköpfe).

foot *noun* Fuß *der* (PL die Füße); **Lucy came on foot** Lucy ist zu Fuß gekommen.

football *noun* Fußball *der* (PL die Fußbälle); **to play football** Fußball spielen.

footballer *noun* Fußballspieler *der* (PL die Fußballspieler), Fußballspielerin *die* (PL die Fußballspielerinnen).

footpath *noun* Fußweg *der* (PL die Fußwege).

for *preposition* 1 für (+ACC); **a present for my mother** ein Geschenk für

△ NEW SPELLING: *See page xii*

meine Mutter; **what's it for?** wofür ist das?; **2** (*for a particular occasion or event*) zu (+DAT); **sausages for lunch** Würstchen zum Mittagessen; **Sam got a bike for Christmas** Sam hat ein Rad zu Weihnachten bekommen; **what for?** wozu?; **3** (*time expressions in the past but continuing in the present*) seit (+DAT); **I've been waiting here for an hour** (*and I'm still waiting*) ich warte hier seit einer Stunde; **my brother's been living in Berlin for three years** (*and he still lives there*) mein Bruder wohnt seit drei Jahren in Berlin; **4** (*time expressions in the past or the future*) **I studied French for six years** (*but I no longer do*) ich habe sechs Jahre lang Französisch gelernt; **I'll be away for four days** ich werde vier Tage nicht da sein; **5** (*with a price*) für (+ACC); **I sold my bike for fifty pounds** ich habe mein Rad für fünfzig Pfund verkauft; **6 what's the German for 'bee'?** wie heißt 'bee' auf Deutsch?

forbid *verb* verbieten ✧; **to forbid somebody to do something** jemandem verbieten, etwas zu tun.

forbidden *adjective* verboten.

force *noun* Kraft *die* (PL *die* Kräfte). *verb* zwingen ✧; **to force somebody to do something** jemanden zwingen, etwas zu tun.

forecast *noun* Vorhersage *die* (PL *die* Vorhersagen).

forehead *noun* Stirn *die* (PL *die* Stirnen).

foreign *adjective* **1** ausländisch; **in a** **foreign country** im Ausland; **from a foreign country** aus dem Ausland; **2 foreign language** *die* Fremdsprache.

foreigner *noun* Ausländer *der* (PL *die* Ausländer), Ausländerin *die* (PL *die* Ausländerinnen).

forest *noun* Wald *der* (PL *die* Wälder).

forever *adverb* **1** immer; **I'd like to stay here forever** ich möchte immer hier bleiben; **2** (*non-stop*) ständig; **he's forever asking questions** er fragt ständig.

forget *verb* vergessen ✧; **to forget about something** etwas vergessen; **we've forgotten the bread** wir haben Brot vergessen; **to forget to do something** vergessen, etwas zu tun; **I forgot to phone** ich habe vergessen anzurufen.

forgive *verb* verzeihen ✧ (+DAT); **to forgive somebody** jemandem verzeihen; **I forgave him** ich habe ihm verziehen; **to forgive somebody for doing something** jemandem verzeihen, dass er/sie etwas getan hat; **I forgave her for losing my ring** ich habe ihr verziehen, dass sie meinen Ring verloren hat.

fork *noun* Gabel *die* (PL *die* Gabeln).

form *noun* **1** Formular *das* (PL *die* Formulare); **to fill in a form** ein Formular ausfüllen; **2** (*shape or kind*) Form *die* (PL *die* Formen); **in the form of** in Form von; **to be on form** gut in Form sein; **3** (*in school*)

✧ IRREGULAR VERB: *See the verb table in the centre of the dictionary*

Klasse *die* (PL *die* Klassen).
verb bilden.

formal *adjective* formell (*invitation, event*).

format *noun* Format *das* (PL *die* Formate).

former *adjective* ehemalig; **a former pupil** ein ehemaliger Schüler, eine ehemalige Schülerin.

fortnight *noun* vierzehn Tage (*plural*); **we're going to Spain for a fortnight** wir fahren vierzehn Tage nach Spanien.

fortunately *adverb* glücklicherweise.

forty *number* vierzig.

forward *noun* (*in sport*) Stürmer *der* (PL *die* Stürmer). *adverb* (*to the front*) nach vorn; **to move forward** vorrücken SEP (PERF *sein*); **a seat further forward** ein Platz weiter vorn.

foster child *noun* Pflegekind *das* (PL *die* Pflegekinder).

foul *noun* (*in sport*) Foul *das* (PL *die* Fouls).
adjective scheußlich; **the weather's foul** das Wetter ist scheußlich.

fountain *noun* Brunnen *der* (PL *die* Brunnen).

fountain pen *noun* Füllfederhalter *der* (PL *die* Füllfederhalter).

four *number* vier; **it's four o'clock** es ist vier Uhr; ★ **on all fours** auf allen vieren.

fourteen *number* vierzehn.

fourth *number* vierter/vierte/viertes; **the fourth of July** der vierte Juli; **on the fourth floor** im vierten Stock.

fox *noun* Fuchs *der* (PL *die* Füchse).

frame *noun* **1** Rahmen *der* (PL *die* Rahmen); **2** (*of spectacles*) Gestell *das* (PL *die* Gestelle).

franc *noun* **1** Franc *der* (PL *die* Francs); **a fifty-franc note** ein Fünfzig-Franc-Schein; **2** (*Swiss*) Franken *der* (PL *die* Franken).

France *noun* Frankreich *das*; **to France** nach Frankreich.

frantic *adjective* **1** (*very upset*) **to be frantic** außer sich ←(DAT) sein; **I was frantic with worry** ich war außer mir vor Sorge; **2** (*desperate*) hektisch (*effort or search*).

freckle *noun* Sommersprosse *die* (PL *die* Sommersprossen).

free *adjective* **1** (*when you don't pay*) kostenlos; **a free ride** eine kostenlose Fahrt; **a free ticket** eine Freikarte; **2** (*without charge*) umsonst; **to do something for free** etwas umsonst machen; **3** (*not occupied*) frei; **are you free on Thursday?** sind Sie am Donnerstag frei?; **4** sugar-free ohne Zucker; **lead-free** bleifrei.
verb befreien.

freedom *noun* Freiheit *die*.

free gift *noun* Werbegeschenk *das* (PL *die* Werbegeschenke).

freeze *verb* **1** (*in a freezer*) einfrieren ◇ SEP; **to freeze raspberries** Himbeeren einfrieren;

△ NEW SPELLING: *See page xii*

2 (*in cold weather*) frieren ✧; **it's freezing** es friert; **3** (*become covered with ice*) zufrieren ✧ SEP (PERF *sein*); **the pond is frozen** der Teich ist zugefroren.

freezer *noun* Gefrierschrank *der* (PL *die* Gefrierschränke).

freezing *noun* **below freezing** unter Null; **three degrees above freezing** drei Grad über Null.
adjective **1** **I'm freezing** ich friere sehr; **2 it's freezing outside** es ist eiskalt draußen.

French *noun* **1** (*the language*) Französisch *das*; **2** (*the people*) **the French** die Franzosen.
adjective **1** französisch; **Jean-Marc is French** Jean-Marc ist Franzose; **2** (*teacher or lesson*) Französisch-; **the French class** der Französischunterricht.

French bean *noun* grüne Bohne *die* (PL *die* grünen Bohnen).

French dressing *noun* Vinaigrette *die*.

French fries *plural noun* Pommes frites (*plural*).

Frenchman *noun* Franzose *der* (PL *die* Franzosen).

French window *noun* Verandatür *die* (PL *die* Verandatüren).

Frenchwoman *noun* Französin *die* (PL *die* Französinnen).

fresh *adjective* frisch; **fresh eggs** frische Eier; **I'm going out for some fresh air** ich gehe ein bisschen frische Luft schnappen.

Friday *noun* **1** Freitag *der* (PL *die* Freitage); **next Friday** nächsten Freitag; **last Friday** letzten Freitag; **on Friday** (am) Freitag; **I'll phone you on Friday evening** ich rufe dich Freitagabend an; **every Friday** jeden Freitag; **Good Friday** Karfreitag; **2 on Fridays** freitags; **closed on Fridays** freitags geschlossen.

fridge *noun* Kühlschrank *der* (PL *die* Kühlschränke); **put it in the fridge** stell es in den Kühlschrank.

friend *noun* **1** Freund *der* (PL *die* Freunde), Freundin *die* (PL *die* Freundinnen); **a friend of mine** ein Freund von mir; **2 to make friends** sich anfreunden; **he made friends with Danny** er hat sich mit Danny angefreundet; **he is friends with Danny** er ist mit Danny befreundet.

friendly *adjective* freundlich.

fries *plural noun* Pommes frites (*plural*).

fright *noun* **1** Schreck *der* (PL *die* Schrecke); **to have** *or* **get a fright** einen Schreck bekommen; **2 you gave me a fright!** du hast mich erschreckt!

frighten *verb* **1** (*of an explosion or shot*) erschrecken; **2** (*scare or threaten*) **to frighten somebody** jemandem Angst machen.

frightened *adjective* **to be frightened** Angst haben; **Martin's frightened of snakes** Martin hat Angst vor Schlangen.

frightening *adjective* beängstigend.

✧ IRREGULAR VERB: *See the verb table in the centre of the dictionary*

fringe noun 1 (*hairstyle*) Pony der (PL die Ponys); 2 (*on clothes or a curtain*) Fransen (*plural*).

frog noun Frosch der (PL die Frösche).

from preposition 1 von (+DAT); **ten metres from the cinema** zehn Meter vom Kino; **a letter from Tom** ein Brief von Tom; **from Monday to Friday** von Montag bis Freitag; **from now on** von jetzt an; 2 aus (+DAT); **he comes from Dublin** er kommt aus Dublin; **the train from London** der Zug aus London; 3 **from seven o'clock onwards** ab sieben Uhr; **from then on** von da ab.

front noun 1 (*of a building*) Vorderfront die (PL die Vorderfronten); (*of a cupboard, card, or envelope*) Vorderseite die (PL die Vorderseiten); 2 (*of a garment or in an interior*) Vorderteil das (PL die Vorderteile); 3 (*at the seaside*) Strandpromenade die (PL die Strandpromenaden); 4 (*of a car*) **to sit in (the) front** vorne sitzen; 5 (*of a train or queue*) vordere Ende das; 6 (*of a procession or in a race*) Spitze die; 7 **in/at the front** vorne; **in/at the front of** vorne in (+DAT, *or* +ACC *with movement towards a place*); **there are still seats at the front of the train** es gibt noch Plätze vorne im Zug; **we got on at the front of the train** wir sind vorne in den Zug eingestiegen; 8 **in front of** vor (+DAT, *or* +ACC *with movement towards a place*); **in front of the TV** vor dem Fernseher; **in front of me** vor mir. adjective 1 vorderer/vordere/vorderes; **in the front rows** in den vorderen Reihen; 2 Vorder-; **front seat** (*of a car*) der Vordersitz; **front wheel** das Vorderrad.

front door noun Haustür die (PL die Haustüren).

frontier noun Grenze die (PL die Grenzen).

frost noun Frost der.

frosty adjective frostig.

frown verb die Stirn runzeln; **he frowned at us** er runzelte die Stirn.

frozen adjective (*in a freezer*) tiefgekühlt; **a frozen pizza** eine tiefgekühlte Pizza.

fruit noun 1 (*a single fruit or type of fruit*) Frucht die (PL die Früchte); 2 (*various fruits*) Obst das; **we bought cheese and fruit** wir haben Käse und Obst gekauft.

fruit juice noun Fruchtsaft der (PL die Fruchtsäfte).

fruit machine noun Spielautomat der (PL die Spielautomaten).

fruit salad noun Obstsalat der (PL die Obstsalate).

frustrated adjective frustriert.

fry verb braten ✧; **we fried fish** wir haben Fisch gebraten; **fried potatoes** Bratkartoffeln; **fried egg** das Spiegelei.

frying pan noun Bratpfanne die (PL die Bratpfannen).

fuel noun (*for a car*) Kraftstoff der.

△ NEW SPELLING: *See page xii*

full *adjective* **1** voll; **the glass is full** das Glas ist voll; **I'm full** ich bin voll (*informal*); **2** full of voller (+GEN); **the train was full of tourists** der Zug war voller Touristen; **3 at full speed** in voller Fahrt; **4 to write something out in full** etwas voll ausschreiben.

full stop *noun* Punkt *der* (PL *die* Punkte).

full-time *adjective* **a full-time job** eine Ganztagsstelle.

fully *adverb* voll.

fun *noun* **1** Spaß *der*; **have fun!** viel Spaß!; **we had fun catching the ponies** wir hatten Spaß daran, die Ponys einzufangen; **skiing is fun** Skifahren macht Spaß; **I do it for fun** ich mache es aus Spaß; **2 to have fun** sich amüsieren; ★ **to make fun of somebody** sich über jemanden lustig machen.

funds *plural noun* Geldmittel (*plural*).

funeral *noun* Beerdigung *die* (PL *die* Beerdigungen).

funfair *noun* Jahrmarkt *der* (PL *die* Jahrmärkte).

funny *adjective* **1** (*amusing*) lustig; **he's so funny** er ist so lustig; **a funny story** eine lustige Geschichte; **2** (*strange*) komisch; **a funny noise** ein komisches Geräusch; **that's funny, I'm sure I paid** das ist komisch, ich bin mir sicher, dass ich gezahlt habe.

fur *noun* **1** (*on an animal*) Fell *das* (PL *die* Felle); **2** (*for a coat*) Pelz *der* (PL *die* Pelze); **fur coat** *der* Pelzmantel.

furious *adjective* wütend; **she was furious with Steve** sie war wütend auf Steve.

furniture *noun* Möbel (*plural*); **to buy some furniture** Möbel kaufen; **piece of furniture** *das* Möbelstück.

further *adverb* weiter; **further than the station** weiter als der Bahnhof; **ten kilometres further on** zehn Kilometer weiter; **further off** weiter entfernt; **further forward** weiter vorn; **further back** weiter hinten.

fuse *noun* Sicherung *die* (PL *die* Sicherungen).

fuss *noun* Theater *das*; **to make a fuss** ein Theater machen; **to make a big fuss about the bill** ein großes Theater um die Rechnung machen.

fussy *adjective* **to be fussy about something** wählerisch in etwas ←(DAT) sein (*food, for example*).

future *noun* Zukunft *die*; **in future** in Zukunft.

G g

gadget *noun* Gerät *das* (PL *die* Geräte).

gain *verb* **1** gewinnen ✧; **in order to gain time** um Zeit zu gewinnen; **2** profitieren; **to gain by something** von etwas profitieren.

✧ IRREGULAR VERB: *See the verb table in the centre of the dictionary*

gale noun Sturm der (PL die Stürme).

gallery noun Galerie die (PL die Galerien).

gamble verb spielen (for money).

game noun 1 Spiel das (PL die Spiele); **game of chance** das Glücksspiel; **board game** das Brettspiel; 2 **to have a game of cards** eine Partie Karten spielen; 3 **to have a game of football** Fußball spielen; 4 **games** (at school) Sport der.

gang noun Bande die (PL die Banden); **all the gang were there** die ganze Bande war da.

gap noun 1 (hole) Lücke die (PL die Lücken); 2 (in time) Pause die (PL die Pausen); **a two-hour gap** eine zweistündige Pause; 3 **age gap** der Altersunterschied.

garage noun 1 (for keeping your car) Garage die (PL die Garagen); 2 (for repairing cars) Autowerkstatt die (PL die Autowerkstätten); 3 (for petrol) Tankstelle die (PL die Tankstellen).

garden noun Garten der (PL die Gärten).

gardener noun Gärtner der (PL die Gärtner), Gärtnerin die (PL die Gärtnerinnen).

gardening noun Gartenarbeit die.

garlic noun Knoblauch der.

garment noun Kleidungsstück das (PL die Kleidungsstücke).

gas noun Gas das.

gas cooker noun Gasherd der (PL die Gasherde).

gas fire noun Gasofen der (PL die Gasöfen).

gas meter noun Gaszähler der (PL die Gaszähler).

gate noun 1 (in garden) Pforte die (PL die Pforten); 2 (in field) Gatter das (PL die Gatter); 3 (at an airport) Flugsteig der (PL die Flugsteige).

gather verb 1 (of people) sich versammeln; 2 sammeln (fruit, vegetables, flowers); 3 **as far as I can gather** soweit ich weiß.

gay adjective (homosexual) schwul (informal).

gaze verb **to gaze at something** etwas anstarren SEP.

gear noun 1 (in a car) Gang der (PL die Gänge); **to change gear** schalten; 2 (equipment) Ausrüstung die; **camping gear** die Campingausrüstung; 3 (things) Sachen (plural); **I've left all my gear at Gary's** ich habe alle meine Sachen bei Gary gelassen.

gear lever noun Schalthebel der (PL die Schalthebel).

gel noun Gel das (PL die Gele).

Gemini noun Zwillinge (plural); **Steph's Gemini** Steph ist Zwilling.

gender noun (of a word) Geschlecht das (PL die Geschlechter); **what is the gender of 'Haus'?** welches Geschlecht hat 'Haus'?

△ NEW SPELLING: See page xii

general *noun* General *der* (PL *die* Generäle).
adjective allgemein; **in general** im Allgemeinen; **the general election** die allgemeinen Wahlen.

general knowledge *noun* Allgemeinwissen *das*.

generally *adverb* im Allgemeinen △.

generation *noun* Generation *die* (PL *die* Generationen).

generous *adjective* großzügig.

genetics *noun* Genetik *die*.

Geneva *noun* Genf *das*; **Lake Geneva** der Genfer See.

genius *noun* Genie *das* (PL *die* Genies); **Lisa, you're a genius!** Lisa, du bis ein Genie!

gentle *adjective* sanft.

gentleman *noun* Herr *der* (PL *die* Herren); **ladies and gentlemen!** meine Damen und Herren!

gently *adverb* sanft.

gents *noun* (*lavatory*) Herrentoilette *die* (PL *die* Herrentoiletten); (*on a sign*) 'Gents' 'Herren'; **where's the gents?** wo ist die Toilette?

genuine *adjective* 1 (*real, authentic*) echt; **a genuine diamond** ein echter Brillant; 2 aufrichtig (*person*); **she's very genuine** sie ist sehr aufrichtig.

geography *noun* Geographie *die*; (*at school*) Erdkunde *die*.

germ *noun* 1 Keim *der* (PL *die* Keime); 2 (*causing a cold*) **germs** Bazillen (*plural*).

German *noun* (*person*) 1 Deutsche *der/die* (PL *die* Deutschen); 2 (*language*) Deutsch *das*; **in German** auf Deutsch.
adjective deutsch; **he is German** er ist Deutscher; **she is German** sie ist Deutsche; **our German teacher** unser Deutschlehrer, unsere Deutschlehrerin.

Germany Deutschland *das*; **to Germany** nach Deutschland; **from Germany** aus Deutschland.

get *verb* 1 (*obtain, receive*) bekommen ✧, kriegen (*informal*); **I got a bike for my birthday** ich habe ein Rad zum Geburtstag bekommen; **Fred got the job** Fred hat die Stelle bekommen; **she got a shock** sie hat einen Schreck gekriegt; **I got a good mark for my German homework** ich habe eine gute Note für meine Deutschhausaufgaben gekriegt; 2 **he's got lots of money** er hat viel Geld; **she's got long hair** sie hat lange Haare; **I've got a headache** ich habe Kopfschmerzen; 3 (*fetch*) holen; **I'll get some bread** ich hole Brot; **I'll get your bag for you** ich hole dir deine Tasche; 4 **to have got to do something** etwas tun müssen ✧; **I've got to phone before midday** ich muss vor Mittag anrufen; 5 **to get (to) somewhere** irgendwo ankommen ✧ SEP (PERF *sein*); **when I got to London** als ich in London ankam; **we got here this morning** wir sind heute Morgen angekommen; **what time did they get there?** wann sind sie angekommen?; 6 (*become*) werden ✧ (PERF *sein*); **it's getting**

late es wird spät; **it's getting dark**
es wird dunkel; **7 to get something
done** etwas machen lassen ✧; **I'm
getting my hair cut today** ich lasse
mir heute die Haare schneiden.

● **to get back** zurückkommen ✧ SEP
(PERF *sein*); **Mum gets back at six**
Mutti kommt um sechs zurück.

● **to get something back** etwas
zurückbekommen ✧ SEP, etwas
zurückkriegen SEP (*informal*); **did
you get your books back?** hast du
deine Bücher zurückbekommen?

● **to get into something** (*a vehicle*) in
etwas ←(ACC) einsteigen ✧ SEP (PERF
sein); **he got into the car** er ist ins
Auto eingestiegen.

● **to get off something** (*a vehicle*) aus
etwas ←(DAT) aussteigen ✧ SEP (PERF
sein); **I got off the train at Banbury**
ich bin in Banbury aus dem Zug
ausgestiegen.

● **to get on: how's Amanda getting
on?** wie geht's Amanda?

● **to get on something** (*a vehicle*) in
etwas ←(ACC) einsteigen ✧ SEP (PERF
sein); **she got on the train at
Reading** sie ist in Reading in den
Zug eingestiegen.

● **to get on with somebody** sich mit
jemandem verstehen ✧; **she
doesn't get on with her brother** sie
versteht sich nicht mit ihrem Bruder.

● **to get out of something** (*a vehicle*)
aus etwas ←(DAT) aussteigen ✧ SEP
(PERF *sein*); **Laura got out of the car**
Laura ist aus dem Auto ausgestiegen.

● **to get together** sich wieder sehen ✧
SEP Δ; **we must get together soon**
wir müssen uns bald mal wieder
sehen.

● **to get up** aufstehen ✧ SEP (PERF *sein*),
I get up at seven ich stehe um
sieben auf.

ghost *noun* Geist *der* (PL *die*
Geister).

gift *noun* **1** Geschenk *das* (PL *die*
Geschenke); **a Christmas gift** ein
Weihnachtsgeschenk;
2 Begabung *die*; **to have a gift for
something** für etwas ←(ACC) begabt
sein; **Jo has a real gift for
languages** Jo ist richtig
sprachbegabt.

gigantic *adjective* riesig.

gin *noun* Gin *der* (PL *die* Gins).

ginger *noun* Ingwer *der* (PL *die*
Ingwer).

girl *noun* Mädchen *das* (PL *die*
Mädchen); **three boys and four girls**
drei Jungen und vier Mädchen; **when
I was a little girl I had** ... als kleines
Mädchen hatte ich ...

girlfriend *noun* Freundin *die* (PL *die*
Freundinnen).

give *verb* **1** geben ✧; **to give
something to somebody**
jemandem etwas geben; **I'll give you
my address** ich gebe dir meine
Adresse; **give me the key** gib mir
den Schlüssel; **Yasmin's dad gave
her the money** Yasmins Vater hat
ihr das Geld gegeben; **2** (*give as a
gift*) schenken; **to give somebody a
present** jemandem etwas
schenken.

● **to give something away** etwas
weggeben ✧ SEP; **she's given away
all her books** sie hat alle ihre Bücher
weggegeben.

Δ NEW SPELLING: *See page xii*

- **to give something back to somebody** jemandem etwas zurückgeben ✧ SEP; **I gave her back the keys** ich habe ihr die Schlüssel zurückgegeben.

- **to give in** nachgeben ✧ SEP; **my mum said no but she gave in in the end** meine Mutti hat nein gesagt, aber schließlich hat sie nachgegeben.

- **to give up** aufgeben ✧ SEP; **I give up!** ich gebe auf!

- **to give up doing something** etwas aufgeben ✧ SEP; **she's given up smoking** sie hat das Rauchen aufgegeben.

glad *adjective* froh; **I'm glad to hear he's better** ich bin froh, dass es ihm besser geht; **I'm glad to be back** ich bin froh, dass ich wieder zurück bin.

glass *noun* Glas *das* (PL *die* Gläser); **a glass of water** ein Glas Wasser; **a glass table** ein Glastisch.

glasses *plural noun* Brille *die* (PL *die* Brillen); **to wear glasses** eine Brille tragen.

glove *noun* Handschuh *der* (PL *die* Handschuhe); **a pair of gloves** ein Paar Handschuhe.

glove compartment *noun* Handschuhfach *das* (PL *die* Handschuhfächer).

glue *noun* Klebstoff *der* (PL *die* Klebstoffe).

go *noun* 1 (*in a game*) **whose go is it?** wer ist dran?; **it's my go** ich bin dran; 2 **to have a go at doing something** versuchen, etwas zu tun; **I'll have a go at mending it** ich versuche, es zu reparieren.

verb 1 (*on foot*) gehen ✧ (PERF *sein*); **to go to school** in die Schule gehen; **Mark's gone to the dentist's** Mark ist zum Zahnarzt gegangen; **to go shopping** einkaufen gehen; 2 (*in a vehicle*) fahren ✧ (PERF *sein*); **we're going to London** wir fahren nach London; **we're planning to go early** wir wollen früh fahren; **to go on holiday** in die Ferien fahren; 3 (*by plane*) fliegen ✧ (PERF *sein*); 4 **to go for a walk** spazieren gehen △ ✧ SEP (PERF *sein*); 5 (*with another verb*) **I'm going to do it** ich werde es tun; **I'm going to make some tea** ich mache Tee; **he was going to phone you** er wollte dich anrufen; 6 (*leave*) gehen ✧ (PERF *sein*); **Pauline's already gone** Pauline ist schon gegangen; 7 (*on a journey*) abfahren ✧ SEP (PERF *sein*); **when does the train go?** wann fährt der Zug ab?; 8 (*turn out*) verlaufen ✧ (PERF *sein*) (*event*); **how did your evening go?** wie ist dein Abend verlaufen?; **the party went well** die Party war gut.

- **to go away** 1 weggehen ✧ SEP (PERF *sein*); **go away!** geh weg!; 2 (*on holiday*) verreisen (PERF *sein*).

- **to go back** 1 zurückgehen ✧ SEP (PERF *sein*); **I'm going back to Germany in March** ich gehe im März nach Deutschland zurück; **I'm not going back there again!** ich gehe da nicht wieder zurück!; 2 **I went back home** ich bin nach Hause gegangen.

- **to go down** 1 hinuntergehen ✧ SEP (PERF *sein*); **she's gone down to the kitchen** sie ist in die Küche

✧ IRREGULAR VERB: *See the verb table in the centre of the dictionary*

hinuntergegangen; **to go down the stairs** die Treppe hinuntergehen; **2** (*price, temperature*) fallen ◇ (PERF *sein*); **3** (*tyre, balloon, airbed*) Luft verlieren ◇.

- **to go in** hineingehen ◇ SEP (PERF *sein*); **he went in and shut the door** er ist hineingegangen und hat die Tür zugemacht.

- **to go into 1** (*person*) gehen in (+ACC) (PERF *sein*); **Fran went into the kitchen** Fran ging in die Küche; **2** (*object*) passen in (+ACC); **this book won't go into my bag** dieses Buch passt nicht in meine Tasche.

- **to go off 1** (*bomb*) hochgehen ◇ SEP (PERF *sein*); **2** (*alarm clock*) klingeln; **my alarm clock went off at six** mein Wecker hat um sechs geklingelt; **3** (*fire or burglar alarm*) losgehen ◇ SEP (PERF *sein*); **the fire alarm went off** der Feuermelder ging los.

- **to go on 1** what's going on? was ist los?; **2 to go on doing something** weiter etwas tun; **she went on talking** sie hat weiter geredet; **3 to go on about something** stundenlang von etwas ←(DAT) reden; **he's always going on about his dog** er redet stundenlang von seinem Hund.

- **to go out 1** (*for an evening*) ausgehen ◇ SEP, weggehen ◇ SEP (PERF *sein*) (*informal*); **we're going out tonight** wir gehen heute Abend aus; **2** (*leave*) **she went out of the kitchen** sie ist aus der Küche gegangen; **3 to be going out with somebody** mit jemandem gehen ◇ (PERF *sein*) (*informal*); **she's going out with my brother** sie geht mit

meinem Bruder; **4** (*light, fire*) ausgehen ◇ SEP (PERF *sein*); **the light went out** das Licht ist ausgegangen.

- **to go past something** an etwas ←(DAT) vorbeigehen ◇ SEP; **we went past your house** wir sind an eurem Haus vorbeigegangen.

- **to go round: to go round to somebody's house** jemanden besuchen; **we went round to Fred's last night** wir haben gestern Abend Fred besucht.

- **to go round something 1** um etwas ←(ACC) herumgehen ◇ SEP (PERF *sein*) (*building, park, garden*); **2** besichtigen (*museum, monument*).

- **to go through 1** the train goes through Cologne der Zug fährt durch Köln; **2 to go through a room** durch ein Zimmer gehen; **3** (*search*) durchsuchen.

- **to go up 1** (*person*) hinaufgehen ◇ SEP (PERF *sein*); **she's gone up to her room** sie ist in ihr Zimmer hinaufgegangen; **to go up the stairs** die Treppe hinaufgehen; **2** (*prices*) steigen ◇ (PERF *sein*); **the price of petrol has gone up** die Benzinpreise sind gestiegen.

goal *noun* Tor *das* (PL *die* Tore); **to score a goal** ein Tor schießen.

goalkeeper *noun* Torwart *der* (PL *die* Torwarte).

goat *noun* Ziege *die* (PL *die* Ziegen).

god *noun* Gott *der* (PL *die* Götter).

God *noun* Gott *der*; **to believe in God** an Gott glauben.

△ NEW SPELLING: *See page xii*

godchild *noun* Patenkind *das* (PL die Patenkinder).

goddaughter *noun* Patentochter *die* (PL die Patentöchter).

goddess *noun* Göttin *die* (PL die Göttinnen).

godfather *noun* Pate *der* (PL die Paten).

godmother *noun* Patin *die* (PL die Patinnen).

godson *noun* Patensohn *der* (PL die Patensöhne).

gold *noun* Gold *das*; **a gold bracelet** ein Goldarmband.

goldfish *noun* Goldfisch *der* (PL die Goldfische).

golf *noun* Golf *das*; **to play golf** Golf spielen.

golf club *noun* 1 (*place*) Golfklub *der* (PL die Golfklubs); 2 (*iron*) Golfschläger *der* (PL die Golfschläger).

golf course *noun* Golfplatz *der* (PL die Golfplätze).

good *adjective* 1 gut; **she's a good teacher** sie ist eine gute Lehrerin; **the cherries are very good** die Kirschen sind sehr gut; 2 **to be good for you** gesund sein; **tomatoes are good for you** Tomaten sind gesund; 3 **good at** gut in (+DAT); **she's good at maths** sie ist gut in Mathe; **he's good at drawing** er ist gut im Zeichnen; 4 (*well-behaved*) brav; **be good!** sei brav!; 5 (*kind*) nett; **she's been very good to me** sie ist sehr nett zu mir gewesen; 6 **for**

good endgültig; **I've stopped smoking for good** ich habe das Rauchen endgültig aufgegeben.

good afternoon *exclamation* guten Tag!

goodbye *exclamation* auf Wiedersehen!

good evening *exclamation* guten Abend!

Good Friday *noun* Karfreitag *der* (PL die Karfreitage).

good-looking *adjective* gut aussehend △.

good morning *exclamation* guten Morgen!

goodness *exclamation* meine Güte!; **for goodness sake!** um Himmels willen!

good night *exclamation* gute Nacht!

goods *plural noun* Waren (*plural*).

goods train *noun* Güterzug *der* (PL die Güterzüge).

goose *noun* Gans *die* (PL die Gänse).

gorgeous *adjective* herrlich; **it's a gorgeous day** es ist ein herrlicher Tag.

gorilla *noun* Gorilla *der* (PL die Gorillas).

gosh *exclamation* Mensch!

gossip *noun* 1 (*person*) Klatschbase *die* (PL die Klatschbasen); 2 (*scandal*) Klatsch *der*. *verb* klatschen.

✧ IRREGULAR VERB: *See the verb table in the centre of the dictionary*

government *noun* Regierung *die* (PL *die* Regierungen).

grab *verb* 1 packen; **she grabbed my arm** sie packte mich am Arm; **2 to grab something from somebody** jemandem etwas ←(ACC) entreißen ✧; **he grabbed the book from me** er hat mir das Buch entrissen.

grade *noun* (*mark*) Note *die* (PL *die* Noten); **to get good grades** gute Noten bekommen.

gradual *adjective* allmählich.

gradually *adverb* allmählich; **the weather got gradually better** das Wetter wurde allmählich besser.

graffiti *plural noun* Graffiti (*plural*).

gram *noun* Gramm *das*; **100 grams of salami** hundert Gramm Salami.

grammar *noun* Grammatik *die*.

grammar school *noun* Gymnasium *das* (PL *die* Gymnasien).

gran *noun* Oma *die* (PL *die* Omas).

grandchildren *plural noun* Enkelkinder (*plural*).

granddad *noun* Opa *der* (PL *die* Opas).

granddaughter *noun* Enkelin *die* (PL *die* Enkelinnen).

grandfather *noun* Großvater *der* (PL *die* Großväter).

grandma *noun* Oma *die* (PL *die* Omas).

grandmother *noun* Großmutter *die* (PL *die* Großmütter).

grandpa *noun* Opa *der* (PL *die* Opas).

grandparents *plural noun* Großeltern (*plural*).

grandson *noun* Enkel *der* (PL *die* Enkel).

granny *noun* Omi *die* (PL *die* Omis).

grape *noun* Weintraube *die* (PL *die* Weintrauben); **a grape** eine Weintraube; **to buy some grapes** Weintrauben kaufen; **do you like grapes?** magst du Weintrauben?; **a bunch of grapes** eine ganze Weintraube.

grapefruit *noun* Grapefruit *die* (PL *die* Grapefruits).

grasp *verb* festhalten ✧ SEP.

grass *noun* 1 Gras *das*; **to lie on the grass** im Gras liegen; **2** (*lawn*) Rasen *der* (PL *die* Rasen); **to cut the grass** den Rasen mähen.

grasshopper *noun* Heuschrecke *die* (PL *die* Heuschrecken).

grate *verb* reiben ✧; **grated cheese** geriebener Käse.

grateful *adjective* dankbar; **to be grateful to somebody** jemandem dankbar sein.

grater *noun* Reibe *die* (PL *die* Reiben).

grave *noun* Grab *das* (PL *die* Gräber).

△ NEW SPELLING: *See page xii*

graveyard *noun* Friedhof *der* (PL die Friedhöfe).

gravy *noun* Soße *die* (PL die Soßen).

grease *noun* Fett *das*.

greasy *adjective* 1 fettig; **to have greasy skin** fettige Haut haben; 2 (*food*) fett.

great *adjective* 1 groß; **a great poet** ein großer Dichter; 2 (*terrific*) großartig; **it was a great party** das war eine großartige Party; **great!** großartig!, prima! (*informal*); 3 **a great deal of** sehr viel; **a great many** sehr viele.

Great Britain *noun* Großbritannien *das*.

Greece *noun* Griechenland *das*.

greedy *adjective* gierig; (*with food*) gefräßig.

Greek *noun* 1 (*person*) Grieche *der* (PL die Griechen), Griechin *die* (PL die Griechinnen); 2 (*language*) Griechisch *das*. *adjective* griechisch; **she's Greek** sie ist Griechin.

green *noun* 1 (*colour*) Grün *das*; **a pale green** ein Hellgrün; 2 **the Greens** (*ecologists*) die Grünen. *adjective* 1 grün; **a green door** eine grüne Tür; 2 **the Green Party** die Grünen (*plural*).

greengrocer *noun* Obst- und Gemüsehändler *der* (PL die Obst- und Gemüsehändler).

greenhouse *noun* Gewächshaus *das* (PL die Gewächshäuser).

greenhouse effect *noun* Treibhauseffekt *der*.

greetings *plural noun* Grüße (*plural*); **Season's Greetings** fröhliche Weihnachten und ein glückliches neues Jahr.

greetings card *noun* Glückwunschkarte *die* (PL die Glückwunschkarten).

grey *adjective* grau.

grief *noun* Trauer *die*.

grill *noun* Grill *der* (PL die Grills). *verb* grillen; **I'm going to grill the sausages** ich grille die Würstchen.

grin *verb* grinsen.

grind *verb* mahlen.

grip *verb* (*hold on to*) festhalten ✧ SEP.

groan *noun* Stöhnen *das*. *verb* stöhnen.

grocer *noun* Lebensmittelhändler *der* (PL die Lebensmittelhändler).

groceries *plural noun* Lebensmittel (*plural*).

grocer's *noun* Lebensmittelgeschäft *das* (PL die Lebensmittelgeschäfte).

groom *noun* Bräutigam *der* (PL die Bräutigame); **the bride and groom** das Brautpaar.

gross *adjective* 1 **a gross injustice** ein schreiendes Unrecht; 2 grob; **a gross error** ein grober Fehler; 3 (*disgusting*) ekelhaft; **the food was gross!** das Essen war ekelhaft!

✧ IRREGULAR VERB: *See the verb table in the centre of the dictionary*

ground *noun* 1 Boden *der*; **to sit on the ground** auf dem Boden sitzen; 2 (*for sport*) Sportplatz *der* (PL die Sportplätze); **football ground** *der* Fußballplatz.
adjective gemahlen; **ground coffee** gemahlener Kaffee.

ground floor *noun* Erdgeschoss △ *das*; **they live on the ground floor** sie wohnen im Erdgeschoss.

group *noun* Gruppe *die* (PL die Gruppen).

grow *verb* (*get bigger*) 1 wachsen ✧ (PERF *sein*); **your hair grows very quickly** deine Haare wachsen sehr schnell; **my little sister's grown quite a bit this year** meine kleine Schwester ist dieses Jahr ein ganzes Stück gewachsen; **the number of students is still growing** die Zahl der Studenten wächst noch; 2 anbauen SEP (*fruit, vegetables*); 3 **to grow a beard** sich ←(DAT) einen Bart wachsen lassen; 4 (*become*) werden ✧ (PERF *sein*); **to grow old** alt werden.
▸ **to grow up** 1 erwachsen werden; **the children are growing up** die Kinder werden erwachsen; 2 aufwachsen ✧ SEP (PERF *sein*); **she grew up in Scotland** sie ist in Schottland aufgewachsen.

growl *verb* knurren.

grown-up *noun* Erwachsene *der/die* (PL die Erwachsenen).

growth *noun* Wachstum *das*.

grudge *noun* **to bear a grudge against somebody** etwas gegen jemanden haben; **she bears me a grudge** sie hat etwas gegen mich.

grumble *verb* 1 murren; **he's always grumbling** er murrt immer; 2 **to grumble about something** sich über etwas ←(ACC) beklagen; **what's she grumbling about?** worüber beklagt sie sich?

guarantee *noun* Garantie *die* (PL die Garantien); **a year's guarantee** ein Jahr Garantie.
verb garantieren.

guard *noun* 1 **prison guard** *der* Gefängniswärter, *die* Gefängniswärterin; 2 (*on a train*) Zugführer *der* (PL die Zugführer), Zugführerin *die* (PL die Zugführerinnen); 3 **security guard** *der* Wächter, *die* Wächterin.
verb bewachen.

guard dog *noun* Wachhund *der* (PL die Wachhunde).

guess *noun* **have a guess!** rate mal!; **it's a good guess** gut geraten.
verb 1 raten ✧; **guess who I saw last night** rate mal, wen ich gestern Abend gesehen habe; 2 (*guess something correctly*) es erraten ✧; **you'll never guess!** du errätst es nie!

guest *noun* Gast *der* (PL die Gäste); **we've got guests coming tonight** wir haben heute Abend Gäste; **a paying guest** ein zahlender Gast.

guide *noun* 1 (*person*) Führer *der* (PL die Führer), Führerin *die* (PL die Führerinnen); 2 (*book*) Reiseführer *der* (PL die Reiseführer);

△ NEW SPELLING: *See page xii*

3 (*girl guide*) Pfadfinderin *die* (PL *die* Pfadfinderinnen).

guidebook *noun* **1** Reiseführer *der* (PL *die* Reiseführer); **2** (*to a museum or monument*) Handbuch *das* (PL *die* Handbücher).

guide dog *noun* Blindenhund *der* (PL *die* Blindenhunde).

guilty *adjective* **1** schuldig; **2 to feel guilty** ein schlechtes Gewissen haben; **I felt guilty about the noise** ich hatte ein schlechtes Gewissen wegen des Lärms.

guinea pig *noun*
1 (*pet*) Meerschweinchen *das* (PL *die* Meerschweinchen);
2 (*in an experiment*) Versuchskaninchen *das* (PL *die* Versuchskaninchen).

guitar *noun* Gitarre *die* (PL *die* Gitarren); **to play the guitar** Gitarre spielen.

gum *noun* **1** (*in your mouth*) Zahnfleisch *das*; **2** (*chewing gum*) Kaugummi *der* (PL *die* Kaugummi).

gun *noun* **1** Pistole *die* (PL *die* Pistolen); **2** (*rifle*) Gewehr *das* (PL *die* Gewehre).

guy *noun* Typ *der* (PL *die* Typen) (*informal*); **he's a nice guy** er ist ein netter Typ; **that guy from Newcastle** der Typ aus Newcastle.

gym *noun* **1** (*school lesson*) Turnen *das*; **2** (*building*) Turnhalle *die* (PL *die* Turnhallen); **3** (*health club*) Fitnesscenter △ *das* (PL *die* Fitnesscenter); **to go to the gym** ins Fitnesscenter gehen.

gymnasium *noun* Turnhalle *die* (P die Turnhallen).

gymnast *noun* Turner *der* (PL *die* Turner), Turnerin *die* (PL *die* Turnerinnen).

gymnastics *noun* Turnen *das*.

gym shoe *noun* Turnschuh *der* (PL die Turnschuhe).

H h

habit *noun* Gewohnheit *die* (PL *die* Gewohnheiten); **it's a bad habit** es ist eine schlechte Gewohnheit.

haddock *noun* Schellfisch *der*; **smoked haddock** *der* Haddock.

hail *noun* Hagel *der*.

hailstone *noun* Hagelkorn *das* (PL *die* Hagelkörner).

hailstorm *noun* Hagelschauer *der* (PL *die* Hagelschauer).

hair *noun* **1** Haare (*plural*); **to comb your hair** sich ←(DAT) die Haare kämmen; **to wash your hair** sich ←(DAT) die Haare waschen; **to have your hair cut** sich ←(DAT) die Haare schneiden lassen; **she's had her hair cut** sie hat sich die Haare schneiden lassen; **2 a hair** ein Haar.

hairbrush *noun* Haarbürste *die* (PL *die* Haarbürsten).

haircut *noun* **1** Haarschnitt *der* (PL *die* Haarschnitte); **2 to have a haircut** sich ←(DAT) die Haare schneiden lassen.

◇ IRREGULAR VERB: *See the verb table in the centre of the dictionary*

hairdresser *noun* Friseur *der* (PL die Friseure), Friseuse *die* (PL die Friseusen); **at the hairdresser's** beim Friseur.

hair drier *noun* Föhn △ *der* (PL die Föhne).

hair gel *noun* Haargel *das* (PL die Haargele).

hairgrip *noun* Haarklemme *die* (PL die Haarklemmen).

hairslide *noun* Haarspange *die* (PL die Haarspangen).

hairspray *noun* Haarspray *das* (PL die Haarsprays).

hairstyle *noun* Frisur *die* (PL die Frisuren).

half *noun* 1 Hälfte *die* (PL die Hälften); **half of** die Hälfte von (+DAT); **I gave him half of the money** ich habe ihm die Hälfte von dem Geld gegeben; **half of it** die Hälfte davon; 2 **half an apple** ein halber Apfel; 3 **to cut something in half** etwas halbieren; 4 (*as a fraction*) halb; **three and a half** dreieinhalb; 5 (*in time*) halb; **half an hour** eine halbe Stunde; **an hour and a half** anderthalb Stunden; **it's half past three** es ist halb vier (*literally: half on the way to four*); 6 (*in weights and measures*) halb; **half a litre** ein halber Liter.

half hour *noun* halbe Stunde *die*; **every half hour** jede halbe Stunde.

half price *adjective, adverb* zum halben Preis; **half-price CDs** CDs zum halben Preis.

half-time *noun* Halbzeit *die*; **at half-time the score is 0–0** zur Halbzeit steht es null zu null.

halfway *adverb* 1 auf halbem Weg; **halfway to Frankfurt** auf halbem Weg nach Frankfurt; 2 **to be halfway through doing something** halb fertig mit etwas sein; **I'm halfway through my homework** ich bin halb fertig mit meinen Hausaufgaben.

hall *noun* 1 (*in a house*) Diele *die* (PL die Dielen); 2 (*public*) Saal *der* (PL die Säle); **village hall** *der* Gemeindesaal; **concert hall** *der* Konzertsaal.

Hallowe'en *noun* der Tag vor Allerheiligen (*in Germany there are no particular customs for this date*).

ham *noun* Schinken *der*; **a ham sandwich** ein Schinkenbrot.

hamburger *noun* Hamburger *der* (PL die Hamburger).

hammer *noun* Hammer *der* (PL die Hammer).

hamster *noun* Hamster *der* (PL die Hamster).

hand *noun* 1 Hand *die* (PL die Hände); **to have something in your hand** etwas in der Hand haben; **to hold somebody's hand** jemandes Hand halten; 2 **to give somebody a hand** jemandem helfen ◇; **can you give me a hand to move the table into the corner?** kannst du mir helfen, den Tisch in die Ecke zu rücken?; **do you need a hand?** kann ich dir helfen?; 3 **on the other hand** … andererseits …; 4 (*of a watch or clock*) Zeiger *der* (PL die Zeiger); **the**

hour hand der Stundenzeiger.
verb **to hand something to somebody** jemandem etwas geben ✧; **I handed him the keys** ich gab ihm die Schlüssel.
- **to hand something in** etwas abgeben ✧ SEP; **hand in your homework** gebt eure Hausaufgaben ab.
- **to hand something out** etwas austeilen SEP.

handbag *noun* Handtasche *die* (PL die Handtaschen).

handcuffs *plural noun* Handschellen (*plural*).

handful *noun* **a handful of** eine Hand voll △.

handicapped *adjective* behindert.

handkerchief *noun* Taschentuch *das* (PL die Taschentücher).

handle *noun* **1** (*of a door, drawer, bag, or knife*) Griff *der* (PL die Griffe); **2** (*on a cup, jug, or basket*) Henkel *der* (PL die Henkel); **3** (*of a frying pan or broom*) Stiel *der* (PL die Stiele).
verb **1** erledigen; **Gina handles the correspondence** Gina erledigt die Korrespondenz; **2** umgehen ✧ SEP (PERF *sein*) mit; **she's good at handling people** sie kann gut mit Menschen umgehen; **3** fertig werden △ ✧ (PERF *sein*) mit; **he can't handle problems** er kann mit Problemen nicht fertig werden.

handlebars *plural noun* Lenkstange *die* (PL die Lenkstangen).

hand luggage *noun* Handgepäck *das*.

handmade *adjective* handgemacht▪

handsome *adjective* gut aussehend △; **he's a handsome guy** er ist ein gut aussehender Typ.

handwriting *noun* Handschrift *di*▪ (PL die Handschriften).

handy *adjective* **1** praktisch; **this little knife's very handy** dieses kleine Messer ist sehr praktisch; **2** griffbereit; **I always keep a notebook handy** ich habe immer ein kleines Notizbuch griffbereit.

hang *verb* **1** hängen ✧; **there was a mirror hanging on the wall** an der Wand hing ein Spiegel; **2** aufhängen▪ SEP; **to hang a mirror on the wall** einen Spiegel an der Wand aufhängen.
- **to hang around** rumhängen ✧ SEP (PERF *sein*) (*informal*); **we were hanging around outside the cinema** wir haben vor dem Kino rumgehangen.
- **to hang on** warten; **hang on a second!** warten Sie einen Moment!
- **to hang up** (*on the phone*) auflegen SEP; **she hung up on me** sie hat einfach aufgelegt.
- **to hang something up** etwas aufhängen SEP.

hangover *noun* Kater *der* (PL die Kater).

happen *verb* **1** passieren (PERF *sein*); **what happened?** was ist passiert?; **it happened in June** es ist im Juni passiert; **2** what's happening? was ist los?; **what's happened to Jill?** was ist mit Jill los?; **3** what's happened to the can-opener?** wo ist der Dosenöffner?; **4** if you happen to see him wenn du ihn

---

✧ **IRREGULAR VERB:** *See the verb table in the centre of the dictionary*

zufällig triffst, **Leila happened to be there** Leila war zufällig da.

happily *adverb* 1 glücklich; 2 (*willingly*) gerne; **I'll happily do it for you** ich tu es gerne für dich.

happiness *noun* Glück *das*.

happy *adjective* glücklich; **a happy child** ein glückliches Kind; **Happy Birthday** herzlichen Glückwunsch zum Geburtstag.

harbour *noun* Hafen *der* (PL *die* Häfen).

hard *adjective* 1 hart; 2 (*difficult*) schwer; **a hard question** eine schwere Frage; **it's hard to know** ... es ist schwer zu wissen ...
adverb 1 **to work hard** hart arbeiten; 2 **to try hard** sich sehr bemühen.

hard disk *noun* Festplatte *die* (PL *die* Festplatten).

hardly *adverb* 1 kaum; **I can hardly hear him** ich kann ihn kaum hören; **there was hardly anybody there** es war kaum jemand da; **we've got hardly any milk** wir haben kaum Milch; **hardly anything** kaum etwas; **he ate hardly anything** er hat kaum etwas gegessen; 2 **hardly ever** fast nie; **I hardly ever see him** ich sehe ihn fast nie.

hard up *adjective* **to be hard up** knapp bei Kasse sein.

harm *noun* **it won't do any harm** es kann nichts schaden.
verb 1 **to harm somebody** jemandem etwas tun; **they didn't harm him** sie haben ihm nichts

getan; 2 schaden (+DAT) (*health, environment, reputation*); **a cup of coffee won't harm you** eine Tasse Kaffee schadet nicht.

harmful *adjective* schädlich.

harmless *adjective* unschädlich.

hat *noun* Hut *der* (PL *die* Hüte).

hate *verb* hassen; **I hate geography** ich hasse Erdkunde.

hatred *noun* Hass △ *der*.

have *verb* 1 haben ◇; **Anna has three brothers** Anna hat drei Brüder; **how many sisters do you have?** wie viele Schwestern hast du?; 2 **what have you got in your hand?** was hast du in der Hand?; **he has (got) flu** er hat die Grippe; 3 (*to form past tenses, some verbs in German take 'haben' and others 'sein'*) **I've finished** ich bin fertig; **have you seen the film?** hast du den Film gesehen?; **Rosie hasn't arrived yet** Rosie ist noch nicht angekommen; 4 **to have to do something** etwas tun müssen ◇; **I have to phone my mum** ich muss meine Mutter anrufen; 5 (*'have' is often translated by a more specific German verb*) **we had a coffee** wir haben einen Kaffee getrunken; **what will you have?** was nehmen Sie?; **I'll have an omelette** ich nehme ein Omelett; **I'm going to have a shower** ich dusche jetzt; **to have lunch** zu Mittag essen; **to have dinner** (*in the evening*) zu Abend essen; 6 (*get*) bekommen ◇; **Emma had a letter from Sam yesterday**

gestern bekam Emma einen Brief von Sam; **she had a baby** sie hat ein Baby bekommen; **7 to have something done** etwas machen lassen ✧; **I'm going to have my hair cut** ich lasse mir die Haare schneiden; **8 to have on** (*be wearing*) anhaben ✧ SEP; **to have nothing on** nichts anhaben.

hay fever *noun* Heuschnupfen *der*.

hazelnut *noun* Haselnuss Δ *die* (PL *die* Haselnüsse).

he *pronoun* er; **he lives in Manchester** er wohnt in Manchester.

head *noun* **1** Kopf *der* (PL *die* Köpfe); **he shook his head** er schüttelte den Kopf; **2** (*of a school*) Direktor *der* (PL *die* Direktoren), Direktorin *die* (PL *die* Direktorinnen); **3** (*of a firm*) Chef *der* (PL *die* Chefs), Chefin *die* (PL *die* Chefinnen); **4** (*when tossing a coin*) **'heads or tails?'** 'Kopf oder Zahl?'.
- **to head for something** auf etwas ←(ACC) zusteuern SEP (PERF *sein*); **Liz headed for the door** Liz steuerte auf die Tür zu.

headache *noun* Kopfschmerzen (*plural*); **I've got a headache** ich habe Kopfschmerzen.

headlight *noun* Scheinwerfer *der* (PL *die* Scheinwerfer).

headline *noun* Schlagzeile *die* (PL *die* Schlagzeilen).

headmaster *noun* Direktor *der* (PL *die* Direktoren).

headmistress *noun* Direktorin *die* (PL *die* Direktorinnen).

headphones *noun* Kopfhörer *der* (PL *die* Kopfhörer).

headteacher *noun* Direktor *der* (PL *die* Direktoren), Direktorin *die* (PL *die* Direktorinnen).

health *noun* Gesundheit *die*.

health centre *noun* Ärztezentrum *das* (PL *die* Ärztezentren).

healthy *adjective* gesund.

heap *noun* Haufen *der* (PL *die* Haufen); **I've got heaps of work** ich habe einen Haufen Arbeit (*informal*).

hear *verb* hören; **I can't hear anything** ich kann überhaupt nichts hören; **I hear you've bought a dog** ich habe gehört, dass ihr einen Hund gekauft habt.
- **to hear about something** von etwas ←(DAT) hören; **have you heard about the concert?** hast du von dem Konzert gehört?
- **to hear from somebody** von jemandem hören.

heart *noun* **1** Herz *das* (PL *die* Herzen); **2 to learn something by heart** etwas auswendig lernen; **3** (*in cards*) Herz *das*; **the jack of hearts** der Herzbube.

heat *noun* Hitze *die*.
verb **1 to heat something** etwas heiß machen; **I'll go and heat the soup** ich mache die Suppe heiß; **2 the soup's heating** die Suppe wird warm; **3** heizen (*a room*);

✧ IRREGULAR VERB: *See the verb table in the centre of the dictionary*

to **heat something up** etwas aufwärmen SEP; **I'm heating the sauce up** ich wärme die Soße auf.

eater noun Heizgerät das (PL die Heizgeräte).

eather noun Heidekraut das.

eating noun Heizung die.

eatwave noun Hitzewelle die (PL die Hitzewellen).

eaven noun Himmel der.

eavy adjective 1 schwer; **my rucksack's really heavy** mein Rucksack ist sehr schwer; 2 (busy) **I've got a heavy day tomorrow** ich habe morgen viel zu tun; 3 (in quantity) stark; **heavy rain** starker Regen.

hectic adjective hektisch; **a hectic day** ein hektischer Tag.

edge noun Hecke die (PL die Hecken).

edgehog noun Igel der (PL die Igel).

eel noun 1 (of foot or sock) Ferse die (PL die Fersen); 2 (of a shoe) Absatz der (PL die Absätze).

eight noun 1 (of a person) Größe die; **what height are you?** wie groß bist du?; 2 (of a building, mountain) Höhe die; **what height is it?** wie hoch ist es?

helicopter noun Hubschrauber der (PL die Hubschrauber).

hell noun Hölle die; **hell!** verdammt! (informal).

hello exclamation 1 (polite) guten Tag!; 2 (informal, and on the phone) hallo!

helmet noun Helm der (PL die Helme).

help noun Hilfe die; **do you need any help?** kann ich dir helfen?; (in a shop) kann ich Ihnen behilflich sein?
verb 1 helfen ✧ (+DAT); **to help somebody (to) do something** jemandem helfen, etwas zu tun; **can you help me lay the table?** kannst du mir helfen, den Tisch zu decken?; 2 **to help yourself to something** sich ←(DAT) etwas nehmen ✧; **help yourself to vegetables** nimm dir Gemüse; **help yourself!** greif zu!; 3 **help!** Hilfe!; 4 **he can't help it** er kann nichts dafür.

helpful adjective (person) hilfsbereit.

hen noun Henne die (PL die Hennen).

her pronoun (in German this pronoun changes according to the function it has in the sentence or the preposition it follows) 1 (as a direct object in the accusative) sie; **I know her** ich kenne sie; **I saw her last week** ich habe sie letzte Woche gesehen; 2 (after prepositions +ACC) sie; **without her** ohne sie; **we've heard a lot about her** wir haben viel über sie gehört; 3 (as an indirect object or after verbs that take the dative) ihr; **I gave her my address** ich habe ihr meine Adresse gegeben; **we helped her** wir haben ihr

△ NEW SPELLING: See page xii

geholfen; **4** (*after prepositions* +DAT)
ihr; **with her** mit ihr; **5** (*in comparisons*) sie; **he's older than her** er ist älter als sie; **6** (*in the nominative*) sie; **it was her** sie war es.
adjective **1** (*before a masculine noun*) ihr; **her brother** ihr Bruder; **2** (*before a feminine noun*) ihre; **her sister** ihre Schwester; **3** (*before a neuter noun*) ihr; **her house** ihr Haus; **4** (*before a plural noun*) ihre; **her children** ihre Kinder; **5** (*with parts of the body*) der/die/das, die (*plural*); **she had a glass in her hand** sie hatte ein Glas in der Hand; **she's washing her hands** sie wäscht sich die Hände.

herb *noun* Kraut *das* (PL *die* Kräuter).

here *adverb* **1** (*in or at this place*) hier; **not far from here** nicht weit von hier; **here's my address** hier ist meine Adresse; **I want to stay here** ich möchte hier bleiben; **2** (*to this place*) hierher; **when Peter came here** als Peter hierher kam; **3 here they are!** da sind sie!; **Tom isn't here at the moment** Tom ist im Moment nicht da.

hero *noun* Held *der* (PL *die* Helden).

heroin *noun* Heroin *das*.

heroine *noun* Heldin *die* (PL *die* Heldinnen).

herring *noun* Hering *der* (PL *die* Heringe).

hers *pronoun* **1** (*for a masculine noun*) ihrer; **my coat is blue and hers is red** mein Mantel ist blau und

ihrer ist rot; **I took my hat and she took hers** ich nahm meinen Hut und sie nahm ihren; **2** (*for a feminine noun*) ihre; **I gave Ann my address and she gave me hers** ich habe Ann meine Adresse gegeben und sie hat mir ihre gegeben; **3** (*for a neuter noun*) ihr(e)s; **my bike is new but hers is old** mein Rad ist neu, aber ihrs ist alt; **4** (*for masculine/ feminine/neuter plural nouns*) ihre; **I showed Emma my photos and she showed me hers** ich habe Emma meine Fotos gezeigt und sie hat mir ihre gezeigt; **5 the CDs are hers** die CDs gehören ihr; **it's hers** das gehört ihr.

herself *pronoun* **1** (*reflexive*) sich; **she's hurt herself** sie hat sich wehgetan; **2** (*stressing something*) selbst; **she said it herself** sie hat es selbst gesagt; **3 she did it by herself** sie hat es ganz allein gemacht.

hesitate *verb* zögern.

heterosexual *adjective* heterosexuell.
noun Heterosexuelle *der/die* (PL *die* Heterosexuellen).

hi *exclamation* hallo!

hiccups *plural noun* **to have the hiccups** einen Schluckauf haben.

hidden *adjective* verborgen.

hide *verb* **1** sich verstecken; **she hid behind the door** sie hat sich hinter der Tür versteckt; **2 to hide something** etwas verstecken.

hi-fi *noun* Hi-Fi-Anlage *die* (PL *die* Hi-Fi-Anlagen).

high *adjective* 1 hoch; **how high is the wall?** wie hoch ist die Mauer?; **the wall is two metres high** die Mauer ist zwei Meter hoch; **the shelf is too high** das Regal ist zu hoch; (*the adjective 'hoch' loses its c when it has an ending, becoming hoher/hohe/hohes*) **a high tower** ein hoher Turm; **a high wall** eine hohe Mauer; **at high speed** mit hoher Geschwindigkeit; **a high voice** eine hohe Stimme; 2 **high winds** starker Wind.
adverb hoch.

high-heeled *adjective* hochhackig.

high jump *noun* Hochsprung *der*.

hijack *verb* **to hijack a plane** ein Flugzeug entführen.

hijacker *noun* Entführer *der* (PL *die* Entführer).

hike *noun* Wanderung *die* (PL *die* Wanderungen).

hilarious *adjective* lustig.

hill *noun* 1 (*large hill*) Berg *der* (PL *die* Berge); **you can see the hills** man kann die Berge sehen; 2 (*smaller*) Hügel *der* (PL *die* Hügel); **to walk up the hill** den Hügel hinaufgehen; 3 (*hillside*) Hang *der* (PL *die* Hänge); **the house on the hill** das Haus am Hang.

him *pronoun* (*in German this pronoun changes according to the function it has in the sentence or the preposition it follows*) 1 (*as a direct object in the accusative*) ihn; **I know him** ich kenne ihn; **I saw him last week** ich habe ihn letzte Woche gesehen; 2 (*after prepositions* +ACC) ihn; **he fought against him** er hat gegen ihn gekämpft; **without him** ohne ihn; 3 (*as an indirect object or after verbs that take the dative*) ihm; **I gave him my address** ich habe ihm meine Adresse gegeben; **you must help him** du musst ihm helfen; 4 (*after prepositions* +DAT) ihm; **with him** mit ihm; 5 (*in comparisons*) er; **she's older than him** sie ist älter als er; 6 (*in the nominative*) er; **it was him** er war es.

himself *pronoun* 1 (*reflexive*) sich; **he's hurt himself** er hat sich wehgetan; 2 (*stressing something*) selbst; **he said it himself** er hat es selbst gesagt; 3 **he did it by himself** er hat es ganz allein gemacht.

Hindu *adjective* hinduistisch.

hip *noun* Hüfte *die* (PL *die* Hüften).

hippie *noun* Hippie *der* (PL *die* Hippies).

hire *noun* 1 Vermietung *die*; **car hire** *die* Autovermietung; 2 **for hire** zu vermieten.
verb mieten.

his *adjective* 1 (*before a masculine noun*) sein; **his brother** sein Bruder; 2 (*before a feminine noun*) seine; **his sister** seine Schwester; 3 (*before a neuter noun*) sein; **his house** sein Haus; 4 (*before a plural noun*) seine; **his children** seine Kinder; 5 (*with parts of the body*) der/die/das, die (*plural*); **he had a glass in his hand** er hatte ein Glas in der Hand; **he's washing his hands** er wäscht sich ←(DAT) die Hände.

△ NEW SPELLING: *See page xii*

pronoun **1** (*for a masculine noun*) seiner; **my hat is red and his is blue** mein Hut ist rot und seiner ist blau; **2** (*for a feminine noun*) seine; **I gave him my address and he gave me his** ich habe ihm meine Adresse gegeben und er hat mir seine gegeben; **3** (*for a neuter noun*) sein(e)s; **my book is new but his is old** mein Buch ist neu, aber seins ist alt; **4** (*for masculine/feminine/neuter plural nouns*) seine; **I've invited my parents and Steve's invited his** ich habe meine Eltern eingeladen und Steve hat seine eingeladen; **5 the green car's his** das grüne Auto gehört ihm; **it's his** das gehört ihm.

history *noun* Geschichte *die*.

hit *noun* **1** (*song*) Hit *der* (PL *die* Hits); **their latest hit** ihr neuester Hit; **2** (*success*) Erfolg *der* (PL *die* Erfolge); **the film is a huge hit** der Film ist ein großer Erfolg.
verb **1** treffen ✧; **to hit the ball** den Ball treffen; **2 to hit your head on something** sich ←(DAT) den Kopf an etwas ←(DAT) stoßen; **I hit my head on the door** ich habe mir den Kopf an der Tür gestoßen; **3** prallen gegen (+ACC) (PERF *sein*); **the car hit a wall** das Auto ist gegen eine Wand geprallt; **4 to be hit by a car** von einem Auto angefahren werden.

hitch *noun* Problem *das* (PL *die* Probleme); **there's been a slight hitch** ein kleines Problem ist aufgetaucht.
verb **to hitch a lift** per Anhalter fahren ✧ (PERF *sein*).

hitchhike *verb* per Anhalter fahren ✧ (PERF *sein*); **we hitchhiked to Heidelberg** wir sind per Anhalter nach Heidelberg gefahren.

hitchhiker *noun* Anhalter *der* (PL *die* Anhalter), Anhalterin *die* (PL *die* Anhalterinnen).

HIV-negative *adjective* HIV-negativ.

HIV-positive *adjective* HIV-positiv.

hobby *noun* Hobby *das* (PL *die* Hobbys).

hockey *noun* Hockey *das*.

hockey stick *noun* Hockeyschläger *der* (PL *die* Hockeyschläger).

hold *verb* **1** halten ✧; **to hold something in your hand** etwas in der Hand halten; **can you hold the torch?** kannst du die Taschenlampe halten?; **2** (*be able to contain*) fassen; **the jug holds a litre** der Krug fasst einen Liter; **3 to hold a meeting** eine Versammlung abhalten ✧ SEP; **4 can you hold the line, please?** bleiben Sie bitte am Apparat; **5 hold on!** (*wait*) warten Sie!; (*on the phone*) bleiben Sie am Apparat.
● **to hold on to something** (*to stop yourself from falling*) sich an etwas ←(DAT) festhalten ✧ SEP.
● **to hold somebody up** (*delay*) jemanden aufhalten ✧ SEP; **I was held up at the dentist's** ich bin beim Zahnarzt aufgehalten worden.
● **to hold something up** (*raise*) etwas hochhalten ✧ SEP.

hold-up *noun* **1** Verzögerung *die* (PL

✧ IRREGULAR VERB: *See the verb table in the centre of the dictionary*

die Verzögerungen); 2 (*traffic jam*) Stau der (PL die Staus); 3 (*robbery*) Überfall der (PL die Überfälle).

hole noun Loch das (PL die Löcher).

holiday noun 1 Ferien (*plural*), Urlaub der (PL die Urlaube) (*students, schoolchildren, and families usually have 'Ferien'; people in paid employment usually have 'Urlaub'*); **where are you going for your holiday?** wo fahrt ihr in den Ferien hin?; **have a good holiday!** schöne Ferien!, schönen Urlaub!; **to be away on holiday** auf Urlaub sein, in Ferien sein; **to go on holiday** in Urlaub fahren, in die Ferien fahren; **the school holidays** die Schulferien; 2 (*day off work*) freie Tag der (PL die freien Tage); **I'm taking two days' holiday next week** ich nehme mir nächste Woche zwei Tage frei; 3 **public holiday** der Feiertag; **Monday's a holiday** Montag ist ein Feiertag.

Holland noun Holland das.

holy adjective heilig.

home noun 1 **I was at home** ich war zu Hause; **to stay at home** zu Hause bleiben; 2 **make yourself at home** mach es dir bequem.
adverb 1 (*to home*) nach Hause; **Susie's gone home** Susie ist nach Hause gegangen; **on my way home** auf dem Weg nach Hause; **to get home** nach Hause kommen; **we got home at midnight** wir sind um Mitternacht nach Hause gekommen; 2 (*at home*) zu Hause; **I'll be home in the afternoon** ich bin am Nachmittag zu Hause.

homeless adjective obdachlos; **the homeless** die Obdachlosen.

homemade adjective selbst gemacht △; **homemade biscuits** selbst gebackene Kekse.

homeopathic adjective homöopathisch.

homesick adjective **to be homesick** Heimweh haben.

homework noun Hausaufgaben (*plural*); **I did my homework** ich habe meine Hausaufgaben gemacht; **my German homework** meine Deutschhausaufgaben.

homosexual adjective homosexuell.
noun Homosexuelle der/die (PL die Homosexuellen).

honest adjective ehrlich.

honestly adverb ehrlich.

honesty noun Ehrlichkeit die.

honey noun Honig der (PL die Honige).

hood noun 1 Kapuze die (PL die Kapuzen); 2 (*on a car*) Verdeck das (PL die Verdecke).

hook noun 1 Haken der (PL die Haken); 2 **to take the phone off the hook** das Telefon aushängen SEP.

hooligan noun Hooligan der (PL die Hooligans).

hooray exclamation hurra!

hoover verb saugen; **I hoovered my bedroom** ich habe mein Schlafzimmer gesaugt.

△ NEW SPELLING: *See page xii*

Hoover™ *noun* Staubsauger *der* (PL *die* Staubsauger).

hope *noun* Hoffnung *die* (PL *die* Hoffnungen); **to give up hope** die Hoffnung aufgeben.
verb **1** hoffen; **we hope you'll be able to come** wir hoffen, ihr könnt kommen; **I'm hoping to see you on Friday** ich hoffe, dich am Freitag zu sehen; **2 I hope so** hoffentlich; **I hope not** hoffentlich nicht.

hopefully *adverb* hoffentlich; **hopefully, the film won't have started** hoffentlich hat der Film noch nicht angefangen.

hopeless *adjective* miserabel (*informal*); **I'm hopeless at geography** ich bin miserabel in Erdkunde.

horn *noun* **1** (*of an animal, instrument*) Horn *das* (PL *die* Hörner); **2** (*of a car*) Hupe *die* (PL *die* Hupen).

horoscope *noun* Horoskop *das* (PL *die* Horoskope).

horrible *adjective* **1** furchtbar; **the weather was horrible** das Wetter war furchtbar; **2** (*person*) gemein; **she's really horrible** sie ist richtig gemein; **he was really horrible to me** er war richtig gemein zu mir.

horror *noun* Entsetzen *das*.

horror film *noun* Horrorfilm *der* (PL *die* Horrorfilme).

horse *noun* Pferd *das* (PL *die* Pferde).

hospital *noun* Krankenhaus *das* (PL *die* Krankenhäuser); **in hospital** im Krankenhaus; **to be taken into hospital** ins Krankenhaus kommen

hospitality *noun* Gastfreundschaft *die*.

host *noun* **1** Gastgeber *der* (PL *die* Gastgeber); **2** (*on a TV programme*) Moderator *der* (PL *die* Moderatoren)

hostage *noun* Geisel *die* (PL *die* Geiseln).

hostel *noun* **youth hostel** die Jugendherberge.

hostess *noun* **1** Gastgeberin *die* (P *die* Gastgeberinnen); **2** (*on a TV programme*) Moderatorin *die* (PL *die* Moderatorinnen); **3 air hostess** die Stewardess.

hot *adjective* **1** heiß; **be careful, the plates are hot** sei vorsichtig, die Teller sind heiß; **it's hot today** heute ist es heiß; **2** (*person*) **I'm very hot** mir ist sehr heiß; **3** (*spicy*) scharf; **the curry's too hot for me** das Curry ist mir zu scharf; **4 a hot meal** ein warmes Essen.

hotel *noun* Hotel *das* (PL *die* Hotels).

hour *noun* Stunde *die* (PL *die* Stunden); **two hours later** zwei Stunden später; **we waited for two hours** wir haben zwei Stunden lang gewartet; **I've been waiting for hours** ich warte schon seit Stunden; **two hours ago** vor zwei Stunden; **to be paid by the hour** pro Stunde bezahlt werden; **every hour** jede Stunde; **half an hour** eine halbe Stunde; **a quarter of an hour** eine Viertelstunde; **an hour and a half** anderthalb Stunden.

house *noun* **1** Haus *das* (PL *die*

✧ IRREGULAR VERB: *See the verb table in the centre of the dictionary*

Häuser); **2 at somebody's house**
bei jemandem; **I'm at Judy's house**
ich bin bei Judy; **I'm going to Sid's
house tonight** ich gehe heute Abend
zu Sid; **I phoned from Jill's house**
ich habe von Jill angerufen.

housewife *noun* Hausfrau *die* (PL
die Hausfrauen).

housework *noun* Hausarbeit *die*;
he does the housework er macht
den Haushalt (*informal*).

hovercraft *noun*
Luftkissenfahrzeug *das* (PL *die*
Luftkissenfahrzeuge).

how *adverb* 1 wie; **how did you do
it?** wie hast du das gemacht?; **how
are you?** wie geht es dir?; **how
many?** wie viele?; **how many
brothers do you have?** wie viele
Brüder hast du?; **how old are you?**
wie alt bist du?; **how far is it?** wie
weit ist es?; **how far is it to York?**
wie weit ist es bis York?; **how long
will it take?** wie lange dauert es?;
how long have you known her? wie
lange kennst du sie?; **2 how much?**
wie viel?; **how much money do you
have?** wie viel Geld hast du?; **how
much is it?** wie viel kostet das?

however *adverb* 1 jedoch; **2** (*in
questions*) **however did she do it?**
wie hat sie das nur gemacht?;
3 however famous he is wie
berühmt er auch sein mag.

hug *noun* **to give somebody a hug**
jemanden umarmen; **she gave me
a hug** sie hat mich umarmt.

huge *adjective* riesig.

hum *verb* summen.

human *adjective* menschlich.

human being *noun* Mensch *der*
(PL *die* Menschen).

humour *noun* Humor *der*; **to have
a sense of humour** Humor haben.

hundred *number* hundert; **two
hundred** zweihundert; **two
hundred and ten** zweihundertzehn;
a hundred people hundert
Menschen; **about a hundred** um die
hundert; **hundreds of people**
hunderte von Menschen.

Hungary *noun* Ungarn *das*.

hunger *noun* Hunger *der*.

hungry *adjective* **to be hungry**
Hunger haben; **I'm hungry** ich habe
Hunger.

hunting *noun* Jagd *die*; **fox-
hunting** *die* Fuchsjagd.

hurry *noun* **to be in a hurry** es eilig
haben; **I'm in a hurry** ich habe es
eilig; **there's no hurry** es eilt nicht.
verb 1 sich beeilen; **I must hurry** ich
muss mich beeilen; **hurry up!** beeil
dich!; **2 he hurried home** er ging
schnell nach Hause.

hurt *verb* 1 **to hurt somebody**
jemandem wehtun ◇ SEP; **you're
hurting me!** du tust mir weh!; **that
hurts!** das tut weh!; **2 my arm
hurts** der Arm tut mir weh; **3 to hurt
yourself** sich ←(DAT) wehtun ◇ SEP;
did you hurt yourself? hast du dir
wehgetan?
adjective 1 (*in an accident*) verletzt;
three people were hurt drei
Menschen wurden verletzt; **2** (*in

△ NEW SPELLING: *See page xii*

feelings) gekränkt; **she felt hurt** sie
fühlte sich gekränkt.

husband *noun* Ehemann *der* (PL *die*
Ehemänner).

hymn *noun* Kirchenlied *das* (PL *die*
Kirchenlieder).

hypermarket *noun*
Großmarkt *der* (PL *die* Großmärkte).

hyphen *noun* Bindestrich *der* (PL
die Bindestriche).

I i

I *pronoun* ich; **I have two sisters** ich
habe zwei Schwestern.

ice *noun* Eis *das*.

ice cream *noun* Eis *das*; **two
chocolate ice creams** zwei
Schokoladeneis.

ice hockey *noun* Eishockey *das*.

ice rink *noun* Eisbahn *die* (PL *die*
Eisbahnen).

ice-skating *noun* **to go ice-
skating** Schlittschuh laufen ✧
(PERF *sein*).

icy *adjective* **1** vereist (*road*); **2** (*very
cold*) eiskalt.

idea *noun* **1** Idee *die* (PL *die* Ideen);
what a good idea! was für eine gute
Idee!; **2 I've no idea** ich habe keine
Ahnung.

ideal *adjective* ideal.

identical *adjective* identisch.

identification *noun*
1 Identifizierung *die*; **2** (*proof of
identity*) Ausweispapiere (*plural*).

identity card *noun*
Personalausweis *der* (PL *die*
Personalausweise).

idiot *noun* Idiot *der* (PL *die* Idioten).

idiotic *adjective* idiotisch.

i.e. *abbreviation* d.h. (*das heißt*).

if *conjunction* **1** wenn; **if it rains**
wenn es regnet; **if I won the lottery**
wenn ich in der Lotterie gewinnen
sollte; **if not** wenn nicht; **if only**
wenn nur; **if only you'd told me**
wenn du mir das nur gesagt hättest;
2 even if selbst wenn; **even if it
snows** selbst wenn es schneit;
3 if I were you an deiner Stelle;
4 (*whether*) ob; **I wonder if he'll
come** ich bin gespannt, ob er
kommt; **as if** als ob.

ignore *verb* **1** ignorieren;
2 überhören (*what somebody says*).

ill *adjective* krank; **to fall ill, to be
taken ill** krank werden; **I feel ill** ich
fühle mich krank.

illegal *adjective* illegal.

illustration *noun* Illustration *die*
(PL *die* Illustrationen).

image *noun* Bild *das* (PL *die* Bilder);
★ **he's the spitting image of his
father** er ist das Ebenbild seines
Vaters.

imagination *noun* Phantasie *die*.

imaginative *adjective*
phantasievoll.

✧ IRREGULAR VERB: *See the verb table in the centre of the dictionary*

imagine *verb* sich ←(DAT) vorstellen; **imagine that you're very rich** stell dir vor, du bist sehr reich; **you can't imagine how hard it was** du kannst dir nicht vorstellen, wie schwer es war.

imitate *verb* nachahmen SEP.

immediate *adjective* 1 (*without delay*) unmittelbar; 2 **the immediate family** die engste Familie.

immediately *adverb* 1 sofort; **I rang them immediately** ich habe sie sofort angerufen; 2 **immediately before** unmittelbar davor; **immediately after** unmittelbar danach.

immigrant *noun* Einwanderer *der* (PL *die* Einwanderer), Einwanderin *die* (PL *die* Einwanderinnen).

immigration *noun* Einwanderung *die*.

impatience *noun* Ungeduld *die*.

impatient *adjective* 1 ungeduldig; 2 **to be impatient with somebody** ungeduldig mit jemandem sein.

impatiently *adverb* ungeduldig.

importance *noun* Wichtigkeit *die*.

important *adjective* wichtig.

impossible *adjective* unmöglich; **it's impossible to find a telephone** es ist unmöglich, ein Telefon zu finden.

impressed *adjective* beeindruckt; **to be impressed by something** von etwas ←(DAT) beeindruckt sein.

impressive *adjective* eindrucksvoll.

improve *verb* 1 **to improve something** etwas verbessern; 2 (*get better*) besser werden; **the weather is improving** das Wetter wird besser.

improvement *noun* Verbesserung *die* (PL *die* Verbesserungen).

in *preposition* 1 in (+DAT *or, with movement into*, +ACC); **it is in my pocket** es ist in meiner Tasche; (*with movement*) **he put it in his pocket** er hat es in die Tasche gesteckt; **she sat in the sun** sie saß in der Sonne; **I read it in the newspaper** ich habe es in der Zeitung gelesen; **in Oxford** in Oxford; **in Germany** in Deutschland; 2 **the biggest city in the world** die größte Stadt auf der Welt; **a house in the country** ein Haus auf dem Land; **in the street** auf der Straße; 3 (*wearing and with colours*) in (+DAT); **the girl in the pink shirt** das Mädchen im rosa Hemd; 4 **in German** auf Deutsch; 5 (*time expressions*) in (+DAT); **in May** im Mai; **in 1994** (im Jahre) 1994; **in winter** im Winter; **in summer** im Sommer; **in the night** in der Nacht; **I'll phone you in ten minutes** ich rufe dich in zehn Minuten an; **she was ready in five minutes** sie war in fünf Minuten fertig; 6 **in the morning** am Morgen; **at eight in the morning** um acht Uhr morgens; 7 (*among people or in literature*) bei (+DAT); **it's rare in children** das ist selten bei Kindern; **in Shakespeare** bei

Shakespeare; **in the army** beim Militär; **8 in time** rechtzeitig.
adverb **1** (*inside*) hinein-, herein-, rein- (*informal*); (*Herein-, hinein-, and rein-* form prefixes to separable verbs. 'Herein-' is used with verbs like kommen, which have the sense of moving towards the speaker. 'Hinein-' is used with verbs like gehen, which have the sense of going away from the speaker. The informal 'rein-' can be used with either movement.) **to come in** hereinkommen ✧ SEP (PERF *sein*); **to go in** hineingehen ✧ SEP (PERF *sein*); **he was not allowed to go into the room** er durfte nicht ins Zimmer reingehen; **to run in** reinlaufen ✧ SEP (PERF *sein*) (*informal*); **2 to be in** da sein; **Mick's not in at the moment** Mick ist im Moment nicht da; **3** (*at home*) zu Hause; **4** (*indoors*) drinnen; **in here** hier drinnen; **in there** da drinnen.

include *verb* einschließen ✧ SEP; **service is included in the price** die Bedienung ist im Preis inbegriffen.

including *preposition*
1 einschließlich (+GEN); **everyone, including the children** alle, einschließlich der Kinder; **£50 including postage** fünfzig Pfund einschließlich Porto; **including Sundays** einschließlich sonntags; **2 not including Sundays** außer sonntags.

income *noun* Einkommen *das* (PL *die* Einkommen).

income tax *noun* Einkommenssteuer *die* (PL *die* Einkommenssteuern).

increase *noun* Erhöhung *die* (PL *die* Erhöhungen) (*in price, for example*). *verb* **1** steigen ✧ (PERF *sein*); **the price has increased by £10** der Preis ist um zehn Pfund gestiegen; **2** erhöhen (*salary*).

incredible *adjective* unglaublich.

incredibly *adverb* (*very*) unwahrscheinlich; **the film's incredibly boring** der Film ist unwahrscheinlich langweilig.

indeed *adverb* **1** (*to emphasize*) wirklich; **she's very pleased indeed** sie hat sich wirklich sehr gefreut; **2** (*certainly*) natürlich; **'can you hear the radio?' – 'indeed I can!'** 'kannst du das Radio hören?' – 'ja, natürlich!'; **3 thank you very much indeed** vielen herzlichen Dank.

indefinite article *noun* unbestimmte Artikel *der*.

independence *noun* Unabhängigkeit *die*.

independent *adjective* unabhängig; **independent school** *die* Privatschule.

India *noun* Indien *das*.

Indian *noun* **1** Inder *der* (PL *die* Inder), Inderin *die* (PL *die* Inderinnen); **2** (*a Native American*) Indianer *der* (PL *die* Indianer), Indianerin *die* (PL *die* Indianerinnen).

✧ IRREGULAR VERB: *See the verb table in the centre of the dictionary*

adjective **1** indisch; **he's Indian** er ist Inder; **2** (*Native American*) indianisch; **she's Indian** sie ist Indianerin.

indicate *verb* **1** zeigen auf (+ACC) (*a person or a thing*); **2** (*of a car or driver*) blinken.

indigestion *noun* Magenverstimmung *die* (PL *die* Magenverstimmungen).

individual *noun* Einzelne △ *der/die* (PL *die* Einzelnen). *adjective* **1** einzeln (*serving, contribution*); **2 individual tuition** *der* Einzelunterricht.

indoor *adjective* **an indoor swimming pool** ein Hallenbad; **indoor games** Spiele im Haus; (*in sports*) Hallenspiele.

indoors *adverb* drinnen; **it's cooler indoors** drinnen ist es kühler; **to go indoors** ins Haus gehen.

industrial *adjective* industriell.

industrial estate *noun* Industriegebiet *das* (PL *die* Industriegebiete).

industry *noun* Industrie *die* (PL *die* Industrien); **the car industry** die Autoindustrie.

inevitable *adjective* unvermeidlich.

inevitably *adverb* zwangsläufig.

inexperienced *adjective* unerfahren.

infant school *noun* Vorschule *die* (PL *die* Vorschulen).

infection *noun* Infektion *die* (PL *die* Infektionen); **eye infection** *die* Augeninfektion; **throat infection** *die* Halsentzündung.

infectious *adjective* ansteckend.

infinitive *noun* Infinitiv *der* (PL *die* Infinitive).

inflammable *adjective* feuergefährlich.

inflatable *adjective* **inflatable mattress** *die* Luftmatratze; **inflatable boat** *das* Schlauchboot.

influence *noun* Einfluss △ *der* (PL *die* Einflüsse); **to be a good influence on somebody** einen guten Einfluss △ auf jemanden haben. *verb* beeinflussen.

inform *verb* informieren; **to inform somebody of something** jemanden über etwas ←(ACC) informieren.

informal *adjective* **1** zwanglos (*meal or event*); **2** ungezwungen (*language, tone*).

information *noun* Auskunft *die*; **where can I get information about flights to Berlin?** wo kann ich Auskunft über Flüge nach Berlin bekommen?

information desk, information office *noun* Auskunftsbüro *das* (PL *die* Auskunftsbüros).

information technology *noun* Informatik *die*.

ingredient *noun* Zutat *die* (PL *die* Zutaten).

△ NEW SPELLING: *See page xii*

inhabitant *noun* Einwohner *der* (PL die Einwohner), Einwohnerin *die* (PL die Einwohnerinnen).

initials *plural noun* Initialen (*plural*).

injection *noun* Spritze *die* (PL die Spritzen).

injure *verb* verletzen.

injury *noun* Verletzung *die* (PL die Verletzungen).

ink *noun* Tinte *die* (PL die Tinten).

in-laws *noun* Schwiegereltern (*plural*).

innocent *adjective* unschuldig.

insane *adjective* 1 geisteskrank; 2 (*foolish*) wahnsinnig.

insect *noun* Insekt *das* (PL die Insekten); **insect bite** *der* Insektenstich.

insect repellent *noun* Insektenvertilgungsmittel *das*.

inside *noun* **on the inside** innen; **the inside of the oven is black** innen ist der Herd schwarz. *preposition* in (+DAT, *or, with movement towards a place,* +ACC); **inside the cinema** im Kino; **to go inside (the house)** ins Haus gehen. *adverb* drinnen; **she's inside, I think** ich glaube, sie ist drinnen.

inside out *adjective, adverb* (*clothing*) links.

insist *verb* darauf bestehen ✧; **if you insist** wenn du darauf bestehst; **to insist on doing something** darauf bestehen, etwas zu tun; **he insists on paying** er besteht darauf zu zahlen; **to insist that** ... darauf bestehen, dass ...; **Ruth insisted I was wrong** Ruth hat darauf bestanden, dass ich Unrecht hatte.

inspector *noun* 1 (*on a bus or train*) Kontrolleur *der* (PL die Kontrolleure), Kontrolleurin *die* (PL die Kontrolleurinnen); 2 (*in the police*) Kommissar *der* (PL die Kommissare), Kommissarin *die* (PL die Kommissarinnen).

install *verb* installieren.

instalment *noun* (*of a story or serial*) Folge *die* (PL die Folgen).

instance *noun* **for instance** zum Beispiel.

instant *noun* Augenblick *der* (PL die Augenblicke); **come here this instant!** komm sofort her! *adjective* 1 Instant- (*coffee, tea*); 2 (*immediate*) sofortig.

instantly *adverb* sofort.

instead *adverb* 1 **Ted couldn't come, so I came instead (of him)** Ted konnte nicht kommen, also bin ich an seiner Stelle gekommen; 2 **instead of** statt (+GEN *or* +DAT); **he bought a bike instead of a car** er hat ein Fahrrad statt eines Autos gekauft; **instead of cake I had cheese** statt Kuchen habe ich Käse genommen; **instead of playing tennis we went swimming** statt Tennis zu spielen, sind wir schwimmen gegangen.

instinct *noun* Instinkt *der* (PL die Instinkte).

✧ IRREGULAR VERB: *See the verb table in the centre of the dictionary*

institute *noun* Institut *das* (PL *die* Institute).

instructions *plural noun* Anweisung *die* (PL *die* Anweisungen); **follow the instructions on the packet** befolgen Sie die Anweisung auf der Packung; **'instructions for use'** 'Gebrauchsanweisung'.

instructor *noun* Lehrer *der* (PL *die* Lehrer), Lehrerin *die* (PL *die* Lehrerinnen); **my skiing instructor** mein Skilehrer.

instrument *noun* Instrument *das* (PL *die* Instrumente); **to play an instrument** ein Instrument spielen.

insulin *noun* Insulin *das*.

insult *noun* Beleidigung *die* (PL *die* Beleidigungen). *verb* beleidigen.

insurance *noun* Versicherung *die* (PL *die* Versicherungen); **travel insurance** *die* Reiseversicherung.

intelligence *noun* Intelligenz *die*.

intelligent *adjective* intelligent.

intend *verb* beabsichtigen; **as I intended** wie beabsichtigt; **to intend to do something** beabsichtigen, etwas zu tun; **we intend to spend the night in Rome** wir beabsichtigen, in Rom zu übernachten.

intention *noun* Absicht *die* (PL *die* Absichten); **I have no intention of paying** ich habe nicht die Absicht zu zahlen.

interest *noun* 1 Interesse *das* (PL *die* Interessen); **to have lots of interests** viele Interessen haben; **he has an interest in jazz** er hat Interesse an Jazz; 2 (*financial*) Zinsen (*plural*). *verb* interessieren; **that doesn't interest me** das interessiert mich nicht.

interested *adjective* **to be interested in something** sich für etwas ←(ACC) interessieren; **Sean's interested in cooking** Sean interessiert sich für Kochen.

interesting *adjective* interessant.

interfere *verb* 1 **to interfere with something** (*to fiddle with it*) sich ←(DAT) an etwas ←(DAT) zu schaffen machen; **don't interfere with my computer!** mach dir nicht an meinem Computer zu schaffen!; 2 **to interfere in something** sich in etwas ←(ACC) einmischen SEP (*somebody else's affairs*).

interior designer *noun* Innenarchitekt *der* (PL *die* Innenarchitekten), Innenarchitektin *die* (PL *die* Innenarchitektinnen).

international *adjective* international.

Internet *noun* Internet *das*; **on the Internet** im Internet.

interpret *verb* (*act as an interpreter*) dolmetschen.

interpreter *noun* Dometscher *der* (PL *die* Dolmetscher), Dolmetscherin *die* (PL *die* Dometscherinnen).

interrupt *verb* unterbrechen ♦.

△ NEW SPELLING: *See page xii*

interruption *noun*
Unterbrechung *die* (PL *die* Unterbrechungen).

interval *noun* (*in a play or concert*)
Pause *die* (PL *die* Pausen).

interview *noun* 1 (*for a job*)
Vorstellungsgespräch *das* (PL *die* Vorstellungsgespräche); **to go for an interview** sich vorstellen SEP; 2 (*in a newspaper, on TV, or radio*)
Interview *das* (PL *die* Interviews).
verb interviewen (*on TV, radio*).

interviewer *noun* Interviewer *der* (PL *die* Interviewer), Interviewerin *die* (PL *die* Interviewerinnen).

into *preposition* 1 in (+ACC); **he's gone into the garden** er ist in den Garten gegangen; **I put the ball into the bag** ich habe den Ball in die Tasche getan; **we all got into the car** wir sind alle ins Auto eingestiegen; **to go into town** in die Stadt gehen; **to get into bed** ins Bett gehen; **to translate into German** ins Deutsche übersetzen; **to change pounds into marks** Pfund in Mark wechseln; 2 (*against*) gegen (+ACC); **he drove into the wall** er ist gegen die Wand gefahren; **to be into jazz** auf Jazz abfahren ✧ SEP (PERF *sein*) (*informal*).

introduce *verb* vorstellen SEP; **she introduced me to her brother** sie hat mich ihrem Bruder vorgestellt; **she introduced her brother to me** sie hat mir ihren Bruder vorgestellt; **can I introduce you to my mother?** darf ich Sie meiner Mutter vorstellen?

introduction *noun* (*in a book*)
Einleitung *die* (PL *die* Einleitungen).

invade *verb* einfallen ✧ SEP in (PERF *sein*) (+ACC).

invalid *noun* Kranke *der/die* (PL *die* Kranken);

invent *verb* erfinden ✧.

invention *noun* Erfindung *die* (PL *die* Erfindungen).

inverted commas *plural noun*
Anführungszeichen (*plural*);
in inverted commas in Anführungszeichen.

investigation *noun*
Untersuchung *die* (PL *die* Untersuchungen); **an investigation into the incident** eine Untersuchung des Vorfalls.

invisible *adjective* unsichtbar.

invitation *noun* Einladung *die* (PL *die* Einladungen); **an invitation to dinner** eine Einladung zum Abendessen.

invite *verb* einladen ✧ SEP; **Kirsty invited me to lunch** Kirsty hat mich zum Mittagessen eingeladen; **he's invited me out on Tuesday** er hat mich eingeladen, Dienstag mit ihm auszugehen; **they invited us round** sie haben uns zu sich eingeladen.

inviting *adjective* verlockend.

involve *verb* 1 erfordern; **it involves a lot of time** es erfordert viel Zeit; 2 (*include*) beteiligen; **the game will involve everybody** alle können sich an dem Spiel beteiligen; **to be involved in something** an etwas ←(DAT) beteiligt sein; **I am involved in the new project** ich bin an dem

✧ IRREGULAR VERB: *See the verb table in the centre of the dictionary*

neuen Projekt beteiligt;
3 (*implicate*) verwickeln; **to get involved in something** in etwas ←(ACC) verwickelt werden; **two cars were involved in the accident** zwei Autos waren in den Unfall verwickelt; **4 to get involved with somebody** sich mit jemandem einlassen ◇ SEP.

Iran *noun* Iran *der*.

Iraq *noun* Irak *der*.

Ireland *noun* Irland *das*; **the Republic of Ireland** die Republik Irland.

Irish *noun* **1** (*the language*) Irisch *das*; **2** (*the people*) **the Irish** die Iren.
adjective irisch; **he's Irish** er ist Ire; **she's Irish** sie ist Irin.

Irishman *noun* Ire *der* (PL die Iren).

Irish Sea *noun* Irische See *die*.

Irishwoman *noun* Irin *die* (PL die Irinnen).

iron *noun* **1** (*for clothes*) Bügeleisen *das* (PL die Bügeleisen); **2** (*the metal*) Eisen *das*.
verb bügeln.

ironing *noun* Bügeln *das*; **to do the ironing** bügeln.

ironing board *noun* Bügelbrett *das* (PL die Bügelbretter).

ironmonger's *noun* Haushaltswarengeschäft *das* (PL die Haushaltswarengeschäfte).

irregular *adjective* unregelmäßig.

irritable *adjective* reizbar.

irritate *verb* ärgern.

irritating *adjective* ärgerlich.

Islam *noun* Islam *der*.

Islamic *adjective* islamisch.

island *noun* Insel *die* (PL die Inseln).

isolated *adjective* **1** (*remote*) abgelegen; **2** (*single*) einzeln; **isolated cases** Einzelfälle.

Israel *noun* Israel *das*.

Israeli *noun* Israeli *der/die* (PL die Iraelis).
adjective israelisch.

issue *noun* **1** (*something you discuss*) Frage *die* (PL die Fragen); **a political issue** eine politische Frage; **2** (*of a magazine*) Ausgabe *die* (PL die Ausgaben).
verb (*hand out*) ausgeben ◇ SEP.

it *pronoun* **1** (*as the subject*) er (*standing for a masculine noun*), sie (*standing for a feminine noun*), es (*standing for a neuter noun*); **'where's my key?' – 'it's in the kitchen'** 'wo ist mein Schlüssel?' – 'er ist in der Küche'; **'where's my bag?'- 'it's in the living-room'** 'wo ist meine Tasche?' – 'sie ist im Wohnzimmer'; **'how old is your car?' – 'it's five years old'** 'wie alt ist dein Auto?' – 'es ist fünf Jahre alt'; **2** (*as the direct object, in the accusative*) ihn (*standing for a masculine noun*), sie (*standing for a feminine noun*), es (*standing for a neuter noun*); **'where's your umbrella?' – 'I've lost it'** 'wo ist dein Regenschirm?'- 'ich habe ihn verloren'; **'have you seen my bag?'** –

'I saw it in the kitchen' 'hast du meine Tasche gesehen?' – ' ich habe sie in der Küche gesehen'; **'have you read his new book?' – 'I've just bought it'** 'hast du sein neues Buch gelesen?' – 'ich habe es gerade gekauft'; **3 to it** ihm (*masculine*), ihr (*feminine*), ihm (*neuter*); **4 yes, it's true** ja, das stimmt; **it doesn't matter** das macht nichts; **5 who is it?** wer ist da?; **it's me** ich bins; **what is it?** was ist los?; **6 it's raining** es regnet; **it's Monday** es ist Montag; **it's two o'clock** es ist zwei Uhr; **7 of it** davon; **8 out of it** daraus.

Italian *noun* **1** (*the language*) Italienisch *das*; **2** (*person*) Italiener *der* (PL die Italiener), Italienerin *die* (PL die Italienerinnen). *adjective* **1** italienisch; **Italian food** die italienische Küche; **2 my Italian class** mein Italienischunterricht.

italics *noun* Kursivschrift *die*; **in italics** kursiv.

Italy *noun* Italien *das*.

itch *verb* **1 my back's itching** mein Rücken juckt; **2 this jumper itches** dieser Pullover kratzt.

item *noun* **1** Gegenstand *der* (PL die Gegenstände); **2** (*for sale in a shop*) Artikel *der* (PL die Artikel).

its *adjective* **1** sein (*for a masculine noun*), ihr (*for a feminine noun*), sein (*for a neuter noun*); **the dog has lost its collar** der Hund hat sein Halsband verloren; **the cat's in its basket** die Katze ist in ihrem Korb; **the horse is brown and its mane is black** das Pferd ist braun und seine

Mähne ist schwarz; **2** (*for a plural noun*) seine (*standing for a masculine noun*), ihre (*standing for a feminine noun*), seine (*standing for a neuter noun*); **its toys** seine Spielsachen, ihre Spielsachen.

itself *pronoun* **1** (*reflexive*) sich; **the cat's washing itself** die Katze wäscht sich; **2 he left the dog by itself** er hat den Hund allein gelassen.

ivy *noun* Efeu *der*.

J j

jack *noun* **1** (*in cards*) Bube *der* (PL die Buben); **the jack of clubs** der Kreuzbube; **2** (*for a car*) Wagenheber *der* (PL die Wagenheber).

jacket *noun* Jacke *die* (PL die Jacken).

jackpot *noun* Jackpot *der* (PL die Jackpots); **to win the jackpot** das große Los ziehen.

jam *noun* **1** Marmelade *die* (PL die Marmeladen); **raspberry jam** die Himbeermarmelade; **2 traffic jam** *der* Stau.

January *noun* Januar *der*; **in January** im Januar.

Japan *noun* Japan *das*.

Japanese *noun* **1** (*the language*) Japanisch *das*; **2** (*person*) Japaner *der* (PL die Japaner),

Japanerin *die* (PL *die* Japanerinnen); **the Japanese** die Japaner. *adjective* japanisch.

jar *noun* **1** (*small*) Glas *das* (PL *die* Gläser); **a jar of jam** ein Glas Marmelade; **2** (*large*) Topf *der* (PL *die* Töpfe).

javelin *noun* Speer *der* (PL *die* Speere).

jaw *noun* Kiefer *der* (PL *die* Kiefer).

jazz *noun* Jazz *der*.

jealous *adjective* eifersüchtig; **to be jealous of somebody** eifersüchtig auf jemanden sein.

jeans *plural noun* Jeans (*plural*); **my jeans** meine Jeans; **a pair of jeans** ein Paar Jeans.

jelly *noun* **1** Gelee *das* (PL *die* Gelees); **2** (*dessert*) Götterspeise *die* (PL *die* Götterspeisen).

jellyfish *noun* Qualle *die* (PL *die* Quallen).

jersey *noun* **1** (*jumper*) Pullover *der* (PL *die* Pullover); **2** (*for football*) Trikot *das* (PL *die* Trikots).

Jesus *noun* Jesus *der*; **Jesus Christ** Jesus Christus.

jet *noun* (*a plane*) Jet *der* (PL *die* Jets).

Jew *noun* Jude *der* (PL *die* Juden), Jüdin *die* (PL *die* Jüdinnen).

jewel *noun* Edelstein *der* (PL *die* Edelsteine).

jeweller *noun* Juwelier *der* (PL *die* Juweliere).

jeweller's *noun* Juweliergeschäft *das*.

jewellery *noun* Schmuck *der*.

Jewish *adjective* jüdisch.

jigsaw *noun* Puzzlespiel *das* (PL *die* Puzzlespiele).

job *noun* **1** (*paid work*) Stelle *die* (PL *die* Stellen), Job *der* (PL *die* Jobs) (*informal*); **a job as a secretary** eine Stelle als Sekretärin; **2** (*a task*) Arbeit *die* (PL *die* Arbeiten); **it's not an easy job** das ist keine leichte Arbeit; **3 she made a good job of it** sie hat es gut gemacht.

jobless *adjective* arbeitslos.

jog *verb* joggen ✧ (PERF *sein*).

join *verb* **1** (*become a member of*) beitreten ✧ SEP (+DAT) (PERF *sein*); **I've joined the tennis club** ich bin dem Tennisklub beigetreten; **2** (*to meet up with*) treffen ✧; **I'll join you later** ich treffe euch später.
● **to join in 1** mitmachen SEP; **Kylie never joins in** Kylie macht nie mit; **2 to join in something** bei etwas ←(DAT) mitmachen SEP; **won't you join in the game?** willst du bei dem Spiel nicht mitmachen?

joint *noun* **1** (*of meat*) Braten *der* (PL *die* Braten); **a joint of beef** ein Rinderbraten; **2** (*in your body*) Gelenk *das* (PL *die* Gelenke).

joke *noun* Witz *der* (PL *die* Witze); **to tell a joke** einen Witz erzählen. *verb* Witze machen; **you must be joking!** du machst wohl Witze!

joker *noun* (*in cards*) Joker *der* (PL *die* Joker).

△ NEW SPELLING: *See page xii*

journalism *noun*
Journalismus *der*.

journalist *noun* Journalist *der* (PL
die Journalisten), Journalistin *die* (PL
die Journalistinnen); **Sean's a
journalist** Sean ist Journalist.

journey *noun* **1** (*a long one*)
Reise *die* (PL *die* Reisen); **on our
journey to Italy** auf unserer Reise
nach Italien; **2** (*shorter; to work or
school*) Fahrt *die* (PL *die* Fahrten);
bus journey *die* Busfahrt.

joy *noun* Freude *die* (PL *die* Freuden).

judge *noun* **1** (*in court*) Richter *der*
(PL *die* Richter); **2** (*in sporting
events*) Schiedsrichter *der* (PL *die*
Schiedsrichter); **3** (*in a
competition*) Preisrichter *der* (PL *die*
Preisrichter).
verb schätzen (*time or distance*).

judo *noun* Judo *das*; **he does judo**
er macht Judo.

jug *noun* Krug *der* (PL *die* Krüge).

juice *noun* Saft *der*; **two orange
juices please** zwei Orangensaft
bitte.

juicy *adjective* saftig.

jukebox *noun* Jukebox *die* (PL *die*
Jukeboxes).

July *noun* Juli *der*; **in July** im Juli.

jumble sale *noun* Basar *der* (PL *die*
Basare).

jump *noun* Sprung *der* (PL *die*
Sprünge); **parachute jump** *der*
Fallschirmsprung.
verb springen ◇ (PERF *sein*).

jumper *noun* Pullover *der* (PL *die*
Pullover).

June *noun* Juni *der*; **in June** im
Juni.

jungle *noun* Dschungel *der*.

junior *adjective* jünger; **junior
school** *die* Grundschule; **the
juniors** (*at primary school*) die
Grundschüler, die
Grundschülerinnen.

junk *noun* Trödel *der*.

junk food *noun* ungesunde
Essen *das*.

just *adverb* **1** (*very recently*) gerade;
to have just done something
gerade etwas getan haben; **Tom has just
arrived** Tom ist gerade
angekommen; **2 to be just doing
something** gerade dabei sein, etwas
zu tun; **I'm just doing the food** ich
bin gerade dabei, Essen zu machen;
3 just before midday kurz vor
Mittag; **just after 4 o'clock** kurz
nach vier Uhr; **4** (*only*) nur; **just for
fun** nur zum Vergnügen; **he's just a
child** er ist doch nur ein Kind; **just
me and Justine are coming** nur ich
und Justine kommen; **5 just a
minute!** einen Moment!; **6 just
coming!** ich komme schon!;
7 (*exactly*) **just as** genauso wie;
he's got just as many friends
er hat genauso viele Freunde.

justice *noun* Gerechtigkeit *die*.

◇ IRREGULAR VERB: *See the verb table in the centre of the dictionary*

K k

kangaroo *noun* Känguru △ *das* (PL die Kängurus).

karate *noun* Karate *das*.

kebab *noun* Kebab *der* (PL die Kebabs).

keen *adjective* 1 (*enthusiastic or committed*) begeistert; **he's a keen photographer** er ist ein begeisterter Fotograf; **you don't seem too keen** du scheinst nicht gerade begeistert zu sein; 2 **to be keen on** mögen ✧; **I'm not keen on fish** ich mag Fisch nicht; 3 **to be keen on doing** (*or* **to do**) **something** etwas gerne tun.

keep *verb* 1 behalten ✧; **you can keep the book** du kannst das Buch behalten; **to keep a secret** ein Geheimnis für sich behalten; 2 **will you keep my seat?** können Sie meinen Platz freihalten?; 3 **to keep somebody waiting** jemanden warten lassen; 4 (*store*) aufbewahren SEP; **can I keep my watch in your desk?** kann ich meine Uhr in deinem Schreibtisch aufbewahren?; **where do you keep saucepans?** wo hast du die Töpfe?; 5 (*not throw away*) aufheben ✧ SEP; **I kept all his letters** ich habe alle seine Briefe aufgehoben; 6 **to keep on doing something** etwas weiter tun; **she kept on talking** sie hat weitergeredet; **keep straight on** weiter geradeaus gehen; 7 **to keep on doing something** (*time after time*) dauernd etwas tun; **he keeps on ringing me up** er ruft mich dauernd an; 8 (*maintain*) halten ✧; **to keep the food warm** das Essen warm halten; **to keep a promise** ein Versprechen halten; 9 (*stay*) bleiben ✧ (PERF sein); **to keep calm** ruhig bleiben; **to keep out of the sun** im Schatten bleiben.

kerb *noun* Randstein *der*.

kettle *noun* Kessel *der* (PL die Kessel); **to put the kettle on** Wasser aufsetzen.

key *noun* 1 (*for a lock*) Schlüssel *der* (PL die Schlüssel); **bunch of keys** das Schlüsselbund; 2 (*on a piano or keyboard*) Taste *die*.

keyboard *noun* (*for a computer*) Tastatur *die* (PL die Tastaturen).

keyring *noun* Schlüsselring *der* (PL die Schlüsselringe).

kick *noun* 1 (*from a person or a horse*) Tritt *der* (PL die Tritte); **to give somebody a kick** jemandem einen Tritt geben; 2 (*in football*) Schuss △ *der* (PL die Schüsse); ★ **to get a kick out of doing something** etwas nur zum Spaß tun.
verb 1 **to kick somebody** jemandem einen Tritt geben; 2 **to kick the ball** den Ball schießen.
● **to kick off** anstoßen ✧ SEP.

kick-off *noun* Anstoß *der*.

kid *noun* (*child*) Kind *das* (PL die Kinder); **Dad's looking after the kids** Vati passt auf die Kinder auf.

kidnap *verb* entführen.

△ NEW SPELLING: *See page xi*

kidney *noun* Niere *die* (PL *die* Nieren).

kill *verb* 1 töten (*an animal*); 2 (*murder*) umbringen ◇ SEP; **he killed the girl** er brachte das Mädchen um; 3 **she was killed in a car accident** sie kam bei einem Autounfall ums Leben.

killer *noun* Mörder *der* (PL *die* Mörder), Mörderin *die* (PL *die* Mörderinnen).

kilo *noun* Kilo *das* (PL *die* Kilo); **a kilo of sugar** ein Kilo Zucker; **ten marks a kilo** zehn Mark das Kilo.

kilogram *noun* Kilogramm *das*.

kilometre *noun* Kilometer *der* (PL *die* Kilometer).

kilt *noun* Kilt *der* (PL *die* Kilts).

kind *noun* 1 Art *die* (PL *die* Arten); **this kind of book** diese Art Buch; **all kinds of people** alle möglichen Leute; 2 (*brand*) Sorte *die* (PL *die* Sorten).
adjective nett; **she was very kind to me** sie war sehr nett zu mir.

kindness *noun* Freundlichkeit *die*.

king *noun* König *der* (PL *die* Könige); **the king of hearts** der Herzkönig.

kingdom *noun* Königreich *das* (PL *die* Königreiche); **the United Kingdom** das Vereinigte Königreich.

kipper *noun* Räucherhering *der* (PL *die* Räucherheringe).

kiss *noun* Kuss △ *der* (PL *die* Küsse); **to give somebody a kiss** jemandem einen Kuss geben.
verb küssen; **kiss me!** küss mich!;

we kissed each other wir haben uns geküsst.

kit *noun* 1 (*of tools*) Werkzeug *das*; 2 (*in a box*) **a tool kit** ein Werkzeugkasten; 3 (*clothes*) Sachen (*plural*); **where's my football kit?** wo sind meine Fußballsachen?; 4 (*for making a model, a piece of furniture, etc.*) Bausatz *der* (PL *die* Bausätze).

kitchen *noun* Küche *die* (PL *die* Küchen); **the kitchen table** der Küchentisch.

kitchen foil *noun* Alufolie *die*.

kitchen roll *noun* Küchenrolle *die* (PL *die* Küchenrollen).

kite *noun* Drachen *der*; **to fly a kite** einen Drachen steigen lassen.

kitten *noun* Kätzchen *das* (PL *die* Kätzchen).

kiwi fruit *noun* Kiwi *die* (PL *die* Kiwis).

knee *noun* Knie *das* (PL *die* Knie); **on (your) hands and knees** auf allen vieren.

kneel *verb* knien; **to kneel (down)** sich hinknien SEP.

knickers *plural noun* Schlüpfer *der* (PL *die* Schlüpfer); **two pairs of knickers** zwei Schlüpfer.

knife *noun* Messer *das* (PL *die* Messer).
verb einstechen ◇ SEP auf (+ACC); (*kill*) erstechen ◇.

knight *noun* (*in chess*) Springer *der* (PL *die* Springer).

knit *verb* stricken.

◇ IRREGULAR VERB: See the verb table in the centre of the dictionary

knitting *noun* Strickerei *die*.

knob *noun* **1** (*on a door or walking stick*) Knauf *der* (PL *die* Knäufe); **2** (*control on a radio or machine*) Knopf *der* (PL *die* Knöpfe); **3 knob of butter** *das* Butterklümpchen.

knock *noun* Schlag *der* (PL *die* Schläge); **a knock on the head** ein Schlag auf den Kopf; **a knock at the door** ein Klopfen an der Tür. *verb* **1** (*to bang*) stoßen ✧; **I knocked my arm on the table** ich habe mir den Arm am Tisch gestoßen; **2 to knock on something** an etwas ←(ACC) klopfen.

● **to knock down 1** (*in a traffic accident*) anfahren ✧ SEP (*a person*); **2** (*to demolish*) abreißen ✧ SEP (*an old building*).

● **to knock out 1** (*to make unconscious*) bewusstlos Δ schlagen ✧; **2** (*in sport, to eliminate*) k.o. schlagen ✧.

knot *noun* Knoten *der* (PL *die* Knoten); **to tie a knot** einen Knoten machen.

know *verb* **1** (*know a fact*) wissen ✧; **do you know where Tim is?** weißt du, wo Tim ist?; **I know they've moved house** ich weiß, dass sie umgezogen sind; **yes, I know** ja, weiß ich; **you never know!** man kann nie wissen!; **I know how to get to town** ich weiß, wie man in die Stadt kommt; **2** (*be personally acquainted with*) kennen ✧; **do you know the Jacksons?** kennst du die Jacksons?; **all the people I know** alle Leute, die ich kenne; **I don't know his mother** ich kenne seine Mutter

nicht; **3 to know how to do something** etwas tun können; **Steve knows how to make potato salad** Steve kann Kartoffelsalat machen; **Liz knows how to mend it** Liz kann es reparieren; **4 to know about** Bescheid wissen über (+ACC) (*items in the news*); **5 to know about** sich auskennen ✧ SEP mit (*machines, cars, etc.*); **Lindy knows about computers** Lindy kennt sich mit Computern aus; **6 to get to know somebody** jemanden kennen lernen Δ.

knowledge *noun* Wissen *das*.

Koran *noun* Koran *der*.

kosher *adjective* koscher.

L l

lab *noun* Labor *das* (PL *die* Labors).

label *noun* Etikett *das* (PL *die* Etikette).

laboratory *noun* Labor *das* (PL *die* Labors).

lace *noun* **1** (*for a shoe*) Schnürsenkel *der* (PL *die* Schnürsenkel); **to tie your laces** sich ←(DAT) die Schnürsenkel binden; **2** (*fabric or trimming*) Spitze *die*.

ladder *noun* **1** (*for climbing*) Leiter *die* (PL *die* Leitern); **2** (*in your tights*) Laufmasche *die* (PL *die* Laufmaschen).

ladies *noun* (*lavatory*)
Damentoilette *die* (PL *die*
Damentoiletten); (*on a sign*)
'Ladies' 'Damen'.

lady *noun* Dame *die* (PL *die* Damen);
ladies and gentlemen meine
Damen und Herren.

lager *noun* helle Bier *das* (PL *die*
hellen Biere), Helle *das* (PL *die*
Hellen) (*informal*); **a lager, please**
ein Helles bitte.

laid-back *adjective* gelassen.

lake *noun* See *der* (PL *die* Seen); **Lake
Geneva** der Genfer See.

lamb *noun* Lamm *das* (PL *die*
Lämmer); **leg of lamb** *die*
Lammkeule.

lamp *noun* Lampe *die* (PL *die*
Lampen).

lamp-post *noun*
Laternenpfahl *der* (PL *die*
Laternenpfähle).

lampshade *noun*
Lampenschirm *der* (PL *die*
Lampenschirme).

land *noun* 1 (*when at sea*) Land *das*;
2 (*property*) Grundstück *das*; **piece
of land** *das* Grundstück.
verb 1 (*plane, passenger*) landen
(PERF *sein*); 2 (*leave a ship*) an Land
gehen.

landing *noun* 1 (*between flights of
stairs*) Treppenabsatz *der* (PL *die*
Treppenabsätze); (*passage*)
Treppenflur *der*; 2 (*of a plane or
ship*) Landung *die* (PL *die*
Landungen).

landlady *noun* 1 (*of a house or
room*) Vermieterin *die* (PL *die*

Vermieterinnen); 2 (*of a pub*)
Gastwirtin *die* (PL *die*
Gastwirtinnen).

landlord *noun* 1 (*of a house or room*)
Vermieter *der* (PL *die* Vermieter);
2 (*of a pub*) Gastwirt *der* (PL *die*
Gastwirte).

lane *noun* 1 (*small road*) Weg *der*
(PL *die* Wege); 2 (*of a motorway*)
Spur *die* (PL *die* Spuren).

language *noun* 1 (*German, Italian,
etc.*) Sprache *die* (PL *die* Sprachen);
foreign language *die*
Fremdsprache; 2 (*way of speaking*)
Ausdrucksweise *die*; **bad language**
Kraftausdrücke (*plural*).

lap *noun* 1 Schoß *der* (PL *die*
Schöße); 2 (*in races*) Runde *die* (PL
die Runden).

laptop *noun* Laptop *der* (PL *die*
Laptops).

larder *noun* Speisekammer *die* (PL
die Speisekammern).

large *adjective* groß.

last *adjective* letzter/letzte/letztes;
last week letzte Woche; **for the last
time** zum letzten Mal; **last night**
gestern Nacht.
adverb 1 (*in final position*) als
Letzter/als Letzte/als Letztes; **Rob
arrived last** Rob kam als Letzter an;
2 **at last!** endlich!; 3 (*most
recently*) zuletzt; **I last saw him in
May** ich habe ihn zuletzt im Mai
gesehen.
verb dauern; **the film lasted two
hours** der Film dauerte zwei
Stunden.

✧ IRREGULAR VERB: See the verb table in the centre of the dictionary

late *adjective, adverb* **1** spät; **I'm late** ich bin spät dran; **we were five minutes late** wir haben uns fünf Minuten verspätet; **they arrived late** sie sind zu spät angekommen; **to be late for something** zu spät zu etwas ←(DAT) kommen; **we were late for the party** wir kamen zu spät zur Party; **2 to be late** (*of a bus or train*) Verspätung haben; **the train was an hour late** der Zug hatte eine Stunde Verspätung; **3** (*late in the day*) spät; **we got up late** wir sind spät aufgestanden; **the chemist is open late** die Apotheke hat bis spät auf; **late last night** gestern spät in der Nacht; **too late!** zu spät!

lately *adverb* in letzter Zeit.

later *adverb* später; **I'll explain later** ich erkläre es später; **see you later!** bis später!

latest *adjective* **1** neuester/neueste/neuestes; **the latest news** die neuesten Nachrichten; **2 at the latest** spätestens.

Latin *noun* Latein *das*.

laugh *noun* Lachen *das*; **to do something for a laugh** etwas aus Spaß machen.
verb **1** lachen; **everybody laughed** alle haben gelacht; **to laugh about something** über etwas ←(ACC) lachen; **2 to laugh at somebody** jemanden auslachen SEP; **they'll only laugh at me** sie lachen mich bestimmt aus.

launderette *noun* Waschsalon *der* (PL *die* Waschsalons).

lavatory *noun* Toilette *die* (PL *die* Toiletten); **to go to the lavatory** auf die Toilette gehen.

lavender *noun* Lavendel *der*.

law *noun* **1** Gesetz *das* (PL *die* Gesetze); **to break the law** gegen das Gesetz verstoßen; **2 it's against the law** das ist verboten; **3** (*subject of study*) Jura (*plural*).

lawn *noun* Rasen *der* (PL *die* Rasen).

lawnmower *noun* Rasenmäher *der* (PL *die* Rasenmäher).

lawyer *noun* Rechtsanwalt *der* (PL *die* Rechtsanwälte), Rechtsanwältin *die* (PL *die* Rechtsanwältinnen).

lay *verb* **1** (*put*) legen; **she laid the cards on the table** sie legte die Karten auf den Tisch; **2 to lay the table** den Tisch decken.

lay-by *noun* Parkplatz *der* (PL *die* Parkplätze).

layer *noun* Schicht *die* (PL *die* Schichten).

lazy *adjective* faul.

lead¹ *noun* **1** (*when you are ahead*) Führung *die*; **to be in the lead** in Führung liegen; **Baxter's in the lead** Baxter liegt in Führung; **to take the lead** in Führung gehen; **2** (*electric*) Schnur *die* (PL *die* Schnüre); **3** (*for a dog*) Leine *die* (PL *die* Leinen); **on a lead** an der Leine; **4** (*role*) Hauptrolle *die* (PL *die* Hauptrollen); **5** (*an actor*) Hauptdarsteller *der* (PL *die* Hauptdarsteller), Hauptdarstellerin *die* (PL *die* Hauptdarstellerinnen).

△ NEW SPELLING: *See page xii*

verb 1 führen; **the path leads to the sea** der Weg führt zum Meer; **to lead by three points** mit drei Punkten führen; 2 **to lead the way** vorangehen ✧ SEP (PERF *sein*); 3 **to lead to something** zu etwas ←(DAT) führen (*an accident or problems, for example*).

lead² *noun* (*metal*) Blei *das*.

leader *noun* 1 (*of a political party*) Vorsitzende *der/die* (PL *die* Vorsitzenden); 2 (*of an expedition or group*) Leiter *der* (PL *die* Leiter), Leiterin *die* (PL *die* Leiterinnen); 3 (*in a competition*) Erste *der/die* (PL *die* Ersten); 4 (*of a gang*) Anführer *der* (PL *die* Anführer), Anführerin *die* (PL *die* Anführerinnen).

lead singer *noun* Leadsänger *der* (PL *die* Leadsänger), Leadsängerin *die* (PL *die* Leadsängerinnen).

leaf *noun* Blatt *das* (PL *die* Blätter).

leaflet *noun* 1 (*with instructions*) Merkblatt *das* (PL *die* Merkblätter); 2 (*for advertising*) Reklameblatt *das* (PL *die* Reklameblätter).

leak *noun* 1 (*in a roof, tent*) undichte Stelle *die* (PL *die* undichten Stellen); 2 **gas leak** *der* Gasausfluss △; 3 (*in a boat*) Leck *das* (PL *die* Lecks).
verb (*of a bottle or a roof*) undicht sein.

lean *adjective* (*meat*) mager.
verb 1 **to lean on something** sich an etwas ←(ACC) lehnen; **he leaned against the door** er hat sich gegen die Tür gelehnt; 2 sich lehnen; **she was leaning out of the window** sie

lehnte sich aus dem Fenster; 3 **to lean forward** sich vorbeugen SEP.

leap year *noun* Schaltjahr *das* (PL *die* Schaltjahre).

learn *verb* lernen; **to learn German** Deutsch lernen; **to learn (how) to drive** Auto fahren lernen.

learner *noun* 1 Lerner *der* (PL *die* Lerner); **to be a fast learner** schnell lernen; 2 (*beginner*) Anfänger *der* (PL *die* Anfänger), Anfängerin *die* (PL *die* Anfängerinnen).

least *adjective, pronoun*
1 wenigster/wenigste/wenigstes; **to have least time** am wenigsten Zeit haben; **Tony has the least money** Tony hat das wenigste Geld;
2 (*the slightest*) geringster/geringste/geringstes; **I haven't the least idea** ich habe nicht die geringste Ahnung.
adverb 1 am wenigsten; **I like the blue shirt least** ich mag das blaue Hemd am wenigsten; 2 **the least expensive hotel** das billigste Hotel; 3 **at least** (*at a minimum*) mindestens; **at least twenty people** mindestens zwanzig Leute; 4 **at least** (*at any rate*) wenigstens; **she's a teacher, at least I think she is** sie ist Lehrerin, glaube ich wenigstens.

leather *noun* Leder *das*; **leather jacket** *die* Lederjacke.

leave *noun* Urlaub *der*; **three days' leave** drei Tage Urlaub.
verb 1 (*go away*) gehen ✧ (PERF *sein*); (*by car*) fahren ✧ SEP (PERF *sein*); (*a train or bus*) abfahren ✧ SEP

✧ IRREGULAR VERB: *See the verb table in the centre of the dictionary*

(PERF *sein*); **they're leaving tomorrow evening** sie fahren morgen Abend; **we left at six** wir sind um sechs Uhr gegangen; **the train leaves Munich at ten** der Zug fährt um zehn Uhr von München ab; **2** (*go away from or go out of*) verlassen ✧; **I left the office at five** ich habe das Büro um fünf verlassen; **he left his wife** er hat seine Frau verlassen; **3** (*deposit or allow to remain in the same state*) lassen ✧; **you can leave your coats in the hall** Sie können Ihre Mäntel in der Diele lassen; **to leave the door open** die Tür offen lassen; **leave it until tomorrow** lass es bis morgen; **4 to leave somebody something** jemandem etwas hinterlassen ✧ (*a message or money*); **he didn't leave a message** er hat keine Nachricht hinterlassen; **5** (*not do*) stehen lassen ✧ △; **leave the washing up** lass den Abwasch stehen; **6** (*forget*) vergessen ✧; **he left his umbrella on the train** er hat seinen Regenschirm im Zug vergessen; **7 be left** übrig sein (PERF *sein*); **there are two pancakes left** zwei Pfannkuchen sind noch übrig; **I don't have any money left** ich habe kein Geld mehr übrig; **we have ten minutes left** wir haben noch zehn Minuten Zeit.

ecture *noun* **1** (*at university*) Vorlesung *die* (PL *die* Vorlesungen); **2** (*public*) Vortrag *der* (PL *die* Vorträge).

eek *noun* Lauch *der*.

eft *noun* **on the left** links; **to drive on the left** links fahren; **on my left** links von mir.
adverb links; **turn left at the church** an der Kirche links abbiegen.
adjective linker/linke/linkes; **his left foot** sein linker Fuß.

left-hand *adjective* **the left-hand side** die linke Seite.

left-handed *adjective* linkshändig.

leg *noun* **1** Bein *das* (PL *die* Beine); **my left leg** mein linkes Bein; **to break your leg** sich ←(DAT) das Bein brechen; **2** (*in cooking*) Keule *die* (PL *die* Keulen); **leg of lamb** die Lammkeule; ★ **to pull somebody's leg** jemanden auf den Arm nehmen.

leggings *plural noun* Leggings (*plural*).

leisure *noun* Freizeit *die*; **in my leisure time** in meiner Freizeit.

lemon *noun* Zitrone *die* (PL *die* Zitronen).

lemonade *noun* Limonade *die* (PL *die* Limonaden).

lemon juice *noun* Zitronensaft *der* (PL *die* Zitronensäfte).

lend *verb* leihen ✧; **to lend something to somebody** jemandem etwas leihen; **I lent Judy my bike** ich habe Judy mein Rad geliehen; **will you lend it to me?** kannst du es mir leihen?

length *noun* Länge *die* (PL *die* Längen).

lens *noun* **1** (*in a camera*) Objektiv *das* (PL *die* Objektive); **2** (*in spectacles*) Brillenglas *das* (PL *die* Brillengläser); **3 contact lenses** Kontaktlinsen (*plural*).

△ NEW SPELLING: *See page xii*

Lent *noun* Fastenzeit *die*.

lentil *noun* Linse *die* (PL *die* Linsen).

less *pronoun, adjective, adverb*
weniger (*'weniger' never changes*);
Ben eats less Ben isst weniger; **less
time** weniger Zeit; **less than**
weniger als; **less than three hours**
weniger als drei Stunden; **you spent
less than me** du hast weniger als ich
ausgegeben; **less and less** immer
weniger.

lesson *noun* (*class*) Stunde *die* (PL
die Stunden); **German lesson** *die*
Deutschstunde; **driving lesson** *die*
Fahrstunde.

let[1] *verb* 1 (*allow*) lassen ✧; **to let
somebody do something**
jemanden etwas tun lassen; **she lets
me drive her car** sie lässt mich mit
ihrem Auto fahren; **the police let us
through** die Polizei hat uns
durchgelassen; **let me in** lass mich
herein; 2 (*as a suggestion or a
command*) **let's go !** gehen wir !;
let's not talk about it reden wir
nicht mehr darüber; **let's eat out**
essen wir im Restaurant.
● **to let off** 1 hochgehen lassen ✧
(*fireworks*); 2 (*to excuse from*)
befreien von (+DAT) (*homework*).

let[2] *verb* (*to rent out*) vermieten; **'flat
to let'** 'Wohnung zu vermieten'.

letter *noun* 1 Brief *der* (PL *die*
Briefe); **a letter for you from Delia**
ein Brief für dich von Delia; 2 (*of the
alphabet*) Buchstabe *der* (PL *die*
Buchstaben).

letter box *noun* Briefkasten *der* (PL
die Briefkästen).

lettuce *noun* Salat *der*; **two
lettuces** zwei Kopf Salat.

level *noun* Höhe *die*; **at eye level**
in Augenhöhe.
adjective 1 eben (*ground or floor*);
2 (*horizontal*) waagerecht (*shelf*);
3 (*at the same height*) auf gleicher
Höhe; **to be level with the ground**
auf gleicher Höhe mit dem Boden
sein.

level crossing *noun*
Bahnübergang *der* (PL *die*
Bahnübergänge).

lever *noun* Hebel *der* (PL *die* Hebel).

liar *noun* Lügner *der* (PL *die* Lügner),
Lügnerin *die* (PL *die* Lügnerinnen).

liberal *adjective* 1 tolerant; 2 (*in
politics*) liberal; **the Liberal
Democrats** *die* Liberaldemokraten.

Libra *noun* Waage *die*; **Sean's Libra**
Sean ist Waage.

librarian *noun* Bibliothekar *der* (PL
die Bibliothekare), Bibliothekarin
die (PL *die* Bibliothekarinnen).

library *noun* Bibliothek *die* (PL *die*
Bibliotheken); **public library** *die*
öffentliche Bücherei.

licence *noun* 1 (*for a TV*)
Genehmigung *die* (PL *die*
Genehmigungen); 2 (*driving
licence*) Führerschein *der* (PL *die*
Führerscheine).

lick *verb* lecken.

lid *noun* Deckel *der* (PL *die* Deckel).

lie *noun* Lüge *die* (PL *die* Lügen); **to
tell a lie** (or **lies**) lügen ✧.
verb 1 (*to be stretched out*) liegen ✧

✧ IRREGULAR VERB: *See the verb table in the centre of the dictionary*

he's lying on the sofa er liegt auf dem Sofa; **my coat lay on the bed** mein Mantel lag auf dem Bett; **2 to lie down** (*for a rest*) sich hinlegen SEP; **I'm going to lie down for a little** ich lege mich ein bisschen hin; **3** (*tell lies*) lügen ♦.

lie-in *noun* **to have a lie-in** ausschlafen ♦ SEP.

life *noun* Leben *das* (PL die Leben); **all her life** ihr ganzes Leben lang; **full of life** voller Leben; **that's life!** so ist das Leben!

life-style *noun* Lebensstil *der* (PL die Lebensstile).

lift *noun* **1** Aufzug *der* (PL die Aufzüge); **let's take the lift** fahren wir mit dem Aufzug; **2** (*a ride*) **to give somebody a lift to the station** jemanden zum Bahnhof mitnehmen ♦ SEP; **Khaled's giving me a lift** Khaled nimmt mich mit; **would you like a lift?** möchtest du mitfahren?
verb hochheben ♦ SEP; **he lifted the box** er hob die Kiste hoch.

light *noun* **1** Licht *das*; **will you turn the light on?** kannst du das Licht anmachen?; **to turn off the light** das Licht ausmachen; **are your lights on?** hast du Licht an?; **2** (*in the street*) Straßenlampe *die* (PL die Straßenlampen); **3** (*a lamp*) Lampe *die* (PL die Lampen); **4 traffic lights** *die* Ampel (*singular*); **the lights are green** die Ampel ist grün; **5** (*for a cigarette*) **have you got a light?** hast du Feuer?
adjective **1** (*not dark*) hell; **a light blue dress** ein hellblaues Kleid; **it

gets light at six** es wird um sechs hell; **2** (*not heavy*) leicht; **a light coat** ein leichter Mantel; **a light breeze** eine leichte Brise.
verb **1** anzünden SEP (*the fire, a match, the gas*); **we lit a fire** wir zündeten ein Feuer an; **2 to light a cigarette** sich ←(DAT) eine Zigarette anzünden.

light bulb *noun* Glühbirne *die* (PL die Glühbirnen).

lighter *noun* Feuerzeug *das* (PL die Feuerzeuge).

lightning *noun* Blitz *der*; **flash of lightning** *der* Blitz; **to be struck by lightning** vom Blitz getroffen werden.

like[1] *preposition, conjunction* **1** wie; **like me** wie ich; **like a duck** wie eine Ente; **like I said** wie gesagt; **what's it like?** wie ist es?; **what was the weather like?** wie war das Wetter?; **2 like this/that** so; **3** ähnlich (+DAT); **to look like somebody** jemandem ähnlich sehen; **Cindy looks like her father** Cindy sieht ihrem Vater ähnlich.

like[2] *verb* **1** mögen ♦; **I like vegetables** ich mag Gemüse; **I don't like meat** ich mag Fleisch nicht; **I like Dürer best** ich mag Dürer am liebsten; **2 to like doing something** etwas gerne tun; **Mum likes reading** Mutti liest gerne; **3 I would like ...** ich möchte gerne ...; **would you like a coffee?** möchten Sie einen Kaffee?; **what would you like to eat?** was möchten Sie essen?; **yes, if you like** ja, wenn du willst; **4 I like the dress das Kleid gefällt mir; **how do you like it?** wie gefällt es dir?

likely *adjective* wahrscheinlich; **she's likely to phone** wahrscheinlich ruft sie an.

lime *noun* Kalk *der*.

limit *noun* Grenze *die* (PL *die* Grenzen); **speed limit** *die* Geschwindigkeitsbeschränkung.

limp *noun* **to have a limp** hinken.

line *noun* 1 Linie *die* (PL *die* Linien); **a straight line** eine gerade Linie; **to draw a line** eine Linie ziehen; 2 (*in writing*) Zeile *die* (PL *die* Zeilen); **six lines of text** sechs Zeilen Text; 3 (*railway*) Bahnlinie *die* (PL *die* Bahnlinien) (*from one place to another*); **on the line** (*the track*) auf der Strecke; 4 (*a queue of people or cars*) Schlange *die* (PL *die* Schlangen); **to stand in line** Schlange stehen; 5 (*telephone*) Leitung *die* (PL *die* Leitungen); **the line's bad** die Verbindung ist schlecht; **hold the line, please** bitte bleiben Sie am Apparat.
verb füttern (*a coat*).

linen *noun* Leinen *das*; **a linen jacket** eine Leinenjacke.

lining *noun* Futter *das* (PL *die* Futter).

link *noun* Verbindung *die* (PL *die* Verbindungen); **what's the link between the two?** was für eine Verbindung besteht zwischen den beiden?
verb verbinden ✧ (*two places*); **the two towns are linked by a railway line** die beiden Städte sind durch

eine Bahnlinie miteinander verbunden.

lion *noun* Löwe *der* (PL *die* Löwen).

lip *noun* Lippe *die* (PL *die* Lippen).

lip-read *verb* von den Lippen lesen ✧.

lipstick *noun* Lippenstift *der* (PL *die* Lippenstifte).

liquid *noun* Flüssigkeit *die* (PL *die* Flüssigkeiten).
adjective flüssig.

list *noun* Liste *die* (PL *die* Listen).

listen *verb* 1 zuhören SEP; **I wasn't listening** ich habe nicht zugehört; **to listen to somebody** jemandem zuhören; **you're not listening to me** du hörst mir nicht zu; 2 **to listen to something** etwas ←(ACC) hören; **to listen to the radio** Radio hören.

listener *noun* (*to the radio*) Hörer *der* (PL *die* Hörer), Hörerin *die* (PL *die* Hörerinnen).

litre *noun* Liter *der* (PL *die* Liter); **a litre of milk** ein Liter Milch.

litter *noun* (*rubbish*) Abfall *der*.

litter bin *noun* Abfalleimer *der* (PL *die* Abfalleimer).

little *adjective, pronoun* 1 (*small*) klein; **a little boy** ein kleiner Junge; **a little break** eine kleine Pause; 2 (*not much*) wenig; **we have very little time** wir haben sehr wenig Zeit; 3 **a little** ein wenig; **we have a little left** wir haben ein wenig übrig; 4 **just a little, please** nur ein bisschen, bitte; **it's a little late** es ist ein bisschen spät;

✧ IRREGULAR VERB: *See the verb table in the centre of the dictionary*

a little more ein bisschen mehr; **a little less** ein bisschen weniger; ★ **little by little** nach und nach.

ve¹ *verb* **1** (*in a house or town*) wohnen; **she lives in York** sie wohnt in York; **we live in a flat** wir wohnen in einer Wohnung; **2** (*be or stay alive, spend one's life*) leben; **we're living in the country now** wir leben jetzt auf dem Land; **they live on fruit** sie leben von Obst; **they live apart** sie leben getrennt.

ve² *adjective, adverb* **1** live (*broadcast*); **a live programme** eine Livesendung; **live music** die Livemusik; **a broadcast live from Wembley** eine Übertragung live aus Wembley; **to broadcast a concert live** ein Konzert live senden; **2** (*alive*) lebend.

ively *adjective* lebhaft.

iver *noun* Leber *die* (PL *die* Lebern).

iving *noun* Lebensunterhalt *der*; **to earn a living** sich ←(DAT) seinen Lebensunterhalt verdienen.

iving room *noun* Wohnzimmer *das* (PL *die* Wohnzimmer).

oad *noun* **1** (*on a lorry*) Ladung *die* (PL *die* Ladungen); **a (lorry-)load of bricks** eine Ladung Ziegelsteine; **2 a bus-load of tourists** ein Bus voll Touristen; **3 loads of** massenhaft (*informal*); **loads of tourists** massenhaft Touristen; **they've got loads of money** die haben einen Haufen Geld (*informal*). *verb* **1** beladen ✧ (*a vehicle*);

2 to load a camera einen Film einlegen SEP.

loaf *noun* Brot *das* (PL *die* Brote); **a loaf of white bread** ein Weißbrot.

loathe *verb* hassen; **I loathe getting up early** ich hasse es, früh aufzustehen.

local *noun* **1** (*a pub*) Stammkneipe *die* (PL *die* Stammkneipen); **2 the locals** (*people*) die Einheimischen. *adjective* **1** hiesig; **the local library** die hiesige Bücherei; **2 local newspaper** die Lokalzeitung.

lock *noun* Schloss △ *das* (PL *die* Schlösser). *verb* abschließen ✧ SEP (*a door, room, or bicycle*); **have you locked the door?** hast du abgeschlossen?

lodger *noun* Untermieter *der* (PL *die* Untermieter), Untermieterin *die* (PL *die* Untermieterinnen).

loft *noun* Dachboden *der* (PL *die* Dachböden).

log *noun* **1** Baumstamm *der* (PL *die* Baumstämme); **2** (*as firewood*) Holzscheit *das* (PL *die* Holzscheite); **a log fire** ein offenes Feuer.

lollipop *noun* Lutscher *der* (PL *die* Lutscher).

London *noun* London *das*.

Londoner *noun* Londoner *der* (PL *die* Londoner), Londonerin *die* (PL *die* Londonerinnen).

lonely *adjective* einsam; **to feel lonely** sich einsam fühlen.

long *adjective, adverb* **1** lang; **a long film** ein langer Film; **a long day** ein langer Tag; **it's five metres long** es ist fünf Meter lang; **the film is an hour long** der Film dauert eine Stunde; **2 a long time** lange; **he stayed for a long time** er ist lange geblieben; **I've been here for a long time** ich bin schon lange hier; **a long time ago** vor langer Zeit; **this won't take long** das dauert nicht lange; **3 how long?** wie lange?; **how long have you been here?** wie lange sind Sie schon hier?; **long ago** vor langer Zeit; **4 a long way** weit; **it's a long way to the cinema** bis zum Kino ist es weit; **5 all night long** die ganze Nacht; **6 no longer** nicht mehr; **he doesn't work here any longer** er arbeitet nicht mehr hier.
verb **to long to do something** sich danach sehnen, etwas zu tun; **I'm longing to see you** ich sehne mich danach, dich zu sehen.

long jump *noun* Weitsprung *der*.

longlife milk *noun* H-Milch *die*.

loo *noun* Klo *das* (PL *die* Klos) (*informal*).

look *noun* **1** (*a glance*) Blick *der* (PL *die* Blicke); **to take a look at somebody** einen Blick auf jemanden werfen; **2** (*a tour*) **to have a look at the school** sich ←(DAT) die Schule ansehen; **to have a look round the town** sich ←(DAT) die Stadt ansehen; **3 to have a look for** suchen.
verb **1** sehen ✧; **to look out of the window** aus dem Fenster sehen; **I**

wasn't looking ich habe nicht hingesehen; **2 to look at** ansehen ✧ SEP; **he looked at the gir** er hat das Mädchen angesehen; **to look at something** sich ←(DAT) etwas ansehen; **I'm looking at the photos** ich sehe mir die Fotos an; **3** (*to seem*) aussehen ✧ SEP; **she looks sad** sie sieht traurig aus; **the salad looks delicious** der Salat sieht köstlich aus; **to look like** aussehen wie; **what does the hous look like?** wie sieht das Haus aus?; **4** (*resemble*) **to look like somebody** jemandem ähnlich sehen; **she look like her aunt** sie sieht ihrer Tante ähnlich; **they look like each other** sie sehen sich ähnlich.

● **to look after 1** sich kümmern um (+ACC); **Dad's looking after the children** Vati kümmert sich um die Kinder; **2** aufpassen SEP auf (+ACC) (*luggage*).

● **to look for** suchen; **I'm looking for my keys** ich suche meine Schlüssel

● **to look forward to** sich freuen auf (+ACC) (*a party or a trip, for example*).

● **to look out** (*to be careful*) aufpasse SEP; **look out, it's hot!** pass auf, das ist heiß!

● **to look up** nachschlagen ✧ SEP (*in a dictionary or directory*); **he's looking it up in the dictionary** er schlägt es im Wörterbuch nach.

loose *adjective* **1** (*screw or knot*) locker; **2** (*garment*) weit; **3 loose change** *das* Kleingeld; ★ **I'm at a loose end** ich habe nichts zu tun.

lorry *noun* Lastwagen *der* (PL *die* Lastwagen).

✧ **IRREGULAR VERB:** *See the verb table in the centre of the dictionary*

•rry driver *noun*
Lastwagenfahrer *der* (PL *die*
Lastwagenfahrer).

•se *verb* 1 verlieren ✧; **we lost** wir
haben verloren; **we lost the match**
wir haben das Spiel verloren; **Sam's
lost his watch** Sam hat seine Uhr
verloren; 2 **to get lost** sich
verlaufen ✧; **we got lost in the
woods** wir haben uns im Wald
verlaufen; 3 **to lose weight**
abnehmen ✧ SEP.

•ss *noun* Verlust *der* (PL *die*
Verluste).

•st property *noun* Fundsachen
(*plural*).

•ot *noun* 1 **a lot** viel; **Wilbur eats a
lot** Wilbur isst viel; **I spent a lot** ich
habe viel ausgegeben; **he's a lot
better** es geht ihm viel besser; **a lot
of** viel; **a lot of coffee** viel Kaffee;
2 (*many*) **a lot of** viele; **a lot of
books** viele Bücher; 3 **lots of** eine
Menge (*informal*); **lots of people**
eine Menge Leute.

•ottery *noun* Lotterie *die* (PL *die*
Lotterien); **to win the lottery** in der
Lotterie gewinnen.

•oud *adjective* 1 laut; **in a loud voice**
mit lauter Stimme; 2 **to say
something out loud** etwas laut
sagen.

•oudly *adverb* laut.

•oudspeaker *noun*
Lautsprecher *der* (PL *die*
Lautsprecher).

•ounge *noun* 1 (*in a house*)
Wohnzimmer *das* (PL *die*
Wohnzimmer); 2 (*in a hotel or an*
airport) Halle *die* (PL *die* Hallen);
departure lounge *die* Abflughalle.

love *noun* 1 Liebe *die*; **for love** aus
Liebe; 2 **to be in love with
somebody** in jemanden verliebt
sein; **she's in love with Jake** sie ist
in Jake verliebt; 3 **Gina sends her
love** Gina lässt grüßen; **with love
from Charlie** herzliche Grüße von
Charlie; 4 (*in tennis*) null.
verb 1 lieben (*a person*); **I love you**
ich liebe dich; 2 sehr gerne
mögen ✧ (*a place or food*); **she loves
London** sie mag London sehr gerne;
Wayne loves chocolate Wayne mag
Schokolade sehr gerne; 3 **to love
doing something** etwas sehr gerne
tun; **I love dancing** ich tanze sehr
gerne; 4 **I'd love to come** ich würde
sehr gerne kommen.

lovely *adjective* schön; **a lovely
dress** ein schönes Kleid; **we had a
lovely weather** wir hatten schönes
Wetter; **we had a lovely day** es war
sehr schön.

low *adjective* 1 niedrig; **a low table**
ein niedriger Tisch; **at a low price**
zu einem niedrigen Preis; 2 (*not
loud*) leise; **in a low voice** mit leiser
Stimme.

lower *adjective* (*not as high*) tiefer.
verb senken.

luck *noun* 1 Glück *das*; **good luck!**
viel Glück!; **with a bit of luck** wenn
wir Glück haben; 2 **bad luck!** so ein
Pech!

luckily *adverb* zum Glück; **luckily
for them** zu ihrem Glück.

Δ NEW SPELLING: *See page xii*

lucky *adjective* **1 to be lucky** Glück haben; **we were lucky** wir haben Glück gehabt; **2 to be lucky** (*bringing luck*) Glück bringen; **it's supposed to be lucky** es soll Glück bringen; **my lucky number** meine Glückszahl.

luggage *noun* Gepäck *das*; **my luggage is in the boot** mein Gepäck ist im Kofferraum.

lump *noun* **1** Klumpen *der* (PL die Klumpen); **2** (*of sugar or butter*) Stück *das* (PL die Stücke).

lunch *noun* Mittagessen *das* (PL die Mittagessen); **to have lunch** zu Mittag essen; **we had lunch in Oxford** wir haben in Oxford zu Mittag gegessen.

lunch break *noun* Mittagspause *die* (PL die Mittagspausen).

lunch hour, lunch time *noun* Mittagszeit *die*.

lung *noun* Lungenflügel *der*; **lungs** die Lunge (*singular*).

luxurious *adjective* luxuriös.

lyrics *plural noun* Text *der*.

M m

mac *noun* Regenmantel *der* (PL die Regenmäntel).

macaroni *noun* Makkaroni (*plural*).

machine *noun* **1** Maschine *die* (PL die Maschinen); **2** (*a slot machine*) Automat *der* (PL die Automaten).

mackerel *noun* Makrele *die* (PL die Makrelen).

mad *adjective* **1** verrückt; **she's completely mad!** sie ist total verrückt!; **2** (*angry*) wütend; **to be mad at somebody** wütend auf jemanden sein; **3 to be mad about something** ganz verrückt auf etwas ←(ACC) sein; **she's mad about horses** sie ist ganz verrückt auf Pferde.

madman *noun* Verrückte *der* (PL die Verrückten).

madness *noun* Wahnsinn *der*.

magazine *noun* Zeitschrift *die* (PL die Zeitschriften); (*with mostly photos*) Magazin *das* (PL die Magazine).

magic *noun* Zauber *der*; (*conjuring tricks*) Zauberei *die*. *adjective* **1** Zauber-; **magic wand** der Zauberstab; **2** (*great*) super (*informal*).

magician *noun* **1** (*wizard*) Zauberer *der* (PL die Zauberer); **2** (*conjurer*) Zauberkünstler *der* (PL die Zauberkünstler).

magnifying glass *noun* Lupe *die* (PL die Lupen).

maiden name *noun* Mädchenname *der* (PL die Mädchennamen).

mail *noun* Post *die*.

mail order *noun* Bestellung per Post *die*; **to buy something by mail**

order etwas bei einem Versandhaus bestellen; **mail order catalogue** der Versandhauskatalog.

main adjective Haupt-; **main entrance** der Haupteingang.

mainly adverb hauptsächlich.

main road noun Hauptstraße die (PL die Hauptstraßen).

major adjective 1 (important) groß; 2 (serious) schwer; **a major accident** ein schwerer Unfall.

Majorca noun Mallorca das.

majority noun Mehrheit die.

make noun Marke die (PL die Marken); **the make of a car** die Automarke.
verb 1 machen; **to make a meal** Essen machen; **I made breakfast** ich habe Frühstück gemacht; **she made her bed** sie hat ihr Bett gemacht; **to make somebody happy** jemanden glücklich machen; **it makes you tired** das macht einen müde; 2 herstellen SEP; **they make computers** sie stellen Computer her; **'made in Germany'** 'in Deutschland hergestellt'; 3 **he made me wait** er ließ mich warten; **she makes me laugh** sie bringt mich zum Lachen; 4 verdienen; **he makes forty pounds a day** er verdient vierzig Pfund pro Tag; **to make a living** seinen Lebensunterhalt verdienen; 5 (force) zwingen ◇; **to make somebody do something** jemanden zwingen, etwas zu tun; **she made him give the money back** sie hat ihn gezwungen, das

Geld zurückzugeben; 6 (the verb 'make' is often translated by a more specific verb) **to make a cake** einen Kuchen backen; **to make a phone call** telefonieren; **to make a dress** ein Kleid nähen; 7 **to make friends with somebody** sich mit jemandem anfreunden SEP; 8 **I can't make it tonight** ich kann heute Abend nicht kommen; 9 **two and three make five** zwei und drei ist fünf.
• **to make something up** 1 etwas erfinden ◇; **she made up an excuse** sie hat eine Ausrede erfunden; 2 **to make it up** (after a quarrel) sich versöhnen; **they've made it up again** sie haben sich wieder versöhnt.

make-up noun 1 Make-up das; **I don't wear make-up** ich trage kein Make-up; 2 **to put on your make-up** sich schminken; **Jo's putting on her make-up** Jo schminkt sich.

male adjective 1 männlich; **male voice** die Männerstimme; 2 **male animal** das Männchen; **male rat** das Rattenmännchen; 3 **male student** der Student.

male chauvinist noun Chauvi der (PL die Chauvis) (informal).

man noun 1 Mann der (PL die Männer); **an old man** ein alter Mann; 2 (the human race) der Mensch.

manage verb 1 leiten (a business, team); **she manages a travel agency** sie leitet ein Reisebüro; 2 (cope) zurechtkommen ◇ SEP (PERF sein); **I can manage** ich

△ NEW SPELLING: *See page xii*

komme schon zurecht; **3 to manage
to do something** es schaffen, etwas
zu tun; **he managed to push the
door open** er hat es geschafft, die
Tür aufzustoßen; **I didn't manage to
get in touch with her** ich habe es
nicht geschafft, sie zu erreichen.

management noun
1 Management das (PL die
Managements); **management
course** der Managementkurs;
2 Leitung die.

manager noun 1 (of a company or
bank) Direktor der (PL die
Direktoren); 2 (of a shop or
restaurant) Geschäftsführer der (PL
die Geschäftsführer); 3 (in football)
Trainer der (PL die Trainer); 4 (in
entertainment) Manager der (PL die
Manager).

manageress noun (of a shop or
restaurant) Geschäftsführerin die
(PL die Geschäftsführerinnen).

mania noun Manie die (PL die
Manien).

maniac noun Wahnsinnige der/die
(PL die Wahnsinnigen); **she drives
like a maniac** sie fährt wie eine
Wahnsinnige.

man-made adjective **man-made
fibre** die Kunstfaser.

manner noun 1 **in a manner of
speaking** mehr oder weniger;
2 **manners** Manieren (plural); **to
have good manners** gute Manieren
haben; **it's bad manners to talk like
that** es gehört sich nicht, so zu reden.

mantelpiece noun Kaminsims der
(PL die Kaminsimse).

manual noun Handbuch das (PL d
Handbücher).

manufacture verb herstellen SEP.

manufacturer noun
Hersteller der (PL die Hersteller).

many adjective, pronoun 1 viele;
does she have many friends? hat
sie viele Freunde?; **we didn't see
many people** wir haben nicht viele
Leute gesehen; **not many** nicht
viele; **many of them forgot** viele
haben es vergessen; **there were too
many people** es waren zu viele
(Leute) da; **how many?** wie viele?;
how many were there? wie viele
waren da?; **how many sisters have
you got?** wie viele Schwestern hast
du?; **how many are there left?** wie
viele sind übrig geblieben?; **I've
never had so many presents** ich
habe noch nie so viele Geschenke
bekommen; 2 (a lot) **so many** so
viel; **I have so many things to do**
ich habe so viel zu tun; 3 (as much
as) **as many as** so viel wie; **take as
many as you like** nimm so viel wie
du willst; 4 (too much) **that's far too
many** das ist viel zu viel.

map noun 1 Karte die (PL die
Karten); 2 (of a town) Stadtplan (PL
die Stadtpläne).

marathon noun Marathonlauf der
(PL die Marathonläufe).

marble noun 1 Marmor der;
2 (for playing) Murmel die (PL die
Murmeln); **to play marbles**
Murmeln spielen.

March noun März der; **in March** im
März.

◇ IRREGULAR VERB: See the verb table in the centre of the dictionary

larch noun Marsch der (PL Ue Märsche).
verb marschieren (PERF sein).

hare noun Stute die (PL die Stuten).

margarine noun Margarine die.

margin noun Rand der (PL die Ränder).

marijuana noun Marihuana das.

mark noun 1 (at school) Note die (PL die Noten); **I got a good mark in German** ich habe eine gute Note in Deutsch bekommen; 2 (stain) Fleck der (PL die Flecke); 3 (German money) Mark die (PL die Mark).
verb 1 korrigieren; **the teacher marks our homework** die Lehrerin korrigiert unsere Hausaufgaben; 2 (in sports) decken.

market noun Markt der (PL die Märkte).

marketing noun Marketing das.

marmalade noun Orangenmarmelade die.

maroon adjective kastanienbraun.

marriage noun 1 Ehe die; 2 (wedding) Hochzeit die (PL die Hochzeiten).

married adjective 1 verheiratet; **they've been married for twenty years** sie sind seit zwanzig Jahren verheiratet; 2 **married couple** das Ehepaar.

marry verb 1 **to marry somebody** jemanden heiraten; **she married a Frenchman** sie hat einen Franzosen geheiratet; 2 **to get married**

heiraten, **they got married in July** sie haben im Juli geheiratet.

marvellous adjective wunderbar.

marzipan noun Marzipan das.

mascara noun Wimperntusche die.

masculine noun (in German and other grammars) männlich.

mash verb stampfen.

mashed potatoes plural noun Kartoffelbrei der (singular).

mask noun Maske die (PL die Masken).

mass noun 1 **a mass of** eine Menge; 2 **masses of** massenhaft (informal); **they've got masses of money** sie haben massenhaft Geld; **there's masses left over** es ist massenhaft übrig geblieben; 3 (religious) Messe die (PL die Messen); **to go to mass** zur Messe gehen.

massage noun Massage die (PL die Massagen).

massive adjective riesig.

master verb 1 meistern; 2 **to master a language** eine Sprache beherrschen.

mat noun 1 (doormat) Matte die (PL die Matten); 2 (to put under a hot dish) Untersetzer der (PL die Untersetzer); 3 **table mat** das Platzdeckchen.

match noun 1 (for lighting) Streichholz das (PL die Streichhölzer); **box of matches** die Streichholzschachtel; 2 (in sports)

Spiel *das* (PL *die* Spiele); **football match** *das* Fußballspiel; **to watch the match** das Spiel sehen; **to win the match** das Spiel gewinnen; **to lose the match** das Spiel verlieren.
verb passen zu (+DAT); **the jacket matches the skirt** die Jacke passt zu dem Rock.

mate *noun* Freund *der* (PL *die* Freunde); **I'm going to the pub with my mates** ich gehe mit meinen Freunden in die Kneipe.

material *noun* 1 (*fabric, also information*) Stoff *der* (PL *die* Stoffe); 2 (*substance*) Material *das* (PL *die* Materialien).

mathematics *noun* Mathematik *die.*

maths *noun* Mathe *die* (*informal*); **I like maths** ich mag Mathe gerne; **Anna's good at maths** Anna ist gut in Mathe.

matter *noun* **what's the matter?** was ist los?
verb 1 **that's what matters most** das ist am wichtigsten; **it matters a lot to me** es ist mir sehr wichtig; **does it really matter?** ist das wirklich so wichtig?; 2 **it doesn't matter** es macht nichts; **it doesn't matter if it rains** es macht nichts, wenn es regnet; 3 **you can write it in German or English, it doesn't matter** du kannst es auf Deutsch oder Englisch schreiben, das ist egal; 4 **to matter to somebody** jemandem etwas ausmachen SEP; **does it matter to you if I leave earlier?** macht es dir etwas aus, wenn ich früher gehe?

mattress *noun* Matratze *die* (PL *d* Matratzen).

May *noun* Mai *der*; **in May** im Ma

may *verb* 1 **she may be ill** vielleic ist sie krank; **we may go to Spain** wir fahren vielleicht nach Spanien; 2 (*expressing permission*) dürfen ✧ **may I close the door?** darf ich die Tür zumachen?

maybe *adverb* vielleicht; **maybe they've got lost** vielleicht haben s sich verlaufen.

May Day *noun* der Erste Mai.

mayonnaise *noun* Majonäse △ *die*

mayor *noun* Bürgermeister *der* (PL *die* Bürgermeister), Bürgermeisteri *die* (PL *die* Bürgermeisterinnen).

me *pronoun* (*in German this pronou changes according to the function it has in the sentence or the prepositior it follows*) 1 (*as a direct object in th accusative*) mich; **she knows me** sie kennt mich; 2 (*after a preposition that takes the accusative*) mich; **they left without me** sie sind ohne mich abgefahren; **wait for me** warte auf mich!; 3 (*as an indirect object or following a verb that takes the dative*) mir; **can you give me your address?** kannst du mir deine Adresse geben?; **he helped me** er hat mir geholfen; 4 (*after a preposition that takes the dative*) mir; **she never talks to me** sie redet nie mit mir; 5 (*in comparisons*) than me als ich; **she's older than me** sie ist älter als ich; 6 (*in the nominative*) ich; **it's me** ich bin's; **not me** ich nicht.

✧ IRREGULAR VERB: *See the verb table in the centre of the dictionary*

meal *noun* **1** Essen *das* (PL *die* Essen); **to cook a meal** Essen kochen; **2 to go for a meal** essen gehen.

mean *verb* **1** (*signify*) bedeuten; **what does that mean?** was bedeutet das?; **2** (*intend to say*) meinen; **3 what do you mean?** was meinst du?; **that's not what I meant** das habe ich nicht gemeint; **4 to mean to do something** etwas tun wollen; **I meant to phone my mother** ich wollte meine Mutter anrufen; **5 to be meant to do something** etwas tun sollen; **she was meant to be here at six** sie sollte um sechs hier sein. *adjective* **1** (*with money*) geizig; **2** (*unkind*) gemein; **she's really mean to her brother** sie ist richtig gemein zu ihrem Bruder; **what a mean thing to do!** das ist gemein!

meaning *noun* Bedeutung *die* (PL *die* Bedeutungen).

means *noun* **1** Mittel *das* (PL *die* Mittel); **means of transport** *das* Verkehrsmittel; **2 a means of** eine Möglichkeit; **a means of earning money** eine Möglichkeit, Geld zu verdienen; **3 by means of** mit Hilfe (+GEN); **4 by all means!** selbstverständlich!

meantime *adverb* **for the meantime** einstweilen; **in the meantime** in der Zwischenzeit.

measles *noun* Masern (*plural*).

measure *verb* messen ◇.

measurements *plural noun* Maße (*plural*); **the measurements of the room** die Maße des Zimmers; **my measurements** meine Maße.

meat *noun* Fleisch *das*.

mechanic *noun* Mechaniker *der* (PL *die* Mechaniker), Mechanikerin *die* (PL *die* Mechanikerinnen).

mechanical *adjective* mechanisch.

medal *noun* Medaille *die* (PL *die* Medaillen); **the gold medal** die Goldmedaille.

media *noun* **the media** die Medien (*plural*).

medical *noun* **1** ärztliche Untersuchung *die* (PL *die* ärztlichen Untersuchungen); **2 to have a medical** sich untersuchen lassen. *adjective* **1** medizinisch; **2** ärztlich (*examination, treatment*).

medicine *noun* **1** (*drug*) Medikament *das* (PL *die* Medikamente); **2** (*subject of study*) Medizin *die*; **she's studying medicine** sie studiert Medizin; **3 alternative medicine** die Alternativmedizin.

Mediterranean *noun* **the Mediterranean (Sea)** das Mittelmeer.

medium *adjective* mittlerer/mittlere/mittleres.

medium-sized *adjective* mittelgroß.

meet *verb* **1** (*by chance*) treffen ◇; **I met Rosie at the baker's** ich habe Rosie beim Bäcker getroffen; **2** (*by appointment*) sich treffen mit (+DAT); **I'll meet you outside the cinema** ich treffe mich mit dir vor dem Kino; **3** sich treffen; **we're**

meeting at six wir treffen uns um sechs; **4** (*get to know*) kennen lernen△; **I met a German girl last week** ich habe letzte Woche eine Deutsche kennen gelernt; **5 I've never met Oskar** ich kenne Oskar nicht; **6** (*off a train or bus, for example*) abholen SEP; **my dad's meeting me at the station** mein Vater holt mich vom Bahnhof ab.

meeting *noun* **1** (*by arrangement*) Treffen *das* (PL die Treffen); **2** (*in business*) Besprechung *die* (PL die Besprechungen); **she's in a meeting** sie ist in einer Besprechung; **3** (*by chance, in sports*) Begegnung *die* (PL die Begegnungen).

melon *noun* Melone *die* (PL die Melonen).

melt *verb* **1** schmelzen ✧ (PERF *sein*); **the snow has melted** der Schnee ist geschmolzen; **2** (*in cookery*) zerlassen ✧ (*butter, fat*); **melt the butter in a saucepan** Butter im Topf zerlassen.

member *noun* Mitglied *das* (PL die Mitglieder).

Member of Parliament *noun* Abgeordnete *der/die* (PL die Abgeordneten).

membership *noun* Mitgliedschaft *die*.

membership card *noun* Mitgliedskarte *die* (PL die Mitgliedskarten).

membership fee *noun* Mitgliedsbeitrag *der* (PL die Mitgliedsbeiträge).

memorize *verb* **to memorize something** etwas auswendig lernen.

memory *noun* **1** (*of a person*) Gedächtnis *das*; **you have a good memory** du hast ein gutes Gedächtnis; **2** (*of the past*) Erinnerung *die* (PL die Erinnerungen); **I have good memories of our stay in Italy** ich habe schöne Erinnerungen an unseren Urlaub in Italien; **3** (*of a computer*) Speicher *der*.

mend *verb* **1** reparieren; **2** (*by sewing*) ausbessern SEP.

mental *adjective* **1** geistig; **2 mental illness** die Geisteskrankheit; **mental hospital** die psychiatrische Klinik.

mention *verb* erwähnen.

menu *noun* **1** (*in a restaurant*) Speisekarte *die* (PL die Speisekarten); **2** (*in computing*) Menü *das* (PL die Menüs).

meringue *noun* Baiser *das* (PL die Baisers).

merit *noun* **1** Verdienst *das* (PL die Verdienste); **2** (*good feature or advantage*) Vorzug *der* (PL die Vorzüge).

merry *adjective* **1** fröhlich; **Merry Christmas** fröhliche Weihnachten; **2** (*from drinking*) angeheitert.

mess *noun* **1** Durcheinander *das*; **my papers are in a complete mess** meine Unterlagen sind ein einziges Durcheinander; **what a mess!** was für ein Durcheinander!; **2 to make**

✧ IRREGULAR VERB: *See the verb table in the centre of the dictionary*

a mess Unordnung machen; **3 to clear up the mess** aufräumen SEP.

to mess about herumalbern SEP; **stop messing about!** hör auf herumzualbern!

to mess about with something mit etwas ←(DAT) herumspielen SEP; **it's dangerous to mess about with matches** es ist gefährlich, mit Streichhölzern herumzuspielen.

to mess something up 1 etwas durcheinander bringen △ ✧; **you've messed up all my papers** Sie haben meine Unterlagen völlig durcheinander gebracht; **2** (*make dirty*) etwas schmutzig machen; **3** (*botch*) etwas verpfuschen.

message *noun* **1** Nachricht *die* (PL die Nachrichten); **a telephone message** eine telefonische Nachricht; **2 to give somebody a message** jemandem etwas ausrichten SEP.

messy *adjective* **1** (*dirty*) **it's a messy job** das ist ein dreckiger Job; **2 he's a messy eater** er bekleckert sich beim Essen; **3 her writing's really messy** sie hat eine furchtbare Schrift; **4** (*untidy*) **she's very messy** sie ist sehr unordentlich.

metal *noun* Metall *das* (PL die Metalle).

meter *noun* **1** (*electricity, gas, taxi*) Zähler *der* (PL die Zähler); **to read the meter** den Zähler ablesen ✧ SEP; **2 parking meter** *die* Parkuhr.

method *noun* Methode *die* (PL die Methoden).

Methodist *noun* Methodist *der* (PL die Methodisten), Methodistin *die* (PL die Methodistinnen).

metre *noun* Meter *der* (PL die Meter).

metric *adjective* metrisch.

microphone *noun* Mikrofon *das* (PL die Mikrofone).

microscope *noun* Mikroskop *das* (PL die Mikroskope).

microwave (oven) *noun* Mikrowellenherd *der* (PL die Mikrowellenherde).

midday *noun* Mittag *der*; **at midday** mittags.

middle *noun* **1** Mitte *die*; **in the middle of the room** in der Mitte des Zimmers; **in the middle of June** Mitte Juni; **in the middle of the night** mitten in der Nacht; **2 to be in the middle of doing something** gerade dabei sein, etwas zu tun; **when she phoned I was in the middle of washing my hair** als sie anrief, war ich gerade dabei, mir die Haare zu waschen.

middle-aged *adjective* mittleren Alters; **a middle-aged lady** eine Dame mittleren Alters.

middle-class *adjective* der Mittelschicht; **a middle-class family** eine Familie der Mittelschicht.

Middle-East *noun* **the Middle East** der Nahe Osten.

midge *noun* Mücke *die* (PL die Mücken).

midnight *noun* Mitternacht *die*; **at midnight** um Mitternacht.

△ NEW SPELLING: *See page xii*

Midsummer's Day *noun*
Sommersonnenwende *die*.

might *verb* 1 'are you going to
phone him?' – 'I might' 'rufst du
ihn an?' – 'vielleicht'; I might invite
Jo vielleicht lade ich Jo ein; he
might have forgotten vielleicht hat
er es vergessen; 2 she might be
right sie könnte Recht haben.

mike *noun* (*microphone*) Mikro *das*
(PL *die* Mikros) (*informal*).

mild *adjective* mild.

mile *noun* 1 Meile *die* (PL *die* Meilen)
(*Germans use kilometres for
distances; to convert miles to
kilometres, multiply by 8 and divide
by 5*); it's ten miles to Oxford es
sind sechzehn Kilometer bis Oxford;
2 it's miles better das ist viel besser.

milk *noun* Milch *die*; full-cream
milk *die* Vollmilch; skimmed milk
die Magermilch; semi-skimmed
milk *die* fettarme Milch.
verb melken.

milk chocolate *noun*
Milchschokolade *die*.

milkman *noun* Milchmann *der* (PL
die Milchmänner).

milk shake *noun*
Milchmixgetränk *das* (PL *die*
Milchmixgetränke).

millimetre *noun* Millimeter *der* (PL
die Millimeter).

million *noun* Million *die* (PL *die*
Millionen); a million people eine
Million Menschen; two million
people zwei Millionen Menschen.

millionaire *noun* Millionär *der* (PL
die Millionäre), Millionärin *die* (PL
die Millionärinnen).

mince *noun* Hackfleisch *das*.

mind *noun* 1 Sinn *der*; it never
crossed my mind to ask them for
help es kam mir überhaupt nicht in
den Sinn, sie um Hilfe zu bitten;
2 Meinung *die*; to change your
mind seine Meinung ändern; I've
changed my mind ich habe meine
Meinung geändert; 3 to make up
your mind to do something sich
entschließen ✧, etwas zu tun; I can'
make up my mind which dress to
wear ich kann mich nicht
entschließen, welches Kleid ich
anziehe; 4 I've made up my mind
ich habe mich entschieden.
verb 1 aufpassen SEP auf (+ACC); can
you mind my bag for me? können
Sie auf meine Handtasche
aufpassen?; could you mind the
baby for ten minutes? könntest du
zehn Minuten auf das Baby
aufpassen?; 2 do you mind closing
the door? würden Sie bitte die Tür
zumachen?; 3 do you mind if ...?
würde es Ihnen etwas ausmachen SEP
wenn ...?; do you mind if I open the
window? würde es Ihnen etwas
ausmachen, wenn ich das Fenster
aufmache?; I don't mind es macht
mir nichts aus; I don't mind the heat
die Hitze macht mir nichts aus;
4 never mind macht nichts.

mine¹ *noun* Bergwerk *das* (PL *die*
Bergwerke); coal mine *das*
Kohlenbergwerk.

mine² *pronoun* 1 (*for a masculine*

✧ IRREGULAR VERB: *See the verb table in the centre of the dictionary*

noun) mein, she took her coat and I took mine sie hat ihren Mantel genommen und ich habe meinen genommen; **2** (*for a feminine noun*) meine; **she gave me her address and I gave her mine** sie hat mir ihre Adresse gegeben und ich habe ihr meine gegeben; **3** (*for a neuter noun*) meins; **her dress is red and mine is blue** ihr Kleid ist rot und meins ist blau; **4** (*for masculine/feminine/neuter plural nouns*) meine; **she showed me her photos and I showed her mine** sie hat mir ihre Fotos gezeigt und ich habe ihr meine gezeigt; **5 a friend of mine** ein Freund von mir; **it's mine** das gehört mir.

miner *noun* Bergarbeiter *der* (PL *die* Bergarbeiter).

mineral water *noun* Mineralwasser *das*.

minibus *noun* Kleinbus *der* (PL *die* Kleinbusse).

minimum *noun* Minimum *das* (PL *die* Minima); **a minimum of** ein Minimum von.
adjective Mindest-; **the minimum age** das Mindestalter; **minimum wage** *der* Mindestlohn.

miniskirt *noun* Minirock *der* (PL *die* Miniröcke).

minister *noun* **1** (*in government*) Minister *der* (PL *die* Minister), Ministerin *die* (PL *die* Ministerinnen); **2** (*of a church*) Geistliche *der/die* (PL *die* Geistlichen).

ministry *noun* Ministerium *das* (PL *die* Ministerien).

mint *noun* **1** (*herb*) Minze *die* (PL *die* Minzen); **2** (*sweet*) Pfefferminzbonbon *der* (PL *die* Pfefferminzbonbons).

minus *preposition* minus (+GEN); **seven minus three is four** sieben minus drei ist vier; **it was minus ten this morning** es war minus zehn heute Morgen.

minute[1] *noun* **1** Minute *die* (PL *die* Minuten); **I'll be ready in two minutes** ich bin in zwei Minuten fertig; **it's five minutes' walk from here** es ist fünf Minuten zu Fuß von hier; **2** Moment *der*; **just a minute!** einen Moment bitte!; **3 in a minute** gleich.

minute[2] *adjective* winzig; **the bedrooms are minute** die Schlafzimmer sind winzig.

miracle *noun* Wunder *das* (PL *die* Wunder).

mirror *noun* Spiegel *der* (PL *die* Spiegel); **he looked at himself in the mirror** er hat sich im Spiegel betrachtet.

misbehave *verb* sich schlecht benehmen ◇.

miserable *adjective* **1** unglücklich; **he was miserable without her** er war unglücklich ohne sie; **2 I feel really miserable today** ich fühle mich heute richtig elend; **3** mies; **it's miserable weather** das Wetter ist mies; **she gets paid a miserable salary** sie bekommt ein mieses Gehalt.

△ NEW SPELLING: *See page xii*

miss *verb* 1 verpassen; **she missed her train** sie hat ihren Zug verpasst; **I missed the film** ich habe den Film verpasst; **to miss an opportunity** eine Gelegenheit verpassen; 2 nicht treffen ✧; **the stone missed me** der Stein hat mich nicht getroffen; **the ball missed the goal** der Schuss ging am Tor vorbei; **missed!** nicht getroffen!; 3 versäumen; **he's missed his classes** er hat den Unterricht versäumt; 4 vermissen (*a person or thing*); **I miss you** ich vermisse dich; **she's missing her sister** sie vermisst ihre Schwester; **I miss England** ich vermisse England.

Miss *noun* Fräulein *das*; **Miss Jones** Fräulein Jones, Frau Jones (*adult women are usually addressed as 'Frau', whether or not they are married*).

missing *adjective* 1 fehlend; **she's found the missing pieces** sie hat die fehlenden Teile gefunden; **the missing link** das fehlende Glied; 2 **to be missing** fehlen; **there's a plate missing** ein Teller fehlt; **there are three forks missing** drei Gabeln fehlen; 3 **to go missing** verschwinden ✧ (PERF *sein*); **several things have gone missing lately** mehrere Sachen sind kürzlich verschwunden; 4 **three children are missing** drei Kinder werden vermisst.

missionary *noun* Missionar *der* (PL *die* Missionare), Missionarin *die* (PL *die* Missionarinnen).

mist *noun* Nebel *der*.

mistake *noun* 1 Fehler *der* (PL *die* Fehler); **spelling mistake** *der* Rechtschreibfehler; **you've made lots of mistakes** du hast viele Fehler gemacht; 2 **to make a mistake** (*be mistaken*) sich irren; **sorry, I made a mistake** Entschuldigung, ich habe mich geirrt; 3 **by mistake** aus Versehen.
verb **I mistook you for your brother** ich habe dich mit deinem Bruder verwechselt.

mistaken *adjective* **to be mistaken** sich täuschen; **you're mistaken** du täuschst dich.

mistletoe *noun* Mistel *die* (PL *die* Misteln).

misty *adjective* dunstig; **a misty morning** ein dunstiger Morgen.

misunderstand *verb* missverstehen △ ✧; **I misunderstood** ich habe es missverstanden.

misunderstanding *noun* Missverständnis △ *das* (PL *die* Missverständnisse); **there's been a misunderstanding** da liegt ein Missverständnis vor.

mix *noun* Mischung *die* (PL *die* Mischungen); **a good mix** eine gute Mischung; **cake mix** *die* Backmischung.
verb 1 vermischen; **mix the ingredients together** die Zutaten vermischen; **mix the cream into the sauce** die Sahne in die Soße rühren; 2 **to mix with** verkehren mit (+DAT); **she mixes with lots of interesting people** sie verkehrt mit vielen interessanten Leuten.

✧ IRREGULAR VERB: *See the verb table in the centre of the dictionary*

to mix up 1 durcheinander bringen △ ✧; **you've mixed up all the papers** du hast alle Unterlagen durcheinander gebracht; **you've got it all mixed up** du hast alles durcheinander gebracht; 2 (*confuse*) verwechseln; **I get him mixed up with his brother** ich verwechsele ihn mit seinem Bruder.

mixed *adjective* 1 bunt; **a mixed programme** ein buntes Programm; 2 gemischt; **a mixed salad** ein gemischter Salat.

mixture *noun* Mischung *die* (PL *die* Mischungen); **it's a mixture of jazz and rock** es ist eine Mischung aus Jazz und Rock.

moan *verb* (*complain*) jammern; **stop moaning!** hör auf zu jammern!

mobile home *noun* Wohnwagen *der* (PL *die* Wohnwagen).

mobile phone *noun* Mobiltelefon *das* (PL *die* Mobiltelefone), Handy *das* (PL *die* Handys).

mock *noun* (*mock exam*) Übungsprüfung *die* (PL *die* Übungsprüfungen). *verb* sich lustig machen über (+ACC); **stop mocking me** hör auf, dich über mich lustig zu machen.

model *noun* 1 Modell *das* (PL *die* Modelle); **his car is the latest model** sein Auto ist das neueste Modell; **a model of Westminster Abbey** ein Modell von der Westminsterabtei; 2 (*fashion model*) Mannequin *das* (PL *die* Mannequins); **she's a model** sie ist Mannequin.

model aeroplane *noun* Modellflugzeug *das* (PL *die* Modellflugzeuge).

model railway *noun* Minieisenbahn *die* (PL *die* Minieisenbahnen).

modem *noun* Modem *der* (PL *die* Modems).

modern *adjective* modern.

modernize *verb* modernisieren.

modern languages *noun* neuere Sprachen (*plural*).

modest *adjective* bescheiden.

modify *verb* abändern SEP.

moisture *noun* Feuchtigkeit *die*.

moisturizer *noun* Feuchtigkeitscreme *die*.

mole *noun* 1 (*animal*) Maulwurf *der* (PL *die* Maulwürfe); 2 (*on the skin*) Leberfleck *der* (PL *die* Leberflecke).

moment *noun* 1 Moment *der* (PL *die* Momente); **at any moment** jeden Moment; **at the moment** im Moment, im Augenblick; **at the right moment** im richtigen Moment; 2 Augenblick *der* (PL *die* Augenblicke); **wait a moment!** einen Augenblick!; 3 **he'll be ready in a moment** er ist gleich fertig.

monarchy *noun* Monarchie *die*.

Monday *noun* 1 Montag *der*; **on Monday** am Montag; **I'm going to**

△ NEW SPELLING: *See page xii*

see him on Monday ich sehe ihn am Montag; **see you on Monday!** bis Montag!; **every Monday** jeden Montag; **last Monday** letzten Montag; **next Monday** nächsten Montag; **2 on Mondays** montags; **the museum is closed on Mondays** das Museum ist montags geschlossen.

money *noun* Geld *das*; **I don't have enough money** ich habe nicht genug Geld; **to make money** Geld verdienen.

monitor *noun* (*of a computer*) Monitor *der* (PL die Monitoren).

monkey *noun* Affe *der* (PL die Affen).

monotonous *adjective* eintönig.

monster *noun* Ungeheuer *das* (PL die Ungeheuer).

month *noun* Monat *der*; **in the month of May** im Mai; **this month** diesen Monat; **next month** nächsten Monat; **last month** letzten Monat; **for three months** drei Monate lang; **every month** jeden Monat; **every three months** alle drei Monate; **in two months' time** in zwei Monaten; **at the end of the month** am Monatsende.

monthly *adjective* monatlich; **monthly payment** *die* monatliche Zahlung; **monthly ticket** *die* Monatskarte.

monument *noun* Denkmal *das* (PL die Denkmäler).

mood *noun* **1** Laune *die* (PL die Launen); **to be in a good mood**

gute Laune haben; **to be in a bad mood** schlechte Laune haben; **2 I'm not in the mood** ich habe keine Lust dazu; **I'm not in the mood for working** ich habe keine Lust zum Arbeiten.

moon *noun* Mond *der* (PL die Monde); **by the light of the moon** im Mondschein; ★ **to be over the moon** im siebten Himmel sein (*literally: to be in seventh heaven*).

moonlight *noun* Mondschein *der*; **by moonlight** im Mondschein.

moped *noun* Moped *das* (PL die Mopeds).

moral *noun* Moral *die*; **the moral of the story** die Moral der Geschichte. *adjective* moralisch.

morals *noun* Moral *die*.

more *adverb* **1** (*followed by an adjective*) (*in German the ending '-er' is added to the adjective to show the comparative*) **more interesting** interessanter; **the book's more interesting than the film** das Buch ist interessanter als der Film; **more difficult** schwieriger; **more slowly** langsamer; **more easily** einfacher; **books are getting more and more expensive** Bücher werden immer teurer; **2 not any more** (*no longer*) nicht mehr; **she doesn't live here any more** sie wohnt nicht mehr hier. *adjective* **1** mehr (*'mehr' never changes*); **more friends** mehr Freunde; **more ... than** mehr ... als; **they have more money than we do** sie haben mehr Geld als wir; **2 no more** kein; **there's no more milk**

es ist keine Milch mehr da; **3** (*of something you have already*) noch; **would you like some more cake?** möchtest du noch etwas Kuchen?; **a few more glasses** noch ein paar Gläser.

pronoun **1** mehr; **he eats more than me** er isst mehr als ich; **no more, thank you** nichts mehr, danke; **2** (*of something you have already*) noch; **we need three more** wir brauchen noch drei; **any more?** noch etwas?; **3 more and more** immer mehr; **it takes more and more time** es beansprucht immer mehr Zeit; **4 more or less** mehr oder weniger; **it's more or less finished** es ist mehr oder weniger fertig.

morning *noun* **1** Morgen *der* (PL *die* Morgen); **in the morning** am Morgen; **this morning** heute Morgen; **tomorrow morning** morgen früh; **yesterday morning** gestern Morgen; **on Friday morning** am Freitagmorgen; **2 in the morning** (*regularly*) morgens; **she doesn't work in the morning** sie arbeitet morgens nicht; **on Friday mornings** freitagmorgens; **at six o'clock in the morning** um sechs Uhr morgens; **3** (*as opposed to afternoon*) Vormittag *der* (PL *die* Vormittage); **I spent the whole morning waiting for him** ich habe den ganzen Vormittag auf ihn gewartet.

Moscow *noun* Moskau *das*.

Moslem *noun* Moslem *der* (PL *die* Moslems), Moslime *die* (PL *die* Moslimen).

mosque *noun* Moschee *die* (PL *die* Moscheen).

mosquito *noun* Mücke *die* (PL *die* Mücken); **mosquito bite** *der* Mückenstich.

most *adjective, pronoun* **1** (*followed by a plural noun*) die meisten; **most children like chocolate** die meisten Kinder mögen Schokolade; **most of my friends** die meisten von meinen Freunden; **2** (*followed by a singular noun*) der meiste/die meiste/das meiste; **they've eaten most of the ice-cream** sie haben das meiste Eis gegessen; **3 the most** (*followed by a noun or a verb*) am meisten; **I've got the most time** ich habe am meisten Zeit; **4 most of the time** die meiste Zeit; **most of them** die meisten.

adverb **1** (*followed by an adjective*) (*in German the ending '-(e)st' is added to the adjective to show the superlative*) **the most interesting film** der interessanteste Film; **the most exciting story** die spannendste Geschichte; **the most boring book** das langweiligste Buch; **2** am meisten; **the noise bothers me most** der Lärm stört mich am meisten; **3** (*very*) höchst; **it's most unlikely** es ist höchst unwahrscheinlich.

moth *noun* **1** Nachtfalter *der* (PL *die* Nachtfalter); **2** (*clothes moth*) Motte *die* (PL *die* Motten).

mother *noun* Mutter *die* (PL *die* Mütter); **Kate's mother** Kates Mutter.

△ NEW SPELLING: *See page xii*

mother-in-law *noun*
Schwiegermutter *die* (PL *die*
Schwiegermütter).

Mother's Day *noun* Muttertag *der*
(PL *die* Muttertage).

motor *noun* Motor *der* (PL *die*
Motoren).

motorbike *noun* Motorrad *das* (PL
die Motorräder).

motorcyclist *noun*
Motorradfahrer *der* (PL *die*
Motorradfahrer), Motorradfahrerin
die (PL *die* Motorradfahrerinnen).

motorist *noun* Autofahrer *der* (PL
die Autofahrer), Autofahrerin *die* (PL
die Autofahrerinnen).

motor racing *noun*
Autorennen *das*.

motorway *noun* Autobahn *die* (PL
die Autobahnen).

mouldy *adjective* schimmelig.

mountain *noun* Berg *der* (PL *die*
Berge); **in the mountains** in den
Bergen.

mountain bike *noun*
Mountainbike *das* (PL *die*
Mountainbikes).

mountaineer *noun*
Bergsteiger *der* (PL *die* Bergsteiger),
Bergsteigerin *die* (PL *die*
Bergsteigerinnen).

mountaineering *noun*
Bergsteigen *das*; **to go
mountaineering** Bergsteigen gehen.

mountainous *adjective* gebirgig.

mouse *noun* Maus *die* (PL *die*
Mäuse) (*also for a computer*).

moustache *noun* Schnurrbart *der*
(PL *die* Schnurrbärte).

mouth *noun* **1** (*of a person*)
Mund *der* (PL *die* Münder); **2** (*of an
animal*) Maul *das* (PL *die* Mäuler);
3 (*of a river*) Mündung *die* (PL *die*
Mündungen).

mouthful *noun* (*food*) Happen *der*
(PL *die* Happen) (*informal*).

mouth organ *noun*
Mundharmonika *die* (PL *die*
Mundharmonikas); **to play the
mouth organ** Mundharmonika
spielen.

move *noun* **1** (*to a different house*)
Umzug *der* (PL *die* Umzüge); **2** (*in a
game*) Zug *der* (PL *die* Züge); **your
move!** du bist am Zug!
verb **1** sich bewegen; **she didn't
move** sie hat sich nicht bewegt; **2 to
move up** vorrücken SEP (PERF *sein*);
move up a bit rücken Sie etwas vor;
3 wegnehmen ✧ SEP; **can you move
your bag, please?** können Sie Ihre
Handtasche bitte wegnehmen?; **4 to
move something somewhere else**
etwas woandershin stellen; **I've
moved the chest into the cellar** ich
habe die Truhe in den Keller gestellt;
5 (*car*) fahren ✧ (PERF *sein*);
6 (*traffic*) vorwärtskommen ✧ SEP
(PERF *sein*); **7** (*driver*) wegfahren ✧
SEP; **could you move your car,
please?** würden Sie bitte Ihr Auto
wegfahren?; **8 to move forward**
(*person*) vorrücken SEP (PERF *sein*);
(*vehicle*) vorwärts fahren ✧ (PERF
sein); **9** (*move house*) umziehen ✧
SEP (PERF *sein*); **we're moving on
Tuesday** wir ziehen am Dienstag

✧ IRREGULAR VERB: *See the verb table in the centre of the dictionary*

um; **they've moved to London** sie sind nach London umgezogen; **10 to move away** (*live somewhere else*) wegziehen ✧ SEP (PERF *sein*); **11 to move in** einziehen ✧ SEP (PERF *sein*); **she's moving in with friends** sie zieht bei Freunden ein.

movement *noun* Bewegung *die* (PL *die* Bewegungen).

movie *noun* Film *der* (PL *die* Filme); **to go to the movies** ins Kino gehen.

moving *adjective* **1** fahrend; **a moving car** ein fahrendes Auto; **2** (*emotionally*) ergreifend.

mow *verb* mähen.

mower *noun* Rasenmäher *der* (PL *die* Rasenmäher).

MP *noun* Abgeordnete *der/die* (PL *die* Abgeordneten).

Mr *noun* Herr *der*; (*in an address*) **Mr Angus Brown** Herrn Angus Brown; (*in a letter*) **Dear Mr Brown** Sehr geehrter Herr Brown.

Mrs *noun* Frau *die*; **Mrs Mary Hendry** Frau Mary Hendry; (*in a letter*) **Dear Mrs Hendry** Sehr geehrte Frau Hendry.

Ms *noun* Frau *die* (*there is no direct equivalent to 'Ms' in German, but 'Frau' may be used whether the woman is married or not*).

much *adjective, adverb, pronoun* **1** viel; **she doesn't eat much for breakfast** sie isst nicht viel zum Frühstück; **much more** viel mehr; **much quicker** viel schneller; **we**
don't have much time wir haben nicht viel Zeit; **2 not much** nicht viel; **'do you have a lot of work?'** – **'no, not much'** 'hast du viel Arbeit?' – ' nein, nicht viel'; **3 so much** so viel; **I have so much to do** ich habe so viel zu tun; **you shouldn't have given me so much** du hättest mir nicht so viel geben sollen; **4 as much as** so viel; **take as much as you like** nimm so viel du willst; **5 too much** zu viel Δ; **she gets too much money from her parents** sie bekommt zu viel Geld von ihren Eltern; **that's far too much** das ist viel zu viel; **6 how much?** wie viel? Δ; **how much is it?** wie viel kostet es?; **how much do you want?** wie viel möchten Sie?; **how much money do you need?** wie viel Geld brauchst du?; **7** (*greatly*) sehr; **he loved her very much** er hat sie sehr geliebt; **too much** zu sehr; **so much** (so) sehr; **we liked it so much** es hat uns sehr gefallen; **8** (*often*) oft; **I don't watch television much** ich sehe nicht oft fern; **we don't go out much** wir gehen nicht oft aus; **9 thank you very much** vielen Dank.

mud *noun* Schlamm *der*.

muddle *noun* **1** Durcheinander *das*; **2 to be in a muddle** durcheinander sein.

mug *noun* Becher *der* (PL *die* Becher); **a mug of milk** ein Becher Milch. *verb* **to mug somebody** jemanden überfallen ✧; **to be mugged** überfallen werden.

multiplication *noun*
Multiplikation *die*.

multiply *verb* multiplizieren; **six multiplied by four** sechs multipliziert mit vier.

mum, mummy *noun* Mutti *die* (PL die Muttis); **Tom's mum** Toms Mutti; **I'll ask my mum** ich frage die Mutti.

mumps *noun* Mumps *der*.

Munich *noun* München *das*.

murder *noun* Mord *der* (PL die Morde).
verb ermorden.

murderer *noun* Mörder *der* (PL die Mörder), Mörderin *die* (PL die Mörderinnen).

muscle *noun* Muskel *der* (PL die Muskeln).

muscular *adjective* muskulös.

museum *noun* Museum *das* (PL die Museen); **to go to the museum** ins Museum gehen.

mushroom *noun* Pilz *der* (PL die Pilze), Champignon *der* (PL die Champignons); **mushroom salad** *der* Champignonsalat.

music *noun* Musik *die*; **pop music** *die* Popmusik; **classical music** *die* klassische Musik.

musical *noun* Musical *das* (PL die Musicals).
adjective **1** **musical instrument** *das* Musikinstrument; **2** **they're a very musical family** sie sind eine sehr musikalische Familie.

musician *noun* Musiker *der* (PL die Musiker), Musikerin *die* (PL die Musikerinnen).

Muslim *noun* Moslem *der* (PL die Moslems), Moslime *die* (PL die Moslimen).

mussel *noun* Muschel *die* (PL die Muscheln).

must *verb* **1** müssen ✧; **we must leave now** wir müssen jetzt gehen; **you must learn the vocabulary** du musst die Vokabeln lernen; **2** (*with a negative*) dürfen ✧; **you mustn't do that** das darfst du nicht tun; **3** (*expressing probability*) müssen ✧; **you must be tired** ihr müsst müde sein; **it must be five o'clock** es muss fünf Uhr sein; **he must have forgotten** er muss es vergessen haben.

mustard *noun* Senf *der* (PL die Senfe).

mutter *verb* murmeln.

my *adjective* **1** (*before a masculine noun*) mein; **my brother** mein Bruder; **they don't like my dog** sie mögen meinen Hund nicht; **2** (*before a feminine noun*) meine; **my sister** meine Schwester; **3** (*before a neuter noun*) mein; **that's my new car** das ist mein neues Auto; **we can go in my car** wir können mit meinem Auto fahren; **4** (*before masculine/feminine/neuter plural nouns*) meine; **my children** meine Kinder; **5** (*with parts of the body*) der/die/das (*plural:* die); **I had a glass in my hand** ich hatte ein Glas in der Hand; **I'm washing my hands** ich wasche mir die Hände.

✧ IRREGULAR VERB: *See the verb table in the centre of the dictionary*

myself *pronoun* **1** (*reflexive and after a preposition taking the accusative*) mich; **I've cut myself** ich habe mich geschnitten; **I've addressed the letter to myself** ich habe den Brief an mich adressiert; **2** (*reflexive and after a preposition taking the dative*) mir; **I've hurt myself** ich habe mir wehgetan; **I said to myself** ich habe mir gesagt; **3** (*stressing something*) selbst; **I said it myself** ich habe es selbst gesagt; **4 by myself** allein.

mysterious *adjective* rätselhaft.

mystery *noun* **1** Rätsel *das* (PL die Rätsel); **2** (*book*) Krimi *der* (PL die Krimis) (*informal*).

mythology *noun* Mythologie *die* (PL die Mythologien).

N n

nail *noun* (*on your finger or toe, also metal*) Nagel *der* (PL die Nägel). *verb* nageln.

nailbrush *noun* Nagelbürste *die* (PL die Nagelbürsten).

nailfile *noun* Nagelfeile *die* (PL die Nagelfeilen).

nail polish *noun* Nagellack *der*.

nail polish remover *noun* Nagellackentferner *der*.

name *noun* **1** Name *der* (PL die Namen); **I've forgotten her name** ich habe ihren Namen vergessen;

what's your name? wie heißt du?; **my name's Joy** ich heiße Joy; **2** (*of a book or film*) Titel *der* (PL die Titel).

napkin *noun* Serviette *die* (PL die Servietten).

nappy *noun* Windel *die* (PL die Windeln).

narrow *adjective* schmal; **a narrow street** eine schmale Straße.

nasty *adjective* **1** (*mean*) gemein; **that was a nasty thing to do** das war gemein; **2** (*unpleasant, bad*) scheußlich; **that's a nasty job** das ist eine scheußliche Arbeit; **a nasty smell** ein scheußlicher Geruch.

nation *noun* Nation *die* (PL die Nationen).

national *adjective* national.

national anthem *noun* Nationalhymne *die* (PL die Nationalhymnen).

nationality *noun* Nationalität *die* (PL die Nationalitäten).

national park *noun* Nationalpark *der* (PL die Nationalparks).

natural *adjective* natürlich.

naturally *adverb* natürlich.

nature *noun* Natur *die*.

nature reserve *noun* Naturschutzgebiet *das* (PL die Naturschutzgebiete).

naughty *adjective* unartig.

△ NEW SPELLING: *See page xii*

navy *noun* Marine *die*; **my uncle's in the navy** mein Onkel ist bei der Marine.

navy-blue *adjective* marineblau.

near *adjective* 1 nah(e); 2 (*the superlative of nah(e) is der/die/das nächste*) **the nearest park** der nächste Park; **the nearest bank** die nächste Bank; **the nearest shop** das nächste Geschäft.
preposition nahe an (+DAT); **near (to) the station** nahe am Bahnhof.
adverb 1 nah(e) (*in spoken German 'nah' is more common*); **they live quite near** sie wohnen ganz nah; 2 **to come nearer** näher kommen.

nearly *adverb* fast; **nearly empty** fast leer.

neat *adjective* 1 (*well organized, tidy*) ordentlich; **a neat room** ein ordentliches Zimmer; 2 adrett (*clothes or the way you look*).

necessarily *adverb* **not necessarily** nicht unbedingt.

necessary *adjective* nötig; **if necessary** falls nötig.

neck *noun* 1 (*of a person*) Hals *der* (PL *die* Hälse); 2 (*of a garment*) Kragen *der* (PL *die* Kragen).

necklace *noun* Halskette *die* (PL *die* Halsketten).

need *noun* **there's no need, I've already done it** das ist nicht nötig, ich habe es schon gemacht; **there's no need to wait** du brauchst nicht zu warten.
verb 1 brauchen; **we need bread** wir brauchen Brot; **everything you need** alles, was man braucht; 2 (*to have to*) müssen ◇; **I need to go to the bank** ich muss zur Bank gehen; 3 (*with a negative*) **you needn't wait** du brauchst nicht zu warten.

needle *noun* Nadel *die* (PL *die* Nadeln).

negative *noun* (*of a photo*) Negativ *das* (PL *die* Negative).

neighbour *noun* Nachbar *der* (PL *die* Nachbarn), Nachbarin *die* (PL *die* Nachbarinnen); **we're going round to the neighbours'** wir besuchen die Nachbarn.

neighbourhood *noun* Nachbarschaft *die*; **in our neighbourhood** in unserer Nachbarschaft.

neither *conjunction* 1 **neither ... nor** weder ... noch; **I have neither the time nor the money** ich habe weder die Zeit noch das Geld; 2 **neither do I** ich auch nicht; **'I don't like fish' – 'neither do I'** 'ich mag keinen Fisch' – 'ich auch nicht'; **'I didn't like the film' – 'neither did Kirsty'** 'mir hat der Film nicht gefallen' – 'Kirsty hat er auch nicht gefallen'.
pronoun keiner von beiden/keine von beiden/keins von beiden; **'which do you like?' – 'neither'** 'welches gefällt dir?' – 'keins von beiden'.

nephew *noun* Neffe *der* (PL *die* Neffen).

nerve *noun* Nerv *der* (PL *die* Nerven); 1 **to lose your nerve** die Nerven verlieren; **you've got a nerve!** du hast Nerven! (*informal*);

2 what a nerve! so eine Frechheit!; ★ **he gets on my nerves** er geht mir auf die Nerven (*informal*).

nervous *adjective* **1** (*afraid*) ängstlich; **to feel nervous about something** Angst vor etwas ←(DAT) haben; **2** (*highly strung*) nervös (*person*).

net *noun* Netz *das* (PL die Netze).

Netherlands *noun* Niederlande (*plural*); **in the Netherlands** in den Niederlanden.

nettle *noun* Nessel *die* (PL die Nesseln).

neutral *noun* (*neutral gear*) Leerlauf *der*; **to be in neutral** im Leerlauf sein.
adjective neutral.

never *adverb* **1** nie; **Ben never smokes** Ben raucht nie; **I've never told him** ich habe es ihm nie gesagt; **never again** nie wieder; **2** noch nie; **'have you ever been to Spain?' – 'no, never'** 'warst du schon mal in Spanien?' – 'nein, noch nie'; **3 never mind** macht nichts.

new *adjective* neu; **have you seen their new house?** hast du ihr neues Haus gesehen?

news *noun* **1** (*new information*) Nachricht *die* (PL die Nachrichten); **I've got good news** ich habe gute Nachrichten; **2 a piece of news** eine Neuigkeit; **any news?** was gibt es Neues?; **3** (*on TV or the radio*) Nachrichten (*plural*); **we saw it on the news** wir haben es in den Nachrichten gesehen.

newsagent *noun* Zeitungshändler *der* (PL die Zeitungshändler).

newspaper *noun* Zeitung *die* (PL die Zeitungen).

newsreader *noun* Nachrichtensprecher *der* (PL die Nachrichtensprecher), Nachrichtensprecherin *die* (PL die Nachrichtensprecherinnen).

New Year *noun* Neujahr *das*; **Happy New Year!** ein gutes neues Jahr!

New Year's Day *noun* Neujahr *das*.

New Year's Eve *noun* Silvester *der*.

New Zealand *noun* Neuseeland *das*.

next *adjective* **1** nächster/nächste/nächstes; **the next train leaves at ten** der nächste Zug fährt um zehn ab; **next week** nächste Woche; **next Thursday** nächsten Donnerstag; **next year** nächstes Jahr; **next time I see you** nächstes Mal, wenn ich dich sehe; **2** (*following*) **next please!** der Nächste bitte/die Nächste bitte; **the next thing** das Nächste; **the next day** am nächsten Tag; **the letter arrived the next day** der Brief kam am nächsten Tag an; **3 the week after next** übernächste Woche; **4** (*next-door*) nebenan; **I'm in the next room** ich bin nebenan.
adverb **1** (*afterwards*) danach; **what did he say next?** was hat er danach gesagt?; **2** (*now*) als Nächstes; **what**

shall we do next? was machen wir als Nächstes?; **3 next to** neben (+DAT, *or* +ACC *with movement towards a place*); **the house next to the baker's** das Haus neben dem Bäcker's; **I sat down next to her** ich habe mich neben sie gesetzt.

next door *adverb* nebenan; **they live next door** sie wohnen nebenan; **the girl next door** das Mädchen von nebenan.

nice *adjective* **1** (*pleasant*) schön; **we had a nice evening** wir haben einen schönen Abend verbracht; **Brighton's a nice town** Brighton ist eine schöne Stadt; **we had nice weather** wir hatten schönes Wetter; **2 to have a nice time** sich amüsieren; **have a nice day!** viel Spaß!; **3** (*attractive to look at*) hübsch; **that's a nice dress** das ist ein hübsches Kleid; **4** (*kind, friendly*) nett (*person*); **she's really nice** sie ist wirklich nett; **5 to be nice to somebody** nett zu jemandem sein; **she's been very nice to me** sie war sehr nett zu mir; **6** (*tasting good*) gut; **it tastes nice** es schmeckt gut.

niece *noun* Nichte *die* (PL *die* Nichten).

night *noun* **1** (*after bedtime*) Nacht *die* (PL *die* Nächte); **during the night** während der Nacht; **Sunday night** Sonntag Nacht; **it's cold at night** nachts ist es kalt; **to stay the night** über Nacht bleiben; **I stayed the night at Emma's** ich habe bei Emma übernachtet; **2** (*before you go to bed*) Abend *der*

(PL *die* Abende); **what are you doing tonight?** was macht ihr heute Abend?; **one night** eines Abends; **tomorrow night** morgen Abend; **I met Greg last night** ich habe Greg gestern Abend getroffen; **on Friday night** am Freitagabend; **see you tonight!** bis heute Abend!

night club *noun* Nachtklub *der* (PL *die* Nachtklubs).

nightie *noun* Nachthemd *das* (PL *die* Nachthemden).

nightmare *noun* Alptraum *der* (PL *die* Alpträume).

nil *noun* (*in sport*) null; **they won four-nil** sie haben vier zu null gewonnen.

nine *number* neun.

nineteen *number* neunzehn.

ninety *number* neunzig.

ninth *number* neunter/neunte/neuntes; **on the ninth floor** im neunten Stock; **on the ninth of June** am neunten Juni.

no *adverb* nein; **I said no** ich habe nein gesagt; **no thank you** nein danke.
adjective **1** kein; **we've got no bread** wir haben kein Brot; **no problem!** kein Problem!; **2** (*on a notice*) **'no smoking'** 'Rauchen verboten'; **'no parking'** 'Parken verboten'.

nobody *pronoun* niemand; **'who's there?' – 'nobody'** 'wer ist da?' – 'niemand'; **there's nobody in the kitchen** es ist niemand in der

Küche; **nobody was at home**
niemand war zu Hause.

nod *verb* nicken; **he nodded in
agreement** er hat zustimmend
genickt.

noise *noun* Lärm *der*; **to make a
noise** Lärm machen.

noisy *adjective* laut.

none *pronoun* 1 (*not one*)
keiner/keine/keins; **none of us**
keiner von uns/ keine von uns; **'how
many students failed the exam?'** –
'none' 'wie viele Schüler sind durch
die Prüfung gefallen?' – 'keine';
none of the boys knows him keiner
der Jungen kennt ihn; 2 **there's
none left** es ist nichts mehr übrig.

nonsense *noun* Unsinn *der*; **to talk
nonsense** Unsinn reden;
nonsense! Unsinn!

non-stop *adjective* durchgehend
(*train*); Nonstop- (*flight*).
adverb ununterbrochen;
she talks non-stop sie redet
ununterbrochen.

noon *noun* Mittag *der*; **at (twelve)
noon** um zwölf (Uhr mittags).

no-one *pronoun* niemand; **'who's
there?'** – **'no-one'** 'wer ist da?' –
'niemand'; **there's no-one in the
kitchen** es ist niemand in der
Küche; **no-one was at home**
niemand war zu Hause.

nor *conjunction* 1 **neither ... nor**
weder ... noch; **I have neither the
time nor the money** ich habe weder
die Zeit noch das Geld; 2 **nor do I**
ich auch nicht; **'I don't like fish'** –

'nor do I' 'ich mag keinen Fisch' –
'ich auch nicht'; **nor do we** wir
auch nicht.

normal *adjective* normal.

normally *adverb* 1 (*usually*)
normalerweise; 2 (*in a normal way*)
normal.

north *noun* Norden *der*; **in the
north** im Norden.
adjective nördlich, Nord-; **the north
side** die Nordseite; **north wind** *der*
Nordwind.
adverb 1 (*towards the north*) nach
Norden; **to travel north** nach
Norden fahren; 2 **north of London**
nördlich von London.

North America *noun*
Nordamerika *das*.

northeast *noun* Nordosten *der*.
adjective **in northeast England** in
Nordostengland.

Northern Ireland *noun*
Nordirland *das*.

North Pole *noun* Nordpol *der*.

North Sea *noun* **the North Sea** die
Nordsee.

northwest *noun* Nordwesten *der*.
adjective **in northwest England** in
Nordwestengland.

Norway *noun* Norwegen *das*.

Norwegian *noun* 1 (*person*)
Norweger *der* (PL *die* Norweger),
Norwegerin *die* (PL *die*
Norwegerinnen); 2 (*language*)
Norwegisch *das*.
adjective norwegisch.

nose *noun* Nase *die* (PL *die* Nasen);
to blow your nose sich ←(DAT) die
Nase putzen.

not *adverb* 1 nicht; **not on Sundays**
sonntags nicht; **not all alone!** nicht
ganz allein!; **not bad** nicht schlecht;
not at all überhaupt nicht; **not yet**
noch nicht; **Sam didn't phone** Sam
hat nicht angerufen; **I hope not**
hoffentlich nicht; **2 not a**
kein/keine; **he's not a specialist** er
ist kein Fachmann; **not a bit** kein
bisschen.

note *noun* 1 (*a short letter*)
Zettel *der* (PL *die* Zettel) (*informal*),
Brief *der* (PL *die* Briefe); 2 (*in a class*)
Notiz *die* (PL *die* Notizen); **to take
notes** sich ←(DAT) Notizen machen;
3 (*a banknote*) Schein *der* (PL *die*
Scheine); **a ten-pound note** ein
Zehnpfundschein; 4 (*in music*)
Note *die* (PL *die* Noten).

notebook *noun* Notizbuch *das* (PL
die Notizbücher).

notepad *noun* Notizblock *der* (PL
die Notizblöcke).

nothing *pronoun* nichts; **'what did
you say?' – 'nothing'** 'was hast du
gesagt?' – 'nichts'; **nothing special**
nichts Besonderes; **nothing new**
nichts Neues; **I saw nothing** ich
habe nichts gesehen; **there's nothing
left** es ist nichts mehr übrig.

notice *noun* 1 (*a sign*) Anschlag *der*
(PL *die* Anschläge); 2 (*an
advertisement*) Anzeige *die* (PL *die*
Anzeigen); 3 (*advance warning*)
Ankündigung *die*; 4 **don't take any**

notice of her nimm keine Notiz von
ihr; 5 **at short notice** kurzfristig.
verb bemerken; **I didn't notice
anything** ich habe nichts bemerkt.

notice board *noun*
Anschlagbrett *das* (PL *die*
Anschlagbretter).

nought *noun* Null *die* (PL *die*
Nullen).

noun *noun* Substantiv *das* (PL *die*
Substantive).

novel *noun* Roman *der* (PL *die*
Romane).

novelist *noun* Romanautor *der* (PL
die Romanautoren), Romanautorin
die (PL *die* Romanautorinnen).

November *noun* November *der*; **in
November** im November.

now *adverb* 1 jetzt; **where is he
now?** wo ist er jetzt?; **from now on**
von jetzt an; 2 **he left just now** er
ist gerade eben gegangen; **I saw her
just now in the corridor** ich habe
sie gerade eben im Gang gesehen;
3 **do it right now!** mach es sofort!;
4 **now and then** hin und wieder.

nowhere *adjective* nirgends;
there's nowhere to park man kann
nirgends parken.

nuclear *adjective* Kern-; **nuclear
power** *die* Kernenergie; **nuclear
power station** *das* Kernkraftwerk.

nude *noun* **in the nude** nackt.
adjective nackt.

nuisance *noun* **it's a nuisance** das
ist ärgerlich; **what a nuisance!** wie
ärgerlich!

✧ IRREGULAR VERB: *See the verb table in the centre of the dictionary*

numb *adjective* 1 (*with cold*) gefühllos; 2 (*emotionally*) benommen.

number *noun* 1 (*of a house, telephone, or account*) Nummer *die* (PL *die* Nummern); **I live at number five** ich wohne Nummer fünf; **my new phone number** meine neue Telefonnummer; 2 (*a written figure*) Zahl *die* (PL *die* Zahlen); 3 (*amount*) Anzahl *die*; **the number of visitors** die Anzahl der Besucher.

number plate *noun* Nummernschild *das* (PL *die* Nummernschilder).

nun *noun* Nonne *die* (PL *die* Nonnen).

nurse *noun* Krankenschwester *die* (PL *die* Krankenschwestern); **Janet's a nurse** Janet ist Krankenschwester.

nursery *noun* 1 (*for children*) Kindertagesstätte *die* (PL *die* Kindertagesstätten); 2 (*for plants*) Gärtnerei *die* (PL *die* Gärtnereien).

nursery school *noun* Kindergarten *der* (PL *die* Kindergärten).

nut *noun* 1 Nuss ∆ *die* (PL *die* Nüsse); 2 (*for a bolt*) Mutter *die* (PL *die* Muttern).

nylon *noun* Nylon *das*.

O o

oak *noun* Eiche *die* (PL *die* Eichen).

oar *noun* Ruder *das* (PL *die* Ruder).

oats *noun* Hafer *der*; **porridge oats** Haferflocken (*plural*).

obedient *adjective* gehorsam.

obey *verb* 1 gehorchen (+DAT); **to obey somebody** jemandem gehorchen; 2 **to obey the rules** sich an die Vorschriften halten ✧.

object *noun* 1 (*thing*) Gegenstand *der* (PL *die* Gegenstände); 2 (*aim*) Zweck *der*; 3 (*in grammar*) Objekt *das* (PL *die* Objekte). *verb* etwas dagegen haben ✧; **if you don't object** wenn Sie nichts dagegen haben.

objection *noun* Einwand *der* (PL *die* Einwände).

observe *verb* beobachten.

obsessed *adjective* besessen; **she's really obsessed with her diet** sie ist von ihrer Schlankheitskur ganz besessen.

obstinate *adjective* starrsinnig.

obtain *verb* erhalten ✧.

obvious *adjective* eindeutig.

obviously *adverb* 1 (*of course*) natürlich; 2 (*looking at something*) offensichtlich; **the house is**

obviously empty das Haus steht offensichtlich leer.

occasion *noun* Gelegenheit *die* (PL *die* Gelegenheiten); **on special occasions** zu besonderen Gelegenheiten.

occasionally *adverb* gelegentlich.

occupation *noun* Beruf *der* (PL *die* Berufe).

occupied *adjective* 1 (*taken*) besetzt; **the seat is occupied** der Platz ist besetzt; 2 (*lived in*) bewohnt.

occur *verb* 1 **to occur to somebody** jemandem einfallen ✧SEP (PERF *sein*); **it occurs to me that …** mir fällt ein, dass …; 2 **it never occurred to me** darauf wäre ich nie gekommen; 3 (*happen*) sich ereignen.

ocean *noun* Ozean *der* (PL *die* Ozeane).

o'clock *adverb* **at ten o'clock** um zehn Uhr; **it's three o'clock** es ist drei Uhr.

October *noun* Oktober *der*; **in October** im Oktober.

odd *adjective* 1 (*strange*) komisch; **that's odd, I'm sure I heard the bell** das ist komisch, ich habe es bestimmt klingeln gehört; 2 (*number*) ungerade; **three is an odd number** drei ist eine ungerade Zahl; 3 **the odd one out** die Ausnahme.

odds and ends *plural noun* Kleinkram *der*.

of *preposition* 1 von (+DAT); (*instead of translating 'of' with 'von', the*

genitive case can be used) **the parents of the children** die Eltern von den Kindern, die Eltern der Kinder; **the name of the flower** der Name der Blume; **it's very kind of you** das ist sehr nett von Ihnen; 2 (*with quantities 'of' is not translated*) **a kilo of tomatoes** ein Kilo Tomaten; **a bottle of milk** eine Flasche Milch; **the three of us** wir drei; 3 **of it/them** davon (*things*); **of them** von ihnen (*people*); **how many of them didn't pay?** wie viele von ihnen haben nicht gezahlt?; **Ray has four cars but he's selling three of them** Ray hat vier Autos, aber er verkauft drei davon; **half of it** die Hälfte davon; **we ate a lot of it** wir haben viel davon gegessen; 4 **the sixth of June** der sechste Juni; 5 **made of** aus; **a bracelet made of silver** ein Armband aus Silber.

off *adverb, adjective, preposition* 1 (*switched off*) aus; **is the telly off?** ist der Fernseher aus?; **to turn off the lights** das Licht ausmachen SEP; 2 (*electricity, water, gas*) abgestellt; **the gas and electricity were off** Gas und Strom waren abgestellt; **to turn off the tap** den Wasserhahn zudrehen SEP; 3 **to be off** (*to leave*) gehen ✧ (PERF *sein*); (*in a vehicle*) fahren ✧ (PERF *sein*); **I must be off** ich muss gehen; 4 **on my day off** an meinem freien Tag; **to take three days off work** sich ←(DAT) drei Tage frei nehmen; **we were given two days off school** wir hatten zwei Tage schulfrei; **to be off sick** wegen Krankheit fehlen; **Maya's off school today** Maya fehlt heute in der

Schule; **5** (*cancelled*) abgesagt; **the match is off** das Spiel ist abgesagt worden; **6 '20% off shoes'** 'Schuhe 20% reduziert'.

offence *noun* **1** (*crime*) Straftat *die* (PL *die* Straftaten); **2 to take offence** beleidigt sein; **he takes offence easily** er ist schnell beleidigt.

offer *noun* **1** Angebot *das* (PL *die* Angebote); **job offer** *das* Stellenangebot; **2 on special offer** im Sonderangebot.
verb anbieten ◇ SEP (*a present, a reward, or a job*); **he offered her a chair** er bot ihr einen Stuhl an; **to offer to do something** anbieten, etwas zu tun; **he offered to drive me to the station** er hat angeboten, mich zum Bahnhof zu fahren.

office *noun* Büro *das* (PL *die* Büros); **he's still at the office** er ist noch im Büro.

office block *noun* Bürohaus *das* (PL *die* Bürohäuser).

official *adjective* offiziell.

off-licence *noun* Wein- und Spirituosenhandlung *die* (PL *die* Wein- und Spirituosenhandlungen).

often *adverb* **1** oft; **he's often late** er kommt oft zu spät; **how often?** wie oft?; **2 more often** öfter; **couldn't you come more often?** könntest du nicht öfter kommen?

oil *noun* **1** (*crude oil*) Öl *das*; **2 olive oil** *das* Olivenöl; **suntan oil** *das* Sonnenöl.

ointment *noun* Salbe *die* (PL *die* Salben).

okay *adjective* **1** okay (*informal*); **tomorrow at ten, okay?** morgen um zehn, okay?; **is it okay if I don't come till Friday?** ist es okay, wenn ich erst Freitag komme?; **2** (*person*) in Ordnung; **Daisy's okay** Daisy ist in Ordnung; **3** (*nothing special, not ill*) ganz gut; **the film was okay** der Film war ganz gut; **I've been ill but I'm okay now** ich war krank, aber jetzt geht es mir ganz gut; **'how are you?' – 'okay'** 'wie geht's?' – 'ganz gut'; **4 it's okay by me** mir ist es recht.

old *adjective* **1** (*not young, not new, previous*) alt; **an old man** ein alter Mann; **an old lady** eine alte Dame; **an old tree** ein alter Baum; **old people** alte Leute; **bring some old clothes** bring ein paar alte Sachen mit; **I've only got their old address** ich habe nur ihre alte Adresse; **2** (*talking about age*) **how old are you?** wie alt bist du?; **James is ten years old** James ist zehn Jahre alt; **3 a two-year-old child** ein zweijähriges Kind; **4 my older sister** meine ältere Schwester; **she's older than me** sie ist älter als ich; **he's a year older than me** er ist ein Jahr älter als ich.

old age *noun* Alter *das*.

old age pensioner *noun* Rentner *der* (PL *die* Rentner), Rentnerin *die* (PL *die* Rentnerinnen).

old-fashioned *noun* altmodisch.

olive *noun* Olive *die* (PL *die* Oliven).

△ NEW SPELLING: *See page xii*

olive oil noun Olivenöl das (PL die Olivenöle).

Olympic Games, Olympics plural noun Olympische Spiele (plural).

omelette noun Omelett das (PL die Omelette); **a cheese omelette** ein Käseomelett.

on preposition 1 auf (+DAT, or +ACC with movement towards a place); **it's on the desk** es ist auf dem Schreibtisch; 2 (attached to) an (+DAT, or +ACC with movement towards a place); **on the wall** an der Wand; 3 **on the beach** am Strand; **on the right/left** rechts/links; 4 (in expressions of time) **on March 21st** am 21. März; **he's arriving on Tuesday** er kommt am Dienstag an; **it's shut on Sundays** es ist sonntags geschlossen; **on rainy days** an Regentagen; 5 (for buses, trains, etc.) **to go on the bus** mit dem Bus fahren; **I met Jackie on the train** ich habe Jackie im Zug getroffen; **let's go on our bikes** fahren wir mit dem Rad; 6 **on TV** im Fernsehen; **on the radio** im Radio; **on video** auf Video; 7 **on holiday** in den Ferien. adjective 1 (switched on) **to be on** an sein; **the lights are on** das Licht ist an; **is the radio on?** ist das Radio an?; 2 (happening) **what's on TV?** was gibt's im Fernsehen?; **what's on this week at the cinema?** was läuft diese Woche im Kino?

once adverb 1 einmal; **I've tried once already** ich habe es schon einmal versucht; **try once more** versuch es noch einmal; **once a day**

einmal täglich; 2 **more than once** mehrmals; 3 **at once** (immediately) sofort; **the doctor came at once** der Arzt kam sofort; 4 **at once** (at the same time) gleichzeitig; **I can't do two things at once** ich kann nicht zwei Sachen gleichzeitig machen.

one number (when counting) eins; (with a noun) ein; **one son** ein Sohn; **one apple** ein Apfel; **if you want a biro I've got one** falls du einen Kugelschreiber brauchst, habe ich einen; **at one o'clock** um ein Uhr. pronoun 1 einer/eine/eins; **I saw the photos, can I have one of them?** ich habe die Fotos gesehen, kann ich eins davon haben?; 2 **this one** dieser/diese/dieses; **I'd prefer that bike, but this one's cheaper** ich würde lieber das Rad haben, aber dieses ist billiger; 3 **that one** der da/die da/das da; **'which video?'** – **'that one'** 'welches Video?' – 'das da'; 4 **which one?** welcher/welche/welches?; **'my foot's hurting'** – **'which one?'** 'mir tut der Fuß weh' – 'welcher?'; **'she borrowed a skirt from me'** – **'which one?'** 'sie hat sich einen Rock von mir geliehen' – 'welchen?'; 5 (you) man; **one never knows** man kann nie wissen.

one's adjective sein/seine/sein; **one pays for one's car** man zahlt für sein Auto.

oneself pronoun 1 (reflexive) sich; **to wash oneself** sich waschen; 2 (stressing something) selbst; **one**

✧ IRREGULAR VERB: See the verb table in the centre of the dictionary

has to do everything oneself man muss alles selbst machen.

one-way street *noun* Einbahnstraße *die* (PL *die* Einbahnstraßen).

onion *noun* Zwiebel *die* (PL *die* Zwiebeln).

only *adjective* 1 einziger/einzige/einziges; **the only free seat** der einzige freie Platz; **the only thing you could do** das Einzige, was du machen könntest; 2 **an only child** ein Einzelkind.
adverb, conjunction 1 nur; **they've only got two bedrooms** sie haben nur zwei Schlafzimmer; **Anne's only free on Fridays** Anne ist nur freitags frei; **there are only three left** es sind nur noch drei übrig; **I'd walk, only it's raining** ich würde zu Fuß gehen, nur regnet es; 2 (*very recently*) gerade erst; **he's only just got the message** er hat die Nachricht gerade erst bekommen; 3 (*barely*) gerade noch; **we've only just made it on time** wir sind gerade noch rechtzeitig angekommen.

onto *preposition* auf (+ACC).

open *noun* **in the open** im Freien.
adjective 1 offen; **the door's open** die Tür ist offen; **the baker's is not open** die Bäckerei ist nicht geöffnet; 2 **in the open air** im Freien.
verb 1 aufmachen SEP; **can you open the door for me?** kannst du mir die Tür aufmachen?; **the bank opens at nine** die Bank macht um neun auf; 2 (*open up*) sich öffnen; **the door opened slowly** die Tür öffnete sich langsam.

opera *noun* Oper *die* (PL *die* Opern).

operation *noun* 1 Operation *die* (PL *die* Operationen); 2 **to have an operation** operiert werden.

opinion *noun* Meinung *die* (PL *die* Meinungen); **in my opinion** meiner Meinung nach.

opinion poll *noun* Meinungsumfrage *die* (PL *die* Meinungsumfragen).

opportunity *noun* Gelegenheit *die* (PL *die* Gelegenheiten); **to have the opportunity of doing something** die Gelegenheit haben, etwas zu tun.

opposite *noun* Gegenteil *das* (PL *die* Gegenteile); **no, quite the opposite** nein, ganz im Gegenteil.
adjective 1 entgegengesetzt (*direction*); **she went off in the opposite direction** sie ging in die entgegengesetzte Richtung; 2 (*facing*) gegenüberliegend; **in the house opposite** im gegenüberliegenden Haus.
adverb gegenüber; **they live opposite** sie wohnen gegenüber.
preposition gegenüber (+DAT); **opposite the station** gegenüber dem Bahnhof.

optician *noun* Optiker *der* (PL *die* Optiker), Optikerin *die* (PL *die* Optikerinnen).

option *noun* Wahl *die*; **we have no option** wir haben keine andere Wahl.

optional *adjective* auf Wunsch erhältlich; **optional subject** *das* Wahlfach.

△ NEW SPELLING: *See page xii*

or *conjunction* **1** oder; **English or German?** Englisch oder Deutsch?; **today or Tuesday?** heute oder Dienstag?; **2** (*in negatives*) noch; **I don't have a cat or a dog** ich habe weder eine Katze noch einen Hund; **not in June or July** weder im Juni noch im Juli; **3** (*or else*) sonst; **phone Mum, or she'll worry** ruf Mutti an, sonst macht sie sich Sorgen.

oral *noun* (*an exam*) Mündliche *das* (*informal*); **my German oral** mein Deutschmündliches.

orange *noun* (*the fruit*) Orange *die* (PL *die* Orangen); **orange juice** *der* Orangensaft.
adjective orange (*'orange' never changes*); **my orange socks** meine orange Socken.

orchestra *noun* Orchester *das* (PL *die* Orchester).

order *noun* **1** (*sequence*) Reihenfolge *die* (PL *die* Reihenfolgen); **in the right order** in der richtigen Reihenfolge; **in the wrong order** nicht in der richtigen Reihenfolge; **in alphabetical order** in alphabetischer Reihenfolge; **2** (*in a restaurant, café, or shop*) Bestellung *die* (PL *die* Bestellungen); **3 'out of order'** 'außer Betrieb'; **4 in order to do something** um etwas zu tun.
verb **1** (*in a restaurant or a shop*) bestellen; **we ordered soup** wir haben Suppe bestellt; **have you ordered?** haben Sie schon bestellt?; **2** bestellen (*a taxi*).

ordinary *adjective* normal.

organ *noun* **1** (*the instrument*) Orgel *die* (PL *die* Orgeln); **2** (*of the body*) Organ *das* (PL *die* Organe).

organic *adjective* Bio- (*food*); **organic food** *die* Biokost.

organization *noun* Organisation *die* (PL *die* Organisationen).

organize *verb* **1** organisieren; **2** veranstalten (*a conference or festival*).

original *adjective* **1** ursprünglich; **the original plan was better** der ursprüngliche Plan war besser; **2** originell; **it's a really original novel** das ist ein wirklich originelle Roman.

originally *adverb* ursprünglich; **originally we wanted to go by car** ursprünglich wollten wir mit dem Auto fahren.

other *adjective* **1** anderer/andere/ anderes; **we took the other road** wir haben die andere Straße genommen; **where are the others?** wo sind die anderen?; **the other two cars** die anderen beiden Autos; **2 give me the other one** gib mir den anderen/die andere/das andere (*the translation of 'the other one' depends on the gender of the noun it refers to*); **3 the other day** neulich; **4 every other week** jede zweite Woche; **5 somebody or other** irgendjemand; **something or other** irgendetwas; **somewhere or other** irgendwo; **6 any other questions?** sonst noch Fragen?

✧ IRREGULAR VERB: *See the verb table in the centre of the dictionary*

therwise *adverb, conjunction*
sonst.

ught *verb* (*'ought' is usually
translated by the subjunctive of
'sollen'*) **I ought to go** ich sollte
eigentlich gehen; **they ought to
have known the address** sie
hätten die Adresse kennen sollen;
**you oughtn't to have any
problems** du solltest keine
Probleme haben.

our *adjective* **1** (*before a masculine
noun*) unser; **our father** unser
Vater; **2** (*before a feminine noun*)
unsere; **our mother** unsere Mutter;
3 (*before a neuter noun*) unser; **our
house** unser Haus; **4** (*before
masculine/feminine/neuter plural
nouns*) unsere; **our parents** unsere
Eltern; **5** (*with parts of the body*)
der/die/das (*plural:* die); **we'll go
and wash our hands** wir waschen
uns die Hände.

ours *pronoun* **1** (*for a masculine
noun*) unserer; **their garden's
bigger than ours** ihr Garten ist
größer als unserer; **2** (*for a feminine
noun*) unsere; **their kitchen is
smaller than ours** ihre Küche ist
kleiner als unsere; **3** (*for a neuter
noun*) unsers; **their child is younger
than ours** ihr Kind ist jünger als
unsers; **4** (*for plural nouns*) unsere;
**they've invited their friends and
we've invited ours** sie haben ihre
Freunde eingeladen und wir haben
unsere eingeladen; **5 the green car
is ours** das grüne Auto gehört uns;
it's ours es gehört uns; **a friend of
ours** ein Freund von uns.

ourselves *pronoun* **1** (*reflexive*)
uns; **we introduced ourselves** wir
haben uns vorgestellt; **2** (*for
emphasis*) selbst; **in the end we did
it ourselves** schließlich haben wir
es selbst gemacht.

out *adverb* **1** (*outside*) draußen; **it's
cold out there** es ist kalt da
draußen; **they're out in the garden**
sie sind draußen im Garten; **2 to go
out** hinausgehen ◇ SEP (PERF *sein*),
rausgehen ◇ SEP (PERF *sein*)
(*informal*); **to go out shopping**
einkaufen gehen; **3 get out!** raus!
(*informal*); **4 the ball is out** der Ball
ist aus; **5** (*absent*) **to be out** nicht
da sein; **Mr Barnes is out** Herr
Barnes ist nicht da; **6 to go out** (*for
an evening or to the theatre or
cinema*) ausgehen ◇ SEP (PERF *sein*),
weggehen ◇ SEP (PERF *sein*)
(*informal*); **are you going out this
evening?** gehst du heute Abend
weg?; **to be going out with
somebody** mit jemandem gehen;
Alison's going out with Danny now
Alison geht jetzt mit Danny; **7 to ask
somebody out** jemanden
einladen ◇ SEP; **he's asked me out**
er hat mich eingeladen; **8** (*light,
fire*) aus; **are all the lights out?** ist
das Licht aus?
preposition **out of** aus (+DAT); **to go
out of the room** aus dem Zimmer
gehen; **he threw it out of the
window** er hat es aus dem Fenster
geworfen; **to drink out of a glass**
aus einem Glas trinken; **she took the
photo out of her bag** sie hat das
Foto aus der Tasche genommen.

△ NEW SPELLING: *See page xii*

outdoor *adjective* (*activity or sport*) im Freien; **outdoor games** Spiele im Freien.

outdoors *adverb* draußen; **to go outdoors** nach draußen gehen.

outing *noun* Ausflug *der* (PL *die* Ausflüge); **to go on an outing** einen Ausflug machen.

outline *noun* (*of an object*) Umriss *der* (PL *die* Umrisse).

out-of-date *adjective* 1 (*no longer valid*) ungültig; **my passport's out of date** mein Pass ist ungültig; 2 (*old-fashioned*) altmodisch (*clothes, music*).

outside *noun* Außenseite *die*; **it's blue on the outside** auf der Außenseite ist es blau.
adjective Außen-.
adverb draußen; **it's cold outside** es ist kalt draußen.
preposition vor (+DAT); **I'll meet you outside the cinema** ich treffe mich vor dem Kino mit dir.

oven *noun* Ofen *der* (PL *die* Öfen); **to put something in the oven** etwas in den Ofen tun.

over *preposition* 1 (*above*) über ←(DAT); **there's a mirror over the sink** über dem Waschbecken hängt ein Spiegel; 2 (*involving movement*) über (+ACC); **he threw the ball over the wall** er hat den Ball über die Mauer geworfen; 3 **over here** hier drüben; **the food is over here** das Essen ist hier drüben; 4 **over there** da drüben; **she's over there** sie ist da drüben; 5 (*more than*) über; **it will cost over**

a hundred pounds es wird über hundert Pfund kosten; **he's over sixty** er ist über sechzig; 6 (*during*) über (+ACC); **over Christmas** über Weihnachten; **over the weekend** übers Wochenende; 7 (*finished*) zu Ende; **when the meeting's over** wenn die Besprechung zu Ende ist; **it's all over** es ist vorbei; 8 **over th* phone** am Telefon; **to ask someone over** jemanden einladen ✧ SEP; **to come over** herüberkommen ✧ SEP; **come over on Saturday** komm am Samstag zu uns herüber; 9 **all over the place** überall; **I've been looking for it all over** ich habe überall danach gesucht.

overtake *verb* überholen.

overtime *noun* **to work overtime** Überstunden machen.

overweight *adjective* **to be overweight** Übergewicht haben.

owe *verb* schulden; **I owe him ten pounds** ich schulde ihm zehn Pfund.

owing *adjective* 1 (*outstanding*) ausstehend; **there's five pounds owing** fünf Pfund stehen aus; 2 **owing to** wegen (+GEN); **owing to the snow** wegen des Schnees.

owl *noun* Eule *die* (PL *die* Eulen).

own *adjective* 1 eigen; **my own computer** mein eigener Computer; **I've got my own room** ich habe mein eigenes Zimmer; 2 **on your own** allein; **Annie did it on her own** Annie hat es allein gemacht.
verb besitzen ✧.

wner *noun* Besitzer *der* (PL *die* Besitzer), Besitzerin *die* (PL *die* Besitzerinnen).

xygen *noun* Sauerstoff *der*.

zone layer *noun* Ozonschicht *die*.

P p

pace *noun* 1 (*a step*) Schritt *der* (PL *die* Schritte); 2 (*the speed you walk at*) Tempo *das* (PL *die* Tempos).

Pacific *noun* the Pacific (Ocean) der Pazifik.

pack *noun* 1 Packung *die* (PL *die* Packungen); 2 pack of cards *das* Kartenspiel.
verb 1 packen (*your case*); I haven't packed yet ich habe noch nicht gepackt; I'll pack my case tonight ich packe meinen Koffer heute Abend; 2 einpacken SEP (*clothes, shoes, etc.*); have you packed my red shirt? hast du mein rotes Hemd eingepackt?

package *noun* Paket *das* (PL *die* Pakete).

packed lunch *noun* Lunchpaket *das* (PL *die* Lunchpakete).

packet *noun* 1 Päckchen *das* (PL *die* Päckchen); a packet of tea ein Päckchen Tee; 2 (*box*) Schachtel *die* (PL *die* Schachteln); 3 (*bag*) Tüte *die* (PL *die* Tüten); a packet of crisps eine Tüte Chips.

pad *noun* (*of paper*) Block *der* (PL die Blöcke).

page *noun* Seite *die* (PL *die* Seiten); on page seven auf Seite sieben.

pain *noun* Schmerz *der* (PL *die* Schmerzen); to be in pain Schmerzen haben; I've got a pain in my leg ich habe Schmerzen im Bein; ★ Eric's a real pain (in the neck) Eric geht einem richtig auf den Wecker (*informal*).

painful *adjective* schmerzhaft.

paint *noun* Farbe *die* (PL *die* Farben); 'wet paint' 'frisch gestrichen'.
verb malen (*a picture*); streichen ✧ (*a room*); to paint a room pink ein Zimmer rosa streichen.

paintbrush *noun* Pinsel *der* (PL *die* Pinsel).

painter *noun* Maler *der* (PL *die* Maler), Malerin *die* (PL *die* Malerinnen).

painting *noun* (*picture*) Gemälde *das* (PL *die* Gemälde); a painting by Picasso ein Gemälde von Picasso.

pair *noun* 1 Paar *das* (PL *die* Paare); a pair of socks ein Paar Socken; 2 a pair of scissors eine Schere; 3 a pair of trousers eine Hose; a pair of knickers eine Unterhose; 4 to work in pairs paarweise arbeiten.

Pakistan *noun* Pakistan *das*.

palace *noun* Palast *der* (PL *die* Paläste).

pale *adjective* blass △; to turn pale blass werden; pale green zartgrün.

△ NEW SPELLING: *See page xii*

palm *noun* **1** (*of your hand*) Handfläche *die* (PL *die* Handflächen); **2** (*a palm tree*) Palme *die* (PL *die* Palmen).

pan *noun* **1** (*saucepan*) Topf *der* (PL *die* Töpfe); **a pan of water** ein Topf Wasser; **2** (*frying-pan*) Pfanne *die* (PL *die* Pfannen).

pancake *noun* Pfannkuchen *der* (PL *die* Pfannkuchen).

panel *noun* **1** (*for a discussion*) Diskussionsrunde *die*; (*for a quiz*) Rateteam *das*; **2** (*a piece of wood*) Tafel *die* (PL *die* Tafeln).

panic *noun* Panik *die*. *verb* in Panik geraten ✧; **don't panic!** keine Panik!

pantomime *noun* Märchenvorstellung *die* (PL *die* Märchenvorstellungen).

pants *plural noun* Unterhose *die* (PL *die* Unterhosen).

paper *noun* **1** Papier *das*; **a sheet of paper** ein Blatt Papier; **2 paper hanky** *das* Papiertaschentuch; **3 paper cup** *der* Pappbecher; **4** (*newspaper*) Zeitung *die* (PL *die* Zeitungen); **it was in the paper** es stand in der Zeitung; **5 papers** (*documents*) Unterlagen (*plural*).

paperback *noun* Taschenbuch *das* (PL *die* Taschenbücher).

paperclip *noun* Büroklammer *die* (PL *die* Büroklammern).

paper towel *noun* Papierhandtuch *das* (PL *die* Papierhandtücher).

parachute *noun* Fallschirm *der* (P die Fallschirme).

parade *noun* Umzug *der* (PL *die* Umzüge).

paragraph *noun* Absatz *der* (PL *die* Absätze); **'new paragraph'** 'Absatz

paralysed *adjective* gelähmt.

parcel *noun* Paket *das* (PL *die* Pakete).

pardon *noun* **I beg your pardon** (*a an apology*) Entschuldigung!; **pardon?** wie bitte?

parent *noun* Elternteil *der*; **parents** Eltern (*plural*); **my parents live in Germany** meine Eltern wohnen in Deutschland; **parents' evening** *der* Elternabend.

park *noun* **1** Park *der* (PL *die* Parks); **theme park** *der* (thematische) Freizeitpark; **2 car park** *der* Parkplatz. *verb* **1** parken; **you can park outside the house** du kannst vor dem Haus parken; **2 to find somewhere to park** einen Parkplatz finden.

parking *noun* Parken *das*; **'no parking'** 'Parken verboten'.

parking meter *noun* Parkuhr *die* (PL *die* Parkuhren).

parking space *noun* Parklücke *die* (PL *die* Parklücken).

parking ticket *noun* Strafzettel *der* (PL *die* Strafzettel).

parliament *noun* Parlament *das* (PL *die* Parlamente).

parrot *noun* Papagei *der* (PL *die* Papageien).

✧ IRREGULAR VERB: *See the verb table in the centre of the dictionary*

parsley *noun* Petersilie *die*.

part *noun* **1** Teil *der* (PL *die* Teile); **part of the garden** Teil des Gartens; **the last part of the book** der letzte Teil des Buches; **2 that's part of your job** das gehört dazu; **3 to take part in something** an etwas ←(DAT) teilnehmen ✧ SEP; **4** (*spare part*) Teil *das* (PL *die* Teile) (*for a machine or an engine*); **5** (*a role in a play*) Rolle *die* (PL *die* Rollen).

particular *adjective* besonderer/besondere/besonderes; **nothing in particular** nichts Besonderes.

particularly *adverb* besonders; **not particularly interesting** nicht besonders interessant.

partly *adverb* teilweise.

partner *noun* Partner *der* (PL *die* Partner), Partnerin *die* (PL *die* Partnerinnen).

part-time *adjective* Teilzeit-; **part-time work** die Teilzeitarbeit. *adverb* **to work part-time** Teilzeit arbeiten.

party *noun* **1** (*small, private*) Party *die* (PL *die* Partys), Feier *die* (PL *die* Feiern); **a Christmas party** eine Weihnachtsfeier; **to have a birthday party** eine Geburtstagsparty machen; **2** (*more formal, in the evening*) Gesellschaft *die* (PL *die* Gesellschaften); **we've been invited to a party at the Smiths' house** wir sind zu einer Gesellschaft bei Smiths eingeladen worden; **3** (*group*) Gruppe *die* (PL *die* Gruppen); **a party of schoolchildren** eine Gruppe

Schulkinder; **4** (*in politics*) Partei *die* (PL *die* Parteien).

party game *noun* Gesellschaftsspiel *das* (PL *die* Gesellschaftsspiele).

pass *noun* **1** (*to let you in*) Ausweis *der* (PL *die* Ausweise); **2 bus pass** *die* Buskarte; **3** (*over the mountains*) Pass △ *der* (PL *die* Pässe); **4** (*in an exam*) **to get a pass in maths** die Mathematikprüfung bestehen. *verb* **1** (*walk past*) vorbeigehen ✧ SEP (PERF *sein*) an (+DAT) (*a place or building*); **we passed your house** wir sind an deinem Haus vorbeigegangen; **2** (*drive past*) vorbeifahren ✧ SEP (PERF *sein*) an (+DAT) (*a place or building*); **3** (*overtake*) überholen (*a car*); **4** (*give*) reichen; **could you pass me the sugar please?** könnten Sie mir bitte den Zucker reichen?; **5** (*time*) vergehen ✧ (PERF *sein*); **the time passed slowly** die Zeit verging langsam; **6** bestehen ✧ (*an exam*); **to pass an exam** eine Prüfung bestehen; **did you pass in German?** hast du die Deutschprüfung bestanden?

passenger *noun* **1** (*in a plane or ship*) Passagier *der* (PL *die* Passagiere); **2** (*in a train or bus*) Fahrgast *der* (PL *die* Fahrgäste); **3** (*in a car*) Mitfahrer *der* (PL *die* Mitfahrer).

Passover *noun* Passah *das*.

passport *noun* Reisepass △ *der* (PL *die* Reisepässe), Pass △ *der* (PL *die* Pässe).

△ NEW SPELLING: *See page xii*

password noun Kennwort das (PL die Kennwörter).

past noun Vergangenheit die; **in the past** in der Vergangenheit.
adjective **1** (recent) letzter/letzte/letztes; **in the past few weeks** in den letzten paar Wochen; **2** (over) vorbei; **winter is past** der Winter ist vorbei.
preposition, adverb **1** **to walk past something** an etwas ←(DAT) vorbeigehen ◇ SEP (PERF sein); **we went past the school** wir sind an der Schule vorbeigegangen; **to go past** vorbeifahren ◇ (PERF sein); **2** (after) nach (+DAT); **it's just past the post office** es ist kurz nach der Post; **3** (talking about time) **ten past six** zehn nach sechs; **half past four** halb fünf; **a quarter past two** Viertel nach zwei.

pasta noun Nudeln (plural); **I don't like pasta** ich mag keine Nudeln.

pastry noun **1** (for baking) Teig der; **2** (cake) Gebäck das.

path noun Weg der (PL die Wege); (very narrow) Pfad der (PL die Pfade).

pathetic adjective (useless, hopeless) jämmerlich.

patience noun **1** Geduld die; **2** (card game) Patience die.

patient noun Patient der (PL die Patienten), Patientin die (PL die Patientinnen).
adjective geduldig.

patiently adverb geduldig.

patio noun Terrasse die (PL die Terrassen).

pattern noun **1** (on wallpaper or fabric) Muster das (PL die Muster); **2** (dressmaking, knitting) Schnitt der (PL die Schnitte).

pause noun Pause die (PL die Pausen).

pavement noun Bürgersteig der (P die Bürgersteige); **on the pavement** auf dem Bürgersteig.

paw noun Pfote die (PL die Pfoten).

pawn noun (in chess) Bauer der (PL die Bauern).

pay noun (wage) Lohn der (PL die Löhne); (salary) Gehalt das (PL die Gehälter).
verb **1** zahlen; **I'm paying** ich zahle **to pay cash** bar zahlen; **to pay by credit card** mit Kreditkarte zahlen; **they pay £8 an hour** sie zahlen acht Pfund pro Stunde; **to pay by cheque** mit Scheck zahlen; **2** bezahlen ('bezahlen' is used when you pay a person, a bill or for something); **to pay for something** etwas bezahlen; **Tony paid for the drinks** Tony hat die Getränke bezahlt; **it's all paid for** es ist alles bezahlt; **3** **to pay somebody back** (money) jemandem Geld zurückzahlen SEP; **4** **to pay attention** aufpassen SEP; **5** **to pay a visit to somebody** jemanden besuchen.

payment noun **1** Bezahlung die (of sum, bill, debt, or fine); **2** Zahlung die (PL die Zahlungen) (of interest, tax, or fee).

pay phone noun Münzfernsprecher der (PL die Münzfernsprecher).

◇ IRREGULAR VERB: See the verb table in the centre of the dictionary

C noun (*computer*) PC der (PL die PC).

ea noun Erbse die (PL die Erbsen).

eace noun Frieden der.

eaceful adjective friedlich.

each noun Pfirsich der (PL die Pfirsiche).

eak period (*for holidays*) Hauptferienzeit die (PL die Hauptferienzeiten).

eak rate noun (*for phoning*) Höchsttarif der (PL die Höchsttarife).

eak time noun (*for traffic*) Stoßzeit die (PL die Stoßzeiten).

eanut noun Erdnuss △ die (PL die Erdnüsse).

eanut butter noun Erdnussbutter △ die.

ear noun Birne die (PL die Birnen).

earl noun Perle die (PL die Perlen).

ebble noun Kieselstein der (PL die Kieselsteine).

eculiar adjective komisch.

edal noun Pedal das (PL die Pedale).
verb (*on a bike*) **to pedal off** (mit dem Rad) wegfahren ✧ (PERF *sein*).

pedestrian noun Fußgänger der (PL die Fußgänger), Fußgängerin die (PL die Fußgängerinnen).

pedestrian crossing noun Fußgängerüberweg der (PL die Fußgängerüberwege).

pedestrian precinct noun Fußgängerzone die (PL die Fußgängerzonen).

pee noun **to have a pee** pinkeln (*informal*).

peel noun Schale die (PL die Schalen).
verb schälen (*fruit, vegetables*).

peg noun 1 (*hook*) Haken der (PL die Haken); 2 **clothes peg** der Kleiderhaken; 3 (*for a tent*) Pflock der (PL die Pflöcke).

pen noun (*ball-point*) Kugelschreiber der (PL die Kugelschreiber); **felt pen** der Filzstift.

penalty noun 1 (*a fine*) Geldstrafe die (PL die Geldstrafen); 2 (*in football*) Elfmeter der (PL die Elfmeter).

pence plural noun Pence (*plural*).

pencil noun Bleistift der (PL die Bleistifte); **to write in pencil** mit Bleistift schreiben.

pencil case noun Federmäppchen das (PL die Federmäppchen).

pencil sharpener noun Bleistiftanspitzer der (PL die Bleistiftanspitzer).

penfriend noun Brieffreund der (PL die Brieffreunde), Brieffreundin die (PL die Brieffreundinnen); **my German pen-friend is called Heidi** meine deutsche Brieffreundin heißt Heidi.

penis noun Penis der (PL die Penisse).

penny *noun* Penny *der* (PL *die* Pence).

pension *noun* Rente *die* (PL *die* Renten).

pensioner *noun* Rentner *der* (PL *die* Rentner), Rentnerin *die* (PL *die* Rentnerinnen).

people *plural noun* 1 Leute (*plural*), Menschen (*plural*); ('*Menschen' is used in a more formal context*); **most people round here** die meisten Leute hier; **several people** verschiedene Leute; **nice people** nette Leute; **all the people in the world** alle Menschen auf der Welt; **a crowd of people** eine Menschenmenge; 2 (*when you're counting them*) Personen (*plural*); **for ten people** für zehn Personen; **how many people have you invited?** wie viele Personen hast du eingeladen?; 3 **people say that ...** man sagt, dass ...

pepper *noun* 1 (*spice*) Pfeffer *der*; 2 (*vegetable*) Paprikaschote *die* (PL *die* Paprikaschoten).

peppermill *noun* Pfeffermühle *die* (PL *die* Pfeffermühlen).

peppermint *noun* (*plant*) Pfefferminze *die*; **peppermint tea** der Pfefferminztee.

per *preposition* pro (+ACC); **ten pounds per person** zehn Pfund pro Person.

per cent *adverb* Prozent *das*; **sixty per cent of students** sechzig Prozent der Studenten.

percentage *noun* Prozentsatz *der* (PL *die* Prozentsätze).

percussion *noun* Schlagzeug *das* **to play percussion** Schlagzeug spielen.

perfect *adjective* 1 perfekt; **she speaks perfect English** sie spricht perfekt Englisch; 2 (*ideal*) herrlich (*day or weather*).

perfectly *adverb* 1 (*absolutely*) vollkommen; 2 (*faultlessly*) perfekt

perform *verb* 1 spielen (*a piece of music or a part*); 2 singen ✧ (*a song*); 3 **to perform a play** ein Theaterstück aufführen SEP.

performance *noun* 1 (*playing or acting*) Darstellung *die* (PL *die* Darstellungen); **his performance as Hamlet** seine Darstellung des Hamlet; 2 (*show or film*) Vorstellung *die* (PL *die* Vorstellungen); **the performance starts at eight** die Vorstellung fängt um acht Uhr an; 3 (*of a play or opera*) Aufführung *die* (PL *die* Aufführungen).

performer *noun* Künstler *der* (PL *die* Künstler), Künstlerin *die* (PL *die* Künstlerinnen).

perfume *noun* Parfüm *das* (PL *die* Parfüme).

perhaps *adverb* vielleicht; **perhaps he's missed the train** vielleicht hat er den Zug verpasst.

period *noun* 1 (*length of time*) Zeit *die* (PL *die* Zeiten); **trial period** die Probezeit; 2 (*a portion of time*) Zeitraum *der*; **a two-year period**

✧ IRREGULAR VERB: *See the verb table in the centre of the dictionary*

ein Zeitraum von zwei Jahren;
3 (*in school*) Stunde die (PL die
Stunden); **4** (*menstruation*)
Periode die (PL die Perioden).

perm *noun* Dauerwelle die (PL die
Dauerwellen).

permanent *adjective* **1** ständig;
2 fest (*job or address, for example*).

permanently *adverb* **1** dauernd;
2 to be permanently employed fest
angestellt sein.

permission *noun* Erlaubnis die; **to
get permission to do something**
Erlaubnis zu etwas ←(DAT) erhalten.

permit *noun* Genehmigung die (PL
die Genehmigungen).
verb **1** erlauben; **to permit
somebody to do something**
jemandem erlauben, etwas zu tun;
smoking is not permitted Rauchen
ist nicht gestattet; **2 weather
permitting** bei entsprechendem
Wetter.

person *noun* **1** Person die (PL die
Personen); **there's still room for
one more person** wir haben noch
Platz für eine Person; **2 in person**
persönlich.

personal *adjective* persönlich.

personality *noun*
Persönlichkeit die (PL die
Persönlichkeiten).

personally *adverb* persönlich;
personally, I'm against it ich
persönlich bin dagegen.

perspiration *noun* Schweiß der.

persuade *verb* überreden; **to
persuade somebody to come**
jemanden überreden zu kommen.

pessimistic *adjective*
pessimistisch.

pest *noun* **1** (*greenfly, for example*)
Schädling der (PL die Schädlinge);
2 (*annoying person*) Nervensäge die
(PL die Nervensägen) (*informal*).

pet *noun* **1** Haustier das (PL die
Haustiere); **do you have a pet?**
habt ihr Haustiere?; **a pet dog** ein
Hund; **2 Julie is teacher's pet** Julie
ist der Liebling des Lehrers.

petrol *noun* Benzin das (PL die
Benzine); **to fill up with petrol**
tanken; **to run out of petrol** kein
Benzin mehr haben.

petrol station *noun* Tankstelle die
(PL die Tankstellen).

pharmacy *noun* Apotheke die (PL
die Apotheken).

pheasant *noun* Fasan der (PL die
Fasane).

phone *noun* Telefon das (PL die
Telefone); **she's on the phone** sie
telefoniert; **I was on the phone to
Sophie** ich habe mit Sophie
telefoniert; **you can book by phone**
du kannst telefonisch buchen.
verb **1** telefonieren; **while I was
phoning** während ich telefonierte;
2 to phone somebody jemanden
anrufen ◇ SEP; **I'll phone you
tonight** ich rufe dich heute Abend
an.

phone book *noun* Telefonbuch
das (PL die Telefonbücher).

△ NEW SPELLING: *See page xii*

phone box noun Telefonzelle die (PL die Telefonzellen).

phone call noun 1 Anruf der (PL die Anrufe); **to get a phone call** einen Anruf erhalten; 2 **to make a phone call** ein Telefongespräch führen; **phone calls are free** Telefongespräche sind gebührenfrei.

phone card noun Telefonkarte die (PL die Telefonkarten).

phone number noun Telefonnummer die (PL die Telefonnummern).

photo noun Foto das (PL die Fotos); **to take a photo** ein Foto machen; **to take a photo of somebody** ein Foto von jemandem machen.

photocopier noun Fotokopiergerät das (PL die Fotokopiergeräte).

photocopy noun Fotokopie die (PL die Fotokopien). verb fotokopieren.

photograph noun Fotografie die (PL die Fotografien); **to take a photograph** ein Foto machen. verb fotografieren.

photographer noun Fotograf der (PL die Fotografen), Fotografin die (PL die Fotografinnen).

photography noun Fotografie die.

physics noun Physik die.

physiotherapist noun Physiotherapeut der (PL die Physiotherapeuten), Physiotherapeutin die (PL die Physiotherapeutinnen).

physiotherapy noun Physiotherapie die.

piano noun Klavier das (PL die Klaviere); **to play the piano** Klavier spielen; **piano lesson** die Klavierstunde.

pick noun **to take your pick** sich ←(DAT) etwas aussuchen SEP. verb 1 (to select) wählen; **he picked his words carefully** er wählte seine Worte mit Bedacht; 2 (choose for oneself) sich ←(DAT) aussuchen SEP; **pick any book** such dir irgendein Buch aus; 3 **to pick a team** eine Mannschaft aufstellen; 4 pflücken (fruit); **to pick strawberries** Erdbeeren pflücken.
● **to pick up** 1 (lift) (in die Hand) nehmen ✧; **he picked up the papers** er hat die Unterlagen genommen; 2 (collect) abholen SEP; **I'll pick you up at six** ich hole dich um sechs Uhr ab; **I'll pick up the keys tomorrow** ich hole die Schlüssel morgen ab.

pickpocket noun Taschendieb der (PL die Taschendiebe).

picnic noun Picknick das (PL die Picknicke); **to have a picnic** ein Picknick machen.

picture noun 1 Bild das (PL die Bilder); 2 **to go to the pictures** (the cinema) ins Kino gehen.

pie noun 1 (sweet) Kuchen der (PL die Kuchen); **apple pie** der Apfelkuchen; 2 (savoury) Pastete die (PL die Pasteten).

piece noun 1 (a bit) Stück das (PL die Stücke); **a big piece of cheese**

✧ IRREGULAR VERB: See the verb table in the centre of the dictionary

ein großes Stück Käse, **2** (*that you fit together*) Teil *das* (PL *die* Teile); **the pieces of a jigsaw** die Teile von einem Puzzle; **to take something to pieces** etwas in Einzelteile zerlegen; **3 piece of furniture** *das* Möbelstück; **a piece of information** eine Information; **a piece of luck** ein Glücksfall; **4** (*coin*) Stück *das* (PL *die* Stücke); **a five-pence piece** ein Fünf-Pence-Stück.

pierce *verb* **1** durchstechen ✧ SEP; **2 to have pierced ears** Löcher in den Ohrläppchen haben.

pig *noun* Schwein *das* (PL *die* Schweine).

pigeon *noun* Taube *die* (PL *die* Tauben).

pigtail *noun* Zopf *der* (PL *die* Zöpfe).

pile *noun* **1** (*a neat stack*) Stapel *der* (PL *die* Stapel); **a pile of plates** ein Stapel Teller; **2** (*a heap*) Haufen *der* (PL *die* Haufen).

to pile something up (*neatly*) etwas aufstapeln SEP; (*in a heap*) etwas auftürmen SEP.

pill *noun* Pille *die* (PL *die* Pillen).

pillow *noun* Kopfkissen *das* (PL *die* Kopfkissen).

pilot *noun* Pilot *der* (PL *die* Piloten), Pilotin *die* (PL *die* Pilotinnen).

pimple *noun* Pickel *der* (PL *die* Pickel).

pin *noun* **1** (*for sewing*) Stecknadel *die* (PL *die* Stecknadeln); **2 a three-pin plug** ein dreipoliger Stecker.

to pin up 1 hochstecken SEP (*a hem*), **2** anschlagen ✧ SEP (*a notice*).

PIN *noun* (*personal identification number*) Geheimnummer *die*.

pinball *noun* Flippern *das*; **to play pinball** flippern; **pinball machine** *der* Flipper.

pinch *noun* (*of salt, for example*) Prise *die* (PL *die* Prisen).
verb **1** kneifen ✧; **she pinched my arm** sie hat mich in den Arm gekniffen; **2** klauen; **somebody's pinched my bike** jemand hat mein Rad geklaut.

pine *noun* Kiefer *die* (PL *die* Kiefern); **pine furniture** Kiefernmöbel (*plural*).

pineapple *noun* Ananas *die* (PL *die* Ananas).

ping-pong *noun* Tischtennis *das*; **to play ping-pong** Tischtennis spielen.

pink *adjective* rosa (*'rosa' never changes*); **pink hats** rosa Hüte.

pip *noun* (*in a fruit*) Kern *der* (PL *die* Kerne).

pipe *noun* **1** (*for gas or water*) Rohr *das* (PL *die* Rohre); **2** (*for smoking*) Pfeife *die* (PL *die* Pfeifen); **he smokes a pipe** er raucht Pfeife.

Pisces *noun* Fische (*plural*); **Amanda is Pisces** Amanda ist Fisch.

pitch *noun* Platz *der* (PL *die* Plätze); **football pitch** *der* Fußballplatz.
verb **to pitch a tent** ein Zelt aufstellen SEP.

△ NEW SPELLING: *See page xii*

pity noun **1** (*feeling sorry for somebody*) Mitleid das; **2 what a pity!** wie schade!; **it would be a pity to miss the beginning** es wäre schade, den Anfang zu verpassen.
verb **to pity somebody** jemanden bemitleiden.

place noun **1** Ort der (PL die Orte); **Salzburg is a wonderful place** Salzburg ist ein schöner Ort; **in place** an Ort und Stelle; **2 all over the place** überall; **3** (*a space*) Platz der (PL die Plätze); **a place for the car** ein Platz für das Auto; **is there a place for me?** gibt es Platz für mich?; **will you keep my place?** kannst du mir den Platz freihalten?; **to change places** die Plätze tauschen; **4** (*spot*) Stelle die (PL die Stellen); **this is a good place to stop** das ist eine gute Stelle zum Halten; **5** (*in a race*) Platz der (PL die Plätze); **to gain first place** den ersten Platz belegen; **6 at your place** bei dir; **we'll go round to Zafir's place** wir gehen zu Zafir; **7 to take place** stattfinden ✧ SEP; **the competition will take place at four** der Wettbewerb findet um vier Uhr statt.
verb (*upright*) stellen; (*lying flat*) legen.

plain noun Ebene die (PL die Ebenen).
adjective **1** einfach; **plain food** einfaches Essen; **2** (*unflavoured*) Natur-; **plain yoghurt** der Naturjoghurt; **3** (*not patterned*) einfarbig; **plain curtains** einfarbige Vorhänge.

plait noun Zopf der (PL die Zöpfe).

plan noun Plan der (PL die Pläne); **we've made plans for the summer** wir haben Pläne für den Sommer gemacht; **to go according to plan** nach Plan gehen; **everything went according to plan** alles ist nach Plan gegangen.
verb **1 to plan to do something** etwas vorhaben ✧ SEP; **we're planning to leave at eight** wir haben vor, um acht abzufahren; **2** (*make plans for, organize, design*) planen; **she's planning a trip to Italy** sie plant eine Reise nach Italien.

plane noun Flugzeug das (PL die Flugzeuge); **we went by plane** wir sind geflogen.

planet noun Planet der (PL die Planeten).

plant noun Pflanze die (PL die Pflanzen); **a house plant** eine Topfpflanze.
verb pflanzen.

plaster noun **1** (*sticking plaster*) Pflaster das (PL die Pflaster); **2** (*for walls*) Verputz der; **3** Gips der; **to have your leg in plaster** das Bein in Gips haben.

plastic noun Plastik das; **plastic bag** die Plastiktüte.

plate noun Teller der (PL die Teller).

platform noun **1** (*in a station*) Bahnsteig der (PL die Bahnsteige); **2 the train is arriving at platform six** der Zug fährt auf Gleis sechs ein; **3** (*for lecturing or performing*) Podium das (PL die Podien).

play noun (*in the theatre*) Stück das (PL die Stücke); **television play** das

✧ IRREGULAR VERB: *See the verb table in the centre of the dictionary*

Fernsehspiel; **we are putting on a play by Brecht at school** wir führen ein Stück von Brecht in der Schule auf.

verb 1 spielen; **the children are playing with a ball** die Kinder spielen Ball; **they play the piano and the guitar** sie spielen Klavier und Gitarre; **who's playing Hamlet?** wer spielt Hamlet?; **to play tennis** Tennis spielen; **they were playing cards** sie haben Karten gespielt; 2 (*in sport*) **to play somebody** gegen jemanden spielen; **Italy are playing Germany** Italien spielt gegen Deutschland; 3 spielen (*a tape, CD, or record*); **play your new CD** spiele mal deine neue CD.

player *noun* 1 Spieler *der* (PL *die* Spieler), Spielerin *die* (PL *die* Spielerinnen); **football player** *der* Fußballspieler; 2 (*in the theatre*) Schauspieler *der* (PL *die* Schauspieler), Schauspielerin *die* (PL *die* Schauspielerinnen).

playground *noun* Spielplatz *der* (PL *die* Spielplätze); **school playground** *der* Schulhof.

playgroup *noun* Kindergarten *der* (PL *die* Kindergärten).

playing field *noun* Sportplatz *der* (PL *die* Sportplätze).

pleasant *adjective* angenehm.

please *adverb* bitte; **two coffees, please** zwei Kaffee bitte; **could you turn the TV off, please?** könntest du bitte den Fernseher ausmachen?

pleased *adjective* 1 erfreut; **I'm really pleased!** das freut mich wirklich!; 2 **she was pleased with**

her present sie hat sich über ihr Geschenk gefreut; 3 **pleased to meet you!** freut mich!

pleasure *noun* 1 (*amusement*) Vergnügen *das*; 2 (*joy*) Freude *die*; **to get a lot of pleasure out of something** viel Freude an etwas ←(DAT) haben.

plenty *pronoun* 1 (*lots*) viel; **he's got plenty of money** er hat viel Geld; 2 (*enough*) genug; **that's plenty!** das ist genug!; **we've got plenty of time left** wir haben noch genug Zeit.

plot *noun* (*of a film or novel*) Handlung *die*.

plug *noun* 1 (*electrical*) Stecker *der* (PL *die* Stecker); 2 (*in a bath or sink*) Stöpsel *der* (PL *die* Stöpsel); **to pull out the plug** den Stöpsel herausziehen.

plum *noun* Pflaume *die* (PL *die* Pflaumen); **plum tart** *der* Pflaumenkuchen.

plumber *noun* Installateur *der* (PL *die* Installateure).

plural *noun* Mehrzahl *die*, Plural *der*; **in the plural** in der Mehrzahl, im Plural.

plus *preposition* plus (+DAT); **three children plus a baby** drei Kinder und ein Baby.

p.m. *abreviation* nachmittags (*for times up to 6 p.m.*); abends (*for times after 6 p.m.*); **at two p.m.** um zwei Uhr nachmittags, um vierzehn Uhr; **at nine p.m.** um neun Uhr abends, um einundzwanzig Uhr (*in German you usually express times after*

△ NEW SPELLING: *See page xii*

midday in terms of the 24-hour clock).

pocket *noun* Tasche *die* (PL *die* Taschen).

pocket money *noun* Taschengeld *das*.

poem *noun* Gedicht *das* (PL *die* Gedichte).

poet *noun* Dichter *der* (PL *die* Dichter), Dichterin *die* (PL *die* Dichterinnen).

poetry *noun* Dichtung *die*.

point *noun* 1 (*tip*) Spitze *die* (PL *die* Spitzen); **the point of a nail** die Spitze eines Nagels; 2 (*a tiny mark or dot*) Punkt *der* (PL *die* Punkte); 3 (*in time*) Zeitpunkt *der* (PL *die* Zeitpunkte); **at that point** zu diesem Zeitpunkt; **to be on the point of doing something** gerade etwas tun wollen; 4 **that's not the point** darum geht es nicht; **there's no point phoning, he's out** es hat keinen Sinn anzurufen, er ist nicht da; **what's the point?** wozu?; 5 **that's a good point!** das stimmt!; **the point is …** es geht darum …; 6 **point of view** *der* Standpunkt; **from my point of view** von meinem Standpunkt aus; 7 **her strong point** ihre Stärke; 8 (*in scoring*) Punkt *der* (PL *die* Punkte); **to win by fifteen points** mit fünfzehn Punkten Vorsprung gewinnen; 9 (*in decimals*) 6 **point 4** sechs Komma vier (*in German, a comma is used for the decimal point*).
verb 1 hinweisen ⧫ SEP auf (+ACC); **a notice pointing to the station** ein Schild, das auf den Bahnhof

hinweist; 2 (*with your finger*) zeigen auf (+ACC); **he pointed at Tom** er zeigte auf Tom.

pointless *adjective* sinnlos; **it's pointless to keep on ringing** es ist sinnlos, dauernd zu klingeln.

poison *noun* Gift *das* (PL *die* Gifte). *verb* vergiften.

poisonous *adjective* giftig.

Poland *noun* Polen *das*.

pole *noun* 1 (*for a tent*) Stange *die* (PL *die* Stangen); 2 (*for skiing*) Stock *der* (PL *die* Stöcke); 3 **the North Pole** *der* Nordpol.

Pole *noun* (*a Polish person*) Pole *der* (PL *die* Polen), Polin *die* (PL *die* Polinnen).

police *noun* **the police** die Polizei; **the police are coming** die Polizei kommt.

police car *noun* Streifenwagen *der* (PL *die* Streifenwagen).

policeman *noun* Polizist *der* (PL *die* Polizisten).

police station *noun* Polizeiwache *die* (PL *die* Polizeiwachen).

policewoman *noun* Polizistin *die* (PL *die* Polizistinnen).

polish *noun* 1 (*for furniture*) Politur *die*; 2 (*for shoes*) Schuhcreme *die*; 3 (*for the floor*) Bohnerwachs *das*. *verb* 1 polieren (*furniture, silver*); 2 **to polish your shoes** seine Schuhe putzen.

⧫ IRREGULAR VERB: *See the verb table in the centre of the dictionary*

Polish *noun* (*language*)
Polnisch *das*.
adjective polnisch.

polite *adjective* höflich; **to be polite
to somebody** höflich zu jemandem
sein.

political *adjective* politisch.

politician *noun* Politiker *der* (PL *die*
Politiker), Politikerin *die* (PL *die*
Politikerinnen).

politics *noun* Politik *die*.

polluted *adjective* verschmutzt.

pollution *noun*
Verschmutzung *die*.

polo-necked *adjective* Rollkragen-;
a polo-necked jumper ein
Rollkragenpullover.

pond *noun* Teich *der* (PL *die* Teiche).

pony *noun* Pony *das* (PL *die* Ponys).

ponytail *noun* Pferdeschwanz *der*
(PL *die* Pferdeschwänze).

poodle *noun* Pudel *der* (PL *die*
Pudel).

pool *noun* 1 (*swimming pool*)
Schwimmbecken *das* (PL *die*
Schwimmbecken); 2 (*pond*)
Tümpel *der* (PL *die* Tümpel);
3 (*puddle*) Lache *die* (PL *die*
Lachen); 4 (*game*) Poolbillard *das*;
5 **the football pools** das Toto; **to do
the pools** Toto spielen.

poor *adjective* 1 arm; **a poor country**
ein armes Land; **a poor family** eine
arme Familie; 2 **poor Tanya's failed
her exam** die arme Tanya ist durch
die Prüfung gefallen; 3 (*bad*)

schlecht; **that's a poor result** das
ist ein schlechtes Ergebnis; **the
weather was pretty poor** das Wetter
war ziemlich schlecht.

pop *noun* Popmusik *die*; **pop
concert** das Popkonzert; **pop star**
der Popstar; **pop song** *der* Schlager.
● **to pop into: I'll just pop into the
bank** ich gehe kurz auf die Bank.

popcorn *noun* Puffmais *der*.

pope *noun* Papst *der* (PL *die* Päpste).

poppy *noun* Mohn *der*.

popular *adjective* beliebt.

population *noun* Bevölkerung *die*
(PL *die* Bevölkerungen).

porch *noun* Vorbau *der* (PL *die*
Vorbauten).

pork *noun* Schweinefleisch *das*;
pork chop *das* Schweinekotelett.

porridge *noun* Haferbrei *der*.

port *noun* 1 Hafen *der* (PL *die*
Häfen); 2 (*wine*) Portwein *der* (PL
die Portweine).

porter *noun* 1 (*at a station or an
airport*) Gepäckträger *der* (PL *die*
Gepäckträger); 2 (*in a hotel*)
Portier *der* (PL *die* Portiers).

portion *noun* (*of food*) Portion *die*
(PL *die* Portionen).

portrait *noun* Porträt *das* (PL *die*
Porträts).

Portugal *noun* Portugal *das*.

Portuguese *noun* 1 (*language*)
Portugiesisch *das*; 2 (*a person*)
Portugiese *der* (PL *die* Portugiesen),

△ NEW SPELLING: See page xii

Portugiesin *die* (PL *die* Portugiesinnen).
adjective portugiesisch.

posh *adjective* vornehm; **a posh area** eine vornehme Gegend.

position *noun* 1 Platz *der* (PL *die* Plätze); 2 (*situation*) Lage *die* (PL *die* Lagen); 3 (*status, job*) Stellung *die* (PL *die* Stellungen).

positive *adjective* 1 (*sure*) sicher; **I'm positive he's left** ich bin mir sicher, dass er gegangen ist; 2 (*enthusiastic*) positiv; **her reaction was very positive** ihre Reaktion war sehr positiv.

possessions *plural noun* Sachen (*plural*); **all my possessions are in the flat** alle meine Sachen sind in der Wohnung.

possibility *noun* Möglichkeit *die* (PL *die* Möglichkeiten).

possible *adjective* möglich; **it's possible** es ist gut möglich; **if possible** wenn möglich; **as quickly as possible** so schnell wie möglich.

possibly *adverb* 1 (*maybe*) möglicherweise; **'will you be at home at midday?' – 'possibly'** 'bist du mittags zu Hause?' – 'möglicherweise'; 2 **how can you possibly believe that?** wie kannst du das nur glauben?; **I can't possibly arrive before Thursday** ich kann unmöglich vor Donnerstag ankommen.

post *noun* 1 Post *die*; **to send something by post** etwas per Post schicken; (*letters*) **is there any post for me?** ist Post für mich

gekommen?; 2 (*a pole*) Pfosten *der* (PL *die* Pfosten); 3 (*a job*) Stelle *die* (PL *die* Stellen).
verb **to post a letter** einen Brief abschicken SEP.

postbox *noun* Briefkasten *der* (PL *die* Briefkästen).

postcard *noun* Postkarte *die* (PL *die* Postkarten).

postcode *noun* Postleitzahl *die* (PL *die* Postleitzahlen).

poster *noun* 1 (*for decoration*) Poster *das* (PL *die* Poster); **I've bought an Oasis poster** ich habe ein Poster von Oasis gekauft; 2 (*advertising*) Plakat *das* (PL *die* Plakate); **I saw a poster for the concert** ich habe ein Plakat für das Konzert gesehen.

postman *noun* Briefträger *der* (PL *die* Briefträger).

post office *noun* Post *die*; **the post office is on the right** die Post ist auf der rechten Seite.

postpone *verb* verschieben ✧; **we've postponed the meeting until next week** wir haben die Besprechung auf nächste Woche verschoben.

postwoman *noun* Briefträgerin *die* (PL *die* Briefträgerinnen).

pot *noun* 1 (*jar*) Topf *der* (PL *die* Töpfe); **a pot of honey** ein Topf Honig; 2 (*teapot*) Kanne *die* (PL *die* Kannen); 3 **the pots and pans** die Töpfe und Pfannen.

✧ IRREGULAR VERB: *See the verb table in the centre of the dictionary*

potato *noun* Kartoffel *die* (PL *die* Kartoffeln); **fried potatoes** Bratkartoffeln (*plural*); **mashed potatoes** *der* Kartoffelbrei.

potato crisps *plural noun* Kartoffelchips (*plural*).

pottery *noun* 1 (*craft*) Töpferei *die*; 2 (*objects*) Töpferwaren (*plural*).

pound *noun* 1 (*money*) Pfund *das* (PL *die* Pfunde); **fourteen pounds** vierzehn Pfund; **three marks to the pound** drei Mark für ein Pfund; **a five pound note** ein Fünfpfundschein; 2 (*in weight*) Pfund *das*; **two pounds of apples** zwei Pfund Äpfel.

pour *verb* 1 gießen ◇ (*liquid*); **he poured milk into the pan** er hat Milch in den Topf gegossen; 2 eingießen ◇ SEP (*a drink*); **to pour the tea** den Tee eingießen; **I poured him a drink** ich habe ihm zu trinken eingegossen; 3 (*with rain*) **it's pouring** es gießt.

poverty *noun* Armut *die*.

powder *noun* 1 Pulver *das* (PL *die* Pulver); 2 (*for face or body*) Puder *der* (PL *die* Puder).

power *noun* 1 (*electricity*) Strom *der*; **a power cut** eine Stromsperre; 2 (*energy*) Energie *die*; **nuclear power** die Kernenergie; 3 (*strength*) Kraft *die*; 4 (*over other people*) Macht *die*; **to be in power** an der Macht sein.

powerful *adjective* (*strong*) stark; (*influential*) mächtig.

power station *noun* Kraftwerk *das* (PL *die* Kraftwerke).

practical *adjective* praktisch.

practice *noun* 1 (*for sport*) Training *das*; **hockey practice** *das* Hockeytraining; 2 Übung *die*; **to do your piano practice** Klavier üben; **to be out of practice** außer Übung sein.

practise *verb* 1 üben (*an instrument, exercise, or skill*); **to practise the piano** Klavier üben; 2 anwenden SEP (*a language*); **a week in Berlin to practise my German** eine Woche in Berlin, um mein Deutsch anzuwenden; 3 (*in sport*) trainieren; **the team practises on Wednesday** die Mannschaft trainiert Mittwoch.

praise *verb* loben; **to praise somebody for something** jemanden für etwas ←(ACC) loben.

pram *noun* Kinderwagen *der* (PL *die* Kinderwagen).

prawn *noun* Garnele *die* (PL *die* Garnelen).

pray *verb* beten.

prayer *noun* Gebet *das* (PL *die* Gebete).

precinct *noun* **shopping precinct** *das* Einkaufszentrum; **pedestrian precinct** *die* Fußgängerzone.

precisely *adverb* genau; **at eleven o'clock precisely** um genau elf Uhr.

prefer *verb* 1 vorziehen ◇ SEP; **I prefer Anna to her sister** ich ziehe Anna ihrer Schwester vor; 2 **to prefer to do something** etwas lieber tun; **I prefer to stay at home** ich bleibe lieber zu Hause.

△ NEW SPELLING: *See page xii*

pregnant *adjective* schwanger.

prejudice *noun* Vorurteil *das* (PL *die* Vorurteile); **to fight against racial prejudice** gegen Rassenvorurteile ankämpfen.

prejudiced *adjective* **to be prejudiced** voreingenommen sein.

prep *noun* Hausaufgaben (*plural*); **my English prep** meine Englischhausaufgaben.

preparation *noun* Vorbereitung *die* (PL *die* Vorbereitungen); **in preparation for something** in Vorbereitung auf etwas ←(ACC); **our preparations for Christmas** unsere Weihnachtsvorbereitungen.

prepare *verb* 1 vorbereiten SEP; **to prepare somebody for something** jemanden auf etwas ←(ACC) vorbereiten; 2 **to be prepared for the worst** sich auf das Schlimmste gefasst machen.

prepared *adjective* bereit; **I'm prepared to pay half** ich bin bereit, die Hälfte zu zahlen.

preposition *noun* Präposition *die* (PL *die* Präpositionen).

prep school *noun* private Grundschule *die*.

prescription *noun* Rezept *das* (PL *die* Rezepte); **on prescription** auf Rezept.

present *noun* 1 (*a gift*) Geschenk *das* (PL *die* Geschenke); **to give somebody a present** jemandem ein Geschenk machen; 2 (*the time now*) Gegenwart *die*; **in the present (tense)** in der Gegenwart; 3 **that's all for the present** das ist vorläufig alles. *adjective* 1 (*attending*) anwesend; **Mr Blair is not present** Herr Blair ist nicht anwesend; **to be present at something** bei etwas ←(DAT) anwesend sein; **fifty people were present at the funeral** fünfzig Personen waren bei der Beerdigung anwesend; 2 (*existing now*) gegenwärtig; **the present situation** die gegenwärtige Lage; 3 **at the present time** zur Zeit. *verb* 1 überreichen (*a prize*); 2 (*introduce*) vorstellen SEP; 3 (*on TV, radio*) moderieren (*a programme*).

presenter *noun* (*on TV*) Moderator *der* (PL *die* Moderatoren), Moderatorin *die* (PL *die* Moderatorinnen).

president *noun* Präsident *der* (PL *die* Präsidenten), Präsidentin *die* (PL *die* Präsidentinnen).

press *noun* **the press** die Presse. *verb* 1 (*to push*) drücken; **press here!** hier drücken!; 2 drücken auf (+ACC) (*a button or switch*); **she pressed the button** sie hat auf den Knopf gedrückt.

press conference *noun* Pressekonferenz *die* (PL *die* Pressekonferenzen).

pressure *noun* Druck *der*; **to put pressure on somebody** jemanden unter Druck setzen.

pressure group *noun* Interessengruppe *die* (PL *die* Interessengruppen).

✧ IRREGULAR VERB: *See the verb table in the centre of the dictionary*

pretend *verb* **to pretend that** ... so tun, als ob ...; **he's pretending not to hear** er tut so, als ob er nicht hört.

pretty *adjective* hübsch; **a pretty dress** ein hübsches Kleid.
adverb ziemlich; **it was pretty silly** das war ziemlich blöd.

prevent *verb* **to prevent somebody from doing something** jemanden daran hindern, etwas zu tun; **there's nothing to prevent you from leaving** niemand kann dich daran hindern wegzugehen.

previous *adjective* **1** (*earlier*) früher (*years, opportunity, or job*); **2** (*immediately preceding*) vorig; **on the previous Tuesday** am vorigen Dienstag.

price *noun* Preis *der* (PL *die* Preise); **the price per kilo** der Preis pro Kilo; **CDs have gone up in price** CDs sind im Preis gestiegen; **what is the price of this?** was kostet das?

price list *noun* Preisliste *die* (PL *die* Preislisten).

price ticket *noun* Preisschild *das* (PL *die* Preisschilder).

prick *verb* stechen ✧; **to prick your finger** sich in den Finger stechen.

pride *noun* Stolz *der*.

priest *noun* Priester *der* (PL *die* Priester).

primary school *noun* Grundschule *die* (PL *die* Grundschulen).

primary (school) teacher *noun* Grundschullehrer *der* (PL *die* Grundschullehrer),

Grundschullehrerin *die* (PL *die* Grundschullehrerinnen).

prime minister *noun* Premierminister *der* (PL *die* Premierminister), Premierministerin *die* (PL *die* Premierministerinnen).

prince *noun* Prinz *der* (PL *die* Prinzen).

princess *noun* Prinzessin *die* (PL *die* Prinzessinnen).

principal *noun* (*of a college*) Direktor *der* (PL *die* Direktoren), Direktorin *die* (PL *die* Direktorinnen).
adjective (*main*) Haupt-.

principle *noun* Prinzip *das* (PL *die* Prinzipien); **on principle** im Prinzip; **that's true in principle** im Prinzip stimmt das.

print *noun* **1** (*letters*) Druck *der*; **in small print** klein gedruckt; **2** (*a photo*) Abzug *der* (PL *die* Abzüge); **colour print** *der* Farbabzug.

printer *noun* (*for a computer*) Drucker *der* (PL *die* Drucker).

print-out *noun* Ausdruck *der* (PL *die* Ausdrucke).

prison *noun* Gefängnis *das* (PL *die* Gefängnisse); **in prison** im Gefängnis.

prisoner *noun* Gefangene *der/die* (PL *die* Gefangenen).

private *adjective* **1** Privat-, privat; **private school** *die* Privatschule; **private property** *das* Privateigentum; **to have private**

lessons Privatstunden nehmen;
2 in private privat.

prize *noun* Preis *der* (PL *die* Preise);
to win a prize einen Preis
gewinnen.

prize-giving *noun*
Preisverleihung *die* (PL *die*
Preisverleihungen).

prizewinner *noun* Gewinner *der*
(PL *die* Gewinner), Gewinnerin *die*
(PL *die* Gewinnerinnen).

probable *adjective* wahrscheinlich.

probably *adverb* wahrscheinlich.

problem *noun* Problem *das* (PL *die*
Probleme); **it's a serious problem**
das ist ein ernstes Problem; **no
problem!** kein Problem!

process *noun* 1 Prozess △ *der* (PL *die*
Prozesse); **2 to be in the process of
doing something** dabei sein, etwas
zu tun.

produce *noun* (*food*) Erzeugnisse
(*plural*).
verb 1 herstellen SEP (*goods, food*);
2 vorzeigen SEP (*a ticket, document*);
I produced my passport ich habe
meinen Pass vorgezeigt; **3** erzeugen
(*interest, tension*); **it produces heat**
es erzeugt Wärme; **4 to produce a
film** einen Film produzieren; **5 to
produce a play** ein Theaterstück
inszenieren.

producer *noun* (*of a film or
programme*) Produzent *der* (PL *die*
Produzenten).

product *noun* Produkt *das* (PL *die*
Produkte).

production *noun* 1 (*of a film or an
opera*) Produktion *die* (PL *die*
Produktionen); **2** (*of a play*)
Inszenierung *die* (PL *die*
Inszenierungen); **a new production
of Hamlet** eine neue Inszenierung
von Hamlet; **3** (*by a factory*)
Produktion *die*.

profession *noun* Beruf *der* (PL *die*
Berufe).

professional *noun* 1 (*a trained
person*) Fachmann *der* (PL *die*
Fachleute); **2** (*in sport*) Profi *der* (PL
die Profis).
adjective 1 professionell (*work,
sportsman*); **a professional
footballer** ein professioneller
Fußballer; **2** beruflich (*career,
success*); **she's a professional
singer** sie ist Sängerin von Beruf.

professor *noun* Professor *der* (PL
die Professoren), Professorin *die* (PL
die Professorinnen).

profile *noun* Profil *das* (PL *die*
Profile).

profit *noun* Gewinn *der* (PL *die*
Gewinne).

profitable *adjective* rentabel.

program *noun* **computer program**
das Programm.

programme *noun* 1 (*for a play or an
event*) Programm *das* (PL *die*
Programme); **2** (*on TV or radio*)
Sendung *die* (PL *die* Sendungen).

progress *noun* 1 Fortschritt *der* (PL
die Fortschritte); **to make progress**
Fortschritte machen; **2 to be in
progress** im Gange sein.

✧ IRREGULAR VERB: *See the verb table in the centre of the dictionary*

project *noun* **1** (*at school*) Arbeit *die* (PL *die* Arbeiten); **2** (*a plan*) Projekt *das* (PL *die* Projekte); **a project to build a bridge** ein Brückenbauprojekt.

promise *noun* Versprechen *das* (PL *die* Versprechen); **to make somebody a promise** jemandem ein Versprechen geben; **to keep a promise** ein Versprechen halten; **it's a promise!** ganz bestimmt! *verb* **to promise something** etwas versprechen ✧; **I've promised to ring my mother** ich habe versprochen, meine Mutter anzurufen.

promote *verb* **to be promoted** (*in football*) aufsteigen ✧ SEP (PERF *sein*); (*at work*) befördert werden.

promotion *noun* **1** Beförderung *die*; **2** (*in football*) Aufstieg *der*; **3** (*in advertising*) Reklame *die*.

pronoun *noun* Pronomen *das* (PL *die* Pronomen).

pronounce *verb* aussprechen ✧ SEP; **you don't pronounce the 'c'** das 'c' spricht man nicht aus.

pronunciation *noun* Aussprache *die*.

proof *noun* Beweis *der* (PL *die* Beweise); **there's no proof that ...** es gibt keine Beweise dafür, dass ...

propaganda *noun* Propaganda *die*.

propeller *noun* Propeller *der* (PL *die* Propeller).

proper *adjective* **1** (*correct, real, genuine*) richtig; **the proper answer** die richtige Antwort; **he's not a proper doctor** er ist kein richtiger Arzt; **2** (*decent*) anständig; **I need a proper meal** ich brauche ein anständiges Essen; **3 in its proper place** an Ort und Stelle.

properly *adverb* **1** richtig; **2** (*decent*) anständig.

property *noun* **1** (*your belongings*) Eigentum *das*; **2** (*land, premises*) Besitz *der*; **'private property'** 'Privatbesitz'; **3** (*house*) Haus *das* (PL *die* Häuser).

propose *verb* **1** (*suggest*) vorschlagen ✧ SEP; **2** (*marriage*) **he proposed to her** er hat ihr einen Heiratsantrag gemacht.

protect *verb* schützen; **to protect somebody from something** jemanden vor etwas ←(DAT) schützen.

protection *noun* Schutz *der*.

protein *noun* Protein *das* (PL *die* Proteine).

protest *noun* **1** Beschwerde *die* (PL *die* Beschwerden); **to make a protest** eine Beschwerde einlegen SEP; **2** (*disapproval*) Protest *der* (PL *die* Proteste); **in protest against something** aus Protest gegen etwas ←(ACC). *verb* protestieren; **to protest about something** gegen etwas ←(ACC) protestieren.

Protestant *noun* Protestant *der* (PL *die* Protestanten), Protestantin *die* (PL *die* Protestantinnen). *adjective* protestantisch.

△ NEW SPELLING: *See page xii*

protest march *noun*
Protestmarsch *der* (PL *die*
Protestmärsche).

proud *adjective* stolz; **to be proud
about something** stolz auf etwas
←(ACC) sein.

prove *verb* beweisen ✧.

provide *verb* zur Verfügung stellen.

provided, providing *conjunction*
vorausgesetzt; **provided it doesn't
rain** vorausgesetzt, es regnet nicht.

prune *noun* Backpflaume *die* (PL *die*
Backpflaumen).

psychiatrist *noun* Psychiater *der*
(PL *die* Psychiater), Psychiaterin *die*
(PL *die* Psychiaterinnen).

psychological *adjective*
psychologisch.

psychologist *noun*
Psychologe *der* (PL *die*
Psychologen), Psychologin *die* (PL
die Psychologinnen).

psychology *noun* Psychologie *die*.

PTO *abbreviation* b.w. (*bitte
wenden*).

pub *noun* Kneipe *die* (PL *die*
Kneipen) (*informal*).

public *noun* **the public** die
Öffentlicheit; **in public** in aller
Öffentlichkeit.
adjective öffentlich.

public holiday *noun* gesetzliche
Feiertag *der* (PL *die* gesetzlichen
Feiertage); **January 1st is a public
holiday** der erste Januar ist ein
gesetzlicher Feiertag.

publicity *noun* **1** Publicity *die*;
2 (*advertising*) Werbung *die*.

public school *noun*
Privatschule *die* (PL *die*
Privatschulen).

public transport *noun* öffentliche
Verkehrsmittel (*plural*).

publish *verb* veröffentlichen.

publisher *noun* **1** Verleger *der* (PL
die Verleger), Verlegerin *die* (PL *die*
Verlegerinnen); **2** (*company*)
Verlag *der* (PL *die* Verlage).

pudding *noun* (*dessert*)
Nachtisch *der* (PL *die* Nachtische);
**for pudding we've got
strawberries** zum Nachtisch gibt es
Erdbeeren.

puddle *noun* Pfütze *die* (PL *die*
Pfützen).

puff *noun* (*of smoke*) Wölkchen *das*
(PL *die* Wölkchen).

puff pastry *noun* Blätterteig *der*.

pull *verb* **1** ziehen ✧; **to pull a cart**
einen Wagen ziehen; **2** ziehen an
(+DAT); **to pull a rope** an einem Seil
ziehen; **he pulled a letter out of his
pocket** er hat einen Brief aus der
Tasche gezogen; ★ **he's pulling
your leg!** er nimmt dich auf den Arm
(*literally: he's picking you up in his
arms*).

● **to pull down 1** herunterziehen ✧
SEP; **2** (*demolish*) abreißen ✧ SEP (*a
building*).

● **to pull in** (*at the roadside*) an den
Straßenrand fahren ✧ (PERF *sein*).

pullover *noun* Pullover *der* (PL *die*
Pullover).

pump *noun* Pumpe *die* (PL *die*
Pumpen); **bicycle pump** *die*

✧ **IRREGULAR VERB: See the verb table in the centre of the dictionary**

Fahrradpumpe.
verb pumpen.
● **to pump up** aufpumpen SEP.

punch *noun* **1** (*in boxing*)
Faustschlag *der* (PL *die*
Faustschläge); **2** (*drink*) Bowle *die*
(PL *die* Bowlen).
verb **1** he punched me in the
stomach er hat mich in den Magen
geboxt; **2** lochen (*a ticket*).

punctual *adjective* pünktlich.

punctuation *noun*
Interpunktion *die*.

punctuation mark *noun*
Satzzeichen *das* (PL *die*
Satzzeichen).

puncture *noun* (*flat tyre*)
Reifenpanne *die* (PL *die*
Reifenpannen).

punish *verb* bestrafen.

punishment *noun* Strafe *die* (PL *die*
Strafen).

pupil *noun* Schüler *der* (PL *die*
Schüler), Schülerin *die* (PL *die*
Schülerinnen).

puppet *noun* Puppe *die* (PL *die*
Puppen).

puppy *noun* junge Hund *der* (PL *die*
jungen Hunde); **a boxer puppy** ein
junger Boxer.

pure *adjective* rein.

purple *adjective* lila (*'lila' never
changes*).

purpose *noun* **1** Zweck *der* (PL *die*
Zwecke); **what's the purpose of it?**
was hat das für einen Zweck?; **2 on
purpose** absichtlich; **she did it on
purpose** das hat sie absichtlich
getan; **he closed the door on
purpose** er hat die Tür absichtlich
zugemacht.

purr *verb* schnurren.

purse *noun* Portemonnaie *das* (PL
die Portemonnaies).

push *noun* **to give something a
push** etwas schieben ✧.
verb **1** schubsen; **he pushed me** er
hat mich geschubst; **2** (*to press*)
drücken auf (+ACC) (*a bell or button*);
**3 to push somebody to do
something** jemanden zu etwas
drängen; **his teacher is pushing him
to sit the exam** sein Lehrer drängt
ihn, die Prüfung zu machen; **4 to
push your way through the crowd**
sich durch die Menge drängen.
● **to push something away** etwas
wegschieben ✧ SEP; **she pushed her
plate away** sie schob ihren Teller
weg.

pushchair *noun* Sportwagen *der*
(PL *die* Sportwagen).

put *verb* **1** (*place generally*) tun ✧;
put some milk in your tea tu etwas
Milch in den Tee; **you can put the
butter in the fridge** du kannst die
Butter in den Kühlschrank tun; **2** (*lay
flat*) legen; **she put the pencil on the
desk** sie hat den Bleistift auf den
Schreibtisch gelegt; **3** (*place
upright*) stellen; **where did you put
my bag?** wo hast du meine
Handtasche hingestellt?; **4** (*write*)
schreiben ✧; **put your address
here** schreiben Sie Ihre Adresse
hierhin.
● **to put away** wegräumen SEP; **put**

away your things räume deine
Sachen weg.
- **to put back 1** zurücklegen SEP,
zurückstellen SEP, zurücktun SEP (*the
translation of 'put back' depends on
the way it is done: if it's placed lying
down, use 'zurücklegen', if placed
upright use 'zurückstellen' and if it
could be either, use 'zurücktun'*); **I put
it back in the drawer** ich habe es in
die Schublade zurückgetan; **2**
(*postpone*) verschieben ✧; **the
meeting has been put back until
Thursday** die Besprechung ist auf
Donnerstag verschoben worden.
- **to put down** (*lying down*) hinlegen
SEP; (*upright*) hinstellen SEP; **where
can I put the vase down?** wo kann
ich die Vase hinstellen?
- **to put off 1** (*postpone*)
verschieben ✧; **he's put off my
lesson till Thursday** er hat meine
Stunde auf Donnerstag verschoben;
2 (*turn off*) ausmachen SEP; **don't
forget to put off the lights** vergiss
nicht, das Licht auszumachen; **3 to
put somebody off something**
jemandem die Lust an etwas ←(DAT)
verderben ✧; **it really put me off my
food** das hat mir wirklich die Lust
am Essen verdorben; **4 to put
somebody off doing something**
jemanden davon abbringen ✧ SEP,
etwas zu tun; **don't be put off** lass
dich nicht davon abbringen.
- **to put on 1** anziehen ✧ SEP (*clothes*);
I'll just put my shoes on ich ziehe
nur schnell meine Schuhe an;
2 auflegen SEP (*a CD or record*); **I'm
putting on Oasis** ich lege Oasis auf;
3 (*switch on*) anmachen SEP (*a light

or the heating*); **could you put the
lamp on?** kannst du die Lampe
anmachen?
- **to put out 1** (*put outside*)
hinaustun ✧ SEP, raustun ✧ SEP
(*informal*); **have you put the
rubbish out?** hast du den Müll
rausgetan?; **2** ausmachen SEP (*a light
or cigarette*); **I've put the lights out**
ich habe das Licht ausgemacht; **3 to
put out your hand** die Hand
ausstrecken SEP.
- **to put up 1** heben ✧ (*your hand*);
2 aufhängen SEP (*a picture or poster*);
**I've put up some posters in my
room** ich habe ein paar Poster in
meinem Zimmer aufgehängt;
3 anschlagen ✧ SEP (*a notice*);
4 erhöhen (*the price*); **they've put up
the fare** sie haben den Fahrpreis
erhöht; **5** (*for the night*) **friends put
me up** ich habe bei Freunden
übernachtet; **can you put me up on
Friday?** kann ich Freitag bei euch
übernachten?
- **to put up with something** etwas
aushalten ✧ SEP; **I don't know how
she puts up with it** ich weiß nicht,
wie sie das aushält.

puzzle *noun* (*jigsaw*) Puzzle *das* (PL
die Puzzles).

puzzled *adjective* verdutzt.

pyjamas *plural noun*
Schlafanzug *der* (PL *die*
Schlafanzüge); **a pair of pyjamas**
ein Schlafanzug; **where are my
pyjamas?** wo ist mein Schlafanzug?

✧ IRREGULAR VERB: *See the verb table in the centre of the dictionary*

Q q

qualification *noun* 1 (*ability, experience*) Qualifikation *die* (PL *die* Qualifikationen); 2 (*on paper*) Zeugnis *das* (PL *die* Zeugnisse).

qualified *adjective* 1 ausgebildet; **she's a qualified ski instructor** sie ist eine ausgebildete Skilehrerin; 2 (*having a degree or a diploma*) Diplom-; **a qualified engineer** ein Diplomingenieur.

quality *noun* Qualität *die*; **good quality products** Waren von guter Qualität.

quantity *noun* Menge *die* (PL *die* Mengen).

quarrel *noun* Streit *der* (PL *die* Streite); **to have a quarrel** Streit haben.
verb sich streiten ✧; **they're always quarrelling** sie streiten sich dauernd.

quarter *noun* 1 Viertel *das* (PL *die* Viertel); **a quarter of the price** ein Viertel des Preises; **three quarters of the class** drei Viertel der Klasse; **it's a quarter past ten** es ist Viertel nach zehn; **it's a quarter to ten** es ist Viertel vor zehn; 2 **we meet at quarter to eight** wir treffen uns um Viertel vor acht; 3 **a quarter of an hour** eine Viertelstunde; 4 **three quarters of an hour** eine Dreiviertelstunde; 5 **an hour and a quarter** eineinviertel Stunden.

queen *noun* 1 Königin *die* (PL *die* Königinnen); 2 (*in chess, cards*) Dame *die* (PL *die* Damen).

question *noun* Frage *die* (PL *die* Fragen); **to ask somebody a question** jemandem eine Frage stellen; **I asked her a question** ich habe ihr eine Frage gestellt; **it's out of the question** das kommt nicht in Frage.
verb befragen (*a person*).

question mark *noun* Fragezeichen *das* (PL *die* Fragezeichen).

questionnaire *noun* Fragebogen *der* (PL *die* Fragebögen).

queue *noun* (*of people, cars*) Schlange *die* (PL *die* Schlangen); **to stand in a queue** Schlange stehen; **a queue of cars** eine Autoschlange.

quick *adjective* schnell; **to have a quick lunch** schnell etwas zu Mittag essen; **it's quicker on the motorway** auf der Autobahn geht es schneller; **to have a quick look at something** sich ←(DAT) schnell etwas ansehen; **be quick!** mach schnell!

quickly *adverb* schnell; **I'll just quickly phone my mother** ich rufe schnell meine Mutter an.

quiet *adjective* 1 (*silent*) still; **to keep quiet** still sein; **please keep quiet** sei bitte still; 2 (*not loud*) leise; **the children are very quiet** die Kinder sind ganz leise; **in a quiet voice** mit leiser Stimme; 3 (*peaceful*) ruhig; **a quiet street** eine ruhige Straße.

△ NEW SPELLING: *See page xii*

quietly adverb **1** (*speak, move*) leise; **he got up quietly** er ist leise aufgestanden; **2** (*read or play*) ruhig; **to sit quietly** ruhig sitzen.

quilt noun Steppdecke die (PL die Steppdecken).

quite adverb **1** (*fairly*) ziemlich; **it's quite cold outside** es ist ziemlich kalt draußen; **quite often** ziemlich oft; **quite a few** ziemlich viele; **quite a few of our friends came** ziemlich viele unserer Freunde sind gekommen; **quite a few people** ziemlich viele Leute; **that's quite a good idea** das ist eine ganz gute Idee; **2** (*completely*) völlig; **it was quite amazing** es war einfach fantastisch; **not quite** nicht ganz; **she's not quite ready** sie ist noch nicht ganz fertig; **3** genau; **I don't quite know what he wants** ich weiß nicht genau, was er will; **quite!** genau!

quiz noun Quiz das (PL die Quiz).

quotation noun (*from a book*) Zitat das (PL die Zitate).

quotation marks plural noun Anführungszeichen (*plural*); **in quotation marks** in Anführungszeichen.

quote noun **1** (*from a book*) Zitat das (PL die Zitate); **2** (*estimate*) Kostenvoranschlag der (PL die Kostenvoranschläge). verb zitieren.

R r

rabbi noun Rabbi der (PL die Rabbis).

rabbit noun Kaninchen das (PL die Kaninchen).

race noun **1** (*a sports event*) Rennen das (PL die Rennen); **cycle race** das Radrennen; **2 to have a race** (*running*) um die Wette laufen ✧ (PERF sein); (*swimming*) um die Wette schwimmen ✧ (PERF sein); **3** (*an ethnic group*) Rasse die (PL die Rassen).

racetrack noun Rennbahn die (PL die Rennbahnen).

racial adjective rassisch, Rassen-; **racial discrimination** die Rassendiskriminierung.

racing car noun Rennwagen der (PL die Rennwagen).

racing driver noun Rennfahrer der (PL die Rennfahrer).

racism noun Rassismus der.

racist noun Rassist der (PL die Rassisten), Rassistin die (PL die Rassistinnen). adjective rassistisch.

racket noun **1** (*for tennis*) Schläger der (PL die Schläger); **my tennis racket** mein Tennisschläger; **2** (*noise*) Krach der.

radiator noun Heizkörper der (PL die Heizkörper).

✧ IRREGULAR VERB: *See the verb table in the centre of the dictionary*

radio *noun* Radio *das* (PL *die* Radios); **to listen to the radio** Radio hören; **to hear something on the radio** etwas im Radio hören.

radioactive *adjective* radioaktiv.

radio station *noun* Rundfunkstation *die* (PL *die* Rundfunkstationen).

radish *noun* Radieschen *das* (PL *die* Radieschen).

rag *noun* Lumpen *der* (PL *die* Lumpen).

rage *noun* Wut *die*; **to fly into a rage** in Wut geraten ✧ (PERF *sein*); **she's in a rage** sie ist wütend; ★ **it's all the rage** das ist der letzte Schrei (*literally: it's the last scream*).

rail *noun* **1** (*for a train*) Schiene *die* (PL *die* Schienen); **2** (*the railway*) **to go by rail** mit der Bahn fahren; **3** (*on a balcony, bridge, or stairs*) Geländer *das* (PL *die* Geländer).

rail card *noun* Bahnpass △ *der* (PL *die* Bahnpässe).

railing(s) *noun* Geländer *das* (PL *die* Geländer).

railway *noun* **1** (*the system*) Bahn *die*; **the railways** die Bahn; **2 railway line** (*from one place to another*) die Bahnstrecke; **3 on the railway line** (*the track*) auf dem Gleis.

railway carriage *noun* Eisenbahnwagen *der* (PL *die* Eisenbahnwagen).

railway station *noun* Bahnhof *der* (PL *die* Bahnhöfe).

rain *noun* Regen *der*, **in the rain** im Regen.
verb regnen; **it's raining** es regnet; **it's going to rain** es wird regnen.

rainbow *noun* Regenbogen *der* (PL *die* Regenbogen).

raincoat *noun* Regenmantel *der* (PL *die* Regenmäntel).

rainy *adjective* regnerisch.

raise *verb* **1** (*lift up*) hochheben ✧ SEP; **2** (*increase*) erhöhen (*prices*); **3 to raise money for something** Geld für etwas aufbringen ✧ SEP.

raisin *noun* Rosine *die* (PL *die* Rosinen).

rally *noun* **1** (*a meeting*) Versammlung *die* (PL *die* Versammlungen); **2** (*for cars*) Rallye *die* (PL *die* Rallyes); **3** (*in tennis*) Ballwechsel *der* (PL *die* Ballwechsel).

rambler *noun* Wanderer *der* (PL *die* Wanderer), Wanderin *die* (PL *die* Wanderinnen).

rambling *noun* Wandern *das*.

range *noun* **1** (*a choice*) Auswahl *die*; **a wide range of travel brochures** eine große Auswahl an Reiseprospekten; **2 a range of subjects** verschiedene Fächer; **in a range of colours** in verschiedenen Farben; **3 a computer in this price range** ein Computer in dieser Preislage; **that's out of my price range** das kann ich mir nicht leisten.

rap *noun* Rap *der* (*music*).

△ NEW SPELLING: *See page xii*

rape *noun* Vergewaltigung *die* (PL
die Vergewaltigungen).
verb vergewaltigen.

rare *adjective* 1 selten; **a rare bird**
ein seltener Vogel; 2 englisch
gebraten (*steak*).

rarely *adverb* selten.

rash *noun* Ausschlag *der* (PL die
Ausschläge).
adjective voreilig.

raspberry *noun* Himbeere *die* (PL
die Himbeeren); **raspberry jam** *die*
Himbeermarmelade.

rat *noun* Ratte *die* (PL die Ratten).

rate *noun* 1 (*a charge*) Gebühren
(*plural*); **postage rates**
Postgebühren; 2 **are there special
rates for children?** gibt es
Sonderpreise für Kinder?; **at
reduced rates** zu ermäßigten
Preisen; 3 **rate of exchange** *der*
Wechselkurs; 4 **rate of pay** *der*
Lohnsatz; 5 (*a level*) Rate *die* (PL die
Raten); **a high cancellation rate**
eine hohe Absagerate; 6 **at any rate**
auf jeden Fall.

rather *adverb* 1 lieber; **I'd rather
wait** ich warte lieber; **I'd rather you
didn't go** es wäre mir lieber, wenn
du nicht gingst; 2 ziemlich; **I'm
rather busy** ich habe ziemlich viel
zu tun; **I've got rather a lot of
shopping to do** ich muss noch
ziemlich viel einkaufen; 3 **rather
than** eher als; **in summer rather
than winter** eher im Sommer als im
Winter.

rave *noun* (*party*) Fete *die* (PL die
Feten) (*informal*).

raw *adjective* roh.

razor *noun* Rasierapparat *der* (PL die
Rasierapparate).

razor blade *noun* Rasierklinge *die*
(PL die Rasierklingen).

RE *noun* Religionsunterricht *der*.

reach *noun* Reichweite *die*; **out of
reach** außer Reichweite; **within
reach** leicht erreichbar; **to be within
easy reach of Munich** von
München aus leicht erreichbar sein.
verb 1 ankommen ◇ SEP (PERF *sein*)
an (+DAT) (*a place or point*),
ankommen ◇ SEP (PERF *sein*) in
(+DAT) (*a town or country*); **when
you reach the station** wenn du am
Bahnhof ankommst; 2 kommen ◇
(PERF *sein*) zu (+DAT) (*an agreement,
a conclusion*); **to reach a decision**
zu einer Entscheidung kommen;
3 **to reach for something** nach
etwas ←(DAT) greifen ◇.

react *verb* reagieren.

reaction *noun* Reaktion *die* (PL die
Reaktionen).

read *verb* 1 lesen ◇; **what are you
reading at the moment?** was liest
du zur Zeit?; **I'm reading a detective
novel** ich lese einen Krimi; 2 **to
read out** vorlesen ◇ SEP; **he read
out the list to the students** er hat
die Liste den Studenten vorgelesen.

reading *noun* 1 (*action*) Lesen *das*;
2 (*reading matter*) Lektüre *die*;
some easy reading for the holidays
eine leichte Lektüre für die Ferien.

ready *adjective* 1 fertig; **supper's not
ready yet** das Essen ist noch nicht

◇ IRREGULAR VERB: *See the verb table in the centre of the dictionary*

fertig; **we are not quite ready** wir sind noch nicht ganz fertig; **are you ready to leave?** seid ihr fertig?; (*on a journey*) seid ihr reisefertig?; **to get ready** sich fertig machen; **I'm getting ready to play tennis** ich mache mich zum Tennisspielen fertig; **I was getting ready for bed** ich war gerade dabei, ins Bett zu gehen; **2 to get something ready** (*complete*) etwas fertig machen, etwas vorbereiten SEP (*a room or food*); **I'll get your room ready** ich bereite dein Zimmer vor.

real *adjective* **1** (*genuine*) echt; **it's a real diamond** das ist ein echter Brillant; **he's a real coward** er ist ein echter Feigling; **2** (*true*) richtig; **is that her real name?** ist das ihr richtiger Name?; **3** (*not imagined*) wirklich; **it's a real pity you can't come** es ist wirklich schade, dass du nicht kommen kannst.

realistic *adjective* realistisch.

realize *verb* wissen ◇; **I hadn't realized** das wusste ich nicht; **I didn't realize he was French** ich habe nicht gewusst, dass er Franzose ist; **do you realize what time it is?** weißt du, wie viel Uhr es ist?

really *adverb* **1** wirklich; **the film was really good** der Film war wirklich gut; **really?** wirklich?; **2 not really** eigentlich nicht.

reason *noun* Grund *der* (PL *die* Gründe); **for that reason** aus diesem Grund; **the reason why I phoned** der Grund meines Anrufs.

reasonable *adjective* vernünftig.

receipt *noun* Quittung *die* (PL *die* Quittungen).

receive *verb* erhalten ◇.

receiver *noun* Hörer *der* (PL *die* Hörer); **to pick up the receiver** den Hörer abnehmen ◇ SEP.

recent *adjective* **1** kürzlich erfolgter/kürzlich erfolgte/ kürzlich erfolgtes; **the recent closure** die kürzlich erfolgte Schließung; **2 in recent years** in den letzten Jahren.

recently *adverb* **1** (*at a time not long ago*) kürzlich; **2** (*over the recent period*) in letzter Zeit.

reception *noun* **1** Rezeption *die* (PL *die* Rezeptionen); **he's waiting at reception** er wartet in der Rezeption; **2** Empfang *der* (PL *die* Empfänge); **a big wedding reception** ein großer Hochzeitsempfang; **3 to get a good reception** gut aufgenommen werden.

receptionist *noun* **1** Empfangsdame *die* (PL *die* Empfangsdamen); **2** (*in a doctor's surgery*) Sprechstundenhilfe *die* (PL *die* Sprechstundenhilfen).

recipe *noun* Rezept *das* (PL *die* Rezepte).

reckon *verb* glauben; **I reckon it's a good idea** ich glaube, das ist eine gute Idee.

recognize *verb* erkennen ◇.

recommend *verb* empfehlen ◇; **can you recommend a dentist?** kannst du mir einen Zahnarzt empfehlen?; **I recommend the fish soup** ich empfehle die Fischsuppe.

record noun 1 Rekord der (PL die Rekorde); **it's a world record** das ist ein Weltrekord; **record sales** Verkaufsrekorde; 2 (*of events*) Aufzeichnung die (PL die Aufzeichnungen); **on record** aufgezeichnet; **to keep a record of something** sich ←(DAT) etwas notieren; 3 (*music*) Platte die (PL die Platten); **a Miles Davis record** eine Platte von Miles Davis; 4 **records** (*office files*) Unterlagen (*plural*); **I'll just check your records** ich prüfe nur Ihre Unterlagen.
verb (*on tape*) aufnehmen ✧ SEP; **I'm recording it on cassette** ich nehme es auf Kassette auf.

recorder noun 1 Blockflöte die (PL die Blockflöten); **to play the recorder** Blockflöte spielen; 2 **cassette recorder** der Kassettenrekorder; **video recorder** der Videorekorder.

recording noun (*on tape or CD*) Aufnahme die (PL die Aufnahmen); (*on video*) Aufzeichnung die (PL die Aufzeichnungen).

record player noun Plattenspieler der (PL die Plattenspieler).

recover verb sich erholen; **she's recovered now** sie hat sich wieder erholt.

recovery noun (*from an illness*) Erholung die; **to make a good recovery** sich gut erholen.

recycle verb recyceln.

red adjective rot; **a red car** ein rotes Auto; **to go red** rot werden; **to have red hair** rote Haare haben.

Red Cross noun **the Red Cross** das Rote Kreuz.

redcurrant noun Johannisbeere die (PL die Johannisbeeren); **redcurrant jelly** das Johannisbeergelee.

redecorate verb (*with paint*) neu streichen ✧; (*with wallpaper*) neu tapezieren; **they've redecorated the kitchen** sie haben die Küche neu gestrichen.

redo verb noch einmal machen.

reduce verb 1 **to reduce prices** die Preise herabsetzen SEP; 2 **to reduce speed** die Geschwindigkeit verringern.

reduction noun 1 (*in price*) Ermäßigung die (PL die Ermäßigungen); 2 (*in speed or number*) Verringerung die.

redundant adjective **to be made redundant** entlassen werden.

referee noun (*in sport*) Schiedsrichter der (PL die Schiedsrichter), Schiedsrichterin die (PL die Schiedsrichterinnen).

reference noun Referenz die (PL die Referenzen); (*for a job*) **she gave me a good reference** sie hat mir gute Referenzen ausgestellt.

reference book noun Nachschlagewerk das (PL die Nachschlagewerke).

refill verb nachfüllen SEP.

✧ IRREGULAR VERB: *See the verb table in the centre of the dictionary*

reflect verb spiegeln, to be reflected sich spiegeln.

reflection noun 1 (in a mirror or on water) Spiegelung die (PL die Spiegelungen); to see your reflection in the mirror sich im Spiegel sehen; 2 (thought) Überlegung die; on reflection nach nochmaliger Überlegung.

reflexive adjective a reflexive verb ein reflexives Verb.

refreshing adjective erfrischend.

refrigerator noun Kühlschrank der (PL die Kühlschränke).

refugee noun Flüchtling der (PL die Flüchtlinge).

refund noun Rückzahlung die (PL die Rückzahlungen). verb zurückerstatten SEP.

refusal noun 1 Weigerung die (PL die Weigerungen); 2 (for a job) Absage die (PL die Absagen); to get a refusal eine Absage bekommen.

refuse noun (rubbish) Abfall der. verb sich weigern; I refused ich habe mich geweigert; he refuses to help er weigert sich zu helfen.

regards plural noun Grüße (plural); regards to your parents viele Grüße an deine Eltern; Nat sends his regards Nat lässt grüßen.

reggae noun Reggae der.

region noun Gebiet das (PL die Gebiete).

regional adjective regional.

register noun (in school) Anwesenheitsliste die (PL die Anwesenheitslisten), Klassenbuch das (PL die Klassenbücher) (kept by the teacher, it also contains notes about students' achievements). verb 1 eintragen ✧ SEP (a name); 2 (report) anmelden SEP.

registered letter noun Einschreiben das (PL die Einschreiben).

registration number noun Autonummer die (PL die Autonummern).

regret verb bedauern.

regular adjective regelmäßig; regular visits regelmäßige Besuche.

regularly adverb regelmäßig.

regulation noun Vorschrift die (PL die Vorschriften).

rehearsal noun Probe die (PL die Proben).

rehearse verb proben.

reheat verb aufwärmen SEP.

reject verb ablehnen SEP.

related adjective verwandt; we're not related wir sind nicht verwandt.

relation noun Verwandte der/die (PL die Verwandten).

relationship noun Beziehung die (PL die Beziehungen); I have a good relationship with my parents ich habe eine gute Beziehung zu meinen Eltern.

△ NEW SPELLING: See page xii

relative noun Verwandte der/die (PL die Verwandten).

relatively adverb relativ.

relax verb entspannen; **I'm going to relax and watch telly tonight** heute Abend entspanne ich und sehe fern.

relaxed adjective entspannt.

relaxing adjective entspannend.

relay race noun Staffel die (PL die Staffeln).

release noun (a film, CD, or book) **1** Neuerscheinung die (PL die Neuerscheinungen); **this week's new releases** die neuen Filme der Woche; **2** (of a prisoner or hostage) Freilassung die (PL die Freilassungen).
verb **1** herausbringen ✧ SEP (a record, film, or video);
2 freilassen ✧ SEP (a person).

reliable adjective zuverlässig.

relief noun Erleichterung die; **what a relief!** da bin ich aber erleichtert!

relieve verb stillen (pain).

relieved adjective erleichtert; **I was relieved to hear you'd arrived** es hat mich erleichtert zu hören, dass du angekommen bist.

religion noun Religion die (PL die Religionen).

religious adjective religiös.

rely verb **1** (trust) **to rely on somebody** sich auf jemanden verlassen ✧; **I'm relying on your help for Saturday** ich verlasse mich darauf, dass du mir am Samstag

hilfst; **2** (be dependent on) **to rely on** angewiesen sein auf (+ACC).

remain verb (be left over) übrig bleiben ✧ ∆ (PERF sein); (stay) bleiben ✧ (PERF sein).

remark noun Bemerkung die (PL d Bemerkungen); **to make remarks about something** Bemerkungen über etwas ←(ACC) machen.

remarkable adjective bemerkenswert.

remarkably adverb bemerkenswert.

remember verb **1** sich erinnern an (+ACC) (a person or an occasion); **I don't remember** daran kann ich mich nicht erinnern; **do you remember the holiday in Italy?** erinnerst du dich noch an die Ferien in Italien?; **2 I can't remember his number** seine Nummer fällt mir nicht ein; **3 to remember to do something** daran denken ✧, etwas zu tun; **remember to lock the door** denk daran abzuschließen; **I remembered to bring the CDs** ich habe daran gedacht, die CDs mitzubringen.

remind verb **1** erinnern; **to remind somebody to do something** jemanden daran erinnern, etwas zu tun; **remind your mother to pick me up** erinnere deine Mutter daran, mich abzuholen; **he reminds me of my brother** er erinnert mich an meinen Bruder; **2 oh, that reminds me ...** dabei fällt mir ein, ...

remote adjective abgelegen.

✧ IRREGULAR VERB: See the verb table in the centre of the dictionary

remote control *noun* **1** (*for a car or plane*) Fernsteuerung *die* (PL *die* Fernsteuerungen); **2** (*for TV or video*) Fernbedienung *die* (PL *die* Fernbedienungen).

remove *verb* **1** entfernen (*a stain, mark, or obstacle*); **2** ausziehen ◇ SEP (*clothes*).

renew *verb* verlängern (*a passport or licence*).

rent *noun* Miete *die* (PL *die* Mieten).
verb mieten; **Simon's rented a flat** Simon hat eine Wohnung gemietet.

reorganize *verb* umorganisieren.

repair *noun* Reparatur *die* (PL *die* Reparaturen).
verb reparieren; **to get something repaired** etwas reparieren lassen; **we've had the television repaired** wir haben unseren Fernseher reparieren lassen.

repay *verb* zurückzahlen SEP.

repeat *noun* Wiederholung *die* (PL *die* Wiederholungen).
verb wiederholen.

repeatedly *adverb* wiederholt.

repetitive *adjective* eintönig.

replace *verb* ersetzen.

reply *noun* Antwort *die* (PL *die* Antworten); **I didn't get a reply to my letter** ich habe keine Antwort auf meinen Brief bekommen; **there's no reply** niemand antwortet.
verb antworten; **I still haven't replied to the letter** ich habe immer noch nicht auf den Brief geantwortet.

report *noun* **1** (*of an event*) Bericht *der* (PL *die* Berichte); **2** (*school report*) Zeugnis *das* (PL *die* Zeugnisse).
verb **1** melden (*a problem or an accident*); **we've reported the theft** wir haben den Diebstahl gemeldet; **2** sich melden; **I had to report to reception** ich musste mich an der Rezeption melden; **3** (*in the news*) berichten; **to report on the strike** über den Streik berichten.

reporter *noun* Reporter *der* (PL *die* Reporter), Reporterin *die* (PL *die* Reporterinnen).

represent *verb* **1** darstellen SEP (*a word, a thing, an idea*); **2** verteten ◇ (*a group or company*).

representative *noun* Vertreter *der* (PL *die* Vertreter), Vertreterin *die* (PL *die* Vertreterinnen).

republic *noun* Republik *die* (PL *die* Republiken).

reputation *noun* **1** Ruf *der*; **to have a good reputation** einen guten Ruf haben; **2 she has a reputation for honesty** sie gilt als ehrlich.

request *noun* Bitte *die* (PL *die* Bitten); **at my mother's request** auf Bitte meiner Mutter.
verb bitten ◇; **to request something** um etwas ←(ACC) bitten.

rescue *noun* Rettung *die*; **rescue operation** *die* Rettungsaktion; **to come to somebody's rescue** jemandem zu Hilfe kommen.
verb retten; **they rescued the dog** sie haben den Hund gerettet.

△ NEW SPELLING: *See page xii*

rescue party *noun*
Rettungsmannschaft *die* (PL *die* Rettungsmannschaften).

research *noun* 1 Forschung *die*; **for research into Aids** für die Aidsforschung; 2 **to do research** forschen.
verb **to research into something** etwas erforschen.

resemblance *noun*
Ähnlichkeit *die* (PL *die* Ähnlichkeiten).

reservation *noun* (*a booking*) Reservierung *die* (PL *die* Reservierungen); **to make a reservation (for a room)** (ein Zimmer) reservieren lassen.

reserve *noun* 1 Reserve *die* (PL *die* Reserven); **we have a few in reserve** wir haben ein paar in Reserve; 2 **nature reserve** *das* Naturschutzgebiet; 3 (*for a match*) Reservespieler *der* (PL *die* Reservespieler), Reservespielerin *die* (PL *die* Reservespielerinnen).
verb reservieren; **this table is reserved** dieser Tisch ist reserviert.

resident *noun* Bewohner *der* (PL *die* Bewohner), Bewohnerin *die* (PL *die* Bewohnerinnen).

residential *adjective* Wohn-; **a residential area** eine Wohngegend.

resign *verb* 1 (*from your job*) kündigen; 2 (*from an official post*) zurücktreten ✧ SEP.

resignation *noun* 1 Kündigung *die* (PL *die* Kündigungen); 2 (*from an official post*) Rücktritt *der*.

resist *verb* widerstehen ✧ (+DAT) (*an offer or temptation*).

resit *verb* wiederholen (*an exam*).

resort *noun* 1 (*for holidays*) holiday resort *der* Urlaubsort; **ski resort** *der* Skiurlaubsort; **seaside resort** *das* Seebad; 2 **as a last resort** als letzter Ausweg.

respect *noun* Respekt *der*.
verb respektieren.

respectable *adjective* anständig.

responsibility *noun*
Verantwortung *die* (PL *die* Verantwortungen).

responsible *adjective*
1 verantwortlich; **he was responsible for the accident** er war für den Unfall verantwortlich; **I'm responsible for booking the rooms** ich bin für die Zimmerreservierung verantwortlich; 2 (*reliable*) verantwortungsbewusst △; **he's not very responsible** er ist nicht sehr verantwortungsbewusst.

rest *noun* 1 **the rest** der Rest; **the rest of the day** der Rest des Tages; **the rest of the bread** der Brotrest, der Rest von dem Brot; 2 (*the others*) **the rest** die Übrigen; **the rest have gone home** die Übrigen sind nach Hause gegangen; 3 Erholung *die*; **he's going to the mountains for a rest** er fährt zur Erholung ins Gebirge; **ten days' rest** zehn Tage Erholung; **to have a rest** sich ausruhen SEP; 4 (*a short break*) Pause *die* (PL *die* Pausen); **to stop for a rest** eine Pause machen.
verb (*have a rest*) sich ausruhen SEP.

✧ IRREGULAR VERB: *See the verb table in the centre of the dictionary*

restaurant *noun* Restaurant das (PL *die* Restaurants).

restful *adjective* erholsam.

restless *adjective* unruhig.

restrain *verb* zurückhalten ✧ SEP.

result *noun* 1 Ergebnis *das* (PL *die* Ergebnisse); **the exam results** die Prüfungsergebnisse; 2 **as a result** infolgedessen; **as a result we missed the train** infolgedessen haben wir den Zug verpasst.

retire *verb* 1 (*from work*) aufhören zu arbeiten; (*civil servant, teacher, soldier*) sich pensionieren lassen; **she retires in June** sie lässt sich im Juni pensionieren; 2 **to be retired** nicht mehr arbeiten.

retirement *noun* Ruhestand *der*; **since his retirement** seitdem er in den Ruhestand gegangen ist.

return *noun* 1 (*coming back*) Rückkehr *die*; **the return journey** die Rückreise; 2 **by return of post** postwendend; 3 **in return for** für; **in return for his help** für seine Hilfe; 4 **in return** dafür; ★ **many happy returns!** herzlichen Glückwunsch zum Geburtstag.
verb 1 (*come back*) zurückkommen ✧ SEP (PERF *sein*); **he returned ten minutes later** er kam zehn Minuten später zurück; **to return from holiday** aus den Ferien zurückkommen; 2 (*go back*) zurückgehen ✧ SEP (PERF *sein*); (*drive*) zurückfahren ✧ SEP (PERF *sein*); **we are planning to return in the evening** wir wollen am Abend zurückfahren; 3 (*to give back*)

zurückgeben ✧ SEP, **Gemma's never returned the video** Gemma hat das Video nie zurückgegeben.

return fare *noun* Preis für eine Rückfahrkarte *der*; (*for a flight*) Preis für einen Rückflugschein *der*.

return ticket *noun* Rückfahrkarte *die* (PL *die* Rückfahrkarten); (*for a flight*) Rückflugschein *der* (PL *die* Rückflugscheine)

reveal *verb* enthüllen.

reverse *verb* 1 (*in a car*) rückwärts fahren ✧ (PERF *sein*); 2 **to reverse the charges** ein R-Gespräch führen.

review *noun* (*of a book, play, or film*) Kritik *die* (PL *die* Kritiken).
verb rezensieren (*a book, play, or film*).

revise *verb* 1 lernen (*for an exam*); **Tessa's busy revising for her exams** Tessa lernt jetzt für ihre Prüfung; 2 wiederholen; **to revise maths** Mathe wiederholen.

revision *noun* Wiederholung *die*.

revolting *adjective* eklig.

revolution *noun* Revolution *die* (PL *die* Revolutionen).

reward *noun* Belohnung *die* (PL *die* Belohnungen).
verb belohnen.

rewind *verb* zurückspulen SEP (*a cassette or video*).

rhubarb *noun* Rhabarber *der*.

rhyme *noun* Reim *der* (PL *die* Reime).

rhythm *noun* Rhythmus *der* (PL *die* Rhythmen).

ribbon *noun* Band *das* (PL *die* Bänder).

rice *noun* Reis *der*; **rice pudding** *der* Milchreis.

rich *adjective* **1** reich; **they are very rich** sie sind sehr reich; **2 the rich** die Reichen.

rid *adjective* **to get rid of something** etwas loswerden ◇ SEP (PERF *sein*) (*informal*); **we got rid of the car** wir sind das Auto losgeworden.

riddle *noun* Rätsel *das* (PL *die* Rätsel).

ride *noun* Fahrt *die* (PL *die* Fahrten); **to go for a ride (on a bike)** eine Fahrt machen; **to go for a ride (on a horse)** reiten gehen ◇ (PERF *sein*). *verb* **1 to ride a bike** Rad fahren ◇ △ (PERF *sein*); **can you ride a bike?** kannst du Rad fahren?; **I've never ridden a bike** ich bin noch nie Rad gefahren; **2 to ride (a horse)** reiten ◇ (PERF *sein*); **I've never ridden a horse** ich bin noch nie auf einem Pferd geritten.

ridiculous *adjective* lächerlich.

riding *noun* Reiten *das*; **to go riding** reiten gehen.

riding school *noun* Reitschule *die* (PL *die* Reitschulen).

right *noun* **1** (*not left*) rechte Seite *die*; **on the right** auf der rechten Seite; **on my right** rechts von mir; **2** (*to do something*) Recht *das* (PL *die* Rechte); **to have the right to something** ein Recht auf etwas ←(ACC) haben; **the right to work** das Recht auf Arbeit; **you have no right to say that** du hast kein Recht, das zu sagen. *adjective* **1** (*not left*) rechter/rechte/ rechtes; **my right hand** meine rechte Hand; **2** (*correct*) richtig; **the right answer** die richtige Antwort; **is this the right address?** ist das die richtige Adresse?; **3 to be right** (*of person*) Recht haben; **you see, I was right** siehst du, ich hatte Recht; **4 you were right not to say anything** du hattest Recht, nichts zu sagen; **5 the clock is right** die Uhr geht richtig; **6 yes, that's right** ja, das stimmt; **is that right?** stimmt das? *adverb* **1** (*direction*) rechts; **turn right at the lights** biege an der Ampel rechts ab; **2** (*correctly*) richtig; **you're not doing it right** du machst das nicht richtig; **3** (*completely*) ganz; **right at the bottom** ganz unten; **right at the beginning** ganz am Anfang; **4** (*exactly*) genau; **right in the middle** genau in der Mitte; **5 right now** sofort; **6** (*okay*) gut; **right, let's go** gut, gehen wir.

right-hand *adjective* **on the right-hand side** rechts.

right-handed *adjective* rechtshändig.

ring *noun* **1** (*on the phone*) **to give somebody a ring** jemanden anrufen ◇ SEP; **2** (*for your finger*) Ring *der* (PL *die* Ringe); **3** (*circle*) Kreis *der* (PL *die* Kreise); **4 there was a ring at the door** es hat geklingelt.

◇ IRREGULAR VERB: *See the verb table in the centre of the dictionary*

verb 1 *(a bell or phone)* klingeln; **the phone rang** das Telefon hat geklingelt; 2 *(phone)* anrufen ✧ SEP; **I'll ring you tomorrow** ich rufe dich morgen an; 3 **to ring for a taxi** ein Taxi rufen.
to ring back zurückrufen ✧ SEP; **I'll ring you back later** ich rufe dich später zurück.
to ring off auflegen SEP.

ring road *noun* Ringstraße *die* (PL die Ringstraßen).

rinse *verb* spülen.

riot *noun* Aufstand *der* (PL die Aufstände).

rioting *noun* Unruhen *(plural)*.

rip *verb* zerreißen ✧.

ripe *adjective* reif; **are the tomatoes ripe?** sind die Tomaten reif?

rip-off *noun* **it's a rip-off** das ist Nepp *(informal)*.

rise *noun* 1 Anstieg *der*; **a rise in temperature** ein Temperaturanstieg; 2 **pay rise** die Gehaltserhöhung.
verb 1 *(the sun)* aufgehen ✧ SEP (PERF *sein*); 2 *(prices)* steigen ✧ (PERF *sein*).

risk *noun* Risiko *das* (PL die Risiken); **to take a risk** ein Risiko eingehen.
verb riskieren; **he risks losing his job** er riskiert es, seine Stelle zu verlieren.

river *noun* Fluss △ *der* (PL die Flüsse).

road *noun* 1 Straße *die* (PL die Straßen); **the road to London** die Straße nach London; 2 **the baker's is on the other side of the road** die Bäckerei ist auf der anderen Straßenseite; 3 **across the road** gegenüber; **they live across the road from us** sie wohnen bei uns gegenüber.

road accident *noun* Verkehrsunfall *der* (PL die Verkehrsunfälle).

road map *noun* Straßenkarte *die* (PL die Straßenkarten).

roadside *noun* **by the roadside** am Straßenrand.

road sign *noun* Straßenschild *das* (PL die Straßenschilder).

roadworks *plural noun* Straßenarbeiten *(plural)*.

roast *noun* Braten *der* (PL die Braten).
adjective gebraten; **roast potatoes** Bratkartoffeln; **roast beef** *der* Rinderbraten.

rob *verb* 1 berauben *(a person)*; 2 ausrauben SEP *(a bank)*.

robber *noun* Räuber *der* (PL die Räuber).

robbery *noun* Raub *der* (PL die Raube); **bank robbery** *der* Bankraub.

rock *noun* 1 *(a big stone)* Felsen *der* (PL die Felsen); 2 *(the material)* Fels *der*; 3 *(music)* Rock *der*; **rock band** die Rockband; **to dance rock and roll** Rock'n'Roll tanzen.

rock climbing *noun* Klettern *das*; **to go rock climbing** zum Klettern gehen.

rock star *noun* Rockstar *der* (PL *die* Rockstars).

rocky *adjective* felsig.

rod *noun* **a fishing rod** eine Angel.

role *noun* Rolle *die* (PL *die* Rollen); **to play the role of Hamlet** die Rolle des Hamlet spielen.

roll *noun* 1 Rolle *die* (PL *die* Rollen); **a roll of film** eine Rolle Film; **a toilet roll** eine Rolle Toilettenpapier; 2 **bread roll** *das* Brötchen, *die* Semmel (*South German*). *verb* rollen (PERF *sein*).

roller *noun* 1 (*for hair*) Lockenwickler *der* (PL *die* Lockenwickler); 2 (*for paint*) Rolle *die* (PL *die* Rollen).

rollerblades *plural noun* Inlineskates (*plural*), Inliners (*plural*).

roller skates *plural noun* Rollschuhe (*plural*).

Roman Catholic *adjective* römisch-katholisch.

romantic *adjective* romantisch.

roof *noun* Dach *das* (PL *die* Dächer).

roof rack *noun* Gepäckträger *der* (PL *die* Gepäckträger).

room *noun* 1 Zimmer *das* (PL *die* Zimmer); **she's in the other room** sie ist im anderen Zimmer; **a three-room flat** eine Dreizimmerwohnung; 2 (*space*) Platz *der*; **enough room for two** genug Platz für zwei; **very little room** wenig Platz; **to make room** Platz machen.

root *noun* Wurzel *die* (PL *die* Wurzeln).

rope *noun* Seil *das* (PL *die* Seile).

rose *noun* Rose *die* (PL *die* Rosen).

rot *verb* verfaulen (PERF *sein*).

rotten *adjective* verfault.

rough *adjective* 1 (*scratchy*) rau △; 2 (*vague*) grob (*plan or estimate*); 3 **a rough idea** eine vage Vorstellung; 4 (*stormy*) stürmisch; **a rough sea** eine stürmische See; 5 (*difficult*) **to have a rough time** e schwer haben; 6 **to sleep rough** ir Freien schlafen.

roughly *adverb* (*approximately*) ungefähr; **roughly ten per cent** ungefähr zehn Prozent; **it takes roughly three hours** es dauert ungefähr drei Stunden.

round *noun* Runde *die* (PL *die* Runden); **a round of talks** eine Gesprächsrunde; **a round of drinks** eine Runde. *adjective* rund; **a round table** ein runder Tisch. *preposition* 1 um (+ACC); **round the city** um die Stadt; **round my arm** um meinen Arm; **they were sitting round the table** sie haben um den Tisch gesessen; **it's just round the corner** es ist gleich um die Ecke; 2 **to go round a museum** ein Museum besuchen. *adverb* 1 **to go round to somebody's house** jemanden besuchen←(DAT); 2 **to invite somebody round** jemanden zu sich←(DAT) einladen ◇ SEP; **we invited Sally round for lunch** wir

◇ IRREGULAR VERB: *See the verb table in the centre of the dictionary*

haben Sally zum Mittagessen eingeladen; **3 to look round the shops** sich in den Geschäften umsehen ✧ SEP; **4 all the year round** das ganze Jahr hindurch.

roundabout *noun* **1** (*for traffic*) Kreisverkehr *der*; **2** (*in a fairground*) Karussell *das* (PL *die* Karussells).

route *noun* **1** (*that you plan*) Route *die* (PL *die* Routen); **the best route is via Calais** die beste Route ist über Calais; **2 bus route** *die* Linie.

row[1] *noun* **1** Reihe *die* (PL *die* Reihen); **in the front row** in der ersten Reihe; **in the back row** in der letzten Reihe; **2 in a row** hintereinander; **four times in a row** viermal hintereinander.
verb (*in a boat*) rudern (PERF *sein/haben*); **we rowed across the lake** wir sind über den See gerudert; **he rowed us across the lake** er hat uns über den See gerudert.

row[2] *noun* **1** (*a quarrel*) Krach *der* (*informal*) (PL *die* Kräche); **to have a row** Krach haben; **they've had a row** sie haben Krach gehabt; **I had a row with my parents** ich habe Krach mit meinen Eltern gehabt; **2** (*noise*) Krach *der*; **they were making a terrible row** sie haben einen furchtbaren Krach gemacht.

rowing *noun* Rudern *das*; **to go rowing** rudern gehen.

rowing boat *noun* Ruderboot *das* (PL *die* Ruderboote).

royal *adjective* königlich; **the royal family** die königliche Familie.

rub *verb* reiben ◊, **to rub your eyes** sich ←(DAT) die Augen reiben.
● **to rub something out** etwas ausradieren SEP.

rubber *noun* **1** (*an eraser*) Radiergummi *der* (PL *die* Radiergummis); **2** (*material*) Gummi *der*; **rubber soles** Gummisohlen.

rubbish *noun* **1** (*for the bin*) Müll *der*; **2** (*nonsense*) Quatsch *der* (*informal*); **you're talking rubbish!** du redest Quatsch. *adjective* blöd; **the film was rubbish** der Film war blöd; **they're a rubbish band** sie sind eine blöde Band.

rubbish bin *noun* Mülleimer *der* (PL *die* Mülleimer).

rucksack *noun* Rucksack *der* (PL *die* Rucksäcke).

rude *adjective* **1** unhöflich; **that's rude** das ist unhöflich; **2** unanständig; **a rude joke** ein unanständiger Witz.

rug *noun* **1** Teppich *der* (PL *die* Teppiche); **2** (*a blanket*) Decke *die* (PL *die* Decken).

rugby *noun* Rugby *das*.

ruin *noun* (*remains*) Ruine *die* (PL *die* Ruinen); **in ruins** in Trümmern. *verb* **1** ruinieren; **you'll ruin your jacket** du ruinierst dir die Jacke; **2** verderben ✧ (*day, holiday*); **it ruined my evening** das hat mir den Abend verdorben.

rule *noun* **1** Regel *die* (PL *die* Regeln); **the rules of the game** die

△ NEW SPELLING: *See page xii*

Spielregeln; **as a rule** in der Regel;
2 (*administrative*) Vorschrift *die*
(PL *die* Vorschriften); **according to
the school rules** nach den
Schulvorschriften.

ruler *noun* Lineal *das* (PL *die*
Lineale); **I've lost my ruler** ich habe
mein Lineal verloren.

rumour *noun* Gerücht *das* (PL *die*
Gerüchte).

run *noun* **1** (*in games, sport, and for
fitness*) Lauf *der* (PL *die* Läufe); **to
go for a run** einen Lauf machen,
joggen (PERF *sein*); **2** (*of a play*)
Laufzeit *die*; **3** (*in skiing*)
Abfahrt *die* (PL *die* Abfahrten);
4 in the long run auf lange Sicht.
verb **1** laufen ✧ (PERF *sein*); **I ran ten
kilometres** ich bin zehn Kilometer
gelaufen; **he ran across the pitch**
er ist über das Spielfeld gelaufen;
2 (*run fast*) rennen ✧ (PERF *sein*);
Kitty ran for the bus Kitty rannte,
um den Bus zu kriegen; **3** (*drive*)
fahren ✧; **I'll run you home later**
ich fahre dich später nach Hause;
4 (*organize*) veranstalten (*a course
or competition*); **who's running this
competition?** wer veranstaltet
diesen Wettbewerb?; **5** (*manage*)
leiten (*a business*); **she's been
running the firm for years** sie leitet
die Firma schon seit Jahren; **to
run a shop** ein Geschäft führen;
6 (*a train or a bus*) fahren ✧ (PERF
sein); **the buses don't run on
Sundays** sonntags fahren keine
Busse; **7 to run a bath** ein Bad
einlaufen lassen.
● **to run away** weglaufen ✧ SEP (PERF
sein).

● **to run into something** gegen etwas
←(ACC) fahren ✧ (PERF *sein*); **the car
ran into a tree** das Auto ist gegen
einen Baum gefahren.
● **to run out of something: we've run
out of bread** wir haben kein Brot
mehr; **I'm running out of money** ich
habe kaum noch Geld.
● **to run somebody over** jemanden
überfahren ✧; **he nearly got run
over** er ist beinahe überfahren
worden.

runner *noun* Läufer *der* (PL *die*
Läufer), Läuferin *die* (PL *die*
Läuferinnen).

runner-up *noun* Zweite *der/die* (PL
die Zweiten).

running *noun* (*for exercise*)
Laufen *das*, Jogging *das*.
adjective **1 running water**
fließendes Wasser; **2 three days
running** drei Tage hintereinander;
to win three times running dreimal
hintereinander gewinnen.

runway *noun* **1** (*for take-off*)
Startbahn *die* (PL *die* Startbahnen);
2 (*for landing*) Landebahn *die* (PL
die Landebahnen).

rush *noun* (*a hurry*) **to be in a rush**
in Eile sein; **sorry, I'm in a rush**
Entschuldigung, ich bin in Eile.
verb **1** (*hurry*) sich beeilen; **I must
rush!** ich muss mich beeilen;
2 (*run*) rasen (PERF *sein*); **she rushed
out** sie raste raus (*informal*);
3 Louise was rushed to hospital
Louise ist schnellstens ins
Krankenhaus gebracht worden.

✧ IRREGULAR VERB: *See the verb table in the centre of the dictionary*

rush hour *noun* Stoßzeit *die* (PL *die* Stoßzeiten); **in the rush hour** während der Stoßzeit.

Russia *noun* Russland △ *das*.

Russian *noun* 1 (*a person*) Russe *der* (PL *die* Russen), Russin *die* (PL *die* Russinnen); 2 (*the language*) Russisch *das*. *adjective* russisch; **he's Russian** er ist Russe.

rust *noun* Rost *der*.

rusty *adjective* rostig.

rye *noun* Roggen *der*.

S s

Sabbath *noun* 1 (*Jewish*) Sabbat *der* (PL *die* Sabbate); 2 (*Christian*) Sonntag *der* (PL *die* Sonntage).

sack *noun* 1 Sack *der* (PL *die* Säcke); 2 **to get the sack** rausgeschmissen werden (*informal*). *verb* **to sack somebody** jemanden rausschmeißen ♦ SEP (*informal*).

sad *adjective* traurig.

saddle *noun* Sattel *der* (PL *die* Sättel).

sadly *adverb* 1 traurig; **she looked at me sadly** sie hat mich traurig angesehen; 2 (*unfortunately*) leider.

safe *adjective* 1 (*out of danger*) sicher; **to feel safe from something** sich vor etwas ←(DAT) sicher fühlen;

2 **she's safe** sie ist in Sicherheit, 3 (*not dangerous*) ungefährlich; **the path is safe** der Weg ist ungefährlich; **it's not safe** das ist gefährlich.

safety *noun* Sicherheit *die*.

safety belt *noun* Sicherheitsgurt *der* (PL *die* Sicherheitsgurte).

safety pin *noun* Sicherheitsnadel *die* (PL *die* Sicherheitsnadeln).

Sagittarius *noun* Schütze *der*; **Kylie's Sagittarius** Kylie ist Schütze.

sail *noun* Segel *das* (PL *die* Segel).

sailing *noun* Segeln *das*; **to go sailing** segeln.

sailing boat *noun* Segelboot *das* (PL *die* Segelboote).

sailor *noun* Seemann *der* (PL *die* Seeleute).

saint *noun* Heilige *der/die*.

sake *noun* 1 **for your mother's sake** deiner Mutter zuliebe; 2 **for heaven's sake** um Gottes willen.

salad *noun* Salat *der* (PL *die* Salate); **tomato salad** *der* Tomatensalat.

salad dressing *noun* Salatsoße *die* (PL *die* Salatsoßen).

salary *noun* Gehalt *das* (PL *die* Gehälter).

sale *noun* 1 (*selling*) Verkauf *der* (PL *die* Verkäufe); **the sale of the house** der Verkauf des Hauses; **'for sale'** 'zu verkaufen'; 2 **the sales**

△ NEW SPELLING: *See page xii*

der Ausverkauf; **I bought it in the sales** ich habe es im Ausverkauf gekauft.

sales assistant *noun* Verkäufer *der* (PL *die* Verkäufer), Verkäuferin *die* (PL *die* Verkäuferinnen).

salesman *noun* Verkäufer *der* (PL *die* Verkäufer).

saleswoman *noun* Verkäuferin *die* (PL *die* Verkäuferinnen).

salmon *noun* Lachs *der* (PL *die* Lachse).

salt *noun* Salz *das*.

salty *adjective* salzig.

same *adjective* **the same** der gleiche/die gleiche/das gleiche; **she said the same thing** sie hat das gleiche gesagt; **her birthday's the same day as mine** sie hat am gleichen Tag Geburtstag wie ich; **at the same time** zur gleichen Zeit; **their car's the same as ours** sie haben das gleiche Auto wie wir. *adverb* **1 the same** gleich; **the two bikes look the same** die beiden Fahrräder sehen gleich aus; **2 all the same** trotzdem.

sample *noun* Muster *das* (PL *die* Muster); **a free sample** ein unverkäufliches Muster, eine Warenprobe.

sand *noun* Sand *der*.

sandal *noun* Sandale *die* (PL *die* Sandalen); **a pair of sandals** ein Paar Sandalen.

sandwich *noun* Sandwich *das* (PL *die* Sandwichs), belegte Brot *das* (PL *die* belegten Brote); **ham sandwich** *das* Schinkenbrot.

sanitary towel *noun* Damenbinde *die* (PL *die* Damenbinden).

Santa Claus *noun* der Weihnachtsmann.

sarcastic *adjective* sarkastisch.

sardine *noun* Sardine *die* (PL *die* Sardinen).

satchel *noun* Ranzen *der* (PL *die* Ranzen).

satellite *noun* Satellit *der* (PL *die* Satelliten).

satellite dish *noun* Satellitenschüssel *die* (PL *die* Satellitenschüsseln).

satellite television *noun* Satellitenfernsehen *das*.

satisfactory *adjective* befriedigend.

satisfied *adjective* zufrieden.

satisfy *verb* befriedigen.

satisfying *adjective* **1** befriedigend; **2 a satisfying meal** ein sättigendes Essen.

Saturday *noun* **1** Samstag *der* (PL *die* Samstage), Sonnabend *der* (*North German*) (PL *die* Sonnabende); **on Saturday** am Sonnabend/am Samstag; **I'm going out on Saturday** ich gehe Sonnabend aus; **see you on Saturday!** bis Samstag!; **every Saturday** jeden Samstag; **last**

✧ IRREGULAR VERB: *See the verb table in the centre of the dictionary*

Saturday vorigen Sonnabend; **next Saturday** nächsten Sonnabend; **2 on Saturdays** samstags, sonnabends (*North German*); **the museum is closed on Saturdays** das Museum ist sonnabends/ samstags geschlossen; **to have a Saturday job** sonnabends/ samstags arbeiten.

sauce *noun* Soße *die* (PL *die* Soßen).

saucepan *noun* Kochtopf *der* (PL *die* Kochtöpfe).

saucer *noun* Untertasse *die* (PL *die* Untertassen).

sausage *noun* Wurst *die* (PL *die* Würste).

save *verb* **1** retten (*life*); **to save somebody's life** jemandem das Leben retten; **the doctors saved his life** die Ärzte haben ihm das Leben gerettet; **2** sparen (*money*); **I've saved £60** ich habe sechzig Pfund gespart; **I cycle to school to save money** ich fahre mit dem Rad zur Schule, um Geld zu sparen; **we'll take a taxi to save time** um Zeit zu sparen, nehmen wir ein Taxi; **3** (*on a computer*) speichern; **4** (*stop*) abwehren SEP (*a shot*); **to save a penalty** einen Elfmeter abwehren.

● **to save up** sparen; **I'm saving up for a car** ich spare auf ein Auto.

savings *plural noun* Ersparnisse (*plural*).

savoury *adjective* (*not sweet*) pikant.

sax *noun* Saxophon *das* (PL *die* Saxophone).

saxophone *noun* Saxophon *das* (PL *die* Saxophone); **to play the saxophone** Saxophon spielen.

say *verb* **1** sagen; **what did you say?** was hast du gesagt?; **she says she's tired** sie sagt, dass sie müde ist; **he said to wait here** er hat gesagt, wir sollen hier warten; **they say** man sagt; **2 to say something again** etwas wiederholen; **3 that's to say** das heißt.

saying *noun* Redensart *die* (PL *die* Redensarten); **it's just a saying** das ist so eine Redensart; **as the saying goes** wie man so sagt.

scale *noun* **1** (*of a map or model*) Maßstab *der* (PL *die* Maßstäbe); **2** (*extent*) Ausmaß *das* (PL *die* Ausmaße); **the scale of the disaster** das Ausmaß der Katastrophe; **3** (*in music*) Tonleiter *die* (PL *die* Tonleitern).

scales *noun* Waage *die* (PL *die* Waagen); **bathroom scales** *die* Personenwaage.

scandal *noun* **1** Skandal *der* (PL *die* Skandale); **2** (*gossip*) Klatsch *der* (*informal*).

Scandinavia *noun* Skandinavien *das*.

Scandinavian *adjective* skandinavisch.

scar *noun* Narbe *die* (PL *die* Narben).

scarce *adjective* knapp.

scare *noun* **1** Schrecken *der* (PL *die* Schrecken); **to give somebody a scare** jemandem einen Schrecken einjagen SEP; **2** (*general alarm*)

Panik *die* (PL *die* Paniken); **to cause a scare** eine Panik auslösen; **3 bomb scare** *die* Bombendrohung. *verb* **to scare somebody** jemanden erschrecken; **you scared me!** du hast mich erschreckt!

scared *adjective* **1 to be scared** Angst haben; **I'm scared** ich habe Angst; **to be scared of something** vor etwas ←(DAT) Angst haben; **he's scared of dogs** er hat vor Hunden Angst; **2 to be scared of doing something** sich nicht trauen, etwas zu tun; **I'm scared of telling him the truth** ich traue mich nicht, ihm die Wahrheit zu sagen.

scarf *noun* **1** (*silky*) Tuch *das* (PL *die* Tücher); **2** (*long, warm*) Schal *der* (PL *die* Schals).

scary *adjective* unheimlich.

scene *noun* **1** (*of an incident or event*) Schauplatz *der* (PL *die* Schauplätze); **to be on the scene** am Schauplatz sein; **the scene of the crime** der Tatort; **2** (*world*) **the music scene** die Musikszene; **on the fashion scene** in der Modewelt; **3** (*argument*) Szene *die* (PL *die* Szenen); **to make a scene** eine Szene machen.

scenery *noun* **1** (*landscape*) Landschaft *die*; **2** (*in the theatre*) Bühnenbild *das*.

schedule *noun* Programm *das* (PL *die* Programme).

scheme *noun* Projekt *das* (PL *die* Projekte).

scholarship *noun* Stipendium *das* (PL *die* Stipendien).

school *noun* Schule *die* (PL *die* Schulen); **at school** in der Schule; **to go to school** zur Schule gehen.

schoolbook *noun* Schulbuch *das* (PL *die* Schulbücher).

schoolboy *noun* Schüler *der* (PL *die* Schüler).

schoolchildren *plural noun* Schulkinder (*plural*).

schoolfriend *noun* Schulfreund *der* (PL *die* Schulfreunde), Schulfreundin *die* (PL *die* Schulfreundinnen).

schoolgirl *noun* Schülerin *die* (PL *die* Schülerinnen).

science *noun* Wissenschaft *die* (PL *die* Wissenschaften).

science fiction *noun* Sciencefiction △ *die*.

scientific *adjective* wissenschaftlich.

scientist *noun* Wissenschaftler *der* (PL *die* Wissenschaftler), Wissenschaftlerin *die* (PL *die* Wissenschaftlerinnen).

scissors *plural noun* Schere *die* (PL *die* Scheren); **a pair of scissors** eine Schere.

scooter *noun* **1** (*motor scooter*) Motorroller *der* (PL *die* Motorroller); **2** (*for a child*) Roller *der* (PL *die* Roller).

score *noun* Spielstand *der* (PL *die* Spielstände); **the score was three two** es stand drei zu zwei. *verb* **1 to score a goal** ein Tor schießen ◇; **2 to score three**

◇ IRREGULAR VERB: *See the verb table in the centre of the dictionary*

points drei Punkte erzielen; **3** (*keep score*) zählen.

Scorpio *noun* Skorpion *der*; **Neil is Scorpio** Neil ist Skorpion.

Scot *noun* Schotte *der* (PL *die* Schotten), Schottin *die* (PL *die* Schottinnen); **the Scots** die Schotten.

Scotland *noun* Schottland *das*; **from Scotland** aus Schottland; **Pauline's from Scotland** Pauline kommt aus Schottland; **to Scotland** nach Schottland.

Scots *adjective* schottisch.

Scotsman *noun* Schotte *der* (PL *die* Schotten).

Scotswoman *noun* Schottin *die* (PL *die* Schottinnen).

Scottish *adjective* schottisch; **he's Scottish** er ist Schotte.

scout *noun* Pfadfinder *der* (PL *die* Pfadfinder).

scrambled eggs *noun* Rührei *das*.

scrap *noun* Stück *das* (PL *die* Stücke); **a scrap of paper** ein Stück Papier.

scrapbook *noun* Album *das* (PL *die* Alben).

scrape *verb* **1** schaben (*potatoes or carrots*); **2** (*remove dirt or paint*) abkratzen SEP; **3** (*damage*) verschrammen.

scratch *noun* (*on your skin or a surface*) Kratzer *der* (PL *die* Kratzer); ★ **to start from scratch** von vorn anfangen ✧ SEP.

verb (*scratch yourself*) sich kratzen; **to scratch your head** sich am Kopf kratzen.

scream *noun* Schrei *der* (PL *die* Schreie).
verb schreien ✧.

screen *noun* **1** Bildschirm *der* (PL *die* Bildschirme) (*of a TV or computer*); **on the screen** auf dem Bildschirm; **2** (*in the cinema*) Leinwand *die* (PL *die* Leinwände).

screw *noun* Schraube *die* (PL *die* Schrauben).
verb schrauben.

screwdriver *noun* Schraubenzieher *der* (PL *die* Schraubenzieher).

scribble *verb* kritzeln.

scrub *verb* scheuern (*a saucepan or the floor*); **to scrub your nails** sich ←(DAT) die Nägel bürsten.

sculptor *noun* Bildhauer *der* (PL *die* Bildhauer), Bildhauerin *die* (PL *die* Bildhauerinnen); **Rebecca's a sculptor** Rebecca ist Bildhauerin.

sculpture *noun* Skulptur *die* (PL *die* Skulpturen).

sea *noun* Meer *das* (PL *die* Meere), See *die*; **by the sea** am Meer, an der See.

seafood *noun* Meeresfrüchte (*plural*); **I love seafood** ich esse Meeresfrüchte sehr gern.

search *verb* **1** absuchen SEP; **I've searched my desk but I can't find the letter** ich habe meinen Schreibtisch abgesucht, aber ich

kann den Brief nicht finden;
2 durchsuchen; **they searched the
building for him** sie haben das
Gebäude nach ihm durchsucht;
3 suchen; **to search for something**
nach etwas ←(DAT) suchen; **I've been
searching everywhere for my
scissors** ich habe überall nach
meiner Schere gesucht.

seasick *adjective* **to be seasick**
seekrank sein.

seaside *noun* **at the seaside** am
Meer.

season *noun* 1 Jahreszeit *die* (PL *die*
Jahreszeiten); **the four seasons** die
vier Jahreszeiten; 2 (*period of social
or sporting activity*) Saison *die* (PL
die Saisons); **the tennis season** die
Tennissaison; **off-season prices**
Preise außerhalb der Saison;
3 strawberries are not in season at
the moment jetzt ist nicht die
richtige Zeit für Erdbeeren.

season ticket *noun*
Dauerkarte *die* (PL *die*
Dauerkarten).

seat *noun* 1 Sitz *der* (PL *die* Sitze);
the front seat (*in a car*) der
Vordersitz; **the back seat** der
Rücksitz; **take a seat** nehmen Sie
Platz (*formal*); setz dich (*informal*);
2 (*on a bus, in the theatre, etc.*)
Platz *der* (PL *die* Plätze); **to book a
seat** einen Platz reservieren; **can
you keep my seat?** kannst du mir
meinen Platz freihalten?

seatbelt *noun* Sicherheitsgurt *der*
(PL *die* Sicherheitsgurte).

second *noun* Sekunde *die* (PL *die*
Sekunden); **can you wait a
second?** kannst du eine Sekunde
warten?
adjective 1 zweiter/zweite/zweites;
for the second time zum zweiten
Mal; 2 the second of July der
zweite Juli.

secondary school *noun* 1 höhere
Schule *die* (PL *die* höheren Schulen)
(*Germans define the type of secondary
school*); 2 Gymnasium *das* (PL *die*
Gymnasien) (*grammar school, from
age 10 to 19 when Abitur is taken*);
3 Realschule *die* (PL *die*
Realschulen) (*from age 10 to 16, less
academic than a Gymnasium*).

secondhand *adjective, adverb*
gebraucht; **a secondhand bike** ein
gebrauchtes Fahrrad; **secondhand
car** *der* Gebrauchtwagen; **I bought
it secondhand** ich habe es
gebraucht gekauft.

secondly *adverb* zweitens.

secret *noun* Geheimnis *das* (PL *die*
Geheimnisse); **to tell somebody a
secret** jemandem ein Geheimnis
verraten; **in secret** heimlich.
adjective geheim; **a secret plan** ein
geheimer Plan; **to keep something
secret** etwas geheim halten.

secretary *noun* Sekretär *der* (PL *die*
Sekretäre), Sekretärin *die* (PL *die*
Sekretärinnen); **the secretary's
office** das Sekretariat.

secretly *adverb* heimlich.

sect *noun* Sekte *die* (PL *die* Sekten).

section *noun* Teil *der* (PL *die* Teile).

security *noun* Sicherheit *die*.

✧ IRREGULAR VERB: *See the verb table in the centre of the dictionary*

security guard *noun* Wächter *der* (PL *die* Wächter), Wächterin *die* (PL *die* Wächterinnen).

see *verb* 1 sehen✧; **I saw Lindy yesterday** ich habe Lindy gestern gesehen; **have you seen the film?** hast du den Film gesehen?; **I can't see anything** ich kann überhaupt nichts sehen; 2 **to go and see** nachsehen ✧ SEP; **I'll go and see** ich sehe nach; 3 (*visit*) besuchen; **why don't you come and see us in the summer?** warum besucht ihr uns nicht im Sommer?; 4 **to see somebody home** jemanden nach Hause begleiten; 5 **see you!** tschüs! (*informal*); **see you on Saturday!** bis Samstag!; **see you soon!** bis bald!
● **to see to something** sich um etwas ←(ACC) kümmern; **Jo's seeing to the drinks** Jo kümmert sich um die Getränke.

seed *noun* Samen *der* (PL *die* Samen).

seem *verb* 1 scheinen✧; **his story seems odd to me** seine Geschichte kommt mir komisch vor; **he seems shy** er scheint schüchtern zu sein; **the museum seems to be closed** das Museum scheint geschlossen zu sein; 2 **it seems (that)** ... anscheinend ...; **it seems he's left** anscheinend ist er weggegangen; **it seems that there are problems** anscheinend gibt es Probleme.

select *verb* auswählen SEP.

self-confidence *noun* Selbstbewusstsein Δ *das*; **she doesn't have much self-confidence** sie hat sehr wenig Selbstbewusstsein.

self-employed *adjective* **to be self-employed** selbstständig Δ sein; **my parents are self-employed** meine Eltern sind selbstständig.

selfish *adjective* egoistisch.

self-service *adjective* **a self-service restaurant** ein Selbstbedienungsrestaurant.

sell *verb* 1 verkaufen; **to sell something to somebody** jemandem etwas verkaufen; **I sold him my bike** ich habe ihm mein Rad verkauft; **the house sold for a million** das Haus wurde für eine Million verkauft; 2 **the concert's sold out** das Konzert ist ausverkauft; **the tickets sold out very quickly** die Karten waren schnell ausverkauft.

sell-by date *noun* Verfallsdatum *das* (PL *die* Verfallsdaten).

Sellotape™ *noun* Tesafilm™ *der*. *verb* **to sellotape something** etwas mit Tesafilm kleben.

semi *noun* Doppelhaushälfte *die* (PL *die* Doppelhaushälften).

semi-detached house *noun* Doppelhaushälfte *die* (PL *die* Doppelhaushälften).

semi-final *noun* Halbfinale *das* (PL *die* Halbfinale).

send *verb* schicken; **to send something to somebody** jemandem etwas schicken; **I sent her a present for her birthday** ich habe

ihr zum Geburtstag ein Geschenk
geschickt.

● **to send somebody back** jemanden
zurückschicken SEP.

● **to send something back** etwas
zurückschicken SEP.

sender *noun* Absender *der* (PL *die*
Absender).

senior citizen *noun* Senior *der* (PL
die Senioren), Seniorin *die* (PL *die*
Seniorinnen).

sensational *adjective* sensationell.

sense *noun* 1 (*common sense*)
Verstand *der*; 2 (*faculty*) Sinn *der*
(PL *die* Sinne); **sense of smell** *der*
Geruchssinn; **sense of touch** *der*
Tastsinn; **to have a sense of humour**
Humor haben; **she has no sense of
humour** sie hat keinen Sinn für
Humor; 3 (*meaning*) Sinn *der*; **this
sentence makes no sense** dieser
Satz ergibt keinen Sinn; **it doesn't
make sense to do that** es ist
Unsinn, das zu machen; **it makes
sense to collect her first** es ist
sinnvoll, sie erst abzuholen.

sensible *adjective* vernünftig; **be
sensible** sei vernünftig; **that's a
sensible suggestion** das ist ein
vernünftiger Vorschlag.

sensitive *adjective* empfindlich; **for
sensitive skin** für empfindliche
Haut.

sentence *noun* 1 (*words*) Satz *der*
(PL *die* Sätze); 2 (*prison*) Strafe *die*
(PL *die* Strafen); **the death sentence**
die Todesstrafe.
verb verurteilen; **to be sentenced
to death** zum Tode verurteilt

werden; **to sentence somebody to
a year in prison** jemanden zu einem
Jahr Gefängnis verurteilen.

separate *adjective* 1 extra (*'extra'
never has an ending*); **a separate
pile** ein extra Stapel; **she wrote it on
a separate sheet of paper** sie hat
es auf ein anderes Blatt Papier
geschrieben; **the drinks are
separate** die Getränke gehen extra;
2 (*different*) verschieden; **two
separate problems** zwei
verschiedene Probleme; 3 **they
have separate rooms** sie haben
getrennte Zimmer.
verb 1 trennen; 2 (*a couple*) sich
trennen.

separately *adverb* 1 extra;
2 getrennt; **they live separately** sie
leben getrennt.

separation *noun* Trennung *die* (PL
die Trennungen).

September *noun* September *der*;
in September im September.

sequel *noun* Folge *die* (PL *die*
Folgen).

sergeant *noun* 1 (*in the police*)
Polizeimeister *der* (PL *die*
Polizeimeister), Polizeimeisterin *die*
(PL *die* Polizeimeisterinnen); 2 (*in
the army*) Feldwebel *der* (PL *die*
Feldwebel).

serial *noun*
1 Fortsetzungsgeschichte *die* (PL *die*
Fortsetzungsgeschichten); 2 (*on TV
or radio*) Serie *die* (PL *die* Serien).

series *noun* Serie *die* (PL *die* Serien);
television series *die* Fernsehserie.

✧ IRREGULAR VERB: *See the verb table in the centre of the dictionary*

serious *adjective* **1** ernst; **a serious discussion** eine ernste Unterhaltung; **to be serious about something** etwas ernst nehmen; **are you serious?** ist das dein Ernst?; **2** schwer (*accident or mistake*).

seriously *adverb* **1** im Ernst; **seriously, I have to go now** im Ernst, ich muss jetzt gehen; **seriously?** im Ernst?; **2 to take somebody seriously** jemanden ernst nehmen; **3** (*gravely*) schwer; **she is seriously ill** sie ist schwer krank.

serve *noun* (*in tennis*) Aufschlag *der* (PL *die* Aufschläge); **it's my serve** ich habe Aufschlag. *verb* **1** (*in tennis*) aufschlagen ✧ SEP; **Becker is serving** Becker schlägt auf; **2** servieren; **can you serve the vegetables, please?** können Sie bitte das Gemüse servieren?; ★ **it serves him right** das geschieht ihm recht.

service *noun* **1** (*in a restaurant, shop, etc.*) Bedienung *die*; **service is included** inklusive Bedienung; **2** (*from a company or firm to a customer*) Service *der*; **3 the emergency services** der Notdienst; **4** (*church service*) Gottesdienst *der* (PL *die* Gottesdienste); **5** (*of a car or machine*) Wartung *die* (PL *die* Wartungen).

service charge *noun* Bedienung *die*; **there is no service charge** die Bedienung wird nicht extra berechnet.

service station *noun* Tankstelle *die* (PL *die* Tankstellen).

serviette *noun* Serviette *die* (PL *die* Servietten).

session *noun* Sitzung *die* (PL *die* Sitzungen).

set *noun* **1** (*for playing a game*) Spiel *das* (PL *die* Spiele); **chess set** *das* Schachspiel; **2 train set** *die* Spielzeugeisenbahn; **3** (*in tennis*) Satz *der* (PL *die* Sätze). *adjective* **1** fest (*hours, habits*); **a set date** ein festes Datum; **at a set time** zu einer festgesetzten Zeit; **2 set menu** *das* Menü. *verb* **1** festlegen SEP (*a date, time*); **2** aufstellen SEP (*a record*); **3 to set the table** den Tisch decken; **to set an alarm clock** einen Wecker stellen; **I've set my alarm for seven** ich habe meinen Wecker auf sieben gestellt; **4 to set your watch** seine Uhr richtig stellen; **5** (*sun*) untergehen ✧ SEP;

● **to set off** aufbrechen ✧ SEP (PERF *sein*); **we're setting off at ten** wir brechen um zehn auf; **they set off for Vienna yesterday** sie sind gestern nach Wien aufgebrochen.

● **to set off something 1** etwas auslösen SEP (*an alarm, reaction*); **2** etwas abbrennen ✧ SEP (*a firework*); **3** etwas explodieren lassen (*a bomb*).

● **to set out** aufbrechen ✧ SEP (PERF *sein*); **they set out for Hamburg at ten** sie sind um zehn nach Hamburg aufgebrochen.

settee *noun* Sofa *das* (PL *die* Sofas).

△ NEW SPELLING: *See page xii*

settle *verb* 1 bezahlen (*a bill*);
2 lösen (*a problem*); 3 beilegen SEP
(*an argument*).

seven *number* sieben; **Rosie's
seven** Rosie ist sieben.

seventeen *number* siebzehn; **I'm
seventeen** ich bin siebzehn.

seventh *adjective*
siebter/siebte/siebtes; **on the
seventh floor** im siebten Stock; **the
seventh of July** der siebte Juli.

seventies *plural noun* **the
seventies** die Siebzigerjahre △; **in
the seventies** in den
Siebzigerjahren.

seventieth *adjective*
siebzigster/siebzigste/siebzigstes;
it's her seventieth birthday es ist
ihr siebzigster Geburtstag.

seventy *number* siebzig; **my
granny's seventy** meine Oma ist
siebzig.

several *adjective, pronoun*
1 mehrere; **I've read several of her
novels** ich habe mehrere ihrer
Romane gelesen; 2 **I've seen her
several times** ich habe sie
mehrmals gesehen.

sew *verb* nähen.

sewing *noun* Nähen *das*; **I like
sewing** ich nähe gern.

sewing machine *noun*
Nähmaschine *die* (PL *die*
Nähmaschinen).

sex *noun* 1 (*gender*) Geschlecht *das*
(PL *die* Geschlechter); 2 (*sexuality*)
Sex *der*.

sex education *noun*
Aufklärungsunterricht *der*.

sexism *noun* Sexismus *der*.

sexist *adjective* sexistisch; **sexist
remarks** sexistische Bemerkungen.

sexual *adjective* sexuell.

sexual harassment *noun*
sexuelle Belästigung *die*.

sexuality *noun* Sexualität *die*.

sexy *adjective* sexy.

shabby *adjective* schäbig.

shade *noun* 1 Ton *der* (PL *die* Töne);
a shade of green ein Grünton;
2 Schatten *der*; **in the shade** im
Schatten.

shadow *noun* Schatten *der* (PL *die*
Schatten).

shake *verb* 1 (*tremble*) zittern; **I was
shaking with fear** ich zitterte vor
Angst; 2 **to shake something** etwas
schütteln; **to shake your head**
(*meaning no*) den Kopf schütteln;
3 **to shake hands with somebody**
jemandem die Hand geben ✧; **she
shook hands with me** sie hat mir
die Hand gegeben; **we shook hands**
wir gaben uns die Hand.

shaken *adjective* erschüttert; **I was
shaken by the news** die Nachricht
hat mich erschüttert.

shall *verb* **shall I come with you?**
soll ich mitkommen?; **shall we stop
now?** sollen wir jetzt aufhören?

shallow *adjective* flach; **stay in the
shallow end of the pool** bleib am
flachen Ende des Beckens.

✧ IRREGULAR VERB: *See the verb table in the centre of the dictionary*

shambles *noun* Chaos *das*; **it was a total shambles!** es war ein völliges Chaos!

shame *noun* 1 Schande *die*; **the shame of it!** was für eine Schande!; 2 **what a shame!** wie schade!; **it's a shame she can't come** schade, dass sie nicht kommen kann.

shampoo *noun* Shampoo *das* (PL die Shampoos), Schampon *das* (PL die Schampons); **I bought some shampoo** ich habe Shampoo gekauft.

shamrock *noun* Klee *der*.

shandy *noun* Radler *der* (PL die Radler) (*South German*), Alsterwasser *das* (PL die Alsterwasser) (*North German*).

shape *noun* Form *die* (PL die Formen).

share *noun* 1 Anteil *der* (PL die Anteile); **your share of the money** dein Anteil am Geld; **he paid his share** er hat seinen Anteil gezahlt; 2 (*in a company*) Aktie *die* (PL die Aktien).
verb teilen; **I'm sharing a room with Lucy** ich teile ein Zimmer mit Lucy.

sharp *adjective* 1 (*knife*) scharf; **this knife isn't very sharp** dieses Messer ist nicht sehr scharf; 2 (*pointed*) spitz; **a sharp pencil** ein spitzer Bleistift; 3 **a sharp bend** eine scharfe Kurve; 4 (*clever*) clever.

shave *verb* 1 (*have a shave*) sich rasieren; 2 **to shave your legs** sich ←(DAT) die Beine rasieren; 3 **to shave off your beard** den Bart abrasieren SEP.

shaver *noun* Rasierapparat *der* (PL die Rasierapparate); **electric shaver** *der* Elektrorasierer.

shaving cream *noun* Rasiercreme *die* (PL die Rasiercremes).

shaving foam *noun* Rasierschaum *der*.

she *pronoun* sie; **she's a student** sie ist Studentin; **she's a very good teacher** sie ist eine sehr gute Lehrerin.

shed *noun* Schuppen *der* (PL die Schuppen).

sheep *noun* Schaf *das* (PL die Schafe).

sheepdog *noun* Schäferhund *der* (PL die Schäferhunde).

sheet *noun* 1 (*for a bed*) Laken *das* (PL die Laken); 2 **a sheet of paper** ein Blatt Papier; **a blank sheet** ein leeres Blatt; 3 (*of glass or metal*) Platte *die* (PL die Platten); ★ **to be as white as a sheet** leichenblass △ sein.

shelf *noun* 1 (*in the home or a shop*) Regal *das* (PL die Regale); **a set of shelves** ein Regal; 2 (*in an oven*) Schiene *die* (PL die Schienen).

shell *noun* 1 (*of an egg or a nut*) Schale *die* (PL die Schalen); 2 (*seashell*) Muschel *die* (PL die Muscheln).

shellfish *noun* 1 Schalentier *das* (PL die Schalentiere); 2 (*in cookery*) Meeresfrüchte (*plural*).

shelter *noun* Schutz *der*; **in the shelter of** im Schutz (+GEN); **to take**

shelter from the rain sich unterstellen SEP.

sherry *noun* Sherry *der* (PL *die* Sherrys).

Shetland Islands *noun* Shetlandinseln (*plural*).

shift *noun* Schicht *die* (PL *die* Schichten); **the night shift** die Nachtschicht; **to be on night shift** Nachtschicht haben.
verb **to shift something** etwas verrücken.

shifty *adjective* verschlagen; **he looks shifty** er sieht verschlagen aus; **a shifty-looking guy** ein verschlagener Typ.

shine *verb* scheinen ✧; **the sun is shining** die Sonne scheint.

shiny *adjective* glänzend.

ship *noun* Schiff *das* (PL *die* Schiffe).

shipyard *noun* Werft *die* (PL *die* Werften).

shirt *noun* 1 (*man's*) Hemd *das* (PL *die* Hemden); 2 (*woman's*) Bluse *die* (PL *die* Blusen).

shiver *verb* zittern.

shock *noun* 1 Schock *der* (PL *die* Schocks); **to get a shock** einen Schock bekommen; **it gave me a shock** das hat mir einen Schock versetzt; 2 **electric shock** *der* Schlag.
verb (*upset*) erschüttern; (*cause scandal*) schockieren.

shocked *adjective* schockiert.

shocking *adjective* schockierend.

shoe *noun* Schuh *der* (PL *die* Schuhe); **a pair of shoes** ein Paar Schuhe.

shoelace *noun* Schnürsenkel *der* (PL *die* Schnürsenkel).

shoe polish *noun* Schuhcreme *die* (PL *die* Schuhcremes).

shoe shop *noun* Schuhgeschäft *das* (PL *die* Schuhgeschäfte).

shoot *verb* 1 (*fire*) schießen ✧; **to shoot at somebody** auf jemanden schießen; **she shot him in the leg** sie hat ihm ins Bein geschossen; **he was shot in the arm** er wurde am Arm getroffen; 2 (*kill, execute*) erschießen ✧; **he was shot by terrorists** er wurde von Terroristen erschossen; 3 (*in football, hockey*) schießen ✧; 4 **to shoot a film** einen Film drehen.

shop *noun* Geschäft *das* (PL *die* Geschäfte), Laden *der* (PL *die* Läden); **shoe shop** *das* Schuhgeschäft; **to go round the shops** einen Ladenbummel machen.

shop assistant *noun* Verkäufer *der* (PL *die* Verkäufer), Verkäuferin *die* (PL *die* Verkäuferinnen).

shopkeeper *noun* Ladenbesitzer *der* (PL *die* Ladenbesitzer), Ladenbesitzerin *die* (PL *die* Ladenbesitzerinnen).

shoplifter *noun* Ladendieb *der* (PL *die* Ladendiebe), Ladendiebin *die* (PL *die* Ladendiebinnen).

✧ IRREGULAR VERB: *See the verb table in the centre of the dictionary*

shoplifting noun
Ladendiebstahl der.

shopping noun 1 Einkäufe (plural);
can you put the shopping away?
kannst du die Einkäufe wegräumen?;
2 (activity) Einkaufen das;
shopping is fun Einkaufen macht
Spaß; **to go shopping** einkaufen
gehen.

shopping trolley noun
Einkaufswagen der (PL die
Einkaufswagen).

shop window noun
Schaufenster das (PL die
Schaufenster).

short adjective 1 kurz; **a short dress**
ein kurzes Kleid; **she has short hair**
sie hat kurze Haare; 2 **a short break**
eine kurze Pause; **to go for a short
walk** einen kurzen Spaziergang
machen; **it's a short walk from the
bus stop** es ist nicht weit zu Fuß von
der Bushaltestelle; 3 **to be short of
something** knapp mit etwas ←(DAT)
sein; **we're a bit short of money at
the moment** wir sind im Moment
etwas knapp mit Geld; **we're getting
short of time** wir sind knapp mit der
Zeit.

shortage noun Mangel der.

shortbread noun
Buttergebäck das.

shortcrust pastry noun
Mürbeteig der.

short cut noun Abkürzung die (PL
die Abkürzungen).

shortly adverb gleich; **shortly
before I left** kurz bevor ich ging;
shortly after kurz danach.

shorts plural noun Shorts (plural);
a pair of shorts ein Paar Shorts; **my
red shorts** meine roten Shorts.

short-sighted adjective
kurzsichtig; **I'm short-sighted** ich
bin kurzsichtig.

shot noun 1 (from a gun)
Schuss △ der (PL die Schüsse);
2 (a photo) Aufnahme die (PL die
Aufnahmen).

should verb 1 sollen ✧ ('should' is
usually translated by the imperfect
subjunctive of 'sollen'); **you should
ask Simon** du solltest Simon fragen;
the potatoes should be ready now
die Kartoffeln sollten jetzt fertig
sein; 2 ('should have' is translated by
'hätte sollen') **you should have told
me** du hättest es mir sagen sollen;
I shouldn't have stayed ich hätte
nicht bleiben sollen; **you shouldn't
have said that** das hättest du nicht
sagen sollen; 3 ('should' meaning
'would' is translated by 'würde')
I should forget it if I were you an
deiner Stelle würde ich es vergessen;
4 **I should think** ich würde sagen;
I should think he's forgotten ich
würde sagen, er hat's vergessen;
5 **this should be enough** das
müsste eigentlich reichen.

shoulder noun Schulter die (PL die
Schultern).

shoulder bag noun
Umhängetasche die (PL die
Umhängetaschen).

shout noun Schrei der (PL die
Schreie).
verb 1 schreien ✧; **stop shouting!**

hör auf zu schreien!; **2** (*call*)
rufen ◇; **he shouted at us to come
back** er rief uns zu, wir sollten
zurückkommen.

show *noun* **1** (*on stage*) Show *die* (PL
die Shows); **we went to see a show**
wir haben eine Show gesehen; **2** (*on
TV, radio*) Sendung *die* (PL *die*
Sendungen); **3** (*exhibition*)
Ausstellung *die* (PL *die*
Ausstellungen); **fashion show** *die*
Modenschau.
verb **1** zeigen; **to show something
to somebody** jemandem etwas
zeigen; **I'll show you my photos** ich
zeige dir meine Fotos; **to show
somebody how something works**
jemandem zeigen, wie etwas
funktioniert; **he showed me how to
make pancakes** er hat mir gezeigt,
wie man Pfannkuchen macht; **2 it
shows!** das sieht man!
● **to show off** angeben ◇ SEP.

shower *noun* **1** (*in a bathroom*)
Dusche *die* (PL *die* Duschen); **to have
a shower** duschen; **2** (*of rain*)
Schauer *der* (PL *die* Schauer).

show-jumping *noun*
Springreiten *das*.

show-off *noun* Angeber *der* (PL *die*
Angeber), Angeberin *die* (PL *die*
Angeberinnen).

shriek *verb* kreischen.

shrimp *noun* Krabbe *die* (PL *die*
Krabben).

shrink *verb* **1** schrumpfen (PERF
sein); **2** (*clothes*) einlaufen ◇ SEP
(PERF *sein*); **my sweater has shrunk**
mein Pullover ist eingelaufen.

Shrove Tuesday *noun*
Fastnachtsdienstag *der*.

shrug *verb* **to shrug your shoulders**
die Achseln zucken.

shuffle *verb* **to shuffle the cards**
die Karten mischen.

shut *adjective* zu; **the shops are
shut** die Geschäfte haben zu.
verb zumachen SEP; **can you shut
the door please?** kannst du die Tür
bitte zumachen?; **the shops shut at
six** die Geschäfte machen um sechs
zu.
● **to shut up** den Mund halten ◇
(*informal*); **shut up!** halt den
Mund!

shuttlecock *noun* Federball *der*
(PL *die* Federbälle).

shy *adjective* schüchtern.

shyness *noun* Schüchternheit *die*.

Sicily *noun* Sizilien *das*.

sick *adjective* **1** (*ill*) krank; **2 to be
sick** (*vomit*) sich übergeben ◇; **I
was sick several times** ich habe
mich mehrmals übergeben; **3 I feel
sick** mir ist schlecht; **4** übel; **a sick
joke** ein übler Witz; **5 to be sick of
something** etwas satt haben; **I'm
sick of staying at home every day**
ich habe es satt, jeden Tag zu Hause
zu sitzen.

sickness *noun* Krankheit *die* (PL *die*
Krankheiten).

side *noun* **1** Seite *die* (PL *die* Seiten);
on the other side of the street auf
der anderen Straßenseite; **on the
wrong side** auf der falschen Seite;

I'm on your side (*I agree with you*) ich bin auf deiner Seite; 2 (*edge*) Rand *der* (PL *die* Ränder) (*of a pool, river*); **at the side of the road** am Straßenrand; 3 (*team*) Mannschaft *die* (PL *die* Mannschaften); **the winning side** die siegreiche Mannschaft; **she plays on our side** sie spielt bei uns mit; 4 **to take sides** Partei ergreifen ◇; **he always takes sides against her** er ergreift immer gegen sie Partei; 5 **side by side** nebeneinander.

sideboard *noun* Anrichte *die* (PL *die* Anrichten).

sideburns *noun* Koteletten (*plural*).

side-effect *noun* Nebenwirkung *die* (PL *die* Nebenwirkungen).

side street *noun* Seitenstraße *die* (PL *die* Seitenstraßen).

sieve *noun* Sieb *das* (PL *die* Siebe).

sigh *noun* Seufzer *der* (PL *die* Seufzer).
verb seufzen.

sight *noun* 1 Anblick *der*; **it was a marvellous sight** es war ein herrlicher Anblick; 2 **at first sight** auf den ersten Blick; 3 (*eyesight*) **to have poor sight** schlechte Augen haben; **to know somebody by sight** jemanden vom Sehen kennen; **out of sight** außer Sicht; **to lose sight of somebody** jemanden aus den Augen verlieren; 4 **the sights** die Sehenswürdigkeiten; **to see the**

sights die Sehenswürdigkeiten besichtigen.

sightseeing *noun* Sightseeing *das*; **to do some sightseeing** einige Sehenswürdigkeiten besichtigen.

sign *noun* 1 (*notice*) Schild *das* (PL *die* Schilder); **there's a sign on the door** da hängt ein Schild an der Tür; 2 (*trace, indication*) Zeichen *das* (PL *die* Zeichen); 3 (*of the zodiac*) Sternzeichen *das* (PL *die* Sternzeichen); **what sign are you?** was für ein Sternzeichen bist du? *verb* 1 unterschreiben ◇; **to sign a cheque** einen Scheck unterschreiben; 2 (*using sign language*) sich durch Zeichen verständigen.
● **to sign on** sich arbeitslos melden.

signal *noun* Signal *das* (PL *die* Signale).

signature *noun* Unterschrift *die* (PL *die* Unterschriften).

significant *adjective* bedeutend.

sign language *noun* Zeichensprache *die* (PL *die* Zeichensprachen).

signpost *noun* Wegweiser *der* (PL *die* Wegweiser).

silence *noun* Stille *die*.

silent *adjective* still.

silk *noun* Seide *die* (PL *die* Seiden). *adjective* Seiden-; **a silk blouse** eine Seidenbluse.

silky *adjective* seidig.

silly

546 **ENGLISH–GERMAN**

silly *adjective* dumm; **it was a really silly thing to do** das war wirklich dumm.

silver *noun* Silber *das*.
adjective Silber-; **a silver medal** eine Silbermedaille.

similar *adjective* ähnlich; **it looks similar to my old bike** es sieht so ähnlich wie mein altes Rad aus.

similarity *noun* Ähnlichkeit *die* (PL die Ähnlichkeiten).

simple *adjective* einfach.

simply *adverb* einfach.

sin *noun* Sünde *die* (PL die Sünden).

since *preposition* 1 seit (+DAT); (*notice that German uses the present tense for an action starting in the past and still going on in the present*) **I have been in Berlin since Saturday** ich bin seit Samstag in Berlin; **since when?** seit wann?; 2 (*with a negative the perfect tense is used*) **I haven't seen her since Monday** ich habe sie seit Montag nicht gesehen. *conjunction* 1 seit; **since I have known him** seit ich ihn kenne; **since I've been learning German** seitdem ich Deutsch lerne; 2 (*because*) da; **since it was raining, the match was cancelled** da es regnete, wurde das Spiel abgesagt. *adverb* seitdem; **I haven't seen him since** ich habe ihn seitdem nicht mehr gesehen.

sincere *adjective* aufrichtig.

sincerely *adverb* **Yours sincerely** Mit freundlichen Grüßen.

sing *verb* singen ✧.

singer *noun* Sänger *der* (PL die Sänger), Sängerin *die* (PL die Sängerinnen).

singing *noun* 1 Singen *das*; **a singing lesson** eine Singstunde; 2 **I like singing** ich singe gern.

single *noun* 1 (*ticket*) einfache Fahrkarte *die* (PL die einfachen Fahrkarten); **a single to Munich, please** eine einfache Fahrkarte nach München bitte; 2 (*record, CD*) Single *die* (PL die Singles). *adjective* 1 (*not married*) allein stehend △; **a single woman** eine allein stehende Frau; (*on forms*) ledig; 2 (*just one*) einzig; **I haven't had a single reply** ich habe keine einzige Antwort bekommen; 3 **not a single one** kein Einziger/keine Einzige/kein Einziges △; 4 **single room** *das* Einzelzimmer; **single bed** *das* Einzelbett.

single parent *noun* allein Erziehende △ *der/die* (PL die allein Erziehenden); **she's a single parent** sie ist allein erziehende Mutter; **a single-parent family** eine Einelternfamilie.

singles *plural noun* (*in tennis*) Einzel *das* (PL die Einzel); **the women's singles** das Dameneinzel; **the men's singles** das Herreneinzel.

singular *noun* Einzahl *die*; **in the singular** in der Einzahl.

sink *noun* Spülbecken *das* (PL die Spülbecken). *verb* sinken ✧ (PERF *sein*).

✧ IRREGULAR VERB: *See the verb table in the centre of the dictionary*

sir *noun* Herr der (PL die Herren); (*in German,' Sir' is usually not translated*) **would you like another one, sir?** möchten Sie noch eins?; **yes, sir** ja, mein Herr.

sister *noun* Schwester die (PL die Schwestern); **my sister's ten** meine Schwester ist zehn.

sister-in-law *noun* Schwägerin die (PL die Schwägerinnen).

sit *verb* 1 (*to sit down*) sich setzen; **you can sit on the sofa** ihr könnt euch aufs Sofa setzen; **sit on the floor** setz dich auf den Boden; 2 (*to be sitting*) sitzen ◇; **Leila was sitting on the sofa** Leila saß auf dem Sofa; **to sit on the floor** auf dem Boden sitzen; 3 **to sit an exam** eine Prüfung machen.
• **to sit down** sich setzen; **he sat down on the chair** er setzte sich auf den Stuhl; **do sit down** setzen Sie sich.

sitcom *noun* Situationskomödie die (PL die Situationskomödien).

site *noun* 1 **building site** die Baustelle; 2 **camping site** der Campingplatz; 3 **archaeolological site** die archäologische Stätte.

sitting room *noun* Wohnzimmer das (PL die Wohnzimmer).

situated *adjective* **to be situated** liegen ◇; **the house is situated in a small village** das Haus liegt in einem kleinen Dorf.

situation *noun* 1 (*location*) Lage die (PL die Lagen);

2 (*circumstances*) Situation die (PL die Situationen).

six *number* sechs; **Harry's six** Harry ist sechs.

sixteen *number* sechzehn; **Alice is sixteen** Alice ist sechzehn.

sixth *adjective* sechster/sechste/sechstes; **on the sixth floor** im sechsten Stock; **on the sixth of July** am sechsten Juli.

sixty *number* sechzig; **she's sixty** sie ist sechzig.

size *noun* 1 Größe die (PL die Größen); **it depends on the size of the house** es kommt auf die Größe des Hauses an; 2 **what size is the window?** wie groß ist das Fenster?; 3 (*in clothes*) Größe die (PL die Größen); **what size do you take?** welche Größe haben Sie?; 4 (*of shoes*) Schuhgröße die (PL die Schuhgrößen); **I take a size thirty-eight** ich habe Schuhgröße achtunddreißig.

skate *noun* 1 (*an ice skate*) Schlittschuh der (PL die Schlittschuhe); 2 (*a roller skate*) Rollschuh der (PL die Rollschuhe). *verb* 1 (*ice-skate*) Schlittschuh laufen ◇ (PERF *sein*); 2 (*roller-skate*) Rollschuh laufen ◇ (PERF *sein*).

skateboard *noun* Skateboard das (PL die Skateboards).

skateboarding *noun* Skateboardfahren das; **to go skateboarding** Skateboard fahren ◇ (PERF *sein*).

skating *noun* 1 (*on ice*) Schlittschuhlaufen das; **to go**

skating Schlittschuh laufen ✧ (PERF *sein*); 2 (*roller-skating*) Rollschuhlaufen *das*; **to go roller-skating** Rollschuh laufen ✧ (PERF *sein*).

skating rink *noun* 1 (*ice rink*) Eisbahn *die* (PL *die* Eisbahnen); 2 (*for roller-skating*) Rollschuhbahn *die* (PL *die* Rollschuhbahnen).

sketch *noun* 1 Skizze *die* (PL *die* Skizzen); 2 (*comedy routine*) Sketch *der* (PL *die* Sketche).

ski *noun* Ski *der* (PL *die* Skier). *verb* Ski fahren ✧ (PERF *sein*); **he can ski** er kann Ski fahren.

ski boot *noun* Skistiefel *der* (PL *die* Skistiefel).

skid *verb* schleudern (PERF *sein*); **the car skidded** das Auto ist geschleudert.

skiing *noun* Skifahren *das*; **to go skiing** Ski fahren ✧ (PERF *sein*).

ski lift *noun* Skilift *der* (PL *die* Skilifte).

skin *noun* Haut *die* (PL *die* Häute).

skinhead *noun* Skinhead *der* (PL *die* Skinheads).

skinny *adjective* dünn.

skip *noun* (*for rubbish*) Container *der* (PL *die* Container). *verb* 1 auslassen ✧ SEP (*a meal, part of a book*); **I skipped a few chapters** ich ließ ein paar Kapitel aus; 2 **to skip a lesson** ein Stunde schwänzen (*informal*).

skirt *noun* Rock *der* (PL *die* Röcke); **a long skirt** ein langer Rock; **a tight skirt** ein enger Rock; **a mini-skirt** ein Minirock.

sky *noun* Himmel *der* (PL *die* Himmel).

skyscraper *noun* Wolkenkratzer *der* (PL *die* Wolkenkratzer).

slam *verb* zuknallen SEP; **she slammed the door** sie hat die Tür zugeknallt; **the door slammed** die Tür ist zugeknallt.

slang *noun* Slang *der* (PL *die* Slangs).

slap *noun* Klaps *der* (PL *die* Klapse); (*in the face*) Ohrfeige *die* (PL *die* Ohrfeigen). *verb* **to slap somebody** (*across the face*) jemanden ohrfeigen; (*on the bottom*) jemandem einen Klaps geben.

sledge *noun* Schlitten *der* (PL *die* Schlitten).

sledging *noun* **to go sledging** Schlitten fahren ✧ (PERF *sein*).

sleep *noun* Schlaf *der*; **you need more sleep** du brauchst mehr Schlaf; **I had a good sleep** ich habe gut geschlafen; **to go to sleep** einschlafen ✧ SEP (PERF *sein*); **he's gone back to sleep** er ist wieder eingeschlafen. *verb* schlafen ✧; **she's sleeping** sie schläft.

sleeping bag *noun* Schlafsack *der* (PL *die* Schlafsäcke).

sleeping pill *noun* Schlaftablette *die* (PL *die* Schlaftabletten).

✧ IRREGULAR VERB: *See the verb table in the centre of the dictionary*

sleepy *adjective* **to be sleepy** schläfrig sein; **he was getting sleepy** er wurde schläfrig.

sleet *noun* Schneeregen *der*.

sleeve *noun* Ärmel *der* (PL die Ärmel); **a long-sleeved jumper** ein Pullover mit langen Ärmeln; **a short-sleeved shirt** ein Hemd mit kurzen Ärmeln; **to roll up your sleeves** die Ärmel hochkrempeln.

slice *noun* Scheibe *die* (PL die Scheiben); **a slice of bread** eine Scheibe Brot.
verb **to slice something** etwas in Scheiben schneiden ✧.

slide *noun* 1 (*photo*) Dia *das* (PL die Dias); 2 (*hairslide*) Haarspange *die* (PL die Haarspangen); 3 (*for sliding down*) Rutschbahn *die* (PL die Rutschbahnen).

slight *adjective* klein; **there is a slight problem** es gibt ein kleines Problem.

slightly *adverb* etwas.

slim *adjective* schlank.
verb abnehmen ✧ SEP; **I'm slimming** ich mache eine Schlankheitskur.

sling *noun* Schlinge *die* (PL die Schlingen); **to have your arm in a sling** den Arm in der Schlinge haben.

slip *noun* 1 (*mistake*) Fehler *der* (PL die Fehler); 2 (*petticoat*) Unterrock *der* (PL die Unterröcke).
verb 1 (*slide*) ausrutschen SEP (PERF *sein*); 2 **it slipped my mind** es ist mir entfallen.
● **to slip up** einen Fehler machen.

slipper *noun* Hausschuh *der* (PL die Hausschuhe).

slippery *adjective* glatt.

slope *noun* Hang *der* (PL die Hänge).

slot *noun* Schlitz *der* (PL die Schlitze).

slot machine *noun* 1 (*vending machine*) Automat *der* (PL die Automaten); 2 (*games machine*) Spielautomat *der* (PL die Spielautomaten).

slow *adjective* 1 langsam; **the service is a bit slow** die Bedienung ist etwas langsam; 2 (*of a clock or watch*) **to be slow** nachgehen ✧ SEP (PERF *sein*); **my watch is slow** meine Uhr geht nach.
● **to slow down** langsamer werden.

slowly *adverb* langsam; **he got up slowly** er ist langsam aufgestanden; **can you speak more slowly, please?** können Sie bitte etwas langsamer sprechen?

sly *adjective* gerissen (*a person*);
★ **on the sly** heimlich.

smack *noun* Klaps *der* (PL die Klapse).
verb **to smack somebody** jemandem einen Klaps geben ✧.

small *adjective* klein; **a small dog** ein kleiner Hund.

smart *adjective* 1 (*well-dressed, posh*) elegant; **a smart restaurant** ein elegantes Restaurant; 2 (*clever*) clever.

smash *noun* (*collision*) Zusammenstoß *der* (PL die Zusammenstöße).

△ NEW SPELLING: *See page xii*

verb 1 (*break*) zerschlagen ✧; **they smashed a window pane** sie haben eine Fensterscheibe zerschlagen; 2 (*get broken*) zerbrechen ✧ (PERF *sein*); **the plate smashed** der Teller ist zerbrochen.

smashing *adjective* klasse (*informal*).

smell *noun* Geruch *der* (PL *die* Gerüche); **a nasty smell** ein scheußlicher Geruch; **a smell of gas** ein Gasgeruch.
verb 1 riechen ✧; **I can't smell anything** ich kann nichts riechen; **to smell of perfume** nach Parfüm riechen; 2 (*smell bad*) stinken ✧; **the drains smell** der Abfluss stinkt.

smelly *adjective* 1 stinkend; **her smelly dog** ihr stinkender Hund; 2 **to be smelly** stinken ✧.

smile *noun* Lächeln *das*.
verb lächeln; **to smile at somebody** jemanden anlächeln SEP.

smoke *noun* Rauch *der*.
verb rauchen; **she doesn't smoke** sie raucht nicht.

smoking *noun* 'no smoking' 'Rauchen verboten'; **to give up smoking** mit dem Rauchen aufhören.

smooth *adjective* 1 glatt; **a smooth surface** eine glatte Oberfläche; 2 (*person*) aalglatt.

smug *adjective* selbstgefällig.

smuggle *verb* **to smuggle something** etwas schmuggeln.

smuggler *noun* 1 Schmuggler *der* (PL *die* Schmuggler), Schmugglerin *die* (PL *die* Schmugglerinnen); 2 **drugs smuggler** *der* Drogenschmuggler.

snack *noun* Snack *der* (PL *die* Snacks).

snail *noun* Schnecke *die* (PL *die* Schnecken).

snake *noun* Schlange *die* (PL *die* Schlangen).

snap *noun* (*card game*) Schnippschnapp *das* (PL *die* Schnippschnapp).
verb 1 (*break*) brechen ✧ (PERF *sein*); 2 **to snap something** etwas zerbrechen ✧; 3 **to snap your fingers** mit den Fingern schnalzen.

snapshot *noun* Schnappschuss △ *der* (PL *die* Schnappschüsse).

snarl *verb* knurren.

snatch *verb* 1 entreißen ✧; **to snatch something from somebody** jemandem etwas entreißen; **she had her bag snatched** man hat ihr die Handtasche entrissen; 2 **he snatched it out of my hand** er hat es mir aus der Hand gerissen.

sneak *verb* 1 **to sneak in** sich hineinschleichen ✧ SEP; **to sneak out** sich hinausschleichen ✧ SEP; 2 **to sneak on somebody** jemanden verpetzen (*informal*).

sneeze *verb* niesen.

sniff *verb* schnüffeln.

snob *noun* Snob *der* (PL *die* Snobs).

✧ IRREGULAR VERB: *See the verb table in the centre of the dictionary*

snobbery *noun* Snobismus *der*.

snooker *noun* Snooker *das*.

snore *verb* schnarchen.

snow *noun* Schnee *der*.
verb schneien; **it's snowing** es
schneit.

snowball *noun* Schneeball *der* (PL
die Schneebälle).

snowman *noun* Schneemann *der*
(PL *die* Schneemänner).

so *conjunction, adverb* **1** so; **he's so
lazy** er ist so faul; **not so** nicht so;
**our house is a bit like yours, but not
so big** unser Haus ist so ähnlich wie
eures, aber nicht so groß; **2 so much**
so sehr; **I hate it so much** ich hasse
es so sehr; **3 so much** so viel; **I have
so much work** ich habe so viel
Arbeit; **4 so many** so viele; **we've
got so many problems** wir haben
so viele Probleme; **5** (*therefore*) also;
**he got up late, so he missed his
train** er ist spät aufgestanden, also
hat er den Zug verpasst; **so what
shall we do?** also, was machen wir?;
6 so what? na und?; **7** (*also*) **so do
I, so did I** ich auch; **'I live in Leeds' –
'so do I'** 'ich wohne in Leeds' – 'ich
auch'; **I liked the film and so did he**
ich fand den Film gut und er auch; **so
am I** ich auch; **so do we** wir auch;
8 I think so ich glaube schon;
9 I hope so hoffentlich.

soak *verb* einweichen SEP.

soaked *adjective* patschnass △;
★ **to be soaked to the skin**
patschnass sein.

soap *noun* **1** Seife *die* (PL *die* Seifen);
2 (*soap opera*) Seifenoper *die* (PL *die*
Seifenopern).

soap powder *noun*
Seifenpulver *das*.

sober *adjective* nüchtern.
● **to sober up** nüchtern werden ✧
(PERF *sein*).

soccer *noun* Fußball *der*.

social *adjective* **1** sozial; **social
problems** soziale Probleme;
2 gesellschaftlich (*engagement,
ambition*); **social engagements**
gesellschaftliche Verpflichtungen;
social class *die* gesellschaftliche
Schicht; **3** (*sociable*) gesellig
(*evening, person*).

socialism *noun* Sozialismus *der*.

socialist *noun, adjective*
Sozialist *der* (PL *die* Sozialisten),
Sozialistin *die* (PL *die*
Sozialistinnen).

social security *noun*
1 Sozialhilfe *die*; **to be on social
security** Sozialhilfe bekommen;
2 (*the system*) Sozialversicherung
die.

social worker *noun*
Sozialarbeiter *der* (PL *die*
Sozialarbeiter), Sozialarbeiterin *die*
(PL *die* Sozialarbeiterinnen).

society *noun* Gesellschaft *die* (PL
die Gesellschaften).

sociology *noun* Soziologie *die*.

sock *noun* Socke *die* (PL *die* Socken);
a pair of socks ein Paar Socken.

socket *noun* (*power point*)
Steckdose *die* (PL *die* Steckdosen).

△ NEW SPELLING: See page xii

sofa *noun* Sofa *das* (PL *die* Sofas).

sofa bed *noun* Schlafcouch *die* (PL *die* Schlafcouchs).

soft *adjective* **1** weich; **2** **a soft option** eine bequeme Lösung; ★ **to have a soft spot for somebody** eine Vorliebe für jemanden haben.

soft drink *noun* alkoholfreie Getränk *das* (PL *die* alkoholfreien Getränke).

soft toy *noun* Stofftier *das* (PL *die* Stofftiere).

software *noun* Software *die*.

soil *noun* Erde *die*.

solar energy *noun* Sonnenenergie *die*.

soldier *noun* Soldat *der* (PL *die* Soldaten).

solicitor *noun* **1** (*dealing with lawsuits*) Rechtsanwalt *der* (PL *die* Rechtsanwälte), Rechtsanwältin *die* (PL *die* Rechtsanwältinnen); **2** (*dealing with property or documents*) Notar *der* (PL *die* Notare), Notarin *die* (PL *die* Notarinnen).

solid *adjective* **1** (*not flimsy*) stabil; **a solid structure** ein stabiler Bau; **2** massiv; **a table made of solid oak** ein Tisch aus massiver Eiche; **solid silver** massives Silber.

solo *noun* Solo *das* (PL *die* Solos); **guitar solo** *das* Gitarrensolo. *adjective* Solo-; **a solo act** eine Solonummer. *adverb* solo.

soloist *noun* Solist *der* (PL *die* Solisten), Solistin *die* (PL *die* Solistinnen).

solution *noun* Lösung *die* (PL *die* Lösungen).

solve *verb* lösen.

some *adjective, adverb* **1** (*followed by a singular noun*) etwas; **would you like some salad?** möchtest du etwas Salat?; **can you lend me some money?** kannst du mir etwas Geld leihen?; **have you got some bread?** (*some is often not translated*) hast du Brot?; **2** (*followed by a plural noun*) (*a few*) ein paar; **I've bought some apples** ich habe ein paar Äpfel gekauft; **3** (*followed by a plural noun*) (*a certain number but not all*) einige; **some of his films are too violent** einige von seinen Filmen sind zu brutal; **4** (*referring to something that has been mentioned*) **'would you like tea?'** – **'thanks, I've got some'** 'möchten Sie Tee?' – 'nein danke, ich habe schon welchen'; **he's eaten some of it** er hat etwas davon gegessen; **I'd like some** ich möchte etwas; (*with a plural noun*) ich möchte welche; **5** (*certain people or things*) manche; **some people think he's right** manche Leute glauben, dass er Recht hat; **6** **some day** eines Tages.

somebody, someone *pronoun* jemand; **there's somebody in the garden** da ist jemand im Garten.

somehow *adverb* irgendwie; **I've got to finish this essay somehow** ich muss diesen Aufsatz irgendwie fertig schreiben.

✧ IRREGULAR VERB: *See the verb table in the centre of the dictionary*

something *pronoun* 1 etwas; **there's something I've got to tell you** ich muss dir etwas erzählen; **something new** etwas Neues; **something interesting** etwas Interessantes; **there's something wrong** irgendetwas stimmt nicht; 2 **their house is really something!** ihr Haus ist einfach Klasse!

sometime *adverb* irgendwann; **give me a ring sometime next week** ruf mich irgendwann nächste Woche an.

sometimes *adverb* manchmal; **I sometimes take the train** manchmal fahre ich mit der Bahn.

somewhere *adverb* 1 (*in a place*) irgendwo; **I've left my bag somewhere here** ich habe meine Handtasche hier irgendwo liegen lassen; 2 (*to a place*) irgendwohin; **I'd like to go somewhere warm** ich möchte irgendwohin fahren, wo es warm ist.

son *noun* Sohn *der* (PL *die* Söhne).

song *noun* Lied *das* (PL *die* Lieder).

son-in-law *noun* Schwiegersohn *der* (PL *die* Schwiegersöhne).

soon *adverb* 1 bald; **we'll soon be on holiday** wir haben bald Ferien; **see you soon!** bis bald!; 2 **as soon as she arrives** sobald sie ankommt; **as soon as possible** so bald wie möglich; 3 **it's too soon** es ist zu früh.

sooner *adverb* 1 früher; **we should have started sooner** wir hätten früher anfangen sollen; **sooner or later** früher oder später; 2 **I'd sooner wait** ich würde lieber warten.

soprano *noun* Sopran *der* (PL *die* Soprane).

sore *noun* wunde Stelle *die* (PL *die* wunden Stellen). *adjective* 1 (*inflamed*) wund; **to have a sore throat** Halsschmerzen haben; 2 **he has a sore leg** ihm tut das Bein weh; **my arm's sore** mir tut der Arm weh; ★ **it's a sore point** das ist ein wunder Punkt.

sorry *adjective* 1 **I'm really sorry** es tut mir wirklich Leid △; **sorry to disturb you** es tut mir Leid, dass ich dich störe; **I'm sorry I forgot your birthday** es tut mir Leid, dass ich deinen Geburtstag vergessen habe; **I'm sorry, were closing** es tut mir Leid, aber wir machen jetzt zu; 2 **sorry!** Entschuldigung!; 3 **sorry?** wie bitte?; 4 **I feel sorry for him** er tut mir Leid △.

sort *noun* Art *die* (PL *die* Arten); **a sort of dance music** eine Art Tanzmusik; **what sort of car have you got?** was für ein Auto hast du?; **all sorts of people** alle möglichen Leute; **for all sorts of reasons** aus allen möglichen Gründen.
● **to sort something out** 1 Ordnung schaffen ◇ in (+DAT) (*papers, desk, room, possessions*); **I must sort out my room tonight** ich muss heute Abend in meinem Zimmer Ordnung schaffen; 2 klären (*a problem, arrangement*); **Liz is sorting it out** Liz klärt es.

△ NEW SPELLING: *See page xii*

so-so *adjective* so lala (*informal*); **'how was the film?' – 'so-so'** 'wie war der Film?'- 'so lala'.

soul *noun* 1 Seele *die* (PL *die* Seelen); 2 (*music*) Soul *der*.

sound *noun* 1 (*noise*) Geräusch *das* (PL *die* Geräusche); 2 (*of voices, laughter, bell*) Klang *der*; **the sound of her voice** der Klang ihrer Stimme; **I can hear the sound of voices** ich kann Stimmen hören; 3 **without a sound** lautlos; 4 (*volume*) Lautstärke *die*; **to turn the sound down** leiser stellen. *verb* 1 **it sounds easy** es hört sich einfach an; 2 **it sounds as if she's happy** sie scheint glücklich zu sein.

sound asleep *adverb* **to be sound asleep** fest schlafen ✧.

sound effect *noun* Geräuscheffekt *der* (PL *die* Geräuscheffekte).

soundtrack *noun* Soundtrack *der* (PL *die* Soundtracks).

soup *noun* Suppe *die* (PL *die* Suppen); **mushroom soup** *die* Pilzsuppe.

soup plate *noun* Suppenteller *der* (PL *die* Suppenteller).

soup spoon *noun* Suppenlöffel *der* (PL *die* Suppenlöffel).

sour *adjective* sauer.

south *noun* Süden *der*; **in the south** im Süden. *adjective* Süd-, südlich; **the south side** die Südseite; **south wind** *der* Südwind.

adverb **south of Berlin** südlich von Berlin; **they went south** sie sind nach Süden gefahren.

South Africa *noun* Südafrika *das*.

South America *noun* Südamerika *das*.

southeast *noun* Südosten *der*. *adjective* **in southeast England** in Südostengland.

South Pole *noun* Südpol *der*.

southwest *noun* Südwesten *der*. *adjective* **in southwest England** in Südwestengland.

souvenir *noun* Souvenir *das* (PL *die* Souvenirs).

soya *noun* Soja *die*.

space *noun* 1 (*room*) Platz *der*; **there's enough space** es ist genug Platz da; **we've got enough space for two** wir haben genug Platz für zwei; 2 (*gap*) Zwischenraum *der* (PL *die* Zwischenräume); **to leave a large space between lines** einen großen Zwischenraum zwischen den Zeilen lassen; 3 (**parking**) **space** *die* Lücke; 4 (*outer space*) Weltraum *der*; **in space** im Weltraum.

spacecraft *noun* Raumschiff *das* (PL *die* Raumschiffe).

spade *noun* 1 Spaten *der* (PL *die* Spaten); 2 (*in cards*) Pik *das*; **the queen of spades** die Pikdame.

Spain *noun* Spanien *das*; **from Spain** aus Spanien; **to Spain** nach Spanien.

✧ IRREGULAR VERB: *See the verb table in the centre of the dictionary*

Spaniard *noun* Spanier *der* (PL *die* Spanier), Spanierin *die* (PL *die* Spanierinnen).

spaniel *noun* Spaniel *der* (PL *die* Spaniels).

Spanish *noun* 1 (*language*) Spanisch *das*; **I'm learning Spanish** ich lerne Spanisch; **2 the Spanish** (*people*) die Spanier. *adjective* spanisch; **Pedro is Spanish** Pedro ist Spanier.

spare *adjective* Extra-; **we have a spare ticket** wir haben eine Extrakarte. *verb* **to have time to spare** Zeit haben; **can you spare a moment?** hast du einen Moment Zeit?

spare room *noun* Gästezimmer *das* (PL *die* Gästezimmer).

spare time *noun* Freizeit *die*; **in my spare time** in meiner Freizeit.

spare wheel *noun* Reserverad *das* (PL *die* Reserveräder).

sparkling *adjective* **sparkling mineral water** Mineralwasser mit Kohlensäure; **sparkling wine** *der* Schaumwein.

sparrow *noun* Spatz *der* (PL *die* Spätze).

speak *verb* 1 sprechen ✧; **do you speak German?** sprechen Sie Deutsch?; **spoken German** gesprochenes Deutsch; **to speak to somebody about something** mit jemandem über etwas ←(ACC) sprechen; **she's speaking to Mike about it** sie spricht mit Mike

darüber; **2 who's speaking?** (*on the phone*) wer ist am Apparat?

speaker *noun* 1 (*on a music system*) Lautsprecher *der* (PL *die* Lautsprecher); **2** (*at a public lecture*) Redner *der* (PL *die* Redner), Rednerin *die* (PL *die* Rednerinnen).

special *adjective* 1 besonderer/ besondere/besonderes; **on special occasions** bei besonderen Anlässen; **2 special offer** *das* Sonderangebot.

specialist *noun* Fachmann *der* (PL *die* Fachleute), Fachfrau *die* (PL *die* Fachfrauen).

specially *adverb* 1 besonders; **not specially** nicht besonders; **it's specially good for babies** es ist besonders gut für Babys; **2** (*specifically*) speziell; **I made this cake specially for you** ich habe diesen Kuchen speziell für dich gebacken.

spectacles *noun* Brille *die* (PL *die* Brillen).

spectacular *adjective* spektakulär.

spectator *noun* Zuschauer *der* (PL *die* Zuschauer), Zuschauerin *die* (PL *die* Zuschauerinnen).

speech *noun* Rede *die* (PL *die* Reden); **to make a speech** eine Rede halten.

speed *noun* 1 Geschwindigkeit *die* (PL *die* Geschwindigkeiten); **at top speed** mit Höchstgeschwindigkeit; **what speed was he doing?** wie schnell ist er gefahren?; **2** (*gear*) Gang *der* (PL *die* Gänge); **a twelve-speed bike** ein Rad mit zwölf Gängen.

△ NEW SPELLING: *See page xii*

- **to speed up** 1 beschleunigen (*a car*); 2 (*of a person, car*) schneller werden.

speeding *noun* zu schnelle Fahren *das*; **he was fined for speeding** er hat wegen zu schnellen Fahrens einen Strafzettel bekommen.

speed limit *noun* Geschwindigkeitsbeschränkung *die*.

spell *noun* 1 (*of time*) Weile *die*; **for a spell** eine Weile; 2 **cold spell** *die* Kälteperiode; **sunny spells** sonnige Wetterabschnitte.
verb 1 (*in writing*) schreiben ✧; **how do you spell it?** wie schreibt man das?; **how do you spell your surname?** wie schreibt man Ihren Nachnamen?; 2 (*out loud*) buchstabieren.

spelling *noun* Rechtschreibung *die*; **spelling mistake** *der* Rechtschreibfehler.

spend *verb* 1 ausgeben ✧ SEP (*money*); **I've spent all my money** ich habe mein ganzes Geld ausgegeben; 2 verbringen ✧ (*time*); **we spent three days in Munich** wir haben drei Tage in München verbracht; **she spends her time reading** sie verbringt ihre Zeit mit Lesen.

spice *noun* Gewürz *das* (PL *die* Gewürze).

spicy *adjective* scharf; **he doesn't like spicy food** er mag kein scharfes Essen.

spider *noun* Spinne *die* (PL *die* Spinnen).

spill *verb* verschütten; **I've spilled my wine on the carpet** ich habe meinen Wein auf dem Teppich verschüttet.

spinach *noun* Spinat *der*.

spire *noun* Kirchturm *der* (PL *die* Kirchtürme).

spirit *noun* 1 (*energy*) Energie *die*; 2 **in the right spirit** mit der richtigen Einstellung.

spirits *noun* 1 (*alcohol*) Spirituosen (*plural*); 2 **to be in good spirits** guter Laune sein.

spit *verb* 1 spucken; 2 **to spit something out** etwas ausspucken SEP; **spit it out!** spuck es aus!

spite *noun* 1 **in spite of** trotz (+GEN); **we decided to go in spite of the rain** wir beschlossen trotz des Regens zu gehen; 2 (*nastiness*) Boshaftigkeit *die*; **to do something out of spite** etwas aus Boshaftigkeit tun.

spiteful *adjective* gehässig.

splash *noun* 1 (*noise*) Platsch *der*; 2 **splash of colour** *der* Farbfleck. *verb* bespritzen.

splendid *adjective* herrlich.

split *verb* 1 (*with an axe or a knife*) spalten; **to split wood** Holz spalten; 2 (*come apart*) zerreißen ✧ (PERF *sein*); **the lining has split** das Futter ist zerrissen; 3 (*divide up*) teilen; **they split the money between**

them sie haben das Geld untereinander geteilt.

to split up 1 (*a group or crowd*) sich auflösen SEP; **2** (*a couple*) sich trennen; **she's split up with her husband** sie hat sich von ihrem Mann getrennt; **she's split up with Sam** sie hat mit Sam Schluss gemacht (*informal*).

spoil *verb* verderben ✧; **it completely spoiled our evening** das hat uns den Abend völlig verdorben; **to spoil sombody's fun** jemandem den Spaß verderben.

spoiled *adjective* verwöhnt; **a spoiled child** ein verwöhntes Kind.

spokesman *noun* Sprecher *der* (PL die Sprecher).

spokeswoman *noun* Sprecherin *die* (PL die Sprecherinnen).

sponge *noun* Schwamm *der* (PL die Schwämme).

sponge cake *noun* Rührkuchen *der* (PL die Rührkuchen).

sponsor *noun* Sponsor *der* (PL die Sponsoren).
verb sponsern.

spooky *adjective* gruselig; **a spooky story** eine gruselige Geschichte.

spoon *noun* Löffel *der* (PL die Löffel); **a spoon of sugar** ein Löffel Zucker; **soup spoon** *der* Suppenlöffel; **teaspoon** *der* Teelöffel.

spoonful *noun* Löffel *der* (PL die Löffel).

sport *noun* **1** Sport *der*; **to be good at sport** gut im Sport sein; **my favourite sport** mein Lieblingssport; **2** (*in games*) **to be a good sport** ein guter Verlierer sein.

sports bag *noun* Sporttasche *die* (PL die Sporttaschen).

sports car *noun* Sportwagen *der* (PL die Sportwagen).

sports centre *noun* Sportzentrum *das* (PL die Sportzentren).

sports club *noun* Sportverein *der* (PL die Sportvereine).

sportsman *noun* Sportler *der* (PL die Sportler).

sportswear *noun* Sportbekleidung *die*.

sportswoman *noun* Sportlerin *die* (PL die Sportlerinnen).

spot *noun* **1** (*pattern in fabric*) Punkt *der* (PL die Punkte); **a red shirt with black spots** ein rotes Hemd mit schwarzen Punkten; **2** (*on your skin*) Pickel *der* (PL die Pickel); **I've got spots** ich habe Pickel; **to be covered in spots** völlig verpickelt sein; **3** (*stain*) Fleck *der* (PL die Flecke); **you've got a spot on your shirt** du hast einen Fleck auf dem Hemd; **4** (*spotlight*) Scheinwerfer *der* (PL die Scheinwerfer); (*in the home*) Spot *der* (PL die Spots); **5 on the spot** (*immediately*) auf der Stelle; **we'll do it for you on the spot** wir machen es Ihnen auf der Stelle; **6** (*at hand*) **on the spot** zur Stelle; **7** (*at the same place*) **on the spot** an Ort

△ NEW SPELLING: *See page xii*

und Stelle.
verb entdecken; **he spotted his friend in the crowd** er entdeckte seinen Freund in der Menge.

spotlight *noun* 1 Scheinwerfer der (PL die Scheinwerfer); 2 (*in the home*) Spot der (PL die Spots).

spotty *adjective* (*pimply*) pickelig.

sprain *noun* Verstauchung die (PL die Verstauchungen).
verb **to sprain your ankle** sich ←(DAT) den Fuß verstauchen.

spray *noun* (*spray can*) Spray das (PL die Sprays).
verb sprühen.

spread *noun* Brotaufstrich der; **cheese spread** der Streichkäse.
verb 1 (*of news or a disease*) sich verbreiten; 2 streichen ✧ (*butter, jam, glue*).

spreadsheet *noun* (*on a computer*) Tabellenkalkulation die.

spring *noun* 1 (*the season*) Frühling der (PL die Frühlinge); **in the spring** im Frühling; **spring flowers** Frühlingsblumen; 2 (*made of metal*) Feder die (PL die Federn); 3 (*providing water*) Quelle die (PL die Quellen).

springtime *noun* Frühjahr das; **in springtime** im Frühjahr.

spring water *noun* Quellwasser das.

sprint *noun* Sprint der (PL die Sprints).
verb rennen ✧ (PERF *sein*).

sprinter *noun* Sprinter der (PL die Sprinter), Sprinterin die (PL die Sprinterinnen).

sprout *noun* (*Brussels sprout*) Rosenkohl der; **he likes sprouts** er mag Rosenkohl.

spy *noun* Spion der (PL die Spione), Spionin die (PL die Spioninnen).
verb **to spy on somebody** jemandem nachspionieren SEP; **he's spying on me** er spioniert mir nach

squabble *verb* sich zanken.

square *noun* 1 (*shape*) Quadrat das (PL die Quadrate); 2 (*in a town or village*) Platz der (PL die Plätze); **the village square** der Dorfplatz.
adjective quadratisch; **a square box** eine viereckige Schachtel; **three square metres** drei Quadratmeter; **the room is four metres square** das Zimmer ist vier mal vier Meter; ★ **to go back to square one** noch einmal von vorn anfangen.

squash *noun* 1 (*drink*) Saft der; **orange squash** der Orangensaft; 2 (*sport*) Squash das.
verb zerquetschen.

squeak *verb* 1 (*door, hinge*) quietschen; 2 (*person, animal*) quieken.

squeeze *verb* 1 **to squeeze somebody's hand** jemandem die Hand drücken; 2 drücken (*toothpaste*).

stab *verb* stechen ✧; **to stab somebody** (*kill*) jemanden erstechen ✧.

✧ IRREGULAR VERB: *See the verb table in the centre of the dictionary*

stable *noun* Stall *der* (PL *die* Ställe).
adjective stabil.

stack *noun* **1** Stapel *der* (PL *die* Stapel); **2 stacks of** ein Haufen; **she's got stacks of CDs** sie hat einen Haufen CDs.

stadium *noun* Stadion *das* (PL *die* Stadien).

staff *noun* **1** (*of a company*) Personal *das*; **2** (*in a school*) Lehrkräfte (*plural*).

stage *noun* **1** (*for a performance*) Bühne *die* (PL *die* Bühnen); **on stage** auf der Bühne; **2** (*phase*) Phase *die* (PL *die* Phasen); **at this stage of the project** in dieser Phase des Projekts; **at this stage it's hard to say** im Augenblick ist es schwer zu sagen.

staggered *adjective* (*amazed*) verblüfft.

stain *noun* Fleck *der* (PL *die* Flecke). *verb* beflecken.

stainless steel *noun* Edelstahl *der*; **a stainless steel sink** ein Spülbecken aus Edelstahl.

stair *noun* **1** (*step*) Stufe *die* (PL *die* Stufen); **2 the stairs** die Treppe (*singular*); **I met her on the stairs** ich habe sie auf der Treppe getroffen.

staircase *noun* Treppe *die* (PL *die* Treppen).

stale *adjective* alt.

stalemate *noun* (*in chess*) Patt *das* (PL *die* Patts).

stall *noun* **1** (*at a market or fair*) Stand *der* (PL *die* Stände); **2** (*in a theatre*) **the stalls** das Parkett.

stammer *noun* **to have a stammer** stottern.

stamp *noun* Briefmarke *die* (PL *die* Briefmarken). *verb* **1** frankieren (*a letter*); **2 to stamp your foot** mit dem Fuß aufstampfen.

stamp album *noun* Briefmarkenalbum *das* (PL *die* Briefmarkenalben).

stamp collection *noun* Briefmarkensammlung *die* (PL *die* Briefmarkensammlungen).

stand *verb* **1** stehen ✧; **several people were standing** viele Leute standen; **we stood outside the cinema** wir haben vor dem Kino gestanden; **2** (*bear*) ausstehen ✧ SEP; **I can't stand her** ich kann sie nicht ausstehen; **I can't stand waiting** ich kann es nicht ausstehen, wenn man warten muss; **3** (*keep going*) aushalten ✧ SEP; **I can't stand it any longer** ich halte es nicht mehr aus. *noun* (*in a stadium*) Tribüne *die* (PL *die* Tribünen).
● **to stand for something** (*be short for*) bedeuten; **UN stands for United Nations** UN bedeutet United Nations.
● **stand up** aufstehen ✧ SEP (PERF *sein*); **everybody stood up** alle standen auf.

standard *noun* **1** (*level*) Niveau *das*; **of high standard** von hohem Niveau; **2 standard of living**

der Lebensstandard; **3 she sets
herself high standards** sie stellt
hohe Ansprüche an sich selbst.
adjective normal; **the standard size**
die Normalgröße.

staple *noun* Heftklammer *die* (PL *die*
Heftklammern).
verb heften; **to staple the pages
together** die Seiten
zusammenheften.

stapler *noun* Hefter *der* (PL *die*
Hefter).

star *noun* **1** (*in the sky*) Stern *der* (PL
die Sterne); **2** (*person*) Star *der* (PL
die Stars); **he's a film star** er ist ein
Filmstar.
verb **to star in a film** in einem Film
die Hauptrolle spielen; **starring** ...
in der Hauptrolle ...

stare *verb* **1** starren; **what are you
staring at?** was starrst du so?; **2 to
stare at somebody** jemanden
anstarren SEP; **he's staring at the
wall** er starrt die Wand an.

start *noun* **1** Anfang *der*; **at the
start** am Anfang; **at the start of the
film** am Anfang des Films; **from the
start** von Anfang an; **we knew from
the start that it was dangerous** wir
wussten von Anfang an, dass es
gefährlich war; **2 to make a start on
something** mit etwas ←(DAT)
anfangen ◇ SEP; **I've made a start on
my homework** ich habe mit meinen
Hausaufgaben angefangen; **3** (*of a
race*) Start *der* (PL *die* Starts).
verb **1** anfangen ◇ SEP; **the film
starts at eight** der Film fängt um
acht an; **I've started the book** ich
habe das Buch angefangen; **to start**

doing something anfangen, etwas
zu tun; **I've started learning
Spanish** ich habe angefangen,
Spanisch zu lernen; **to start crying**
anfangen zu weinen; **2 to start a
business** ein Geschäft gründen;
3 to start a car ein Auto starten;
she started the car sie hat das Auto
gestartet; **4 the car won't start** das
Auto springt nicht an.

starter *noun* (*first course*)
Vorspeise *die* (PL *die* Vorspeisen).

starve *verb* verhungern; **I'm
starving!** ich bin schon am
Verhungern!

state *noun* **1** Zustand *der* (PL *die*
Zustände); **the house is in a very
bad state** das Haus ist in einem sehr
schlechten Zustand; **2** (*country*)
Staat *der* (PL *die* Staaten); **the state**
der Staat; **3 the States** (*USA*) die
Staaten; **they live in the States** sie
leben in den Staaten.
verb **1** erklären (*intention, reason*);
2 angeben ◇ SEP (*an address,
income, a reason*).

stately home *noun* Schloss △ *das*
(PL *die* Schlösser).

statement *noun* Erklärung *die* (PL
die Erklärungen).

station *noun* **1** Bahnhof *der* (PL *die*
Bahnhöfe); **at the railway station**
am Bahnhof; **bus station** *der*
Busbahnhof; **2 police station** *die*
Polizeiwache; **3 radio station** *der*
Rundfunksender.

stationer's *noun*
Schreibwarengeschäft *das* (PL *die*
Schreibwarengeschäfte).

◇ IRREGULAR VERB: *See the verb table in the centre of the dictionary*

tatistics *noun* (*subject*)
Statistik *die*; **the statistics** (*figures*)
die Statistik.

tatue *noun* Statue *die* (PL *die*
Statuen).

tay *noun* Aufenthalt *der* (PL *die*
Aufenthalte); **our stay in Cologne**
unser Aufenthalt in Köln; **enjoy your
stay!** einen schönen Aufenthalt!
verb 1 bleiben ✧ (PERF *sein*); **I'll stay
here** ich bleibe hier; **how long are
you staying?** wie lange bleibst du?;
2 (*spend the night*) **you can stay
with us** du kannst bei uns
übernachten; **to stay the night with
friends** bei Freunden übernachten;
3 (*be temporarily lodged*) wohnen;
where are you staying? wo wohnst
du?; **I'm staying in a hotel** ich
wohne im Hotel; 4 (*be on a visit*)
sein ✧ (PERF *sein*); **I'm going to stay
with my sister this weekend** ich bin
am Wochenende bei meiner
Schwester; **I stayed in Munich for a
couple of days** ich war ein paar
Tage in München.
● **to stay in** zu Hause bleiben ✧ (PERF
sein); **I'm staying in tonight** heute
Abend bleibe ich zu Hause.

steady *adjective* 1 fest; **a steady job**
eine feste Stelle; 2 gleichmäßig; **at a
steady pace** mit gleichmäßiger
Geschwindigkeit; 3 (*hand, voice*)
ruhig; **to hold something steady**
etwas ruhig halten; 4 (*dependable*)
zuverlässig.

steak *noun* Steak *das* (PL *die* Steaks);
steak and chips Steak mit Pommes
frites.

steal *verb* stehlen ✧.

steam *noun* Dampf der.

steel *noun* Stahl *der*.

steep *adjective* steil; **a steep slope**
ein steiler Hang.

steeple *noun* (*spire*) Kirchturm *der*
(PL *die* Kirchtürme).

steering wheel *noun*
Lenkrad *das* (PL *die* Lenkräder).

step *noun* 1 Schritt *der* (PL *die*
Schritte); **to take a step forwards**
einen Schritt nach vorn machen; **to
take a step backwards** einen
Schritt zurück machen; 2 (*stair*)
Stufe *die* (PL *die* Stufen);
● **to step back** zurücktreten ✧ SEP
(PERF *sein*).
● **to step forward** vortreten ✧ SEP (PERF
sein).

stepbrother *noun* Stiefbruder *der*
(PL *die* Stiefbrüder).

stepdaughter *noun*
Stieftochter *die* (PL *die* Stieftöchter).

stepfather *noun* Stiefvater *der* (PL
die Stiefväter).

stepladder *noun* Trittleiter *die* (PL
die Trittleitern).

stepmother *noun* Stiefmutter *die*
(PL *die* Stiefmütter).

stepsister *noun* Stiefschwester *die*
(PL *die* Stiefschwestern).

stepson *noun* Stiefsohn *der* (PL *die*
Stiefsöhne).

stereo *noun* Stereoanlage *die* (PL *die*
Stereoanlagen).

sterling *noun* Sterling *der*; **in
sterling** in Pfund (Sterling).

△ NEW SPELLING: *See page xii*

stew noun Eintopf der (PL die Eintöpfe).

steward noun Steward der (PL die Stewards).

stewardess noun Stewardess △ die (PL die Stewardessen).

stick noun 1 Stock der (PL die Stöcke); 2 **hockey stick** der Hockeyschläger.
verb 1 (with glue) kleben; 2 (put) tun ✧; **stick them on my desk** tu sie auf meinen Schreibtisch.

sticker noun Aufkleber der (PL die Aufkleber).

sticky adjective 1 klebrig; **I've got sticky hands** ich habe klebrige Hände; 2 **a sticky label** ein Aufkleber.

sticky tape noun Klebestreifen der.

stiff adjective 1 steif; **to feel stiff** steif sein; (after exercise) Muskelkater haben; **to have a stiff neck** einen steifen Hals haben; 2 **to be bored stiff** sich zu Tode langweilen; 3 **to be scared stiff** furchtbare Angst haben.

still adjective 1 **sit still!** sitz still!; **keep still!** halt still!; 2 **still mineral water** Mineralwasser ohne Kohlensäure.
adverb 1 noch; **do you still live in London?** wohnst du noch in London?; **I've still not finished** ich bin immer noch nicht fertig; **he's still working** er arbeitet noch; 2 (nevertheless) trotzdem; **I told her not to, but she still did it** ich habe

es ihr verboten, aber sie hat es trotzdem gemacht; 3 **better still** noch besser.

sting noun Stich der (PL die Stiche).
verb stechen ✧.

stink noun Gestank der.
verb stinken ✧; **it stinks of fish in here** es stinkt hier nach Fisch.

stir verb rühren.

stitch noun 1 (in sewing, surgical) Stich der (PL die Stiche); 2 (in knitting) Masche die (PL die Maschen); 3 (pain) Seitenstechen das.

stock noun 1 (in a shop) Warenbestand der; **to have something in stock** etwas auf Lager haben; **to be out of stock** ausverkauft sein; 2 (supply) Vorrat der (PL die Vorräte); **I always have a stock of pencils** ich habe immer einen Bleistiftvorrat; 3 (for cooking) Brühe die; **chicken stock** die Hühnerbrühe.
verb (in a shop) führen; **they don't stock books** sie führen keine Bücher.

stock cube noun Brühwürfel der (PL die Brühwürfel).

stocking noun Strumpf der (PL die Strümpfe).

stomach noun Magen der (PL die Mägen).

stomach-ache noun Magenschmerzen (plural); **to have stomach-ache** Magenschmerzen haben.

✧ IRREGULAR VERB: See the verb table in the centre of the dictionary

stone *noun* Stein *der* (PL die Steine); **stone wall** *die* Steinmauer.

stool *noun* Hocker *der* (PL die Hocker).

stop *noun* Haltestelle *die* (PL die Haltestellen); **bus stop** *die* Bushaltestelle.
verb 1 halten ✧; **does the train stop in Stuttgart?** hält der Zug in Stuttgart?; 2 **to stop somebody/ something** jemanden/etwas anhalten ✧ SEP; **the police stopped the car** die Polizei hielt den Wagen an; 3 (*cease*) aufhören SEP; **the noise has stopped** der Lärm hat aufgehört; **to stop doing something** aufhören, etwas zu tun; **he's stopped smoking** er hat aufgehört zu rauchen; **she never stops asking questions** sie hört nie auf, Fragen zu stellen; **stop it!** hör auf!; 4 **to stop somebody doing something** jemanden daran hindern, etwas zu tun; **I can't stop her ringing him** ich kann sie nicht daran hindern, ihn anzurufen; 5 (*prevent*) verhindern (*an accident, a crime*).

stopwatch *noun* Stoppuhr *die* (PL die Stoppuhren).

store *noun* (*shop*) Geschäft *das* (PL die Geschäfte); **department store** *das* Kaufhaus.
verb 1 aufbewahren SEP; (*in a warehouse*) lagern; 2 (*on a computer*) speichern.

storey *noun* Stockwerk *das* (PL die Stockwerke); **a four-storey house** ein vierstöckiges Haus.

storm *noun* 1 Sturm *der* (PL die Stürme); 2 (*thunderstorm*) Gewitter *das* (PL die Gewitter).

stormy *adjective* stürmisch.

story *noun* Geschichte *die* (PL die Geschichten); **to tell a story** eine Geschichte erzählen.

stove *noun* (*cooker*) Herd *der* (PL die Herde).

straight *adjective* 1 gerade; **a straight line** eine gerade Linie; 2 **to have straight hair** glatte Haare haben.
adverb 1 (*in direction*) **straight ahead** geradeaus; **to go straight ahead** geradeaus gehen; 2 (*immediately, directly*) sofort; **straight away** sofort; **he went straight to the doctor's** er ging sofort zum Arzt.

straightforward *adjective* einfach.

strain *noun* Stress △ *der*; **the strain of the last few weeks** der Stress in den letzten Wochen; **to be a strain** anstrengend sein.
verb 1 zerren (*a muscle*); 2 verrenken (*your arm, back*); **he's strained his back** er hat sich ←(DAT) den Rücken verrenkt.

strange *adjective* seltsam; **his strange behaviour** sein seltsames Verhalten.

stranger *noun* Fremde *der/die* (PL die Fremden).

strap *noun* 1 (*on a case, bag, camera*) Riemen *der* (PL die Riemen); 2 (*on a garment*) Träger *der* (PL die Träger);

△ NEW SPELLING: *See page xii*

3 (*of a watch*) Armband *das* (PL *die* Armbänder).

strapless *adjective* trägerlos.

straw *noun* **1** (*for drinking*) Strohhalm *der* (PL *die* Strohhalme); **2** (*the material*) Stroh *das*; **straw hat** *der* Strohhut.

strawberry *noun* Erdbeere *die* (PL *die* Erdbeeren); **strawberry jam** *die* Erdbeermarmelade.

stray *adjective* **a stray dog** ein streunender Hund.

stream *noun* Bach *der* (PL *die* Bäche).

street *noun* Straße *die* (PL *die* Straßen); **I met Simon in the street** ich habe Simon auf der Straße getroffen.

streetlamp *noun* Straßenlampe *die* (PL *die* Straßenlampen).

street map *noun* Stadtplan *der* (PL *die* Stadtpläne).

streetwise *adjective* gewieft.

strength *noun* Kraft *die* (PL *die* Kräfte).

stress *noun* Stress △ *der*. *verb* betonen; **to stress the importance of something** die Wichtigkeit von etwas betonen.

stretch *verb* **1** (*garment, shoes*) sich dehnen; **this jumper has stretched** der Pullover hat sich gedehnt; **2 to stretch your legs** sich ←(DAT) die Beine vertreten ✧.

stretcher *noun* Trage *die* (PL *die* Tragen).

stretchy *adjective* elastisch.

strict *adjective* streng.

strike *noun* Streik *der* (PL *die* Streiks); **to go on strike** in den Streik treten ✧ (PERF *sein*); **to be/go on strike** streiken. *verb* **1** (*hit*) schlagen ✧; **the clock struck six** die Uhr schlug sechs; **2** (*be/go on strike*) streiken.

striker *noun* **1** (*in football*) Stürmer *der* (PL *die* Stürmer), Stürmerin *die* (PL *die* Stürmerinnen); **2** (*person on strike*) Streikende *der/die* (PL *die* Streikenden).

string *noun* **1** (*for tying*) Schnur *die* (PL *die* Schnüre); **2** (*on a musical instrument*) Saite *die* (PL *die* Saiten).

strip *noun* Streifen *der* (PL *die* Streifen). *verb* **1** (*undress*) sich ausziehen ✧ SEP; **2** (*remove paint from*) abbeizen SEP.

strip cartoon *noun* Comicstrip △ *der* (PL *die* Comicstrips).

stripe *noun* Streifen *der* (PL *die* Streifen).

striped *adjective* gestreift.

stroke *noun* **1** (*style of swimming*) Stil *der* (PL *die* Stile); **2** (*medical*) Schlaganfall *der* (PL *die* Schlaganfälle); **to have a stroke** einen Schlaganfall bekommen; ★ **a stroke of luck** ein glücklicher Zufall; **to have a stroke of luck** Glück haben. *verb* streicheln.

✧ IRREGULAR VERB: *See the verb table in the centre of the dictionary*

strong *adjective* 1 (*person, drink, feeling*) stark; 2 (*sturdy*) stabil (*furniture*); **strong shoes** feste Schuhe.

strongly *adverb* 1 (*believe, oppose*) fest; 2 (*support*) nachdrücklich; 3 (*advise, recommend*) dringend; 4 **she smelt strongly of garlic** sie hat stark nach Knoblauch gerochen.

struggle *noun* Kampf der (PL die Kämpfe); **the struggle for freedom** der Kampf für die Freiheit; **it's been a struggle** es war ein Kampf. *verb* 1 (*to obtain something*) kämpfen; **to struggle to do something** kämpfen, um etwas zu tun; **she struggled for a place** sie kämpfte um einen Platz; 2 (*physically, in order to escape or reach something*) sich wehren; 3 (*have difficulty in doing something*) sich abmühen SEP; **they are struggling to pay the rent** sie mühen sich ab, ihre Miete zu zahlen; **he's struggling with his homework** er müht sich mit seinen Hausaufgaben ab.

stub *noun* **cigarette stub** die Kippe.
● **to stub out** ausdrücken SEP.

stubborn *adjective* stur.

stuck *adjective* 1 (*jammed*) **it's stuck** es klemmt; **the drawer's stuck** die Schublade klemmt; 2 **to get stuck** (*person*) stecken bleiben △ ✧ (*in a lift, traffic jam, or place*).

stud *noun* 1 (*on clothes*) Niete die (PL die Nieten); 2 (*on a boot*) Stollen der (PL die Stollen);

0 (*earring*) Ohrstecker der (PL die Ohrstecker).

student *noun* 1 (*at college or university*) Student der (PL die Studenten), Studentin die (PL die Studentinnen); 2 (*at school*) Schüler der (PL die Schüler), Schülerin die (PL die Schülerinnen).

studio *noun* 1 (*film, TV*) Studio das (PL die Studios); 2 (*artist's*) Atelier das (PL die Ateliers).

study *verb* 1 lernen; **he's busy studying for his exams** er lernt fleißig für seine Prüfung; 2 studieren; **she's studying medicine** sie studiert Medizin.

stuff *noun* (*things, personal belongings*) Zeug das (*informal*); **we can put all that stuff in the attic** wir können das ganze Zeug auf den Boden bringen; **you can leave your stuff at my house** du kannst dein Zeug bei mir lassen. *verb* 1 (*shove*) stopfen; **she stuffed some things into a suitcase** sie hat ein paar Sachen in einen Koffer gestopft; 2 füllen (*vegetables, turkey*); **stuffed peppers** gefüllte Paprikaschoten.

stuffing *noun* (*in cooking*) Füllung die (PL die Füllungen).

stuffy *adjective* (*airless*) stickig.

stunned *adjective* sprachlos.

stunning *adjective* toll (*informal*).

stunt *noun* (*in a film*) Stunt der (PL die Stunts).

stuntman *noun* Stuntman der (PL die Stuntmen).

△ NEW SPELLING: *See page xii*

stupid *adjective* blöd; **that was really stupid** das war so blöd; **I did something stupid** ich habe etwas Blödes gemacht.

stutter *noun* **to have a stutter** stottern.
verb stottern.

style *noun* 1 Stil *der* (PL *die* Stile); **style of living** *der* Lebensstil; **he has his own style** er hat seinen eigenen Stil; 2 (*fashion*) Mode *die*; **it's the latest style** das ist die neueste Mode.

subject *noun* 1 Thema *das* (PL *die* Themen); **the subject of my talk** das Thema meiner Rede; 2 (*at school*) Fach *das* (PL *die* Fächer); **my favourite subject is biology** mein Lieblingsfach ist Biologie.

subscription *noun* Abonnement *das* (PL *die* Abonnements); **to take out a subscription to a magazine** eine Zeitschrift abonnieren.

subsidize *verb* subventionieren.

subsidy *noun* Subvention *die* (PL *die* Subventionen).

substance *noun* Substanz *die* (PL *die* Substanzen).

substitute *noun* (*in sport*) Ersatzspieler *der* (PL *die* Ersatzspieler), Ersatzspielerin *die* (PL *die* Ersatzspielerinnen).
verb ersetzen.

subtitled *adjective* mit Untertiteln.

subtitles *plural noun* Untertitel (*plural*).

subtract *verb* abziehen ✧ SEP.

suburb *noun* Vorort *der* (PL *die* Vororte); **a suburb of Edinburgh** ein Vorort von Edinburgh; **in the suburbs of London** in den Londoner Vororten.

suburban *adjective* Vorort-; **a suburban train** ein Vorortzug.

subway *noun* (*underpass*) Unterführung *die* (PL *die* Unterführungen).

succeed *verb* gelingen ✧ (PERF *sein*); **we've succeeded in contacting her** es ist uns gelungen, sie zu erreichen.

success *noun* Erfolg *der* (PL *die* Erfolge); **a great success** ein großer Erfolg.

successful *adjective* 1 erfolgreich; **he's a successful writer** er ist ein erfolgreicher Schriftsteller; 2 **to be successful in doing something** etwas mit Erfolg tun.

successfully *adverb* mit Erfolg.

such *adjective, adverb* 1 so; **they're such nice people** das sind so nette Leute; **I've had such a busy day** ich habe so einen hektischen Tag gehabt; **it's such a long way** es ist so weit; **it's such a pity** es ist so schade; 2 **such a lot of** (*followed by a singular noun*) so viel; **they've got such a lot of money** sie haben so viel Geld; 3 **such a lot of** (*followed by a plural noun*) so viele; **she's got such a lot of problems** sie hat so viele Probleme; 4 **such as** wie; **in big cities such as Glasgow** in großen Städten wie Glasgow;

✧ IRREGULAR VERB: *See the verb table in the centre of the dictionary*

6 there's no such thing so etwas gibt es nicht.

suck *verb* lutschen; **to suck your thumb** am Daumen lutschen.

sudden *adjective* plötzlich; ★ **all of a sudden** plötzlich.

suddenly *adverb* plötzlich; **he suddenly started to laugh** plötzlich hat er angefangen zu lachen; **suddenly the light went out** plötzlich ging das Licht aus.

suede *noun* Wildleder *das*; **suede jacket** *die* Wildlederjacke.

suffer *verb* leiden✧; **to suffer from asthma** an Asthma leiden.

sufficiently *adverb* genug.

sugar *noun* Zucker *der*; **do you take sugar?** nimmst du Zucker?

suggest *verb* vorschlagen✧ SEP; **he suggested I should speak to you about it** er hat vorgeschlagen, dass ich mit dir darüber sprechen soll.

suggestion *noun* Vorschlag *der* (PL *die* Vorschläge); **to make a suggestion** einen Vorschlag machen.

suicide *noun* Selbstmord *der* (PL *die* Selbstmorde); **to commit suicide** Selbstmord begehen.

suit *noun* 1 (*man's*) Anzug *der* (PL *die* Anzüge); 2 (*woman's*) Kostüm *das* (PL *die* Kostüme).
verb 1 (*be convenient*) passen (+DAT); **does Monday suit you?** passt Ihnen Montag?; 2 (*look good on*) stehen✧ (+DAT); **hats suit her** ihr stehen Hüte gut.

suitable *adjective* 1 geeignet; **to be suitable for something** für etwas geeignet sein; **it's suitable for children** es ist für Kinder geeignet; 2 (*convenient*) passend; **at a suitable time** zur passenden Zeit; **Saturday is the most suitable day for me** Samstag passt mir am besten; 3 (*for a social occasion*) angemessen (*clothes*).

suitcase *noun* Koffer *der* (PL *die* Koffer).

sulk *verb* schmollen.

sum *noun* 1 Summe *die* (PL *die* Summen); **a sum of money** eine Geldsumme; 2 (*calculation*) Rechenaufgabe *die* (PL *die* Rechenaufgaben).
● **to sum up** zusammenfassen SEP.

summarize *verb* zusammenfassen SEP.

summary *noun* Zusammenfassung *die* (PL *die* Zusammenfassungen).

summer *noun* Sommer *der* (PL *die* Sommer); **in summer** im Sommer; **summer clothes** *die* Sommerkleidung; **the summer holidays** die Sommerferien.

summertime *noun* Sommer *der*; **in summertime** im Sommer.

summit *noun* Gipfel *der* (PL *die* Gipfel).

sun *noun* Sonne *die* (PL *die* Sonnen); **in the sun** in der Sonne.

sunbathe *verb* sich sonnen.

△ NEW SPELLING: *See page xii*

sunblock *noun* Sun-Block-Creme
die (PL die Sun-Block-Cremes).

sunburned *adjective* **to get
sunburned** einen Sonnenbrand
bekommen.

Sunday *noun* **1** Sonntag *der* (PL die
Sonntage); **on Sunday** am Sonntag;
I'm going to the cinema on Sunday
ich gehe (am) Sonntag ins Kino; **see
you on Sunday!** bis Sonntag!; **every
Sunday** jeden Sonntag; **last
Sunday** vorigen Sonntag; **next
Sunday** nächsten Sonntag; **2 on
Sundays** sonntags; **the museum is
closed on Sundays** das Museum ist
sonntags geschlossen.

sunflower *noun* Sonnenblume die
(PL die Sonnenblumen); **sunflower
oil** das Sonnenblumenöl.

sunglasses *plural noun*
Sonnenbrille die (PL die
Sonnenbrillen).

sunlight *noun* Sonnenlicht das.

sunny *adjective* sonnig; **a sunny day**
ein sonniger Tag; **sunny intervals**
Aufheiterungen.

sunrise *noun* Sonnenaufgang der
(PL die Sonnenaufgänge).

sunscreen *noun*
Sonnenschutzcreme die (PL die
Sonnenschutzcremes).

sunset *noun* Sonnenuntergang der
(PL die Sonnenuntergänge).

sunshine *noun* Sonnenschein der.

sunstroke *noun* Sonnenstich der
(PL die Sonnenstiche); **to get
sunstroke** einen Sonnenstich
bekommen.

suntan *noun* Bräune die; **to have a
suntan** braun sein; **to get a suntan**
braun werden.

suntan lotion *noun*
Sonnenmilch die.

suntan oil *noun* Sonnenöl das.

super *adjective* klasse (*informal*)
('klasse' *never changes*); **we had a
super time** es war wirklich klasse.

supermarket *noun*
Supermarkt der (PL die
Supermärkte).

supernatural *adjective*
übernatürlich.

superstitious *adjective*
abergläubisch.

supervise *verb* beaufsichtigen.

supper *noun* Abendessen das (PL
die Abendessen); **I had supper at
Sandy's** ich war bei Sandy zum
Abendessen.

supplement *noun* **1** (*to newspaper*)
Beilage die (PL die Beilagen); **2** (*to
fare*) Zuschlag der (PL die
Zuschläge).

supply *noun* **1** (*stock*) Vorrat der (PL
die Vorräte); **2 to be in short supply**
knapp sein.
verb **1** stellen; **the school supplies
the books** die Schule stellt die
Bücher; **2** (*deliver*) liefern; **to
supply somebody with something**
jemandem etwas liefern.

supply teacher *noun*
Aushilfslehrer der (PL die
Aushilfslehrer), Aushilfslehrerin die
(PL die Aushilfslehrerinnen).

support *noun* Unterstützung *die*;
in support zur Unterstützung.
verb **1** (*back up*) unterstützen; **her
teachers have really supported
her** die Lehrer haben sie sehr
unterstützt; **to support somebody
financially** jemanden finanziell
unterstützen; **2 Will supports
Chelsea** Will ist ein Chelsea-Fan;
what team do you support? für
welche Mannschaft bist du?; **3** (*keep,
provide for*) ernähren; **to support a
family** eine Familie ernähren.

supporter *noun* **1** Fan *der* (PL *die*
Fans); **she's a Manchester United
supporter** sie ist ein Manchester-
United-Fan; **2** (*of a party or cause*)
Anhänger *der* (PL *die* Anhänger),
Anhängerin *die* (PL *die*
Anhängerinnen).

suppose *verb* annehmen ◇ SEP;
I suppose she's forgotten ich
nehme an, sie hat es vergessen.

supposed *adjective* **to be
supposed to do something** etwas
tun sollen; **you were supposed to
be here at six** du solltest um sechs
hier sein.

sure *adjective* **1** sicher; **are you
sure?** bist du sicher?; **are you sure
you saw her?** bis du sicher, dass du
sie gesehen hast?; **2 sure!** klar!

surely *adverb* doch sicherlich;
surely she hasn't forgotten sie hat
es doch sicherlich nicht vergessen.

surface *noun* Oberfläche *die* (PL *die*
Oberflächen).

surfboard *noun* Surfbrett *das* (PL
die Surfbretter).

surfing *noun* Surfen *das*.

surgeon *noun* Chirurg *der* (PL *die*
Chirurgen), Chirurgin *die* (PL *die*
Chirurginnen).

surgery *noun* **1 to have surgery**
operiert werden; **2** (*doctor's*)
Praxis *die* (PL *die* Praxen); **the
dentist's surgery** die
Zahnarztpraxis; **3** (*surgery hours*)
Sprechstunde *die*.

surname *noun* Nachname *der* (PL
die Nachnamen).

surprise *noun* Überraschung *die*
(PL *die* Überraschungen); **what a
surprise!** was für eine
Überraschung!

surprised *adjective* überrascht; **I
was surprised to see her** ich war
überrascht, sie zu sehen.

surprising *adjective* überraschend.

surround *verb* umgeben;
surrounded by umgeben von (+DAT);
she was surrounded by friends sie
war von Freunden umgeben.

survey *noun* Umfrage *die* (PL *die*
Umfragen).

survive *verb* überleben.

survivor *noun*
Überlebende *der/die* (PL *die*
Überlebenden).

suspect *noun* Verdächtige *der/die*
(PL *die* Verdächtigen).
adjective verdächtig.
verb verdächtigen.

suspend *verb* **1 to be suspended**
(*from school*) vom Unterricht
ausgeschlossen werden; **2** (*from a*

△ NEW SPELLING: *See page x*ⁱ

team) sperren; **to suspend a player for four weeks** einen Spieler für vier Wochen sperren.

suspense *noun* Spannung *die*.

suspicious *adjective*
1 misstrauisch △; **to be suspicious of somebody** jemandem misstrauen; 2 (*suspicious looking*) verdächtig.

swallow *noun* (*bird*) Schwalbe *die* (PL *die* Schwalben).
verb schlucken.

swan *noun* Schwan *der* (PL *die* Schwäne).

swap *verb* tauschen; **do you want to swap?** willst du tauschen?; **he swapped his bike for a computer** er hat sein Rad gegen einen Computer getauscht; **we swapped seats** wir tauschten die Plätze.

swear *verb* (*use bad language*) fluchen.

swearword *noun* Kraftausdruck *der* (PL *die* Kraftausdrücke).

sweat *noun* Schweiß *der*.
verb schwitzen.

sweater *noun* Pullover *der* (PL *die* Pullover).

Swede *noun* Schwede *der* (PL *die* Schweden), Schwedin *die* (PL *die* Schwedinnen).

Sweden *noun* Schweden *das*; **from Sweden** aus Schweden; **to Sweden** nach Schweden.

Swedish *noun* (*the language*) Schwedisch *das*.

adjective schwedisch; **he's Swedish** er ist Schwede; **she's Swedish** sie ist Schwedin.

sweep *verb* fegen.

sweet *noun* 1 Bonbon *der* (PL *die* Bonbons); 2 (*dessert*) Nachtisch *der* (PL *die* Nachtische).
adjective 1 süß; **I try not to eat sweet things** ich versuche nichts Süßes zu essen; **she looks really sweet in that hat** sie sieht richtig süß mit dem Hut aus; 2 (*kind*) lieb; **she's a really sweet person** sie ist wirklich ein sehr lieber Mensch; **how sweet of him** wie lieb von ihm.

sweetcorn *noun* Mais *der*.

swell *verb* (*part of the body*) anschwellen ✧ SEP (PERF *sein*).

swim *noun* **to go for a swim** schwimmen gehen ✧ (PERF *sein*).
verb schwimmen ✧ (PERF *sein*); **can he swim?** kann er schwimmen?; **to swim across a lake** über einen See schwimmen.

swimmer *noun* Schwimmer *der* (PL *die* Schwimmer), Schwimmerin *die* (PL *die* Schwimmerinnen); **she's a strong swimmer** sie ist eine gute Schwimmerin.

swimming *noun* Schwimmen *das*; **to go swimming** schwimmen gehen.

swimming cap *noun* Badekappe *die* (PL *die* Badekappen).

swimming costume *noun* Badeanzug *der* (PL *die* Badeanzüge).

✧ IRREGULAR VERB: *See the verb table in the centre of the dictionary*

swimming pool *noun*
Schwimmbecken *das* (PL *die* Schwimmbecken).

swimming trunks *noun*
Badehose *die* (PL *die* Badehosen).

swimsuit *noun* Badeanzug *der* (PL *die* Badeanzüge).

swing *noun* Schaukel *die* (PL *die* Schaukeln).

Swiss *noun* (*person*) Schweizer *der* (PL *die* Schweizer), Schweizerin *die* (PL *die* Schweizerinnen); **the Swiss** die Schweizer.
adjective schweizerisch; **she is Swiss** sie ist Schweizerin.

switch *noun* (*for a light, radio, etc*). Schalter *der* (PL *die* Schalter).
verb (*change*) wechseln; **to switch places** die Plätze wechseln.
● **to switch something off** etwas ausschalten SEP.
● **to switch something on** etwas anschalten SEP.

Switzerland *noun* die Schweiz; **from Switzerland** aus der Schweiz; **in Switzerland** in der Schweiz; **to Switzerland** in die Schweiz.

swollen *adjective* geschwollen.

swop *verb* SEE **swap**.

syllabus *noun* Lehrplan *der* (PL *die* Lehrpläne); **to be on the syllabus** auf dem Lehrplan stehen.

symbol *noun* Symbol *das* (PL *die* Symbole).

sympathetic *adjective* verständnisvoll.

sympathize *verb* **to sympathize with somebody** mit jemandem mitfühlen SEP; **I sympathize with you** ich kann mit Ihnen mitfühlen.

sympathy *noun* Mitleid *das*.

symptom *noun* Symptom *das* (PL *die* Symptome).

synthesizer *noun* Synthesizer *der* (PL *die* Synthesizers).

synthetic *adjective* synthetisch.

syringe *noun* Spritze *die* (PL *die* Spritzen).

system *noun* System *das* (PL *die* Systeme).

T t

table *noun* Tisch *der* (PL *die* Tische); **to lay the table** den Tisch decken; **to clear the table** den Tisch abräumen SEP.

tablecloth *noun* Tischdecke *die* (PL *die* Tischdecken).

tablespoon *noun* Esslöffel △ *der* (PL *die* Esslöffel); **a tablespoon of flour** ein Esslöffel Mehl.

tablet *noun* Tablette *die* (PL *die* Tabletten).

table tennis *noun* Tischtennis *das*.

tackle *verb* **1** (*in football or hockey*) angreifen ◇ SEP; **2** angehen ◇ SEP (PERF *sein*) (*a job or a problem*).

tact *noun* Takt *der*.

△ NEW SPELLING: *See page x*

tactful *adjective* taktvoll; **that wasn't very tactful** das war nicht sehr taktvoll.

tail *noun* 1 Schwanz *der* (PL *die* Schwänze); 2 **'heads or tails?'** – **'tails'** 'Kopf oder Zahl?' - 'Zahl'.

take *verb* 1 nehmen ✧; **he took a sweet** er nahm einen Bonbon; **take my hand** nimm meine Hand; **I took the bus** ich habe den Bus genommen; **do you take sugar?** nimmst du Zucker?; 2 (*with time*) dauern; **it takes two hours** es dauert zwei Stunden; 3 (*react to*) aufnehmen ✧ SEP; **he took the news calmly** er hat die Nachricht gelassen aufgenommen; 4 (*take to a place*) bringen ✧; **I'm taking Jake to my parents** ich bringe Jake zu meinen Eltern; **I must take the car to the garage** ich muss das Auto in die Werkstatt bringen; **to take somebody home** jemanden nach Hause bringen; 5 **to take something up(stairs)** etwas heraufbringen ✧ SEP; **could you take the towels up?** könntest du die Handtücher heraufbringen?; 6 **to take something down(stairs)** etwas herunterbringen ✧ SEP; **Cheryl's taken the cups down** Cheryl hat die Tassen heruntergebracht; 7 (*carry with you*) mitnehmen ✧ SEP; **she's taken some of the files home** sie hat einige der Akten mit nach Hause genommen; **I'm taking my Walkman** ich nehme meinen Walkman mit; **I'll take him next time** nächstes Mal nehme ich ihn mit; 8 annehmen ✧ SEP (*a credit card or a*

cheque); **do you take cheques?** nehmen Sie Schecks an?; 9 machen (*an exam, a holiday, or a photo*); **she's taking her driving test tomorrow** sie macht morgen ihre Fahrprüfung; **to take a holiday** Ferien machen; 10 (*need*) brauchen; **it takes a lot of courage** dazu braucht man viel Mut; **it takes me at least two hours to read it** ich brauche mindestens zwei Stunden, um es zu lesen; 11 haben ✧ (*clothes size*); **what size do you take?** welche Größe haben Sie?

- **to take something apart** etwas auseinander nehmen ∆ ✧.
- **to take something back** etwas zurückbringen ✧ SEP.
- **to take off** 1 (*plane*) abfliegen ✧ SEP (PERF *sein*); 2 ausziehen ✧ SEP (*clothes, shoes*); **take your jacket off** zieh die Jacke aus; **to take your clothes off** sich ausziehen; 3 abziehen ✧ SEP (*money*); **he took five pounds off the price** er hat fünf Pfund vom Preis abgezogen.
- **to take out something** (*from a bag or pocket*) etwas herausnehmen ✧ SEP; **Eric took out his wallet** Eric nahm seine Brieftasche heraus.
- **to take somebody out** jemanden einladen ✧ SEP; **to take somebody out for a meal** jemanden zum Essen einladen ✧ SEP.

takeaway *noun* 1 (*meal*) Essen zum Mitnehmen *das* (PL *die* Essen zum Mitnehmen); **an Indian takeaway** ein indisches Essen zum Mitnehmen; 2 (*where you buy it*) Restaurant mit Straßenverkauf *das* (PL *die* Restaurants mit Straßenverkauf).

✧ IRREGULAR VERB: *See the verb table in the centre of the dictionary*

take-off *noun* (*of a plane*) Abflug *der* (PL *die* Abflüge).

talent *noun* Talent *das* (PL *die* Talente); **to have a talent for painting** ein Talent zum Malen haben.

talented *adjective* talentiert; **he's really talented** er ist wirklich talentiert.

talk *noun* 1 (*a chat*) Gespräch *das* (PL *die* Gespräche); **we had a serious talk about it** wir hatten ein ernstes Gespräch darüber; 2 Vortrag *der* (PL *die* Vorträge); **she's giving a talk on Hungary** sie hält einen Vortrag über Ungarn.
verb 1 reden; **to talk to somebody** mit jemandem reden; **we talked about football** wir haben über Fußball geredet; **what's he talking about?** wovon redet er?; **we'll talk about it later** darüber reden wir später; **they're always talking** sie reden immer; 2 **to talk to somebody on the phone** mit jemandem telefonieren.

tall *adjective* 1 groß; **she's very tall** sie ist sehr groß; **I'm 1.7 metres tall** ich bin ein Meter siebzig groß; 2 hoch (*building or tree*).

tampon *noun* Tampon *der* (PL *die* Tampons).

tan *noun* Bräune *die*; **to have a tan** braun sein; **to get a tan** braun werden.

tank *noun* 1 (*for petrol or water*) Tank *der* (PL *die* Tanks); 2 **fish tank** *das* Aquarium; 3 (*army*) Panzer *der* (PL *die* Panzer).

tanned *adjective* braun.

tap *noun* Wasserhahn *der* (PL *die* Wasserhähne); **to turn on the tap** den Wasserhahn aufdrehen SEP; **to turn off the tap** den Wasserhahn zudrehen SEP; **the hot tap** der Warmwasserhahn.
verb klopfen; **to tap on the door** an die Tür klopfen.

tap-dancing *noun* Stepptanzen *das*.

tape *noun* 1 Kassette *die* (PL *die* Kassetten); **my tape of the Stones** meine Kassette von den Stones; **I've got it on tape** ich habe es auf Band; 2 **sticky tape** *der* Klebestreifen.
verb aufnehmen ◇ SEP; **I want to tape the film** ich will den Film aufnehmen.

tape measure *noun* Metermaß *das* (PL *die* Metermaße).

tape recorder *noun* Tonbandgerät *das* (PL *die* Tonbandgeräte).

target *noun* Ziel *das* (PL *die* Ziele).

tart *noun* Kuchen *der* (PL *die* Kuchen); **apple tart** *der* Apfelkuchen.

tartan *adjective* Schotten-; **a tartan skirt** ein Schottenrock.

task *noun* Aufgabe *die* (PL *die* Aufgaben).

taste *noun* 1 Geschmack *der* (PL *die* Geschmäcke); **a taste of onions** ein Zwiebelgeschmack; **she's got no taste** sie hat keinen Geschmack; 2 **in bad taste** geschmacklos.
verb 1 schmecken; **the soup tastes**

△ NEW SPELLING: *See page*

horrible die Suppe schmeckt
furchtbar; **2 to taste of something**
nach etwas ←(DAT) schmecken; **it
tastes of garlic** es schmeckt nach
Knoblauch; **3** (*try a little*)
probieren; **do you want to taste?**
möchtest du mal probieren?

tasty *adjective* schmackhaft.

tattoo *noun* Tätowierung *die* (PL *die*
Tätowierungen); **he's got a tattoo
on his arm** er hat eine Tätowierung
am Arm.

Taurus *noun* Stier *der*; **Josephine's
Taurus** Josephine ist (ein) Stier.

tax *noun* Steuer *die* (PL *die* Steuern)
(*on goods, income*).

taxi *noun* Taxi *das* (PL *die* Taxis);
to go by taxi mit dem Taxi fahren;
to take a taxi ein Taxi nehmen.

taxi driver *noun* Taxifahrer *der* (PL
die Taxifahrer), Taxifahrerin *die* (PL
die Taxifahrerinnen).

taxi rank *noun* Taxistand *der* (PL *die*
Taxistände).

tea *noun* **1** Tee *der* (PL *die* Tees); **a
cup of tea** eine Tasse Tee; **to have
tea** Tee trinken; **2** (*evening meal*)
Abendessen *das* (PL *die*
Abendessen).

teabag *noun* Teebeutel *der* (PL *die*
Teebeutel).

teach *verb* **1** beibringen ✧ SEP; **she's
teaching me to drive** sie bringt mir
das Autofahren bei; **2 to teach
yourself something** sich ←(DAT)
etwas beibringen ✧ SEP; **I taught
myself Italian** ich habe mir
Italienisch beigebracht; **3 that'll**

teach you! das wird dir eine Lehre
sein!; **4** unterrichten; **her mum
teaches maths** ihre Mutter
unterrichtet Mathematik.

teacher *noun* Lehrer *der* (PL *die*
Lehrer), Lehrerin *die* (PL *die*
Lehrerinnen).

teaching *noun* Unterrichten *das*.

team *noun* Mannschaft *die* (PL *die*
Mannschaften); **football team** *die*
Fußballmannschaft.

teapot *noun* Teekanne *die* (PL *die*
Teekannen).

tear[1] *noun* (*a rip*) Riss △ *der* (PL *die*
Risse).
verb **1** zerreißen ✧; **she tore up my
letter** sie hat meinen Brief
zerrissen; **2** reißen ✧ (PERF *sein*); **the
net has torn** das Netz ist gerissen;
be careful, it tears easily sei
vorsichtig, es reißt leicht.

tear[2] *noun* (*when you cry*) Träne *die*
(PL *die* Tränen); **to be in tears** in
Tränen aufgelöst sein; **to burst into
tears** in Tränen ausbrechen.

tease *verb* **1** necken (*a person*);
2 quälen (*an animal*).

teaspoon *noun* Teelöffel *der* (PL *die*
Teelöffel); **a teaspoon of vinegar**
ein Teelöffel Essig.

teatime *noun* (*evening meal*)
Abendessenszeit *die* (PL *die*
Abendessenszeiten); **it's teatime!**
es gibt Abendessen!

tea towel *noun* Geschirrtuch *das*
(PL *die* Geschirrtücher).

technical *adjective* technisch.

IRREGULAR VERB: *See the verb table in the centre of the dictionary*

technical college noun Fachhochschule die (PL die Fachhochschulen).

technician noun Techniker der (PL die Techniker), Technikerin die (PL die Technikerinnen).

technique noun Technik die (PL die Techniken).

techno noun (music) Techno der.

technology noun 1 Technologie die; 2 **information technology** die Informatik.

teddy bear noun Teddybär der (PL die Teddybären).

teenage adjective 1 Teenage-; 2 **they have a teenage son** sie haben einen Sohn im Teenageralter; 3 (films, magazines, etc.) für Teenager; **a teenage magazine** eine Zeitschrift für Teenager.

teenager noun Teenager der (PL die Teenager); **a group of teenagers** eine Gruppe von Teenagern.

teens plural noun **the teens** die Teenagerjahre; **he's in his teens** er ist ein Teenager.

tee-shirt noun T-Shirt das (PL die T-Shirts).

telephone noun Telefon das (PL die Telefone); **on the telephone** am Telefon.
verb anrufen ◇ SEP; **I'll telephone the bank** ich rufe die Bank an.

telephone box noun Telefonzelle die (PL die Telefonzellen).

telephone call noun Telefongespräch das (PL die Telefongespräche).

telephone directory noun Telefonbuch das (PL die Telefonbücher).

telephone number noun Telefonnummer die (PL die Telefonnummern).

televise verb im Fernsehen übertragen ◇; **they're televising the match** sie übertragen das Spiel im Fernsehen.

television noun 1 Fernsehen das; **I saw it on television** ich habe es im Fernsehen gesehen; 2 **to watch television** fernsehen ◇ SEP; **I'm watching television** ich sehe fern.

television programme noun Fernsehsendung die (PL die Fernsehsendungen).

tell verb 1 sagen; **to tell somebody something** jemandem etwas sagen; **if she asks, tell her** sag's ihr, wenn sie fragt; 2 **to tell somebody to do something** jemandem sagen, er/sie soll etwas tun; **he told me to do it myself** er hat mir gesagt, ich soll es selbst machen; **she told me not to wait** sie hat mir gesagt, ich soll nicht warten; 3 (explain) **can you tell me how to do it?** kannst du mir sagen, wie man das macht?; 4 erzählen (a story); **tell me about your holiday** erzähl mir von deinen Ferien; 5 (to see) sehen ◇; **you can tell it's old** man sieht, dass es alt ist; **I can't tell them apart** ich kann sie nicht unterscheiden.

△ NEW SPELLING: See page y

telly *noun* **1** (*set*) Fernseher *der* (PL die Fernseher); **2 to watch telly** fernsehen ⬦ SEP; **I saw her on telly** ich habe sie im Fernsehen gesehen.

temp *noun* Aushilfskraft *die* (PL die Aushilfskräfte).

temper *noun* **to lose your temper** wütend werden.

temperature *noun* **1** Temperatur *die* (PL die Temperaturen); **what is the temperature?** wie viel Grad sind es?; **2 to have a temperature** Fieber haben.

temporary *adjective* vorübergehend.

temptation *noun* Versuchung *die* (PL die Versuchungen).

tempted *adjective* versucht; **I'm really tempted to come** ich bin wirklich versucht zu kommen.

tempting *adjective* verlockend.

ten *number* zehn; **Harry's ten** Harry ist zehn.

tend *verb* **to tend to do something** dazu neigen, etwas zu tun.

tender *adjective* **1** (*loving*) zärtlich; **2** (*painful*) empfindlich.

tennis *noun* Tennis *das*; **to play tennis** Tennis spielen.

tennis ball *noun* Tennisball *der* (PL die Tennisbälle).

tennis court *noun* Tennisplatz *der* (PL die Tennisplätze).

tennis player *noun* Tennisspieler *der* (PL die Tennisspieler), Tennisspielerin *die* (PL die Tennisspielerinnen).

tennis racket *noun* Tennisschläger *der* (PL die Tennisschläger).

tenor *noun* Tenor *der* (PL die Tenöre).

tenpin bowling *noun* Bowling *das*.

tense *noun* Zeit *die*; **the present tense** das Präsens; **in the future tense** im Futur.
adjective gespannt.

tent *noun* Zelt *das* (PL die Zelte).

tenth *number* zehnter/zehnte/ zehntes; **on the tenth floor** im zehnten Stock; **the tenth of April** der zehnte April.

term *noun* (*in school*) Halbjahr *das* (PL die Halbjahre); (*at university*) Semester *das* (PL die Semester).

terminal *noun* **1** (*at an airport*) Terminal *der* (PL die Terminals); **2 bus terminal** *die* Endstation; **3** (*computer terminal*) Terminal *das* (PL die Terminals).

terrace *noun* **1** (*outside a house*) Terrasse *die* (PL die Terrassen); **2** (*row of houses*) Häuserreihe *die* (PL die Häuserreihen); **3 the terraces** (*at a stadium*) die Ränge (*plural*).

terrible *adjective* furchtbar.

terribly *adverb* **1** (*very*) sehr; **not terribly clean** nicht sehr sauber; **2** (*badly*) furchtbar; **I played terribly** ich habe furchtbar gespielt.

terrific *adjective* **1** irre (*informal*); **a terrific amount** eine irre Menge; **2 terrific!** super! (*informal*).

⬦ IRREGULAR VERB: See the verb table in the centre of the dictionary

terrified *adjective* verängstigt, **to be terrified** furchtbare Angst haben.

terrorism *noun* Terrorismus *der*.

terrorist *noun* Terrorist *der* (PL *die* Terroristen), Terroristin *die* (PL *die* Terroristinnen).

test *noun* 1 (*in school*) Klassenarbeit *die* (PL *die* Klassenarbeiten); **we've got a maths test tomorrow** wir schreiben morgen eine Mathearbeit; 2 (*medical check, trial*) Test *der* (PL *die* Tests); **eye test** *der* Sehtest; **blood test** *die* Blutprobe; 3 **driving test** *die* Fahrprüfung; **she's taking her driving test on Friday** sie macht am Freitag ihre Fahrprüfung; **he passed his driving test** er hat seine Fahrprüfung bestanden.
verb (*in school*) prüfen; **can you test me?** kannst du mich abfragen?

test tube *noun* Reagenzglas *das* (PL *die* Reagenzgläser).

text *noun* Text *der* (PL *die* Texte).

textbook *noun* Lehrbuch *das* (PL *die* Lehrbücher).

Thames *noun* **the Thames** die Themse.

than *conjunction* als; **they have more money than we do** sie haben mehr Geld als wir; **more than forty** mehr als vierzig; **more than thirty years** mehr als dreißig Jahre.

thank *verb* 1 **to thank somebody for something** sich bei jemandem für etwas ←(ACC) bedanken; 2 **thank you** danke; **thank you for looking after the children** danke, dass du auf die Kinder aufgepasst hast.

thanks *plural noun* 1 Dank *der*; **thanks a lot!** vielen Dank!; **many thanks** vielen Dank; 2 **no thanks** nein danke; **thanks for your letter** danke für deinen Brief; 3 **thanks to** dank (+DAT); **it was thanks to him that we made it** dank ihm haben wir es geschafft.

thank you *adverb* danke; **thank you very much for the cheque** herzlichen Dank für den Scheck; **no thank you** nein danke; **a thank-you letter** ein Dankbrief.

that *adjective* 1 dieser/diese/dieses; **that boy** dieser Junge; **that woman** diese Frau; **that house** dieses Haus; 2 **that one** der da/die da/das da; **'which cake would you like?' – 'that one, please'** 'welchen Kuchen möchten Sie?' – 'den da, bitte'; **I like all the dresses but I'm going to buy that one** mir gefallen alle Kleider, aber ich kaufe das da.
adverb so; **it's not that easy** es ist nicht so einfach.
pronoun 1 das; **what's that?** was ist das?; **who's that?** wer ist das?; **where's that?** wo ist das?; **is that Mandy?** ist das Mandy?; 2 das; **did you see that?** hast du das gesehen?; **that's my bedroom** das ist mein Schlafzimmer; 3 (*in relative clauses*) der/die/das (*depending on the gender of the noun 'that' refers to*); **the train that's leaving now** der Zug, der jetzt abfährt; **the flower that I picked** die Blume, die ich gepflückt habe; **the car that's red** das Auto, das rot ist.
conjunction dass ∆; **I knew that he was lying** ich wußte, dass er log.

∆ NEW SPELLING: *See page* ›

the *definite article* **1** der/die/das (*the article changes according to the gender of the noun*); (*before a masculine noun*) **the dog** der Hund; (*before a feminine noun*) **the cat** die Katze; (*before a neuter noun*) **the car** das Auto; **2** (*before all plural nouns*) die ; **the windows** die Fenster.

theatre *noun* Theater *das* (PL *die* Theater); **to go to the theatre** ins Theater gehen.

their *adjective* ihr; (*plural*) ihre; **their son** ihr Sohn; **their daughter** ihre Tochter; **their car** ihr Auto; **their presents** ihre Geschenke.

theirs *pronoun* **1** ihrer (*when standing for a masculine noun*); **our garden's smaller than theirs** unser Garten ist kleiner als ihrer; **2** ihre (*when standing for a feminine noun*); **your flat is bigger than theirs** deine Wohnung ist größer als ihre; **3** ihrs (*when standing for a neuter noun*); **our car was cheaper than theirs** unser Auto war billiger als ihrs; **4** ihre (*when standing for a plural noun*); **our children are older than theirs** unsere Kinder sind älter als ihre; **5 the yellow car's theirs** das gelbe Auto gehört ihnen; **it's theirs** das gehört ihnen.

them *pronoun* **1** (*as a direct object in the accusative*) sie; **I know them** ich kenne sie; **I don't know them** ich kenne sie nicht; **2** (*after prepositions* +ACC) sie; **it's for them** das ist für sie; **3** (*as an indirect object or following a verb that takes the dative*) ihnen; **I told them a story** ich habe ihnen eine Geschichte erzählt; **4** (*to them*) ihnen; **I gave them my address** ich habe ihnen meine Adresse gegeben; **5** (*after prepositions* +DAT) ihnen; **I'll go with them** ich gehe mit ihnen mit; **6** (*in comparisons*) **he's older than them** er ist älter als sie.

themselves *pronoun* **1** sich; **they enjoyed themselves** sie haben sich amüsiert; **2** (*for emphasis*) selbst; **the boys can do it themselves** die Jungen können es selbst machen.

then *adverb* **1** (*next*) dann; **I get up and then I make the bed** ich stehe auf und dann mache ich das Bett; **I went to the post office and then the bank** ich bin zur Post und dann auf die Bank gegangen; **2** (*at that time*) damals; **we were living in York then** wir haben damals in York gewohnt; **3** (*in that case*) dann; **then why worry?** warum machst du dir dann Sorgen?; **4 since then** seitdem; **5 from then on** von da an.

theory *noun* **1** Theorie *die* (PL *die* Theorien); **2 in theory** theoretisch.

there *adverb* **1** (*in a fixed location*) da; **up there** da oben; **down there** da unten; **in there** da drin; **stay there** bleib da; **2 over there** da drüben; **she's over there with Mark** sie ist da drüben mit Mark; **3** (*with movement to a place*) dahin; **put it there** leg es dahin; **we're going there on Tuesday** wir fahren am Dienstag dahin; **4** (*further away*) dort; **I've seen photos of Oxford but I've never been there** ich habe Fotos von Oxford gesehen, aber ich war noch nie dort; **5 there is** (*there exists*) da ist, es ist; **there's a cat in the garden** da ist eine Katze im Garten; **there's enough bread** es ist genug Brot da; **no, there's not enough** nein, es ist nicht genug da; **6 there is** es gibt; **there's only one hospital in this town** in dieser Stadt gibt es nur ein Krankenhaus; **7 there are** da sind, es sind; **there were lots of people in town** es waren viele Leute in der Stadt; **8 there are** (*there exist*) es gibt; **there are lots of museums here** es gibt hier viele Museen; **9** (*when drawing attention*) da; **there they are!** da sind sie!; **there's the bus coming!** da kommt der Bus!

therefore *adverb* deshalb.

thermometer *noun* Thermometer *das* (PL *die* Thermometer).

these *adjective* diese; **these glasses** diese Gläser.
pronoun die; **these are cheaper** die sind billiger.

they *pronoun* **1** sie; **'where are the knives?' – 'they're in the drawer'** 'wo sind die Messer?' – 'sie sind in der Schublade'; **2** man; **they say** man sagt.

thick *adjective* dick; **a thick layer of butter** eine dicke Schicht Butter.

thief *noun* Dieb *der* (PL *die* Diebe), Diebin *die* (PL *die* Diebinnen).

thin *adjective* dünn.

thing *noun* **1** (*an object*) Ding *das* (PL *die* Dinge); **they have lots of nice things** sie haben viele schöne Dinge;

she told me some strange things sie hat mir ein paar seltsame Dinge erzählt; **that thing next to the hammer** das Ding da neben dem Hammer; **2 things** (*belongings*) Sachen (*plural*); **you can leave your things in my room** du kannst deine Sachen in meinem Zimmer lassen; **3 the best thing to do is …** am besten wäre es …; **4** (*subject, affair*) Sache *die* (PL *die* Sachen); **the thing is, I've lost her address** die Sache ist die, ich habe ihre Adresse verloren; **5 how are things?** wie geht's?

think *verb* **1** (*believe*) glauben; **do you think they'll come?** glaubst du, sie kommen?; **no, I don't think so** nein, ich glaube nicht; **I think so** ich glaube schon; **I think he's already paid** ich glaube, er hat schon gezahlt; **2** denken ◇; **I'm thinking about you** ich denke an dich; **what are you thinking about?** woran denkst du?; **3 what do you think of that?** was halten Sie davon?; **I don't think much of her proposal** ich halte nicht viel von ihrem Vorschlag; **4 what do you think of my new jacket?** wie findest du meine neue Jacke?; **5** (*remember*) **to think to do something** daran denken, etwas zu tun; **he didn't think of locking the door** er hat nicht daran gedacht, die Tür abzuschließen; **6** (*to think carefully*) nachdenken ◇ SEP; **he thought for a moment** er hat einen Moment lang nachgedacht; **think about it!** denk darüber nach!; **7 I've thought it over carefully** ich habe es mir genau überlegt;

△ NEW SPELLING: *See page* ↗

8 (*imagine*) sich ←(DAT) vorstellen
SEP; **just think, we'll soon be in
Spain!** stell dir nur vor, bald sind wir
in Spanien!; **I never thought it
would be like this** ich habe mir nie
vorgestellt, dass es so sein würde.

third *noun* Drittel *das* (PL *die*
Drittel); **a third of the population**
ein Drittel der Bevölkerung.
adjective dritter/dritte/drittes; **on
the third floor** im dritten Stock; **on
the third of March** am dritten März.

thirdly *adverb* drittens.

Third World *noun* Dritte Welt Δ *die*.

thirst *noun* Durst *der*.

thirsty *adjective* durstig; **to be
thirsty** Durst haben; **I'm thirsty** ich
habe Durst; **we were all thirsty** wir
hatten alle Durst.

thirteen *number* dreizehn;
Ahmed's thirteen Ahmed ist
dreizehn.

thirty *number* dreißig.

this *adjective* 1 dieser/diese/dieses;
this boy dieser Junge; **this flower**
diese Blume; **this car** dieses Auto;
at the end of this week Ende dieser
Woche; 2 **this morning** heute
Morgen; **this evening** heute Abend;
this afternoon heute Nachmittag;
3 **this one** der/die/das; (*with more
emphasis*) dieser/diese/dieses; **if
you need a pen you can have this
one** wenn du einen Kugelschreiber
brauchst, kannst du den haben; **I'll
take this one** ich nehme diesen.
pronoun 1 das; **can you hold this?**
kannst du das festhalten?; **what's**

this? was ist das?; 2 **this is my sister
Carla** (*in introductions*) das ist
meine Schwester Carla; 3 **this is
Tracy speaking** (*on the phone*) hier
spricht Tracy.

thistle *noun* Distel *die* (PL *die*
Disteln).

those *adjective* diese; **those books**
diese Bücher.
pronoun die da; **if you need more
knives you can take those** wenn
du mehr Messer brauchst, kannst du
die da nehmen.

though *conjunction* obwohl;
though it's cold obwohl es kalt ist.
adverb aber; **it was a good idea,
though** es war aber eine gute Idee.

thought *noun* Gedanke *der* (PL *die*
Gedanken).

thousand *number* 1 tausend; **a
thousand** eintausend; **three
thousand** dreitausend;
2 **thousands of** Tausende von;
**there were thousands of tourists in
Venice** Tausende von Touristen
waren in Venedig.

thread *noun* Faden *der* (PL *die*
Fäden).
verb einfädeln (*a needle*).

threat *noun* Drohung *die* (PL *die*
Drohungen); **is that a threat?** soll
das eine Drohung sein?

threaten *verb* drohen (+DAT); **he
threatened her** er hat ihr gedroht;
to threaten to do something damit
drohen, etwas zu tun.

three *number* drei; **Oskar's three**
Oskar ist drei.

three-quarters *noun*
Dreiviertel *das*.
adverb **three-quarters full** drei
viertel △ voll.

thrilled *adjective* **to be thrilled** sich
wahnsinnig freuen.

thriller *noun* Thriller *der* (PL *die*
Thriller).

thrilling *adjective* spannend.

throat *noun* Hals *der* (PL *die* Hälse);
to have a sore throat
Halsschmerzen haben.

through *preposition* 1 (*across, via*)
durch (+ACC); **through the forest**
durch den Wald; **the train goes
through Leeds** der Zug fährt durch
Leeds; **through the window** durch
das Fenster; 2 **to let somebody
through** jemanden durchlassen ◇
SEP; **the police let us through** die
Polizei ließ uns durch; 3 **I know
them through my cousin** ich kenne
sie über meinen Vetter.

throw *verb* 1 werfen ◇; **I threw the
letter in the bin** ich habe den Brief
in den Mülleimer geworfen; 2 **to
throw something to somebody**
jemandem etwas zuwerfen ◇ SEP;
throw me the ball wirf mir den Ball
zu; **to throw something at
somebody** etwas nach jemandem
werfen.
● **to throw something away** etwas
wegwerfen ◇ SEP; **I'm throwing
away the old newspapers** ich werfe
die alten Zeitungen weg.
● **to throw somebody out** jemanden
rauswerfen ◇ SEP.

● **to throw something out** etwas
wegwerfen ◇ SEP (*rubbish*).

thumb *noun* Daumen *der* (PL *die*
Daumen).

thunder *noun* Donner *der*; **peal of
thunder** *der* Donnerschlag.

thunderstorm *noun* Gewitter *das*
(PL *die* Gewitter).

Thursday *noun* 1 Donnerstag *der*
(PL *die* Donnerstage); **on Thursday**
(am) Donnerstag; **I'm leaving on
Thursday** ich fahre am Donnerstag
ab; **see you on Thursday** bis
Donnerstag; **every Thursday** jeden
Donnerstag; **last Thursday** vorigen
Donnerstag; **next Thursday**
nächsten Donnerstag; 2 **on
Thursdays** donnerstags; **the
museum is closed on Thursdays**
das Museum ist donnerstags
geschlossen.

thyme *noun* Thymian *der*.

tick *verb* 1 (*clock, watch*) ticken;
2 (*on paper*) abhaken SEP.

ticket *noun* 1 (*for an exhibition,
theatre, or cinema*) Karte *die* (PL *die*
Karten); **two tickets for the concert**
zwei Karten für das Konzert; 2 (*for
the underground, a bus, or a train*)
Fahrkarte *die* (PL *die* Fahrkarten); **a
plane ticket** ein Flugschein, ein
Ticket; 3 (*for left luggage, parking*)
Schein *der* (PL *die* Scheine); 4 (*for a
lottery or raffle*) Los *das* (PL *die*
Lose); 5 **parking ticket** *der*
Strafzettel.

ticket office *noun* (*at a station*)
Fahrkartenschalter *der* (PL *die*
Fahrkartenschalter).

△ NEW SPELLING: *See page*

tickle *verb* kitzeln.

tidy *adjective* ordentlich.
verb aufräumen SEP; **I'll tidy (up) the kitchen** ich räume die Küche auf.

tie *noun* **1** (*necktie*) Krawatte *die* (PL die Krawatten); **2** (*in a match*) Unentschieden *das*.
verb **1** binden ◇; **to tie your shoelaces** sich ←(DAT) die Schnürsenkel binden; **2 to tie a knot in something** einen Knoten in etwas ←(ACC) machen; **3** (*in a match*) **we tied two all** wir haben zwei zu zwei gespielt.

tiger *noun* Tiger *der* (PL die Tiger).

tight *adjective* (*close-fitting*) eng; **the skirt's a bit tight** der Rock ist etwas eng; **these shoes are too tight** diese Schuhe sind zu eng; **she was wearing tight jeans** sie hatte enge Jeans an.

tightly *adverb* fest.

tights *plural noun* Strumpfhose *die* (PL die Strumpfhosen); **a pair of purple tights** eine lila Strumpfhose.

tile *noun* **1** (*on a floor*) Fliese *die* (PL die Fliesen); **2** (*on a wall*) Kachel *die* (PL die Kacheln); **3** (*on a roof*) Ziegel *der* (PL die Ziegel).

till[1] *preposition, conjunction* **1** bis; **they're staying till Sunday** sie bleiben bis Sonntag; **till then** bis dann; **till now** bis jetzt; **2** (*when 'till' is followed by a noun it is usually translated as 'bis zu' +*DAT) **till the evening** bis zum Abend; **3 not till** erst; **she won't be back till ten** sie kommt erst um zehn zurück; **we**

won't know till Monday wir werden erst am Montag Bescheid wissen.

till[2] *noun* Kasse *die* (PL die Kassen); **please pay at the till** bitte zahlen Sie an der Kasse.

time *noun* **1** (*on the clock*) Zeit *die*; **it's time for breakfast** es ist Zeit zum Frühstücken; **2 what time is it?** wie viel △ Uhr ist es?; **at what time does it start?** um wie viel Uhr fängt es an?; **ten o'clock German time** zehn Uhr, deutsche Zeit; **3 on time** pünktlich; **4** (*an amount of time*) Zeit *die*; **we've got lots of time** wir haben viel Zeit; **I haven't got time now** ich habe jetzt keine Zeit; **there's no time left to do it** dafür bleibt keine Zeit mehr; **from time to time** von Zeit zu Zeit; **for a long time** lange; **5** (*moment*) Moment *der* (PL die Momente); **this isn't a good time to discuss it** das ist kein guter Moment, um sich darüber zu unterhalten; **at the right time** im richtigen Moment; **for the time being** im Moment; **any time now** jeden Moment; **6 at times** manchmal; **7** (*in a series*) Mal *das* (PL die Male); **eight times** achtmal; **for the first time** zum ersten Mal; **the first time I saw you** das erste Mal, als ich dich sah; **three times a year** dreimal jährlich; **8 three times two is six** drei mal zwei ist sechs; **9 to have a good time** sich amüsieren; **we had a really good time** wir haben uns richtig gut amüsiert; **have a good time!** viel Vergnügen!

timetable *noun* **1** (*in school*) Stundenplan *der* (PL die

Stundenpläne), **2** (*for trains or buses*) Fahrplan *der* (PL *die* Fahrpläne); **bus timetable** *der* Busfahrplan.

tin *noun* Dose *die* (PL *die* Dosen); **a tin of tomatoes** eine Dose Tomaten.

tinned *adjective* in Dosen; **tinned peas** Erbsen in Dosen.

tin opener *noun* Dosenöffner *der* (PL *die* Dosenöffner).

tiny *adjective* winzig.

tip *noun* **1** (*end*) Spitze *die* (PL *die* Spitzen); **2** (*money*) Trinkgeld *das*; **3** (*useful hint*) Tipp △ *der* (PL *die* Tipps) (*informal*).
verb (*give money*) ein Trinkgeld geben ✧ (+DAT); **we tipped the waiter** wir haben dem Kellner ein Trinkgeld gegeben.

tired *adjective* **1** müde; **I'm tired** ich bin müde; **you look tired** du siehst müde aus; **2 to be tired of something** etwas satt haben; **I'm tired of London** ich habe London satt; **I'm tired of watching TV every evening** ich habe es satt, jeden Abend fernzusehen.

tiring *adjective* ermüdend.

tissue *noun* (*a paper hanky*) Papiertaschentuch *das* (PL *die* Papiertaschentücher).

tissue paper *noun* Seidenpapier *das*.

title *noun* Titel *der* (PL *die* Titel).

to *preposition* **1** (*to a country or town*) nach; **to go to London** nach London fahren; **the motorway to** italy die Autobahn nach Italien; **they're going to Switzerland** sie fahren in die Schweiz; **2** (*to the cinema, theatre, school, office*) in (+ACC); **I'm going to school** ich gehe in die Schule; **she's gone to the office** sie ist ins Büro gegangen; **we want to go to town** wir wollen in die Stadt gehen; **3** (*to a wedding, party, university, the toilet*) auf (+ACC); **she's gone to the toilet** sie ist auf die Toilette gegangen; **4** (*addressed or attached to*) an (+ACC); **a letter to my parents** ein Brief an meine Eltern; **5 give the book to her** gib ihr das Buch; **he said to me that …** er hat mir gesagt, dass …; **6** (*to somebody's house, a particular place, or person*) zu (+DAT); **I went round to Paul's house** ich bin zu Paul nach Hause gegangen; **we're going to the Browns' for supper** wir gehen zu Browns zum Abendessen; **I'm going to the dentist tomorrow** morgen gehe ich zum Zahnarzt; **7** (*talking about the time*) **it's ten to nine** es ist zehn vor neun; **from eight to ten** von acht bis zehn; **from Monday to Friday** von Montag bis Freitag; **8** (*in order to*) um … zu (+ *infinitive*); **he gave me some money to buy a sandwich** er hat mir Geld gegeben, um ein Sandwich zu kaufen; **9** (*in verbal phrases with the infinitive*) zu; **I have nothing to do** ich habe nichts zu tun; **have you got something to eat?** hast du etwas zu essen?

toast *noun* **1** Toast *der* (PL *die* Toasts); **two slices of toast** zwei Scheiben Toast; **2** (*to your health*)

△ NEW SPELLING: *See page*

Toast der (PL die Toasts); **to drink a toast to somebody** auf jemanden trinken.

toaster noun Toaster der (PL die Toaster).

tobacco noun Tabak der.

tobacconist's noun Tabakladen der (PL die Tabakläden).

today adverb heute; **today's her birthday** sie hat heute Geburtstag.

toe noun Zeh der (PL die Zehen).

toffee noun Karamell Δ der.

together adverb 1 zusammen; **we did it together** wir haben es zusammen gemacht; 2 (at the same time) gleichzeitig; **they all left together** sie sind alle gleichzeitig weggegangen.

toilet noun Toilette die (PL die Toiletten); **she's gone to the toilet** sie ist auf die Toilette gegangen.

toilet paper noun Toilettenpapier das.

toilet roll noun Rolle Toilettenpapier die (PL die Rollen Toilettenpapier).

token noun 1 (for a machine or game) Marke die (PL die Marken); 2 (voucher) Gutschein der (PL die Gutscheine); **gift token** der Geschenkgutschein.

toll noun Gebühr die (PL die Gebühren).

tomato noun Tomate die (PL die Tomaten); **tomato salad** der Tomatensalat; **tomato sauce** die Tomatensoße.

tomorrow adverb 1 morgen; **I'll do it tomorrow** ich mache es morgen; **tomorrow afternoon** morgen Nachmittag; **tomorrow morning** morgen früh; **tomorrow night** morgen Abend; 2 **the day after tomorrow** übermorgen.

tone noun (on an answerphone, of a voice, or letter) Ton der (PL die Töne).

tongue noun Zunge die (PL die Zungen); **to stick your tongue out at somebody** jemandem die Zunge herausstrecken; ★ **it's on the tip of my tongue** es liegt mir auf der Zunge.

tonic noun Tonic das (PL die Tonics); **a gin and tonic** ein Gin Tonic.

tonight adverb 1 (this evening) heute Abend Δ; **I'm going out with my friends tonight** ich gehe heute Abend mit meinen Freunden weg; 2 (after bedtime) heute Nacht Δ.

tonsillitis noun Mandelentzündung die; **Ahlem's got tonsillitis** Ahlem hat eine Mandelentzündung.

too adverb 1 zu; **it's too expensive** es ist zu teuer; **too often** zu oft; 2 **too much** zu viel; **I've spent too much** ich habe zu viel ausgegeben; **too many** zu viele; 3 (as well) auch; **Karen's coming too** Karen kommt auch; **me too!** ich auch!

tool noun Werkzeug das (PL die Werkzeuge).

tool kit noun Werkzeug das.

tooth noun Zahn der (PL die Zähne);

to brush your teeth sich (DM) die
Zähne putzen.

toothache noun Zahnschmerzen
(plural).

toothbrush noun Zahnbürste die
(PL die Zahnbürsten).

toothpaste noun Zahnpasta die
(PL die Zahnpasten).

top noun 1 (highest part) Spitze die
(PL die Spitzen) (of a tree); 2 **at the
top of** oben auf (+DAT); **at the top of
the ladder** oben auf der Leiter; **it's
on top of the chest of drawers** es
liegt oben auf der Kommode; 3 **at
the top** oben; **there are four rooms
at the top** oben sind vier Zimmer;
from top to bottom von oben bis
unten; 4 (of a container, jar, or box)
Deckel der (PL die Deckel); 5 (of a
mountain) Gipfel der (PL die
Gipfel); 6 (a lid) Kappe die (PL die
Kappen) (of a pen); Verschluss △ der
(PL die Verschlüsse) (of a bottle);
7 (of a garment) Oberteil das (PL die
Oberteile); 8 (in sport) **the top of
the table** die Tabellenspitze; ★ **and
on top of all that** obendrein; ★ **it
was a bit over the top** es war leicht
übertrieben.
adjective oberster/oberste/oberstes
(step or floor); **on the top floor** im
obersten Stockwerk.

topic noun Thema das (PL die
Themen).

torch noun Taschenlampe die (PL
die Taschenlampen).

torn adjective zerrissen.

tortoise noun Schildkröte die (PL
die Schildkröten).

torture noun 1 Folter die (PL die
Foltern); 2 **the exam was torture**
die Prüfung war die Hölle
(informal).
verb quälen.

Tory noun Konservative der/die (PL
die Konservativen).

total noun 1 (number)
Gesamtzahl die (PL die
Gesamtzahlen); 2 (result of
addition) Summe die (PL die
Summen).
adjective gesamt.

totally adverb völlig.

touch noun 1 (contact) **to get in
touch with somebody** sich mit
jemandem in Verbindung setzen; **to
stay in touch with somebody** mit
jemandem in Verbindung bleiben;
2 **we've lost touch** wir haben
keinen Kontakt mehr miteinander;
I've lost touch with Peter ich habe
keinen Kontakt mehr mit Peter; 3 (a
little bit) **a touch of salt** eine Spur
Salz; **it was a touch embarrassing**
es war ein bisschen peinlich.
verb 1 berühren; 2 (get hold of)
anfassen SEP; **don't touch that** fass
das nicht an.

touched adjective gerührt.

touching adjective rührend.

tough adjective 1 hart; **she's had a
tough time** sie hat eine harte Zeit
hinter sich; **a tough guy** ein harter
Kerl; 2 zäh; **the meat's tough** das
Fleisch ist zäh; 3 fest (material,
shoes, etc).; 4 **tough luck!** Pech!;
tough, you're too late so'n Pech, du
bist zu spät dran.

△ NEW SPELLING: See page

tour *noun* **1** Besichtigung *die* (PL *die* Besichtigungen); **a tour of the city** eine Stadtbesichtigung; **we did a tour of the castle** wir haben das Schloss besichtigt; **2 guided tour** *die* Führung; **3 package tour** *die* Pauschalreise; **4** (*by a band or theatre group*) Tournee *die* (PL *die* Tournees); **to go on tour** auf Tournee gehen. *verb* (*performer*) auf Tournee sein ✧ (PERF *sein*); **they're touring America** sie sind auf Tournee in Amerika.

tour guide *noun* Reiseleiter *der* (PL *die* Reiseleiter), Reiseleiterin *die* (PL *die* Reiseleiterinnen).

tourism *noun* Tourismus *der*.

tourist *noun* Tourist *der* (PL *die* Touristen), Touristin *die* (PL *die* Touristinnen).

tourist information office *noun* Fremdenverkehrsbüro *das* (PL *die* Fremdenverkehrsbüros).

tournament *noun* Turnier *das* (PL *die* Turniere); **tennis tournament** *das* Tennisturnier.

tow *verb* **to be towed away** abgeschleppt werden ✧ (PERF *sein*).

towards *preposition* zu (+DAT); **she went off towards the lake** sie ist zum See gegangen; **to come towards somebody** auf jemanden zukommen ✧ SEP (PERF *sein*).

towel *noun* Handtuch *das* (PL *die* Handtücher).

tower *noun* Turm *der* (PL *die* Türme).

tower block *noun* Hochhaus *das* (PL *die* Hochhäuser).

town *noun* Stadt *die* (PL *die* Städte); **to go into town** in die Stadt gehen.

town centre *noun* Stadtmitte *die* (PL *die* Stadtmitten).

town hall *noun* Rathaus *das* (PL *die* Rathäuser).

toy *noun* Spielzeug *das*.

toyshop *noun* Spielzeuggeschäft *das* (PL *die* Spielzeuggeschäfte).

trace *noun* Spur *die* (PL *die* Spuren); **there was no trace of the thieves** es fehlte jede Spur von den Dieben. *verb* **1** (*find*) finden ✧; **2** (*follow*) verfolgen; **3** (*copy*) durchpausen SEP.

tracing paper *noun* Pauspapier *das*.

track *noun* **1** (*for sport*) Bahn *die* (PL *die* Bahnen); **cycling track** *die* Radrennbahn; **racing track** (*for cars*) *die* Rennstrecke; **2** (*a path*) Weg *der* (PL *die* Wege); **3** (*song*) Stück *das* (PL *die* Stücke); **this is my favourite track** das ist mein Lieblingsstück.

track suit *noun* Trainingsanzug *der* (PL *die* Trainingsanzüge).

tractor *noun* Traktor *der* (PL *die* Traktoren).

trade *noun* **1** (*a profession*) Gewerbe *das*; **2** (*skill, craft*) Handwerk *das*; **to learn a trade** ein Handwerk erlernen.

trade union *noun*
Gewerkschaft *die* (PL *die*
Gewerkschaften).

tradition *noun* Tradition *die* (PL *die*
Traditionen).

traditional *adjective* traditionell.

traffic *noun* Verkehr *der*.

traffic jam *noun* Stau *der* (PL *die*
Staus).

traffic lights *plural noun*
Ampel *die* (PL *die* Ampeln).

traffic warden *noun*
Hilfspolizist *der* (PL *die*
Hilfspolizisten), Politesse *die* (PL *die*
Politessen).

tragedy *noun* Tragödie *die* (PL *die*
Tragödien).

tragic *adjective* tragisch.

trailer *noun* Anhänger *der* (PL *die*
Anhänger).

train *noun* Zug *der* (PL *die* Züge);
he's coming by train er kommt mit
dem Zug; **I met her on the train** ich
habe sie im Zug getroffen; **the train
for York** der Zug nach York.
verb 1 (*for a career*) ausbilden SEP;
2 she's training to be a nurse sie
lässt sich als Krankenschwester
ausbilden; **3** (*in sport*) trainieren;
the team trains on Wednesdays die
Mannschaft trainiert mittwochs.

trainer *noun* 1 (*of an athlete or
horse*) Trainer *der* (PL *die* Trainer),
Trainerin *die* (PL *die* Trainerinnen);
2 trainers Trainingsschuhe
(*plural*).

training *noun* 1 (*for a career*)
Ausbildung *die*; **2** (*for sport*)
Training *das*.

train ticket *noun* Fahrkarte *die* (PL
die Fahrkarten).

train timetable *noun*
Bahnfahrplan *der* (PL *die*
Bahnfahrpläne).

tram *noun* Straßenbahn *die* (PL *die*
Straßenbahnen).

tramp *noun* Landstreicher *der* (PL
die Landstreicher), Landstreicherin
die (PL *die* Landstreicherinnen).

transfer *noun* Abziehbild *das* (PL
die Abziehbilder).

transform *verb* verwandeln.

transistor *noun* Transistor *der* (PL
die Transistoren).

translate *verb* übersetzen; **to
translate something into German**
etwas ins Deutsche übersetzen.

translation *noun* Übersetzung *die*
(PL *die* Übersetzungen).

translator *noun* Übersetzer *der* (PL
die Übersetzer), Übersetzerin *die* (PL
die Übersetzerinnen).

transparent *adjective*
durchsichtig.

transport *noun* Transport *der* (PL
die Transporte); **the transport of
goods** der Warentransport; **public
transport** öffentliche
Verkehrsmittel (*plural*).

trap *noun* Falle *die* (PL *die* Fallen).

travel *noun* Reisen *das*; **foreign
travel** Auslandsreisen (*plural*).
verb reisen (PERF *sein*).

△ NEW SPELLING: *See page*

travel agency noun
Reisebüro das (PL die Reisebüros).

travel agent's noun
Reisebüro das (PL die Reisebüros).

traveller noun 1 Reisende der/die
(PL die Reisenden); 2 (gypsy)
Zigeuner der (PL die Zigeuner),
Zigeunerin die (PL die
Zigeunerinnen).

traveller's cheque noun
Reisescheck der (PL die
Reiseschecks).

tray noun Tablett das (PL die
Tabletts).

tread verb to tread on something
auf etwas ←(ACC) treten ✧ (PERF sein);
she trod on my foot sie ist mir auf
den Fuß getreten.

treasure noun Schatz der (PL die
Schätze).

treat noun 1 I took them to the
circus as a treat ich habe ihnen
eine besondere Freude gemacht und
sie in den Zirkus eingeladen;
2 (food) Leckerbissen der (PL die
Leckerbissen).
verb 1 behandeln; he treats his dog
well er behandelt seinen Hund gut;
the doctor who treated you der
Arzt, der dich behandelt hat; 2 to
treat somebody to something
jemandem etwas spendieren; I'll
treat you to an ice cream ich
spendiere euch ein Eis.

treatment noun Behandlung die
(PL die Behandlungen).

tree noun Baum der (PL die Bäume).

tremble verb zittern.

trend noun 1 (a fashion) Trend der
(PL die Trends); 2 (a tendency)
Tendenz die (PL die Tendenzen).

trendy adjective modern.

trial noun (in court) Prozess △ der
(PL die Prozesse).

triangle noun Dreieck das (PL die
Dreiecke).

trick noun 1 (a joke) Streich der (PL
die Streiche); to play a trick on
somebody jemandem einen Streich
spielen; 2 (a knack or by a conjuror)
Trick der (PL die Tricks); there must
be a trick to it da muss ein Trick
dabei sein.
verb hereinlegen SEP; he tricked
me! er hat mich hereingelegt!

tricky adjective verzwickt; it's a
tricky situation das ist eine
verzwickte Situation.

trim verb schneiden ✧ (hair).

trip noun 1 Reise die (PL die Reisen);
a trip to Florida eine Reise nach
Florida; he's going on a business
trip er macht eine Geschäftsreise;
2 (a day out) Ausflug der (PL die
Ausflüge); a day trip to France ein
Tagesausflug nach Frankreich.
verb (to stumble) stolpern (PERF
sein); Nicky tripped over a stone
Nicky ist über einen Stein gestolpert.

trolley noun 1 (for shopping)
Einkaufswagen der (PL die
Einkaufswagen); 2 (for luggage)
Kofferkuli der (PL die Kofferkulis).

trombone noun Posaune die (PL die
Posaunen).

IRREGULAR VERB: See the verb table in the centre of the dictionary

roops *plural noun* Truppen (*plural*).

rophy *noun* Trophäe die (PL die Trophäen); (*in competitions*) Pokal der (PL die Pokale).

rot *verb* traben (PERF *sein*).

rouble *noun* 1 (*general difficulties*) Ärger der; **to make trouble** Ärger machen; **to get into trouble** Ärger bekommen; **we had trouble with the travel agency** wir hatten Ärger mit dem Reisebüro; 2 (*problem*) Problem das (PL die Probleme); **the trouble is, I've lost his phone number** das Problem ist, dass ich seine Telefonnummer verloren habe; **Steph's in trouble** Steph hat Probleme; **what's the trouble?** was ist los?; **it's no trouble!** das ist kein Problem; 3 (*difficulty, effort*) Mühe die; **to have trouble doing something** Mühe haben, etwas zu tun; **I had trouble finding a seat** ich hatte Mühe, einen Platz zu finden; **it's not worth the trouble** das ist nicht der Mühe wert.

trousers *plural noun* Hose die (PL die Hosen); **my old trousers** meine alte Hose; **a new pair of trousers** eine neue Hose.

trout *noun* Forelle die (PL die Forellen).

truck *noun* Lastwagen der (PL die Lastwagen).

true *adjective* 1 wahr; **a true story** eine wahre Geschichte; 2 **is that true?** stimmt das?; **it's true she's absent-minded** das stimmt, sie ist sehr vergesslich.

trump *noun* Trumpf der (PL die Trümpfe); **hearts are trumps** Herz ist Trumpf.

trumpet *noun* Trompete die (PL die Trompeten).

trunk *noun* 1 (*of a tree*) Stamm der (PL die Stämme); 2 (*of an elephant*) Rüssel der (PL die Rüssel).

trust *noun* Vertrauen das. *verb* 1 (*believe*) **to trust somebody** jemandem vertrauen; 2 (*rely on*) **you can trust him** man kann sich auf ihn verlassen.

truth *noun* Wahrheit die.

try *noun* Versuch der (PL die Versuche); **it's my first try** es ist mein erster Versuch; **to have a try** es versuchen; **give it a try!** versuch's doch mal! *verb* 1 versuchen; **to try to do something** versuchen, etwas zu tun; **I'm trying to open the door** ich versuche, die Tür aufzumachen; 2 (*taste*) probieren.
● **to try something on** etwas anprobieren SEP (*a garment*).

T-shirt *noun* T-Shirt das (PL die T-Shirts).

tube *noun* 1 Tube die (PL die Tuben); 2 (*the Underground*) **the Tube** die U-Bahn.

Tuesday *noun* 1 Dienstag der (PL die Dienstage); **on Tuesday** (am) Dienstag; **I'm going to the cinema on Tuesday** ich gehe Dienstag ins Kino; **see you on Tuesday!** bis Dienstag!; **every Tuesday** jeden Dienstag; **last Tuesday** vorigen Dienstag; **next Tuesday** nächsten

△ NEW SPELLING: *See page* ⟩

Dienstag; **2 on Tuesdays** dienstags; **the museum is closed on Tuesdays** das Museum ist dienstags geschlossen.

tuition *noun* **1** Unterricht *der*; **piano tuition** *der* Klavierunterricht; **2 extra tuition** Nachhilfestunden (*plural*).

tulip *noun* Tulpe *die* (PL *die* Tulpen).

tumble-drier *noun* Wäschetrockner *der* (PL *die* Wäschetrockner).

tuna *noun* Thunfisch *der*.

tune *noun* Melodie *die* (PL *die* Melodien).

tunnel *noun* Tunnel *der* (PL *die* Tunnel); **the Channel Tunnel** der Eurotunnel.

turkey *noun* Pute *die* (PL *die* Puten).

Turkey *noun* die Türkei; **from Turkey** aus der Türkei; **in Turkey** in der Türkei; **to Turkey** in die Türkei.

Turkish *noun* (*language*) Türkisch *das*. *adjective* türkisch; **he is Turkish** er ist Türke; **she is Turkish** sie ist Türkin.

turn *noun* **1** (*in a game*) **it's your turn** du bist an der Reihe; **whose turn is it?** wer ist an der Reihe?; **it's Jane's turn** Jane ist an der Reihe; **2 to take turns** sich abwechseln; **to take it in turns to do something** abwechselnd etwas tun; **3** (*in a road*) Kurve *die* (PL *die* Kurven); **to take a right/left turn** nach rechts/links abbiegen. *verb* **1** drehen; **turn the key to the**

right dreh den Schlüssel nach rechts; **turn your chair round** dreh deinen Stuhl herum; **2** (*person, car*) abbiegen ◇ SEP (PERF *sein*); **turn left at the next set of lights** biegen Sie an der nächsten Ampel links ab; **3** (*become*) werden ◇ (PERF *sein*); **she turned red** sie ist rot geworden.

- **to turn back** umkehren SEP (PERF *sein*).
- **to turn off 1** (*from a road*) abbiegen ◇ SEP (PERF *sein*); **2** (*switch off*) ausmachen SEP (*a light, an oven, a TV, or radio*); zudrehen SEP (*a tap*); abstellen SEP (*gas, electricity, or water*); ausschalten SEP (*an engine*).
- **to turn on** anmachen SEP (*a TV, radio or light*); aufdrehen SEP (*a tap*); anschalten SEP (*an oven*); anlassen ◇ SEP (*an engine*).
- **to turn out 1 to turn out well** gut ausgehen ◇ SEP (PERF *sein*); **the discussions turned out badly** die Gespräche sind schlecht ausgegangen; **it all turned out all right in the end** am Ende ging alles gut aus; **2 it turned out that I was right** es stellte sich heraus, dass ich Recht hatte.
- **to turn up 1** (*to arrive*) aufkreuzen SEP (PERF *sein*); **they turned up an hour later** sie sind eine Stunde später aufgekreuzt; **2** (*to make louder*) lauter machen.

turquoise *adjective* türkis.

turtle *noun* Schildkröte *die* (PL *die* Schildkröten).

TV *noun* Fernsehen *das*; **I saw her on TV** ich habe sie im Fernsehen gesehen.

weezers *noun* Pinzette *die* (PL *die* Pinzetten).

welfth *number* zwölfter/zwölfte/ zwölftes; **on the twelfth floor** im zwölften Stock; **the twelfth of May** der zwölfte Mai.

:welve *number* 1 zwölf; **Tara's twelve** Tara ist zwölf; 2 **at twelve o'clock** um zwölf Uhr.

:wenty *number* zwanzig; **Marie's twenty** Marie ist zwanzig; **twenty-one** einundzwanzig.

:wice *adverb* 1 zweimal; **I've asked him twice** ich habe ihn zweimal gefragt; **twice a day** zweimal täglich; 2 **twice as much** doppelt so viel.

twin *noun* Zwilling *der* (PL *die* Zwillinge); **Helen and Tim are twins** Helen und Tim sind Zwillinge; **her twin sister** ihre Zwillingsschwester. *verb* **Richmond is twinned with Konstanz** Richmond und Konstanz sind Partnerstädte.

twist *verb* 1 (*bend out of shape*) verbiegen ◇; 2 verdrehen (*words, meaning*); 3 **to twist your ankle** sich ←(DAT) den Knöchel verrenken.

two *number* zwei; **Ben's two** Ben ist zwei; **two by two** zu zweit.

type *noun* Art *die*; **what type of computer is it?** welche Art Computer ist es? *verb* (*on a typewriter*) Schreibmaschine schreiben ◇, tippen (*informal*); **I'm learning to type** ich lerne Schreibmaschine schreiben; **I'm just typing some**

letters ich tippe gerade ein paar Briefe.

typewriter *noun* Schreibmaschine *die* (PL *die* Schreibmaschinen).

typical *adjective* typisch.

tyre *noun* Reifen *der* (PL *die* Reifen).

U u

ugly *adjective* hässlich △.

UK *noun* (*United Kingdom*) Vereinigte Königreich *das*.

Ulster *noun* Ulster; **from Ulster** aus Ulster.

umbrella *noun* Regenschirm *der* (PL *die* Regenschirme).

umpire *noun* Schiedsrichter *der* (PL *die* Schiedsrichter), Schiedsrichterin *die* (PL *die* Schiedsrichterinnen).

UN *noun* (*United Nations*) UN (*plural*).

unable *adjective* **to be unable to do something** etwas nicht tun können; **he's unable to come** er kann nicht kommen.

unavoidable *adjective* unvermeidlich.

unbearable *adjective* unerträglich.

unbelievable *adjective* unglaublich.

△ NEW SPELLING: *See page ›*

uncertain *adjective* 1 (*not sure*) **to be uncertain whether** ... sich ←(DAT) nicht sicher sein, ob ...; 2 (*unpredictable*) ungewiss △ (*future or result*).

uncle *noun* Onkel *der* (PL *die* Onkel).

uncomfortable *adjective* 1 unbequem (*shoes, chair, or journey*); 2 unangenehm (*situation, heat*).

unconscious *adjective* (*out cold*) bewusstlos △.

under *preposition* 1 (*underneath*) unter (+DAT, *or* +ACC *when there is movement towards a place*); **the dog's under the bed** der Hund ist unter dem Bett; **the ball rolled under the bed** der Ball ist unter das Bett gerollt; 2 **under there** da drunter; **perhaps it's under there** vielleicht ist es da drunter; 3 (*less than*) unter (+DAT); **under £20** unter zwanzig Pfund; **children under five** Kinder unter fünf.

under-age *adjective* **to be under-age** minderjährig sein.

undercooked *adjective* nicht gar.

underestimate *verb* unterschätzen.

underground *noun* (*railway*) U-Bahn *die* (PL *die* U-Bahnen); **I saw her on the underground** ich habe sie in der U-Bahn gesehen; **shall we go by underground?** fahren wir mit der U-Bahn? *adjective* unterirdisch (*cave*);

underground car park *die* Tiefgarage.

underline *verb* unterstreichen ✧.

underneath *preposition* unter (+DAT, *or* +ACC *when there is movement towards a place*); **it's underneath the newspaper** es ist unter der Zeitung; **I put it underneath the newspaper** ich habe es unter die Zeitung gelegt. *adverb* darunter; **check underneath** sieh darunter nach.

underpants *plural noun* Unterhose *die* (PL *die* Unterhosen); **my underpants** meine Unterhose.

underpass *noun* Unterführung *die* (PL *die* Unterführungen).

understand *verb* verstehen ✧; **do you understand?** verstehst du?; **I couldn't understand what he was saying** ich konnte ihn nicht verstehen; **I can't understand why she doesn't want to see him** ich kann nicht verstehen, warum sie ihn nicht sehen will.

understandable *adjective* **that's understandable** das ist verständlich.

understanding *noun* Verständnis *das*. *adjective* verständnisvoll.

underwear *noun* Unterwäsche *die*.

undo *verb* aufmachen SEP.

undone *adjective* **to come undone** aufgehen ✧ SEP (PERF *sein*).

undress *verb* **to get undressed** sich ausziehen ✧ SEP.

unemployed noun the **unemployed** die Arbeitslosen (*plural*).
adjective arbeitslos.

unemployment noun Arbeitslosigkeit die.

unexpected adjective unerwartet.

unexpectedly adverb (*to happen, arrive*) überraschend.

unfair adjective unfair; **it's unfair on young people** es ist jungen Leuten gegenüber unfair.

unfashionable adjective unmodern.

unfasten verb aufmachen SEP.

unfit adjective nicht fit; **I'm terribly unfit** ich bin nicht sehr fit.

unfortunate adjective unglücklich.

unfortunately adverb leider.

unfriendly adjective unfreundlich.

ungrateful adjective undankbar.

unhappy adjective 1 unglücklich; 2 (*not satisfied*) unzufrieden; **to be unhappy about something** mit etwas unzufrieden sein.

unhealthy adjective ungesund.

uniform noun Uniform die (PL die Uniformen).

union noun (*trade union*) Gewerkschaft die (PL die Gewerkschaften).

Union Jack noun **the Union Jack** die britische Nationalflagge.

unique adjective einzigartig.

unit noun 1 (*for measuring, for example*) Einheit die (PL die Einheiten); 2 (*in a kitchen*) Einbauschrank der (PL die Einbauschränke); 3 (*a department*) Abteilung die (PL die Abteilungen); **the research unit** die Forschungsabteilung.

United Kingdom noun Vereinigte Königreich das.

United Nations noun Vereinte Nationen (*plural*).

United States (of America) plural noun Vereinigte Staaten (von Amerika) (*plural*).

universe noun Universum das, Weltall das.

university noun Universität die (PL die Universitäten); **to go to university** auf die Universität gehen.

unkind adjective unfreundlich.

unknown adjective unbekannt.

unleaded petrol noun bleifreie Benzin das.

unless conjunction es sei denn; **unless he does it** es sei denn, er macht es; **unless you write** es sei denn, du schreibst.

unlike adjective 1 im Gegensatz zu (+DAT); **unlike me, she hates dogs** im Gegensatz zu mir hasst sie Hunde; 2 **it's unlike her to be late** es sieht ihr gar nicht ähnlich, zu spät zu kommen.

unlikely adjective unwahrscheinlich.

unload verb 1 ausladen ✧ SEP (*luggage, car*); 2 entladen ✧ (*lorry*).

△ NEW SPELLING: *See page*

unlock *verb* aufschließen ✧ SEP.

unlucky *adjective* **1** **to be unlucky** (*person*) Pech haben; **I was unlucky, the shop was shut** ich hatte Pech, das Geschäft war zu; **2** (*bringing bad luck*) Unglücks-; **thirteen is an unlucky number** dreizehn ist eine Unglückszahl; **it's unlucky** es bringt Unglück.

unnecessary *adjective* unnötig.

unpack *verb* auspacken SEP; **I'm just unpacking my rucksack** ich packe gerade meinen Rucksack aus; **I'll just unpack and then come down** ich packe nur noch aus und dann komme ich runter.

unpaid *adjective* unbezahlt.

unpleasant *adjective* unangenehm.

unplug *verb* **to unplug the lamp** den Stecker von der Lampe herausziehen ✧ SEP.

unpopular *adjective* unbeliebt.

unreasonable *adjective* uneinsichtig; **he's being really unreasonable** er ist so uneinsichtig.

unreliable *adjective* unzuverlässig; **he's unreliable** er ist unzuverlässig.

unsafe *adjective* gefährlich (*wiring, for example*).

unsatisfactory *adjective* unbefriedigend.

unscrew *verb* aufschrauben SEP.

unshaven *adjective* unrasiert.

unsuccessful *adjective* **1** erfolglos; **an unsuccessful attempt** ein erfolgloser Versuch; **2** **to be unsuccessful** keinen Erfolg haben; **I tried, but I was unsuccessful** ich habe es versucht, aber ich hatte keinen Erfolg.

unsuitable *adjective* unpassend.

untidy *adjective* unordentlich; **the house is always untidy** das Haus ist immer unordentlich.

until *preposition, conjunction* **1** bis; **until Monday** bis Montag; **until now** bis jetzt; **until then** bis dahin; **2** (*when 'until' is followed by a noun it is usually translated as 'bis zu' +DAT*) **until the tenth** bis zum Zehnten; **until the morning** bis zum Morgen; **3** not until erst; **not until September** erst im September; **it won't be finished until Friday** es wird erst Freitag fertig sein.

unusual *adjective* ungewöhnlich; **an unusual face** ein ungewöhnliches Gesicht.

unwilling *adjective* **to be unwilling to do something** etwas nicht tun wollen.

unwrap *verb* auspacken SEP.

up *preposition, adverb* **1** (*out of bed*) **to be up** auf sein △ ✧ (PERF *sein*); **Liz isn't up yet** Liz ist noch nicht auf; **I was up late last night** ich war gestern bis spät auf; **2** **to get up** aufstehen ✧ SEP (PERF *sein*); **we got up at six** wir sind um sechs aufgestanden; **3** (*higher up*) auf (+DAT, *or* +ACC *when there is movement towards a place*); **up on the roof** auf

dem Dach, 1 up have hier oben; up
there da oben; to go up (*upstairs*)
nach oben gehen; I went up ich bin
nach oben gegangen; 5 to go up the
road die Straße entlanggehen ◇ SEP
(PERF *sein*); it's further up the road
es ist weiter die Straße entlang; 6 to
go up the hill (*on foot*)
hinaufgehen ◇ SEP (PERF *sein*); (*in a
vehicle*) hinauffahren ◇ SEP (PERF
sein); (*in spoken German the prefix
'rauf-' is most common*) does the
bus go up the hill fährt der Bus
den Berg rauf?; 7 to come up
heraufkommen ◇ SEP (PERF *sein*),
raufkommen ◇ SEP (PERF *sein*)
(*informal*); 8 (*wrong*) what's up?
was ist los? (*informal*); what's up
with him? was ist mit ihm los?; 9 up
to bis; up to here bis hier; up to last
week bis zur letzten Woche; 10 she
came up to me sie kam auf mich
zu; 11 what's she up to? was hat
sie vor?; 12 it's up to you (*it's for
you to decide*) das hängt von dir ab;
(*it concerns only you*) das ist deine
Sache; ★ time's up! die Zeit ist um.

upheaval *noun* Unruhe *die* (PL *die*
Unruhen).

upper-class *adjective* der
Oberschicht; an upper-class family
eine Familie der Oberschicht.

upright *adjective* aufrecht; put it
upright stell es aufrecht; to stand
upright aufrecht stehen.

upset *noun* stomach upset *die*
Magenverstimmung.
adjective 1 (*annoyed*) ärgerlich;
he's upset er ist ärgerlich;
2 (*distressed*) bestürzt; (*sad*)

verb to upset somebody (*hurt*)
jemanden kränken; (*annoy*)
jemanden ärgern.

upside down *adjective* verkehrt
herum.

upstairs *adverb* 1 oben; Mum's
upstairs Mutti ist oben; 2 (*with
movement*) nach oben; to go
upstairs nach oben gehen.

up-to-date *adjective* 1 (*in fashion*)
modern; 2 (*information*) aktuell.

upwards *adjective* nach oben.

urgent *adjective* dringend.

US *noun* USA (*plural*).

us *pronoun* uns; she knows us sie
kennt uns; they saw us sie haben
uns gesehen; with us mit uns.

USA *noun* USA (*plural*).

use *noun* 1 Gebrauch *der*;
instructions for use *die*
Gebrauchsanweisung (*singular*);
2 it's no use es hat keinen Zweck;
it's no use phoning es hat keinen
Zweck anzurufen.
verb benutzen; we used the
dictionary wir haben das
Wörterbuch benutzt; to use
something to do something etwas
zu etwas ←(DAT) benutzen; I used a
towel to dry myself ich habe ein
Handtuch zum Abtrocknen benutzt.

• to use up 1 aufbrauchen SEP (*food*);
2 verbrauchen (*money*).

used *adjective* 1 to be used to
something an etwas ←(ACC) gewöhnt
sein; I'm used to cats ich bin an
Katzen gewöhnt; I'm not used to it!

△ NEW SPELLING: *See page*

ich bin nicht daran gewöhnt!; **I'm not used to eating in restaurants** ich bin nicht daran gewöhnt, in Restaurants zu essen; **2 to get used to something** sich an etwas ←(ACC) gewöhnen; **you'll soon get used to the new car** du wirst dich schnell an das neue Auto gewöhnen; **I've got used to living here** ich habe mich daran gewöhnt, hier zu wohnen; **you'll get used to it** du wirst dich schon daran gewöhnen.
verb **they used to live in the country** sie haben früher auf dem Land gewohnt; **she used to smoke** sie hat früher geraucht.

useful *adjective* nützlich.

useless *adjective* **1** unbrauchbar; **this knife's useless** dieses Messer ist unbrauchbar; **you're completely useless!** du bist wirklich zu nichts zu gebrauchen!; **2** nutzlos (*advice, information, or facts, for example*); **useless knowledge** nutzloses Wissen; **3** (*pointless*) zwecklos.

user-friendly *adjective* benutzerfreundlich.

usual *adjective* **1** üblich; **it's the usual problem** es ist das übliche Problem; **as usual** wie üblich; **2 it's colder than usual** es ist kälter als gewöhnlich.

usually *adjective* normalerweise; **I usually leave at eight** normalerweise gehe ich um acht weg.

V v

vacancy *noun* **1** (*in a hotel*) **'vacancies'** 'Zimmer frei'; **'no vacancies'** 'belegt'; **2 job vacancy** die freie Stelle.

vacant *adjective* frei.

vaccination *noun* Impfung *die* (PL die Impfungen).

vacuum *verb* saugen; **I'm going to vacuum my room** ich sauge mein Zimmer.

vacuum cleaner *noun* Staubsauger *der* (PL die Staubsauger).

vagina *noun* Vagina *die* (PL die Vaginen).

vague *adjective* vage.

vain *adjective* eitel; **in vain** vergeblich.

Valentine's Day *noun* Valentinstag *der* (PL die Valentinstage).

valid *adjective* gültig.

valley *noun* Tal *das* (PL die Täler).

valuable *adjective* wertvoll.

value *noun* Wert *der* (PL die Werte). *verb* schätzen.

van *noun* Lieferwagen *der* (PL die Lieferwagen).

vandal *noun* Rowdy *der* (PL die Rowdies).

vandalism *noun*
Wandalismus Δ *der*.

vandalize *verb* mutwillig zerstören.

vanilla *noun* Vanille *die*; **vanilla ice cream** *das* Vanilleeis.

vanish *verb* verschwinden ✧ (PERF *sein*).

variety *noun* 1 Abwechslung *die* (*in a routine, diet, or style*); **for the sake of variety** zur Abwechslung; 2 (*kind*) Sorte *die* (PL *die* Sorten); **a new variety of apple** eine neue Apfelsorte; 3 (*assortment*) Auswahl *die*.

various *adjective* verschieden; **there are various ways of doing it** man kann es auf verschiedene Art und Weise machen.

vary *verb* 1 (*become different*) sich ändern; 2 **it varies a lot** es ist sehr unterschiedlich; 3 (*make different*) ändern (*a programme or method*).

vase *noun* Vase *die* (PL *die* Vasen).

VAT *noun* Mehrwertsteuer *die* (PL *die* Mehrwertsteuern).

VCR *noun* Videorecorder *der* (PL *die* Videorecorder).

VDU *noun* Bildschirm *der* (PL *die* Bildschirme).

veal *noun* Kalbfleisch *das*.

vegan *noun* Veganer *der* (PL *die* Veganer), Veganerin *die* (PL *die* Veganerinnen).

vegetable *noun* Gemüse *das*; **fresh vegetables** frisches Gemüse.

vegetarian *noun* Vegetarier *der* (PL *die* Vegetarier), Vegetarierin *die* (PL *die* Vegetarierinnen).
adjective vegetarisch.

vehicle *noun* Fahrzeug *das* (PL *die* Fahrzeuge).

vein *noun* Vene *die* (PL *die* Venen).

velvet *noun* Samt *der*.

vending machine *noun* Automat *der* (PL *die* Automaten).

verb *noun* Verb *das* (PL *die* Verben).

verdict *noun* Urteil *das* (PL *die* Urteile).

verge *noun* 1 (*roadside*) Bankette *die* (PL *die* Banketten); 2 **to be on the verge of doing something** im Begriff sein, etwas zu tun; **I was on the verge of leaving** ich war im Begriff zu gehen.

version *noun* Version *die* (PL *die* Versionen).

versus *preposition* gegen (+ACC); **Arsenal versus Chelsea** Arsenal gegen Chelsea.

very *adverb* sehr; **it's very difficult** es ist sehr schwer; **very much** sehr viel.
adjective 1 **the very person I need!** genau der Mann, den ich brauche; genau die Frau, die ich brauche; **the very thing he's looking for** genau das, was er sucht; **in the very middle** genau in der Mitte; 2 **at the very end** ganz am Ende; **at the very front** ganz vorne.

vest *noun* Unterhemd *das* (PL *die* Unterhemden).

Δ NEW SPELLING: *See page*

vet *noun* Tierarzt *der* (PL *die* Tierärzte), Tierärztin *die* (PL *die* Tierärztinnen); **she's a vet** sie ist Tierärztin.

via *preposition* über (+ACC); **we're going to Frankfurt via Brussels** wir fahren über Brüssel nach Frankfurt.

vicar *noun* Pfarrer *der* (PL *die* Pfarrer).

vicious *adjective* 1 bösartig (*dog*); 2 brutal (*attack*).

victim *noun* Opfer *das* (PL *die* Opfer).

victory *noun* Sieg *der* (PL *die* Siege).

video *noun* 1 (*film, cassette*) Video *das* (PL *die* Videos); **to watch a video** ein Video ansehen; **I've got it on video** ich habe es auf Video; **it's out on video** das gibt's als Video; 2 (*video recorder*) Videorecorder *der* (PL *die* Videorecorder). *verb* aufzeichnen SEP; **I'll video it for you** ich zeichne es für dich auf.

video camera *noun* Videokamera *die* (PL *die* Videokameras).

video cassette *noun* Videokassette *die* (PL *die* Videokassetten).

video game *noun* Videospiel *das* (PL *die* Videospiele).

video recorder *noun* Videorecorder *der* (PL *die* Videorecorder).

video shop *noun* Videothek *die* (PL *die* Videotheken).

Vienna *noun* Wien *das*; **to Vienna** nach Wien.

view *noun* 1 Aussicht *die*; **a room with a view of the lake** ein Zimmer mit Aussicht auf den See; 2 (*opinion*) Meinung *die* (PL *die* Meinungen); **in my view** meiner Meinung nach; **point of view** *der* Standpunkt.

viewer *noun* Zuschauer *der* (PL *die* Zuschauer), Zuschauerin *die* (PL *die* Zuschauerinnen).

vile *adjective* ekelhaft.

villa *noun* Villa *die* (PL *die* Villen).

village *noun* Dorf *das* (PL *die* Dörfer).

vine *noun* Weinrebe *die* (PL *die* Weinreben).

vinegar *noun* Essig *der*.

vineyard *noun* Weinberg *der* (PL *die* Weinberge).

violence *noun* Gewalt *die*.

violent *adjective* 1 gewalttätig (*person, film, behaviour*); 2 heftig (*jolt, punch*).

violin *noun* Geige *die* (PL *die* Geigen); **to play the violin** Geige spielen.

violinist *noun* Geiger *der* (PL *die* Geiger), Geigerin *die* (PL *die* Geigerinnen).

virgin *noun* Jungfrau *die* (PL *die* Jungfrauen).

Virgo *noun* Jungfrau *die*; **Robert's Virgo** Robert ist Jungfrau.

virtual reality *noun* virtuelle Realität *die*.

virus *noun* Virus *das* (PL *die* Viren).

visa *noun* Visum *das* (PL *die* Visa).

visit *noun* Besuch *der* (PL *die* Besuche); **I was in Berlin on a visit to friends** ich war in Berlin bei Freunden zu Besuch; **my last visit to Germany** mein letzter Deutschlandbesuch.
verb **1** besuchen (*a person*); **2** besichtigen (*a building, town*).

visitor *noun* **1** Besucher *der* (PL *die* Besucher), Besucherin *die* (PL *die* Besucherinnen); **2 we've got visitors tonight** wir haben heute Abend Besuch; **3** (*in a hotel*) Gast *der* (PL *die* Gäste).

visual *adjective* visuell.

vital *adjective* unbedingt erforderlich; **it's vital to book** man muss unbedingt buchen.

vitamin *noun* Vitamin *das* (PL *die* Vitamine).

vivid *adjective* lebhaft (*colours, memory*); **to have a vivid imagination** eine lebhafte Phantasie haben.

vocabulary *noun* Wortschatz *der*.

vocational *adjective* beruflich.

vodka *noun* Wodka *der* (PL *die* Wodkas).

voice *noun* Stimme *die* (PL *die* Stimmen).

volcano *noun* Vulkan *der* (PL *die* Vulkane).

volleyball *noun* Volleyball *der*; **to play volleyball** Volleyball spielen.

volume *noun* **1** Lautstärke *die*; **could you turn down the volume?** könntest du etwas leiser stellen?, **2** (*book*) Band *der* (PL *die* Bände).

voluntary *adjective* **1** freiwillig; **a voluntary worker** ein freiwilliger Helfer, eine freiwillige Helferin; **2 to do voluntary work** für einen wohltätigen Zweck arbeiten.

volunteer *noun* Freiwillige *der/die* (PL *die* Freiwilligen).
verb **to volunteer to do something** sich anbieten, etwas zu tun.

vote *verb* wählen; **to vote for somebody** jemanden wählen.

voucher *noun* Gutschein *der* (PL *die* Gutscheine).

vowel *noun* Vokal *der* (PL *die* Vokale).

vulgar *adjective* vulgär.

W w

wage(s) *noun* Lohn *der* (PL *die* Löhne).

waist *noun* Taille *die* (PL *die* Taillen).

waistcoat *noun* Weste *die* (PL *die* Westen).

waist measurement *noun* Taillenweite *die*.

wait *noun* Wartezeit *die*; **an hour's wait** eine Stunde Wartezeit.
verb **1** warten; **they're waiting in the car** sie warten im Auto; **she kept me waiting** sie hat mich warten lassen; **2 to wait for somebody** auf jemanden warten; **wait for me**

△ NEW SPELLING: *See page*

warte auf mich; **to wait for
something** auf etwas ←(ACC) warten;
we waited for a taxi wir haben auf
ein Taxi gewartet; **3 to wait for
somebody to do something** darauf
warten, dass jemand etwas tut; **I'm
waiting for him to ring** ich warte
darauf, dass er anruft; **4 I can't wait
to open it** ich kann's kaum
erwarten, es aufzumachen.

waiter *noun* Kellner *der* (PL *die*
Kellner); **waiter!** Herr Ober!

waiting room *noun*
Wartezimmer *das* (PL *die*
Wartezimmer); (*at a station*)
Warteraum *der* (PL *die* Warteräume).

waitress *noun* Kellnerin *die* (PL *die*
Kellnerinnen); **waitress!** Fräulein!

wake *verb* **1** wecken (*somebody*);
Jess woke me at six Jess hat mich
um sechs geweckt; **2** aufwachen SEP
(PERF *sein*); **I woke (up) at six** ich
bin um sechs aufgewacht; **wake up!**
wach auf!

Wales *noun* Wales *das*; **from Wales**
aus Wales; **to Wales** nach Wales.

walk *noun* **1** Spaziergang *der* (PL *die*
Spaziergänge); **to go for walk** einen
Spaziergang machen; **we'll go for a
little walk round the village** wir
machen einen kleinen Spaziergang
durchs Dorf; **2 to take the dog for
a walk** mit dem Hund spazieren
gehen ✧ (PERF *sein*); **3 it's about
five minutes' walk from here** es ist
ungefähr fünf Minuten zu Fuß von
hier.
verb **1** (*go, not run*) gehen ✧ (PERF
sein); **he walks very slowly** er geht

sehr langsam; **I'll walk to the bus
stop with you** ich gehe mit dir zur
Bushaltestelle; **2** (*on foot rather than
by car or bus*) zu Fuß gehen ✧ (PERF
sein); **it's not far, we can walk** es ist
nicht weit, wir können zu Fuß
gehen; **3** (*walk around*) spazieren
gehen ✧ △ (PERF *sein*); **we walked
around the old town** wir sind in der
Altstadt spazieren gegangen;
4 (*move on foot*) laufen ✧ (PERF
sein); **to learn to walk** laufen
lernen; **the child can't walk yet** das
Kind kann noch nicht laufen.

walking *noun* (*hiking*)
Wandern *das*; **to go walking**
wandern (PERF *sein*).

walking distance *noun* **to be
within walking distance** zu Fuß zu
erreichen sein; **it's within walking
distance of the sea** man kann das
Meer zu Fuß erreichen.

walkman™ *noun* Walkman™ *der*
(PL *die* Walkmen).

wall *noun* **1** (*inside a building*)
Wand *die* (PL *die* Wände); **there's a
picture on every wall** an jeder Wand
hängt ein Bild; **2** (*outside*)
Mauer *die* (PL *die* Mauern).

wallet *noun* Brieftasche *die* (PL *die*
Brieftaschen).

wallpaper *noun* Tapete *die* (PL *die*
Tapeten).

walnut *noun* Walnuss △ *die* (PL *die*
Walnüsse).

wander *verb* **to wander around
town** durch die Stadt bummeln

(PERF *sein*); **to wander off**
weggehen ✧ SEP (PERF *sein*).

want *verb* **1** wollen ✧; **do you want
to come?** willst du mitkommen?;
what do you want to do? was willst
du machen?; **I don't want to bother
him** ich will ihn nicht stören;
2 (*more polite*) mögen ✧ ('*ich
möchte' is much politer than 'ich
will*'); **do you want some more
coffee?** möchtest du noch Kaffee?;
I want two pounds of apples please
ich möchte gern zwei Pfund Äpfel
('*möchte gern' is particularly used
when shopping*).

war *noun* Krieg *der* (PL *die* Kriege).

wardrobe *noun*
Kleiderschrank *der* (PL *die*
Kleiderschränke).

warm *adjective* **1** warm; **a warm
coat** ein warmer Mantel; **it's warm
today** heute ist es warm; **I'll keep
your dinner warm** ich halte dir das
Essen warm; **it's warm inside**
drinnen ist es warm; **I am warm** mir
ist warm; **2** (*friendly*) herzlich; **a
warm welcome** ein herzlicher
Empfang.
verb wärmen; **to warm the plates**
die Teller wärmen.

● **to warm up** **1** (*weather*) warm
werden; **2** (*an athlete*) sich
aufwärmen SEP; **3** (*to heat up*)
aufwärmen SEP; **I'll warm the soup
up for you** ich wärme dir die Suppe
auf.

warmth *noun* Wärme *die*.

warn *verb* **1** warnen; **I warn you, it's
expensive** ich warne dich, es ist
teuer; **to warn somebody not to do
something** jemanden davor

warnen, etwas zu tun; **she warned
me not to let him drive** sie hat mich
davor gewarnt, ihn fahren zu lassen;
2 he warned me to lock the car er
hat mich ermahnt, das Auto
abzuschließen.

warning *noun* Warnung *die* (PL *die*
Warnungen).

wash *noun* **to give something a
wash** etwas waschen ✧; **to have a
wash** sich waschen.
verb **1** waschen ✧; **I've washed your
jeans** ich habe deine Jeans
gewaschen; **2** (*have a wash*) sich
waschen ✧; **to get washed** sich
waschen; **3 to wash your hands**
sich ←(DAT) die Hände waschen; **I
washed my hands** ich habe mir die
Hände gewaschen; **to wash your
hair** sich ←(DAT) die Haare waschen;
4 to wash the dishes abwaschen ✧
SEP.

● **to wash up** abwaschen ✧ SEP.

washbasin *noun*
Waschbecken *das* (PL *die*
Waschbecken).

washing *noun* Wäsche *die*; **to do
the washing** Wäsche waschen.

washing machine *noun*
Waschmaschine *die* (PL *die*
Waschmaschinen).

washing powder *noun*
Waschpulver *das*.

washing-up *noun* Abwasch *der*; **to
do the washing-up** den Abwasch
machen.

washing-up liquid *noun*
Spülmittel *das* (PL *die* Spülmittel).

wasp *noun* Wespe *die* (PL *die* Wespen).

waste *noun* Verschwendung *die*; **it's a waste of time** das ist eine Zeitverschwendung. *verb* verschwenden.

waste-bin *noun* Mülltonne *die* (PL *die* Mülltonnen).

waste-paper basket *noun* Papierkorb *der* (PL *die* Papierkörbe).

watch *noun* Uhr *die* (PL *die* Uhren); **my watch is fast** meine Uhr geht vor; **my watch is slow** meine Uhr geht nach. *verb* 1 (*to look at*) sich ←(DAT) ansehen ✧ SEP; **I was watching a film** ich habe mir einen Film angesehen; **2 to watch TV** fernsehen ✧ SEP; **3** (*keep a check on, look after*) achten auf (+ACC); **watch the children** achte auf die Kinder; **4** (*to be careful*) aufpassen SEP; **watch you don't spill it** pass auf, dass du es nicht verschüttest; **watch out!** pass auf!; **5** (*observe*) beobachten; **they were being watched** sie wurden beobachtet.

water *noun* Wasser *das*. *verb* gießen ✧ (*plants*).

waterfall *noun* Wasserfall *der* (PL *die* Wasserfälle).

watering can *noun* Gießkanne *die* (PL *die* Gießkannen).

waterproof *adjective* wasserdicht.

water-skiing *noun* Wasserskifahren *das*; **to go water-skiing** Wasserski fahren.

wave *noun* 1 (*in the sea*) Welle *die* (PL *die* Wellen); **2** (*with your hand*) **to give somebody a wave** jemandem zuwinken SEP; **she gave him a wave from the bus** sie winkte ihm vom Bus zu. *verb* 1 (*with your hand*) winken; **2** (*flap*) schwenken (*a flag, for example*).

wax *noun* Wachs *das*.

way *noun* 1 (*a route or road*) Weg *der* (PL *die* Wege); **the way to town** der Weg in die Stadt; **we asked the way to the station** wir haben gefragt, wie man zum Bahnhof kommt; **on the way back** auf dem Rückweg; **on the way** unterwegs; **to be in the way** im Weg sein; **to be in somebody's way** jemandem im Weg sein; **to get out of the way** aus dem Weg gehen; **2 to lose your way** sich verlaufen ✧; (*in a car*) sich verfahren ✧; **3 'way in'** 'Eingang'; **'way out'** 'Ausgang'; **4** (*direction*) Richtung *die* (PL *die* Richtungen); **which way did he go?** in welche Richtung ist er gegangen?; **this way** in diese Richtung; **5** (*side*) **the right way up** richtig herum; **the wrong way round** falsch herum; **the other way round** andersherum; **6** (*distance*) **it's a long way** es ist weit weg; **we still had a little way to go** wir mussten noch ein kleines Stück gehen; **7** (*manner*) Art und Weise *die*; **my way of learning German** meine Art und Weise, Deutsch zu lernen; **he does it his way** er macht es auf seine Art und Weise; **I've done it the wrong way** ich habe es falsch gemacht; **in a way**

✧ IRREGULAR VERB: *See the verb table in the centre of the dictionary*

in gewisser Weise; **8 no way!** auf
keinen Fall!; **9 by the way** übrigens.

we *pronoun* wir; **we're going to the
cinema tonight** wir gehen heute
Abend ins Kino.

weak *adjective* **1** (*feeble*) schwach;
in a weak voice mit schwacher
Stimme; **2** dünn (*coffee or tea*).

wealthy *adjective* reich.

weapon *noun* Waffe *die* (PL *die*
Waffen).

wear *noun* **children's wear** *die*
Kinderkleidung; **sports wear** *die*
Sportkleidung.
verb tragen✧, anhaben✧ SEP
(*informal*); **she often wears red** sie
trägt oft Rot; **Tamsin's wearing her
jeans** Tamsin hat ihre Jeans an.

weather *noun* **1** Wetter *das*; **what's
the weather like?** wie ist das
Wetter?; **in fine weather** bei
schönem Wetter; **the weather is
terrible** das Wetter ist furchtbar;
2 in wet weather wenn es regnet;
the weather was cold es war kalt.

weather forecast *noun*
Wettervorhersage *die*; **the weather
forecast says it will rain** der
Wettervorhersage zufolge soll es
regnen.

wedding *noun* Hochzeit *die* (PL *die*
Hochzeiten).

Wednesday *noun* **1** Mittwoch *der*
(PL *die* Mittwoche); **on Wednesday**
(am) Mittwoch; **I'm going to the
cinema on Wednesday** ich gehe
Mittwoch ins Kino; **see you on
Wednesday!** bis Mittwoch!; **every**

Wednesday jeden Mittwoch; **last
Wednesday** vorigen Mittwoch; **next
Wednesday** nächsten Mittwoch;
2 on Wednesdays mittwochs; **the
museum is closed on Wednesdays**
das Museum ist mittwochs
geschlossen.

weed *noun* Unkraut *das*.

week *noun* Woche *die* (PL *die*
Wochen); **last week** vorige Woche;
next week nächste Woche; **this
week** diese Woche; **for weeks**
wochenlang; **a week today** heute in
einer Woche; **in three weeks' time**
in drei Wochen.

weekday *noun* **on weekdays**
wochentags.

weekend *noun* Wochenende *das*
(PL *die* Wochenenden); **last
weekend** voriges Wochenende;
next weekend nächstes
Wochenende; **they're coming for
the weekend** sie kommen übers
Wochenende; **I'll do it at the
weekend** ich mache es am
Wochenende; **have a nice
weekend!** ein schönes
Wochenende!

weigh *verb* **1** wiegen✧; **to weigh
something** etwas wiegen; **to weigh
yourself** sich wiegen; **2 how much
do you weigh?** wie viel wiegst du?; **I
weigh 50 kilos** ich wiege fünfzig
Kilo.

weight *noun* **1** Gewicht *das* (PL *die*
Gewichte); **2 to put on weight**
zunehmen✧ SEP; **3 to lose weight**
abnehmen✧ SEP.

weird *adjective* seltsam.

welcome *noun* **1 they gave us a warm welcome** sie haben uns herzlich empfangen; **2 welcome to Oxford!** herzlich willkommen in Oxford!
adjective willkommen; **you're welcome any time** du bist immer willkommen; **'thank you!' – 'you're welcome!'** 'danke!' – 'bitte!'.
verb begrüßen; **to welcome somebody** jemanden begrüßen.

well *adverb* **1 to be well** gesund sein; **I'm very well, thank you** danke, es geht mir gut; **get well soon!** gute Besserung!; **2** gut; **Terry played well** Terry hat gut gespielt; **it's well paid** es wird gut bezahlt; **well done!** gut gemacht!; **3 as well** auch; **Kevin's coming as well** Kevin kommt auch; **4** na ja; **well, never mind** na ja, macht nichts; **5** gut; **it may well be that …** es ist gut möglich, dass …; **very well then, you can go** also gut, du kannst gehen.

well-behaved *adjective* artig.

well-done *adjective* durchgebraten (*steak*).

wellington (boot) *noun* Gummistiefel *der* (PL *die* Gummistiefel).

well-known *adjective* bekannt.

well-off *adjective* wohlhabend.

Welsh *noun* **1 the Welsh** (*people*) die Waliser (*plural*); **2** (*language*) Walisisch *das*.
adjective walisisch; **he's Welsh** er ist Waliser; **she's Welsh** sie ist Waliserin.

Welshman *noun* Waliser *der* (PL *die* Waliser).

Welshwoman *noun* Waliserin *die* (PL *die* Waliserinnen).

west *noun* Westen *der*; **in the west** im Westen.
adjective West-; **the west side** die Westseite; **west wind** *der* Westwind; **west of** westlich von; **it's west of Munich** es liegt westlich von München.
adverb nach Westen.

western *noun* (*film*) Western *der* (PL *die* Western).

West Indian *noun* Westinder *der* (PL *die* Westinder), Westinderin *die* (PL *die* Westinderinnen).
adjective westindisch.

West Indies *plural noun* die Westindischen Inseln (*plural*); **in the West Indies** auf den Westindischen Inseln.

wet *adjective* **1** nass △; **we got wet** wir sind nass geworden; **2 a wet day** ein regnerischer Tag.

whale *noun* Wal *der* (PL *die* Wale).

what *pronoun, adjective* **1** (*in questions*) was; **what did you say?** was hast du gesagt?; **what's she doing?** was macht sie?; **what did you buy?** was hast du gekauft?; **what is it?** was ist das?; **what's the matter?** was ist los?; **what's happened?** was ist passiert?; **what?** was?; **2 what's your address?** wie ist Ihre Adresse?; **what's her name?** wie heißt sie?; **what was it like?** wie war's?; **3** (*asking for an amount*) wie viel △;

✧ IRREGULAR VERB: *See the verb table in the centre of the dictionary*

at what time! um wie viel Uhr?;
4 (*that which*) was (*relative
pronoun*); **she told me what had
happened** sie hat mir gesagt, was
passiert ist; **do what I tell you** tu,
was ich dir sage; 5 (*which*)
welcher/welche/welches; **what
country is it in?** in welchem Land
ist es?; **what colour is it?** welche
Farbe hat es?; **what make is it?**
welche Marke ist es?; 6 **what for?**
wozu?

wheat *noun* Weizen *der*.

wheel *noun* Rad *das* (PL *die* Räder);
the spare wheel das Reserverad;
the steering wheel das Lenkrad.

wheelbarrow *noun*
Schubkarre *die* (PL *die*
Schubkarren).

wheelchair *noun* Rollstuhl *der* (PL
die Rollstühle).

when *adverb* wann; **when is she
arriving?** wann kommt sie an?;
when's your birthday? wann hast
du Geburtstag?
conjunction 1 (*with the past*) als;
I was out shopping when you rang
ich war beim Einkaufen, als du
anriefst; 2 (*with the present or
future*) wenn; **when she comes I'll
ring** wenn sie kommt, rufe ich an.

where *adverb, conjunction* wo;
where do you live? wo wohnst du?;
where are you going? wo gehst du
hin?; **I don't know where they live**
ich weiß nicht, wo sie wohnen.

whether *conjunction* ob; **I don't
know whether he's back** ich weiß
nicht, ob er schon zurück ist.

which *adjective, pronoun*
1 welcher/welche/welches; **which
CD did you buy?** welche CD hast du
gekauft?; 2 **which (one)**
welcher/welche/welches
(*depending on the gender of the noun
the question refers back to*); **'I met
your brother' – 'which one?'** 'ich
habe deinen Bruder getroffen' –
'welchen?'; **'I met your sister' –
'which one?'** 'ich habe deine
Schwester getroffen' – 'welche?';
**'have you seen my book?' – 'which
one?'** 'hast du mein Buch
gesehen?' – 'welches?'; 3 (*relative
pronoun*) der/die/das (*depending
on the gender of the noun 'which'
refers to*); (*plural*) die; **the film
which is showing now** der Film, der
gerade läuft; **the lamp which is on
the table** die Lampe, die auf dem
Tisch steht; **the book which I lent
you** das Buch, das ich dir geliehen
habe; **the books which I've read**
die Bücher, die ich gelesen habe.

while *noun* **for a while** eine Weile;
she worked here for a while sie hat
eine Weile hier gearbeitet; **after a
while** nach einer Weile.
conjunction während; **you can
make some coffee while I'm
finishing my homework** du kannst
Kaffee kochen, während ich meine
Hausaufgaben fertig mache.

whip *noun* Peitsche *die* (PL *die*
Peitschen).
verb schlagen ◈ (*cream*); **whipped
cream** *die* Schlagsahne.

whisky *noun* Whisky *der* (PL *die*
Whiskys).

△ NEW SPELLING: *See page xii*

whisper noun Flüstern das; **in a whisper** im Flüsterton.
verb flüstern.

whistle noun Pfeife die (PL die Pfeifen).
verb pfeifen ◈.

white noun Weiß das; **egg white** das Eiweiß.
adjective weiß; **a white shirt** ein weißes Hemd.

white coffee noun Kaffee mit Milch der (PL die Kaffees mit Milch).

Whitsun noun Pfingsten das (PL die Pfingsten).

who pronoun 1 (in questions) wer; **who wants some chocolate?** wer möchte Schokolade?; 2 (in the accusative) wen; **who did you ring?** wen hast du angerufen?; 3 (in the dative) wem; **who did you give it to?** wem hast du es gegeben?; 4 (relative pronoun) der/die/das (depending on the gender of the noun 'who' refers to); (plural) die; **my boy friend who lives in Liverpool** mein Freund, der in Liverpool wohnt; **my girl friend who lives in Berlin** meine Freundin, die in Berlin wohnt; **the child who's staying with us** das Kind, das bei uns wohnt; **the friends who are coming to see us tonight** die Freunde, die heute Abend kommen.

whole noun **the whole of the class** die ganze Klasse; **the whole of Germany** ganz Deutschland; **on the whole** im Großen und Ganzen.
adjective ganz; **the whole family** die ganze Familie; **the whole**

morning den ganzen Morgen; **the whole time** die ganze Zeit; **the whole world** die ganze Welt.

wholemeal adjective Vollkorn-; **wholemeal bread** das Vollkornbrot.

whom pronoun 1 den/die/das; (plural) die; **the man whom I saw** der Mann, den ich sah; **the woman whom I saw** die Frau, die ich sah; **the child whom I saw** das Kind, das ich sah; 2 (in the dative) dem/der/dem; (plural) denen; **the girl to whom I wrote** das Mädchen, dem ich geschrieben habe; 3 (in questions) wen; **whom did you see?** wen haben Sie gesehen?; 4 **to whom did you give it?** wem haben Sie es gegeben?

whose pronoun, adjective 1 (in questions) wessen; **whose is this jacket?** wessen Jacke ist das?; **whose shoes are these?** wessen Schuhe sind das?; 2 **whose is it?** wem gehört das?; **I know whose it is** ich weiß, wem es gehört; 3 (as a relative pronoun) dessen/deren/dessen (depending on the gender of the noun 'whose' refers to); (plural) deren; **the man whose car I'm buying** der Mann, dessen Auto ich kaufe; **the woman whose bag I found** die Frau, deren Tasche ich gefunden habe; **the girl whose sister I know** das Mädchen, dessen Schwester ich kenne; **the people whose children he teaches** die Leute, deren Kinder er unterrichtet.

why adverb 1 warum; **why did she phone?** warum hat sie angerufen?; **why not?** warum nicht?; 2 **that's**

why i don't want to come darum will ich nicht kommen.

wicked *adjective* 1 (*bad*) böse; 2 (*brilliant*) geil (*informal*).

wide *adjective* 1 breit; **it's a very wide road** es ist eine sehr breite Straße; **the shelf is 30 cm wide** das Regal ist dreißig Zentimeter breit; **wide screen** *das* Breitbild; 2 groß; **a wide range** eine große Auswahl. *adverb* **the door was wide open** die Tür stand weit offen.

wide awake *adjective* hellwach.

widow *noun* Witwe *die* (PL *die* Witwen).

widower *noun* Witwer *der* (PL *die* Witwer).

width *noun* Breite *die*.

wife *noun* Ehefrau *die* (PL *die* Ehefrauen).

wig *noun* Perücke *die* (PL *die* Perücken).

wild *adjective* 1 wild; **wild animals** wilde Tiere; 2 (*crazy*) verrückt (*idea, party, person*); 3 **to be wild about something** scharf auf etwas ←(ACC) sein.

wildlife *noun* Tierwelt *die*; **a programme on wildlife in Africa** eine Sendung über die afrikanische Tierwelt.

wildlife park *noun* Wildpark *der* (PL *die* Wildparks).

will *verb* 1 (*in German the present tense is often used to express future actions and intentions*) **I'll wait for you at the bus stop** ich warte an

der Bushaltestelle auf dich; **he'll be pleased to help you** er hilft dir gern; **that won't be a problem** das ist kein Problem; **I'll phone them at once** ich rufe sie sofort an; 2 (*the German future tense is used when firm intention is stressed, when referring to the more distant future and when some doubt about the future is expressed*) werden ◇; **he will definitely come** er wird ganz bestimmt kommen; **she'll probably ring before leaving** sie wird wahrscheinlich anrufen, bevor sie geht; 3 (*in questions and requests*) **will you have some more tea?** möchten Sie noch Tee?; **will you help me?** hilfst du mir?; **'will you write to me?' – 'of course I will!'** 'schreibst du mir?' – 'ja, natürlich'; **'he won't like it' – 'yes he will'** 'es wird ihm nicht gefallen' – 'doch'; 4 wollen ◇; **he won't help us** er will uns nicht helfen; **the car won't start** das Auto will nicht anspringen.

willing *adjective* **to be willing to do something** bereit sein, etwas zu tun; **I'm willing to pay half** ich bin bereit, die Hälfte zu zahlen.

willingly *adverb* gern.

win *noun* Sieg *der* (PL *die* Siege); **our win over Everton** unser Sieg über Everton. *verb* 1 gewinnen ◇; **we won!** wir haben gewonnen!; 2 **to win a prize** einen Preis bekommen.

wind [1] *noun* Wind *der* (PL *die* Winde).

wind [2] *verb* 1 wickeln (*a wire or rope, for example*); 2 aufziehen ◇ SEP (*a clock*).

△ NEW SPELLING: *See page x*

wind instrument *noun*
Blasinstrument *das* (PL *die*
Blasinstrumente).

window *noun* 1 Fenster *das* (PL *die*
Fenster); **to look out of the window**
aus dem Fenster sehen; 2 (*in a shop*)
Schaufenster *das* (PL *die*
Schaufenster).

windscreen *noun*
Windschutzscheibe *die* (PL *die*
Windschutzscheiben).

windscreen wiper *noun*
Scheibenwischer *der* (PL *die*
Scheibenwischer).

windy *adjective* windig; **it's windy
today** heute ist es windig.

wine *noun* Wein *der* (PL *die* Weine);
a glass of white wine ein Glas
Weißwein.

wing *noun* Flügel *der* (PL *die* Flügel).

wink *verb* **to wink at somebody**
jemandem zuzwinkern SEP.

winner *noun* Sieger *der* (PL *die*
Sieger), Siegerin *die* (PL *die*
Siegerinnen).

winning *adjective* siegreich.

winnings *plural noun* Gewinn *der*.

winter *noun* Winter *der* (PL *die*
Winter); **in winter** im Winter.

wipe *verb* 1 abwischen SEP; **I'll just
wipe the table** ich wische schnell
den Tisch ab; **to wipe your nose** sich
←(DAT) die Nase abwischen; 2 **to wipe
the floor** den Boden wischen; 3 **to
wipe your feet** sich ←(DAT) die
Schuhe abtreten SEP.
●**to wipe up** abtrocknen SEP (*dishes*).

wire *noun* Draht *der* (PL *die* Drähte);
electric wire *die* Leitung.

wise *adjective* weise.

wish *noun* 1 Wunsch *der* (PL *die*
Wünsche); **to make a wish** sich
←(DAT) etwas wünschen; **make a
wish!** wünsch dir was!; 2 **best
wishes on your birthday** alles Gute
zum Geburtstag; 3 (*in a letter*) **with
best wishes** mit freundlichen
Grüßen.
verb 1 **I wish she were here** ich
wünschte, sie wäre hier; 2 **to wish
for something** sich ←(DAT) etwas
wünschen; 3 **to wish somebody a
happy Christmas** jemandem frohe
Weihnachten wünschen; **I wished
him happy birthday** ich habe ihm
alles Gute zum Geburtstag
gewünscht.

with *preposition* 1 mit (+DAT); **with
me** mit mir; **with pleasure** mit
Vergnügen; **he went on holiday with
his friends** er ist mit seinen
Freunden in die Ferien gefahren; **a
girl with red hair** ein Mädchen mit
roten Haaren; 2 (*at the house of*) bei
(+ACC); **we're staying the night with
friends** wir übernachten bei
Freunden; 3 vor (+DAT); **to shiver
with cold** vor Kälte zittern; **to
tremble with fear** vor Angst zittern;
4 **I haven't got any money with me**
ich habe kein Geld dabei.

without *preposition* ohne (+ACC);
without you ohne dich; **without a
sweater** ohne einen Pullover;
without knowing ohne zu wissen.

✧ IRREGULAR VERB: *See the verb table in the centre of the dictionary*

witness *noun* Zeuge *der* (PL die Zeugen), Zeugin *die* (PL die Zeuginnen).

witty *adjective* geistreich.

woman *noun* Frau *die* (PL die Frauen); **a woman friend** eine Freundin; **a woman doctor** eine Ärztin.

wonder *noun* Wunder *das* (PL die Wunder); **it's no wonder you're tired** es ist kein Wunder, dass du müde bist.
verb 1 sich fragen; **I wonder why she did that** ich frage mich, warum sie das getan hat; **2 I wonder who?** wer wohl?; **I wonder where Jake is** wo Jake wohl ist?; **3** (*in polite requests*) **I wonder if you could tell me ...?** könnten Sie mir vielleicht sagen ...?

wonderful *adjective* wunderbar.

wood *noun* Holz *das*; **the lamp is made of wood** die Lampe ist aus Holz.

wooden *adjective* Holz-, hölzern; **wooden toys** *das* Holzspielzeug.

woodwork *noun* (*craft*) Tischlerei *die*.

wool *noun* Wolle *die*.

word *noun* 1 Wort *das* (PL die Wörter) (*the plural 'Wörter' is used when the words are unrelated*); **a long word** ein langes Wort; **what's the German word for 'window'?** wie heißt 'window' auf Deutsch?; **I've learned ten German words today** ich habe heute zehn deutsche Wörter gelernt; **words in the dictionary** Wörter im Wörterbuch; **2** Wort *das* (PL die Worte) (*the plural 'Worte' is used when the words are connected in a text or conversation*); **he wanted to say a few words** er wollte nur ein paar Worte sagen; **in other words** mit anderen Worten; **to have a word with somebody** mit jemandem sprechen; **3** (*promise*) Wort *das*; **to keep your word** sein Wort halten; **he broke his word** er hat sein Wort gebrochen; **4 the words of a song** der Text von einem Lied.

word processing *noun* Textverarbeitung *die*.

word processor *noun* Textverarbeitungssystem *das*.

work *noun* Arbeit *die*; **I enjoy my work** meine Arbeit macht mir Spaß; **she's looking for work** sie sucht Arbeit; **I've got some work to do** ich habe noch etwas Arbeit; **he's out of work** er hat keine Arbeit; **to be off work** nicht arbeiten; **Ben's off work** (*sick*) Ben ist krank; **to go to work on the tube** mit der U-Bahn zur Arbeit fahren.
verb 1 arbeiten; **she works in an office** sie arbeitet in einem Büro; **Mum works as a dentist** Mutti ist Zahnärztin; **he works part-time** er arbeitet halbtags; **2** (*to operate*) sich auskennen ◆ SEP mit; **can you work the video?** kennst du dich mit dem Videorecorder aus?; **3** (*function*) funktionieren; **the washing machine's not working** die Waschmaschine funktioniert nicht; **4** (*a plan or idea*) klappen; **that worked really well** das hat prima geklappt.

△ NEW SPELLING: *See page xii*

- **to work out 1** (*understand*)
verstehen✧; **I can't work out why**
ich kann nicht verstehen, warum;
2 (*exercise*) trainieren; **3** (*to go well*)
klappen; **4** (*calculate*) ausrechnen
SEP (*a sum*); **I'll work out how much
it would cost** ich rechne aus, wie
viel es kosten würde; **5** (*solve*) lösen
(*a problem*).

worker *noun* Arbeiter *der* (PL *die*
Arbeiter), Arbeiterin *die* (PL *die*
Arbeiterinnen).

work experience *noun*
Praktikum *das* (PL *die* Praktika); **to
do work experience** ein Praktikum
machen.

working-class *adjective* der
Arbeiterschicht; **a working-class
family** eine Familie der
Arbeiterschicht.

workshop *noun* Werkstatt *die* (PL
die Werkstätten).

world *noun* Welt *die*; **the biggest
tree in the world** der größte Baum
der Welt; **all over the world** auf der
ganzen Welt; **the Western world** die
westliche Welt.

World Cup *noun* **the World Cup**
die Weltmeisterschaft.

world war *noun* Weltkrieg *der* (PL
die Weltkriege); **the Second World
War** der Zweite Weltkrieg.

worm *noun* Wurm *der* (PL *die*
Würmer).

worn out *adjective* **1** (*person*)
erschöpft; **2** (*clothes or shoes*)
abgetragen.

worried *adjective* **1** besorgt; **his**

worried parents seine besorgten
Eltern; **2 to be worried about
somebody** sich ←(DAT) um
jemanden Sorgen machen; **we're
worried about Susan** wir machen
uns um Susan Sorgen.

worry *noun* Sorge *die* (PL *die*
Sorgen).
verb sich ←(DAT) Sorgen machen;
don't worry! keine Sorge!; **don't
worry about it** mach dir darum
keine Sorgen.

worrying *adjective* beunruhigend.

worse *adjective* **1** (*more unpleasant*)
schlimmer (*problem, pain, illness*);
things couldn't be worse es kann
nicht schlimmer kommen; **2** (*less
good*) schlechter; **it was even worse
than the last time** es war noch
schlechter als letztes Mal; **to get
worse** schlechter werden; **the
weather's getting worse** das Wetter
wird schlechter; **she's getting
worse** (*in health*) es geht ihr
schlechter.

worst *adjective* **1** (*most unpleasant*)
schlimmster/schlimmste/
schlimmstes; **the worst** der/die/das
Schlimmste; **it was the worst day
of my life** es war der schlimmste
Tag meines Lebens; **if the worst
comes to the worst** wenn es zum
Schlimmsten kommt; **2** (*least good*)
schlechtester/schlechteste/
schlechtestes; **it's his worst film** das
ist sein schlechtester Film; **French is
my worst subject** in Französisch
bin ich am schlechtesten.

worth *adjective* **to be worth** wert
sein; **how much is it worth?** wie
viel ist es wert?; **it's worth buying**

✧ IRREGULAR VERB: *See the verb table in the centre of the dictionary*

das lohnt sich zu kaufen; **it's worth it** das lohnt sich; **it's not worth it** es lohnt sich nicht.

would *verb* **1 would you like something to eat?** möchtest du etwas essen?; **what would you like?** was möchten Sie?; **2 I wouldn't do it** ich würde das nicht machen; **I would buy it, but I haven't got any money at the moment** ich würde es kaufen, aber ich habe zur Zeit kein Geld; **I'd like to go to the cinema** ich würde gern ins Kino gehen; **she said she'd help us** sie hat gesagt, sie würde uns helfen; **3 that would be a good idea** das wäre ein gute Idee; **if we had asked her she would have helped us** wenn wir sie gefragt hätten, hätte sie uns geholfen; **4 he wouldn't answer** er wollte nicht antworten; **the car wouldn't start** das Auto wollte nicht anspringen.

wound *noun* Wunde *die* (PL *die* Wunden).
verb verwunden.

wrap *verb* einwickeln SEP; **I'm going to wrap (up) my presents** ich wickele meine Geschenke ein; **could you wrap it for me please?** können Sie es bitte in Geschenkpapier einwickeln?

wrapping paper *noun* Geschenkpapier *das*.

wreck *noun* **1** Wrack *das* (PL *die* Wracks); **2 I feel a wreck** ich bin völlig kaputt.
verb **1** zerstören (*a building or machinery*); **2** kaputtfahren ✧ SEP (*a car*); **3** verderben ✧ (*a party, holidays*); **it completely wrecked**

my evening das hat mir den Abend völlig verdorben; **4** zunichte machen (*plans*).

wrestler *noun* Ringer *der* (PL *die* Ringer), Ringerin *die* (PL *die* Ringerinnen).

wrestling *noun* Ringen *das*.

wrist *noun* Handgelenk *das* (PL *die* Handgelenke).

write *verb* schreiben ✧; **to write to somebody** jemandem schreiben; **I'll write her a letter** ich schreibe ihr einen Brief; **to write to a firm** an eine Firma schreiben.
●**to write down** aufschreiben ✧ SEP; **I wrote down her name** ich schrieb ihren Namen auf; **she wrote it down for me** sie hat es mir aufgeschrieben.

writer *noun* Schriftsteller *der* (PL *die* Schriftsteller), Schriftstellerin *die* (PL *die* Schriftstellerinnen).

writing *noun* Schrift *die*.

wrong *adjective* **1** (*not correct*) falsch; **the wrong answer** die falsche Antwort; **it's the wrong address** das ist die falsche Adresse; **2 you've got the wrong number** Sie haben sich verwählt; **3 to be wrong** (*be mistaken*) sich irren; **I must have been wrong** ich muss mich geirrt haben; **4** (*out of order*) **to be wrong** nicht stimmen; **there's something wrong** etwas stimmt nicht; **5** (*dishonest*) unrecht; **it's wrong to make him pay for it** es ist unrecht, dass er dafür zahlen muss; **he's wrong** er hat Unrecht; **you're quite wrong there, cars pollute the**

environment da haben Sie aber Unrecht, Autos verschmutzen die Umwelt; **6 what's wrong?** was ist los?

adverb **1** (*false*) falsch; **he's got it wrong** er hat es falsch gemacht; **2 to go wrong** (*break*) kaputtgehen ✧ SEP (PERF *sein*) (*informal*); **3 to go wrong** schief gehen △ ✧ (*plan*).

X x

xerox™ *noun* Fotokopie *die* (PL *die* Fotokopien).
verb fotokopieren.

X-ray *noun* Röntgenaufnahme *die* (PL *die* Röntgenaufnahmen); **to have an X-ray** geröntgt werden ✧ (PERF *sein*).
verb röntgen; **they X-rayed her ankle** sie haben ihren Knöchel geröntgt.

Y y

yacht *noun* **1** (*sailing boat*) Segelboot *das* (PL *die* Segelboote); **2** (*large luxury boat*) Jacht *die* (PL *die* Jachten).

yawn *verb* gähnen.

year *noun* **1** Jahr *das* (PL *die* Jahre); **six years ago** vor sechs Jahren; **the whole year** das ganze Jahr; **2 they lived in Moscow for years** sie haben jahrelang in Moskau gewohnt; **3 to be seventeen years old** siebzehn Jahre alt sein; **a two-year-old child** ein zweijähriges Kind; **4** (*in school*) Klasse *die* (PL *die* Klassen) (*in German secondary schools the years go from the 'fünfte Klasse' to the 'dreizehnte Klasse'*); **I'm in Year 10** (*in Britain*) ich gehe in die zehnte Klasse; **he'll be in Year 11** (*in Britain*) er kommt in die elfte Klasse.

yellow *adjective* gelb.

yes *adverb* **1** ja; **yes please** ja bitte; **'is Tom in his room?' – 'yes, he is'** 'ist Tom im Zimmer?' – 'ja'; **2** (*answering a negative*) doch; **'you don't want to come with us, do you?' – ' yes, I do !'** 'du willst nicht mitkommen?' – 'doch!'; **'you haven't finished, have you?' – 'yes, I have'** 'Sie sind noch nicht fertig, oder?' – 'doch!'.

yesterday *adverb* **1** gestern; **I saw her yesterday** ich habe sie gestern gesehen; **yesterday afternoon** gestern Nachmittag; **yesterday morning** gestern früh; **2 the day before yesterday** vorgestern.

yet *adverb* **1 not yet** noch nicht; **it's not ready yet** es ist noch nicht fertig; **2** (*in questions*) schon; **has she mentioned it yet?** hat sie es schon erwähnt?

yoghurt *noun* Joghurt *der* (PL *die* Joghurt).

✧ IRREGULAR VERB: *See the verb table in the centre of the dictionary*

yolk noun Eigelb das (pl die Eigelbe).

you pronoun 1 (*as the subject of the sentence and in comparisons*) du (*familiar form, singular*); Sie (*polite form, singular and plural*); ('*du' is the familiar way of talking to family members, close friends, and people of your own age; 'Sie' is more polite*) **do you want to go to the cinema tonight?** möchtest du heute Abend ins Kino gehen?; **can you tell me where the station is, please?** können Sie mir bitte sagen, wo der Bahnhof ist?; **he's older than you** er ist älter als du, er ist älter als Sie; 2 (*the object form of 'du' and 'Sie', in the dative*) dir (*familiar form, singular*); Ihnen (*polite form, singular and plural*); **I'll lend you my bike** ich leihe dir mein Rad; **I'll write to you** ich schreibe Ihnen; **I'll come with you** ich komme mit Ihnen mit; 3 (*the object form of 'du' and 'Sie', in the accusative*) dich (*familiar form, singular*); Sie (*polite form, singular and plural*); **I saw you** ich habe dich gesehen, ich habe Sie gesehen; 4 (*as the subject of the sentence*) ihr (*familiar form, plural*); **do you all want to come?** wollt ihr alle kommen?; 5 (*the object form, in the accusative and the dative*) euch; **I'll invite you all!** ich lade euch alle ein!; **I'll give it to you later** ich gebe es euch später.

young adjective jung; **young people** junge Leute; **he's younger than me** er ist jünger als ich; **Tessa's two years younger than me** Tessa ist zwei Jahre jünger als ich.

your adjective 1 (*familiar form singular*) dein; (*this is the familiar way of talking to family members, close friends, and people of your own age; 'Ihr' is more polite*) **I met your brother** ich habe deinen Bruder getroffen; **I met your sister** ich habe deine Schwester getroffen; **I drove your car** ich bin mit deinem Auto gefahren; **I know your brothers** ich kenne deine Brüder; 2 (*familiar form, plural*) euer; **your brother** euer Bruder; **your sister** eure Schwester; **your car** euer Auto; **your friends are waiting downstairs** eure Freunde warten unten; 3 (*polite form, singular and plural*) Ihr; **your brother** Ihr Bruder; **your sister** Ihre Schwester; **your car is in the garage** Ihr Auto ist in der Garage; **you can all bring your friends** Sie können alle Ihre Freunde mitbringen.

yours pronoun 1 (*familiar form, singular*) deiner/deine/deins; (*this is the familiar way of talking to family members, close friends, and people of your own age; 'Ihrer/Ihre/Ihrs' is more polite*) **my brother's younger than yours** mein Bruder ist jünger als deiner; **my sister is older than yours** meine Schwester ist älter als deine; **I enjoyed that book – is it yours?** das Buch hat mir gefallen – ist es deins?; **my shoes are more expensive than yours** meine Schuhe sind teurer als deine; 2 (*familiar form, plural*) euer/eure/eures; **my children are younger than yours** meine Kinder sind jünger als eure; 3 (*polite form, singular and*

△ NEW SPELLING: *See page xii*

plural) Ihrer/Ihre/Ihrs; **his father must be older than yours** sein Vater muss älter als Ihrer sein; **4 she's a friend of yours** sie ist eine Freundin von Ihnen; **these books are yours** diese Bücher gehören Ihnen; **5** (*in letters*) **Yours sincerely** Mit freundlichen Grüßen.

yourself *pronoun* **1** (*when translated by a reflexive verb in German*) dich; (*formal*) sich; **ask yourself** frage dich, fragen Sie sich; **2** (*as a reflexive dative pronoun*) dir; (*formal*) sich; **did you hurt yourself?** hast du dir wehgetan?, haben Sie sich wehgetan?; **3** (*for emphasis*) selbst; **did you do it yourself?** hast du es selbst gemacht?; **4 all by yourself** ganz allein.

yourselves *pronoun* **1** euch; (*formal*) sich; **make yourselves comfortable** macht es euch gemütlich, machen Sie es sich gemütlich; **2** (*for emphasis*) selbst; **did you do it yourselves?** habt ihr es selbst gemacht?; **3 by yourselves** allein.

youth hostel *noun* Jugendherberge *die* (PL *die* Jugendherbergen).

Yugoslavia *noun* Jugoslawien *das*; **in the former Yugoslavia** im ehemaligen Jugoslawien.

Z z

zany *adjective* verrückt.

zebra *noun* Zebra *das* (PL *die* Zebras).

zebra crossing *noun* Zebrastreifen *der* (PL *die* Zebrastreifen).

zero *noun* Null *die* (PL *die* Nullen).

zigzag *verb* **1** im Zickzack laufen ◇(PERF *sein*); **2** (*in a car*) im Zickzack fahren ◇(PERF *sein*).

zip *noun* Reißverschluss △ *der* (PL *die* Reißverschlüsse).

zodiac *noun* Tierkreis *der*; **the signs of the zodiac** *die* Sternzeichen (*plural*).

zone *noun* Zone *die* (PL *die* Zonen).

zoo *noun* Zoo *der* (PL *die* Zoos).

zoom lens *noun* Zoomobjektiv *das* (PL *die* Zoomobjektive).

◇ **IRREGULAR VERB:** *See the verb table in the centre of the dictionary*

USEFUL LISTS

Deutschland

DEUTSCHLAND	GERMANY
Bundesland	**State**
Baden-Württemberg	Baden-Württemberg
Bayern	Bavaria
Berlin	Berlin
Brandenburg	Brandenburg
Bremen	Bremen
Hamburg	Hamburg
Hessen	Hessen
Mecklenburg-Vorpommern	Mecklenburg-West Pomerania
Niedersachsen	Lower Saxony
Nordrhein-Westfalen	North Rhine-Westphalia
Rheinland-Pfalz	Rhineland-Palatinate
Saarland	Saarland
Sachsen	Saxony
Sachsen-Anhalt	Saxony-Anhalt
Schleswig-Holstein	Schleswig-Holstein
Thüringen	Thuringia

618

Europa

Reykjavik · ISLAND

Europäisches Nordmeer

NORWEGEN
SCHWEDEN
FINNLAND

Oslo · · Stockholm · Helsinki

Nordsee

SCHOTTLAND
NORDIRLAND

Tallinn · ESTLAND

Riga · LETTLAND

RUSSLAND

Moskau ·

REPUBLIK IRLAND

Dublin · GROSSBRITANNIEN

WALES

ENGLAND

London ·

DÄNEMARK

Kopenhagen ·

Ostsee

LITAUEN
Wilna ·

RUSSLAND

Minsk ·

Kiew ·

Amsterdam ·

Hamburg ·

Berlin ·

POLEN

WEISSRUSSLAND

Ärmelkanal

Brüssel ·

NIEDERLANDE

DEUTSCHLAND

Bonn ·

Warschau ·

BELGIEN

LUXEMBURG

Prag ·

UKRAINE

Atlantischer Ozean

Paris ·

LIECHTENSTEIN

München ·

TSCHECHISCHE REPUBLIK

SLOWAKEI

FRANKREICH

Bern ·

SCHWEIZ

Wien ·

Bratislava ·

MOLDAWIEN

Chișinău ·

ÖSTERREICH

Budapest ·

UNGARN

RUMÄNIEN

Mailand ·

SLOWENIEN

Ljubljana ·

Zagreb ·

Belgrad ·

Bukarest ·

MONACO

SAN MARINO

KROATIEN

BOSNIEN – HERZEGOWINA

BULGARIEN

PORTUGAL

Lissabon ·

Madrid ·

ANDORRA

Korsika

ITALIEN

Rom ·

Sarajevo ·

JUGOSLAWIEN

Sofia ·

Skopje ·

SPANIEN

Ibiza

Menorca

Mallorca

Sardinien

ALBANIEN

Tirana ·

MAZEDONIEN

TÜRKEI

GRIECHENLAND

Athen ·

Sizilien

Kreta

| 0 | 200 | 400 | 600 | 800 km |

| 0 | 100 | 200 | 300 | 400 | 500 Meilen |

Mittelmeer

EUROPA	EUROPE
Land	**Country**

Albanien	Albania
Andorra	Andorra
Belgien	Belgium
Bosnien-Herzogowina	Bosnia-Herzegovina
Bulgarien	Bulgaria
Dänemark	Denmark
Deutschland	Germany
Estland	Estonia
Finnland	Finland
Frankreich	France
Griechenland	Greece
Großbritannien	United Kingdom;
	Great Britain
England	England
Nordirland	Northern Ireland
Schottland	Scotland
Wales	Wales
Kroatien	Croatia
Island	Iceland
Italien	Italy
Jugoslawien	Yugoslavia
Lettland	Latvia
Liechtenstein	Liechtenstein
Litauen	Lithuania
Luxemburg	Luxembourg

EUROPA	EUROPE
Land	**Country**
Mazedonien (Ehmalige Jugoslawische Republik Mazedonien)	FYROM (Former Yugoslav Republic of Macedonia)
Monaco	Monaco
Moldawien	Moldavia
Niederlande	Netherlands
Norwegen	Norway
Österreich	Austria
Polen	Poland
Portugal	Portugal
Republik Irland	Republic of Ireland
Rumänien	Romania
Russland	Russia
San Marino	San Marino
Schweden	Sweden
Schweiz	Switzerland
Slowakei	Slovakia
Slowenien	Slovenia
Spanien	Spain
Tschechische Republik	Czech Republic
Türkei	Turkey
Ukraine	Ukraine
Ungarn	Hungary
Weißrussland	Belarus

NUMBERS

null	0	einundzwanzig	21
eins	1	zweiundzwanzig	22
zwei	2	dreiundzwanzig	23
drei	3	vierundzwanzig	24
vier	4	fünfundzwanzig	25
fünf	5	sechsundzwanzig	26
sechs	6	siebenundzwanzig	27
sieben	7	achtundzwanzig	28
acht	8	neunundzwanzig	29
neun	9		
zehn	10		
elf	11	dreißig	30
zwölf	12	vierzig	40
dreizehn	13	fünfzig	50
vierzehn	14	sechzig	60
fünfzehn	15	siebzig	70
sechzehn	16	achtzig	80
siebzehn	17	neunzig	90
achtzehn	18		
neunzehn	19	hundert	100
zwanzig	20	tausend	1 000
		eine Million	1 000 000

DATES

am ersten Januar	on January 1st
der erste Januar	the 1st of January
zweite (2.)	2nd
dritte (3.)	3rd
vierte (4.)	4th
fünfte	5th
sechste	6th
siebte	7th
achte	8th
neunte	9th
zehnte	10th
elfte	11th
zwölfte	12th
dreizehnte	13th
vierzehnte	14th
fünfzehnte	15th
sechzehnte	16th
siebzehnte	17th
achtzehnte	18th
neunzehnte	19th
zwanzigste	20th
einundzwanzigste	21st
dreißigste	30th

IMPORTANT DATES

Feiertag	public holiday
Fasching/Fastnacht	carnival time
Heiligabend	Christmas Eve
Karfreitag	Good Friday
Maifeiertag	May Day
Neujahr	New Year
Ostern	Easter
Pfingsten	Whitsun
Silvester	New Year's Eve
Weihnachten	Christmas
1. Weihnachtstag	Christmas Day
2. Weihnachtstag	Boxing Day

DAYS

Montag	Monday
Dienstag	Tuesday
Mittwoch	Wednesday
Donnerstag	Thursday
Freitag	Friday
Samstag/Sonnabend	Saturday
Sonntag	Sunday

MONTHS

Januar	January
Februar	February
März	March
April	April
Mai	May
Juni	June
Juli	July
August	August
September	September
Oktober	October
November	November
Dezember	December

SEASONS

der Winter	winter
der Frühling	spring
der Sommer	summer
der Herbst	autumn

NOTES

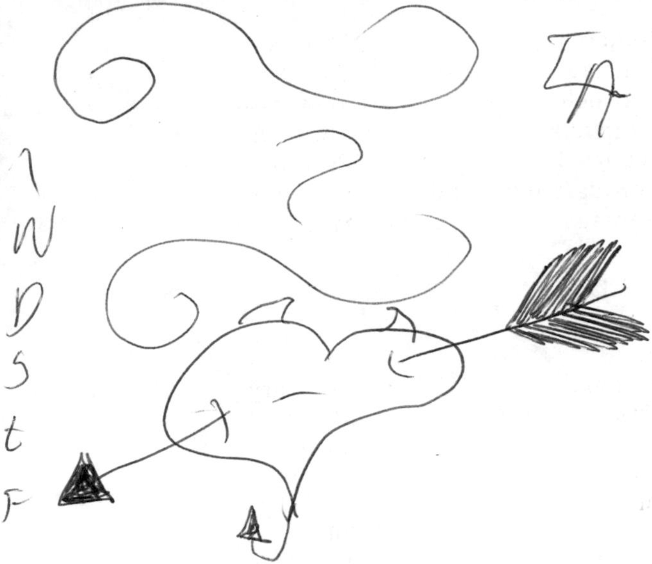

Martin Handley

Chaz ❤ Ewen.

Chaz ❤ Nicky.

4eva.

Chaz ❤ Ewen F

4eva.

I D S T.

I D S T